Jas. Burgess

The Indian Antiquary

Volume I, 1872

Jas. Burgess

The Indian Antiquary
Volume I. 1872

ISBN/EAN: 9783742837561

Manufactured in Europe, USA, Canada, Australia, Japa

Cover: Foto ©Thomas Meinert / pixelio.de

Manufactured and distributed by brebook publishing software
(www.brebook.com)

Jas. Burgess

The Indian Antiquary

THE

INDIAN ANTIQUARY,

A JOURNAL OF ORIENTAL RESEARCH

IN

ARCHÆOLOGY, HISTORY, LITERATURE, LANGUAGES, FOLKLORE, &c. &c.

EDITED BY

JAS. BURGESS, M.R.A.S., F.R.G.S.

VOL. I. 1872.

BOMBAY:

PRINTED AT THE "TIMES OF INDIA" OFFICE.

LONDON: TRÜBNER & Co. PARIS: E. LEROUX. BERLIN: ASHER & Co. LEIPZIG: F. A. BROCKHAUS.
NEW YORK: WESTERMANN & Co. BOMBAY: THACKER, VINING & Co.

1872.

CONTENTS.

Authors' names arranged Alphabetically.

SELECTIONS & MISCELLANEA.

ILLUSTRATIONS.

THE INDIAN ANTIQUARY,

A JOURNAL OF ORIENTAL RESEARCH.

PREFATORY.

JUDGING from many private communications received from all parts of India, it would appear that such a Journal as the *Indian Antiquary* was much wanted; and if it be considered that almost every branch of scientific research possesses, not merely the transactions of societies specially devoted to its culture, but also weekly, monthly, and quarterly journals, publishing all sorts of information, for all classes of readers, it is surely not too much to expect that *Indian Research* should be of sufficient interest to Europeans resident in India, or interested in it, and to the intelligent and educated natives of the country, to support one journal devoted to its promotion. The scope of this will be as wide as possible—addressing the general reader with information on Manners and Customs, Arts, Mythology, Feasts, Festivals and Rites, Antiquities and History,—in which every one, in any way connected with the country, ought to feel an intelligent interest,—and, at the same time, it is intended to be a *medium of communication* between Archæologists in the East and the West. Its Correspondence columns will afford ample opportunity for the amicable discussion of many questions, on which more information is yet required before any fixed opinion can be formed, and for propounding *Queries* on all matters fairly within the domain of Oriental Research. By presenting its readers with abstracts of the most recent researches of savans in India, Europe and America, and by its translations from German, French, and other European languages—it will make fully accessible to the many Native Scholars, unacquainted with these languages, the latest results arrived at by the greatest continental scholars. It will be the aim of the *Indian Antiquary* to supplement the Journals of the various Asiatic Societies by directing the attention of its readers to the best articles in each, and supplying a variety of such articles, notes, and memoranda as never find their way to the pages of these publications.

Among the many subjects we wish and hope to see discussed, we may enumerate—Architectural and other Lithic remains—of the extent and variety of which, in India, the world is only beginning to form a vague idea. And as attention has been specially directed to this branch of late years, and Government has at last very properly responded to the demand for an Archæological Survey, we may hope to aid it by the early publication of all the information respecting its progress and discoveries communicated to us by its officers, and aid it by information respecting localities and remains as yet but imperfectly known. Then there are old Native Engineering works of no small interest—of which, scarcely one satisfactory account of a single work has yet appeared in type. Local legends and Folklore, Proverbs and Songs, are subjects at every one's door who can speak a vernacular tongue, and, besides their intrinsic interest, they often shed a most instructive light on the habits of thought of the people. When ready to go to press, we have had the pleasure of receiving a contribution to this department that we feel sure all our readers will welcome with delight.

Mr. Gover's "Folk-songs of Southern India" is not only an instructive book, it is probably without exception, the most interesting work relating to India and the social character of its people, that has appeared for years; and it shows what a patient worker may effect.

Then the History, Chronology and Genealogies of the many provinces, races, and royal families are all but exhaustless subjects. On the costumes ancient and modern; on implements of domestic use, husbandry, and war; on Sports and Pastimes; and on the Arts and Handicrafts, of India, volumes might be filled. The Ethnology of the various tribes and the connections of their languages, &c., may well occupy many enquirers. Topography and Geography—ancient and modern,—are only beginning to attract attention, and are susceptible of very extensive elucidation. The Indian Governments have at length taken up the compilation of Provincial Gazetteers; but such works can at first be only approximately complete, and the compilers—however talented and energetic—cannot be expected to obtain the best possible information, in more than a majority of cases. Here, again, our contributors may be of public service, by supplying our pages with articles on points of local geography and history.

Numismatology is another branch for which much remains to be done. There are coinages—Sah, Gupta, Bactrian, Hindu, and Mughal, of various ages and dynasties, that will amply reward patient study, and respecting which we expect to be aided with remarks and outline figures.

Inscriptions abound in some districts more than in others, and if *fac-similes* are sent to the *Indian Antiquary*, we hope to find the means of publishing them for decipherment and translation by those among our correspondents best skilled in such studies.

Then there are the subjects of Mythology and Religions—with their sects, rites and ceremonies; Literature and Bibliography; Philology and Grammar; Astronomy; Medicine; Geology and Natural History,—which will all supply themes interesting to the scholar, the man of science, the politician, the educationist, the missionary, the general reader and the tourist.

We are gratified to find that so ready a response has been made by so many eminent scholars in India to our request for aid, and we have to thank many others for voluntarily offering very valuable contributions to our pages. We invite all our readers to aid us with their pens; there is no country where fresh information of the most varied sort lies so near to every one's hand as in India; and whoever tries to write, we feel sure, will find the field widen and deepen in interest the oftener he makes the attempt to put it into form for the interest and instruction of others.

Finally, by inducing subscribers to join our ranks, and thereby obtaining for us the pecuniary means of which, as yet, we necessarily stand in need, our readers and first supporters will enable us to accomplish the objects at which we aim; and no pains will be spared on our part in endeavouring to stimulate that literary spirit and power which very many of those who have first welcomed our proposals are known to possess, and which not a few are ready to exert for the instruction of all who will join us.

ON THE PRESENT POSITION OF OLD HINDI IN ORIENTAL PHILOLOGY.

BY JOHN BEAMES, B.C.S., M.R.A.S., &c., BALASORE.

ORIENTAL scholars in Europe, as a rule, devote their time and attention exclusively to Sanskrit and its off-shoots, Pali and the Prakrits. With the exception of the veteran Professor, M. Garcin de Tassy, I know of none who have considered the Indian vernaculars of the mediæval and modern periods worthy of their study, and even that eminent scholar's labours have been chiefly directed to Urdu, and other quite modern branches of the Hindi group of dialects. Manuscripts of works by Hindi writers from the twelfth to the sixteenth century are very rare, and those that exist are seldom complete. On the occasion of my recent visit to England, I found that the British Museum contained none, the Bodleian had one bad manuscript of Chand, (which was entered in the catalogue as a Sanskrit poem!) and the library of the Royal Asiatic Society had not more than half-a-dozen works of this class. I found only three or four imperfect copies of some of the latest and most common of these poets in the India Office library, and I believe continental collections are entirely destitute of them, though I had no time during my short stay in Paris to verify the fact.

A wide field is then awaiting attention. Its

interest and importance for the student of comparative philology will be apparent, when I say that the modern Aryan group of languages has been developed from the Sanskrit, or rather from that old Aryan *ursprache*, of which Sanskrit is our only surviving type, by precisely the same processes as those by which the Romance group in Europe has evolved itself from the Latin. We see in both groups exactly parallel developments, marvellously synchronous, and precisely similar in point of structure. So also with the German group; readers of Grimm might almost take his rules and the skeleton of his German Grammar, and fill up the details with examples drawn from Hindi, Marathi, and other Indian languages. Inasmuch then, as what we want, more especially in philology at present, is an absolute parallelism of all developments in groups of languages of the same family, to enable us to give to our science that mathematical precision which it is at present reproached with lacking, there can be few more important lines of study for the enquirer to follow, than a thorough elucidation of the principles of development of the Aryan languages of India. The first requisite for this task is, that there should exist an accessible and trustworthy series of texts. As long as the Indian authors remain in manuscript, no real work can be done. We must have Chand in print, just as readily procurable as Otfried or Notker, so that he may be analysed and commented upon, and the lessons which his rude style teaches, as fully understood as those of the old and middle-German writers.

It is generally supposed, that, to translate an old Hindi work, is as easy as it is to translate a modern German or French novel. This is a very great mistake, and entails much undeserved neglect and some little contempt, upon scholars who undertake the task. I wish therefore, as one who has had occasion to spend many a weary hour over the dark and mystic pages of those knotty old poets, to say a few words with a view to putting the importance and difficulty of these studies in a truer light, and winning some sympathy and recognition for those who are engaged in, what seems to them at present, a task of almost disheartening difficulty.

The earliest Hindi poem extant, as far as we know at present, is the great epic of CHAND BARDAI, [*Baroth*] called the *Prithirája Rásau*, which was written about A. D. 1200, and records the life and exploits of Prithiráj of the Chauhán tribe of Rájputs, the last Hindu sovereign of Dehli. This is followed by a long string of writers of religious poetry, whose names are too well known to need repetition here, but whose works are, perhaps, not so familiar as their names.* In spite of occasional dialectic differences, and although a gradual modernization of style and vocabulary is discernible in them, these poets are all of one type as regards grammatical construction, and general characteristics. And this type is about the most enigmatical that can possibly be imagined.

In the first place, as though peculiarities of grammar and syntax were not enough to bewilder the student, a mechanical stumbling-block of the gravest description meets him at the outset. All the words in one line are written together without any break; thus—

[illegible] ॥

Chand.

[illegible] ॥

Kabir.

which is much as if one should write in one word, the line—

[illegible].

Milton.

This is the universal custom in Indian manuscripts of all ages, but in Sanskrit the practice causes no difficulty, because the inflexional terminations of the words themselves supply a guide to their proper division.

In old Hindi, however, the inflexional terminations of nouns and verbs (as I shall point out presently more in detail) have almost entirely disappeared; so, that, we have frequently no clue at all to help us in dividing the words. Take for instance the following lines from Chand:—

[illegible] ॥

[illegible] ॥

[illegible] ॥

The above lines are not consecutive, but are taken at random, from different parts of the poem. It will be observed, that each one of them admits of being divided in more than one way; as, for instance, the first from a hymn in praise of Sarasvati. We may take it thus—

छत्र आ, मढ़ेरो धरु &c.

"Whose is the umbrella, holder of the drum."

(मढ़ेरो for मुढ़ेरो a common change), or we may perhaps more correctly divide—

छत्र आ मढ़े [illegible]

* See Garcin de Tassy's valuable Histoire de la Littérature Hindoui et Hindoustani, vol. I. passim.

"Whose is the umbrella, smelling of wine, brilliant in wrath." The remaining part of the line भ्रमि भूरि भाराहिता "canopied with a cloud of bees," is clear enough.

If it be objected that the context and general sense of the passage will generally decide which of several possible ways is the right one, I am constrained to reply, that these rhapsodical old authors are often so very vague that little help can, in most instances, be obtained from the context. Their verses were, especially in the case of bards like Chand, meant to be sung, and the tone and gestures of the singer were relied upon to express the meaning as much as, if not more than, the strict grammatical construction of the words. Chand's epic is in the main historical, though often extravagantly legendary and hyperbolical. In his tamer passages some connected sense may be traced, but when he soars into religious or descriptive altitudes, one may say of him with Bassanio; "Gratiano speaks an infinite deal of nothing, more than any man in all Venice. His reasons are as two grains of wheat hid in two bushels of chaff: you shall seek all day ere you find them, and when you have them, they are not worth the search."

It is still worse when we come to purely mythical or quasi-philosophical poems like Kabir's Rekhtas, where there is no regular narrative or chain of events to guide us. In such cases the luckless translator flounders in deep mire with no landmarks by which to direct his course.

The value of this old Hindi literature consists, to my mind, almost entirely in the assistance it renders to philology: for purposes of philosophy, history, or anything else, it is not of much worth.

Secondly, even if the task of dividing the words rightly be at last achieved, *tant bien que mal*; leaving only one or two doubtful places to be settled hereafter, the translator's troubles have after all only begun. The language of all but the most modern of these poets is in a transitional stage.

Sanskrit and the Prakrits are, as every one knows, purely inflexional languages, while the modern vernaculars are all more or less analytical. In the Indo-Aryan, as in the European cognate groups, a time came when the case and tense-endings of the old synthetical system had become so abraded and corrupted that they no longer sufficed to distinguish clearly the relations between words in a sentence. After a time a remedy was unconsciously found for this difficulty in the introduction of particles, pre- or post-positions, and auxiliaries, whose use constitutes the distinguishing characteristic of the analytical stage. But between the decay of the old and the rise of the new system, there intervenes a period of the greatest obscurity, and it is unfortunately just at this period, both in India and in Europe, that modern literature takes its rise. This period in Europe is occupied by the Trouvères and Troubadours, of the tongues of *Oïl* and *Oc*, by the Juglars of Spain, the Minnesinger of Germany and the like, and occurs, historically, from the twelfth to the fourteenth century. In Germany, (where however the synthetical system never suffered so much decay as in other countries,) the rise to power of the Swabian dynasty in the person of Konrad III. in 1138 A. D. marks the commencement, as Walther von der Vogelweide (1230), the Nibelungenlied, and Wolfram von Eschilbach mark the zenith, and a host of minor writers the decay of this brilliant period. Almost exactly contemporaneous with these writers, as also with the unknown Juglars, who wrote the Romance of the Cid in Spain, are our early Hindi poets, and their language is in the same transitional and undefined stage, as that of their European compeers. It is marked by a great scarcity, at times by a total absence, of what the Germans call Verhältnisswörter, and by a general neglect, and capricious misuse of tense-endings in the verb and case-endings in the noun. It abounds with archaisms which are only to be rendered at all intelligible by the tedious process, impossible to all but experts in philology, of restoring them by reversing the order of phonetic corruption, and so tracing them back to some known Sanskrit word.

But here occurs another difficulty. Sanskrit as a language, does not cover the whole ground of Aryan speech. Many old Aryan words remained in use among the lower orders but were never admitted into literary composition, either because they were stigmatised as vulgar, or because Brahmanical literature, confined to religion, philosophy and ritual, had no need of them. The Hindi poets, however, receiving such words Prakritised by lapse of time, from their fathers, make no scruple of using them, and if, as often happens, they are no longer in use in modern times, their meaning is excessively difficult of discovery, because neither the ancient Sanskrit nor the modern Hindi afford any clue to their origin or sense.

To illustrate this point, I will here give the

first few lines of Paradise Lost, first in Milton's own words, and then in such a form of old English as shall bear the same relation to the real words, as Chand's style bears to modern Hindi, and I will then leave the impartial reader to judge of the difficulty of the task.

1. Milton's own words.

Of man's first disobedience, and the fruit
Of that forbidden tree, whose mortal taste
Brought death into the world, and all our woe,
With loss of Eden, till one greater Man
Restore us, and regain the blissful seat,
Sing, heavenly Muse! &c.

2. The same, in "Chandesque" English.

[illegible]
[illegible]
[illegible]
[illegible]
[illegible]
[illegible]

The reader may well ask for an explanation of No. 2. All I have done is to put Milton's lines into eleventh-century English—the English spoken at the time of Chand—and to make the resemblance to the 'Chandesque' style still more complete, I have written all the words in one, and have inserted here and there a word of a still older period, either from the old High German, or from the Moeso-Gothic of Ulfilas, such as "aigawith." The high German words represent those words in Chand which are derived from lost Aryan roots, and the Moeso-Gothic pure Sanskrit tatsamas, such as are to be found in his writings. I have inserted an e or an a here and there to imitate Chand's habit of inserting such vowels needlessly, and I have omitted them in one or two places where they ought to be found, just as he does. Especially, to make an exact parallel, in nine out of ten cases all inflexions have been dispensed with, both in noun and verb, and I have used the rarest words to be found in English works of that century, in preference to the simpler and commoner. With this explanation, the ordinary English reader will have, of course, no difficulty in deciphering my translation. If he should find any difficulty in this, a specimen from his own language, he will perhaps not be too ready to believe in the easy and trifling nature of similar work in a foreign language like Hindi.

In conclusion, to show that I have not overdrawn the picture, I append a short extract from Chand in his own words, and a translation of the same into ordinary modern Hindi. The extract selected is not by any means so difficult as some others, the exact rendering of which I must confess to being still in doubt about, and which the Pandits and Bhâts have given up as unintelligible long ago.

1. Chand's own words,—

प्रथमभुजङ्गीसुधारीग्रहनं । जिनिनामैकअनेककहनं ॥ दुतीयंलभ्यौदेवतंजीवतेसं । जिनैविश्वराख्यौबलीमन्तसेसं ॥ चवेवेदब्रह्मंहरीकित्तिभाखी । जिनैधम्मसाधम्मसंसारसाखी ॥

2. Modern Hindi translation,—

पहले भुजङ्गी सुधारी ग्रहण किये आवे । जिसका एकही नाम अनेक प्रकार से कहा जावे ॥ दुसरे लिये सीरा देवता को जीवन के ईसको । जिस ने रखा सब संसार को शेष पर बली बैठे के भारा । चारों वेद के ब्राह्मणों ने हरिकी कीर्त्ति को भाखा । जिसके धर्मा ले अधर्म संसार साखी है ॥

Balasore, Dec. 2, 1871.

THE ÂPASTAMBA SÛTRA OF THE BLACK YAJUR VEDA,

AND THE COMMENTARIES &c. BELONGING TO IT.

BY A. C. BURNELL, M.C.S., M.R.A.S. &c.

The most important perhaps, though not the oldest of the Black Yajur Veda Sûtras is the one attributed to Âpastamba. The first three *praśnas* which describe the Darśa and Pûrṇamâsa sacrifices are not uncommon in Southern India, and there are a few manuscripts which contain fifteen or sixteen *praśnas*, but it is only after several years of search I have been able to find a complete manuscript, and to ascertain for certain that the whole work contains thirty *praśnas*. This manuscript belongs to a Brahman in the Tanjor district, and, as it is most likely unique, and there is, I fear, little chance of his parting with it or even allowing a copy to be made, an account of the contents may be useful. *Praśnas* I—III describe the

Darśapûrṇamâsa sacrifices, P. IV—VIII, the initiation agnyâdheya and remaining haviryajña rites; P. IX contains the prâyaśchitta for these ceremonies; P. X—XVII describe the Soma sacrifices &c.; P. XVIII, the Vâjapeya and Râjasûya; P. XIX, the Sautrâmaṇî, Kâṭhakachitî, and Kâmyeshṭi; P. XX, the Aśvamedha and Purushamedha; P. XXI, the Dvâdaśâha and Mahâvrata; P. XXII, the Utsargiṇâm-ayana; and P. XXIII, the Sattrâyaṇa. In Praśna XXIV, there are three sections: the Paribhâshâsûtras (translated by Professor Max Müller in the German Oriental Society's Journal, IX.), the Pravarakhaṇḍa and the Hautraka. Praśnas XXV and XXVI contain the mantras for the gṛihya rites, and P. XXVII contains the Gṛihyasûtra. Of this section Dr. Eggeling has an edition in hand. Praśnas XXVIII and XXIX contain the Dharmasûtra which has been edited by Dr. Bühler. The last praśna contains the Śulva sûtra.

The manuscript described is of the early part of the last century, and is in the Grantha character.

To these thirty praśnas may be added two more which treat of the Pitṛimedha &c. and nearly agree with parts of the Hiraṇyakeśi (Praśnas XXVIII and XXIX) and Bhâradvâja Sûtra. In Chaṇḍapa's commentary on the Âpastamba Sûtra they are not mentioned, though in his introduction he gives the order of the chapters as described above, and expressly states that the work contains thirty sections.

There are several commentaries on the Âpastamba Sûtra. Rudradatta was one of the earliest who attempted to explain this large work but there is every reason to believe that he only finished fifteen praśnas. Kapardisvâmin and Dhûrtasvâmin most probably commented on the first twenty-four praśnas, and Kauśika Râma has annotated the work of the last. Gurudevasvâmin is also said to have written on this sûtra (v. Max Müller As. Soc. Jour., p. 366 note), but I have not seen his work. In the fourteenth century Chaṇḍapa wrote a very diffusive commentary, but I have only seen the first three sections. There is also a commentary by Âhobala which appears to be of the seventeenth century. Haradatta Miśra explained the XXVth, XXVIth, XXVIIIth, and XXIXth, sections, and on the last two there seems to have been another commentary, as there is a quotation from such a work in the Smṛiti-chandrikâ, which I cannot find in any copy of Haradatta's commentary accessible to me. There is a comment on P. XXVII by Sudarśanârya or Sudarśanâchârya. On praśna XXX there are comments by Karavindasvâmin, Kapardisvâmin, and Sundararâja. As I have several good manuscripts of all these works, I hope sometime to bring out an edition and translation of this interesting section which I have long had nearly ready. Very useful for the understanding of the Śrauta and Gṛihya (ritual) parts are the two prayogas by Tâlavṛintanivâsin. The whole of these may, I believe, be found, but in fragments, and generally very incorrectly copied. Few Brahmans care to get more of the work than they require for the time, and very few śrotriyas are grammarians, or well acquainted with modern Sanskrit. As there is very little chance that it will be ever possible to bring out an edition of the whole of this immense sûtra, it is satisfactory to be able to add that it does not appear to differ materially from the Kâtyâyana Sûtra edited by Dr. Weber.

Tanjore, Nov. 1871

A LEGEND OF SERPENT WORSHIP.

From BHAUNAGAR IN KÂTHIÂWÂD.

There was once a king who had seven wives, of whom six were favoured but one was disliked by him. No member of her father's family being alive, she was obliged to take such food as was given her by her mother-in-law and *derâni jethâni*.* This poor creature was content to take the refuse of the food left by the other members of the family. One day when all the others cooked and ate *khir* (rice boiled in milk) she longed to have some of it, but alas! whence could she hope to obtain it? She took all the cooking pots, which were given her to wash, to the river, and scraping out what adhered to their sides, she collected it all into one pot and then went to bathe. Meanwhile a *Nâgan* (female snake) coming out of its *rafâfâl* (or

* The younger brother's wife is so called [illegible] an elder brother's wife,—who, in turn, is so called in the former.

burrow) close by the river, ate up all that was in the pot, and entering her hole sat there resolved to bite the woman if she should curse her, but not otherwise. The woman returned to the spot, and finding the pot empty exclaimed "May the stomach of the eater be cooled!" Hearing these words the *Nágun* coming out of her hole said "Well done! I now regard you as my daughter, and as you are pregnant at present, go and inform the members of your family to perform the *Shrímanas* (pregnancy) ceremonies, and tell them that the *mobo-ádá** and *pháshawant*† presents will be sent from your parents' house. The *kankotari* (the letter inviting the guests to the festive meeting) you should tie to this *A'kash* tree near the *sifasla*." Hearing these words she returned and spoke as she had been told, asking the members of the family to write *kankotaris* to her brothers that she might send them to them. At these words they were all surprised and began to laugh at her; but at length they wrote a *kankotari* and gave it to her. This she took and tied to the *A'kash* tree. Next day the young of the *Nágun* assuming human form, came to the village attended with music. An escort from the king went out to receive them; and they gave large *presentments* to their adopted sister, and to other members of her father-in-law's family; while their sister had previously arranged to have two earthen pots (*kalsias*) filled with milk and placed in a room for them to drink. Next day they took their sister home with them to be confined. When she reached the burrow the snake who was sitting outside took her in. At first she was much afraid, but when she found that there were large drawing-rooms and halls inside, she was delighted. There she gave birth to her child and was well treated during the month-and-half. Afterwards the time for the *Nágun* to bear young arrived, and the lady was told to hold a lamp beside her. This she did, but was rather frightened, so that her hand shook a little, and the consequence was that the *Nágun* as usual devoured her offspring except two which were left half eaten, whence they were called *Khándia* and *Bándia*. The *Nágas* after this gave the queen presents of gold toys, and many other things to carry to her home, and said to her, "here is your father sitting, put your hand into his mouth"; she was petrified with fear, but at length thrust her left and half her right arm into his mouth, when both her arms were covered with gold *chudá* (bangles). Now *Khándia* and *Bándia* asked their mother to bite her who called them by such names, but they were refused. The queen then returned to her father-in-law's house, where she was greatly honoured because of her wealth. One day, however, her mother-in-law, seeing her send for milk from the bazar for her baby, said tauntingly—"Why don't you get cows from your parent's house." Hearing this she went to the *A'kash*-tree and began to cry. She was heard by the *Nágun* who came out and asked her what was the matter with her that she wept. She related what had been stated, and the *Nágun* said "go home and get a large yard made and it shall be filled with cows and buffaloes." This excited the envy of the snake brothers *Khándia* and *Bándia*, and they resolved to lie in wait, the one in the *paniara* (where the water-vessels stand) and the other in the kitchen, that they might bite her as she passed. Now it happened as she went to fill a *kalsiya* with water that she struck her foot against the door step, when she exclaimed "may my *Khándia* and *Bándia* be safe and sound!—they who are brothers to her who has no brothers." She again repeated the same words in the kitchen. At this the brothers were greatly pleased with her, and next day they gave her many presents and took their way home, and the queen passed the rest of her life in happiness and enjoyment.

J. B.

MANNERS AND CUSTOMS OF THE DARDS.

[*Being part of Dr. Leitner's forthcoming work—Part III. of "Dardistan."*]

(a.)—AMUSEMENTS.

THE Changhan Bazi, or Hockey-on-horseback, so popular everywhere north of Kashmir, and which is called Polo by the Baltis and Ladakis, who both play it to perfection and in a manner which I shall describe elsewhere, is also well known to the Ghilgiti and Astori sub-divisions of the Shina people. On great general holydays as well as on any special occasion of rejoicing, the people meet on these grounds, which are usually near the larger villages, and pursue

* Presents from the wife's father for her child.

† From the wife's father to her husband and his family.

the game with great excitement and at the risk of casualties. The first day I was at Astor, I had the greatest difficulty in restoring to his senses a youth of the name of Rustom Ali who, like a famous player of the same name at Mardo, was passionately fond of the game, and had been thrown from his horse. The place of meeting near Astor is called the 'Idgah. The game is called Tora in Astor, and the grounds for playing it are called Shajaran. At Ghilgit the game is called Bulla, and the place Shawaran. The latter names are evidently of Tibetan origin.

The people are also very fond of target practice, shooting with bows, which they use dexterously, but in which they do not excel the people of Nagyr and Hunza. Game is much stalked during the winter. At Astor any game shot on the three principal hills—*Tabhoni*, a high hill opposite the fort, *Dashkin* and *Talibahal*—belongs to the Nawab of Astor (the sportsman receiving only the head, legs and a haunch) or to his representative, now the Tahsildar Munshi Rum Khan. At Ghilgit everybody claims what he may have shot, but it is customary for the Nawab to receive some share of it. Men are especially appointed to watch and track game, and when they discover their whereabouts notice is sent to the villages from which parties issue, accompanied by musicians, and surround the game. Early in the morning, when the "Lobo" dance, the musicians begin to play and a great noise is made, which frightens the game into the several directions where the sportsmen are placed.

The guns are matchlocks and are called in Ghilgit *turmul* and in Astor *tumak*. At Ghilgit they manufacture the guns themselves or receive them from Badakhshan. The balls have only a slight coating of lead, the inside generally being a little stone. The people of Hunza and Nagyr invariably place their guns on little wooden pegs, which are permanently fixed to the gun and are called *dugaza*. The guns are much lighter than those manufactured elsewhere, much shorter, and carry much smaller bullets than the matchlock of the Mahârâja's troops. They carry very much farther than any native Indian gun, and are fired with almost unerring accuracy. For "small shot" little stones of any shape —the longest and oval ones being preferred—are used. There is one kind of stone especially which is much used for that purpose; it is called "Balish Batt," which is found in Hunza, Nagyr, Skardo, and near the *Demâlahha* hill already noticed, at a village called Paradingbl near Astor. It is a very soft stone, and large cooking utensils are cut out from it, whence the name, "balish" kettle, "batt" stone,—"Balish Batt." The stone is cut out with a chisel and hammer; the former is called "[illegible]" in Astori and "[illegible]" in Ghilgiti; the hammer "[illegible]" and "[illegible]," and in Ghilgiti "[illegible]." The gunpowder is manufactured by the people themselves.*

The people also play at backgammon, [called in Astori *Patshis*, and *Takh* in Ghilgiti,] with dice [called in Astori and also in Ghilgiti *dall*.]

Fighting with iron wristbands is confined to the Chilasi women, who bring them over their fists, which they are said to use with effect.

The people are also fond of wrestling, of butting each other whilst hopping &c.*

To play the Jew's-harp is considered unbecoming, as King David played it. All other sound-good Mussulmans are told to avoid.

The "Sitara" [the Eastern Guitar] is said to be much played in Yasen, the people of which country, as well as of Hunza and Nagyr excel in dancing, singing and playing. After them come the Ghilgitis, then the Astoris, Chilasis &c., &c. The people of Nagyr are a comparatively mild race. They carry on gold-washing, which is constantly interrupted by kidnapping parties from the opposite Hunza. The language of Nagyr and Yasen is the Non-Aryan Khajuna, and no affinity between that language and any other has yet been traced. The Nagyris are mostly Shiahs. They are short and stout, and fairer than the people of Hunza (the Kunjutis) who are described as "tall skeletons," and are desperate soldiers. The Nagyris understand Tibetan, Persian and Hindustani. Badakhshan merchants are the only ones who can travel with perfect safety through Yasen, Chitral and Hunza.

Dances fall into two main Divisions: slow or "Bâti Harip"—Slow Instrument, and quick "Damal Harip," = Quick Instrument. The

* "Powder" is called *[illegible]* in Astori, and in Ghilgiti *[illegible]*, which is, in [illegible] [illegible], also the word used for [illegible] powder. It is made of sulphur, saltpetre and coal. Sulphur = [illegible] = [illegible] in Astori, and [illegible] in Ghilgiti. Coal = [illegible]. The general proportion of the composition is, as my informant put it, after dividing the whole into six and a half parts to give 5 of saltpetre, 1 of coal, and ½ of sulphur. Some [illegible] [illegible] [illegible] it is generally believed that more than the [illegible] proportion of sulphur would make the powder too explosive.

Yassen, Nagyr and Hunza people dance quickest; then come the Ghilgitis; then the Astoris; then the Balais, and slowest of all are the Ladakis.

When all join in the dance, cheer or sing with gesticulations, the dance or recitative is called "thajeatt" in Ghilgiti, and "lurrō" in Astori.

When there is a solo dance it is called "nātt" in Ghilgiti, and "nots" in Astori. Cheering is called "halamush" in Ghilgiti, and "halamdah" in Astori. Clapping of hands is called "tas." Cries of "Yā, Yā dea; tas thoē, Hiā Hiā Jea; Halamdah thoē; shabāsh" accompany the performance.

There are several kinds of Dances. The *Prusulld nats* is danced by ten or twelve people ranging themselves behind the bride as soon as she reaches the bridegroom's house. This custom is observed at Astor. In this dance men swing about sticks, or whatever they may happen to hold in their hands.

The *Bard natt* is a dance performed on the Nao holyday, in which both men and women engage—the women forming a ring round the central group of dancers, which is composed of men. This dance is called *Toppuatunn* Ghilgit. In Daryl there is a dance in which the dancers wield swords and engage in a mimic fight. This dance the Ghilgitis and Astoris call the *Darold nats*, but what it is called by the Darylis themselves I do not know.

The mantle dance is called *Gojo nat*. In this popular dance the dancer throws his cloth over his extended arm.

When I sent a man round with a drum inviting all the Dards that were to be found at Ghilgit to a *festival*, a large number of men appeared, much to the surprise of the invading Dogras, who thought that they had run to the hills. A few sheep were roasted for their benefit; bread and fruit were also given them, and when I thought they were getting into good humour, I proposed that they should sing. Musicians had been procured with great difficulty, and after some demur, the Ghilgitis sang and danced. At first, only one at a time danced, taking his sleeve well over his arm so as to let it fall over, and then moving it up and down according to the cadence of the music. The movements were, at first, slow, one hand hanging down, the other being extended with a commanding gesture. The left foot appeared to be principally engaged in moving or rather jerking the body forward. All sorts of *pas seuls* were danced; sometimes a rude imitation of the Indian Nāchh; the bystanders clapping their hands and crying out "Shabāsh;" one man, a sort of Master of Ceremonies, used to run in and out amongst them, brandishing a stick, with which, in spite of his very violent gestures, he only lightly touched the bystanders, and exciting them to cheering by repeated calls, which the rest then took up of "Hiā, Hiā." The most extraordinary dance, however, was when about twelve men came to dance, of whom six went on one side and six on the other. Both sides then, moving forward, jerked out their arms so as to look as if they had all crossed swords, then receded and let their arms drop. This was a war dance, and I was told that properly it ought to have been danced with swords, which however, out of suspicion of the Dogras, did not seem to be forthcoming. They then formed a circle, again separated, the movements becoming more and more violent till almost all the bystanders joined in the dance, shouting like fiends and literally *kicking* up a frightful amount of dust, which, after I had nearly become choked with it, compelled me to retire.* I may also notice that before a song is sung the rythm and melody of it are given in "solo" by some one, for instance,—

Dand-dang dāng-dāngeh
nadang dung, &c., &c., &c.

(b.)—DEVKHAURS.

Beer.—Fine corn (about five or six seers in weight) is put into a kettle with water and boiled till it gets soft, but not pulpy. It is then strained through a cloth, and the grain retained and put into a vessel. Then it is mixed with a drug that comes from Ladak which is called "Papps," and has a salty taste, but in my opinion is nothing more than hardened dough with which some kind of drug is mixed. It is necessary that "the marks of four fingers" be impressed upon the "Papps." The mark of "four fingers" make one stick, 'two fingers' mark half a stick, and so forth. This is scraped and mixed with the corn. The whole is then put into an earthen jar with a narrow neck, after it has received an infusion of an amount of water equal to the proportion of corn. The jar is put out into the sun—if summer—for twelve days, or under the fireplace if in winter—

* The drawing and description of this scene were given in the *Illustrated London News* of the [illegible] February [illegible], under the heading of "A Dance at Ghilgit."

(where a separate vault is made for it) for the same period. The orifice is almost hermetically closed with a skin. After twelve days the jar is opened and contains a drink possessing intoxicating qualities. The first infusion is much prized, but the corn receives a second and sometimes even a third supply of water, to be put out again in a similar manner and to provide a kind of Beer for the consumer. This Beer is called "Mō," and is much drunk by the Astoris and Chilasis—(the latter are rather stricter Mussulmans than the other Shina people.) After all strength has been taken out of the corn it is given away as food to sheep, &c., which they find exceedingly nourishing.

*Wine.**—The Ghilgitis are great wine-drinkers, though not so much so as the people of Hunza. In Nagyr little wine is made. The mode of preparation of the wine is a simple one. The grapes are stamped out by a man who, fortunately before entering into the wine press, washes his feet and hands. The juice flows into another reservoir, which is first well laid round with stones, over which a cement is put of chalk mixed with sheep-fat which is previously heated. The juice is kept in this reservoir; the top is closed, cement being put round the edges, and only in the middle an opening is made over which a loose stone is placed. After two or three months the reservoir is opened, and the wine is used at meals and festivals. In Gurēyz (and not in Ghilgit, as was told to Vigne,) the custom is to sit round the grave of the deceased and eat grapes, nuts, and Tshilgōzas (edible pine). In Astor (and in Chilas?) the custom is to put a number of Ghi (clarified butter) cakes before the Mulla, (when the earth has been put on the deceased) who, after reading prayers over them, distributes them to the company who are standing round with their caps on. In Ghilgit, three days after the burial, bread is generally distributed to the friends and acquaintances of the deceased. To return to the wine presses, it is to be noticed that no one ever interferes with the store of another. I passed several of them on my road from Chakerkot onward, but they appeared to have been destroyed. This brings me to another custom which all the Dards seem to have of burying provisions of every kind in cellars that are scooped out in the mountains or near their houses, and of which they alone have any knowledge. The Maharaja's troops when invading Ghilgit often suffered severely from want of food, when, unknown to them, large stores of grain of every kind,—butter, ghi, &c., were buried close to them. The Ghilgitis and other so-called rebels, generally, were well off, knowing where to go for food. Even in subject Astor, it is the custom to lay up provisions in this manner. On the day of birth of any one in that country, it is the custom to bury a stock of provisions, which are opened on the day of betrothal of the young man and distributed. The ghi, which by that time turns frightfully sour and (to our taste) unpalatable, and the colour of which is red, is esteemed a great delicacy, and is said to bring much luck.

The skin used for containing the wine is called "Mau kuli." Grapes are called "dachh," and are said, together with wine, to have been the principal food of Ghazanfar, the Raja of Hunza, of whom it is reported that when he heard of the arrival of the first European in Astor (probably Vigne) he fled to a fort called Gojal and shut himself up in it with his flocks, family and retainers. He had been told that the European was a great sorcerer, who carried an army with him in his trunks, and who had magicians at his command that stretched themselves over any river on his way to afford him a passage. I found this reputation of European sorcery of great use, and the wild mountaineers looked with respect and awe on a little box which I carried with me, and which contained some pictures of clowns and soldiers belonging to a small magic lantern. The Ghilgitis consider the use of wine as unlawful; probably it is not very long since they have become so religious and drink it with remorse. My Ghilgiti told me that the Maulai—a sect living in Hunza, Gojal, Yassin and Punyal—considered the use of wine with prayers to be rather meritorious than otherwise. A drunkard is called "Mato."

(c)—BIRTH CEREMONIES.

As soon as a child is born, the father or the Mulla repeats the "bāng" in his ear "Allah Akbar" (which an Astori, of the name of Mirza Khan, said was never again repeated in one's life!). Three days after the reading of the "bāng" or "namāz" in Ghilgit, and seven days after that ceremony in Astor, a large company assembles, when the father or grand-father of the newborn child gives him a name, or the Mulla fixes on a name by putting his

* Wine is called in Ghilgit by the same name as beer is by the Astoris, viz "Mo". The wine press is called "Mō Kurr." The reservoir into which it flows is called "Mōs Bas."

hand on some word in the Koran which may serve the purpose, or by getting somebody else to fix his hand at random on a passage or word in the Koran. Men and women assemble at that meeting. There appears to be no *purdah* whatsoever in Dardu land, and the women are remarkably chaste. The little imitation of *purdah* amongst the Ranis of Ghilgit was a mere fashion imported from elsewhere. Till the child receives a name the woman is declared impure for the seven days previous to the ceremony. In Ghilgit twenty-seven days are allowed to elapse till the woman is declared pure. Then the bed and clothes are washed and the woman is restored to the company of her husband and the visits of her friends.

Men and women eat together everywhere in Dardu land. In Astor, cow milk alone cannot be drunk together with a woman, unless thereby it is intended that she should be a sister by faith, and come within the prohibited degrees of relationship. When men drink of the same raw milk they thereby swear each other eternal friendship. In Ghilgit this custom does not exist, but it will at once be perceived that much of what has been noted above belongs to Mussulman custom generally. When a son is born great rejoicings take place, and in Ghilgit a musket is fired off by the father whilst the "bang" is being read.

(V.)—MARRIAGE.

In Ghilgit marriage appears to be a more simple ceremony than in Chilas and Astor. The father of the boy goes to the father of the girl and presents him with a knife about 1½ foot long, 4 yards of cloth, and a pumpkin filled with wine. If the father accepts the present the betrothal is arranged. It is generally the fashion that after the betrothal, which is named *Shile gutu wigr. baili piyu*, i.e., "4 yards of cloth and a knife he has given, the pumpkin he has drunk," the marriage takes place. A betrothal is inviolable, and is only dissolved by death as far as the woman is concerned. The young man is at liberty to dissolve the contract. When the marriage day arrives, the men and women who are acquainted with the parties range themselves in rows at the house of the bride, the bridegroom, with her at his left, sitting together at the end of the row. The Mulla then reads the prayers, the ceremony is completed, and playing, dancing and drinking begin. It is considered the proper thing for the bridegroom's father, if he belongs to the same Shin race, to pay 12 tolas of gold of the value [at Ghilgit] of 13 Rupees Nanakshahi, (10 annas each), to the bride's father, who, however, generally returns it with the bride, in kind—dresses, ornaments, &c., &c. The 12 tolas are not always, or even generally taken in gold, but oftener in kind—clothes, provisions and ornaments. At Astor the ceremony seems to be a little more complicated. There the arrangements are managed by third parties,—an agent being appointed on either side. The father of the young man sends a present of a needle and three real (red) "mungo" called "lajum" in Chilasi, which, if accepted, establishes the betrothal of the parties. Then the father of the bride demands *pro forma* 12 tolas, which in Astor and Chilas are worth 24 Rupees of the value of ten annas each.

All real Shin people must pay this dowry for their wives in money, provisions, or in the clothes which the bride's father may require. The marriage takes place when the girl reaches puberty, or perhaps rather the age when she is considered fit to be married. It may be mentioned here in general terms that those features in the ceremony which remind one of Indian customs are undoubtedly of Indian origin, introduced into the country since the occupation of Astor by the Maharaja's troops. Ghilgit, which is further off, is less subject to such influences, and whatever it may have of civilization is indigenous, or more so than is the case at Astor, the roughness of whose manners is truly Chilasi, whilst its apparent refinement in some things is a foreign importation. When the marriage ceremony commences the young man, accompanied by twelve of his friends and by musicians, sits in front of the girl's house. The mother of the girl brings out bread and ghi-cakes on plates, which she places before the bridegroom, round whom she goes three times caressing him and finally kissing his hand. The bridegroom then sends her back with a present of a few rupees or tolas in the emptied plates. Then, after some time, as the evening draws on, the agent of the father of the boy sends to say that it is time that the ceremony should commence. The mother of the bride then stands in the door-way of her house with a few other platefuls of cakes and bread, and the young man accompanied by his bridesman ("Shunér" in Astori and "Shamaderr" in Ghilgiti,) enters the house. At his approach the girl, who also has her particular friend, the "Shanerey" in Astori, and "Shamaderey" in Ghilgiti, rises. The boy is seated at her right, but both in Astor and in Ghilgit, it is considered indecent for the boy to turn round and look at her. Then a particular friend, the "Dharm-bhai"* of the girl's brother asks her if she consents to the marriage. In receiving or imagining an affirmative he turns round to the Mulla, who, after asking three times whether he, she, and the bridegroom, as well as all present are satisfied, reads the prayers and completes the ceremonial. Then some rice boiled in milk is brought in, of which the boy and the girl take a spoonful. They do not retire the first night, but grace the company with their presence. The people assembled then amuse themselves by hearing the musicians, eating, &c., &c.

It appears to be the custom that a person leaves an entertainment whenever he likes, which is generally the case after he has eaten enough.

It must not, however, be imagined that the sexes are secluded from each other in Dardistan. Young people have continual opportunities of meeting each other in the fields, at their work, or at festive gatherings. Love declarations often take place on these occasions, but if any evil intention is perceived the seducer of a girl is punished by this [illegible] with death. The Dards know and speak of the existence of "pure love," "[illegible]." Their love songs show sufficiently that they are capable of a deeper, than mere sensual feeling. No objection to lawful love terminating in matrimony is ever made, unless the girl or the boy is of a lower caste. In Ghilgit, however, the girl may be of a lower caste than the bridegroom. In Astor it appears that a young man, whose parents—to whom he must mention his desire for marrying any particular person—refuse to intercede, often attains his point by threatening to live in the family of the bride and become an adopted son. A Shin of true race at Astor may live in concubinage with a girl of lower caste, but the relatives of the girl, if they discover the intrigue, revenge the insult by murdering the paramour, who, however, does not lose caste by the alliance.

The bridegroom dances as well as his twelve companions. The girl ought not to be older than 15 years; but at twelve girls are generally engaged.†

The Balti custom of having merely a *claim to dowry* on the part of the woman—the prosecution of which claim so often depends on her satisfaction with her husband, or the rapacity of her relatives—in spite of the intercourse of the Baltis with the Shin people, is never observed by the latter—not even by the Shin colonists of little Tibet, who are called "Brokhpa."

When the bridegroom has to go for his bride to a distant village, he is furnished with a bow. On arriving at his native place, he crosses the breast of his bride with an arrow, and then shoots it off. He generally shoots three arrows off in the direction of his home.

At Astor the custom is sometimes to fire guns as a sign of rejoicing. This is not done at Ghilgit.

When the bridegroom on the second day fetches his bride to his own home, the girl is crying with the women of her household, and the young man catches hold of her dress in front (at Ghilgit by the hand) and leads her to the door. If the girl cannot get over embracing her people and crying with them quickly, the twelve men who have come along with the bridegroom (who in Astor are called *[illegible]*, bridegrooms, and [illegible] in Ghilgit) sing the following song:—

INVITATION TO THE BRIDE.

[illegible] [illegible] ("[illegible]" is added to the [illegible]).
Come out, [illegible] daughter.
[illegible] [illegible] [illegible] ("[illegible]," in Ghilgit).
Come out, why delayest thou?
[illegible] [illegible] [illegible].
Come out from thy father's land.
[illegible] [illegible] [illegible].
Come out, why [illegible] thou.
[illegible] [illegible] [illegible].
Do not weep! [illegible]'s [illegible].
[illegible] [illegible] [illegible].
Do not weep! thy [illegible] will go.
[illegible] [illegible] [illegible].
Do not weep! brother's beloved.
[illegible] [illegible] [illegible].
Do not weep! thy [illegible] will go.
[illegible] [illegible] [illegible].
Do not weep! father's beloved.
[illegible] [illegible] [illegible].
Do not weep! thy [illegible] will go.

TRANSLATION.

Come out, O daughter of the [illegible],
Come out, why dost thou delay?
Come forth from thy father's land.

* The "brother in the faith" with whom vows [illegible] has been drunk, [illegible]

[illegible]	= [illegible]	[illegible] in Ghilgit; [illegible] Astori
[illegible]	[illegible]	[illegible] Astori
[illegible]	= [illegible]	
Bridegroom's [illegible]	= [illegible]	[illegible] Astori
Marriage ([illegible])	= [illegible]	[illegible] Astori
Dowry	= "[illegible],"	[illegible] and Astori

[illegible] "[illegible]"

Husband	= [illegible]	[illegible] Astori
Wife	= [illegible]	[illegible] Astori

[illegible] in Ghilgit, "[illegible]" in Astori ([illegible] "[illegible]" is [illegible], "[illegible]" [illegible] — [illegible].]

† The Turks say "a girl of 15 years of age should be either married or buried."

Come out and do not delay.
Weep not! O fairy of the waterfall!
Weep not! thy colour will fade:
Weep not; thou art the beloved of us all who are thy brethren,
Weep not! thy colour will fade
Oh weep not! thou beloved of fathers, [or "thy father's darling"]
For if thou weepest, thy face will grow pale.

Then the young man catches hold of her dress, or in Ghilgit of her arm, puts her on horseback, and rides off with her, heedless of her tears and of those of her companions.

(e)—FUNERALS.

Funerals are conducted in a very simple manner. The custom of eating grapes at funerals I have already touched upon in my allusion to Daroyl in the chapter on "Wine." Three days after the funeral, bread is commonly distributed together with ghi, &c., to people in general, which is called "Nashi" by the Astoris, and "Khatm" by the Ghilgitis. When a person is dead, the Mulla, assisted generally by a near friend of the deceased, washes the body which is then placed in a shroud. Women assemble, weep, and relate the virtues of the deceased. The body is conveyed to the grave the very day of the decease. In Astor there is something in the shape of a bier for conveying the dead. At Ghilgit two poles, across which little bits of wood are placed sideways and then fastened, serve the same purpose. The persons who carry the body think it a meritorious act. The women accompany the body for some fifty yards and then return to the house to weep. The body is then placed in the earth, which has been dug up to admit of its interment. Sometimes the grave is a pucka one, and a kind of small vault is made over it with pieces of wood closely jammed together. A Pir or saint receives a hewn stone, standing as a sign-post from the tomb. I have seen no inscriptions anywhere. I do not believe there are any in the whole of Dardistan proper. The tomb of one of their famous saints at Ghilgit has none. I have heard people there say that he was killed at that place in order to provide the country with a shrine. My Ghilgiti, who, like all his countrymen, was very patriotic, denied it, but I heard it at Ghilgit from several persons, among whom was one of the descendants of the saint. As the saint was a Kashmiri, the veracity of his descendant may, however, justly be doubted. To return to the funeral. The body is conveyed to the cemetery, which is generally at some distance from the village, accompanied by friends. When they reach the spot the Mulla reads the prayers standing—as in the 'Jenaza'—any genuflexion, 'ruku,' and prostration are of course, inadmissible. After the body has been interred the Mulla recites the Fatiha, or opening prayer of the Koran, all the people standing up and holding out their hands as if they were reading a book. The Mulla prays that the deceased may be preserved from the fire of hell as he was a good man, &c. Then after a short benediction the people separate. For three days at Ghilgit, and seven days at Astor, the near relatives of the deceased do not eat meat. After that period the grave is again visited by the deceased's friends, who, on reaching the grave, eat some ghi and bread, offer up prayers, and, on returning, slaughter a sheep, whose kidney is roasted and divided into small bits amongst those present. Bread is distributed amongst those present, and a little feast is indulged in, in memory of the deceased. I doubt, however, whether the Ghilgitis are very exact in their religious exercises. The mention of death was always received with shouts of laughter by them, and one of them told me that a dead person deserved only to be kicked. He possibly only joked, and there can be little doubt that the Ghilgit people are not very communicative about their better feelings. It would be ridiculous however, to deny them the possession of natural feelings, although I certainly believe that they are not overburdened with them. In Astor the influence of Kashmir has made the people attend a little more to the ceremonies of the Musulman religion.

In Chilás rigour is observed in the maintenance of religious practices, but elsewhere there exists the greatest laxity. In fact, so rude are the people, that they have no written character of their own, and till very recently the art of writing (Persian) was confined to, perhaps, the Rajas of these countries, or rather to their Munshis, when they had any. Some of them may be able to read the Koran. Even this I doubt, as of hundreds of people, I saw at Ghilgit only one who could read, and he was a Kashmiri who had travelled far and wide, and had at last settled in that country. Grave-inscriptions, or indeed inscriptions of any kind, I did not see in the country, and the report that they kill saints in order to have shrines where to worship, has been repeated to me so often, and from so many different quarters as almost to deserve credence.

(f.) HOLIDAYS.

The great holiday of the Shin people happened, in 1867, during the month succeeding the

Ramazan, but seems to be generally on the sixth of February. It is called the "Shino nao," "the new day of the Shin people." The Gilgitis call the day "Shino basdus," the spring of the Shin people. The year, it will be remembered, is divided into basunn, spring; walo, summer; shero, autumn; yono, winter. The snow is now becoming a little softer, and out-of-door life is more possible. The festivities are kept up for twelve days. Visits take place, and men and wife are invited out to dinner during that period. Formerly when the Shins had a Raja or Nawáb of their own it used to be the custom for women to dance during these twelve days. Now the advent of the sipahis, and the ridiculous pseudo-morality of the Kashmiris who have introduced a kind of *purdah*, and the Kashmiri Shin women do not like to expose themselves to strangers. Then there is the Nosalo which is celebrated for three, and sometimes for six days.

There are five great holidays in the year:

The 'Id of Ramazan.
The Shin-i-Nao.
The Nosalo.
Kurbani 'Id.
The Baly Bás,* Asauj. }
Dawaiká Chilkis. }

On the last-named holiday the game of Polo is played, good clothes are put on, and men and women amuse themselves in public meetings.

The Shin people are very patriotic. Since the Maharaja's rule, many of their old customs have died out, and the separation of the sexes is becoming greater.

* Is celebrated in Autumn when the fruit and corn are brought in.

A TÁMRA PATRA OR ANCIENT COPPER-PLATE GRANT FROM KATHIAWAD

TRANSLATED BY RAMKRISHNA GOPAL BHANDARKAR, M.A.

WELFARE! From Valabhi. From Bhatárka the great *Máheśvara*† who obtained greatness by a hundred wounds received in the midst of a circle of friends of matchless might, who, with main force, had subjugated their enemies,—who won the attachment [of kings] by his gifts, respectful treatment and upright conduct,—the result of that greatness—who, by the power of the kings so attached to him, obtained sovereignty, and whose royal race is unbroken,—sprang *Śrí*‡ *Guhasena* the great *Máheśvara*,—who had all his sins washed away by bowing at the lotus-like feet of his mother and father,—who, sword in hand, from his childhood manifested great prowess, by breaking the ranks of the maddened elephants of his enemy,—the rays of the nails of whose feet were mixed with the light of the crown jewels of the enemies laid prostrate [at his feet] by his valour,—who delighted the hearts of his subjects by excellently protecting them, thoroughly, according to the method prescribed in the *Smritis*‖ and thus rendered his title of *Rája* literally true,—who in beauty, lustre, firmness, depth, genius and wealth, excelled *Káma*,§ the moon, the King of mountains,¶ the ocean, the preceptor of the Gods,** and the Lord of wealth,††—who sacrificed his own interests as if they were as worthless as straw, by his readiness to extend protection from danger to those who sought an asylum with him,—and, who delighted the hearts of learned men, friends and favourites, by giving them more wealth than was asked, and who was the very incarnate [moving on legs] delight of the whole extent of the world. His son was *Śrí Dharasena* the great *Máheśvara* whose stains of sin were wholly washed away by the water of the *Gangá** in the shape of the rays from the nails of his father's feet,—whose wealth was fed on by hundreds of thousands of favourites,—who was resorted to as it were, out of love for his beauty, by many acquired virtues,—who astonished all archers by his innate power and acquired skill,—who continued the charitable grants made by former kings,—who averted the evils destructive to his subjects,—who showed himself to be the common abode of *Śrí*† and *Sarasvatí*,‡—whose exploits placed him in the enjoyment of the wealth and power of his united enemies, and who, by his exploits, obtained unsullied royal dignity. His son was *Śíláditya*, the great *Máheśvara*, who meditated on his father's feet,—who filled the circle of all the quarters by extraordinary virtues which were united in him, and

† Devotee of Maheśvara or Shiva. The Valabhi kings probably belonged to the Máheśvara Sect.

‡ This is an honorific, prefixed to the names of kings.

‖ Law-books. § The God of Love. ¶ Himálaya.

** Brihaspati. †† Kubera.

* The water of the Ganges is white, according to Hindu poets, and rays of light are also white; hence the resemblance.

† The Goddess of wealth.

‡ Goddess of learning. These two are supposed always to live apart.

which delighted the whole world,—the burden of whose great desires was borne successfully by his shoulders, which were brighter than those of others, in consequence of his conspicuousness amongst the allies, who had obtained distinction by winning a hundred battles,—whom it was always very easy to please by writing sane epigrams, though his own mind was purified by the study of all sciences, in all their branches,—who, though transcending all people in the unfathomable depth [of his heart], was of a very benevolent disposition, as shown by his good deeds,—who obtained great fame by clearing the obstructed path trodden on by kings of the *Krita** age,—whose enjoyment of the sweets of affluence was refined by his adherence to justice, and thus procured for him his other name of *Dharmâditya*.† His younger brother was *Shrî Kharagraha*, the great *Maheshvara*, who meditated on his (brother's) feet, who bore the sovereign power though it was an object of desire to the loving elder one, who was like the elder one of Upendra,‡ as a bullock (bearer of the yoke) bears on his shoulders something that is great, simply on account of the pleasure he took in executing his (brother's) commands, and while doing so he did not allow his virtue to be diminished, either by love of pleasure or vexation, whose mind,—though his foot-stool was enveloped in the lustre of the crown jewels of the hundred kings subjugated by his prowess—was not affected by arrogance, or a fondness to treat others with indignity,—to counteract whom (whose power), cutting aside submission, there was no way even for enemies reputed for manliness and pride,—who by a number of pure virtues which perfumed the whole world, resisted with main force the progress of the sport of Kali,‖—whose heart was noble and untouched by all the faults which little men are prone to,—and who obtained the first place amongst men of valour by the royal Lakshmî,§ of a host of inimical kings voluntarily embracing him, on account of his well-known valour and skill in the management of weapons.

His son who meditated on his feet was *Shrî Dharasena*, the great *Maheshvara*,—who gave exceedingly great delight to the hearts of learned men by the acquisition of all the sciences,—who in his stock of virtue and liberality in giving away, found a device, by which was effected the defeat of the desires of his enemies, who, though his thoughts were deep (in his breast), in consequence of his having been thoroughly acquainted with various sciences, arts, and with the ways of the world, was of a very benevolent disposition,—whose unaffected humility and chastened manners, were his ornaments,—who destroyed the pride of all enemies by his powerful and massive arm, which carried the flag of victory in a hundred battles,—and whose commands were obeyed by the whole circle of kings, whose skill in the management of weapons he had defeated by the might of his bow. His younger brother who meditated on his feet was the great *Maheshvara Dhruvasena*, who surpassed all previous kings by his good deeds,—who accomplished things that were very difficult to accomplish,—who was valour itself in a human form,—who was respected as if he were Manu himself by his subjects, with hearts full of love for his great virtues,—who was the very lord of lotuses‖ without the spots, full-moon,* shining, and the cause of joy to others,—who was the ever shining sun, the dispeller of darkness by filling all quarters with the bright lustre [of his great prowess] —who, inspiring confidence† in his subjects, as to the acquisition of wealth, the furtherance of a great many purposes, and the increase of prosperity [*Gram.* prescribing the addition to bases of a termination with a certain sense, having letters indicatory of a great many changes, and with the augment added on to it]; proficient in determining matters about peace,‡ war, and alliance [*Gram.* well-versed in *Sandhi* or phonetic rules—dissolution of compounds and compounds], issuing‖ commands proper for the occasion [*Gram.* prescribing a substitute for the original]; and doing§ honour to the good by raising

* The kings of the Krita or the first age of Hindu Mythology were very virtuous; and their ways and manners were forgotten. Shîlâditya trod in their first steps.

† Literally—'the Sun of justice or virtue.'

‡ Upendra is a name of Vishnu; and the allusion here is probably to Krishna, in whose favour Balarâma, his elder brother, or *pûrva*,—the word in the original,—resigned the kingdom.

‖ The principle of evil. Kali is supposed to have full swing in the present age, which is called Kali-yuga.

§ The triumph of a lover consists in his mistress giving him a voluntary embrace. The royal power and state of Kharagraha's enemies are personified as Lakshmî, who is attracted by his valour.

‖ i.e. The moon.

* There is a play here on the word, Kalâ which means 'a digit of the moon' and 'an art.' The moon had all her digits i.e. was full, and the king was versed in all the arts.

† There is a play here on the words prakriti, pratyaya, anubandha, âgama and vidadhâna, which are technical terms used by Pâṇini. The grammatical meaning is enclosed within brackets in the text.

‡ Here the words Samâsa, Vigraha and Sandhi are used in a double sense.

‖ Sthâna and âdeśa are the words here.

§ Here the words with a double meaning are Samâhâra, Sâdhu, Guṇa, Vriddhi, and Vidhâna.

them from a subordinate position [Guna, giving correct forms to words by prescribing *Guna* and *Vriddhi* changes] was thoroughly versed in the art of Government, and of the *Shâlâturiya*.* Though of great valour, he possessed a heart softened by compassion; though learned, he was not boastful,—though he was a lover, his passions were subdued; though his kindness was unchanging, he rejected those who were guilty. He rendered his well-known second name of Bâlâditya (morning sun) literally true, by the warm† love which he engendered in men at the time of his accession,‡ and which overspread the earth. His son is *Shrî Dhara*sena who bears on his forehead, a crescent of the moon, in the shape of the mark of scars produced by rubbing his head on the earth, when prostrating himself at his father's lotus-like feet—whose great learning is as pure as the pearl ornament put on his graceful ear in his childhood,—the lotus-like palm of whose hand is always washed by the water (poured in the making) of gifts,—whose joy is heightened by the levy of taxes‖ as light as the soft grasp of the hand of a maiden,—who, like the revealed science of archery,§ has dealt by means of his bow with all the aims in the world (takes aims),—whose commands are treated by the circle of subject kings as the jewels worn on the head,¶ who meditates on his grandfather's feet and who is the great *Mâheshvara*, the great lord, the king of kings, the great ruler, the universal sovereign. He, enjoying good health, commands all whom it may concern:—" Be it known to you, that for the increase of the religious merit of my mother and father, I have given in charity, by pouring water, a field of the area of 86 paces** at the southern extremity of *Sharkarâpadraka*, a district of *Kikkatapatra*, a village in *Kâlâpakapatha* in *Surashtra*, to the Brahman *Ajvaa*, son of the Brahman *Onkadhara*, residing in *Kikkatapatra*, formerly of *Sinhapura*, honoured among the Brahmans of *Sinhapura* knowing the four Vedas, of the *Bhâradvâja gotra*, and student of the *Chhandoga Veda*. The boundaries of the field are, to the east the well *Vrakatavâlika*,—to the south, the field *Vatiakaratthika*,—to the west, the field *Kutumbi-Vehala-Satkâ*,—to the north, the field of *Brahmana-shashti-bhara Satka*:—And also to the Brahman *Manka-Sedanta* son of the Brahman *Guhadhya* residing in the village of *Kikkatapatra*, formerly of *Sinhapura*, honoured among the *Brahmans* of *Sinhapura* knowing the four Vedas of the *Bhâradvâja gotra*, student of the *Chhandoga Veda*: a well of the area of sixteen paces, at the western extremity of *Kikk*... a village in *Kalap*...in *Surashtra*. The boundaries are:—To the east, the well *Chaura-vatika*,—to the south and west, the field *Kutumbi Chandra-Satka*, and to the north the field *Makk*... And also at the western extremity of the village of *Sharkarâpadraka* a district of *Kikkatapatra*, a field of the area of 28 paces, the boundaries of which are,..............and also a field measuring fourteen paces, the boundaries of which are.. and also six *pattalas*†† whose boundaries are: —to the east .... to the south .... to the west .... and to the north, at the boundary of the village of *Vapdanaka*, the field of *Vâpi*, of the extent of 182 paces. All these are granted, along with their appurtenances, and whatever is on them, together with the revenue in kind, or gold, and with whatever may be grown on them, except what may have been granted to Gods or Brahmans before. The whole is not to be meddled with by any officer of the king, and is to be enjoyed from son to grandson, and to last as long as the sun, the moon, the ocean, the earth, rivers and mountains endure. On this account no one shall obstruct any one, who, in virtue of this Brahman-gift, enjoys the land, ploughs it, or allows it to be ploughed, or assigns it over to another person. All future kings, whether of our race or others, should, bearing in mind that power is transitory, and humanity frail, and knowing the good fruits arising from the grant of land, recognise this our grant, and continue it. It is said this earth has been enjoyed by many kings, such as Sagara and others, each one obtains the fruit when he is in possession. The things given in charity by kings who were afraid of poverty, are like flowers which have been used. What good man will

* Pânini was a native of Shalâtura, in the country to the west of the Indus; and he is known by the name of Shâlâturiya or native of Shalâtura.

† There is a play on the word *anurâga* here, which means 'redness' as well as 'love.' The light of the morning sun is reddish.

‡ Udaya is the word here which means 'rise' as applied to the sun or the king.

‖ A pun on the word Kara which means a 'tax' and the 'hand'.

§ The Dhanurveda as translated here, teaches how to take all sorts of aims; and the king had actually taken all aims, hence the comparison.

¶ i. e. worn, reverentially obeyed.

** The word in the original is pâdâvarta, which appears to have been a square measure.

†† Probably a certain square measure.

resume them? The grantor of land dwells in Heaven for sixty thousand years, and he who takes it away or allows it to be taken away lives in hell for as many years. The prince *Dhruvasena* is minister (executive officer) here. Engraved by *Divirapati Skanda-bhaṭa* the son of *Divirapati Vatsa* [?] *bhaṭa*, minister for peace and war. 326* In the bright half of Ashâḍha. My own hand [sign manual].

REMARKS.

Three copperplates of the Valabhi Dynasty have been hitherto deciphered and translated. Two of these were discovered by Mr Wathen, and the third by Dr. Burns of Kaira. Mr. Wathen's translation of one of the two and his remarks on the other are given in the fourth volume of the Bengal Asiatic Society's Journal. One leaf of the latter was afterwards deciphered and translated by the Rev. P. Anderson. The translation, a Devanâgarî transcript, and a lithographed copy are given in the third volume of the Bombay Asiatic Society's Journal. A transcript and translation of Dr. Burn's copperplate are to be found in the seventh volume of the Bengal Society's Journal. We shall distinguish these by the numbers 1, 2, and 3. No. 1 records a grant of land by Dharasena II, the great grandson of the founder of the dynasty and the seventh in Mr. Anderson's list; and Nos. 2 and 3 are said to be from Dhruvasena, the thirteenth in the list. The copperplates now translated were put into my hands by the Editor.† The grantor, in this case, is Dharasena IV., the twelfth in Mr Anderson's list and consequently the immediate predecessor of the king who is considered as the grantor in Nos. 2 and 3.

Dr. Bhau Dâjî gives, in one place, the dates of five copperplate grants of this dynasty,‡ while in another he mentions seven dates professedly derived from copperplates. But he does not say when or by whom so many grants of the Valabhi kings were discovered, nor who deciphered and translated them, or where the plates or their transcripts and translations are to be found. Mr. Thomas, as appears from his edition of Prinsep's Essays, knows only of the three I have mentioned.

The descriptions of the several kings in all these plates are given in the same words; so that, so far as they go, they may be considered to be copies of each other. There are a few *variæ lectiones* but some of these at least must be ascribed to the ignorance or carelessness of the engraver. The published transcript of No. 1 is generally correct; but those of the other two are full of mistakes, and it is difficult or impossible in a great many places to make out any sense. Any one well acquainted with Sanskrit may ascertain the truth of this for himself by comparing the several transcripts with that of the present one. Many instances of this might be given, but I shall confine myself here to one: The plays on certain grammatical terms, and Shâlâturîya, the name of Pâṇini, were not at all made out by previous decipherers; Guṇavṛiddhi was read by Mr. Anderson and the Calcutta scholar as Guṇabhividdhiḥ, and Shâlâturîya as Shâlâgurîyaḥ. But these mistakes are not in the original copperplates. Nos. 1 and 2 are preserved in the museum of the Bombay Asiatic Society and I have collated them (in original) with the present one. I did not find there the mistakes I speak of, and which are to be ascribed to the transcribers. The translations based upon such transcripts must, of course, be equally wrong.

The genealogy of the Valabhi kings as gathered from the present grant is as follows:—

From Bhaṭârka sprang
- Guhasena.
  - Dharasena II.
    - Shîlâditya I.
    - Kharagraha I.
      - Dharasena III.
      - Dhruvasena.
        - Dharasena IV.

This genealogy agrees in every respect, as far as it goes, with that in Nos 2 and 3. The exact relationship between Bhaṭârka and Guhasena is not given; but in No. 1 he is represented as his great grandson. No. 1 gives also the names of the several sons of Bhaṭârka who succeeded each other.

The name of the grandfather of Dharasena IV and brother of Shîlâditya I. is given as Ishvaragraha by the translators of Nos. 2 and 3. In the present plate it is clearly Kharagraha and I find it so even in No. 2. Mr. Wathen's reading of it was Charagraha which is nearer to the true name than Ishvaragraha.

From a passage in the description of Kharagraha, the younger brother of Shîlâditya, it appears that during the life time of the latter, the former held the reins of government. For he is there spoken of as having administered the affairs of the kingdom in obedience to the orders of his *guru* which word must, from the analogy of the *guru* of Upendra or Kṛishṇa mentioned there, as well as for other reasons, be taken to mean 'elder brother.' Mr. Anderson has entirely misunderstood this passage. The Calcutta translator gives the substance of it though the bearing of the analogy does not seem to have been clearly comprehended. There appears to have been a sort of usurpation here, for Shîlâditya's children were passed over and the

* Remarks on this reading of the date will be made in a future number.

† They were kindly lent me by Major J. W. Watson.—Ed.

‡ Jour. Bomb. B. R. Asiat. Soc. Vol. VIII. p. [illegible].

kingdom was governed by Kharagraha, and after him, by his lineal descendants. The line of Shiláditya was restored after the death of Dharasena IV., as is evident from Nos. 2 and 3.

According to the translators of these, the immediate successor of this king made the grants Nos. 2 and 3, and his name was Dhruvasena. There is here a double mistake. The grantor's name was evidently Shiláditya, as may be ascertained by comparing the passage in No. 2 with the corresponding one in the transcript of No. 3, and he was not the immediate successor of Dharasena IV. He was great grandson to Shiláditya I. as shown in the following genealogy gathered from the original of No. 2, now in the museum of the Bombay Asiatic Society :—

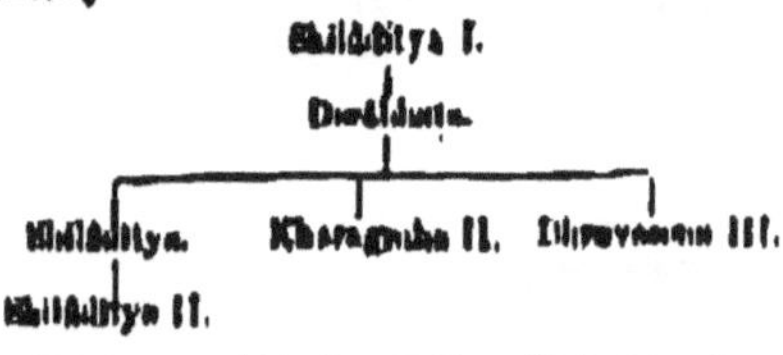

This last, marked—Shiláditya II. is the grantor in Nos. 2 and 3.

This genealogy differs from that given by all the writers on the Valabhi dynasty except Dr. Bhau Daji* who does not give his authorities; but if they are not the same as mine, the order of names given above receives confirmation from what may, for the present, be called an independent source.

In another list† given by the same writer,‡ I find another Shiláditya, placed below Shiláditya II. But here again I must complain of his silence as to his authorities.

It is not likely, though there is nothing impossible in it, that Derabhata, the son of Shiláditya, should have lived to succeed Dharasena IV, the grandson of his uncle. It appears to me that those only whose names in the plates are in the nominative case and have the epithet paramamáheśvara prefixed to them were reigning kings. The names of Derabhata, and Shiláditya, the father of Shiláditya II are in the genitive case in No. 2 and they are not styled paramamáheśvara. They do not seem, therefore, to have sat on the throne.

In a few places, in the latter part of the present copperplate, the letters are not distinct, so that I am not sure of the readings I have given of the names of the fields mentioned as boundaries of the pieces of land conveyed. But these names cannot be of any importance.

* Ibid. p. 713. † Jour. Bomb. B. R. Asiat. Soc. Vol VII. p. 116 ‡ Ibid. Vol VIII. p. 245.

ON THE INDENTIFICATION OF VARIOUS PLACES IN THE KINGDOM OF MAGADHA VISITED BY THE PILGRIM CHI-FAH-HIAN (A.D. 400-415.)

BY A. M. BROADLEY, C.S., ASSISTANT MAGISTRATE IN CHARGE OF SUBDIVISION BIHAR, IN PATNA.

PART, I.

The travels of Chi-Fah-Hian were first translated into French by MM. Remusat, Klaproth and Landresse. An English version of this work* was published by Mr. Laidlay in Calcutta in 1848. In 1869, the Rev. S. Beal published an original translation from the Chinese text.† Great doubts are entertained as to the correctness of portions of the French work, and M. Julien points out that it cannot be safely used by persons unable to verify the translation by comparison with the original. Under these circumstances I make reference only to the edition of Mr. Beal.

A constant residence of many months in the midst of the places visited by the pilgrim and consequently a very familiar acquaintance, not only with the ruined temples, topes and cities themselves, but with the geography of the surrounding country, must be my apology for publishing my notes, differing as they often do with former identifications of these spots. I maintain that no satisfactory identification can be made without a lengthened stay in the neighbourhood of the places in question, and a careful survey of the ruins themselves. No amount of antiquarian knowledge, however profound, can compensate for an imperfect or second-hand acquaintance with the places professed to be identified.

Throughout Fah-Hian's work, distances are computed by "lis" and "yojanas." Mr. Beal allows four or five "lis" to the mile, General Cunningham six, and their estimate is doubtless correct. As to the second measure Mr. Beal allows seven miles to a "yojana" in the North-West Provinces, and only four in Magadha. General Cunningham counts *uniformly* 7½ or 8 miles as equal to a "yojana". From a comparison of the distances given in Bihar, *the very centre of the kingdom of Magadha*, I do not see how more than five

* "The Pilgrimage of Fah-Hian; From the French edition of the Foe Koue Ki. By J. W. Laidlay, Esq. Calcutta: 1848.

† Travels of Fah-Hian and Sung-Yun Buddhist Pilgrims from China to India. By Samuel Beal, B.A., Chaplain in H. M. Fleet. London: 1869.

or six miles can, by any possibility be allowed, *e.g.* Bihár to Nálanda "one yojana" actual distance 5½ or 6 miles; Patna to Bihár 9 yojanas—actual distance about 54 miles; Nálanda to Rajgir one yojana, actual distance—5½ or 6 miles. For these reasons I consider a yojana as equivalent to a distance of between 5 and 6 miles.

I now proceed to follow the text of Mr. Beal page 110, chapter 28. "From this city [Patna] proceeding in a south-easterly direction nine yójanas, we arrive at a *small rocky hill standing by itself*, on the top of which is a stone cell facing the south. On one occasion, when Buddha was sitting in the middle of this cell, the divine Sekra took with him his attendant musicians, each one provided with a five-stringed lute, and caused them to sound a strain in the place where Buddha was seated. Then the divine Sekra proposed forty-two questions to Buddha, writing each one of them singly with his finger upon a stone. The traces of these questions yet exist. There is also a Sangharáma built upon this spot. Going *south-west* from this one yójana we arrive at the village of Ná-lo."

This hill is identified by General Cunningham with Giryak. "The remains of Giryak" he writes* "appear to me to correspond exactly with the accounts given by Fa-hian of the Hill of the Isolated Rock." His reasons are twofold, 1st the position, and 2nd the supposed etymology, of Giryak, *i.e.*, giri-eka *ek giri*. I think I shall be able to show beyond doubt that this identification is entirely erroneous.

Firstly, at Giryak *there is no solitary hill at all*, nor any hill which can be described as resembling in any way an eminence of that description. At Giryak terminates the rocky range of the Rajgir hills, which stretch from the neighbourhood of Gya to the banks of the Panchana, on which the village of Giryak stands, and, as a matter of fact, the hill which rises above the village—so far from being solitary—is a mere offshoot of Vipulagiri at Rajgir and is not less than six miles in length.

Secondly, from the "solitary hill" Fah-Hian proceeded SOUTH-WEST, one yójana, to Nála. Now Nála has been identified most satisfactorily with Bargáon [Cunningham page 469] by position and by the aid of inscriptions, but strange to say, Bargáon is exactly six miles NORTH-WEST of Giryak. If General Cunningham's identification of Giryak be right, Nálanda must have been situated somewhere to the *south* of the Rajgir hills, in the middle of the Nowádá valley, but, strange to say, he identifies it with Bargáon which is exactly north-west of the Rajgir hills in the centre of the Bihár valley. For this reason it is clear that "the hill of the solitary rock" could not be Giryak. The two identifications involve a dilemma, because no amount of argument can make Bargáon six miles south-west of Giryak, when physically it is six miles in the very opposite direction. The identification of Nálanda with Bargáon (Vihára-gráma) is undoubtedly right, and as a consequence, that of the "solitary hill" with Giryak—undoubtedly wrong. Strange to say, General Cunningham writes as one reason for identifying Nálanda with Bargáon (page 469)—"Fah Hian places the hamlet of Ná-lo at one yojana, or seven miles from the hill of the isolated rock, *i.e.* from Giryak, and also the same distance from new Raja Griha. This *account agrees exactly with the position of Bargáon with respect to Giryak and Rajgir*." Now in reality both translators agree in placing Nálanda to the *south-west* of the hill, and as a matter of fact Bargáon is *north-west* of Giryak.

I have no hesitation in identifying the "solitary hill" with the rocky peak at Bihár, which rises by itself in the midst of the plain covered with rice and poppy fields, and which gently slopes from the northern foot of the Rajgir hills to the banks of the Ganges itself. My reasons for so doing are: first,—correspondence of the relative distance and position of the Bihár rock and Patna, and of the solitary hill and Pataliputra; second,—the agreement of the relative distance and position of the Bihár rock and Bargáon, and the "solitary hill" and Nálanda; third,—natural appearance of the Bihár rock.

Of Nálanda, Fah says, "this was the place of Sáriputra's birth. Sáriputra returned here to enter Nirvána. A town therefore was erected on this spot which is still in existence."

Nálanda corresponds with Bargáon, a spot still marked with the ruins of vast topes and temples.

"Going west from this one yójana we arrive at the new Rajgir." This corresponds with the large circuit of fortifications at the foot of the Baibhár and Vipula hills, *exactly* six miles to the *south* of the Bargáon ruins. I therefore think the direction given by the translators must be a mistake.

* Ancient Geography of India, page 452.

Fah-Hian continues; "this was the town king Ajâsat built. There are two Sanghârâmas in it. Leaving the town by the west gate and proceeding 300 paces (we arrive at) the tower which king Ajâsat raised over the share of Buddha's relics which he obtained. Its height is very imposing."

The walls of the town and its gates are distinctly traceable at the distance of about half a mile from the foot of the mountain and directly facing the northern entrance of the valley of the five hills. Its form is somewhat difficult to describe and authors have varied in their attempts to do so, but after careful inspection from all points of view, and, what is still better, after studying its form from two of the hills above, I am of opinion it cannot be correctly called a pentagon, but is rather a parallelogram having, as measured from the top of the ramparts, three equal sides, viz., the north, west, and south, each measuring 1,[illegible] feet, and one unequal viz., the east measuring 1,[illegible] feet. The wall appears to have had a uniform thickness of about 14 feet and is composed of masses of stone about four feet square, the faces of which are made uniform and placed one upon the other in close contiguity, without any mortar or cement whatever. Starting from the north-east corner, where a stone bastion still exists in tolerable entirety, the wall remains unbroken for 200 feet, at the end of which distance a second bastion appears to have existed and similar traces are seen at the 300th foot. The remains of the wall now almost entirely disappear, but at the distance of 1100 feet from the north-east corner there is portion of entire wall measuring 20 feet by 14. Further on the wall appears clearly to have been removed and hardly a trace of it remains till towards the north-west corner, where its elevation considerably increases and there are enormous masses of brick which lead me to the conclusion that a tower must have once existed here. At this place the bricks are very small and of remarkable solidity. At a distance of 110 feet from the corner there are clear marks of a bastion, and the same feature is observable at similar distances up to the great west door, some 500 or 600 feet from the north-west corner of the fort. The rampart throughout this distance presents an average elevation of 25 or 30 feet above the plain beneath. Just before the west door, a fine piece of wall still remains intact measuring 26 feet by 14. Passing out by the west gate and going 300 feet in a direct line to the south-west, and crossing about midway the Sarasvati rivulet one arrives at a circular mound having an elevation of some 30 feet and a diameter of 100. The centre is considerably depressed and seems to consist simply of masses of bricks similar to those on the ramparts and inside the fort. From the west side of the ruins a sort of terrace leads to a semi-circular heap of somewhat less elevation than the first, in the centre of this I discovered three large statues of Buddha all headless but otherwise little mutilated, they are all seated on lotus-leaf thrones supported by bases ornamented by different devices. In one, several figures are seen in the act of making an offering; the centre of the second is occupied by the "Wheel of the Law" with a deer on either side, and the third bears the representations of two lions couchant. These mounds are undoubtedly the ruins of the great tower mentioned in the text. I hope to make a complete excavation of them during the cold season. I have made at the present time two incisions in the side of the tower, and have recovered from them some Buddhist idols of remarkable beauty, as well as a tablet covered with the representations of the nine planets.

From the west door the ramparts still increase in height, but the wall is hidden by masses of brush. Not far from the end of the western side, there is another break in the wall exactly opposite which is a small temple containing a Buddhist idol, now worshipped by the Hindus as the image of [illegible]. At each side of the Sarasvati stream is a pucca ghât and the ceremonies of "Mundan" and "Pindadân" are constantly performed here. At a short distance from this opening, the south rampart commences and has an elevation nearly equal to that on the west. The wall is not straight, but inclines towards the north-east. At about the 600th foot from the south-west corner, there are unmistakable traces of an enormous brick tower, and [illegible] feet farther on there is a long piece of wall still intact, and terminating in the southern gate. From this point to the south-east angle the wall is clearly visible. It has an elevation of some 30 or 40 feet above the valley, and there appears to have been bastions at distances varying from 100 to 110 feet. Opposite the south-east corner and at a distance of 50 or 60 paces there are distinct marks of a ruined tower similar to the one near the western gate already described. The wall towards the east has a total length of nearly 1,200 feet, and the ruins have a very inconsiderable elevation. Bastions are clearly visible at the following distances from the south-east angle, viz., 200, 320, 420, 520, 620, 720, 820, 920, 1,020, 1,120 and 1,200 feet. Montgomery Martin considers the heaps of brick to be the remains of a second set of fortifications built by Shir Shah, but I am rather inclined to regard them as the ruins of the ancient towers, the two monasteries and the royal palace which we know to have existed in the town and parts of which as well as other buildings were doubtless built on the city walls. General Cunningham gives a much larger area to the ruined city, but it must be remembered he made his measurements outside the ditch, very faint traces of which are visible on two sides of the wall. I have endeavoured to trace carefully the rampart and in many places removed the heaps of brick which covered it. In most cases I succeeded in uncovering the original wall, which uniformly presents a thickness of 14 feet. As regards the outer walls which are said to have existed, if the heaps of stone which are found at different distances from the fort are traces of them, they are so imperfect that any attempt to follow them would be simply futile.

(To be continued.)

PANINI AND THE GEOGRAPHY OF AFGHANISTAN AND THE PANJAB.

BY PROF. RAMKRISHNA GOPAL BHANDARKAR, M.A.

The chief native authorities for Ancient Indian Geography hitherto made use of by Antiquarians, are the Purâṇas and the Itihâsas. But there is another, and a very important one, which is not frequently referred to. The great Grammarian Pâṇini and his commentators, often give very useful information in cases where the Purâṇas and the Itihâsas afford no hint. We propose in the following remarks to show by examples, what use may be made of this branch of Sanskrit literature, in illustrating the Ancient Geography of India.

In teaching the formation of the names of places and of the inhabitants thereof, Pâṇini, as is usual with him, gives general rules where possible; and where not, he groups together certain names, in which the grammatical peculiarity is the same. These groups are distinguished from each other by the name of the first in the list, with an expression which is equivalent to 'and others' added to it. In the body of the work, the names of the groups so formed, and the grammatical or etymological changes characteristic of them, are only given, while the words constituting each group are set forth, in what may be considered as an appendix to the work, called *gaṇa-pâṭha*. Instances of the general rules are given by the commentators, but they are not, on that account, to be considered as recent. There is internal evidence to show that most of these must have been handed down from the time of Pâṇini himself. A good many are given by Patanjali, the author of the great commentary on Pâṇini's work. On the other hand, all the words comprised in each group ought not, because the Gaṇa-pâṭha is attributed to Pâṇini, to be regarded as having been laid down by him. Several of the gaṇas, or groups, are what are called *âkṛiti gaṇas*, *i.e.*, such as each subsequent writer has the liberty of adding to; and we have no doubt, that even such as are not now considered to be of this nature, must have fared similarly at the hands of the early successors of Pâṇini. For instance, the name of the mediæval Kâṭhiawâḍ town Valabhi, occurs at the end of the group called Varaṇâdi (Pâṇ. IV-2-82) and of Ujjayinî in the same group, and also at the end of Dhûmâdi (Pâṇ., IV.-2-127). No one would, we believe, push his scepticism, as to the age of Pâṇini so far as to urge that this proves him to have flourished after Valabhi came into importance under the dynasty of Bhaṭârka. And if any one were to do so, it would not be difficult to satisfy him. For, independently of the mass of evidence hitherto brought forward to prove that Pâṇini flourished long before the Christian Era, we may state that in the copperplate grant* of Dharasena IV. we find puns on a good many of the technical terms of Pâṇini, and the great grammarian himself is alluded to under the name of Shâlâturîya, (native of Shalâtura). This shews that Pâṇini was at that time a person of established reputation, and consequently, was even then an ancient author. The groups or *gaṇas*, therefore, seem to have been tampered with by his successors, but we think we are safe in ascribing the first three names at least, in each, to him.

The number of names of towns, villages, rivers,

* Translated at page 14.

mountains, and warlike tribes, occurring in the works of Pāṇini and his commentators, is very large. It would be difficult, or even impossible, to identify them all, but the positions and modern names of a good many can be determined with ease. It is not our purpose in this article to notice all such places, but to confine ourselves to such as may serve to throw new light on some doubtful points connected with the Ancient Geography of Afghanistan and the Panjāb.

The northernmost Kingdom of Afghanistan, in ancient times, was known to some of the Greek and Roman Geographers by the name of Kapisene, and the Chinese traveller Hwan Thsang calls it Kia-pi-she. Pāṇini mentions Kāpiśī (IV-2-99), from which he derives Kāpiśāyanī—the name of a wine manufactured from grapes produced in the district. The country about Kabul is still remarkable for its fine grapes. The name of another kingdom was Arachosia, which was called Arkhaj or Rokhaj by the Arab geographers, and Tsaokuta, supposed to be equivalent to Haukata, by Hwan Thsang. European antiquarians* trace the name, or that of the river Arachotus, in the province, to the Zend Harakaiti, corresponding to the Sanskrit Sarasvati. But we are not aware upon what evidence a river of the name of Sarasvati is found in this district. Sarasvatī is one of the Sapta Sindhavas, or seven rivers of the Vedas, and if assigned a position here, would certainly be far away from the other six. The river Sarasvatī was situated to the east of the Satlej. Perhaps the name Arachosia, Arkhaj, or Rokhaj, is to be derived from that of the mountain Rikshoda, mentioned by Pāṇini's commentators, the Brahmans living about which, were called Ārkshodas. This name is given as one to which Pāṇini's rule (IV-3-91) does not apply.

Another province of Afghanistan is called Fa-la-na by Hwan Thsang, and identified with the modern Vanneh or Wanneh by some, and with Banu, by General Cunningham. The Sanskrit name corresponding to this is not known. Pāṇini, however, mentions a country named Varṇu in several places (IV-2-103, and IV-3-93), which is very likely the same as Hwan Thsang's Fa-la-na. The country of Gandhāra is mentioned in the group Kachchhādi IV-2-133 and in IV-1-169, and the river Suvāstu, the modern Swat, a branch of the Kabul river, (in IV-2-77).

The position of the hill-fort of Aornos in the capture of which Alexander the Great displayed very great valour, is still a matter of uncertainty. The Sanskrit name corresponding to it is also equally unknown. Professor Wilson traces it to the word—āvaraṇa, 'enclosure', which, he thinks, forms the latter part of many names of cities. Whether it was actually so used is more than doubtful, and it would be necessary to suppose that the Greeks, in their Aornos dropped the first part of the name, retaining only the latter. General Cunningham derives it from the name of a king, whom he calls Rājā Vara. May it not be the Varaṇā mentioned by Pāṇini in IV-2-82? It was the name of a city as well as its people. There is a place on the right bank of the Indus, opposite to Atak, still called, we are told, Baraṇa or Varaṇa.

The Ortospana of the classical geographers has been identified with the modern Kabul. The Sanskrit name corresponding to it is not known. Professor Wilson derives it from such an original as Urddhasthāna. But we do not meet with such a name, and the etymology is purely aimless and conjectural. To derive it from the name of a tribe would be more reasonable. Hwan Thsang calls the country about the place Fa-la-shi-tang-na. May not this name be derived from such a compound as Parśusthāna, the country of the Parśus, a warlike tribe mentioned by Pāṇini in V-3-117.

Pāṇini and Patanjali call the Panjab—Vāhīka (IV-2-117 and V-3-114). The historians of Alexander tell us, that after having crossed the Hydraotes or Rāvī in the course of his march through the Panjab, he captured and destroyed a town of the name of Sangala. European antiquarians have identified it with the Sanskrit Śākala. But Śākala, from the evidence to be gathered from the Mahābhārata, and according to Hwan Thsang, who visited the place, was situated to the west of the Rāvī. Professor Wilson, therefore thinks that after Alexander had destroyed the Śākala to the east of the Rāvī, another was founded to the west of the river. This is merely a gratuitous supposition. General Cunningham thinks that Alexander re-crossed the Rāvī to conquer the town. Would it not be better to suppose that the two places were distinct? Alexander destroyed Sangala, while Śākala existed in the time of Hwan Thsang. Sangala belonged to a tribe that had no King,

* See Wilson's Ariana Antiqua.

while Shâkala was the capital of the Madras, who were governed by a king. Sangala is very probably to be traced to Sânkala, a place mentioned by Pâṇini (IV-2-75). Sankala was the name of the person who is said to have founded the city. It stands at the head of the group Sankalâdi, the second name in which is Pushkala, from whom the city of Pushkala, the ancient capital of Gândhâra, and the Peukelas of the ancient European Geographers, derived its name. Sânkala agrees more closely with Sangala than Shâkala. If this identification is to be trusted, the occurrence of the name of Sangala in Pâṇini, may be taken as a proof of his having flourished before Alexander; for the Macedonian Conqueror is said to have destroyed the city, on which account it must have ceased to exist after him.

The central province of the Panjâb is called Po-lo-fa-to by Hwan Thsang, transcribed Parvata by M. Julien. General Cunningham proposes [illegible] for Parvata. But Parvata is given as the name of a country by Pâṇini (IV-2-143) and the group Takshashilâdi, (under IV-3-93).

In the central and lower Panjâb, Alexander met with two tribes of warriors, named the Malli and the Oxydrakæ. The Sanskrit original of the former is unknown; and Professor Wilson identifies the latter with the Shudrakas of the Purâṇas. But there is a rule in Pâṇini (V-3-114) which teaches us to form the singular and dual of the names of warlike tribes in the Panjâb, by adding the termination -ya and changing the vowel of the first syllable to its *vṛiddhi*. Of this rule, his commentators give Mâlavya (pl. Mâlavâs) and Kshaudrakya (pl. Kshudrakâs) as instances. We thus learn that the Mâlavâs and Kshudrakâs, were two tribes of warriors in the Panjâb. The name Mâlavâs corresponds with Malli, and Kshudrakâs with Oxydrakæ. Kshudrakâs is nearer to the latter than Professor Wilson's Shudrakas.

At the confluence of the Panjâb rivers, Alexander came in contact with a tribe which is called Sambracæ or Sabracæ. General Cunningham traces this name to Samvâgri which he considers a Sanskrit word. But we are not aware of the existence of such a word; and it has an unsanskrit look about it, meaning as it does, according to the General, 'united warriors.' The Sabracæ were probably the Shaubhreyas, grouped along with the Yaudheyas, V-3-117.

PROGRESS OF ORIENTAL RESEARCH IN 1869-70.

[From the last published Report of the Royal Asiatic Society.]

The Sanskrit series of the Bibliotheca Indica, which, from various reasons, had for several years made but little progress, has taken a fresh start. Of the Tândya Brâhmaṇa three fasciculi have already been issued, and a number of other important works are reported to be in preparation. The Bombay Sanskrit Series, conducted by the Sanskrit Professors of the Bombay and Puna Colleges, presents also a promising aspect, and though of only a few years' standing, has raised hopes that, with an increased staff of well-trained editors, and commensurate support from Government, it may some day successfully compete with its elder Bengal sister.

The searching for Sanskrit MSS. has also been carried on during the last year with laudable vigour and decided success in several parts of India, particularly in Bengal, by the indefatigable Bâbu Râjendralâla Mitra; and in Bombay by Professors Bühler and Kielhorn, the latter of whom has just published a classified catalogue, containing little short of 600 Titles of Sanskrit Manuscripts, discovered in the southern division of that Presidency.

As regards the Dekhan, the Council cannot, unfortunately, present so favourable a report, as they are not aware that any official steps have as yet been taken by the Madras Government to carry into effect the resolution passed by the Government of India in 1868. This, in the opinion of the Council, is the more to be regretted, as the value of Sanskrit MSS. written in the vernacular alphabets of southern India, is beginning to be better appreciated, furnishing as they do, in many cases, a more correct text than the Devanâgarî MSS. of the north, and supplying, not unfrequently, texts and variant versions which have not hitherto been known to exist. The members of this Society cannot have failed to notice the Descriptive Catalogue, now being published by Mr. A. Burnell, of the Madras C.S., in Mr. Trübner's "American and Oriental Literary Record," of an excellent collection of Sanskrit MSS. made by himself during his residence in various parts of the Dekhan. It must be satisfactory to him to know that the portion of the catalogue which he has already published, exhibits several important works, for the most part belonging to the Black Yajur-veda, which are either entirely new, or of which incomplete MSS. alone have as yet been discovered in the north. Mr. Burnell (like Sir Walter Elliot, Mr. C. P. Brown, and some few scholars of earlier days) thus shows what benefit a civilian in southern India, who earnestly applies himself to the study of Hindu Literature, may be able to confer on Indian Philology, by collecting materials, and placing the results of his researches before European scholars. The Madras Service, however, has of late evinced but little interest in literary pursuits of this kind, and the Literary Society of Madras itself has for years scarcely shown a sign of its existence. It is to be hoped that the few earnest scholars still engaged in Oriental Studies may put an end to this unhappy state of indifference, by showing what important problems of Sanskrit Philology and Indian history are dependent for their solution upon the south, and that Madras will thus not stay behind other local governments in lending its support to the scientific exertions of European and native scholars, but still cordially co-operate in carrying out Mr. Whitley Stokes' scheme of procuring, and compiling lists of MSS. scattered over the whole of India.

The contents of the Sarasvati Bhandaram Library of H. H. the Mahârâja of Maisur, have been made known through a catalogue issued a few months since by the Bangalore Press, and containing the titles of several rare works. Of the Tanjore Library, a list had been printed many years ago, in which unfortunately, an extremely bad, often unintelligible, method of transcription was adopted; of this list there is a copy in the possession of Professor Goldstücker, the only one which is supposed to be now extant in Europe. Many parts of the Dekhan, however, have up to this time remained completely unexplored, and still promise a plentiful harvest to future investigators; although, in many cases, it will, no doubt, require the utmost care to overcome the suspicion and superstitions of the Brahmans. Of the Nambûris in Malabar, for instance, a most interesting, though very retired and secluded class of Brahmans, we know next to nothing; yet they are said to be staunch followers of the Vedic religion, and to have in their possession a great many old Vedic MSS. Some places in the Mahârâshṭra territory also, especially Kaleshvaram on the Upper Godavari, are known as great seats of Rig and Sâma-veda learning, and may be expected, when visited and explored, to add considerably to our knowledge of ancient Sanskrit literature.

There exists already a large collection of Sanskrit MSS. in Madras, which awaits a thorough examination, and the Council of this society have for some years used their best endeavours to get the collections transferred to England for incorporation with the Library of the India Office, with a view not only to rescuing the MSS. from the early destruction with which they are threatened by the ravages of the climate and of the white ants, but also in order to render them more accessible to European scholars. Though their recommendation has not been carried out in full, the Council are gratified in stating that in reply to their application they have been informed by the Government of Madras that it is proposed to build at Madras a Public Library, in which these MSS. will be deposited and properly protected against the ravages of insects, and that the Professor of Sanskrit at Madras has further been instructed to print a list of those MSS. which he may consider of primary importance, with a view of making these works better known than they are through the so-called Catalogue Raisonné. The Council has also been informed that a printed list of MSS. will be communicated to the Asiatic Society, and that any suggestions which may be made by the Society for the transcription of any of these MSS. will receive the attention of the Government.

By a minute in the Public Works Department, in May, 1868, the Government of India authorized the expenditure of sums not exceeding Rupees 10,000 in each of the four political divisions of the country for the purpose of delineating and casting some of the more remarkable antiquities of each presidency with a view to their ultimate conservation. These sums, if properly expended, being quite sufficient to commence upon, great hopes were entertained that the work so long desired by every well-wisher of India, would at last be accomplished by means of this well-timed liberality on the part of the Government.

In pursuance of this policy, Mr. Terry, Superintendent of the School of Design, was despatched from Bombay with a party of modellers, and some of his own pupils, to commence operations on the Temple at Ambernath, near Kalyan, on the other side of the Bombay harbour. Owing to the novelty of the undertaking and the inexperience of the party, nothing else was attempted during the available season of 1868-69, especially as an outbreak of fever and other unexpected difficulties very materially retarded the work; but so much disappointment was felt at the result that no attempt was made to continue operations during the last cold weather. In the meantime so much difficulty has been experienced in transmitting the casts and photographs that no specimens of either have yet reached this country, nor has any satisfactory report of the results obtained from the labours of the party.

At the same time another expedition was organized in Calcutta, with the object of visiting Orissa for the purpose of delineating some of the numerous and interesting antiquities of that province. Owing, however, to dissensions among the members composing it, and other difficulties, it seems to have been as little fruitful in results as that fitted out from Bombay. They did however bring back some casts of sculpture, a few photographs, and several copies of inscriptions, but unfortunately neglected to take casts or photographs of the remarkable sculptures in the Ganesha and Jodev caves, at Udayagiri. These are probably the oldest and most interesting in India, and their attention had been previously specially directed to them. As in the case of the Bom-any expedition, none of the results of their labours have been sent home; and no attempt was made to follow up those experiments during the last cold weather. Nor, so far as is known in this country, have any expeditions been organized, either in Bengal or Bombay, for operations during the next season.

In the meanwhile Dr. Hunter, at Madras, has been most successfully employing the pupils in his school of design in photographing some of the numerous temples which abound in that part of India, and also in casting some of their sculptures; none of the latter have reached this country, but the photographs are a valuable contribution to our knowledge, and, combined with those taken for Government by Captain Lyon, convey a very perfect idea of the enormous architectural wealth of that Presidency.

During the cold weather of 1868-9 Lieut. Cole, R.E., was deputed to Kashmir to photograph and make plans and drawings of the temples in that valley. A work giving the result of his labours is on the eve of publication by the India Office. It promises to be a most valuable contribution to our knowledge of the style of architecture there prevailing, and worthily completes what was so well commenced by General Cunningham in 1848.

During the last cold season the same officer has been employed under the auspices of the Science and Art Department at South Kensington, in casting the eastern gate-way of the great tope at Sanchi. It is understood that he has successfully accomplished this object, and is now on his way home with the moulds. Lieut. Cole took with him from this country a party of draughtsmen, with the intention of drawing all those sculptures which had not hitherto been delineated by General Cunningham and his brother, or by Col. Maisey. We may therefore hope that before long the means will be available in this country for obtaining a perfect knowledge of that remarkable monument.

Besides these expeditions, which are all more or less dependent on Government support, Mr. James Burgess, of Bombay, has just completed a splendid work on the great Temple city of Palitana. This work, which is illustrated by 45 photographs by Mr Sykes, is preceded by an introduction by himself, full of interesting local information and antiquarian knowledge regarding the sect of the Jains, to whom all the temples on that hill belong.

The same author has also published 41 photographs taken by the same artist during an expedition to the caves of Talája and Sana, and the temples of Somnath and Girnar. The text to this book is not so elaborate as that of the previous work, but is sufficient to describe and explain the history of the monuments it illustrates.

Messrs. Sykes and Dwyer have also photographed the caves and temples at Nasik and Kárlí, but no text has yet been added in illustration of them by any such competent hand.

Besides these, Mr. T. C. Hope of the Civil Service, has published a valuable work illustrated with 30 photographs by Mr. Lindley, of "Surat, Bharoch and other old cities of Gujerat with descriptive and architectural notes," by himself.

From the above it will be seen that our knowledge of the architecture and antiquities of some parts of our Indian Empire is progressing, though not so rapidly as might be desired. More, however, may be doing in India than we are aware of here; for unfortunately there is no agency either there or in this country where photographs by amateurs or local societies are collected, or from which a knowledge can be obtained of what is being done in this respect.

In continuation of their report on the present state of literary and antiquarian research on the Indian continent, the Council, now desire to refer to the neighbouring island of Ceylon, and to offer a few remarks on the condition of that seat of Buddhism and Pali learning. They have noticed with no little satisfaction that the Pali language and literature and the religion of Sakya Muni in general have, during the last year or two, received a great amount of attention at the hands of European as well as of Singalese scholars. Several important works bearing on the subjects have been published in England and abroad during the past year; and it is but fair to mention that this Society also has contributed its share to the promotion of these studies as is testified by the communications of Messrs. Childers and Fausböll, printed in its Journal, besides several papers on Buddhistic antiquities. A great and long-felt want will, at last, be supplied by the Pali Dictionary about to be published by Mr. Childers, who, it is to be expected, will by this work give a fresh and more general impulse to Pali studies.

A Singalese scholar, Pandit Devarakkhita, has published, a few months since, an excellent edition of the Balavatara, the most popular Pali Grammar in Ceylon; and the Pali text of the Digha Nikaya has been promised by another native scholar.

The Ceylon branch of the Asiatic Society also, has just issued a new and highly interesting number of its Journal, containing, amongst other articles, the continuation of Mr. James d'Alwis' paper on the Singalese language, the Aryan origin of which he maintains in an able and convincing manner, together with a Lecture on Buddhism, delivered shortly before his death by Mr. Gogerly, the late eminent Pali scholar, and edited, with an introduction and notes, by the Revds. J. Scott and D. de Silva. Another number of that Journal is reported to be already in preparation. It is further gratifying to learn that Mr. T. W. R. Davids, a young promising Pali scholar of the Ceylon C. S., has undertaken to collect the Pali inscriptions which are scattered in great number over the island. Whether he may succeed in deciphering, or whether he may have to content himself with copying and publishing, these ancient historical and religious records, Mr. Davids deserves the encouragement and approbation of all who take an interest in those studies; and the Council have no doubt but that the Ceylon Government, which has recently shown its liberality by granting a sum of money for the searching for, and procuring of MSS., will lend its full support and countenance to so promising and well-timed an undertaking.

As regards our sister societies on the Continent, the Asiatic Society of Paris and the German Oriental Society, their scientific researches have lost nothing of their wonted vigour and efficiency, and their publications embody, as usual, a goodly amount of useful information in the various branches of Oriental knowledge.

The number of the American Oriental Society's Journal, issued during the last year, contains the greater part of an important publication, viz., of Professor W. D. Whitney's Taittirîya Prâtiçâkhya, the Sanskrit Text and Commentary, with a translation of the former, and copious annotations. A new number of the same Journal, which will contain the concluding part of this work, will be issued in the course of the summer.

REVIEWS.

A Catena of Buddhist Scriptures, from the Chinese. By Samuel Beal, Chaplain R.N., Author of "Buddhist Pilgrims," &c. (pp. 436, 8vo.) London, Trübner & Co. 1871.

Of this extensive store-house of Buddhist lore, it is our duty at present merely to give a brief outline. Some of the translations here published have already appeared in the Journal of the Royal Asiatic Society. Having revised them, and added others to complete what he considers to be the cycle of the Buddhist development, the author now publishes the entire series as a contribution towards a more general acquaintance with Buddhist literature in China. It seems that the Buddhist Canon in that country, as was arranged between the years 67 and 1285 A.D., includes 1440 distinct works comprising 5586 books. These however form only an insignificant portion of the whole Buddhist literature which is spread throughout the empire, of which, hitherto the majority, or nearly all of English people, have been content to remain ignorant. In these circumstances, the author may well think that it is difficult to understand how we can claim to have any precise idea of the religious condition of the Chinese people, or even to appreciate the phraseology met with in their ordinary books. The book, we are told, and we can well believe it, represents the results of seven years of patient labour; and that whatever be its fate, the author, or rather editor, has found his reward in the delight which the study has afforded him, and in the insight which he has thereby gained into the character of one of "the most wonderful movements of the human mind in the direction of Spiritual Truth, which is traced in the history of Buddhism." Much has been done within the last thirty years to elucidate Buddhist history and philosophy, and it is certainly extraordinary, that little or no use has been made of the Buddhist Canon as it is accepted in China. In many of the large monasteries, there are to be found not only complete editions of the Buddhist Scriptures in the vernacular, but also the Sanskrit originals from which the Chinese version was made. Yet no effort has hitherto been made, either in this country or elsewhere, to secure for our great libraries copies of these invaluable works. Buddhist books, we learn, began to be translated into Chinese as early as the middle of our first century A.D. "It is one of the singular coincidences which occur in such abundance, between the history of Buddhism and the Christian religion, that whilst the influence of the latter was pervading the Western world, the knowledge of the former was being carried by missionaries—as zealous, though not so well instructed, as the followers of St. Paul—into the vast empire beyond the Eastern deserts; where it took root, long before Germany or England had become Christian, and has flourished ever since." The first complete edition of the Chinese Buddhist Canon dates merely from the seventh century. It was prepared under the direction of Tai Tsung, the second emperor of the Tang dynasty, who reigned from 627 to 650 A.D., and it was published by his successor Kaou-Tsung. Yung-loh, the third emperor of the Ming dynasty, in the year 1410, prepared a second and much enlarged edition of the Canon, writing a royal preface to it. This is called the Southern Edition—nan-tsang. Wan-leih the thirteenth emperor of the same dynasty, caused the publication of a third edition about 1590 A.D., which goes by the name of the Northern Collection, or pih-tsang, and which was renewed and enlarged in 1723, during the reign of Keen-lung, under the auspices of a former governor of Chih-kiang, who wrote a preface to the catalogue of works contained in it, and added a reprint of the royal preface to the first complete edition written by Tai-Tsung. "It is calculated that the whole work of the Indian translators in China, together with that of Hiuen-Thsang, amounts to about seven hundred times the size of the New Testament. The section known as the Mahâprajñâ Pâramitâ alone, is eighty times as large as the New Testament, and was prepared by Hiuen-Thsang, without abbreviation, from the Sanskrit, embracing two hundred thousand stanzas." It is certainly singular, that with a knowledge of this large and complete collection of the Buddhist Scriptures, so little use has been made of it by missionaries and scholars, with the exception of M. Wassiliev. "It would be wrong to state," says Mr.

Beal, "that the 350 or 400 million people who inhabit China are Buddhists, but yet Buddhist modes of thought and phraseology prevail largely amongst them, and it is hardly consistent in us, whilst we deal with religious questions, to overlook the literature which contains the sacred deposit of the faith of so many millions of that population as do strictly belong to the Buddhist faith. Moreover, it must be evident that so long as we are ignorant of the details of their religion, they will not be induced to listen to our denunciation of it; nor can we expect that our indifference to their prejudices will tend to remove them or induce them to overlook ours." Another important service which a careful study of the Chinese version of the Buddhist Scriptures may render to the cause of literature generally, but especially towards a critical acquaintance with the original Sanskrit text of the Tripitaka; as Max Muller suggests: "The analytical structure of the Chinese language imparts to Chinese translations the character of a gloss; and although we need not follow implicitly the interpretations of the Sanskrit originals adopted by Chinese translators, still their antiquity would naturally impart to them considerable value and interest."

Another important consideration is the advantage we may derive from having in China copies of many of the sacred books which are unknown elsewhere. Such are the numerous works of the Northern School, as it is called, and which, so far as is at present known, are not to be met with in their original Sanskrit form, either in India or Nepal. Such are, for example, the Avatamsaka Sûtra, written by Nagarjuna, and which, under the name of the Hwa-yen King, is one of the commonest and most widely circulated Sûtras in China—the Kin-kong and [illegible], the Surangama Sûtra, and many others.

"Incidentally," says the author, "we shall derive from these studies much information relating to the more obscure parts of Indian history, and the struggles of the conflicting Indian sects." In the history of the mission of Sung Yun, for example, we have an account of the effect which a picture of the sufferings of Bodhisatva, when he was born as Vessantara, produced on the rough Indo-Scythic tribes who invaded North India at the beginning of the Christian Era. He tells us they could not refrain from tears when they saw the picture of the sufferings of the Prince. This little incident may very reasonably account for the conversion of the whole tribe of invaders who, under the rule of Kanishka and his successors, became the most devoted patrons of the Buddhist faith, and "the magnificent founders" of Topes and Temples, the ruins of which at present survive. And from this reference of Sung Yun to the Vessantara Jataka, represented in the white Elephant Temple, Varusha, the writer is led to connect the Sang-loh or Shell temple in the neighbourhood of that city with the Sanchi or Sanchi Tope near Bhilsa, where also, over the northern gateway of the great Tope, we find sculptured the same history of Bodhisatva as Vessantara, giving away his whole possessions, his children and his wife, so that there might be no remnant of selfishness left in his nature, and thus he might be fitted to undertake the salvation of men. But it is hardly necessary, recollecting the labours of M. Julien, and the school of French Sinologues amongst whom he is conspicuous, to bring further instances of the manner in which we may derive funds of information from China respecting the civilization of India. The connection is also noted between the history of Buddhism in the East, and the progress of Christianity in the West. In the middle ages there was a favourite legend known throughout Europe, and generally accepted as genuine, under the name of Barlaam and Josaphat. This history is at present widely circulated in the modern editions of the *Lives of the Saints*, by Symeon, the translator. But on examination we find that the life of Josaphat, who has somehow crept into the Roman Martyrology, was but a copy of the well known history of Shakya Buddha, and was appropriated doubtlessly by the early Christian hagiographers as being in itself a very touching and natural account of the struggle of a sensitive conscience with the temptations of a wicked and unsparing world. We quite agree with Mr. Beal too, where he says—"The widest and most interesting result to be derived from such studies as these, is the means they afford us of arriving at a correct judgment in the science of comparative religions"—so far as that is possible. "The scope of the present work is to present the reader with a brief Catena of Buddhist Scriptures arranged, so far as possible, in a chronological order, with a view to exhibit the origin and gradual expansion of the system, and to point out in what particulars it deserves our candid consideration, and in what particulars it fails to deserve either attention or inquiry. The former phase will be found to consist of its primitive purity as a religious system properly so called, whilst the latter will embrace those numerous divergencies of the system from its original character, into a scholastic and vain philosophy, which ended in its ultimate confusion with other sects in India, or in its present lifeless condition in China and Japan. The works here translated are mostly standard ones, and if not, strictly speaking, in the Canon, are yet of great authority, and are found in the libraries of most of the monasteries in the South of China."

Mr Beal's work more than achieves his prefatory anticipations. He has given an elaborate and splendid contribution to our knowledge of early Eastern Mythology. His notes and comments exhibit a wide acquaintance with European orientalism, and his tone of thought a width and liberalism altogether unusual. Mr. Beal's handsome and deeply interesting volume well deserves a place in the library of every one who can read English.

A. H. B.

GOVER'S FOLK SONGS.

THE FOLK SONGS OF SOUTHERN INDIA. By Charles E. Gover, Member of the Royal Asiatic Society and of the Society of Arts, Fellow of the Anthropological Society. Madras: Higginbotham and Co.

This is one of the most attractive and instructive books, relating to the social life of the people of India we have ever read. We think we can safely predict that it will be a favourite in the drawing-room as well as in the study. The introductory remarks, criticisms, &c. are well written, and the many songs rendered with great spirit and in every variety of metre. Some of these have already appeared in the *Cornhill Magazine*, and others were read before the Royal Asiatic Society but have not yet been published.

The Dravidian languages have hitherto been too much overlooked by Orientalists. The Rev. W. Taylor remarks, "It is desirable that the polish of the Telugu and Tamil poetry should be better known in Europe; that so competent judges might determine whether the high distinction accorded to Greek and Latin poetry, as if there were nothing like it in the world, is perfectly just." And Dr. Caldwell remarks, that Tamil is "the only vernacular literature in India which has not been content with imitating the Sanskrit, but has honourably attempted to emulate and outshine it. In one department, at least, that of ethical epigrams, it is generally maintained, and I think must be admitted, that the Sanskrit has been outdone by the Tamil."

But we must let Mr. Gover speak for himself:—"There is," he says, "a great mass of noble writing ready to hand, in Tamil and Telugu folk-literature, especially in the former. Total neglect has fallen upon it. Overborne by Brahmanic legend, hated by the Brahmans, it has not had a chance of obtaining the notice it so much deserves. The people cling to their songs still, and in every pyal-school the people learn the stories of Tiruvalluvar, Auvaiyar, Kapila, Pattanattu and the other early writers. To raise these books in public estimation, to exhibit the true products of the Dravidian mind, would be a task worthy of the ripest scholar, and the most enlightened government. I would especially draw attention to the eighteen books that are said to have received the sanction of the Madura College, and are among the oldest specimens of Dravidian literature. Any student of Dravidian writings would be able to add a score of equally valuable books. If these were carefully edited, they would form a body of Dravidian classics of the highest value."

Nor ought we to pass over the author's history of his book—"the result of an attempt," as he describes it, "to fathom the real feelings of the masses of the people, by gathering and collecting the folk-songs of each family of the great Dravidian nation. It has been the pleasant labour of years to make this collection—in the plains, where dwell the Tamil and Telugu peoples; on the Mysore plateau, the home of Kanarese; among the hills and valleys of the Nilgiris and the Western Ghats, sheltering the stalwart tribes of Koorg, and the humble Badagas of Ootacamund; along the narrow strip of low-lying coast that parts the sea from the western Ghats and gives a home to the Malayalim tongue." And lovingly and honestly has he done his work, and we feel that the vista he has opened up is a picture of reality of no common interest.

Before proceeding to the songs let us quote this picture, so well drawn, of the dasa:—"Their service was first of all poverty; secondly, singing; thirdly, forgetfulness of caste. Their reward lay in human honour and the certainty of a living. None dared to despise the 'slave of God;' none could refuse him a handful of rice or a couple of coppers or chuckrams. At weddings and feasts, at fasts and funerals, at sowing and harvest, at full moon and new moon (the passing of the equinox or the sun changed his dwelling), the dasa must be invited, honoured and rewarded. At weddings, he must sing of Krishna; at funerals of Yama; before soldiers of Rama; before sadhus, of Brama. As he sings his songs of right and duty, which he hears the chink of copper in his skull of benevolence and charity.

"There can be few more pleasant scenes than when in the cool of the evening, the dasa enters some quiet country village, to find and earn his food and quarters for the night. Marching straight to the Mandapam or many-pillared porch of the pagoda, he squats on the elevated basement, takes his drum, places before him his large begging skull. The villagers are just returning from the fields weary with their labours, anxious for some amusement. The word is quickly passed round that the singer has come, and men, women and children turn their steps towards the *Mandapam*. There they sit on the ground before the bard and wait his pleasure. He begins by trolling out some praise to Krishna, Vishnu or Pillaiyarswami. Then he starts with a poem or short song, such as those with which this book commences. There is chorus to every verse. If the song be well known, before the bard has finished the long-drawn-out note with which he ends his verse, the villagers have taken up their part and the loud chorus swells on the evening breeze. If the song be new they soon learn chorus, and every fresh verse bears a louder and louder refrain. Then the skull is carried round and pice are showered into it. When darkness closes in, the headman of the village invites the singer to his house, gives him a full meal and then leaves him with mat, pillow and shawl to sleep in the pyall. In busy towns the singer squats by the roadside and soon collects a crowd to hear his song. The chorus here is less frequently heard. The people cannot stay, their children are at home, they hear a little and then pass on." This is but a specimen of the descriptions of life and manners with which the songs are interspersed and illustrated.

Here is a poem—selected at random from the twenty-eight Kanarese songs with which the book commences:—

"One longs of others for a wife,
 On her bestows both rule and home;
He counts her half of all his life,
 But when death comes, he dies alone.
Chorus.—Of all good things the best are these—
  Wives, lands, and countless gain.
  Which is the dearest friend to thee?
One mounts the throne of mighty kings,
 His palace girds with fort and wall;
Of his great power the whole world rings,
 His lifeless corse in dust shall fall,
  Chorus.—Of all good things the best, &c.
King's grace, good luck, hard work and trade,
 May load with wealth of coin or land,
What friends know, the [illegible];
 For riches fly like desert sand.
  Chorus.—Of all good things, &c.
In vain wives mourn, in vain sons weep,
 Wealth helps who lies in death's last sleep;
Two things alone the past can keep—
 The sin, the good, our life has seen.
  Chorus.—Of all good things, &c.
In this weak frame put not your trust,
 But think on Him with [illegible].
Is your heart clean? For [illegible];—
 Then Vishnu is a healing balm.
  Chorus.—Of all good things, &c.

Of the three Badaga songs translated—the "[illegible]" is of weird and wonderful interest: it is a Vision of Heaven and Hell that might [illegible] another Dante. But it is too long for quotation; its concluding verse reminds us of what will strike most readers, as the prevailing undertone of a large proportion of the translations in this interesting volume.

"Oh brother, how I wish
 To reach that blissful shore!
Why did I ever come
 To see such fearful things!
If when at last I die,
A solemn gathering mourns,
And the devotees my corpse—
It will be paid to him
Who guards the heavenly gate—
If this and more be done,
Can I obtain that bliss,
Or must I sink to hell?"
"Alas! my dear sister, I know not of that."

Here as in very many other instances in these Dravidian songs the note of sorrow is clear enough. And, as the author remarks "no one can fail to be struck with the sadness that prevails. The world and every soul in it are so sinful, so full of all evil, man should give up all to save his life; and even then can hardly hope to succeed. 'How to cross the sea of Sin?' becomes the great question. Its current is so strong, its waves so high, its hidden rocks so many, that none but a strong swimmer can dare to hope to reach the other side. Even he is so battered by storm and rock, so exhausted by the contest or worn by exertion, that when he comes nigh to touch the shore his strength may fail, his heart grow weak, and he sink back into the swirling tide. If things be so with the vigorous scornful few, how can the feeble trembling many ever hope to see the golden feet of the god whose help they crave? It is inexpressibly saddening again and again to read such songs as these, and know that they represent the inmost feelings of the larger part of a great nation."

We must pass over the Kurg Harvest and Wedding songs too—beautiful as they are, and made still more interesting by Mr. Gover's excellent sketches of the ritual ceremonies; the Funeral Song also is full of pathos and striking images, such as—

"Woe! The string of choicest pearls
Round the neck of favoured child
Is for ever burst and lost!
Woe! The clear and brilliant glass,
Fallen from our trembling hands,
Falls—broken to the ground!

But it is too hard to particularise. Nor can we find space for quotations from the Tamil songs, though those by Kapila and Tiruvalluvar, as well as from the Cural of Tiruvalluva—the "typical and immortal book" of the Tamils—will interest and instruct every thoughtful reader. These occupy nearly a third of the volume. Next come Malayalam songs—five in number; and lastly thirteen Telugu songs close the work, which we heartily commend to all readers.

Hindustanian Musafari—or Journal of Travels in India. By Ardaseer Framjee Moos. 8vo. I., Bombay, 1871.

This very elegant volume, dedicated to His Royal Highness the Duke of Edinburgh, is written in Gujarati, and illustrated by a good map, a photograph of His Royal Highness, a steel engraving of the author and his travelling companions, and by a series of sixty-six beautiful chromolithographs, prepared by Messrs. Vincent, Brooks, Day and Sons, from photographs collected by the author, of places visited during his travels. The text occupies [illegible] pages of beautifully printed vernacular, and [illegible] pages of translations spiritedly rendered from what the author considers the most interesting portions of his book. In typography, illustrations, and binding, the book has never been equalled in India.

MISCELLANEA.

MR. RAVENSHAW'S HISTORY OF GAUR.

In reply to a letter from the Government of India to the Director-General of the Archæological Survey of India, asking him to state whether he was prepared to revise and edit Mr. Ravenshaw's historical sketch of the kingdom of Gaur, General Cunningham wrote as follows:—

"I beg to state that I feel some delicacy about meddling with Mr. Ravenshaw's historical sketch without his permission, as he states that he spent much time and labour upon it, and evidently believes that he has made a very good job of it. But if he has no objection to my revision of his sketch, I would undertake to edit the work, merely making the necessary corrections in his text, and adding such notes as are absolutely necessary to illustrate the subject. I would, however, give an introductory chapter, treating of the style of architecture compared with that of Northern India, as shown in the existing buildings at Delhi and Jaunpur.

"I should like also, if possible, to obtain some further illustrations of the Muhammadan architecture of Bengal from the eastern capital of Sonârgaon, which still exists about 20 miles from Dacca."

General Cunningham has been asked to place himself in communication with Mr. Ravenshaw with reference to the proposed editing of the sketch.

We have been favoured with a copy of a letter, dated 6th September, from the Bengal Government to the Commissioner of Dacca, asking that officer to "be so good as to report, for the Lieutenant-Governor's information, whether there is any one in Dacca or its neighbourhood who is willing to take photographs of the Muhammadan architectural ruins of Sonârgaon, and to supply Government with copies of these views at a moderate cost."—*Englishman, Oct. 20.*

SHRI HARSHA.

At the monthly meeting of the Bombay B. R. Asiatic Society, on the 9th Nov. Dr. George Bühler read a paper entitled "A Note on the History of the Sanskrit Literature," of which the following is a brief abstract:—

A Jaina writer, Rajasekhara, gives in his Prabandhakosha, composed A.D. 1348, a life of Shri Harsha. He states that Shri Harsha, the son of Hira, was born in Benares, and composed the Naishadha-charita at the request of a king of that town, named Jayantachandra the son of Govinda Chandra. Various details which Rajasekhara gives regarding Jayantachandra, especially the statement that he had the surname Panjula, that he was contemporary of Kumarapala of Anahillapattana, and that he and his dynasty were destroyed by the Musalmans, show that Raja Sekhara's Jayantachandra is nobody else than the Rashtrakuta prince, Jayachandra, who reigned over Kanyakubja and Benares, in the latter half of the 12th century, probably from 1168-1194.

Rajasekhara's account of the age of the Shri Harsha is confirmed by the fact, that the latter states, at the end of his Naishadhiyakavya, that he was honoured by a king of Kanyakubja.

THE SELUNS.

COLONEL BROWNE, the Deputy Commissioner of the Mergui district, British Burmah, gives a very interesting account of the Selung, a peculiar race of people living under our rule. This they have been doing ever since Mergui became ours, some fifty years ago, and yet they are described as perfectly uncivilized, and not a bit the better for our rule. The number of this race living in British territory is about 1,000. They have no written language, nor have they any traditions regarding their origin. Dr Mason, the well known American Missionary of the Karens, is of opinion that they have a Polynesian origin, but their Mongolian cast of features completely upsets this theory. Their spoken language is quite distinct from the Burmese. They are divided into families; these we are told, are free to intermarry with each other, but the bride becomes a part of her husband's family. The wealth consists of boats and fishing apparatus. Each family appears to understand its own boundaries, and no encroachment is allowed by one into the preserves of another. The race is described as strong and well-built but very ugly. They go about almost naked. They live in small huts of a most primitive description, in which the whole family is huddled together. Their principal weapon appears to be the spear, with which they capture fish and wild pigs, which constitute their principal articles of food. Turtles and shell-fish also afford them subsistence, together with yams, which grow on the islands, and are sometimes found of 50 pounds weight. They are very fond, we are told, of opium, arrak and tobacco. Weaving cloth is unknown to them, but they manufacture neat sleeping mats of a certain kind of leaf, and the walls of their huts are constructed of the same material. They are without religion of any sort, and have no idea of a future existence. Like the Dyaks of Borneo they believe in the existence of spirits which haunt streams, forests, &c. When a Selun dies, his body, with his spear, &c., is placed on a mat on the sea beach. His friends then vacate the spot, and return after a year to bury the bones and the weapons. They are said to be very truthful, and polygamy and conjugal infidelity are unknown among them. They are moreover of a mild and peaceable nature, and offer no resistance to the attacks frequently made upon them by Malay pirates.—*Delhi Gazette.*

ROCK TEMPLE AT HARCHOKA.

AT the last meeting of the Asiatic Society at Calcutta, an interesting letter was read from Captain W. L. Samuells, Assistant Commissioner, Parharnba, Chord Line, regarding a rock-cut temple which he discovered at Harchoka in the Chota Nagpur Tributary Mahal of Chang Bhaker. Tracings, plans, and inscriptions were exhibited, and Captain Samuells has promised to send descriptive notes for the next meeting. There appear to be several rock-cut temples in the neighbourhood. Captain Blunt, in 1795, visited those at Mara, a village in Rewa.

COIN OF FIRUZ SHAH ZAFAR.

In March last, Mr. E. C. Bayley presented the Asiatic Society of Bengal with a unique coin bearing the name of Firuz Shah Zafar. A woodcut had just been prepared when the first copy of Mr. Thomas's Chronicles of the Pathan Kings of Dehli reached this country. Mr. Thomas (p. 300) enumerates four coins that bear the name of that prince, among them one gold coin, a "unique specimen in the possession of Col. Guthrie," and "one silver coin, a new variety, belonging to Mr. Bayley," &c. They are all posthumous coins, as Zafar died before his father. The original is identical with Col. Guthrie's specimen, of which, however, the margin has been cut away. The coin bears date, A. H. 791, which agrees with the third coin described by Mr. Thomas. During the year 791, Abubakr, son of Zafar, ascended the throne of Dehli, which accounts perhaps for the issue, or re-issue of coins with Zafar's name. The weight of the coin cannot be determined, as it is attached to a necklace. It bears the following legend:—"The great Sultan Firuz Shah Zafar, son of Firuz Shah, the Royal, in the time of the Imam, the Commander of the Faithful, Abdullah,—may his *Khilafat* be perpetuated!"

ORIENTAL STUDIES AT CAMBRIDGE.

The Board of Oriental Studies at Cambridge has presented the following Report on Oriental Studies to the Vice-Chancellor. (Dated Nov. 8, 1871).

"The Board of Oriental Studies are unanimously of opinion that the time has now arrived for assigning to the Oriental languages a more prominent position among the studies of the University. These form at present the only great branch of learning which, though long recognised in the University by the foundation of Professorships, fails to take its proper place in our great examinations. The impulse given in the last few years to the Moral and Natural Sciences by the establishment of Triposes suggests to the Board similar examinations in their department as the best method, in accordance with the present University system, for fostering the early growth of Oriental Studies.

As the Oriental Languages, now represented in the University, naturally separate into two main groups the Board beg to recommend the establishment of two independent Oriental Triposes: (1) the *Semitic*, and (2) the *Aryan*. In each of these two great divisions, it would probably be found expedient to confine the attention of the student to a few of the leading languages rather than to encourage a superficial knowledge of many. Hebrew (together with Chaldee), Syriac and Arabic might be taken as the best representatives of the first group. It seems superfluous to urge the importance of an accurate knowledge of Hebrew in a great Christian University; this study has always flourished to some extent at Cambridge, and it is hoped that many who have already devoted themselves to it might be induced to extend their researches to the sister dialects. The connection of Syriac with the early Christian Literature, and the revival of its study in the present generation, to which the large addition of Syriac MSS. to the British Museum has in no slight degree contributed, would justify the position proposed for it in a Semitic examination. In Arabic, the intricacies of the Grammar and the extent of the Vocabulary render an early systematic training especially necessary. Its literature is rich and varied in poetry, history and science, and indispensable to all who would fully understand the spirit of the Muhammadan religion. Not only is Arabic the spoken language of that part of the East most interesting to Europeans, but it enters largely into the composition of Persian and Turkish.

In the Aryan group, Sanskrit holds the first and foremost place. Independently of its vast literature which embraces the authoritative theological works of the Brahmans, it is the oldest sister of the Indo-European tongues, and is now acknowledged to be an indispensable aid in unravelling the structure of Greek and Latin as well as of the German, Keltic and Slavonic tongues. It is the parent of most of the spoken languages of Northern India, and also of Pali, the sacred language of the Buddhists. Persian also possesses an extensive literature of especial value for historic and theosophic investigations; it is cultivated by the Muhammadans in India, as well as in Persia itself, and might therefore be introduced with advantage into the Tripos.

The Members of the Board feel that it would be presumptuous to expect any great result from the establishment of Oriental Triposes, until these studies have won a due share of the College endowments; yet they confidently hope that the University will grant, as far as lies in its power, a fair field for the growth and development of studies so intimately connected with Biblical and Ecclesiastical Literature, with the Religion of our Indian fellow-subjects, with the Science of Language, and the history of the human Mind."

The Vice-Chancellor invited the attendance of Members of the Senate in the Arts School, on Monday, Nov. 20 at 2 p.m., for the discussion of this Report.

REVISION OF THE SINHALESE BUDDHIST SCRIPTURES.

In the year 1867, through the exertions of a Sinhalese nobleman named Iddamalgoda, a Synod of the Buddhist clergy, was convened at the town of Palmadulla for the purpose of correcting the Tripitaka. The Synod was under the joint presidency of two eminent prelates, Sumangala and Dhirânanda.

and its members were priests selected for their learning and scholarship, from the principal Ceylon monasteries. The procedure was as follows:—After the formal opening of the Synod, each member was furnished with a manuscript in the Sinhalese character, which he took to an apartment assigned to him, and collated with a number of Ceylon, Burmah and Siam copies of the same work. All obvious errors in his manuscript he corrected at once, but where a passage was doubtful, he merely marked it. On an appointed day each member carried his corrected manuscript to the hall of assembly, where in a public sitting of the Synod all the corrected manuscripts were compared together. When the corrections were identical in all the manuscripts, they were generally adopted without much loss of time, but in many doubtful or difficult passages the reading was not finally fixed without long and anxious discussion. The first session of the Synod lasted seven months, and was devoted exclusively to the Vinaya, a revised and authorised version of which, together with its Atthakathâ and Tîkâs, was deposited in safe hands. The next meeting of the Synod was held after a considerable interval, and was devoted to the correction of the Sutra Pitaka. On this occasion a somewhat different plan was followed, for the members had been instructed to correct at their own monasteries the manuscripts intrusted to them, and when the Synod met, it was able to sit daily until the work of fixing the text of the Sutras was ended. The Abhidharma Pitaka is now undergoing revision, and the labours of the Synod are drawing to a close. When they are completed, a palm-leaf copy of the authorised version of the sacred texts will be deposited in one of the Ceylon monasteries, and the public will be permitted to inspect and transcribe the different books. In the very extensive collation of MSS. made by the Synod, it was found that the Ceylon MSS. were generally more accurate than those of Burmah and Siam.—*The Academy.*

DISCOVERY OF ANCIENT COINS.

ABOUT a month and a half ago, some of the villagers of Hanjori, while digging out a rain in the vicinity of an old tank, discovered an earthern pot, (not unlike a common *surai*) containing three *sirs* and a half of silver-coin. The earthern pot was buried about seven feet underground; the coins at the bottom of the pot were completely defaced by corrosion, though nearly three-fourths of its contents were in a very good state of preservation. On examination the coins were found to belong to Græco-Baktrian Kings. The coins of Menander are certainly more numerous than those of any other king, though by far the best impressions are on the coins of King Philoxenus. The following are the names of the kings whose coins have been deciphered:—Menander, Philoxenus, Diomedes, Antialkides, Apollodotus, Hermæus, Heliokles, Straton, Antimachus, Hermæus and Kalkalliope. A description of the coins and the circumstances of their discovery, is being prepared for the London *Academy.*—*Delhi Gazette*, Oct. 11.

DISCOVERY OF COPPER AXES.

AT the last meeting of the Asiatic Society of Bengal, a letter was read from the Assistant Commissioner, Fattehabad, describing two ancient copper axes which he has presented to the Society. The narrative of their discovery is very curious. It appears that they had been found by a villager just below the surface of a hillock, round which he was cultivating land. But where this hillock is, he steadily refuses, in spite of an offer of twenty rupees, to tell to any one, lest the demon of the spot should revenge itself upon him. He has, he declares, already suffered at his hands. The night after he found the things, he had a dream in which a *genius* of terrible aspect appeared before him. He was no ordinary looking spirit, but of prodigious proportions, his skin being red and his clothes black, whilst a profusion of hair hung down his back from his head to his heels, each hair being as thick as a man's wrist. Having dismounted from a tiger, which had carried him to the villager's door, he entered the hut and, pointing to the copper pieces, informed the trembling man that they were his (the genius's) property. The man at once expressed his willingness to give them up, but the genius would have none of them. He wanted in exchange four babes of the villager's right hand, and in return offered to relinquish all claim to the treasure which, he said, lay buried under the other hillocks in that locality. But the man objected to lose the man would not part with at any price. So the genius mounted his tiger, and rushed off in high dudgeon. When the day broke, the villager proceeded to do a little ploughing before continuing his excavations at the hillock, but as he passed that spot, one of his bullocks dropped down stone-dead; and within a few days the remaining two bullocks which he possessed died also. Upon this he deserted that place, and took up his residence in the village where he now lives. This, he says, happened three years ago, and till last year he concealed the copper pieces, which he believed to be gold; but thinking he might then realize something by them, he carried them off in great secrecy to a European official, to whom he imparted the information of where he had found them. But this little indiscretion brought fresh troubles on him; for when he returned home, his little girl sickened and died. For these valid reasons he refuses to point out the hillock where the demon's treasures lie hidden.—*Pioneer.*

QUERY.

Will any of the correspondents of the *Indian Antiquary* help me by obtaining the consonant alphabet of the ancient characters used in the Maldivian islands? The form of each consonant changes completely according to the affixed vowel, and the late Captain Christopher, I. N., only published the consonants with the short *a*. The *present* Maldivian characters are sufficiently known.

ANTOINE D'ABBADIE,
Membre de l'Institut de France.

Hendaye, Basses Pyrenées, Nov. 29, 1871.

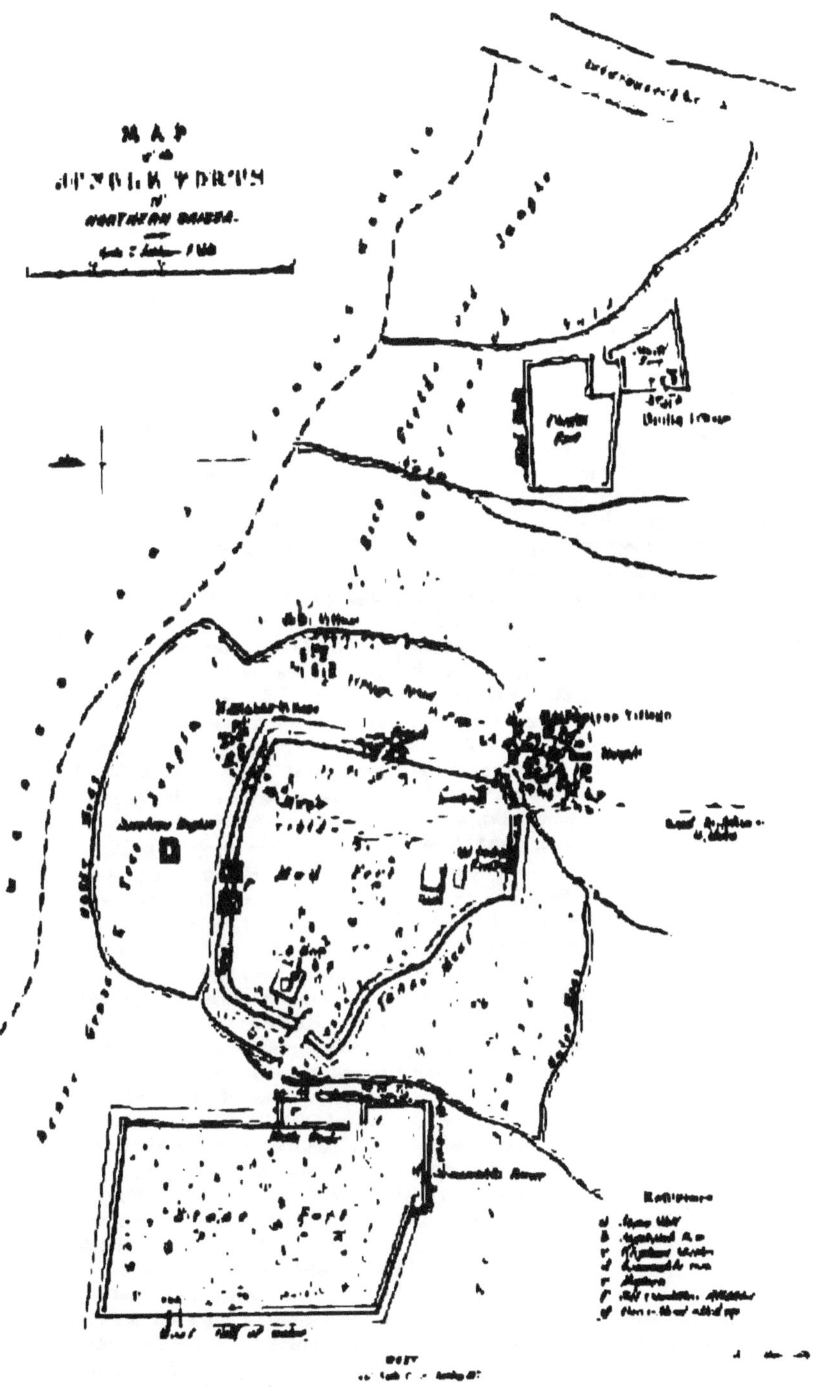

THE JUNGLE FORTS OF NORTHERN ORISSA.

BY JOHN BEAMES, B.C.S., M.R.A.S., MAGISTRATE OF BALASORE.

NORTHERN ORISSA is, considering its situation within 150 miles of Calcutta, very isolated and little known. There is however a good historical reason for this. The Kings of Orissa fixed their capital always in the southern part of the province, and the long narrow strip of country between the hills and the sea was only at times, and never for long periods, under their sway. It was covered with dense jungle, which extended apparently with hardly any break to the banks of the Hooghly.* The Kings of Bengal, on the other hand, held their court either at Gaur, or some other place far to the north, and the lower Gangetic delta was to them also almost a *terra incognita*. The English settlement of Calcutta pushed out feelers along the course of the Ganges, and the wave of conquest and commerce followed the same path, leaving Midnapore and Balasore comparatively unheeded and unexplored. In the present day the great Imperial high road from Calcutta to Madras has opened up a portion of this country, and is much frequented, especially by the thousands and tens of thousands of pilgrims who annually visit the great shrine of Jagannâth at Purî. But the line of traffic, and the road of invading armies in former times, did not follow the course of the present great avenue of communication, and it is not therefore along the Madras and Calcutta road that we must look for relics of past times.

One hundred and fifteen miles S.W. of Calcutta, at the town of Jellasore (J a l e s h w a r) the road crosses the river Subanrekha (S u v a r n a r e k h â—"streak of gold") at a spot on the confines of British territory and the territory of the tributary Raja of Mohurbhunj (M a y û r a b h a n j). The river here winds so as to run for about five miles nearly parallel to the road on the northern side. Crossing the river we come into the isolated pargana of N a t t i b â b â d, one of the so-called Jungle Mehals, which is now included in the district of Balasore (B â l e s h w a r). Nine miles north of Jellasore, and about two from the right bank of the river, amidst dense grass and tree jungle, which is here and there in course of being brought into cultivation, stands the group of forts which I propose to describe. I hope the above details will enable the reader to form a clear idea of their actual position on the map of India, in case however the ordinary maps should not show the road, or the little town of Jellasore, I would add that the forts are distant from the sea at the mouth of the Subanrekhâ, twenty-six miles as the crow flies.

I propose first to describe the forts themselves, and secondly to endeavour to arrive at an approximation to the date of their foundation, and to collect such few facts respecting their past history as I can. This enquiry will, if successful, throw considerable light on the relations between the Kings of Orissa and their northern neighbours, as well as on the somewhat obscure subject of the Musalman invasions of the province, in addition to the more purely archæological interest which it may present.

It will be seen from the annexed map that the forts are four in number, the two larger ones being close to the large village of R â i b a n i y â, and the two smaller ones at the village of P h u l j h â, or more correctly P h u l b a t t â. Of these two small forts nothing now remains save the outline of mud walls, with here and there a scattered mass of laterite stones.

The whole soil of this neighbourhood for many miles is composed of laterite, a dark brick-red stone full of holes like a sponge, but very hard. All these forts are built of this stone, though in many cases the stones have either, from having been originally loosely put together, or owing to some subsequent violence, become scattered or sunk in the soil. The stones are all hewn and of various sizes, the largest and most regularly shaped being found in the most important and probably most ancient portions of the work, the smaller and less carefully hewn in the walls and outworks. The largest stones are about 3 feet in length by a foot in depth, and the same in breadth; while in some of the pettier and more modern works, stones not bigger than ordinary bricks are found. Owing to the denseness of the jungle, and the great number of tigers and bears which find shelter there, it is very difficult to explore these forts thoroughly. In three visits which I have recently made to them, I obtained from the Zamindar some thirty or forty coolies armed with the useful little Sonthal axe, and these together with my own Police and Chaukidars were ac-

* In writing native names I follow Dr. Hunter's rule of using the received (although often incorrect) spelling for well-known places and the strictly correct Wilsonian system for those that are unknown to the general public.

occupied many hours every day in cutting a path through the thick tangle of underwood.

The most accessible and fortunately also the most interesting of the forts is that which I have marked as the "Mud fort" on the map, at the north-west angle of the Baibaniyan village. This fort is in shape an irregular pentagon, having the following dimensions:—

Eastern wall	1,6[illegible]	English yards.
Northern	1,6[illegible]	" "
North-western	900	(about)
South-western	1,320	(about)
Southern	[illegible]	

There seems to be some sort of order even in the irregularity as the eastern and northern walls are the same length, as also the north-western and southern. The north and south-western, however, are so covered with jungle that it is impossible to arrive at more than an approximate measurement.

Though called the 'Mud fort,' the walls of this fort are not really of mud. The peasants of the neighbouring villages have made breaches through the walls in some places to enable them to get at their rice-fields in the inside, and in entering the fort by one of these breaches a sort of section is obtained which reveals the nature of the construction. The following section will explain how the wall is made. The centre or heart consists of layers of stone

AB. Base of the Wall. C. Moat. DD. Earth.

gradually diminishing to a point, and this is covered and entirely hidden with about four feet of earth closely rammed. The breadth at the base from A to B is by measurement 112 feet, and the height we guessed to be about 50 feet.

The wall is surrounded by a deep and broad moat, and a slight but continuous ridge, evidently artificial, runs parallel to the moat on its outer edge. Outside all this again, at a distance in some places of as much as half a mile, runs a nalld which by a little dexterous cutting and deepening has been made into a very efficacious outer moat lined here and there with a wall of laterite.

The interior of the fort is a large plain covered with debris of stone buildings, tanks, and patches of jungle; a considerable portion of it is now cultivated, and near the south wall is the remains of a small indigo factory which was conducted by a European for some years, but has now long ago been abandoned.

The natives have a tradition that the north-western corner contained the palace of the Raja, and this is partially confirmed by the greater height and strength of the works in that corner, and by the numerous remains of buildings still traceable. The principal of these I have called the "keep" on the map, as the natives assert that it was the highest and strongest part of the fort. It is a strong square tower of which about 20 feet only now remain; the stones are carefully hewn and placed together, but without any traces of cement or mortar. A simple but graceful style of ornament is effected by a straight moulding running round the middle of each course, above which the top of each stone is sloped inwards with a small pine-apple shaped projection in the centre. The effect of this arrangement cannot be fully seen owing to the jungle, but when perfectly visible, the broken

light and shade produced by it must have lent a peculiar grace and elegance to the otherwise massive and solid building. In spite of the native idea of its being a keep or citadel, I am disposed to think this building must have been a Shiva-temple, as the architecture is precisely similar to the other ancient temples to that deity in other parts of Orissa, and the dimensions of the building, which is not more than 100 feet square, are too small for the purposes of a citadel. On the top, half hidden by trees, are the capitals of some pillars of the dark coloured stone known as mugani pathar or chlorite: none of the columns however remain. In the centre is a well or tank—similar to the square enclosure round the linga-stone in Shiva-temples; so that I imagine the stone walls must have formed a lofty platform surmounted by an open hall surrounded by pillars, in the centre of which was the linga in its sunken square enclosure. The capitals, though massive, are quite plain and without ornament.

At the foot of this building on the south side is a curious little hollow where the trees and jungle are perhaps more dense than in any other part. This is called the Jaychandi Ban or Jaychand's jungle. Who Jaychand was nobody knows. In the heart of this jungle, approached by a narrow winding path, is a small platform

2 feet high on which have been set up, in quite modern times, some beautiful pieces of sculpture which have probably fallen from the temple above. There is the lower half of a female figure bedecked with jewels, and the legs of a man running—both in high relief. There is also an exquisite piece of arabesque carving—probably the moulding or edge of the frame enclosing the relievo. Though much defaced the general design is clearly traceable.* There is a freedom and graceful play of outline in the rounded foliage which is rare in ancient remains in this part of India. The rest of this moulding is probably hidden beneath the masses of laterite, stones, and debris of all kinds. If I have an opportunity of visiting the spot at any future time, I may succeed in unearthing more of it. The people said they remembered in their youth having seen stones with inscriptions in the Nagari character, but unfortunately knew not where to find them. The Nagari character is not understood by any one except a very few Pandits in this part of the country, and as far as I know was never used in inscriptions, which are all in a bad form of Kutila, but the difference between Kutila and Nagari would not be appreciable by the natives here.

The idols and carvings in the Jayachandi Ban are still worshipped, and in consequence, are smeared all over with that mixture of oil and vermilion (*sindur*), which is so freely applied to all sacred buildings and trees. A small plot of rent free land has been assigned to some Brahmans who carry on the worship at stated seasons, but do not seem able to specify what god the shrine is sacred to. This Jayachandi Ban is evidently a modern arrangement. Some one found these mutilated bits of sculpture and set them up and invited people to worship them, partly as a bit of Brahmanical speculation, and probably the speculator's name was Jayachand. This sort of thing goes on even at the present day: an Uriya will worship anything, especially if he does not know what it is, and a Brahman tells him it is a *debata*.

The western gate of the fort which is close to the Ban, was probably only a sort of postern, as it is only wide enough for one horseman at a time. The sketch below represents its present appearance. In the wall will be noticed the

sockets of the hinges of the doors which at one time stood there. Crossing the moat by a strong though narrow bridge, we come to a second doorway, precisely similar to the first. This is merely a gateway in a sort of *tete de pont*, protecting the bridge across the moat.

Moving round to the north wall of the fort we come upon the largest and most perfect group of remains in the whole building. It is called the Sat Gambhira Attalika—literally "Palace of the seven deeps," this name however is a mere modern corruption of *sat gumbaz* or 'the seven domes'†. The building consists of six large rooms which have evidently at one time been vaulted, and the passage through them or gateway counted as a seventh room,—which was probably covered in and vaulted like the others. The ground plan is—

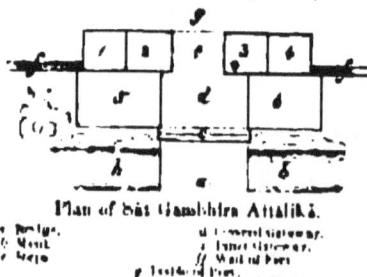

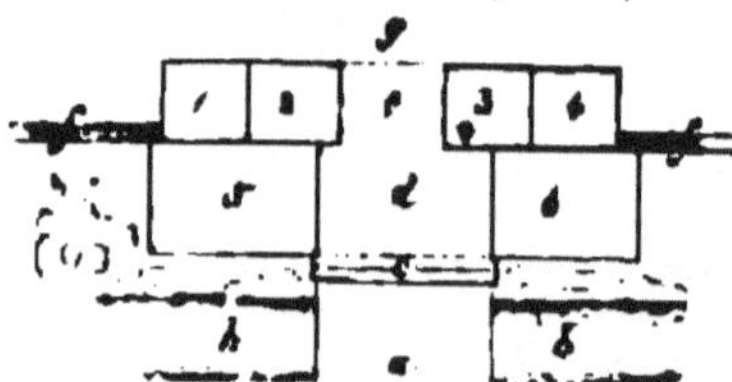

Plan of Sat Gambhira Attalika.

a Bridge. b, h Moat. c Steps. d Central Gateway. e Inner Gateway. ff Wall of Fort. g Inside of Fort.

as far as could be made out from the top of the wall at *; but as a big black bear was sleep-

* I have represented the broken and undecipherable portions by cross-shading and dotted spaces.

† The Uriyas, have soon changed the comparatively little known Persian word *gumbaz* 'a dome,' into their own perso-

ing at the foot of the wall in No. 3, and I had unfortunately no gun with me, having brought a sketch-book and measuring rod instead, it was not thought prudent to remain long in that neighbourhood. For the same reason there was not time to make more than a plan of the building with a rough measurement. The covered gateway is about 40 feet wide and 25 feet deep, and rooms Nos. 5 and 6, though so encumbered with rubbish as to be quite inaccessible were judged to be about the same size. This approximation will enable the reader to judge of the size of the other rooms. The rest of the palace was probably, as usual in Bengal, built of mud with thatched roofs,—which mode of construction would account for its total disappearance.

The last fort of the group is that which I have called the "Stone Fort," as its walls, as far as they could be seen, are built of hewn stone not covered, as in the other, with mud. It seems more modern than the mud fort, and may either have been originally a mere out-work to the other, which seems improbable from its nearly equalling it in size, or was more likely—as I shall show presently—a comparatively modern erection, built when the old fort had become so far ruined as to be no longer tenable.

The eastern entrance is through a vast hall or yard, with walls of hewn stone in which are still to be seen the staples to which, in native tradition, the Rájá's elephants were fastened. This gateway is called the *Háthí dwár* or *Háthí bandhá dwár*, (elephant gate, or elephant-enclosure gate.) The southern door-way,—of which only a crumbled heap of stones remains,—is called the *Sona mukhi*, or golden faced gate, the origin of which name I cannot trace; but as many places in northern Orissa are called Soná-mukhi,—even bare salt-marshes washed by the sea, thus the appellation must be very ancient, and the allusion which it was meant to convey has become obscure. The only suggestion offered is—that it refers to the golden face of the idol Jagannáth at Puri—miniature copies of which are to be seen in many parts of Orissa. Such an idol may have stood in or near this gateway.

THE SO-CALLED DASYUS OF SÁNCHI.

By BABU RÁJENDRALÁLA MITRA, Hon. M.R.A.S.

Mr. Fergusson, in his magnificent work on "Tree and Serpent Worship," has discussed at great length the ethnology of a race of men represented on the Sánchi bas reliefs, whom he designates the Dasyus or aborigines of India. The deductions he has drawn, however, are not warrantable from the premises on which he has argued. As the subject is of some importance in connexion with the history of the Sánchi Tope, a summary of it will perhaps not be uninteresting.

The people who are called Dasyus or aborigines, as distinct from the Aryans, are generally represented as people of the woods, living in thatched huts, wearing a small dhuti wrapped round the waist, and possessing no ornaments. Their head dress consists occasionally of a plain skull-cap, but frequently of plaited or matted hair wound round the head, and tied on the crown in a conical form. Occasionally they allow the hair to hang behind in loose tresses. Most of them have beards: a few appear with shaven chins. They sit with their knees raised and legs crossed and tied round with a strip of cloth or a napkin, and are occupied in splitting wood or other domestic tasks; occasionally navigating in rude canoes; but they never seem to mix with the community at large, except for the observance of religious rites. They have invariably by them a chafing dish with a blazing fire, a pair of tongs, and a bowl which, from its shape, appears to be made of the hard shell of the gourd. It was carried about hanging from the left hand. In one instance a man has a stand of the shape of a mord, over which he holds something which appears to us, from the tracing of writing on it, to be a scroll or a mass of written paper; a companion of his is folding or unfolding a similar scroll or bundle, and a third is taking up some burning charcoal with his tongs. Mr. Fergusson, following General Cunningham, takes the first scroll to be a flagon from which the man is pouring something into his fire pot, and the second a fan with which the owner is enlivening his fire; but the appearance of the scrolls and the position and action of the hands according to several intelligent European gentlemen including two professional artists, are entirely against

---

line position. The change was probably caused by their approaching the building from the top of the walls, as they took me; seen from this position the rooms look like deep vaults, and it was not till I had the jungle cleared from the northern face that I convinced them the rooms were not underground.

this supposition. Mr. Fergusson himself half suspects the persons to be hermits, and attributes their rarity in the A m a r á v a t i sculptures, to the scarcity of D a s y u s at the time.*

Some of these figures are repeated on the temples of B h u v a n e s h v a r a. They appear old and emaciated, having by their sides a pair of tongs, a gourd pot, and a chafing dish. The scene is scrupulously true to life, and may be found to this day not only in every part of India, but even beyond it, and everywhere it represents an Aryan of the third order, *i. e.*, a hermit or ascetic (V á n a p r a s t h a) seated at his ease, reading his prayer book, or attending to his domestic occupations, and not a non-Aryan. Adverting to some of these houseless hermits on the shores of the Caspian Sea, M. de Pauly observes—"On trouve encore à Bakou quelques adorateurs du feu, dont la personnalité est particulièrement intéressante. L'aspect de ces feux perpétuels, sortant spontanément de la terre offre au coup d'œil vraiment magique, surtout pendant la nuit; dans le voisinage de ces feux se trouve une sorte de temple ou de couvent dans lequel les derniers débris des antiques adorateurs du feu, représentés par quelques vieux Indous desséchés, presque nus, semblables à des fantômes ambulants, pratiquent sur eux-mêmes leurs macérations contre nature, et célèbrent leur culte idolâtre, triste et misérable parodie de la doctrine de Zerdoucht."†

General Cunningham, from his thorough knowledge of Indian life, at once took the S á n c h i D a s y u s for ascetics, and no one who has once seen a group of S a n n y á s í s at H a r d w á r, B a n a r a s, or other sacred places, could for a moment mistake them. The head gear, the style of sitting, the tongs, the gourd, and the blazing fire, are so peculiar and characteristic that I, as a Hindu—perfectly familiar with the scene—cannot possibly mistake it, and I have no hesitation in asserting that the D a s y u s in such scenes are entirely imaginary. It might be said that the hermits of the present day are generally celibates, whereas the D a s y u s of the S á n c h i T o p a have women and children about them. But the objection is of no moment, as we have ample evidence to show that the ancient Aryan hermits or sages were not altogether free from domestic ties. According to M a n u, "when the father of a family perceives his muscles become flaccid, and his hair grey, and sees the child of his child, let him seek refuge in a forest, abandoning all food eaten in towns and his household utensils, let him repair to the lonely wood, committing the care of his wife to her sons, or accompanied by her if she choose *to attend him*. Let him take up his consecrated fire, and all his domestic implements for making oblations to it, and departing from the town to the forest, let him dwell in it, with complete power over his organs of sense and of action." This state of hermitage or V á n a p r a s t h a was subsequently exchanged for that of the S a n n y á s í, or houseless mendicant, but the distinction was rarely very rigidly observed; and the transition, when it did take place, was so gradual as to be imperceptible. Hence it is that we find the ancient sages generally described as living in woods and retired places, but not without women and children about them. K á l i d á s a makes the sage K a n v a live in a wood, with about half a dozen maidens—including S h a k u n t a l á, in his hermitage. K á s h y a p a, in the same way, has his retreat full of women of different ranks and a boy. S í t á is said to have lived in the hermitage of V a s i s h t h a, with her two sons who were borne there; and almost every ancient story book has its tale of hermitages having feminine and juvenile residents. No doubt these works treat of several fictions, but it is not to be supposed that their authors outraged the sense of propriety of their readers by describing hermits having wife and children and female lodgers in their cells, if they had not found such things to be common in their times. The Vedas, the Upanishads, the great epics, and the Puránas, also describe sages, rishis, and munis, having females about them; and the presence of such persons cannot, therefore, be taken as inconsistent with ancient Indian ascetic life.

The same practice also prevailed among the Buddhists, and priestesses or female mendicants—the Σεμναί of Clement of Alexandria—are frequently named in the Avadánas the Játakas and other legendary writings. In Mr. James D'Alwis's translation of the *Attanagalu Vansa* we have a remarkable instance of this. As the story there given is of importance, in connexion with the question at issue, and cannot readily be had for reference, I shall quote it entire. It forms a part of the Sáma Játaka, and runs as follows:—

* *Tree and Serpent Worship*, p. 1[illegible].

† *Peuples de la Russie*, p. 14[illegible].

"Once upon a time when Pillyuk was king of Baranes, Gotama was born unto a hermit, named Dukûla, and was named Sâma. After the son had grown up, Dukûla and his wife Parikâ went one day into the jungle in quest of roots and fruits. There they encountered a storm, and being much wet, were obliged to take shelter under a tree close to a hole inhabited by a malignant serpent. Whilst the venerable pair were standing there, dripping from their garments, a cobra issued a venomous blast, whereby they were instantly struck blind. In this helpless condition their son discovered and conducted them home, and began to nourish and maintain them with the affection of a dutiful son. Sometime afterwards the king went upon a hunting expedition, and rested on the banks of the Migasammata, not far from the hermitage. He had not, however, been long there before he saw the footsteps of deer that came down to the river to drink; and, thinking that he could kill them, lay in ambush. Immediately a remarkably handsome person with a pitcher came down to the river surrounded by a flock of deer. Amazed at the sight and wishing to ascertain whether it was a nymph of the forest whom he thus beheld, he loosed a dart which, alas! severely wounded him. In the agonies of death the wretched man put his pitcher by him, and, falling on the ground, began to exclaim, 'Who can be the enemy of a person that was devoted to the religious duties of the eight sîlas and ten kusalas? Who, indeed, could desire the death of an innocent person like myself?' Hearing these cries the king approached his victim, proclaimed that he was Pillyuk, king of Baranes, explained the motive with which he had shot him, and desired to know who or what he was. Whereupon Sâma replied, 'I was born in this forest, I am the only prop and support of two parents, both aged and blind. Little do they know of the mishap that has happened to me. They will indeed be much grieved and distressed when they find me thus delaying. I alone gave them what they desired. Twice daily have I washed them and thrice have I fed them. Who indeed will give them a drop of water even after asking ten times? They will be parched like fishes out of water. Who, alas! will succour and help those, who, probably, at this very moment are anxiously waiting my return and are watching for the first sounds of my footsteps?' Thus lamenting, he began to weep, not for himself, but for the destitution in which he would leave his feeble parents. Horror seized the king at the reflection that his conduct was calculated to deprive of life three persons who had exercised the duties of Brahmachariyâ, and that he could not escape the torments of hell if they all died; and touched by the lamentations of the youth, he promised to succour and help his parents until his death. Sâma, relying upon his faithful promises, blessed the king, and desiring him to convey his respects and the sad tidings of his death to his blind parents, closed both his eyes and dropped down as if he had expired.

"Instantly a goddess named Bahusundari, who had been Sâma's mother in his tenth birth before the present, perceiving the danger to the hermit-boy and also to his parents, as well as the king, made her appearance on the spot; and, after rebuking the king for his conduct and advising him how he should behave towards Sâma's parents, watched over Sâma.

"The king sorely afflicted with grief, picked up the pitcher which had been filled up by Sâma, and taking the path which he had been directed, reached the humble cottage of the blind pair, who sat anxiously watching the return of their son. They now heard the sound of advancing footsteps, but, knowing that they were not those of their son, inquired, 'who approached the door?' The stranger announced that he was Pillyuk, the king of Baranes; and entered with them into a conversation, in the the course of which he delicately disclosed their son's fate and the particulars connected with it, offering at the same time to succour them through life. Unbounded was now the grief of the hapless parents, to which they gave utterance in the language of despair, falling down, and each bitterly crying, 'Oh, son Sâma! from the day I have lost my sight, have I, by thy unceasing attentions, felt that I have acquired divine eyes. Where hast thou now gone? How shall I henceforth live? Son, thou hast never done nor conceived any evil towards us, or any other being. Thou hast never uttered a falsehood. Thou hast never committed life-slaughter; ever hast thou maintained the observance of the pancha sîla.' The king tried his utmost to console them but without success. Afterwards, turning to the king, the blind parents addressed him, saying, that they had no faith in his proffered protection, and that all the favour they desired was to be led to the place where Sâma lay. The king

compelled by leading the point of a stick which the blind ones held in their hands. When they reached their destination, the bereaved parents again gave vent to their feelings by much weeping, and praying to the titular gods. The mother, on examination, finding that all signs of life had vanished, gave utterance to the following *Satya Kiriyá*:—'If it be true that my son Sáma unceasingly devoted himself to the duties of Brahmachariya and that he has ever maintained the ordinances of the *Atthasila*; and if it be also true that I have entertained no other faith except Buddhism, and that I have ever performed *[illegible] Bhávana*, may, by the power of these truths, my son receive life.' By the influence of this *Satya Kiriyá* and by the might of the gods, Sáma moved from one side to another. When the father had also uttered a similar *Satya Kiriyá*, Sáma again moved to a side, and by the power of the goddess already named he revived, and the parents received their lost sight. Instantly the morning sun arose, and Sáma dismissed the astonished king, after preaching to him on the merits of nourishing one's parents, and above all of leading a religious life, as they were testified to by his miraculous restoration to life."—p. 167 et seqq.

This story will no doubt appear as a Buddhist adaptation of the anecdote of Dasaratha and the blind sage Andhaka; but it has been reproduced in stone on the standing pillar of the western gateway of the Sánchi Tope, and we see in it Gautama as Sáma wounded by the King, and his parents, the hermit and his wife, dressed in the same garb which has been assigned to the Dasyus. According to the Játaka, Sáma recovered from his wounds and was restored to his parents, as we see in the sculpture. The *Rámáyana* kills the boy and sends his parents to the funeral pyre, to immolate themselves.

The following is Mr. Griffith's version of the Rámáyana story* as related by the king to the blind hermits:—

"High-minded saint, not I thy child,
A warrior, Dasaratha styled,
I bear a grievous sorrow's weight,
Born of a deed which good men hate.
My lord, I came to Sarju's shore
And in my hand my bow I bore,
For elephant or beast of chase,
That sought by night his drinking place.
There from the stream a sound I heard,
As if a jar the water stirred.
An elephant, I thought, was nigh:
I aimed and let an arrow fly.
Swift to the place I made my way,
And there a wounded hermit lay
Gasping for breath; the deadly dart
Stood quivering in his youthful heart.
I hastened near with pain oppressed,
He faltered out his last behest,
And quickly, as he bade me do,
From his pierced side the shaft I drew.
I drew the arrow from the rent,
And up to heaven the hermit went,
Lamenting, as from earth he passed,
His aged parents to the last.
Thus unawares the deed was done,
My hand, unwitting, killed thy son:
For what remains, O, let me win,
Thy pardon for my heedless sin."

Mr. Fergusson has published this scene in his great work,† but says that it represents one of those transactions between the Hindus and Dasyus which have probably only a local meaning, and to which, therefore, it is improbable we shall ever be able to affix a definite meaning. To those, however, who are familiar with the story of the Rámáyana and the Játaka, the indefiniteness will give place to unmistakable certainty, the only difficulty being the presence of a companion of the king in the scene of action, due probably to the Buddhist version having included such a personage in the tale—whose name has been omitted in Mr. D'Alwis's abstract as unimportant. According to the Rámáyana, the king went to the wood in his car, and was attended by his charioteer. General Cunningham, as already observed, takes the blind hermits of Sánchi to be ascetics, and adds—"I am unable to offer any explanation of this curious scene, but it may possibly have reference to some event in the early life of Shakya." Mr. Fergusson appeals to this scene as an evidence of the Aryans or Hindus having formerly indulged in the wicked pastime of shooting the inoffensive Dasyus; but if our identification be correct it will of course lose its only foothold.

Exception might also be taken to our identification of the so-called Dasyus with Vánaprastha ascetics on the ground of its being inconsistent in such people to engage in domestic and pastoral occupations. But the laws of Manu do not at all prohibit such pursuits. On the contrary, they ordained that the retired hermit should not only live in a hut and go about dressed, but even horde food sufficient to last for a year (vi. 18). He should also provide means for the performance of various rites

* Rámáyana, vol. II. p. 241, and compare another version in his *Specimens of Old Indian Poetry*, p. 12.

† Fergusson's Tree and Serpent Worship, Plate XXX. page 133.

and ceremonies, make oblations on the hearth to the three sacred fires, not omitting in due time the ceremonies to be performed at the conjunction and opposition of the moon, and also to "perform the sacrifice ordained in honour of the Lunar asterisms, make the prescribed offering of new grain, and solemnize holy rites every four months, and at the winter and summer solstices." Nothing has been said by Manu as to the propriety or otherwise of ascetics keeping cattle; but the epics and the the Purânas clearly show that the ancient sages were partial to milk, and the saintly character of Vasishtha was not in any way opposed to his keeping the famous cow Nandini. The rites enjoined them could not be performed without an ample supply of milk. The Buddhist ascetics, likewise, lived in huts, and not unfrequently collected money enough to dedicate images and topes built at their cost. During their four months cases they lived in monasteries together, with their religious sisterhood.

Some of the hermits in the Sânchi bas-reliefs are engaged in worshipping the five-headed, Nâga, but as the Hindu recognised in it an emblem of the sempiternal divinity, Ananta, and the the Buddhist a race of superhuman beings worthy of adoration,—devotion to it would not be by any means unbecoming a hermit, who is required to observe all the necessary regular and periodical rites and ceremonies.

The last and most important argument of Mr. Fergusson in support of the non-Aryan origin of the Dasyus is founded upon their features; but at Sânchi the figures are generally so small, so rough, and so weather-worn, that their indications of the aboriginal broad face and flat nose cannot be relied upon. That the appearance of youth and beauty, and rank and wealth, should be different from that of age, decay, decrepitude, and squalid poverty, is a fact which none will question, and therefore what are taken in the sculptures for ethnic peculiarities, may be entirely due to a desire to mark the distinctions of condition.

It may be added that the term Dasyu itself is Aryan, and indicates an Aryan and not a non-Aryan race. According to Manu, all those tribes of men who sprung from the mouth, the arm, the thigh, and the foot of Brahma, but who became out-castes by having neglected their duties, are called Dasyus or plunderers (X 45); and the designation therefore fails to convey the idea which the learned author of the History of Architecture wishes to attach to it.

THE TEMPLE AT HALABÍD.

By CAPT. J. S. F. MACKENZIE.

Sixteen miles north of Hassan, in the Mysore province, is Halabid, or as Ferishtah the Muhammadan historian calls it, Dhur Samudra, once the capital of the Belála kings, who ruled one of the minor states into which Southern India was formerly divided. Fables and the dimness of a remote period throw illusive shadows over the traditions of these kings of a bye-gone age. Doubt and uncertainty haunt the enquirer into their unilluminated history.

From inscriptions and other sources it appears, however, that the Belála kings held the sceptre from about 950 A. D. to 1310 A. D. when a Muhammadan army, led by Kafur, plundered their capital for the first time. An expedition sent by Muhammad III. in 1326 finally destroyed Halabid. The seat of a declining government was removed by Vishnu Verdhana, the then reigning sovereign, to Joour, better known by the name of the Moti Taláv (Lake of Pearls), 12 miles north of the famous Seringapatam. Vishnu Verdhana was converted from the Jaina religion—the religion of his forefathers—by the celebrated Vaishnava reformer, Rámánujácháryá, a reformer who—protected by the king—hesitated not at using physical force to convert the followers of the heterodox Jaina religion, and by grinding their priests in an oil mill effectually did away with anything like active opposition. After his conversion, Vishnu Verdhana is said to have resided at Belúr (the present head-quarters of the taluqa, and distant 10 miles from Halabid); and, from an inscription there, it appears he rebuilt the temple Keshava Perumal in the year 1116 A. D.

Such is the account given, of the most important event in the history of the Belála kings by Buchanan in his *Journey through Mysore and Canara.** A cursory examination of known dates, however, proves that the Verdhana, who became a Vaishnava, was not the same Verdhana who fled before the Musalman invasion of 1362.

---

* Conf. Buchanan, *Journey*, &c. vol. II. p. 81, and vol. III. p. 391.

The latest date assigned to the birth of Rama nuja A'charyá is A. D. 1025. The final Muhammadan conquest of the Belála capital was in 1326. In order that these statements might agree, we should be compelled to allow that the great Vaishnava reformer lived for a period of 300 years. Nowhere in the whole of Halebíd do we find a vestige of its having been at any time the seat of the Vaishnava religion. The temples are either Jaina *bastis* or dedicated to Shiva. It is therefore clear that they were erected by kings professing one of these two religions, and the date of their building cannot be later than 1025 A. D. How long they were erected before, it is impossible now to determine, for the history of the builders is buried under the dust of bye-gone ages, and has been forgotten in the lapse of centuries. The inscriptions on the walls of the Hoisala Ishwara, or larger temple, prove it must have been in existence at a time when the Norman conquest of England was a hardly-established fact, and long before many of England's grandest Cathedrals were thought of.

Tradition—a people's history—has preserved for us the story connected with the capital. In the reign of the ninth king it happened that his favourite concubine fell greatly in love with his nephews, who are said to have been remarkably handsome men. Each in his turn treated all her advances and overtures with contempt. Her love now changed to hate. In order to be revenged, she did not scruple to charge the nephews with having made overtures to her. Furious on hearing this, the king ordered them to be impaled, and their bodies, like those of common thieves, exposed at the city gates. The gate to the south of the Jaina *bastis* is pointed out as being the one where this was done. Hearing what had happened, their unfortunate mother ran to the palace to demand justice. Not only was she refused admittance, but the inhabitants of the city were commanded not to give her assistance of any sort or kind. Weary and worn, the unfortunate woman wandered from street to street, only to find that every door was closed against her, and every helping hand withheld. At length a poor potter took compassion upon the bereaved mother, drew her aside, and supplied her with the refreshment of which she was so much in want. Refreshed, she turned round and cursed the king, prophesying that his race would soon be extinct and his capital fall into ruins. She, however, out of gratitude for the kindness shown her by the potter, spared the street in which he lived. Her prophecy was soon fulfilled. A Muhammadan invasion shortly afterwards took place; the whole of the city with the exception of one street was laid in ruins. To this day the street which was saved, goes by the name of the Potter's Street.

The old city was surrounded by an outer wall having nine gates, and close upon 6 miles in length. The stones are cyclopean and were trimmed to fit each other. No mortar was employed. From a comparison of this work with the temples, it is conjectured that the walls are the work of a prior and different race. The popular idea that these walls once enclosed 770 temples of various kinds, is supported by the immense number of broken shafts, pillars, columns, capitals and carvings of every sort, used in forming the bund of a large neighbouring tank.

Of all these temples only five now remain, viz., the Kait Ishwara, Hoisala Ishwara, and three Jaina *bastis*.

Time, assisted by a banian tree, whose roots are embedded in its Vimana (or pyramidal tower over the spot where the god or his emblem is enthroned) is fast reducing the Kait Ishwara to a shapeless mound. In its pristine state this temple must have been a noble specimen of its architect's skill. The carvings, which adorned its walls, though small when compared with those of the larger temple, display a fineness of detail in execution which might be equalled but could scarcely be surpassed.

Mr. Fergusson, in his History of Architecture, when treating of the Chalukya style, has made the following remarks* with regard to Hoisala Ishwara, or larger temple:—

"It (the Kait Ishwara) is however surpassed in size and magnificence by its neighbour, the great temple, which, taking it altogether, is perhaps the building on which the advocate of Hindu architecture would desire to take his stand. Unfortunately it was never finished. ....The general arrangement of the building is.......a double temple.......Such double temples are by no means uncommon in India, but the two sanctuaries usually face each other, and have the porch between them. The dimensions may

* *History of Architecture*, vol. II. pp. 414-418.

be roughly stated as 200 feet square over all, including all the detached pavilions. The temple itself is 160 feet N. and S. by 122 feet E. and W. Its height, as it now remains, to the cornice is about 25 feet from the terrace on which it stands. It cannot, therefore, be considered by any means as a large building, though large enough for effect. This, however, can hardly be judged of as it now stands, for there is no doubt but that it was intended to raise two pyramidal spires over the sanctuaries, four smaller ones in front of these, and two more, one over each of the two central pavilions, ...and if carried out with the richness of detail exhibited in the Kait Iswara would have made up a whole, which it would be difficult to rival anywhere.

"The material out of which the temple is erected is an indurated pot-stone, of volcanic origin, found in the neighbourhood. This stone is said to be soft when first quarried, and easily cut in that state, though hardening on exposure to the atmosphere. Even this, however, will not diminish our admiration of the amount of labour bestowed on the temple, for, from the number of parts still unfinished, it is evident, that, like most others of its class, it was built in block, and carved long after the stone had become hard. As we now see it, the stone is of a pleasing creamy colour, and so close-grained as to take a polish like marble.........The enduring qualities of the stone seem to be unrivalled, for though neglected and exposed to all the vicissitudes of a tropical climate for more than six (eight) centuries, the minutest details are as clear and sharp as the day they were finished . . . .

"It is of course impossible to illustrate so complicated and so varied a design...The building stands upon a terrace from 5 to 6 feet in height, and paved with large slabs. On this stands a *frieze of elephants* following all the sinuosities of the plan and extending to some 710 feet in length, and containing not less than 2000 elephants, most of them with riders and trappings, sculptured as only an Oriental can represent the wisest of brutes. Above these is a *frieze of shardulas*, or conventional lions—the emblems of the Hoisala Belálas who built the temple. Then comes a scroll of infinite beauty and variety of design; over this a frieze of horsemen and another scroll; over which is a bas-relief of scenes from the Râmâyana, representing the conquest of Ceylon and all the varied incidents of that epic. This, like the other, is about 700 feet long. (The frieze of the Parthenon is less than 550 feet.) Then come celestial beasts [crocodiles?] and celestial birds [swans?] and all along the east front a frieze of groups from human life, and then a cornice, with a rail, divided into panels each containing two figures. Over this are windows of pierced slabs like those of Bailur, though not so rich or varied. . . . . In the centre, in place of the windows, is first a scroll and then a frieze, of gods and heavenly apsaras, dancing girls, and other objects of Hindu mythology. This frieze, which is about 5 feet 6 inches in height, is continued all round the western front of the building, and extends to some 400 feet in length. . . . . Every great god of the Hindu Pantheon finds his place. Some of these are carved with a minute elaboration of detail, which can only be reproduced by photography, and may probably be considered as the most marvellous exhibition of patient human labour that the world ever produced.

"It must not, however, be considered that it is only for patient industry that this building is remarkable. The mode in which the eastern face is broken up by the larger masses, so as to give height and play of light and shade, is a better way of accomplishing what the Gothic architects attempted by their transepts and projections. This, however, is surpassed by the western front, where the variety of outline and the arrangement and subordination of the various facets in which it is disposed, must be considered a masterpiece of design in its class. If the frieze of gods were spread along a plain surface, it would lose more than half its effect, and the vertical angles, without interfering with the continuity of the frieze, give height and strength to the whole composition. The disposition of the lower line of friezes is equally effective. Here again the artistic combination of horizontal with vertical lines, and the play of outline and of light and shade, far surpass anything in Gothic art. The effects are just what the mediæval architects were often aiming at, but they never attained them so perfectly as was done at Halabid.

"If it were possible to illustrate the Halabid temple to such an extent as to render its peculiarities familiar, there would be few things more interesting or more instructive than to institute a comparison between it and the Parthenon at Athens. . . . .

"The Halabîd temple...is regular, but with a studied variety of outline in plan, and even greater variety in detail. All the pillars of the Parthenon are identical, while no two facets of the Indian temple are the same; every convolution of every scroll is different. No two canopies in the whole building are alike, and every part exhibits a joyous exuberance of fancy scorning every mechanical restraint. All that is wild in human faith or warm in human feeling is found pourtrayed on these walls; but of pure intellect there is little—less than there is of human feeling in the Parthenon."

Strange to say, both here and at Bailur, this frieze of horsemen appears to have been the more especial object of aversion to the conquerors of the capital. It is with difficulty, and only where concealment has been afforded by some figure in front, that one can find a complete figure of man and horse. All have been more or less mutilated. It appears to have been the custom then, not only among the horsemen but generally, for all men, to wear their hair—like the Sinhalese of the present day—tied up in a knot behind; long boots were always worn by the riders, whose seat is more European than native; in some instances their horses were protected by network, similar in every outward respect to that of the old Norman knight. The cavalry were armed generally with a short Roman-like sword; and from this it is conjectured they usually dismounted to fight; some however are delineated with lances. The saddle-cloth was indispensable, and stirrups were not unknown.

Fah Hian,* (who, as Col. Sykes conjectures,) visited Elura about A. D. 400, found there "a Sangharâma of the former Buddha Kâshyapa. It is constructed out of a great mountain of rock hewn to the proper shape. This building has altogether five stories. The lowest is shaped into the form of an elephant, and has five hundred stone cells in it. The second is in the form of a lion, and has four hundred chambers. The third is shaped like a horse, and has three hundred chambers. The fourth is in the form of an ox, and has two hundred chambers. The fifth story is in the shape of a dove and has one hundred chambers in it."—Now the order of friezes at Halabîd, with an interpolation of scenes from the Râmâyana and Mahâbhârata, is the same, except that in lieu of the ox we have the crocodile, and the dove is represented by the sacred goose or swan. This similarity in order cannot be considered accidental, and must, as its prototype at Elura, signify something.

A study of the frieze, where scenes from the Râmâyana and Mahâbhârata are delineated, well repays any trouble. A clearer and better knowledge of these two great Hindu epic poems is obtained by examining these carvings than hours of tedious weary reading would ever give. Although some of the carvings are to a considerable extent mutilated, yet the attitude of the actors and the position of the scene, with reference to those on its right and left, enable us to state with certainty what the sculptor meant to represent. Here we see that, as to-day, so eight hundred years ago, the Hindu mother carried her child on the hip. Large earrings were the fashion among the women of those days, for the lobe of the ear is distended to an enormous extent. Like the natives of the Western Ghâts of the present day, no covering then concealed a woman's breast. As now, so then, children ran about perfectly naked. Looking-glasses were not unknown; for we find a fair one admiring herself in a circular glass.

Both two and four wheeled chariots appear to have been in use. As is natural, kings affected the four-wheeled one more than the two. The wheels were much lower than the body, which was a sort of raised platform. Each wheel had an independent axle. Improvements in carriage building had, however, taken place, for in one instance the solid circular disc is replaced by spokes. The horses were attached, as bullocks are now, to the pole on which the driver stood. Hirapadma, scorning the more common-place horse, has tamed the lion, which is represented as yoked to his war chariot. In all these eight hundred years, no change has been made in the pounding of rice—the same sort of mortar and pestle is now used.

In the upper and larger frieze, where every Hindu god finds a place, and which consists in all of some 2000 figures, is to be seen one which—from its peculiar Assyrian-like look—cannot fail to attract attention. In his right hand he holds a disc, in his left a wand. The fingers of both hands are adorned with rings. His dress, a simple long robe descending below the knee, is thrown back showing a Brahmanical cord. What

* Beal's Travels of Fah-Hian and Sung-Yun, Buddhist Pilgrims, p. 139. Compare Julien's Voyages de Hiouen Thsang tom II. p. 101., and Cunningham's Anc. Geog. of India, pp. 521–[illegible]. It is not at all probable that the *Po-lo-yu* of Fah Hian was Elura, but some place considerably to the S. E. of it.—Ed.

appears of his hair under the hood, which is one with the robe, is curly. His features are by no means Ethiopian. The attitude is easy and his *tout ensemble*, when compared with his bedecked and bejewelled companions—the gods, pleasingly simple. A peculiarity, observable both in this and the lower frieze where underdelineations of the same figure are to be found, is—that he is always in attendance upon, or attended by, a perfectly nude woman, whose only covering is a few snakes? She wears sandals of uncommon pattern, and has large earrings. Her hair is curly but her features by no means of the negro type. The fact that her companion wears a hood would support the idea that he was an inhabitant of a cold climate, but her want of dress and being entwined by snakes would lead one to think she was some unknown goddess or religious devotee. All enquiries from natives and search among authorities fail to show by what right or title these figures take a place among the gods.

The building was originally protected by curtains of cloth hung all round. These have long ago disappeared, but the carvings have in no way suffered by the atmosphere; and if they had not been wilfully mutilated, would have been as clear and perfect as the day they were finished.

In front of each of the eastern doors and under porticos supported by massive, beautifully turned stone pillars, are splendid specimens of Shiva's vehicle—the Bull. The larger is opposite the upper door, and like its companion, is represented in a lying position watching its master's emblem—the Linga. They are each carved out of a single block of stone. So natural is the position, and so well proportioned the parts, that one does not fully realize the size until the dimensions are examined. The larger, formed of stone similar to that employed in the construction of the temple, is sixteen feet long, ten feet high, and seven broad. The stone used for the other bull is finer and admits of a marble polish. "It seems, also, to be potstone or perhaps a talc impregnated with hornblende, and contains small irregular veins of a green shining matter. Its general colour is black with a greenish tinge."*

The general effect of the inside of the temple is somewhat marred by pillars, which evidently formed no part of the original plan, and which were subsequently erected to prop up some cross beams where the stone has unfortunately cracked. Judging from these pillars, as compared with the original ones, it is clear that architecture, so far as finish is concerned, had already deteriorated. If proof were wanting that the Department of Public Works of to-day either wants the means or skill to produce works equal to those of former ages, we have only to turn to the pillar recently erected by that department. It is a single slab of undressed granite which eke out its length and strength in a rough bed of brick and chunam. The walls inside are covered with inscriptions, in old Kanadi, commemorating donations given at various times by different persons.

Jakanáchárya is the reputed architect of this magnificent building, but he is also credited with having built all the temples, similar in style, throughout the district. The number of these is so great, that—even if we allow him the lakh of masons tradition says he always employed—it would be difficult to believe he could have superintended the building of all. A man of the same name is said to have built the temples at Mudure. Jakanácharyá was a prince who, having accidentally killed a Brahman, employed twenty years of life, with the hope of washing away this great sin, in rebuilding temples between Kasi and Rameshwara (Cape Comorin),—so says tradition. The engineers of the Bellála kings did not confine their attention to building alone, but irrigation works were also taken in hand. Tradition has it that the waters of the Yagachi, which flows through a valley distant 10 miles and divided by a range of hills from the Halebid Valley, were brought by a channel to supply the capital with water and fill the neighbouring tanks: a deep cutting on the Hassan-Bailur road at the 16th mile, marks the spot where the channel crossed the saddle of the hills.

It is difficult, when looking at this fine temple, to believe that the builders of the neighbouring mud huts are the descendants of the great masons whose brains planned, and whose hands fashioned, this monument of their skill and taste. What has become of them, and where have they gone, are questions which, though hard to answer, are none the less interesting, and may well form the subject of antiquarian research.

* Buchanan's *Journey*, vol. III. page [illegible]

ON TWO COPPERPLATES FROM VALABHI,

By PROF. RAMKRISHNA GOPAL BHANDARKAR, M.A.

The following are translations of the second halves of two copperplate grants sent to the Editor from Bhaunagar. The second and smaller one, 12 inches by 8¾, is greatly damaged; and the letters are indistinct in many places. The other is 12¾ inches by 10½ and is in a better state of preservation—the right hand edge only being broken off.

The grantor in No. I. is Dharasena IV., the same as in the one translated at page 14. The date is also the same, viz. 326, the month being Mâgha instead of Ashâḍha. The first nine lines and a half have not been translated, as the description of the kings in them is in almost every respect the same as in the corresponding portion of the last and other Valabhi grants.

The grantor in No. II. is Shilâditya I., the son and successor of Dharasena II., the king in Mr. Wathen's first plate. The figured date is—

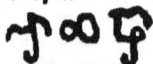

The first figure, having only one side stroke, represents 200. The value of the second we know from Dr. Burn's Châlukya and Gurjara plates to be 80, and the last stands for 6; so that the whole is 286. But the date usually assigned to the father of Shilâditya from Mr. Wathen's plate is 332. I have shown* that this date has been misread and misinterpreted. The first figure in it stands for 200, and the value I have assigned to the second from the evidence available is 70. The date therefore is 272.

These two plates, broken and mutilated as they are, are very interesting. Those hitherto discovered record grants of land to Brâhmaṇs; but both these record grants of land to Buddhist monasteries or vihâras. In the larger plate the village of Yodhâvaka is assigned to a Vihâra constructed by the minister Skandabhaṭa, who appears to have been a pious Buddhist. We see from these, that the Valabhi kings patronised the Buddhists as well as the Brâhmaṇs: Buddhism flourished at the time side by side with Brâhmanism, and the worship of images formed part of the religion.

The genealogy of the Valabhi dynasty has been given at p. 17. The dates gathered from the copper-plate grants I know of are given below. I believe, for reasons elsewhere given, that the era used in these grants is that of the Śaka King.

Dharasena II. ....272 Sh. or 350 A.D.
Shilâditya I. ....286 Sh. „ 364 A.D.
Dharasena IV. (2 grants) 326 Sh. „ 404 A.D.
Shilâditya II. (2 grants) 356 Sh. „ 434 A.D.

PLATE I.

Shrî Dharasena, the great Mâheshvara, the great lord, the king of kings, the great ruler, the universal sovereign, who meditates on his grand-father's feet, enjoying good health, commands all whom it may concern:—Be it known to you that for the increase of the religious merit of my mother and father I have [assigned] to the assembly of the reverend mendicant priests of the Mahâyâna (school) coming from the four quarters to the monastery constructed by Divira-pati Skandabhaṭa in the village of Yodhâvaka in Hastava prâhâra in Surâshṭra, the four divisions of the same village of Yodhâvaka—viz., three for the purpose of [providing] clothing, food,† [means of] sleeping and sitting . . . . and medicine; for the purpose of [providing] the means of worshipping and washing the glorious Buddhas, viz., fragrant ointment, incense flowers, and oil for lamps, and for executing repairs to the monastery (lit. for putting aright the broken parts): and the fourth part of the same village for the further digging, clearing or repairing of the tank dug at the same place by Divirapati Skandabhaṭa, and thus for providing water just at the door, (lit. at the root of the feet). In this manner, by pouring water, the village is assigned as a charity-grant to the monastery, and the tank along with its appurtenances, and whatever is on it, with the creatures living therein, the revenue in grain or gold, the defects* in its condition, and whatever may grow in it spontaneously. The grant is exclusive of whatever may have been given to gods or Brâhmans before; is not to be interfered with by the officers of the king; and is to last on the principle of a hole* in the earth, so long as the moon,

* In a paper recently read at a meeting of the Bombay B. B. R. As. Society. Vide inf.

† Pinda-pâta, is explained as पिण्डपातं भिक्षापात्रपतित ओदनम्, Pinda is a ball, i. e. of rice in this case, and pâta is dropping; hence it means the dropping in of a ball of rice in the Bhikshu's bowl.

* To the list of expressions the senses of which are not accurately known, given by Prof. Dowson, I might add सदशापराधः which occurs in several plates. I have however translated it as in the text.

sun, ocean, earth, rivers, and mountains endure. Therefore, no one shall obstruct the reverend mendicant priests in the act of ploughing the land, causing it to be ploughed or assigning it over [to some person], in virtue of this its condition as an assignment to gods. All future kings, whether of our race or others, bearing in mind that power is transitory and humanity frail, and knowing the good fruits ordinarily arising from grants of land, should recognize this our grant and continue it. It is said, &c. (the rest as in the translation of the plate at page 16.) The prince Dhruvasena is executive officer here.

Engraved by Divirapati Skandabhata, the son of Divirapati Vatsa(?)bhatti, minister for peace and war. S. 330, the fifth day of the dark half of Mâgha.

My own hand.

PLATE II.

Transcript of the second half of another grant to a Buddhist Monastery, found in the ruins of Valabhi.

[illegible] ... ।१।

...[illegible] ... ... ।२।

...[illegible] ... ... ।३।

[illegible] ... ... ।४।

[illegible] ।५।

[illegible] [?] [illegible] [?] [illegible] ... ... ।६।

[illegible] .... [illegible] ।७।

[illegible] &c. [The rest as usual, a word or two only differing].

[illegible] [?] [illegible] ... ... ।१२।

.... [illegible] ... ... ।१३।

स्वहस्तो मम.

Shri Shila . . . the great Maheśvara, whose noble name, procured for him by the enjoyment . . . was Dharmâditya, commands persons in office or holding commissions . . . great [and small] and others . . . . 'Be it known to you, that for the increase of the religious merit of my mother and father, I [have assigned] a field named . . . . on the northern side of the river, in the village of Bahabaenpura (?) in Palatiralakhma [?]; and also a field . . . . in the village of Udrapadraka, to the assembly of the reverend mendicant priests coming from the four quarters, and residing in the monastery constructed by . . . . for [providing] clothing, food, and [the means of] sleeping and sitting, ... and for the purpose of [providing] fragrant ointments, incense, flowers, and for lamps for the glorious Buddhas, and for the repairing of the monastery [lit. putting aright the broken parts]. These fields are granted by pouring water, along with their appurtenances, &c. &c.' [the rest as usual].

The son Dharâdityayashah is executive officer here. Written . . . . . [illegible] on the 6th day of Vaisâkha vadya. My own hand.

MANDARA HILL.

BY BABU RASBIHARI BOSE, BANKA.

This hill stands in the midst of a large plain near Bausi which was lately the head quarters of a sub-division of the district of Bhâgalpur in Bihar. It is of granite and almost devoid of vegetation except near the summit and on one side where it is generally overgrown with low jungle. The ascent has been rendered easy by steps cut in the rock, which run up about two-thirds of the way; but as the hill is upwards of 700 feet high, and is extremely steep and rugged near the top, very few persons can reach the summit without halting in the middle of the journey.

This hill occupies a large place in the ancient

---

* भूमिच्छिद्रन्याय —This expression Bhûmichchhidranyâya, which occurs in a great many copperplates, and which no one has yet attempted to explain, may have some reference to the circumstance that holes in the earth are not permanent but are filled up in the course of time. That this fact was often the subject of thought and remark is shown by the story (in the [illegible] Sec. II. i, and in the Bhâgavata VI. 9 and other works) that Indra transferred the sin he incurred by killing Viśvarûpa, the son of Tvashṭṛi—among other objects and persons—to the earth, and in consideration of her having taken it, gave her a boon, that all holes made in her would be filled up in time. The sense of the expression then is—that 'a grant is to last as long as the sun, the moon, &c. shall endure on the principle of holes in the earth (nyâya means a principle cf. the [illegible] Kâkatâlîya and other nyâyas) that is, as holes in the earth are filled up in time and the earth is whole again and as unchanged, so a grant should survive all revolutions &c. and last unchanged for ever.

† It is on the east side of the river [illegible], 30 miles N. of Bausi and 32 ft. Bhâgalpur [illegible] lat. 24° 50′ N., Long. 87° 4′ E.—Ed.

mythology of the Hindus. It is even mentioned in the accounts of the great deluge, when Vishnu floated on the waters in a state of profound slumber. The Purânas state that a giant of enormous stature then sprung from the secretions of his ears, and having advanced to destroy Brahmâ, Vishnu, and Shiva—the Hindu Triad, who had been produced from other parts of his body, Vishnu gave him battle and, after a protracted struggle of ten thousand years' duration, succeeded in cutting off his head; but the giant's headless trunk having proved equally powerful in the work of destruction, Vishnu was obliged not only to pile Mandara over it, but to keep the hill pressed under his foot, that it might not rise up again to destroy creation. Vishnu is therefore supposed to be always present in the hill under the title of Madhusûdana so-called from Madhukaitabha—the name of the giant thus killed.

The hill is also believed to be the one that was used by the gods and Asurs in churning the ocean. This, as recorded in the Mahâbhârata, was done partly to obtain the *Amrita* which confers immortality, and partly to recover the goddess of Fortune who, in obedience to the curse of a sage, had forsaken heaven and descended into the bosom of the sea. The great serpent who supports the earth on his thousand heads having, on that occasion, consented to act as a string, Mandara hill was selected as the only churning-rod that was capable of withstanding the mighty movement.* The learned are divided as to this hill being identical with the gigantic Mandara that is compared in their books with the fabulous Sumeru which supports the heavens on its head, the earth on its navel, and the nether world on its base, and round whose sides the sun, moon, and stars roll in their accustomed orbits. But the ignorant pilgrims who annually flock to the hill entertain no doubt on this point, especially when they behold with wonder and awe the coil of the great serpent traced round its enormous girth.

Having such memories associated with the Hill, the great sanctity attached to it by the Hindus need not excite wonder. But besides being a place of pilgrimage, the hill possesses great value in the eye of the antiquarian, abounding, as it does, in interesting ruins as well as in natural and artificial curiosities. For a mile or two around its base are to be seen numerous tanks, several old buildings, some stone figures, and a few large wells—which attest the remains of a great city that has long since disappeared. A common saying among the people in the neighbourhood is, that this city contained fifty-two bazars and fifty-three streets besides four times twenty-two tanks. Near the foot of the hill, there is a building, now in ruins, which has an immense number of square holes evidently designed for lamps or *Chirags*. The tradition runs that on the night of the Dewâli festival, there were a hundred thousand lighted *Chirags* placed in these holes by the inhabitants of the city,—each householder being allowed to place there only a single *Chirag*.

About a hundred yards from the above structure may be observed a large building of stone, which is generally ascribed to Râjâ Chola. As the Râjâ is said to have flourished twenty-two centuries ago, the building must be very old. It is built without mortar, and the walls are made of large stones laid upon one another. The roof, which is composed of long and spacious marble slabs, is supported upon huge stone beams 18 inches by 18, and the *Verandah* rests upon massive posts of the same material. The building consists of a large hall in the centre, with an adjoining verandah in front and six dark rooms on the sides—only lighted through small apertures in the perforated windows, which are of various devices.

The rise of the city, like many other ancient Hindu cities, is no doubt due to the sanctity attached to the place, or the great veneration felt for Madhusûdana on the Mandara, which was not inferior to what is inspired by Krishna at Mathurâ, by Jagannâth at Purî, or by Râma at Nâsik. It is said it subsequently became the capital of Râjâ Chola. However when the city fell into ruins, it is difficult to say; but popular tradition ascribes its destruction as well as that of Madhusûdana's temple on the hill to Kâlâpahar, who is charged, rightly or wrongly, with the demolition of every sacred relic of Hindu antiquity throughout the length and breadth of Hindustan. Not far from the building with the square holes, previously mentioned, there is a triumphal arch built of stone containing an inscription in Sanskrit† which seems to show that

* See a spirited rendering of this tale from the Mahâbhârata in Griffith's *Specimens of Old Indian Poetry*, pp. 33-48.—Ed.

† It is written in the old Bengali character of the Tirhut type and in the Sanskrit language. The following is a translation of it by Babu Râjendralâla Mitra:—

'The well disposed and [illegible] Ugrabhairava, son of the [illegible] Thâkura, dedicated his pure and noble place of [illegible] on earth for Srî Madhusûdana in the Śaka year 1461, when the noble Brâhmana [illegible] was the officiating priest. Śaka 1461.'—[A. D. 1539.] *Proceedings of the Asiatic Society of Bengal for November* 1870, page 288.

the city was in existence 270 years ago; for the inscription is dated in the Shaka year 1521, and records the victory of one Chhatrapati and the dedication of the arch to Madhusúdana. This victory evidently marks a series of struggles between Hindu conservatism and Muhammadan fanaticism under which the city must have been gradually depopulated. This must have been the work of time, and could not have been simultaneous with the demolition of Madhusúdana's temple on the hill to which Kálápahár's invasion must have been directed. It may be presumed that Chhatrapati would hardly have thought of dedicating the triumphal arch to Madhusúdana for the purpose of swinging, had not the city been in existence in his time. This supposition finds corroboration in the well known fact, that, after the destruction of the temple on the hill, the image of Madhusúdana was brought down to the plains and located in a new temple built near the arch. The present Zamindars of Mahalpur, who claim to be descended from Chhatrapati, assert that the image was removed to Bausi only when the city was wholly abandoned by the inhabitants. The precise date of this depopulation cannot be ascertained; but it is clear that though the Muhammadans under Kálápahár may have plundered the city when demolishing the temple on the hill, it continued to flourish, though not in its former splendour, for a considerable time afterwards. It is worthy of notice that, according to immemorial custom, the image of Madhusúdana, continues to be brought annually from Bausi to the foot of the hill on the Paush-Sankranti day for the purpose of being swung on the triumphal arch built by Chhatrapati.

The removal of the image to Bausi has no doubt lessened the sanctity of the hill in the estimation of the Hindus; but on the above mentioned day there is annually an immense gathering of pilgrims, ranging from thirty to forty thousand, who come from different parts of the country to bathe in a tank at the foot of the hill. The consequence is a large *mela* or fair which lasts for fifteen days. The origin of the fair is accounted for by the following legend:—

A Rájá of Kanchipur called Cholá was afflicted with leprosy, a disease which, according to the Hindus, visits only those who are especially accursed of heaven. In accordance with this belief he paid visits to all the sacred shrines in India but could nowhere find relief. At last he came to the Mandara. Happening to wash his feet in the water of a spring at the foot of the hill he was surprised to find his leprous ulcers disappear. He next washed his hands with the water, when lo! the disease disappeared from them also. He then widened and deepened the spring which was then called Manohar Kunda, and named it Pápharni, or what cleanses men from sin. In commemoration of the event he instituted the *mela* or fair which was to take place on the last day of Paush, because it was on that day that he used the water of the spring with such miraculous results.

It is also believed that Brahma spent millions and millions of years on the top of this hill in contemplation and prayers to the Supreme. When it was at last over, he offered, according to custom, a betel-nut and other things to the burning pile, but the betel-nut came rolling down the side of the hill and fell into the spring at its base. Thus the waters of the Manohar-kunda or Pápharni became especially sacred, and had the merit of curing Rájá Chola of his leprosy. Dead bodies from the neighbourhood are burnt on its banks, and the bones thrown into it, as if its waters were as holy as those of the Ganges. It is indeed cleared at the time of the fair, but it is impossible for the water to be freed from the stench arising from the putrefaction of the half-burnt bodies that are seen floating on its surface throughout the rest of the year. In spite of of this, the immense host of pilgrims on the day of the fair bathe in it, in the hope of obtaining salvation in a life to come. Women from the most respectable families in the neighbourhood come to perform their ablutions at night that they may not be the objects of vulgar gaze.

As usual on such occasions, the pilgrims also offer oblations to the manes of their deceased ancestors. This is generally done at one of the Ghâts which is deemed especially sacred to the memory of Ráma. For this deified hero is believed to have visited the hill during his twelve years exile from Oudh, and performed the funeral obsequies of Dasaratha his father, at the Ghât which after him is called Dasarathi.

After his miraculous cure, Rájá Chola is said not only to have fixed his capital in the city near the famous spring, but to have spent his immense wealth in beautifying and adorning the hill with marble figures, stone temples, spacious tanks, and deep reservoirs. To him is also attributed the pious fraud of tracing the coil of the great serpent round its sides, so as to induce the belief that the hill was used by the gods in churning the ocean. This, as well as the steps cut in the rock, must have cost enormous sums. But an inscription at the side of the steps which has lately been deciphered* seems to show that they were the work of a Buddhist king named Ugrabhairava. It is however probable that the inscription does not refer to the steps cut in the rock, but, as supposed by the decipherer,† commemorates the dedication of a statue. Though there is at present no statue near the inscription, there are still to be seen many Buddhist and Hindu images lying here and there on the left side of the steps, which have evidently been transported from their original places and mutilated and disfigured by Muhammadan bigotry. There is also a Buddhist temple near the summit of the hill which is held in great veneration by people of the Jains. But even if the honour of cutting the steps in the rock really belongs to Ugrabhairava—as a Buddhist, he would not have traced the coil of the great serpent on the body of the hill in order to keep up the memory of a Hindu superstition.

The steps do not go much higher than Sítákuṇḍa. This is the name of a beautiful oblong tank, about 100 feet by 50, excavated in the body of the rock, nearly 500 feet above the surrounding plain. Every hot spring in India is known by the name of Sítákuṇḍa, it being supposed that Sítá bathed in it after passing through the fiery ordeal to which she was subjected by her husband with a view to test her purity, and thereby imparted to its water the heat which she had imbibed in the flaming pile. But the water in the Sítákuṇḍa on the Mandara is almost as cold as ice. Whether there was formerly a hot spring, the heat of which has become extinct, it is not easy to say. The Mandara Mahátmya, an old Sanskrit work which gives an account of the hill from a religious point of view, describes several springs existing at the place which appear to have been subsequently amalgamated and converted into a tank by Rájá Cholá. That the Sítákuṇḍa has undergone extensive changes within the memory of man is apparent from Col. Francklin's account of it. For when he visited the hill in 1814, there was a cascade or waterfall from the Sítákuṇḍa to the Pápharni (which he calls *Pouphar*).‡ The passage of the cascade may still be clearly traced a few yards from the steps by the smooth surface, abrupt declivities, and deep gorges left by it on that portion of the hill where it fell. But at present the Sítákuṇḍa, instead of overflowing, is scarcely full even during the rains. The pilgrims who visit it are persuaded to believe that it has derived its name from Sítá —who used to bathe in it during her stay in the hill with her husband when banished from Oudh.

On the northern bank of the Sítákuṇḍa, stood the temple of Madhusúdana, said to have been built by Rájá Cholá, now entirely in ruins. The temple appears to have been pulled down, its stones hurled down the sides of the hill to the plain, and the image of Madhusúdana reduced to dust by Muhammadan fanatics. But according to the Bráhmans, Kálápahár could not destroy the image of Madhusúdana, for it leaped into the Sítákuṇḍa on his approach, and cutting a subterranean passage, proceeded to the large tank at Kajrélí near Bhágalpur, where it remained concealed for many years. At length Madhusúdana appeared to a Paṇḍá in a dream and told him of the place of his concealment, whence it was accordingly conveyed back to the Mandára and lodged in a new temple at the foot of the hill. But the Zamindars of Sukdalpur, by whose ancestors the new temple was built, affirm that the image of Madhusúdana, after its plunge into the Sítákuṇḍa, went direct to Paubhi, and thence appeared to one of their ancestors in a dream, and that it was not till they had waited in vain upon the Rájá of that place for recovery of the image, that Madhusúdana condescended to appear in the tank at Kajrélí.

A few feet above the Sítákuṇḍa is another spring which is called Shankha Kuṇḍa from a monster *Shankha* or oyster reposing beneath its waters. The Shankha, to judge of its size by the impression left on the bank, where it was formerly kept, is about 3 feet by 1½. It is said to be the same identical Shankha that is designated in the Mahábhárata as Panchajanya—whose sound used to fill the ranks of the enemy with dismay. The Shankha Kuṇḍa is believed to be very deep. It has been very irregularly excavated, not presenting the appearance of any symmetrical figure, but rather resembling the shape of the oyster which is preserved in it; and

* Vide page 34, note †.

† It is just to state that at the time of deciphering, he was not aware that the inscription occurred near the side of the steps.

‡ Vide his *Inquiry concerning the Site of Ancient Palibothra*, Part II.—As Francklin's work is now scarce, his account is appended in full.—Ed.

at the surface it is hardly four times the size of the oyster.

A perpendicular ridge of rock rises abruptly from the Shankhakuṇḍa and stretches towards the north and east. On the north-west corner of this ridge, about five feet from the base, is a small cave hewn out in the solid rock. It is about four feet square and high enough to allow a person to sit at his ease in it. It is just like one of the rock-cut caves to be met with in different parts of India, where Buddhist ascetics used to retire for the purpose of contemplation and prayer. But from an inscription on a large cave in the neighbourhood, to be presently noticed, it appears doubtful whether it does not rather owe its origin to Hindu devotees.

Further north, about half way to the summit of the ridge above mentioned, is situated a spring named Akáshgangá, meaning the Gangá of the sky. The only approach to this is by a wooden ladder about 15 feet high. The water, which is contained in a cavity in the shape of a cone, cut in the body of the rock, is only about three feet deep, and is so transparent that the smallest objects at the bottom appear distinctly. This cavity, to which no rain-water can find access, fills itself as often as it is emptied, being supplied from a source which no eye has ever seen.

The following legend accounts for the existence of the sacred Gangá at Mandara.

The Mandara having been blessed by the presence of all the principal deities, was anxious to have Shiva also. With this object, it offered prayer to the sage Nárada, who thereupon undertook a journey to Kailása for the purpose. On his way he met an ascetic who, having propitiated Shiva by his prayers, had just been promised the sovereignty of Banáres. Nárada told him he was a fool to desire the sovereignty of Banáres as long as Shiva himself was there, since the latter would be considered the real Rájá and the ascetic only so in name. So under the guise of friendship, Nárada advised him to go back and ask Shiva to leave Banáres as long as he reigned. The ascetic did so; and Shiva, being unable to refuse the prayer of a devoted votary, consented to leave Banáres; and as Nárada happened just then to prefer his own prayer, towards the accomplishment of which he had played so deep a game, the deity agreed to spend the time on Mandara. He would not go however unless he had the water of the Gangá to drink, in order to quench the irritating sensation occasioned by the poison in his throat. At Nárada's suggestion he went to Brahma, and having brought some water from his famous basin in which the Gangá is said to have taken its birth, deposited it on Mandara for his own use.

On the left side of the Akáshgangá, is the colossal figure of Madhukaiṭabha traced on the rock. This, according to the Mandara Mahátmya, was done by Ráma during his residence on the hill. About 15 feet below, is a vaulted cave, cut into the body of a smaller ridge of rock which rises like an inclined plane from near the base of the perpendicular ridge before mentioned. The chamber is about 15 feet by 10, and, like the veranda of a bangalo, gets higher as it recedes from the entrance, owing to the inclination of the vaulted roof with which it is covered. On this roof there is an inscription in large letters which has not yet been deciphered. The only approach to the cave is by a small door which just enables a person to enter in a sitting posture, but does not admit sufficient light to perceive what it contains. The ascetic residing on the hill, who has his cottage contiguous to the cave, however, assists pilgrims with lamps to observe the representation of one of the incarnations of Vishṇu—carved in stone—on the middle of the floor. The image in the centre, is that of Vishṇu in the shape of the man-lion, its eyes almost glaring with unearthly lustre and its claws tearing into pieces the body of a Titan thrown over his thigh, while a child stands underneath with half-shut eyes trembling at the fearful scene. There are other figures such as those of Lakshmí, Sarasvatí, Ráma, &c.; but the cave goes under the name of the central image—to which it is principally dedicated.

The following is the legend to which the central image alludes. There were two brothers Asuras or Titans by birth who by the favour of Shiva, became very powerful and, expelling the gods, usurped the throne of heaven. In the pride of victory the elder brother, named Hiraṇyáksha, thought himself even equal to Vishṇu in power, and so sought him in the nether world to give him battle, but was killed in the encounter. The younger Hiraṇyakaśipu therefore hated Vishṇu so intensely that he could not even bear to hear his name pronounced in his presence. But in course of time a son was born to him, who became a devoted follower of his antagonist, and who, forsaking the studies and pursuits suited to his age, began to pray to Vishṇu night and day. The king became highly incensed, and finding it impossible to shake his son's belief, or make him forsake his devotion, ordered him to be put to death. But though Prahláda, (for so the son was named) was successively hurled to the earth from the summit of a high hill, put upon a flaming pile, thrown into the sea with weights fastened round his neck, and trampled under the feet of an elephant, yet he escaped uninjured? The monarch then asked his son how he had survived such fearful perils, to which Prahláda answered that Vishṇu had preserved his life. "But where is your Vishṇu?," demanded the king in a rage. "He is," replied the son, "present everywhere." "Is he present in that impervious and solid body," asked Hiranyakaśipa, pointing with his finger to a large crystal globe that stood before him. "Yes, father" replied Prahláda. "He must be there, since He is omnipresent and nothing can exist without Him." Scarcely were these words uttered when Hiranyakaśipa's scimitar descended like a thunderbolt and broke the crystal into a thousand fragments; but at the same instant, a terrific figure, with the head and fore-claws of a lion and under part of a man, issued out of the broken crystal, and throwing Hiranyakaśipa over his thigh, tore him into pieces. This took place at the twilight. He was killed in this manner, because by the blessing of Shiva, he was not to die by the hands of god or demigod, of man or beast, in the water or in the sky, during the glare of day or during the shades of night.

The three caves above mentioned are situated on the left of the Shankhakuṇḍa and on the eastern bank of the Sítákuṇḍa, while the way to the summit lies just over the right margin of these two springs. Beyond Shankhakuṇḍa, it runs for a considerable distance over a slightly inclined plane till it reaches the base of a conical ridge of rock which leads to the summit. By the side of this road, about ten feet above the Shankhakuṇḍa, there is an empty temple, now the abode of bats and mice, in which Shiva is said to have resided during his self-imposed exile from Benares. Probably the original image having been reduced to dust by Kálápahár, was not replaced by another, owing at first to the frequent incursions of the Muhammadans, and afterwards to the removal of Madhusúdana's image to Bausi.

Far to the right, separated by a waterway through which the rains falling on the summit find their way to the foot of the hill, is the temple of the Jains already mentioned. From Shiva's temple up to the base of the conical ridge, there is nothing else to arrest the attention. Thence to the summit, the ascent is very difficult owing to the rugged and uneven rock, loose and disjointed stones, abrupt precipices, and thick jungle that obstruct the way. On the highest summit of the hill, stands a very old temple of stone, said to have been built by Ráma. It contains only the footprints of Vishṇu, thereby indicating that he still holds the hill over the headless giant, with the weight of the universe embodied in his divine frame.

COL. FRANCKLIN'S ACCOUNT OF MANDARA HILL.

(From his "Inquiry concerning the Site of Ancient Palibothra," Part II., pp. 15-26 and 73-79.)

(November 22, 1814.) Moved at 20 minutes past 7, quitted the *Chandan*, and proceeded on into the interior, to visit *Mandara* hill E. by N., *Chandan* river W.......... Passed the village of *Beliya*, which stands on elevated ground, the surrounding scenery beautiful and fertile, the cottages of the inhabitants very neatly and compactly built, in patches detached from each other: *Mandara* hill N., passed several *talaos* (or large tanks of water); *Madusúdan Math*, a Hindu place of worship. N. At 5 minutes past 9, reached the village of *Bonsi* near *Mandara*, at a spacious *talao* with high banks. *Mandara* hill N. *Barbari* hill S., *Malida* SE. Distance 8 miles 5 furlongs.

(November 23.) Halted and visited *Mandara* hill. The south side of the hill presents on the approach to it a singular appearance, it consisting of a range of five distinct hills rising one above the other, till they are terminated by the summit of *Mandara*, which is of an oval form, and very much resembles the *Gola* at *Patna*; the summit is surmounted by a stone *math* whither the idols that are kept in the plain below, at a *math* of the same name, are carried at the annual *jatras*, two in each year, to be worshipped in the temple. At the south foot of the hill is a spacious *talao*, called by the natives *Poquhur* [Pápharni], the descent to which is by a stone staircase of seven steps, each step being 14 feet in length by 1½ in breadth. Near this flight of steps are great quantities of broken stones of different dimensions, mutilated idols, fragments of pillars, and other irrugular masses. The circumference of the *talao*, as measured by a perambulator, is 4 furlongs 40 yards. Three sides of it are covered with trees and jungle; the fourth embraces the south-eastern base of the mountain, which trends away in a sloping direction.

A stone channel or watercourse, formed from a natural fissure in the rock, runs in a direction from N.W. to S.E. along the centre of the hill, which it divides into two parts. The sides of this channel are very steep, and formed of hard black rock, having a coal-like appearance resembling the crater of a volcano; the channel itself is deep and hollow. From this channel, in the rainy season, a torrent of water pours down, and is discharged into the tank in the plain below. It is called by the natives *Patalabandara*, and perfectly answers to the description of that place, as detailed by the learned Wilford in the Asiatic Researches; though he has applied the circumstances to the neighbourhood of *Rájmahál*, and the *Motijharna*, or pearl cascade of that place.*

The mountain *Mandara*, though in its general features, barren and rugged, is yet occasionally interspersed with trees and jungle growing out of the fissures on its rocky base and sides.

(Nov. 24). The ascent to *Mandara* is by a winding road or staircase cut in the rock, with landing places of rock at intervals. Near the first staircase is a small stone image of the bull *Nandi*, but badly executed; the head is broken. About 200 yards from the foot of the hill is a heap of ruins, apparently the remains of a small temple. Adjoining to this the second staircase, consisting of 87 steps, continues the ascent. All these stairs are carved out from the rock, 3 feet 7 inches in length and 1 foot 8 inches in breadth. On the right hand of the second flight is a colossal figure of *Mahâkâlî* cut in the rock. The goddess is bestriding a demon, whom she has subdued in combat; she is armed with a battle-axe in one hand and a sword in the other, and has three faces and ten arms, with a *mala* or necklace of human skulls.

A short distance from this place, continuing the ascent, you meet with a sight extremely beautiful: a natural cascade, which issuing from the spring called *Sitá Kunda*, flows over the black and rugged surface of the rock, and discharges itself into the *Patala Kundara*, or channel below, from whence it is conveyed to the *talao* of *Paphara* at the foot of the mountain. From this place you ascend the third range of stairs, being a flight of 30 steps, and presently after, the fourth which has 101 steps, and then a fifth of 35 steps; the whole forming, as it were, a magnificent natural ladder.

In our road up we observed many images and fragments of stone lying scattered on each side of the way, the latter appearing to be the remains of small temples, to be visited by the pilgrims in progressive ascent to that on the summit. From the last landing place the *Chir Nala* on the left bore E., the river *Chandan* on the right W., the mountain *Mandara* being in the centre between the two. From hence you proceed up the sixth range of stairs 11 in number, when, turning round a corner to the N. W., you come to a beautiful enclosure of mango trees, and behold the cistern called *Sitá Kunda*, or well of Sítá, being a square enclosure faced on three sides with large stones, the scarp of the rock forming the fourth, and containing sweet and transparent water. This water, issuing from apertures in the rock, flows down the side of the mountain, and is finally discharged into the *talao* at the bottom, and from the brightness of its appearance it may truly be called a *moti jharna*, or pearl-dropping spring. Here the scenery is romantic and picturesque, the green and flourishing trees forming a most remarkable contrast to the black and barren rock over which they grow.

A short distance from *Sitá Kunda* is another well or cistern, called '*Sankar*' *Kunda*, of a triangular shape, cut between two parts of the rock, which divides at this place. On the side of this cistern future travellers may recognize a figure of *Shankha* cut in the rock. Close to *Shankha Kunda* commences the seventh series of stairs, consisting of 88 steps, after passing which you come to the well or cistern called *Lakshmana Kunda*, or well of *Lakshman*.† This is situated in a niche of the rock to the eastward; beyond which, by an ascent of 87 steps, you are conducted to the summit of the mountain and the *Mandara Math* (or temple) dedicated to *Mahâdeva*. The *Patal Kandara*, or channel, so frequently mentioned, runs along the north-west side of this temple, and preserves the same features as at the bottom of the mountain, viz. a deep rugged channel of coal-black rock, of volcanic appearance. Here a magnificent prospect bursts upon the view; the whole range of hills in the *Jangal Tarai* extending from S.E. to N.W., the *Chandan* river and its numerous arms or *nalas*, and the dark and impervious forests stretching towards the south as far as the eye can reach, altogether form a picture that at once contributes to warm the imagination and to elevate the mind. Though we viewed the prospect to disadvantage, the weather being hazy, yet the coup-d'œil made an impression on our minds that will not be easily eradicated. Descending from the summit we returned to *Shankha Kunda*, and from thence proceeded to view some figures cut in the rock on the north-west side of the hill; their appearance was singular. After descending a range of 18 steps, we entered the rocky bed of a watercourse,

* See Asiatic Res. vol. V.

† See note p. 55.

extending along the side of the mountain, and presently reached an assemblage of projecting rocks that overhung us. In the centre of this assemblage was a huge and hideous figure, or rather its head only, for the body does not appear below the neck; it is of larger dimensions than life, cut out of the rock, which has been hollowed on both sides for the purpose, and a flight of stone steps leads up to it from the channel below. The native *pandits* who inhabit the mountain, as likewise some *pandits* whom we brought from the *Mandar Math* in the plain below, informed me that the figure was a demon, and was called in their *Purânas* by the name of *Madhu Kaitabha*. It is stated in the *Markandeya Purâna*, that this demon was produced on the mountain *Mandara* from the ears of the god *Vishnu* at the creation of the world, and having shortly after his birth attempted the life of *Brahma*, or the creating power, was, together with another demon, punished for his presumption, and driven from the world above to the depths below. The figure now seen was cut to represent this occurrence, but by whom I could not learn. Near the figure of the demon is another large figure cut in the rock, called by the natives *Vâman*; it is connected with one of the Hindu *avatâras*, or incarnations of the divinity, which is named from the dwarf, whose form *Vishnu* had assumed. Another figure, lower down the rock, is also to be seen, called *Narasinha*.

About 50 yards eastwards of *Madhu Kaitabha* is an excavation in the rocks, forming one of the *Kundas* or cisterns, which abound in this singular mountain.* It is called *Akâsh Ganga* (or sky river). In it is a perpetual spring of clear and sweet water, but of shallow depth. The natives affirm that it is never dry, but that, if it be completely emptied, it will fill again of itself: a curious circumstance, if correct, for the bed of the nearest river must be at least a thousand feet from the place where this cistern is found. The name is emphatic, meaning in Sanskrit "sky river." Near this cistern is a cave on the side of a rock, in which a *faqir* [yogi] constantly resides.†

* The following are the names of the *Kundas* (or cisterns) that adorn this singular mountain:—

1. *Gambhîra Kunda.*	7. *Akâsh Ganga.*
2. *Kâshava Kunda.*	8. *Kumâr Kunda.*
3. *Homa Kunda.*	9. *Suraj Kunda.*
4. *Lakshman Kunda.*	10. *Nath Kunda.*
5. *Kak Kunda.*	11. *Mangala Kunda.*
6. *Sita Kunda.*	12. *Pâpahar* (*Papharni*) *Kund.*

† *Extract from the Mandara Mahâtmya, or Eulogium of Mandara, from the Varâha Purâna, or Legend of the Fourth Incarnation of Vishnu.*

After salutation and obeisance to *Krishna* (it is asked by *Shuka*, son of *Mahadeva*,) "O *Bhagavan*, thou hast spoken already of all things, of *Tirtha* (places of pilgrimage) and *Hari Tirtha*, *Gangasagar Tirtha* (Kapil), of *Ayodhya*, of *Prayaga*, and of *Chandra Tirtha*. I am now desirous to learn from thee the nature and situation of *Mandara*; relate this at full length, O chief of the *Devatas*, for thou art worthy to relate it!"

Shri Mahesvara, the divinity, replied, "O son, who art acceptable, by this inquiry thou wilt gratify thy heart. Know thou that amongst the places of worship, *Mandara* is the greatest in the world. It is the place of residence of (various) holy persons of pure dispositions; of *Jagdish*, with eyes like the lotus and heart-attracting. This place is the end or destruction of the malignant demon *Madhu*, whose fall was celebrated with songs of joy from the holy *Vedas* by all the *Devatas*, therefore no place of worship is superior in sanctity to *Mandara*. *Mandara* covered with beautiful flowers, the place where the *Jogies* reverence the footstep of thee, O *Vishnu*! Where *Brahma* himself was produced from the lotus, and where he paid worship and adoration at the feet of *Mahadeva* and *Vishnu*. There also dwells the goddess *Sree*, beautiful as the flower of the lotus and delicate as the plant thereof. *Kapila Muni*, after reciting the praises of the mountain, has here taken up his abode. Verily [illegible] thee of everything, O my son, and ask thy desire. The praises of *Vishnu* are a thousand-fold. *Kapila Muni*, sitting in the esteemed place, performing his reverence to the asylum of the world (*Vishnu*), the prince thus says, 'O *Bhagavan* (*Mahadeva*), by strenuous exertions, aided by those of my own family, I have subdued the whole world, and brought its seven divisions under obedience. The works which I have performed would be difficult to detail. Those deeds which I have made manifest are inscribed at the palace gate. Often have the princes of my family, clad in bright armour, destroyed their enemies; they have punished the presumption of the princes of the earth. Now I am growing old and infirm, and am therefore desirous of worshipping thy footsteps, O *Vishnu*! From decay of my strength I have lost that activity which I was wont to possess: my accustomed sense of hearing as likewise my eye-sight, have failed me, and neither wisdom nor understanding remain; my body is wasted and my flesh and blood decay! Acquaint me, therefore, O *Bhagavan*, in what manner I shall obtain relief from these infirmities."

Bhagavan replied, "Know, O Raja, that there is a heart-attracting place of worship, where the wind blows with vigour on all sides; a temple as yet hidden from the view of mankind. It is *Mandara*, the greatest in the world; there *Vishnu* resides for ever; he who destroyed the well-known malignant demon *Madhu*. It was *Bhagavan* who cast him under ground, and without difficulty placed the mountain *Mandara* on his head, an everlasting burden! Therefore, O Raja, is *Vishnu* the sovereign of all the *Devatas*. *Mandar Math* is also well known; it is renowned as the very summit of *Mandara*; the [illegible] and the [illegible] shall find equal absolution at *Mandara*.

"Whoever, O Raja, shall in future visit *Mandara* with reverence, that person shall be acceptable to the god, and be absolved from his sins by the grace of *Vishnu*. In *Jambudwipa* there are many places of worship. *Bhagavan* remains everywhere; he resides in no particular place; neither here in *Mandara*, nor in *Kasi*, nor [illegible] nor *Gomati*, nor *Dwaraka*, nor in *Prayag*, but everywhere. At this place the spirit of *Bhagavan* was gladdened, where he assumed the form of *Hansa*, [illegible] in the house of *Dasaratha*; here he released [illegible] from these [illegible] and slew the demons. [illegible] therefore, O Raja, for thine own benefit."

The Raja answered, "O *Bhagavan*, in what manner shall I reach there? Relate this to me at length, thou who art the [illegible] of those who reverence thee."

Bhagavan replied, "*Mandara* is conspicuous for a spacious reservoir, situated at the foot of the mountain, whereby those who bathe shall become united to *Vishnu*. The water flows from the rock of holy quality, glittering like light derived from the moon. O Raja, that reservoir is *Manohar* (heart-attracting). At that place, sinners who bathe therein, shall, with their relatives and dependants, be absolved from sin and sickness. Fast therefore, O Raja! for one day, and then bathe, and be united to *Vishnu*. The act of ablution at this place is equivalent to the sacrifice of an *Aswamedha yaga* at the place where *Rama* [illegible] his deceased father. Here is, half way up the mountain, another reservoir, whose waters glitter like gold; at sight of that water grief is dispelled from the heart. It flows from the mountain. Whosoever thou visitest this reservoir, be thou abstemious in thy soul, O Raja, and bathe therein before the great guardian of mankind (*Jagat guru*), whose residence is on the summit on the south side of the mountain. He who shall yield up his soul at this place shall be absolved from his sins; and he who shall voluntarily relinquish the pleasures of this world, shall acquire

At 11 A. M., reached our breakfast tent at the foot of the mountain, highly pleased and gratified with the day's work. It may be better imagined than described what an appearance the collected waters of these respective reservoirs, when overflowed at the period of the solstitial rains, must present to the view, traversing the sides of the mountain in all directions, dashing with a violence totally irresistible, over the surface of the rocky declivities and other parts, until their final discharge into the 'Pamphar' and other receptacles in the plain below.*

Kamdhenu or the Parent Cow.—About a mile to the east, on the skirts of the hill, stands the *Kamdhenu Math* or pagoda, being a small square temple built of stone with a roof of brick. The temple contains the figure of *Kamdhenu*, or the parent cow of the Hindus, well known in Sanskrit records to have been one of the fourteen ratnas (or gems) produced by the churning of the ocean in the white sea, in which operation the mountain *Mandara* served as a churning-staff.

The figure of the cow is in height 2 feet 4 inches; in length, from the forehead to the tip of the tail, 6 feet 3 inches; in girth 5 feet. Round the hump of the animal is a necklace of flowers by way of ornament; two small calves, in alto, are taking milk from the mother. The figure is cut out of a solid block of light grey stone, and stands on a pedestal; its execution, though proportionate in its parts, is rude, and evidently of high antiquity. The temple is now mouldering fast to ruin.

Near this temple is another in ruins, which consists of large blocks of stone: the emblem of *Mahadeva* is to be seen in the remains of a small stone chamber. The building is called *Kamdhenu Math*, and is connected with the worship of the other temple. To a considerable extent around the mountain are the remains of ruined temples, which in ancient times, and during the splendour of the Hindu Government, must have greatly contributed to enhance the beauty and amenity of the situation of *Mandara* hill. The tradition prevalent asserts, that there was a large city in the neighbourhood. East of the *Math Kamdhenu* is a mutilated image of the goddess *Kali*, of blue stone, near 7 feet in height. Though the principal figure in the centre has been destroyed by bigot hands, the head only remaining, several of the figures of smaller dimensions on the sides remain entire; some of them are well executed.

A thick forest encompasses the hill *Mandara* on three sides; it is only accessible from the south-east. I conjecture its circumference to be about 4 miles, and its height from the base to the summit 1 mile 3 furlongs.

Near '*Pamphar*' tank, a short distance up the rock to the N.W., are several very large inscriptions cut in the rock, but in a character of which I could procure no account†...... There are other inscriptions to be seen, both above and below, in different parts of the mountain. I should suspect, if they are ever deciphered, that they will be found to relate to the worship of the temple called *Madhusudan Math*. The natives call them *Devata Khat* or the character of the gods.

NOTES ON THE GONDS MET WITH IN THE SÂTHPURÂ HILLS, CENTRAL PROVINCES.

BY MR. C. SCANLAN, ASSISTANT SURVEYOR.

The Sathpuras extend to a mean breadth of about seventy miles. They are inhabited by the Gonds and Kirkus, who are a shy, ignorant, and very primitive race of men; their predilection for hilly and forest ridden tracts is so great, that I think nothing could induce them to leave their abodes. The Kirku is a perfect Hindu, though he indulges in fowls; while the Gond, who styles himself a Hindu, is a hybrid between him and a Musalman, for he appreciates his beef. The Gond

a true knowledge of the divine being. The *Gandharvas*, or heavenly choristers, then approaching, bathed therein, near the seven fountains, as [illegible] superior to the triple ablutions [illegible], at morning, noon, and evening]. At this place, turning your face to the eastward, bathe and worship Vishnu; at which act the three worlds (*tri loka*) will rejoice, and every desire will be fulfilled. He who shall worship in this manner shall not return to earth again. So commanded Vishnu. The *Gandharvas* then commenced a melodious concert, singing and praising the deity. Then go, O Raja! and casting away all cares and passions, repair to the quadrangular reservoir [*Lakshmi Kund*], beautiful as Lakshmi of divine form; there fast three or five days, since whoever bathes therein, after fasting shall become courageous and worthy to assume sovereign authority. Whilst traversing the sides of this reservoir should he (the penitent) perceive Vishnu sitting on his throne, grief shall then be expelled from his heart. Finally, O Raja! whoever shall perform the funeral rites of his deceased ancestors or relatives at this place, their souls shall thereby be gratified for a hundred years."

* Of these *Kunds* the first six are on the sides and near the summit of the hill, the others are below.

† The author here gives "a fac-simile on a smaller scale than the original for the investigation of the learned." Of this inscription, Babu Rajendralala Mitra remarks, that "judging from its character and subject, he is satisfied that it was a Buddhist record and commemorated the dedication of a statue or a chaitya. The character is intermediate between the Gupta and Kutila, and was inscribed probably in the sixth century of the Christian era. The 8th letter of the 3rd line was doubtful, as were the last two letters of the last line, but he read the record as follows:—

Paramabhattâr-
ka mahârâjâdhirâ-
ja shri ugrabhai (?)ra.
vasya deyindhya (?) ar deya dharmmo.

"The highly venerated, the great king, the king of kings, Shri Ugrabhairava dedicated this."—*Proc. Asiat. Soc. Ben.* Nov. 1870, pp. 294, 295.—Ed.

claims his descent from a deity. It is said that while a Rájput prince was once out hunting, he espied a goddess perched on a rock enjoying the wild scenery of the country. They became enamoured of each other, and were blessed with a son. From this man the Gonds are supposed to be descended, and since he claimed his origin from a goddess and a Rájput prince, they style themselves Raj-Gonds and Gond-Thakurs. Both the men and women, especially the latter, have a peculiar cast of countenance, which is broad and high-cheeked, with oblique eyes and a rather flattish nose. They appear to be of a very lively disposition, and are honest and well-behaved to us. During the Holi festival, the women throw off all reserve, and do not scruple to detain for *bakshish* any one going through their villages or encamped near them; they will surround him and keep dancing and singing in a ring till their claims are complied with. On a moonlight night both men and women assemble round their village fires and enjoy themselves by discoursing music.

The Bhumkas are the constituted priests of the Gonds and Kirkus, and preside at all their religious ceremonies. Each village has its Bhumka. These men have their special Lares and Penates, which are called the Bhumka and Phatak Devas,—the latter being the gods they place in a road over which visitors to shrines pass, and through these tutelar deities, they levy a sort of black-mail on all who go that way. The chief gods of the people appear to be Bara Deo, Mahádeo, Narayandeo, Máta, and Khanderáo; in fact, almost every hill-top has on it the shrine individuality of some one of their many mythological powers. To these are offered up the *nariel*, *khajur*, *sindur*, *pan-khaja*, *chandal*, incense, eggs, limes, and fowls. The last named god plays a prominent part during the Holi festival. He is to be seen in almost every village, represented by a long red-coloured pole, which is driven vertically into the ground. A ladder leads to the top of the pole, a few feet below which is a platform made of bamboo work, on which two men can take their places. On the extremity of the pole is placed a cross-piece which revolves round; to the ends of it men and women allow themselves to be attached and swung round—fanatics submitting to the hook. This is what they call the Gal. At the foot of this pole are placed stone or earthen images, which are called Kham and Khami, the former being the male, the latter the female representation. As I said before, it is during the Holi this god calls his votaries in large numbers, when they bring their offerings, which are alway cocks and hens—men presenting the former and women the latter. The Bhumka decapitates them; the offerer takes the trunk and sprinkles the posts and stones with the warm blood, when, from a basket, little pieces of cake are broken and put before the deities. On the Gál day each village sends out its men and women in procession, the men ahead beating their drums, and the women behind singing—the former lustily sending totally different airs. When they reach Khanderáo and his wife, the men sit down in a ring and keep chaunting on, while the women form their usual arc of a circle and gyrate round the pole.

The birth ceremonies of the Gonds and Kirkus are alike, both give a dinner; but in their death ceremonies they differ. I can best draw the distinction by describing each. The Gonds burn their adults and bury their children. After a few days they offer up to their memory a bull or cow, which they place right over the threshold and knock over with a blow from the blunt end of a hatchet. This they call the Pat. The widows are not allowed to marry without the consent of the Patia, who is the high priest of the Baradeva, and one is attached to every Gat (*gotra*), which I shall hereafter describe. The Patia, in technical language, sells the widow for five rupees to the man seeking her hand; in other words, five rupees are used in the ceremony.

The Kirkus, like the Gonds, burn their adults and bury their children. They offer goats and fowls to their Gata-Paria—which are their Lares and are made of wood—supposed representations of the deceased, who are thus incorporated into their polytheistic category. The ceremony itself is called Sidoli or Phuljhari. On the day appointed, friends are invited, a great deal of eating, drinking, dancing, and merry-making is gone through. From the cross beam of the roof a thread is suspended, and its lower end hangs directly over a small cup of brass or clay, and to the upper end a finger ring is attached so as to run down at the slightest oscillation; after a short time it begins to move and drops into the receptacle below, with a clanging sound, then the wandering spirit is supposed to have returned to his former haunts, and ceases to molest any one; for so long as his relations do not propitiate him, the restless spirit, they say, will annoy them—either sickness, want, or ravages by wild animals on their cattle will keep afflicting them.

When Gonds marry, a dinner is given, and the food consists of *dál* and *kutki*. The bride gets, as a present, a cloth and a pair of anklets. When a man makes his overtures and is accepted, if able, he gives the bride's parents 9 rupees, 160 sers of *kutki*, 40 sers *dál*, 160 sers *kodo*; if not able to supply these, he makes terms of servitude for a period of 5, 7 or 12 years, and though he may soon get married afterwards, still he goes on working at his father-in-law's house. This is called *lamjhana*.

When among the Kirkus a marriage is settled on, the asker gives a good supply of liquor to the bride-elect's father; this binds the contract. If he cannot give 20 rupees or their value (if he be a widower Rs. 40, or their equivalent), he is obliged also to do *langhana*. At the marriage, the bridegroom gives the paternal aunt and the mother of the bride a cloth each, and the paternal uncle a *pagri*. Among both the Gonds and Kirkus, the money is not given to defray the expenses of the marriage dinner and paraphernalia of the bride but for the marriage contract.

The Kirkus are divided into four chief divisions of caste: The Bapcha, Beoria, Rumba and Bundoi,—the last being the highest. These castes do not intermarry, eat, drink, nor smoke the *hukka* amongst themselves.

The Gonds divide into two sections, which call themselves Raj Gonds and Khatola Wala Gonds,—the latter wearing the Brahmanical thread or *jânvi* across the shoulder. These two divisions hold nothing common among them.

The Gots which I have alluded to above, I find to be clans, something after the manner of those among our Scottish brethren, and in no instance is intermarriage permitted between men and women of the same clan, but cousins are permitted to marry each other. How this finds sanction I shall explain: I shall instance a brother and sister of the Wika Got. The sister marries, say, a Dhurwa: she accordingly becomes of the Dhurwa clan, while her brother, of course, still retains his clanship; thus the sister's children being Dhurwas and the brother's Wikas, they can intermarry. From this precise explanation it will at once be seen that the marriage of two brothers' children is interdicted, because they are of the same clan.

I was not successful in collecting the names of many of the Gondi Gots worth recording, but I think I have got a good number of the Kirku clans which are as follows:—Kasda, Botha, Chuthar, Masal, Basson, Dharma, Salmoos, Atakar, Akhandi, Tota, Bhasaira, Tandil, Kolsa, Savali, Selu, and Athwa.

This year I met with no archæological remains which invited my attention; there is only one place which has its local tradition.

I have briefly attempted to enter into the chief points of interest regarding these wild tribes, without detailing the many other minutiæ which relate to them, such as their dancing, their dress, their villages, and many of their customs.—*Report on the Topographical Surveys for 1869-70.*

EXPLANATION OF VEDIC WORDS.

BY PROF. TH. AUFRECHT.

(*Translated from the Zeitschrift der Deutschen Morgenländischen Gesellschaft Bd. XXIV.* pp. [illegible].)

1. Nishṭura.

Nishṭur is found in the Rigveda only in the two forms nishṭurâ and nishṭurah. The pada divides thus, nih-turâ and nih-turah, and thus it is regarded as compounded of tur and the preposition nis. Roth takes this view, and translates it, "He who has no conqueror (the unvanquished one)." He forgets that this translation yields no sense in VIII. 32, 27, and that no passage occurs in the Veda, in which the root tur is combined with nis. In my opinion it should be resolved into nish-ṭar, which I derive from nishṭar, to strike to the ground, *prosternere*. In the former passage nishṭar is active, "felling to the ground"; in the latter, passive, "to fall to the ground." VIII. 32, 27.

"To the mighty conqueror, to the unvanquished victor arise

Your god-suggested hymn."

VIII. 66, 2.—

"Then spake to him Çavasî: the deadly hater, the rined-one

My child, thou cast to ground do thou."

This interpretation receives confirmation also from anishṭṛitâ in VIII. 33, 9.—

"The gallant, never-vanquished hero, fearlessly equipped for fight,

Hears Indra gladly the singer's call, no longer tarrying he draws nigh to us."

Also from the use of nishṭar, II. 11, 20.—

Asyâ suvânasya mandinas tritasya ny arbudam vâvṛidhâno astah |

"Arbuda, the enemy of this lavish, joyous Trita, he violently strikes down." VII. 18, 11.—

ekam cha yo vimçatim cha çravasyâ vaikarṇayor janân râjâ ny astah |

"As the king from desire for fame slew one and twenty men of the two Vaikarṇa."

2. Açvabudhya.

This word occurs three times, and indeed only in the first Ashṭaka. Roth translates it, "notable on account of horses—distinguished," and Benfey, "recognizable by horses." This interpretation, in which budhya is derived from the root budh, is unsatisfactory both etymologically and with reference to the sense. Etymologically, because the analogous formations brahmacharya, pûrbhidya, prakâmodya, brahmodya, brahmavâdya, mantraçrutya, adhmasadya, talpasadya, râjasûya, devahûya, and others, have the accent on the last portion. As regards the sense,—because in 92, 7 the distinction between açvabudhya and gomagra is unmistakable. The true account of the matter is, that budhya is either directly a corruption from budhnya or it comes from a form budha—no longer extant, but corresponding in meaning to the word budhna. Açvabudhya means "grounded (established) on horses depending on horses." I. 92, 7.—

prajávato nrivato áçvabudhyán usho
gógrán úpa mási váján |

"Aurora, bestow upon us, together with posterity and sons, possessions which shall have their foundation in horses, and their summit in cows." Agra and budhna are also opposed to each other in III. 55, 7. X. 111, 8. 135, 6 and Agni in I. 96, 6, is called the foundation of all property and the procurer of treasures. In I, 92, 8 we have—

úshas tám açyám yaçásam suvíram
dásápravargam rayím áçvabudhyam |

"O Dawn, may I attain to the glorious prosperity which is accompanied by excellent sons and numerous slaves, and is supported on horses."

I. 121, 14.—

prá no vájân rathyò áçvabudhyân
ishé yandhi çrávase sûnṛitâyai |

"Give us possessions accompanied with chariots, supported on horses, for power and renown and delight."

REVIEWS.

The Daśaratha Jâtaka, being the Buddhist Story of King Râma. The original Pâli text, &c. by V. Fausböll. Copenhagen: 1871. 48 pp. 8vo.

Prof. Weber's essay Über das Râmâyaṇa, published about a year and a half ago, proved almost beyond doubt that the well known Indian epic, the Râmâyaṇa, is based on a Buddhist legend, and drawn up in its present form, not more than 1800 years ago, chiefly under Greek influences. The result of his researches must have startled many, and though the argument is supported by vast learning and copious quotations, it must be a great satisfaction to all interested in Indian literature to see the authentic text critically edited and translated by so well known a scholar as Dr. Fausböll.

The original Râma-saga forms one of the numerous Jâtaka stories which Buddha is said to have related in illustration of his doctrine, and which get their name from the events related having occurred during former existences of Buddha. In this case Buddha had existed as Râma. Among the Jâtakas are to be found most of the legends we meet with in Sanskrit literature, and even tales which exist in the Sanskrit Panchatantra; the value of the collection is thus very great, and especially because these tales here occur in a much older and less corrupt form than can be found elsewhere.

This Buddhist Râma-saga forms a striking contrast to the complicated and perverted version of the Râmâyaṇa with its supernatural trumpery. Daśaratha is here said to have had three children, Râma, Lakkhaṇa, and Sîtâ by his first, and a son Bharata by a second wife. By intrigues in in favour of Bharata, the second wife gets Râma banished for twelve years. His brother and sister attend him and serve him dutifully. In the ninth year Daśaratha dies, and Bharata, refusing to profit by his mother's wickedness, goes in search of Râma, and tells him the news of his father's death. The philosophic Râma displays the apathetic disposition assigned to him in the Râmâyaṇa, but breaks the news gently to Lakkhaṇa and Sîtâ who give way to grief. Bharata asks Râma the cause of his indifference, and is answered by some Gathás, which are evidently intended to be sung to a simple accompaniment, and thus to relieve the monotony of the prose recital for a popular audience. One cannot help comparing the Jâtakas to the Arabic romances of 'Antar, &c., which may be still heard in Cairo and Algiers, and which, like the Jâtakas, are essentially popular as opposed to the exclusive spirit of the general literature. The most striking, perhaps, are—

3. "What cannot be preserved
by man, even if much bewailed,
for such a thing's sake why should the intelligent (and) wise (man)
distress himself."

. . . .

5. "As ripe fruits
always are in danger of falling,
so born mortals
always (are) tending to death."

6. "In the evening some are not seen (any more),
(although) in the morning many were seen,
(and) in the morning some are not seen,
(although) in the evening many were seen."

7. "If by lamenting
The fool, who (only) injures himself,
gains anything,—
let the wise (man) do the same too."

8. "(But) he (only) becomes lean (and) sallow,
(while) injuring his own self,
(and) the dead are not saved,
lamentation (therefore) is of no avail," &c.*

Lakkhaṇa tries to persuade Râma to return as king; he, however, refuses to do so before the end of the twelve years, and sends his straw shoes which are placed on the throne, and by their striking together the ministers know when injustice was done. At the end of the twelfth year, he returns, is throned as king, and makes his sister his queen. The statement that Sîtâ was at once Râma's sister

* Compare Yâjnavalkyasmṛiti, III. 8—11, where similar gáthás occur.

and wife is a striking proof of the authenticity of of the Buddhist Saga, and agrees entirely with the results of recent research regarding primitive marriage.

It is thus evident that the Rāmāyaṇa consists of an original saga as above, with the addition of a mythological fiction chiefly consisting of the rape of Sītā and war with Rāvaṇa. As the paltry results of the sectarian interpreters are based on the last part, they deserve but little attention; if the original saga has any historical basis, the additions are certainly recent and spurious. It is much to be regretted that Orientalists habitually content themselves with a far lower standard of historical evidence, than their fellow-students who occupy themselves with Classical and European antiquities. Few in the East have got beyond the long exploded euhemerism, and they have not spared the two Indian epics. To extract history out of them at present, when the texts and recensions have not been critically edited, is at least premature, even though the inferences were legitimate in method; but recourse to a vicious system is inexcusable when means are at hand, such as Professor Weber's essay and the work now noticed, by which the historical development of the Saga may be studied.

Though Professor Weber has been able to fix pretty nearly the oldest date for the redaction of the Rāmāyaṇa, it is by no means so easy to say how late this may have occurred.

The story of Rāma is told in a number of works, of which Professor Weber has noticed several (p. 33ff.); but in every case, it is the Rāmāyaṇa version. The Kathāsarit-sāgara (12th cent.) and the perhaps still older Bṛihatkathā of Kshemendra evidently copy the Rāmāyaṇa with the Uttarakāṇḍa. The Tamil Rāmāyaṇa of Kampan, assigned to the 11th cent. by Dr. Caldwell (*Comparative Grammar*, p. 88) is divided precisely like the Sanskrit poem. The story must, therefore, have been thus told before the 10th cent. but the remark in the Kataka commentary (the oldest we now possess, but which is certainly by no means an old work) that "the nectar of the tīrtha of the Rāmāyaṇa has been made muddy by the dust of unsuitable comments"—proves that a difference of text was early noticed. The author of this, being a Telugu, cannot be put earlier than the 11th century. He follows the usual Southern text,* but does not include the Uttarakāṇḍa. The number of verses he puts at 24,000. It is remarkable that there is no allusion to Rāma in Hiouen-Thsang, except the name Rāma-grāma be held to refer to the hero of the saga.

Dr Fausböll has added an admirable critical commentary, to justify his renderings of the many difficulties in the text. To his remarks (on p. 25) regarding lancha, it may be added that this is probably a Dravidian word; it is current everywhere in the South of India with the meaning of bribe.

Short as Professor Weber's essay and Dr. Fausböll's Dasaratha-Jātaka are, it would be difficult to mention two more important contributions to a critical study of Sanskrit literature since 1861, when Professor Goldstücker's Pāṇini appeared.

A. BURNELL.

THE SAPTASATI OR CHANDI PATH, being a portion of the Mārkaṇḍeya Purāṇa, translated into Gujarati from the English version of Kavali Venkat Rāmaswami Pandit. 79 pp. sm. 8vo. Bombay: 1871.

This Sapta Shati is held in great esteem by the devotees of Kāli, and was translated into English and published at Calcutta in 1823. From this version it has now been rendered into Gujarati by a Parsi—Merwanji Nasarwanji Wādia, who does not seem to be aware of the Gujarati poetical version made long ago by the famous Ranchodji Diwan of Junagadh.

THE ASIATIC SOCIETIES.

"*Journal of the Ceylon Branch of the Royal Asiatic Society*, 1870-71."

This part of the Journal contains:—1, A paper "On methods of taking impressions of Inscriptions," by T. W. Rhys Davids, C. C. S.; 2. A Prose Translation of the Introductory Stanzas of the 'Kusa Jātaka' by Lionel F. Lee, C. C. S.; 3, Notes on a Sannas, by the same. This Sannas, the writer says, is a copper-plate 15 by 4 inches, with an ornamental border of silver, having the sun and moon in the margin on one side and the royal sign Sri between them, and on the other side the figures of the lion and leopard. Among the interpretations assigned to the leopard "the most remarkable seems to be that the figure stands for the word *Jivi*, signifying 'life' as well as 'leopard.' The interpretation then of the four figures would be 'as long as the sun and moon endures, and as long as life remains to the Royal Lion race.' The *Sri* or royal sign, is of gold, and so are portions of the other figures." The translation runs thus:—

"The command issued from the grandeur and light of divine knowledge and benevolence of our most excellent, most gracious, and most high lord, exalted king of all men. 'Whereas Vijjasundara Rājā Karunayaka Herat Mudiyanselâ has from his earliest youth remained most true and faithful to the most high royal family, and has also contracted

* The South Indian MSS. agree with one another far more than those from other parts of India, and differ but little from Schlegel's text.

an auspicious marriage in obedience to our royal instructions, with the view of perpetuating hereafter the Kshatriya caste, of which the line has remained unbroken since we established our sovereignty over men at Siriwardanapura, formerly Jambudiva, the most prosperous and wealthy of all cities; and whereas Vijiyasundara Rájakaruṇayaka Herat Mudiyanselé is descended from the Brahman Shri-Vána Chandraya, who was a descendant from the Brahmans summoned from Jambudiva by the King Dappulusenanam, and was afterwards called by his majesty Bhuwaneka Bahu who reigned at Dambadeniya, after having built the temple of Vishnu at Alut-nuwara, and removed there the divine image from the city of the gods, and was appointed Basnayaka Nilame of the Mahá-dewala, as instructed by Vishnu in a dream, after having received a grant of land and an elephant and various offices of state, together with lands at Lewuke, and having married a lady of the family of Walagama Tennakóon—a favourite of the great and victorious Shri-Prákrama-Báhu on account of his faithful services, and the recipient of many emoluments and offices, lived at Lewuke to be [*here follow the names of the lands and their boundaries*] possessed by Mudiyanselé and his children and grand-children from generation to generation free of all taxes and tolls.

'This copper sannas was granted in the Shaka year 1646, in the month Medindina on the 6th Wednesday after the full moon, Mars being in the ascendant.'

Next follow—4, "Notes on the Geological origin of South Western Ceylon, together with its relation to the rest of the Island," by Hugh Nevill, Esq., F. Z. S.; 5, "Inscription at Weligama Vihára: text, translation, and notes," by T. W. Rhys Davids, C.C.S. At Weligama—the half way village between Galle and Matara, there are two Viháras; "one called Agra Bodhi—a fine Vihára on the top of a hill, whose founder is unknown, and which has a Dewalaya of very modern date; the other is called Weligama Gane Vihára and is on the plain. There is a very ancient Bó-tree and large Dagoba at this place, but for a Vihára only a small modern building, corresponding to the wording of the sannas, which speaks only of a Sakmana or covered corridor for priests to walk in—corresponding to the ancient cloisters. From this Sakmana is derived the name of the village of Hakmana. The inscription is on a stone built into the wall round the dagoba, and is translated by Mr. Davids as follows:—

"In the sixth year of the revered Lord Emperor Siri Sangabo Siri Bhuwanaika Báhu,* the minister named Kala Parákrama having given wages to the workmen, and having given in perpetuation the four gifts to the two priests who reside continuing in this (cloister) common to the priesthood; and also —in order that the gifts might be given for a day to the reverend priesthood coming from the four directions—(having given) ten amunas sowing extent of paddy-field which he had bought and a fruit-bearing cocoa-nut garden, and ten slaves and a yoke of oxen, and round torches and goblets with spouts, and a row of lamp-stands (for illumination) and palanquins, doli-baskets and leather, and cushions, and mattresses, and cloths woven with silk and hemp to spread over (seats for guests), and tubs and iron basins together with other things of this kind proper for the priesthood . . . . . . It is proper for all good men who in the future shall be, to maintain without dispute this cloister (Sakmana) or vihára, improved by the king's family, which (cloister) has been made to add merit to the revered king Bhuwanaika Báhu who brought me up, and (thus) to obtain the bliss (moksha) of release in heaven."

6, "Dondra Inscription No. I, Text, Translation and Notes," by the same. This inscription was on an upright slab of granite resembling a gravestone, and standing under the cocoanut palms on the sea shore at Dondra. It was removed by Mr. Davids to a place of safety. The translation records the grant of lands "in Nawadunna (now Naotunna) and Patégama, and the produce of Hatgama, where the Alapatta Arachchi made the dam," that it might continue for ever as the places "now included in the Parawésara" (now Paramedera) in the Nagárisa Nila (Vishnu) temple in Dondra, by Siri Sangabo Siri Vijaya Báhu in the Shaka year 1432."

7, "On the second species of Zosterops inhabiting Ceylon," by W. V. Legge, Hon. Sec.; 8, "Further notes on the Ornithology of Ceylon," by the same; 9, "On various Birds of the Western Province," by the same; 10, "On the Origin of the Shri Páda or Sacred Foot-print on the summit of Adam's Peak," by W. Skeen, Esq. This is an elaborate paper of fifty pages. 11, "The Romanized Text of the first five chapters of the Bálávatára, a Pali Grammar, with translation and explanatory notes," by L. F. Lee, C.C.S.; 12, "Specimens of Sinhalese Proverbs," by Louis de Zoysa, Mudaliyar. These are one hundred in number, from which we may give as specimens: 'Like the mad-woman's basket of herbs,'—an ill assorted mixture; 'Cannot drink as it is hot, and cannot throw away as it is Kanji'—an unpleasant dilemma; 'The idle man has divine (prophetic) eyes'—forbodes and magnifies difficulties as enemies are. 'He murders saints but drinks water after straining'—straining out a gnat and swallowing a camel; 'When the deer trespasses on his field he comes home and beats the deer's skin'—not able to punish the real offender he vents his anger on the inoffensive; 'One puts on the head to pluck out the eyes'—flatters to injure; 'If the dog bites your leg would you bite his?' 'The rat who was returning home drunk with toddy, said, If I meet a cat, I will tear him to pieces;' 'If one possesses a dog he must go where he is whistled for?' 'Like placing a ladder to the jumping monkey'. 'Even

* It is uncertain—"which Bhuwaneka Báhu this was: but judging from the form of the letters it must be either the sixth, who came to the throne, according to Turnour, in 1464, but according to Sadagama lankára (quoted in Alwis's Sidat Sangárawa pp. 32,300) in 1469;—or the seventh, who came to the throne in 1534, and was shot by accident by a Portuguese sportsman."

when a donor raises his step, it is a commensal'; 'Why feed with your finger the bag that you will have to open?'

18. "Translations of certain Documents, Family and Historical, found in the possession of the descendants of M. Nanclars de Lanerolle, French Envoy to the Court of Kandi" contributed by L. Ludovici, Esq. These documents are:—(1) an account of the French embassy to the Court of Kandi in 1685 and some particulars of the De Lanerolles Ceylon—translated from the Sinhalese; (2) Extracts of a Resolution passed in the Council of Ceylon on the 24th September 1765, granting maintenance to the descendants of Laisne de Nanclars de la Nerolle, followed by a most amusingly sarcastic endorsement by the late Mr. O'Brady, Government Agent of Galle, on a petition presented by one of the Lanerolles (a police Vidahn at Kattaluwa) applying for the rank of Mohandiram; (3) A letter from Holland giving an account of the siege of Vienna in 1683; (4) Letter from John Sobieski, King of Poland, to the Queen informing her of his victory; (5) The muster roll of the Turkish Army; (6) The spoil of the Turks carried into Vienna; and (7) a letter relating to trade in Amsterdam. These last five were probably intercepted at Trinkomali on their way to the Dutch Governor at Colombo by the emissaries of Raja Sinha, and translated into Sinhalese for his information.

Bombay Branch Royal Asiatic Society.

THE OLD SANSKRIT NUMERALS.

At the monthly meeting of the Bombay B. R. Asiatic Society, held Thursday, 11th January, Prof. Ramkrishna Gopal Bhandarkar, M.A. presented a Devanâgarî transcript of a Valabhi copperplate grant,* with a paper of considerable length on the reading of the ancient Indian numerals. The following is an abstract of his remarks:—

In this copperplate, put into his hands, he said, by Mr. Burgess, the date is given in figures thus—

The first figure in this was formerly understood to signify 300 in all cases; but Mr. Thomas found variations in the form and number of the side strokes, whence he inferred that the value of the symbol was in some way modified by them.† The exact signification of these was given by Dr. Bhau Daji,‡—who has pointed out that this symbol without the right hand strokes represents 100; with one stroke, it signifies 200; and with two, 300. His conclusions are based chiefly on the numerals found in the Nâsik cave inscriptions. He (Mr. Bhandarkar) had examined Mr. West's copies of these,§ and was convinced of the truth of this opinion, which is also confirmed by the numerals on the Sâh coins.‖ And in the *fac-simile* of one of Dr. Bura's Gurjara plates, given by Prof. Dowson,¶ in which the date 385 is given in words as well as figures, the first symbol has a loop at the lower end similar to that in the present plate. For these reasons the first figure in the present case stands for 300.

Now, as to the value of the second figure:—We know the symbols for 10, 40, 60, and 90. Dr. Bhau Daji quotes an inscription from Kârlen in which a symbol somewhat resembling the second in this plate is given with the value in words as 'twenty', and it occurs twice in the Nâsik inscription No. 26** which is considered to be a deed of sale, executed at the orders of Gotamiputra in some year represented by this and another symbol. In another inscription (No. 26), in which Gotamiputra's exploits are enumerated, his wife assigns the cave in which it occurs for the use of religious mendicants in the 19th year of Pulumayi. And as these events took place shortly after each other, the symbol most probably stands for 20. The same figure occurs on a coin of Vishva Sâh, the 18th king in Mr. Newton's list,‡ while the second figure on his father's coin on hand represents 10, the whole date being 217,—the other symbol, therefore, must stand for 20. The last figure in this grant resembles our modern ६ = 6, and that has generally been considered its value.* The date of the present grant is therefore 326.

This grant is by Dharasena IV., the great grandson of Dharasena II.; but the figured date—

on the copper plate of this latter monarch as deciphered by Mr. Wathen, was considered by Prinsep† and Mr. Thomas‡ as equal to 300 + some undetermined quantity, and the Rev. P. Anderson thinks it to be 3?4.§ Dr. Bhau Daji‖ has given five dates from Valabhi plates, but none of them resembles the date in any of the three known grants, though one, which somewhat resembles that on Mr Wathen's plate, is interpreted by him as 332, while in another paper,¶ he assigns to Dharasena II. the dates 322 and 328. If, then, the date in the present case is correctly interpreted, these readings would make Dharasena IV. to have reigned *four* or *six* years *before* his great grandfather, or in the *same* year, or only *four* years after him. But on examining Mr. Wathen's plate in the Bombay Asiatic Society's Museum, it is found that the figure representing hundreds has only one side stroke.** It thus appears that the first figure in the grant of Dharasena II. represents 200. Now the same minister Skandabhata executed the grant of Dharasena IV. and

---

* A fac-simile and translation of this grant has been given at pp. 16 17.

† Jour. R. Asiat. Soc., Vol. XII., pp. 33, Note 1.

‡ Jour. Bom. B. R. As. Soc. Vol. VIII., pp. 225-233.

§ Ib., Vol. VII., pp. 37-52.

‖ Ib., Vol. VII., pp. 71-88.

¶ Jour. R. As. Soc. N. S., Vol. I., p. 267.

** Conf. Jour. Bomb. B. R. As. Soc., Vol. V., p. 46; and Vol. VII. p. 233, where the second occurrence of the same symbol appears to have escaped Dr. Bhau's attention, though he remarks the second symbol as 4.

‡ Jour. Bom. B. R. As. Soc., Vol. VII., p. 15, and Mr. Thomas, Jour. R. As. Soc., Vol. XII., p. 55.

* Jour. B. B. R. As. Soc., Vol. VIII., p. 233, under 'Cave No. 4.'

† Jour. As. Soc. Beng., Vol. VII., p. 356.

‡ Jour. R. As. Soc., Vol. XII., p. 8, Note.

§ Jour. Bom. B. R. As. Soc., Vol. III., p. 213.

‖ Ib., Vol. VIII., p. 230.   ¶ Ib., Vol. VIII., p. 246.

** Jour. As. Soc. Beng., Vol. VII., p. 968.

the present one; and we now know the values of the symbols for 10, 20, 40, 80, and 90. The second figure in Mr. Wathen's plate which resembles none of these, must then be 30, 50, 60, or 70, and, as the last figure in it consisting of two simple strokes clearly represents 2, the most probable date would be 272—giving a value of 70 to the second symbol. A tenure of 84 years would not be too long for a single holder of a hereditary office. The symbol too bears a sufficient resemblance, making allowance for the difference of age, to that for 70 in Rudra Dáma's Girnar inscription, in which the date 72 is given in words and figures.*

Mr. Wathen's second plate, in the Museum of the Bombay Society, resembles Dr. Burn's No. 4; the granter in both cases is the same—Shiláditya II., the third king after Dharasena IV. and the date in both† is the same, viz.—

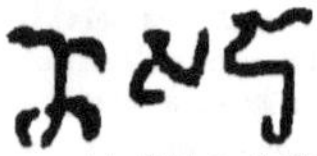

The first figure is equal to 300, and the second symbol has generally been taken for 70—a value just assigned to a different one. Now the minister who prepared Shiláditya's deed was Madana Hála, the son of Skandabhata; but there is probably no instance in history of a father and son holding an office for 104 years,—which period the date 376 here would place between Dharasena II. and Shiláditya II.; and the only tens now available for the symbol are 30, 50, and 60. Now 30 would limit the duration of three reigns to ten years; 60 would give too long a period to Skandabhata's son; but if 50, the dates on the Sáh coins support the interpretation of the symbol as 50 rather than 60. For after Rudra Sáh, the 13th in Mr. Newton's list‡ reigned his two sons Vishva Sinha and Atri Dáma, then Vishva Sáh the son of Atri Dáma, and, after an interval, Rudra Sáh's third son, Asha Dáma. One of Rudra Sáh's coins is dated 197, one of Atri Dáma's 210, one of Vishva Sáh's 227, and one of Asha Dáma's a date, the second symbol in which is the one under consideration. The value of 60 has been rejected on other grounds; 50 ranks next in probability, as 60 would render Asha Dáma's reign too long and make him live at least 33 years after his second brother. The date on Mr. Wathen's 2nd plate and of Dr. Burn's thus appears to be 356. The conclusions here drawn are—that [symbol] stands for 50, and [symbol] for 70; that the date of the grant of Dharasena II. discovered by Mr. Wathen is 272; of Dharasena IV, 326; and of Shiláditya II. is 356. The interval between Dharasena II. and Shiláditya II. is thus 84 years,—and there is no impossibility in the circumstance of a father and son holding between them the office of minister to all the kings for 84 years.

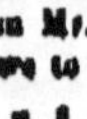

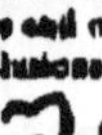

Mr. Thomas and Dr. Bhau Dáji think the era used in these dates is the Shaka, and we find the words Shaka-Kála used in those records of the period in which the era is specified; and the name Shaka-nripa-kála and the very existence of such an epoch show that there was a great king from whom it originated and who belonged to a tribe known as Shakas. Now from cave inscriptions and coins, it appears that Gujarát and a great part of Maháráshṭra were for about three centuries governed by kings calling themselves Kshatrapas—a name of foreign origin, and the same as the Persian word Satrap. The earliest known of these is Nahapana, the Kshatrapa of a king named Kshaharáta, and another was called Chashṭana—all three names of foreign origin, as is also the name Sáh of the Satrap dynasty of Suráshṭra. Nahapana or his sovereign, or whoever conquered this part of the country, and established the dynasty, must have been the Shaka king with whom the era originated. And Ushavadáta, the son-in-law of Nahapana, is called a Shaka in one of the Násik inscriptions.§ When the Satraps were superseded by the Valabhis in Suráshṭra, the same era must have continued in use. From what has taken place in later times, after the Maráthas succeeded the Muhammadans, we should also expect to find the Valabhis and the Chálukyas using the era of the Satraps whom they succeeded—especially when they had no other.

And if we refer the Valabhi dates to the era of the Shaka king, we arrive at an intelligible starting point for the Valabhi era itself, ascertained by Col. Tod to have commenced in 319 A.D. If the date 272 of the grant of Dharasena II be referred to the Shaka-kála it corresponds to 350 A.D., and shows that he was reigning in the 31st year of the family era. Now Bhaṭárka and his first son did not assume the title of king, but were called Senápatis or 'commanders of forces.' Dronasinha the second son is the first to whom the title of Mahárája is given in Mr. Wathen's first plate, and he is spoken of as having been crowned by 'the only sovereign of the whole world'—whoever he may have been. The independence of the Valabhi kings therefore dates from this event. Dronasinha also must have received the title of Mahárája some years after he succeeded his brother, and therefore 31 years is a sufficiently long period for a portion of the reign of Drona-sinha and the reigns of his two brothers and Guhasena.

The conclusions then are,—that the date of the grant of Dharasena II. discovered by Mr. Wathen is 272 Shaka, or 350 A.D., that of the present grant is 326 Shaka, or 404 A.D., and that of those of Shiláditya II. is 356 Shaka or 434 A.D.

* Jour. Beng. As. Soc., Vol. VII., p. 350 lith.; Jour. Bom. B. B. As. Soc., Vol. I., p. 148, lith. 4; and Vol. VII., p. 118, lith.

† Jour. Beng. As. Soc., Vol. VII., p. 968.

‡ Jour. Bom. B. B. A. Soc., Vol. VII., p. 28.

§ No. 14, Jour. Bom. B. B. A. Soc., Vol. VII., p. 53.

MISCELLANEA.

THE HILL TRIBES OF THE NORTH-EAST FRONTIER.

It will not be out of place perhaps to give some account of the various wild tribes that inhabit our North-East frontiers, regarding whom very little is known by many. We will commence with the tribes occupying North Kachar and the hills round Munipur. This tract, which lies wholly within the watershed of the Brahmaputra on its left bank, is bounded on the North, East and West by large branches of that river, and on the South by the Barail, a ramification of the great mountain chain which stretches from Asam to Cape Negrais. The whole country is one vast jungle of bamboos, called *Mali* or *Tula* with a few patches of cultivated ground, on which some of the tribes temporarily establish their villages. The Barail has several enormously high peaks, the summits of which are cloud-capped, and through the gorges of the whole range a strong southerly wind generally blows over North Kachar. In the lower ranges and the valleys, dense fogs and mists are common, and there is a general dampness throughout the year. The consequence of this is that malaria, breeding the most deadly epidemics, makes them the most insalubrious places in India. The jungle throughout the country abounds with apes, buffaloes, elephants, tigers, bears, leopards, and hyenas; there are snakes in infinite variety, and leeches, gnats, and flies in swarms. In North Kachar, there are several wild tribes, but they are all supposed to be the branches of the principal ones called Cacharis, Kukis, Lohupas, Mikirs, and Nagas. It is, however, a curious fact that several of the smaller tribes, or clans, not only differ from each other in manners and customs, but also in language. In the valleys of the Brahmaputra alone, there are no less than twenty different clans, each speaking a dialect unintelligible to the others, as among the wild tribes of Africa. The Kacharis differ little from the Asamese not only in appearance and customs, but also in dress and accommodation, except in remote parts where both are rude and scanty. The Kukis are subdivided into two classes, the Old and the New. The Old Kukis, physically the most powerful in Kachar, dress decently, and affect a modesty unknown to the other tribes. They are very fond of ornaments, and wear rings, bracelets, armlets, necklaces, and ear-rings in great numbers. Instead of boring the ears, they, in common with two or three clans of the New Kukis, cut off a piece of flesh in a circular form from the lower lobe, and insert into the hole thus made an elastic sheave of bamboo, so as to form a powerful spring acting equally on all sides of the lobe, which is thus gradually enlarged until it is made to reach enormous dimensions,—the outer flesh and skin of the lobe being sufficiently stretched out to admit of a brass or silver ring four or five inches in circumference. The ear is also turned round so as to make the ear-ring be at right angles to the side of the head, and both through the ear and the ring are hung other ornaments. Among the Old Kukis, marriage is as much a religious as a civil rite. The Ghalim or headman of the village must be present, and in the presence of the congregation he blesses the young couple, who stand with a foot each upon a large stone in the centre of the village. The custom of entering into bondage in the house of the parents of the bride before marriage, is also prevalent among them as among the New Kukis. Courtship is well understood and delicately managed. When wooing has gone on for some time, the lover sends a friend to the parents of the damsel with a stoup of liquor: if they quaff it, the omen is favourable; if they decline, the sentimental lover must give up all hope and seek his bride elsewhere, a fact which demonstrates that parental authority is a natural law, as distinctly defined and understood among these savages as amongst the most civilized nations. It is superfluous to state that early marriage is unknown among the wild tribes. Old Kukis have a long list of deities, many of whom are malignant. The feeling against the gods is intense; they are mere objects of terror, and if the savages could only get a chance, they would most likely bestir themselves in beating the gods. New Kukis are a short sturdy race, the women more squat even than the men, but strong and lusty. The face is broad as it is long; the cheek bones high, broad, and prominent; the eyes small and almond-shaped; and the nose short and flat, with wide nostrils. New Kukis differ slightly in manners from the Old Kukis. Their marriage costs the parents two or three years of bondage, or about thirty rupees in gifts. There is a solemn marriage ceremony preceded by feasting and games, especially among the rich. The parties, clothed in their best, both drink from a stoup of liquor,—that being the common mode among these tribes of pledging truth and fidelity. A stoup is presented to the couple by the thempu or priest, who mutters over them some words in an unknown tongue, and ties round the bride's neck two small threads of cotton, and one round that of the bridegroom. The threads are allowed to wear out, and are never replaced. After the threads are put on, the thempu presents the happy pair with a small [illegible], again mutters something in the unknown tongue, and the marriage is complete. A New Kuki can put away his wife though she be faultless, but in such a case, she is allowed to take away all his property, except his drinking vessel and the cloth round his waist. Wives, however, are generally the slaves of their husbands, and may be sold or pawned at the will of the latter. A husband will even sometimes sell or pawn his wife to purchase a Mithun. This practice extends to all the North-Eastern Tribes, even among the Munipuris, Asamese, and Nagas. New Kukis believe in a future state. The dead amongst them are supposed to assume their former shapes, and continue their lives in a land lying to the North, where the good men of the tribes are said to congregate, and this is their heaven. The leading joys in it are those of war and the chase, and in which rice grows without cultivation, and the jungles abound in game. In this particular, the New Kukis much resemble the North American Indians. The practice of burial prevails in all countries where the belief of the resurrection is entertained. Among the New Kukis, Puthen is the Supreme Deity, the creator of the universe. His wife is named Nongi, and his son Thila. Thila's wife is named [illegible], and she has the power of causing slight distempers, such as headache, toothache, &c. As their system of medicine is closely connected with their theology, the physician is generally the priest, whose business it is to offer sacrifices in addition to administering medicine. The Lohupas, who reside near Munipur, are not very savage. They are of superior stature to the tribes around them. They shave off their hair on both sides of the head, leaving a ridge on the top like that of a helmet. In war, they wear a head-dress like that of the Tangkhuls, and as ornaments, tresses of women are allowed to dangle on all sides. They use generally long spears, in wielding which they are very expert, being with these and shields more than a match for all the neighbouring tribes with their spears, bows, and poisoned arrows. The name of the Lohupas spreads terror even into the far Burmese territories. In other respects, they nearly resemble the Mikirs and the Munipuris. The Mikirs wear moustaches, and have a peculiar dress. It is a sack put on like a shirt, consisting of two pieces of cotton cloth, each about three feet long by one and a half broad, dyed with red stripes and fringed at both ends, sewed together like a bag with holes for the head and arms. They look upon marriage as a matter purely of civil contract, unconnected with any religious rite, a feast to all the villagers being the chief part of the ceremony. The Nagas, so called from the plural *nanga* or naked, are a lazy and savage race. They go almost undressed, their sole covering being a small piece of cloth tied round the waist. They load themselves, however, with ornaments made mostly of brass wire, shells, or cowries. An armlet which they wear is peculiar to them though it has now been adopted also by the Kukis. It is a brass rod twisted some eight or ten times in the shape of a wire-spring, and fitting tightly on to the flesh between the shoulder and the elbow. They all wear ear-rings of brass wire, and their chief weapon is the spear. They have a great many deities, one of whom is blind, and he is systematically cheated by his worshippers. He is worshipped at stone mounds, where the Nagas place large baskets with small offerings in them, trusting that he judges of the quantity of the contents from the largeness of the receptacles. It is supposed that the population of the hills in North Kachar has accumulated from the successive waves, from the north side, of fugitive Tatars; and from the south and west sides from similar waves, of the inhabitants of Chittagong and Tipura, and the plains of India, giving place to conquerors, and retreating into the hills and jungles before them. They would appear to be either of pure Tatar origin, or an intermixture of Tatar and Malay.* Such are the hill tribes of North Kachar and the Barél.—*Bengal Times, Dec. 28.*

THE MINES OF MEWAR.

About twenty miles from Udaypur, towards the south, you enter the beautiful Valley of *Jawara*, more famed for its mineral wealth than for its natural beauty. Yet, in truth, rarely does one see a more magnificent vale than this. In the centre a foaming river runs past a ruined town, temples of great antiquity, and many a spot hallowed by associations of past heroism and glory. Here it was that the noble Pratap Singh, the saviour of his country, paused awhile to recruit his strength, ere he made a [illegible] upon the fort, which was as unexpected as it was irresistible; and, as the result, he planted the new standard of his race in the new capital—the beautiful city of Udaypur. Around *Jawara*, hills, clothed with verdure, rise to a great height on every side, and the eye is attracted by a picturesque fort, temple, or watch-tower on almost every prominent elevation. Yet, though there are so many indications of a large population, life is wanting; for *Jawara* was deserted when the fortunes of the country fell. At the south corner of the valley stands a temple dedicated to a Devi, a goddess (so her votaries say) of wonderful power; but some are found to own that they have their doubts as to her being present in this particular shrine in these days of degeneracy and dissolution. The high priest is there, than whom it would be difficult to find one of more clerical cut. But he, with doleful countenance, because of glory departed, will assure you in trembling accents, that the goddess has withdrawn her patronage from the caste of miners, hence they have forgotten their business. Be this true or not, the miners no longer exist—probably enough because they fled when the war-cry of the Maratha invader re-echoed through the land. There remains in *Jawara* a temple which is well worth examination. The dome of the ante-chamber is of considerable beauty, and the carving is in wonderful preservation, although the building is close upon three hundred years old. But this is not the oldest temple. At the north-east of the valley stands a temple older than this by a hundred years, and it, too, though standing amid the ruins of the town, is in a good state of preservation. Râmnâth and Bhairavnâth occupy the most prominent positions whilst Hanuman, Râma's monkey-general, is placed in front, in a posture of adoration. A noble tank, surrounded by smaller shrines, spreads out in front of the principal entrance. All around lie ruins of temples and houses. The walls of the latter must have been constructed of the earthen pots used by the smelters, and the slag remaining after the ore had been extracted.

But let us to the mines, which may yet be again laid under contribution by the rulers of Mewar. Immense heaps of refuse point the road to the principal of them. The path leads through the thickest and most beautiful jungle, over rivulets, through nallas, through thickets which electrify the botanist, and dense jungle which afford the huntsman true earnest that royal game is well within reach of his rifle. The mines themselves are mere shafts in the solid rock—apparently natural, yet doubtless, superficial. In some places, attempts at regular work appear to have been made; but, as a rule, the miners were contented with boring only far enough into the hill to obtain ore without trouble, never venturing where the natural solidity of the stone would not suffice for the support of the rock above. Veins of almost pure lead ramify through the primitive rock; whilst beautifully coloured ores of the mineral sparkle overhead. Silver is obtained in small quantities, whilst gold has been found, it is said, on several occasions. A very short time sufficed to find numerous valuable specimens; no doubt more extended research would have shown that these mines could be worked with profit. A hundred years ago, in 1780, *Jawara* alone poured two lakhs of rupees into the Maharána's treasury. About the beginning of this century an attempt was made to re-work these mines, but it failed—it may have been from an imperfect knowledge of the science of mining, or from the fear that increase of wealth would attract the spoiler from the plains. Such a feeling still exists. When these mines were visited, with a view to obtaining some little material for this letter, they had not been visited by any native for five or six years, although the hill is almost entirely perforated. There the tiger had its lair, and the panther its habitation. Towards the south there are smaller mines, which are better-known.

A steep and rugged path winds up the grand hill overlooking the Temple of Kali, crosses a wall of [illegible] of enormous thickness, and finally is lost on a plain which is surrounded by a girdle of other hills, wherein are dug the mines. Traces of walls are to be found all round, and ruins of forts on every prominent spur. It was here that Pratap Singh held out when driven from his capital, and here he lived with those trusty followers who still preferred patriotism to ease, until the dawn of better days. Aided they were by the trusty Bhils, lords of the Passes and Monarchs of the Wood. In these caves there were preserved, for generations, the rings and bolts to which the cradles of Pratap Singh's children had been attached; and even now, the inhabitants of the village on this elevated plain speak of their being there still. Shafts and mines are innumerable. There are traces of steps, walls, and outlets for water which show that more attention had been paid to the working—probably because the ore was not so abundant. Perhaps Pratap himself opened the mines when in exile here. However that may be, the extensive ruins show that he must have had a large host with him.

The highest point on the hill commands a magnificent view of the country for many miles around; but more magnificent and grander far is the view from the summit of the Hill of [illegible]—ten miles further south. To the north-west and south stretch ranges upon ranges of "everlasting hills." Dungarpur, the capital of the Aharia Prince of Dungarpur, the head of the eldest branch of the royal race of Mewar, is distinctly visible. Salumbra can also be seen, the chief town of the descendant of the elder son of a former Rána.

who gave away his birthright to a younger, and, as yet unborn brother, to please an imbecile father. You can also see Chawand, another home of Pratap. The palace on the summit at Udaipur, and many an ancient place seem to lie at one's feet when he stands on the peak of Pratab. Dense jungle circles hill and dale, and affords shelter to many a wild beast and shade to thousands of cattle—the property of the valiant Bhil, whose hand is against every man, and against whom all are prepared to fight; for this hardy mountaineer levies rakwali, or black mail, upon all who pass through his territory, and who are unable to protect themselves—a difficult matter, seeing that the Bhil's war cry will bring an armed man from behind every bush and rock:—

"Wild as the scream of the curlew,
From crag to crag the signal flew—
Instant, thro' copse and heath, arose
Bonnets and spears and bended bows;
On right, on left, above, below,
Sprung up at once the lurking foe."

Not sooner sprung the belted clansman into view at the whistle of Roderick Dhu than answers the Bhil to his leader's call.

At Jawar we lived in temples, the delicate tracery of whose ornamentation would afford a model for more than one architect.—*Times of India, Jan.*

DISCOVERY OF FORGOTTEN RECORDS.

A curious discovery of neglected and forgotten records has lately been made by the Commissioner of the Burdwan Division, and, singularly enough, the treasure has been unearthed in a collectorate, the records of which had already been searched by Dr. Hunter. While inspecting the Collector's office, Mr. Buckland found a number of old English manuscript books lying in an open rack in the clerk's room, where they had been exposed for an unknown period to the ravages of time and white-ants, and undisturbed by any previous explorer, having by some accident been left out of the treasury almirahs. Among them, the most neglected, have been found what are probably the oldest records of Birbhum; for Mr. Keating is mentioned in the "Rural Annals" as the first Collector of that district whose records survived, and here we have the correspondence of Messrs. Foley and Sherburne, the former of whom was Collector in November 1786, two years before Mr. Keating, and the latter in April 1787. Indeed, the correspondence contains a complete account of the eighteen months' administration of the latter officer, and furnishes a clue to the cause of his removal and subsequent trial. The letters of Mr. Foley's time are chiefly between that officer and the Board of Revenue. One of them is remarkable as presenting an early existence of recourse to the sale of land for arrears of revenue, and showing that the step was most reluctantly taken. In 1787 wild elephants were so numerous in Birbhum that the whole district was in danger of being overrun by them; and shikaris were sent from Sillet and Chittagong to aid in their capture.—*Englishman.*

QUERIES.

Mode of Dating in Orissa.

2. In Orissa, it is the custom in all Zemindary accounts, receipts, leases, and other documents to denote the month by the sign of the Zodiac, instead of by the familiar names of asterisms used by the whole Aryan race in India. Thus—

Baisakh is called	मेष ...	Mesha.	Aries.
Jesht	वृष ...	Vrisha.	Taurus.
Asharh	मिथुन ..	Mithuna.	Gemini.
Shraban	कर्कट.	Karkata.	Cancer.
Bhadrab	सिंह ...	Sinha.	Leo.
Asin	कन्या ..	Kanya.	Virgo.
Kartik	तुला ...	Tula.	Libra.
Margsir (Aghan)	वृश्चिक..	Brischik.	Scorpio.
Push (Pus)	धनु ...	Dhanu.	Sagittarius.
Magh	मकर ..	Makara.	Capricornus.
Phagun	कुम्भ ..	Kumbha.	Aquarius.
Chaitra	मीन ...	Mina.	Pisces.

I should be glad to know if this curious custom prevails in any other part of India. The singular thing is that the months are lunar, although thus indicated by solar names. Weber, in a valuable essay on the Vedic Nakshatras, reprinted from the *Journal of the Berlin Scientific Society*, points out the existence of several systems of names for the months, which I have hitherto believed to be obsolete. It may be, however, that some of them are still preserved in remote corners of India. Chand, in one of his earlier chapters, speaks of the month of Sahas (सहस), which I believe to be Kartik. As I am writing from camp I cannot give the reference either to Chand or Weber.

JOHN BEAMES.

Balasore, January 15th, 1872.

Clearing Inscriptions.

3. In deciphering inscriptions on stone tablets my efforts have often been completely frustrated by a practice that the natives have of smearing the stones with oil. The oil forms a cake on the stone, often a quarter of an inch thick, thus obliterating all traces of the writing underneath.

Can you or any of your readers inform me of any application by means of which the oil may be successfully removed without any risk of injury to the inscribed tablet?

25th January 1872. F.

All fats and oxidised oils may be removed by Benzine, and were the crust nothing more, that solvent would answer; but no doubt contact of lime, red-lead, &c. has converted it almost into a mineral incrustation, and the best plan would be to apply carefully either concentrated acetic or nitric acid—having first ascertained that the stone will not be acted on by them. Constant application of a mixture of turpentine and benzine is very good for searching out and removing traces of oil. But if the stone could be kept for some time in a hot solution of washing soda or pearl ashes, it would take out almost anything. D. S. K.

SÂT GAMBHIRA ATTÂLIKA.
BALASORE

SKETCHES OF MATHURÂ.

By F. S. GROWSE, M.A., B.C.S.

I.—THE BRAJ MANDAL.

THE modern district of Mathurá is in its form the result of political exigencies, and consists of two tracts of country which have little or nothing in common beyond the name which unites them. Its outline is that of a carpenter's square, of which the two parallelograms are nearly equal in extent, the upper one lying due north and south, and the other at right angles to it, stretching eastward below. The head-quarters of the local administration are situated on the line of junction, and are therefore more accessible from the border district of Aligarh and the independent state of Bharatpur than from the greater part of their own territory. Yet the position is the most central that could be determined in an area of such eccentric outline.

The eastern parallelogram, comprising the parganas of Jalesar,* Sa'dábád,† and half of Mahá-ban, is a fair specimen of the ordinary character of the Doáb. Its luxuriant crops and fine orchards indicate the fertility of the soil, and render the landscape not unpleasing to the eye, but, though far the most valuable part of the district for the purposes of the farmer and the economist, it possesses few historical associations to detain the antiquary. On the other hand, the western parallelogram, though comparatively poor in natural products, is rich in mythological legend, and contains a series of the master-pieces of Hindu architecture. Its still greater wealth in earlier times is attested by the one solitary specimen which has survived the torrent of Muhammadan barbarism. Yet widely as the two tracts of country differ in character, there is reason to believe that their first union dates from a very remote period. The Chinese pilgrim Hwen Thsang, who visited India in the seventh century after Christ, describes the circumference of the kingdom of Mathurá as 5,000 li, i.e. 833 miles, taking the Chinese li as almost ⅙ of an English mile. The soil, he says, was rich and fertile, and specially adapted to the cultivation of grain and cotton, while the mango trees were so abundant that they formed complete forests. The fruit was of two varieties; the smaller kind turning yellow as it ripened, the larger remaining always green. From this description it would appear that the then kingdom of Mathurá extended east of the capital along the Doáb in the direction of Mainpuri, for there the mango flourishes most luxuriantly and almost every village boasts a fine grove, whereas in western Mathurá it will not grow at all, except under the most careful treatment. In support of this inference it may be observed that, notwithstanding the number of monasteries and stupas mentioned by the Buddhist pilgrims as existing in the kingdom of Mathurá, no traces of any such buildings have been discovered in the western half of the modern district, except in the immediate neighbourhood of the capital. In Mainpuri, on the contrary, and more especially on the side where it touches Mathurá, fragments of Buddhist sculpture may be seen lying in heaps in almost every village. In all probability the territory of Mathurá, at the time of Hwen Thsang's visit, included not only the eastern half of the modern district, but also some small part of Agra, and the whole of the Shikohábád and Mustafábád parganas of Mainpuri; while the remainder of the present Mainpuri district formed a portion of the kingdom of Sankisa, which extended to the borders of Kanauj. But all local recollection of this exceptional period has absolutely perished, and the mutilated effigies of Buddha and Máyá are replaced on their pedestals, and adored as Brahma and Devi by the ignorant villagers, whose forefathers, after long struggles, had triumphed in their overthrow.

It is only the western half of modern Mathurá, considered as the birth-place and abid-

* Jalesar, a slight modification of the original form Jalesvar, "Lord of water," is very appropriate to the position of the town, which stands between two branches of the river Sarsa, on an artificial hill formed by excavation of the surrounding country. Hence in the rains it is often a complete island. The fort, which rises from its centre, is locally said to date from the time of Kutb-ud-din (which should probably be corrected to Ala-ud-din), and to have been founded by the Rana of Chitor, the then capital of Mewar, who, being vanquished by the Muhammadans in his own country, fled into these parts where the Jadaun name Mahában, [illegible] the local Governor, in a pitched battle, and took possession of the town. The tomb of [illegible], who fell on the field, is still shown and venerated as a sacred shrine, an annual fair called 'the [illegible]' being celebrated at it in the month of Sáwan.

† Sa'dábád was founded by an eminent historical character, Sa'dullah Khán, the able minister of the Emperor Shahjahán. He died in 1655 A.D.

ing home of Vaishnava Hinduism, that forms the subject of the present papers. It is about 42 miles in length, with an average breadth of 30 miles, and is intersected throughout by the river Jamuná. On the right bank of the stream are the parganas of Kosí* and Chhátá,† so named after their principal towns, with the home pargana below them to the south; and on the left bank the united parganas of Noh-jhíl‡ and Mát§ with half the pargana of Mahában as far east as the town of Baldeva. This extent of country is almost absolutely identical with the Braj-mandal of Hindu topography, the circuit of 84 kos¶ in the neighbourhood of Gokul and Brindában, where the divine brothers Krishna and Balarám grazed their herds. On the west a low range of sandstone hills forms a barrier between English territory and the independent state of Bharatpur; and one of the twelve sacred woods, viz., Káman, is beyond the border. To a very recent period almost the whole of this large area was pasture and woodland, and to the present day many of the villages are environed by broad belts of trees variously designated as *ghand*, *jhári*, *rakhyá*, *ban*, or *khandí*. These tracts are often of considerable extent: thus the Kokila ban at Great Bathan covers 798 acres; the rakhyá at Kámar‖ more than 1000, and in the contiguous villages of Pisáyo* and Karhela† the *rakhyá* and *kadamb-khandí* together amount to nearly as much. The year of the great famine Samvat 1894, that is, 1838 A.D., is invariably given as the date when the land began to be largely reclaimed; the immediate cause being the number of new roads then opened out for the purpose of affording employment to the starving population. Almost every spot is traditionally connected with some event in the life of Krishna or of his mythical mistress Rádhá, sometimes to the prejudice of an earlier divinity. Thus two prominent peaks in the Bharatpur range are crowned with the villages of Nandgánw and Barsána, of which, the former is venerated as the home of Krishna's foster-father Nanda, and the latter as the residence of Rádhá's parents Brikhabhán and Kírat.‡ Both legends are now as implicitly credited as the fact that Krishna was born at Mathurá; while in reality the name Nandgánw, the sole foundation for the belief, is an ingenious substitution for Nandíshvar, a title of Mahádeva, and Barsána is a corruption of *Brahma-sánu*, the hill of Brahma. Only the Giriráj at Gobardhan was according to the original distribution, dedicated to Vishnu, the second person of the triad, who is now recognized

* Kosí is a populous and thriving municipal town on the high road to Delhi, with the largest cattle market in that part of the country. The name is said to be a corruption of Kusasthali, though it may be conceived to have rather some connexion with the sacred grove of Kokila which is close by.

† The local pandits, who are determined to find a reference to Krishna in every name throughout the circle of Braj, derive Chhátá from the [illegible], which they say the god [illegible] there. But the town has no genuine tradition nor reputed sanctity, nor appearance of antiquity, and more probably derives its name from the clumsy Chhattris which surmount the lofty gateway of the Imperial Sarái, and form prominent objects from a very considerable distance.

‡ Noh-jhíl is a decayed town about 30 miles from Mathurá, situate on the borders of a very large *jhíl*, some 8 miles in length, which is said to have been the original bed of the Jamuná. The banks of the river are now some 4 or 5 miles distant. The name of the patriarch Noh may have been given to the place with a reference to its flooded appearance. There is a ruinous Fort with high and massive earthen ramparts constructed by the Játs, and also a Muhammadan dargáh which includes in its precincts a covered colonnade, consisting of some 20 or 30 Hindu pillars, the spoils of an older temple.

§ Mát, though the head of a pargana, is merely a small and meanly built village on the left bank of the Jamuná, a little above Brindában. It is one of the stations in the *ban játrá*, and is the reputed scene of Krishna's childish frolic in upsetting Jasodá's milk-pails (*mát*). Close by are the more famous *tirthas*—Bhándir-ban and Bel-ban: both mentioned in all the Vaishnava Puránas.

¶ The number 84 seems originally to have been selected as a sacred number in consequence of its being the multiple of the number of months in the year with the number of days in the week. Its connection with the Braj-mandal is therefore peculiarly appropriate, if Krishna be regarded as the Indian Apollo. Thus the magnificent temple in Kashmír dedicated to the sun under the title of Mártand has a colonnade of exactly 84 pillars.

‖ Kámar in the Kosí pargana is still a populous Ját town, but in the early part of last century was a place of much greater wealth and importance, when a daughter of one of the principal families was taken in marriage by Thákur Badan Sinha of Sahár, the father of the famous Suraj Mal, the first of the Bharatpur Rajas. On the outskirts of the town is a large walled garden with some monuments to his mother's relations, and in connection with it a spacious masonry tank filled with water brought by aqueducts from the surrounding *rakhyá*. At a little distance is an artificial lake with unfinished stone ghats, the work of the Raja; this is called [illegible] kund, after the [illegible] saint of that name, but there is no tradition to connect him with the locality.

* *Bhúkhe piyáse* is, in the local patois, a common expression for hungry and thirsty; and Pisáyo is said to be so called because Rádhá one day met Krishna there fainting with thirst, and relieved him with a draught of water.

† Karhela is locally derived from *kar-khel*, the movements of the hands in the *Rás-lílá*. At the village of [illegible] a pond bears the same name—Karhela kund—which is there explained as [illegible] equivalent to [illegible]. But in the Mainpuri district is a large town called Karhal—the same name in a slightly modified form—where neither of the above etymologies would hold. In each case the name is probably connected with a simple natural feature, there being at all these places dense thickets of the *karil* plant.

‡ Kírat is the only name popularly known in the locality, but in the Brahma Vaivarta Purána it is given as Kalávati.

as the tutelary divinity at all three hill places. A similar displacement would seem to have occurred at another locality in yet earlier times; for one of the twelve sacred woods, mentioned even in the *Bhágavat Purána*, viz., Bhadraban betrays, in the name, its original dedication to Mahádeva, but now acknowledges the presence of no god but Krishna. Again, Bhangáow, on the bank of the Jamuná, was clearly so called from Bhava, one of the eight manifestations of Shiva; but the name is now generally modified to Bhay-gáow, and is supposed to commemorate the alarm (*bhay*) felt in the neighbourhood at the time when Nanda, bathing in the river, was carried off by the god Varuna. A masonry landing-place and temple on the water's edge, called Nand-ghát, dating only from last century, are the foundation and support of the local legend. The village names of Shivdál and Bisambhara may also be quoted as showing that Mahádeva was once a more popular divinity in the country than at present. Of a still more absolute origin, viz. snake-worship, faint indications may be detected in a few local names and customs. Thus at Jait, on the high-road to Delhi, an ancient five-headed Nága, carved in stone, rises beside a small tank in the centre of a low plain, to the height of some four feet above the surface of the ground, while its tail is supposed to reach away to the Káliya-mardan Ghát at Brindá-ban, a distance of 8 miles. A slight excavation at the base of the figure has, for a few years at least, dispelled the local superstition. So again at the village of Paigáow, a grove and lake called respectively Pai-ban and Pai-ban-kund, are the scene of an annual fair known as the *Nág-mela*. The name is probably derived from the large offerings of milk (*payas*) with which it is usual to propitiate the serpent-god.

It was towards the close of the 16th century A.D., under the influence of the celebrated Bengali Gosains at Brindában that the Vaishnava cultus was first developed in its present form, and it is not improbable that they were the authors of the *Brahma Vaivarta Purána*,* the recognized authority for all the modern local legends. It was then that every lake and grove in the circuit of Braj received a distinctive name, in addition to the some seven or eight spots which alone are mentioned in the earlier *Puránas*. In the course of time small villages sprang up in the neighbourhood of the different shrines bearing the same name though perhaps in a slightly modified form. Thus the *Khadira-ban*, or acacia grove, gives its name to the village of Khaira, and the *anjan-pokhar*, on whose green bank Krishna pencilled his lady's eyebrows with *anjan*, gives its name to the village of Ajnokh, occasionally written at greater length Ajnokhari. Similarly when Krishna's home was fixed at Nandgáow and Rádhá's at Barsána, a grove half way between the two hills was fancifully selected as the spot where the youthful couple used to meet to enjoy the delights of love. There a temple was built with the title Rádhá-Raman, and the village that grew up under its shelter was called Sanket, that is, the place of rendezvous. Thus we may readily fall in with Hindu prejudices, and admit that many of the names on the map are etymologically connected with events in Krishna's life, and yet deny that these events have any real connexion with the spot, inasmuch as neither the village nor the local name has had any existence for a longer period than at the most 300 years. The really old local names are almost all derived from the character of the country, which has always been celebrated for its wide extent of pasture-land and many herds of cattle. Thus Gokul means originally 'a herd of kine'; Gobardhan, 'a nurser of kine'; Mát is so called from *mat*, 'a milk pail'; and Dadhi-gáow, (contracted into Dahgáow,) in the Kosi Pargana, from *dadhi*, 'curds.' Thus too Mathurá is probably connected with the Sanskrit root *math* 'to churn,' the churn forming a prominent feature in all poetical descriptions of the local scenery; and 'Braj' in the first instance means 'a herd' from the root *vraj*, 'to go,' in allusion to the constant moves of nomadic tribes. In many cases a false analogy has suggested a legendary derivation, thus all native scholars see in Mathurá an allusion to *Madhumathan* a title of Krishna. Again the word Bajhan is still current in some parts of India to designate a pasture-ground, and in that sense has given a name to a very extensive parish in Kosi; but as the term is not a familiar one thereabouts, a legend has been invented

* The *Brahma Vaivarta Purána* is, to all intents, an essentially modern composition. Prof. Wilson believed it to have emanated from the sect of Vallabháchárya, or Gosains of Gokul, about four centuries ago. In so writing he was probably unaware of the exact date of the Mathurá propaganda. The popular Hindi authority for Rádhá's Life and Loves is the Braj Bilás, a poem written by one Brajbási Dás in the year 1743 A.D.

in explanation, and it is said that here Balarám sat down (*baitha*) to wait for Krishna. The myth was accepted; a lake immediately outside the village was styled Balbhadra Kund, was furnished with a handsome masonry ghát by Rúp Rám, Katára of Barsána, about the middle of last century, and is now regarded as positive proof of the popular etymology which connects the place with Balarám. Of Rúp Rám, the Katára, further mention will be made in connection with his birth-place Barsána. There is scarcely a sacred site in the whole of Braj which does not exhibit some costly memorial in the shape of temple or tank of his unbounded wealth and liberality. His successor in the fourth descent, a most worthy man, by name Lachhman Dás, lives in a corner of one of his ancestor's palaces, and is dependent on charity for his daily bread. The present owners of many of the villages, so munificently endowed by Rúp Rám, are four brothers, residents of Calcutta, the representatives of a Bengali Kayath by name Krishn Chandra, less better known as the Lála Bábu, who, in the year 1810, made a disastrous visit to this district, and by an affected regard for the holy places and assumption of the character of an ascetic cajoled the old Zamindárs out of their landed estates, in several cases purchasing them outright for a sum which is less than the rental of a single year. Property so lightly acquired is, it seems, lightly esteemed; and its present condition pointedly illustrates the evils supposed to be inseparable from absenteeism.

As might be inferred from the above sketch, the country possesses no relics of hoary antiquity. Excluding for the present any reference to the four large towns, Mathurá, Brindában, Gobardhan and Mahában, the earliest buildings are probably the three Saráis, along the line of the imperial road from Agra to Delhi; at Chaumuhá, Chhátá, and Kosí. These are generally ascribed by local tradition to Shír Sháh, whose reign extended from 1540 to 1545 A.D.; though it is also said that the one at Kosí was built by Itibár Khán, and that at Chhátá by Abd-ul-Majíd, better known by his honorary title of Asaf Khán. He was first Humáyún's Díwán and subsequently Governor of Delhi under Akbar. The style of architecture is in exact conformity with that of similar buildings known to have been erected in Akbar's reign, such for example as the Fort at Agra; and, on other grounds also it may be inferred that the whole series is due to that monarch rather than to his predecessor Shír Sháh. For at the entrance of the civil station of Mathurá is a fourth Saraí, now much modernized and of somewhat inferior character to the other three, though probably of the same date. This, with the little hamlet outside its walls, is known by the name of Jalálpur in honour of Jalál-ud-dín Akbar, who was therefore, presumably, its founder. Similarly the Chaumuhá Saráí is always described in the old topographies as at Akbarpur. This latter name is now restricted in application to a village some three miles distant; but in the 16th century local divisions were few in number and wide in extent, and beyond a doubt the foundation of the imperial saráí was the origin of the local name which has now deserted the actual spot that suggested it. The formation of Chaumuhá into a separate village dates from a very recent period, when the name was bestowed in consequence of the discovery of an ancient sculpture, supposed by the ignorant rustics to represent the four-headed (Chaumunha) god Brahma. The stone is in fact the base of a Jaina pillar or statue, with a lion projecting at each corner and a rude figure in each of the four intermediate spaces. The upper margin is rudely carved with the pattern commonly known as the Buddhist rail.

From the description given by John de Laet, in his *India Vera*, written in the year 1631, we find these saráis were managed precisely as our modern Dák Bungalos. He says—"They occur at intervals of five or six kos, built either by the king or by some of the nobles, and in them travellers can find bed and lodging: when a person has once taken possession he may not be turned out by any one." They are fine fort-like buildings, with massive battlemented walls and bastions, and high-arched gateways. Though primarily built merely from selfish motives, on the line of road traversed by the imperial camps, they were at the same time enormous boons to the general public; for the highway was then beset with gangs of robbers, with whose vocations the law either dared not, or could not interfere: and on one occasion, in the reign of Jahángír, we read of a caravan having to stay six weeks at Mathurá, before it was thought strong enough to proceed to Delhi, no smaller number than 500 or 600 men being deemed adequate to encounter the dangers of the road. Now, the solitary traveller is so confident of legal protection, that, rather than drive his cart up the steep ascent that conducts to the portals of the fortified enclosure, he prefers to spend the night unguarded on the open plain. Hence it comes that not one of the saráis is now applied to the precise purpose for which it was constructed. At Chhátá one corner is occupied by a school, and another by the offices of the Tahsildar and local police, while the rest of the broad area is nearly deserted; at Chaumuhá, the solid walls have in past years been undermined and carried away for building materials; and at Kosí, the whole area is occupied with streets and bazars forming the nucleus of the town.

Till the close of the 16th century, except in the neighbourhood of the one great thoroughfare, the country was unreclaimed wood-land, with only here and there a scattered hamlet. The tanks and temples which now mark the various legendary sites were either constructed by Rúp Rám of Barsána, about the year 1740, or are of still more recent date. Many of the sacred groves however, though occasionally disfigured by the too close proximity of the village, are pleasant and picturesque spots; one of the most striking being the Rohila-ban at great Bathan. The prevalent trees are the *pílu*, *ber*, *chhonkar*, *kadamb*, *pasendu*, *papri*, and other species of the fig tribe, which are always intermingled with clumps of *karil*, the special product of Braj, with its leaf-less evergreen twigs and bright-coloured flower and fruit. Somewhat less common are the *aral*, *hingot*, *ajún*, *rúkh*, *gondi*, *barna* and *dhák*; though the last named, the Sanskrit *dhava*, clothes the whole of the hill-side at Barsána. In the month of Bhádon these woods are the scene of a series of *melas*, where the *rás-lila* is celebrated in commemoration of Krishna's sports with the Gopis; and the arrangement of these dances forms the recognized occupation of a class of Bráhmans very numerous in some of the villages, who are called Rásdháris, and have no other profession or means of livelihood.

The number of sacred places, woods, groves, ponds, wells, hills and temples, which have all to be visited in the course of the annual perambulation, is very considerable; but the twelve *bans* or woods and twenty-four groves or *upabans* are the characteristic feature of the pilgrimage, which is thence called the *Banjatra*. Further notice of this popular devotion must be reserved till our next chapter.

(*To be continued.*)

ON THE IDENTIFICATION OF VARIOUS PLACES IN THE KINGDOM OF MAGADHA VISITED BY THE PILGRIM CHI-FAH-HIAN.

BY A. M. BROADLEY, B.C.S., BIHAR.

(*Continued from page* 31.)

PART II.

"LEAVING the south side of the city and proceeding southwards four *li*, we enter a valley between five hills. These hills encircle it completely like the walls of a town. This is the site of the old city of king Bimbisára."* This valley is clearly identical with the narrow tract of country surrounded by the five mountains of Rájgir, a little less than a mile due south of the fortifications previously described. This spot is of the greatest archaeological interest. Here once stood, according to tradition, the impregnable fortress of Jarásandha, outside whose walls was fought the celebrated battle of the Mahábhárata; centuries later the valley was the scene of many of the episodes in the life of the Tathágata; and lastly—during the palmiest days of Muhammadan rule in Bihár—its solitudes became the abiding place of Makhdum Sharif-ud-din, one of the greatest saints amongst the faithful in Hindustán.

These five hills are by no means solitary; they form a portion of a rocky mountain chain stretching nearly thirty miles from the neighbourhood of Gayá, north-west as far as Giryak in Bihár. Their sides are rugged and precipitous, and are mostly covered with an impenetrable jangal, broken only by irregular pathways overgrown with brushwood, which are yearly trodden by hundreds of Jaina pilgrims from Murshidábád, Banáres, and even Bombay, who throng to Rájgir during the cold and dry seasons to do homage to the sacred *charanas* or 'foot-prints' of their saints enshrined in the temples which crown the mountain tops.

* Beal's Fah Hian, Chapter xxviii. p. 112.

The north side of the valley is bounded by Mount Baibhâr—a rocky hill running three or four miles north-west, and terminating at its eastern side in the hot wells of Râjgir. Here the valley is entered by a narrow ravine through the midst of which the Sarasvati rivulet forces its way into the low country to the north of the hills. On the eastern side of the stream rises the lofty ascent of Mount Vipula, a branch of which runs as far as Giryak, a distance of six miles. Hardly a quarter of a mile from the eastern side of the hill it is joined at right angles by a third mountain running from the north called Ratnagir. This hill is of inconsiderable length and terminates in a narrow ravine branching away to the east. On the opposite side of this ravine rises Mount Udayagir, a less important hill, running due south and terminating in the ancient wall and fort of Bânganga—the southern gate of the ancient capital of Magadha. To the west of the torrent is the fifth and largest hill—Mount Sonagir. It first takes a course to the west, then turns northwards, and finally, exactly opposite the narrow valley between Mounts Ratnagir and Udayagir, stretches away to the west, and forms the southern boundary of this natural fortress, being only separated at its western extremity by a narrow ravine from an offshoot of Mount Baibhâr, commonly called the 'Chhata'. These five hills are called in the Mahabharata*—Vaihâra, Varâha, Vrishabha, Rishigiri, and Chaityaka; and in the Pali annals of Ceylon—Gijjhakuta, Isigili, Webhâra,† Wepulo, and Pandawo.‡

Speaking of the valley, Fah-Hian§ goes on to say: "From east to west it is about five or six *li*, from north to south seven or eight *li*." It is evident Fah-Hian excluded from his computation the eastern and western inflexions of the valley, and even then its dimensions are slightly understated.

The north side of the valley is watered by two streams, both bearing the name of Sarasvati, which rise, the one at the foot of Ratnagir, and the other at the western extremity of Mount Sonâr. These rivulets join a short distance to the south of the ravine which forms the entrance to the valley. The sides of the hills and the plain at their feet are covered mostly by a tangled mass of flowering shrubs and wild *kulsi* grass, broken only by some protruding escarpment or the white cupola of a Jaina pagoda in the one case, and in the other, by heaps of bricks—the ruins of temples and topes, and the huge piles of stones which still mark the ancient ramparts of the city. The form of the walls can, with a little difficulty, be traced with tolerable accuracy. Strictly speaking, these ramparts formed an irregular pentagon about four miles in circumference. One side faced the west, and was about a mile in length, extending along the western branch of the Sarasvati; a second ran south to the foot of the Sonagir, a third east to the entrance of the ravine between Udayagir and Ratnagir; a fourth north, towards the junction of the streams; and the fifth and smallest joins the first and fourth. A road seems to have run through the city from the new town to Bânganga. The northern side of the city, facing the ravine, appears to have been protected by a lofty tower composed of stones of irregular shape, placed one upon the other (not squared and arranged in courses as in the walls of new Râjgir). Near the stream appears to have been another tower of great height and of similar appearance, and close under it an outer gate towards the north. From this place an enormous wall, 18 or 20 feet thick and 15 or 20 feet high, stretched itself to the summit of Mount Vipula, and protected the city from attacks on the mountain side. There were doubtless similar fortifications on the side of Mount Baibhâr, but their traces are very faint, whereas those on the western slope of Mount Vipula are remarkably perfect and distinct. Over the whole surface of the interior of the city is spread a mass of débris covered by brushwood and shrubs, and here and there are piles of bricks and stones, denoting the site of some house or temple. Near the south-west corner of the city is a lofty tumulus, somewhat higher than the ruins of the eastern entrance. This is covered by a small Jaina cupola of brick and plaster. The sides of the tumulus are strewn with bricks and fragments of granite pillars. I also discovered some pieces of cornice covered with representations of Buddhas and Nâgas. I made an excavation on the north side of the tumulus, and uncovered a considerable portion of the northern side of a Buddhist building, of which the entrance seems to have faced the

* Mahâbhârata, II. 20 v. 798,800.

† Lassen suspects the reading Webhâra by Turnour to be incorrect and proposes to read Vaibhâra in accordance with the Mahâbhârata. 'It is surprising,' he adds, 'that the first and last names are Buddhistic, and we may, therefore, suspect they were given to these mountains only after the time of Buddha.—*Alterth.* vol. II, p. 79.—Ed.

‡ Turnour, in Jour. Beng. As. Soc. vol. VI, p. 991.

§ Beal's Fah Hian, as sup. Chapter xxviii. p. 112.

north—a feature I have not before met with in any similar ruin,—for the numerous temples which I have seen at Rájgir and other places are, without exception, approached from the east. A staircase of brick, with walls on either side, led to the inner hall. The walls appear to have been strengthened, and the roof at the same time provided with supports, by the erection of gray stone pillars, about four feet apart, with plain square bases and capitals. This passage led to a room about 12 feet square, containing twelve pillars similar to those in the staircase—ten of which are imbedded in the brickwork and two support the roof in the centre of the chamber. The centre hall is directly underneath the Jaina temple, and it consequently has been impossible to uncover it. I think the precise nature of the original building is doubtful; the position of the entrance leads me to the conclusion that it was most likely a house or tower—not a religious edifice. The doorway seems to have been surmounted by a long basalt slab containing figures twelve inches high. I brought away two pieces of this to Bihár. Several other figures were found in this place years ago, when it was pierced by an avaricious road-contractor in the hope of finding treasure. If he ever learned the Jaina traditions connected with the place, his hopes must have been high, for they make out the remains to be the ruin of the house of Dhanaji and Sálibhadraji, two seths or bankers, in whose honour, they say, a small temple still exists on the eastern slope of Mount Baibhár. If the priests made their story known to this enterprising scion of the Department of Public Works, they cannot safely blame him for the disaster which followed on his researches, namely, the collapse of the stucco pagoda and its sacred 'chaumukh,' towards the end of the succeeding rains.

About a mile to the south-east of the mound is a long piece of rampart known as "Burgháti." In the centre of this was the southern gate of Kusâgarapura—flanked by two towers. The view from the top of the ruin is very striking, for you see at once both entrances of the valley and all the five hills. A little to the west of this, at the foot of Sonágir, is a ridge of rock called the wrestling ground of Bhim, and various indentations in its surface are pointed out as the marks of the feet of the combatants. Beneath this, to the west of the city walls, and between Mounts Baibhár and Sonár is Ranabhúm, the traditionary scene of the great battle of the Mahábhárata.

A rugged path leads from this place to the southern outlet of the valley at Bánganga. Certain marks on the stones are considered by Captain Kittoe to be inscriptions, but if this be the case, the letters are far too imperfect to admit of being deciphered. The valley terminates in a rocky ravine of the most inconsiderable width, having Sonágir to the west and Udayagir to the east. The Bánganga torrent, which rises at the foot of the former, rushes over the slippery rocks into the southern plain of Hasua-Nawáda. The pass is literally only a *few feet* wide, and its entrance was jealously guarded by fortifications of enormous strength, which will be fully described when I come to speak of the antiquities of the hills.

The first mountain I ascended was Baibhár to the north-west of the northern entrance of the valley. At the foot of the hill rises the Sarasvati, from the banks of which a large stone staircase leads to the sacred wells and temples, which, though still venerated by the Hindus of Bihár, yield but a scanty subsistence to the numerous Bráhmans who attend them. The wells are vaults of stone, about 10 feet square and 12 deep, approached by steps; and the temples are quite modern, and of the poorest proportions and workmanship. Most of them contain fragments of Buddhist idols, mouldings, cornices, &c. and here and there I noticed a *chaitya*, now doing duty as a *lingam*. All of these carvings, however, are very inferior to those found by me in the mounds of Bargáon, Rohoi, and Kulyanpur. The wells at the foot of Baibhár are seven in number, and are all clustered round the great Brahma-kund which is larger, deeper and more highly esteemed than the rest. The one nearest the ascent of the mountain is the *Ganga-Jamuna-Kund*. The water is warm, and enters the vault by means of two stone shoots, the ends of which are carved to represent the heads of tigers or lions. They remind one strangely of the *gargoyles* of early English Architecture. These pipes were clearly mentioned by Hwen Thsang in the narrative of his travels. He says "à toutes les ouvertures par où s'échappe l'eau des sources, on a posé des pierres sculptées. Tantôt on a figuré des têtes de lions, etc."* Below this are the Anan-

* Mémoires sur les Contrées Occidentales traduit du Sanskrit en Chinois en l'an 648 A. D. par Hiouen Thsang, et du Chinois en Français par M. Stanislas Julien. Paris 1857. Tom. II. p. 22.

Kokhi, Mârkanda, and *Byâs Kund* springs. Next to them comes the *Sât dhâra*—a vault some 60 feet long by 10 feet wide, which receives seven distinct streams on the west side, from the mountain above. Several of these springs enter the reservoir through "tuyeaux suspendus,"* and at the south end is a small subterranean temple containing rude and, apparently, very modern images of the 'Seven Rishis.' At the east side of the *Sât dhâra* is the celebrated *Brahma kund*. The temperature of the water is about 108 deg. Fahr. It is in this that several hundred thousand persons bathe at the recurrence of every thirty-first lunation. Below this is the *Kâsi tirth*, which is in reality a mere outlet for the waters of the Brahma kund, which escape through it, still warm and steaming, into the Sarasvati Nâla. Climbing a distance of 270 feet to the south-west of the Mârkanda kund, one arrives at an enormous stone platform projecting from the face of the hill. It is composed of huge masses of unhewn stone piled one upon the other, and is about 30 feet square and 20 high. At its base there are a number of small grottoes six or eight feet square, of which two are on the eastern and five on the northern side. These were evidently caves or chambers of meditation, and are up to this day inhabited at times by 'nagas' or 'chilâs,' a *fakir* whose body is perpetually smeared with ashes, and whose wardrobe seems to consist merely of a very small waist-cloth, a tattered umbrella, and a necklace of enormous beads. These beggars flock in thousands from all parts of India to Râjgir during the great fair, and are fed by the *Mahants* or abbots of the monasteries of Râjgir and Râjâvali, who alone exercise the jealously-guarded right of raising their crimson standards during the month in which the gathering takes place.

To return to the stone platform: it is generally known as the *Jarâsandha-ka-baithak*, and on the summit are three Muhammadan tombs, one of which is said to be that of Râja Kamdar Khan Mai, whose life and adventures during the end of the 17th and beginning of the 18th centuries form the subject of many a rude ballad and story in Bihâr, and which occupy almost the same place in the heart of the people as the tales of Robin Hood and his followers do at home. Behind this platform is a large cave. I searched for it in vain in September, but owing to the dense brushwood and jungal which covered it during the rainy season, I failed to find it. General Cunningham, however, was fortunate enough to light on it during his recent visit, and I have since completely cleared and excavated it. It is of oval shape, and has an opening to the east. Its floor was considerably below the surface, and was reached by a flight of eight or nine brick steps, several of which I uncovered almost entire. The chamber measured 36 feet from east to west, and 20 from north to south. The roof (most of which has fallen in) was 18 or 20 feet high. The whole was lined, as it were, by a brick wall about 2 feet thick. In the midst of the rubbish which filled up the bottom of the cave I found a very perfect standing figure of Buddha in black basalt. I can, I think, satisfactorily identify this cave and platform with the account of Fah-Hian and also with that of Hwen Thsang. Fah-Hian says—"skirting the southern hill" (and it is to be noted that this part of Baibhâr runs almost due south) "and proceeding westward 300 paces, there is a stone cell called the *Pippal Cave*, where Buddha was accustomed to sit in deep meditation after his mid-day meal."†

This corresponds exactly with the position of the cave in question, and this view is supported strongly by the succeeding sentence,—"going still in a westerly direction five or six *li*, there is a stone cave situate in the northern shade of the mountain, and called Che-ti." This description applies with singular accuracy to the Son-bhandâr Cave in the northern shade of Mount Baibhâr, and almost exactly a mile from the *baithak* of Jarâsandha. Hwen Thsang's account is still more striking.—"A l'ouest des sources thermales, on voit la maison en pierre du *Pi-po-lo* (Pippala). Jadis, l'honorable du siècle y faisait son séjour habituel. La caverne *profonde* qui s'ouvre derrière ses murs était le palais des '*O-sou-lo*—Asuras'"‡ [of Jarâsandha?]

Pushing 900 feet further up the mountain side, I found another platform or *baithak*, almost identical in size and shape with that of Jarâsandha. The Râjwar call it *Sitâmari*, but I could discover no special legend concerning it. Leaving it and climbing up a steep ascent to the west for a distance of about 1300 feet, one comes, quite suddenly, on a small Jaina temple built some few years ago by one Hukumat Rai

* Idem. † Beal's Fah-Hian, Ch. xxx. p. 117. ‡ Mémoires, Tom. II. p. 21.

Between the last *baithak* and this temple there are marks of an enormous wall 14 or 15 feet thick, and this forms the pathway which leads up the mountain side. The Rájwars—the almost sole inhabitants of the wilds of Rájgir—call it Jarásandha's staircase, and tell you that he built it in a single day to assemble his troops on the mountain tops on the approach of his enemies from the west. The temple contains (besides the usual *charans* or footprints) two very fine and perfect figures of Buddha. The first is three feet high. Buddha is represented sitting on the lotus throne (*padmásana*) in the attitude of meditation. Beneath this, the *Sinhásana* is divided into three compartments—the two outer containing lions and the middle one the 'Wheel of the Law,' (very elaborately carved,) supported by two shells. The second figure is a smaller one and is surmounted by a canopy.

Eight hundred feet to the west of this temple is a similar building containing nothing of interest. Twelve or fourteen paces to the south of it, I found the ruins of a very small Buddhist temple covered with the densest jangal. It appears to have contained twelve gray stone columns about six feet high. The entrance was to the east, and in digging out the centre I found a very curious image of Buddha—very roughly carved. The main figure was surrounded by smaller ones, each depicting some chief episode in his life. Piercing the jangal 400 feet to the south-west of this ruin, I found the remains of a very large temple almost perfect. The cupola had fallen down on all sides, forming a mound about 300 feet in circumference and 16 or 17 feet high. The entrance to the east is about 6 feet wide, and leads to a passage some 14 or 15 feet long, the roof of which was formerly supported by gray stone pillars about 8 feet high. This leads to a square chamber or hall some 23 or 24 feet square. Its roof is supported by twelve columns in the chamber, and eighteen more let into the brick work. These columns are each 7 feet high, with square bases and capitals and octagon shafts. They rested on a detached square plinth a foot high. A sur-capital, separate from the shaft, and cruciform in plan, supported the roof which was composed of enormous granite slabs laid transversely. From this room a massive doorway and a flight of three steps leads to the inner chamber—somewhat less in size than the other, but considerably loftier—the total height of its roof being 18 feet. The columns are of the same description as those in the outer hall, but more lofty. The detached capital are each a foot high, the base is 2, the octagonal shaft 6, and the second capital 3 feet in height. The lintel of the doorway is 3 feet broad and is carved with a rude moulding. In the centre of the lintel, is a figure of Buddha. I found no images in the temple, but it is by far the most perfect building of the kind I have yet seen. Its situation is magnificent, commanding at once a view of the highly cultivated plain of Bihár, the "military rock," the topes and temples of Nalanda, the walls of new Rajgir, the five hills, and the valley of Kusánagarapura.

A short distance to the south of this is a very small Jaina temple dedicated to Dharmanátha and Shantinátha, the 15th and 16th *Tirthankaras*. It contains two images and a *charana*, with an inscription about 200 years old. The *pujári* has corrupted the names to 'Dhanaji' and 'Sathadraji', and describes them as two wealthy bankers who lived in the house at the Nirmal Kund, *i. e.* the mound in the south-west corner of the ancient city.

Continuing to ascend the eastern slope of the hill for nearly a quarter of a mile, we arrive at a Jaina temple of very considerable dimensions. It is square in form, and is surmounted by four handsome minarets and a cupola. It was built by one Pratáp Singh of Murshidábád, and a passage (*pradakshina*) encircles the central shrine. There is also a small octagon chapel containing charanas at each corner. The doorway has been taken from a Buddhist temple, and is covered with exquisite carving. The temple is 51 feet by 58. Some two hundred yards to the west of this is the largest temple of the group, built by one Mánikchand Seth in the middle of the last century. Mánikchand was a well known character in Calcutta, and his dedication is recorded on the *charana*. The building consists almost entirely of Buddhist materials. It has a vestibule, the roof of which is supported by pillars somewhat smaller in size, though of the same shape as those in the temple I have described above in detail. At the north side are the remains of a Buddhist temple, probably larger than any other on the hill. Its pillars, &c., lie about in all directions, and it seems to have served as the quarry from which Mánikchand built his. A quarter of a mile further on, and near the crest of the hill, I had the good fortune to find another Buddhist temple in the jangal, about five paces to the north of the path. Its details resemble very much those of the great temple below, but a figure of Buddha still occupies the centre, and the foundations of a court-yard can still be traced.

Proceeding still westwards for nearly half a mile, the highest peak of the hill is gained, where is an enormous tope, covered with brushwood, and crowned with a Jaina temple. The view from the top is magnificent, especially towards the valley, the whole of which Baibhâr commands.

Descending the almost precipitous southern face of the mountain, I arrived at the Sonbhândâr cave, which is situated in the "northern shade" of the hill, as nearly as possible a mile to the south-west of the hot wells. I have little difficulty in identifying this with the Sattapanni cave spoken of both by Fah-Hian and Hwen Thsang. In doing so it must be borne in mind that the Baibhâr hill runs due south-west—and 'west,' and that the Sonbhândâr is near the northern end of the mountain. Fah Hian* says, that "going in a westerly direction five or six *li*" (*i. e.* from just above the hot-springs) "there is a stone cave situate in the northern shade of the mountain, and called *Cheti*. This is the place where 500 Rahats assembled after the *Nirvâna* of Buddha to arrange the collection of sacred books." This coincides exactly with the position of the Sonbhândâr cave, and it also agrees with Hwen Thsang,† who places it five or six *li* to the south-west of the Karandavênouvana clump of bamboos, which both authors represent as being close to the hot-springs. The words of Hwen Thsang are as follows—"au sud-ouest du Bois des Bambous, il fit cinq à six lis. Au nord d'une montagne située au midi," (this I have previously explained) "au milieu d'un vaste bois de bambous il y a une grande maison en pierre. Ce fut là qu'après le *Nirvâna* de *Joulaï*, le vénérable Mahâ Kâshyapa et neuf cent quatre-vingt-dix-neuf grands Arhats formèrent la collection des trois Recueils sacrés. Devant de cette maison, on voit encore d'anciens fondements. Le roi Ajâtasatru avait fait construire cet édifice, &c."

The cave appears to have been formerly approached from the south by a staircase or sloping path, which has now almost entirely disappeared, and to have been faced by a broad platform nearly 100 feet square. The space was occupied by an extensive hall, the rafters supporting the roof of which rested in cavities in the rock that still exist. Piles of bricks and stones lie in all directions. The face of the cave has a naked surface of rock, as smooth and even as if built of brick. It is 44 feet in breadth and 14 feet high, and is bounded on the west by a protruding rock and on the east by a narrow staircase of twenty steps cut in the cliff. The rock is pierced in the centre by a door 6 feet 4 inches high and about 3½ feet wide. The thickness of the wall of rock is exactly 3 feet. At 11 feet 10 inches west from the door, and in a line with it is an opening in the cliff 3 feet high by 2 feet wide, which serves to light the vault. The interior is a vaulted chamber 34 feet long by 17 feet wide, with a semicircular roof 11 feet high. The floor has been spoiled by the water which constantly falls from the roofs. Outside the door, and three feet to the west of it, is a headless figure of Buddha cut in the rock, and close to it, an inscription, in the Asoka character, recording the visit of some holy man to the cave in search of quiet and solitude. There are also some Devanâgarî inscriptions inside. Inside there is a square "chaitya" three and a half feet high, on each side of which is a figure of Buddha and various emblems.

Leaving the cave and going a mile to the north-east we again come to the banks of the Sarasvatî and the hot-springs.

(*To be continued.*)

THE JUNGLE FORTS OF NORTHERN ORISSA.

By JOHN BEAMES, B.C.S., M.R.A.S., MAGISTRATE OF BALASOR.

(*Continued from Page 36.*)

The date of the building of these forts is, like that of every building in India which has no marked architectural features and contains no inscriptions, very uncertain. In the present case, however, the uncertainty is to some extent limited by considerations derived from their geographical position. If it be assumed that they were the work of kings of Orissa,—an assumption which I shall consider immediately,—then there are only two brief periods within which they could have

* Beal, c. c. p. 116.

† Mémoires, Tom. II. p. 33.

been built—those, namely, in which the limits of the Oriyá monarchy extended so far to the northward as the banks of the Subarnarekha river. The general absence of historical data in India prior to the coming of the Muhammadans is, in Orissa, relieved by the scanty and untrustworthy *pánji* or daily record of occurrences kept in the national temple of Jagannáth,—the omissions or inaccuracies of which may occasionally be corrected or supplied from the *pánjis* and *Vansávalis* kept in the minor temples and monasteries throughout the province, and by one or two connected histories written on palm-leaf, which are in the possession of private families.

The chief interest of Oriyá history centres round the great cities of the southern part of the province—Katak, Jájpur, and Purí. Northern Orissa is seldom mentioned. Only twice in the annals of the country is it asserted that its boundaries extended beyond the Kánsbáns, a small stream near Soro at that point where the hill ranges trend eastward to the sea. The long narrow slip between the Kánsbáns and Subarnarekhá appears to have been for centuries a forest. This supposition is confirmed by the frequency of names of places in which the word *ban* (Sansk. *vana*) occurs as Banchás, *i.e.* "forest-hills," Banáhár, *i.e.* "forest-enclosure," Bampadda, *i.e.*, Ban-paddá—"forest-clearing," Banhátí—"forest-sitting," and the like.

In the reign of Gangeshwar Deb (A.D. 1151), the Orissan monarchy is said to have extended from the Ganges to the Godávarí. By the Ganges is here of course meant, as always in Oriyá history, the branch which flows by Húglí. Whether this is merely an exaggeration or not we cannot tell; it probably is so, as in the celebrated speech of his great-grandson Anang Bhím Deb, the most illustrious prince of the Gangábansi dynasty (A.D. 1196), recorded by Stirling, the king is reported to have said that he had extended the boundaries of his kingdom on the north from the Kánsbáns to the Dantái Buchi river (the modern Burá Balang, which flows past the town of Balasor). The Gangábansis were great builders, and their temples, palaces and tanks still adorn the southern part of the province. I do not think it probable that they would have been contented with so comparatively clumsy and inartistic forts as these now under consideration. I shall show presently another reason for assigning these forts to a much later epoch.

In 1550 the throne of Orissa was occupied by a prince from the Telugu or Telinga country, celebrated under the name of Telinga Mukund Deb. He was the last independent sovereign of Orissa, and of him again it is recorded that his sway extended to Tribeni Ghát on the Húglí river, where he built a temple and bathing-steps. In his reign northern Orissa became for the first time important, for then the invasions of the Musalmans, hitherto few and far between, just began to be constant and successful. "Sulimán Gurzani, the Afghan King of Bengal," waged a long war with Mukund Deb, who, to oppose him, built a strong fort in a commanding position in the northern frontier. This fort, or chain of forts, I apprehend to have been those we are now discussing. No more commanding situation could well be found than Ráibaniyán on its laterite ridge overlooking the passage of the Subarnarekha, and backed by the impenetrable forest. This position too is on the edge of the country inhabited by the Oriya-speaking race. The situation of the main entrance, and the much greater strength of the fortifications on the northern side, seem to show that it was from that direction that the danger came. Seven miles west of Ráibaniyán is the fort of Deulgaon "temple-village" which—as will be seen from the appendix—is in still better preservation than Ráibaniyán, and, as evidence of the date, contains the two stone horsemen so celebrated in Orissan legend. It is related that when Rájá Purshottam Deb was marching (circa A.D. 1490) southwards to the conquest of Kanjivaram (Kanjikaveri), his army was preceded by two youths, one on a black and the other on a white horse, by whose auspicious aid he gained the victory. The youths then disappeared after declaring themselves to be Krishna and Balaram.* The fort which contains these two images cannot well be older than the legend which they preserve.

Further, it may be urged that, in the early times of Gangeshwar Deb, there existed no necessity for strong forts on the northern frontier, which was then inhabited only by wild forest tribes, and whose possession seems to have been little cared for by the Rájás themselves. It was not till the encroachments of the Musal-

* The similarity of this legend to that of the appearance of "the great twin-brethren," Castor and Pollux, so vividly related in Macaulay's *Lays of Ancient Rome*, must strike every classical reader.

mans of Bengal rendered some resistance necessary that forts would be built and garrisoned so far away from the capital, nor in the earlier times had the Oriya race penetrated so far to the north as to have settlements on the banks of the Subarnarekha.'

On the other hand, if we cannot place the date of the erection of these forts earlier than 1568, we cannot assign to them any later date. After the ravages of the terrible Kálápahár* Orissa sank into a condition of anarchy and disorganization. Neither the invaders from Bengal nor the national rulers had any interest in keeping up forts at a place which was no longer important to either, and we find the Afghans immediately afterwards, and for a long period, firmly established at the strong post of Garhpadá, fifteen miles to the south of Ráibaniyan.

An important result follows from the above considerations, namely, that the Oriya language is not—as a certain party among the Bengalis would persuade us—an offshoot of their own tongue, but an independent variety of Aryan speech. We have every reason to believe that the march, or frontier between the two provinces, was occupied by a dense forest peopled by non-Aryan tribes, and that there was absolutely no communication between Orissa and Bengal in that direction; when the forest was penetrated and the communication opened, the Oriya language was already formed, and Upendra Bhanj and Dín Krishna Dás had written many of their still celebrated poems. Orissa had more intimate dealings with her southern neighbours, and one at least of her dynasties came from the banks of the Són-Gangá or Godávarí. Even to this day the course of trade from the ports of Orissa tends more towards Madras than Bengal.

APPENDIX.

After returning from Ráibaniyan I received the following note from the Revd. J. Phillips, the well-known missionary to the Santhals, whose settlement is at Sántipur, two miles south of Ráibaniyan:—

"*Camp Balidohiba, Dec* 11, 1871.

"On the 2nd instant we were at [illegible], about 7 miles to the north-west of Sántipur, where are the remains of an old stone fort. It is 75 paces long and 60 broad inside the walls. The walls are 12 feet in height composed of the common laterite, hewn as are the stones in Ráibaniyan. The walls are perforated on all sides with loopholes near the top, and there were entrances on the four sides with bastions over the gateways. In one corner of the enclosure there is a small tank and a walled up well in the opposite corner.

A large laterite stone was pointed out to me as containing inscriptions, but if such ever existed, it had become quite too much defaced to be at all legible. Two large stone images of horses with their riders, cut from solid blocks of the "Mugani" stone (chlorite), stand near the centre of the fort. When we were there two years ago these lay partially covered with rubbish, but have since been exhumed, and now they receive some attention, though I did not discover signs of their being worshipped. The natives told us that these were living animals in the *Satya Yug*, and engaged in battle, and pointed out scars and bullet marks on their mutilated bodies. The fact of gunpowder being a modern invention seemed no obstacle to their theory so far as I saw."

BIOGRAPHICAL NOTICES OF GRANDEES OF THE MUGHUL COURT.

By H. BLOCHMANN, M.A., CALCUTTA MADRASAH.

The greater part of the following notes, which I hope to continue, are taken from a Persian work entitled *Maásir ul Umará*, or the 'Deeds of the Amirs,' by Shah Nawáz Khán of Aurangábád, whose family had come, during the reign of Akbar, from Khawáf in Khurásán. The work underwent several editions. The original compilation was enlarged by the renowned Ghulám 'Ali Ázád, and the third edition, which contains the lives of 730 nobles, was written in A. H. 1194, or A. D. 1780, by 'Abdul Hai Khán Çamçám-ul Mulk, son of Shah Nawáz Khán. MSS. are very rare. The library of the Royal Asiatic Society of London possesses one (No. CIII. of Morley's Catalogue); the Asiatic Society of Bengal has two, of which one (MS. No. 77) is very excellent. It is so free from errors and so carefully corrected, that it looks like an autograph. "The biographies," says Mr. Morley, "are very ably written, and full of important historic detail; and, as they include those of all the most eminent men who flourished in the time of the Mughul Emperors of the house of Timúr, down to A. H. 1194 (A. D. 1780), the *Maásir ul Umará* must always hold its place as one of the most valuable books of reference for the student of Indian history." There are but few notices of the Amirs who

* Vide ante p. 67.

served under Bábar and Humáyún; most of them refer to the period between the reigns of Akbar and Farrukh Siyar. Many of the biographies, however, are not merely biographies of one grandee, but of his whole family. The last edition, which is the only valuable one, "enumerates no less than thirty histories and biographical treatises, from which 'Abdul Hai has drawn the materials for his own portion of the work;" he has also added numerous incidental notices from inscriptions on tombs and family histories.

The biographies of the Amirs who served under Akbar have nearly all been given in my translation of the *Á'ín*. I shall therefore select biographies of the Amirs that belong to the subsequent reigns.

The grandees of the Mughul Court were divided into two classes, of which the first comprised the *Umará i kibár*, or great Amirs. The emperor's service was strictly military, and the titles of the several ranks indicated the strength of the contingent which each Amir had to furnish. As commanders of contingents the Amirs were called *Mançabdárs*. The lowest *mançab*, or command, which entitled an officer to the title of Amir, was, under Akbar, a command of Two Hundred, and from the time of Sháhjahán, a command of Five Hundred. Commanders of Two Thousand and upwards were looked upon as 'great Amirs.' The highest command was that of Five Thousand; but the princes, several Maharájahs, and grandees related to the emperors, held higher commands. The princes often held commands of Thirty Thousand. Under Akbar, commands of Seven Thousand were given to a few, as to Mánsingh and Mirzá Sháhrukh. Under Sháhjahán the highest command was that of Áçaf Khán, the father of Mumtáz Mahall, Sháhjahán's wife who lies buried in the Táj at Agrá. He held a command of Nine Thousand; but on his death, no grandee was promoted to his post. Jai Singh held, only towards the very end of Sháhjahán's reign, a command of Seven Thousand. The weak emperors after Aurangzíb again conferred high *mançabs*.

During the time of war, many grandees kept up much larger contingents than their rank indicated. Thus Áçaf Khán I., the conqueror of Gondwána, had under Akbar for some time a contingent of 20,000 men, recruited by himself. In times of peace, the rule was to maintain only the fourth part of the nominal command, so that a commander of Five Thousand kept up 1250 men. On account of the frequent rebellions of powerful Amirs, the emperors continually lowered the actual commands, and increased the strength of the standing or imperial army. Thus Sháhjahán, during the Balkh war, lowered the strength of the contingents from one-fourth to one-fifth. The troops of the Amirs were called *tábínán*, or followers. Cavalry alone was counted. The recruiting and officering of the contingents rested entirely with the Amirs. The men of the standing army of the emperor were called *Ahadí* troops. For the payment of their contingents the Amirs received lands as *tuyúl*, or *jágír*. The former term is generally restricted to lands held exclusively for military purposes; the word *jágír* has a more general meaning, and refers usually to lands granted as rewards to distinguished officers. Hence we often find in histories that Amirs held certain lands as *tuyúl* and other lands, often far away, as *jágír*.

The contingents of the Amirs consisted mostly of troopers who joined their service with one horse each. Troopers who furnished two horses were called *duaspah*, and such as came with three, *sihaspah*. This will explain such titles as *Panjhazárí, chahár hazár sawár, sihazár duaspah sihaspah*, 'a commander of five thousand, four thousand horse, three thousand Duaspah and Sihaspah troopers,' which means that the Amir held a personal rank of 5,000, with a contingent not exceeding 4,000 horse, of which 3,000 should be troopers with two and three horses. Horses killed when on service were replaced by the state.

When grandees were old, they were excused attendance at court ([illegible]), they lost their *tuyúls*, and were sent to their *jágírs*, or received pensions in cash. At death, their whole property lapsed to the emperor.

There are several other points of interest connected with the salaries, promotions, and titles of the Amirs, and certain court-ceremonies, which will be described hereafter.

I now commence the biographical notices with

I. SHAIKH DÁÚD QURAISHÍ.

Shaikh Dáúd was the son of Bhíkan Khán, and belonged to a family of *Shaikhzádahs* settled in Hiçár Fírúzah. The word 'Quraishí' signifies 'tracing his descent from the Arabian tribe of Quraish,' to which the Prophet belonged; but the term is often applied in this country to Hindú converts to Islám. Dáúd's father had been in the service of the renowned Khán Jahán Lodi, and was killed in the beginning of the rebellion of his master, in the fight near Dholpur. Dáúd entered the service of Prince Dárá Shikoh, and distinguished himself in the field and in council. In the 20th year of Sháhjahán's reign, when the executive of the government was in Dárá's hands, Dáúd was *Faujdár* of Mathurá, Mahában, Jalesar, and several other districts. On the death of Sa'dullah, he was put in charge of the Prince's *tuyúl*, and received orders to guard, with two thousand horse, the roads between Agra and Shahjahánábád. In the same year, at the request of the Prince, the emperor made him a Khán; hence he is best known in history as *Dáúd Khán*. At the outbreak of the war between Dárá and Aurangzíb, Dáúd held an important post and, together with Satr Sál Hárá, commanded Dárá's vanguard. In the first battle, which was fought near Samugar, 9 miles east of Agra, (6th Ramazán 1068, or 26th May 1658, A.D.) Dáúd's brother Shaikh Ján Muhammad was killed. Dárá was defeated and retreated to the Panjáb, and ordered Dáúd to guard the Guzar i Talwan, a well-known ford of the Satlaj south of Jálandhar; but when Dárá fled from Láhor to Multán, Dáúd crossed the river, burned and sunk the ships, and joined the Prince. Seeing that his cause was hopeless, he left him near Bhakkar, and went through Jaisalmír to Firúzah, his ancestral home. He had not been there long, when Aurangzíb sent him a *khil'at*, in order to win him over to his party. Dáúd accepted it, and, on Aurangzíb's return from Multán to the capital, paid his respects at Court, when he was appointed to a command of Four Thousand with 3000 horse. He served immediately afterwards in the war with Shujá', and pursued that Prince under Mír Jumlah. When Shujá' had fled, Dáúd was sent to occupy Patna, and during his stay there was appointed Governor of Bihár. For some time he continued his operations against Shujá', who was forced to retreat from Tándah, near Gaur, to Eastern Bengal; but when the Prince had withdrawn beyond the frontiers of the empire, Dáúd returned to Patna, and prepared to subject several refractory zamíndárs of Bihár. He also received orders to invade Palámau, which he finally conquered in the end of December 1660.* Dáúd had scarcely returned from Palámau to Patna, when he was called to Court. On his arrival, he was appointed, together with Mirzá Rájah Jai Singh, to take the field against Sivá Bhonslah. Aurangzíb also raised him to the rank of a commander of Five Thousand, with 4000 horse, 3000 duaspah and sihaspah troopers, and made him governor of Khándesh. He conquered Fort Rudramal, and marched with Jaisingh to Fort Purandhar, during the siege, devastating Sivá's country with 7000 horse, especially the districts of Rájgarh and Kundanah. Returning from his excursions to Jai Singh, he took the command of the right wing of the Imperial army, and attacked A'dil Shah of Bíjápur.

In the 9th year of Aurangzíb's reign, he was recalled from Khándesh to Court, but was in the following year sent as Governor to Barár, and not long afterwards to Burhánpur. In the 14th year, he went again to Court, and was appointed Governor of Iláhábád.

'The date of his death is not recorded.'—*Madsir*.

His son Hamíd Khán also distinguished himself as a brave soldier. He died in the 25th year of Aurangzíb's reign (beginning of A. H. 1093, or A. D. 1682). The Bibl. Indica edition of the *Madsir 'Alamgiri* calls him (on p. 217, l. 6) *Hámid Khán*, and in the last line, *Jamshed Khán*.

Colonel E. D. Dalton lately favoured me with a short biography of Dáúd Khán, written by one of Dáúd's descendants. According to this biography, Dáúd is the son of Kabir Khán, son of Farid Khán, and the (younger) brother of Bhikan Khán. The *Madsir ul Umará* makes Bhikan Khán Dáúd's father. The paper contains no notice of the various services which Dáúd performed; but it mentions that the town of Dáúdnagar in Bihár was founded by him in A. H. 1083, or 1672-73 A.D., and that he died at Rohtásgarh on the 29th Zil Hajjah 1084, or 17th March 1674. It concludes with a few verses in the long *hazaj* metre, the last of which contains the *Táríkh* of Dáúd's death.

Chu ján bispard o burda burd dar rah i jawánmardí,
Bat árikhash khirad guft ba-rindí raft mardánah.

As he gave his life, but carried off his faith, on the road of valour,

The mind (of the poet) selected as *táríkh* the words '*Ba-rindi raft mardánah*' (he left the world bravely and piously.)

The values of the letters in the last three words, when added up, will be found to give 1084.

* The details of the conquest are given in the Journal of the Asiatic Society of Bengal for 1871, p. 127.

Dáúd's descendants exist in Bihár to this day. Colonel Dalton speaks of a large *fresco* in Dáúdnagar representing the battles fought by Dáúd, especially the conquest of Palámau. There is also a series of family portraits taken from life.

Dáúdnagar is thus mentioned in Thornton's Gazetteer. "It lies on the banks of the Son, forty miles west of Gaya. About eight miles lower down the Son from Dáúdnagar, there is a considerable village, called Shamsheranagar, founded by Shamsher Khán, a nephew of Dáúd Khán, and a very pleasing structure built by him as his tomb. It is now rapidly falling to pieces, although still in possession of his descendants."*

THE INDIGENOUS LITERATURE OF ORISSA.

BY JOHN BEAMES, B.C.S., M.R.A.S., BALASOR.

THERE is a general impression abroad amongst scholars that the modern Indian vernaculars are mere jargons which suffice for the colloquial needs of imperfectly civilized races, but that they possess nothing which can fairly be called a literature. Even those who are better informed are prone to disparage the mediæval poems which are to be found in most, if not all of these languages, though in Panjábí and Hindhí they do not rise above the rank of ballads. Now, before a judgment is delivered on this class of books, it may fairly be demanded that they be read. I fancy very few European or Indian scholars have any practical acquaintance with the real middle-age literature of the Hindus. In fact the very names of the books themselves are hardly known. Three characteristics are common to them all, and deprive them of much of the interest that would otherwise attach to them. Firstly, they are all of inordinate length; secondly, they are mere repetitions, more or less embellished, of the old fables of the Brahmanical religion,—*réchauffés* of the Puráṇas and Mahábhárata; thirdly, they are all in verse. But with all these drawbacks they are often valuable for the light they throw on the growth of the languages in which they are written. They are in many cases still intensely popular in rural districts, and a study of them will often supply the key to curious and apparently inexplicable peculiarities of native thought and manners. Some few indeed possess higher merits, and may be read with pleasure for the beauty of their poetry, their stores of history and geography, or the purity and loftiness of their morality. Under the first head come such works as Tulsí Dás's Rámáyaṇa, and the Satsai of Bihárí Lál, under the second Chand and the other Rajput bards, under the third Kabír, Námdeva, Tukarám, and occasionally Vidyapati and other writers of the Chaitanya school.

On the whole, then, it may be said that this literature is worth preserving. It shows us the people as they are and were,—not as the English schoolmaster would have them be,—and possesses a value even in its faults, quite above and apart from the spurious unnatural literature composed of works written to order by Fort William pandits and maulavis, such as the Prem Ságar, a farrago of nonsense in equal parts of bad Hindi and disguised Gujarátí.

What we want is, first to find out what books exist in the various languages; secondly, to have them read with a view to finding out which are worth preserving and printing; and thirdly, to get scholars to edit such as may be worth the trouble.

We should then be able to place in the hands of the student real genuine native works from which he could learn what the language he was studying really was, instead of, as at present, misleading him by trash like the Bagh-o-Bahar or Baitál Pachísí, composed in a language which no native ever spoke, and which he can with difficulty understand. The change which this would cause in, and the impetus it would give to, the study of Indian languages would probably be comparable only to the new life which was imparted to the schools of Europe when Virgil and Cicero first began to supersede, as text books, the crabbed Latin of Cassiodorus and Erigena.

As a contribution to the above objects I here append a list of works known to exist in Oriya, and propose, as opportunity offers, to read the most celebrated, and see what they are worth, and to report my discoveries from time to time through the medium of the *Indian Antiquary*. I am aware that Oriya holds a low place in its group of languages, but this is owing chiefly to its obscurity. I consider it in many respects one of the most interesting languages of the

* *From Mr. T. F. Peppé's Report*, Proceedings As. Soc. Bengal, December, 1871, p. 252.

Aryan group, especially because, owing to its long isolation from the rest, it has preserved words and forms which have perished from them, and exhibits at times very singular developments of its own.

The following list is the result of much enquiry, and is believed to be nearly, if not quite, exhaustive. The RASAKALLOLA or "Waves of Delight" by Dinakrishna Dás, a work of the early part of the sixteenth century, is the most celebrated Oriya poem, and is still well-known; its songs are even now frequently heard at village meetings, and most educated Oriyas know whole cantos by heart. I propose to give some notices of it at a future time.

List.

[N.B.—The following ancient Oriya works are known to be in existence, and copies of them written on palm-leaf, may probably be procured in different parts of the province. Those marked * can be obtained at Balasor, but Puri and Katak are better places to search for them in, especially Puri.]

No.	Work	Description
[illegible]	[illegible]	An epic poem.
[illegible]	[illegible]	do.
[illegible]	[illegible]	A tale.
[illegible]	[illegible]	do.
[illegible]	[illegible]	[illegible]
[illegible]	[illegible]	do.
[illegible]	[illegible]	do.
[illegible]	[illegible]	A [illegible] poem.
[illegible]	[illegible]	[illegible]
[illegible]	[illegible]	[illegible]
[illegible]	[illegible]	[illegible]
[illegible]	[illegible]	do.
[illegible]	[illegible]	[illegible] story in verse.
[illegible]	[illegible]	A sort of [illegible].
[illegible]	[illegible]	[illegible]
[illegible]	[illegible]	Epic poem.
[illegible]	[illegible]	do.
[illegible]	[illegible]	do.
[illegible]	[illegible]	Poetry.
[illegible]	[illegible]	do.
[illegible]	[illegible] Mahátmya	Religious poem on Krishna.
[illegible]	[illegible]	Religious poem.
[illegible]	[illegible]	do.
[illegible]	[illegible]	do.
[illegible]	[illegible]	do.
[illegible]	[illegible]	do.
[illegible]	[illegible]	do.
[illegible]	[illegible]	do.
[illegible]	[illegible]	do.
[illegible]	[illegible]	Dictionary

The above thirty works are by the celebrated Upendra Bhanj of Gumsur.

No.	Work	Description
[illegible]	Rasakallola	Poem on Krishna by Dinakrishna Dás.
[illegible]	[illegible]	do. do.
[illegible]	[illegible]	—The well-known [illegible] by Jagannáth Dás.

No.	Work	Author	Description
[illegible]	Mahábhárata,	by Sáralá Dás	Versions of the great Epic.
[illegible]	do.	[illegible] Dás	
[illegible]	do.	[illegible]	
[illegible]	[illegible]	[illegible]	Version of the Sanskrit poem.
[illegible]	[illegible]	[illegible] Dás	do.
[illegible]	Rámáyana	Balarám Dás	Version of the Sanskrit Epic.
[illegible]	[illegible]	[illegible] Dás	Version of the [illegible].
[illegible]	[illegible] Mahátmya	[illegible] Dás	Religious poem.
[illegible]	[illegible]	[illegible] Dás	do.
[illegible]	[illegible] Mahátmya	[illegible] Dás	do.
[illegible]	[illegible] Mahátmya	[illegible] Dás	do.
[illegible]	[illegible] Mahátmya	do.	do.
[illegible]	[illegible]	[illegible] Dás	do.
[illegible]	[illegible]	[illegible] Dás	do.
[illegible]	[illegible]	[illegible]	do.
[illegible]	[illegible]	[illegible]	Poetical [illegible]
[illegible]	[illegible]	[illegible]	[illegible] poem.
[illegible]	[illegible]	[illegible]	[illegible] of the Sanskrit [illegible].
[illegible]	[illegible]		[illegible]
[illegible]	[illegible]	Jagannáth Dás	[illegible]
[illegible]	[illegible]	do.	do.
[illegible]	[illegible]	[illegible] Dás	[illegible]
[illegible]	[illegible]	do.	do.
[illegible]	[illegible]	do.	do.
[illegible]	[illegible]	do.	Version of the [illegible].
[illegible]	[illegible]	unknown	[illegible]
[illegible]	[illegible]	do.	[illegible]
[illegible]	[illegible]	[illegible]	[illegible]
[illegible]	[illegible]	[illegible]	[illegible]
[illegible]	[illegible]	[illegible]	Commentary [illegible]
[illegible]	[illegible]	[illegible]	[illegible]
[illegible]	[illegible]	do.	do.
[illegible]	[illegible]	do.	[illegible]
[illegible]	[illegible]	do.	[illegible]
[illegible]	[illegible]	do.	[illegible]
[illegible]	[illegible]	[illegible] Dás	[illegible]
[illegible]	[illegible]	[illegible]	[illegible]
[illegible]	[illegible]	[illegible] Dás	[illegible]
[illegible]	[illegible]	[illegible]	[illegible]
[illegible]	[illegible]	[illegible] Dás	[illegible]
[illegible]	[illegible]	[illegible] Dás	[illegible]
[illegible]	[illegible] Purána	[illegible] Dás	A Purána.
[illegible]	[illegible]	[illegible] Dás	Religious work.
[illegible]	[illegible]	[illegible] Dás	Life of [illegible]
[illegible]	[illegible]	[illegible]	Religious poem.
[illegible]	[illegible]	[illegible] Dás	From the Sanskrit.
[illegible]	[illegible]		History of the [illegible]
[illegible]	[illegible]	[illegible]	Version of the Sanskrit.

TRANSLATION AND REMARKS ON A COPPER-PLATE GRANT DISCOVERED AT TIDGUNDI IN THE KALÁDGI ZILLA.

BY SHANKAR PANDURANG PANDIT, M.A., ACTING PROFESSOR OF SANSKRIT, PUNÁ.

THE following inscription is engraven on three thick rectangular sheets of copper, each 12½ by 9¼ inches, strung together by a ring about the middle of one of the shorter sides, and weighing in all a little more than seventeen pounds. The ring passes through the handle of a solid hemispherical seal, about the size of half of an ordinary orange; and upon the flat side of the seal are the figures, in distinct relievo, of a lion, the sun, a half moon, the palm of an expanded hand, a cobra di capella with its hood expanded, a swastika cross, a palm tree, and what appears to me to be a spear. The inscription is engraved on four of the six sides, the two outer ones being left blank.

This copper-plate grant was found about twelve years ago, by a Māng in tilling his field, at the village of Tidgundi, about twelve miles to the north of Bijāpur, in the district of Kalādgi. It was shown about by the Māng in hopes that it might be deciphered, being supposed by him to relate to a hidden treasure; but not finding any one who could read and explain it, though it was taken as far as Nipāni and Kolhāpur, he pawned it to a Mārvāḍī at Managoli in the Bāgevāḍi Tāluka. When I accidentally heard about it,* it had changed hands several times, and I had not a little difficulty in getting possession of it, by finding out the several persons through whose hands it had passed, and by satisfying the claims of all concerned. The set of plates is now in my possession. The inscription is well preserved, except in one or two places at the edge of one side, where a few letters are somewhat worn out, though they offer no difficulty to the reader.

Translation.

Victory to that body of Vishṇu, which was manifested in the form of a Boar, that agitated the ocean, and on the tip of the right tusk of which, raised for the purpose, rested the world. Victory to that Hari,† who, when he attempted to crush the body of his enemy, and the latter crouched in the hollow of his (Hari's) nails lest he should be destroyed, looked in all directions, surprised at his disappearance—and who shook off his hand in disappointment, and then laughed, seeing the Demon,‡ his foe, fallen before him on the ground like a grain of dust. He,§ who has a throat resembling a white lotus, perched upon by a line of bees,—that one, wearing a garland of human skulls—may he confer prosperity upon thee.

Welfare! At the time when the victorious reign of *Śrī Tribhuvana Malla Deva*, the Refuge of the whole world, the Lord of the Earth, Mahārāja among the Mahārājas, the *Paramesvara*, the *Bhaṭṭāraka*, the flower of the race of *Satyāśraya*, the ornament of the dynasty of the Chālukyas is, from the long-standing city of Śrī Kalyāṇa, protecting the earth,—six years of the era of Śrī Vikrama having passed, and there having commenced the seventh by name Dundubhi,—on the first day of the *Shuddha* fortnight of the month of Kārtika of that year, being Sunday. Dependent for his subsistence upon his (Tribhuvana Malla's) lotus-like feet, the ancestor of king *Munja*, the ruler of four thousand *pratyandakas* of land, sprung from the race of *Sinda*, and of incalculable dread in the fields of battle, (is) by name *Bhīma*. His eldest son, by name *Sindarāja*, of renowned fame, dear to great victory won on battle fields. Of his son King *Munja* the series of titles is:—*Prosperity (svasti), He who has obtained the five great words*‖ *Lord of the great circle*,¶ *Lord of the city of Bhogavati, descendant of the king of the Snakes, flower of the race of the Snakes, delight of the Sinda race, like the sun to the lotuses, destruction like the submarine fire to the Gurjaras*,** *the Mandalika, adorned by a series of names that purifies the world*,† *Lord of the great circle*.

This is a benediction on king *Śrī Munja Rāja*:—This king *Munja* is not [like] that Vāmana, who, for the purpose of entrapping king Bali, assumed poverty though for a time, but he is the crown jewel of all kings. Nor is he [like] him that eated the Boar, whose destruction from its enemies throughout the world. He, the lord of earth, victorious among numbers of resplendent kings—may he be victorious! It is strange O king Munja, that though the hearts of your enemies are always exceedingly heated, your Fame, who is your consort, loves to wander among them (the hearts) dreadful as the deep ocean!‡ But ah! yes, I see the reason. There resides in you the power of the knowledge of making fire and poison harmless.§ Hence it is that she incessantly roams among your enemies living between the Himālaya and the Bridge.‖

* The writer was then District Deputy Collector in the Kalādgi Collectorate.

† Here there is a play upon the word *Hari*, which means both Vishṇu and a lion, and the allusion is to the Man-lion avatara of Vishṇu.

‡ This was *Hiraṇyakaśipu*, an demon whom Vishṇu became incarnate as the Man-lion or half man and half lion.

§ This refers to Śiva, who attempted to swallow the poison churned out of the ocean, by which his throat was blackened.

‖ *Samadhigatapanchamahāśabda*: It is usual to render this to mean 'who has obtained the five great sounds,' viz. of certain musical instruments. But it seems more probable that *Mahā Śabda* refers to certain five titles, though I am not certain what those titles were. The word *Mahāśabda* appears to refer to five words or titles beginning with *Mahā*, such as *Mahārāja*, *Mahāmaṇḍaleśvara*, &c.

¶ *Maṇḍala* is the circle of the vassals and chiefs paying tribute to a king.

** *Gurjaravaḍavānala* in the original. It is not certain whether Gurjara is the name of an individual or of a people. The translation given above is a guess.

† The original is *Jagatpāvananāmāvalīvirājita*, which appears to be a mistake for *Jagatpāvananāmāvalīvirājita*.

‡ The original has clearly *rudra*—*sa hhidhīra*. The latter word is clear, but I have not been able to decypher it. It may be due

§ *Śikhi-viṣa-vidyā-siddhi*,—This is used to mean an art or magical power, whereby the effects of fire are averted, and by the help of which one may rush into fire and come out unscathed. And so also is *viṣasiddhi*, which is applied to the magical powers supposed to be possessed by snake-charmers.

‖ The bridge here referred to is the bridge-like range of rocks connecting Lanka or Ceylon with India, supposed to have been built by the hero of the Rāmāyaṇa. "From the Himālaya to the bridge" is ordinarily used to signify "from one end of India to the other."

by him. In the circle of his vassals [there is Kanna Sâmanta] whose titles are *Prosperity*, he who has obtained the *five great words*, the *Mahâsâmanta*, *beloved of victory*, *death to the forces of his enemy*, *disperser* * *of hostile feather-vassals as a gust of wind is of the clouds*, *a lion among his elephant-like inimical Sâmantas*, *the Boolelâva*,† *Mayurakirti* [illegible],‡ *the* [illegible]§ *destroyer*‖ *of Rovama*, ...¶ *pure in his family*, *the chief friend of the good worshipper of Truth like the son of Yama*,** *Tunnyasvarola*,†† *brave as a lion*, *propitiator of the feet of Shrîmat Tribhuvana Malladeva*,—Kanna Sâmanta [to wit]. This is a benediction for him:—Victory to *Shrî Kanna Sâmanta*, devoted to the worship of the feet of Hara, who manipulates the breasts of the Princess of the Isles, and who is ever death to his enemies.

To him are sold‡‡ for the full consideration and delivered (*literally given*) the twelve villages of *Vâgvâdi*, the village called *Tâkkolid* being excepted from them. His (*Munja's*) ministers [being] *Shrî Khambhayya Nayaka*, *Mudduvi Nâyaka* the minister entrusted with War and Peace, *Bhamayya Nâyaka*, *Nimbayo Nâyaka*, in their presence, having caused this copper plate grant to be written by *Narayana*, the minister in the Ministry of War and Peace, King *Shrî Munja* by his own hand delivered it to *Kanna Sâmanta*. [Now] that stated: 'Whoever should resume land whether given by himself or by others lives as an insect in filth for sixty thousand years.'

Remarks.

At first sight the words *Shrî Vikramâditya* [illegible] *chakra* [illegible] *saptame* [illegible] *pravartamâne* might be supposed to indicate the *Samvat* era of Vikrama, and the inscription states that the 6th year of these having passed, and the seventh having commenced on the first day of the *Shukla* half of the month of Kârtika, the grant was made on that day. Now the *Samvat* year commences from the first of the *Shukla* half of the month of Kârtika; further more this day falls on Sunday in the seventh year of the era, and *Dundubhi* is also the name of the seventh year of the cycle according to the method of naming the cycle of years followed north of the Narmadâ. I am assured by Prof. Keru Lakshman Chhatre that the calculations by which he arrived at these results were carefully made, and admit of no doubt as to their accuracy. If, then, the date given in the grant be according to the old Vikrama era, it corresponds to the 29th of September 51, B.C. (N.S.) But to set against this coincidence, there is, in the first place, the appearance of the characters which is decidedly modern. In fact with the exception of the letters [illegible] and [illegible], and so many compounded letters, the whole of the inscription may be read with little difficulty by any one acquainted only with the modern form of the Devanâgarî alphabet used in the Dekhan. I have seen, in the district of Kaladgi, several inscriptions in Devanâgarî characters about ten or eleven centuries old, and I invariably found the characters present a much more ancient appearance than those in the present inscription. Of course it will not always be safe in assigning dates to ancient inscriptions and documents, to be guided entirely by the appearance of the characters, when it is often found that one and the same alphabet presents considerable variety in the shape of the letters as used in different parts of the country even at the same time, and that individual peculiarities of a writer's or engraver's style of writing may account for a great deal of variety of form. But the forms of the letters in the many inscriptions of the seventh, eighth and ninth centuries after Christ, still extant in the Kaladgi district, which formed part of the Châlukya territories, are so much more ancient than those of the present Devanâgarî alphabet, and even than those of this copper plate, that if the latter really belonged to the first century before Christ, its letters should be of far more ancient forms than those of the above inscriptions.

In the second place, the King of the Châlukya dynasty, in whose reign the grant is stated to have been made is well known, and belongs to the branch of that dynasty, which reigned at Kalyâna from about the end of the tenth to near the end of the twelfth century of the Christian era. Mr Elliot's paper§§ on *Hindu Inscriptions* mentions a King Vikramâditya II. or Kali Vikrama, or Permâdirâya, who assumed the title of Tribhuvana Malla.

---

* The original distinctly reads [illegible], of which the translation given above is an approximate guess, but is open to correction. If the epithet is not corrupt, it seems difficult how *Sabbata* should mean *feather*. It is possible that [illegible] may be a mistake for [illegible].

† This is an ancient Canarese word, the modern form of which is *bolgâra* or *bolldra*. It means a sportsman, a hunter.

‡ I do not know what this epithet means. *Literally* it signifies 'the new moons of the lives of an alligator.'

§ [illegible]—[illegible] is a Canarese word, and means a [illegible]. [illegible] is its genitive plural, and with the Sanskrit [illegible], the epithet seems to mean the 'demon-like [illegible]' or rather 'the *demon* ([illegible]) *of the horses*,' i. e. the greatest hero.

‖ [illegible] in the original, which may be a mistake for [illegible], and if so, [illegible] stand for the name of some local deity. [illegible] is not unfrequently a proper name among the lower classes in the Karnâṭaka.

¶ Here there occurs a long expression which I read as [illegible], but which I cannot translate intelligibly.

** The original [illegible] appears to a mistake for [illegible] or [illegible]. The son of Yama is Dharma, the eldest of the Pândavas. Yama is also called Dharma.

†† Rich in breasts?

‡‡ The original [illegible] for [illegible] is rather doubtful if not corrupt. The letters, however, are perfectly clear in the inscription.

§§ Published in the *Journal Royal Asiatic Society*, vol. IV.

and the date of his accession to the throne is given as Shaka 998. This K a l i V i k r a m a is described in one of Mr. Elliot's inscriptions as having set aside the ancient Shaka, and established the *Vikrama Shaka* in his own name,* &c. Tribhuvana Malla, therefore, mentioned twice in this grant is most probably the same as that of Mr. Elliot's list, and the *Vikrama Samvat* of the grant is the era established by that prince. From the fact that he called himself Vikramâditya, gave the name of *Vikrama Samvat* to the era he established, and lastly, that he began it on the first *tithi* of the Shukla fortnight of Kârtika, the day on which the year of the old *Vikrama* epoch commences—one of two inferences may be drawn. He may have set his era in opposition to that of the Shaka King, Shâlivâhana, which was then, as now, prevalent in the Dekhan, and attempted to supersede it the more effectually by giving his own the appearance of a revival of the older era of Vikrama, the great rival of the Shaka King,—*i. e.* by calling himself K a l i V i k r a m a or Vikrama of the *Kali* or modern age, and commencing it on the same day of the month of Kârtika as the older era of Vikramâditya. This is probable from the fact, that, according to Mr. Elliot, he is described in an inscription as "rubbing out the *Shaka*," and instituting the *Vikrama Era* in its stead. The other inference is, that wishing to perpetuate his own memory by the establishment of a new era, he set himself in opposition to the older Vikramâditya, and attempted to blot out the older era. But whatever might be his object, the fact of its institution is placed beyond all doubt by some of the inscriptions collected by Mr. Elliot.

Referring then the date given in the grant to the era commenced by Tribhuvana Malla, we find that the cycle year *Dundubhi*, which is mentioned in the grant as falling in the seventh year of the era [illegible] in Shaka 1004, according to the Dekhan or Telingana method of calculation; and in that year the first of the *Shukla* fortnight of Kârtika falls on Tuesday. The coincidence of Sunday on the first *tithi* of Kârtika takes place in 1005, but the year Dundubhi cannot be made to agree with the Shaka year 1005. As, however, the coincidence of the day of the week with the *tithi* of the month is more important, as not being likely to have been wrongly stated, than the coincidence of a given year of any era with a certain year of the Bârhaspatya cycle, which, at different courts of kings, has from time to time been subjected to different methods of calculation,—it may safely be assumed that the grant was dated upon the first *tithi* of Kârtika of the Shaka year 1005, or 15th of October, 1083, *N. S.* The choice of Shaka 1005 as corresponding with the *seventh* year of the new Vikrama epoch of the Châlukya prince is strengthened by a statement that, according to Mr. Elliot, appears to be contained in an inscription at Galaganâtha,† that the Shaka year 1003 corresponds with the fifth year of his reign, in which "he overcame B a l l a v a r â j a of the P a l a v a n y a or P a l a v a s."

The inscription purports to record a grant of twelve villages made by M u n j a M a h î p a t i, or King M u n j a to K a n n a S â m a n t a. B h î m a is the first mentioned ancestor of King M u n j a, and is described as born of the race of the S i n d a kings. His eldest son was S i n d a R â j a. His son M u n j a R â j a is the grantor of the *Shâsana*. The grant accordingly makes mention only of the father and the grand-father of M u n j a. B h î m a is further described as being *pratyaṇḍakachatuh sahasrâdhipati*, about the meaning of which I am not quite certain. *Pratyaṇḍaka* might be a square measure of land, and the epithet may mean, 'lord of four thousand *pratyaṇḍakas* of land.'

One of the titles of M u n j a is '*Bhogavatîpura-parameshvara*,'—'lord of the city of Bhogâvatî.' As no other place is mentioned that appears to have been his capital; but I have not been able to identify this city with any town in the Dekhan. Another epithet of King M u n j a is *Phaṇîndravaṁshodbhava*, or 'born in the family of the serpents' or the 'Nâgas.' B h î m a, the grand-father of M u n j a, is described as depending for his subsistence on the lotus-like feet of King T r i b h u v a n a M a l l a D e v a, from which, as also from the manner that that prince is mentioned in the grant, it appears that he was a chief under, or a Râja paying tribute to, T r i b h u v a n a M a l l a D e v a.

The grantee is K a n n a S â m a n t a, one of the chiefs subordinate to King Munja, and is also described as being a worshipper of the feet of Tribhuvana Malla Deva, from which it appears, that, besides being subordinate to Munja, he also owed allegiance to the Châlukya king. He is further described as a devotee of S h i v a and was married to a daughter of the L â ḍ a s. The grant is silent as to the country or residence of Kanna Sâmanta, though he probably belonged to the Karnâṭaka, as some of his titles are taken from the Canarese language.

The grant records the conveyance by sale of twelve villages which, if I am not mistaken, went by the collective name of V â y v a ḍ a, which appears quite distinct in the plate. Out of the V â y v a ḍ a villages, the grant states that one village named T o h k a l i k â is excepted. It is interesting to note that there is still a village called T â k a l k i in the B â g e v â ḍ i Tâluka of the Kalâdgi district, not far from the place where the copper-plate was discovered. There is also a village called *Tâkli* on the northern bank of the Bhîmâ about fifteen miles north of T i ḍ g u n d i, and near the village of D h â ḷ i k h e ḍ.

* Gadag inscription No. 7, VII, p. 156 of Mr. Elliot's collection.

† Noticed by Mr. Elliot in his paper on *Hindu Inscriptions*, printed in the *Journal Royal Asiatic Society* vol. IV.

However strange it might appear, from the inscription being a mere deed of sale—if the interpretation of [illegible] [illegible] be correct—it appears that the grantee was more than a mere thief; otherwise the mention of his Ministers, and among them a Minister of Peace and War, could hardly be satisfactorily explained. It is probable, however, that the grantee Kauna Sâmanta was no more than a petty chief.

DARDU LEGENDS, PROVERBS AND FABLES.*

By G. W. LEITNER, M.A. Ph. D.

I.—DARDU LEGENDS.

A—Demons—Yatsh.†

Demons are of a gigantic size, and have only one eye which is in the forehead. They used to rule over the mountains and oppose the cultivation of the soil by man. They often dragged people away into their recesses. Since the adoption of the Muhammadan religion, the Demons have relinquished their possessions, and only occasionally trouble the believers.

They do not walk by day, but confine themselves to perambulating at night. A spot is shown near Astor at a village called Bulent, where five large mounds are pointed out which have somewhat the shape of huge baskets. Their existence is explained as follows. A Zemindár at Grukôt, a village further on, on the Kashmir road, had with great trouble sifted his grain for storing, and had put it into baskets and sacks. He then went away. The Demons came—five in number—carrying huge leather sacks, into which they put the grain. They then went to a place which is still pointed out and called "[illegible] Yatshoyn gau bahl," or "the place of the demons' loads at the hollow"—that being the Shina name for the present village of Grukôt. There they brought up a huge flat stone—which is still shown—and made it into a kind of pan (tawa) for the preparation of bread. But the morning dawned and obliged them to disappear; they converted the sacks and their contents into earthen mounds which have the shape of baskets and are still shown.

1.—*The Wedding of Demons.*‡

"A Shikari was once hunting in the hills. He had taken provisions with him for five days. On the sixth day he found himself without any food. Excited and fatigued by his fruitless expedition, he wandered into the deepest mountain recesses, careless whither he went so long as he could find water to assuage his thirst, and a few wild berries to allay his hunger. Even that search was unsuccessful and, tired and hungry, he endeavoured to compose himself to sleep. Even that comfort was denied him, and, nearly maddened with his situation, he again arose and looked around him. It was the first or second hour of night, and at a short distance he descried a large fire blazing—a most cheerful welcome to the hungry and now chilled, wanderer. He approached it quietly, hoping to meet some other sportsman who might provide him with food. Coming near the fire, he saw a very large and curious assembly of giants, eating, drinking and singing. In great terror he wanted to make his way back, when one of the assembly who had a squint in his eye, got up for the purpose of fetching water for the others. He overtook him and asked him whether he was a "child of man." Half dead with terror, he scarcely could answer that he was, when the Demon invited him to join them at the meeting which was described to be a wedding party. The Shikari replied, "You are a Demon and will destroy me;" on which the spirit took an oath by the sun and the moon, that he certainly would not do so. He then hid him under a bush and went back with the water. He had scarcely returned when a plant was torn out of the ground and a small aperture was made into which the giants managed to throw all their property, and, gradually making themselves thinner and thinner, themselves vanished into the ground through it. Our sportsman was then taken by the hand by the friendly demon, and, before he knew how, he himself glided through the hole and found himself in a huge apartment, which was splendidly illuminated. He was placed in a corner where he would not be observed. He received some food and gazed in mute astonishment on the assembled spirits. At last he saw the mother of the bride taking her daughter's head into her lap and weeping bitterly at the prospect of her departure into another household. Unable to control her grief, and in compliance with an old Shin custom, she began the singing of the evening by breaking into the following strains:—

Song of the Mother.

Ajaye Biraneì [illegible], [illegible] [illegible],
(Thy) mother's Biraneì my little darling ornaments will wear,
[illegible] Baldar Basha [illegible] [illegible] [illegible],
[Whilst] here at Baldar Basha the heavens dark will become,
Nagyré Phal Chacha Kuní [illegible],
The Nagyr (of men) Phal Chacha of Khuni, the prince will come,

* Committed to writing for the first time in 1866 from the [illegible] of Dards. This race has no written character of its own.

† "Yatsh" means "bad" in Kashmiri.

‡ This Legend and that of the origin of Ghagit have appeared before, but without annotations.

‡ The father's name was Mir Khan; the daughter's name was Biranì; the bridegroom's name was Khade Mach of Nagyr of Phal Chachanosh; and the place of the wedding was Baldar Basha.

Thy Mirkan father [illegible] *begis,*
Thy Mirkan father from, new corn will be distributed.
Sati [illegible] [illegible] *Malik* [illegible]
Seven rivers' water be * Shadu Malek a-going will make,
Thy Mirkan [illegible] [illegible] *bego,*
Thy Mirkan, father, now ghee will distribute.

Translation.—"Oh Birani, thy mother's own; thou little darling will wear ornaments, whilst to me, who will remain here at Buldas Dache, the heavens will appear dark. The prince of Lords of that Chache race is coming from Nagyr and Mirkan thy father, now distributes corn [as an act of welcome.]

"Be (as fruitful and pleasant) as the water of seven rivers, for Shadu Malik [the prince] is determined to start, and now thy father Mirkan is distributing ghi" [as a compliment to the departing guest.]

The Shikari began to enjoy the scene, and would have liked to have staid, but his equivocating friend told him now that he could not be allowed to remain any longer. So he got up, but before again vanishing through the above mentioned aperture into the human world, he took a good look at the Demons. To his astonishment he beheld on the shoulders of one, a shawl which he had safely left at home. Another held his gun; a third was eating out of his own dishes; some had his many-coloured stockings on, and another disported himself in Pyjamas (drawers) which he only ventured to put on on great occasions. He also saw many of the things that had excited his admiration among the property of his neighbours in his native village being most familiarly used by the Demons. He scarcely could be got to move away, but his friendly guide took hold of him and brought him again to the place where he had first met him. On taking leave he gave him three loaves of bread. As his village was far off he consumed two of the loaves on the road. On reaching his home, he found his father who had been getting rather anxious at his prolonged absence. To him he told all that had happened and showed him the remaining loaf of which the old man ate half. His mother, a good housewife, took the remaining half and threw it into a large granary, where, as it was the season of harvest (autumn), a sufficient store of flour had been placed for the use of the family during the winter. Strange to say, that half loaf brought luck, for demons mean it sometimes kindly to the children of men, and only hurt them when they consider themselves offended. The granary remained always full, and the people of the village rejoiced with the family for they were liked and were good people. It also should be told that as soon as the Shikari came home he looked after his costly shawl, dishes, and clothes, but he found all in their proper places and perfectly uninjured. On enquiring amongst his neighbours he also found that they too had not lost anything. He was much astonished at all this, till an old woman who had a great reputation for wisdom, told him that this was the custom of demons, and that they invariably borrowed the property of mankind for their weddings and as invariably restored it. On occasions of rejoicings amongst them, they felt kindly towards mankind. Thus ends one of the prettiest tales that I have ever heard.

2.—*The Demon's Present of Coals turned into Gold.*

Something similar to what has just been related is said to have happened at Doyur on the road from Ghilgit to Nagyr. A man of the name of Phidhu had a son, named Lachir, who, one day, going out to fetch water, was caught by a Yach who tore up a plant (reeds?) "[illegible]" and entered with the lad into the fissure which was thereby created. He brought him to a large palace, in which a number of goblins, male and female, were diverting themselves. He there saw all the valuables of the inhabitants of his village. A wedding was being celebrated and the mother sang:—

[illegible]
[illegible]
[illegible]
[illegible]
[illegible]
[illegible]
[illegible] &c. &c.

Translation.

[illegible] is being distributed, daughter of [illegible].
[illegible] is being distributed, hurrah! hurrah! (Chorus)
[illegible] is being distributed, &c. &c. (Chorus)
Meat is being distributed, &c. &c. (Chorus)
Wine is being distributed, &c. &c. &c. &c. (Chorus)

On his departure, the demon gave him a sackful of coals, and conducted him, through the aperture made by the tearing up of the reed, towards his village. The moment the demon had left, the boy emptied the sack of the coals and went home, when he told his father what had happened. In the emptied sack they found a small bit of coal which, as soon as they touched it, became a gold coin, very much to the regret of the boy's father who would have liked his son to have brought home the whole sackful.

B.—DARAI—[illegible] ON FAIRIES.

They are handsome, in contradistinction to the Yachas or demons, and stronger; they have a beautiful castle on the top of the Nanga Parbat or Dyarmul (so called from being inaccessible). This castle is made of crystal, and the people fancy they can see it. They call it "[illegible]" or "Castle of Glass-stone."

1.—*The Sportsman and the Castle of the Fairies.*

Once a sportsman ventured up the Nanga Parbat. To his surprise he found no difficulty, and venturing farther and farther, he at last reached the top. There he saw a beautiful castle made of glass, and pushing one of the doors, he entered it, and found himself in a most magnificent apartment. Through it he saw an open space that appeared to be the garden of the castle, but there was in it only one tree of excessive height and which was entirely composed of pearls and corals. The delighted* sportsman filled his sack in which he carried his corn and left the place, hoping to enrich himself by the sale of the pearls. As he was going out of the door he saw an innumerable crowd of serpents following him. In his agitation he shouldered the sack and attempted to run, when a pearl fell out. This a serpent at once swallowed and disappeared. The sportsman, glad to get rid of his pursuers at any price, threw pearl after pearl to them, and in every case it had the desired effect. At last, only one serpent remained, but for her (a fairy in that shape?) he found no pearl, and, urged on by fear, he hastened to his village—Tarsing, which is at the very foot of the Sanga Parbat. On entering his house he found it in great agitation: bread was being distributed to the poor as they do at funerals, for his family had given him up as lost. The serpent still followed and stopped at the door. In despair, the man threw the corn-sack at her, when lo! a pearl glided out, which was eagerly swallowed by the serpent which immediately disappeared. However, the man was not the same being as before. He was ill for days, and in about a fortnight after the events narrated, died,—for fairies never forgive a man who has surprised their secrets.

2.—*The Fairy who Punished Her Human Lover.*

It is not believed in Astor that fairies ever marry human beings, but in Ghilgit there is a legend to that effect. A famous sportsman, Kibá Lori, who never returned empty-handed from any excursion, kept company with a fairy to whom he was deeply attached. Once in the hot weather, the fairy told him not to go out shooting during "the seven days of the summer,"—the "Cholelars"—which are called *Bardi*, and are supposed to be the hottest days in Dardistan. "I am," said she, "obliged to leave you for that period, and mind you do not follow me." The sportsman promised obedience and the fairy vanished, saying that he would certainly die if he attempted to follow her. Our love-intoxicated Nimrod, however, could not endure her absence. On the fourth day he shouldered his gun and went out with the hope of meeting her. Crossing a range he came upon a plain, where he saw an immense gathering of game of all sorts and his beloved fairy milching a "Kill" [*markhor*], and collecting the milk in a silver vessel. The noise which Kibá Lori made caused the animal to start and to strike out with its legs, which upset the silver vessel. The fairy looked up, and to her anger behold the disobedient lover. She went up to him and, after reproaching him, struck him in the face. But she had scarcely done so when despair mastered her heart, and she cried out in the deepest anguish, that "he now must die within four days." "However," she said, "do shoot one of these animals, so that people may not say that you have returned empty-handed." The poor man returned crest-fallen to his home, lay down and died on the fourth day.

C.—Dayals—Wizards and Witches.

The gift of second sight, or rather the intercourse with fairies, is confined to a *few families* in which it is hereditary. The wizard is made to inhale the fumes of a fire which is lit with the wood of the *chili*† (Panjâbî. *padam*) a kind of firewood which gives much smoke. Into the fire the milk of a white sheep or goat is poured. The wizard inhales the smoke till he apparently becomes insensible. He is then taken on the lap of one of the spectators who sings a song which restores him to his senses. In the meanwhile, a goat is slaughtered and the moment the fortune-teller jumps up, its bleeding neck is presented to him, which he sucks as long as a drop remains. The assembled musicians then strike up a great noise and the wizard rushes about in the circle, which is formed round him, and talks unintelligibly. The fairy then appears at some distance and sings, which, however, only the wizard hears. He then communicates her sayings in a song to one of the musicians who explains its meaning to the people. The wizard is called upon to foretell events and to give advice in cases of illness, &c., &c. The people believe that in ancient times these Dayals invariably spoke correctly, but that now scarcely one saying in a hundred turns out to be true. Wizards do not now make a livelihood by their talent which is considered its own reward.

D.—Historical Legend of the Origin of Ghilgit.

There are few legends so exquisite as the one which chronicles the origin or rather the rise of Ghilgit. The traditions regarding Alexander the Great, which Vigne and others have imagined to exist among the people of Dardistan are unknown to, at any rate, the Shina race, excepting in so far as some Munshi accompanying the Mahárájá's troops may, perhaps, accidentally have referred to it in conversation with a Shin. Any such information would have been derived from the Sikandarnáma of Nizámi, and would therefore possess no original value. There exist no ruins, so far as I have gone, to point to an occupation of Dardistan by the soldiers of Alexander. The following legend, however, which not only lives in the memories of all the Shin people, whether they be Chiláskis, Astoris, Ghilgitis, or Brokpas—[the latter, as I discovered, living actually side by side with the Baltis in Little Tibet], but which also an annual festival comme-

* Elsewhere called "ghi."

morning, is not devoid of interest either from an historical or a purely literary point of view:—

"Once upon a time there lived a race at Gilgit whose origin is uncertain. Whether they sprung from the soil or had immigrated from a distant region is doubtful; so much is believed that they were Gayupi, *i.e.*, spontaneous aborigines, unknown. Over them ruled a monarch who was a descendant of the evil spirits, the Yach, who terrorized over the world. His name was Shiri-badat, and he resided at a castle in front of which was a course for the performance of the manly game of Polo. His tastes were capricious, and in every one of his actions his fiendish origin could be discerned. The natives bore his rule with resignation, for what could they effect against a monarch at whose command even magic aids were placed? However, the country was rendered fertile, and round the capital bloomed attractive gardens.

"The heavens, or rather the virtuous Peris, at last grew tired of his tyranny, for he had crowned his iniquities by indulging in a propensity for cannibalism. This taste had been developed by an accident. One day his cook brought him some mutton broth, the like of which he had never tasted. After much inquiry as to the nature of the food on which the sheep had been brought up, it was eventually traced to an old woman, its first owner. She stated that her child and the sheep were born on the same day, and losing the former, she had consoled herself by suckling the latter. This was a revelation to the tyrant. He had discovered the secret of the palatability of the broth, and was determined to keep a never-ending supply of it. So he ordered that his kitchen should be regularly provided with children of a tender age, whose flesh, when converted into broth, would remind him of the exquisite dish he had once so much relished. This cruel order was carried out. The people of the country were dismayed at such a state of things, and sought slightly to improve it by sacrificing, in the first place, all orphans and children of neighbouring tribes! The tyrant, however, was insatiable, and soon was his cruelty felt by many families at Gilgit, who were compelled to give up their children to slaughter.

"Relief came at last. At the top of the mountain Ko, which it takes a day to ascend, and which overlooks the village of Doyur, below Gilgit, on the other side of the river, appeared three figures. They looked like men, but much more strong and handsome. In their arms they carried bows and arrows, and turning their eyes in the direction of Doyur, they perceived innumerable flocks of sheep and cattle grazing on a prairie between that village and the foot of the mountain. The strangers were fairies, and had come [perhaps from Nagyr?] to this region with the view of ridding Gilgit of the monster that ruled over it. However, this intention was confined to the two elder ones. The three strangers were brothers, and none of them had been born at the same time. It was their intention to make Azru Shemsher, the youngest, Rajah of Gilgit, and, in order to achieve their purpose, they hit upon the following plan. On the already noticed prairie, which is called Didinge, a sportive calf was gambolling towards and away from its mother. It was the pride of its owner, and its brilliant red colour could be seen from a distance. 'Let us see who is the best marksman,' exclaimed the eldest, and saying this, he shot an arrow in the direction of the calf, but missed his aim. The second brother also tried to hit it, but also failed. At last, Azru Shemsher, who took a deep interest in the sport, shot his arrow, which pierced the poor animal from side to side and killed it. The brothers, whilst descending, congratulated Azru on his sportsmanship, and on arriving at the spot where the calf was lying, proceeded to cut its throat and to take out from the body the *titbits, namely, the kidneys and the liver.*

"They then roasted these delicacies, and invited Azru to partake of them first. He respectfully declined, on the ground of his youth, but they urged him to do so, 'in order,' they said, 'to reward you for such an excellent shot.' Scarcely had the meat touched the lips of Azru when the brothers got up, and vanishing into air, called out, 'Brother! you have touched impure food, which Peris never should eat, and we have made use of your ignorance of this law, because we want to make you a human being* who shall rule over Gilgit; remain, therefore, at Doyur.' Azru, in deep grief at the separation, cried, 'Why remain at Doyur, unless it be to grind corn?' 'Then,' said the brothers, 'go to Gilgit.' 'Why,' was the reply, 'go to Gilgit, unless it be to work in the gardens?' 'No, no,' was the last kind consoling rejoinder, 'you will eventually become the king of this country, and deliver it from the monstrous oppressor.' No more was heard of the departing fairies, and Azru remained by himself, endeavouring to gather consolation from the great mission which had been bestowed on him. A villager met him, and, struck by his appearance, offered him shelter in his house. Next morning he went on the roof of his host's house, and calling out to him to come up, pointed to the Ko mountain, on which, he said, he plainly discerned a wild goat. The incredulous villager began to fear he had harboured a maniac, if not a worse character; but Azru shot off his arrow, and, accompanied by the villager (who had assembled some friends for protection as he was afraid his young guest might be an associate of robbers, and lead him into a trap) went in the direction of the mountain. There, to be sure, at the very spot that was pointed out though many miles distant, was lying the wild

* Eating meat was the process of "incarnation."

goat, with Azru's arrow transfixing its body. The astonished peasants at once hailed him as their leader, but he exacted an oath of secrecy from them; for he had come to deliver them from their tyrant, and would keep his *incognito* till such time as his plans for the destruction of the monster should be matured.

"He then took leave of the hospitable people of Dayur, and went to Gilgit. On reaching the place, which is scarcely four miles distant from Dayur, he amused himself by prowling about in the gardens adjoining the royal residence. There he met one of the female companions of Shiribadat's daughter—(*gori* in Hill Panjabi, *chaiboy* in Gilgiti) fetching water for the princess. This lady was remarkably handsome and of a sweet disposition. Her companion rushed back and told the young lady to look from over the ramparts of the castle at a wonderfully handsome young man whom she had just met. The princess placed herself in a place from which she could observe any one approaching the fort. Her maid then returned and induced Azru to come with her to the Polo ground—the Shawaran—in front of the castle; the princess was smitten with his beauty and at once *fell in love* with him. She then sent word to the young prince to come and see her. When he was admitted into her presence, he for a long time denied being anything else than a common labourer. At last, he confessed to being a fairy's child, and the overjoyed princess offered him her hand and heart. It may be mentioned here that the tyrant Shiribadat had a wonderful horse, which could cross a mile at every jump, and which its rider had accustomed to jump both into, and out of, the fort, over its walls. So regular were the leaps which that famous animal could take, that he invariably alighted at the distance of a mile from the fort, and at the same place. On the very day on which the princess had admitted young Azru into the fort, King Shiribadat was out hunting, of which he was desperately fond and to which he used sometimes to devote a week or two at a time. We must now return to Azru, whom we have left conversing with the princess. Azru remained silent when the lady confessed her love. Urged to declare his sentiments, he said that he would not marry her unless she bound herself to him by the most stringent oath; this she did, and *they became in the sight of God, as if they were wedded man and wife.*[*] He then announced that he had come to destroy her father, and asked her to kill him herself. This she refused; but as she had sworn to aid him in every way she could, he finally induced her to promise that she would ask her father where his *soul was*. 'Refuse food,' said Azru, 'for three or four days, and your father, who is devotedly fond of you, will ask for the reason of your strange conduct; then say, 'Father, you often stay away from me for several days at a time, and I get distressed lest something should happen to you; do reassure me by letting me know where your soul is, and let me feel certain that your life is safe.' This the princess promised to do, and when her father returned refused food for several days. The anxious Shiribadat made enquiries, to which she replied by making the already named request. The tyrant was for a few moments thrown into mute astonishment, and finally refused compliance with her preposterous demand. The love-smitten lady went on starving herself, till at last her father, fearful for his daughter's life, told her not to fret herself about him as his *soul was* [*of snow?*] *in the snows*, and that he could only perish by fire. The princess communicated this information to her lover. Azru went back to Dayur and the villages around and assembled his faithful peasants. These he asked to take twigs of the fir-tree or *chi*, bind them together, and light them—then to proceed in a body with torches to the castle in a circle, keep close together, and surround it on every side. He then went and dug out a very deep hole, as deep as a well, in the place where Shiribadat's horse used to alight, and covered it with green boughs. The next day he received information that the torches (*Lo'o* in Gilgiti and *Lomo* in Astori) were ready. He at once ordered the villagers gradually to draw near the fort in the manner which he had already indicated.

"King Shiribadat was then sitting in his castle; near him his treacherous daughter, who was so soon to lose her parent. All at once he exclaimed, 'I feel very warm; go out, dearest, and see what has happened.' The girl went out and saw torches approaching from a distance, but fearing it to be something connected with the plans of her husband, she went back and said it was nothing. The torches came nearer and nearer, and the tyrant became exceedingly restless. 'Air, air,' he cried, 'I feel very, very ill; do see, daughter, what is the matter.' The dutiful lady went and returned with the same answer as before. At last the torch-bearers had fairly surrounded the fort, and Shiribadat, with a presentiment of impending danger, rushed out of the room, saying 'that he felt he was dying.' He then ran to the stables and mounted his favourite charger, and with one blow of the whip made him jump over the wall of the castle. Faithful to its habit, the noble animal alighted at the same place, but alas! only to find itself engulfed in a treacherous pit. Before the king had time to extricate himself, the villagers had run up with their torches. 'Throw them upon him,' cried Azru. With one accord all the blazing wood was thrown upon Shiribadat, who miserably perished. Azru was then most enthusiastically proclaimed king, celebrated his nuptials with the

[*] The story of the famous horse, the love-making between Azru and the Princess, the manner of their marriage, and other incidents connected with the expulsion of the tyrant, deserve attention.

their tyrant, and, as sole tribute, exacted the offering of one sheep, instead of that of a human child, annually from every one of the natives.* This custom has prevailed down to the present day, and the people of Gilgit, wherever they be, celebrate their delivery from the rule of a monster, and the inauguration of a more humane Government, in the month preceding the beginning of winter—a month which they call [illegible]—after the full moon is over and the new moon has set in. The day of this national celebration is called '[illegible],' the 'feast of fire.' The day generally follows four or five days after the meat provision for the winter has been laid in to dry. A few days of rejoicing precede the special festivity, which takes place at night. Then all the villagers go forth, having a torch in their hands, which, at the sound of music, they swing round their heads, and throw in the direction of Gilgit, if they are at any distance from that place; whilst the people of Gilgit throw it indifferently about the place in which that town, if town it may be called, is situated. When the throwing away of the torches is over, every man returns to his home, when a curious custom is observed. He finds the door locked. The wife then asks, 'Where have you been all night? I won't let you come in now.' Then her husband entreats her and says, 'I have brought you property and children, and happiness, and anything you desire.' Then after some further parley, the door is opened and the husband walks in. He is, however, stopped by a beam which goes across the room, whilst all the females of the family [illegible] to the eldest lady of the place. The [illegible] then [illegible] and [illegible], when the [illegible] into the following song:

Ma tatt [illegible] wai [illegible] [illegible],
Ma tatt [illegible] wai [illegible] [illegible].
Ma tatt [illegible] wai [illegible] [illegible].†
Ma tatt [illegible] wai [illegible] [illegible].
Ma tatt [illegible] wai [illegible] [illegible]
Ma tatt [illegible] [illegible] [illegible] [illegible]
Ma tatt [illegible], wai [illegible] [illegible].
[illegible] [illegible] [illegible] [illegible]
Ma tatt [illegible], wai [illegible] [illegible],
[illegible] [illegible] [illegible]

Translation.—

Thou hast made me glad? thou favourite of the Raja!
Thou hast rejoiced me, oh [illegible]!
I am pleased with thee who so well [illegible]!
Thou hast delighted me, oh thou who art invested with a mantle (of honour)!
Oh great happiness! I will buy it all by giving pleasure's price.
Oh thou [illegible] a heap of [illegible] and a [illegible] of ghee!
Delighted will I buy it all by giving pleasure's price!

My [illegible] thou made glad [illegible]!
Rejoicing, pleasure's price giving, I will buy."

"Then the husband [illegible] and steps over the partition beam. They all sit down, dine together, and thus end the festivities of the '[illegible].' The little domestic scene is not observed at Gilgit; but it is thought to be an essential element in the celebration of the day by people whose ancestors may have been residents of the Gilgit Raja [illegible], and by whom they may have been dismissed to their homes with costly presents.

"The song itself is, however, well-known at Gilgit.

"When [illegible] had safely secured the throne, he ordered the tyrant's place to be levelled to the ground. The willing peasants, manufacturing spades of iron, (*[illegible]*,) [illegible] to accomplish a grateful task, and sang whilst demolishing his castle —

[illegible] [illegible] [illegible] [illegible] [illegible]
[I am] hard and [illegible] and [illegible] my [illegible]!
[illegible] [illegible] [illegible] [illegible]
[illegible] [illegible] Khuon [is] hard;
[illegible] [illegible] [illegible] [illegible] [illegible] [illegible]
[With] this [illegible] spade the [illegible] [illegible] I [illegible]
[illegible] [illegible] [illegible] [illegible] [illegible] [illegible]
[illegible] [illegible] [illegible] [illegible] [illegible] [illegible],
[illegible] [illegible] [illegible] [illegible] [illegible]
[illegible] [illegible] [with] this [illegible] [illegible]
[illegible] [illegible] [illegible] [illegible], [illegible]!
[illegible] [illegible] [illegible] [illegible], [illegible]?

Translation.

"'My nature is of a hard metal,' said [illegible] and [illegible]. 'Why hard? I Khuon, the son of the peasant [illegible], am [illegible] hard; with this iron spade I [illegible] to the ground thy haughty house. [illegible] now, although there art of [illegible] [illegible], of [illegible], [illegible] [illegible]'s son, one of a hard metal; for with this iron spade I [illegible] thy very palace; look out! look out!'"

During the [illegible] [evidently because it is not a national festival] and the [illegible] [illegible] [illegible] [illegible] [illegible] [illegible] [illegible] song. [illegible] are [illegible] in different colours, and people go about [illegible] themselves by trying which eggs are hardest, by striking the end of one against the end of another. The [illegible] of the hardest egg wins the broken one. The women, however, amuse themselves on those days by tying ropes to trees and swinging themselves about on them.

E.—LEGENDS RELATING TO ANIMALS.

1.—*A Bear and a Corpse.*

It is said that bears, as the winter is coming on, are in the habit of filling their dens with grass, and that they eat a plant called *[illegible]*, which has an narcotic effect upon them and keeps them in a state

---

* Possibly this legend is one of the causes of the unfounded reputation of cannibalism which was given by [illegible] and others to the Dards before 1866, and if [illegible] one Dardu tribe accuses another, with which even if it should reside in a neighbouring valley, it may have no intercourse. I refer elsewhere to the custom of drinking a portion of the blood of an enemy, to which my own Kafirs [illegible].

† Evidently a modern interpolation.

‡ Elsewhere called "[illegible]" by [illegible] [illegible].

of torpor during the winter. After three months, when the spring arrives, they awake and go about for food. One of these bears once scented a corpse, which he disinterred. It happened to be that of a woman who had died a few days before. The bear, who was in good spirits, brought her to his den, where he set her upright against a stone, and fashioning a spindle with his teeth and paws, gave it to her into one hand, and placed some wool in the other. He then went on growling "mā-mā-mā" to encourage the woman to spin. He also brought her some nuts and other provisions to eat. Of course, his efforts were useless, and when she, after a few days, gave signs of decomposition he ate her up in despair. This is a story based on the playful habits of the bear.

2.—*A Bear Marries a Girl.*

Another curious story is related of a bear. Two women, a mother and her little daughter, were one night watching their field of Indian corn (*makkay*,) against the inroads of these animals. The mother had to go to her house to prepare the food, and ordered her daughter to light a fire outside. Whilst she was doing this, a bear came and took her away. He carried her into his den, and daily brought her to eat and to drink. He rolled a big stone in front of the den, whenever he went away on his short [illegible] which the girl was not strong enough to remove. When she became old enough to be able to do this he used daily to lick her feet, by which they became swollen and gradually dwindled down to mere shapeless stumps. The girl who had become of age, had to endure the caresses of her guardian by whom she eventually became pregnant. She died in child-birth, and the poor bear, after vain efforts to restore her to life, roamed disconsolately about the fields.

3.—*Origin of Bears.*

It is said that bears were originally the offspring of a man who was driven into madness by his inability to pay his debts, and who took to the hills in order to avoid his creditors.*

4.—*The Bear and the one-eyed Man.*

The following story was related by a man of the name of Ghulám Shah, residing at a village near *Astór*, called Parishing. He was one night looking out whether any bear had come into his *troosho* (field).† He saw that a bear was there, and that he, with his forepaws, alternately took a pawful of *troosho*, blew the chaff away, and ate it heartily. The man was one-eyed (also blind; [illegible] Ghilghiti [illegible] *Kyor* which he said was a Persian word, but which is evidently Turkish) and ran to his hut to get his gun. He came out and pointed it at the bear. The animal, who saw this, ran round the blind side of the man's face, snatched the gun out of his hand and threw it away. The bear and the man then wrestled for a time, but afterwards both gave up the struggle and retired. The man, after he had recovered himself, went to look for the gun, the stock of which he found broken. The match-string by which the stock had been tied to the barrel had gone on burning all night and had been the cause of the gun being destroyed. The son of that man still lives at the village, and tells this story which the people affect to believe.

5.—*Wedding Festival among Bears.*

A Mulla of the name of Lal Muhammad, said that when he was taken a prisoner into Chilas,‡ he and his escort passed one day through one of the loneliest portions of the mountains of that inhospitable [illegible]. There they heard a noise, and quietly approaching to ascertain its cause, they saw a company of bears tearing up the grass and making bundles of it which they [illegible]. Other [illegible] wrapped their heads in grass, and some stood on their hindpaws, holding a stick in their forepaws, and dancing to the sound of the howls of the others. They then ranged themselves in rows, at each end of which was a young bear; on one side a male, on the other a female. These were supposed to celebrate their marriage on the occasion in question. My informant swore to the story, and my Ghilghiti corroborated the truth of the first portion of the account, which he said described a practice held [illegible] to be common to bears.

6.—*The Flying Porcupine.*

There is a curious superstition with regard to an animal called *Hargin* which appears to be more like a porcupine than anything else. It is covered with bristles, its back is of a reddish-brown, and its belly of a yellowish colour. The animal is supposed to be very dangerous, and to contain poison in its bristles. At the approach of any man or animal, it is said to gather itself up for a terrific jump into the air, from which it descends, so as to [illegible] the head of the intended victim. It is said to be generally

---

* The scrupulousness of the Dards in discharging such obligations, when contracted with a member of the same race, is said to be notorious.

† Troosho—Indian corn which must be ground into flour, then boiled in water and placed in the "chandi" [in Astori] or "pepish" [Ghilghiti] a receptacle under the hearth, and has to be kept in this place for one night, after which it is fit for use after being roasted or put on a stove (pan) like a chapati (a thin cake of unleavened bread) [illegible] or [illegible]—[illegible].

‡ Almost every third man I met had, at some time or other, been kidnapped, and dragged off either to Chilas, Chitral, Hindustan, or Bukhara. The surveillance, however, which is exercised over prisoners, as they are being moved by guides over mountains, cannot be a very effective one and, therefore, many of these escape. Some of the Kashmir Maharaja's own sepoys invaded [illegible], had been captured and had escaped. They narrated many stories of the cruelty of these mountaineers, e.g., that they used their captives as [illegible] &c. in order to relieve public [illegible]. Even if this be true, there can be no doubt that the sepoys retaliated in the severest manner whenever they had an opportunity, and the only acts of barbarism that came under my observation, during the war with the tribes in 1866, were committed by the invaders.

about half a yard long and a span broad. Our friend Lal Muhammad, a saintly Akhunzada, but a regular Munchausen, affirmed that he once met with a curious incident with regard to that animal. He was out shooting one day, when he saw a stag, which seemed to look intently in one direction. He fired off his gun, which, however, did not divert the attention of the stag. At last he found out what it was that the stag was looking at. It turned out to be a huge *Hargin* which had swallowed a large *Markhor* with the exception of his horns! There was the porcupine, out of whose mouth protruded the head and horns of the *Markhor*!! My Ghilgiti, on the contrary, said that the *Hargin* was a great snake "like a big fish called *Nang*." Perhaps, *Hargin* means a monster or dragon, and is applied to different animals in the two countries of Ghilgit and Astor.

7.—A Fight between Wolves and a Bear who wanted to dig their Graves.

A curious animal something like a wolf is also described. The species is called *Kô*. These animals are like dogs; their snouts are of a red colour, and are very long; they hunt in herds of ten or twenty, and track game which they bring down,—one herd or one Kô, as the case may be, relieving the other at certain stages. A Shikari once reported that he saw a large number of them asleep. They were all ranged in a single long line. A bear approached, and by the aid of a long branch measured the line. He then went to some distance, and measuring the ground, dug it out to the extent of the line in length. He then went back to measure the breadth of the sleeping troop, when his branch touched one of the animals, which at once jumped up and roused the others. They all then pursued him and brought him down. Some of them harassed him in front, whilst one of them went behind him and sucked his stomach clean out at once. This seems to be a favourite method of these animals in destroying game. They do not attack men, but bring down horses, sheep, and goats.

II.—BIJONI—RIDDLES, PROVERBS AND FABLES.

A.—RIDDLES.

1. The Navel.—*Tichhiroyo sabkirey kaiti*."—"The perpendicular mountain's sparrow's nest—the body's sparrow's hole."

2. A Stick.—*May sasiâ kâyu, sáree poriyu, kâs dáre pató kâju*.*—"Now listen! My sister walks in the day-time and at night stands behind the door;" as *Sás*, sister also means a stick, ordinarily called *kunali* in Astori, the riddle means: 'I have a stick which assists me in walking by day and which I put behind the door at night.'

* Words inviting attention, such as "listen," "explain," &c., &c., are generally put at the end of riddles.

3. The Ghilgitis say '*may kâko tré pay; dushùs*'—'my brother has three feet; explain now.' This means a man's two legs and a stick.

4. A Radish.—*Astori mâ dádo dunn dine-lok; dâyu sarpe-lok, kaje.* My grandfather's body [is] in Hades, his beard [is in] the world; [now] explain!

This riddle is explained by 'a radish,' whose body is in the earth and whose sprouts, compared to a beard, are above the ground. Remarkable above all, however, is that the unknown future state, referred to in this riddle, should be called, whether blessed or cursed, "Dewaloh" (the place of gods) by these nominal Muhammadans. This world is called "Sarpaloh,"—the world of serpents. "Sarpe" is also the name for man, *loh* is "place," but the name by itself is not at present understood by the Shins.

5. A Hooka.—*G. May Dadi shishá(?) agár, käpras*,—'My father's mother on her head fire is burning.' The top of the hooka is the *dadi's* or grandmother's head.

6. A Sword.—*Tshány gúlijo rúi nikai*—'Darkness from the house, the female demon is coming out,' *i.e.* "out of the dark sheath the beautiful, but destructive, steel issues." It is remarkable that the female Yach should be called *Rúi*.

7. Red Pepper.—*Lolo kalaro sha shá ká kâ—kâje!* 'In the red sheep's pen white young ones are many—attend!' This refers to the red pepper husk in which there are many white seeds.

B.—PROVERBS.

8. Dotage.—To an old man people say,—*Tû jarro mûte [illegible]*—thou and old brains delivered. "You are old and have got rid of your senses." Old women are very much dreaded and are accused of creating mischief wherever they go.

9. Duties to the aged—(*Gh.*†) *Juwani [illegible] diguas, jarvale [illegible]*.—In youth's time I gave, in old age I demand. "When young I gave away, now that I am old you should support me."

10. A burnt child, &c.—*Ek dam agáre dáh dagáni shang thé!*—Once in fire you have been burnt, a second time take care!

11. Evil Communications, &c.—*Ek kácho [illegible] bile [illegible] the*.—One bad sheep if there be, to the whole flock is an insult.—"One rotten sheep spoils the whole flock."

12. *Ek kácho manújo [illegible] the*;—'one bad man is to all an insult.'

13. Advice to keep good company.—

A mishta manújo—kaski bayu, to mishta shiki.

Kacho manújo—kaski bayu, to kacho sikhe.

When you [who are bad?] sit near a good man you learn good things: When you sit beside a bad man you learn bad things. This proverb is not very intelligible, if literally translated.

† The abbreviations "G." and "A." stand respectively for "in the Ghilgiti dialect" and "in the Astori dialect."

14. Dimtal [illegible] to [illegible], &c.—*[illegible]*.—"Tell me—my friend is such and such a one, I will tell you who you are."

15. Disappointment.—*[illegible]*.—"He went to acquire horns and got his ears cut off."

16. How to treat an enemy. *[illegible]*—"give the daughter and cut the son," is a Ghilghit proverb with regard to how one ought to treat an enemy. The recommendation given is "marry your daughter to your foe and then kill him," by which you get a male's head which is more valuable than that of a female. The [illegible] have sometimes acted on this maxim in order to lull the suspicions of their Kashmir enemies.*

C.—Fables.

17. The woman and the hen.—*[illegible]*.—A woman had a hen; it used to lay one golden egg; the woman thought that if she gave it much food it would lay two eggs; but she lost even the one, for the hen died, its stomach bursting.

Moral.—*[illegible]*. To gain much the little is lost.

18. The Sparrow and the Mountain.—"*[illegible]*." A sparrow having tried to kick the mountain himself toppled over."

19. The bat supporting the Heavens.—The bat is in the habit of sleeping on its back. It is believed to be very proud. It is supposed to say as it lies down and stretches its legs towards heaven,—"This I do so that when the heavens fall down I may be able to support them."

[illegible]
A bat at night sleeping its legs upwards heaven-
wards them; *[illegible]*
ward them; the heavens when falling with my feet
support them.
uphold I will.

20. "Never walk behind a horse or before a king"—as you will get kicked in either case.
[illegible].
Horse behind not walk; raja in front not walk.

21. Union is Strength.—"A kettle cannot balance itself on one stone; on three however it does.
[illegible]
On one I one stone on a kettle not stops; three
[illegible]
stones on a kettle stops.
The Ghilghitis instead of *[illegible]*—"upon," say *[illegible]*.
[illegible] is, I believe, used for a stone [ordinarily *[illegible]*] only in the above proverb.

22. The Frog in a Dilemma.—"If I speak, the water will rush into my mouth, and if I keep silent I will die bursting with rage."

This was said by a frog who was in the water and angry at something that occurred. If he croaked, he would be drowned by the water rushing down his throat, and if he did not croak he would burst with suppressed rage. This saying is often referred to by women when they are angry with their husbands, who may, perhaps, beat them, if they say anything. A frog is called *[illegible]*.
[illegible]‡ *[illegible]*§ *[illegible]*
When I do—if mouth in water will come; and die
[illegible]
then bursting I will die.

23. The Fox and the universe.—When a man threatens a lot of people with impossible enemies, the reply often is—"Don't act like the fox *[illegible]* who was carried away by the water." A fox one day fell into a river, as he was swept past the shore he cried out, "The water is carrying off the universe." The people on the banks of the river said, "We can only see a fox whom the river is drifting down."

24. The fox and the pomegranate.—
[illegible]
The fox, the pomegranate not reached on account *[illegible]*
sour spitting it is sour.

"The fox wanted to eat pomegranates; as he could not reach them, he went to a distance, and biting his lips [as *[illegible]* was explained by an Astori, although Ghilghitis call it *[illegible]*] spat on the ground, saying, they are too sour." I venture to consider the conduct of this fox more amusing than the one of "sour grapes" memory. His biting his lips and, in consequence, spitting on the ground, would make his disappointed face really look as if he had tasted something sour.

REVIEWS.

Rude Stone Monuments in all Countries; their Age and Uses. By James Fergusson, D.C.L., F.R.S., V.P.R.A.S., F.R.I.B.A., &c., with 234 Illustrations, 540 pp. 8vo. London: John Murray, 1872.

For more than a quarter of a century Mr. Fergusson has been an indefatigable worker in the history of the architecture of all ages and countries, and so thoroughly has he made this branch of investigation his own, and so well has he unravelled the principles of its development, that almost singlehanded he may be said to have founded the science of Comparative Architecture. Indian Architecture,

* Not very many years ago, the Ghilghit [illegible] in attacking [illegible] used to consider [illegible] if they had [illegible] more [illegible] than they had lost.

† "[illegible]" [illegible] is pronounced like "[illegible]."

‡ *[illegible]* mouth; [illegible]—in the mouth; [illegible]—against the mouth.

§ *[illegible]* mouth; [illegible]—in the mouth; [illegible]—against the mouth.

as a study, owes almost everything to him, and since the publication of his "Illustrations of the Rock-Cut Temples of India" in 1845, to the present day, his interest in it and his zeal for its thorough investigation has steadily increased. But few of the many contributions he has made to the cause of his favourite science promise to be more important in their ultimate bearing than the service he has just rendered by the publication of his "Rude Stone Monuments."

The age of the Monuments treated of has long been a mystery, and of late the tendency has been to relegate them almost without exception to "prehistoric" times. Mr. Fergusson, however, is justly dissatisfied with all the theories on this point broached during the last two centuries. Stukeley, as he remarks, "cut the vessel adrift from the moorings of common sense, and she has since been a derelict tossed about by the winds and waves of every passing fancy, till recently, when an attempt has been made to tow the wreck into the misty haven of prehistoric antiquity. If ever she reaches that unknown region, she may as well be broken up in despair, as she can be of no further use for human purposes." Further, as he remarks elsewhere, some of these remains cannot belong to prehistoric, while the others belong to the historic period ;—"all belong to the one epoch or to the other. Either it is that Stonehenge and Avebury and all such are the temples of a race so ancient as to be beyond the ken of mortal man, or they are the sepulchral monuments of a people who lived so nearly within the limits of true historic times, that their story can easily be recovered." And if the author has proved any point, it is that most of the European remains of this class have been erected since the Christian era, and most of those in England, at least, between the fifth and tenth centuries. Stonehenge, for example, belongs to the period of the struggle between the Saxons and the Britons under Ambrosius, and most probably to the years 466 to 470 A. D. The argument he advances is backed by the results of extensive reading, and from the cumulative character of the evidence becomes very powerful. And it perhaps deserves all the more attention because the results are not those of predilection :—"When I first took up the subject," says Mr. Fergusson in his preface, "I hoped that the rude stone monuments would prove to be old,—so old, indeed as to form the 'incunabula' of other styles, and that we might thus, by a simple process, arrive at the genesis of styles. Bit by bit that theory has crumbled to pieces as my knowledge increased, and most reluctantly have I been forced to adopt the more prosaic conclusions of the present volume. If, however, this represents the truth, that must be allowed to be an ample compensation for the loss of any poetry which has hitherto hung round the mystery of the Rude Stone Monuments." Regarding these monuments—whether Tumuli, Dolmens or Cromlechs, Circles, Avenues, or Menhirs,—Mr. Fergusson sets himself to prove—1st, that they "are generally sepulchral, or connected directly, or indirectly, with the rites of the dead; 2nd, that they are not temples in any usual or appropriate sense of the term; and lastly,—that they were generally erected by partially civilised races after they had [in the west] come in contact with the Romans, and most of them may be considered as belonging to the first ten centuries of the Christian Era."

It is not to be expected that all that the author advances will stand the test of a rigid criticism, or be confirmed by future discoveries, but this book has the great merit of, for the first time, presenting a distinct and positive view of the age or use of these megalithic remains, and if suggestions on many minor points have been offered, which it might be difficult to establish by proof, he avows he has put them forth—"because it often happens that such suggestions turn the attention of others to points which would otherwise be overlooked, and may lead to discoveries of great importance ; while if disproved, they are only so much rubbish swept out of the path of truth, and their detection can do no harm to any one but their author." We need scarcely add that a writer who has added so much to our knowledge can afford to be corrected if it should turn out that on some minor point he has not divined the truth.

We cannot attempt to follow the author over the whole of the British Isles, Scandinavia and North Germany, France—so rich in these remains, Southern Europe, Northern Africa, the Mediterranean Islands, and Western Asia, in all of which regions such monuments are found ; but we must pause at India to make a few brief extracts.

"The number of rude-stone monuments in India," says Mr Fergusson, "is probably as great as even greater than that of those to be found in Europe, and they are so similar that, even if they should not turn out to be identical, they form a most important branch of this enquiry. Even irrespective, however, of these, the study of the history of architecture in India is calculated to throw so much light on the problems connected with the study of megalithic monuments in the West that, for that reason alone, it deserves much more attention than it has hitherto received."

The first tribe noticed as erecting rude-stone monuments are the Khasias, in whose country they 'exist in greater numbers than perhaps in any other portion of the globe of the same extent. All travellers who have visited the country have been struck with the fact and with the curious similarity of their forms to those existing in Europe." . . . . "The natives make no mystery about them, and many were erected within the last few years, or are being erected now, and they are identical in form with those which are grey with years, and must have been set up in the long forgotten past." The top of one dolmen "measured 30 feet 4 inches by 10 feet in breadth, and had an average thickness of 1 foot,"

—this great stone weighed 23 tons 16 cwt., and another is described as still larger, probably weighing about 40 tons, and others are of nearly the same dimensions. These "are frequently raised some height from the ground, and supported on massive monoliths or pillars.

"While this is so, we need not wonder at the means employed in the erection of Stonehenge or Avebury, or any of our European monuments. Physically the Khasias are a very inferior race to what we can conceive our forefathers ever to have been. Their stage of civilization is barely removed from that of mere savages, and their knowledge of the mechanical arts is of the most primitive description. Add to all this that their country is mountainous and rugged in the highest degree. Yet with all these disadvantages they move these great stones, and erect them with perfect facility, while we are lost in wonder, because our forefathers did something nearly equal to it some fourteen centuries ago."

In Western India "there are some groups of rude-stone monuments similar to those found in the Khasia hills, and apparently erected for similar purposes. They are, however, much less perfectly known, and are described, or at least drawn, by only one traveller.* The most conspicuous of these is one near Belgâm. It consists of two rows of thirteen stones each, and one in front of them of three stones—the numbers being always uneven, as in Bengal—and on the opposite side four of those small altars, or tables, which always accompany these groups of stones on the Khasia hills. These, however, are very much smaller, the central stone being only about 4 feet high, and falling off to about a foot in height at the end of each row."

When we turn to the sepulchral arrangements of the aboriginal tribes of India, the analogies to those of western Europe "are so striking that it is hard to believe they are accidental, though equally hard to understand how and when the intercourse could have taken place which led to their similarity." The examples adduced by the author are certainly very remarkable.

As the writer remarks—"nothing would tend more to convey clear ideas on the subject of Indian dolmens than a map of their distribution, were it possible to construct one . . . The following sketch, however, is perhaps not very far from the truth regarding them. They do not exist in the valley of the Ganges, or of any of its tributaries, nor in the valleys of the Narmadâ or Tâpî, nor, in fact, in that part of India which is generally described as north of the Vindhya range of hills. They exist, though somewhat sparsely, over the whole of the country drained by the Godâverî and its affluents. They are very common, perhaps more frequent than in any other part of India, in the valleys of the Krishna and its tributaries. They are also found on both sides of the Ghâts, through Koimbatur, all the way down to Cape Comorin; and they are also found in groups all over the Madras presidency, but especially in the neighbourhood of Conjiveram."

To help towards clearing up the question as to the race of the Indian dolmen builders, as well as to throw light on other points connected with the history of Indian architecture in all its stages, we need to know more than we do of the Haidarâbâd territory. As Mr. Fergusson states,—"In so far as the history or ethnography of the central plateau of India is concerned, or its arts or architecture, the Nizam's dominions are absolutely a *terra incognita*. No one has visited the country who had any knowledge of these subjects, and the Indian Government has done nothing to enquire, or to stimulate enquiry, into these questions in that country. Yet, if I am not very much mistaken, the solution of half the difficulties, ethnological or archæological, that are now perplexing us, lies on the surface of that region, for any one who will take the trouble to read them. Till this is done, we must, it is feared, be content with the vaguest generalities."

Leaving these extracts, to speak for themselves, we commend this beautiful and most instructive volume to all who have any real taste for the scientific study of antiquities, in the hope that it will give a fresh and powerful stimulus to research in a field almost new in India and of uncommon interest.

Ruins of the Nalanda Monasteries, at Burgâon, Sub-Division Behar, Zillah Patna. By A. M. Broadley, Esq., Assistant Magistrate and Collector, Patna. [illegible] pp. 8vo. Calcutta, 1872.

Mr. Broadley is an enthusiastic and energetic archæologist, and is, by good fortune, located in the district which, beyond all others, is the richest in India in historic associations and ancient Buddhist remains. His contributions to our pages testify to his earnestness and ability, and this little brochure illustrated with two plates—of an excavated temple at Burgâon, and of a sketch plan of the ruins there, with ten lithographs of inscriptions—is further proof of the extent and thoroughness of his researches. Printed unfortunately at a distance from its author, it is disfigured by many typographical errors. The account of the excavations undertaken by Mr. Broadley occupies little more than 10 pages, and is followed by the description of fully seventy Hindu and Buddhist sculptures found in the ruins; then follows an inscription on a door, in his remarks on which we fear Mr. Broadley has been misled as to a date, which his translator seems to fancy is concealed in the words *agni-naga-srâva*, and which

---

* Colonel Forbes Leslie, 'Early Races of Scotland,' vol. II. pls. [illegible]. They have also been described by Dr. Stevenson, 'J. R. A. S.' vol. V. pp. 192 et seqq. It would be extremely interesting in an ethnographic point of view, if some further information could be obtained regarding these stone rows.

he makes 919 of the Samvat of Vikramâditya. The date is probably either the 1st or 11th of the reign of Śrimat Mahîpâla Deva of Bengal. We hope the examples of Mr. Bradley and the late Mr. Boswell of the Madras Civil Service will be followed by many others, each in his own province adding something to our knowledge of the antiquities of the country.

MISCELLANEA.

THE SEA OF MEWAR.

It is not often that a white face is seen on the *band* at Debar, albeit that marble structure possesses no equal as historians say. The main road through Mewar leads not past Debar, hence the limited number who see those fine places in which the heroes revel, or those placid bays in which sport fish of no great flavour but of enormous size, and alligators said to be possessed of an unbounded stomach.

Travellers wishing to visit the Debar Lake must leave the Ahmadabad and Udepur road at Prasâd, a small *pal*, or village, some twenty miles from Khârwâra. From Prasâd to Debar the way is rough, but on every hand beautiful jungle and beautiful birds fascinate the eye of the artist and the sportsman. A long and narrow *nâl*, or pass, winds round the foot of the great hill at Prasâd, one of the stations of the Trigonometrical Survey of India. Then the road opens out to the plain of Chappan, the South-West Province of Mewar. Chawand, the principal village, is reached in about an hour and a half from Prasâd. Chawand is perhaps hardly worthy of being remembered, except for the circumstance that it at one time afforded refuge to the great Pratâp, the patriot Rânâ of Udepur. At Chawand he lived, after having been driven from the hill fort of Kumalmer, by the treachery of the Thakur of Mount Abu. At Chawand, Pratâp cut to pieces the army of Khan Farid, the trusted general of Akbar, rolling back the tide of invasion towards the plains, and proving to the great Emperor of Dehli that some valour yet remained in the hills of the Rajputs. The ruins of an old palace and fort rise from a ridge a short distance from the village, and here and there stands a fine *chhatrî*, or temple, to show that a large population once occupied the place.

Ten or twelve miles from Chawand, towards the north-west, is the Debar Lake. A few ruined towers, palaces, and temples beyond the village of Jharol are first noticeable, and then the fine palace overlooking Debar itself meets the eye. The whole of the northern side of the plain is bounded by an immense rocky natural wall; towards the east end alone can you discover a break. Across this, a massive barrier of stone has been thrown to keep the waters of the Lake within the bounds prescribed for them by the machinations of man and nature combined. A great pool always existed towards the North: its waters escaped by a large and noble stream through the "fault" in the range. Jaisingh, the ruler of Mewar, about the year 1681, when all his resources were taxed to the utmost, and while Aurangzeb pressed him hard, still found means of executing this splendid work. The name "Jaya-Samudra," or "Sea of Victory," which he gave to the former pool of Debar, served a double purpose: it served alike to celebrate the triumph over the forces of nature, and to immortalize the designer. The enormous proportions of the grand wall strike the observer with wonder and admiration. The outer embankment, 380 paces in length, and some sixty or seventy feet in height, rises abruptly from the plain. A road cut on the left side of the hill leads to the top. Massive stones, one piled above the other, form the wall; yet time has not been idle.

It is a long pull to the top of the inner band. But, once you are there, a view opens out before you which well rewards your toil. You stand upon a magnificent rampart: below you, steps stretch away to the water's edge: right and left, are rugged hills, crowned with ruined forts and palaces; and far away before you, stretches the lake until it touches the outlying spurs of the mighty Aravalis. Islands and hills covered with verdure, [illegible] silent beneath the glorious sky, marble temples, palaces, and terraces on the *band* itself, with the water dashing underneath—where could you look for a more lovely scene! Yet how seldom has an English eye gazed upon it! Thirty-seven steps, by three flights, descend to the water. Pavilions of marble stand at each end of the band, their roofs supported by thirty-two columns. In the space between the two, rises a splendidly carved quadrangular temple; the building has never been completed, yet it is magnificent even now. Eight small *chhatrîs*, once surmounted by domes, fill up the intervening parts, each of these buildings standing upon the uppermost of a tier of platforms. Elephants rear up near the palaces; their trunks are some twelve or fifteen feet above the level of the water. The natives say that when the water in the lake rises so far as to lave these elephants' trunks, an opening in the hills allows the overflow to escape towards the east, upon the plains beneath. In ordinary seasons the rainfall would appear to be some five or six feet below the greatest capacity of the lake. The numerous platforms on the *band* have carved upon them, in bas *relief*, figures of elephants vanquishing wild beasts; and all around the [illegible] stones upon which the images of the gods, in good condition, are engraved. Every stone in the *band* bears upon it the name of the [illegible] mason. In a niche below the great temple is beautifully represented Nârâyana, or Vishnu, reclining on Śesha; the god Brahma springing from a lotus, which rises from his navel, whilst Lakshmî is seated at his feet. It is as though Jaisingh had said —"By the power of the gods this great work has been accomplished; by Vishnu the Preserver, and it shall remain." Yet, alas! as remarked above, neglect bids fair to destroy the noble structure; massive stones have been forced from their places by the roots of the numerous trees and shrubs which spring from every crevice on the steps. The tiger, the panther, and the boar haunt the gardens and palaces of the Lake of Victory, whilst the very lake itself seems anxious to burst its bounds, caring not, apparently, to retain the splendid distinction of being the largest artificial sheet of water in the world.

At the south-west end rises the steeper of the two hills which the embankment unites; on the summit of this hill stands the splendid palace built by Jaisinha for his favourite wife, Umeda Devi, a princess of the Pramara race, strangely also called the Ruta Rani, or "testy queen." She and the elder queen, mother of the heir apparent, naturally quarrelled; and, to make peace, or rather to prevent domestic "scenes," Jaisinha himself retired with his favourite to Dhebar, and lived in seclusion some years of inglorious ease, until the discontent of his regent and heir-apparent at Udaipur compelled him to resume the reins of government. The principal building of the palace rises abruptly from the rock; domes surmount the building, and from these magnificent views can be obtained. Numerous rooms and courts, small and inconvenient, are crowded together. Upon the walls of the apartments devoted to the Rani are paintings still in fair preservation—scenes from the Ramayana, the Great War, &c. A wall of stone surrounds all the attached buildings, as well as the palace itself. On a higher eminence arising from the eastern margin of the principal arm of the lake stands another palace, from the walls of which the grandest view of the lake can be obtained. The greatest length of Dhebar is from east to west, whilst the principal, and deepest arm, runs towards the bund, from the south. This arm is comparatively narrow, so that from the embankment the great mass of water cannot be seen, especially as the view is limited by the presence of a large island stretched across its opening. Away to the north, the waters extend, shut off like arms, almost by the feet of the hills, leaving, as they subside, immense tracts of the finest rice land in Rajputana. In the summer small streams can be seen meandering through the plains, to lose themselves in the lake itself. Twelve villages are dotted along the banks, the inhabitants of which support themselves by cultivation of the soil and fishing, which last is a lively occupation. Casting the eye far away to the south, one can see Salumbra, the home of the most powerful chief present at durbar to do honour to His Highness of Mewar on his installation, and the hereditary councillor of Mewar, whose symbol, the lance, must be borne before every state document that bears his signature.

FAMED RIKHABNATH.

Although Dhebar Lake is so seldom visited, this is not the case with the famous shrine of Rishabhanatha, ten miles south of Frasid, on the Udaipur and Ahmadabad road. Thither flock thousands upon thousands of Hindus from Gujarat, Mewar, Marwar, and all Rajwara, to pay their devotions to the shrine of the presiding lord. Rikhabnath is a walled village in the midst of the hills; it contains numerous houses, and a large dharmasala for the accommodation of strangers. The temple, the centre of attraction, is surrounded by a large stone rampart, and is shut off from the town by successive gates. Tradition states that, nearly a thousand years ago, a husbandman one day found in his field one of his cows giving forth milk lavishly and spontaneously. Upon observation as to why this was, it was ascertained that it occurred only over one spot. There the spade and pick-axe were manfully plied, and there they discovered a statue of the god. Afterwards it was revealed to the priest that it was the wish of the deity to found a home at Rikhabnath. A small temple was first erected; and, as worshippers increased in number, other and more magnificent buildings followed, until the pile is now large, beautiful, and exceedingly wealthy. The Bhil swears by the god, and hence one is led to believe that this is only a temple where Krishna is worshipped under one of his many forms. A large and ancient *naubatkhana* (room for musicians) overhangs the great gate. The temple itself is made up of a series of temples, all connected; in each are images of the Jaina tirthas. Of course the great image is there. The inner shrine is shut off from the rest of the building by gates plated with silver. Each full moon from the *Bhandar*, the high priest brings forth a dress valued at a lakh and a half of rupees, wherewith to deck the god, whilst gold and silver vessels are used in *puja*. All day long devotees lie prostrate before the shrine, whilst others offer saffron upon pillars upon which are engraved impressions of the feet of the god. All the rulers in Rajputana send gifts to Rikhabnath—saffron, jewels, money; and, in return, receive the high priest's blessing.—*Abridged from the Times of India.*

A New Jaina Temple at Palitana.—About three years ago when Mr. Kesavji Nayak, a Bhattia merchant of Bombay, was at Palitana, he contributed Rs 1,00,000 for the erection of a temple there. The temple has now been completed, and the ceremony of opening performed last month.

NOTES AND QUERIES.

Note on Query 2, p. 84.

With regard to Mr. Beames's enquiry as to whether the custom of denoting the months by the signs of the Zodiac prevails in other parts of India, I find that in this part of the country (Hassan District, Mysore) it is the custom among astrologers always to use in documents drawn up by them in addition to the usual month and date, that of the corresponding month according to the "Sankramana" style. For instance the 15th February would be given as the 7th day of the bright half of Mágha, and the 5th day of the month "Kumbha;" the "panchanga" or native almanack gives both styles.

J. S. F. MACKENZIE.

Hassan, 15th Feb. 1872.

Query 4.

Many figures of Buddha holding the bhikshu's bowl, have on the base a monkey making an offering, while another is disappearing, head foremost down a well or bucket! (See plate Jour. Beng. As. Soc. vol. XVI p. 78) What does this mean or allude to?

Bihár, Feb. 6th.

A. M. B.

COPPER-PLATE GRANT of TRIBHUVANA MALLA. A.D. 1083.

Reduced Copy ½ of Original

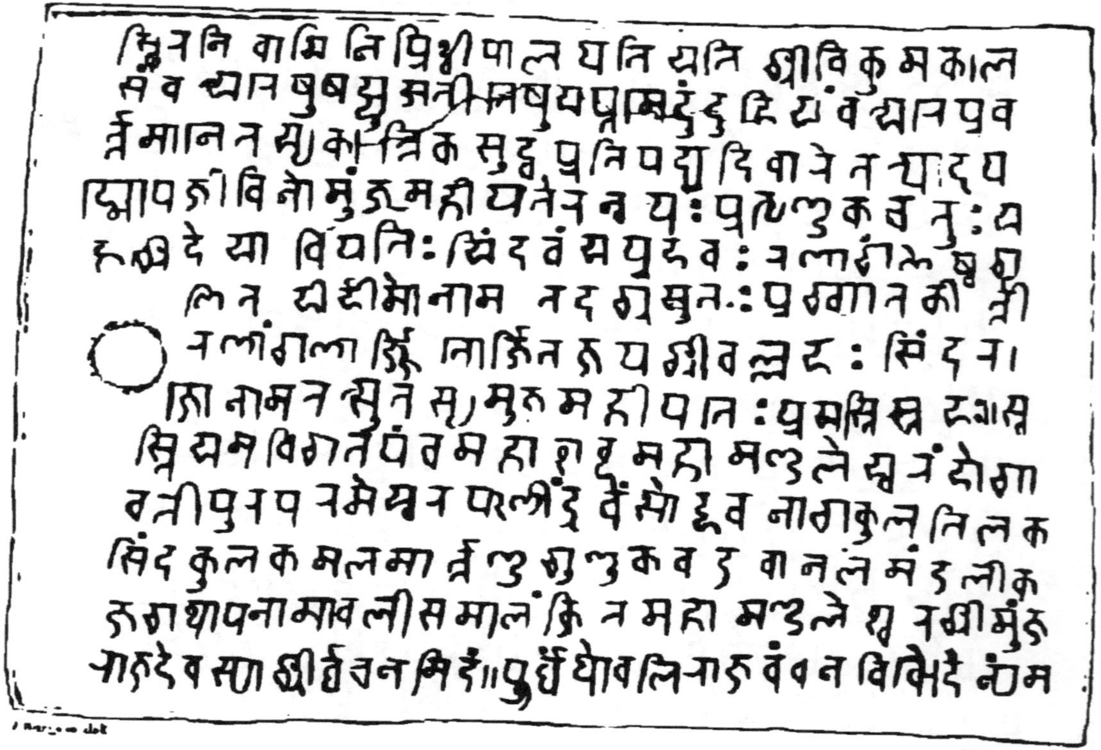

स्थिरनि वामि नि प्रिथ्वीपाल यति यति श्रीविक्रमकाल
संव ध्यान षुषयुक्ती नषुयप्रमुद्रुद्रि यं व ध्यान प्रव
र्त्तमानन म्रा कार्त्तिक सुद्व पुनिपद्य दिवाने न पादप
द्मापद्मी विनो मुंडमही पते रन य: प्रत्येकव नु: प्र
रुक्षदे या विपति: सिंदवं सपुरुव: नलादालेख्रु
लिन घटीमोनाम नदशुसुन: प्रत्यानकी त्री
नलांदाला ठ्ठि लाठिनरुय श्रीवल्लद: सिंदना।
ठ्ठा नामन सुन स्रा मुरु महीपाल: प्रमास्त्रिसूदाास्त्र
स्त्रि यम विठानपं व महा रा टू महा मण्डले स्थनं दोला
वत्ती पुरप नमेयन पालीदु वें सो ढूव नागकुल तिलक
सिंद कुलकमलमार्त्त ण्डु शुण्डुकव ढु वानलमं डलीक
ठणाथापना माव लीसमालं क्रि न महा मण्डले श्रु नश्री मुंठ
नाठदेव सणा श्रीर्थवन मिदं॥ प्रुर्थी धोवलि नाठ वंवन विविमेदे नाम

TAMIL POPULAR POETRY.

BY ROBERT CHARLES CALDWELL, M.R.A.S.

First Paper.

THE number of Europeans in South India possessing a fair knowledge of common Tamil is not inconsiderable. Yet I have always remarked with wonder how few of these have thought it worth their while to make themselves acquainted with one or two of the popular Tamil poets, just to gain thereby a little insight into Hindu customs, Hindu characteristics, Hindu fancies, and Hindu creeds. Now I feel certain that popular Tamil poetry would be far more widely studied by such Tamil-speaking Europeans, were it not for two considerations. In the first place, it is supposed that these poems—merely because they are Tamil poems—do not possess such inherent beauty of thought, fancy, or expression, as we Europeans understand beauty in literary compositions, to repay the labour of their perusal by a cultivated reader acquainted with the splendid and sublime literatures of Europe. In the second place, it is imagined that to peruse, so as to understand and appreciate these poems, is a matter of great difficulty, and that these popular lyrics are couched in the same difficult language as nearly all the great poetical works in Tamil are.

With reference to the latter of these two suppositions, I beg to submit that popular Tamil poetry is written, as a general rule, in clear, plain, mellifluous Tamil. Stanzas here and there may be met with, containing verbal difficulties. But supposing, in the first place, the reader is bent, not upon a critical study of such poems, but upon a lighter course, and merely wishes to run through them for his amusement and information,—then, in the majority of instances, he will find these poems intelligible on their first perusal. Indeed, I have repeatedly noticed that, with scarcely any exceptions, stanzas in the works of popular Tamil poets are most beautiful in the thoughts they contain, when the language in which these thoughts are expressed is simple and not stilted. Poets, such as SIVA VAKKIYAR, PATTANATU PILLAI, and PUTTIRA GIRIYAR generally—as far as it appears to me—betake themselves to difficult phraseology and intricate involutions of style, when they are giving utterance to some trite or trashy sentiment. It seems as if consciousness of poverty and weakness in matter, had the direct effect of urging them to adopt a strained and affected manner.

In the second place, I can assert with confidence, and I trust I shall be able to prove, in this and in a subsequent paper, that Tamil popular poetry is full of really beautiful fancies, similes, metaphors, aphorisms, and thoughts. And I hold—and I trust I shall be able to convince the reader that I am right in holding—that Tamil popular poetry contains gems of art of which any European language might be proud.

In this introductory paper my aim is to prove a portion of this thesis to the best of my ability, without entering at any length into the very wide field of discussion which will present itself in connection with my subject. I shall only take a few—a very few—instances of the beautiful thoughts embodied in poetical language to be found amongst the immense stores at every Tamil scholar's disposal. The difficulty which meets me when about to treat of this subject is, not what specimens of Tamil poetical writing I ought to adopt, but what striking examples I ought not to select. The abundance of materials at my disposal makes me hesitate and almost wish that the garden were smaller from which I have undertaken to cull a few flowers.

But, before proceeding further, I wish the reader to consider one important point regarding my subject. It must be remembered that I am *translating*; and that upon which I base my argument is *translated poetry*. Take up the best translations the English language possesses; take up Chapman's *Homer*, Conington's *Virgil*, or Cary's *Dante*,—suppose these translations had appeared as original poems in English, would they have become celebrated? Perhaps as literary curiosities they might, but would they have passed into the household literature of England and left such a mark upon English literature as their originals have upon the literatures of Greece and of Rome? It is impossible to answer this in the affirmative. And the reason for this lies in the very nature of the case.

In the first place, the subject of such poems is of no national interest to Englishmen. It is like olives—it requires a trained taste in an Englishman to appreciate it, whilst a Greek, or an Italian, might take to it naturally, as it is a natural product of his fatherland. A certain course of education is necessary before an Englishman can appreciate the 'ox-eye' of Athenæ, before he can see any force in Æneas being styled 'father,' and before he can believe in the existence of an Il Purgatorio. And I hope the reader will reflect that if the themes of the poems of Homer, Virgil and Dante do not possess many fascinations for Englishmen, how much less likely are the subjects of the poems of a rude non-European nation to do so. In the second place, the language of Chapman, Connington, and Cary, though undoubtedly very fine, cannot be well supposed to be as good English as Homer's language was good Greek, Virgil's good Latin, and Dante's good Italian. And in my own case, I have keenly and constantly felt, whilst engaged in translating from Tamil popular poems, how utterly impossible it was for me to reproduce the infinite harmonious iteration of sound and sense of the original. I therefore have to ask the reader to judge merely of the poetical thoughts in Tamil popular poetry from my translation; for, if he wishes to ascertain the beauty of the language, he must go to the original and to that alone.

But it has sometimes been considered that there is one certain advantage, amongst many disadvantages, resulting from the judgment of a poet's writings being based upon their accurate translation, and not upon his writings in the original. Without adopting any of the various definitions of poetry, let us consider for a moment what pleases us in any writing and forces our intellectual discriminative faculties to pronounce it *poetry*. The prime source of pleasure always ought to be the *thoughts* contained in the writing—"thoughts that shake mankind,"—original, deep, suggestive, and sublime thoughts,—thoughts fanciful, playful, or grotesque,—thoughts that cheer or thoughts that elevate,—thoughts that in any way exercise a stimulative on the mind of the reader. Such ought to be the prime source of pleasure; but in a great measure it is not. Englishmen now-a-days seem to prefer sound to sense. If a man can dress a trite thought in a novel manner he is a poet. The mysterious utterances of the Delphic Oracle of the past were nothing to the ambiguous phraseology patronised by the Rossettis and Swinburnes of the present. Extraordinary involutions of style, bristling with metaphor and glittering with rhyme, constitute 'poetic diction.' It appears to be the aim of most modern English poets to say a thing "not only as it never has been said before, but as no one else would have been likely to think of saying it." Even a real thinker, like Browning, often clothes his thoughts in language which is anything but plain English. Thus the vicious taste is daily gaining ground in England of regarding the dress more than the person, poetic phraseology more than poetic thought.

But let one of our English poets be translated into a foreign language, or better still, into English prose, and the real value of his writings will be at once apparent. In the crucible of translation all petty adornments of rhyme and rhythm are separated, like dross, from the pure precious metal of the thought. The thought remains, and the reader is obliged to judge by it, and by it alone, of the value of the poet's work, and his real position as one of the sweet singers of the world. "Dryden said of Shakespeare, that if his embroideries were burnt down, there would be silver at the bottom of the melting pot." Göthe says:—"I honour both rhythm and rhyme, by which poetry first becomes poetry; but the properly deep and radical operative—the truly developing and quickening—is that which remains of the poet when he is translated into prose. The inward substance then remains in its purity and fulness; which, when it is absent, a dazzling exterior often deludes with semblance of, and when it is present, conceals."

But, on the other hand, it cannot for a moment be denied that poetic expression is a great gift, a gift necessary to a poet. When beautiful thoughts are couched in beautiful language, there is an additional beauty which springs from the amalgamation of the two. The thought appears lovelier because of the musical language; the language appears lovelier because of the pleasing thought. There is a reflection of bright beauty from one to the other, and this reflection doubles the brilliance which emanates from both. And this is especially the case, so far as regards the thoughts and expressions in the popular poetry of an Asiatic people like the Tamilians. Ardent thoughts are expressed in glowing language: the thoughts breathe of a tropical sky; the words burn with all the fire of oriental imagery.

With these prefatory remarks, I beg to draw the attention of the reader to the following translations from the poems of two Tamil popular poets, SIVAVAKKIYAR and PATTANATTU PILLAI. I have shown these translations to several Tamil scholars. One of the most eminent of such scholars in this Presidency has assured me that, in his estimation, my translation is almost absolutely accurate, although I have written in rhyme. I do not however desire the reader to lay any stress whatever upon this. But I would draw attention to the fact that, in parallel columns with the stanzas of my translation, I have placed the Romanised form of the Tamil text from which I translate. Thus if my translation be in any particular unfaithful, the scholarly reader will be able at once to detect the flaw.

SIVAVAKKIYAM.

Paṇḍu nān parit' eṭutta
 Pū malangal ettanai;
Pāḍi pāḍi vitta
 Mantirangal ettanai;

Tonṇḍanāy vilunt' uruṇḍu
 Kumba kōḍam ettanai;
Tēr iḷukka, vēr alutu,
 Mūr aḷitta ettanai;

Mīṇḍaṇḍy turinta pōtu
 Iraiya vargal ettanai;
Mīlavum Sivālayangal
 Sūlada vandat' ettanai;

Āṇḍavan irupparkalum
 Arint' unarnta gnānigal,
Kaṇḍa kōvil dēvam enḍru
 Kai yeḍuppat' illaiyē.

THE SHEPHERD OF THE WORLDS.

*A Detached Piece from the Poems of Sivavakkiyar.**

How many various flowers
 Did I, in bye-gone hours,
Cull for the god, and in his honour strew;
 In vain how many a prayer
 I breathed into the air,
And made, with many forms obeisance due.

 Beating my breast, aloud
 How oft I called the crowd
To drag the village car; how oft I stray'd
 In manhood's prime to lave
 Sunwards the flowing wave,
And circling Saiva fanes, my homage paid.

 But they, the truly wise,
 Who know and realise [will ne'er
Where dwells the SHEPHERD OF THE WORLDS,
 To any visible shrine,
 As if it were divine,
Deign to raise hands of worship or of prayer.

I would draw the special attention of the reader to these verses. The musical flow of them and their accurate Homeric conclusion cannot be caught in any translation. The beauty of the thoughts they contain, however, must shine through any language. That there may be no misapprehension I shall now give the exact verbal translation of the original.—

"How many various kinds of flowers did I of yore cull and scatter.

How many mantras have I said in vain.

How often, with obeisance, falling, rolling round I accompanied the beautification (of a devotee).

How often have I, beating my breast, called the village to drag the car.

How often, at prime of life, whilst in my wanderings, have I sprinkled water.

How often have I kept encircling Saiva temples.

The wise who have known and inwardly realised the dwelling place of the Shepherd of the Worlds.

To visible temples, as if they were divine, lift their hands—never!"

SIVAVAKKIYAM.

Naṭṭu vaitta dēvarum
 Naḍḍimal vaitta dēvarum,
Suṭṭu vaitta dēvarum
 Suḍḍimal vaitta dēvarum,
Kaṭṭu vaitta dēvarum
 Kaṭṭ' aviḷa vallarō?
Iṭṭa vaitt' iḍattilē
 Kiḍapat' anḍri, yen seyvār?

EXTRACTS FROM THE POEMS OF SIVAVAKKIYAR

Gods set up, Gods not set up,
 Lords baked, and unbaked Lords,
And Deities bound securely
 (To sacred cars) with cords.
Say, are these even able
 To free themselves when tied?
When placed somewhere, what can they
 But in that place abide?

* Notice the beautiful epithet *Shepherd of the Worlds!* This word *Āṇḍavan* is often simply rendered Monarch of the Gods, but I have taken the more magnificent rendering, —a rendering which represents the inner spirit of the original, and which, by the way, has the sanction of my teacher, the Rev. Dr. Caldwell.

Naṭṭu kallai dêvam endru
 Nâlu puṣpam sâttuvîr,
Suttri vantu, muṇu-muṇ' endru,
 Sollum mantram êtadâ?
Naṭṭu kallu pêsumô?
 —Nâtan uḷḷirukkaiyil;
Suṭṭa saṭṭi saṭṭuvam
 Kari suvai ariyumô?

Ousi pottra kallai nîr
 Uḍaiya' mukkal seygirîr,
Pujai* pottra kal atil
 Pûvum nîrum sattuvîr;
Vâsalil padutta kal
 Meḷungavê mettukirîr;
—Iranuḍ' uganta kal
 Iranḍu kallum allavê!

Dêvar dêvar endru nindru
 Têḍukiṛaîr mûḍarkâl,
Dêvar pôvar eṇḍr' ariyâ
 Têḍuvom arikilîr;
Mûvar dêvar endru nîr
 Moḷikiṛaîra? Uṇḍamô?
Mêvatâka ummuḷê
 Viḷittunarntu kollumô.

Kaḷaṭṭai kaṭṭi, ômam ceytu,
 Kaḷuṭṭai annam âkumô?
Paḷuvai kaṭṭra makkaḷâl
 Parama Sivan kartiaṉô?
Meḷuttuḷḷa gnâna rûpa
 Mûrti nimirtu' appuramê,
Yaḍuḷum ilai yanikumê
 Ilay ummum kaḍuntatê.

Aṇu v alla, Avaṉum alla,
 Anavi-u alla,—appuram,
Karumai, veṇmai, vemmaiyum,
 Kaḍanta nindra kâraṇam;
Periyum alla, siriyum alla,
 Peṇṇum âṇum allavê,
Dariśanam kaḍantu nindra—
 Dûra dûra dûramê!

Sâsvâna Tattuva
 Kaḷangu aṟyyum âmaikâl,—
Dêvar kallum avarô?
 Sirippat' andri yen seyvêṉ?

With flowers of bush and creeper,
 Tank-flowers, and flowers from boughs,†
Why deck ye stones, and round them
 Stand, paying mumbled vows?
Can idols speak, though in them
 The Omnipresent dwell?
Say, of the curry's flavour
 Can the pot's ladle tell?

Stones consecrated ye fashion
 To idols; then adore,—
With flowery wreaths adorn them
 With salves smear them o'er:
The stone before your threshold
 Grows worn out, being trod;—
But of these two stones, neither
 Affords delight to God!

Fools! with continual searching,
 "The gods, the gods," ye cry;
Even the way ye know not
 To seek for them whereby.
Tell me, is it religion
 To say "the gods are three"?
To attain to God, within you
 Your search for him must be.

The tailor's son, because it
 A boon if God's beloved?‡
Ye sinful fools, can Siva
 Become the sinless Lord?
A wholly spiritual object
 In the Beneath He stands,
The Original, the Endless,
 Whom no blind understands!

Not Vishnu, Brahma, Siva,
 In the Beyond is He,
Not black, nor white, nor ruddy,
 This Source of things that be:
Not great is he, not little,
 Not female and not male,—
But stands, far, far, and far, beyond
 All beings' utmost pale!§

Dumb fools, whom physical principles,
 The six-and-ninety, guide,‖
Shall I not laugh when ye tell me
 Of deities petrified?

* The Tamil scholar will notice an emendation of the text here, which seems to me absolutely necessary. The stanza, as it stands in all editions of Sivavakkiyar, presents a strange grammatical medley. The alteration I have adopted, though but a slight one, seems sufficient.

† Literally—*the four kinds of flowers.* Tamilians divide all flowers into flowers that grow on low bushes, flowers of creepers, flowers that grow on trees, and flowers that grow in water.

‡ Literally—"By the offering of burnt offerings."

§ The poet here uses the S'aiva-siddhanta word *Darisam.* This term signifies a high state (or the highest) of existence. God, he says, stands beyond *Darisam, far, far, far away.* According to the S'aiva-siddhanta philosophy there are five states of existence:—1. The state of vigilance and activity. 2. The state of suspended mental condition, like that of dreams. 3. The state of inactivity like that of deep dreamless sleep. 4. The state of entire quiescence. 5. The state of supreme quiescence completely free from external entanglements. This stanza is the most beautiful and the most famous one in the writings of Sivavakkiyar.

‖ The literal translation of the words in the beginning of this stanza is as follows:—"O ye dumb persons, who perform the perishable *Tattuva* laws." *Tattuva* primarily signifies the essential nature of things. According to Tamilians there are ninety-six properties of things, or physical principles. There is a good deal of difference of opinion amongst Tamil authors regarding these in detail, although the total number ninety-six is generally agreed to. The knowledge of all these ninety-six physical principles is required in a man who professes to be a genuine ascetic. In other words, the true ascetic must know the *Tattuva Sastiram*, or Hindu Physiology, in all its modifications, and ninety-six divisions. Sivavakkiyar, who is a passionate writer delighting in strong epithets, calls this in the text before the reader "perishable." I apprehend he thereby desires to show his utter scorn of Hindu physics, ontology, and natural philosophy. And certainly the reader would agree with him were I to enumerate the ninety-six divisions of that science.

Mûvardlum ariyonâta
    Muttoñr pegapporul,
Kâvalâka unmalê
    Kalant' iruppat' unmaiyê.

Indra vaîdu tan kalmittil
    Iṭṭa poṭṭanangal pôl,
Mûndru nâlu alleiyal
    Mudiṇt' avilkum mudashil,
Mûndru lingamum kadantu
    Mutal nindra Kâchiyai
Undri, ûndri, nir mudinta
    Unmai yenna unmaiyê ?

Vâjamiṭṭu mani kilukki,
    Mikka tubam iṭṭumê,
Tôdi veitta sembilâm
    Tiraipadapparappiyê ;
Adu komiru, pongu veittu,
    Arattu maru pôlavê,
Pôdu patparu, iṭṭa pujai,
    Pujai yenna pujaiyê ?

Tantirangal attinal !
    Davangal seyta airbimum,
Mantirattal ûdaruttu,
    Mandapangal sudimum,
Antarattil nindra Jôti
    Yâvarum ariṭattâr,
Sin talyil tarim ttiâl
    Siva patangal sêraimê.

Pûvum nirum yen manamum :
    Porunta kôvil yen ullum ;
Avi pôla lingamây
    Aṭavalâlangrum nunâl ;
Mûvakindra avarum
    Vilangu tiba tîbamây,
Adukindra kuttanukkâr
    Andi sandi illeiyê.

Idangal panni sutti ceytê
    Iṭṭa pôla mitilê
Adanga nirum puja ceytu
    Arun tavangal pannuvir
Odungukindra nâthanâr
    Ulikkum Unnam evidam ?
Adangukindra Uvviam ?
    Ariuin pujai seyyumê.

He who createth all things
    Preserveth, layeth low,
The Indivisible Substance,
    Whom the Triad cannot know,
Himself to thy hearts unto keeping
    He truly can bestow.

When cows have calved, with bundles*
    Their throats ye silly deck ;
Thus, fools, your oft-wrapt lingas
    Ye carry round your neck.
Indeed, heart-fixed, thus can ye
    Subdue mischief, and sustain
The Light whom earth and heaven
    And hell cannot contain !

Your garb, your bells' quick tinkle,
    Your incense floating far,
Your copper gods, that by you
    Array'd in order are—
As men arrange in markets
    Mutton in lumps, and bawl !—
The flowers ye cast,—this worship
    What is it after all ?†

How many your devices !
    Although ye mortify
Your bodies, go through mantras,
    To temple-chambers hie,
Ye will not know the Splendour
    Who hath in space his seat ;
They with minds cleared can only
    Reach the true Siva's feet.

My thoughts are flowers and ashes,
    In my breast's fane enshrined,
My breath too is therein is
    A linga unconfined ;
My senses, too, like incense
    Rise, and like bright lamps shine,
There too my soul leaps ever
    A dancing-god divine !‡

Clearing a place, an altar
    Ye raise upon the site,
And heaping ashes on it
    Perform ye many a rite ;
Austerities perform ye ;
    But tell me this I pray,—
The god whom ye thus limit,
    Where dawns his wisdom's ray ?
How localised this wisdom ?
    Know this—then homage pay.

---

* I know of no such custom, but content myself with translating the Tamil word *pottanam* literally. I am inclined to think the word *charms* is meant. Conch-shells are frequently tied round the necks of bullocks as charms to ward off the effects of the evil-eye,—one of which supposed effects is to decrease the flow of milk. I have made enquiries of shepherds, and find three kinds of charms are in use, viz. :— shells, pieces of leather perforated in the middle, and pieces of cocoa-nut shell, but of any "bundles" thus used, I could obtain no information.

† This stanza will be noted as one which describes the worship of gods in some ordinary little village temple briefly yet very felicitously.

‡ This, in my opinion, is one of the finest stanzas penned by Sivavakkiyar. The drift of it is this :—You popular Hindus, you have your temples,—you have your flowers and sacred ashes,—you have your lingas, or emblems of divine creative power,—you have also your incense and lamps, and you have your divine dancer, Siva.—I too have my flowers and ashes, but they are of the mind ! I too have my linga, but it is my breath or spirit ! I too have my incense and lamps, but they are my five senses ! And I too have my deity leaping in divine sport within me, but that is my soul. In a word, mine is the true spiritual worship !

"Kâsi, Kâsi" endru nîr
    Kal kadukka vealerîr,
Kâsi âdi âdinum
    Karuppu vellai akumô?
Aosibusam vittu nîr
    Eivarum odungināal,
Kâsi nîrum sammukhê
    Kândâlum ammaiyê.

To Kasi, still to Kasi *
    Ye haste in foot-sore plight,
Although you go and bathe there
    Will black be changed to white?
If, all allurements shunning,
    Your senses be repressed,
The sacred wave of Kasi
    Will well within your breast!

PUTTIRAGIRIYAR PULAMBAL.

Manatul wern villâkki,
Vân periyol nâdâkki,
Yenatarivvé ambâkki,
    Yeyvatu'ini—Yekkâlam?

Ayum kaluttal ellâm
Ardyntu pârttalippin
Ni andri yeudrum illa
    Nicang kânbat'—Ekkâlam?

Ganjâ abin mayakkam
Kolļundu vâdâmal
Panjâ vamirtam ni
    Pagaruvatum—Ekkâlam?

Pattrattra nirill
Padar Tâmarai ilai pôl
Suttrattâr nibhu manam
    Dûre nirpat'—Ekkâlam?

Angâramum adakki,
Ainbulanai austaruttâ,
Tûngâmal tûngi
    Sugam peruvat'—Ekkâlam?

Mâyâ pirapi
Mayakkattai ûdaruttu
Kâya puri kôttai
    Kai kolvat'—Ekkâlam?

Sattirattai suttu
Sathur maraiyai poy âkki
Sûttirattai kaņdu
    Sugam peruvat'—Ekkâlam?

Sattirattai kaṭṭi
Sathur maraiyai poy âkki
Sûttirattai kaņdu
        Tuyaruruput'—Ekkâlam?

STANZAS FROM THE LAMENTATION OF PATTIRAGIRIYAR.

When, ah when,
Shalt thou, O Lord, bend as a bow, my mind;
And like a string, thereto, my senses† bind;
That all the arrowy thoughts within my heart
To thee alone, by thee impelled, may dart?

When, ah when,
Shall I perceive, after that I have pored
O'er all the wisdom in all writings stored,
The truth—that nothing is, save thee O Lord?

When, ah when,
To me, whose lips narcotic drugs‡ have stain'd,
Who have eat opium, and have spirits drain'd
Wilt thou, that I may without withering live,
The five-fold sweetness§ of thy nectar give?

When, ah when,
Like lotus-leaves, which o'er the water grow
Yet in the water no adherence show,||
From those who my own kith and kindred are,
Shall I in mind stand separate and far?

When, ah when,
Will the blest time of bliss attained arrive
When I annihilate these senses five,
Suppress my pride, and my life's being steep
In that existence which is sleepless sleep?

When, ah when,
Cleaving through all this birth's illusions vain
Shall I to my last spiritual state attain?

When, ah when,
Burning the Shastras, deeming the Vedas four
Mere lies, shall I the Mystery explore,
And perfect bliss attain for evermore?¶

When, ah when,
Laying aside, bound fast,* the Shastra's lore
Wholly distrusting, too, the Vedas four,
Shall I the Mystery know, and grieve no more?

---

* Kasi,—this is the Tamil name for Benares.

† The Tamilians speak of five bodily senses just as we do. 1. The feeling—of the surface of the body. 2. The taste—of the mouth. 3. The seeing—of the eye. 4. The smelling of the nose. 5. The hearing—of the ear.

‡ Literally—Ganja, a plant with narcotic properties.

§ It is supposed that ambrosia contains the following five delicacies:—Milk, ghi, sugar, curds, and honey.

|| The author alludes to a supposed natural fact. Although the leaf of the lotus lies outspread on the surface of the water, yet water adheres not to it, nor interpenetrates it. Water poured upon the leaf leaves no apparent moisture behind. The Tamil scholar would do well to compare with this stanza one in the Naladi beginning,—"Nillappadiyo-ramamainâlirruudambe," &c.

¶ This is the most famous of all Pattiragiriyar's stanzas. In one edition of his Lamentations occurs the same verse in an altered form,—the translation of which I also give. (See the subsequent stanza, and notice that he is made to say not that the Shastras should be burnt, but that they should be bound up.)

* This expression is the Tamil equivalent for our English phrase "shelving a book." The Tamil book is written on palmyra leaves: these leaves are strung together by a cord. When you open the book, you first undo that portion of the cord which is bound round the whole. When you close it, you reverse this operation. Thus when Pattiragiriyar speaks of "binding up the Shastras," he means,—close and shelve them as useless in your search after the great Mystery of Future Existence.

Karaimariya nāl Vēdam
 Kūpiṭṭu kāndan
Parama rahasyattai
 Pārpat'—Ekkālam?

Tāriyin mēl pāl
Sulamiru, manam vāḍāmal,
Ariyanai tēḍi
 Adipaṇivat'—Ekkālam?

Ponmalaiyār neri
Piramaṭṭhanai viṭṭ'ulutu,
Kuppirandu mēḍi,
 Kalant'iruppat'—Ekkālam?

When, ah when,
Though I the Vedas four may loudly* shout,
The secret of the heavens shall I find out?

When, ah when
Shall this poor soul, within this body set
Dissolved like fire within a ...,
Find the true Friend, and after ...
Perpetual homage to his sacred feet.

When, ah when,
Will all my carnal lusts have thus an end,
And I, with symbols dropt, to heaven ascend,
And with God's being my own being blend.

ON THE NON-ARYAN ELEMENT IN HINDI SPEECH.

BY F. S. GROWSE, M.A., OXON, B.C.S.

The precise character of the relationship which connects the modern Braj Bhāshā with the ancient Sanskrit of the Vedas and the mediæval Prākrits of the classic dramatists, and how far its vocabulary has been adulterated by the introduction of a foreign element, are matters regarding which a considerable diversity of opinion still exists among the most eminent philologists. Lassen says:—"The few words in Prākrit which appear to be of extraneous origin can, for the most part, be traced to Sanskrit, if the investigation is pursued on right principles," an opinion which Colebrooke has stated in equally emphatic terms by declaring that "nine-tenths of the Hindi dialect may be traced back to the Sanskrit." On the other hand, a third writer maintains that "the line taken by Professor Lassen of treating all Prākrit words as necessarily modifications of Sanskrit words is one which he has borrowed whole from Vararuchi and Hemachandra, and however excusable in those ancient commentators seems unworthy of an age of critical research." Dr. Muir, in the second volume of his *Original Sanskrit Texts*, republished within the last few months, holds, as is usual with that most impartial of critics, a middle course between the two extreme views. He says:—"Lassen may not under-rate the number of purely indigenous words in the Prākrits, as they are exhibited in the dramas, polished compositions written by Pandits, men familiar with Sanskrit; but his remarks are not certainly correct if applied to the modern vernaculars, in which words not derived from the Sanskrit, and which must have come down to them from the vernacular Prākrits, are very numerous." For my own part, a resident of Braj, and writing of the Braj Bhāshā, the typical form of modern Hindi, which I hear spoken about me, I discover every day stronger arguments for agreeing to the very full both with Lassen and the ancient commentators. The maxim 'stare super antiquas vias' is one which has often proved sound in application, and is never rashly to be discarded. After a lapse of 1800 years the sūtras of Vararuchi, if rightly handled, seem to me as accurate an exponent of the variations from classic form which characterize the modern dialect as they were of the peculiarities of the vulgar speech at the time when they were first enunciated. No more satisfactory proof could be desired of the essential identity of the Indian vernacular from its Vedic birth to its present rustic degradation. Out of Sanskrit arose the Pāli, from that the Sauraseni Prākrit, and from that again the Braj Bhāshā; each supplanting its predecessor so imperceptibly that neither contemporaries were conscious of the transition, nor can critics at the present day determine its period.

I specially omit from the above table of descent the language of the Buddhist Gāthas, which appears to be entirely exceptional. Used by the early teachers of Buddhism, men for the most part sprung from the lower orders of the people, it is described by Bābu Rājendralāla Mitra, who is of all men best competent to speak on the subject, as differing from the Sanskrit more in its neglect of the grammatical rules of the latter than from inherent peculiarities of its own: "it professes to be Sanskrit, and yet does not conform to its rules." A fitting and indeed a singularly close parallel to such a style is afforded by the barbarous Latin of some of the mediæval

* Literally—"Shout till I strain my throat."

ecclesiastical historians. Take for example the following passage from a chronicle of the tenth century:—"Otto rex veniente Italico regno, tanta pene multitudo gentis in Italia, quæ ita impleverunt faciem terræ, sicut situlæ. Habebat autem secum gentes nationes quorum linguæ non agnoscebant gentis. Insuper hoc habebat gens quæ Gamula vocabantur, arcus et carros et machina portantes. Erat enim aspectus eorum orribilis, et turbis properantes, carpentes iter et ad prœlium ut ferro stantes." To use the very words of the learned editor of the *Lalita Vistara*, it professes to be Latin and yet does not conform to its rules: though at the same time the similarity is sufficient to render the meaning of the barbarous jargon tolerably intelligible.

In my present remarks I do not propose an exhaustive discussion, but merely to suggest—1stly, an answer to a prominent argument; 2ndly, to deprecate *prima facie* conclusions on the part of the non-Aryan school; and 3rdly, to indicate a mode of illustration which I conceive may be employed with great effect in support of the opposite theory.

It is asserted that the earliest native grammarians distinctly recognize the presence of a *des'i* or non-Aryan element in the different Prâkrits; as for example, the line in the Kâvya-dars'a: *Tadbhavam, tat-samam, des'yam, anekam prâkritam viduh*, upon which the scholiast's remarks are as follows:—"*Tadbhavah Sanskrita-bhavah, khaggâdi s'abdah*," "*Tad-bhava* means derived from Sanskrit, as *Khagga* for *Khadga*, and so on." *Tatsamah Sanskrita-prâkritayoh samah, hindîra-komalâdi s'abdah*. "*Tatsama* means the words which are alike in Sanskrit and Prâkrit, as *hindîra*, a cuttle fish bone, *komala*, a mode of address, &c." *Des'î iti mahârâshtriyâdi*. "*Des'î* is the name of the Mahârâshtri, &c." We may confine our attention exclusively to the above passage, since it appears to be the original authority upon which the comments of all later writers have been founded. The text is generally understood to mean that Prâkrit words are of three kinds; 1st, *tad-bhava*,—derived from the Sanskrit; 2ndly, *tatsama*,—identical with the Sanskrit; and 3rdly,—*des'î*, i.e. provincial, or rather—to obviate all ambiguity of expression—non-Aryan; since in the sense of local corruptions of correct speech the *tad-bhava* words are considered to be provincial. But the illustrations given by the scholiast appear to me to necessitate a very different conclusion. It may be presumed that in his time no Sanskrit word passed into the Prâkrit without undergoing a change; the large number of purely Sanskrit words in the modern vernacular, and which I imagine the non-Aryan school of philologists would designate as *tat-sama*, never entered into the scholiast's imagination as an element of Prâkrit speech, being all of very recent introduction. The two examples that he gives of *tat-sama* words are such as it would be difficult to connect with any Sanskrit root. The one is the name of a natural object, the other a colloquial exclamation; and both would appear to have been borrowed not from the Sanskrit, but by the Sanskrit from the dialect of the vulgar. In fact they are really what would now be ordinarily called *des'i*; only with this material difference, that although of vulgar descent they have been formally adopted into the Sanskrit family. Thus it will be observed that the scholiast does not, as with the other two classes, give a word as an explanation of the term *des'i*, but a dialect, the Mahârâshtri. Hence I infer that the original text of the *Kâvyâdars'a* involves two orders of subdivision, the one of words into *tatsama* and *tad-bhava*, the other of dialects as Mahârâshtri, Sauraseni and the like, according to the country (*des'*) in which they prevailed.

To sum up, there are in all Prâkrits two kinds of words; the one called *tad-bhava*, corruptions from the Sanskrit; the other called *tatsama*, words of vulgar origin, and usually signifying local customs or productions, adopted into Sanskrit from the want of any exactly equivalent terms in that language. Thus mediæval and ecclesiastical Latin, after it had become a dead tongue, like classical Sanskrit, borrowed from the popular dialect, itself a corruption of Latin, many technical terms, which would be unintelligible to a Roman of the Augustan age, while they have also ceased to correspond with the current forms of every-day speech. Thus if the division is exhaustive, every Prâkrit word, though not necessarily derived from the Sanskrit, still exists there; allowance being made in the modern vernacular for the fact that a Prâkrit term, when once transferred into Sanskrit composition, was stereotyped, while in current speech it continued subject to the influence of progressive phonetic decay. The above considerations clearly explain why it is that Lakshmîdhara in his *Shad-bhâshâ-chandrikâ* treats only of *tad-bhava* and *tatsama* terms; since a third division with the title of *des'ya* had never been recognized. Thus much in answer to the argument drawn from the language of the ancient native grammarians in support of the view that the Indian Prâkrits contain a large non-Sanskritic element. Their language, it is shown, is capable of an exactly opposite interpretation, and rather indicates that the classic and vulgar speech were both confluents from two identical sources. But again it is said all argument and theory may be dismissed as unnecessary, since it is a positive fact, and one obvious at a glance, that the Hindi vocabulary is, to a large extent, essentially different from the Sanskrit. Thus Dr. Muir writes:—"There are in Hindi words which have no resemblance to any vocables discoverable in Sanskrit books, such as *bâp*, father; *beṭâ*, son; *per*, tree; *chaukî*, a chair; *chûk*, a blunder; *khiṛkî*, a window; *jhagrâ*, a dispute; *bakherâ*, a dispute; *âṭâ*, flour; *râvaṭî*, a tent, and a multitude of other instances." A few pages further on he gives a tabular list of such Prâkrit words, with their modern vernacular equivalents, as are not found in classical Sanskrit or are of doubtful origin. This list is composed of the ten words above mentioned, together with fourteen more, viz., *gor* the leg; *peṭ*, the belly; *ṭokrî*, a basket; *khûnṭâ*, a peg; *johnâ*, to look; *thartharânâ* to tremble; *ḍûbnâ*, to sink; *ḍhûṇḍhnâ*, to seek; *ḍhaknâ*, to cover; *pahuṇchnâ*, to arrive; *ghoṭnâ*, to gulp; *khopṛî*, a skull; *jhamaknâ*, to glitter; and *ṭhokar*, a blow or stumble. To this total of 24, he is careful to add at the end of a long comparative vocabulary of Pâli and Prâkrit, extending over 14 pages, two other supplementary words, viz., *os*, dew, and *ḍhonâ*, to carry a load,—thus increasing the specification to 26. Now I am far from asserting that there are not in Hindi many more than 26 words, which it would be difficult, if not impossible, to connect with any Sanskrit forms; but from the pains with which Dr. Muir has made up even so short a list, it may be concluded that "the multitude of instances" did not readily occur to him; and secondly, even though the connection may not be discoverable, it is rash to assert positively that no such connection ever existed; witness the extraordinary manner in which, at the present day, English names are distorted by Indian pronunciation beyond all possibility of recognition. Even among the 26 words, so carefully selected, I detect several that, at a glance, appear to betray their Sanskrit origin; and I cannot doubt that a rigorous scrutiny would yield further results in the same direction. Thus I would connect *os* 'dew' with the Latin *ros*, the Greek *δρόσος*, the English *drop*, and the Sanskrit *drapsa* from the root *dru* or *drava*, 'to run.' Again the derivation of *peṭ*, 'the belly,' from the Sanskrit *peṭa*, 'a basket,' appears to me by no means inconceivable, when we have the English slang term 'bread-basket' applied to that part of the body. *Bakherâ*, again, which also occurs in the verbal form *bakhernâ*, 'to scatter,' as in the phrase *bîj bakhernâ*, 'to sow seed,' is, I think, almost beyond a doubt derived from the Sanskrit *kship* with the prefix *vi*. So too, *chaukî* would seem to be connected with *chatur*, 'four,' a seat being ordinarily of square shape; while an 'outpost' (*chaukî*) is most conveniently situate at a quadrivium or *chaurâhâ*; and a man may be called *chaukas*, 'vigilant,' who keeps a good look-out on all four sides. Again, *chhînṭ* is unquestionably the same word as *chhidra*, 'perforate,' from the root *chhid*; and equally certain the Prâkrit *hâṇo* for 'a dog,' is connected with the Kashmîri *hûn*, the English *hound*, the Greek *κύων*, Latin *canis*, and Sanskrit *śvan*. Nor do I see the slightest improbability in the suggestion which Dr. Muir himself makes, that *gharnâ* or *ghalnâ* is from the root *ghaṭ*, since Vararuchi expressly recognizes the substitution of ḍ for a non-initial ṭ. But, without labouring to establish any further identification, we are justified in declaring that the system of hermeneutics adopted by Lassen, in conformity with the ancient grammarians, is an eminently judicious one, and less likely to result in error than the hasty assumption of the non-Aryan school that every unfamiliar form in vernacular speech is necessarily of barbarous extraction.

A skilful dissection of the village names that prevail in Upper India would probably illustrate in a very interesting manner the successive changes which the language of the country has undergone. And perhaps no district in India better adapted for such a purpose than Mathurâ. A mere glance at the map proclaims it to be of almost exclusively Hindi character. In the two typical parganas of Kosi and Chhâtâ there are 172 villages, not one of which bears a name with the familiar termination of *-âbâd*. Not a score of names altogether betray any admixture of a Muhammadan element, and even these are formed with some Hindi ending, as *-pur*, *-nagar* or *-garhi*; for example Shâhpur, Shernagar, and Shergarh. All the remainder, to any one but a philological student, denote simply such and such a village, but have no connotation whatever and are at once classed as barbarous Hindi. Yet an application of Vararuchi's rules will, in many cases, without any great exercise of ingenuity, suffice to discover the original Sanskrit form, and explain its corruption. Thus Maholi is for Madhu-puri; Paroli for Parasurâma-puri, (Parsa being the ordinary colloquial abbreviation for Parasurâma) Dhan-singha for Dhana-sinha,* Bâti for Bahula-vati; and Khaira for Khadira. So far as I am aware, the true explanation of these common endings *-oli*, *-auli*, *-ori*, *-awar*, has never before been clearly stated. They are merely corruptions of *-puri* or *-pura*, combined with the prior member of the compound, as explained by Vararuchi, in Sûtra II. 2, which directs the elision of certain consonants, including the letter *p*, where they are simple and non-initial; the term 'non-initial' being expressly extended to the first letter of the latter member of a compound. The practical application of the rule was first suggested to me by observing that two large tanks at Barsâna and Govardhan were called indiscriminately in the neighbourhood, the one Kusum-Sarovar or Kusum-okhar (for Kusuma-pushkara), the other Brikhbhân-pokhar or Bhân-okhar. As the rule was laid down by Vararuchi 2000 years ago, I can only claim credit for its practical re-application; but it is of great importance, and at once affords a clue to the formation of an immense number of otherwise unintelligible local names.

The foregoing considerations demonstrate the soundness of the proposition laid down at the outset, viz., that the proportion of words in the Hindi vocabulary not connected with Sanskrit forms is exceedingly inconsiderable; such fact appearing—1st, from the silence of the early grammarians as to the existence of any such non-Sanskritic element; 2ndly, from the discovery that many of the words hastily set down as barbarous are in reality traceable to a classic source; and 3rdly, from the unconscious adherence of the modern vernacular to the same laws of formation as influenced it in an admittedly Sanskritic stage of development.

* This bare adoption of a personal name as a local designation is uncommon, but is paralleled by the name of a village in the Chhâtâ Pargana, which is called simply Umrao, while another village in the Kosi Pargana has the fuller form Umrâora, for Umrao-pura.

ON THE IDENTIFICATION OF VARIOUS PLACES IN THE KINGDOM OF MAGADHA VISITED BY THE CHINESE PILGRIM CHI-FAH-HIAN, IN A. D. 415.

BY A. M. BROADLEY, B.C.S., ASSISTANT MAGISTRATE IN CHARGE OF SUB-DIVISION BIHAR IN PATNA.

(*Continued from page 71.*)

PART III.

Since writing the last part of my notes, I have paid another visit to the Son-bhândâr cave, and carefully examined the *chaitya* I found there. It appears to me so curious that I propose to describe it more particularly. Its form is square with a conical top surmounted by a large knob. Each side is 1 foot 10 inches broad, and its total height is 4 feet 2 inches. On each face there is a pillared canopy, underneath which is a standing figure of Buddha on a lotus-leaf pedestal, with a miniature attendant on either side, each holding a torch. The hair on the head is knotted, and the body is covered by a long cloak. The hands, instead of being raised in the usual attitude, are held down close by the side. The attendant figures are elaborately dressed and ornamented. At each corner of the arch of the canopy are figures holding scrolls. In the centre of the canopy, and immediately above the head of Buddha, rises a pipal tree surmounted by three umbrellas. The bases vary in design; on either side, beneath the pedestal, is depicted the 'Wheel of the Law,' supported on one side by elephants, on another by caparisoned horses, (with saddles of almost European shape), on the third by elephants kneeling, and on the fourth by bulls. The conical top of the *chaitya* resembles the cupola of a temple.

To return to Mount Vipula. This hill rises about three hundred yards to the east of the hot springs previously described. Its direction is due north-east. The northern face of the mountain is a rugged cliff, and its western slope is but a little less precipitous. At the foot of the hill there are six wells,—some of which contain hot, and some cold water. They resemble in shape those of Mount Baibhâr, and are called respectively Nânâ-kund, Sitâ-kund, Sômakund, Ganesh-kund, and Râma-kund. Nearly a quarter of a mile from these wells is a spring immediately under the northern face of the mountain. It is surrounded by a large enclosure, and its water is tepid. Passing through a courtyard, the visitor arrives at a small stone cell in the rock, and immediately above this a flight of some eighty steps leads up the side of the hill to a platform paved with brick. This is the celebrated Makhdum-kund of the Muhammadans, and Sringgi-rikhi-kund of the Hindus. This well is held in extraordinary veneration alike by Hindus and Musalmans, and is thronged by pilgrims all the year round. The spot is celebrated as the residence of Makhdum Shah Shaikh Saraf-ud-din Ahmad, a saint, not only revered by the Muhammadans of Bihár, but by the followers of the Crescent all over India. The date of his sojourn at Rájgir was, as far as I can ascertain, about 715 A.H. The stone cell is said to be his "hujra," i.e., the scene of a forty days' meditation and fast [vu: *chillah*], and the platform above, the place of his morning and evening prayers. General Cunningham has been led into a strange error about this spot, and states it to have been the dwelling of Saint *Chillah*, a converted Hindu. I trust at a future time to be able to give a complete history of the life and writings of Saraf-ud-din, in connexion with the history of Muhammadan rule in Bihár.

About two hundred feet from the foot of the hill, almost immediately above the northern gate of the ancient city, and nearly half a mile south-west of the Makhdum-kund, are the remains of an enormous brick *Stúpa* or "tope," now surmounted by a small temple of Mahádeva. There is a similar ruin opposite this at the foot of Baibhár, and the bed of the ravine is also strewn with débris. I clearly identify these ruins with the description of Hwen Thsang*: "En dehors de la porte septentrionale de la ville, il y a un *Stúpa*. . . . au *nord-est* de l' endroit où fut dompté l'éléphant ivre il y a un *Stúpa*." Leaving this place, and going some few hundred yards to the north-east, one arrives at two small Jaina pagodas, built on a peak of the hill. The first is dedicated to Munisuvrata Sádhu, and the second to Mahávira, the 24th Tirthankara of the Jainas, who is said to have lived, and died at Pawapúri, eight miles north-east of Rájgir. Continuing to ascend the western face of the hill, one looks down on a rocky *defile which separates Mount Vipula from Ratnagir.*

There is little difficulty in identifying this from the remarks of Hwen Thsang as well as by those of Fah-Hian. The former says,† "Au nord de l'endroit où *Che-li-tseu* (Çáriputtra) avait obtenu le fruit du Saint (la dignité d'*Arhat*), tout près il y a une fosse large et profonde à côté de laquelle on a élevé un *Stúpa*. . . . . . . Au nord-est de la fosse susdite, à l'angle de la ville entourée de montagnes il y a un *Stúpa*. En cet endroit, le grand médecin *Chi-po-kia* (Djívika) bâtit en faveur du Bouddha, une salle pour l'explication de la loi." Fah-Hian writes:‡ "To the north-east of the city in the middle of a crooked defile, Djivika erected a Vihara. . . *Its ruins still exist.*" I believe these places to be identical with the remains which I shall presently describe.

Nearly a quarter of a mile to the east of the pagoda of Mahávira one arrives at the summit of the hill, which is exactly above the centre of the "crooked defile." At this place is an enormous platform 180 feet long by 30 wide, and about 6 feet above the surrounding rocks. It is constructed almost entirely of the materials of Buddhist buildings (I counted more than 50 pillars in the floor alone), and this is easily accounted for by a large pile of ruins *at either end of the platform.* The mound to the east is nearly 20 feet high, and its surface is bestrewn with pillars and stone slabs. The ruins to the west are undoubtedly those of a temple or vihára, and several grey stone columns are still erect. The modern Jaina temples on the platform deserve some notice, as all of them abound, more or less, in Buddhist ornamentation. The first of the series of four is only about 10 feet square, and is surmounted by a simple semi-circular cupola. It is dedicated to Chandraprabha, the 8th Tirthankara. The doorway is a fine specimen of Buddhist art. In the centre is a figure of Buddha under a canopy, and three parallel rows of exquisite geometrical pattern run round the sides. Above the door, a large ornamental slab, about five feet long and eight inches wide, is inserted in the masonry. It is divided into seven compartments. The first of which, on either side, contains figures of elephants, and the remainder—groups of figures in the attitude of the dance. This is almost identical with the ornamentation of a very beautiful doorway excavated by me from the mound at Baptha, and which is now in my collection of Buddhist sculp-

* Mémoires, tom. II. p. 16. † Mémoires, tom. II. p. 20-21. ‡ Beal's Translation, chap. xxviii. p. 113.

tures. The next temple is divided into two chambers, and is of considerable size. It is dedicated to Mahâvira, and both the inner and outer doors are very fine. The cornice of the latter is divided into nine compartments, in the first of which a man is represented in the act of dedicating a chaitya. The others are filled with the usual Buddhist devices. The top of the temple is pyramidal in shape. The next pagoda is faced by an open court, to the right and left of which are two slabs, the one covered with the representation of the ten Incarnations of Vishnu, and the other with those of the Nine Planets. The vacant space at the base of the carving is covered with a modern inscription in Nâgarî. The doorway is ornamental by a comparatively plain moulding. This temple is dedicated to Munisuvrata—the 20th Jaina Tirthankara, who is said to have been born in Râjgir. Inside the fourth temple are four charanas—two of them being of white marble. They are dedicated respectively to Mahâvira, [or Vardhamâna] Pârshwanâtha, Shantinâtha, and Kunthunâtha—the 24th, 23rd, 16th and 17th Tirthankaras respectively.

Leaving the temples and skirting the north-side of the ravine, you come a narrow ridge which brings you to Mount Ratnagir. The summit is crowned by a temple decorated with some small black basalt columns, elaborately carved. From this a stone staircase or pathway leads down the western slope of the hill to the plain beneath.

Between Ratnagir and Udayagir lies a narrow valley covered with jungal, situated, as nearly as possible, due north-east of the ancient city, and stretching away as far as Giryak—a distance of six or seven miles. I shall now proceed to establish if possible an identification of this valley, connected with the writings of both the pilgrims. Hwen Thsang writes as follows*: "*Au nord-est* de la ville, il fit de quatorze à quinze li" [2½ or 3 miles]. " et arriva au mont *Ki-li-tho-kiu-tch'a* (Gridhrakoûta Pârvata) qui *touche au midi de la montagne du nord*, et s'élève isolément à une hauteur prodigieuse. . . . Le roi *Pin-pi-so-lo* (Bimbasâra), voulant entendre la loi, leva un grand nombre d'hommes; puis, pour *traverser la vallée* et franchir les ravins, depuis le pied de la montagne jusqu'au sommet, il fit assembler des pierres, et pratiqua des *escaliers* larges d'environ dix pas, et ayant une longueur de cinq à six li. Au milieu du chemin, il y a deux petits *Stoupas*: .... Le sommet de cette montagne est allongé de l'est à l'ouest, et resserré du sud au nord." He then proceeds to speak of a vihâra to the west of the mountain, a colossal stone once trodden by the sacred feet of Śakya Muni, a Stûpa to the *south*, and a second on the summit of the mountain. Fah-Hian's description† is far less minute, but he gives exactly the same distance [viz. 15 *li*] and speaks of two caves on the hill—the colossal stone—the Vihara, and the lofty peak.

On the 26th January, I made an attempt to explore the valley. Clearing the dense brushwood and jungal as I advanced, I skirted the foot of Ratnagir for about a mile from the old city, and then struck across into the centre of the valley, and pushed on two miles further to the east. I then saw that to the east of Ratnagir there is another mountain terminating in a lofty peak, which towers above the summit of the surrounding hills. This mountain is called [illegible], and I unhesitatingly identify it with that mentioned in the text of Fah Hian and Hwen Thsang. It adjoins the southern side of Vipula. In the middle of the valley a stone terrace or staircase, about 20 feet broad, runs due north, towards the foot of the hill, for a distance of 900 feet. At this point it branches off to the east up the mountain side. At the distance of 500 feet from the plain I found a small stûpa in *the very centre of the staircase* about 8 feet square, and in front of it three or four steps are still almost intact, each step being about 18 or 20 feet wide and a foot high. Near this place under a great heap of débris I found three images of Buddha almost perfect, but of the rudest workmanship. They are uniform in size, and bear inscriptions. From the stûpa the staircase continues to traverse the mountain-side for a distance of 800 feet. At this point I discovered a *second stûpa* and a large quantity of bricks, pillars, &c. Of these, the most remarkable are a figure of Buddha seated on a lion, a large seated Buddha with the usual lotus throne, and a standing figure of Buddha with a long inscription. All these idols have been removed to Bihâr, and merit a much more detailed description. The terrace now becomes more broken, but its traces are visible up to the peak. From its commencement in the valley up to the summit of the mountain it measures, as

* Mémoires, Vol. II. p. 20-21

† Beal's Fah-Hian, Ch. xxix, p. 116.

nearly as possible, one mile. The south and west side of the hill are covered with the débris of houses, &c., and the solitary peak which crowns the hill is surmounted by an enormous brick *stûpa*. Though there is no natural cave in the southern face of the hill, as might reasonably be expected, the other features it presents are so remarkable as to put its identification beyond a doubt, and everything tends to show that the caves and grottoes of Râjgir were mostly artificial.

Parallel with Ratnagir and Devaghât runs Udayagir. Two ramparts or walls seem to have traversed the valley. The first to the west now called the Nekpai-bând, and the second stretches from the foot of Devaghât, as before described, to the centre of the valley, and this seems to have been continued as far as the foot of the Udaya hill. The slopes of this hill are more gradual than any of the others, and this accounts for the fortifications which surmount it. The steepest side of the mountain is towards the west, and it is through a narrow ravine at the foot of it, that the valley is entered from the south. The passage is very narrow, and in the centre runs the Bânganga rivulet, which rises from beneath Sonâgir. The pass was strongly fortified, and the ramparts and bastions are still remarkably perfect, although they have been exposed to the devastations of the rain and sun for many centuries. Just within the valley are the remains of the two towers, and at the entrance of the pass, where the width of the ravine is little more than twenty feet, two forts of considerable size—one on the slope of Udayagir, and the other facing it, at the foot of Sonâgir. The former measures 111 feet from the north to south, and 40 from east to west. From this point a massive wall, 16 feet thick, (and still having an elevation of some 10 or 12 feet), stretches in a direct line due east to the summit of the mountain. I measured it to a distance of 2,000 feet from the commencement, and it thus appears to continue its course for more than two miles on the crest of the hill, then to cross over towards the north, and finally to pass down the northern slope, and into the narrow valley between Udayagir and Ratnagir, just opposite the staircase of Bimbisâra, which leads to the summit of the Devaghât hill. The wall is composed of huge stones on either side, closely fitted together without cement, the centre being filled up by a mass of pebbles and rubbish. There are traces of Buddhist ruins on the top of the hill, and I found several images, and the remains of two large stûpas, and one temple similar to that on Baibhâr. There is also a large enclosure containing five modern Jaina temples—the centre one square and the others *triangular* in shape. Each of the small ones contains a figure of Buddha bearing the creed, "*ye dharma hetu* etc." There are large numbers of gray stone columns at the foot of the mounds abovementioned, and the spot has evidently been once the site of a Vihâra.

Although five hills are stated both in poetry and history to have surrounded the ancient capital of Magadha, this can hardly be considered literally correct, and to maintain the old description, several peaks must be considered as forming part of the same mountain. Thus the rocky cliffs of Chhata or Chhatra must be deemed the eastern extremity of Baibhâr, and the various parts of Sonâgir must be considered as portions of one great hill. Sonâgir, the most extensive, though the least lofty of all the hills, begins at the south-east corner of the valley, and runs due east from this point till it reaches the centre of the valley just above the plain of the Banbhûm. From this point three branches stretch eastwards; the first inclining slightly towards the north, and forming the southern boundary of the valley of the five hills, the second runs due east and forms the western side of the ravine which leads into the Hisua-Nawâda plains, and the third turns first south, then again almost due east, and finally terminates, as I have before described, in the rocks and torrents of Bânganga. This was evidently the weakest point in the natural defences of the city, for an enemy who had once gained the entrance of the valley, (which appears to have been still further protected by a semi-circular wall outside it,) could easily pass up the gentle slope between the two last mentioned branches of the hill, and descend by an equally easy road on the northern side of the hill into the very heart of the valley. I ascended the hill on this side, and soon gained the summit, which, like that of Udayagir, is occupied by an enormous pile of ruins, and a modern Jaina temple. Inside the pagoda is a large figure of Buddha, bearing the creed, and also a comparatively modern inscription on the unoccupied portions of the pedestal. Several columns are lying about, and also portions of cornice and other ornamental carving. This was once, evidently, the site of some great vihâra or temple. Thirty paces south of the pagoda, one comes quite suddenly on the great wall—almost unbroken and entire. It is uniformly sixteen feet thick, but its height differs at various places. It commences in the Banbhûm plain, and then runs in a direct line to the summit of the hill, a distance of 2800 feet. From this point an enormous embankment runs across the valley to the foot of Baibhâr, and now bears the name of Jarâsandha's bând. At the top of the mountain the wall turns to the east, following the crest of the central branch of Sonagir, which now takes an almost semicircular form, to a distance of 4100 feet. The wall at this point runs down the ravine, crosses it close to the source of the Bânganga torrent, then ascends the slope of the southern branch of the hill, and passes first along its ridge and then down its western slope till it ends in the fort to the west of the stream, as nearly as possible 12,000 feet from its commencement in the Banbhûm plain. The fort at which it ends is about half the size of the one on the opposite side of the torrent. I have thus succeeded in tracing the great wall which formed the artificial defence of the valley, but strange to say, popular legends, so far from connecting it with any such purpose, make it the evening walk of the Asura king—the spot where he used to enjoy the cool mountain air after the fatigues of the day.

Before giving some account of the wild ravine to the west of the valley, it may be interesting to say something of the Jaina pagodas which still adorn the hills. They are maintained and repaired by subscriptions collected all over India, and are yearly visited by thousands of pilgrims from Gwalior, Bombay, Calcutta and Murshidâbâd. They all contain charanas, or, impressions of the sacred feet of the Tîrthankaras—generally carved in black basalt, but sometimes in marble, and invariably surrounded by a Nâgari inscription. I have taken copies of the whole of them, but many have become very indistinct, on account of the oil, ghi, &c. with which they are anointed. The following are specimens of them.* In the temple dedicated to Munisuvrata, on the Vipula-hill, I found the following :—"On the 7th of the waxing moon in the month of Kârtika, Samvat 1848, the image of the supremely liberated sage who *attained salvation on the Vipula mountain*, together with his congregation, was made and consecrated by Śrî Amrita Dharma Vâchaka." In another of the series of temples :—"On the 9th of the waxing moon in the month of Phâlguna, Samvat 1504, by Sangha Śivarâja, &c. of the noble Jataṭa race." On Sônâgir :—"In the auspicious Kharatara First [*gachchha*], the image of Śrî Adinâtha, &c." The other inscriptions are similar, and the dates 1819, 1823, (on Udayagir) 1816, (Ratnagir) 1800 Samvat occur. I will only give one other at length. It comes from Vipulagir, and runs as follows :—"On Friday, the 11th of the waxing moon, in the month of Âśvina, when the Śaka year 1572 was current, Samvat 1707, [A. D. 1650], Sangama and his younger brother Gobardhana, sons of Lakshmidâsa and his wife Vasantalâlâ, of the Vihâra Vastâvya family, of the Dupada gotra, caused certain repairs to be done to...... in Râjagriha." Bâbu Râjendralâla Mitra remarks, that in this inscription all the proper names have the title 'sangha' prefixed to them, and this shows that the individuals in question belonged to a Buddhist congregation."

In one of the temples at the summit of Vipulagir I found the following :—"On the 7th of the waxing moon in Kartika this statue of Mahâdgupta, the absolutely liberated sage, was made by Śrî Sangha, on the "Śrî Vipulâchala hill, and consecrated by the preachers of salvation." The Charana on Ratnagir bears the following :—"Om, Salvation. On the 6th of the waxing moon in the month of Mâgha, Samvat year 1839, Sâh Manikchand, son of Bulâkhidâs of the Gunghâputra, and Osa family, an inhabitant of Hugli having repaired the temple on the Ratnagiri hill in Râjagriha placed the two lotus-like feet of the Jina Śrî Pârśvanâtha there." I conclude with the oldest inscription, which is on Sonagir—"On the 5th of the waxing moon in the month of Phâlguna, in the Samvat year 1504 . . . . of the Jâtaṭa Gotra, Râmasiṃha Varma Dasa, son of Sangha Manikadeva, son of the wife of Sangha . . . barâja, son of Sangha Bânarâja, son of Sangha Devarâja."

The most recent of the inscriptions is dated so late as Samvat 1912, or A. D. 1855.

I purpose in the next part to trace the route of Hwen Thsang amongst the hills and valleys to the west of Râjagriha.

(To be continued.)

* These readings and translations were made by Babu Râjendralâla Mitra, for whose valuable assistance I cannot be too grateful.

ON THE CHAṆḌIKÂŚATAKA OF BÂṆABHAṬṬA.

By G. BÜHLER, Ph. D.

In the learned preface to his edition of the *Vâsavadattâ*, Dr. Fitz-Edward Hall gives (pp. 8 and 49) extracts from two anonymous Jaina commentaries on the *Bhaktâmarastotra* of Mânatunga, which contain curious details regarding the life of Bâṇabhaṭṭa, the famous author of the *Kâdambarî* and of the *Harshacharita*. Amongst other matters, it is stated there that Bâṇa and Mayûra, the author of the *Sûryaśataka*, were related to each other by marriage, and that each of them composed a *Śataka* or century of verses in honour of a patron deity and obtained thereby liberation from great evils. Mayûra, it is said, who had suddenly become a leper, was cleansed of his disease by Sûrya, whom he propitiated with the *Sûryaśataka*. Bâṇa, jealous of this feat of his brother poet, thereupon cut off his own hands and feet, composed a *Śataka* in honour of Chaṇḍikâ, and through her favour obtained the restoration of his limbs.

Dr. Hall, in giving this story, observes that, whatever its absurdity, it may have an historical basis in making Mayûra and Bâṇa contemporaries, and that it deserves attention for that reason. This surmise has also been confirmed by Bâṇa's own statement in the *Harshacharita*, where he names Mayûraka amongst his friends. I have lately found that it contains another element of truth, viz. that it is right in ascribing to Bâṇabhaṭṭa the composition of a *Chaṇḍikâśataka*.

Not long ago, I acquired for the Government of Bombay a book bearing this title, which, according to its colophon, had been composed by a Mahâkavi Śrîvâṇa or Śrîvâṇabhaṭṭa. As no great poet of this name was known to me, and Dr. Hall's Jainas attributed a *Chaṇḍikâśataka* to Bâṇa, I at once concluded that Śrîvâṇa or Śrîvâṇa must be a mis-spelling for Śrî Bâṇa. This surmise was fully confirmed, shortly afterwards, when I obtained a copy of the commentary mentioned by Dr. Hall at p. 49 of his preface: for the latter work quotes the first verse of Bâṇa's *Chaṇḍikâśataka*, which agrees with the beginning of the *soi-disant* Śrîvâṇa's production.

The manuscript of the *Chaṇḍikâśataka* acquired by me is written on nine folios. Besides the text, which consists of 102 Ślokas, it contains a short commentary on Ślokas 1–44, written on the margin of each page. It has been written by a Jaina Lekhak, who, unfortunately, was neither careful, nor a good Sanskrit scholar. Though clerical errors and even omissions are frequent, still it is possible to restore the text of most verses.

Bâṇa's address to Chaṇḍikâ is composed in the *Śârdûlavikrîḍita vṛitta* and its style, as becomes a poet like the author of the *Kâdambarî*,* is made to harmonize with the difficult metre. The tortuosity of the construction, the double-entendres and puns, and the quaint similes in which it abounds, will make it dear to the heart of every true Paṇḍit. But these qualities make it rather an object of serious study than of enjoyment on first hearing or reading, and they render it improbable that European critics will accord to it the epithet of—'uttamâ kavitâ,'—"first rate poetry," which—according to the opinion of my learned native friends, to whom I showed the poem—is its due.

It is somewhat difficult to give an exact analysis of the contents of the *Śataka*, as the poet himself seems to have followed no fixed plan in its composition. Every stanza contains an allusion to, or a description of an incident from Chaṇḍikâ's great battle with the buffalo-shaped demon Mahishâsura, and winds up with a prayer to the goddess to protect the hearers or readers from evil, to bless them, or to destroy their enemies.

That a *Chaṇḍikâśataka* should celebrate the victory of the goddess over Mahisha, is no more than might be expected; for the Purâṇas state that the Chaṇḍikâ form of Śiva's wife, or *Śakti*, was expressly created for the destruction of that demon. In the *Devîmâhâtmya*,* the story of Chaṇḍikâ's creation, and of her contest with Mahisha and his army of fiends, is narrated at great length. According to that authority, the gods over whom Indra rules, were driven by Mahisha out of heaven. They went to Brahma, Vishṇu, and Śiva to complain and to ask for help. On hearing of the Asura's boldness, those deities were moved by anger and emitted from their bodies a great lustre. That lustre, united with the flames which Indra

* *Mârkaṇḍeya Purâṇa*, Adhy. 80 seqq.

and his followers emitted, and filled the whole world. It then assumed the shape of a three-eyed female, Chaṇḍiká-Deví. The gods, selected her to do battle with Mahisha and provided her with arms for the combat. S'iva drew a new trident forth from his own favourite weapon, Vishṇu produced a new Chakra from his Chakra, Varuṇa gave a conch-shell, Agni a spear, Váyu a bow and arrows, and Indra a thunderbolt forged out of his own Vajra. The Himálaya presented a lion to be the Váhana of the new deity. When Deví had thus been honoured with presents by all the gods, she uttered a great cry which shook the universe. The gods answered it with a shout of victory. "Alarmed by the noise the Asuras sallied forth from Heaven and prepared at once to do battle with their newly created foe. After a furious fight the army of the demons was routed with great slaughter by Chaṇḍiká. Next the goddess had to undergo a series of single combats with Chikshura, the general of the Asura host and other leaders. When they had all been slain, Mahisha himself came forward. He assumed his buffalo-shape, attacked the Pramathas, who accompanied Chaṇḍiká and routed them. Emboldened by this success, the Asura attempted to kill Deví's *Váhana*, the lion. The goddess met his onslaught by entangling him in her *Páśa*, or snare. He then turned himself into a lion. But Deví cut off his head, upon which he assumed human shape. Pierced by the arrows of the goddess, the demon assailed her in the shape of an elephant. Punished again by the loss of his trunk, he returned to his buffalo form and tried to bury Chaṇḍiká under the mountains which he uprooted with his horns. The mountains were rent to pieces by the arrows of the goddess. But, before attacking him more actively, she rested and refreshed herself by repeated draughts of nectar. Thus fortified, she jumped on the monster, drove her trident into his neck and finally cut off his head. The remainder of the Daitya army fled, the gods re-obtained possession of Svarga, and sang the praises of Chaṇḍiká, humbly acknowledging her power and supremacy.

It would seem that Báṇa, when writing his *Chaṇḍikáśataka*, had this legend, or some very similar story before him. He mentions the flight and helplessness of the gods, the circumstance that the goddess jumped on Mahisha and pierced him with the trident, and similar incidents; but he does not describe the combat with Mahisha at full length. He contents himself with taking out some of its most prominent features, and with placing before the mind of his hearers, again and again, the final tableau, where the victorious Deví appears standing on the body of her vanquished enemy. This picture gives him repeated opportunities of exalting the miraculous power of Chaṇḍiká's foot, and of recommending to his hearers the adoration of those limbs. A translation of a few verses will, however, give a better idea of the character and contents of the poem than the most minute analysis. I subjoin, therefore, some of the first S'lokas as well as the concluding one.—

Text.

Má bhánkshír vibhramam bhrúradhara vidhurasá koyam ásyásya rágam

páṇe práṇyeva nayam kalayasi kalahaśraddhayá kiṁ triśúlam |

ityudyatkopaketún prakṛitim avayaván prápayantyeva devyá

nyasto vo múrdhni mushyánmarudasuhṛidasún saṁharann anghrir aṁhaḥ || (1)

Hunkáre nyakkṛitodanvati asati jite śiñjitair núpurasya

ślishyacchákhávaṅgakotáḍitprakháredaṛjit* ni-jálah tatkálakrántibháji |

skandhe vindhyádribuddhyá nikashati mahishasyáhitaránsahárehi

ajñánáveva yasyáścharaṇa iti śívaṁ sá śivá vaḥ karotu || (2)

Jálmaryá yá na jasánunayaparihárakshiptayá kshálayantyá

náuṁ na núpuraṇa glapitaśaśaruchá jyotsnayá vá nakhánám

táṁ śobháṁ ádadháná jayati nijaṁ tráluktakam pádayitvá

pádenaiva kshipanti mahisham asuraśiláná-nishkáryam áryá | (3)

Mṛityos tulyaṁ trilokím grasitumatirasán nishkṛitáḥ kiṁ nu jihváḥ

kiṁ vá krishṇánghripadmadyutibhiraruṇitá vishṇupadyáḥ padavyaḥ |

práptáḥ sandhyáḥ smarárer svayam uta nutibhistisra ityúhyamáná

devair devítriśúláhatamahishajushe raktadhárá jayanti || (4)

* The MS reads, ślishyachháṇungakshitepi, but I am unable to extract any sense out of this reading.

Datte darpât prahâre sapadi padabharotpishṭa-dushṭâvaśishṭâm
ślishṭâm śṛiṅgasya koṭim mahishasuraripor nûpuragranthisîmni |
mohâdyâdvaḥ kalmashâṇi vyatikaraviratâvâ-dadânaḥ kumâro
mâtuḥ prabhrashṭalîlâkuvalayakalikâkarṇapûrâ-vâdaran || (5)

Trailokyâtaṅkanâśe praviśati virase dhâtari dhyânatandrâm
indrâdyeshu dravatsu draviṇapatipayaḥ-pâlakâlânaleshu |
sparśenaivâtra pishṭvâ mahisham atirusham trâsayantam jaganti
pâtu tvâm pañcha chaṇḍyâścharaṇanakhâs tu
ime nâpare lokapâlâḥ || (9)

Kuṇṭe dantairniruddhe dhanushi vimukhitajye vishâṇena mauli-
lâṅgûlena prakoshṭhe valayini patite tatkṛipâṇe svapâṇeḥ* |
śûle bhaṅgâṅghrighâtair lalitakaratalât prachyute dûram urvyâm
sarvâṅgînam lulâyam jayati charaṇaiś chaṇḍikâ chûrṇayantî | (102).

Translation.

1. "O brow, do not interrupt thy coquettish play! O lip, what mean these contortions! O face, throw off the (expression of) passion! O hand, why brandishest thou the trident in expectation of strife! He is no longer alive." Speaking thus Devî reduced, as it were, to their natural state her limbs that showed signs of rising anger. May her foot that stole the vital spirits of the enemy of the gods, being placed on your heads, take away your distress.

2. Whilst his bellowing of defiance, that surpassed the roar of the ocean, was conquered by the jingling of her anklets, and whilst the blood, flowing from the wound inflicted by his encircling horn, was mistaken (by the goddess) for the lac-dye of her foot-soles, she placed, by mistake, her foot on the shoulder that resembled a touch-stone, and took the life of Mahisha. May that female Śiva give you happiness.

3. The worshipful goddess assumes, through her anklets that make the hare-bearer's brightness fade, or through the moon-like brilliancy of her toe nails, such a splendour, which Jahnu's daughter, who was flung into her course by the affection of a son and who certainly purifies us, does never wear,—Glory to her, who crushed with her foot Mahisha like the lac-dye of her soles and who threw him away, when he had become worthless through the taking of his life-juice.

4. Glory to those jets of blood that issued from Mahisha, when he was struck by Devî's trident, and that made the gods ask themselves in perplexity, 'Has Death, greedy to swallow the three worlds put forth his three tongues at once? Or are the roads, which Vishṇu steps on, lit up by the brilliancy of Krishṇa's lotus feet? Or have the three Sandhyâs appeared (at once) in consequence of the devotions of the enemy of Cupid?'

5. When Mahisha, the enemy of the gods, struck out of pride, the tip of his horn, which became the sole remnant of his body, that was crushed by the weight of (Devî's) foot, became entangled in the knot of her anklet,—May Kumâra who at the end of the combat took it up, supposing it to be the bud of a lotus fallen from his mother's ear, take away your sins.

9. May the five toe-nails of Chaṇḍî—not those other guardians of the world—protect you, since by their mere touch they crushed the over-furious Mahisha, who made the worlds tremble, while the Creator, who was to be exiled for the torment of the world, helpless entered weary meditation, and Indra with the other gods, the Lord of Wealth, the Guardian of the Ocean, Yama and Agni, took to flight.

102. His teeth held firmly the spear, his horn had entirely unstrung the bow, his tail, like a bracelet, encircled the elbow, from her hand her sword had fallen, by the spasmodic blows of his feet the trident had been flung from her graceful hand, far away on the ground—Glory to Chaṇḍikâ, who (then) crushed all the limbs of the buffalo with her foot."

As the story of the Jaina commentator† has gained a fresh interest by the recovery of the *Chaṇḍikâ Śataka* and as it is not improbable that other statements which it contains may prove of use to students of Sanskrit literary history, I give in conclusion a translation of the introductory Kathâ which describes the origin of the *Bhaktâmarastotra*, as far as it relates to Mayûra and Bâṇa. It runs as follows:—

"Formerly there lived in Amarâvatî Ujjayinî, Śrî Ujjayinî, a Pandit, named Mayûra, who had

* Lâṅgûlena prakoshṭhe valayite tatkṛipâṇasya pâṇeḥ.—MS. against metre and sense.

† Though the commentator does not mention his name, or time, it is very probable that he lived at the beginning of the 13th century, as he names Śrîtilaka Sûri as the predecessor of the reigning Paṭṭadhâri Guṇachandra, in the Vaṃśâvalî, at the conclusion of the book. Śrîtilaka of the Abhayadevavaṃśa was the teacher of Rajaśekhara, who wrote the Prabandha Kosha in 1347.

studied the S'âstras and was honoured by the *elder Bhoja*. His son-in-law was Bâṇa. The latter also was clever. The two were jealous of each other, for it is said,—

'Donkeys, bulls, stupids, gamblers, Pandits, and rogues cannot bear each other and cannot live without each other.'*

One day they were quarrelling. The king said to them, 'Ho Pandits, go to Kashmir. He is the best whom Bhârati who dwells there, considers to be the better Pandit.†

They took food for their journey and set out. They came on their road to the country of the Madhumatas (Kashmir). Seeing five hundred oxen which carried loads on their backs, they said to the drivers, 'What have you got there?' The latter answered, 'Commentaries on the syllable Om.' Again they saw, instead of five hundred oxen, a herd of two thousand. Finding that all these were laden with different new explanations of the syllable Om, they lost their pride. They slept in some place together. Mayûra was awakened by the goddess Sarasvatî, who gave him this '*theme*' for a verse, '*The sky filled with a hundred moons*.' He half raised himself, yawned and gave the following solution,—

'Chakyaramalli, stunned by the blow of Dâmodara's hand, saw *the sky filled by a hundred moons*.'

The same question was addressed to Bâṇa. He growled and worked the theme in the following manner:—

'In that night, on account of the lotus-faces that moved to and fro on the high terraces, *the sky shone as if filled by a hundred moons*.'‡

The goddess said, 'You are both poets who know the *S'âstras*. But Bâṇa is inferior, because he growled. I have shown you that quantity of commentaries on the syllable Om. Who has ever attained a complete knowledge of the dictionary of the goddess Speech. It has been also said, "Let nobody assume pride saying, 'I am the only Pandit in this age. Others are ignorant.' Greatness of intellect is only comparative.'

Thus Sarasvatî made friendship between the two. When they arrived at the outer wall (of Ujjayini) they went each to his house. One after the other they paid their respects to the King as before. It has been also said,—"Deer herd with deer, kine with kine, steeds with steeds, fools with fools, wise men with wise ones. Friendship (has its root) in the similarity of virtues and of faults."

Once Bâṇa had a lover's quarrel with his wife. The lady, who was proud, did not put off her pride. The greater part of the night passed thus. Mayûra, who was taking his constitutional, came to that place. Hearing the noise, made by the husband and his wife through the window, he stopped. Bâṇa fell at the feet of his wife, and said, "O faithful one, pardon this one fault, I will not again anger thee." She kicked him with her foot which was encircled by an anklet. Mayûra, who stood under the window, became angry on hearing the sound of the anklet, and on account of the disrespect shown to the husband. But Bâṇa recited a new stanza—

"O thin-waisted one, the night that is nearly past, escapes swiftly like a hare, this lamp nods as if it were sleepy; O fair-browed one thy heart also has become hard on account of its enmity to thy breasts, at first. Alas, thou dost not put off thy pride and thy anger at the end of my prostrations."§

Hearing this Mayûra said—"Don't call her fair-browed but passionate, (chaṇḍi) since she is angry." Hearing this harsh speech that faithful wife cursed her father, who revealed the character of his daughter saying, "Mayest thou become a leper by the touch of the betel juice which I now have in my mouth." At that moment leprosy-spots appeared on his body. In the morning Bâṇa went as formerly to the Court dressed as a Varaka and made with reference to Mayûra, who also came, the following speech containing a pun, "The Varakoḍhî has come."‖

The King understanding this, and seeing the leprosy-spots, sent (Mayûra) away, saying, "You must go." Mayûra fixed himself in the temple of the Sun, sat down, keeping his mind concentrated on the deity, and praised the Sun with

---

* Na sahanti ikkamikkam na viṇâ chiṭṭhanti ikkamikkeṇa rāsaha-vasaha-turaṅgā jûyârâ paṇḍiyâ ḍimbhâ.

† A journey to Kashmir and a presentation of books to Sarasvatî is frequently mentioned as a test for poets by the Jaina authors.

‡ Jâgarite tanyâṁ vâpyâṁ s'aśaśatamaṁ nabhastalaṁ samasyâpadaṁ vadantyâ | [illegible]
[illegible] |
[illegible] ||

[illegible] samasyâ pûritâ | Bâṇena tathaiva pûritaḥ | [illegible] krtvâ [illegible].

[illegible] |
[illegible] ||

§ [illegible] [illegible] iva
[illegible] iva |
[illegible]
[illegible] ||

‖ I am unable to translate the term Varaka. The words of the text are—Varakavastraṁ, paridhâya sametaṁ mayûraṁ prati (âyâtaḥ varakoḍhî) iti s'lishṭaṁ vacho avocha.

the hundred verses,* which begins Jambhârâtibhakumbhodbhavam, &c.

When he had recited the sixth verse which begins '*S'îrnaghrânânghripâṇîn*, etc.,'—the witness of the world's deeds appeared visibly. Mayûra, bowing to him, said, 'Lord, deliver me from my leprosy!' The Sun answered, 'Friend, I also suffer even now from leprosy on the feet, in consequence of a curse, because I had sexual intercourse with the horse-shaped Raṇṇâdevî against her will.† Nevertheless, I will cover the leprosy caused by the curse of the faithful wife by giving you one of my rays!' Speaking thus, the Jewel of the Sky went away. That one ray enveloping his (Mayûra's) body destroyed the lepra-spots. The people rejoiced. The King honoured him. Bâṇa, being jealous of Mayûra's fame, caused his hands and feet to be cut off, and making a firm resolution, praised Chaṇḍikâ with the hundred verses, beginning 'Mâ bhânkshîr, etc.,' at the recitation of the sixth syllable of the first verse Chaṇḍikâ appeared and restored his four limbs."

Here I break my translation off. The remainder of the *Kathâ* states that the Jainas who were anxious to show that their holy men could work as great miracles, produced Mânatunga Sûri to uphold their good name. This worthy allowed himself to be fettered with forty-two iron chains, and to be locked up in a house. He then composed the forty-four verses of the *Bhaktâmarastotra*, and freed himself thereby. He of course converted King Bhoja by this miracle to the Jaina religion.

I may add that according to some Jaina *Theràvalis*, Mânatunga lived in the be beginning of the 3rd century A.D. We know, however, that Bâṇa and Mayûra lived four centuries later. It seems that there is great confusion in the earlier parts of the *Theràvalis*. Mânatunga and Bâṇa may after all turn out to be contemporaries. As regards the story of Bâṇa's self-mutilation, I think it not improbable that it has arisen from a misinterpretation of the words of his *Chaṇḍî* "styndyathupahetûn prakṛtim avayavân prâpayantyeva devyâ,"—Devî bringing to their natural state the limbs which showed signs of rising anger.

BENGALI FOLKLORE—A LEGEND FROM DINAJPUR.

By G. H. DAMANT, B.C.S.

There was once a king who had two queens named Duhâ and Suhâ. Suhâ had two sons, but Duhâ had only one lame son. One night the king dreamed that he saw a tree whose stem was silver, its branches were of gold, the leaves were diamonds, the fruits were pearls, and peacocks were playing in the branches and eating the fruits. When the king saw this he lost the sight of both his eyes, and he again dreamed that if he could really see the silver tree with golden branches, diamond leaves, pearly fruits, and peacocks playing in the branches, his eyesight would be restored to him, otherwise he would remain blind for the rest of his life. Then he rose up, and retired to his 'house of anger' and slept there. Early next morning the prime minister with the officers and attendants came to court, and not finding the king sitting on his throne as usual, they went to enquire what had happened, but the king would not speak a single word to any of them. Shortly after that the two sons of queen Suhâ came, and after offering the king much consolation, they asked him why he refused to speak, and why he had slept in 'the house of anger.' Then the king told them all about the dream which he had seen, and how he had become blind, and how he had been told that if any one would shew him a tree like that which he had seen in his dream, he would recover his sight, otherwise he would remain blind for the rest of his life. The king's sons said that they would find some way to shew him the tree, and comforted him, so that he left 'the house of anger' and sat on his throne, and began to attend to his public business as usual. Meanwhile the king's sons mounted their horses, and started to search for the tree. When queen Duhâ's lame son heard of it, he went to his mother, and told her how his father had become blind, and how his brothers had mounted their horses to search for the means of curing their father by bringing the tree with the golden branches, and that he wished to go with them and help to search for the tree. His mother told him

* The *Mayûra S'ataka* which like the *Chaṇḍîs'ataka* is written in the *S'ardûlavikrîḍita* metre, exists now and is being printed with a commentary by my learned friend Yajnes'var S'âstrî.

† This is apparently an allusion to the history of Vivasvata and Saraṇyû, which occurs already in the Rig-veda. Raṇṇâ is possibly a corruption of *Saraṇyû* or *Sanjñâ*, as the goddess is called in the Mahâbhârata and the Purâṇas.

that the king could not bear the sight of him or her, and that he could not go. At this he was very angry and said he was determined to go, so his mother told him that he might go, but he must first obtain leave from the king. So he went into the king's presence, but as he did not dare to approach him, he remained standing in a corner of the court. The prime minister saw him, and went and told the king that the son of queen Duhá had been standing there for some time, but was afraid to come near and tell what he had to say. The king ordered the prime minister to enquire why he had come. So the prince told him that his brothers had gone to search for the silver tree to cure the king, and he wished to go with them. The king said that he was lame, and could not go, but the prime minister replied that in the dream it was only said that somebody must bring the tree, it did not matter who brought it, and that no one's name had been mentioned, and if the prince wished to go the king might allow him to do so. The king told the prime minister to do as he thought best, so he gave the prince some money and a horse, and sent him away.

The prince went to his mother queen Duhá, and as he was taking leave of her, he gave her a plant, and said, "mother, take care of this plant, and look at it every day, and when you see that it is fading, you will know that some misfortune has befallen me, and when it is dead, I shall be dead too, and if it be flourishing you will be sure that I am well." So saying he left his home, and travelled for some distance till he came to a tree where his brothers were sitting with their horses tied near. When his brothers saw him, they said to each other, "Look brother, the lame boy is coming, it is a very lucky thing, we will make him cook for us." So they all met together, and after they had cooked and eaten, they lay down at the foot of the tree, and went to sleep, but the son of queen Duhá sat up wide awake. Now it happened that a pair of birds had built their nest in the tree, and at night the old birds went out to seek food, leaving their young ones in the nest. After they had gone, a great snake climbed up the tree to eat the young birds; they all began to cry out when they saw it, but queen Duhá's son drew a sword from his belt and cut the snake in pieces, he then cut off the snake's hood and tail, and gave them to the young birds to eat. At the end of the night the old birds returned to their nest, and the young birds told their father and mother all that had befallen them, and enquired who the three men were who had come to the foot of the tree. The mother bird told them that the men were the sons of the king of a certain country, and that the lame man who had saved their lives and given them food was the son of queen Duhá, and the king would not bear to look on him. The young birds then enquired why they had come and whither they were going, so the mother bird told them that the king had seen a dream, and become blind, and his sons had come to search for the silver tree to make him well. The young birds then asked if the princes would find the tree, and the mother bird told them that the princes would find it if they would descend into the well which was at the foot of the tree. Now the son of queen Duhá was awake all the time and heard all the talk of the birds, and in the morning he told his brothers, and asked them if they would go down into the well, but they told him to go himself, thinking that he would probably be killed. Queen Duhá's son agreed to go, but told his brothers that they must weave a rope of grass, and lower him down into the well, and draw him up again when he shook the rope, and must not leave the place until he had shaken it. So he fastened the rope round his waist, and was let down into the well; when he reached the bottom he saw a path before him, and walked along it for some distance, till he reached a city built of stone, into which he entered, and found that the whole place was covered with the bones of men,—there was no living thing to be seen, nothing but bones. He could not help thinking to himself that he was very unlucky in having come there. After this he went into one of the houses, and saw a dead woman lying stretched upon a bed; again he wondered what ill luck had brought him there; then he looked again, and found a golden wand and a silver wand lying one on each side of the dead woman; he took them up, and as he was moving them from side to side, he touched her body with the golden wand, then she turned on one side and awoke. When she saw the man she said to him, "Who are you, and why have you come here, this is a city of Rákshasas who will kill and devour you." The prince told her that, now he had come, she could either save him or destroy him as she thought best. So the woman arose, and cooked food, and gave him to eat, and after she had presented him with betel-nut and tobacco, she said, "It is now time for the Rákshasas to return, you must touch my body with the silver wand, and make me dead again, and you go and conceal yourself in that large cauldron which my father used in performing worship." So the prince touched her body with the silver wand, and went and hid himself in the cauldron. When the Rákshasas came they brought her to life, and after she had bathed, she cooked twenty-two maunds of rice and twenty-two buffaloes, and gave to the Rákshasas to eat. At nightfall they all went to their own houses, and the woman began to shampoo the feet of the old Rákshasa with an iron rod of twenty-two maunds weight. In the morning the Rákshasas returned, and made the woman dead as before, and went away. Then the king's son came out of the cauldron and aroused the woman, and she cooked for him, and after they had both eaten, she again presented him with betel-nut and tobacco. As they were talking together, he said that he should be forced to remain in concealment all the time he was in that place, so she must go to the old Rákshasa, and ask him how the Rákshasas could be destroyed. The woman said it would be impossible for her to discover that, but he told her that she must begin to cry when she was shampooing the feet of the old Rákshasa. She asked what she was to do if tears would not come into her eyes, and the prince replied, "you must mix some salt with the water which you pour over the Rákshasa's feet, and put some of it into your eyes, and when the old Rákshasa asks you why you are crying, you must say to him—'you are now very old, and will die soon, and when you are dead, the other Rákshasas will kill me, and eat me, and this is the cause of my tears.'" After the king's son had given her this counsel, he went and concealed himself in the cauldron as before. After a little time the Rákshasas came and ate their food as usual, and went to sleep, then the woman went to the old Rákshasa to shampoo his feet, and as she was doing it, she put the salt water in her eyes and made the tears flow, as the king's son had told her. When the old Rákshasa saw it, he asked her why she was crying, and she said it was because he was old and would die in a few days, and after his death the others would eat her. Then he said: "It is impossible that we should die, but still your father had a tank, and in that tank there is a pillar of crystal and a great knife and a bitter gourd; now in a certain country there is a king who has a queen named Duhá, and she has a lame son; if he were to come and cover his eyes with a cloth folded seven times, and lift all these things out of the tank at one dive, and cut through the crystal pillar at one blow, he would find the gourd in the middle of it, and inside the gourd are two bees; then if any one could smear his hand with ashes, and catch the bees as they fly away, and squeeze them to death we should all die; but if a single drop of their blood were to fall to the ground, we should become twice as numerous as we were before." The woman replied that it was quite impossible that queen Duhá's son could come there and kill them.

When the morning had come, the Rákshasas made the woman dead as before, and went away, but the king's son revived her, and she told him all that she had heard from the old Rákshasa, so they both of them went to the bank of the tank, and the woman bound a cloth seven times over his eyes; then he plunged into the water, and at one dive brought up all the things, and at one blow split open the crystal pillar. Just as the two bees were flying out from the gourd, the woman smeared her hands with ashes, and caught them, and killed them so that not a single drop of their blood fell to the ground, and at that very instant all the Rákshasas died, no matter where they were.

After this the king's son and the woman lived quietly together for some time, till one day he said that, although he had been some time in the country, he had never visited the different parts of it, and that day he would go and see the northern part. The woman told him that he might go and see the northern part of the country if he wished, but he must be careful not to go into the northernmost corner. So the king's son went and saw all the northern part except the farthest corner, but he could not help wondering what there was there, and why the woman had forbidden him to visit it; at last he determined to go and see for himself. When he reached the place he saw a woman sitting weaving a garland, and some sheep were feeding in front of her. As soon as he saw how beautiful she was, he thought that was the reason the woman had forbidden him to come there. When the woman saw him she treated him with great politeness, and said to him, "Prince, here is a garland which I have been weaving for you." With these words she put the garland on his head, but as she was doing so, she rubbed a drug on his forehead, which changed him into a sheep. In the meantime the woman, finding that the king's son was very slow in returning, could not help thinking that he must have gone into the northernmost corner. So she went to search for him, and found that the garland-maker had transformed him into a sheep, so she told her that she had changed her brother-in-law into a sheep. The garland-maker said she did not recognise her brother-in-law when he came to her, and asked the woman to point him out. Then the woman found the right sheep and rubbed the drug from his forehead, and the king's son became himself again, and she told him that he was acting very wrongly in going to the northernmost corner although she had forbidden him. They then went home and had some food.

But after a few days the prince said that he was going to see the southernmost part of the country. The woman told him that he might go, but he must not go into the southernmost corner. After the prince had seen all the southern country, he could not help wondering what was to be seen in the southernmost corner to which he was forbidden to go, so he went and saw a beautiful garden of plantain trees, with plantains of all the best kinds ripening in it. He said to himself, "only look! here are all these ripe plantains, and the woman has never brought me a single one to eat with milk." With these words he took hold of a plantain tree to shake down a ripe fruit, but no sooner had he touched it than he was changed into a monkey, and leaped up into the tree. Meanwhile the woman, seeing his delay in returning, went in search of him, and found that he had been changed into a monkey. So she took an unripe plantain, and showed it to him, and when he came near to smell it, he became a man again, and she told him that he must never disobey her again; he promised never to do so, and they both went home and ate and drank.

After some days the king's son said he would go and see the eastern part of the country, and the woman told him not to go into the easternmost corner; but after he had seen all the eastern country, he thought that just for once he would go and see the easternmost corner; so he went and found a faqir sitting there saying his prayers. The faqir saluted him respectfully, and told him not to remain so far off, but to come a little nearer, and when he came nearer, he put a drug on his forehead, and transformed him into a horse. Then he climbed on his back just as if he was his own horse, and beat him with the whip, and made him gallop at full speed. In the meanwhile the woman saw that he was long in returning, and thought that he must have gone into the corner and met with some misfortune, so she went to look for him, and found that it really was so, and he had been changed into a horse, and the faqir was riding him and making him gallop. Then she told the faqir that it was her own son whom he had transformed into a horse, and was riding, and made him so ashamed of what he had done that he changed the horse to a man again, and she said to the king's son, "For shame, prince, you always do what I forbid you, see what marks the faqir's whip has made on your back." He looked and found that blood was dropping from his back, and he promised that he would never again do what she forbade him. They then went home and ate their food.

After some days had passed, the king's son said he would go and see the western part of the country. The woman told him he might go if he did not go into the westernmost corner. When he had seen the whole of the western country, he said to himself that he had suffered every misfortune which could possibly happen to him, and that there was only one little corner remaining and he must go and see it. So he went and found a well into which a man, a tiger, a snake, and a frog had fallen. When they saw him they all called out to him to come and take them out. He then took the turban from his head and let it down into the well and pulled out the tiger first. The tiger saluted him and said; "Prince, when any misfortune befals you, think on me and I will come and befriend you, but be sure not to give any assistance to any creature which has no tail." After that the prince pulled the snake out of the well and the snake saluted him in the same way as the tiger and went away. He then lifted the frog out, (now a frog has no tail) and the frog spat upon his body and went away. Last of all he drew up the man, (now a man has no tail) and the man seized him and bound him and threw him into the well and went away. Meanwhile the woman seeing the prince's delay, thought that some fresh misfortune must have befallen him, so she went to search for him and found him in the well. She pulled him out, but from that day forth she would not allow him to go out of her sight.

After some time had passed the prince one day thought that, although he had come to try and find a remedy for his father, he had fallen in with the woman and forgotten everything else, so he began to cry. The woman asked him why he was crying, and he told her it was because he had done nothing to obtain the object for which he came, but had spent all his time with her. The woman enquired what his object in coming was, and he told her that his father had seen a silver tree in a dream and become blind, but that if anyone could show him a tree with silver stem, golden branches, pearly fruits, and peacocks playing in the branches, he would recover his sight, otherwise he would remain blind. The woman told him that he must not stay there any longer, and she packed provisions for ten or fifteen days, in the shell of a gourd, but she continued to go into the house and come out of the house and to make such delay that the prince grew very angry and said to himself, "I have suffered all these dangers for the sake of this woman and yet she does not attend to what I say, but continues to say she will come, and goes into the house and comes back again and makes great delay: I will kill her and cut her in pieces." Having determined on this, he took the large knife which he had brought from the tank and cut her asunder at one blow. No sooner had he done so, than her two legs became a silver stem, her two arms were golden branches, the palms of her hands were diamond leaves, all her ornaments were fruits of pearl, and her head was a peacock dancing in the branches and eating the fruits. When the prince saw it, he perceived that it was the very tree for which he was searching, and he thought it was a great pity that he had killed the woman in that place, for if he had taken her to his father he could have cured him, while the tree itself was too large for him to carry, so he was about to cut it in pieces when the knife slipped from his hand, and the moment it touched the ground, the tree was again changed into the woman, who said to him, "Prince, I did not attend to what you said, in order that you might see the tree; now if you kill me you will be able to show your father the silver tree, and if you drop the knife on the ground, I shall again become a woman: come now let us go to my father-in-law and restore him to sight." Then they both went to the well by which the prince had descended and began to shake the rope. The woman said to the prince: "You must go first because if I go first your brothers will see me and will never pull you up afterwards;" but he said,—"If I go first and you do not follow me, my father will not be cured;" so they agreed to go both together.

When they reached the top, the prince's brothers saw how beautiful the woman was, and determined that queen Duhá's lame son should not have her but that they would keep her for themselves, and throw him into the sea when they were in the ship on their way home, and they would tell their father that, although they had searched long for a remedy for him, they could not find it, and had only brought a woman. So they all went into the ship, and when they were on the open sea, the prince's brothers bound him hand and foot and threw him overboard; but the woman, from inside the ship, saw what had happened, and threw him the shell of the gourd which she had brought with her, so the lame prince sat on the gourd and travelled on, and when he was hungry he ate the food which the woman had stored in it. In the meanwhile, when the prince's brothers attempted to touch the woman, she told them that she had made a vow that no man should touch her for twelve years, and that the lame prince had never touched her although he had married her, and that if they used violence to her they would be at once burnt to ashes; so they did not touch her, and after a few days they reached home and told their father that they had found no remedy for him but had brought a woman, and the king was pleased when he heard it.

All this time queen Duhá's son was sitting on the gourd, without any means of escape, till at last he thought over all that had happened to him and remembered the snake; no sooner had he done so than the snake came, and giving him his tail to hold, dragged him through the water to the shore and told him that he must then think of his friend the tiger who would come and unfasten the ropes by which he was bound. Then the prince thought of the tiger, and the tiger came and cut the prince's bonds with his teeth, and he travelled slowly on till he reached home, and went to his mother and told her all about the woman he had found, and how his brothers had thrown him into the sea. She told him that his brothers had brought the woman and invented a long story to satisfy the king, so he determined to go and enquire about it. When he came into the king's presence he asked whether his brothers had brought the silver tree, and the king told him that they had only brought a woman. The prince said that it was he who had found the woman, and that he would change her to a silver tree, but that if his brothers could change her back to a woman he would confess that they had found her and they might keep her. The king promised that if the prince could change the woman to a silver tree and back to a woman again, she should belong to him, and that if he recovered the sight of his eyes he would give him all his kingdom. The prince then called the woman and cut her in pieces with the large knife, and her feet became a silver stem, her two hands were golden branches, her head-ornaments were diamond leaves, all her bracelets and bangles were pearly fruits, and her head was a peacock dancing and playing in the branches and eating the pearls. Directly the king saw it he recovered the sight of his eyes. But the other princes said that they had found the woman and their brother had changed her to a tree by magic. The king told them that if they could change her back to a woman they might keep her, but they could not do it; so the lame prince dropped his knife on the ground, and she instantly became a woman again and did homage to her father-in-law. Then the king gave the whole kingdom to his lame son and banished the wicked princes, and he loved queen Dulâ as much as he used to love Nulâ and took her to his palace and lived with her.

When we had heard and seen all this we came away.

ON THE RÂMÂYANA.

BY PROF. ALBRECHT WEBER, BERLIN.

Translated from the German by the Rev. D. C. Boyd, M.A.

The question regarding the composition of the Râmâyana has assumed an entirely new phase* since the labours of D'Alwis† have made us acquainted with the Buddhistic conception of the Râma-Saga and of one of the legends interwoven with it by Vâlmîki, the Dasaratha-jâtaka. For there are important differences between this Buddhistic account and the representation given by Vâlmîki; and the former bears so plainly the impress of a higher antiquity, that it cannot well be doubted that it belongs to an earlier age. This is indeed the conclusion to which D'Alwis himself has been led. Leaving out of view many minor particulars, the main points of difference are these:—1, That Râma and his brother Lakshmana are sent by their father into exile during his lifetime, with the sole object of protecting them from the intrigues of their step-mother; 2, that Sîtâ, who is here surnamed Devî,‡ and who is the sister, not the wife of Râma, voluntarily joins her two brothers in their banishment; 3, that at the close of his exile, which in this account lasts only twelve years, Râma immediately returns, assumes the reins of government, and only then marries his sister Sîtâ; and consequently, 4, that the rape of Sîtâ by Râvana, and the whole expedition against Lankâ are entirely wanting! And, indeed, we are now in a position to point out that the entire narrative of the exile itself has to a large extent, been developed out of germs furnished by Buddhistic legends. In Buddhaghosa's commentary on the *Dhammapada*,§ for instance, there is found a legend of king Brahmadatta in Benares, who in like manner exiles his two sons, prince Mahimsâsaka and prince Chanda (Chandra), to secure them against their mother, to whom he has granted the fatal permission to choose anything she may wish; and their younger step-brother, prince Suriya (Sûrya), on whose account they are sent away, joins his fortunes to theirs and accompanies them in their exile.‖ Again, as bearing on our subject, we meet with the simply told, yet truly captivating, legend of the origin of Buddha's ancestors, that is of the Sâkya and the Koliya families, which is found in Buddhaghosa's commentary on the *Suttanipâta*, and has been published by the present writer, with a translation, according to Fausböll's edition of

* Cf. *Indische Streifen* II. 232, 264.

† *Attanagaluvansa*, p. 164ff., Colombo 1866, in the *Dasaratha-jâtaka*, Jât. XI. (46), 1, and in the *Sâmajâtaka*, Jât. XXI. (16), 2. Vide *Lawrence* p. 184.

‡ *Devî* seems here to mean simply *Princess*. Cf. *Childers* on Hardy, *Manual of Buddhism*, p. 116ff. also Fausböll, *Dhammapada*, p. 174, 5, 437, 21 (where, indeed, appears—first queen.) Or are we to see here a reflection of the divinely honoured Sîtâ of the gṛihya-ritual?

§ Ed. Fausböll p. 292.

‖ The conclusion of this legend is, that on the death of the father, the three princes return home; the eldest takes possession of the throne, prince Chandra assumes the uparâja-dignity, and prince Suriya becomes commander-in-chief. The narrative, for the sake of which the legend is narrated, is interesting, among other reasons, because it recalls an episode of the *Râmâyana*. In the *Yuddhakânda*, as Hanumant is fetching from the mountain Gandhamâdana, the plant which has the power of bringing to life again, he is attacked by a grâha, which drags every living thing down into the water. Similarly here in Buddhaghosa a daka-(that is an udaka-) rakkhasa, living on *Himavant*, has received from Vessavana (Vaiśravaṇa) the power to drag down into his pond all who do not know the divine command; and this fate befalls the two younger princes; but, by information that satisfies the rakkhasa, the eldest manages to deliver his brothers out of their difficulty.

the text.* In this legend the Ikshvâku king, Ambaṭṭharâjan, to please a young wife, exiles all his elder children, four sons and five daughters. The young princes, when they have reached the forest, intermarry with their sisters, with the view of providing a mutual safeguard against the degeneracy of their race through *mésalliance*; and they install their eldest sister Piyâ in the place of mother. When, after a time, the latter is stricken with leprosy, they remove her to another part of the *forest*; and there she is found by a king Râma, who has also been driven by leprosy into the forest but has *recovered*; and by him she is cured and wedded.† Now, whatever points of difference the legend here presents, the mutual relations of these three forms of the story cannot be mistaken. In the *Dasarathajâtaka*, in addition to the reasons for the exile and the intermarriage of the brothers and sisters, we find mention made of the names Dasaratha, Lakshmana, Bharata, and Sitâ; and Râma is spoken of, not as a prince who was unacquainted with the exiled family, but as one of their number and occupying the chief place among them. And the poet of the *Râmâyana*, following the main idea of the story thus presented, has not only represented Râma and Sitâ as lovers, but, what is most important, has added the rape of Sitâ and the expedition to Lankâ. He has also changed the home of the exiles from Vârânasî to Ayodhyâ, and, on the other hand, he has shifted the scene of the banishment from the Himavant to the Dekhan (*Dandaka forest*, &c.)

Now, when we consider this question of the *change of locality*, it becomes evident that the removal of the place of the exile to the Dekhan can easily be explained by the poet's intention to describe an expedition to Lankâ; while the alteration of Vârânasî into Ayodhyâ is perhaps connected with an older form of the *Saga*, and one no doubt current at the time of the *Dasaratha jâtaka*, according to which both Brahmadatta and Ambaṭṭharâjan lived in Vârânasî, but the exiled children of the latter, or at least their descendants, the Sâkyas and Koliyas, settled in Kapilapura (*Kapilavastu*) and Koliyapura, on opposite banks of the river Rohiṇî;‡ and thus we are brought into the immediate neighbourhood of Ayodhyâ.

And now with regard to the expedition to Lankâ. In opposition to the hitherto received view§ that the poet intended under this representation to depict the spread of Aryan civilization toward the south, and especially to Ceylon, Talboys Wheeler‖ has recently given to the world his opinion that the account of this expedition only gives expression to the hostile feeling entertained by the Brahmans toward the Buddhists of Ceylon, who are to be identified with the *Râkshasas* of the poem. This view receives support from the fact that Râvana and his brothers are represented as having themselves sprung from the Brahmanical race,¶ and as having by their penances won the favour of Brahman, Agni and other gods; and in this representation there may lurk an allusion to the Aryan origin of the royal race of Ceylon.* And it is at least quite as consistent with the circumstances (if not even more so) that an Indian poet writing about the beginning of the Christian era (and the work of Vâlmîki can hardly date earlier than this, as we shall presently see) should have taken as the subject of his representation the conflicts with the Buddhists, which were by that time being fiercely waged, and have depicted a conquest of their chief seat in the South,—as that he should have selected for his theme an idea so abstract as a picture of the "spread of Aryan civilization." The Monkeys of the poem, too, which are undoubtedly to be regarded as the representatives of the aborigines of the Dekhan, appear throughout (with the single exception of *Bâlin*) as the allies of Râma, and therefore as already brought completely within the influence of the Aryan culture. This holds true also of king Guha with his Nishâdas. And though Wheeler certainly presses his theory too far when, for instance, he talks of the molestations which the sages of Chitrakûṭa and of the Daṇḍaka-forest suffered at the hands of the Râkshasas and to save them from which Râma took them under his protection, and makes these refer solely to the Buddhists,† yet it must be allowed that

* Vide *Monatsberichte der K. P. A. d. W.*, 1859 p. 410 ff. *Ind. Stud.* V 410 ff. *Ind. Streifen.* I, 347 ff., and Rogers, "Buddhaghosha's Parables" p. 176. The legend had already been made known by Turnour, Csoma Körösi, and Hardy, if not textually, at all events in substance. See also Emil Schlagintweit, *Die Könige von Tibet* (München, 1866) p. 10 837.

† In the *Mahâvanso*, p. 184-185 mention is made of a place *Râmagâma* on the banks of the Ganges (with a sacred *dâgoba*) as existing in the time of Asoka, and as belonging to the Koliyas (Cf. also Bigandet, *Life of Buddha* p. 310.) Contemporaneously therewith Fa-Hian (Chap. 22, at the end,) and later also Hiwen Thsang mention a land bordering on Kapilavastu called Lanmo; which Stan. Julien (II., 325) and Beal (*Fa-Hian* p. 90) translate by Râmagrâma.

‡ "By Klaproth said to come from the mountains of Nepal, and after uniting with the Mahananda to fall into the Rapti, near Gorakhpur."—*Hardy.*

§ Vide Lassen, *Ind. A. K.* I. 535 and my *Vorles. über Ind. L. G.*, p. 181.

‖ In the second volume of his *History of India* (London 1869), a work which can hardly indeed be said to correspond to its title, but which notwithstanding its extravagant Euhemerism, is rich in valuable views and suggestions.

¶ As grandchildren of *Pulastya*, I. 22, 15, 17. IV. 10, 14.

* In the *Uttarakâṇḍa* it appears pretty certain that in the quite detailed separation of the *Râkshasas* of Lankâ into the Paulastya and the Sukeśavanśa (? VIII. 21) or Salakaṭankaṭâs (? IV. 21, 20) we are to recognise the double peopling of Ceylon by aborigines and by Aryans of the Brahmanical stock.

† While the special description of these *Râkshasas*, for instance in *Muir*, III. 8, 16 ff., points unmistakeably not to the Buddhists, but to hostile aborigines, who were still leading a savage life. *Vide* Muir, *Orig. S. Texts*, II, 426 ff.; Monier Williams, *Ind. Epic Poetry* p. 10.

Sítá's speech in favour of the *ahinsá**, especially the protest which she raises against the attack on the Rákshasas as inconsistent with Ráma's character as a devotee† may be fairly regarded as a relic from an old Buddhistic legend embodying this idea that‡ a *Kshatriya* was not justified "in interfering in the disputes between the Brahmans and the Buddhists," so long as the latter, that is the *Rákshasas* of the poem, have not shown towards him any feeling of hostility. There is nothing, however, in the representation of the town Lanká and its inhabitants that can be regarded as having a direct reference to Buddhism; on the contrary, the same gods§ are invoked alike by Rávaṇa and by Ráma, just as is done by the Greeks and the Trojans in Homer. The red turban and the red garments of the priests who officiated at Indrajit's magical sacrifice|| remind us also of the magic ritual of the *Sámaveda*¶, and they are consequently not to be connected with the *yellowish-red* garments of the Buddhists (*kasháya, raktapaṭa*). And finally, the solitary passage in which Buddha is directly referred to, and then indeed only to be likened to a thief,** has been pointed out by Schlegel as being probably a later interpolation. Any one, therefore, who may be disposed, notwithstanding the preceding considerations, to adopt Wheeler's view must be prepared to draw this further conclusion, from the great caution with which the poet has veiled his intention to depict the struggle with and the conquest of the Buddhists of Ceylon,—that he himself lived under a Buddhistic power, and therefore found himself compelled to conceal his real purpose—and that besides, to insure his own safety, he just took an old Buddhistic legend, and modified it to suit the object he had in view!

In addition to this tendency, whether it be specially political or having reference to the history of cultivation in general, which unquestionably runs through the *Rámáyaṇa*, and secures for it its character as a national Epic, it has still another purpose which may be said to lie on the very surface, namely, to represent Ráma as an incarnation of Vishṇu, and to confirm the supremacy of this god over all the other gods. With respect to this matter, however, it is difficult to decide in how far *Válmíki* himself had this purpose in view, or whether it may not have been introduced in later additions to the poem. On account of the loose connection in which the portions that bring out this idea stand with the general structure of the work, it is well known that the latter view has been most generally adopted.† But if Wheeler's opinion as to the anti-Buddhistic tendency of the poet should be positively established, then the view of those who believe that he had himself given this Vaishṇava complexion to his work‡ would undoubtedly receive no inconsiderable support, inasmuch as this view so completely harmonises with the anti-Buddhistic theory. As a matter of fact, at least, the result was thus by means of the *Rámáyaṇa*, and especially by means of the Vaishṇava elements in it just referred to, assistance of the most important kind was rendered to the efforts of the Brahmans, which were directed, by the clothing of their divinities and of the worship of their gods with new life, to the recovering of the ground which Buddhism had won among the people. And it is at all events a remarkable phenomenon that the old Buddhistic *Saga* of the pious prince Ráma, which glorified him as an ideal of Buddhistic equanimity, should have been cast by the skilful hand of *Válmíki* into a form§ which, whether in accordance with his own plan or through the introduction of subsequent elements, has so powerfully contributed to the suppression and overthrow of Buddhism—the Buddhistic elements so favourable and gratifying to the popular spirit being preserved, and merely clothed in a garb subservient to the Brahmanical pretensions.

In addition to the Buddhistic legend, it is beyond question that *Válmíki* must have had access to other materials for his work, which enter into its composition, and which must from the very first have secured it a favourable reception among the people. It is very obvious, for instance, to trace a connection between Ráma, the hero of his work, and the agricultural demi-god of the same name, the Ráma Halabhṛit of the Brahmans. I have already called attention to this elsewhere||, and have laid special stress on this point, that in the versions of the *Ráma-Saga* which are found in the *Mahábhárata*, and some of which are of considerable antiquity¶, a special prominence is given almost throughout to the fact that the reign of Ráma was a Golden Age, and that cultivation and agriculture were then vigorously flourishing. The

* III, 13, 2 ff.

† [illegible]

‡ Wheeler vol. II. p. 248, 256, 384, 391.

§ Vide Muir, IV, 440 ff.; Cf. also *Rám.* V. 18, 11 ... where Hanumán is the ... in Lanká,—Bhagnaga[illegible] [illegible]

|| VI, 13, 66, 62, 81.

¶ Vide *Ind. Stud.* I, 31, 32, borrowed no doubt from the Puráṇas.

** II, 109, 34, Ed. Schl.

† *Vide* Lassen, *Ind. A. K.* I, 488-489; Muir, *Orig. S. Texts* IV, 149 ff. 377 ff.

‡ Gorresio, vol. X. p. xlvii, is at least undecided.

§ This Buddhistic germ of Ráma's personality is still in fact apparent enough in the *Rámáyaṇa* in its present form: and in opposition to Monier Williams, who supposed that we were to find here later Christian influences, I had already pointed out this fact in my treatise on the *Ráma Táp. Up.* p. 270 (1864,) even before D'Alwis had made us acquainted with the contents of the *Dasaratha-játaka*.

|| Cf. *Ind. Stud.* I, 173, 277. II, 392, 410. *Vorles. über Ind. Lit. Gesch.*, p. 181. *Ráma Tápan. Upan.* p. 275, (where at the same time I have made mention also of the Raman hvástra of the Avesta, that genius of the air who as the friendly genius of taste, but also as a brave hero is represented as wearing golden armour.

¶ *Vide infra.*

cradle of Râma seems intended to represent the winter-time, during which the activity of Nature, and especially the operations of agriculture, are at a stand-still. Any other *direct* evidence, however, of such a connection between these two is not in the meantime forthcoming. But on the other hand, as regards Râma's wife Sîtâ, there are two points that are all the more deserving of notice:—namely, first, her mythical character itself; secondly, and specially her relation to the similarly named goddess of the Vedic ritual, the symbol of the field-furrow (*sîtâ*); and indeed the significance of both these points should be so fully recognised as that it could hardly be called in question. The accounts in the *Râmâyana* regarding her being born from a ploughed field* and regarding her return into the bosom of her Mother Earth†; the name of her sister Urmilâ, which can be explained as "waving seed-field;" finally, the surname‡ of her father Janaka: Sîradhvaja "bearing a plough on a banner;" are clear derivatives of her mythical, agricultural character. Fortunately, besides, for the working out of the conception, there was available the glorified representation of the similarly named spouse of Indra or Parjanya in the *grihya* texts, which picture her appearance§ in such plastic youthful beauty that the pencil of the poet needed only to add a few touches here and there.|| Endowed with these characteristics of the national goddess, the representation of the wife of Râma must have awakened the widest interest;¶ and this conception of her was admirably fitted either for purely poetical uses, or for the purpose of bringing back the hearers to their allegiance to the Brahmanical gods. *Vâlmîki* has besides introduced an additional element into his representation of Sîtâ, by making her the daughter of the pious Videha king, Janaka, highly honoured on account of his wisdom with Yâjnavalkya in the *Brâhmana* of the White *Yajus*, and in various legends of the *Mahâbhârata*, a circumstance which is no doubt partly due to the desire of giving, by means of this paternity, a decidedly Brahmanical colouring to her descent, and which in fact may easily be understood as in some measure favouring an earlier conjecture of my own* namely, that *Vâlmîki* himself belonged to that part of India which corresponds to the kingdom of Kosala, bordering on the region of the Videhas, and standing in the closest relations with them—to the chief city of which kingdom, Ayodhyâ, the scene of *Vâlmîki's* work is laid. It is also deserving of notice that Aśvapati, the king of the Kekayas,† who appears in the *Râmâyana* as the brother-in-law of Daśaratha, is mentioned in the *Brâhmana* of the White *Yajus*‡ as being nearly contemporary with Janaka.§ And the name of Sîtâ herself occurs in a [illegible]|| as even then in use as a proper name though the bearer of it appears there in a relation

* Râm. I. 66, 14, 19, [illegible]

† First mentioned indeed in the *Uttarakâṇḍa*.

‡ First, so far as I have been able to discover, in the *Uttara Râmacharita*.

§ Cf. my Abh. über Omina und Portenta pp. 370, 375.

|| [illegible] are the words used so early as in the *Kauś.* 106, naturally, however, without any reference to the later position of Srî as the wife of Vishnu, or to the identification of Sîtâ, as the wife of Râma, with the latter.

¶ Was it Vâlmîki's finding of the two names, Râma and Sîtâ united in the Buddhistic legend, that suggested to him the idea of making use of them for his contemplated work, which had for its object the restoration of the ancestral gods? We may conjecture that he made such a use of these names with the intention of [illegible] to which Buddha was heir, by glorifying his ancestor Râma?—a question which it is natural to ask, especially if Wheeler's view be adopted with reference to the legend regarding the origin of the Śâkya race. Whether we are also to maintain, with regard to those Buddhistic legends of Râma the progenitor of the Śâkyas, and of Râma and Sîtâ as children of Daśaratha, that there is such a connection between them on the one hand, and Râma Halabhrit and the Sîtâ of the *grihya*-ritual on the other, as I have assumed regarding the representations of Vâlmîki:—this seems to me to be at least, very questionable.

* Vide Akad. Vorles. über Ind. Lit. p. 182.

† The Sopeithes, king of the [illegible] who waited upon Alexander the Great in person, is evidently only the analogue of Aśvapati vide Lassen, Ind. Alt. I, 2nd ed. II. 161. Besides the name which his country also bears, I connect (let me say in passing) with Kaṭha, the name of the Vedic *Yajus*-school. The practice of infanticide is mentioned in the *Kâṭhaka* 27, 9 (Cf. Tâ. VI, 5, 10, 3, *Nir.* III, 4. *Ind. Stud.* IX, 481); it was permitted to expose new-born female children, but not male [illegible], [illegible].

‡ 10, 6, 1, 2 Chând. Up. V. 11, vide Ind. Stud. I, 173, 213, [illegible]

§ With regard to this special reference to [illegible] in the White *Yajus*, it should be added that Vâlmîki's own name, as is well known, appears among the teachers who are mentioned in the *Taittirîya Prât.* And indeed it appears in the passage [illegible] coming next to that of *Agniveśya* vide *Ind. Stud.* I, 167, where I have called attention to the fact that a [illegible] is also ascribed to one Agniveśa. It is apparently, to be sure, quite a modern performance (vide Aufrecht, Catal. Cod. MSS. Sanskrit, 1864) bearing the name [illegible], and composed in the [illegible]; but the [illegible] of this name is certainly significant, especially when we remember that [illegible] (for the form of this name vide [illegible] XIV, 6, [illegible]) the celebrated *Râma's* [illegible] in a dramatic form, belonged to a Brâhmanic family which studied the *Taittirîya* [illegible] IX, 2, 41, ed. [illegible], p. 121 [illegible]); then further there exists a drama called [illegible] (vide Taylor's Catalogue of the MSS. I, 11, Madras 1860) composed by [illegible], and corresponding to the first six Books of the *Râmâyana*, and that, finally, the names of the Sages Bharadvâja and Atri, which are so remarkably prominent in Vâlmîki's description of the exile, appear also among the teachers of the Taitt. Veda. From all this then, it appears to be fairly presumable that the *Râma-Saga* was very carefully preserved among the followers of the *Yajus*, especially of the Black *Yajus*; though this is perhaps to be accounted for only on the ground that *Vâlmîki*, the first who made a poetical use of the *Saga*, was one of themselves, and bore a name peculiar to them. According to the tradition of the *Adhyâtma Râmâyana* II, 6, 64 ff., vide Hall in the *Ind.* [illegible] II, 81 and Wheeler p. 318, *Vâlmîki* was "of low caste"! that neither in his work itself nor in *Bhavabhûti* is there anything to be found that bears out this assertion.

|| Taitt. Br. II, 3, 10, 1-3.

quite different from that which is found both in the gṛihya-ritual and in the *Rámáyaṇa*, namely, as the daughter of Savitar, that is, of Prajápati, and as enamoured of the Moon, who on his part looked with loving eyes on another of the daughters* Sraddhá (Faith); by the help of her father, however, she succeeds in winning his love.† It seems to me that in this *Saga*, too, we may find an element that has been made use of by Válmíki; in so far only, however, as the garland‡ with which her father decks her brows§ (accompanying the action with the recitation of various sentences,) and on account of the virtue of which, as a love-charm, the whole legend has been narrated, may probably have served as a direct model for the angarága (unguent) which Anasúyá, the wife of Atri, poured out in the form of an ointment, over the limbs of Sítá.‖ A still further parallel is indeed offered here to modern mythologists. For since Ráma is, at a later period, called also Rámachandra¶ and indeed is called also by the name Chandra itself,** the mildness, which is so prominent a feature in his character may, perhaps be explained in this way, that originally he was nothing more than a Moon-genius, and that consequently the *Saga* found in the *Taitt. Br.* regarding the love of Sítá (that is, the field-furrow) for the Moon actually represents the first germ out of which the *Saga* of the *Rámáyaṇa* has grown—that the angarága—ointment of the Rámáyaṇa, the ornaments [illegible] of the *Taitt. Br.*, is just the fragrant vapour or the dew which rises out of the furrow, and in which the Moonlight is reflected. This would be indeed genuinely poetical, and perhaps also quite possible, if it were not that the designation of Ráma as Rámachandra, or simply as Chandra is only found for the first time at so late a date, that rather the converse assumption is far more probable, namely, that a poetical spirit among the Bráhmans connected Ráma with the Moon just on account of the gentleness of his character†; though by this view a rollen reference by the learned to the *Sítá-Saga* of the *Taitt. Br.* is by no means excluded.‡

(*To be continued.*)

EXCURSUS.

As the version of the *Ráma-legend* [illegible] by D'Alwis is rarely to be met with, I subjoin an extract from that work (p. 170 ff.), containing the substance of the *Dasaratha-Játaka*. This is evidently based, in part at least, on a metrical version of the story; and the verse quoted at the close about the 16,000 years that Ráma reigned after his happy return from exile has an almost exact counterpart in the *Rámáyaṇa* itself (though the number of years there is only 11,000), as well as in several of the Ráma-legends in the *Mahábhárata*. And it is very possible that an acquaintance with the whole of the Páli text, which is therefore greatly to be desired, might bring to light still further coincidences of a similar nature.

"In aforetime there was at Baranes a king named Dasaratha. He reigned righteously, free from the four causes of agati (favour, anger, fear, and ignorance). His queen-consort, who was at the head of 16,000 wives, became the mother of two sons and a daughter. The eldest was called Ráma paṇḍit (*Doctor*), the second was named Lakkhana, and the daughter Sítá-devi. Some time afterwards the queen-consort died. Upon this event the king was afflicted for some time; and being consoled by his ministers he performed what was necessary to be done, and married another queen. She bore him love and affection, and in process of time conceived and bore him a son

---

* Cf. sraddhá vai sáryasya duhitá, Sat. XII. 7, 3, 11.

† This is no doubt only a variation of the older legends, e.g., for instance, *Ṛ. Saṃh.* X. 19, 1.—Nir. 12, 8, that Savitar gave his daughter Súryá in marriage to the Moon; cf. also the marriage of Saraṇyú, who bears twins (dva mithunau) to the husband Vivasvat (*Ṛik* X. 17, 1-2 Nir. XII 10, 11) just as Sítá does to Ráma.

‡ [illegible]

§ [illegible] *Vide* Colebr. i. 2, 10 [illegible] and Cf. the similar use of [illegible] as denoting a love charm in the *Kaus'*. 35 (Ind. Stud. V, 312.) It cannot be precisely identical with [illegible] (*Kaus.* 79), seeing that both words occur in the *Kaus'*; but perhaps the meaning is something similar. In the *Ráma-prasáda* II, 8, 5 [illegible] the word [illegible] is used quite generally as the name for fragrant ointments, such as sandal-oil and the like [illegible].

‖ *Rám.* III, 4, 18 [illegible] and 19, [illegible].

¶ First, so far as we yet know, in *Bhavabhúti* (for instance, *Mahávíracharita*, III, 14 (Calc. 1857), also in the *Padmapur.*, *Adhyátma-Rám.* In the *Rámáyaṇa*, *Adbhutottarakáṇḍa*, in the tale given in Alwis's work p. 8, &c. Although according to the accounts in recent Burmese writings, the names Rámachandra and Rámasiṃha are found among those of the last princes of Prithivi[illegible], which town is said to have been destroyed in the year 95 A.D., yet Lassen, II, 1101 probably goes somewhat too far when from this circumstance he infers "with tolerable certainty that subsequent to the beginning of the Christian era, Vishṇu was honoured there under the name of Ráma." On the contrary, these names, which are arbitrarily understood as having some relation to the Ráma of the *Rámáyaṇa*, may be supposed rather to raise a very emphatic protest against the authenticity of these Burmese accounts, and especially against their having any validity with regard to the period in question.

** *Vide* *Rámatáp.* p. 340.

† In *Bhavabhúti*, i.e. he is addressed "[illegible]."

‡ In the *Bhágavata Puráṇa*, for instance, it is well known that many similar forced reminiscences can be pointed out. That the disciples of the *Taittiríya-Veda* have even to the most recent times bestowed a remarkable amount of attention on the history of Ráma is, as we have remarked in note p. 123 referred to above,) evident enough. And when, as we find is stated in Wheeler, "the ointment given by Anasúyá to Sítá, which was to render her ever beautiful, is supposed by some pandits to mean piety or faith in Ráma, which renders all women beautiful," it is probable that we are to look here also for a faint reflection of the *Saga* in the *Taitt.* regarding the love of the Moon for Sraddhá.

([illegible]). He was named prince Bharata.* From the love which he bore to the son, the king said to the queen: "Dear (*bhadde*), I shall confer a boon; accept (it)." Behaving as having accepted it,† or as if she were pleased at it, she (was silent for a time) and went up to the king (one day), when the boy was seven or eight years of age, and said to the king: "Please your majesty, a boon was conferred by you upon my son; give it to him now." "Dear, take it," replied the king. "Sire, give the kingdom to my son." The king snapping his fingers wrathfully said: "Wretch (*nassa*), I have two sons as resplendent as two flames of fire, and dost thou wish me to kill them and give the kingdom to thy son?" (Whereupon) terrified, she quietly entered her bed chamber. On subsequent days (nevertheless) she repeatedly asked the king to bestow the very kingdom (on her son). The king, still refusing her the boon, and reflecting,—"that women were ungrateful and envious, and that either by means of forged writings (*kūṭapaṇṇa*)‡ or by means of a dishonest bribe (*kūṭalañcha*), the queen might procure the death of his sons," caused them to be summoned (to his presence), communicated the same (his misgivings) to them, and said: "Children, some calamity might befall you if you live here; go (therefore) to a foreign country or to the woods; return at the time of my funeral obsequies (*dhūmakāle*?), and assume the sovereignty to which you are lineally entitled." So saying, he sent for astrologers (*nemittake*?), and enquired of them how long he would live; and having learnt that he would live a further period of twelve years, said: "Sons, return after twelve years from hence, and ascend the throne." The princes saying: "Well," saluted the king, and went down the mansion weeping. Sītādevī (hearing this) said: "I too will go with my brothers," saluted the king and proceeded with them weeping.§

These three persons, accompanied with a large retinue, left (the city), and dismissing them (after they had gone some distance,) gradually reached Himavanta, and built a dwelling in a locality which had the advantage of water and herbs, and abounded with various fruits; and living on them they dwelt there. Paṇḍita [sic!] Lakkhaṇa and his sister Sītā supplicated Rāma, and obtained his consent (to the following proposal): "You stand to us in the position of a father, therefore tarry you here, we shall fetch herbs and fruits and maintain you."

From thence Rāma was altogether at home and the others nourished him with herbs and fruits. Whilst they were thus dwelling, king Dasaratha, owing to the grief for his sons, died (a premature death) in the ninth year (after the departure of his sons). His queen, after the rites of cremation, said: "Give the kingdom (*chattaṃ*) to my own son prince Bharata." The ministers saying—"those who are entitled to the kingdom are in the forest," did not comply. (Whereupon) prince Bharata (resolving)—"I will bring my brother Rāma from the woods and will set him upon the throne," proceeded with four-bodied army and the five-fold royal insignia (*pañcarājakakudhabhaṇḍa*)‖ to the locality where Rāma dwelt; and pitching their tents near it, Bharata with several ministers went to his residence at a time when Lakkhaṇa and Sītā had gone to the woods. He saw Rāma at the door of his residence, in the enjoyment of health, and quietly seated like a firm golden statue. Having saluted him and taken his respectful distance, Bharata informed him of the news regarding the king, and wept with his ministers falling down at the feet of Rāma. But Rāma neither wept nor answered. In him there was not the slightest emotion.¶ In the evening, whilst Bharata was (yet) weeping, the other two returned with herbs and fruits.

Whereupon Rāma thus pondered:—"These are children. They have not, as I have, the wisdom of *pariggaha*?.* If at once it be said to them, 'your father is dead,' unable to bear the grief, their hearts will be rent. I shall (therefore) by some device get them to descend into the water, and shall then cause the intelligence to be conveyed (to them)." He then, pointing to a pond opposite to them, spoke in a couplet thus: "You have come very late, let this be a punishment for you. Get down into this water and stand. Lakkhaṇa and Sītā come ye both (*etha Lakkhaṇa Sītā cha*) and descend into the water." They at once descended and stood (as desired); when, communicating to them the (sad) intelligence, Rāma gave utterance to the remaining couplet.—"This Bharata says thus:—'King Dasaratha is dead'." The moment they heard the intelligence of their father's death they became insensible. It was again conveyed to them, and they again became insensible. When they had thus fainted for the third time, his ministers raised and lifted them up from the water, and set them down on the ground. After they had recovered, all of them reciprocated their grief.

* D'Alwis has *Baratha* throughout.

† [illegible] (pat-?) [illegible] [illegible].—"behaving as if (she had) accepted it, i. e. inducing him by her manner to believe that she would accept the offer hereafter," [the gerund, [illegible] has usually the meaning, [illegible]: properly, "putting aside."

‡ With reference to this word, conf. *Ind. Streifen*, II. 337-8. In addition to the passages quoted there regarding letters and the like, numerous proofs are to be found in Buddhaghosa's commentary on the *Dhammapada*; vide Fausböll, p. 217, 221, 235, 264, 294, 348, 363-5, 417.

§ In this respect the demeanour of the [illegible] in the *Vessantara-Jātaka* (vide Hardy, *Manual*, p. 117) corresponds much more closely with the account in the *Rāmāyaṇa*.

‖ Conf. Fausböll, *Dhammapada*, p. 321 (where *rājakakudha-bhaṇḍa*).

¶ Contrast Rāmāy. II. 103, [illegible].

* The wisdom of taking things easy, of accepting all things with complaisance, of submitting to every condition of life.

and wept and bewailed. Bharata (however) pondering,—"this brother Lakkhana and sister Sîtâ, from the moment they heard the intelligence of their father's death, are unable to restrain their grief; but Râma sorrows not and weeps not; I shall, therefore, enquire of him the cause of his non-sorrowing"—uttered the second stanza for the (purpose of) that enquiry:—

"Having heard the death of a father, sorrow distresses thee not (*na tam pasahati*)* Râma. By what power (*pabhâvena*) dost thou not grieve for that which should be grieved for?"

Râma then addressing him explained the reason why he sorrowed not:

1.—"If a person by great grief cannot protect (*pâlitum*) a thing, wherefore should a wise (*viññû*) and discreet (*medhâvî*) man distress himself?

2.—"The young as well as (*daharâ cha*) the old, the ignorant as well as the wise, and the poor as well as the rich—all are (alike) subject to death (*machchuparâyanâ*).

3.—"The ripe fruit is ever in danger of dropping down (*papatanâ*); so likewise man that is born (of a woman) is always in danger of death.

4.—"Many people are seen in the morning (of whom) some disappear in the evening (*sâyam*) (and again) many people are seen in the evening (of whom) some disappear in the morning.

5.—"If a stupid person, who weeps afflicting himself, can derive any profit (*kiñchid attham*) then indeed should the wise man do the same (*kayirâ naṃ [?] vichakkhaṇo*).

6.—"He who torments himself (*hiṃsam attano*) (by sorrow) becomes lean and (*vivaṇṇo*) colourless; by sorrow (*tena*) the dead are not saved (*na pâlenti*), it is vain (*niratthâ*) (therefore) to weep.

7.—"As a house (*saraṇam*) involved in flames is extinguished with water, so likewise the steady, well-informed, intelligent and learned man speedily destroys the sorrow that is begotten (the felt sorrow) as the wind (drives away a tuft of) cotton.

8.—Alone is man (*eko va machcho*) born in a family—alone does he depart; the chief end of the enjoyment of all beings is their very association together (for a time) *saṃyogaparamâ tv eva sambhogâ sabbapâṇinaṃ*).

9.—Wherefore the heart (*hadayaṃ manaṃ cha*) of the wise and well-informed, who sees both this and the world to come (*passato imaṃ cha paraṃ cha lokaṃ*), and who knows the *dhamma*† (*aññâya*, i. e. *aññâya dhammaṃ*) is not inflamed even by exceeding sorrow.

10.—Thus I know exactly what should be done shall, seeing and enjoying (*so 'ham dassañ cha bhokkhañ cha*) nourish (my) relations, and protect all the rest."

* * * * * * * * * * *

The attendants who heard this sermon of Pandit Râma, declaring the transientness of things, were consoled. Afterwards prince Bharata, saluting Râma, said: "Accept the kingdom of Bârâṇasî."

"Child, take Lakkhaṇa and Sîtâ and rule the kingdom."

"(Why not) your Highness?"

"Child, my father said to me, 'Assume the kingdom by returning after twelve years.' If I go now, I would not be acting up to his word. I shall therefore go after the expiration of the remaining three years?"

"Who will reign until then?"

"Do ye."

"We cannot."

Then (saying):—"Until I come these shoes‡ will reign," he took off his shoes made of grass (straw), and gave them (to Bharata.) These three people, taking the shoes, and saluting the pandit, went with their retinue to Bârâṇasî. The shoes reigned for three years. The ministers placing the straw shoes on the throne, administered justice. Whenever they committed an act of injustice, the shoes struck each other. From that warning (sign) they released the case. But whenever they adjudicated justly, the shoes remained silent.

The Paṇḍita, after the expiration of three years, left the wood, and, having reached Bârâṇasî, entered the royal park. The princes learning his arrival entered the park attended with ministers, installed Sîtâ (in the office of) queen-consort, and performed the ceremony of consecration on both. The Mahâsatta, who had been thus consecrated, ascended an ornamented carriage, entered the city with a large retinue, and after receiving (reverential) salutation, ascended the upper storey of his magnificent mansion called Sukandaka. From thence he reigned righteously for 16,000 years and went to heaven.

dasa vassasahassâni saṭṭhim vassasatâni cha |
kambugîvo§ mahâbâhu Râmo rajjam akârayi¶ |

Buddha having delivered this sermon, applied

* With *pasahati* compare *parisahati*, Fausböll, *Dhammap.* 301, 5, 6 and *Vikrama* in Westergaard; especially my treatise on *Hâla*, Appendix V. 31. 32.

† Nature of all things, especially the eight realities of life; namely—

lâbho alâbho ayaso yaso cha nindâ pasaṃsâ cha sukham cha dukkham |
Ete cha dhammâ manussesu aniccâ.

‡ *Vide Râm.* II. 112, 21 ff. Schl., 128. 162. Gorr. *Zeit. d. Deut. Morgenl. Gesellsch.* XVI, 267, 268.

§ "Of golden neck"; here *kambugîvo* means 'a neck like golden drum,' *kambu* being used to express gold (!); for the true explanation see Böhtlingk-Roth, s. v. As an epithet given to Râma in the *Râm.* I. 1, 11. V. 32, 10.

¶ The Sanskrit form of this verse differs only in the third pâda, and, as already remarked above, in this respect also, that only ten hundred years are spoken of, instead of sixty hundred (making therefore altogether only 11,000 years instead of 16,000); but as regards the remainder, there is perfect identity. In the Sanskrit version the sentence runs as follows.—

daśa varshasahasrâṇi daśa varshaśatâni cha |
...... *Râmo râjyam akârayat.* ||

This is how it occurs in the last chapter of the *Ra-*

(*anusandhim*) the *jātaka* to the matter in hand: and after the explanation of the four verities, the husbandman* attained the path. Dasaratha of that period is now king Suddhodana, the mother (of Rāma)—Mahāmāyā, Sītā—Rāhulamātā—Bharata, Ānanda, Lakkhana—Sāriputta, the retinue—the attendants of Buddha, and Rāma [am] I."

CORRESPONDENCE, NOTES, AND QUERIES.

Dinajpur, 18th February 1872.

I should be glad if some of the readers of the *Indian Antiquary* would supply some information as to the history of the district of Dinajpur. The only work to which I have access on the subject is Dr. Buchanan's Report, and the writer unfortunately omits to state from what authorities his information was derived, so that I am able to form no estimate of its value. There are scattered about the district numerous pieces of carved stone, hornblende I think, some of them highly ornamented, and apparently of about the same date, which local tradition declares to have been brought from Bân-nagar, a place now a jungle, but said to have been the royal residence of Râja Bâṇa, or Vaṇ, mentioned in the Mahâbhârat. Bân-nagar is situated about sixteen miles south of the town of Dinajpur, on the Purnabhaba river, and four or five miles further down is the mart of Kantahr ("hand-burning"), said to derive its name from the burning of 998 of Bâṇa's thousand arms by Krishna. I know of the remains of at least four highly carved doorways, and some plain ones, besides numerous stones, generally hewn on one or more sides, often with mouldings, and the marks of metal clamps for holding them together. There are also, in different places, some scores of pillars, of similar workmanship, though by no means uniform pattern. Four of them are set up at the four corners of the tomb of Sultan Shah, in the middle of the Bân-nagar jungle, where there are also a number of the carved stones to which I am referring, though evidently not in the position for which they were cut, but taken by the Musalmans from some earlier building.

Some time ago I sent to the Bengal Asiatic Society a transcript of an inscription on a pillar, more richly carved than any of the others that I have seen, now lying at the Rajbari Dinajpur, and to which I hope to find the fellow, as it is said to have been broken when in course of removal in consequence of some alterations, thirty or forty years ago. The inscription,† in three lines, is as follows:—

Durvvârâri-varûthinî-pramathane dâne cha Vidyâdharaiḥ sânandaṁ divi

yasya mârggaṇa-guṇa-grâma-graho gîyate | Kâmbojânvayajena Gauḍa-pati

nâ tenendu-maulerayaṁ prâsâdo niramâyi kuñjara ghaṭa varsheṇa bhûbhûshaṇaḥ. |

Babu Rajendralâla Mitra has been good enough to send me the following translation:—

"By him, whose ability in subduing the forces of his irresistible enemies, and liberality in appreciating the merits of his suitors, are sung by the Vidyâdharas in celestial spheres, by that sovereign of Gauda, by him who is descended from the Kamboja line. This temple, the beauty of the earth, was erected for the moon-crested (Shiva) in the year 888." Babu Rajendralâla further remarks:—"The figures I derive from the words *kunjara ghata*, *kunjara* being equal to 8, the eight elephants of the quarters, and *ghata* three-fold or plural. The two *ghata* at the end might be allowed to remain to make it correspond with the masculine preceded, though the word *bhûshana* does not take the masculine affix. This appears to me to be the true meaning. But if the word *varsha* be a misreading of *varshena*, it would mean a temple which has many elephants carved on it." The pillar in question has eight elephants carved upon it, two on each face, crouching each under a tiger, or some similar animal, which is rampant upon it. The Babu afterwards told me that the date 888 must refer to either the Samvat or the Saka era, and would be either A. D. 832 or A. D. 967, more probably, judging from the style of writing, the later, and that he attributed it to one of the Shaiva dynasty of Bengal.

This, if correct, shows that the remains can have nothing to do with Bâṇa, whose story is told

---

[illegible] (Book VI) in A. (pâda 2, [illegible]) in C. (pâda 6, [illegible]), and in the Bombay edition, VI, 199, 104, in which, likewise, strange to say, only pâdas 1 and 4 are found); it does not occur in Gorr. at all. Further, in the *Mahâbhar.* VII, 2246 (pâda 2; sarvabhûtamanohârî[illegible]), XII, 944 (pâda 3; Ayu[illegible] bhûtvâ), *Hariv.* 1834 (pâda 6; Ayutâ[illegible] [illegible]). In the *Buddh.* III, 1371?, the second hemistich runs somewhat differently; [illegible] Râmas tatah sva(r)bhavanam gatah.—The first hemistich occurs also in the first chapter of the *Ram.*, and indeed in the whole of the texts, in Schlegel (I. 1, 95) and Gorr. (I. 1, 100), also in the editions of Serampore (I. 1, 91) and of Bombay (I. 1, 97), and in ABC.; and it is found in combination with the following second hemistich which, in accordance with the context in which it occurs, is regarded as prophetic:—

Râma-râjyam upâsyâ 'yam brahmalokam gamishyati.

The various readings in which are—for upâsya—upâsyâ [illegible]—upâsitvâ, *Schl. Bomb.*; râjyam upâsitvâ 'yam, *A* sec. m., for brahmalokam—vishnulokam *ABC Ser.*, brahmalokam *Bomb.*, and for gamishyati—prayâsyati *Schl. Bomb.*

* This refers to Buddha's telling the story of Râma (as the introduction of the *Jâtaka* informs us) for the comfort of a husbandman who had lost his father, and who "overcome with grief, left off all his avocations and began to lament"; the story is told as an example from the olden time:—"wise men of old, who knew the eight conditions of life (of the lokadhammas) did not at all sorrow on the death of a parent." We are probably to find here therefore "a text of true Buddhism" (Max Müller on *Buddhist Nihilism*). This subject was undoubtedly a favourite theme in Buddhistic preaching; compare on this point the legend (in Fausböll, *Dhammap.* p. 318, 368) of the father mourning over the death of his son, as also the legend of Kisâgotamî.

† See Plate VII.

in the Mahábhárat, and I should like to know more about the Shaiva dynasty, and its connection with the district of Dinajpur.

I think it quite possible that the original temple to Shiva, of which these are fragments, was erected, not in Dinajpur, but in Gauda, the capital of its founder, and that its fragments were thence brought by the Muhammadans who had a large frontier post at Bán-nagar, or thereabouts, not being in possession of the country to the north. One reason for thinking so would be that there is no tradition of any such great rája as the founder of this temple would be, or of any important personage between Bána and the Muhammadan conquest. On the other hand, it is from Bán-nagar that the fragments have been distributed over the district of Dinajpur, and if it had been a Muhammadan, and not a Hindu building, which was there constructed of them, we should scarcely find, as we do, that the Muhammadans had plundered it for the decoration of the tomb of Sultan Shah. It appears to me possible that in Buchanan's time, 1808, tradition may have confused some Shiva-worshipping Bán-raja, or "King of the Forest," with Bána of the Mahábhárata, and that the date of the former may have been about A. D. 900, or not very long anterior to the Muhammadan occupation. The absence of all written history renders such confusion possible. Then further explanation is required, why a king of Gauda, of the Kanaujan race, should have set up a costly temple to Shiva at Bán-nagar, forty or fifty miles north-east from Gaur. Buchanan tells a curious story of a stone which lay in one of the sacred pools at Bán-nagar, and which was said to be a dead cow thrown in by the infidel Yavans to pollute the water. He had it pulled out, and it proved to be an image of the bull Vrishabha, usually worshipped by the Shaivas. In another place he says that by the protection of Shiva, and the assistance of jungle fever, Bán-raja was enabled to repel the attacks of Krishna, who had a family quarrel with him, but that afterwards Krishna sent the Yavanas, eaters of beef, whom Buchanan believes to have been the Macedonians of Baktria, to attack Bána, and that they succeeded in defeating him, after defiling his sacred ponds by a bit of beef tied to the foot of a kite. This legend of the beef, and the other of the dead cow, correspond curiously with the fact of the finding in 1808 of the image of Vrishabha, and I think point very clearly to the overthrow of the worship of Shiva, and to its previous existence at Bán-nagar. Buchanan says that the story rests on the authority of one of the Puránas attributed to Vyása, and I find from Small's *Handbook of Sanskrit Literature*, that the earliest date ascribed to the Puránas is the 8th or 9th century, while some are as late as the 16th. If Babu Rajendralala Mitra's date is correct, the Shiva temple at Bán-nagar was erected, and presumably the worship of Shiva was at its height, about A.D. 950, and the Muhammadan conquest was in A.D. 1203, or only 250 years later. The image of Vrishabha cannot have been allowed to remain dishonoured, while Shiva worshippers were in the ascendant, and therefore must have been pitched into the water after the erection of the great temple. Who, then, were the Yavanas to whom tradition points as having defeated the Shiva-worshippers, and thrown the image of the sacred bull into the water? Can the author of the Purána have so confused tradition as to indicate by the Yavans the Muhammadan conquerors? or was there a conquest before that of the Muhammadans, and yet subsequent to A.D. 953 or A.D. 967, whichever date is adopted for the Bán-nagar temple?

E. Vesey Westmacott,
Bengal Civil Service, Dinajpur.

Note on the above.

Babu Rájendralála gives no authority for taking g h a ṭ â as equivalent to *threefold*; and supposing that were its meaning,—'threefold eight' would be 24. But the instrumental v a r s h a ṇ a is a serious objection, I think, to his interpretation of k u ñ j a r a-g h a ṭ â-v a r s h a ṇ a,—for if the last word of the compound meant the 'year,' and the other two 888, v a r s h a ought to be in the locative case. When a noun denoting time is in the instrumental case it indicates the period occupied in doing a thing (Pán. II. 3, 6), and thus the sense of the above expression, if it referred to time, would be 'the temple was constructed in 888 years,' or at least that it took the 888th year to be constructed. But the construction is awkward, and if it represented a date the compound would be difficult to separate grammatically. I think the expression means 'he who pours forth an array of elephants',—or, if the va is to be taken as dis-which is not unlikely,—'the destroyer of the ranks of elephants.' V a r s h m a ṇ a does not agree with the metre and is consequently inadmissible: besides the compound would be ungrammatical. The word has two forms v a r s h m a and v a r s h m a n; if the former be taken, the final word of the nominative singular of the compound would be v a r s h m o, if the latter v a r s h m â, but in neither case v a r s h m a ṇ a, but even were it not so—the meaning would be "a temple in which there are bodies or [illegible] of many elephants." The idiom of the language does not admit of such a word as "carved" being understood, except when a double sense is intended.

R. G. Bhandarkar.

Gonds and Kurkus.

Pardi, 24th Feb. 1872.

I would beg to offer a few remarks in reference to a notice of the hill tribes of Gonds and Kurkus, which appeared in the *Indian Antiquary*, pp. 54-56. I have given some account of these tribes in my Settlement Reports on the Baitul and Chindwárá districts of the Central Provinces. Just now I wish only to touch on certain general points as regards these tribes. The Gonds and Kurkus are radically distinct, almost as much so as Hindus and Musalmans. Their languages are quite different, and have hardly anything in common, as I shall show by some examples. In the main, too, they inhabit different localities though they do intermix a good deal along the frontier line. The proper habitat of the Kurku is in the wild country between Asirgarh and the Pachmarî hills. Westward of Asirgarh he is replaced by the Bhill. The chief seat of the Gonds is in the Baitul, Chindwara, and Seoni districts, mostly east of the Pachmarî hills; further east, he is replaced by the Baigas of Mandlâ, a cognate, but still quite distinct, tribe. As regards religion the Kurku is a Hindu, a worshipper of Mahâdeva and the Linga, a venerator of the cow, conforming to certain Hindu usages, and claiming descent from a Rajput race. On the other hand, the Gond admits none of the Hindu divinities into his pantheon, and is moreover bound on occasions of death to slay a cow and pour its blood on the grave to ensure peace and rest for the manes of the departed. In my experience, Gonds almost always bury their dead. Sometimes in the cases of Gonds of good position, who rather ape Hinduism, burning is practised.

The Gond deities are numerous; hill tops deified are the favourite objects of adoration. The whole race is primarily divided into classes according to the gods whom they worship; those of seven, six, and three gods; it is doubtful if there are worshippers of four or five, but it is very difficult to get any accurate information, as even the Pradhâns, or Gond priests, seem to have little knowledge on the subject. These primary divisions are again subdivided into numerous *gots* or clans which do not intermarry. There are said to be 12½ *gots*, after the manner of the Hindu castes, but the number actually existing is very much larger. I have been given the names of upwards of thirty. One god seems common to all the Gonds, viz., Buraipen, or the great god, though he is known by different names in different places.

The Gonds were once a powerful nation, and the Gond Râjâ had his seat on the hill of Deogarh in the Chindwara district; being ousted by the Marâthas of Nâgpur, he became a sort of pensioned prisoner, and he still remains a pensioner of the British Government. In former days the Gond Râjâ averted complete subjugation at the hands of the Delhi Emperors by adopting Muhammadanism, and to this day the Râjâ is apparently a Musalman; he sends for a pure Gond wife from the Chindwara hills, and she conforms to the religion of her husband. It is common to hear of the Gonds as divided into Râj Gonds, viz. those of the royal stock, and common Gonds, but this I believe to be a fanciful distinction; but, on the other hand, there are two well recognized original branches, viz., the Dhurwas and Wikas, each of these has its *got* sub-divisions and its distinctions of worshippers of distinct gods.

With the Kurkus, the sub-division into *gots* is by no means so well established a fact as it is among the Gonds, and the idea was probably derived from the latter. As regards religion, that of the Kurkus is essentially one and the same, the same deities being worshipped under various forms as is the case with all Hindus. Both Kurkus and Gonds worship the manes of their deceased ancestors, and both perform ceremonies analogous to the *Śrâddha* of Hindus. But it is undoubtedly true that customs vary immensely in different places, and what may be a true account of a Baitul Gond would not be equally true of one from the Seoni district, and it is also true that where the Gonds and Kurkus are in immediate juxtaposition, they have mutually borrowed some of each other's customs. And again the Gond Thâkurs of the Chindwârâ hills have adopted many Hindu customs quite unknown to their wilder brethren of the Baitul forests,—hence it may be that notices of the tribe may vary very very much, and yet each present a true picture of the varying circumstances. The social customs of these people are very peculiar, but I cannot enter into an account of them now. As an example I append the numerals up to ten in Gondi and Kurku.—

	Gondi.	Kurku.
1.	Wonde (Undi)*	Miyâ
2.	Rana (Rand)	Baryâ
3.	Mund	Apilyâ
4.	Nâlom (Nalung)	Uphanyâ
5.	Siyum (Saiyung)	Munyâ
6.	Sârum (Sarung)	Turyâ
7.	Yerum (Yelung)	Iyâ
8.	Irmul (Yermud)	Tîâryâ
9.	Anma	Arrya
10.	Pad	Gelya

Some Kurku words are undoubtedly of Aryan origin as *Bap* (father), *Mai* (mother), *Betya* (son), *Beti* (daughter), *gai* (cow),—almost pure Hindi words, but these are exceptional. The corresponding Gond terms are radically different as *Dâo* (father), *Yero* (mother), *Chovâ* (son), *Turi* (daughter), *Tâlo* (cow).

W. Ramsay.

MSS. of the Atharvaveda.

In Lunawâdâ (Revâkânthâ) is a small colony of Atharvavedîs consisting of three families, who are in possession of the books belonging to their Veda. They have already furnished some MSS. to Rao Bahadur Gopalrao Hari of Ahmadabad, who, about two years ago, placed a copy of the *Gopatha-brâhmaṇa*, procured from Lunawâdâ, at the dis-

* The names added in parentheses are those given in Hislop's Vocabulary as the Gondi names of the numerals.—Ed.

posal of the Bengal Asiatic Society. This copy is one of those used for the edition of the *Gopatha* in the Bibliotheca Indica. I have now obtained the consent of the owners of the books to have them catalogued, and the promise of a copy of the *Atharvaveda Prâtiśâkhya*. The copy at Lunawâḍâ is the third known to exist,—one being in the Royal Library at Berlin and one in the Government Collection at Bombay; the latter I obtained last year at Bharoch.

One of the Lunawâḍâ Atharvavedis says that a commentary on four kandas of the Atharvaveda exists in this Presidency, and that he has seen it; he also asserts that a commentary on eight kandas is in the possession of one Pundkar, a pensioner of Sindhia's at Lashkar. Is there any of the readers of the *Indian Antiquary* about Gwalior who can verify this latter statement?

Feb. 22, 1872. G. Bühler.

Note on Query 4, *page* 96.

The allusion apparently is to an incident in Buddha's life, mentioned by Hwen Thsang in connection with one of the Mathurâ stûpas. It is said that while Buddha was pacing the margin of a tank near that city, a monkey came and offered him some honey, which he was graciously pleased to accept. The creature was so delighted at this act of condescension, that in his delight he fell over into the water and was drowned. In his next birth, as a reward he assumed human shape. The supposed scene of the event is within 100 yards of the spot where I am writing.

Mathurâ. F. S. Growse.

Note on Valabhi.

Lunawada Feb. 24.

Sir,—On a late visit to *Walâ*, the supposed site of the ancient Valabhipur, I obtained from one of the officers of the Thakur the accompanying Muhammadan coins, which had been dug up on the morning of the day preceding my visit (Dec. 19, 1871), by the Kolis searching for Charas in the ruins. I am not sufficiently acquainted with Muhammadan coins to fix their age myself, and trust that you will find among your contributors some one able to tell us their exact date. As you are aware, the destruction of Valabhi is an event around which there hangs more than one mystery, and the question when it happened is one of the most difficult to decide. The turning up of Muhammadan coins among the ruins of the city ought to help us to clear away some of the myths regarding its fall. Besides these coins, I brought away some other relics,—one of which, at least, is important from its bearing on the chronological question. This is a small circular seal of clay, that bears on one side the impression of the Buddhist Creed *Ye dharma hetu prabhava hetun*, &c. On the other side the seal shows a distinct impression of the human epidermis. It would seem from this that the maker held the soft mud in the hollow of his hand while stamping it. About three years ago I was shown three similar seals by Mr. Richey, who obtained them also from Walâ, and all of them bore the same inscription. The Walâ officials state that they occur among the ruins in great numbers, and I have seen many in the possession of gentlemen in Kathiawad.

We know that Valabhi was a seat of Buddhism, and the frequent occurrence of these little seals or medals is therefore easily explained, as they were most probably amulets worn by most Buddhists. But the most interesting point is, as Mr. West (who describes similar seals, obtained at Kanheri) correctly observes, that the letters imprinted on them belong to the 9th or 10th century. (Vide *Jour. Bomb. Br. R. As. Soc.* vol. VI. pl. LVII). Does not this show that the ruins at Walâ were inhabited down to a much later date than is usually supposed?—I have, &c. G. Bühler.

Query 5.

Can any reader oblige me with the correct botanical names of the following trees, all common in the Mathurâ district, viz., the *pilu* or *dhungar*, *chhonkar*, *pasendu*, *piyari*, *arni*, *hingot*, *anjan-rukh*, *gondi*, *barna* and *dho*? The names given are the Hindi names in common use.

F. S. Growse.

Pilu or Dhungar is *Salvadora Persica*.
Chhonkar is *Prosopis Spicigera*.
Pasendu is *Diospyros Cordifolia*.
Piyari is *Holoptelea integrifolia*. It is also the name of *Pongamia glabra*.
Arni is *Clerodendron phlomoides*.
Hingot is *Balanites Ægyptiaca*.
Anjan rukh is *Hardwickia binata*?
Gondi is *Cordia myxa* and *spinosa*.
Barna is *Cratæva Roxburghii*.
Dho is *Conocarpus latifolia*.

16*th March* 1872. Narayan Daji.

The *pilu* is mentioned in the Amarakosha, Bk. II ch. iv. sec. 2 śl. 9,—with the synonyms *Guḍaphala* and *Sransi*, and, according to Wilson, is the name applied in some provinces to the *Careya arborea* of Roxburgh, in others to the *Salvadora persica*. The *Barna* is also mentioned in the second half of śloka 5, of the same section—

Varuṇo varaṇaḥ setus tiktaśâkaḥ kumârakaḥ |

and is translated as the *Cratæva tapia* or *Capparis trifoliata*.

In śloka 57, we have the *karîl*,—

. . karîre tu krakara-granthilâv ubhau |

and in śl. 15, the *Gondi*,—

Śeluḥ śleshmâtakaḥ śita uddâla vahuvârakaḥ |

Ed.

THE SRIRANGAM JEWELS.

The wealth of a native temple, like the wealth of a Hindu, consists of gold, lands, and women. The landed property which has at various times been in the possession of the Brahmans of Srirangam is well known to have been prodigious. Dancing-girls, too, who play a conspicuous part in the ceremonial observances of Hindus, are not scarce at Srirangam. Gold, too, flows into the temple year by year in various ways. Not only do monetary offerings from the vast crowds of devotees which yearly visit the temple, flow into the Srirangam coffers, but the pagoda possesses considerable stores of gold vessels and ornaments which have been presented from time to time by individual votaries. The oldest jewels possessed by the temple were presented by a personage, once of great importance in these parts, namely, Vijianagra Chokanatha Naidu. Of these, and of other more recent and more valuable pieces of ornament possessed by the temple, we will now proceed to speak.

First, as to their character. A great number of these ornaments are merely vessels of pure gold. Others are chiefly gold, with an occasional setting of a precious stone in them. Others are mere masses of jewels set one gold—diamonds, emeralds, rubies, sapphires, carbuncles, and pearls. Others are specimens of pearl-embroidery.

Secondly, the value. What is it? This is a very difficult question to answer, as it is almost impossible to ascertain the value—even the approximate value—of jewels cut clumsily and but indifferently set. The natives assert that several of the individual ornaments are worth nearly a lakh of rupees each, and estimate the value of the whole collection at about eight or nine lakhs. This is probably an exaggerated valuation.

And now, in the third place, before proceeding to give a description of the individual ornaments, let us refer to a curious history connected with several of the most valuable of them. During our visit to Srirangam we were especially struck by this fact, that the most valuable ornaments were also the newest. We were greatly surprised. It is a well known fact that Hinduism has greatly decayed since the time of those great native rājās who delighted in rivalling each other as to who would make the most splendid offerings to notable shrines. Under the prestige conferred by royal favour, thousands of temples were enriched by offerings. Such offerings have lately greatly fallen off, of course, and indeed the ruinous condition of innumerable temples through the length and breadth of Southern India bears witness to the decay of Hinduism. Rather the rulers' devotees have grown cold, or the number of rich devotees has greatly diminished. How then is the strange fact that of all the famous Srirangam jewels, the most valuable perhaps are those which have been presented during the last thirty years? The natives of Srirangam gave us the explanation of this strange fact, and it is an interesting one.

There lives now in Srirangam a rather remarkable personage, a Brahman. This man is a beggar, a mendicant. About thirty years ago he gave out that he had made a vow that he would not eat on any day of the year in which he did not receive the sum of ten rupees as alms. He also, no doubt, gave out that with the money daily given him, he intended to make a handsome offering to the great Edvari Rangan, as Vishnu is termed in Srirangam. Of course, rather than that so very holy a devotee should die, herds of pious Hindus were ready to give him ten rupees daily. Some, to gain additional religious merit through the superior holiness of this ascetic, gave him 1,000 rupees and more. So in a few years this Brahman beggar gave a present to the Srirangam pagoda of several ornaments, studded with diamonds, emeralds, rubies, and pearls. One of these ornaments alone is probably worth about 30,000 Rs.! Thus the munificence of one modern ascetic beggar has outdone the munificence of ancient rājās! This man, by name Vembu-batālsi, is in Srirangam, still living. We will now give an enumeration and description of the principal Srirangam jewels.

I. A diamond covered head-piece, in three parts, with an extra diamond-headed pin and screw. The chief stones contained in this piece of jewelry are diamonds, rubies and emeralds. One large emerald, well cut, is perhaps the most valuable stone in this crown. Some of the rubies and diamonds also are very fine. The great majority of the larger diamonds are shockingly badly cut, and are flat stones, which fact detracts from their value. Their worth is said to be about a lakh of rupees; probably half a lakh would be nearer the mark. These were presented by Vembusastri, the Brahman beggar.

II. Another similar crown, much older. The stones are also, as in the other crown, emeralds, diamonds and rubies. In this ornament, the rubies are the most valuable stones. However, in appearance they look very dim, being badly cut, badly set, and covered with the dirt of years. They are probably worth about 30,000 Rs.—or even less.

III. A magnificent necklace, worth fully 7,000 Rs., in all probability, containing a great number of splendid pearls, besides good rubies, diamonds, emeralds, &c. This necklace was also presented to the idol by the beggar Brahman.

IV. Another and similar necklace, presented by Vijianagra Chokanatha Naidu.

V. Three or four small necklaces, chiefly of pearls.

VI. Large emerald ear drops. One of these is a pear-shaped emerald probably worth about 1,000 Rs.

VII. A number of head and foot ornaments for the god. Some of these are very richly decked with small but brilliant gems. These ornaments are chiefly the [illegible] of the god, namely, his two [illegible] weapons, the chank and the chakra.

IX. A pair of pearl ear-rings containing each fully a hundred fine pearls of various sizes.

X. The most [illegible] ornament in the whole collection is undoubtedly the [illegible] or "body covering of jewels." This ornament is in several pieces. The stones it contains are very badly cut—some not cut at all, only smoothed by friction—but they are very large, and some very brilliant. The ground work which the gems are set in is of pure gold. The whole ornament is intended as a covering for the idol. It is probably worth more than a lakh of rupees. Of course here again we guess at the value, but we do not think we are far wrong. When stones are so badly cut and badly set the temptation is simple to under-value them.

XI. A number of pans, vessels, stools, &c., all of pure gold. Most of these vessels bear [illegible] engraved words taken in Telugu literature. One single pot was of such size and weight that we enquired the value of it. This we were informed was exactly [illegible]. These golden vessels are used for the daily service of the god, they are used in bearing the water for the divine ablutions.

XII. Two canopies, with thousands of fine small pearls embroidered on black velvet,—for holding before the idol on state occasions.

XIII. Two large pearl-embroidered umbrellas for the god. The pearls are embroidered on black velvet, the top of the umbrella [illegible] being covered with yellow silk. In the embroidery of the umbrella, and in that of the two banners, tens of thousands of small pearls have been employed; and although the work is old, the pearls have wonderfully retained their original creamy lustre.

XIV. One large set, and one small set, of golden [illegible] and hands for the god. Several very large rubies have been placed, so as to imitate rings, on the fingers and one of these also a cluster of [illegible] rubies is placed in the palm of one of the hands.

XV. A gold [illegible] for the god, entirely composed of very fine chased work. In this alone are about 1,000 rupees worth of gold alone.

XVI. A golden crown containing 3,000 Rs. worth of gold. A single large ruby is set in the front of this crown.

XVII. An ornament representing the mark which the Tengalai class of Vaishnava devotees wear on their foreheads. This ornament contained several valuable rubies and other precious stones.

Abridged from the Madras Athenæum, Jan. 17.

THE LATE PROFESSOR GOLDSTÜCKER.

It is with deep regret that we have to chronicle the death of Professor Theodor Goldstücker, which sad event occurred at his house, 14 St. George's-square, Primrose Hill, London, on 6th March. This eminent Sanskrit scholar was of Jewish parentage, and was born at Königsberg in the early part of the century, being at his death somewhere about 50 years old—for on careful enquiry we find that none of his friends accurately knew his age, and the excessive labour to which he subjected his wiry frame gave him a premature look of being older than he really was.

His university career was at Bonn, and among his distinguished rivals was the eminent scholar Westergaard. He subsequently qualified for the Professorial career at Berlin. This ended, he moved to Paris, where he enjoyed the inestimable privilege of the friendship of the distinguished Eugene Burnouf. So far back as 1839, we find some of the fruits of his Oriental studies in an article on the introductory stanzas of the Amaru Sataka, which appeared in *Die Zeitschrift für die Kunde des Morgenlandes*, a periodical widely known through the able editing of Prof. Christian Lassen. This might be looked upon as a forerunner of the great Lexicographical work he was afterwards to undertake.

His earliest separate work is a translation of the allegorical, or as he styled it, the 'theologico-philosophical drama' Prabodha Chandrodaya, "the Moon of Intellect." This appeared in 1842 with a preface from his learned friend Professor Karl Rosenkranz. Years ago he mentioned his intention of publishing the Mahâbhârata in a German dress. This intention, so far as the MS. was concerned, was, we believe, nearly completed at the time, though no part of the translation has ever been printed.

The accidental discovery, in the India Office Library, of a MS. of the Mânava Kalpa Sûtra, a rare and valuable work on the Vedic ritual, led to his preparing a splendid Introduction to the publication of a fac-simile of the manuscript, and which was subsequently published separately under the title of '*Pânini and his place in Sanskrit Literature*.' His later works, apart from the enormous labour bestowed on a revised edition of Wilson's *Sanskrit Dictionary*, consists of some five parts of the Jaiminîya Nyâya Mâlâ Vistara,—the principal work of the Mimânsa philosophy. This, as well as the Dictionary, is left incomplete by his sudden demise.

It is alleged that this worthy scholar has left behind him but slight memorials of his extraordinary powers; this is perhaps partly owing to his almost fanatic desire to state only the naked truth, and partly to an extreme fastidiousness for elegant forms of expression. This he carried to such a degree that though he read many papers before the Royal Asiatic Society, not one of them was ever allowed to appear in its Journal.

We cannot part from his Dictionary, carried as it is only to the first letter of the Sanskrit Alphabet, without characterizing it as it truly deserves, as an encyclopædia of Sanskrit lore. But though his lexicographical labours are those by which he will be best remembered, still his studies were not confined to Sanskrit philology. His knowledge of medicine, especially of Hindu medicine, is evidenced by the remarkable collection of notes to be found in his copy of Suśruta's work; and his article on *Indian Epic Poetry*, written for the *Westminster Review* in 1868, was another brilliant effort of his genius. His pamphlet on the method of dealing with Indian appeals on questions of Hindu law, shows another phase of his many-sided mind; and it is known that he rendered valuable services to the Privy Council on abstruse points of Indian jurisprudence.

It has been stated that he has "left instructions that every scrap of his vast possessions, the labour of so many years, shall be burned." This we believe to be entirely unfounded,—no will having been found. His nearest and only relative is a half brother—Dr. William Tobias, of Berlin.

Professor Goldstücker was a man of private fortune, and occupied the chair of Sanskrit in University College, London, more with a view of giving an impulse to the study of that ancient tongue than for any personal profit. At the time of his death Professor Goldstücker was President of the Philological Society, a member of the Council of the Royal Asiatic Society, &c. &c. His chief characteristics were, a generosity seldom witnessed in the world, fearlessness in the assertion of what he felt to be right, and an honest scorn of anything approaching to humbug or sham. In looking back at his active career, we find an excessive zeal for absolute accuracy of statement was a principal cause of his leaving behind him so much unfinished work. His kindness to novices in philological study was proverbial; his vast stores of knowledge were ever at the disposal of any one who showed a tolerably fair claim to their use. In politics he was a liberal; "in private life he was a model of honour and truth and a firm and generous friend."

On the 6th of February he wrote promising to contribute to the *Indian Antiquary*: but the news of his death reached India before the letter. "An attack of bronchitis, at first neglected, then treated by himself, till medical aid—at last called in—was of no avail," has deprived us of this great master of Sanskrit scholarship. His loss will be felt in all the intellectual centres of the world.

C. Maybee.

London, 8 March 1872.

SKETCHES OF MATHURÁ.

By F. S. GROWSE, M.A., OXON, B.C.S.

II.—THE BAN-JATRA.

THOUGH the number of *bans* is invariably stated as twelve, and of *upabans* as twenty-four, there is often considerable difference in the specification, and probably few of the local pandits, if required to enumerate either group off-hand, would be able to complete the total without some recourse to guess work. A little Hindi manual for the guidance of pilgrims has been published at Mathurá, and is considered to embody the most authentic traditions on the subject. The compiler, however great his local knowledge and priestly reputation, has certainly no pretensions to accuracy of scholarship. His attempts at etymology are as a rule absolutely grotesque; as for example in the two sufficiently obvious names Khaira and Shergarh, the one of which he derives from *khedna*, 'to drive cattle,' and the other, still more preposterously, from *sihara*, 'a marriage wreath.' The list which he gives is as follows, his faulty orthography in some of the words being corrected:—

The 12 Bans: Madhu-ban; Tál-ban; Kumud-ban; Bahulá-ban; Kám-ban; Khadira-ban; Brindá-ban; Bhadra-ban; Bhándir-ban; Bel-ban; Loha-ban; and Mahá-ban.

The 24 Upabans: Gokul, Gobardhan, Barsána, Nand-gánw, Sanket, Paramadra, Aring, Sessái, Mát, Uncha-gánw, Khel-ban, Srí kuṇḍ, Gandharv-ban, Parsoli, Bilchhu, Bachh-ban, Ádi-badri, Karahla, Ajnokh, Pisáya, Kokila-ban, Dadhi-gánw, Koṭ-ban and Rával.

This list bears internal evidence of some antiquity in its want of close correspondence with existing facts; since some of the places, though retaining their traditionary repute, have now nothing that can be dignified with the name either of wood or grove; while others are known only by the villagers in the immediate neighbourhood, and have been supplanted in popular estimation by rival sites of more easy access or greater natural attractions. But first to take in order the twelve Bans:—

Madhu-ban is situate in a village, now called Maholi, some 4 or 5 miles to the south west of Mathurá. This forest, according to the Puráṇas, was the stronghold of the giant Madhu, and from him derived its name. On his decease it passed to his son Lavaṇa, who, inflamed with the lust of universal conquest, presumed to send an insolent challenge to the most powerful monarch of the time, the great Ráma, then reigning at Ayodhyá. The god-like hero disdained the easy victory for himself, but sent his youngest brother Śatrughna to Madhu-vana, who vanquished and slew the monster, hewed down the wood in which he had trusted for defence, and on its site founded the city of Madhu-purí. This is uniformly regarded by native scholars as merely another name for Mathurá, regardless of the fact that the forest is several miles from the river, while Mathurá has always, from the earliest period, been described as situate on its immediate bank. The confusion between the two places runs apparently through the whole of classical Sanskrit literature; as for example in the *Harivansa*, (canto) 95, where we find the city founded by Śatrughna distinctly called, not Madhu-purí, but Mathurá which, it is said, Bhíma subsequently annexed, Bhíma's own original capital being, according to this isolated legend, Gobardhan.

Śatrughna Lavaṇam hatwá chichchheda tan Madhor vanam
Tasmin Madhu-vane sthâne purím cha Mathurám imám
Niveśayámása vibhuḥ Sumitrá-nandi-vardhanaḥ
Paryáye chaiva Rámasya Bharatasya tathaiva cha
Sumitrá-sutayoś chaiva práptayor Vaishṇavam padam
Bhímeneyam purí tena rájya-sambandha-káraṇát
Svavanśe sthápitá púrvam svayam-adhyásitá tathá.

But there are many very clear indications that the writer of the *Harivansa* was a complete stranger to the country of Braj, the scene of his poem; for almost all the topographical descriptions are utterly irreconcileable with facts. Thus he states that Kṛishṇa and Balaráma were brought up at a spot selected by Nanda on the bank of the Jamuná near the hill of Gobardhan (canto 61.) Now Gobardhan is some 15 miles from the river and the neighbourhood of Gokul and Mahában, which all other written authorities and also ancient tradition agree in declaring to have been the scene of Kṛishṇa's infancy is several miles further distant from the ridge and on the other side of the Jamuná

Again, Tál-ban is described (canto 70) as lying north of Gobardhan:—

Govarddhanasyottarato Yamuná-tíram áśritam
Dadṛiśáte tato víram ramyam Tala-vanam mahat.

In the *Bhágavat* it is said to be close to Brinda-ban; while in fact it is south-east of Gobardhan and, with the city of Mathurá, half-way between it and Brinda-ban. So also Bhándír-ban is represented as being on the same side of the river as the Káli-mardan Ghát, being in reality nearly opposite to it.

But to return from this digression; it is clear on etymological no less than topographical considerations that Mathurá and Madhu-purí were always distinct places; for Maholi, the traditional site of the Madhu-vana, is simply the Prakrit corruption of the Sanskrit Madhu-purí. By Vararuchi, II. 27, *h* is substituted for *dh*, (as *bahira* for *badhira*, 'deaf') which gives us Mahupurí; and by Sútra II. 2, the *p* of *purí* is elided (the initial letter of the last member of a compound being considered non-initial for the purposes of the rule), and thus we get Mahurí, easily convertible into Maholi. Some faint reminiscence of its ancient importance would seem to have long survived; for though so close to Mathurá, it was in Akbar's time and subsequently for many years the head of a local division. By the sacred wood is a pond called Madhu-kuṇḍ, and a temple dedicated to Kṛishṇa under his title of Chatur-bhuj, where a *mela* is held on the 11th of the dark fortnight of Bhádon.

Tál-ban is about 5 miles from Mathurá on the road to Bharatpur. The village in which it is situate is called Tárasí, probably in allusion to the ancient-wood, though locally it is *referred* only to the name of the *founder*, one Tárá-chand, a Kachhwáhá Thákur, who, in quite modern times, moved to it from Satoha,* a place a few miles off. The annual *mela* is held on the 11th of the light fortnight of Bhádon, in commemoration of Balaráma's victory over the demon Dhenuk, who, as described in the *Puráṇas*, attacked the two boys in the form of an ass, as they were shaking down the fruit from the palm trees.

Kumud-ban and Bahulá-ban are in close proximity to each other, the one at Unchá-gánw, the other at Bátí, a contraction for Bahulá-vati. The former has no special legend attaching to it, and the latter is only said to have been the scene of a terrific encounter between a cow and a lion, in which the cow came off victorious. There is a pond called Kṛishṇa-kuṇḍ, with a temple dedicated to Bahulá Gáe on its margin. Kám-ban is by the town of Káma, the head of a Tahsíl in the Bharatpur territory, 39 miles from Mathurá.

Khadira-ban is some 4 or 5 miles from Chhátá, immediately outside the village of Khaira, which derives its name from it; the letter *d*, when simple and non-initial, being elided in accordance with Vararuchi's rule (II. 2,) as for example† *bor* for *badara*, the Zizyphus jujuba. The wood is at present of small extent, and consists of *kadamb*, *pilu* and *chhonkar* trees without a single specimen of the *khadira*, i.e., the acacia. Hence probably the popular misconception of the name, which is commonly spelt *Khadir*, and derived from the Hindi root *khod*. Adjoining it is a large pond called Kṛishṇa Kuṇḍ, with a temple of Baldeva, and in the village another temple dedicated to Gopináth, said to have been founded by the famous Todar Mal of Akbar's reign. Bhadra-ban occupies a high point on the left bank of the Jamuná, some 8 miles above Mát. With the usual fate of Hindi words under the present Muhammadanising regime, it is transformed in the official map of the district into Bahádur-ban. It is the traditional scene of the Dávánala, or forest conflagration, which Kṛishṇa is described in the *Bhágavat* as miraculously extinguishing. The neighbouring village is called Bhadáura, i.e. Bhadra-pura. Close by, in the hamlet of

* At Satoha is a sacred tank called Sántanu-kuṇḍ, after king Sántanu, who, it is said, for many years practised the severest religious austerities here in the hope of obtaining a son. His wishes were at last gratified by a union with the goddess Gangá, who bore him Bhíshma, one of the famous heroes of the *Mahábhárat*. Every Sunday the tank is frequented by women who are desirous of issue, and a large *mela* is held there on the 6th of the light fortnight of Bhádon. The tank, which is of very considerable dimensions, was faced all round with stone, early last century, by Sawai Jay Sinh of Amber, but is now somewhat dilapidated. In its centre is a high hill, connected with the mainland by a bridge. The sides of the mound are covered with fine [illegible] trees, and on the summit, which is approached by a flight of 30 stone steps, is a small temple. Here it is incumbent upon the female devotees, who would have their prayers effectual, to make some offering to the shrine, and inscribe on the ground or wall the mystic device of the Satiya. Raja Santanu is mentioned in several of the Puráṇas as the father of Bhíshma by the river Gangá, and his name also occurs in the Nirukta; but the legend there related of him has nothing to do with his desire of progeny. The local superstition has probably arisen from a confusion of the king's name Sántanu with the Sanskrit word for 'children,' *santána*. Satoha is similarly supposed on the spot to be derived from *Satta*, as that was the royal ascetic's only diet; it is really a corruption of Sántanu.

† This illustration has not the authority of Vararuchi, who most unnecessarily, as it would seem, invents a special rule to explain the formation of bor from badara.

Chháhiri, is Bhándir-ban, a dense thicket of ber and hins and other low prickly shrubs. In its centre is an open space with a small modern temple bearing the title of Bihári Jí, and a well and rest house; and at the distance of a few hundred yards outside is a venerable Ficus Indica, called the Bhándir-bat, with a small shrine under it, dedicated to Śrídáma. This was the favourite tree for the herdsmen's children to meet and take their midday repast under, and derives its name from the cups and plates (bhándi) used on such occasions. One day, according to the Puránas, the boys had made it their goal in a race, when the demon Pralamba, disguised as one of themselves, came to join them, and getting Sankarshana to mount on his back, ran off with him in hopes to destroy him. But the sturdy lad so crushed him with his knees and belaboured him with his fists that he soon brought the monster lifeless to the ground, and in commemoration of his prowess he was ever afterwards known by the title of Bala-Ráma,* or Ráma the strong.

Bel-ban is on the left bank of the Jamuná in the village of Jahángír-pur, part of the endowment of the Bengáli temple of Sringár-bat in Brindá-ban,—that town being just on the other side of the water. Loha-ban, in the Mahá-ban Pargana, some 3 miles from Mathurá, across the river, probably derives its name from the lodh or lodhra tree. On the spot it is said to commemorate Krishna's defeat of an otherwise unknown demon called Lohásur. In consequence of the similarity of sound, offerings of iron (loha) are always made by the pilgrims. Of the two remaining bans—Brindá-ban and Mahá-ban more detailed notices will be given hereafter.

All the twelve bans are mentioned by name in the *Mathurá Máhátmya*, and most of them, it will be observed, are connected with the Pauránik legends of Krishna and Balaráma. On the other hand, the twenty-four *upabans* refer mainly to Rádhá's adventures, and have no ancient authority whatever. Of the entire number only three were, till quite recent times, places of any note, viz., Gokul, Gobardhan, and Rádhá-kund. Of these, Gokul in all classical Sanskrit literature is the same as Mahá-ban, which is included among the bans; Gobardhan is as much a centre of sanctity as Mathurá itself, and is only for the sake of uniformity inserted in either list; while Rádhá-kund, as the name denotes, is the one primary source whence the goddess derives her modern reputation. We propose to pass them all briefly in review, excepting for the present the four first—Gokul, Gobardhan, Barsána and Nand-gánw, which will each in turn form the subject of a separate sketch. 5, Sanket, 'the place of assignation,' is half way between Rádhá's home Barsána and Nand-gánw the residence of Krishna's foster father Nanda; 6, Paramadra is an obscure point in the Bharatpur hills. 7, Aring is a small town on the high road from Mathurá to Dig. Till 1868 it was the head-quarters of a tahsíli, though only 9 miles distant from the capital of the district. At the present time there is no vestige of any grove, and the only spot accounted sacred is a pond called Kilolkund. 8, Sessái, for Śesha-sáya, is a village in the Kosi Pargana, where Krishna and Balaráma are said to have revealed themselves to the Gopis under their heavenly form of Náráyana and Śesha. This is a good illustration of the disregard for ancient authorities which characterizes the modern cycle of local legends; since the transfiguration in question is described in the Puránas, not as worked for the benefit of the Gopis, but as a vision vouchsafed to Akrúr, on the bank of the Jamuná, the day he fetched the two boys from Brindában to attend the tourney of arms at Mathurá. Sessái ought thus to be between those two towns, whereas it is in fact far away to the north of them both. 9, Mát.—In the town itself there is nothing whatever of interest or antiquity, though the two sacred woods, Bhándir-ban and Bhadra-ban, are both on its borders. 10, Unchá-gánw is the old village site not far from the foot of the hill, the crest and slopes of which are now crowned by the temple of Larliji and the comparatively modern town of Barsána. Unchá-gánw, corresponding to the English Higham, must originally have included in its limits the hill whence it derives its name. 11, Khel-ban is not far from the town of Shergarh. 12, Rádhá-kund, or as it is occasionally called Śrí-kund, i. e. Holy Well, is a small town adjoining Gobardhan, 13 miles to the west of Mathurá. It has grown up on the margin of the sacred lakes, prepared according to the legend for Krishna's expiatory ablution after he had

* Balaráma, under the title of Belus, is described by the Greek and Latin historians as the Indian Hercules, and said to be one of the tutelary divinities of Mathurá, a proof that the local cultus has a higher antiquity than is sometimes allowed it.

slain the bull Arishta. To avert the consequences of so ill-omened a deed, all the sacred streams and places of pilgrimage, obedient to the summons of the god, assembled in bodily form at the foot of the Giri-ráj and poured from their holy urns into two deep basins, excavated for the purpose, now known as Krishan-kuṇḍ and Rádhá-kuṇḍ. There Krishṇa bathed, and—by the efficacy of such concentrated essence of sanctity, was washed clean of the pollution he had incurred. And still, at midnight on the 8th day of the dark fortnight of the month Kártik, the same spirits renew their visit to the auspicious spot; and every devout Hindu who then plunges beneath the wave acquires by the single act as much merit as if he had laboriously made a separate pilgrimage to each of the shrines there represented. The town which has arisen on the margin of these two famous lakes is of considerable extent, and is crowded with religious edifices, the pious foundations of princes and pilgrims from the most remote parts of India. One temple in particular may be mentioned as erected by the Rájá of Manipur from the far east of Bengal. The two lakes are only parted by a broad stone terrace, and are both supplied on all four sides with long unbroken flights of steps of the same material. Ordinarily the water is so abundant that it reaches nearly the highest tier, being the whole drainage of the adjoining jhand, or woodland, a tract of very considerable extent; and the charm of the broad and brimming basin is much enhanced by the unusual care that is taken to preserve it from all pollution. Till the beginning of this century the two reservoirs were simply as nature had designed them; the present stone Ghats were completed in the year 1817 at the sole cost of the Lálá Bábú, whom we have before had occasion to mention. The whole quarter of the town most immediately adjoining is exclusively occupied by a colony of Bangális.

The 13th on the list of upabans is Gandharv-ban, of which the precise locality is uncertain. 14, Parsoli, near Gobardhan, is styled on the maps and in the Revenue Roll, Mahmúdpur, a name barely recognised at all on the spot. On its borders is the Chandra-sarovar, a fine octagonal sheet of water with stone gháts, the work of Rájá Nahar Sinh of Bharatpur. Here Brahma, joining with the Gopis in the mystic dance, was so enraptured with delight, that all unconscious of the fleeting hours he allowed the single night to extend over a period of six months. 15, Bilchha, 16, Bachh-ban, and 17, Ádibadri are obscure places on the Bharatpur border. 18, Karahla, or Karhela in the Chhátá Pargana, has been already mentioned for its magnificent Kadamb-Khandi. 19, Ajnokh or Ajnokhari, derives its name from the Anjan-pokhar, but is now often corrupted, both in writing and pronunciation, into the unmeaning form Ajnot. 20, Pisáyo, 21, Kokila-ban in Great Bathan, and 22, Dadhi-gánw or Dahi-gánw have already been incidentally mentioned. 23, Koṭ-ban, beyond the town of Kosi, is the most northern point in the modern perambulation, and from the name would appear always to have been so; the extreme limit of a series of holy places being ordinarily designated Koṭ. Thus the city of Mathurá has twenty-four tírthas along the bank of the Jamuná, the highest up the stream called Uttar-koṭ, the lowest simply Koṭ-tírath. 24. Ráwal, (for Rabh-kula?) Rádhá's reputed birth-place, according to a half obsolete legend, is a small village in the Mahában Pargana, with a temple of Larliji, the sanctity of which has been entirely eclipsed by the greater preeminence of its more modern rival at Barsána.

In the *Váráha Purána*, or rather in the interpolated section known as the *Mathurá Máhátmya*, the Mathurá-Mandal is described as 20 yojanas in extent.

Vinsati yojanánám cha Máthuram mama mandalam
Yatra yatra narah snáto muchyate sarva-pátakaih.

And taking the yojana as 7 miles, and the kos as 1½ miles, 20 yojanas would be nearly equal to 84 kos, the popular estimate of the distance traversed. In computing the length of the way, full allowance must be made for the constant incidents, turns and returns, which result in the ultimate perambulation of a comparatively circumscribed area. It is however sometimes said that the circle originally must have been of much wider extent, since the city of Mathurá, which is described as its centre, is some 30 miles distant from the most northern point Koṭ-ban, and only 6 from Társi to the south. Elliot moreover quotes in his Glossary the following couplet as fixing the limits of the Braj-mandal:

'It Bar-hadd, ut Sona-hadd, ut Súrasen ká gánw,
Braj chaurási kos men Mathurá mandal tháṇh.'

According to this authority, the original area has been diminished by more than a half; for

Bar is in the Agra district; Sona, famous for its hot sulphur springs, is in Gurgânw; while the 'Sûrasena kâ gânw' is supposed to be Batesar, a place of some note on the Jamunâ below Agra, the scene of a very large horse-fair held on the full moon of Kartik. But the lines above quoted cannot be of any great antiquity, seeing that they contain the Persian word *hadd*, the exact locality of an ideal centre need not be very closely criticised; and certainly all the places of legendary reputation fall well within the limits of the modern pari-krama.

Attempts have been made to establish a connection between the earlier chapters of St. Matthew's Gospel and the legends of Krishna as commemorated by the ceremonies of the Ban-jâtra. There is an obvious similarity of sound between the names Krishna and Christ; Herod's massacre of the innocents may be compared with the massacre of the children of Mathurâ by Kansa; the flight into Egypt, with the flight to Gokul; as Christ had a fore-runner of supernatural birth in the person of St. John Baptist, so had Krishna in Balarâma; and as the infant Saviour was cradled in a manger and first worshipped by shepherds, though descended from the royal house of Judah, so Krishna, though a near kinsman of the reigning prince, was brought up among cattle and first manifested his divinity to herdsmen.* The inference drawn from these coincidences is corroborated by an ecclesiastical tradition that the Gospel which St. Thomas the Apostle brought with him to India was that of St. Matthew, and that when his relics were discovered, a copy of it was found to have been buried with him. It is, on the other hand, absolutely certain that the name of Krishna, however late the full development of the cycle of legends, was celebrated throughout India long before the Christian era. Thus the only possible hypothesis is that some Pandit, struck by the marvellous circumstances of our Lord's infancy, as related in the Gospel, transferred them to his own indigenous mythology, and on account of the similarity of name, selected Krishna as their hero. It may be added that the Harivansa, which possibly is as old† as any of the Vaishnava Purânas, was certainly written by a stranger to the country of Braj; and not only so, but it further shows distinct traces of a southern origin, as in its description of the exclusively Dakhini festival, the Pongal; and it is only in the south of India that a Brahman would be likely to meet with Christian traditions. But after all that can be urged, the coincidences though curious are too slight, in the absence of any historical proof, to establish a connection between the two narratives. Probably they would never have attracted attention had it not been for the similarity of name; and it is thoroughly established by literary criticism that the two names had each an independent origin. Thus the speculation may be dismissed as idle and unfounded. To many persons it will appear profane to institute a comparison between the inspired oracles of Christianity and the Hindu scriptures. But if we fairly consider the Indian legend, and allow for a slight element of the grotesque and that tendency to exaggerate which is inseparable from Oriental imagination, we shall find it not incongruous with the primary idea of a beneficent divinity, manifested in the flesh in order to relieve the world from oppression and restore the practice of true religion.‡ As to those wayward caprices of the child-god, for which no adequate explanation can be offered, the Brahman may regard them as the sport of the wind; in western phraseology—*sapientia Indicus omni tempore, Indus in orbe terrarum.*

* Hindu pictures of the infant Krishna in the arms of his foster-mother Jasodâ, with a glory encircling the heads both of mother and child and a back ground of Oriental scenery, are indistinguishable, except in name, from representations of Christ and the Madonna.

† It is quoted by Birûni (born 970, died 1039 A.D.) as a standard authority even in his time.

‡ Conf. Trench, *Hulsean Lectures*, 1846, Lect. III., 4th ed. 1862, pp. 204-6, &c.—Ed.

ON THE TREATMENT OF OXYTONE NOMINAL BASES IN SANSKRIT AND ITS DERIVATIVES.

By JOHN BEAMES, B.C.S., M.R.A.S., MAGISTRATE OF BALASOR.

The following remarks are intended to direct attention to a hitherto neglected point in the formation of nominal bases. It has been observed that the -*a* base in Sanskrit, as in *naras*, *putra*, &c., divides itself into two separate sets of bases in the mediæval and modern Aryan languages and investigators seem to have been puzzled by this fact. Dr. Trumpp, writing on Sindhi, in the

Journal of the German Oriental Society, thus expresses the difficulty: "The old Prakrit ending in -o has, in Sindhi, been split up into two great classes, one of which has corrupted the Prakrit -o into -u, the other has preserved it unchanged. No rule seems to have influenced this separation, at least I have not yet discovered any, but daily usage seems to have decided in favour of the one or the other ending. It is however noteworthy that many words which in Sindhi end in o, in Hindi end in á, the same remark holds good of Maráthi, Bengali, and Panjábi, while on the other hand the short final u in Sindhi has in those languages been thrown away, or become quiescent."*

The rule which Dr. Trumpp professes himself unable to discover appears to me to be this. A Sanskrit noun in -a which bears the accent on the last syllable, or, in other words, is oxytone, generally ends in the mediæval languages in ao, and in the moderns in o or á; while a noun in a which has its final syllable unaccented, or is barytone, ends in the mediæval languages in u, and in the moderns in u, or a, or entirely rejects the final vowel.

With regard to the practice in each language —Hindi, Bengali, Panjábi, Uriya, and Maráthi take á in oxytones, Gujaráti and Sindhi take o.

It cannot however be said that every oxytone substantive in Sanskrit gives rise to a noun in á or o in the modern languages. On the contrary, the exceptions to the rule are as numerous as the illustrations of it. This leads to a further definition of much practical importance. The class of words called early Tadbhavas is, as a rule, faithful to the accent. This class consists of those words which were in existence in Sanskrit, and continued to be used in Prakrit, and have uninterruptedly retained their position in the mouths of the people down to the present time. These words may be recognised by their appearance. They have undergone the regular and usual phonetic corruptions and abrasions of all Prakrit words, and are often now only recognisable as of Sanskrit origin by the application to them of the rules of Vararuchi or other Prakrit and Pali grammarians. Inasmuch however as their use has been continuous, and as they were derived from the Sanskrit at a time when it was still spoken, they have always, so to speak, been pronounced by ear, and were so long before they were committed to writing. Consequently they have retained the accent which they bore in the older language.

In late Tadbhavas however the case is different; late Tadbhavas are those words which had entirely dropped out of use, and were only resuscitated and brought into vogue again at a period when Sanskrit had ceased to be known to the people. Being revived from books, they were spoken by the eye, if such an expression may be permitted; that is to say, they were pronounced as they seemed destined to be, the accent generally lying on a syllable already long by nature or position. These words are recognisable by the much smaller amount of corruption they have undergone, and by the corruptions which do exist being of a different nature from those demanded by the rules of Prakrit Grammar.

Moreover, these late Tadbhavas are generally words which are synonymous with already existing earlier words. They are the grand, high-flown words of the language, not so frequently used or so expressive of simple ideas as the early Tadbhavas.

The proportion of these two classes to each other varies in the different languages. In those which have been less cultivated, and which have been most under Muhammadan influence, they are not so frequent as in the more cultivated and more Bráhmanical languages.

There are many other collateral and subsidiary considerations which further complicate this difficult question, a question which is rendered all the more difficult by the absence of continuous literature. When the mediæval poets began to write, the languages were already so far fixed as to have passed the stage of formation of either early or late Tadbhavas, and to have got into the stage when the vast crowd of Tatsamas began to make its appearance.

The line of investigation thus briefly sketched in outline is of the utmost importance in the elucidation of the origin and formation of the modern noun, and I hope on a future occasion to give examples and illustrations.

It will be seen that it is in the determination of the treatment of the oxytone -a base that the real crux of the question lies, because the barytones naturally lose their final vowel, and thus fall under the the same head as the late Tadbhava oxytones, except in Sindhi, where they retain the obscure final -u for masculines, and -a for feminines.

* Journal of Germ. Or. Soc. vol. XVI p. 131.

THE CAVE OF THE GOLDEN ROCK, DAMBULA, CEYLON.

By T. W. RHYS DAVIDS, C.C.S., ANURADHAPURA,

Sir Emerson Tennent has eloquently and yet very justly described this wonderful hill of stone "underneath which the temple has been hollowed out, which from its antiquity, its magnitude, and the richness of its decorations, is by far the most renowned in Ceylon."* He has given two woodcuts which afford a good idea of its front and its entrance, but fail altogether to do justice to the effect created by its enormous size; and he has all the more strongly, because inadvertently, testified to the curious success of the paintings within, when he states that "the ceiling of this gloomy vault is concealed with painted *cloths*," for what seemed, even to so educated an observer, to be cloths is, in reality, the rock painted in fresco, and this is the more remarkable as those paintings were undoubtedly executed hundreds of years ago.†

Sir Emerson Tennent mentions one inscription which was translated for Turnour by Mr. Armour,‡ but I have discovered eleven others, and believe that still more would reward a careful search, and I venture to submit the oldest and for some reasons the most interesting.

From this inscription it may be considered proved that the temple was originally founded, not by Walagam Bâhu about 86 B.C., as stated by Tennent,§ but in the time of Dewânampiya Tissa (B.C. 245)|| the ally of Asoka and the friend and patron of Mahinda who introduced Buddhism into Ceylon.

It is possible that Walagam Bâhu repaired the temple, and it is certain that he built the Soma dâgoba, in honour of his queen,¶ in the plain to the south of the sacred hill; but the authority adduced by Tennent for his statement that that king first endowed it is of little value, being merely Upham's translation of the Râja Ratnâkari, a grossly inaccurate translation of a very useful but late and unreliable work. The ignorance of the translator having been so cruelly exposed by Turnour,* I quote the words of the original on the point in question. Upham† says:—

"He (Wattagâmini, or Sinhalese Walagam Bâhu) afterwards caused to be built *the temple Dambulla*, *and a monument* 140 cubits high, and five temples; he also caused many hundreds of *stone houses to be built*, and did many other things *of public utility*."

The original words are‡ * * * * nawata Dambulu wihâraya da karawâ, nawata Soma nam ek siya hatalis riyan maha weherak karawâ, nawata pas maha wihârayak da karawâ, boho siya ganan gal lenawal kapâra koṭawâ, anik ŝâsanopakâri wâseka:—which literally translated is—

"And furthermore having made the Dambulla wihâra, and also having made the *great Dâgoba* 140 cubits high *called Soma*, and also having made five large wihâras, and having *cut ledges in* many hundred *stone caves*, he was of great assistance in other ways also to 'the Doctrine.'"

It is difficult to find the source from which Abhayarâja, the author of *Râja Ratnâkara*, derived the first statement, for nothing is said either in the *Mahâwanso* or in the *Dîpawanso* about Dambulla Wihâra being made by Wattagâmini although in the former§ the names of five, and in the latter|| the names of seven comparatively unimportant ones, made by his eight strong men, are given: but nothing is said about it in *Râjâwaliya*, although a comparatively large space is devoted to that king's reign.

The inscription referred to is cut in the face of the rock, in one line, under the ledge or eaves called 'katâra' in Ceylon—formed to cause the rain to drop off instead of trickling down into the cave. Owing to this position the inscription is in perfect preservation, and is only difficult to read from its great height above the ground, the katâra being half way up a precipice 200 feet high. My copy is therefore only an eye copy taken with an opera glass; but the characters being so simple it may, I think, be relied upon.

* Sir E. Tennent, Ceylon, Vol. II. pp. 575–578, 2nd edition. A detailed account of the Dambulla temple is given in Forbes's *Eleven Years in Ceylon*, vol. I. ch. xvi. pp. 367–376; and by Mr. Knighton, *Jour. As. Soc. Ben.* vol. XVI. (1847) pt. I. pp. 340–350.—Ed.

† The engraving in Forbes's *Eleven Years in Ceylon*, Frontispiece, Vol. II. is a striking but inaccurate view of one of the interiors.

‡ Appendix to Turnour's *Epitome*, p. 95, and Forbes, Ceylon, Vol. II. pp. 367, 368.

§ Loc cit. p. 578.

|| I have ventured to substitute this date for B.C. 307 according to the Sinhalese chronology, by which Asoka is placed 60 years before the date usually assigned to him.—Ed.

¶ This building is mentioned in Mahâwanso 205–6, but it has not been previously known where the dagoba was: the Revd. C. Alwis writes to me that it is supposed to enshrine the left canine tooth of Buddha, and to be somewhere near Trincomali.

* Mahâwanso pp. v. seqq.

† *Sacred and Historical Books*, Vol. II. p. 42.

‡ From the MS. in my possession, verse 32.

§ Page 206, 12.

|| Verses 1142 and 1143 of the MS. in my possession.

The letters are a slight variation of the old Páli alphabet deciphered by Prinsep.

The first sign is a symbol consisting of the swastika and another symbol joined thus follows:—

Dewaná piya maha rajasa Gamini Tissa maha lene agata anágata chatu disa sagasa dine.

Taking each word separately the first de may possibly be de? but we should expect neither, dewánam being the Páli form, and dewaná the Sinhalese; the third letter [illegible] ná may possibly be ± na, but what appears to be the vowel stroke before the upright is probably a natural mark in the rock. Even in regular Páli the m at the end of genitive plurals being often dropt, its absence here needs no remark; and possibly the long vowel ná is in compensation for the loss of the nasal.

The [illegible] of piya is, at least in Ceylon, an older form than [illegible], which also occurs here, and is the only form given in Thomas's edition of Prinsep.

The word rája is remarkable. In the first place rája is the more usual form in the dialect of Ceylon cave inscriptions in which the vowel is seldom, I believe never, written separately as it is here, and the j is the sign given by Prinsep for the aspirate jh: but there is not the slightest doubt about the reading.

In Gamini Tisa the first letter may possibly be ga instead of ∧ ga. The Sinhalese form of the Páli name Gámini is Gemunu (e to be pronounced like English a in bat, gap, &c.). The name Tissa, so common in Páli, is now unknown, except among a low caste of tom-tom beaters (berawa), and among these only in the Anurádhapura district, and only in the form Tisará, which is probably derived immediately from the Sanskrit Tishya. Who this Gámini Tissa was is not mentioned in the books. He must be some relation to Dewánampiya Tissa, or the use of the genitive would be inexplicable, but it is expressly stated in Maháwanso* that the king left no son: as, however, he reigned for 40 years, it is possible that he had a son who may have been sub-king of the Dambula district. Duṭṭha Gámini, Sinhalese Dutu Gemunu, calls himself in inscriptions Gámini Abhaya; and uses a later form of the alphabet.

The sa of the genitive in this word is most remarkable, and was one of the greatest obstacles to a decipherment of the inscription: it is not given by Prinsep, and has not I think been found in India, but I have since found it in many places in Ceylon, and there can be no doubt about the meaning of the sign. There is a slight mark at the bottom of the letter which may be a vowel mark for u, if so Sumaha Lene must be taken as the name of the cave. For the expression agata anágata, one would expect ágatánágata, but I have subsequently found it in many places, and it is usually agata anágata; the Sinhalese understand the corresponding expression áwida nowida in the sense of all those who have come to this place, and those who have not come, but it may also mean all—in the sense of present and future. The expression is not noticed either in Böhtlingk-Roth or in Mr. Childers' Páli Dictionary. A'gatánágata in Fausböll's Dasaratha Játaka, p. 31, means passers by.†

Chatudisa is the form always found on the caves for chátuddisa translated by Turnour‡ "who had come from the four quarters of the globe," but it seems that the idea "who had come" is not contained in the word, for in the Wadigama Inscription§ the corresponding Sinhalese expression is satara digin wadana (sanghaya wahansé) which gives a general sense. In sagasa the first sa is the same as the genitive of Tisa noticed above, and the genitive case sa is expressed by the letter given by Prinsep. These two characters are therefore interchangeable, and do not represent श and ष. The more usual sign of the genitive is ha, and in the double inscription at Mánâ Kanda at the Mahindana Piriveṇa (built by Agra Bodhi I. about A. D. 600) sa occurs on one and ha on the other side of the cave. There is no sign whatever for the nasal, and I have not found either the nasal or the aspirate expressed anywhere, either in the cave dialect, or in the later flat rock inscriptions of Ceylon. At first I thought that sagho in the Maháwanso|| might be a transitional form, but it must be merely a misprint, for two MSS. in my possession, one belonging to Yátrámulla Unnánsé, and the one in the newly formed Government Library at Colombo all read saṅgho.

It is not easy to state with certainty what part of the Páli verb is represented by dine, but it is probable the p.p.p. In a double inscription at Diwulwewa in Anurádhapura district, dine

* Turnour, Mahawanso, p. 124. † Maháwanso, 186. 2.

‡ Journal of Ceylon As. Soc. 1870-71, p. 21; and vide note p. 141.

§ Page 207, 6.

|| Whose recent death is an irreparable loss to Oriental literature, see p. 152.

Plate VII

INSCRIPTION UNDER THE KATÁRA OF DAMBULA CAVE TEMPLE, CEYLON. p. 130.

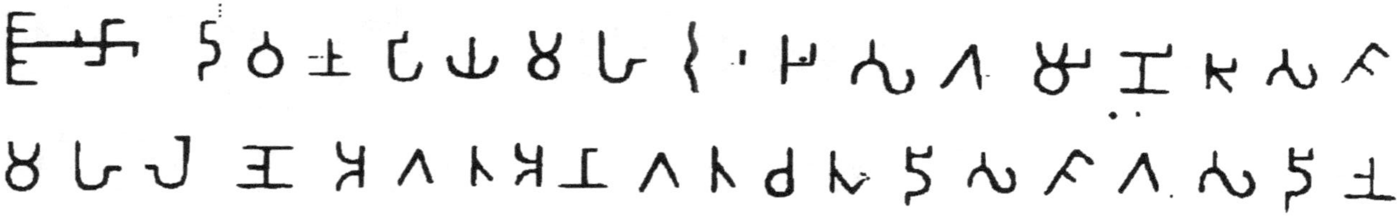

INSCRIPTION FROM DINAJPUR. p. 127.

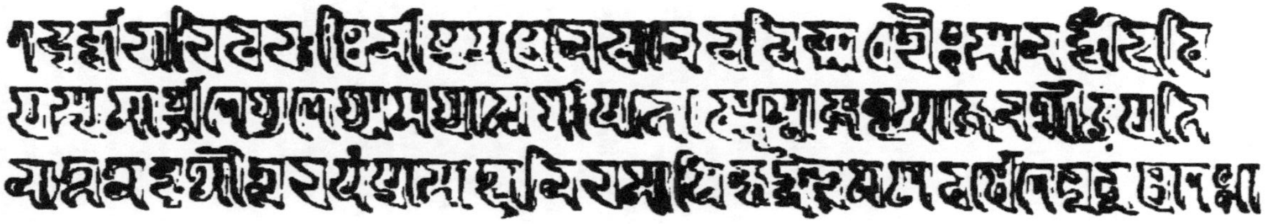

in one case is distinctly *dini* on the other. In a cave inscription at *Kiriinduwela* near Dambulla *dine* is found, and at Koratota in the Colombo, Tonigala in the Puttalam, and Mihintale in the Anuradhapura districts, *niyate* which looks like the third person singular present *Âtmanepadam*, is the corresponding word. If *dine* be taken as a nominative to agree with *lene* the translation will be—

The great cave of Gamini Tisa (son) of Devanampiya Tisa is given to the priesthood present and future of the four quarters (of the world).

It is an interesting circumstance that the courteous and much respected chief priest of the temple, Giranegama Unnanse, was one of the leaders in the rebellion of 1848, but after being many years in hiding, is now a loyal though perhaps regretful subject of the English Government.

Anuradhapura, 26th Feb. 1872.

AN OLD CANARESE INSCRIPTION FROM THE BELGÂM DISTRICT.

By J. F. FLEET, C.S.

The stone tablet from which the accompanying inscription has been transcribed stood originally in front of a small and ruinous temple of Sankaradeva in the bed of the river Malaprabhâ near Kâdaroli, which is about three miles from Mughatkhânhubli in the Sampgâm Taluka of the Belgâm Collectorate. As the temple is completely submerged during the rains, and the stone tablet was every year becoming further buried in the ground, I have had the latter removed from its original site to a place of security in the village of Kâdaroli.

The tablet bears at the top the usual Châlukya emblems, viz.,—in the centre a linga on its pedestal, with a priest officiating at it; to the right of it, a figure of Basava with the sun above it, and to the left of it, a cow and calf with the moon above them. The average length of the lines is from 18 to 19½ inches, and the average height of the letters, which are old Canarese,* and are excellently preserved in spite of the stone having been so often submerged, is from one half to three quarters of an inch. The language, it will be seen, is almost entirely Sanskrit, but the idioms and inflections are old Canarese.

Translation.

Reverence to Sambhu, the foundation-pillar for the erection of the city of the three worlds, who is resplendent with his *chámara*, which is the moon that kisses his lofty head.

Hail! While the victorious rule of the fortunate Bhuvanaikamalladeva,†—the asylum of the whole world, the favourite of the earth, the great king of kings, the supreme lord, the most venerable, the forehead-ornament of the‡ Satyâśrayakula, the glory of the Châlukyas,—was flourishing with perpetual increase so as to endure as long as the moon and sun and stars might last, he who flourished on the lotuses that were his feet (was):—

The fortunate prime minister, Someśvarabhatta, the chief of the houses of Heri, Sandhi, and Vigraha, the commander of the forces, who was possessed of all the glory of the names of 'The great chief of chieftains who has attained the five great sabdas, the bold Dandanâyaka (commander of troops), the conferrer of happiness on good people, he who abounds in fame, he whose ornament is the welfare of others (or who labours for the good of others), the moon of the ocean of affability, he who abounds in the quality of bravery, he who restrains the fury of his foes, Nayanadevar, Ayyanargandhavâraṇa,' and others also.

As his nominee the fortunate commander of the forces, Kesavâdityadeva, possessed of all the glory of the names of "The great chief of chieftains who has attained the five great sabdas, the bold Dandanâyaka, he who confers boons upon Brahmans, he who is pure of lineage, the best friend of good people, the granter of all the desires of his relations, the crest-jewel of good people, he who is terrible to the forces of his foes, he who is a very mine for the jewel of truth, the impetuous Mâvanasinga," and others, in the year of the Saka era 997, being the Râkshasa samvatsara, at the moment of the conjunction of a vyatipâta, with the sun's commencement of his northward progress, on Sunday, the day of the full-moon of Pushya, gave as a yearly grant

* The accompanying transcript corresponds line for line with the original, but corrections and emendations are inserted within brackets. Here and there the requisite marks of punctuation have been supplied, where they are wanting in the original.

† The Châlukya king Someśvaradeva II. Śaka 991 ? to 998.

‡ The Châlukya race; the name of Satyâśrayakula is derived from that of one of the early Châlukya kings,—Satyâśraya, or Satyâśraya.

five golden gadyâṇas of Gaṅga in (out of) the customs of Vaḍḍarâvula* for the purpose of the aṅgabhoga† of the god Śankaradeva of Kâdaravalli.

Whosoever preserves this act of piety, his reward is as great as if he had, at Vâraṇâsi, or at Prayâga, at Arghyatîrtha, or at Kurukshetra, fashioned out of the five jewels the horns and hoofs of twelve thousand cows of a tawny colour, and given to Brahmans who are well-versed in the Vedas the gift called Ubhayamukhîdâna.‡ But he who destroys this act of piety, commits a sin as great as if, at these same holy places, he had destroyed the same number of tawny cows.

He who appropriates land that has been bestowed either by himself or by another is born for sixty thousand years as a worm in ordure. "This general bridge of piety, which belongs in common to all rulers of mankind, should at all times be preserved by you,"—thus does Râmachandra make his earnest request to all future kings.

This is the writing of Singoja, the son of Rainoja, a very bee at the lotuses which are the feet of the god Śankaradeva. May the greatest prosperity attend it!

THE HOT SPRINGS OF UNAI.

By W. RAMSAY, BOM. C.S.

Unai is a small hamlet in the territory of the Rájá of Bánsdá near the hills east of the Surat district. It is remarkable for a very copious hot spring, rising in a stone built tank about 110 feet square; it is the scene of a large fair held every year at the full moon of the month of Chaitra. There is also a temple dedicated to a divinity locally known as "Unai Mátá." The water is too hot for the hand to be held in it for above a second or two; yet at the time of the fair crowds enter it and bathe. A miraculous agency is of course attributed. On the afternoon of the 13th of the month the god descends and cools the waters, which remain so until the day after the full, after which period the heat returns. The more matter-of-fact interpretation of the phenomenon is, that the bathers enter the water in large numbers simultaneously, thus expelling from the tank the bulk of the water, and assimilating the temperature of the remainder to that of the human body. The water is strongly impregnated with sulphur, but is not otherwise unpleasant. Cattle drink of the stream that issues from the tank, and grass and sedges grow on its banks in unusual vigour. The origin of the spring as told by the Sádhu or holy man who guards the mysteries of Unai Mátá was as follows:—Ráma on his return from the conquest of Ceylon halted at a place called Pátarwádá in the hills of Wánsdá, and held a "Jugna" (*Yajna*) or sacrifice. No Brahmans however were forthcoming, so the god collecting at once 18,000 men of the hill tribes created them Brahmans. This done, he commanded them to wash and be clean, but these new 'neolytes,' unused from birth to the use of cold water save as a drink, stoutly refused. Ráma promised them hot water, and thereupon created the Unai spring. Still another difficulty arose: the men refused to walk to the bath. This was overcome by Hanuman taking the whole of the men on his tail, and conveying them to the spring, whence after the due performance of ablutions he carried them back to Pátarwádá, where Ráma awaited them. A *Hom* or sacrifice was now offered, a recitation from the Vedas was made, and a feast given. Last of all, Ráma told the new Brahmans to go forth into the world, and to beg after the manner of the rest of their sect, but to this they had no mind, and positively refused, so Ráma relenting gave them permission to go and till the ground, and this they have done to the present day. Their descendants are the Anáwalá Brahmans, so called from the town of Anáwal in the Wánsdá territory. They are the wealthiest of the cultivating classes in the Surat district, and are not found in any other part of India: they are otherwise called Bhátelás or Bhathelás, i. e. cross-grained Bhats, also Mástán, i. e. proud, overbearing. They are a corrupt intriguing set, ever at feud among themselves, and well bearing out the sobriquets they enjoy. They are looked down upon by other sects of Brahmans, and are themselves divided into two sects, who do not intermarry, viz., those termed Desáis or hereditary district officers, and ordinary Bhátelás.

* It is not clear whether this is the name of a locality or the name of a particular tax.

† The decoration of the image of the god with clothes, ornaments, &c.

‡ Lit. "the gift of (a cow) that has two faces;" this ceremony is performed by fashioning out of the five jewels,—a diamond, a pearl, a sapphire, an emerald, and a piece of coral, the image of a cow in the act of bringing forth a calf, when of course there are two heads to apparently only one body, and presenting it to a Brahman.

ನಮಸ್ತುಂಗಶಿರಶ್ಚುಂಬಿಚಂ(ದ್ರ)ಚಾಮರಚಾರವೇ (ತ್ರೈ)ಲೋಕ್ಯನಗರಾರಂಭಮೂ

ಳಸ್ತಂಭಾಯ ಸಂ(ಶಂ)ಭವೇ ॥

ಸ್ವಸ್ತಿ ಸಮಸ್ತಭುವನಾ(ಶ್ರ)ಯಂ (ಶ್ರೀ) (ಪೃ)(ಪೃ) ಥ್ವೀವಲ್ಲಭ-

ಮಹಾರಾಜಾಧಿರಾಜಪರಮೇಶ್ವರಂ ಪರಮಭಟ್ಟಾರಕಂ

ಸತ್ಯಾ(ಶ್ರ)ಯಕುಳತಿಳಕಂ ಚಾಳುಕ್ಯಾಭರಣಂ (ಶ್ರೀ)ಮತ್ತ್ರೈ

ಲೋಕ್ಯಮಲ್ಲದೇವರ ವಿಜಯರಾಜ್ಯಮುತ್ತರೋತ್ತರಾಭಿವೃದ್ಧಿ

(ಪ್ರ) ವರ್ಧಮಾನಮಾಚ(ನ್ದ್ರಾ)ರ್ಕತಾರಂ ಬರಂ ಸಲುತ್ತಮಿರೆ ॥

ತತ್ಪಾದಪದ್ಮೋಪಜೀವಿ ಸಮಧಿಗತಪಂಚಮಹಾಶಬ್ದ(ಬ್ದ)ಮ-

ಹಾಸಾಮನ್ತಾಧಿಪತಿ ಮಹಾ(ಪ್ರ)ಚಣ್ಡದಣ್ಡನಾಯಕಂ ಸುಜನಸು-

ಖದಾಯಕಕೀರ್ತ್ತಿಕಾನ್ತಿ ಸ್ತುತಿರಪರಿಚಿತಾಭಾ(ಭ್ರ)ರವನೆ(ಗ)ಯಾಬ್ಧಿಚ(ನ್ದ್ರ)ಧೈ-

ರ್ಯ್ಯಗುಣಾಕರ(ಗ್ರ) ಸಹಿತ ಮಹಾವಿರಾಜಸ್ಥಾನಗಸ್ಥಾನ (ರ)-

ಣಾನಾಮಾದಿಸಮಸ್ತ(ಪ್ರ)ಶ(ಶ)ಸ್ತಿಸಹಿತ (ಶ್ರೀ)ಮನ್ಮಹಾ(ಪ್ರ)ಧಾನಹೆ(?ಹೊ)

ರಿಸನ್ಧಿವಿ(ಗ್ರ)ಹಿ ಮನೆವೆಗ್ಗಡೆ ದಣ್ಡನಾಯಕಂ ಸೋಮೇಶ್ವರಭಟ್ಟರ ಚೆ

ಸದಿಂ ಸಮಧಿಗತಪಂಚಮಹಾಶಬ್ಧ(ಬ್ದ)ಮಹಾಸಾಮನ್ತಾಧಿಪತಿ-

ಮಹಾ(ಪ್ರ)ಚಣ್ಡದಣ್ಡನಾಯಕಂ ಪಿ(ಪ್ರ)ಪರದಾಯಕಂ ಗೋ(ತ್ರ)ಪ-

ವಿ(ತ್ರ)ಂ ಸುಜನಸ್ಯ(ಸ್ಯೈ)ಮಿ(ತ್ರ) ಬನ್ಧುಜನಚಿನ್ತಾಮಣಿ ಸುಜನಚೂ-

ಡಾಮಣಿ ಪರಬಳಭೀಕರಂ ಸತ್ಯರತ್ನಾಕರಂ ಸಾಹಸೋತ್ತುಂಗಮಾ-

ವನ ಸಿಂಗನಾಮಾದಿ ಸಮಸ್ತ(ಪ್ರ)ಶ(ಶ) ಸ್ತಿಸಹಿತ (ಶ್ರೀ)ಮದ್ದಣ್ಡ

ನಾಯಕಂ ಕೇಶವಾದಿತ್ಯದೇವ(ವಂ) ಸ(ಶ)ಕವರ್ಷ ಸಸ್ರಗೆಯ ರಾಕ್ಷ-

ಸಗಂವತ್ಸರದ ಪುಷ್ಯದ ಪುಣ್ಣಮೆ ಆದಿತ್ಯವಾರ ಉತ್ತರಾಯ

ಣಸಂ(ಸಂ)ಕ್ರಾಂತಿ ವ್ಯತಿಪಾತದಂದು ಕಾದರ ಪಳ್ಳಿಯ ಶಂಕರದೇವರ

ಗಭೋಗಕ್ಕೆ ಪಡ್ಡರಾವೆ(?ವು)ಳದ ಮೊದಲ ವರ್ಷ(ಕ್ಷೇ)ತ್ರ ಹೊ-

ಲ ಗಂಗ ಪೊಂಗಣ್ಣಾಣವಯ್ದು ॥ ಈ ಧರ್ಮ್ಮವುಗಾದ

ಸೋ ವ್ಯರಂ ಕ್ಷೇತ್ರ ಹೊಳಲದವಗ್ಗರ ವಾರಣಾಸಿಯುಲುಂ

ಪ್ರಯಾಗೆಯುಲುಮರ್ಘ್ಯಂ ತ್ತಗ(ಕ್ಷಗ) ದಲಂ ಕುರುಕ್ಷೇತ್ರ

ದಲು(ಲೂ) ಪಿಸಿಟ್ಟಾಸಿರ ಕವಿಲೆಯ ಕೋಡು ಕುಳಗೂ(ಗು)

ಪಂಚರಕ್ತಂ ದಲ ಕಟ್ಟಿ ಪೇದಪಾರಗ ಗಷ್ಟಿ ಗಾತ್ರ

ಣಗ್ಗಂಸ್ತ್ಯಂಯುವು ಬಿಂದಾನವಂ ಕೊಟ್ಟ ದ(ಧ)ಲವನೆಯ್ದು

ವರ್ ಈ ಧರ್ಮ್ಮವ ನಾವಸುಂಕ್ಷರಗಳವದಗಾ ಕ್ಷೇ(ಕ್ರ)ದ

ಲಸಿ ಹು ಕವಿಲೆಯಂ ಕೊಂದ ಪಾಪವು ನೆಯ್ದುಗು ॥

ಸ್ವದತ್ತಂ(ತ್ತಾಂ) ಪರದತ್ತಂ(ತ್ತಾಂ) ವಾ ಯೋ ಹರೇತಿ ವಸುಂಧ

ರಾಂ ಷಷ್ಟಿರ್ವರ್ಷಸಹಸ್ರಾಣಿ ವಿಷ್ಠಾಯಾಂ ಜಾಯ

ತೇ ಕ್ರಿಮಿಃ ॥ ಸಾಮಾನ್ಯೋಯಂ ಧರ್ಮಸೇ(ಸೇ)ತುರ್ನೃ(ನೃ)ಪಾ

ಣಾಂ ಕಾಲೇ ಕಾಲೇ ಪಾಲನೀಯೋ ಭವದ್ಭಿಃ ಸರ್ವಾನ

ನೇತಾಂ ಭಾ(ನ್ಭಾ)ವಿ(ವಿ)ನಃ ಪಾರ್ತ್ಥಿ(ರ್ಥಿ)ವೇಂದ್ರಾ ಭೂ(ನ್ಭೂ)ಯೋ ಭೂಯೋ

ಯಾಚತೇ ರಾಮಚಂದ್ರಃ ॥

ಸಂಬರ(ಶಬರ)ದೇವಪಾದ(ದ)ಪದ್ಮ(ದ್ಮೋ)ಪಜೀವಿ ಸಂಭೋಗೆಜಗ ಮನ(ಗಂ) ಸಿಂ

ಗೋಜಗ ಬರೆದ(ದಂ) ಮಂಗಳಮಹಾ ಶ್ರೀ ಶ್ರೀ ಶ್ರೀ ॥

OUDH FOLKLORE—A LEGEND OF BALRAMPUR.

BY W. C. BENETT, B.C.S., GONDA.

Not many generations ago there was a great Pahlwán in Balrámpur named Bhawan Misr. He was passing the Sembar tree* to the north of the town, and broke off a twig. Immediately Mirchi Dáno, whose home the tree was, attacked him. For a day and a night they wrestled, and the demon was finally beaten. He promised his conqueror a mán of wheat every day if he would let him go, on the condition that he would tell no one whom it came from. On the next day Dáno left a big bag with a mán of wheat at the wrestler's house. Now Dáno had a sister's son bigger and stronger than himself, and was persuaded by him to leave off the disgraceful tribute. The wrestler, missing his grain, went to the Sembar tree, and began to break it down, challenging the perfidious goblin to interfere. On this the goblin's sister's son came out, and offered to fight for his uncle. For two days and two nights they fought, and the sister's son was beaten. He bought his liberty by promising to grind the mán of corn provided by his uncle, with the same condition as to secrecy. For several days the flour was left at the wrestler's house, and he lived in great plenty. But he had a foolish wife who plagued him till he told her how he had got it. From that time he could neither get his flour again, nor induce Dáno or his sister's son to fight. As the Sembar tree is still standing, he does not seem to have taken his revenge by destroying that.

Such is the story, reminding one strongly of Grimm's Hausmärchen, which was told me by a Kurmi of Balrámpur, a town on the Rápti in Gondá district, as we passed the fabled cotton tree. Dáno Baitál is a personification of the *ignis fatuus*. His sthána are found in many places along the crest of the lower range of hills which divides Gondá from Nepál, and he is appeased by offerings of milk and rice. This terrible demon feeds chiefly on dung beetles, and sallying forth at dusk with a fire between his lips, tempts unwary travellers from their path, and destroys their senses.

BHAVABHÚTI IN ENGLISH GARB.

BY THE REV. K. M. BANERJEA, HON. M.R.A.S.

BHAVABHÚTI is deservedly reckoned among the great poets. This is a title which the Sanskrit *Ars poetica* (for such in reality is the Alankára S'ástra) would not allow to be conferred on any writer as a mere compliment: it must be won, like an academical honour or diploma, by literary merits which satisfy certain definite rules.

But though universally allowed to be a great poet, but little is known of Bhavabhúti's personal history. We have no biographical tradition or anecdotes about him such as we have in the case of Kálidása, Bhartrihari, &c. In the preludes to his two dramatic works, his lineage and parentage are given, and that is almost all we know of his personal history. The prelude to the *Mahá-Víra Charita* informs us "that in the south there is a city named Padma-pura; in it dwell certain followers of the Black Yajur-Veda, descendants of Kas'yapa, chiefs of their school, making holy the company, keeping the five fires, holding vows, drinking the soma, most excellent, repeating the Veda. From their illustrious descendant who is highly esteemed, and makes the Vájapeya sacrifice, and is a great poet, the fifth in order, the grandson of one whose well selected name is Bhattagopála, and the son of the pure in fame Nílakantha, is the poet whose appellation is Bhavabhúti, surnamed S'ríkantha (whose voice is eloquent), and whose mother is Jatukarní, a friend of ours." The prelude of the *Uttara Ráma Charita* gives the poet's lineage to the same effect but more briefly: "There is truly a poet of the name of Bhavabhúti, of the race of Kas'yapa, having as surname the word S'ríkantha. The *Uttara Ráma Charita* will now be represented, composed by him, on whom being a Brahman this goddess Speech attends like an obedient wife."

Bhavabhúti's reputation is founded on his works.

The Sanskrit drama, like everything else in that language, is regulated by prescribed rules. The first ceremony is the devotional invocation of the gods for the successful issue of the play about to be acted. This is performed by the manager in the theatre itself, before the assembled audience, and is called Nándí. It is something like the prayers which precede the business of Parliament, and testifies to the sentiment of piety animating the nation and the age, even though the ceremony itself may be perfunctorily gone through or indifferently listened to. The sentiment is observed in all branches of the Sanskrit literature, there being scarcely a single author who commences his work without a salutation to some god or supernatural power. And

* In Marâthî, Sâmvar or Sâmval, Sans. S'âlmali, the *Bombax heptaphyllum* or *ceiba*.—ED.

the technical name for this is mangalâcharana. The nândî being concluded, the manager says audibly—"Enough, no need of enlarging on this." (Alamdyante sâtmodihârah alam ati vistarena.) He then commences the prastâvanâ—or the prologue, i.e. the propounding of what is going to be undertaken. He gives utterance to this not as addressing the audience, but as speaking to his own actors. The prastâvanâ gives him the opportunity of manifesting his programme—in which he gives a succinct account of the author and subject of the drama about to be acted. After the prastâvanâ, commences the actual performance of the play. But notwithstanding the prastâvanâ which is a general introduction to the whole play, every anka or act, after the first, has its own peculiar prelude called the "vishkambhaka," which prepares the audience for what is coming on in the Act itself. The 'vishkambhaka' in this sense somewhat corresponds to the Chorus in a Greek play.

The Sanskrit ars poetica does not lay down distinct rules for tragedies and comedies. There is, in fact, no Sanskrit tragedy in the proper sense of the term. The destruction of Râvana and his host in the *Mahâ Vîra Charita* might have been considered a tragedy, if the actors and auditors had been Râkshasas: but as the play is for the amusement of the followers of Brahmanism, that catastrophe of the demon race is celebrated as one of the most joyous events in Indian history or tradition. And except the death of the celestial bird Jatâyu, there is no other really tragical event to produce any sensation in the audience.

The late Professor Wilson was the first to introduce the Sanskrit drama to the notice of the European public, though Sir William Jones had preceded him as the translator of *Śakuntalâ*. But Professor Wilson only gave extracts from the dramas he summarized, and his translations were too free representations of the original.

We are now in a position to congratulate the Indian public on two translations from Bhavabhûti,—Professor Pickford's *Mahâ-Vîra-Charita*, and Professor Tawney's *Uttara Râma Charita*.*

The principle Professor Pickford has observed in his translation is thus explained by himself:—"Desirable as it doubtless is to give a translation the best form of which circumstances will allow, still it would be wrong to give up fidelity to the original for a specious affectation of elegance. The sense and character of the author's work must be retained as much as possible, even at the cost of the translator's style. The literature of one modern language may be translated into another with little difficulty, and the turn of expression retained without awkwardness, as it is generally possible to find words and phrases to denote the same conceptions and connote the same attributes. To translate a Greek or Latin author into English is, as every scholar is aware, a far harder task, yet an essentially true rendering may, in most cases, be obtained in good idiomatic English. The chasm is not too great to be bridged over. Oriental, and especially Sanskrit works, will not, however, admit of the same kind of treatment."

Professor Tawney's object was to supply a local and a temporary desideratum, and, as he states in his Preface, his object has been "to give the literal meaning of the original in tolerable English prose."

Notwithstanding these modest apologies of the two accomplished translators, however, we think that the one has rendered the original Sanskrit quite as closely as any author has ever translated Greek, and the other has presented the public with a book that scholars will value for its abiding merits.

We cannot admit without qualification Professor Pickford's implication that it is easier to give a literal translation of Greek than of Sanskrit into idiomatic English; and we need no other evidence to justify our dissent than his own *Mahâ-Vîra-Charita* as compared with an ordinary version of a Greek play. Elegant as it is, his translation cannot be charged with want of fidelity to the original. If disposed to find fault, we might criticise his views regarding some words and phrases in the original which we would interpret in a different sense; but where we have so much to admire we need not stop to notice what we consider to be a few errors. One, however, we must notice since it pervades the whole volume. The translator confounds the word siddha with prasiddha, and has invariably rendered the former in the sense of "famous;"—that may be the signification of prasiddha, but the meaning of siddha is very different. Its proper sense is *perfected*. When applied to persons, it implies the perfection or the accomplishment of the exercises or efforts they had undertaken. In theology it would denote those who had been *perfected* by their devotion, and would be equivalent to the English *Saint*. The word siddhâśrama is therefore wrongly rendered "famous hermitage." Taking the expression as a *tatpurusha samâsa*, we would interpret it, "the hermitage of the Saints," or 'the sacred hermitage.' Professor Tawney has in a parallel passage (siddhakshetre Janasthâne) rendered it, "the *holy* Janasthâna." In another place Professor Pickford has rendered siddha "well-known" (p. 12), but there the context itself drove him to explain by a foot note what he correctly guessed was the true meaning. He says "the meaning, I think, is—'for the family of Raghu is great already.'" This explanation would have been unnecessary if the proper meaning

* Mahâ Vîra Charita, translated into English prose from the Sanskrit of Bhavabhûti, by John Pickford, M.A., Professor of Sanskrit, Madras.

Uttara Rama Charita, a Sanskrit Drama by Bhavabhûti, translated into English prose by C. H. Tawney, M.A. Professor of English Literature, Pres. Col. Calcutta.

of siddha had been given in the text, thus,—"the excellence of the family of Raghu is indeed *perfected.*"

If we take exception to the rendering of another word, it is to invite discussion as to its proper representation in English, of the Sanskrit vocable tapas. This word has been rendered *penance* by both translators in their translation of tapovana 'penance-grove.' We submit that :—(1) If tapas is *penance* then tâpasa must be *penitent* ; but this derivative has been translated "ascetic" by both of them. (2) Students are often in the habit of rendering tapas "penance ;" but should this rendering be stereotyped in scholarly versions? (3) The Hindu notion of tapas is simply, *hard exercises of body or mind, or of both*—*i.e.* self-inflictions, asceticism,—the very idea which the translators have given expression to in their rendering of tâpasa. The root *tap* is doubtless the same as the root of the Greek τέρπω, and the radical meaning is also identical. Where a *penitent* submits to *tapas* (in the Roman Catholic sense) for the remission of sin, it may of course be called "penance," but where a god or a Rishi, held to be sinless and pure practises *tapas*, and mortifies himself, it cannot be called 'penance' according to Hindu notions. It is then a work of supererogation—prolific of great merit and high supernatural power. The tapovana was never looked upon as a penitentiary ; and although it might occasionally admit what might be called penance, yet it was venerated as a holy site—the scene of self-inflictions and mortifications in the sense of supererogatory works by which Rishis of great repute obtained large accretions of merit and righteousness, calculated to exalt them to an equality with the gods themselves.

The drama of *Maha-Vîra-Charita* is founded on the story of Râma concluding with his return to Ayodhya after the destruction of Râvana and the installation of Vibhishana as king of Lankâ. The sequel of the story forms the subject of the *Uttara Râma Charita.*

The story of Râma down to the death of Râvana and the recovery of Sîtâ is so well known that it is unnecessary to repeat it here. Râma's conflict with the demon-chief is recounted by the Hindus in all parts of India. It has occasioned the greatest annual festival in Bengal, the Durgâpujâ, when, for a whole fortnight, all business is suspended. Even thieves and rogues allow themselves a vacation at that period, for magistrates and policemen get but little custom during those holidays. On the day that the Bengalis consign their Durgâ to the waters, Hindus of other provinces perform the Râma-lîlâ, concluding with the death of Râvana, of which that day is the anniversary.

The sequel of the story is neither so popularly known nor are all the legends of it concurrent. The topic has always appeared to devout Hindus one of extreme delicacy. The banishment of Sîtâ, without the slightest fault in her, and while she was in a condition requiring the tenderest care, is too solemn a subject for popular merriment or mimic shows. The description in the *Uttara Râma Charita* is equally affecting and graphic. Râma had scarcely returned to Ayodhya and resumed the reins of government amid the congratulations of his relatives, ministers, and spiritual guides, when Rishyasringa proclaimed a great sacrifice, which took away Vasishtha and his wife from the capital of the empire. The king received from them benedictory messages and injunctions—on the one hand (Arundhatî pressing the advice) to pay to his queen Sîtâ all the tender attention which a virtuous wife in a delicate state of health, could claim from a husband, and on the other hand (Vasishtha himself laying the command) to govern the kingdom consistently with popular approbation. Râma was a good king as well as an affectionate husband, and willingly promised hearty compliance with both the precepts. Meanwhile, with a view to ascertain the popular will and the opinion of the public on his measures, he had employed a confidential emissary to bring him daily reports of the town-talk in his capital. He was thunder-struck on learning, immediately after his receipt and acceptance of Vasishtha's commands, that the citizens talked scandal about Sîtâ, because of her capture by Râvana and compulsory stay at Lankâ. Râma, a little before this awfully scandalous report reached his ears, had answered Vasishtha's message by promising to guide himself according to the wishes of his subjects, to propitiate whom (ârâdhanâya lokasya) he was ready to sacrifice everything—"affection, pity, and happiness," yes and if fate so will, the daughter of Janaka herself, his beloved queen.

Bhavabhûti has represented, with all the pathos which the refined versatility of Sanskrit could impart, and his own extraordinary genius could conceive, the distractions produced in Râma's mind on receiving the report of his Brahman emissary to the prejudice of his honoured and beloved queen. The indignation of posterity has affixed to the reporter of such a defamatory gossip the appellation of "Durmukha," or *foul-mouthed.* The poet, however, represents him as reluctantly and regretfully communicating the awful intelligence in the faithful discharge of a disagreeable office which he had undertaken at the king's own desire. With inexpressible mental pain, Râma decided on following what policy and worldly honour required, rather than what real justice and conjugal obligations demanded. Pilate-like, he abandoned one whom he knew to be innocent, and stole away from a wife sleeping by his side, as guileless, as she was dutiful, and directed his brother Lakshmana to conduct her to the woods. Sîtâ was thus banished to the forests, and left unprotected in the midst of noxious animals and "raw-flesh eating" cannibals, when she was about to become a mother. By the interference of supernatural agencies, Sîtâ was both preserved and also safely delivered of twin sons, who were entrusted to the fostering care of Vâlmîki, the author of the Râmâyana. Meanwhile an incident occurred, itself an index of social manners of the age, which led Râma to a second visit of the forests of Dandaka, the scene of his previous exile. An infant son of a Brahman expired by an untimely, and therefore an unaccountable, death. His body, together with the guilt of his death, was laid at Râma's door. It could not be believed that such a life would be cut off in its very bloom, without some national sin pressing on the empire through the king's misrule. Nor could Râma himself disown a responsibility, which the sense of the age attached to the royal office. But then where was the misrule? What official neglect could be attributed to a monarch who had gone the length of sacrificing the wife of his bosom for the sake of the commonwealth? While he was thus musing in his mind, an "aerial voice" declared that a Sudra of the name of Sambûka was practising religious austerities on the earth. "His head must be struck off by thee O Râma! by slaying him, raise thou the Brahman to life."

Râma now discovered the cause of the Brahman boy's untimely death. A Sudra, who should have devoted his whole time to the service of the twice-born orders, had undertaken religious exercises which were forbidden to his class. Even a Brahman was subject to ex-communication if he performed any spiritual services for the benefit of a Sudra. This invasion of the privileges of twice-born men by Sambûka, was a sin which infected the whole community, and threw the kingdom under the ban of the divine displeasure. Râma set out, sword in hand, in search of the audacious Sudra who was aspiring after heavenly felicity. This brings the king a second time to the Dandaka forest, where he found Sambûka in the act of spiritual devotion, and, having thus caught him in the fact, struck off his head without a question.

By an extraordinary combination of circumstances, brought about through supernatural agency, and after many painful and tantalizing adventures, Râma at last discovers his much injured wife and recognizes his princely sons. The drama concludes with their happy reunion.

The most touching descriptions in this tragi-comic drama are those pourtrayed in the scenes where the banished Sîtâ meets, and, herself being invisible, recognizes Râma, who hears her voice and recognizes her touch, but (the supernatural powers having so managed it) without optical perception of her form. His distractions on the occasion are vividly—perhaps too vividly described—for it is impossible to read the description without the most affecting emotions.

And here we must notice our author's incidental representation of an ancient Hindu custom which may surprise some of our readers. The learned Brahmans knew how to relish beef long before the English came into the country.

In the *Vishkambhaka* (or prelude) of the 4th Act, two Brahman pupils of Vâlmîki are introduced—one of whom was an attentive student, the other, fonder of jests and witticisms than of lessons, and unable even to speak Sanskrit. The boys had got a holiday in consequence of the arrival of Vasishtha on the very day which was to terminate with the happy re-union of Râma and Sîtâ. The jester asks his more learned companion the name of "the guest that came to-day at the head of this great troop of reverend seniors." He was told it was Vasishtha.

"*Saudhâtaki*—Ah, Vasishtha is his name.

Bhândâyana. Certainly.

S. I was thinking he must be a tiger or a wolf

B. What do you mean?

S. Why, the moment he arrived he gobbled up that poor little calf that was only a month old

B. Householders reverencing the holy text—"An offering of curds and honey must be accompanied with flesh"—when a sage, learned in the Vedas, arrives, slay in his honour a calf, a bull, or a goat, for that is what the writer on ceremonial law ordains.

S. Ha! you are caught out.

B. How do you mean?

S. Why, when Vasishtha and his companions came, the calf was slaughtered, whereas this very day when the royal sage Janaka arrived, an offering consisting of curds and honey only was presented to him by the Reverend Vâlmîki himself and the calf was let go unharmed.

B. The ceremony first mentioned is appointed by sages for those who do not abstain from flesh, but the revered Janaka is under a vow of abstinence."

Abbe du Bois despaired of the extension of Christianity in India, simply because he thought the parable of the prodigal son, exhibiting the killing of the "fatted calf" on the return of the penitent, would itself disgust the Brahmans, and close their ears against the preaching of Christianity. But the Abbe did not know of the ancient Hindu custom of entertaining reverend sages in the identical way. The slaughter of a calf or bull on the arrival of a distinguished guest was as generally practised in India, as the slaughter of a horse among the Arabians for the purposes of hospitality. The custom was indeed so widely prevalent that goghna or "cow-killer" passed as a recognised term for "guest." Pâṇini the grammarian had to give the etymology of "cow-killer" in the sense of a guest. He did so in the Sutra (III. 4, 73) Dâsa-goghnau sampradâne, which is thus expounded in the *Siddhánta Kaumudí ghá hanti tasmai goghna*, atithi, "One kills a cow for him—hence 'cowkiller,' meaning a guest." The practice doubtless fell into desuetude as the Aryans occupied the warmer latitudes of the country, but the *litera scripta* continues to remind the Brahmans of what their sanátana dharma was in the days of their ancestors.

The story of Rama to the death of Rávana as contained in the *Mahá Víra Charita* is considered by Professor Pickford as an allegory. He says in his preface—"either that the powers of night, Rávana and his followers, conquer the bright powers of day, and put an end to the labours of agriculture, until the sun with its increasing rays drives away the darkness, and restores all things as before; or that winter, from the time that the seed is sown in the ground, robs the earth of its splendour until it is dispelled by the glowing sun of summer, when the grain springs up once more." The appellative niśáchara or nightstalker, as a synonym for Rákshasa, and the legends of Ráma's being a lineal descendant of the Sun, and of Sítá having sprung from the ploughing of a field, and therefore identified with the labours of agriculture, are of course arguments favouring the Professor's allegorical explanation of the capture of Sítá by the chief of the night stalkers, who was therefore the prince of darkness, and her subsequent recovery by the might of the solar hero. But the events of the Rámáyana seem intimately connected with the national tradition of the actual conquest of the Dakhan by the Aryans, that we cannot reconcile ourselves to reduce the whole narrative to an allegorical myth, representing either the succession of day and night, or a casual stoppage of cultivation by inclement weather and its restoration by returning sunshine, or of the annual rotation of winter and summer. Night and day, winter and summer, again, are ideas which must be very different in the latitudes of the Indian Dakhan from what they are in Southern Europe. Night has the agreeable association of 'rajani,' which is one of the words expressive of it in Sanskrit, and summer is called 'nidágha.' The sun is 'tapana' or 'tigmáṃśu' burning or fierce-rayed, the moon is 'śítáṃśu' or cool-rayed, and clouds are "mudira" or delightful, being looked upon as causes of hilarity, and eagerly waited for, both for the relief they afford to exhaustion, and the growth they give to the fruits of the earth.*

There is one legend in the story of Ráma on which we must say a few words before we conclude. Although we are loath to reduce the Rámáyana to a mere allegorical myth, and although we incline to the theory of its having had a historical substratum, yet we agree with Professor Pickford that the struggle at Lanka, which we believe not to be devoid of some historical element, "takes the form of a combat between good and evil in the world. Ráma is the champion of holiness, Rávana the type of wickedness, and though the evil is allowed to flourish for a time, yet his reign is short, and goodness in the end triumphs." And we cordially join him in saying "this, then, is no new story." We may add that in this story of Ráma we discover something, embedded like a fossil in human traditions of primitive events, which reminds us of a remarkable prediction, that in the great struggle between the principles of good and evil, the seed of the woman, itself bruised in the heel, would bruise the serpent's head. When the demon-chief, Rávana, representing the principle of evil, had become the dread and scourge of the world, the gods had to deliberate about his destruction. Brahma said that Rávana had a charmed life as against gods and demi-gods, and could only die at the hands of men. Man excepted, he could be in no peril from any other species. He could only be subdued by human agency and Vishnu (the second person of the Hindu Triad) was requested to go down to the earth in human form and destroy the monster.†

REVIEW.

NÁGÁNANDA, OR THE JOY OF THE SNAKE WORLD: A Buddhist Drama in Five Acts. Translated into English Prose with explanatory notes, from the Sanskrit of Śrí-Harshadeva. By PALMER BOYD, B.A., Sanskrit Scholar of Trinity College, Cambridge. With an Introduction by Professor COWELL. (pp. xii and 100). London, Trübner and Co. 1872.

THE learned Professor of Sanskrit in the University of Cambridge has added an interesting preface to this translation made by one of his students. The *Nágánanda* was edited in Calcutta in 1864 by Mádhava Chandra Ghosha. MS. copies are scarce; and it is not mentioned in Prof. Wilson's list of untranslated plays. Prof. Cowell, however, with Dr Hall's assistance, got two copies from the North-West; and these with one or two MSS. from Bengal enabled him to print an accurate text. Mr. Boyd translated this text, and the Professor, in his preface, gives an account of the date and authorship of the work.

The play is quoted in the *Sáhitya-darpana* on pages 89, 106, 109 and 249; also in the *Das'a-rúpa* on pages 64, 65, 74, and 178. Now the author of the *Das'a-rúpa* lived at the court of King Munja, uncle of Bhoja of Dhará, about the year 985 (see

* In the Meghadúta—"Sentaptánám tvamasi saranam." Again "Tvayyáyattam Krishiphalamiti."

† The Rámáyana of Válmíki says: (Báláhánda 16 Chap.) "Mánushaṃ ripunávásádya Rávanaṃ jahi saṃyuge, Samtruddhaḥ pradadau tasmai [illegible] varam prabhuḥ Nánávidhebhyo bhútebhyo bhayaṃ [illegible] Tasmát tasya badho drishto mánushebhyaḥ parantapa."

Colebrooke, *Essays*, Vol. II. p. 53). Other considerations shew that the Nāgānanda and the Ratnāvalī and king Śrī Harsha Deva, who is mentioned as their author, must be dated anterior to the time of Bhoja or his uncle Muñja. Professor Cowell argues that the Nāgānanda and the Ratnāvalī could not have been produced by the same author, and that while he agrees with Mr. Hall that Bāṇa wrote the former, the latter, he thinks, must be attributed to Dhāvaka. He thinks there can be no doubt that the King Śrī Harsha Deva of these two plays is a different person from the Śrī Harsha who wrote the *Naishadha*. His age is uncertain. Bābu Rājendralāla Mitra (Journ. Beng. As. Soc. 1864) conjectures he lived in the tenth century. "But I find," says Prof. Cowell, "from a notice in the first number of the *Indian Antiquary* (p. 30), that Dr. Bühler of Bombay has recently fixed his date in the twelfth century."

This delightful little volume is beautifully printed, and every line of the translation, the preface and the notes bears the traces of learning and conscientious accuracy.

In the first act, which has a prologue wherein, according to custom, some blessing from a deity is invoked upon the audience, and in which alone in Sanskrit literature the person thus invoked is Buddha, Jīmūtavāhana falls upon the "tranquil charms of an ascetic grove." The herons and fowl are all right, whilst doubtful passages of the Veda are constantly discussed by the Munis. "Even these trees, taught respect for a guest, seem to utter a sweet welcome, with the murmuring of bees and make, so to speak, an obeisance with their heads bowed down with fruit; sprinkling rains of flowers, they present one a propitiatory offering. I think we shall have peace while living here." Then enters the graceful Malayavatī, daughter of Viśvāvasu, who, after some talk with her maid, begins to sing, whereupon the hero and his friend begin to peep—the former exclaiming—"If she be a goddess, the thousand eyes of Hari have all they can wish. If she be a woman of the Nāgas, then whilst her face is there, the lowest hell is not without its moon. If she be of the Vidyādharas, then our race surpasses all others. If she be born of a family of Siddhas, then in the three worlds are the Siddhas glorious." His Vidūshaka is of a similar opinion, and love-making immediately proceeds apparently to the satisfaction of all present. The entry of an ascetic announcing that the head of the family requires the heroine at the time of mid-day oblation closes the first act by separating the sighing lovers. In the second scene both are in great distress, raving about in love, till they overhear and matters become worse; the heroine thinks the hero is talking about somebody else, and gets a noose over her neck to hang herself. The hero comes to the rescue, and a full understanding and the Gāndharva marriage takes place. The third act gives a very graphic picture of the marriage merry-makings. The Vidūshaka gets very much pulled about by a *Viṭa* or *parasite*, who is so drunk that he mistakes him for his sweet-heart. This is the more ludicrous because the jester is a Brahman. There is a garden scene which closes with the entry of Mitrāvasu, son of the king of the Siddhas, who announces to the hero that Mataṅga has attacked his kingdom. The action in Act IV. is stirring. The hero's companion explains how, lest the whole snake world should be destroyed through fear of the furious descent of Garuḍa, king of birds, the king of the lower world arranged with his implacable foe that, at the spot where the event took place, a Nāga should be ready daily for his dinner. "How well," says the hero, "were the snakes defended by their king! Amongst his thousand double tongues was there not one with which he could say—'myself is given by me this day to save the life of a snake?'" and again, on seeing the heaps of Nāga bones he exclaims, "Wonderful! Fools commit sin even for the sake of a worthless body, which once perishes, is ungrateful, and a storehouse of all uncleanness. Well, this destruction of the Nagas will assuredly bring some judgment. Would that by giving up my own body I might save the life of a single Nāga!" An opportunity easily presents itself, for hereupon enters a victim Nāga Prince with his mother and servant, whom no entreaty will dissuade from assuming the red badge by which Garuḍa recognizes his daily victim. The scene between the prince, the old woman, and the hero is pathetically put, and ends by the prince going to "walk round the southern Gokarṇa which is close at hand," so as to be better prepared to be born into a new state. He however leaves the red garment behind him, and this the hero joyfully seizes, for he says "through the merit that I gain to-day by protecting a Nāga at the sacrifice of myself, may I still obtain in succeeding existences a body to be sacrificed for others!" Natural enough, as Mr. Boyd observes, for "to escape from the necessity of future birth and to obtain Nirvana is the supreme end of the Buddhist system." Here descends Garuḍa in blackness of darkness, and asserts that he must take the hero, "and ascend the Malaya mountain, there to eat him at my pleasure," and the curtain falls.

The fifth Act is by far the most striking. It opens with a universal lamentation for the disappearance of the hero on the part of his parents and wife and his father-in-law's ambassador and others—with whom the delivered Nāga prince at last consorts and explains how matters stand. They all proceed to the hill home of Garuḍa where they see "the enemy of the Nāgas, on a pinnacle of the Malaya, making new gullies in the mountain-side as he rubs his gory beak. The woods around are all uprooted and burnt by the streaks of flaming fire from his eyes, and the ground is hollowed round him by his dreadful adamantine claws." Garuda has half eaten the hero whose body is lying before him. Here ensues another series of lamentations joined in by Garuda himself when he finds he has wronged the hero:—"What a terrible sin, I have committed," says Garuda! "In a word this is a *Bodhi-sattwa* whom I have slain. I see no way of expiating my sin except by entering the fire." The king also laments—"Alas! Son Jîmûtavâhana, whence came this exalted degree of compassion? How was it that the thought did not occur to you—*Are many to be saved, or one?* For by giving up your life to save a Nâga from Garuda, yourself, your parents, your wife—yes, the whole family is destroyed." Various lamentations follow, and Garuda wants to know what he can do. The hero directs him to "cease for ever from destroying life; repent of thy former deeds; labour to gather together an unbroken chain of good actions by inspiring confidence in all living beings; so that this sin, which has its origin in the destruction of living beings, may not ripen to bear fruit, but may be all absorbed in thy merits, as a morsel of salt thrown into the depths of yonder ocean." Garuda promises to do so, nor trouble the Nâgas any more, and the victorious hero sinks in a dying state. Garuda thereupon bethinks himself of a way to wipe out his disgrace—"I will pray to Indra and persuade him by a shower of ambrosia to restore to life not only Jîmûtavâhana, but all those lords of Nâgas that have been eaten by me and are now mere skeletons." The goddess Gauri now descends a *dea ex machina*, and sprinkles the hero; the repentant lord of birds sends his shower of ambrosia; the hero is restored to life, and, in conclusion, makes a neat little speech wherein he expresses his unbounded satisfaction in seeing his worthy parents and wife, in having performed the feat of taming the lord of birds, and in rendering the Nâgas safe for ever, and also in being honoured by the bodily presence of the goddess Gauri.

A. H. B.

ON THE ANCIENT REMAINS IN THE KRISHNA DISTRICT.

(*From the Report of the late J. A. C. [illegible], Esq., M.C.S., Offg. Collector Krishna District.*)

The archæological remains in this district represent well the successive periods of the country's history and civilization, each period having its own distinct relics. These I classify as follows:—

I.—Natural caves enlarged by the hand of man and used as dwelling places probably by the aborigines.

II.—Very ancient sculptures of serpents belonging probably to the Takshaks or Dragons.

III.—Cromlechs, sepulchral tumuli, and stone circles, the remains of the early Scythic or Turanian races before the Aryan invasion.

IV.—The rock caves and temples and topes of the Buddhist era.

V.—The relics of the transition period when Brahmanism triumphed over Buddhism, represented by Brahmanical sculptures introduced into the old Buddhist caves, and sculptured stones taken from Buddhist buildings and used in the construction of temples to Vishnu and Shiva.

VI.—Temples of the Brahmanical period, with inscriptions which purport to be from 800 to 600 years old.

VII.—Forts illustrating the periods of the Uriya sovereigns, the Reddi Chiefs, the Bijayanagar or Royals dynasty, the Muhammadan conquest, the rise of Zamindars, and the power of the Marâṭhas and Rohillas.

VIII.—The mahals or palaces of Zamindars constructed within the last century.

IX.—European remains—Portuguese, Dutch, French, and English.

I. *Aboriginal Caves.*—These remains are to be chiefly found in the Palnad—a wild rocky country, but sparsely inhabited. The chief caves are those of Guttikonda and Gamagalla, both within a few miles of Karempudi. The one at Guttikonda I visited. It is about two miles from the village of that name. At the bottom of the hill a large artificial pond has been made. The ascent of the hill is rendered easy by a flight of loose stone-steps, and at the top, facing the approach, a small Śivâlaya stands. On the top is the grave of the late Karnam of the village, who was a Lingayat, and, at his particular request, was buried here with an altar-seat of stone-slabs over his remains, and close by, a tombstone with a Linga carved on it, and an inscription in Telugu. I mention these particulars to show how religious associations gradually accumulate and invest with new ideas an old cave like this. Immediately facing the grave, is the entrance to the cave, which is high and wide. On entering, one finds oneself in a spacious natural chamber, with an artificial dais or altar. Out of this hall, a gallery proceeds in a downward direction. The passage is in some places very low, so that one is compelled to stoop or crawl. The air is very oppressive, and respiration difficult. Lighted by torches, the visitor proceeds a considerable way down, and then the passage gradually ascends. At the end of about 100 yards, there is a perennial

* This Report, from the Proceedings of the Madras Government, Revenue Department, of 7th Nov. [illegible], contains so much interesting matter, that most of it seems deserving of being reproduced. We do not agree, however, with some of the lamented author's theories; for example the ethnological and chronological place assigned to the first three classes of remains does not seem tenable. Some paragraphs have been omitted (p. 151) as unnecessary: otherwise the report is given without material alteration.—ED.

spring, filling a large basin in the rock, about 14 yards across. The place is now resorted to for sacred ablutions. The water is clear and limpid, but there floats on the surface a white powder or formation of lime, which, when collected in a cloth and dried, resembles white sand. Beyond this point the cave has not been penetrated in the memory of man, but there are galleries running further on into the rock, and local traditions tell of under-ground passages to Benares and Rameshwaram. The rock through which the cave extends is disintegrated, and readily crumbles away, which will probably account for the natural formation of the cave by the action of water. It may be surmised that it was used as a place of habitation by the aboriginal races, whose descendants we probably see in the Yenadis and Yerukalas. There is also a tradition that it was at one time inhabited by a band of recluses, probably during the Buddhist era. About twenty years ago a Sanyasi, by name Lakshmi Nârâyaṇa, took up his abode here, and improved the passage leading to the spring, and revived its celebrity. Brahmanism found it desirable to give it a sacred tradition which runs to the following effect:—Muchukundudu was a royal saint who belonged to the Solar race in the age before Râma. Wearied out with his exertions in carrying on a war with the Râkshasas—a term always used here as designating the Buddhists—he retired to this cave, and, like Rip van Winkle, indulged himself in a sleep for some centuries. Meantime, the war between the Devatas and Râkshasas continued, and, in course of time, the Râkshasas beset Krishna, who took refuge in the depths of this cave and disappeared. The Râkshasas entering the cave in pursuit of Krishna, disturbed the rest of Muchukundudu, who arose like a giant refreshed and extirpated the descendants of his old foes.

The cave at Ramagallu I have not visited, but it is said to be entered by descending a sort of well. The galleries are said to run an immense length into the rock, but the passage is over-grown and has not been entered for many years.

At Sitanagaram there is a rock-spring which never runs dry, and a natural reservoir. It is much resorted to on sacred days for bathing.

There are also other caves in the Palnad. I saw several in the banks of the Krishna, on the Haidarabad side, as I came down the river in a boat.

In other parts of the district the only other natural caves I have come across are at Mangalagiri and Undavalli in the Guntur Taluqa. These two places, seven miles apart, are said to be connected by an under-ground passage. All that is to be seen is a passage going into the rock, but it has not been explored in the memory of man, and is said to be infested with snakes.

II. Very ancient sculptures of Snakes, belonging probably to the Takshakas or Dasyus, or whoever may have been the races that inhabited the country before the Scythic or Turanian immigration. Of their great antiquity I believe there can be no doubt. They may be found in the enclosures of many temples. A number of them are either collected around a tree—very often the *Ficus religiosa*—affording corroborative evidence of the antiquity of tree and serpent-worship in this part of the country, or they are ranged along the outer wall of the temple, and are regarded with peculiar veneration by the lower classes of the people. In some villages I have seen an old serpent-stone which has probably been turned up in cultivating the ground, installed in a shrine of its own as the popular object of worship. These sculptures are of the roughest and rudest description; the forms of the snakes are very varied, and an interesting collection of photographs might be made from these stones, which are probably the earliest representations of native art existing in the country.

III. Scythic remains of Sepulture.—These consist of cromlechs, sepulchral tumuli, and stone circles, and are found in several parts of the Palnad, etc. My researches were made in the neighbourhood of Nermpalli. I found the cairns much resembling those in the Koimbatur district and on the Nilgiris. There is a large field covered with these cairns, many of which have been opened and examined. It may be desirable to issue some orders for the preservation of those that remain, as they are very interesting relics.

In every instance there is a large flat stone upon the top of the *kist-vaen*, which is formed with carefully selected flat stones placed on edge, so as to form a square or oblong chamber. In one of the sides there is often a sort of entrance left. Sometimes there is a hole in one of the side slabs, communicating with an adjacent chamber in which pottery, etc., is found. The *kist-vaen* is entirely under-ground, the upper slab being all that is visible. On removing this slab it is necessary to excavate about four or five feet through sand and stones. Then, if the *kist-vaen* be a large one, it will usually be found divided into two or four cells or compartments. In each of these is found a quantity of burnt human bone, and beside them—but not holding them—a collection of cinerary urns and vessels of baked clay of various shapes and sizes—pottery resembling the common *chatties* of the present day, as well as vases, basins, and cups of antique and graceful forms now quite out of use. In some cases the pottery is burnt red throughout; in some burnt black throughout; in some half burnt—in some red outside and black within; and sometimes it is hand-glazed. These vessels were probably used to contain offerings or provisions for the dead. They are generally found in an inverted position. In one tomb I opened there was a portion of an ivory or bone bracelet, but I came across no iron implements, such as I have found in the Koimbatur cairns. The size of the bones, teeth, etc., show the race of men who employed this means of sepulture to have been, in physical configuration, much on the same scale as the present natives of the country, and gives no support to the local tradition, which is, that they are the remains of an extinct race of Pigmies who, being threatened with a storm of fire from heaven, built these stone structures and retired into them when the anticipated danger arrived, but were overwhelmed, buried, and burnt alive in the surrounding conflagration. The position in which the bones are found show, however, also, that the corpse was first burnt, and the bones collected and heaped in the stone cells.

It is said that many years ago a ryot dug up in this field of tombs a large bell-metal wheel, but he kept his discovery a secret, and had the wheel broken up. There are persons still living who say they have seen pieces of it. This must have been a Buddhist relic.

The *kist-vaens* are of all sizes from about three feet square to twenty feet square. One of the largest may be seen immediately behind the District Munsiff's Court. The converging slab is an enormous mass about a foot thick.

These evidently appear to be the remains of the Scythian or Turanian race who first conquered the aborigines and settled in India, and must therefore be of very great antiquity. We do not know of any race of a subsequent period in this part of India, who employed both cremation and interment in their mode of disposing of the dead.

To the westward of Amravati on the Krishna, celebrated for its Buddhist remains, and near an unexplored mound known as *Ivarhi-dibba*, there are a great number of rude circles of stones which have been noticed by Mr. Fergusson in his *Tree and Serpent-worship*. A still greater number of these remains are found at a distance of four or five miles to the south-east, where they cover the roots of the hills. They range apparently from twenty-four to thirty-two feet in diameter, and when dug into, have always yielded cinerary urns, burnt bones, and other indications of being burning places.

On the left bank of the Krishna also in the Nandigâma Taluqa these monuments are to be found in great numbers, extending for many miles in all directions, as noticed in a review of Mr. Fergusson's work in the *Edinburgh Review*.*

IV. Buddhist remains.—The most celebrated Buddhist remains in this district are the antique marble sculptures of Amrâvati, recently brought to the notice of the public, and illustrated by Mr. James Fergusson in his *Tree and Serpent Worship*. Amrâvati is situated on the right bank of the river Krishna, about twenty miles above Bejwâḍâ.

These sculptures were first discovered by Captain C. Mackenzie in 1797. Some years previous to Captain Mackenzie's visit, the Vasereddi Râja of Chintapalli, attracted by the sanctity of the temple dedicated to Shiva under the title of Amareshwarasvâmi, determined to build a town here and a residence for himself. He had recourse for stone to the walls of Dharanikota, the ruins of an ancient city, about half a mile to the westward of Amrâvati. He also opened several mounds adjoining the spot, and among them the one known as *Dipaldinne-Kaṇu* or the Hill of Lights, when the remains of an ancient Buddhist dagoba were found. Large quantities of the stone he removed and employed in building new temples and palaces, and many of the fine marble sculptures perished, being burnt for lime. The Râja discovered in his excavations a small relic-casket of stone with a lid—on opening which a crystal was found containing a small pearl, some gold leaf, and other things of no value. This was sent to the Madras Museum.

Captain (afterwards Colonel) Mackenzie, Surveyor General, first saw Amrâvati in 1797. He visited the spot again in 1816, and had eighty drawings made of the sculptures. He selected a number of the stones which were forwarded to Calcutta in 1819. Subsequently a number were brought to Masulipatam, with the view, it is said, of erecting some building, and they lay there for more than eighteen years before they were given to Mr Alexander, Master Attendant. Some were removed to the temple of Shivagaṅgâ.

Sir Walter Elliot resumed the excavations at Amravati in 1840, and discovered a portion of the monument not before touched. These slabs had, however, all been probably removed in the twelfth or thirteenth centuries from their original positions, Mr. Fergusson surmises, and built into a little chapel, of which they formed the walls. Sir Walter Elliot sent a large number of the sculptures to Madras, where they lay till they were sent home to England in 1856. In London they were put out of the way into a coach-house attached to Fife-house, where they were at last discovered by Mr. Fergusson, who was able to appreciate their value.

Besides the sculptures sent to England, there were others deposited in the Central Museum, Madras. Some are to be found in the Bejwâḍâ Museum, and a few are in the possession of Captain Maiden, Master Attendant, Masulipatam.†

Such inscriptions as have been found at Amravati are in Pali, the form of letters being those of the Gupta alphabet, as used immediately before or after 319, A.D.

Colonel Mackenzie collected a considerable number of coins about Dharanikota, some of these were Roman and others of the Baktrian Kadphises type affording additional evidence as to the fact that the place was of some importance about the Christian era. Some were gold coins. Small lead coins are still to be found there in great numbers, and may

* Vol. CXXX. (Oct. 1869,) p. 501.—Ed.

† We omit Mr. Boswell's outline of Mr. Fergusson's restoration of the Amravati tope, which follows here in the original report.—Ed.

be picked up on the surface of the ground after a shower of rain, but the impressions are almost entirely obliterated.

Coins of a similar description, and probably of the same period, are also to be found at Gudivâdâ about the elevated mound on which a former Collector built a bungalo. The soil is thickly impregnated with broken pottery and bricks. There are also other places in the district where similar coins are met with—

(1.) Bakhipala dibba near Bokkevala in Najivid Zamindari.

(2.) On the mounds in the Dalamarta field near Marivâdâ, also in the Najivid Zamindari.

(3.) In the Pati lands in the village of Pamuganchiprol in Nandigama Taluqa.

(4.) In the Ravatapaya and Lavallapalli swamps of the Pundraka Salt Division.

In connection with these leaden coins, I may mention that lead is found in considerable quantities near Karempudi in the Palnad, but the mines are not now worked. Copper is found both in the Palnad and Vinukonda Taluqas.

The next most important Buddhist remains are the rock caves of Bejwâdâ on the left, and Undavalli on the right bank of the Krishnâ. In 1868, when several scientific parties visited the Krishna district to make observations on the great Solar Eclipse of that year, Mr J. Fergusson, the author of the well known work on the Rock Temples of India, drew the particular attention of the savans to the cave temples of Bejwâdâ, with a view to obtaining fuller information for the determination of the question as to their Buddhist origin. These caves are but little known and seldom visited. Those at Bejwâdâ are hollowed out of the eastern side of the great hill, at the foot of which the town stands, and from the summit of which the telegraph wire is carried across the river Krishna to a hill on the opposite side, a distance of about 3290 feet, without any support. At the foot of the hill at the north-east corner of the town, we come upon a small rock-temple which, in the wet season, is a foot or two deep in water. At the entrance is a representation of Venayakudu or Ganesha, showing that, if it had a Buddhist origin, it has been subsequently transformed into a Brahmanical shrine. Further on there are several solitary caves cut out of the rock, like anchorite cells, some of which are only large enough for a man to crawl into. Going on still in a north-east direction, near the base of the hill, there is a good-sized mandapam, or porch, cut out of the rock with solid pillars of stone. Behind the mandapam, and opening out of it, there is a chamber, and there are also several other chambers adjoining, which have been converted into shrines at one time, but subsequently deserted. In some there are still images. In the mandapam I found an old man and two old women had taken up their permanent abode. Old and infirm, without the means of supporting themselves, they found here an asylum for which they had to pay no rent, and which required no repairs.

Ascending the hill from this spot, there is still another cave which was lately occupied by a Bairagi, or wandering devotee. He has divided the cave into several separate chambers with mud walls. The most interior one he appears to have devoted to culinary purposes, which, as it has no chimney, must have filled the other apartments with smoke. The Bairagi in question appears to have been a species of salamander, for his special penance was to sit in the centre of a circle, about eight feet in diameter having a trench all round (which is still to be seen), in which fires were lighted. In this magic circle he performed his mantras or incantations. He had a reputation of his own, and was much resorted to by women of all classes to whom nature had denied the much coveted joys of maternity. The cave is now empty, but there is little about it to indicate traces of its early origin. There is still another cave about half way up the hill just over the town and behind a later temple of Shiva.

In the temple of Malleshwaraswâmi in the town itself, there are some figures and columns of much older date than the temple itself. These appear to be of Buddhist origin. One capital of a pillar is quite different from those of ordinary Hindu architecture.

At the Library in Bejwâdâ there is a colossal figure of Buddha, cut out of black stone. It is said to have been discovered buried near the base of the hill, on the top of which stands a bungalo built by Colonel Orr. This image has, however, lost its features, which appear to have been wilfully defaced probably by the Muhammadans in their iconoclastic zeal. There is another perfect colossal figure of Buddha in the enclosure of a chawltry at Gudiwâdâ, which much resembles the one at Bejwâdâ. The features are very fine, the hair woolly, and it has a seven-headed serpent over the head. There is no one who claims any property in this image, and it is well worthy of preservation.

At Gudiwâdâ there is a circular mound resembling the one at Amrâvati. It is known as lanja dibba or harlot's mound. It is reported to have been raised by a dancing girl who lived on the top, and confined herself to one meal a-day, of which she delayed to partake till she could see the lights at Akurupalli Pagoda. The mound, however, evidently covers the ruins of a Buddhist dagoba. Well burnt bricks are found in large quantities. As there is no stone available in this neighbourhood, sculptures probably do not exist, but the people tell of a stone casket dug up here containing a pearl, some gold leaf, and other relics. There are several other mounds in the neighbourhood, on one of which a former Collector built a bungalo. There are said to have been formerly ninety-nine Buddhist or Jaina temples here and ninety-nine tanks. There are similar mounds also known as *lanja dibbalu* covering similar Buddhist remains at Ghantasalapalem in Bandar Taluqa, and Bhattiprolu in Repalli Taluqa.

There are also a number of copper Buddhist figures in the Library at Bejwâdâ. These were found buried at Buddhavaram in the Repalli Taluqa—a place which retains traces of its origin in its name. There are three images of Buddha, one seated under a triple umbrella, two standing with the head surrounded by a wheel or circle. There are also two copper [illegible] of which the images are wanting. Besides these there are a number of copper images of the Buddhist saints, varying in size from one to two feet in height. These are beautifully executed, and might bear comparison with Grecian or Roman figures for symmetry and design. Most of the figures have the caste thread, and the folds of the dresses are very gracefully represented. Each figure formerly stood on a pedestal of its own, but I am informed that, as these pedestals bore certain characters, probably the names of the saints, they were sent to Madras to be deciphered. They have never, however, been returned. I presume they are in the Government Central Museum. I would recommend bringing the figures and these pedestals together again. Each figure has a spike below the feet to fit into the pedestal. The features are finely cut, the hair woolly, and the lobes of the ears unnaturally extended and pendant. In one of the images the eyes are of silver. The positions are very natural, easy, and graceful.

Crossing the river Krishna at Bejwâdâ, about a mile and-a-half above and west of Sitânagaram, is the village of Undavalli, at the foot of a high hill, along whose base and sides there are the remains of a considerable number of rock caves and temples, evidently of Buddhist origin. There is a rock temple of two storeys close to the village which has been recently utilized as a granary. There are several hermit cells scattered about with more or less carved stone about the entrances, in some of which pigs have taken up their abode. In various places the figures of elephants and other animals in the Buddhist style of representation are to be seen depicted. A pathway along the side of the mountain, at some elevation, leads to more of these remains. At one place there is a *mandapam* cut out of the rock and supported by seven pillars, more solitary cells, and, lastly, a rock temple of four storeys of considerable proportions. The two lower storeys are completely buried in *debris*. From the first floor there runs an unexplored gallery far into the rock, which is said to be an under-ground means of communication with Mangalagiri, seven miles off.

The four storied temple, although it bears many evident traces of its original Buddhist origin, has subsequently been transferred into a temple of Vishnu under the designation of Anantasayana. On the third storey is a large hall, supported by solid stone columns, and on each of these is represented, as far as they can be deciphered, scenes from the history of Râma. There is the rape of Sitâ by Râvana, her search and rescue by Hanuman, the fight between Râma and Râvana, the defeat of Râvana, etc. At one end of the hall is a gigantic figure representing Vishnu as Narayanaswami stretched at length upon the seven-headed serpent, whose heads rise above him. There are two gigantic figures at his feet in *bas relievo*, and a number of others of smaller dimensions. These appear to have been originally painted, for there are remains of paint in spots, representations of flowers between the figures, which have been completely done with Pre-Raphaelite minuteness. The only Buddhist sculpture of figures I could trace was the representation of Buddha seated with a row of disciples on either side. This, however, the Brahmans affirmed was a representation of Vishnu and the Rishis.

Leading out of the central hall, there are other smaller chambers with more sculpture upon the walls. Many of these have become quite obliterated owing to the disintegration of the rock on which they were cut. Others have been obliterated by modern [illegible] with a free use of whitewash. On the fourth storey is another hall with chambers leading out of it, with more sculpture, but all the sculptures here are much inferior to those of Amravati, and, with few exceptions, of the Brahmanical period. The legend of Râma and Râvana is considered to represent the feud between Brahmanism and Buddhism, and the final triumph of the former over the latter. Here we have the story represented in the living rock. The winning party, having got these temples of their old rivals, have sought to obliterate the traces of the old religion, and have substituted in their place the symbols and legends of the triumphant form of worship.

Near the large temple there is an inscription on a rock in Telugu nearly obliterated with whitewash, but, from the form of the letters, I infer that it is not of any very ancient date.

I have alluded to the term Râkshasa as being commonly used to designate the Buddhists, and various remains have been traditionally handed down, associated with these Râkshasas. The chief traditions of the Puranas relate to the wars between the Devatas and Râkshasas, and the country is spoken of as the land of the Râkshasas. The names, too, have their own significance as evidence to this fact. Karempudi is said to be derived from Karra, one of the Râkshasa leaders, Dusari after his brother Dushana. The ancient legends are all localized. Thus it is said that when Râma killed the two brothers Karra and Dushana, the news was conveyed to Râvana, who was in great grief. Then it was suggested to him by Marichudu (from whom the village of [illegible] derives its name) that he should carry off Sitâ, the wife of Râma, which he accomplished, transporting her to Ceylon. Râma first heard the news of Sitâ's rape, it is said, at Vinukonda (th

(Hill of Hearing). Another of the Rákshasa leaders, Balayyudam, gives his name to a village just across the Krishna, opposite Sarrasala, on the Haidarabad side. The cave temples are always pointed out as remains of the Rákshasas, and the people continually speak of Rákshasas and Jainas in connection with each other.

Mr. Fergusson has noticed an extensive excavation near Darhapalli, covered with sculpture in a most masterly style, and another on the road leading from the river to the Pagoda of Srisailam. The former I have not been able to find; the latter is said to be in the Karnul district. There are also rock temples at Ittipotala, Jaterpalem, Kishwaram, and at other places along the banks of the Krishna in the Palnad, of which at present but little is known and which would doubtless repay investigation.

V. *Relics of the transition period, when Brahmanism triumphed over Buddhism.*—This period is represented by Brahmanical sculptures introduced into the old Buddhist caves, and sculptured stones taken from Buddhist buildings, and used in the construction of temples dedicated to Vishnu and Shiva.

The solar race entered India about 1,000 years before the lunar race, which was about the fifteenth century B.C. Both these were Aryans.

From this time till the third or fourth century B.C., no hordes of any sort, so far as we know, crossed the Indus. By this time the blood of the Aryans had become so mixed and impure that the Veda was no longer possible as a rule of faith, and when Śakya Muni attempted to revive, in Buddhism, the religion of the aboriginal Turanians, the call found a ready response. Buddha is ordinarily asserted to have been born at Kapilavastu, a small principality north of the Ganges, B.C. 623, [and to have died] at Kusinagara in the same neighbourhood about B.C. 543. Mr. Fergusson has fixed the first century after Christ for the building of the Buddhist tope at Sanchi between Bhilsa and Bhopal, Central India.

Amravati he places in the fourth century, A.D., and the caves of Ajanta in the seventh century, A.D. From this period the decline of Buddhism dates. Shankara Acharya, the principal teacher of Shaivism, lived about the eighth or ninth century, A.D., and out of Buddhism rose the Jaina and Vaishnava faiths; these are both direct products of Buddhism; indeed Buddha is recognized as the ninth Avatar of Vishnu.

In many parts of this district is to be noticed the employment of sculptured stones of very ancient date in the construction of Vaishnava and Shaiva temples. The sculptures usually represent animals, elephants, horses, deer, boars, tigers, alligators, and various sorts of birds and fishes. The anatomical proportions of these representations are excellent, but in the fabrics in which they are found, they are quite out of keeping with the more recent buildings; thus there is at Vinukonda an ancient mantapam, around whose basement is an entablature representing all sorts of animals. In the interior are some of the most beautifully shaped pillars I have seen anywhere in this part of the country. The old edifice is full of interest, but it is used as a common choultry now by beggars of the lowest castes, and has been disfigured by the erection of a modern travellers' bungalow with two rooms on the top. The bungalow has in its turn been abandoned. One room is used for a school, and the other has been recently applied for, for a Post Office.

Other instances of the use of stones taken from older Buddhist structures for the construction of later temples may be seen at Paritala in the Bapatla Taluq, and at Gurjala and Pidugurala in the Palnad. Near the latter village are a number of mounds forming a sort of large circle, which the people believe to be the remains of an old fort. The appearance of these mounds bears, however, a very strong resemblance to the *dipaladinne* at Amravati, beneath which the Amravati sculptures were discovered. They have never been opened. Scattered all around are great quantities of broken pottery, but no coins are known to have been found here.

A careful examination of existing temples would lead to the discovery of many ancient relics of Buddhism; indeed, one comes across them continually, and the transition from the old to the newer form of faith seems to be very clearly marked on the archaeological remains of this district.

VI. *Temples of the Brahmanical periods, with inscriptions which purport to be from 300 to 800 years old.*—The number of temples dedicated to Vishnu and Shiva in this district is very considerable, and what is strange, we find the most ancient ones abandoned, and their materials used in raising new buildings. The people seem to entertain but few ideas of veneration with regard to the ancient structures, and brick and mortar plastered outside is the description of architecture that finds most favour for temples in the present day. When we do find worship maintained in an old temple, we are sure to find the ancient sculptures and inscriptions effaced and disfigured by a thick coat of whitewash, and the images smeared with oil or red lead.

The principal temples dedicated to Vishnu are at Mangalagiri, Akiripalli, Shrikakulam, Vedadri, and Gollapalli. Attached to the one at Akiripalli there are some cave-temples.

The principal temples dedicated to Shiva are at Kotappa Konda, Bejwada, Kalepalli, Shivaganga, Mopidevi, Chejerla, and Macherla.

I have not personally visited all these, and in some the priests object to admit European visitors. I have, however, visited a large number of temples in the district. An interesting collection might be made of the stone inscriptions, where such are to be found, and which, according to the Telugu dates, appear to extend for about 300 to 800 years back

Sir Walter Elliot made, I understand, a collection of these, but I am not aware what he did with them. It is a work which will require much care to select these inscriptions or dânaśâsanas, as some are no doubt spurious, but those which are genuine would afford much information as to the old dynasties.

Mangalagiri is a town situated about eight miles south of Bejwada. It has a Vaishnava temple dedicated to Narasimhaswâmi of considerable repute. The annual festival or celebration of the *Kalyana Utsavam* in the month of Phalgunam draws great crowds. The chief temple is situated on the side of a high hill. The approach is by steps cut out of the rock. The old caves are evidently of Buddhist origin, and have been transformed to suit the worship of Vishnu. At the foot of the approach is a pillar of black granite with inscriptions in Telugu on all four sides. This was blown down some years ago, exhibiting a cavity in the lower stone or pediment in which coins or other valuables were probably deposited. The temple is of two stories cut out of the rock, and there are also many rock-chambers. Sugar-water is the offering here made to the divinity. It is poured into a cavity in the rock and disappears. The god is supposed to take half of every offering and the other half goes to his priests. Behind the principal chamber is a passage into the hill, which has never been explored, but is said to afford subterraneous communication with Undavalli. In the town of Mangalagiri is another temple (old), though of more recent date, also dedicated to Narasimhaswâmi. It has a very high gopuram of ten stories, but the priests are very exclusive, and will not admit visitors. Some of the carving on the temple car which is kept outside is good, but much of it is abominably disgusting. The difference in the style of work, according as the subject is one worthy or not the study of art, is very marked. The grosser representations are evidently the work of inferior artists. There is a very large koneru or tank, having four sides of cut-stone steps. This is very much esteemed, and greatly resorted to for every sort of purpose, for bathing, for the washing of foul linen, as a receptacle for dirt, and also very largely for drinking purposes. The tank is very deep, and never dries up. It has been proposed to have it cleaned out, but the expense would be great. It is supposed to have a rich deposit of bangles and all sorts of native jewellery, which persons have lost when bathing.

At Macherla in the Palnad there is an ancient stone temple of much fame. On the surrounding walls are a series of sculptures representing scenes from the Mahâbhârat and Bhâgavatam. There are also sculptures in the temples at Sankarapuram, Gamalapad, and Dachepalli.

At Sattenapalle also in the Palnad, on the southern bank of the Krishna, there are a number of stone temples dedicated to Siva. Many of these are in ruins, but worship is still kept up.

At Gurzala in the Palnad there is ancient mantapam or portico, with regular Muhammadan arches cut in stone, but evidently of a date long before the Muhammadan era. An old temple here is said to have been built by Nalagama Râjâ Narasimha Raya (Velamah), of which many of the stones appear to have been taken from more ancient structures of Buddhist origin.

(*To be continued.*)

THE ASIATIC SOCIETIES.

Asiatic Society of Bengal.

A PARTY of draughtsmen and moulders who had been especially trained for the work by Mr. H. H. Locke, Principal of the Calcutta Government School of Art, went to Bhuvaneshwar in 1869,* and there executed casts of the more remarkable of the mouldings and sculptured figures which form the decoration of the exterior of the ancient temples. Bâbu Râjendralâla Mitra accompanied this field party, and during the short time he was with them, selected subjects for their earlier operations. From Bhuvaneshwar he visited the neighbouring rock temples or caves of Khandagiri, on which he has since communicated his observations to the Bengal Asiatic Society.

A second expedition—also a party of Mr. Locke's students, this time under his own personal superintendence—proceeded to Orissa in the end of December last. Mr. Locke's principal object on this second occasion, was to obtain casts and drawings of the best and most characteristic carvings in the Khandagiri caves. He, however, made use of an opportunity which occurred to him, to go to Jâjpur, and to procure some photographs of the celebrated monolithic figures, and column at that place.

Such expeditions serve the double purpose of placing, so to speak, original materials within easy reach of every enquirer, and of taking evidence, as it were *de bene esse*, which otherwise might pass irrecoverably away. This risk of disappearance is by no means imaginary, for Mr. Locke infers from a comparison of the sketch of Bhuvaneshwar given in Stirling's paper on Orissa,† with the present features of the ground, that as many as eight or ten or even more of the smaller temples have, within say the last forty years, sunk into confused masses, or ill-defined jungle covered mounds of ruins. No one will doubt that the tale, which would be told by the archaic remains of Khandagiri and Bhu-

* *Vide ante* pp. 24, 25.

† Asiatic Researches vol. XV. (1825.)

Bhuvaneswar, if they could be rightly interpreted, would be historically most important. The Khandagiri caves bear ample indicia of a Buddhist origin. But Mr. Locke considers there is also a Greek element plainly perceptible in the ornament; I do not now refer to the dress worn by the booted figure of the Rani's cave, which, notwithstanding its foreign appearance, Bábu Rájendralála supposes to be indigenous to this country.—I speak of the conventional ornament on the mouldings and friezes. And then, if we pass to Bhuvaneswar, we find ourselves in the presence of a type of Hindu art, which is, at any rate in this sense, archaic, namely, that the forms assumed by the temples were developed in the infancy of structural resource. The lofty pyramidal tower, gradually rounded in at the top, and surmounted by a lotus-shaped crown, is not at first sight, I think, pleasing to the eye; but it is easy to understand how it might have grown out of the exigencies under which the builder worked. Without the aid of cement, and in the absence of any knowledge of the arch, the horizontal section which could be effectually covered over by overlapping slabs of stone would necessarily be small, and therefore it would be by height alone that the designer could give any imposing character to his buildings. In those cases where the wealth of decorative ornament is striking, a close examination shows that, after all, the whole is little more than repetition on repetition of certain comparatively few forms, examples of each of which appear on almost every temple.—From the President's Address, Proc. As. Soc. Beng. Feb. 1872.

"Journal of the Bombay Branch of the Royal Asiatic Society (No. 27), 1870."

This part of the Journal has just been published and contains:—(1) a paper "On some Sanskrit copper-plates found in Belgám Collectorate;" by J. F. Fleet, C.S. No. 9. of these plates is in possession of a weaver at Bágwádi in the Belgám taluqa. It is in three sheets, written in a corrupted form of the Káyastha character, and bears on the seal a figure of Hanumán. It gives us the names of three kings of the Yádava dynasty.—1. Kanhára, the son of Jaitugi, the son of Simhana. The date of the latter is given by Mr. Elliot as S'aka 1132 to 1170? with a note to the effect that the exact date of his death has not been ascertained. His successor is Kandarae Deva, Kandaráya Deva, or Kanera Deva, S'aka 1170? to 1182, who is evidently the same as Kanhára of this inscription. The last inscription of Simhana that Mr. Elliot obtained bore the date of S'aka 1169. In the present inscription the name of Simhana's son is supplied as Jaitugi, and, the grant being made by Kanhára (his grandson) in S'aka 1171, Mr. Elliot's conjecture as to the date of his accession is thereby confirmed. The remaining plates relate to the family of the Kádambas. From No. 8, we have the following list of kings:—

Jayanta or Trilochanakádamba.

An interval during which eighteen *as'vamedhas* were performed by his descendants.

1. Shashthadeva.
2. Jayakes'i I (his son)
3. Vijayáditya I. (his son.)
4. Jayakes'i II. (his son) md. to Mailamahádevi
5. Permádi or S'ivachitta (his son.)
6. Vijayáditya II or Vikramárka (his brother) md. to [illegible]
7. Jayakes'i III. (his son.)

The inscription records a grant made by Jayakes'i III in the year of the Kaliyuga 4288 (A.D. 1187-8). The first in the list, Jayanta or Trilochanakadamba, 'born from the drops of sweat which flowed from S'iva's forehead to the root of the Kadamba tree, when he conquered the demon Tripura,' seems to be a half mythical personage. He is probably intended for the same as Trinetrakadamba, who is said to have reigned about K.Y. 3210 (A.D. 109, or according to Buchanan, 161-2). The princess Mailalá, whom Jayakes'i II. married, is described as the younger sister of [illegible], and is given in marriage to king Permádi, and as Jayakes'i I. is spoken of as having formed friendship with the Chálukya and Chola kings, this Permádi is evidently identical with Vikramáditya II. or Permádi Ráya of the Chálukya dynasty, whose date Mr. Elliot gives as S'aka 998-1049 (A.D. 1076-1127) which corresponds very well with the position occupied by Jayakes'i II in this list, and who was succeeded by his son Somes'wara Deva III. There is also an inscription at Halsi, dated K.Y. 4270, which agrees with No. 8 in giving Jayanta as the first king. It then proceeds to Jayakes'i, who made Gopakapattana his capital. To him was born Vijayáditya, whose son was Jayadeva or Jayakes'i. Jayadeva married Mailalamahádevi, (?Mailaladevi) and begat S'ivachitta and Vishnuchitta. Mailalamahádevi is said to be the daughter of Vikramárka "the ruby of the Chálukyas."

From plates 1 to 7 is obtained this genealogy of the Kádamba Kings:—

1. Kákusthavarmá (plates 1, 2, 3, 4.)
2. S'ántivarma (his son; 2, 3, 4).
3. Mriges'a (his son; 2, 3, 4).
4. Ravivarmá (his son; 2, 4, 5, 6); his brothers Bhánuvarmá (4); and S'ivaratha (7).
5. Harivarmá (son of Ravivarmá; 6).

They belong to the Mánavyagotra and are the descendants of Háriti; and Palás'iká appears to have been, if not their capital, at least a place of importance. Palás'iká in No. 8 has been corrupted to Palas'ika, and in the Halsi inscription has dwindled to Palasi. Unfortunately we have no direct means of fixing the dates of these kings. Plate 1 tells us that Kákusthavarmá, Yuvaraja of the Kadambas made a grant in the 80th year, possibly referring to some local era. If these Kadambas should prove to be of a different line from the descendants of Elliot's Mayûravarmá, they may be referred to the period before the commencement of the 10th century when the Chálukya dynasty emerged from a temporary obscuration. If they are to be placed before Mayûravarmá, we have the inscription of Yevur, translated by Mr. Elliot, which speaks of Kádamba kings anterior to the first Chálukya king Jayasimha, as "the (?) Kádambas lofty, powerful heroes to conquer, but not to be overcome," &c. Jayasimha, according to inscriptions, flourished about Saka 400, though Mr. Elliot prefers the date Saka 572. All tradition, too, points to Kadambas amongst the very earliest dynasties.

(2.) "The shrine of the river Krishná at the village of Mahábaleśvara;" by Rao Saheb Visvanáth Náráyan Mandlik. "A stone temple built about 125 years ago over the source of the river Krishná is annually resorted to from all parts of the neighbouring country, and every twelfth year, when the planet Jupiter enters the sign of *Virgo*, pilgrims from all parts assemble to bathe in the sacred waters of the Ganges, which river is believed to make her appearance at this shrine at the beginning of that year and to stay there for a twelvemonth on a visit to her younger sister Krishná." The Temple stands at the foot of the hill facing the east. It measures 50½ feet in length by 16½ in depth, having an open courtyard in front 63 ft. 3 in. long and 22 ft. 6 in. wide, in which are two cisterns with steps down to them. Along three sides of the courtyard is an open chavadi 9½ feet deep supported in front on pillars 2 ft. square and about 7 ft. 3 in. from centre to centre. The whole is enclosed by a wall 4 ft. thick, with an entrance door to the east, 4 ft. 9 in. wide, leading into the court. Opposite the entrance and projecting into the outer cistern is a pavilion for Nandi. The temple is formed of two bays separated by four pillars and two corresponding pilasters with a portico in front. Each bay is thus divided into five squares, separately roofed in by domes inside, but outside finished off in slope running longitudinally. The cisterns are similarly roofed. At the back of the temple and behind an inner wall 4ft. thick is the main source of the river. Through this wall, five holes are made to represent the rivers Krishná, Venná, Koyaná, Gáyatri, and Sávitri. The priests say that two others—the Bhágirathi and Sarasvati—also flow from the sides of the other Gangâs or rivers—the former once in 12 years, and the latter once in 60 years; the holes through which they issue being at the N. and S. ends of the temple respectively. The water from these five drains flows into a channel in front, and is thence discharged into the inner cistern in the courtyard through a spout carved to represent a cow's head. Here the visitors bathe and perform all the connected ceremonies. This temple was built by a Sattara Brahman family named Anagala. But the first hereditary officer connected with its management is a Koli or rather a Koli family, from their connection with it, known as Gangâputra, and, as soon as a visitor has bathed all offerings he makes belong to these Kolis. What is offered before bathing only is retained by the Brahmans, who, of course, press visitors to make offerings before bathing. At the temple of Mahábaleśwara also, the Kolis hold a hereditary position, and the Guravas, who worship the Linga there, appear more closely allied to the hill tribes than to the inhabitants of the plains; they have no connection however with the shrine of Krishná, where the Kolis alone are the principal officers in charge. "The serpent," says the writer, "is connected with both these temples; and from the Linga temples he seems to be quite inseparable. In the latter, he is represented as being coiled round the Linga, while in the temple of the Krishná, a living one is supposed to be guarding its source." The priests at both these shrines are primarily the wild or at least Non-Vedic tribes. These wear the Linga, and these do not taste food prepared by a Brahman; and Brahmans are prohibited from becoming officiating priests at Saiva temples, and cannot partake of offerings made there. "There is no doubt that the people do consider that there is something awkward, if not obscene, in Linga worship. Because, so far as I am aware, only young girls who have not arrived at maturity, and old ladies who have passed the period of child-bearing, are permitted to enter a Saiva temple. Others have to perform their worship by deputy."

(3.) "Some further Inscriptions relating to the Kadamba Kings of Goa," by J. F. Fleet, C.S. A large stone tablet in the temple of Narasimha at Halsi records two grants made by Sivachitta and Vishnuchitta in the 23rd and 25th years of their joint reign in K. Y. 4270, and 4272 respectively. The other inscriptions enable us to add a few names to the list of the Kadamba family. The father of Shasthadeva was Guhalladeva; and the wife of Sivachitta was Kamaladevi, daughter of Kámakhúpa of the Somavamsa and Chattaladevi of the Pandya race, according to Nos. 1 and 3, though Nos. 4 and 7 say that Kámakhúpa was of the Súryavamśa and Chattaladevi of the Somakula. "The expression Banavásipuravarádhíśwara would appear to be only a hereditary title and not meant to denote the actual residence* of the Kadamba Kings, as their real capital seems to have been, not Halsi, as I had supposed, but Goa, which is

* Banavási is in N. Lat. 14°. 35', E. Long. 75°; Ptolemy mentions it as Banaousei.—Ed.

mentioned under its modern name in the Gulhalli stone. The Sanskrit inscriptions gives Gopakapattana or Gopakapuri as its equivalent." A Sanskrit copperplate from Mhansi in the Goa territories* is dated Saka 1358, and mentions the "Marathas who had for 12 years usurped the territory of the Kadambas." They do not seem to have been independent sovereigns but rather feudatories of the Chalukyas. With respect to the date of Jayakesi III, the large copperplate of Halsi gives the Siddharthi Samvatsara, the 53rd year of the cycle of Vrihaspati, as corresponding to K.Y. 4288, while the Kittur inscription gives Durmati Sam. as the 55th year, as corresponding to 4290; this calculation moreover differs by 13 years† from the method followed in the other inscriptions and still current in the district. Shivachitta in K.Y. 4275 had been ruling 30 years, and Jayakesi would appear to have succeeded in that year, as K.Y. 4288 is the 13th of his reign. A Canarese inscription from Narendra near Dharwad records a grant made by order of the Mahamandaleswara Jayakesideva II and his wife Mailaladevi, while they were governing the Konkana nine hundred, the Palasige twelve thousand, the Paya (?) five hundred, and Kavadidwipa, in the time of the Chalukya Tribhuvana Malladeva (Vikramaditya II.) The grant was made in Saka 1047.

(4) "Report on Photographic copies of Inscriptions in Dharwad and Mysore," by Dr. Bhau Daji. This is a series of brief notes on the volume of inscriptions photographed by Dr. Pigou and Col. Biggs and printed at the expense of the Committee of Architectural Antiquities of Western India in 1866. From the 60 plates, 57 inscriptions are noticed. No 1, from Iwalli, perhaps of the early part of the 11th century A.D., mentions king Aravudiya of the Sindavansa. No. 2, from Iwalli, is dated Saka 506, K.Y. 3855, and from the Mahabharata war 3730 (A.D. 584.) "The first named king in it is Jayasinha; his son was Ranaraga; his son Pulakesi. He ruled at Vatapipuri and performed the horse-sacrifice. Pulakesi's son was Kirtivarma. He conquered kings of the Nala, Maurya and Kadamba dynasties. After him his younger brother Mangalisa ruled and conquered Revati Dwipa. Pulakesi the son of Kirtivarma was anxious to succeed him, whilst Mangalisa appears to have wished to place his own son on the throne. But Mangalisa appears to have died suddenly and Pulakesi II succeeded. He conquered the Latas, Malavas, Gurjaras, the Pallavas, and defeated king Harsha. He was called Satyasraya (supporter of truth) in addition to the family title of Prithvi Vallabha. The inscription also contains the names of the poets Kalidasa and Bharavi, whose fame is compared to that of Ravikirti the author of the verses of the inscription. No. 6 and 7 are the same, viz. a Sanskrit verse written about the 7th century A.D.—"Peace. No man so skilful in the construction of houses and temples as Matsabha lived, or ever will live, in Jambudvipa." No. 9 contains the name of Sri Prithvi Vallabha, Maharajadhiraja Parameswara, Parama Bhattaraka, Satyasraya Kulatilaka, Chalukya, Bharana, Srimat Tribhuvana (Malla.) This is the Chalukya king who flourished in Saka 1104, A.D. 1182.‡ Subordinate was Mahamandaleswara Mayuravarma Mahamandalesvara, lord of Vanavasi, which was the capital of the Kadambas. No. 24, on a stone at Gadak, is dated S. 1114 (A.D. 1192) and is a grant by Vira Ballaladeva of the Hoysala line. No. 26, Kiwali inscribed stone, is of Tribhuvana Malladeva dated in the 14th year of their era§ (S. 1012). No. 27, Saudatti inscribed stone is dated S. 1151; No. 29 Narapura inscribed stone, is S. 1104; No. 31, from Hampi or Bijanagar, is S. 1121; No. 33, is S. 1130; No. 34, from Telsali, is S. 1100; No. 35, Chandalapur, is of Tribhuvanamalladeva again; and Nos. 36, and 37, also from Chandalapur, in S. 1113, 1186 and 1148. No. 38–43, inscriptions from Harihara dated 1422, and 1456, 1109, 1078, &c. Scarcely any of these are translated in their entirety, and from many only the proper names are picked out.

Journal Asiatique, No. 67, Oct.-Dec. 1871.

This part contains (1) *Extracts from the Paritta*, the text and commentaries in Pali by M. Grimblot, with introduction, translation, notes and notices by *M. Leon Feer.* The *Paritta*, (vulgo *Pirit*) from which the Suttas are extracted, is itself a collection of texts selected from different portions of the *Sutta-pitaka.* It forms a special book well known to the Sinhalese, but appears to be known also to the other southern Buddhists. Seven suttas are given: (1, 2) Chandra and Surya-sutta; (3) Maha Mangala Sutta, or of the highest blessing—already translated by Gogerly and Childers; (4) Parabhava sutta, or of diminution; (5, 6) Metta Sutta and Metta-Anisansa, or of love, and the advantages of love; and (7) Karaniya-Metta Suttam translated by Childers in the Khuddaka-Patha.

(2.) *The Royal Chronicle of Kamboja* by M. Francis Garnier. This is a brief chronology of the kings of Kamboja from Prea-reachea-angca-prea bat-sam-dach-prea-bat who ascended the throne of Anghor in 1346 A.D., till 1787.

(4.) *Memoir on the Ancient History of Japan*, according to the Wen-Hien-Tong-Kao of Ma-tuanlin, by the Marquis D'Hervey de Saint Denys.

(5.) A notice by B. de Meynard of the *Bibliotheca Geographorum Arabicorum, Pars I.—Viae Regnorum,* auctore *Abu Ishak al-Farisi, al Istakhri,* of M. J. de Goeje, now publishing at Leyden.

(6.) Assyrian Tablets, translated by M. Oppert.

(7.) Notice of A. Paspati's *Etudes sur les Tchinghianes ou Bohémiens de l'Empire Ottoman.*

* Given in Courtney and Auld's *Memoir on Sawantwadi*, p. 200.

† See Thomas's Prinsep, vol. II. *Useful Tables*, p. 169.

‡ Prinsep, *Useful Tables*, p. 277.

§ Vide, ante p. 68.

NOTES ON THE BHARIAS.

BY MR. C. SCANLAN, ASSISTANT SURVEYOR.

I had the pleasure of contributing a few fugitive notes on the Gonds and Kurkus of these hills, but this season I have come across a new branch of this family called the Bharias, concerning whom you will perhaps find the following interesting. I have not been able to determine anything of their origin, but I do not hesitate to place them in the great Gond family, of which they form a subdivision. In their language and in some of their customs they differ totally from the Gonds, with whom they neither eat nor drink nor intermarry. I find, however, they acknowledge the law of *Lamjhana*, which I described last year as imposing a servitude of a certain number of years on a man, who, wishing to marry into a family, could not afford to make the usual marriage settlement, and give certain presents to his bride's relatives. In their caste prejudices, they assimilate with the Gond in a hybrid sort of manner to the Hindu; and so they will not eat the cow nor wild buffalo, but do not hold back from making food of the pig, the deer, nilgai, and all such wild animals. In their marriage ceremonies they follow suit with the other hill people, and impose certain dues on the man marrying; for instance, a dowry from the husband consists of 200 seers *kodo*, 20 seers *dal*, Rs. 7, a *pagri* 12 hands long, 2 *saris* and 2 *cholis*, and further, when the wife goes to take possession of her future home, her relatives have to be entertained with a feast of *gur* and a large quantity of liquor to the amount of Rs. 2,—the latter invariably, if to be found. When a marriage is about to be celebrated they proceed to prepare an especial shade in front of the house where the ceremony will take place. A pole of *Salai*-wood (frankincense) is buried, and around it, so as to form a convenient square, are raised eight other props, on which rests the roof, crowned with garlands of leaves and flowers. The middle pole of Salai is called bhaura. Notice is given to all friends when the marriage is to be consummated, and then it is that the bride to be, comes to her intended's village, and takes up her residence opposite to the house he occupies. It will be remembered I explained last year that the villages in these hills are always built in two rows. Both of these are well besmeared with *haldi*, a custom which I found extensively practised in the Dekhan among all classes of the native population. The woman's friends make it a rule to arrive in the morning and the *haldi* is kept on till evening, but any time during the day the couple to be united are summoned and made to walk round the Bhaura seven times with their clothes knotted together. After this, the girl's father gives her a dowry, when the ceremony is supposed to be over. At night, all present are entertained to a dinner, which is called *Bhaura-ki-roti*; *Bayat-ki-roti*, being the first held after arrangements have been entered into to accept the suitor's proposal; the third being called *Chikla Mandi-ki-roti*, given on the morning immediately after the marriage when the girl's relations depart, and it is only after this third feast that the husband gets possession of his wife. It is strange that when the newly married are blessed with an addition to their family, they never even invite the young mother's relatives to come and see the child, but allow them to visit if the wish takes them naturally.

They burn their dead, and also those killed by accident or wild animals, but those killed by a tiger, they will not even so much as touch. They put their relatives out of caste, but re-admit them on their giving a panchayat dinner. While worshipping the other gods of the Gonds, they hold the *Saj* tree as the impersonation of their chief deity. If you want to test the truth of a Bharia's word, break a leaf of the Saj, put it on his head, and ask him to repeat his assertion; if it be true he will at once speak it again, if not, nothing will induce him to do so, at least thus spoke my deponent. Narayan Deva is represented by a copper ring about an inch in diameter; Sabrai Deva by a twisted ring of iron about 2 or 3 inches in diameter; Khauria Khatarpal by a very diminutive stool, about an inch square with four legs and about 1½ inches high. Dulha Deva Durgâ is made of iron, and supposed to be figurative of a peacock; it is hollow, and about 1½ inch long. Khutia Bhimsen exists only in name.

When Gonds, Kurkus or Bharias start together in their *hill* camps, they take with them some ashes and fodder corn meals, and as they go along, they keep making circles with the ashes, and place in their centres the seeds of the corn. This practice is supposed to keep away all the bad will of the Devas. Their women usually dress like the Gonds, but if they can afford it, like the generality of Hindu women, and do not wear the ponderous brass ornaments in vogue amongst the former.

These hill people will not let the *Lamjhana* sleep in the same house where his intended lives, nor do they let them converse more than is good for them; if before they are married, they go astray, they are turned out of caste, and the marriage ceremony is not gone through at all; but on their giving a feast after the expiration of three days to their Panchayat, they are re-installed among their brethren as a wedded couple.

The Bharia Gots, or clans, number eighteen. Thakuria, Chalthia, Angária, Bhardia, Daradia, Mahalia, Bagulia, Rathia, Gangia, Paria, Mehania, Pāchalia, Kurmia, Bijilia, Bagdaria Khamaria, Gaulia, Bagdia, Amaria.

Relating to the Khapa or Belkagarh Jagir, the following was narrated to me:—The Gond dynasty was established at Devagad under Jatwa Râja, who was formerly a servant of the two Gauli brother princes, Ransur and Ghansur. By treason he deposed them and took possession of the Gadi, and then, to his assistance, came the three brothers, Aha Bankha, Phonj Bhankha and Mahâ Bankha, with a force of 2,000 men. During the conflict carried on between the opposing forces, Aha and Mahâ died, and the surviving brother, Phonj Bankha, received as a reward for his services the Balkagarh or Khapa Jâgir. After affairs had been settled, and Jatva made quite secure on his usurped throne, he, together with his ally Phonj Bankha, proceeded to the Nizam at Haidarâbad, and tendered their conjoint aid to him. They were directed to join the attack on Golkonda or Bhâgnagar, whose Rani revelled in the euphonious name of Nakti Rani Ching Muji Sang Moji. They took her possessions, and for this good turn, Jatva received in marriage the Nizam's daughter. He of course turned Muhammadan, and acquired the new title of Bakht Buland, when he returned to Devagad, and assumed the regal purple. His descendant, Suliman Shah Badshah, known as the Gond Râja, now resides at Nâgpur, while Gopal Sing, the descendant of Phonj Bankha, is the present Râja of Khapa, and is put down as in the 14th generation.—*Report of the Topographical Surveys for 1869-70.*

NOTES, QUERIES, &c.

NATIVE TRIBES OF SIKHIM.

THE following account of the principal native tribes inhabiting the hilly country of the Darjiling territory, we get from the local *News*. The mountainous country from 1,500 to 4,000 feet above the level of the sea, is inhabited by a warlike, beardless, Mongolian race, named Limbus, who are by turns Hindus, Buddhists or *Polytheists*, according to circumstances or convenience.

From 4,000 to 8,000 feet, the upper limit of cultivation, the hills are inhabited by *Lepchas*, Bhotias, and Murmis. The Lepchas, who are the aborigines of the Darjiling mountains, are a fair and beardless race, Mongolians, Buddhists, omnivorous, and an amiable and cheerful race of people. They have a written language in their own character. The Bhotias are principally from Bhutan, east of the Tista river; they are a phlegmatic, heavy, quarrelsome race when compared with the Lepchas, many of them have beards and moustaches; they are Mongolians, Buddhists, are omnivorous, have a written language in the Thibetan character; they are an agricultural and pastoral people, depasturing with herds of Yaks on the grassy mountains immediately under the perpetual snow in summer, and the forests in the warm valleys during the winter. They raise crops of rice, buck-wheat, barley and vegetables.

The Murmis are a pastoral and agricultural people, depasturing with flocks of sheep and goats on the grassy mountains near the perpetual snow; they live on the summits and sides of mountains from 4,000 to 6,000 feet, in stone cottages thatched with grass. They are Buddhists, Mongols, and they speak a dialect of Thibetan.

The summit of the great Singalela spur separating Darjiling on the west from Nepal, is occupied during the summer months by a Hindu pastoral race from Nepâl named Gurungs, who from 9,000 up to 14,500 feet depasture their extensive flocks of sheep (which are guarded by large savage black dogs) upon the luxuriously grass-covered summit of this high range. This tribe has not yet settled in the Darjiling district.—*Delhi Gazette, Dec.* 30.

MAULMEIN CAVES.

To one curious in geology or antiquities, there are some interesting natural caves in some lofty limestone rocks, across a river, at the distance of about 10 miles eastward of Maulmein. The rocks extend for two or three miles, and rise perpendicularly to the height of about 500 or 600 feet or even more from the alluvial plain. A few lofty posts were placed in front on the plain, such as are seen sometimes in front of Hindu and Buddhist temples, possibly for hoisting flags. The caves are at a distance of 20 or 30 yards from the foot of the rocks, and extend about that distance into the mountain. The height is very irregular, and in some places may be 30 or 40 feet, with here and there large stalactites hanging down. I struck one of these a smart blow with my stick, and the ringing noise that it gave out made the guide and myself start. This cave is nearly filled with Buddhist images, some are eight or ten yards long, in a reclining posture, but most are sitting. The larger are all of brick and chunam, and the smaller, some of which are not more than two feet high, are of wood, and formerly all were whitewashed. Nearly all are now defaced and in ruins. The breasts of most of the larger had been opened in the hope of finding money or other valuables. A second cave at about a quarter of a mile distant on the N. E. side of the rock is empty of images, and appears never to have had them. This cave extends some 20 yards into the rock, and is 30 or 40 feet high in its highest part. Torches or candles were necessarily used in viewing both these caves, which, whatever they may once have been, are now only the abode of bats. The place is a most lonely one, and is said not to be free from tigers. The only animals seen on my visit were the monkeys, playing and chattering on the trees and rocks near the entrances of both caves, and a large flock of huge storks, nearly as tall as men, which were stalking in the midst of the nearly ripe paddy.—*Abridged from Times of India, Jan. 6.*

RISE OF THE KUKA SECT.

RAM SINGH was originally a carpenter, residing in a small village named Bhaini, situated about seven miles south-east of Ludhiana. He served, however, in the Sikh army as a soldier, I believe, in 1845, but after the breaking up of the Sikh Raj, he retired to his native village, and resumed his occupation as a carpenter. We next hear of him as having undertaken a contract for making the road or a portion of it from Rawal Pindi to Mari. On completing this, he retired again to his village, and is reported to have seen a vision. We next hear of him as the *Guru* called to purify the Sikh faith. In the beginning his ideas were modest, and his following as slender as his ideas were modest. As the Sikhs have ten gurus, so have they ten points of faith—five affirmative and five negative. The first are called five *Ks*, and are—

(A) *Kara, Kachh, Kirpan, Kangha, Kes.*

Iron ornaments, short drawers, iron quoits or weapons, the comb, and hair.

That is to say, they are not to be effeminate nor to shave, and to be always ready for fighting.

The negative points or moral precepts of the faith are contained in the following formula :—

(B) *Nari-mar, Kuri-mar, Sir Gum, Sunnat Kata, Dhir Malia.*

That is to say, they are not to smoke, not to kill their daughters, not to consort with or trust the crown-shorn, nor the circumcised, nor the followers of the Guru of Kartarpur.*

It is of some importance to bear these precepts in mind as they show (although most of them date only from Guru Govind Singh) that the Sikh faith is hostile to both Hindu and Moslem,—naturally much more so to the latter than the former, in consequence of cow-killing.

Ram Singh, however, did not content himself by adhering to the tenets of the faith as left by the last *Guru*. His endeavour appears to have been to bring it back rather to the form in which it took life under Guru Nanak with some modification of his own.

Thus the Kukas reject altogether the Hindu *Shastras*, have separate forms of marriage and burial services, do not drink, do not eat meat, and never eat before bathing; wear the turban above and not over the ears; bathe twice a day; are required strictly to speak the truth; never to eat from the hand of any but a *Kuka*; and, above all, to preserve sacred and inviolate the Cow. The ceremony of initiation consists of the investiture with the sacred string of knotted wool, bathing and the giving of a pass-word never divulged except to a brother *Kuka*. This pass-word or phrase is said to be "*Satnam Kartapurkh*," which are the first words of the *Adi granth*; but hitherto the sect have observed the secrecy of the free-masons, and no certainty prevails on the point. Women are admissable to the sect and to their assemblies; and dancing, is not only allowable, but justified on the ground of the following text from the *Granth*:—

Nachna Kudna Man ka chao
Naam [illegible]

They are consequently noisy in their assemblies, reviving to some extent, it would seem, the ecstacies of of the howling dervishes of Egypt and the dancing dervishes of Constantinople, for so excited do they become that some have been known to fall down in a state of *hal* or *wajd*. At first, votaries of the new religion came in slowly, and Ram Singh had not any difficulty in initiating and baptising all the weavers and carpenters who were prepared to accept him as their *Guru*, but by degrees converts grew more numerous, and he was obliged to appoint lieutenants to aid him in the work. He himself, too, assumed a more important rôle. He rode about on horseback, surrounded by a noisy and numerous following, who continually shouted *Ahal! Ahal!* clear the way! Ram Singh comes. *Ahal! Ahal!* &c., &c. Finally Ram Singh conceived the idea of becoming the tenth *Guru* of the Sikhs, or, if not, the first *Guru* of so powerful a religious and political association. He increased the number of his Subahs to twenty-two, the same number as the king of Delhi had, and commenced a very active system of propagation in the cis and trans-Sutlej States and throughout the Sikh portion of the Panjab. Almost all the carpenters, masons, and weavers joined the new religion, and many *Jats*; but the body of the Sikhs fought very shy of Guru Ram Singh and his followers, and the Chiefs set their faces dead against them. The Sikhs like good meat and strong drink when they can get them, better than shouting *ahal*, and dancing and singing and telling the beads on a woollen string; and the chiefs are not at all in favour of transferring any of the allegiance their subjects owe to them to the *Guru* Ram Singh, the *Guru* of Kartarpur, or any other *Guru* now living or yet to be born. It is quite possible that Ram Singh was at first merely a religious enthusiast; but if so, there can be no doubt that his success turned his head, and that for some years past he entertained visions of becoming the leader of a national movement the ultimate aim of which was power. The Government of the Panjab took little notice of the *Guru's* proceedings for some years, or, indeed, until the movement had made such progress that it would have been difficult to check it. In 1867, however, or when Sir Donald McLeod last visited Ludhiana, he sent for Ram Singh, and demanded from him an explanation of his proceedings. He disclaimed all idea of aspiring to political power, declaring his sole object to be the revival of the Sikh religion in a form more pure than it had attained under any previous *guru*, or at any time in the history of the Sikhs. The tenets of the new faith were no doubt calculated to effect a great moral regeneration, and the strictness with which

---

* This guru is a dissipated man who has been bankrupt twice, and is again over head and ears in debt. He has an original Granth of Govind Singh, and has still a following.

the *Kukas* observed the injunction to speak the truth soon attracted the attention of the courts of law. Sir Donald was satisfied. Ram Singh was dismissed, and continued directly and through his *Subahs* to make converts so fast that their number was once estimated at 100,000 more or less. Still, though no overt act was committed, there was a certain mystery or secrecy about the proceedings of the new sect that discouraged the idea of the movement being purely a religious one, and gave it the semblance rather of a society such as that of the *Carbonari* of western celebrity. Such, too, seems to have been the view of the local authorities for instructions were issued to watch them. Orders were given also not to enlist any more of them in the army; these orders were, however, subsequently withdrawn, but reinforced about eight or nine months ago. The Rájá of Kashmir also finding the Kukas in his service troublesome turned about 400 of them out of his army.—*Times of India*.

BEGGARS.

THE *Lawrence Gazette* gives the following description of the different classes of beggars to be found in the Panjab:—

Dori-walas, so called from their practice of spreading a cord, or rope, before shops, just like a measuring chain. The shops coming within the length of of this rope, they collect money from first, and then proceed to other shops, repeating the same process. In case of any one of the shopkeepers refusing to comply with their demands, they form the rope into a noose and threaten to hang themselves, to make him share the consequences, and compel him to pay something.

Tasmé-walas, so named from their binding a strap of leather round their necks as if in the act of strangling themselves, and then lying on their back on the ground till they are paid, all the while fluttering their hands and feet like one labouring under the agonies of death.

Danda-walas, who, in case of a shopkeeper objecting to meet their demands, blacken their face, and with small bats (*dandas*) in their hands, which they strike together, curse and abuse him in the most scurrilous language, till a crowd of persons gather round the shop to view the sight, thereby interrupting the shop-dealings, which at last compels the owner to satisfy their request.

Tri-maras, or mendicants, who obstinately take their stand before shops, and will not leave them until their demands have been satisfied, even though they should have to stay from morn till eve.

Gurz-maras and *chhuri-maras*, that is, fakirs who carry a knife or a club armed with spikes, with which they wound themselves in order to extort alms from the people. In case of any one happening to stand in their way, they sometimes inflict blows on him in a fit of rage.—*Englishman*, April 12.

MR. WHITLEY STOKES, Secretary to the Government of India in the Legislative Department, has presented to the Bodleian a copy (recently made at Benares) of the Kausika Sûtra of the Sâma-veda. It has been ascertained that no other copy of this sûtra exists in Europe. Mr. Stokes has also presented to the University Library, Cambridge, a Persian MS. containing the Qaṣîdahs of Nazîri of Naishapûr, the Diwan of the same poet, and the largest collection yet found (almost 800) of the celebrated Quatrains (rubâ'iyât) of Omar Khayyâm. This MS. has unfortunately lost a leaf at the end, but seems to be about 200 years old. It formerly belonged to the late Nawâb of the Carnatic, whose seal is on the recto of the third leaf from the beginning.—*Trübner's Literary Record*, Mar. 7.

SANSKRIT MSS.—Pandit Ramanatti, Librarian to the Sanskrit College at Benares, has collected during the last eighteen months the necessary details about more than a thousand Sanskrit manuscripts. In a lately published report on education in the North-West Provinces of India, it is stated that the learned Pandit has visited the districts of Azimgarh, Gorakhpur and Mirzapur, and has found good libraries at Kakhina (district Gorakhpur), and at Dalsa (district Mirzapur). The Pandits entrusted with the care of the libraries put all possible difficulties in his way, believing that the country would, sooner or later, be deprived of its manuscripts. In order to get admission to a library belonging to a Swâmi[illegible], Pandit Ramanatti was obliged to serve the proprietor during several months as a pupil, with ashes on his forehead. In another case an old rich Brahman tried to induce him to buy a number of old account books as a library. The villages Kakhina and Dalsa, in which the most valuable treasures seem to be stored, are in the possession of those Pandits who have inherited the libraries.—*Ibid.*

YATRAMULLE UNNANSE.

The death of the Buddhist Priest Yâtrâmullê Dhammârâma, of Bentota in Ceylon, will be severely felt by Pali scholars. He was not only one of the most learned of the Buddhist priests, but he held such advanced philological views that his assistance was perhaps more valuable to the English Pali student than that of any other monk in Ceylon. A fellow pupil of his was the founder of the now rapidly spreading Ramanna Samâgama, a sect which strives to restore the old purity of life among the Buddhist monks. The following is abridged from a notice of Yâtrâmullê by Mr. Childers in *Trübner's Record*:—

Though far junior to many of the most eminent Pali scholars of his native country, his erudition was perfectly astounding, and his opinion on points of scholarship was treated with universal respect. He lent to the great Synod of Palmadulla,* held for the revision of the Tripitaka, all the aid which his immense range of reading and his critical acumen rendered invaluable to it; and he was a leading promoter of the Tripitaka Society, organized for the purpose of printing the entire Buddhist Scriptures—a scheme which, it is to be feared, will hardly survive his premature death. Yâtrâmullê shrank habitually from publicity, and seldom quitted the retirement of the provincial monastery of his choice, in which he lived a simple and blameless life. Those who have

* Vide ante p. 89, and conf. p. 143.

had the good fortune to know him personally will recollect the singular fascination he exercised upon all with whom he was brought into contact. During the last three or four years he was repeatedly prostrated by the attacks of a torturing malady, to which he had long been a victim, and to one of these attacks he has succumbed after protracted suffering. "The Sthavira Yâtrâmullê Dhammarama, of the Vanavâsa monastery, on the 29th day of this month of January, in the last watch of the night, passed away to another world." Yâtrâmullê, at the time of his death, cannot have been more than fifty years of age.

MR. W. SKEEN.

WE regret to hear of the sudden death of Mr. W. Skeen, the author of "Adam's Peak," and who had in preparation an elaborate work on the history of the Tooth Relic of Ceylon, which could scarcely have failed to throw much light on the history of Buddhism, both in India and Ceylon. His loss to the Ceylon Asiatic Society will be irreparable.

White and Black Yajur Vedas.

IT is worth noticing that the followers of the Black Yajurveda are almost confined to Southern India while the predominant or only Veda among the Gauḍas of the North is the White Yajur. The Gujarat people have got a trace of one S'âkhâ only of the former, the Maitrayaṇîya. Among the Marâṭhâs, the Chitpâvana Brâhmans are nearly equally divided between the Rigveda and the Black Yajurveda, while the Deśasthas are Vâjasaneyins (followers of the White) and Rigvedis. Whether this is to be accounted for by a revolution or some such event enabling the followers of the White Veda to drive their rivals to the South, or by the supposition of that part of India being the country of the origin of the Black Yajur is not determined. But there is a prophecy in the Agni Purâṇa which represents the White Yajurveda as a conquering or triumphant Veda, saying that the only Veda that will prevail in the latter part of the Kaliyuga will be the Vâjasaneyaka*; all others being lost, and the purohita or priest of Kalki, the King that will overthrow the Mlechchhas, who will have overspread the earth, will be Yâjnavalkya.† This latter part of the prophecy occurs in other Purâṇas also. Yâjnavalkya is the founder or first teacher of the White Yajurveda.

Why should not a census be taken of the several Vedas and S'âkhâs, and of the most important sects of Theosophy or religious philosophy?

Publication of Chând.

MR. GROWSE, during the latter part of the rainy season of 1871, had begun an edition of Chand founded on the Agra MS., when his attention was directed to the Baidla MS. as the only one "which the noble families of Râjputâna considered to be of any authority." Finding that he would be unable to do anything towards preparing it for the press before March or April 1873, he wrote a letter to the Secretary of the Bengal Asiatic Society on 3rd February 1872, from which we extract the following:—

"I am convinced that in an *editio princeps* of a work of this peculiar nature, which is mainly interesting to the philologist, it is imperative on an editor, having once secured a good MS., to adhere to its *ipsissima verba*, without the slightest attempt at alteration or correction. If I continue editor, I shall simply make a faithful transcript of the Baidla MS., adding at the foot of the page the various readings which I find in the Agra copy. Now such a task, though laborious, is purely mechanical, requires no special knowledge and can be equally well performed by any one who can read the character. I would therefore suggest to the Philological Committee the desirability of having the two MSS. sent down to Calcutta and there made over to a native writer without engaging any regular editor, but simply having some trustworthy corrector for the press to add the *variæ lectiones* and compare the proofs with the MS. . . . . . I am convinced that the adoption of the plan which I have suggested above, will obviate all cause for delay and secure a result in all respects as satisfactory as if the work had remained under my supervision."

The Philological Committee has resolved to recommend to the Council of the Society "that for the present the edition of Chand be deferred; but they have recommended also that on receipt of the Baidla and Agra MSS. a sum of about Rs. 200 be devoted to the collation of both MSS., the *variæ lectiones* of the Agra MS. are to be entered on the margin of the Society's Baidla MS." But the Committee do not think that it would be of much use to print any portion of Chand in the manner which Mr. Growse suggests, without separating the words, which is of course the greatest difficulty.

Note on 'Arachosia' p. 22.

PROFESSOR Ramkrishna Gopal Bhandarkar doubts if Arachosia ought to be rendered in Zend Harahvaiti or in Sanskrit Sarasvatî. He has the more reason for this doubt because Arachotis does not belong to the Indo-European system at all, but conforms to the great group of ancient river names. Where these have any meaning in Sanskrit, as Śatadru, for instance‡, it is accidental. The river names belong to an older group, and that of Arachotis to a well defined class of roots in

* Dasyavas (?) [illegible] vedo Vâjasaneyakaḥ.

† Kalkeḥ Vishṇuyasaḥ-putra Yâjnavalkya-purohitaḥ.

‡ Śatadru is called in the Vedas S'utudri, which in Sanskrit has no satisfactory Etymology.

DKR or KRD, the root letters being at that epoch interchangeable.

London, 23rd Feb. 1872. HYDE CLARKE.

Query 6—about Tobacco.

COULD any of the readers of the *Indian Antiquary* assist me in obtaining certain Sanskrit ślokas regarding the use of tobacco. I saw the ślokas several years ago, but unfortunately took no note of them. Their object was to prove not only that the tobacco plant is indigenous to India, but that the knowledge of the properties of the plant and its use have been known for centuries.

In my lexicographical studies I came, some time ago, across the following passage in the well-known dictionary of modern Persian, entitled *Bahár i 'Ajam*, by Munshí Tek Chand, who lived about the middle of last century, and though a Hindú, is one of the best Persian scholars that India has produced. He says—

"*Tambákú.* It is known from the *Maásir i Rahímí* that the tobacco came from Europe to the Dakhin, and from the Dakhin to Upper India, during the reign of Akbar Sháh (1556-1605), since which time it has been in general use. You say in Persian *tambákú kashídan*, 'to smoke,'—to which the *Ghiyás ullughát* adds, "it is quite wrong to say *tambákú nakhídan*; for this is a literal and unidiomatic translation of *tambákú píná*."

The 'Maásir i Rahímí' is very rare. It contains the life of Mirzá 'Abdurrahím, Akbar's third Khán Khanán, and was written about 1616. I looked over the copy in the Bengal Asiatic Society's Library—a volume of over 1,200 pages—but have not yet found the passage alluded to.

I do not think that Abulfazl says anything regarding tobacco in the *Akbarnámah*, and we may infer from his silence that the plant must have been introduced into Upper India, after his death, in the very end of Akbar's reign.

Tek Chand's remark seems to imply that it was the Portuguese who introduced tobacco from Europe into Southern India; and it is in accordance with this supposition that the Persian Dictionary entitled Burhán i Qáti', which was written in the *Dakhin* about 1060, is the first Persian Dictionary that mentions the word tambákú, (under *dúdkhwár*, 'smoke-eater').

The *Nafáis ullughát*, an excellent Hindústání Dictionary explained in Persian, states under 'tambákú' that the author of the *Dird Shikohi*—a book not known to me—says, "the tobacco came to Upper India in the very end of Akbar's reign." He mentions 914, but this is a mistake for 1014 A. H. The same book adds, "The Arabians pronounce tambákú with a u, or call it *tutun*; and Hakim 'Ali of Gílán mentions that tobacco is heating and dry, but some doctors look upon it as cooling and dry." Medical authorities, therefore, very early held conflicting opinions.

This Hakim 'Ali of Gílán, on the Caspian Sea, died on the 31st March, 1609, and is the same whom Jahángír accused of having poisoned Akbar (A'in translation, p. 466).

If tobacco came to Upper India in 1014, or A. D. 1605, it must have rapidly found favour; for Jahángír, in 1617, forbade smoking by an imperial edict. He says in his 'Memoirs' (Sayyid Ahmad's Edition of the *Tuzuk*, p. 183)—

"On account of the evils arising from *tambákú*, which has now found favour with so many, I gave the order that no one should henceforth smoke, just as my brother Sháh 'Abbás of Persia recognized the bad consequences of tobacco and forbade it in Irán." He then mentions that one of his nobles, Khan 'Alam, could not exist a moment without smoking.

Sháh 'Abbás's anti-tobacco Edict must, therefore, have been given in Persia, before 1617, but both edicts proved as useless as the well-known Papal bull against the weed.

That smoking was not introduced from Persia is almost proved by the history of the word huqqah, which is only in India used in the sense of a pipe. The Persians use qalyán; in fact the whole Persian tobacco phraseology differs from that of India.

Old John Fryer, M. D., Cantabrig., who travelled in India and Persia between 1672 and 1681, has the following curious passage on p. 8 of his Travels (London, 1698), regarding his visit to the Island of St. Iago, one of the Cape Verde Islands,—"They invite us with an *Hubble-bubble* (so called from the noise it makes) a long Reed as brown as a Nut with use, inserted the Body of a Cocoa-shell filled with Water, and a nasty Bole just pressing the water, they ram Tobacco into it, some of which we may suck as long as we please," &c. And further on, he uses the words 'hubble-bubble' and 'tom-toms,' when he describes India. Is it possible that even hubble-bubble should be a Portuguese onomatopoetikon?

The Portuguese introduced several other things into India. During Akbar's reign, they brought from the Eastern Archipelago the Ananás, or pine-apple; and in 1612, the first turkey found its way from Goa to A'grah, and surprised Jahángír so much that he devotes a whole page to the description of this rare avis.

H. BLOCHMANN.

Query 7—about Gunpowder.

CAN any of the readers of the *Antiquary* supply any information as to Gunpowder was first used in India, and in what native literary work it is first alluded to or mentioned? In old Canarese dictionaries it bears the partly Arab and Hindu names: *bala-mard*, strong powder, and *nakhadaaushadha*, drug of mark.

Mercara, 12th April, 1872. F. KITTEL.

THE MUHARRAM.

A SHIAH HOUSE OF MOURNING IN MADRAS.

By CHARLES E. GOVER, M.R.A.S., &c.

WHILE the outward signs of the Muharram, as they are noticed by a European, are those of the extravagant festivity of an Eastern Carnival, it is known that the Shiahs, to whom the occasion properly belongs, observe it as a fast and as a time of the deepest mourning. The Muharram to them is the anniversary of the foul murder of their revered Imâms, who were cut off at Kerbela by a ruthless usurper. The mourning is both public and private; public at the mosque and in the procession, which, where the Sunnis permit, passes through the streets from Imambarah to Imambarah.

Many persons have seen the procession; few have been permitted to be present at the mosque services. The writer has been honoured with the friendship of influential Shiahs, and was permitted to view the Muharram rites in *every* detail, both public and private. The latter were most interesting on account of their novelty and the peep they afforded into the domestic celebrations of a community which is perhaps the least known in all India. The service takes place on the last day but two of the feast, and is kept strictly private, probably because at this one season alone does the dignified Muhammadan divest himself of the solemn demeanour which is so marked a habit of the more respectable followers of Islâm. My presence was only permitted after considerable discussion, and on the distinct understanding that no alteration whatever in the mode of conducting the service should be made in supposed deference to the feelings of a Christian stranger.

The place chosen for the ceremony is an ordinary native house, selected for the purpose because of its unusually large courtyard and deep verandas round it. Enter then with me this house of mourning. The door is guarded by fierce followers of the martyrs, whose business it is to see that none but those who love the Imâms are admitted. We are challenged, but a guide pacifies the guards, and leads us within,—not into the court where the people are assembled, but into a close and dingy room from whence we may see the whole proceedings. This portends a terrible evening for ourselves, and we ask permission to sit with the people in the court. A glance at our shoes and the remark that their people are very prejudiced, tell us the reason of our imprisonment. We protest that boots are removeable, that we are unwilling to hurt the feelings of a houseful of people merely because our rules of politeness are somewhat different from theirs. This wins the day. In our stocking feet we enter the court, pass into the middle of the assembly, and wait for our chairs. Then we learn that chairs are also tabooed in a sacred place. So down we sit, tailor-fashion on the mat and carpet that cover the floor of the court.

The court-yard is large, some thirty feet square. On the East side is a deep double veranda, on the other three sides ordinary single verandas. The walls are draped with black cloth—even the very wall in the centre of the court has its wall draped. On the north and west sides the funeral cloth hangs from the front of the veranda, enclosing behind it a sort of long narrow room, where the women hide from the men, though able to hear all and see much of the proceedings. On a sort of frieze that passes round the walls and also conceals the rugged tile edges of the veranda roof, are written in large characters verses from the more favourite songs in honour of the martyrs; while on the east wall there hangs a frame enclosing the names of the martyrs, their children, their mother, and grand-father. This frieze greatly relieves the dim blackness of the place, and is aided in this respect by two long narrow strips of paper, on which are painted pictures of the greater tombs of the martyrs in the Shiah cities of the East. On the northern side of the double veranda is a pulpit, if so it may be called, where the preacher merely sits, and has no front board. We might better call it a sort of rude throne; this too is covered from top to bottom with black cloth. In the centre of the east wall is the *punja* or standard of the martyrs. It is of peculiar form, having an immense brass head in the shape of a heart upside down, and from the apex project the five spear heads which give the standard its name. In the centre of the brass heart is written a sentence from the Koran. The lower part of the *punja* is also hidden in black cloth. Right opposite, in the centre of the west side, is a stand adorned with coloured glass globes, candlesticks with glass drops, handsome water jugs, and everything else that can make it look tempting and gorgeous. On this stand are vessels of water and sherbet, sufficient to relieve the thirst of a couple of hundred people. With these exceptions the room is quite bare.

One of the most beautiful features of the Muharram is the charitable and free distribution of water and sherbet to all comers. In every street in Triplicane (the Musalman quarter of Madras) during the ten days of the feast, there were water pandals, to which any thirsty passer-by might go and drink to his heart's content. During the evenings, when the streets are crowded with eager sight-seers, these water stands are much frequented, and are of great service. It will be seen that the martyrs were greatly tortured by thirst, as they were for three days cut off from the Euphrates—their only supply of water. In pity for their sufferings, the water is thus freely distributed to all that ask, whatever their creed or nationality.

The court and its verandahs are well filled by men, besides the women we cannot see. They are friends of the family who have provided the house. All sit upon the floor in the mode most comfortable to them. We can see all, for the place is well lighted with handsome chandeliers, while two candles are fixed to the pulpit and others glisten on the water-stand.

Seated in the middle of the floor is a band of about six singers. In the centre is the chief performer, and he is chanting line by line a song describing the conduct and sufferings of Husain at the battle of Kerbela. The verses are rather long, but each is closed by a sort of chorus, in which all the performers join, the audience taking no part in the actual song. They have an important duty, however, the painful and trying one of listening to the harrowing details of the death of their beloved chief. With every passage of the song, come cries, shrieks, and every sign of deepest sorrow from behind the cloth that hides the women. How they beat their breasts and weep, as the more touching passages are recited! The men are less noisy, but are evidently very deeply impressed. Just in front of us is an old and weather-beaten Arab—a most truculent looking fellow. He sits in an attitude of eager listening, resting his chin upon his knees. As the singer proceeds, he is more and more engrossed. At the more touching passages he raises his hand to his forehead, and gently strikes the open palm upon it—just as I have seen a European father do when he was dazed and broken with the loss of his darling son. There was no display, no shouting, or anything else that could invite attention, but it was plain to see how deeply moved he was.

Presently the singer narrated the death of Husain, here the Arab's fortitude gave way altogether, he buried his face in both his hands, bowed down upon his knees, and wept as if his heart would break. It was no mean study of human nature to see this Arab, who would probably think it no wrong to rob and perhaps murder the lonely traveller in the desert, and yet he had a place so soft somewhere within that stormy heart, that he could not listen to the story—most skilfully related be it remembered—of agony and shameful death without being as much melted as any tender mother. There were many here more unmoved than we were and seemed very perfunctory mourners, but the greater part of the assembly were like our Arab.

Two songs were thus sung, and then one of the assembly mounted the pulpit and delivered an extempore address, dwelling mainly on the incidents in the life and death of Ali Akbar, Husain's eldest son. He entered minutely into all the details with which a loving reverence has surrounded the story—few of them historically true probably. But he presented them as if they were true, and as if he fully sympathised with every pain that befel his hero. One incident out of many can alone be given here to show both the kind of myth which has enveloped the history and the pathos which renders it so touching. Ali Akbar went to the fight by his father's side, and fought, as he had promised, like ten men. In the tide of battle he was separated from his father, but fought on. No water had passed his lips for three days, a blazing sun burnt overhead, his raging energy in the fight had increased the torment of his thirst, and at length he is tired of killing. Unable longer to lift his wearied arm, he forces his way back to his father who, too, has for the moment driven back his foes. Ali Akbar falls fainting at Husain's feet, crying for water. In a moment he revives somewhat, and says, "O father, I said that I could fight for you and die with you, and see how God hath helped us this day. No arrow hath hurt me, no sword has prevailed against mine, I cannot let them slay me. Yet would God I could, for it is better to die in the fight, than to die of thirst. Father! I die with you, I said I would." Husain lifts his son, and gently supports him, saying—"Oh my son, would God that I might die for you, there is not one drop of water in all our camp, let us die. Oh God! forgive them that slay us." Ali Akbar's youth rebels against his pain, he cries "Water, water, who will give me water! My tongue is black and parched, and yet it swells as if it would fill my mouth. Water, water, or I shall die! Father, can you not help your son!" The father's love cannot bear this, he stoops to his boy, and whispers, "My son, my Ali Akbar, have I tried thee too far? there is water, drink my son." "Where? I see none, and look, the enemies approach," moans the dying youth. "There is water, come, my son, put up thy mouth to mine, my mouth is full of water, my tongue is bathed within, drink! my darling, my son!" The youth cannot for the moment appreciate the noble love of his father, and does as he is bid; he puts his mouth to his father's, Husain puts forth his tongue, and the youth sucks it. In a moment he starts back in horror,—"Oh my father! Good God! your tongue is worse than mine, you are more thirsty than I. Oh! that I should dare to think of myself when Husain can only think of me." In awful horror at his own impatience, in deepest affection for so true a father, he rushes away into the battle, fighting with renewed strength. It is not for long; an arrow pierces him, his sword arm fails. Fighting to the last like some wounded lion, he is surrounded and cut to pieces, dying as he had lived, a brave, noble, and loving youth.

Imagine these lines told with every grace of action and every sign of fervent faith to a sympathetic and believing crowd. We may not stay to describe the effect of it upon the audience.

Another preacher took the place of the first. His discourse was mainly upon the deeds and sufferings of Abbas, Husain's youngest brother. The three days' thirst had told upon the women and children in the camp, and his sister-in-law, Husain's wife, was apparently dying. She begged and prayed for water, but there was none to give. In her delirium she called for Abbas. Seeing their agony, he resolved to bring them water. Taking a small brass vessel, he started for the river, the way to which was barred by a host of foes. Armed with new strength by the thought of the suffering women, he fought his way through to the river side. With eager haste he dipped the vessel in the river, and raised the life-giving liquid to his lips. Just as it reached his mouth and before he tasted it, he thought "What! shall I drink when all the rest are faint! No!" He poured the water on his hands, and dipping the vessel again in the river, started off on his perilous journey back to the camp. It had been dangerous before, it was more so now. Then he had two hands available, for the vessel was in his bosom; now he must carry it, lest the water should spill. Fighting on, he had almost broken through, when an arrow pierced his left shoulder. Before the vessel could fall he had caught it with his right hand. Another arrow entered his right wrist. Again he caught the vessel with his teeth, and pushed on in a mad but defenceless rush to the tents he was never again to reach. His foes dared not come near him, but poured in their arrows. A third struck him in the mouth, passing through both cheeks; still he held on, until a last arrow destroyed the vessel, spilling all the water. It was enough—the gallant soul could strive no longer, and fell dead upon the sand. In the course of the subsequent fighting, Husain passed that way, and learnt the fate of Abbas by seeing on the ground the two hands of his beloved brother, which, in their cruel rage, his slayers had severed from the body.

The regular service now abruptly ends, for the audience have been so worked up that they spring to their feet, draw up in a double line across the court, take off their turbans and upper garments, and scream. Now commences the strangest scene it has been my lot to witness. One cries "Husain!" "Husain!" and in a moment the air is rent with shouts of "Husain!" "Husain!" As they shout, they beat their breasts with all their savage force. They leap into the air, they madly dance, they gasp for breath, they stare wildly up to the stars. Ever and anon they surge backwards and forwards, they stand entranced, they fall fainting to the ground. Still goes up to heaven that dreadful cry—"Husain!" "Husain!" "Ali!" "Ali!" shouted at full pitch by nearly a hundred maddened men. The breasts of many are bleeding, completely flayed by excessive flagellation, with the bare hand,—every touch on such a spot must be agony, but still goes on that deep heavy thud, thud, thud, with which the whole house reverberates. Down comes the heavy hand on the wound,—no shrinking, no useless crying, no sign that pain is felt. "Husain" fills every mouth, and causes every heart to pant in pain for him, and not for itself. The worst sight of all is when the frenzied stalwart men fall senseless to the ground in deathly faint. The contrast between the ecstatic frenzy and the senseless mass that a moment before was maddened in the strife and now lies apparently dead is very awful. For a moment the beating ceases, the hoarse shouts of "Husain," "Hasan," lulls. Two or three men dart in to carry off the collapsed mourner. They throw water over him, lay him in the breeze and wait till he comes to. Then swells again the bitter cry, the deadened thuds. It was bad enough to see such things in the crowded street; it is more horrible now in the retired house. Husain has had a long mourning.

When all are too faint, when the body will no longer aid the spirit, this dance of the passional comes to an end. Water and sherbet are liberally distributed. The house-owner brings out his hoqah and composes his feelings with a smoke. The assembly breaks up, and we go home wondering why Christians, who have a still more saddening story, as the key of their hopes, should fail so grievously in realizing its intense interest, should seem to a heathen and Muhammadan world as if the mystery of their faith were but a series of empty words.

FOLKLORE OF ORISSA.

By JOHN BEAMES, B.C.S., M.R.A.S., &c., BALASOR.

Owing to the isolation in which their country has remained for so many ages, the peasantry of Orissa have retained old world ideas and fancies to a greater extent than any other Aryan people of India. They are shy of imparting these ideas to strangers, and a man might live among them for years without finding out the singular views and original processes of reasoning on which many of their habits are based. This shyness arises, I suppose, from the gradual infiltration of modern ideas. The men are beginning to be ashamed of these antiquated fancies, and though in their hearts believing in them, would rather not talk about them, and would prefer to pass for men of the world, bland indifferent free-thinkers to whom all ideas of religion are childish inventions fit only to be smiled at. The women however are still bigotedly attached to the traditions of the past, and the ruder peasantry are in the same primitive stage of credulity.

I do not propose to classify these strange superstitions, but merely to string them together as I hear them, noting here and there curious parallelisms between them and those of our own English peasantry. Students of comparative mythology may draw their own conclusions, but as I do not feel convinced that every one we read of in ancient history represents the sun, nor that all heathen religions are "myths of the dawn," I do not wish to complicate my simple remarks by plunging into the misty regions of the early Aryans, or those of Baal, Bel, Belus and so forth. Human nonsense, like human sense, is very much the same everywhere, and it is only because in ruling men one must take their nonsense into consideration quite as earnestly as their sense, that these scraps of folk-lore are worth recording at all.

Witches abound in Orissa and are called dâinî, (Sanskr. डाकिनी or डाइनी) a word in use in all the Aryan languages of India. They have the power of leaving their bodies and going about invisibly, but if you can get a flower of the pân, or betel-leaf, and put it in your right ear, you will be able to see the witches, and talk to them with impunity. The pân however never flowers, or rather the witches always cause the flower to be invisible, so you are not likely to find it. This is like the English peasants' belief in the virtues of fern-seed.

Witches congregate under banian or pipal trees (in Oriya the first is bôr, बर, Skr. वट —the second ashôth अश्वत्थ, Skr. अश्वत्थ) which grow on the margin of a tank, and if you sit under such a tree in such a position at either of the dawns, that is in the grey of morning or at evening twilight, you will come to grief, especially if the day be Saturday, when the influence of the planet Saturn prevails, or Tuesday when that of Mars is strong. On these days the witches are most powerful, and you will be struck with sickness, or blindness, or suffer loss of property.

A favourite pastime of witches is to get inside the body of a person, who then becomes insensible. In this case you must repeat the following very powerful mantrô or spell, and then ask the witch her name, which she will be obliged to tell you. You may then go to her house, where you will find her walking about as usual. After a severe beating she will be obliged to leave the body of her victim, who will then recover.

This is the mantrá, but care must be taken never to speak it except when a witch has actually taken possession of a person, because if you repeat the spell to any one, all sorts of terrible things will happen. For this reason my informant wrote it out for me.* It looks quite harmless, not to say meaningless, to the uninitiated eye.

Mantra.

Take a handful of dust, and while reciting the following, drop it softly on the crown of the head of the person afflicted.

Bhaj nám koitúni ta puá nám Mahábírá,
Háte gheni kátí buli atek bhágurai
Mo jála parilá asi jojan ghiri
Mo dehare puli pase Mahadeb trisul sakti
Chiá goudá basilá mápi
Swargúru dui angulá chhápi
Ki Chhámula kumbháruni pali
Lakhye Sib basile chhá
Móte chháro nábadwár,
Aho! dáhani rakshasi
Chorgong Rájá mor bhái
Debi Parbati mor mái
Swargúru álá deiá pái
Lolo lolo jibhá bhayangkar múrti
To dekhi Hara Parbati
Jeuthi pesile temhi jibi
Amuká angóru bhitáre thán, [illegible] thán, [illegible] thán, chhákupi thán.
Gharó drushti, báhár drushti, mátá pitá drushti, [illegible] drushti, ehi angóre jo karithibi chhárá! chhárá!
Na chhárí boli káhár ágyá
Sri Churangi koti ágyá.

Then blow three times between the joined hands into the afflicted person's mouth and face.

Translation.

The Koit woman's name is Bhaj, her son's name is Mahábírá,

Holding a dagger in his hand he walks at midnight
My net when dipped extends eighty yojans.
The power of the trident of Mahádeb comes into my body.
The [illegible] has come he sits crouching
Two fingers' breadths from heaven.
What wouldst thou, hag of a potter's wife?
Siva standing by beholds thee.
Leave me by the nine doors,
O blood-sucking witch!
Chorgong Rájá is my brother,
Parbati Debi is my mother;
She has come from heaven planting her foot.
With wagging tongue, of fearful shape
Hara and Parbati look at thee,
Wherever they shall send thee, there thou shalt go.
In so and so's (*naming the person afflicted*) body be there [illegible], be there [illegible], be there witch, be there chhikuni, glance in the house, glance outside, father and mother's glance, glance at market or road, in his body whatsoever there may be
Leave! Leave!

I won't leave, it says, whose order is it?
The myriad orders of Sri Chorangi †

In building a house you must be careful to begin with the southern wall and build northwards, and it is very unlucky to add to a house on the south side. If you are obliged to do so you must leave a cubit and a quarter of clear space between the new house and the old.

There is a verse about this,

Púba bána, pachhim báns
Dakhin chhera, uttar bera

That is—

East grass, west bamboo,
South left, north hedge.

Which may be thus interpreted:—on the east of the house there should be a bána (bána is a grass, and grows in tanks), on the west a grove of bamboos, the south should be left open, and the north enclosed with a hedge. A rationalizing pandit of Balasore thus expounds: There should be a tank on the east side of the house so as to catch the morning sun, and make it comfortable while you sit and wash your

* Mantras must be written in red ink on the leaves of the [illegible].

† It is not to be supposed that anything like connected sense should be made of this rhapsody: the translation is as literal as the corrupted and vulgar nature of the Oriya will permit.

Koituni a female kewt or fisherman's wife. This is the vulgar form of the Sanskrit Kaivartta.

Púa, and fem. puli, are from Skr. [illegible]. Nabadwar—the nine doors, are the nine orifices of the body—eyes, ears, mouth &c.

Chorang Raja is the celebrated king of Orissa who founded the Gangavansi dynasty in A. D. 1131. He is supposed to have been the son of the Sun Ganga or Godavari river, and was a celebrated magician in his life-time.

Chhikuni is a little witch who lurks under bushes in lonely places, and bewitches the cows as they come home in the evening.

Glance, of course, refers to the evil eye, the look by which the witch has done the mischief.

In the transliteration á stands for a as short u, as the Oriyas pronounce it. This short a is only sounded as o in unaccented or final syllables. In all other respects the words are transliterated on the usual Jonesian system, but allowance must be made for many vulgarisms which would not be found in classical Oriya. ṅ is the anuswára.

teeth with a stick, and wash yourself, and rinse your rice, and so on. There should be a grove of bamboos on the west to shelter the house from the hot afternoon sun, and the terrible dust-storms which come from that quarter. The south should be open to allow the delicious sea breeze to blow from the south, as it does all the hot weather, and the north should be fenced and planted with trees to keep off the nasty raw northwind which comes in the rains and gives every one fever and rheumatism. This is ingenious but *ex post facto*, because the same superstition prevails in upper India, where there are no tanks, and where the conditions of wind and seasons are very different; moreover, the rhyme is not in Uriya, but something which looks like bad Hindi of Behar.

You must take care never to call a man back when he is leaving the house, or the business on which he was going will come to naught. His mother may call him back without harm. If you ask why his mother has this privilege, you are told it is because when Krishna was setting forth to kill Kansa, his mother Jasoda called him back, and gave him some curds, and as he was successful on that occasion, as everybody knows, a mother's recall has been harmless ever since.

You must not leave empty water-jars about in the front of a house, or else any one who sees them when starting on a journey will suffer some accident.

If you knock your head against the lintel of the door when going out, you must sit down for a time before going on. This you might be inclined to do naturally, especially if you get a hard crack.

If you are hit by the pankha used to fan the fire, you must spit thrice, because he who is hit by the pankha dies within the year, unless he transfers the curse to the earth by spitting three times.

In the same way, if you hit yourself on the foot with the chhanchuni, a broom made of palm leaves, while you are sweeping the house, you must break off a piece of the leaf, chew, and spit it out.

When a man sneezes, his male friends ought to say "Bhagwān rakhyā karunta," i. e. "May God preserve you!" but women say "Jiu," i. e. "live!" or "achamar hu," a phrase whose meaning is not certain, in consequence of which it is more used than the other.

The ceremonies and precautions necessary to be observed by and towards ladies when in an interesting condition are so numerous and complicated that they must be left for another article. I will merely, in conclusion, observe that rice when growing is also considered as a pregnant woman, and the same ceremonies are observed with regard to it, as in the case of human females.

(To be continued.)

BENGALI FOLKLORE.

BY G. H. DAMANT, B.C.S.

(Continued from page 120.)

THE SECOND STORY.

THERE were once seven brothers, labourers, who were all ploughing together. Feeling very thirsty they sent the youngest brother to bring some water from a pond in a cup. Seeing that he did not return, another brother went in search of him, but he did not return either. At last six of the brothers went one after the other, but none of them came back. Then the seventh brother thought that some misfortune must certainly have befallen them, so he went and looked at the pond from a distance, and saw a goat grazing, and the cup lying near where it had fallen, he then went to give information to the king, and the goat assumed the form of a beautiful woman, and followed him. The labourer called to the king for justice, and told him that the woman was a Rākshasa, who had eaten his six brothers, and wished to eat him, but she replied that he had married her, and now wished to desert her. Directly the king saw the woman he fell in love with her, and said to the labourer, "If you wish to give her up, I will marry her myself." The labourer did all he could to dissuade the king from doing so, but he paid no attention, and was about to marry her on the spot, when she said, "If you really wish to marry me, place the eyes of your present queen in my hands, and send her to live in the forest; if you promise to do that, I will marry you." The king being enchanted by the wiles of the Rākshasa, took out the eyes of his first queen, and placed them in her hands, and then sent the old queen to live in the forest. After a short time the old queen bore a son, who grew up along with her in the forest, till one day he asked his mother why they lived in that solitary place, and why they had no kinsfolk or friends. His mother began to weep, and told him that he had plenty of kinsfolk, and then related the whole story to him.

In the mean time the Rākshasa queen had discovered everything concerning the blind queen's son, so one night she went over the sea to the island of Ceylon, and said to her fellow Rākshasas, "I have married a king, but there is a son of his first wife living, I will make some excuse to send him to you, and you must kill him when he comes," so saying she returned home. After this the son of the blind queen took a sharp sword and went to his father, and the king loved him directly he saw him, and enquired who he was and why he had come. The boy replied that he had left his own country, and was seeking service. The king then asked him what he could do, and he said he could do anything that the other servants considered impossible, so the king took him into his service.

Now the Rākshasa queen had not tasted man's flesh for many days, so she went to the boy's house, and said, "Where are you going? I will kill you." With these words she returned home, and put some dry stalks of hemp under her bed, and lay down on them. When her servants came to enquire what was the matter, she rolled from side to side, and the hemp stalks made a crackling noise. At that the servants became alarmed, and went and told the king, who came and asked the queen what was the matter, and she said she felt great pain in her bones, and then rolled from side to side and made the crackling noise. The king sent for a great many doctors, but none of them did any good, at last she said, "None of these doctors can cure me, but if you can procure me some foam from the sea, I shall be well." The king replied, "How can foam of the sea be procured? it is perfectly impossible for man to do it," but she said that the new servant could bring it, so the king asked him, and he said that he would undertake to procure it, but a large sum of money would be necessary. The king gave him the money, and he gave it all to the blind queen, and went empty-handed to fetch the foam of the sea. In the course of his journey he came to a temple, and there met with a Sanyasi, who received him graciously, and said, "I know why you have come, I will change you into a kingfisher, and you must go and fetch the foam of the sea, and then come back to me." So the boy took the shape of a bird, and flew away till he found the foam, which he brought to the Sanyasi, who restored him to his proper form again, and he went back to the king, and gave him the foam. When the queen had taken the foam as medicine she felt much better, and she perceived that the boy was no ordinary person, and she must use every effort to destroy him. So she again pretended to be ill, and when the king asked how her pain could be cured, she said, "In the island of Ceylon there is a kind of rice which ripens the same day that it is sown, and can be boiled the same day, if I could obtain some of it, my pain would be cured." So the king called the boy, and asked him if he could get it, he replied that he could, but said that a very large sum of money would be wanted. The king gave it him, and he put it in his house, and went to the Sanyasi, who changed him into a parrot, and he went and brought the rice in his beak and came back to the Sanyasi, who transformed him to a man, he then went and gave the rice to the queen, and she boiled it and recovered from her pain.

After a few days the pain again returned, and when the king asked what ailed her, she said, "All the Rākshasas live in the island of Ceylon, they have a cow a cubit in length and half a cubit in height, if it can be brought, and I can drink its milk, I shall be cured." The king told the boy that he must bring the cow, and he undertook to do so, but said that still more money than before would be needed. What could the king do? he was forced to sell his kingdom, and give the proceeds to the boy, who deposited it in his house, and went to the Sanyasi. The Sanyasi told him to go to the place, and say, "aunt, aunt, your sister has married a king, and I am her son, my mother has had no news of you for a long time, so she has sent me, and she wishes to know why you have not killed her enemy who came to fetch the foam of the sea and the rice;" by saying this he would be received as a guest, and would be able to get the cow. The boy went and did as the Sanyasi had told him, and all the Rākshasas believed that he was their nephew, and treated him kindly. After he had lived with them for some time, he said that he was very much afraid lest they should die, and he should have nowhere to live. They replied "We cannot easily die, for the cause of our death is in this house; this lemon which you see is our life, if any one were to cut it, we should all be cut to pieces; the two eyes which you see are the eyes of your father's first wife." The boy enquired the use of the eyes, and they said, "If they are fixed in the eye sockets of a blind man with clay from this place, he will be able to see as before." There was also a young bird kept there, and he enquired what its use was. The Rākshasas answered, "This is the life of your mother, if its wing be broken your mother's arm will be broken, and if its throat be cut, her throat will be cut too." On hearing all this he said boldly, "What danger is there then? no one can know of these things, you will never die, and I can live here without fear." So the Rākshasas, believing he was really their nephew, went out as before to search for food, and when the boy saw that they were at a distance, he cut the lemon to pieces, and they all died. He then took his mother's eyes, and the young bird and the cow, and went back to the Sanyasi, who ordered him to go home and kill the Rākshasa. He first restored his mother to sight, and then went to the king. As soon as he arrived the Rākshasa queen, seeing that she could remain disguised no longer, assumed her own terrible shape, and came forward to devour every one. So he broke the two wings of the young bird, and her two arms were instantly broken, and then he killed the bird and she died too. The king was full of amazement at the sight, till his son told him the whole story, and after that he put on the dress of a king's son, and the king fetched his first wife from the forest, and they all lived happily together for the rest of their lives.

THE THIRD STORY.

THERE was once a Brahman who had no son, he used to go every day to the king's palace, and say, "As thy liberality, so thy virtue." He did this daily for a year and six months, and received a rupee each time. At last the king wondered what was the use of giving a rupee every day, so he asked the Brahman, what was the meaning of the saying "As thy liberality, so thy virtue," which he repeated every day. The Brahman went home, and reflected about it, but the king gave him nothing that day, and moreover told him that it would be well for him to give the interpretation of the saying, for if he failed to do so, he would sacrifice him before the goddess Durga.

Now that very day a daughter was born to the childless Brahman, and directly she came from the womb, she smiled and stood up, and said, "Father, why is your face so sad?" The Brahman replied, "What is the use of telling you? You were only born to-day." but his little daughter again said, "My father, let me hear your story, why is your face so sad?" So the Brahman answered, "Every day since I was a boy, I have been to the king's palace, and said, 'As thy liberality, so thy virtue,' and received a rupee, but to-day the king has threatened to sacrifice me to the goddess Durga, if I do not explain the meaning of the saying to him, and therefore my face is sad." His daughter told him to go and bathe, and she would give him the interpretation; so he went and bathed with a glad countenance; after he had eaten, he came back and asked his daughter to tell him as she had promised. She told him to go to the court, and if the king made any enquiry of him to say, "Sir, two and a half days ago, a daughter was born in my house, and she will tell you the meaning of the saying." So the Brahman went and told the king, who was exceedingly astonished, and declared that it was nonsense to suppose that a child of that age could explain the meaning, but nevertheless he took elephants, horses, and soldiers, and went to the Brahman's house. When the little child saw him, she stood up, and asked him smiling who he was, and why he had come to her house. He told her that he had come to try and find the interpretation of the saying, and she said, "I could tell you if I would, but I will only say this much: in the southern corner of your village lives an oilman, and his red ox will tell you." So the king took away his elephants, horses and soldiers, and went to the oilman's house, and asked him whether he kept a red ox to turn his oil mill. The oilman replied, "Yes, Sir, there he is in that field." Then the king went and said,—"Ho, Mr. Oilman's ox, what is the meaning of the saying, 'As thy liberality, so thy virtue?'" The ox replied weeping, "Listen, Sir, I could tell you if I would, but I will only say that there is a clump of Shahura trees[*] to the east of your house, and they will tell you." Then the king took his elephants, horses and soldiers, and went to the clump of Shahura trees and said, "Clump of Shahura trees, tell me the meaning of the saying 'As thy liberality so thy virtue.'" The genius of the Shahura tree replied, "Listen, king of the world, you have been made a king, because in your former state of existence you were very liberal, and gave your whole mind to charity; the woman who was then your wife was very pure in heart, and she has now been born in the house of the childless Brahman, and the oilman's red ox was formerly your son. Now since you have come to me, last of all, I must explain the meaning of the saying. I was once your son's wife, but my heart was hardened against every one, and I was most unwilling to bestow anything in charity, therefore I have become the genius of this grove of trees." On hearing this the king returned home, and every day after that the Brahman went to the palace, and repeated the saying, and received a rupee.

Tailor-bird, my story is ended, let me hear yours.

ON THE RÂMÂYANA.[*]

BY PROF. ALBRECHT WEBER, BERLIN.

Translated from the German by the Rev. D. C. Boyd, M.A.

(*Continued from p. 124.*)

WE come now to consider the principal question that arises out of the relation in which Vâlmîki's version of the Râma-Saga stands to that which is found in the old Buddhistic legends. Seeing that in this latter there is no mention made of the rape of Sîtâ, we naturally ask—where did the poet of the *Râmâyana* get the idea? Is it merely the offspring of his own imagination, taking shape in accordance with his intention to describe the expedition to Lankâ and the battles fought in front of that city, whether these were really waged with the abo-

[*] [illegible]

rigines, or with the Buddhists, as Wheeler imagines? or has he borrowed the materials for this part of the poem from some other quarter? Let me say at once that I consider the latter alternative to be the true account of the matter, and that the rape of Helen and the siege of Troy have served as a model for the corresponding incidents in the poem of Vâlmîki.* I do not indeed imagine that he had himself studied Homer, or even that he must have been aware of the existence of the Homeric poems. Nor am I inclined to go so far as to attach importance (though the idea is by no means far-fetched, as even Monier Williams admits†) to the apparent analogies between Agamemnon and Sugrîva, Patroklos and Lakshmaṇa, Nestor and Jâmbavant, Odysseus and Hanumant, Hektor and Indrajit,—analogies which have led Hippolyte Fauche, who has translated the *Râmâyaṇa* into French, to adopt the converse theory that Homer has borrowed the materials for his work from that of Vâlmîki! I pass over the coincidences also noticed by Monier Williams himself,‡—the consoling of the forsaken Sîtâ by means of a dream; the surveying and enumerating of the hostile troops from the battlements of Lankâ; and the appearing of Sîtâ before the army.§ Nor do I wish to discuss the very wide and far-reaching question,||—In how far an acquaintance with the Greek epic may have exercised an influence on the development of the Indian one? I content myself rather with the simple assumption that in consequence of the mutual relations, which Alexander's expedition into India brought about, between the inhabitants of that country and the Greeks (and which, in so far as the Buddhists are concerned, have found remarkable expression, for instance in the *Milindapanha*),¶ some kind of knowledge of the substance of the Homeric story found its way to India. And I feel all the more justified in assuming this by the fact that, in addition to the combinations suggested by the rape of Sîtâ and the war before Lankâ, two other Homeric incidents are found, not indeed in the *Râmâyaṇa* itself, but in the Pâli texts of Ceylon*—namely, the adventures of Odysseus and his companions on the island of Kirke, in the *Mahavansa*,† and the Trojan

* Without questioning the possible anti-Buddhistic design in the selection of Lankâ as the scene of the conflict.

† *Ind. Ep. Poetry*, p. 10. ‡ P. 74, 82, 86.

§ As Monier Williams (p. 8) assumes that the greater part of the *Mahâbhârata*, if not the entire work, dates from a period as early as the fifth century B.C., he regards these details as well as those which he [illegible] are borrowed from [illegible] (p. 74) [illegible] only later embellishments—that is, if he sees in them anything more than purely accidental coincidences.

|| Vide *Ind. Stud.* II. 166.

¶ It is greatly to be desired that this important work were given to the public with the least possible delay. It contains the conversations held by the Yavana king of Sagala, Milinda (Menandros, cf. *Ind. Skizzen* p. 83, reigned according to Lassen, *Ind. Alt.* II. 327 and p. xxxiv. from 144 B.C.), with the Buddhist priest Nâgasena; but as yet we have been made acquainted only with extracts from it, in Hardy. Cf. *Ind. Stud.* III. 120.

* Vide *Ind. Streifen* II, 226. I. 370.

† Cap. VII. vide Turnour, p. 48. I think it advisable to give here the Indian version in detail. When Vijaya, sent into exile on account of his insolence by his father Sîhabâhu, King of Lâla, landed on Lankâ with 700 companions exhausted by the fatigues of the voyage, they immediately fell in with the tutelary divinity of the island, the god Uppalavaṇṇa (Vishṇu), who was sitting, in the form of a paribbâjaka ("devotee," Turnour), at the foot of a tree, for the purpose of receiving them and providing them with a counter-charm against enchantment (*cf. Od.* X. 277, 287. Lane, *Arabian Nights* III. 299, 307). In reply to their enquiry, he told them the name of the island, then besprinkled them with water out of his pitcher, tied "(charmed) threads on their arms" (suttam tesam hatthesu laggetvâ) and vanished. Immediately thereafter there appeared to them a Yakkha female attendant in a canine form. Although the Prince warned him not to do so, yet one of the men followed her, saying to himself, "Where you see dogs, you may look for a village." And so by-and-bye he found himself in the presence of her mistress, the Yakkhinî Kuvaṇṇâ ("with bad plaited hair"? or "bad, wickedly plaiting"?) who (near a tank) was sitting spinning (*Od.* X. 120) under a tree, "in the character of a devotee" (tâpasî viya). When he saw the tank and the anchoress sitting beside it, he bathed and drank from it, and collected (edible) roots, as well as water with lotus flowers. Thereupon she stood up and said to him, "Thou art my food (prey)!" Then he stood spell-bound; but because the (charmed) thread was tied (on his hand), she could not devour him; and although she begged him to give her the thread, he would not. She thereupon laid hold of him, and cast him bellowing loudly (*Od.* X. 241) into an underground cave (v. 17 tam gahetvâ surungâyam rudantam yakkhinî khipi). And so [illegible] the whole 700 companions (of the Prince) were gradually, one by one, caught and shut up in the cave. Seeing that none of them came back, Vijaya became anxious, went after them, and on arrival at the tank [illegible] he saw that there were no footsteps of any that had come out [illegible] Turnour has "he could perceive footsteps leading down only into the tank", but there is nothing of the sort in the Pâli), saw he now the anchoress, and he thought, "I shouldn't wonder if she has caught hold of my attendants." So he asked her, "Now, hast thou not seen my attendants?" She said, "What are thy attendants to me, Prince? Drink and bathe!" Then he perceived—"She is a Yakkhinî (enchantress) [illegible] my rank;" and, resolved in a moment, [illegible] his bow and naming his own name, he sprang on her, caught her by the neck with a narâcha noose, seized her hair with his left hand, drew his sword with his right (*Od.* X. 321, 322) and said: "Slave, deliver up my attendants! or I will put thee to death." Struck with terror, she begged for her life: "Lord, grant me life! I will give thee a kingdom, I will serve thee as thy wife, and do everything that thou mayest wish." In order to avoid the risk of a similar danger being repeated he made her swear an oath (*Od.* X. 343, 345). Forthwith she restored to him his attendants, and because she saw that they were exhausted (*Od.* X. 463), she set before them rice and other food, and all kinds of ships' stores, once the property of merchants who had formerly fallen a prey to her. The attendants prepared the rice, &c., and they enjoyed, with the Prince, a delicious meal. The Yakkhinî also received some of it to taste; and she was in consequence so delighted, that she changed her form into that of a maiden of sixteen. Having adorned her person with splendid attire, the Mâra-wife (Mâramganâ: Turnour has erroneously: "lovely as Mâra's own self"), approached the Prince, and speedily conquered his heart. Under a tree she caused a sumptuous bed to arise, enclosed with curtains as with a wall, and perfumed with the most fragrant odours

home (though certainly transformed into an elephant) in Buddhaghosa's *Comm. on the Dhammapada.*[*] Just as so many Æsopic fables have found a place in the Jâtaka-collection, which forms a part of the sacred *Tipitaka*,[†] so also from various other sources, western tales, sagas and other forms of popular thought have found their way into India by means of that direct intercourse with the Greeks to which we have already referred.[‡] The Saga of the ... of Simonides appears indeed to have found admission into an *Upanishad* belonging to the *Rig-veda*.[§] And perhaps we can point to certain elements of the same kind even in the *Râmâyana*

---

and Vijaya spent the night with her there (*Ib.* X. 617), while his companions slept around him outside. While he was thus with her on the couch, he heard singing and music, and in reply to his question, she told him what was the state of affairs and gave him such directions as would enable him to make himself master of the island; and by means of her counsel and with her help, he succeeded in this. After a time, however, he put her away again, when the opportunity presented itself of winning "a queen consort of royal rank to himself" in the daughter of the Pandava-king of Madhura; and the Yakkhini met her death by the hand of one of her Yakkha relations, ... at her as ... of his treachery.—With regard to this story, I remark that the word surunga [illegible] (according to Gorresio) used in v. 14, is of itself sufficient to demonstrate, what indeed requires no further proof, the existence of Greek influence in the time at which the *Mahâvanso* was composed (cf. *Ind. Streifen* II. 340). Though this sacred document indeed but sparingly made use of the determining the relation that exists between the above ... and that which is found in the *Odyssey*, seeing that the word ... "underground passage" is not used ... in the corresponding portion of the latter work, or elsewhere at all in the poem, still it is certainly a significant circumstance that in a story which has so many points of resemblance with one in the *Odyssey*, we should find a word which can be easily recognised as Greek, though altered in form through the influence of oral tradition. The difficulties which prevented Turnour (*Introd.* p. [illegible]) from recognising in the story told in the *Mahâvanso* an echo of the Homeric saga certainly do not exist for us.

[*] Vide Fausböll, p. 158, and in Rogers, *Buddhaghosha's Parables*, p. [illegible]. In the same way, [illegible] be made to [illegible] these correspondences with the *Odyssey*, which Schiefner has pointed out as existing in the later Mongolian version of the Saga of Gesser Khan (*Abh. d. K. A. d. W. zu Berlin*, for the year 1851, p. 270, or p. 17 of the separate impression); see also Jolg in the *Verhandlungen der Würzburger Philologen Versammlung* (1868), p. [illegible]. (A Tibetan recension of the same has recently, [illegible] Schiefner in the *Mélanges Asiatiques of the Petersb. Acad.* V. 67, 1863) come into the possession of E. Schlagintweit; but so far as I am aware nothing more exactly relating to this subject has yet been published.) The Indian account, corresponding to the story of the Trojan horse, of the artificial elephant inside of which a number of warriors were concealed for the purpose of effecting the capture of king Udayana, appears to have formed also the subject of a drama, devoted to the fortunes of this king; vide *Sâhitya-darpaṇa* § 197 : vatsa Udayanacharita [illegible].

[†] Cf. *Ind. Stud.* III. 368. In Buddhaghosa, too (Fausböll, *Dhamma.* p. 1[illegible]) an Æsopic fable is found; that of the flight of the tortoise through the air (cf. *Ind. Stud.* III. 339).

[‡] On this subject, compare, for instance, what I have said in the *Zeitschr. der Deutsch. Morgenl. Gesellsch.* XIV. 269, in the *Monatsberichte der Akademie* for the year 1860, p. [illegible] ff., and in the *Ind. Streifen* I. 1[illegible], II. [illegible]. Perhaps we should class also with these materials the parable quoted by M. Müller in his paper on *Buddhist Nihilism*, p. 10, from Buddhaghosa's *Comm.* on the *Dhammapada*, of the mother mourning the death of her only son, whom Buddha comforted by bidding her bring him as a medicine that would procure the boy's restoration to life, a grain of mustard-seed "from a house to which neither a son, nor a father, nor a slave had died." The fruitless search brought home to her the passing nature of all earthly things, and raised her above her individual sorrow. This parable, which M. M. calls "a test of true Buddhism," appears in Lucian's *Demonax*, Cap. 25 (Paris: 1840 ed. Dindorf, p. 391), identical in substance, but so far changed in form, that Demonax, whom Lucian speaks of as his contemporary, promised the philosopher Herodes, in similar circumstances, that his child would be restored to life "if he would only name to him three men, who had never mourned for any one lost (dead)" (εἰ μόνον αὐτῷ τρεῖς τινας ἀνθρώπους ὀνομάσειεν μηδένα πώποτε πεπενθηκότας). Similarly also the emperor Julian, in his 37th epistle (ed. Heyler, Mainz, 1828, p. 64, 65, 401), in which he seeks to console his friend Amerius (var. Himerius) on the death of his young wife, tells the same story, in this form, that Democritus of Abdera promised Darius to restore life to his dead queen, if he should succeed in finding, throughout his wide dominions, three names of persons who had not yet been called to mourn (τριῶν ἀπενθήτων ὀνόματα; ... Heyler translates, but according to the [illegible] text, this is is decidedly incorrect). The imperial letter-writer alludes also to the "tomb that becomes barren" (Βαγώαου ...) in the *Odyssey* IV. 720 [illegible], which, raised in the view of any one, doubtless has for ... ... forget his mourning for mother, father, brother, and son; and he speaks of the story as coming to his friend "probably not pleasant, though to the most of people, as he believed, unknown" (λόγον ... ... οὐκ ἐπ᾽ ἴσης ... ...). Buddhaghosa wrote about 420 A. D., consequently about 400 years after the emperor Julian (363), and some 250 years after Lucian. If therefore any connection is to be looked for here, which can hardly indeed be called in question, the probability of the borrowing having taken place from the West is certainly greater than, or is, at all events, as great as that of the converse supposition; and this opinion is not materially affected by the circumstance that, according to M. M. (though a kind [illegible] ... regarding both of these passages, the "Democritus" is really a pseudo-Lucianic work; for the emperor's letter is certainly genuine, and at the same time it appeals to the fact that although the story in question was "to most people unknown," yet it was "probably not new" to the person addressed—an evident proof that it had come down from an earlier time, though to be sure the assertion of the connection of the story with Darius or with Democritus (in whose biography in Diogenes Laertius, according to Heyler p. 409, nothing of the kind is to be found) has no claim to be received as true. And besides, as M. M.'s account is not taken direct from the Pali text, but from the Burmese translation of the same, translated into English by Capt. Rogers (vide p. 100, 101 of his book), it is quite natural to expect that an investigation of the original might show that it stands in a still closer relation to the Greek form of the story (the corresponding section is unfortunately not given in Fausböll's extracts from Buddhaghosa's Commentary; vide ibid p. [illegible]; a legend of similar import, however, is found at p. [illegible]). In fact we have already seen that Buddhaghosa shows an acquaintance with Greek elements from other sources also. At all events, just as the legends regarding Christ that were current in the sixth or tenth centuries of the Christian era have little weight with reference to the times at which Christ lived, if they are not supported by evidence from other sources, so these legends of Buddhaghosa's, which occupy, almost throughout, the standpoint of the most credulous superstition, and give evidence of the full development of Buddhist doctrine, have as little claim as *Ipso* to be regarded as "parables of Mahinda, if not of Buddha himself" (an opinion toward which M. Müller evidently leans, in his preface to Capt. Rogers' book, p. xvii), so long as this conclusion is not supported by other evidence out of the *Tipitaka* itself; though indeed they often enough refer at least to the *gâthâ*, *padas*, *sâtras*, [illegible], &c. That they contain much legendary matter that is really ancient, and of the highest value, I do not mean for a moment to deny; and in regard to their antiquity, Fausböll himself has pointed out that they seem to be borrowed in part from an ancient metrical version (l. c. p. [illegible]).

[§] Vide *Ind. Stud.* IX, 42.

itself. Here for instance seems to be a further instance of the occurrence of a directly Homeric element:—in the first book of the *Rámáyaṇa*,* we are told how Janaka, king of Mithilá, had given out that his daughter Sítá should be the prize of the man who should show the greatest prowess (víryaśulká), and how Ráma won her hand by bending an enormous bow which none of her previous suitors had been able to bend; how these latter, feeling ashamed at their defeat, laid siege to Mithilá, and how Janaka succeeded, by the help of the gods, in conquering them and driving them away. Such an incident† naturally reminds us of the bow of Odysseus; and the coincidence gains additional significance from the fact that we are able to bring forward another Indian form of the same saga. This is found, namely, according to Bigandet, in the *Janaka-jātaka*;‡ and it has already been made use of by Ernst Kuhn§ as a proof that there are points of agreement between the Buddhist writings and the Odyssey. "In a *Jātaka* quoted by Bigandet," says Kuhn, "we find an account of one who is shipwrecked being rescued by a sea-goddess,∥ who carries him to land, into a mango-garden, where he immediately falls asleep. On his awaking he is, in consequence of a divine decision, elected as king; and he marries the queen of the country, when, by bending an enormous bow, and by other proofs,¶ he has shown that he is her appointed husband." The rescuing of Odysseus by Leukothea seems here to be combined with the bending of the bow which the other suitors were unable to bend; and while by this combining of the two incidents, we are involuntarily reminded of Homer, the second of them at once recalls the incident at the court of Janaka, King of Mithilá, which, as we have seen, is described in the *Rámáyaṇa*; and with regard to this latter there cannot be the least doubt, for the story in this *Jātaka*, as quoted by Bigandet, is of a young prince of Mithilá of the same name as the father of Sítá (Janaka), who set out from that country in order to win back the throne of his ancestors, and so met with the adventures described. If these incidents, then, be really capable of being referred to Homer (and the combining of the two hardly leaves any room for doubt on this point), it seems to follow that the scene in the *Rámáyaṇa* may also be assigned to the same source! It is true that the evidence thus furnished by Bigandet is derived only from a Burmese translation; but since his testimony regarding other matters has proved to be trustworthy and reliable, there is no ground for suspecting it in reference to this question. There can be no doubt, at the same time, that it would be peculiarly interesting to obtain some acquaintance with the Pali text of this *Jātaka*.*—The two other apparently western elements that find a place in the *Rámáyaṇa* are:—Hanumant's commanding the sun, *à la Joshua*, to stand still;† and Ráma's satisfying the ritual requirements of the horse-sacrifice regarding chastity by sleep-

---

* Cap. lxvi, lxvii, Schlegel.

† In the *Mahábhárata*, too, the same story occurs pretty nearly in the same form:—Drupada offers his daughter as a prize to him who excels in archery (I, 6961); no one is able to bend the bow, except Karṇa whom Draupadí, however, despises, because he is a sûta (7017), and Arjuna (7053), who has consequently to engage in a severe conflict with the other suitors, in which his brother Bhíma stands faithfully by him.

‡ *The Life or Legend of Gaudama*, first edition, Rangoon, 1858, p. 409 ff., second edition, ibid. 1866, p. 415 ff. In [illegible] *Jainaka-Jāta*[illegible], which is evidently identical with *Janaka-jātaka*, though in another passage, (p. [illegible]) Bigandet gives [illegible] as also the equivalent of the name [illegible].

§ In the *Lit. Centralblatt*, 1869, [illegible], p. 1316.

∥ Janaka is the only one rescued out of 700 who were in the ship. He "swims [illegible] of a day, even with all his strength" (vide *Od.* V, 371). At last a sea-nymph seeing "his generous and courageous behaviour, took pity on him (ibid. v. 333) and came to his assistance. These followed a sort of dialogue." (ibid v. 339 ff.).

¶ "He was to be able to bend and unbend an enormous bow, a feat that the united efforts of a thousand soldiers could scarcely achieve, and find the place where he" that is, the former king "had concealed 16 golden cups."

* The *Catalogue of the Copenhagen Pali MSS.* gives two *Jātakas* of this name:—a *Chulla-Janaka-jātaka*, I (VI) 52, and a *Mahā-*, XXI (LVI) 531.

† More exactly, 'not to rise', and consequently it must be admitted, a very different circumstance, so much so as to make it on the whole questionable whether any foreign influence is here to be looked for. The same prohibition addressed to the sun is also found in [illegible], vide Meyer l. c. p. 24 ff. and [illegible], in [illegible] the only request of the maiden addressed to the night, that it would not come to a close.—Besides, our only information on this point as regards Hanumant is derived from Wheeler, p. 100; did he obtain his from the North-West Recension? Gorresio's edition makes no mention of the incident, in either of the accounts which it furnishes of Hanumant's expedition (VI. 35 and VI. 84). The Bombay edition, too, which contains altogether (and no doubt correctly) only one such account (VI. 74. 33 ff.; cf. VI. 42, 36 ff.), is entirely silent on the point, although it several times refers to the sun's path:—thus 74, 59 [illegible]; 74, 60 [illegible]. It is exactly the same also in A (Fol. [illegible]) and in C (Fol. [illegible]). According to a notice in the *Magazin f. d. Lit. d. Ausl.* 1870, p. 207, the command of Joshua, in precisely analogous circumstances, belongs also to Japan; and the incident is assigned to the year 200 of our era. "Before the battle was decided, the sun was in the act of setting. Then the Princess, the consort of the Mikado Tsin Ai, drew her sword, and waved it toward the sun, which turned back on its course; and once more it became mid-day. . . ."

ing with the golden statue of Sîtâ, whom he had abandoned in the forest,*—with reference to which Wilson† has called attention to the similar‡ situation in the Alkestis of Euripides (v. 341-345).§ And in view of what has been advanced, regarding Western influences, the supposition that the Sopeithes, king of the Kekaya, who entered into friendly personal relations with Alexander the Great, may be identified with the Aśvapati, king of the Kekaya, who is mentioned in the *Râmâyaṇa* as the brother-in-law of Daśaratha, may not appear, as a mere question of literary history, so absolutely untenable as Lassen is inclined to regard it; though undoubtedly there seems to be greater probability in the view (v. supra p. 123) that Vâlmîki introduced this name into his poem simply because he found it already in use in the *Vêda*-text.

Are we able, then, to fix approximately the *date* at which the work of Vâlmîki was composed? It is known that we have accounts in Greek writers—first in Dio Chrysostom (in the time of Trajan), and then in Ælian—of an Indian translation of Homer. I have already expressed my opinion elsewhere‖ that we must not take this statement in too literal a sense, but that we should accept it rather as a testimony, that at the time when it was made the people of India, equally with those of Greece, were in possession of an epic, conceived in the style of the Homeric poems. And in the same place I have pointed out that the more detailed statements of Dio Chrysostom—namely, that the people of India were well acquainted with the sorrows of Priam, with the dirges and lamentations of Andromache and Hekabe, and with the bravery of Achilles and Hektor—point to a Greek influence in the *Mahâbhârata*, quite as much as in the *Râmâyaṇa*, and that in fact this may be seen even in larger measure in the former than in the latter; that at the same time, however, the expedition to the distant Laṅkâ and the siege of that city in the *Râmâyaṇa* certainly offer a closer analogy with the expedition to the distant [and similarly transmarine] Troy and the siege thereof, than is presented by the conflict on the open battle-field between the neighbouring Kuru and Pañchâla described in the *Mahâbh.*; but that on the other hand the absence of any mention in Dio Chrysostom of a similarity so striking (and, I ought to have added, the omission of any reference to the similar origin of the war in the two cases, the abduction, namely, of the wife of the hero of the one party by the hero of the other) was a convincing proof that under the title of "the Indian Homer" we were to understand, not a poem on the Saga of the *Râmâyaṇa*, but a poem on the Saga of the *Mahâbhârata*. It may no doubt be said, in opposition to this opinion, that as Dio Chrysostom proceeds on the assumption that Homer had actually been translated into the language of India, he would take it as a matter of course that the origin and the locality of the conflict were the same, that he would not think it necessary therefore to call special attention to this, and that he would content himself with mentioning only what seemed to him to be most suitable for the rhetorical purpose which he had in view. In accordance with this theory, it would certainly be possible that his account of the matter was founded on some actual intimation of the existence of the *Râmâyaṇa*. Nor indeed do I mean absolutely to deny such a possibility; but on the other hand it evidently does not allow of being used, even remotely, as a proof of that existence, or

* First, it must be owned, in the *Uttarakâṇḍa* (sarga 99, vol. 8, vide Wheeler, p. [illegible]), which does not indeed belong to the *Râmâyaṇa* proper, but is a later addition; it occurs besides in Bhavabhûti in the *Uttararâmacharita*, and also in the *Jaimini-Bhârata*, xxix. 47, 68. Attention should, however, be called to the reference to this, as early as in the [illegible] III. 1, 14, [illegible] This work bears the name of Râmâyaṇa, and is regarded as a pariśishṭa to the *Sâma Veda*; vide *Ind. Stud.* I, 50. *Verz. d. Berl. S. H.* p. 82. (I remark here, in passing, that [illegible] is found only in [illegible] and there, too, only [illegible]; it is changed, on the other hand, [illegible] into achyutah. [illegible] reads it thus in his Comm., [illegible] and explains this word by Vishṇuḥ. This is evidently a hypercritical emendation of the text, in which Râma is regarded only as a man.

† In the *Hindu Theatre*, I. 337.

‡ The incident in Euripides however, undoubtedly, differs in important respects from that referred to here. In the anguish caused by the approaching loss of his wife, who is about to die for him, Admetos exclaims—

"The beauteous figure by the artists' hand
Skilfully wrought, shall in my bed be laid;
By that reclining I will clasp it to me,
And call it by thy name, and think I hold
My dear wife in my arms, though far she dwells." (*Potter*).

But he receives her back again alive, through the intervention of Herakles, who rescues her from Thanatos.—As the Greek settlers in the frontier lands of India, for instance in Bactria, seem to have kept up their acquaintance with the Greek drama (cf. the accounts from Plutarch in my translation of the Mâlavikâ, p. xlvi., note 50) it may readily be supposed that the substance of a passage from Euripides might easily find its way into India.

§ We might also perhaps have pointed out with Wheeler [p. 331] the similarity to which he calls attention "between the seven-walled city of Laṅkâ and the seven-walled city of Ecbatana" (Herod. I. 98). But the editions of the *Râmâyaṇa* contain nothing of the kind; on the contrary, mention is made in the poem of only one great golden prâkâra (V. 2, 16 Gorr., V. 2, 16, 3, 6 Bomb.), and besides, in general, only of earth walls and trenches (vapraiś [illegible] parikhâbhiś cha, Gorr. V. 2, 14).

‖ *Ind. Stud.* II. 162.

of being employed as chronological capital for determining the time of the composition of the poem itself.*

And with reference to this part of the subject, I think it desirable that we should, in the first place, investigate such data bearing on the time of the composition of the *Rámáyaṇa* as can be furnished by internal evidence, and that we should then collect the external data for the existence of the poem, so far as these are to be found in Indian literature and elsewhere.

The *first* point then which meets us in connection with the internal evidence furnished by the *Rámáyaṇa* (and it is a very perplexing one) is the great extent of the work, which shows that it cannot have been the composition of one poet only, but that centuries must have contributed to mould it into its present form. The natural result of this has been that the text has been split up into several distinctly separate recensions. Indeed we can say with almost perfect truth that there are as many texts as there are manuscripts or editions.† And a further consequence has been that even within these individual recensions there have been found numerous contradictions and obvious additions, which afford sufficient evidence of

---

* We are unfortunately unable to determine exactly the time to which the account given in Dio Chrysostom ought to be assigned. My own view, which I have stated in the *Ind. Stud.* pp. 160 and 161, and which has received the approval of Benfey (*Gött. Gel. Anz.* 1858 p. [illegible]), that it should be assigned to the time after Pliny, who would hardly have left so important a fact unnoticed, still seems to me preferable to that of Lassen, *Ind. Alt.* II., Anhang p. [illegible], namely, that we are indebted to Megasthenes for the report in question. But at least I can no longer support my opinion as I endeavoured to do there, by the argument that the account given by Dio Chrysostom in the same passage, to the effect that the Great Bear is not visible to the people of India is to be regarded as a mistaken report brought to Europe (from the South of India), after the time of Pliny. For as Lassen has justly pointed out in the place already quoted, this report is mentioned at least as early as by Onesikritos and by Megasthenes. (On this subject, see also *Ind. Stud.* II. [illegible].) And in any case, the circumstance that Pliny makes no mention of the Indian Homer is at least no proof that up till that time no information on the subject had reached Europe; for he might have omitted to mention this just in the same way as he left unmentioned the information regarding the Great Bear. It must be admitted at the same time that such omissions are remarkable enough in a man like Pliny.

† With reference to the various recensions of the *Rámáyaṇa*, we are hardly able to say with certainty at present, which of them should be considered as most closely corresponding with the original. The so-called Bengal recension has found the warmest opponent in Hall, who speaks of it, in his edition of Wilson's translation of the *Vishṇu Puráṇa* (II. 190), as "a modern depravation," and even characterizes it as "spurious" (ibid III. [illegible]). Gorresio, too, in his [illegible] (p. [illegible]), refers to it as a production of the 12th century. Hall justly describes Schlegel's edition as "composite," and, in his opinion, the "genuine *Rámáyaṇa*" is contained only in the editions of Calcutta (which unfortunately I am acquainted with only through Muir's extracts), and of Bombay. [He has seen in India no fewer than seven commentaries "on the real *Rámáyaṇa*;" and one of these was a manuscript nearly 300 years old, with accompanying text.]—At the same time, I have made it, I hope, sufficiently clear by the arguments I have adduced from the Berlin MSS.,—partly in my *Catalogue of the Berlin Sanskrit MSS.* p. 119 ff., partly in the *Indische Streifen*, II. [illegible] ff., partly in the present paper *passim*,—that these views of Hall's must undergo considerable modification. These Berlin MSS., written throughout in Devanágarí, partly correspond to a large extent with Gorresio's text, and therefore lend it additional authority; and partly they represent, as compared with Gorresio and with the Bombay edition, a perfectly independent text; in other words they form a recension for themselves. And there is no reason to doubt that the same result will be frequently repeated as further new MSS. are brought to light and compared with one another. In fact, it could hardly be otherwise, considering the manner in which so national and popular a poem must have been handed down, beyond a doubt merely by means of oral tradition (in the *Uttarakáṇḍa* mention is made continually and expressly of recitation of the poem): the wonder really is that after all there is so much substantial harmony among the different versions. And this is the more surprising when we consider also that the different provinces of India had each their own peculiar styles (*ríti*), which differed from one another in important respects, and that consequently the work of Válmíki, as it gradually spread over the whole of India, would be exposed to the modifying influences which such a state of things would naturally exert. For our earliest and at the same time most detailed information regarding this variety of style, we are indebted to the (*Kávyádarśa* v. 1. [illegible]) of Daṇḍin, who in all probability lived as far back as the 6th century; and Paṇḍit Premachandra Tarkavágíśa, in the commentary with which he has accompanied his edition of this work (in the *Bibliotheca Indica*, Calc. 1863), has made a most valuable collection of what is known on this subject from other sources, namely, from the works of Vámana, Bhojadeva (*Sarasvatíkaṇṭhábharaṇa*, II. [illegible]) and Viśvanátha (*Sáhityadarpaṇa*, Chap. IX. [illegible]). Compare on this subject the detailed statements from the works of the first two of these authors, namely, the *Kávyálaṅkáravṛitti* of Vámana, and the *Sarasvatíkaṇṭhábharaṇa* of Bhojarája as found in Aufrecht's *Catalogus*, &c. [illegible]; according to [illegible], the same subject is specially treated also in Chap. IX. of the [illegible] of [illegible]. And in this matter it so happens that the Bengalis (Gauḍas) play quite a conspicuous part. Daṇḍin recognises only two kinds of style, that of the Bengalis (Gauḍí) and that of the Vidarbha (Vaidarbhí). Vámana and Viśvanátha mention also the style of the Páñchálas (Páñchálí), [illegible], and Bhojadeva adds to these the Ávantiká and the Mágadhí styles [illegible]; while he designates the Vaidarbhí style as that of the [illegible]. It is greatly to be wished that some one would work up carefully and thoroughly the details that are furnished in such abundance by these passages. I content myself with remarking here that the style of the Vaidarbhas is described as having the preference on account of its being smooth, simple and universally intelligible, while that of the Gauḍas is characterised as having the opposite qualities. Whether the latter, and especially the detailed statements in Daṇḍin &c. are to be understood as having in some way a reference to the recension of the *Rámáyaṇa* edited by Gorresio, and by him, following the example of Schlegel, designated as "Gauḍana"—and if so, to what extent—are questions that cannot be answered without further special research. (The same remark holds good also of the so-called Bengal recension of the *Śakuntalá*, for the authenticity of which, and especially for its being truer to the original than the so-called Devanágarí recension, Dr. R. Pischel has recently been contending very earnestly, in what is at all events a very valuable dissertation (Breslau 1870, De Kálidásae Çákuntali recensionibus, pp. 117); though to be sure Stenzler had expressed his opinion to the same effect a long time ago (vide Zarncke's *Literar. Centralblatt*, 1861, p. 811 ff.). Gorresio's recension received the name "Gauḍana" on two grounds: 1. Because the MSS. on which it was founded are written for the most part in the Bengali character; 2. Because the statement in Carey and Marshman, I. p. 212 that the text from this place in the book (I. 15, 1–10 in Gorresio) is to be found only in the copies of the Gauḍa Paṇḍits and not in those of the south or west"—is especially pertinent to this recension (v. Gorr. I. 15, 1—10), while the verses in question are wanting in Schlegel (in I. between 18 and 19)

revisions and interpolations by different hands.* So that though this may no doubt be a proof of the great popularity of the work, on the other hand it seriously complicates the critical questions which arise as to the value of the constituent elements of which the poem is made up. And in addition to the hitherto known recensions,† we have now a new one introduced by Wheeler, which he calls the North-West (?) Recension, but which is evidently stamped as quite modern by its omissions and its very recent additions.‡ It is not so easy to determine, in the other recensions, what should be recognized as original, and what should be regarded as merely the result of later accretions. What are we to say, for instance, regarding the well-known episode of Viśvâmitra in the first book?§ It wears an unmistakably antique aspect, referring as it does to the elevation of a Kshatriya to the dignity of a Brâhman,—a circumstance which though it is handled with all possible delicacy as regards the Brahmans, must yet have been exceedingly humiliating to the pride of the Brâhmanical hierarchy. And the same difficulty meets us in the story of the defeat of Râma Jâmadagnya, the representative and champion of the Brâhmanical caste, by Dâśarathi, the hero of the epic.‖ Looking at the tenor of these episodes, we are not justified, in my opinion, in considering that they are later additions to the poem;¶ whatever may be their want of connection with the general narrative. They are found, it ought to be observed, in all the existing recensions. But then, in the episode of Viśvâmitra (the substance of which its narrator Śatânanda, the Purohita of Janaka, describes as having come down from the olden primitive times) there is found, as is well-known, that catalogue* of the Pahlava, of the Śaka mingled with the Yavana, of the Yavana-Kâmboja—that is of the Kâmboja, Pahlava, Yavana, Śaka, Varvara, Mlechha, Tushâra, Hârîta and Kirâta,‡ who were produced, at the command of Vasishtha, by his cow of plenty in order to defeat the army of Viśvâmitra. And the introduction of these names in such a connection could evidently be thought of as possible only at a time when, in point of fact, the hosts of the Pahlava, Śaka, and Yavana appeared actually almost to swarm up out of the earth and to sweep victoriously down upon the Indian Kshatriya, (for they annihilate the army of Viśvâmitra);§—in other words, just at the time when the Graeco-Bactrian and after them the Indo-Scythian kings held sway in the north-west of India.‖—And in perfect accord with what has been now stated, we find the following notices that are taken from the fourth book. When Sugrîva sends out his Monkeys to the four quarters of the

and in the Bombay edition (in I. 18, between 2 and 3). They are wanting, however, elsewhere also, as far as I [illegible] there, namely in A B C, see the Verz. der Berl. S. H. p. [illegible] [illegible] (Râm. II, [illegible] Bomb. II [illegible], A. [illegible]) is according to Schlegel (vol. I, pag. [illegible]) [illegible] as being wanting in the [illegible]. It is wanting also in [illegible]; at least the corresponding chapter there (II. 109) has a different beginning; but it will hardly do on this account to identify, as Gorresio seems inclined to do (vol. I. p. [illegible]), the [illegible] with this [illegible]. In that case the connection between the name [illegible] and the [illegible] in question would be given up; for the [illegible] are themselves [illegible]! And besides, the corresponding chapter in Schlegel (II. 101) agrees in this respect with Gorresio's text; it also has a different beginning,—[illegible].

* Cf. on this subject, Holtzmann Ueber den griechischen Ursprung des indischen Thierkreises, p. 31 ff.

† See, for instance, Muir, Original S. Texts, IV. 148ff. [illegible], and so also my notice of the Bombay edition of the Râmâyana in the Ind. Streifen II. [illegible]. We have to add to the statements there made regarding the extent of the work, that from the [illegible] (I, [illegible]), according to which it contains 500 sargas with 24,000 ślokas (a round number!)

‡ Vide Wheeler, p. lxxxv, 58, 65, 104, 208.

§ Cap. 51—65 in Schlegel.

‖ Ibid. Cap. 74—76.

¶ They might rather be regarded as ancient fragments incorporated by Vâlmîki into his work.

* Regarding the decisive circumstance in the matter (namely, that under the name Yavana we are to understand the Bactrian Greeks, or rather perhaps, by this time their successors) vide Ind. Streifen, II. 321. The name Yavana passed from the Greeks over to their Indo-Scythian successors, and finally to the Arabs.

† May we suppose that the words [illegible] (in ABC), have possibly a direct reference to the [illegible]? (Conf. [illegible] Ind. [illegible] p. [illegible].)

‡ Vide I. 55, 18—23, B, Gorr., I. 56, 18—23, A, Schlegel and Bomb., I. 55, 1—[illegible], Gorresio, and the relative passages in A B C (by A B C, I mean those manuscripts which are designated by these letters in my Catalogue of the Sanskrit manuscripts in the Royal Library at Berlin, p. 119 ff.) they show, in the passage under consideration, a very special reference to the Greek recension. In B C there is another verse added which brings in also the [illegible] and [illegible]. [Prof. Weber collates here for purposes of comparison, the texts of all the recensions, taking B C as a basis. These need not be reproduced.—Ed.] § I, 55, [illegible].

‖ It is known that this very extended for a considerable time into India; at the time of the Periplus, Barygaza was the southern limit of Aryan India (vide Ind. Streifen, II. 371.) The passage in which Sîtâ says to Râvana, "between thee and Râma there is a difference wide as that between Saurâshtra and Sauvîraka" (Râm. III. [illegible] Gorr., cf. Mbhar. III. [illegible]) perhaps has reference to this subject, and illustrates the hatred felt towards the Sauvîras (who in the Mbhar. also are reckoned among the non-Brâhmanical peoples), and their Greek or Indo-Scythian government, and especially toward their Buddhistic proclivities (vide Ind. Stud., where however, a somewhat different view is taken). But also regarding Surâshtra as subject to Greek influence, see Ind. Stud. IV. [illegible] IX. [illegible]. The Greek feeling of nationality and especially the Greek culture, probably maintained their hold on the people in the parts of India referred to for a considerable time after the overthrow of the Greek kings.

earth, that they may search for the lost Sîtâ, the various regions are briefly described in their order, and the description is accompanied by an enumeration of the inhabitants. Regarding the west, for instance, we are told that the Monkeys are to search through the cities of the Yavana, the dwelling place of the Pahlava, and, in the neighbourhood of the same, the whole Pañchanada (Panjâb), Kashmir, (the Pârada, C.), Takshaśilâ, Śâkala, Pushkalâvatî, the Śâlva, and the mountain Maṇimant (Aratta, Kapiśa, Vâlhi, in AC.), the country of the Gândhâra &c.; and with regard to the north they are similarly directed to explore among the Gândhâra and the Yavana, the Śaka, Odra and Pârada (G., Chîna, Paurava, Mâlava AC.), the Vâhlîka, Ṛishika, Paurava, Kiṅkara (Kâmatha AC.), Chîna, Apara-Chîna (Parama-Chîna AC.), Tukhâra, Varvara, Kâmboja, (and Khasa? C.), also the Darada, and Himavant.* Here also the texts to which I have had access harmonize in the main;† and it is obvious that such notices‡ could belong only to a time in which the Yavana (that is, the Greeks), the Pahlava, Pârada, Śaka, &c. were settled in the north-west of India, and were consequently neighbours, as specified, of the Kâmboja, Bâhlika, Darada, Gândhâra, &c. In another passage, in the second book,§ the Yavana at least appear in the immediate neighbourhood of the Śaka; this occurs, however, in addition to Gorresio, only in A, while the other texts show a variety of readings.

A second point that calls for examination here is one that has already been largely discussed, namely, the horoscope of the birth of Râma and his brothers: more specifically, the names given to the zodiacal figures,‖ karkata (with kulîra) and mîna. It will be remembered that A. W. von Schlegel looked on the mention of these names as a proof not only of the high antiquity but even of the Indian origin of the Zodiac.¶ But since the appearance of Holtzmann's admirable memoir *Ueber den griechischen Ursprung des indischen Thierkreises*, (Karlsruhe 1841), it is hardly possible for any one longer to doubt that the truth is quite the other way, and that the converse position is the correct one. The evidence brought forward, to use my own words on a former occasion,* "furnishes only an additional proof of what has been made sufficiently clear from other sources, namely, the late date of the composition of the *Râmâyaṇa* itself, though certainly only of that recension,' in which the passage in question occurs. For as the Zodiac, in the particular form in which it is found among the people of India, "was completed by the Greeks only in the first century B.C. it could not possibly have found its way into India earlier than this age, we may be pretty sure, until several decades later; and a considerable time must have elapsed before this new conception could have so become, as it were, the possession of the people so that the poet could refer to it as something perfectly well-known."† And although the horoscope is certainly wanting‡ in the Bengal recension and also in A. B. C.,§ yet it is found without any material variations in the [illegible], in Schlegel's

* IV. 43, 12 ff. Gorr.

† The Bombay edition gives nothing corresponding to the first passage (in IV. 43, 12 Gorresio's v. 9 comes immediately after his v. 17); and in the second passage which fully agrees with Gorr. as far as the matter in question is concerned, it reads thus: Kâmboja-Yavanâṁś chaiva Śakânâṁ pattanâni cha | anvîkshya Varadâṁś (Daradâṁś?) chaiva Himavantaṁ vichinvatha (?) || [The detailed statements in G. A. C. taking up so a table given by the author, need not be detailed here.—Ed.]

In Gorresio, vol. IV. p. 301, we find the following various reading of the verse IV. 42, 21, represented as occurring in Cod. G.—

[illegible] Pahlavasthânam [illegible] |
[illegible] chaiva [illegible] ||

And here perhaps we may find a still further direct trace of the Greek dominion. In case the reading which occurs here, and which is certainly very doubtful (see the *Varietas lectionis* given by Prof. Weber—Ed.), should need to be confirmed from other sources, we might very fairly cite (vide *Ind. Stud.* V., 150) the name of the city Dattâmitrî, in the Sauvîra, in Pân. IV. 2, 76, which there appears to have been founded by the Sauvîra-king Dattâmitra, who is mentioned in the Mahâbhârata as the contemporary and the opponent of Arjuna, but regarding whom Lassen (vide *Ind. Alterth.* I. 653n.) seems not disinclined, following Tod's example, to believe that we are to find in him a trace of the Bactrian King Demetrius (the son of Euthydemus), who reigned (according to Lassen, II., 298-300, xliv.) from about 200 to 165 B.C. With reference to a conjecture, which certainly receives considerable support from the [illegible] that have just been quoted regarding the city Dattâmitrî, [illegible] made use of [illegible] to the effect that a city in Arachosia moreover, bore his name (Demetrias), and was probably founded by him, vide Lassen, II. 301. It should be added that inscriptions [illegible] with regard to the city Dattâmitrî that it numbered Yavanas i. e. Greeks among its inhabitants. This has been confirmed by the mention of a Dhâtamitiyaka Yonaka; vide *Journal Bombay Branch R. As. S.* V. 54, *Indische Skizzen* p. 87, 88.

‡ A similar use has already been made of these notices by the Abbé Gorresio in a note on the Râmâyaṇa (p. 227—31) in his curious book *[illegible] Indienne* (Paris, 1847).

§ II. 3, 10, Gorr.

‖ I. 19, 2, 3; II. 18, 9, Schlegel.

¶ Vide *Z. für die Kunde des Morgenl.* I. 3[illegible] ff.; 373 [illegible] ff.

* Vide *Ind. Stud.* II. 240, 241. 1852.

† See my Preface to the translation of *Mâlavikâ* p. xxxiv v. 1856.

‡ Vide Kern, Preface to Varâhamihira's *Bṛihatsaṁhitâ* p. 49.

§ All three manuscripts agree here also; and indeed the first two verses of the chapter in question, quoted in the *Catalogue of the Berlin Sanskrit Manuscripts*, follow the closing verse of Chapter 18 in Gorresio.—Conf. the verses following Gorr. 18. 6, in MSS. A, B, & C.

and in the Bombay editions. It is certainly remarkable, however, that throughout the remainder of the work, so far at least as I can at present remember, although astronomical facts are frequently mentioned, there is no further reference to the Zodiac.* And therefore the suspicion naturally suggests itself, that the particulars regarding the horoscope of the nativity were introduced at a later period by zealous astrologers, who were anxious both to obtain and to impart exact information regarding an event of so great importance.† But even if we refrain, on account of this uncertainty, from insisting on the validity of the inferences which might otherwise be legitimately drawn from the mention of the Zodiacal signs, and do not therefore press their bearing on the question as to the time at which the *Ramayana* was composed, yet the notices in the poem of other astronomical matters furnish also at least some support to the opinion already indicated. For, besides the mention of the zodiac,‡ there are also frequent references to the planets; and we know that the Indian astronomers acquired their knowledge of the planets at a comparatively late period—considerably subsequent, at least, to the dates hitherto assigned to the *Ramayana*—the first mention of them occurring in the *Atharvaparis'ishta* and in Yajnavalkya (I. 294 ff.).§ And the peculiar relations which exist, just in three oldest passages in which the planets are mentioned, between Mars and War, between Mercury and Commerce, between Jupiter and Sacrificial Ritual,‖ appear to point with certainty to the fact that the Indian astronomers were indebted to the Greeks for their knowledge of the planets; for neither their Indian names, nor the deities associated with them, afford the smallest explanation of such relations.

Reverting now to what I have said under the first head, regarding the politico-geographical aspect of the question, as to the time when the poem was composed, I beg in the *third* place to call attention to the fact that in the *Ramayana*, Ceylon¶ is never called Tâmraparṇî or Sinhala (or—though it is true that this was hardly to be looked for—Pâlisimunta),* by which names alone the island was known to the Greeks (Taprobane in the earliest times, Palaesimundu at the time of the *Periplus*, Salike or Sielediba in the time of Ptolemy and of Kosmas Indicopleustes),—but that throughout the poem it is designated only by the name Lañkâ, which was unknown to the Greeks, and which we meet with (except in the *Mahawanso*—p. 67, for instance) for the first time in an *Atharvaparis'ishta* (on the Kûrmavibhâga; and indeed in the form Lañkâpurî connected with Sinhala†) and next in Âryabhaṭa, Varâhamihira, &c.—The geographical horizon of the *Ramayana* (which may also be referred to here) is naturally more extensive than that of the *Mahabharata*, inasmuch as the original story of the latter confines itself to the description of a little bit of Hindustan, while the *Ramayana* carries us as far south as to Ceylon. But it has already been remarked by others, that the *Ramayana* shows by no means an exact acquaintance with the geography of the Dakhan.‡ It is evident, on the other hand, from passages here and there, that the poet possessed a special acquaintance with the North-West of India. This appears, for instance, in the episode of Vis'vâmitra (vide

* Even in the second passage, although one of the zodiacal signs is mentioned in Schlegel's edition, and with reference to the nativity (II. 15, 3, [illegible] (sic!) [illegible]), yet the Bengal recension has nothing corresponding, but merely (II. 15, 3, [illegible]).

† It is perfectly evident that we have to do here with a purely arbitrary guessing at the time and not with an actual date. See my *Abh. über die Naksh.* I. 394. Bentley, among others, has also attempted to calculate from Râma's horoscope the year in which he was born, the result being the year 961 B. C.—and for the time of the composition of the *Ramayana* the year 285 A. D. (*Hindu Astronomy*, London, 1825 p. 14 ff.). Gaskin, in his *Astronomia Indicana*, p. 214, fixes the latter event more exactly as having taken place in 146 A. D. The notices regarding the horoscope do indeed furnish a certain groundwork for calculations regarding the latter event; but they can hardly be used for this purpose of course, so as to determine exactly the precise year in question (compare what is said e. g. in the *Ind. Stud.* X. 238 ff. regarding what is essentially the same calculation). Besides, the notices referred to have after all a bearing only on those texts (that is, manuscripts) in which they occur—and not on the time at which the *Ramayana* itself was composed.

‡ Vide e. g. I. 21, 24, 72, 18; II. 4, 20, II, Schl.; V. 80, 1, 3, 74, 15, 16, ff., Gorr.

§ Cf., however, Manu, I. 24; VII, 121. Regarding the late period at which mention is made of the planets by Indian writers, see *Ind. Stud.* II, 260, 261, IX. 363; X. 319, *Indian and European*, p. 339, 340; *Jyotisha*, p. 14. Regarding the recent origin of the verse in the *Yajus*-recension of the *Jyotisha*, in which the Zodiac and Jupiter are mentioned, see my Treatise on that work, p. 11, 22; and on a passage ascribed to Baudhâyana, see my *Abh. über die Naksh.* II. 390.

‖ Vide *Ind. Stud.* VIII, 413, X, 319.

¶ Vide Lassen, *Ind. Alt.* I. 200-201. Gorresio, Introd. to vol. I. p. c.

* The name of the rakshasî Siñhikâ, on the island between Ceylon and the mainland, IV. 41, 44, V. 8, 1 Gorr. appears to contain a play upon the name Sinhala.

† Vide *Verz. der S. H. der Ber. Bibl.*, p. 94.

‡ An excellent opportunity offered itself for showing such an acquaintance in the description of the regions to be visited by the messengers sent out by Sugrîva (IV. 40, 17 ff. Gorr.)—This digvijaya of the *Ramayana* deserves to receive special treatment (cf. Hall's Edition of Wilson's *Vishnu*. II. 156 ff.). Gorresio's Text and the Bombay edition differ materially in this matter; A C follow Gorr., in the main; in this respect, for instance that instead of Yavadvîpa, the island of Java, IV. 40, 30 (cf. Kern, Introd. to the *Brihats.* p. 10) they read Jaladvîpa (A, owing to a clerical error, has only Jadvîpa).

supra), in Bharata's return journey from his uncle, and in the journey of the messengers who were sent to fetch him.* In Râvana's palace in Lankâ, Hanumant sees† noble horses from the North-West: Âraṭṭajâṅś cha Kâmbojân Vâhlikân śubhalakshaṇân, | śukânasâṅś cha turagân . . . . ; and the powerful hounds which Bharata takes home with him as a present from Aśvapati‡ re-appear in the accounts of the Greeks regarding the country of the Kekaya.§

I remark further, in the fourth place, that although the word saṃskṛita is applied in the Râmâyaṇa‖ in a manner which shows that it had not yet come to be used in its technical meaning as the name of the "Sanskrit"¶ language, yet it is evident that the use of the latter name was just about to come into existence. And accordingly we find frequent reference made to a literature already very widely developed, and designated by names that are comparatively modern (śâstra, for instance, used throughout as the name for a treatise, both standing alone,** and as the second part of compound words, as shown in the examples given below). Thus, in addition to the Veda,†† and the vedâṅga, consisting of six aṅga,‡‡ specially the śikshâ§§ (mantrâḥ śikshâkshara[illegible]vitâḥ) in addition to the sûtra and bhâshya,‖‖ sûtra and kalpa¶¶, kalpasûtra,* the following are also mentioned by name: the dhanurveda with sûtra, upâṅga, upanishad and rahasya,† the gândharvavidyâ,‡ astronomy§ (jyotirgaṇitâ[illegible]

nishyâtâḥ), gaṇakâḥ‖ writing and reckoning (lekhya-saṃkhyâ),¶ the arthaśâstra,** and all kinds of arts (śilpa†† and kalâ),‡‡ the nâṭaka,§§ but especially the dharmaśâstram,‖‖ the nîtiśâstram,¶¶ the nyâyaśâstram,* (cf. naiyâyika,† and the ânvîkshikî buddhi,)‡ In this place also may be noticed the frequent references to the heretical views of the materialists and the unbelievers, laukâyatika,§ and nâstika.‖ In addition to these, there are direct quotations: e.g., the Hastibhir gîtâḥ ślokâḥ¶ (regarding enmity among relatives), Kaṇḍuṇâ gâthâ[illegible]** (regarding those that pray for help), paurâṇî gâthâ,†† imam purâṇam dharmasaṃhitam . . . . Rikshena gîto yaḥ ślokaḥ‡‡ Finally, we may also refer here to the mention of Dhanvantari as king of the physicians,§§ and father of Suśruta,‖‖ as also to the representing of Jaimini,¶¶ Kâtyâyana,* Jâbâli and Mârkaṇḍeya as among the royal counsellors,† in Ayodhyâ.—Although these literary data, which I have taken, for the sake of unity, exclusively from the Gauḍa recension,‡ by no means enable us to determine the precise time at which the poem was composed, yet they certainly furnish, on the other hand, decisive evidence against so high an antiquity as has hitherto been assigned to the Râmâyaṇa.

Nor, fifthly, do the data relating to the history of religion, which are furnished by the Râmâyaṇa, give any certain evidence that a high antiquity should be assigned to the poem. Specially noticeable in this connection is the

* I. 68, 18 ff., II. 70, 9. 11—19, 73, 9 ff. Gorr. Lassen Ind. Alt. II. 520.

† V. 12, 36.

‡ II. 72, 24.

§ Alexander receives from Sopeithes as a present 150 of such hunting dogs; vide Lassen, Ind. Alt. II. 14).

‖ Vide Ind. Streifen, II. 52.

¶ As distinguished from the deśabhâshâ; I. 41, 8, Gorr.

** E. g. I. 12, 19. II. 108, 60, 68.

†† The prasthâpada is the month for the ad[illegible]dhyâya of the Sâmaga IV. 27, 10.

‡‡ E. g. I. 5, 20 6, I. 71. 6, 18, 72. 89, 4. V. 18 41. 32, 5.

§§ I. 13, 18. ‖‖ I. 11, 6. ¶¶ I. 13, 21.

* I. 14, 3. † I. 34, 10, 70, 20. 80, 27. V. 72, 8.

‡ I. 79, 21. 82, 4. § I. 80, 23. ‖ I. 12, 7.

¶ I. 80, 2, 20.

** I. 80, 28. V. 1. 83. In this class also, e. g., hastiśikshâ and rathaśikshâ,—treatises (? or merely: information ?) regarding the management of elephants, and the preparation (guiding ? Vide I. 78, 21) of war-chariots; cf. Kâdambarî, I. 67; Wilson, Hindu Theatre, I. 14.

†† I. 80, 4. ‡‡ I. 79, 22.

§§ II. 71, 4. nâṭakânyapare chakrur (prâhur Schl. II, 69, 4) hâsyâni vividhâni cha; cf. naṭa in combination with nartaka I. 12, 7 (Schl. and Gorr.) II. 67, 15 (Schl., not in Gorr. II. 69).

‖‖ I. 79, 28.

¶¶ I. 78, 23. 80, 6, 27. Cf. the reference to the [illegible] vaśam, III. 60, 17.

* I. 80, 4. † II. 116, 1.

‡ II. 109, 29. (in the Kachchha-Sarga, however).

§ II. 109, 32, (also in the Kachchha-Sarga).

‖ I. 5, 12, Ramâyaṇa II. 109, 34 (ibid.) 110, 36 (of Jâbâli). III. 49, 6. IV. 66, 46.

¶ V. 86, 9. ** VI. 91, 7. †† VI. 116, 2.

‡‡ VI. 99, 22. §§ I. 46, 22. ‖‖ I. 86, 22.

¶¶ II, 83, 14. * I. 71, 4. VI, 112, 78.

† Similarly the old Vedic rishi, Vasishṭha, Vâmadeva, Gautama or Gautama, Maudgalya, Kâśyapa, Suyajña (I. 73, 6), and other names that have merely an etymological significance such as Suyajña, Sumantra, Vijaya—are mentioned among the royal gurus or counsellors; the former evidently only to enhance glories! Sumitrâ, the third wife of Daśaratha, is even spoken of as the daughter of Vâmadeva (by a boon!) I. 13, 6.—The passages regarding Vâlmîki's being contemporary with Râma are wanting in the Gauḍa recension, and are found besides only in some MSS. It is only when we come to the Uttarakâṇḍa (and Râm.-Bomb.) that the MSS. agree in recording (III. 47, 31, 1 f.) that Sîtâ came into his hermitage and there gave birth to her two sons, whom he afterwards taught to repeat the Râmâyaṇa. Vâlmîki thus appears to be a new acquaintance of Râma; so that those passages in the previous books which speak of an earlier meeting having taken place between them, must evidently have been added at a later period.—In the peculiar position which Jâbâli occupies in the Râm., I am inclined to recognise a slight trace of the pique which probably animated our poet, a follower of the black Yajus (vide supra p. 123 b, n.§) against the Jâbâla-school of the white Yajus.

‡ Regarding the mention of Buddha, in II. 109, 33 (ed. Schlegel), vide supra p. 122 a, n.**

absence of any reference to Krishṇa or the Krishṇa-worship,* though of course the only legitimate inference to be drawn from this silence is that we must not push the date of the work too far back.† The same remark applies to the absence of any mention of the Dâkinî and (if I do not mistake) of the Vidyâdhara. The Vedic gods, however—for instance, Indra, Vâyu, Agni, Rudra—are repeatedly mentioned, and frequently as taking part in the action of the poem; but alongside of them, and decidedly ranking as the principal deities, we find Brahman, Vishṇu (Nârâyaṇa), and Śiva; and, as we have already seen, one of the chief tendencies of the poem, in its present form at least, is a distinctly implied desire to exalt Vishṇu above the other gods. Whether the legends that specially serve to favour this and other aims, regarding the pious Śavarî, and regarding Śarabhanga, Kabandha and Virâdha, are to be ascribed to a Christian origin (as Monier Williams thinks)‡ or to a Buddhist one (which is my own opinion)§ is a question which must probably be left in the meantime undecided; but, in any case, completely to strike them all out of the original text, and to regard them only as later additions, would certainly be attended with considerable difficulties.‖

I refer, in the sixth and last place, to the diction of the work, as exhibiting on the whole decidedly less of a tendency to take liberties with the grammar, than is shown in the earlier parts of the *Mahâbhârata*. There is an important difference also in the form of the composition in the two works, and in this the *Râmâyaṇa* is at a disadvantage, as in it the concluding verses of the chapters (and the remark holds true of all the recensions) are constructed in various metres, more artificial than the simple epic śloka-measure. From this it is quite evident that a more artistically correct kâvya-form was aimed at; and accordingly the *Râmâyaṇa* is frequently designated as mahâkâvya.¶ The title of the chapters, sarga (not adhyâya), probably furnishes additional evidence in the same direction.

(*To be continued.*)

* Vide Gorresio: Introd. to Vol. I. 1843, p. xciii.

† It ought also to be said that this silence is capable of explanation by the rivalry of these two incarnations of Vishṇu, or rather by that of their respective followers. Râma undoubtedly represents an earlier stage of Vishṇuism; but it is certainly possible that his becoming the deity of a sect is due to some previous development of the Krishṇa-worship.

‡ Śavarî, indeed, recalls the "woman of Samaria."

§ Râm. Tâp. Up. p. 276.

‖ In connection with this part of the subject we may refer also to Śambuka in the Raghuvaṁśa and in Bhavabhûti; differently in the Uttarakâṇḍa 82, 2.

¶ See my Acad. Vorl. über Ind. Lit. G. p. 180, 181.

ON THE ANCIENT REMAINS IN THE KRISHNA DISTRICT.

(*From the Report of the late J. A. C. Boswell, Esq., M. C. S., offg. Collector Krishna District.*)

(*Concluded from page 155.*)

VII. *Forts illustrating the periods of the Oriya sovereigns, the Reddi Chiefs, the Vijayanagar or Narsinga dynasty, the Muhammadan conquest, the rise of the Zamindars, and the powers of the Marathas and Rohillas.* The most important forts in this district are those of Kondavid, Kondapalli, and Bellamkonda. These have interesting associations, and are worthy of preservation. The stones have been largely removed of late years, and used for building purposes. I would propose in future only to allow the loose stones to be removed, and to preserve the walls and buildings at present existing.

Kondavid.—This is a small range of hills about 1,500 feet high about 12 miles to the west of Guntur. There are two ghâts, that on the north is much the shortest, but very steep, there being an ascent of steps the whole way, the other ghât is more circuitous about two miles, but it is not so steep, and persons can be carried up by bearers. There are three forts of successive periods, the ruins of which still exist.

(1.) *The Puttakota.*—This, the most ancient fort, is said to have been built by Odiya sovereigns when they held this part of the country. It is situated in a valley between two spurs of the hill, and the mouth of the valley was closed by a high embankment of earth and stone. A stone wall was also raised across the top of the valley. The area of the old fort is overgrown with jungle, but hid among the bushes and trees are to be found remains of temples, mosques, wells, rice-pounding mortars of stone, &c. The opening of the valley, where the wall was raised, faces the north-east. The whole drainage of the valley was let out through this wall by a sluice which may still be seen. The tradition of the place is, that this sluice having become choked, the heavy fall of rain during a single night inundated the whole fort, and drowned all the inhabitants.

(2.) *The Durgam or Kila.*—The second fort is situated on the top of the hill, the longer ghât is through the Puttakota, and on the top of the hill there is a gate known as *kattel dibbi* or firewood gate. By this ascent all supplies were brought up to the fort. The gate was originally surmounted by a building of four stories, each supported on rows of stone-pillars, but the two upper stories have fallen down. The third was in existence within the memory of those still living. The other gate known as *pedda darwaja* is on the north-west side towards Narasaraopet. It became the principal gate in later times, but there is reason to suppose that the other was originally the main gate. This fort is said to have been built by the Reddis. On entering the fort by the *kottal diddi*, there face one the two bungalows erected by Messrs. Rohde and Newill, which, however, are both considerably dilapidated.

The area of this higher fort is very extensive. There are high towers and battlements, ramparts loop-holed for musketry along every commanding eminence, overhanging the edge of deep precipices. The views from many of these forts looking over the low country is very fine. One of these points of vantage has been availed of for the erection of a colonnade or long mandapam known as *nirdyala tokkam*. Tradition says that this was the favourite resort of one of the old Reddi Chieftain who held the fort. There are the remains of the old treasury, magazine, granaries, and all sorts of stone godowns. One of these is a bomb-proof building, the interior of which is a well cut in the rock eleven feet by seven and four feet six inches deep. This was the receptacle used for the storing of ghee. Everywhere may be seen the foundations of dwelling houses, and the number of rice-pounding stone mortars is very great, giving evidence that a large number of persons must have, at one time been quartered in this hill fort. There are many springs on the top of the hill, and three large tanks, one leading into the other, so that when the first is filled, the second begins to receive its supply, and similarly again the third. There is also the remains of a *picota* showing that this was the method of raising water then employed. There are on the hill a number of temples, but all the images have been broken, or had their features chipped off through the iconoclastic zeal of the Mahommedans, who have also turned several of the temples into Mosques. One of these Mosques was transformed in this way by one Gulab Ghazi, and close beside it is the dargah or tomb, for the repairs of which there is an endowment of four Kuchelas of land in a village in Repalle Taluq. The holder of the Inam is bound to look after the repairs of the Mosque and tomb, and ascends the hill every Friday to light a lamp, as well as on the occasion of the principal festivals.

But the time when the Mahommedans gained possession of this fort was subsequent to the date when the third or lower fort on the south side was built. This is known as simply Kota, and owes its origin to the dynasty of Bijayanagar, better known as the Royals. Tradition goes that about the beginning of the sixteenth century the race of the Reddi sovereigns came to an end. The last old king died childless, and his seventy-two chiefs could not agree upon the selection of a successor. Krishna Deva Royalu, the most illustrious ruler of his race, heard of this state of things, and at once conceived the idea of acquiring for himself the old Reddi's kingdom and fort. His strong idea was to make religion the support of the throne, and his pious memory is still revered throughout the Northern Circars and Ceded Provinces, as the founder or restorer of many Hindu temples and Pagodas. Krishna Deva Royalu's idea on the subject of a union between Church and State was a worldly-wise policy, and for the protection afforded by the sovereigns to religion, he expected as a return that the priesthood, whom he endowed with wealth, should use all their influence to carry out his political views. Accordingly, it is said on the present occasion, he selected a wily and unscrupulous member of the sacerdotal fraternity, as his tool for the accomplishment of his ambitious designs. The Brahman was furnished with money, and directed to restore a magnificent temple of Gopinathaswami at the foot of Kondavid. A new image was to be consecrated and set up, and for the celebration of these rites, the presiding priest invited the seventy-two Chiefs to descend from their hill fortress. They came—the three score and twelve—and were all seated in the great hall. From thence one by one the officiating priest led them to the inner shrine to view the new representation of deity, and to bow before the image that the great Krishna Deva Royalu had set up. As they stepped into the *antaralikam* or inner hall, and bowed at the threshold, two ruffians, who were concealed in the chamber, stepped forward, and before the victim had time to raise a cry, precipitated him into a deep well whose mouth it was impossible to discover amid the surrounding gloom. One by one each Reddi Chieftain approached the shrine, and all shared one common fate, one common grave, and then all was easy for Krishna Deva Royalu to seize the fort. He preferred the plain, however, to the hill, and the third fort, as has been said, owes its origin to him. It has two entrances known as the *Kotapetta Darwaja* and the *Nadella Darwaja*. The ramparts of the fort still remain to a considerable extent, with the gates and streets paved with stone. There are a number of modern houses in the fort, and ruins, and blocks of cut stone, scattered all round. The chief feature of interest, however, in this fort is Gopinathaswami's temple. It is a very large building of stone, and the pillars are very fine, in some cases a cluster of five pillars carved out of a single block. The Mahommedans, however, have destroyed all the images, and converted the great hall into a Mosque. It remains as such to this day. To enter the hinder portion one has to go round to the other side. The *antaralikam* is to be seen where the well is said to have been dug which received the Reddi Chiefs.

The place is inhabited now by a colony of swallows which dazzled with the light of the torch as we entered, fluttered wildly about, and fell with outspread wings on the ground.

Kondavid hill has a considerable extent of pasturage which is leased out, and the contract supplies alone fetch some Rupees 300 a-year. The bamboo grows on the summit, and gives its name to one of the tanks.

The tradition and history of the place has been collected, a copy of the Telugu manuscript of which is in the possession of one of the village Karnams. Sir Walter Elliot is said to have taken the original, and left this copy instead.

Kondapilly.—This is an old hill fort which formerly belonged to the Nizam, it is about ten miles west of Bejwada. All along the road and in the town there are numerous remains of old Masjids, Ashur Khanas, Pirla Chawadis, and Muhammadan burying grounds. Not far from Ibrahimpatnam, on the north of the road, is a well, known as a well of the Minister of Krishna Deva Rayalu who lived about 1520. The fort is entered through three successive massive gates at the foot of the hill, and by the fort walls a considerable space is enclosed, all thickly overgrown with jungle and luxuriant cactus. Within the limits of the old fort were built the English Barracks, which are still standing, consisting of eight large rooms besides outhouses, all in tolerable order. There was formerly a detachment sent here from the Regiment stationed at Masulipatam, but the place is now entirely abandoned as a military post, and the old barracks are used by any visitors as a halting bungalow. Opposite the barracks is an English burying ground, enclosed by a mud wall, but the tombs are all of comparatively recent date. A few hundred yards from the bungalow, the ascent of the hill commences. It is a winding tortuous path between two hills, and the whole way for about three quarters of a mile is a climb by a staircase of stones placed in position to form steps. The labour of constructing this must have been great; many of the stones have the mark of blasting, and many are cut and trimmed as if they had previously been used for some other purpose. The ordinary mode of ascent is on foot, but visitors can be carried up by bearers. The bearers through practice go up with their burden very quickly. As one approaches the summit, the ruins of the old palace appear perched on a crest between the two hills, on either side of the Pass. The heights are fortified with towers, and loopholed ranges of battlemented wall show how strong the place must once have been. On every jutting crag and eminence there are works which completely command the Pass. The upper fort is entered through three enormous gateways in succession. This entrance is known as the *Dargah Darwaja*. The sides of the gateways, about fifteen feet high, are single blocks of granite, and the lintels about twelve feet wide are the same. The gate derives its name from the dargah or tomb of Ghulab Shah, who was killed here in fight. It was endowed with twelve kuchelas of inam land, which has been subsequently reduced to eight, yielding eight puttis of produce. The endowment is for the purpose of keeping the tomb in repair. It is a modern looking edifice, plastered white inside and out, in close proximity to the ruins of an old Masjid.

Immediately above this stands the *Tanisha Mahal* or palace. The fort is said to have been originally built by the Reddis who once ruled this part of the country, but this building is purely Muhammadan. The whole of the ground-floor consists of extensive cloisters, supported by stone-built pillars, and the roofs arched. Between the pillars, in some instances, partitions have been run up, so as to form separate chambers. This ground-floor was probably used as a barrack for troops. The floors are all paved with stone, and the masonry is exceedingly strong and good. At present these cloisters are used at night for the protection of the cattle which are sent up the hill to graze in large numbers. A small stone staircase leads to the upper floor, where there is a great hall over which a thatched roof was lately placed, when a party of gentlemen came up here to spend the Christmas Holidays. There are several bath-rooms with stone cisterns and pipes providing the escape for the water. There are the remains of a number of large and small chambers, but all [illegible]. The walls have been originally plastered, and the ornamental designs are still visible, some in excellent preservation. There is a balcony overhanging a large tank, a terrace leading past what was once the garden to the zenana. These apartments are surrounded by a high wall. There is a court-yard within having a large stone bath, to which water was conveyed by pipes, and there are the remains of various chambers all now [illegible]. The walls are covered with ornamental niches.

Leaving the zenana, a path leads to the great reservoir, which is supplied by a spring, and where the water never fails. It is very cold, and said to produce fever. The reservoir is of great depth. There are also several tanks on the hill which, however, dry up during the hot weather, and in the tanks several wells.

Beyond the reservoir is the granary, a massive building of stone supported on high arches, and so constructed that each compartment might be divided by stone walls, so as to make a number of separate receptacles for grain. There is but one entrance below, but each receptacle has an aperture at the top. The place is now inhabited by millions of bats which, continually flying about, give forth the sound of rushing water. Beyond the granaries are the magazines. All around the hill is strongly defended by towers and ramparts. Besides the

Dargah Darwâja, there is another entrance, known as Gudhunda Darwâja, on the other side of the hill, from which a path leads down towards Jagiapett. On the hill forms abound, and many flowering and odoriferous shrubs. There is a white and purple creeper (*samudrapala* the milk of ocean) which is very luxuriant. There is a good deal of jungle but no forest. One tree *Punugu chettu* grows in considerable abundance, and is much used by the *Moochis* of Kondapalli who are celebrated for the manufacture of figures as representations of all the castes and costumes. Some of these are very good. On the hill there are numbers of monkeys (*kondamuchu*). There is a Telugu manuscript containing the legends and history of this fort.

Bellamkonda.—There is an old fort of stone here, also said to have been built by the Reddis when they ruled the country. The fort is on the top of a high hill, and is termed a durgam or durg. The fortification still remains, and also the ruins of flat roofed dwelling houses, magazines, granaries, etc. There is a perennial spring at the top which supplies a reservoir. The hill is covered with jungle, and there are tamarind trees, custard apple trees, and bamboos. There is a pathway formed for the ascent.

Vinukonda.—This is the Hill of Hearing. Tradition says that here was the spot where, according to the localised legend, Râma first heard of the rape of his wife Sîtâ by Râvana. On the hill, about 600 feet high—a bare rock without vegetation, there is a temple of Siva under the designation of Râmalingeshwaraswâmi. The ascent is a very steep one, by steps cut in the rock, and cut stones piled to form steps. Close to the temple on the summit are two basins or artificial reservoirs of water revetted with cut stone. These never run dry. The larger one is known as Râmagundam, and is much resorted to for bathing. The other, which is much smaller, is known as Sîtâgundam, and it would be considered desecrative to bathe in it, as it is left for the goddess's private use.

There are three lines of fortification around the hill, one above the other, but the walls have been demolished, and the stones are gone for long distances. The fort is said to have been built when the Reddis held the country, and there are still to be seen the foundations of the old dwelling houses on the hill, magazines, granaries, etc. About a quarter of the way up the hill there is a large artificial reservoir with a perennial spring known as Tyga Bhavi. At the foot of the hill there is an old temple dedicated to Kodandarâmaswâmi and another to Prasanna Râmalingaswâmi; all around are the ruins of mantapams, and much cut stone.

There is a curious story attached to a large representation of Hanuman at the foot of the hill. It is known as *Tappal Anjaneyulu*, and it is said that when the country was held by Gunteppalli or Rayani Baskarudu, a Deshapanda, under the Muhammadan Government, he used to deposit his letters for Haidarabad at the foot of this image, and used to return the following day and find the answers. The monkey god is credited with a feat worthy only of the electric telegraph.

There is another fort with walls of mud and stone at the foot of the hill. This formerly belonged to the Malraj Zamindar's family. The fort is entirely in ruins, and the area has been given up for cultivation.

Dharanikota, Amravati, and Chintapalli.—Dharanikota is the site of a very ancient town, "the city of magic" as the name imports. The walls were pulled down by the late Vasireddi Zamindar to build the town of Amravati about a century ago. These buildings have also in time fallen into ruins. There were two hundred two-storied houses built for Brahmans, and the Zamindar's palace is reported to have had gilt and silvered tiles. The whole place is now a mass of ruins. There are to be seen the remains of large reservoirs and fountains and places for pleasure grounds. A long law suit, carried through many years regarding a disputed succession, dissipated the wealth of the family. The estate fell into arrears, and was sold by auction, and bought in by Government for a nominal sum. There are two brothers, the present representatives of this old and ancient Zamindari, who now live in a ruined tenement where their ancestors were once high lords, drawing a revenue of thirty or forty lacs a year. They are dependent on their mother's pension of Rupees 150 a-month. The fort at Chintapalli belonged to the same family, and is now also in ruins. Also another at Rajpett, which is in the same condition.

Gurjala.—At Gurjala in the Palnad there are the ruins of an old fort, the stones of which have been largely taken by the villagers to build their houses. It is said to have been originally ruled by Râja Narendrudu, the 6th descendant of the Pândavas (Kshatriyas).

There are also the remains of other stone forts in the Palnad, at Tummakota (this has lately been pulled down and levelled,) at Kambhampad, Gudi Nagarjunakonda, Tangeda, and Karempudi. At the latter place, outside the fort wall, there are several two storied mantapams or porticos, which are said to have been used by an old Brahmin in former days for the performance of his *japam* (prayers). He would recite his prayers at different quarters of the town at different hours of the day, high up in the second story of these *mantapams* where his devotions might be duly observed.

Agnigundala.—This place, in the Vinukonda Taluq, derives its name from the hot springs which are said to have existed here, but there are no traces of them now. The fort here belonged to the old Malraj family, and is now quite dilapidated, and the site unoccupied.

In the Vinukonda Taluq there are also the ruins of old forts at Vinukonda, which belonged to the

Sekamuri family, at Tangerala and Gummampad, the former an Agraharam, and the latter a Mokhasa village.

In the Nandigama Taluq there is an old Reddi fort or durgam on the north bank of the Krishna, a little to the east of Magetala at Gudimetla, known as Turangarmida. There are the ruins of mud forts built by the Vasereddi Zamindar at Nandigama, Raghavapuram, Ipolupad and Magallu; one built by Chava Narasaya at Krishnavedu, and one built by Chevamandla Venkataramanaiya Vedadi. There is another old fort at Itur, and one at Panugarshapeta, built about a century ago by the Muhammadan Governor or Tandala. The walls of both have fallen down. Jaggayapet is a town of considerable trade and importance in the Nandigama Taluq on the borders of the Haidarabad territory. A band of Rohillas once came here and burnt down the place. The people then built a square tower in the centre of the town for protection provided with narrow loopholes for musketry, but they never added the staircase to ascend to the top, and the tower would practically be of very little use as a means of defence. The town was surrounded by a high wall by the Vasereddi Zamindar of old time, a considerable portion of which remains. At each gate was built a temple. There are also forts in this taluq at Konakanchi, Dabbakupalli, Malkapuram, Mukkapeta, Annegutlapad, and Shir Muhammadpet. Also at Lingagiri, Shri Narasimhapuram, Gomugundla Sarvavaram, Kalampalli, Lakkavaram, and Amaravaram. These villages belong to the Lingagiri Zamindar. In Munagala, Nelamarru, Madhavaram, Repalli, Karivirala, Sripuram, Modugudamuda, Komarabanda, Ambugomula, Barayabudugudam and Brindavanapuram, villages belonging to the Munagala Zamindar there are also forts. In Vinukonda Division there are also forts in the villages of Tiruvur, Kalagara, Gampalagudem, Venagala, and Vishnupett. In the last-mentioned village the fort is not walled, but surrounded by a hedge of bramble; it is called Kampakota.

In the Bejwada Taluq there are two old ruined forts at Valavadam and Vallatur. At Bejwada, too, there was a fort; there are no signs of it at present, and in the Gudiwada Taluq at Kanukolanu, Vemavarapupad, Kaldindi, Venkatapuram, Chigurukota and Koluru; but none of them are worth preservation. In the Devarakota Zamindari of Bandar Taluq there are the ruins of a fort at Lakshmipuram, built about 200 years ago. There are also forts in this taluq at Yendapalli, Nunagegada, Nagayalanka, and Marapalam.

In the villages of Nujid Zamindari there are forts at Katur, Medur Kasbah, Nana Kasbah, Suravaram, Telaprolu, Gollapilli Kasbah, Nujid, Musunur, Vijiarny Kasbah, Rayanapalem, and Mutanapalle. There are also forts in some villages of Chatroy, Pentapad, Bahurjali, Gundugul, Ambarpett, and Elur Haveli Parganas, belonging to the Nedadavol Zamindari, which was transferred to Godavari District at the amalgamation of the late Guntur and Masulipatam Districts.

In the Nizampatam Sarkar of Repalli Taluq, there are also forts at Vellipalem, Kolavakaduru, Gangavaram, Yalaturpalem and Ammulalapalli.

There are also forts at Vallur and Undur belonging to the Vallur Zamindar. One at Avanigadda belonging to the ex-Divi Zamindar, and one at Malluveram belonging to that Zamindar.

There are also ruins of ancient forts in the Palnad Taluq at Kalavarnan, Macherla, Tangeda, Pulagurallu, Tumdalla, Gottalapad, Kanapalli, Pedda Munmaralu, Uldupalli, near Dachepalli, Gottipalli, Pulipadilingodam, Nagarjunakonda or Durg, Karampudi, Kamblampad, Gulli, Pondugal, Pillutla.

In Guntur Taluq at Nambur.

In Narasaraupet Taluq at Chilakalurpad and Kunkalagunta.

In Repalli Taluq at Repalli, Nuduamarru and Bachar.

In Vinukonda Taluq at Gundlapanpad, Konnadapad, and Chintalacheruvu, besides a number of smaller ones, or bastions in the Palnad Taluq at Mandampadu, Jampalla on a pagoda, Pedda Garlapadu, Kunnuhi, in the centre of the village, Pindi on a pagoda, Chilinipalli, Kaleburu, Machavaram, Pattavela, Gundlapad, Gottipalli, Velduru, Rayavaram, Pasvamula, Nangalavaram, Oppicherla, Adigoppala, Miryala, Pedda Kudavagunta, Bhunagalla, Jallepalem, Pulipad, Rentala, Rentachintala, Mandugalla, Pullagunta, Chenlagudepad, Gottimukkala, Nutta.

VIII. *The Mahals or palaces of Zamindars constructed within the last century.*—The best specimens of these are the palace of the ex-Zamindar of Narsaraupet, and the palace of the Devarakota Zamindar of Challapalli. These are each large piles of buildings in the Muhammadan style of architecture, four or five stories high. There is a very large hall on the ground floor and a gallery round it on the second floor, with five ranges of rooms above. The buildings are of brick plastered, with high Muhammadan arches. There are ornamental devices in plaster, and the woodwork is carved and painted in bright colours. There are extensive court-yards with reservoirs and fountains and gardens and shrubberies.

IX. *European remains.*—Tradition exists of the sea coast of this district having formerly been several miles inland of the present shore, and this is supported by a mark of an old beach along the eastern road to Masulipatam from China Ganjam. The black soil here gives place to a belt of sand from 5 to 10 miles in breadth, covering with the drift the elevated ridges generally found above high water mark, and then sloping gradually to the present coast. The general tradition is supported by a *Danda kavali*, describing the sea as having formerly extended nearly to the present town of

China Ganjam, and noting that so far back as A.D. 1234, some *Frangals* or European foreigners, probably Portuguese, carried on considerable traffic with Masulipatam for a time on the coast, and raised a town called *Franguluppetnam*, the remains of which are still to be seen in certain existing mounds *Frangala dinne*.

The Dutch were the first European settlers in Masulipatam, but the old Dutch burial ground at Masulipatam is all that remains to tell of their connection with the country. The Dutch Chapel has been converted into a private house, and that in time has been allowed to fall into ruins. The old Dutch tombs are finely carved with inscriptions and coats of arms in relievo letters. The dates of the tombs are from 1640—1725. In 1611 the English factory at Bantam attempted to open a trade with Pulicat, but were opposed by the Dutch. In the following year, however, they succeeded in establishing a trade at Masulipatam. In 1628 the English were driven from Masulipatam by the oppression of the native Governors, but five years subsequently the place was established as a factory through a *Firman* of the Nizam of Golconda. In 1689, owing to misunderstanding between the English and the great Mughal, the latter seized the factories at Masulipatam and Vizagapatam. In the following year an imperial *Firman* permitted the Company to re-settle in the district, and the following year the kowle for the Madras settlement, including the English factories of Masulipatam, Madapollam, Vizagapatam, etc., within the territories of the Golconda country, was granted, which emanated from Zulfikar Khan, the Mughal General in the Dekhan.

There is a French burying ground in the Town of Masulipatam, but the only tomb that has any inscription left is one to the memory of John Rowland, 1701. The Northern Sarkars were obtained by the French in 1753, and remained in their possession till 1759, when they were transferred to the East India Company, to whom they were finally ceded in 1766. The fort at Masulipatam was built by the English, but the greater part of the ramparts have, within recent years, been entirely levelled. It was designed by Sir Charles Trevelyan to level the walls, and lay out boulevardes and a people's park, but this idea was frustrated by the cyclone of 1864 that carried off some 30,000 souls and depopulated the fort.

FORMS OF GOVERNMENT, &c., AMONG THE DARDS.

By G. W. Leitner M.A., Ph.D., &c.

Chilas, which sends a tribute every year to Kashmir for the sake of larger return-presents, rather than as a sign of subjection, is said to be governed by a council of elders, in which even women are admitted. When I visited Ghilgit, in 1866, it was practically (without a ruler, the invading troops of Kashmir barely) holding their own within a few yards of the Ghilgit Fort—a remarkable construction which was blown up by accident last year.* There is now a Thanadar of Ghilgit, whose rule is probably not very different from that of his rapacious colleagues in Kashmir. The Ghilgitis are kept quiet by the presence of the Kashmir army, and by the fact that their chiefs are prisoners at Srinagar, where other representatives of once reigning houses are also under surveillance. Mahmud Ali Khan, the supposed rightful Râja of Ghilgit is there; he is the son of Azghar Ali Khan, son of Râja Khan, son of Gurtam Khan—but legitimate descent has little weight in countries constantly disturbed by violence, except in Hunza, where the supreme right to rule is hereditary. The Ghilgitis, who are a little more settled than their neighbours to the West, North and South, and who possess the most refined Dardu dialect and traditions, were constantly exposed to marauding parties, and the late ruler of Chitral, Gouhar-Amân, who had conquered Ghilgit, made it a practice to sell them into slavery on the pretext that they were Shiahs and infidels. Yasin was ruled by Mir Wali, the supposed murderer of Mr. Hayward, and is now a dependency of Chitral which is ruled over by Aman-ul-mulk. The Hunza people are under Ghazan Khan, the son of Ghazanfar,† and seem to delight in plundering their Kirghiz neighbours, although all travellers through that inhospitable region, with the exception of Badakhshan merchants, are impartially attacked by these robbers whose depredations have caused the nearest pass from Central Asia to India to be almost entirely deserted. At Ghilgit I saw the young Râja of Nagyr, with a servant, also a Nagyri. He was a most amiable and intelligent lad, whose articulation was very much more refined than that of his companion, who prefixed a guttural to every Khajunâ word beginning with a vowel. The boy was kept a prisoner in the Ghilgit Fort as a hostage to Kashmir for his father's good behaviour, and it was with some difficulty that he was allowed to see me and answer certain linguistic questions which I put to him. If he has not been sent back to his country, it would be a good opportunity for our Government to get him to the

* The only record is the drawing published in the *Illustrated London News* of the 12th February 1870.

† Major Montgomerie remarks "the coins have the word Gujanfar on them, the name, I suppose, of some celebrated animal. I was however unable to find out its meaning." The word is Ghazanfar [which means in *Arabic*: lion-hero] and is the name of the former ruler of Hunza, whose name is on the coins.

Panjáb in the present cold weather with the view of our obtaining more detailed information than we now possess regarding the Khajuná, that extraordinary language to which I have several times alluded.

The names of *Rá*, *Ráeh*, *Rája*, applied to Muhammadans, may sound singular to those accustomed to connect them with Hindu rulers, but it is the ancient name for King at Gilgit (for which Nawáb seems a modern substitute)—whilst Sháh Kator in Chitral, Tham in Hunza and Nagyr, Mihtr and Bakhta in Yassan, and Trakhné, in Gilgit, offer food for speculation. The Hunza people say the King's race is Mughalot (or Mughal); they call the King Ayeshah, and affirm that he is Aishen (this probably means that he is descended from Aisha, the wife of Muhammad). Under the king or chief for the time being, the most daring or intriguing hold office and a new element of disturbance has now been introduced into Dardistan by the Kashmir faction at every court (or rather robber's nest), which seeks to advance the interests or ulterior plans of conquest of the Maharaja, our feudatory. Whilst the name of Vazir is now common for a "minister," we find the names of the subordinate offices of Trangpá, Yarfá, Zeytá, Gaqá, &c., &c., which point to the reminiscence of Tibetan Government.

I need scarcely add that under a Government like that of Chitral, which used to derive a large portion of its revenue from kidnapping, the position of a slave-dealer (Diwan-begi) was a high official one. Shortly before I visited Gilgit, a man used to sell for a good hunting dog (of which the Dards are very fond), two men for a pony, and three for a large piece of patch (a kind of woollen stuff). Women and weak men received the preference, it being difficult for them to escape once they had reached their destination. Practically, all the hillmen are republicans. The name for servant is identical with that of "companion;" it is only the prisoner of another tribe who is a "slave." The progress of Kashmir will certainly have the effect of stopping, at any rate nominally, the trade in male slaves, but it will reduce all subjects to the same dead level of slavery and extinguish that spirit of freedom, and with it many of the traditions that have preserved the Dard races from the degeneracy which has been the fate of the Aryans who reached Kashmir and India. The indigenous Government is one whose occasional tyranny is often relieved by rebellion. I think the Dard Legends and Songs show that the Dards are a superior people to the Dogras, who wish to take their country in defiance of treaty obligations, and I for one would almost prefer the continuance of the present anarchy, which may end in a national solution or in a direct alliance with the British, to the *épicier* policy of Kashmir which, without shedding blood, has drained the resources of that Paradise on earth and killed the intellectual and moral life of its people. The administration of justice and the collection of the taxes in Dardistan are carried on, the former with some show of respect for religious injunctions, the latter with sole regard to whatever the tax-gatherer can immediately lay his hand upon.

HABITATIONS.

The villages, are situated on the main lines of road which, as everywhere in Himalayan countries, generally coincides with the course of rivers. The villages are sometimes scattered, but as a rule, the houses are closely packed together. Stones are heaped up and closely cemented, and the upper story which is often only a space shielded by a cloth or by grass-bundles on a few poles, is generally reached by a stair-case from the outside. Most villages are protected by one or more wooden forts, which—with the exception of the Gilgit fort—are rude block-houses, garnished with rows of beams, behind which it is easy to fight as long as the place is not set on fire. Most villages also contain an open space, generally near a fountain, where the villagers meet in the evening and young people make love to each other. Sometimes the houses contain a subterranean apartment which is used as a cellar or stable—at other times, the stable forms the lower part of the house. In Ladak, a little earth heaped up before the door and impressed with a large wooden seal, was sufficient, some years ago, to protect a house in the absence of its owner. In Dardistan bolts, &c., &c., show the prevailing insecurity. I have seen houses which had a courtyard round which the rooms were built, but generally all buildings in Dardistan are of the meanest description—the mosque of Gilgit, in which I slept one night whilst the sepoys were burying their dead two or three yards away from me, being almost as miserable a construction as the rest. The inner part of the house is generally divided from the outer by a beam which goes right across.

Water-mills and wind-mills are found. Cradles were an unknown commodity till lately. I have already referred to the wine and treasury-cellars excavated in the mountains, and which provided them with food during the war in 1866, whilst the invading Kashmir troops around them were starving. Baths (which were unknown till lately) are sheltered constructions under waterfalls; in fact they are mere sheltered douche-baths. There is no pavement except so far as stones are placed where there are no roads. The rooms have a fire-place, which at Astor, (where it is used for the reception of live coals) is in the middle of the room. The conservancy arrangements are on the slope of the hills close to the villages, in front of which are fields of Indian corn, &c., &c.—*Indian Public Opinion*, Dec. 1.

REVIEW.

THE STORY OF GAUTAMA BUDDHA AND HIS CREED: An Epic by RICHARD PHILLIPS. Longmans, 1871.

WE rise from the perusal of this elegantly got up volume with a feeling of disappointment. We had hoped for a solution of many of the problems which remain to students of Buddhistical literature; but to none of these does the author direct his attention. His sole object is an attempt to give "a reasonable narrative of Buddha and Buddhism, looking at these subjects of course from a poetical standpoint." These are stated so much better in prose by Hardy in his "Manual of Buddhism," that we should have thought the author would have abstained from "slaying the slain." We fully agree with Mr. Phillips in his notion that "the great Ascetic" deserves to be better known; but we cannot add the cheering hope that the present volume will in any degree advance the object most to be desired. The attractive beauty of Buddha's life, and the vast influence exercised by his creed over more than one-half of the human race, are in themselves powerful motives for an attentive study of his career. But the qualifications demanded for the task of able exposition are so numerous, that since the much-to-be-lamented death of Eugene Burnouf, we almost despair of hearing of an equally able commentator. There are Jaina works, Chinese works, Tibetan works, Pali works, and perhaps even Japanese works, to be carefully mastered before we gain full and accurate information as to the results of the teaching of Buddha and his missionaries on the Eastern races. The wonderful exertions made by the apostles of Buddhism, can only be likened to the great efforts put forth by the Jesuits during the earliest period of that great order; and the extraordinary resemblance is heightened by the fact that both employ only celibates as their agents.

From a careful perusal of this volume, we cannot in any way learn that the author has the least acquaintance with any of the Eastern languages; so that at the very outset he is prevented from adding to our store of knowledge. The other course which lay open to him of presenting in a compact form the results attained by the many able scholars who have devoted long years to the study has been utterly ignored. So that as far as the inquiring reader is concerned, he is exactly where he was.

Mr. Phillips tells us that "The poem," as he calls it, "is founded upon a theory; but nothing short of a full conviction of the soundness of that theory would have led the author to represent Gautama as a wilful deceiver, beguiling men to virtue; and thus by impeaching his moral character to lessen him in men's eyes. But if his moral character is lowered by this assumption, as undoubtedly it is, it must be allowed as a slightly compensating fact, that his intellectual status is considerably raised by it."

The work consists of about 600 stanzas spun out with unconscious perseverance, with little regard for rhyme and none at all for rhythm. Thus we take, entirely at random, a specimen which is no better than its neighbours:—

"Yes, unlike many, Sakya-Muni weighed
The Pundit's reasoning, and was not afraid,
Nor did he deem it impious to doubt
The Brahman's doctrines; as he soon found out
The measure of his wisdom; and discerned
Where lay his weakness: thus he soon had learned
All he could teach him. Thence he prepares
To seek for wisdom and for truth elsewhere."

MISCELLANEA, NOTES, AND QUERIES.

KANGRA.

As Jamu is the chief of all the States on the other side of the Ravi, so has Kangra always been regarded as the principal among a large circle of states on this side. The Katoch, or Kangra family, sprang from no mortal stock; the first Raja, Bhum Chand, was created from the perspiration from the brow of the Kangra goddess; not born, like other men, a puling infant, but cast perfect in a mould, a god-like man, prepared for mighty deeds. This appears somewhat startling, but as it occurred some eleven thousand years ago, perhaps we may allow ourselves to believe that things were differently managed in those days. Coming down to more recent days, we find the Greek historians, more than 300 years B.C., alluding to the mountain kings north of the Panjab. Almost all the noble families from the Ravi to the Satlej claim connexion with, or descent from, the Katoch family.

It is this extreme antiquity which makes Kangra, and particularly the Kangra Fort, of such value in the eyes of the natives of the district, who will still tell you that he who holds Kangra holds the Panjab. When the Muhammadans held sway in India, they plundered Kangra of immense treasure; but the idol was restored to the temple, and the Hindus again obtained possession in 1044 A. D. From that time till 1360 A. D., when Firuz Tughlak again plundered the temple, the history is uncertain. This Emperor is supposed by Mr. Barnes, to whose settlement report we are indebted for much of this history, to have resided in the Kangra fort, and to have there received, twenty-eight years after, Prince Muhammad Tughlak, who was a fugitive from Dehli.

Ferishtah tells us that the great Akbar, having subdued Kangra, received the Katoch King, Dharmchand, with kindness. In this reign the Fort at Kangra was held by Imperial troops; and the

Emperor Jehangir, after whom one of the gates of the fort is named, was so delighted with the Kangra valley that he proposed to make it his residence. The natives, who always sought every opportunity to rebel in their conquerors' absence, were naturally much opposed to this scheme, and the present inhabitants of Kangra will tell you that to prevent the Empire from settling there, the people collected an immense crowd of those who were affected with hideous goitres, and bringing them before Jehangir, warned him that as this terrible deformity was so common in the valley, he and his followers could not hope to escape. This is said to have caused him to remove to Kashmir.

In 1752 A.D. the Panjab passed from the Mughals to the Afghans; and from that time to 1764 A.D. it remained attached to the kingdom of Kabul; but Nawab Saifulah Khan, whom the Mughal Court had appointed commandant of Kangra, had still possession of the place, even when the hill chiefs resumed their territories, leaving him nothing but the lands immediately under the fort. In 1764 A.D. the Afghans, defeated by the Sikhs, crossed the Indus, never again to return, and the Panjab fell into the hands of the Sikh Sirdars; but Fort Kangra was not reduced until 1783 A.D. Saifulah Khan, an isolated Mughal governor, having held it all the intervening years, with no resources beyond the range of his guns. This fact proves the value of the fort as a military post in olden times. Even then it could not be taken by assault, and only fell when Saifulah Khan died in the siege, and his followers, disheartened by the loss, surrendered.

Jaya Singh, the conqueror, held the fort for four years, when he was forced to make concessions to a combined army of Sikhs and Katoch Rajputs, at Batala, in the Gurdaspur district, and fort Kangra, after many centuries, came into the hands of Sansar Chand, its legitimate chief. From the possession of this famous fort, Sansar Chand gained the chief power in the hills, and placed Kangra at the head of the eleven Jalandar principalities. Here he reigned for twenty years; but his continued aggressions at last brought him into trouble. He had attacked the hill state of Kalur, and its chief, unable to meet him in person, called in the Gurkhas to his assistance. This led to the terrible Gurkha invasion so much talked of even now by the inhabitants of the valley. The people fled to Chamba and to the plains, not a blade of grass grew in the Kangra valley; but amid all the horrors and confusion of the invasion, fort Kangra remained in the hands of the worsted Katochas, who were at last delivered from the Gurkhas by the interference of Ranjit Singh.

The Sikh, taking a large part of the Katoch dominions as a reward for his assistance, gave Sansar Chand the fort and a number of villages, which had always been allotted for the maintenance of its garrison; but year by year he encroached more and more on the Katoch independence, and in 1828 annexed the whole country. In 1839 Ranjit Singh died, and his disorganized soldiery, invading British territory, were punished. Lahor was occupied and the British army obtained possession of the Jalandar Doab in March, 1846. But even then, in the midst of a conquered country, cut off from all hope of succour and assistance, the native confidence in the strength of the Kangra fort was so great that it held out, in spite of warnings, until a British brigade had actually invested it, when the Sikh Governor agreed to evacuate on condition that he and his men were allowed a free and honourable passage.

It would be difficult to exaggerate the value which natives set on fort Kangra; it is a most sacred place, consecrated by its idols and its antiquity; it is of the highest political value, for any native chief holding Kangra would be paramount in the hills; and the native idea of its military importance is high, and were it unoccupied, it would be immediately seized as a great prize, in case of any disturbance in the Panjab.

After it fell into the hands of the British, the fort was first garrisoned by native troops; and, when the country was supposed to be sufficiently quieted down, they were replaced by a hill corps which was then formed. But in the same year in which this change was made, the Multan insurrection broke out, and it was thought necessary to replace regular troops in the Fort. Ram Singh was only prevented from attacking and perhaps recapturing the garrison there in 1848, by a sudden movement of Captain Davidson's and Major Fisher's irregular horse to its succour. This Ram Singh during his short-lived power was joined by about 600 men, and was only dislodged by Mr. John Lawrence, now Lord Lawrence, bringing up reinforcements and driving him out of the Nurpur Fort.—*Panjab Times*, Nov 21.

A LAKE LEGEND OF THE CENTRAL PROVINCES.

LAKE Tarola in the Chanda district, situated 14 miles east of Segaon, in a basin of the Chimur hills, at a considerable height above the plain, is believed by the natives of the surrounding country to owe its origin to enchantment. It is far from any village, and though artificially embanked at one point, has all the appearance of a natural lake. Its depth is very great and the water is considered to be of peculiar excellence. In the early ages—so runs the legend—a marriage procession of Gavalis was passing through these hills from the west. Hot and thirsty they sought for water but found none, when a strange-looking old man suggested that the bride and bridegroom should join in digging for a spring. Laughingly they consented, and with the removal of a few spadesful of earth a clear fountain leapt to the surface. While all were delightedly drinking, the freed waters rose and spread into a wide lake, overwhelming bride, bridegroom, and procession; but fairy hands soon constructed a temple in the depths, where the spirits of the drowned are supposed to dwell. Afterwards on the lake-side a palm tree grew up, which only appeared during the day, sinking into the earth at twilight. One morning a rash pilgrim seated himself upon the tree-top, and was borne into the skies, where the flames of the sun consumed him. The palm then shrivelled into dust, and in its place appeared an image of the spirit of the lake, which is worshipped under the name of Tandia. Formerly at the call of pilgrims, all necessary vessels rose from the lake, and after being used were washed and returned to the waters. But at last one evil-minded man took those he had received to his home; they quickly vanished, and from that day the mystic provision wholly ceased. In quiet nights the country-folk still hear faint sounds of drum and trumpet passing round the lake.

> " She is not dead, she has no grave,
> She lives beneath Lough Ulle's water,
> And in the murmur of each wave,
> Methinks I catch the songs I taught her."

The old men say that in one dry year, when the waters sank low, golden pinnacles of the fairy temple were seen glittering in the depths.

> " On Lough Neagh's banks as the fisherman strays,
> On a cold calm eve's declining,
> He sees the round towers of other days,
> In the wave beneath him shining."

The lake is much visited, especially during the months of December and January, and the rites of the god are performed by a Gond. Wives seek its waters for their supposed virtue in causing fertility, and sick persons for health. Fish in the lake grow to a large size, the skeleton of one which was stranded some years ago measuring 8 feet in length.

MARCO POLO'S ROUTE FROM YUNAN.

In his report on Western Yunan Dr. Anderson seeks to identify the route traversed by the expedition from Bhamo to Momein with that described by Marco Polo as having been taken by him on his journey from the Court of the Great Khan to the capital of Mien or Burmah. So far as any conclusions can be drawn from so fragmentary a narrative as that of the famous old traveller, the supposition seems probable enough. Marco Polo's route seems to have been from Yunan (Karazan) ten days journey to Talifu (Yachi); and thence five days journey to Yungchan (Vochang). After leaving this province, Marco Polo goes on to say, " you come to a great descent; in fact you ride for two days and a half continually down hill. On all this descent there is nothing worthy of mention except only that there is a large place there where occasionally a great market is held. * * * After you have ridden those two days and a half down hill, you find yourself in a province towards the south which is pretty near to India, and this province is called Amien. You travel therein for fifteen days through a very unfrequented country and through great woods abounding in elephants and unicorns and numbers of other wild beasts. * * * And when you have travelled those fifteen days through such a difficult country as I have described, in which travellers have to carry provision for the road because there are no inhabitants, then you arrive at the capital city of this province of Mien, and it also is called Amien and is a very great and noble city."—(Yule's *Marco Polo*, II., 45, 52, 70 f.) This passage has presented considerable difficulty to Col. Yule in his admirable commentary, because, as it seems to us, he has erroneously counted the 17½ days' journey from Yungchan. Col. Yule is thus driven to the supposition that Marco Polo descended from Yungchan to the Shweli tributary of the Irawadi, and performed the rest of the distance by water. There are many difficulties in the way of this supposition, a supposition however which is rendered necessary on the assumption that Marco Polo's distances are to be calculated from Yungchan. But it will be observed that Marco Polo speaks of leaving the province merely and not the town. This province is called Kardandan, a name however which is probably only used to designate a portion of Karazan, a word which Dr. Anderson would connect with the Kakhyen mountains north-east of Momein, and which probably included most of the country which now goes by the name of Yunan. Of Marco Polo's descent of 2½ days' journey Dr. Anderson writes:—" I do not know of any more accurate description that could be given of the descent from the Shan states over the Kakhyen hills to Burmah. * * * Starting from the Shan-Chinese town of Manwyne at the eastern end of the Sanda valley, where the descent begins, the journey occupies exactly two days and a half. So closely does Marco Polo's account of the route to Burmah coincide with the two roads that follow the valley of the Taping over which I travelled, that I cannot but conclude that it referred to one of these, but his description being devoid of details, it is impossible to say which of the two routes he had in view." Dr. Anderson would further fix the market referred to at Old Bhamo, which, he says, is distant from the capital of Mien or New Pagan in a straight line about 180 miles. Dr. Anderson endeavours to strengthen his position by a reference to certain curious customs which are mentioned by Marco Polo and of which he found traces in the Shan states. Such customs are the use of tallies, the consultation of persons supposed to be possessed of a devil, the docking of horses' tails, and the relative values of gold and silver. But after the lapse of six centuries, we are not inclined to attach much weight to mere coincidences of this nature, at any rate in determining the line of direction of any particular route. All that can be said is that Dr. Anderson's supposition is as probable as any other—he found traces of a substantial bridged road the whole way from Bhamo to Momien,—and more probable than that advanced by Col. Yule. We have no doubt that that eminent savant will find much in Dr. Anderson's report that will serve to illustrate future editions of his exquisite work on the great traveller of the thirteenth century.—*Indian Observer, Jan. 13.*

TEMPLE AT TRIPETTY.

The *Asiatic Journal* furnishes particulars of the Hindu temple of Tripetty, eighty miles from Madras, the precincts of which had never been "profaned" by Christian or Muhammadan till the Madras police invaded it the other day. The exterior even had not been seen but by genuine Hindus. The temple is in a village near the centre of a long range of hills running almost North and South. At different distances round the hills are gates, the last at the top, and the pilgrims all pass through these on their way up. The mere sight of these hills so gratifies Hindus, that leagues off, upon first catching a glimpse of them, they fall prostrate, calling on the idol's name. The idol is worshipped by votaries who pour in from all parts of India, under a thousand names, but the three principal ones are Vengataramana Swami, as the expeller of evil and bestower of good; Sreenewaasaswami, implying the habitation of Sri, the Indian Ceres; Seshachellawasa, implying the habitation of Sesha, Seshachella being the name of the hills, derived from *Sesha*, the king of serpents, and *achala* a mountain. The legend is that Vishnu assumed the appearance of a serpent and transformed himself into the Tripetty hill. The idol in the temple is an erect stone figure almost seven feet in height, with four arms, personifying Vishnu; one right hand contains a *chakra*, or war mace, the other points to the earth, alluding to the sacred origin of the hill; one left hand holds the *shank*, or holy shell; the other holds the lotus. The Brahmans assert that the temple was erected at the commencement of the *kali yuga*. This period is to last 5,000 years, when Vishnu's worship on earth is to cease, and the Hindus are taught to expect his last and most glorious incarnation in person, terminating the days of "contention and baseness." We are further told by the historian of the temple, that it is distinguished by the oblations which are offered to the idol by Vishnu's votaries from all parts of India. Princes send their vakils, or ambassadors, to present their offerings to the shrine; whilst the poorer peasant, who may have little else to offer, wraps up some petty oblation in a piece of wax-cloth. The cause of these offerings is as follows. The idol smitten with love for the charming *Padmavati*, daughter of a certain king, determined to marry her, but wanting money he had to seek the aid of Kuvera. This god however directed that the money thus lent should be repaid annually to the sovereign of the countries lying between the Pálar and Suvarnmukhi rivers, and so it comes to pass that votaries pour in great numbers during the Brahmotsavam, or nine-day celebration of the nuptials, and annually, at this period, two-thirds of the usual collections are made. The Brahmans say that the Hindu rulers allowed the offerings to be entirely employed on the spot in religious ceremonies, but the Musalman rulers appropriated them. During the early wars between the English and the French, this source of revenue was one of the first fruits of our conquests. These offerings are made generally from interested motives, and are of every diversity of articles conceivable; gold and silver lamps, coins of all sorts, bags of rupees, copper money, spices, assafoetida, the hair cut off the head, frequently vowed from infancy, and given up by some beautiful virgin in compliance with her parent's oath. A man who is lame presents a silver leg; if blind, a silver or gold eye. The jewels which a woman has worn with pride from infancy, are voluntarily left before the idol; she appears with a shabby cloth before the stone god, and presents a splendid one, which has never been worn; she tears the bangles from her child's legs and prays that the idol will shower down blessings on her and hers.—*Delhi Gazette*, 28th *Dec.* 1871.

THE SAMLAJI FAIR.

Almost on the border line between Mahi Kanta and Mewar, stands the famous shrine of the much venerated god Samlaji. The river Meshwa meanders over its rocky bed in the valley immediately below, and the waters of a splendid natural lake, of great beauty sparkle amid the well-wooded hills at the foot of which lies the road (if it can be so termed) that leads to [illegible], a village in the territory of the Raja of Dungarpur. To this shrine of Samlaji there used to collect once a year, in the beginning of the cold weather, some seventy or eighty thousand pilgrims and traders. The shrine has existed for 500 years, but the fair unfortunately fell into disfavour, chiefly because of the annoying and often heavy black-mail levied by the petty chiefs and thakurs through whose territories the traders from Rajputana and Gujarât had to pass. The traders had to part freely with his money, and got no return in the shape of roads, and very little return indeed in the shape of protection. Likewise, trading was impossible during the troublous times of the Musalman invasion of Gujarat.

But Sir James Outram (then Colonel Outram) when Political Agent in Mahi Kanta, re-established this important mart. He made arrangements with all these petty robbers, whereby traders should be allowed to pass free through their states, due compensation being given by him in a legitimate way. For a number of years the fair flourished and trade increased rapidly, but of late years it has again begun to decline. The chiefs have resumed their old habits, especially the Thakur of *Barodra*, "a sturdy old man;" and now the numbers attending the fair do not amount to more than fifty thousand.—*Times of India*.

ORIENTAL STUDIES AT CAMBRIDGE.

THE Syndicate, appointed by Grace of the Senate Dec. 4, 1871, to consider the best means of promoting the Study of the Oriental Languages, gave in their report on 13th March, recommending :—

That, recognizing the intrinsic importance of Oriental Literature, its special bearing on the theological and classical training of the University, the close connexion of England with the countries of the East, and the fact that Oriental Studies have as yet failed, for want of due encouragement, to take their proper place in the University System of Education, they are of opinion that these studies should be placed on a level with the other studies of the University by the institution of two Triposes, one for the Semitic languages and the other for the Indian languages.

The Syndicate therefore recommend, that—

I. A Semitic Languages Tripos be established, the first examination to be held in 1875.

All students who shall pass the examination so as to deserve Honours shall be entitled to admission to the degree of Bachelor of Arts. No student shall be admitted to the examination who has not passed the examination in the additional Mathematical subjects of the previous examination. An Undergraduate or Bachelor-designate in Arts may be a candidate for Honours in the Semitic Languages Tripos of any year, if at the time of the examination for such Tripos he shall have entered on his ninth term at least, having previously kept eight terms; provided that not more than ten terms shall have passed after the first of the said eight terms; and, excepting in special cases, no student of a different standing shall be allowed to be a candidate unless he shall have obtained permission from the Council of the Senate.

The subjects of the examination of candidates for Honours in the Semitic Languages Tripos are—

Translation into Arabic; Selected portions of the Kur'án, with Arabic commentary; Arabic Grammar, with passages for translation into English from a selected work of some native Grammarian. At least four Selected Arabic works. Passages for translation into English from unspecified Arabic works.

Translation into Hebrew, and passages for pointing. At least four selected books of the Hebrew Scriptures, with a selected Hebrew commentary on one of the said books. Passages for translation into English from unspecified books of the Hebrew Scriptures. Paper on post-biblical Hebrew.

Translation into Syriac; at least four selected books of the Syriac Versions of the New Testament. Biblical Chaldee, and selected books of the Targums and of the Syriac Versions of the Old Testament. Selected Syriac works. Passages for translation into English from unspecified Syriac works. Comparative Grammar of the Semitic Languages. Literary History of the Semitic Languages.

The papers on selected works shall contain passages for translation into English and questions on the subject-matter and criticism of such works. The paper on selected Arabic works shall include specimens of poetry and rhymed prose, with or without commentary. The Kur'án and Grammatical works shall be excluded from this paper. The paper on post-biblical Hebrew shall contain passages for translation from at least two selected and two unspecified works.

The Board of Oriental Studies will publish a list of books bearing on the subjects of the last day's examination, and will revise such list from time to time. Public notice of all the variable subjects selected for the examination in any year will be given by the Board of Oriental Studies before the beginning of the Lent Term in the year next but one preceding the examination. No student will be placed in the First Class, who has not exhibited a competent knowledge of two of the three languages, Arabic, Hebrew, and Syriac, and also of the Comparative Grammar of the Semitic Languages. The examination in each year shall be conducted by four examiners, who shall be nominated by the Board of Oriental Studies and elected by the Senate.

And that—II. An Indian Languages Tripos be established, the first examination to be held in 1875, under regulations similar to those for the Semitic Languages Tripos.

Subjects :—Translation into Sanskrit. Selected Sanskrit Dramatic and other Poems. Selected Sanskrit Prose works (including a philosophical treatise) and a selected portion of the Rig Veda with Sâyana's Commentary. Passages for translation into English from unspecified Sanskrit works. Paper on Sanskrit Grammar, including a selected portion or portions of a work of some native Grammarian.

Selected Persian works, including a portion or portions of the Masnavî. Translation into Persian. Passages for translation into English from unspecified Persian works. Persian Grammar, and Arabic Grammar with especial reference to the forms occurring in Persian.

Selected Hindustani works, including the Intikhâb-i Kulliyât-i Saudâ. Translation into Hindustani. Passages for translation into English from unspecified Hindustani works. Comparative Grammar of the Indo-European Languages. History of the Indian Languages, Literature and Philosophy.

No student will be placed in the First Class, who has not exhibited a competent knowledge of Sanskrit together with Comparative Grammar, or of Persian (including the Arabic element) together with Comparative Grammar, or of Hindustani together with Sanskrit or Persian.

AN EARLY SANSKRIT PRESS AS YET UNNOTICED BY BIBLIOGRAPHERS.

IT is strange that the earliest editions of a number of Sanskrit books should never as yet have been described, though they were printed in a large town of Southern India, and in a part where Europeans have always been numerous. The first press with Devanagari type, in Southern India, was started about 1805, at Tanjor, by Raja Sarabhoji (Serfoji), the well-known pupil of the great German Missionary Swartz. His object was to print the books required for the elementary Sanskrit and Marâthî schools he had established in the Tanjor district. A small hand press (still in the Tanjor Palace) and a fount of Devanagari type were procured, probably from Madras, and this little office received the rather magniloquent name of Navavidyâkalânidhi. The superintendent was a Brahman named Kuppâ Bhatta. The first production of the press seems to have been a Sanskrit-Marâthî Panchânga, or Almanac, which was continued for several years, till superseded by those of the Bombay lithographic presses. In 1808 (year vibhava) was printed an edition of the Raghuvamśa, the 19 cantos of text complete, 97 pp. 8vo. The verses are numbered, and there are two short perpendicular lines after each half verse. In other respects it is printed like native MSS. This is the earliest edition of this poem by several years; the Calcutta edition (Gildemeister, No. 234) and Stenzler's were both published in 1832. In 1811 was printed on 8 pp. (transv.), an edition of the Tarkasangraha. The copy of this which I have seen is ruled with borders in red ink, and the close of each sentence has been marked in the same way by hand, a vacant space having been left by the compositor for this purpose. On the first page are two rude cuts of Ganeśa and Śiva. In the same year also was printed an edition of Annam Bhatta's Comment on the Tarkasangraha, similar to that of the text, oblong 22 pp. In 1812 was printed an edition of the Bhâshâparichchheda (Kârikâvalî), by Panchânana Bhatta, oblong 10 pp. In 1813 (year Śrîmukha) appeared an edition of the complete text of Mâgha's Śiśupâlavadha, 8vo. 168 pp. In 1814 the Kumârachampû, attributed to Sarabhoji himself, but really composed by one of his Pandits, was printed, 26 pp. transv. Two editions of the Amarakosha (one in 8vo. and the other in folio*) were also early finished; of the dates I am uncertain, as I have only seen imperfect copies. An edition of the Muktâvalî (a comment on the Bhâshâparichchheda) was also begun, but only 45½ pp. (transv.) were finished. Among the Maratha publications of this press is a translation of Æsop's fables, with rude cuts, in 12mo. The type is very good and clear; each letter is however separated, as in many MSS. All the copies I have seen are printed on European hand-made paper. The texts are tolerably correct, in some copies errors have been corrected by hand.—A.C.B. in *Trübner's Lit. Rec.*

DISCOVERY OF IMAGES.

A Native Christian of Velangani (Tanjor) has made a curious and interesting discovery of five very ancient copper figures of Hindu deities. The images were found buried in the man's compound, but he being a Roman Catholic, objections were made by the priest to the sale of the images to the people. It was therefore proposed to break them up and sell them for old copper, when the matter came to the knowledge of the Collector (Mr. H. S. Thomas), who purchased the images for Government at the rate of four annas per seer, or the price of old copper. The figures are as follows:—

Pidari, a village goddess, seated, with four arms; in one an axe, in one a drum. Height 1 foot 9 inches. Breadth at base of pedestal 1 foot 2½ inches. Weight 63 lbs.

Pillayar, called also Ganapati, Ganesa, and Vighneswara, son of Shiva and Parvati, and therefore called *Pillayar*, son. Height 1 foot 8½ inches. Weight 43 lbs.

Nadasha, figure of Shiva, dancing (*Nada* dancing, *isha*, king), enclosed in a horse-shoe arch, ornamented with flowers. Shiva, matted hair, is worked into an ornamental pattern, with four arms. In one hand a small drum such as is used by fortune tellers, with a ball made of cord and wax attached by a string to the middle, which strikes each end of the drum alternately when oscillated. Second arm over a cobra. In one hand a flame. Dances on a prostrate Rakshasa. Height 3 feet 7½ inches; width 3 feet 8 inches.

Sundikeswara (or Chandikeswara), a son of Shiva is deaf, for which reason worshippers snap their hands in his temple to attract his attention. Is placed to the left hand of the figure of Shiva, facing south. Has hair arranged in ornament at each side of neck. Figure standing in devotional attitude. Height 2 feet 2 inches, weight 60 lbs.

Amman, a goddess, standing. Height 2 feet, weight 56 lbs.

The images are believed to have belonged to a Shiva temple which once existed at Velangani. Why or when they were buried is but conjectural. They were found embedded in sand three feet below the surface. The images are believed to be very ancient. They are to be placed in the Museum at Madras for the present.

HIMALAYAN CUSTOM.

Dr. Cowran, in his "Medical History of the Himalayas," speaking of a native tribe in the northern district of the peninsula, says, when a mother goes into a field to work, or is otherwise unable to take her child with her, she selects some sheltered spot near a stream, in which she places a little straw for a bed for her infant, and then directs, by means of a piece of split bamboo, a current of

* Gildemeister's No. 236 must refer to one of these editions.

water, of from one to two or three inches in diameter, on its uncovered occiput and temples. This produces a soporific effect, which generally lasts as long as the water continues to flow. The sleep is said to be very soothing, and children who have been much subjected to its influence are known to have been generally free from the annoyances incidental to the period of dentition.

THE WHITE JEWS OF COCHIN.

It is not surprising to find the blackness of the Jews of Cochin adduced in Manu's Commentary as a proof of the effects of climate, because English ignorance on Indian subjects never is surprising; but though there are black Jews on the Western Coast, (descendants of slaves and native proselytes), the Jews of Cochin—the Jews who profess to have settled in the country 1800 years ago, and hold grants dated in the fourth century A.D., are a handsome and singularly fair race, compared even with European Jews.—*South of India Observer, May 9.*

ORIENTAL NOTES.

We learn that the well-known Mîmâmsâ text-book the Jaiminîya-Nyâya-Mâlâ-Vistara, of which 400 pages in large quarto were completed by Dr. Goldstücker, will be completed by E. B. Cowell, Professor of Sanskrit in the University of Cambridge.

The photo-lithographic fac-simile edition of the celebrated commentary by Patanjali on Sanskrit Grammar entitled the Mahâbhâshya, which the same worthy and much lamented scholar had in hand, has only advanced to the XXth page, i. e. only one-half of the book has been done. Whether this will be completed remains to be seen. As the writing is very small, the exertion required for editing is almost too much for the eyes, and therefore we have considerable doubts about its rapid completion. Should the work be published, we understand that the price will be Rs. 300, which will of necessity place it beyond the reach of most scholars.

Professor Monier Williams' Sanskrit-English Dictionary, we hear, is to be published in June.

A Hindustani Grammar will shortly appear from the pen of Professor Dowson of the Staff College, Sandhurst.

ON MASTA'N BRAHMANS.

In the article by Mr. Ramsay on the hot springs of Unai (p. 142), mention is made of the Mâstân Brahmans. It may be useful to record that in Orissa, also, the majority of Brahmans do not touch the plough. Those that do are called Mastân, and are looked down upon by other sects of Brahmans. They are often to be found holding the post of Sarbarâhkâr, or village headmen, and in that case are called Padhan (*i. e.* प्रधान). They are, like all Oriya Brahmans, a haughty stiff-necked set, distinguished by the most serene indifference to the sufferings of their fellow-creatures. As Padhans therefore they are highly appreciated by the rapacious and tyrannous zamindars, who find them useful tools in their oppression of the ryots.

Balasor, 11th May 1872. JOHN BEAMES.

THE Muhammadan coins mentioned (p. 130) by Dr. Bühler as found in the excavations at Walleh, are, in the opinion of Mr. Justice Gibbs, not older than the 16th century A. D. It is probable they may have been lost or deposited in comparatively recent times by villagers whose huts stood over the site of the buried city.—ED. *I. A.*

CHESS.

THE Burmese game of chess differs slightly from the European game, but only where the Europeans have altered it since they received it from the East, for it was brought into Western Europe by the Crusaders, who appear to have altered the Burmese 'horses' to 'knights,' and 'chariots' to 'castles,' as now found in the European game. The Burmese name *chekturen* has been defined, "the chief ruler or leader of an army," which is not quite correct. The name is derived from the Pali or Sanskrit, *chatur*, 'four,' and *anga* 'a member,' i. e. 'the four members' (of an army), elephants, chariots, cavalry, and infantry; and it is the same name dragged through Persian and Arabic which appears in the English word *chess* which Webster refers to the French. The 'rook' of the English game is the same word as the *ratha* of the Burmese, being the Pali or Sanskrit name for a chariot.—*Dr. F. Mason, 'A Worldly Man's Life.'*

To the Editor of the "Indian Antiquary."

SIR,—A transcript of the Dinajpur inscription (page 127) of which a facsimile is published (plate VI page 140) was sent to me some time ago by the Assistant Secretary to the Asiatic Society of Bengal, together with a translation by him, for my opinion as to the meaning of the words which constitute the date. The appearance of my note in reply in the *I. A.* (p. 127), and the comments made on it by Mr. R. G. Bhandarkar render a few remarks from me necessary.

The text sent to me was a transcript, carefully made, but not a facsimile, and I had every reason therefore to suspect copyist's errors in those parts which were doubtful. A rubbing since sent to me by Mr. Westmacott shows the letters to be in an excellent state of preservation. With this before me all idea of possible errors must be set aside, and the reading published by you must be taken as correct, with the exception of a single misprint in the second line in which the word 'gupa' has been changed to 'gana.'

As regards the translation: in the first half of the śloka there is a *double entendre*; the compound word mârgaṇa-gaṇa-grâmagrâhî meaning "appreciation of the sum total of the merits of beggars," when referring to *dâna* (liberality), and "his hold of the multitude of strings of his arrows," when corresponding to the "overthrow of the irresistible forces of the enemies" (Durvvâri-vairibala-pramathana). In the second half the issue originated in the phrase—kuñjaraghaṭâ-varshena. Word for word it means "elephant," "collection," and "rain," or "year." Being in the instrumental case, if it be taken as an epithet of Dantidurga, the meaning of the reduced compound may be, as suggested by Mr Bhandarkar, "by him who raised a crowd of elephants." But the compound is such an awkward one, it is so far removed from its noun, and the raising of elephants is so unnatural a metaphor, that I feel very unwilling to accept this interpretation as correct. The conjecture about 'varshena' being a mistake of 'varshana' is not supported by the facsimile, and must therefore be at once rejected. I am driven therefore to the necessity of accepting 'varsha' to mean a year, and the two words preceding it for the figures of the year. Now, 'kuñjara' unquestionably is equivalent to eight, the elephant regents of the eight quarters, and 'ghaṭâ' after it can only imply a crowd or several eights the lowest limit of which is three, the plural beginning with three, and is therefore a more fixed quantity than any other number. In connexion with numerals no other meaning is admissible, and I do not think it forced to accept the word for "three-fold," that is three eights standing in a row, and not the multiple of 8 by 3. Against this Mr. Bhandarkar urges the objection that to imply the year in which a work is completed the locative is more appropriate than the instrumental which is used to indicate the total period occupied in completing a work. But he has himself solved the difficulty by the alternative meaning he has suggested in the remark "or at least that it took the 888th year to be constructed." In the absence of all information as to the size of the temple I cannot positively assert that it was completed in course of a year, but the only grammatical objection to my reading of the date thus disappears. Were it otherwise still I do not think the misuse of the instrumental for the locative by a writer who has clearly sinned against grammar by using the neuter 'bhushana' in the masculine gender, is such as to justify the rejection of the interpretation. It is possible also that with a view to indulge in a *double entendre*, similar to what occurs in the first half of the śloka, and make one word serve both for a date and an epithet of his royal patron, the poet has submitted to a slight infraction of the rules of grammar, of which men of his class are generally much less mindful than of rhetoric. Anyhow the date does not appear to be so questionable as Mr. Bhandarkar is disposed to think.

Rajendralala Mitra.

Calcutta, 21st May 1872.

THE JAYA SRI MAHA BODIN WAHANSE IN CHANCERY.

All who have read Sir E. Tennent's charming work on Ceylon, or have glanced into Turnour's Mahawanso, will recollect that the great Bo tree of Anuradhapura is the oldest historical tree in the world, and the highest earthly object of veneration to millions of Buddhists. When it was brought over to Ceylon more than 2,000 years ago, Dewanampiya-Tissa, the then king of Ceylon, appointed the chief who brought it lord over the district, and gave him and his heirs the right to appoint for ever the chief priests of the sacred Bo tree. Like the best among the Rajput chiefs the Nuwara Wewa family traces itself back through chiefs and rulers to that memorable time. The last young chief however died suddenly of cholera, leaving no male issue: and a man has come forward claiming to be descended from the last chief but one; but the descendants in the female line saying that he is no Sir Roger and only some Tom Castro or Arthur Orton, and have elected a rival priest and brought the estates and the most ancient and honourable "family living" in the world into the District Court of Anuradhapura. In historical research the trial is likely to be most interesting. The late young chief's grandfather was beheaded by the last tyrant of Kandy for marrying a Telugu princess, and his father was banished to Galle for high treason against the then newly established English Government. It is in banishment that he is said to have married the daughter of another banished chief and to have had issue the present claimant.

Query 8.—Râmeśvara.

Sir,—Can any of your correspondents tell me who founded the temple of Râmeśvara at Cape Kumârî, and what has been its history? The Tamils say that it was built by Râma B.C. circa 2000, which would be interesting, if probable. On an inscription at Dambulla it is said of Parakrama Bâhu the Great (1153-1186 A.D.) that after his conquest of South India "as there were then no rivals "(pratiwalla) left in all the continent of India, he "staid at Râmeśwara, and filled the hearts of all the "poor by gifts of his own weight in precious things, "and drove not the poor away. *Having put up a "column of victory to endure for many ages, he "built the dêwâla called Nissankeswara*, and surrounded by his four-fold army returned to Ceylon."

The name of the king of Pandi at that time is stated in Sinhalese books (see Turnour, Mahawanso, lxvi) to have been Kulasekara.

I should be glad to have an explanation of the words in italics.

Anuradhapura. T. W. Rhys Davids.

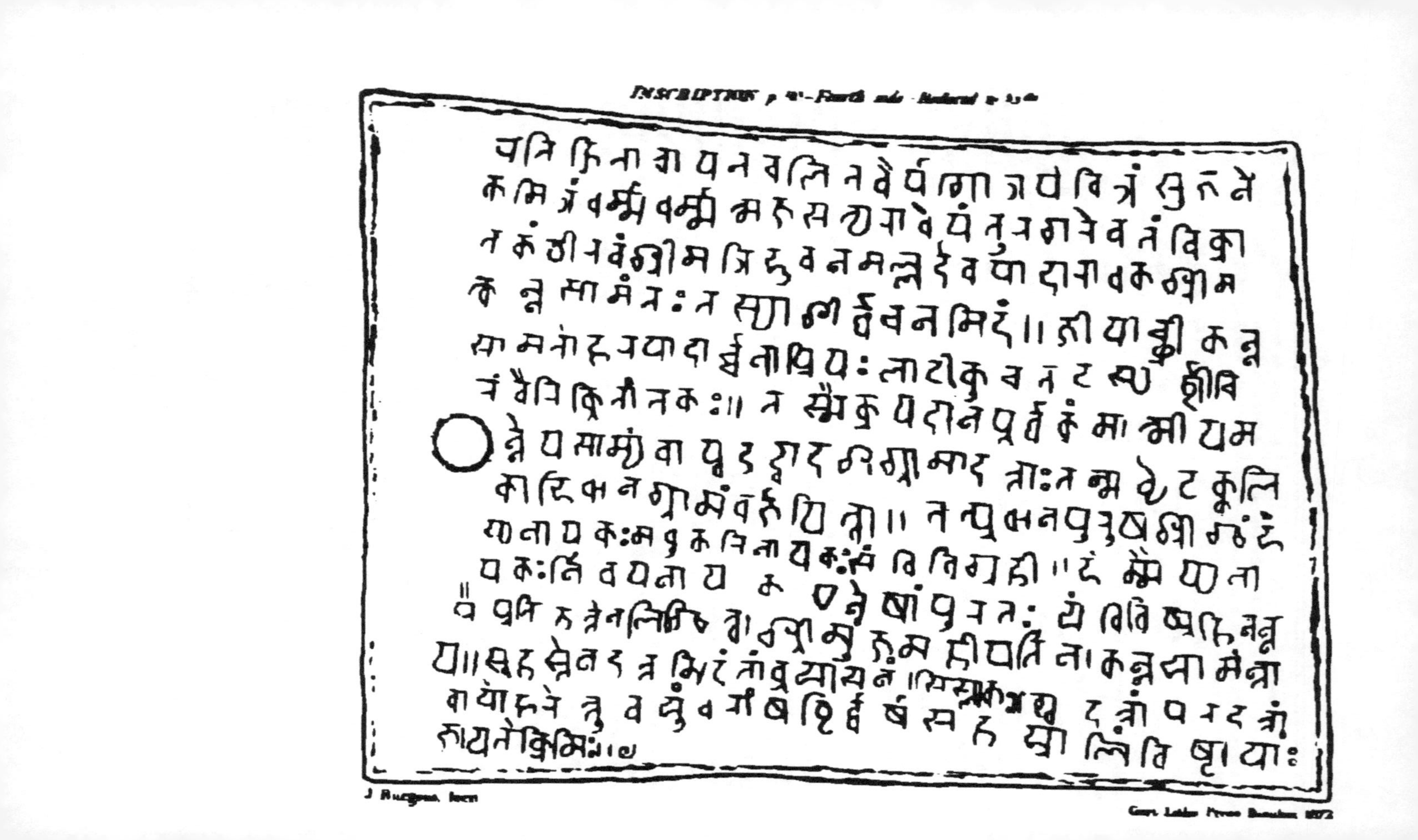

INSCRIPTION, p. [illegible]—Fourth side · Reduced to [illegible]

J Burgess, [illegible]

Govt. Litho Press Bombay 1872

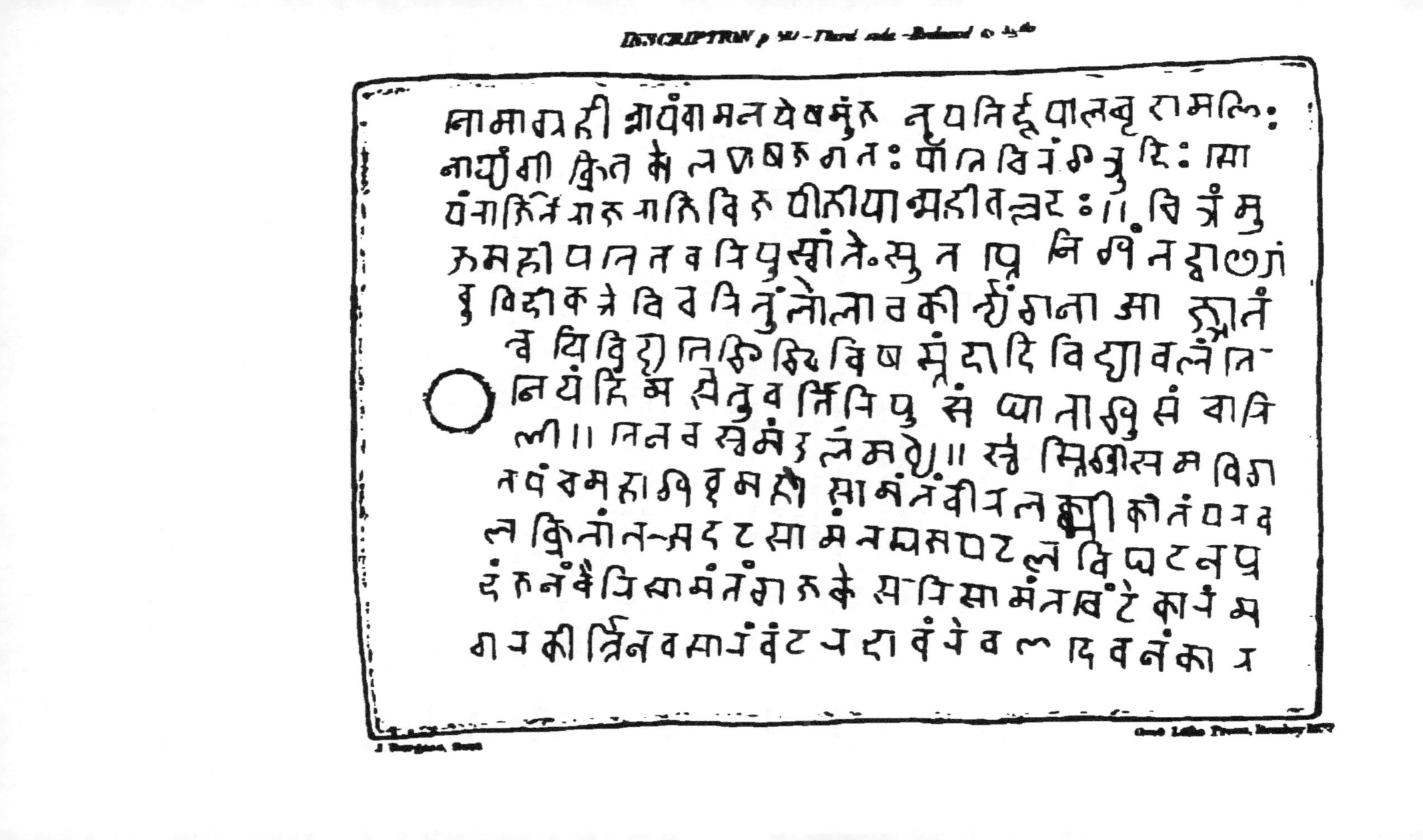

J Burgess, Scott

Govt Litho Press, Bombay 1877

POPULAR TAMIL POETRY.

BY ROBERT CHARLES CALDWELL, M.R.A.S.

Second Paper.

THERE are two phases of Popular Tamil Poetry. SIVAVAKKIYAR, for instance, has written nothing, as far as I know, which may not be classed as popular poetry; and three-fourths of the writings of the classic AVVAIYAR, who has been called the Sappho of Southern India, are strictly of this class. But, beyond this, there is a great deal of difficult and abstruse poetry in high Tamil, which has been popularised. The *Râmâyanam* of KAMBAN, for example, is an elaborate poem, written in a highly polished poetical diction; and yet, if a Hindu were to be asked to point to the first *Popular* poem in the Tamil language, he would, undoubtedly, point to it. Wandering minstrels recite it night by night in the streets of every town in Southern India where Tamil is spoken. There is a subtle and wonderful charm about this poem. It contains by far the finest literal descriptions of scenery to be found in Tamil literature. The magic muse of VIRAMAMUNI was only able to reflect this beauty; for it is well-known that BESCHI wrote his *Tembâvani* in direct imitation of KAMBAN's *Râmâyanam*. Besides this, the palm must be awarded to KAMBAN as the most facile and brilliant of Tamil versifiers. The *Râmâyanam* is written in a metre called the *Viruttam*, one of the most plastic, and perhaps the most harmonious, of Tamil metres. And the whole poem, lit up in every part by alliterations, assonances, mimetic words, and rhymes, leaps and sparkles like a sun-lit sea. There is a ripple in the stanza which describes a running stream, there is a flutter in the verse which depicts a bannerol quivering in the breeze.* For seven centuries KAMBAN's masterpiece has delighted Hindus of all classes. It is *the* Folk-Song of Southern India. And yet, will it be credited that, unless it were explained to him word by word, there is not a single stanza in the whole of the epic, which a common Tamilian labourer or artisan, upon first hearing it, could understand and appreciate! When, therefore, wandering "*Kavirâyar*"—i.e., native minstrels,—sing the *Râmâyanam* to a crowd in bazaars, or upon festive occasions to assemblages in the houses of Hindus, a running comment is kept up, either by the singer or an assistant, explaining the meaning of the verses as they are recited. On the other hand, the most ignorant of Tamilians can understand such a popular poem as the *Vivêka Chintâmani*—a shrewd and plainly-worded poem, possessing a good deal of real artistic merit. Thus in Tamil there are two kinds of popular poems,—poems which require a commentary, and poems which do not. It perhaps may be advisable, ere passing on, to give one brief specimen of classic poetry of the highest order which has been popularised by frequent quotation and common use. Here is a stanza from the *Tembâvani* of VIRAMAMUNI—

> Oli nâkkodu vân mîn pugala,
> Oli nâkkodu pan mani pugala,
> Kali nâkkodu pur pul pugala,
> Kamal nâkkodu kâ malar pugala,
> Teli nâkkodu ninaippunal pugala,—
> Tanaiyâ pugalkuppoy aiyô ini ?—
> Ali nâkkodu nân unai pugala,
> Ariya nûlum uyarttiyê !

It is the most famous verse in a famous poem, and may be thus translated:—

> Whilst Thee, with tongues of splendour, the orbs of heaven praise;
> Whilst gems to Thee their voices, with tongues of brilliance, raise;
> Whilst unto Thee wood-warblers, with tongues of joyance, sing;
> Whilst wood-flowers Thy sweet praises, from tongues of fragrance fling;

---

* Beschi imitated Kamban in the most elaborate manner, and gloried in so doing. The aim of the great Italian was to supplant the Râmâyanam in a measure. He wished to present to Christian natives a poem which would be to them what the Râmâyanam was to other Hindu religionists. So Beschi, called by his admirers Vîramâmunivar, or "the Heroic Devotee," composed his Tembâvani, a poem which reproduces in a fashion the Biblical narrative, and the heroes of which are Christ, the Blessed Virgin, and Joseph. Pursuing his imitation of Kamban to wonderful extremes, Beschi gives us, in one poem, the story of the sun-tongues in Palestine! In the text I allude to another extraordinary imitation. Kamban, in one of his stanzas, makes the flags flutter a warning to Rama, as if motioning him to go away. Beschi reverses this as something similar. When the Holy Family are returning from Egypt, the Italian poet makes the flags flutter the three travellers a welcome, waving their folds as if they say 'come, come!' I have neither the *Râmâyanam* of Kamban, nor the *Tembâvani* of Vîramâmuni before me as I write, or I should verify by quotation these strange matters. As a whole I consider the *Râmâyanam* the greater poem: parts of the *Tembâvani*, however, are superior to any parts of Kamban's poem. And Beschi was undoubtedly the greater genius. These two poems, together with Tiruvalluvar and Tiruvalluvar, must be ranked in the very first class of Tamil poets.

Whilst Thee, with tongues of clearness, the water-floods applaud ;
(Thus, day by day, from all things, dost Thou receive not laud ?)
Wilt Thou not deign to suffer the tongue Thou gavest me—
Though I be dumb and thoughtless—to offer praise to Thee ?

It is, however, impossible in any translation to reproduce the spirit and melody of the original stanza. Even those who have studied Tamil deeply must be struck with the remarkable verbal structure of these eight lines. The measure in which they are written is very frequently employed in Tamil popular verse. In the original, given above in a Romanised form, note that the *first* word of the first, third, fifth, and seventh lines are perfect rhymes to the Tamilian ear, that the *second* word in each of these four lines is identical,—as is also the last ; that the first word of the second line is a perfect rhyme with the first word of the first line ; that the first syllable of the first word of the *fourth* line is an alliteration which chimes with the first syllable of the *third* line : that *Ti* in "Tinamô" alliterates with *Te* in "Teli"—according to the rules of Tamil Syntax ; and that the same vowel begins the last two lines. But this is not all,—the last words of the second and fourth lines are identical, and the same word recurs in the sixth line. Add to all this, a subtle continuous assonance, and a wonderful rhythmic flow,—and the reader may have some conception of what an artistic thing a Tamil Viruttam is when it is the work of a master-poet. The Veṇbâ, a still more intricate measure, is also frequently made use of by popular Tamil poets. There is an old Hindu story about that one of the greatest of Tamil poets took three years to compose one short *Kural* couplet (*i. e.*, two lines) !—and it was so fine a couplet, that, when it was thoroughly finished, the poet himself was the only one who could comprehend it ! Such a story as this is ridiculous enough to our ears, but it is no matter for laughter to any Hindu Pandit. I have often had the pleasure of listening to natives reciting their own compositions in verse : upon such occasions the greatest compliment you can pay is to declare that the poem is couched in such elegant language that it wholly transcends your comprehension !*

Popular Tamil Poetry, however, is for the most part written with some regard to the patience of readers. The well-known works of that really great poetess Avvaiyar (a portion of which was probably written quite nine centuries ago) contain perhaps the oldest specimens of Tamil popular poetry extant. And yet, old as they are, they are written in clear pure Tamil. There is a great and indefinable charm about the style of the *Nalvali and Mudurei*. It is so simple yet so elegant,—sailing along so smoothly, yet freighted with so much weighty sense. Let us take an instance of Avvaiyar's style from the *Vâkkuṇḍam* :—

Nūrāṇḍu palaginum
  Mūrkkar kēṇmai
Nīrkkuḷ pāsipōl
  Vērkoḷḷādē.
Oru nāḷ palaginum
  Periyōr kēṇmai
Iru nilam piḷandu
  Vēr vīḷkkummē.
Kaṟkai nanḍrē
  Kaṟkai nanḍrē
Piccai puginum
  Kaṟkai nanḍrē
Kallā voruvan
  Kulanalam pēsudal
Nellinuṭ piṟanda
  Padarā kummē.

The friendship of the worthless
  Though for a century tried,
Is like the weed which floateth
  All rootless in the tide.
The friendship of the worthy,
  Though proved for but one day,
Is like a root which downwards
  Through good soil cleaves its way.
Right good, right good is learning !
  Though you a beggar be,
The benefits of knowledge
  Will still extend to thee ;
The unlearned man who boasteth
  How nobly he is born,
Is but an empty corn-ear
  Sprung up midst fruitful corn.

* It has proved an irremediable curse to Tamil literature that writers of genius have so generally adopted a Sanskritised phraseology, and intricate involutions of style, which are as unnecessary as they are in bad taste. The writings of *Tâyumânavar*,—who is perhaps really the greatest of Tamil poets,—may be pointed to as an example of the fact that the highest kinds of speculative and philosophical poetry can be written in pure plain Tamil, which at once satisfies the critical taste, and is thoroughly intelligible to the careful reader.

Auvaiyar is chiefly noted as a poetess for her unrivalled collection of brief moral aphorisms. Whilst the genuineness of several of her reputed works is open to the gravest question, the authorship of the Âttisûdi has never been doubted. This remarkable poem, possessed of a sublime simplicity, contains the same number of lines as there are letters in the Tamil alphabet ordinarily in use. Each line begins with a letter of this alphabet. Thus the first line commences with an *Ana*, the next with an *Aavana*, and so on, the proper sequence of letters in the Tamil alphabet being strictly adhered to. It is quite a unique poem, and has been styled by the learned Beschi as "worthy of Seneca himself." The following are the opening lines:—

Aram seya virumbu.
Aruvadu sinam.
Iyalvadu Karavêl.
Ivadu vilakkel.
Udaiyadu vilambel.
Ukkamatu keividêl.
Ennezhuttigazhêl.
Erpat' igalchi.
Aiyamitt' un.
Oppura volugu.
Oduvadoliyêl.
Avviyam pêsêl.

Desire to do thy duty. Cool thy heat
Of wrath. What thou can'st give, do not secrete.
Hinder not alms. Of wealth make not a show.
Of perseverance never let thou go.
Numbers and letters scorn not. 'Tis not meet
To go a-begging. First give alms, then eat.
According to established custom walk.
From learning cease not. Without envy talk.

All Tamil poems, popular or otherwise, begin with a formal invocation of some deity. One of the most famous of such invocations is that prefixed to the *Nalvali* of Auvaiyar. The following is a translation of this invocation and of two subsequent stanzas of the poem:—

Pâlum, telitenum pâgum paruppum,—ivai
Nâlum kalant' unakku nân taruvên.
Kôlam sey
Tungak kari mugattu, tu maniyê, ni yenakku
Sanga Tamil mundrum tâ!

Milk and clear honey, sugar and pulse,—these blent,
To thee, O Holy Gem, will I present,
Thou elephant-visaged, graceful, eminent;
So in return do thou vouchsafe to me
Of sanctioned Tamil the varieties three.*

Âttrup perukkattradi sudumanalilumavv'â
Lattrup perukkâl ulagûttum.
Mettravarkku
Nalla kudippirandâr nalkurndâr ânâlum
'Illai' yena mâttâr, isaintu.

When the dried rivers sands you hap to tread
Your feet are scorched; yet, e'en then, in its bed
Lurk springs, by which the neighbourhood is fed.†
Thus men, of good stock born, will never say,
E'en when impoverish'd, to a beggar—'Nay.'

Âttrang karaiyin maramum arasariya
Vîttirunta vâlvum vilumandrê.
Yêttram
Ulutundu vâlvatark' oppillai, kandir,
Palutundu vêrôr panikku.

Trees, growing by rivers, fall; and fall, too, they
Who in some monarch's favour flourish gay.
Have ye not seen the truth of what I say?
All else is faulty;—naught compared can be
With Agricultural Prosperity.

There is a pretty little legend connected with one of Auvaiyar's most popular verses. The poetess visited the town of Ambal. It happened that a dancing-girl named Chilambi lived in this town. On a former occasion the great Kamban had visited Chilambi's house, and the maiden had given the author of the *Râmâyana* a very large sum of money to write a stanza in her praise. The sum which the unfortunate girl offered the miserly poet was only half of the sum he demanded, so Kamban took the money, dashed off the following incomplete stanza, and went away!—

Tannîrum Kâvêri
Târvêndan Chôlan
Mannâvatum Chôla
Mandalamê,
Pennâval—

Of streams, the stately Kâveri—
Of kings, is Cholan, best;

* Tamil sanctioned by the conclave of learned Tamilians who used to hold their assemblies in the temple at Madura. We speak of "Queen's English"; "Sanga Tamil" is a similar expression.

† This alludes to the well-known native custom of digging small temporary wells in the sandy bed of rivers for water, after the rivers have been dried up in the hot season.

And Chola-land the fairest land
Of all the earth's broad breast:—
And of all women——

Shortly afterwards the poetess Auveiyar visited Chilambi, and found the poor girl in tears. She told the poetess of her sorrow—how she had given Kamban nearly a thousand rupees, and the poet had scribbled an unfinished stanza in charcoal on the wall, and had hastily left her. Upon hearing this Auveiyar rose up, and finished the stanza as follows:—

Ambar Silambi
Yaravinta tēniyum
Sempon silambē
Silambu!

——Chilambi
Of Ambal is most sweet,—
And the best of golden anklets
Those on her lotus-feet!

Auveiyar for these lines would receive nothing but a little rice-water, to assuage her thirst. And to the present day the poetess goes by the name of Kûḷukkuppâḍi, *i.e.*, "She who sang for some rice-water."*

One of the most popular poems in Tamil is the *Mûdurai*. It is perhaps the most wonderful collection of fine *similes*, within a small compass, in any language. The diction is plain, pure, and extremely beautiful. It has all the marks about it of having been composed by the authoress of the *Nalvali* and the *Konraivendan*. Indeed the internal evidence in favour of this is extremely strong. The phraseology, the rhythmic flow, the copious use of similes and metaphors, all point to her as its author. But there is one stanza in the Mûdurai which could not possibly have been written by Auveiyar, viz., the one beginning:—

'Kânamayilâḍa, kaṇḍirunta Vânkoḷi,' &c.

In this stanza a comparison is instituted between the stately peacock and the strutting turkey-cock. It has been pointed out that the turkey was introduced into India by the Portuguese about three hundred years ago.† Auveiyar, the reputed sister of Tiruvalluvar, obviously could not have penned the stanza in question. But on this ground, and it really appears to me on this ground only, some scholars of great learning and undoubted critical acumen, have refused to accredit Auveiyar with the authorship of any portion of the poem containing the stanza. A defence has lately been set up, in the assertion that by "Vânkoḷi" Auveiyar meant a *pea-hen*; but nowhere in classic literature is a pea-hen so denominated. The safest explanation is to reject the stanza as a spurious interpolation. Yet it must be allowed that if the stanza be a spurious one it is a marvellous imitation of Auveiyar's style. In the third line a trick of alliteration, very frequent in the verses of Auveiyar, is skilfully adopted.

Polla siragai viritt'—Âḍinâl *pôlumê*.

The alliteration which, as the stanza is in the Venbâ metre, should occur at the first syllable of *Âḍinâl* is kept in suspension till the last word is reached, without the ear being offended.

But even if it be allowed that the *Mûdurai* is not the work of Auveiyar, it does not affect the main question at issue. Whoever wrote it, and notwithstanding that it is but a short poem, it occupies a foremost place in Tamil literature as a composition dear to every Tamilian. It is full of the brightest of Oriental thoughts, conveyed in language at once classic and highly elegant, and on this account it is perhaps more frequently quoted than any other Tamil writing. I beg the reader carefully to weigh the following five stanzas from the Mûdurai, which, I think, must commend themselves widely to the general English taste:—

Sîriar keṭṭâlum sîriyar sîriyarê
Allâ'âr keṭṭâlum ennâgum? Sîriya
Ponnin kuḍamuḍaintal ponnâgum; ennâgum
Maṇṇin kuḍam uḍaintakkâl?

Gold vessels, broken, still as gold we prize,
And wise men in adversity are wise:
But worthless men, when ruined, what are they?
Vessels of clay, when broken, are but clay!

———

Nellukk' iṟaitta nîr vâykkâl vaḻiyôḍi
Pullukkum angê pasiyumâm. Tol ulagil
Nallâr oruvar uḷarêl avar poruṭṭ'
Ellârukkum peyyum maḻai.

When the tank's water to the rice field flows,
It feeds the grass which by its channel grows;
Thus for the sake of one good man, on all
In this old world, the gracious rain-drops fall.

———

* The story is a mere myth. Auveiyar could not possibly have met Kamban, who probably flourished a couple of centuries after her.

† Vide Dr. Caldwell's *Dravidian Grammar*, p. 67.

Aṭṭâlam palenvelyir kundrâtalavalla
Naṭṭâlum nanballâr naṇbullar. Keṭṭâlum
Meṇmakkal meynmakkalé, sangu suṭṭalum
Tânmikka veṇmai tarum.

Nenjadaimai tanaṛintu nagang karanturaiyum
Anjâ parangkolakkanir pambu. Nenjir
Karavudaiyâr tammai karappar karavâr
Karavillâ nenjattavar.

Aḍakkam udaiyar aṛivillar endr' enṇi
Kaḍakka karutavum vêṇḍâm. Madai taleyil
Oḍum min ôḍa, uru min varum aḷavum
Vâḍi irukkumâng Kokku!

The last of these stanzas has always struck me, as being a good example of the fact that some Tamil poets possess one of those "faculties divine" which is a sure note of genuine inspiration, viz:—the faculty of appreciating nature. The epithet *withered* (Tamil, *Vâḍi*) is an extremely beautiful one, because it is so extremely true to nature. Anyone will recognise the felicity of this epithet who has watched a paddy-bird (*Kokku*) perched on the brim of a tank waiting, perfectly motionless, and as if it were but a piece of withered vegetation, for the rash approach of its finny prey.

PATTANATTU PILLEIYAR PADAL.

Y'en peṭṭra tâyârum yennai piṇam endru
Igaḷndu viṭṭâr.
Pon peṭṭra mâtarum pô vendru solli
Pulambi viṭṭâr.
Kan peṭṭra maintarum piṛakalam vantu
Kuḍam uḍeittar.
Un paṭṭ'oṛiya ore paṭṭrum illei
Uḍeiyavané!

Sollinum, sollin muḍivilum, vêda
Suruti Ilum,
Allinum, mâsattra âgâsa tannilum,
Ayuta viṭṭôr

Illinum, anbariḍattilum, îsan
Iruppiḍattil
Kallinum, sembilum ô iruppânengal
Kaṇṇutalé.

The bad are bad though cherish'd. Yet when
boil'd,
Sweet milk still sweet remains, and is not spoil'd.
And fire but whitens white shells,—Thus we see
Good men remain good in adversity.

The cobra, conscious of its poison, hides;
Abroad the water-snake unfearing glides.
Thus they whose hearts hide guile exposure fear,
But secrecy befits not the sincere.

Esteem not witless, nor with ease o'ercome,
That man whose lips with wise reserve are dumb.
At the sluice-head the stork, whilst fish play by,
All *withered* seems—till the right fish comes nigh!

No notice of Tamil Popular Poetry would be complete without mention being made of PATTANATTU PILLAI'S writings. These are very unequal: in parts they rise to the level of Sivavakkiyar, but as a whole they are productions characterised more by melodious verbiage than striking thought. The most remarkable poem ever penned by this writer is one in which he bewails the loss of his mother. The verses, however, which I have selected here, as far as I know, never been translated before.

VERSES

From various writings of Pattanattu Pillai.

When dead, my mother mourns me
Saying 'But a corpse is he,'
My gold-bought wife with weeping
Cries out 'depart' to me;
My sons, my pyre encircling,
Their water pots let fall;—
There is no love but thy love
O thou who ownest all!*

In speech, and its conclusion,
And in the Vedas too,
In darkness, and in heaven's
Stainless expanse of blue;
In hearts of true ascetics,
And in each loving mind,
The Lord's unbounded presence
Ye certainly may find;
But how in stones and copper,
Can ye the God descry,
Who in his forehead beareth
The terrible one eye! †

* In these remarkable verses, the poet broods over the time when he shall be a corpse. His mother will mourn him a useless thing. The wife, whom he obtained by paying (as is the Hindu custom) a large sum of money, she too with weeping will not desire him to remain by her side when he is a corpse. His children will encircle his funeral pyre, advancing from behind on the *left* side of the corpse, breaking their vessels of water, as if to say, we thus pay our last common service to you! Thy love only is everlasting, unaffected by life or death, O God!"

† S'iva.

Uḷḷiyiṭṭa kalleium opiṭṭa sāntaium
Uttrī ayn
Paḷiṭṭa sembeium poṭṭirukkilēn, ayar
Ponenavē:
Oḷḷiyiṭṭu uḷḷiraṇḍuḷḷē yiruttavaṭ'
Uṇmai endru,
Veḷḷiyiṭṭ'aḍaittu veittēn, iniméi endrum
Veṇḍilanē.

Uṛaṇmanaiyum alla, uṛavar enṛum alla,
Uṛṛa peṭṭra
Pērum antam alla, peṇḍir antam alla,
Piḷḷeigaḷum

Sīrum antam alla, selvamum antam alla,
Tesattilē
Yārum antam alla, nintrai antam, Kacchi
Egambanē!

Kondrēn—anēgam ayiraiyellām, pinbu
Kondru, kondru,
Tindrēn at'andrinum tingu seytēn, adei
Tīrka vendrē
Nindrēn ninsannatikkē, atanāl kuttram
Nī poṛuppāy
Endrē unai nambinēn, iṛaivā, Kacchi
Egambanē.

Nāyāy pirantiṭinnal vēṭṭei āḍi
Nayampaṇṇum
Tāyār vayaṭṭriṇanṛē piṛantu pin
Sambannaṛē

Kāyā maramum vayalām kuḷamum
Kallāvum anna
Iyā manitarai ēn paḍaittāy, Kacchi
Egambanē?

Attrōḍu tumbei aṇintāḍum ambala
Vāṇar tammai
Pōttrāmal evark kaḷaiyālam āyēn inta
Pūtalattil
Sōttrāvariyaḷam ugamattiṛu suttra
Tuṇiyumattrē

Stones chisell'd, temper'd mortar,
And copper furbish'd o'er
By tamarind,—these ne'er shall I
As thee, O God, adore.
But in the world within me
I've planted as is meet—
(Henceforth I lack for nothing,)
Thy twain effulgent feet.

Your habitation fleeteth,
Your friends, they do not stay;
Your fame so dearly gotten,
It too shall pass away;
Your wives remain not ever,
Your offspring leave your side;
Your ornaments, your riches,
They too will not abide:
Not one in all the country
Of his own life is sure,—
But thou, One God of Kanchi,*
Thy feet alone endure.

I slew, I slew and ceased not,
I slew, yea ate the slain!
I sinned, to thee I got me
To cleanse me from my stain:
Therefore wilt thou forgive me;
I trust in thee, O Lord,
Who as a king in Kanchi
Art evermore adored.

One might have skilled hunters
Had one been born a hound,
And thus had not been worthless;
But what good can redound
From men, who're born of women,
Who opulent have grown,
Yet like dried tanks, trees fruitless,
And cows carved out of stone,
Refuse to help the needy?
Why mad'st thou these, O Lord?
Who at the town of Kanchi
Art evermore adored.

To know them who adore not
The dancing-god divine,
(Who's wreath'd with river-blossoms)
Is there no outward sign?
—Such lack even the odour
Of rice! no health have they.
They need a cloth to gird them;
They beg from day to day,

* Kanchi, or Kachi,—i.e., Conjeveram. This and the two following stanzas were addressed by Pattanattu Pillai to the deity (Siva) worshipped at Conjeveram.

Yôttiraiyum picchai kiḷaiyamal ôkkat
 Tiruppargalê,

Eri yenakkennum, puḷuvô yenakkennum,
 Inta mayyam
Sarri yenakkennum, paravaiô yenakkennum,
 Tan puslika
Nari yenakkennum, punnâ yenakkennum, in
 Narudalai

Pilamudan valarttên, itinâl yenna
 Payan sonbê?

But no one e'er relieves them;
 Hopeless they fade away!

Fire claims me, worms too claim me,
 Earth, too, accounts me here.
Kites claim me too, with jackals,
 And despicable curs.
Then wherefore have I cherish'd
 This vile ill-omen'd thing,—
From this my mortal body
 What benefit can spring?

Nêmangal, Nittaigal, vedangal, Âgama
 Nûlanegi
Omangal tarpanam santi jaba mantira
 Yôga nilai

Nêmangal santanam vengiṇu pûsi
 Nalamuḍanê
Sâmangal dôrum ivar seyum pujaigal
 Sorppanamê

Vows, austerities, vedas,
 Puranas, secular law,
Burnt offerings, sacrifices
 To men that are no more;
Prayers said in markets, mantras,
 Fixed postures, names ye say,
Sandal, and smear'd white ashes,—
 Ye who, from day to day,
Deeming these meritorious,
 Observe such things, do ye
Know that all this is nothing
 But [illegible] prolixity!

Some of the most popular poems in Tamil are those of the Sittar (Siddha) school. These writers are the poetical Quietists of Tamil-land. A great deal might be written concerning them and their works, but space forbids. I must content myself with laying before the reader the translation of one—perhaps the most famous—stanza in these writings. This stanza is from the *Gnanam Nuru*, a work ascribed to Agastiyar, the father of the Tamil language. It is a most remarkable stanza, but certainly Agastiyar had no hand in its authorship.

Vañanguvây jagajâti waruruniki
 Ma nilatti waru nodiyil vagutti nagappâ
Gupamana manitharkam padaitta pinbu
 Kuvalayattil tannattu tiruruvây vantu
Jenamana emunaram wendrilâmal
 Sanniyâsi pôl irunta, devattai katti
Avidan Sittargalai irutti pinbu
 Aganda talam sendravarai,—apparvâyê.

Thou shalt adore the World's One Light,
Who at a thought this vast earth framed,
Made noble man, then, dove-like, flamed
 A Priest, upon his sight.

No kin had he of mortal race;
Ascetic-wise hard deeds he wrought;
Then, having made disciples, sought
 The illimitable Place.

One of the most popular little poems in the Tamil language is the *Viveka Chintâmani*,—a comparatively recent production. Ignorant Tamil women, who know almost nothing of any kind of Tamil literature, are fond of learning portions of the poem off by heart. And yet one of its most famous stanzas runs thus—

THE FICKLE SEX.

Alakâla vishattaiyum
 Nambalâm
Atraiyum perungâttaraiyum
 Nambalâm
Kôla mâ mata Yânaiyai
 Nambalâm
Kollum vengai puliyaiyum
 Nambalâm
Kâlanâr viduvum tûtarai
 Nambalâm

Put faith in the deadliest poison,
 In torrent, or hurricane-gust,
And elephants, huge and powerful,
 And murderous tigers fleet;
Confide in the angels of Yama
 The souls of the wicked who fetch,
Place credence in robber, or felon,

Kaḷḷar, veḍar, moṛavarei
Nambalâm,
—Sâlai kaṭṭiya mâtarei
Nambinâl,—
Teruvil aludu tiyangi
Tavippârê!

Or ev'n in some Maravar wretch;
—But if you believe in a woman
More hopeless your case will be,—
You will stand in the street in your anguish,
And wither with agony!

Now that Christianity is year by year becoming more deeply rooted in Tamil-land, a new class of popular poetry is springing up. Some of these Christian lyrics, or *Kirtanais*, especially those penned by a late Christian poet of Tanjore, have attained a wide popularity, even amongst non-Christian Hindus. But as a whole these modern Christian lyrics are wretched productions, and bear the same relation to Tamil popular poetry of the first class, that Tate and Brady's effusions bear to Milton's "Ode on the Nativity." Common Hindu Labour-songs, too, are for the most part extremely destitute of poetic merit.

I must now bring this paper to a close. I trust I have been able to awaken some little interest in the subject, and I hope I have proved from the specimens, few as they are, which I have adduced, that in days gone by, Tamil—the Queen of the Dravidian tongues—was not without some who possessed, in some measure, the vision and the faculty divine. It must be remembered that I have confined myself to culling specimens from a particular class of poetry, and that not of the highest order. The non-Aryans of Southern India cannot for a moment vie with their Aryan masters in the mighty arena of the Epic or the Drama. But I do not think that any Oriental language possesses a richer collection of Folk-songs, than that which is the especial glory of Tamilian literature.

Madras, 14th March, 1872.

ON THE "GAULI RAJ" IN KHANDESH AND THE CENTRAL PROVINCES.

BY W. F. SINCLAIR, BOMBAY C.S., ASSISTANT COLLECTOR IN CHARGE OF KOLABA.

Throughout the Central Provinces and Khandesh there exist traditions more or less shadowy of a *Gauli Raj*,—which have occasioned considerable perplexity as to their origin. Mr. Grant in his Introduction to the Central Provinces Gazetteer, practically gives the question up as insoluble. This power, whatever it was, has left no coins, no inscriptions, nothing but a name attached to a few old buildings. Enquiry has been made among the people now called Gaulis; but they have no memory of their ancient sovereignty; (if it was ever theirs,) and the quotation from Sir R. Jenkins (p. lx. *C. P. Gazetteer*) is too vague to be of any use, and may just as well refer to legends of Krishna and his companions as to anything else.

The past therefore gives us little aid in identifying the Gauli kings, except the rather shaky story of Asa Ahir, the eponymous chief of Asirgarh, spoken of by Ferishtah. Under the circumstances we should, I think, have recourse to the geological method, and seek in the phenomena of the present for the explanation of the past. Is there then in the present day any dynasty in India deriving its title from a common trade, and is there any which would, if it were wiped out to-morrow, leave nothing but its name to show where it had been? Of the first class, the instance nearest to, there are two, and they are both *Gauli Kingdoms*, the Gaikwar of Baroda and the Gorkha (Go-rakha) of Nepal. To the second class belong all the Maratha states. The Gaikwar of Baroda therefore unites the two qualifications, and stands forth the modern analogue of the Gauli Rajas.

The next question is, how did the Gaikwari Raj in Gujarat get its name? From the surname of the ruler. Gaikwar is one of the commonest surnames in the Dekhan; and is generally attached to the profession of a herdsman; but by no means of necessity. Its bearers hold themselves, and are held, pure Marathas:—"My name is Gomaji, father's name Timaji, surname Gaikwar, trade *Gauli*, caste Maratha;" is a heading common enough on depositions in the Dekhan. The surname of Ahir is also common in a small group of villages near the Ane Ghat in Taluka Junnar (*Jooner*) of Puna. Its bearers are held pure Marathas and are cultivators by trade. Now to readers unacquainted with the Dekhan, it may perhaps be necessary to explain that the use of surnames there is almost the same as in the Highlands; I say the Highlands—because a common surname implies a sort of consanguinity, an identity in fact of tribe. The other surnames commonest among Maráthas,—the Smiths and Joneses of the Dekhan,—are Sindé (Scindia), Jádu, Bhonsla, Powár, and Chauhan. It will at once be remarked that the 2nd, 3rd and 5th on this list are the names of noble Rájput races, and the Bhonslas claim descent from the Sisodias of Chitor, the oldest family in India. All the more respectable members of these clans wear the sacred thread, ("*Brahmans*" to the contrary notwithstanding,) and any one who has met with the heads of the Powár and Jádu families (the chiefs of Wadhgaum, Phaltan, and Malegaum) knows that, in the qualities attributed to high descent in India, they are inferior to no Rájput whatever. I shall, therefore, take up the rather bold ground of asserting my belief that the Marátha clans inherit their names from common ancestors with Rájputs and other pure Aryan tribes of Central India. Taking this for granted, we find that there are Chauhans in Rájputana, Chauhan princes of great antiquity in Garhá-Mandla, (Mahâwati) and Chauhan Maráthas in the Dekhan. There are also Powars or Pramaras at Dhar and Dewas in Central India, and Powars in the Dekhan. The expulsion of the Powars from their ancestral seats, their retreat to the Dekhan, and subsequent return to their own, as Marátha commanders, is, I think, historical,—certainly based on their traditions, but I write far from authorities. The Yádavas or Jádus held barren principalities both in the great desert and in the Dekhan. The traditions connecting the Royal house of Bhonsla with that of the Udepur Ránás are well known, and we find the family, when they first came into notice, established as Deshmukhs at Sind-Khera.

I think, therefore, that the most probable explanation of the Gauli Ráj is this,—that Gauli was the surname, or nickname, of a family of princes (and not of a nation) of Aryan race who established themselves in the valleys of the Tapti and Narmadá during the great migration southward which ended in the colonization of the Dekhan by the Aryan Maráthas. This is of course mere conjecture, but if it sets more learned men than myself on a new track it will have served my purpose. Of this I am quite sure, that any attempt to connect the Gauli Ráj with the scattered bands of herdsmen, themselves of various origin and language, that now roam through the pastures of India, would be hopeless, and equally vain any theory of an invasion of pastoral tribes, "Scythians" or what not, after the somewhat mythical Egyptian pattern.

AN INSCRIPTION AT SÁLOTGI IN THE KALÁDGI DISTRICT, DATED SAKA 867 OR A.D. 945, WITH REMARKS.

BY PROF. SHANKAR PANDURANG PANDIT, M.A.

THE inscription, of which a translation is given below, is engraved on a stone pillar about 6 feet 10 inches in height, 1 foot 2 inches thick, and 1 foot 9 inches broad. It is cut in Devanágari characters on three of its four sides, and the letters are well preserved, except in one place, where a slip is broken off, and eleven letters from an important part have unfortunately been lost. This pillar, and another, also bearing an inscription, when visited by me two years ago, were put up at the end of a verandah before the village entrance-gate that the cattle might rub themselves against them.

Sálotgi is a village in the Indi Táluka of the Kaládgi district, and is about forty miles from Solápur and twenty miles south of the Bhímá. It has a Hindu temple, built after the fashion of a Muhammadan rozah, in which is worshipped a grave with a chadder on it like the tomb of a Muhammadan. Neither Muhammadans nor the lower castes of the Hindus are allowed to enter within the outer walls of the temple, except on the occasion of an annual fair held in its honour on the full moon of Chaitra (April), when, within the walls, Brahman, Mahár, Mang, and Musalman, mingle together without scruple about contamination, and, as at the great Jagannátha in Orissa, partake without caste distinction of food cooked for the occasion. In front and behind the temple there are two large wells, with steps descending to the water, and being entirely out of proportion to the size and importance of the present temple, attest the former existence of edifices which have disappeared amidst the many religious and political revolutions that have passed over the land. Part of a very much larger well, by the side of the present one in front of the temple, is now filled up and a garden cultivated on it, but the outer edges of the old well are in some places well preserved, and two or three small rooms in them may still be seen.

The villagers can give no account as to whence the two pillars came. They have a tradition that the nalla (stream) that flows on the south of the temple washed away in one monsoon the side next to the temple, and thereby discovered the two pillars that were till then buried in the earth.

At the top of the present inscription is carved in prominent relief the linga, an image of the Nandi or Bull sacred to Śiva, and the sun and moon. At the bottom of each of the first three sides containing the Sanskrit inscription there are some lines cut in the H a ḷ e or old Canarese.

The Canarese inscription commences at the bottom of that side of the stone on which the Sanskrit inscription begins, is continued at the bottom of the second side, and appears to be finished on the fourth, the whole of which is occupied by Canarese. From what I understand of it at present I can safely say that the Sanskrit inscription is perfectly independent of it, and it appears that the Canarese one was added subsequently, and that it also relates to a grant of land for the same purpose as that recorded in the Sanskrit inscription, by a Mahámandaleśvara. The college to which the Sanskrit inscription records the grant of land, &c., as also the village where it stood are mentioned in the Canarese inscription.

The inscription records that in the year Śaka 867 (A.D. 945), when king K ṛ i s h ṇ a r á j a called A k á l a v a r s h a D e v a, the son of A m o g h a v a r s h a, was reigning at M á n y a K h e ṭ a, C h a k r á y u d h a, the assistant to the minister, by name N á r á y a ṇ a, of king K ṛ i s h ṇ a r á j a, established a college and assigned lands for the maintenance of its inmates and preceptor. The village at which the college is established is called P á v i t t a g e, and is described as situated in the district of Karonpuri. I have not been able to identify this name with any modern one, or ascertain what district or districts of our own times correspond with it, though it is probable it once indicated a revenue district. But it appears beyond doubt that the Pávittage of the inscription is the same as Sálotgi, the village where the inscription is found. It is possible that Sálotgi is a corruption from Sálahattagi, or 'the village where the college is situate,' Sále being the Canarese word for college, and hattagi meaning 'village' at the end of names of villages and towns. The present ruins at Sálotgi as well as the fact that the stone bearing the inscription does not appear to have been brought from elsewhere, would go a great way to identify the latter village with Pávittage.

Náráyaṇa, the Bráhman minister of Krishṇarája, is described as living at Kanchina Maḍeval, which may perhaps be identical with the modern Muddeb[illegible].

Chakráyudha Bodha, the donor, the son of Govinda Bhaṭṭa Bodha, and lord of the village of Pávittage, is described as having gone, accompanied by two hundred Brahmans, to a place on the bank of the Godávari, and there made the grant at mid-day at the time of a solar eclipse. Unfortunately the stone is broken just at the place which contained the name of the sacred spot on the Godávari whither the donor proceeded to bathe and make the grant. The name of the place begins with Prá,—and though the Godávari is expressly mentioned as the great river on whose banks it lay (Godávaryám mahánadyám), it might have really been on the Bhíma, considering that it is not unusual to style small streams by the name of a more celebrated river of greater sanctity.

This word Mánya is repeated four or five times. In M á n y a K h e ṭ a* there can be no doubt that it is part of the name of Krishṇarája's capital, which several inscriptions distinctly mention. But as Mánya is applied to the land, the garden, and the houses or dwellings, given to the scholars and the Preceptor of the college, the word would seem to bear a technical signification, and that signification is preserved to this day in the M á n y a m s of the Madras Presidency. These M á n y a m s mean nearly the same as A g r a h á r a, a gift of charity. In Sanderson's Canarese and English Dictionary Mányam is defined as "lands either liable to a trifling quit-rent or altogether exempt from tax." In the same place the phrase B h a ṭ ṭ a M á n y a m is explained as "a small portion of rent-free land in a village for the use of Brahmans." In this inscription, accord-

* Wathen gives either Mánkya Kheṭa or Mánya Kheṭa as the name of the capital. It appears to me that the optional form Mánkya has its origin in a misreading of the name in one passage of the Kaḍa plate. In the Devanágarí alphabet of from the 9th to 12th centuries A.D. the compound letter [illegible] (nya) was written in a manner that is very like the modern [illegible]. The engraver of the plate, by a very ordinary mistake among writers, having put a dot over the [illegible], Wathen was naturally led into the mistake of reading Mánkya. In the Kharepaṭan plates, as also in this inscription, and even in the Kaḍa plate, farther on than the passage above alluded to, the name given is clearly and invariably Mánya Kheṭa.

ingly. Mânya is clearly used in the sense of 'rent-free for charitable purposes.'

The grant is described as being made in the reign of Kṛishṇarâja, who bore the title of Akâlavarsha Deva. This Kṛishṇarâja is doubtless of the family of the Yâdava kings, known also by the name of Râshṭra Kûṭas, who reigned at Mânya Kheṭa, or the modern Mal-Khed in the Nizam's territory, and whose authority was subverted by Tailapa Deva of the Châlukya dynasty about the end of the tenth century* of the Christian Era.

There would at first sight appear to be some difficulty as to which Amogha Varsha and Kṛishṇarâja Deva of the lists already published of the Yâdava kings of Mânya Kheṭa are represented by the Amogha Varsha and Kṛishṇarâja Deva mentioned in the inscription. The first list published in 1836† from what is known as the Kardâ (or Kardla ?) *copper-plate grant*, contains fourteen princes. In 1842-43 the late Bal Gangadhar Shastri furnished to the Bombay Branch of the Royal Asiatic Society, from a copper plate grant found at Khârepâṭan, another list of the same dynasty, also containing fourteen names.‡ The two lists are as follows :—

The Kardâ plate :

1 Danti Durga.
2 Kṛishṇa Râja (his paternal uncle)
3 Govinda Râja.
4 Nirupama (his youngest brother)
5 Jagat Rudra.
6 Amogha Varsha.
7 Akala Varsha.
8 Jagat Rudra.
9 Indra Nṛipa.
10 Jagat Rudra.
11 Amogha Varsha.
12 Kṛishṇa Deva.
13 Khoṭṭiga Deva.
14 Kâkala Râja.

The Khârepâṭan plate :

1 Danti Durga.
2 Kṛishṇa Râja (his paternal uncle).
3 Govinda Râja.
4 Nirupama.
5 Jagat Tunga.
6 Amogha Varsha.
7 Akâla Varsha.
8 Indra Râja (grandson of Akâla).
9 Amogha Varsha II.
10 Govinda Râja (brother of Amogha).
11 Baddiga (his paternal uncle).
12 Kṛishṇa Râja.
13 Khoṭṭiga (brother of Kṛishṇa).
14 Kakala (brother's son of Khoṭṭiga).

Prof. H. H. Wilson§ suggested that the list in the Kardâ grant represents a series of princes belonging to two different branches of the Yâdava family, reigning concurrently in two different places. He supposes that the last seven princes beginning with Jagat Rudra form a separate branch, and that Kâkala Râja, the last of the branch, was probably contemporary with Akâla Varsha. On this is based his inference that, as the last, Kâkala, made the Kardâ grant in Śaka 894, "the earliest vestiges of the Yâdavas yet met with in the Peninsula are to be placed about A. D. 867 :—for an average of fifteen years to a reign will be rather more than sufficient for the precarious authority and interrupted succession of the Hindu Râjas."

This theory of "two collateral branches" appears to be untenable. Prof. Wilson's principal ground for the supposition of "two collateral branches" is, that in the Kardâ plate to which his remarks relate, Kâkala Râja the donor (entitled Amogha Varsha) is described as "meditating on" Akâla Varsha's "feet," which he construed to mean that Akâla Varsha lived in the time of Kâkala, and that the latter was subordinate to the former. Now the words "meditating on his feet"‖ do not necessarily suggest that Akâla Varsha Deva was then alive, but that Kâkala Deva took Akâla Varsha Deva as the model for his conduct. In the present inscription Kṛishṇa Deva, who was reigning supreme, is described as "devoted to the contemplation of his father's feet," and yet everything in the context goes to show that his father was not living.

Again in the Kardâ inscription Amogha Varsha, the 6th of the above lists, is expressly stated to have had Mânya Kheṭa as his capital; and further on Kâkala Deva Râja is also described as "residing at Śrî

* See Jour. Bom. Br. R. As. Soc. Vol. I. p. 210ff.
† Dr Wathen, Jour. R. As. Soc. Vol. III. p. 103.
‡ See Jour. Bomb. Br. R. As. Soc. Vol. I. p. 211.

§ Journal Royal As. Soc. vol. II., and p. 105 vol. III. pp. 202-4.
‖ S'rimad-Akâla-Varsha-Deva pâdânudhyâta.

Mânya-Kheṭa-Pura." Now if Kâkala Deva Râja, belonging to a different branch of the same Yâdava family, reigned concurrently with Amogha Varsha (the 6th of the lists), as Prof. Wilson supposes, they could not have had the same city for their capital. Besides, in the Karda inscription there is nothing that would justify the theory that the list of fourteen princes forms two branches of the Yâdava family reigning concurrently with each other. The mention of the Chedi family of the Yâdavas shows that the Manya Kheta princes intermarried with the former.

Then, since Prof. Wilson made these remarks, the date of Govinda Râja, the third of the above lists, has been discovered to be Śaka 730 (A. D. 808) from a copper-plate grant found in the Nâsik district.* Now if Kâkala Râja Deva was contemporary with Akâla Varsha, the seventh of the above lists, then the age of that Akâla Varsha must be the same as that of Kâkala Râja, viz., Śaka 894, and the date of Govinda Râja being Śaka 730, leaves an interval of 164 years and three princes; and even allowing ten years, the portions of the reigns of Govinda Râja and Akâla Varsha, included, we have still an average of 18 years for the reign of each of the intervening princes, which is far too much.

Lastly:—If two branches of the Yâdavas had reigned concurrently, the Khârepâṭan inscription would surely have contained some allusion to this, whereas the list on it is essentially the same as that contained in the Kardâ plate.

It seems clear therefore that the fourteen princes belonged to the same Yâdava family that reigned at Mânya-Kheṭa, and that Kâkala Râja, the fourteenth of the lists, and the grantor of the Kardâ copper-plate grant, did not live at the same time with Akâla Varsha the seventh.

Now there can be no doubt that the Kṛishṇa Deva of the present inscription corresponds with No. 12 of the Kardâ plate. Kṛishṇa Râja's title is Akâla Varsha, and at first sight, Amogha Varsha the 6th and Akâla Varsha the 7th of the lists would seem to claim identification with the two princes of this inscription. The claim would also seem to be strengthened by the fact that both the Kardâ and the Khârepâṭan plates agree with it in describing Amogha Varsha (the 6th of the lists) as the father of Akâla Varsha. But if we identify Akâla Varsha with the 7th of the lists, the difference between him and Govinda Râja, whose date is given as Śaka 730, would be 164 years, a period that is too long for five princes. The Amogha Varsha of this inscription is identical with No. 11 and Kṛishṇa Râja with No. 12 of the Karda plate.

The date of Kṛishṇa Râja Deva being then Śaka 867, and that of Kâkala Râja, Śaka 894, there is only a difference of 27 years, which is not too long for three princes.

The objections to this identification are—*1st*, that the Kardâ plate makes Kṛishṇa Râja (the twelfth) not the son, but a brother, of his predecessor Amogha Varsha, whereas this inscription describes him as his son; and *lastly*, that the Khârepâṭan plate does not mention Kṛishṇa Râja as Amogha Varsha's successor, but gives two princes, Govinda Râja and Baddiga, as intervening between them.

The first objection can only be met by supposing that the Kardâ plate is not quite accurate in giving Kṛishṇa Deva as the *brother* of Amogha Varsha. This is not very extraordinary, seeing that the genealogies of kings have often-times been at the mercy of the memory of Sanskrit writers.

As for the discrepancy between this inscription and the Khârepâṭan plate, it is possible that Baddiga, the predecessor, according to the latter, of Kṛishṇa Râja, might have borne the title of Amogha Varsha. For Baddiga is only the name of the king, not his title. And as No. 11 in the Karda plate is put down as Amogha Varsha, i.e., by the title, not by the name of the King, it is possible that No. 11 of the Karda plate was the same as No. 11 of the Khârepâṭan one.†

The testimony of the Karda plate on the score of some Amogha Varsha being the predecessor of Kṛishṇa Deva is more trustworthy than the discredit thrown on that fact by the list of the Khârepâṭan plate, first because the latter list was recorded in Śaka 930 (A. D. 1008), or about 40 years after the reign of Kâkala Raja, and sixty-six years after the date of the present inscription; and secondly, because it occurs in a document relating to a dynasty subordinate to the Châlukyas, who were antagonistic to, and had subverted the authority of the Mânyakheṭa princes.

The Kṛishṇa Râja Deva of this inscription

* At Van-Dindori, and published in No. X of the *Asiatic Society's Journal*.

† The arrangement on page 207 indicates another way of co-ordinating the lists.—Ed.

being identified with Krishṇa Deva, No. 12 of the above list, it can hardly admit of doubt that Amogha Varsha, No. 11 of the Karda plate, must be taken to be the father of Krishṇa Râja Deva as stated by our inscription; which being dated during Krishṇa Râja's own reign was less likely to be in error regarding the relation between the two princes than either the Karda plate, which was dated about twenty-seven years, or a generation after Krishṇa Râja, or the Kharepatan plate, which was given full sixty years after that prince, and in a district far removed from Mânya-khеṭa.

It is to be noticed that the inscription makes mention of **Krishṇa Râja** being intent upon making an expedition of conquest upon **Kalyâṇa**, the capital of the Châlukyas, thus confirming what we already know—that the latter were antagonists to the Râshṭra Kûṭa kings of Mânyakheṭa. The expression "engaged in reducing the prosperous and great Kalyâṇa" might mean that Krishṇa Deva was the first of his dynasty who undertook an expedition upon the city of the Châlukyas during their temporary bereavement of it, or that the hold of the Râshṭra Kûṭa kings over that city, obtained long before his time, had been shaken by some other rival or by the Châlukya family, who must be supposed to have been attempting at this time to recover it, since they actually did recover it about fifty years later under Tailapa Deva.

The solar eclipse recorded in the inscription was calculated for me by Prof. Kero Lakshman Chhatre, and found to correspond with the Śaka year 867, in which year, in Bhâdrapada, there did occur a solar eclipse. But as usual in the Dekhan inscriptions, the Bârhaspatya or cycle year, Plavanga, mentioned in the inscription, does not correspond with Śaka 867, in which the cycle year Viśvâvasu occurred, and between which and Plavanga there intervene two years. Whatever may be the proper explanation of this oft-recurring discrepancy, the agreement between the year Śaka 867 and the solar eclipse leaves no doubt whatever that Śaka 867 is the correct date of the inscription. By Professor Chhatre's calculations, it has been further found that the new moon of Bhâdrapada in Śaka 867 fell upon Tuesday, as mentioned in the inscription.

To recapitulate then what has been said above regarding the Yadava princes of *Mânya Kheṭa*, we find—

1. That the series of fourteen princes given in the Karda copper-plate grant is made up of kings of one and the same family who reigned one after another at Mânya-Kheṭa.

2. That the date of **Govinda Râja**, the third of the lists being Śaka 730, and that the last prince of the list being Śaka 894, it is probable that the reign of **Danti Durga**, the first prince of the lists, might be taken to have commenced about 40 years before that of Govinda Râja, or A.D. 767, and not A.D. 867 as supposed by Prof. Wilson, and that consequently the Mânya-Kheṭa line of kings covers a period of about two centuries.

3. That **Amogha Varsha**, No. 11 of the Karda plate, was the father of **Krishṇa Deva**, No. 12 in the same, and that the title of the latter prince was Akâla Varsha, and that he was on the throne in Śaka 867; and

4. That **Krishṇa Râja Deva**, No. 12 in the Karda list, given above, should have Akâla Varsha added to him as his title, and that he should be put down as the son of **Amogha Varsha**.

Translation.

PROSPERITY! Victorious is the excellent child* born of Vinatâ, and belonging to Vishṇu, and manifested in [visible] form, carrying him,† whose body is the three-fold universe, and pre-eminent among those that are possessed of bodies! From‡ the time of Śaka eight hundred and sixty-seven years having passed, and as many years in figures,§ when the year Plavanga is current, the people being happy, the country abounding in wealth of corn of various kinds, the beloved son of the glorious King **Amoghavarsha Parameśvara**, **Akâlavarsha**‖ **Deva** [by title], the excellent, devoted to the contemplation of his father's (lit. elder's) feet, engaged in reducing the prosperous and great

* This refers to the great Eagle Garuḍa, the conveyance of Vishṇu, and the son of Vinatâ.

† Vishṇu.

‡ Śakakâla. From this it is clear that Śaka was regarded in the tenth century A.D. as a proper name.

§ Śakakâla ... [illegible] ... The words ... show that the figures indicating the number 867 was intended to be put after them. But no numerals are cut on the stone, doubtless through an oversight of the engraver. In documents of the present day it is very usual in the vernaculars to give a certain number in figures, and say also so many in words. The reversion of the order in the inscription is owing to the latter being mainly in verse.

‖ The original being *Pṛithvî-vallabhâkâlavarsha-Deva* the title may be *Akâlavarsha* or *Kâlavarsha*, but as previous inscriptions contain Akâla Varsha as the title of princes of the Yâdava family of Mânya Kheṭa, I take Akâla Varsha as the title here.

Kalyâṇa, beloved of the world, and possessed of prosperity, is living in virtuous happiness in *Mânya Kheṭa*, where his army is stationed, which is full of beautiful palaces, where the banks are adorned by assemblages of millions of the wives of warriors, and is always protecting his subjects: when that compassionate king is giving innumerable articles to Brahmans and others, whose lotus-like feet receive the kisses of the crown-jewels of many kings, when he is shining in glory resplendent, and possessed of eyes like the lotus—the king who has rendered his own (i.e., brought under his sway) the circle (*maṇḍala*) of his enemies by means of the exceeding splendour of the power of his arms (lit. hands), and who has achieved* victory over the quarters of the world Kṛishṇarâja [to wit] reigning: Here in the district called Karpapuri,† the best of [all] districts, in the beautiful village which is well known by the name of Pâvittage. Living in the village known as Kanchana Maduvol in the prosperous country of Mâlisha, belonging to the clan of Kaundinya and the Sâkhâ (recension or branch of the Vedas) of the Vâjasaneyâs, and studying the branch of Kaṇva, is the son of Dammayarya,‡ rich and liberal, who, full of valour, is known by the name of Nârâyaṇa, like another Nârâyaṇa§ himself; who, full of learning, is known by the cognomen of [illegible], who is the minister of Kṛishṇarâja, and being his counsellor is [also] entrusted with the affairs of War and Peace. [Now] he who was his (Nârâyaṇa's) assistant, beloved like his right hand, and powerful, employed by him‖ in negotiating war and peace, thoroughly versed in the sciences concerning government, dear to the poets, agreeable in his conversation, and who believing in religion appears like embodied Dharma¶: By him this college has been caused to be constructed (established), rich, spacious and beautiful, as by** the creator who by his own will has established this three-fold universe. And this college full of intelligence† is resplendent with Brahmans. Here there are scholars born in various districts. For these subsistence is [hereby] provided, the details of which as to place and time shall now be described in order that the fame of it may be spread.

The lord of this village of Pavittage, born in the clan of Kâśyapa, the chief of the Vâjasaneyas, the flower of the followers of the Kaṇva Branch, son of Govindabhaṭṭa, excellent in his conduct as a Brahman, pure and possessing the sacred fire, Chakrâyudha Budha by name, possessed of fortunateness, chief among those who can speak, learned in theology, learned in sacred law, possessed of wisdom, glorious, born to be obeyed, agreeable in his talk, following the dictates of the sacred law, and full of splendour like [illegible] himself,—in the currency of the year mentioned above, and in the good month of Bhâdrapada, on the day‡ sacred to the Manes, corresponding with Tuesday, at the time of a solar eclipse, the sun being in the middle (i.e., on the meridian at noon) on the great river Godâvarî§ . . . . million . . . . . . sacred places . . . . . . which (or who) . . . . . by name Pra . . . . village . . . . that resplendent one (Chakrâyudha) of great virtue, accompanied by two hundred Brahmans, having stood and bathed in the great sacred spot, and having performed his religious duties, gave land rent-free to the scholars of the college, in this village known as Pâvittage, the mine of virtues,—rent-free land measured by five hundred nivartanas.‖ And the excellent son of Govinda Budha piously gave twenty-seven rent-

---

* *Kṛita digvijaya*. This means that the king had compelled the kings of the earth to pay him tribute, an epithet not applied to an ordinary prince, but to an emperor like Raghu, one of the heroes of Kâlidâsa's poem Raghuvaṁśa.

† *Sa karpapurî nâma vishaya*. Karpapuri would appear literally to be the name of a town, but here it is evidently applied to a district. This use of the word is not rare in southern inscriptions and copperplate grants.

‡ *Dâmâpârya-suta*. The name *Dâmapârya* would appear to be a sanskritised form of the Canarese name Damappa or Dâmappayyâ, very common in the Karnâṭaka.

§ Vishṇu.

‖ The original is [illegible]. The repetition of the instrumental case is a slip of the engraver's hand.

¶ This may be taken to signify either Religion, or the god Yama, who presides over justice.

** The original though perfectly legible and clear is here confused apparently through a mistake of the engraver. It reads: [illegible] (*svâyaṁ*), which appears to be a mistake for [illegible].

† [illegible]. It is possible that *manovatî* is here used in the sense of *Sarasvatî*, the wife of Brahmâ. The sense would then be 'The college shines like *Manovatî* united with *Brahmâ*.' The words *Manovatî* and *Brahma* have a double sense; as applied to the college, the former would mean 'full of intelligence,' and the latter 'united with Brahmans,' i.e., having Brahmans for its students. The translation given above is on the supposition that the reading may be somewhat [illegible].

‡ *Pitṛiparvani*, i.e., the *amâvâsyâ*, or day of new moon.

§ Here a chip is broken off from the middle of the stone, and some middle letters of three lines, viz., four syllables of two lines each and three of one, are destroyed.

‖ A nivartana is a square measure of land, equivalent to two hundred square cubits.

SÁLOṬGI INSCRIPTION Side 1.

Govt. Litho Press Bombay

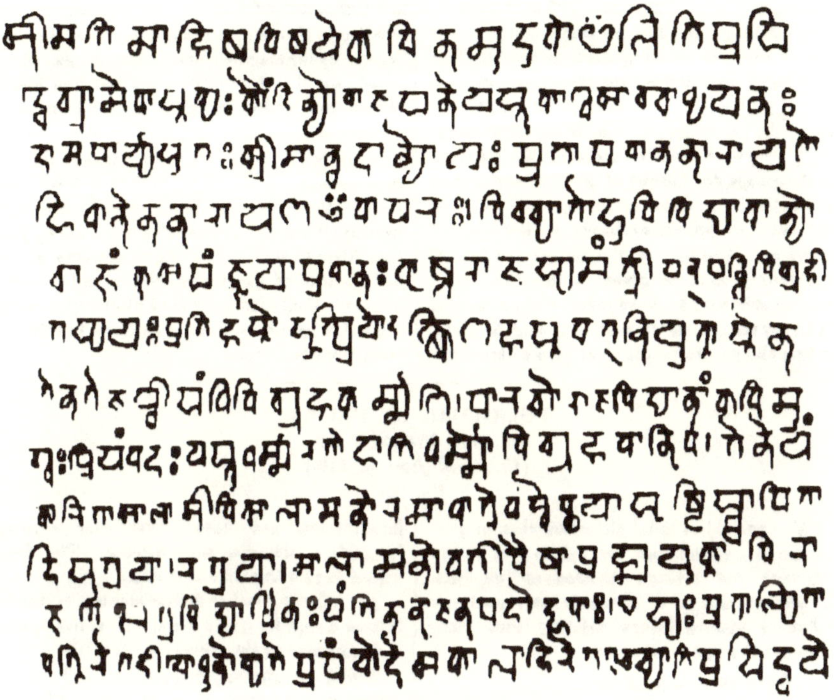

SALOTGI INSCRIPTION Side 1 [illegible]

Side [illegible]

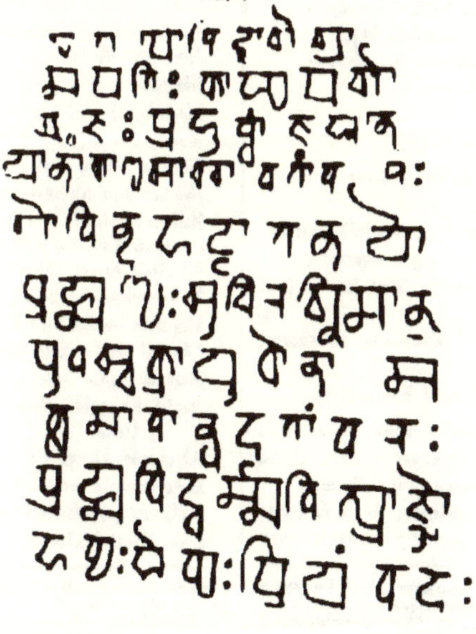

five dwellings, and half as many more* ; and also a rent-free flower garden measuring four nivartanas, and twelve nivartanas [of] rent-free [land] for lamps. On the occasion of a marriage, the [marriage] people, being Brahmans, shall give to the congregation of the scholars of the college five [illegible] of good money.† And at the time of a [illegible] ceremony shall be given the same as prescribed above in the case of marriage. And half of the former and half of the latter‡ shall be given at the time of a [illegible] ceremony by those people who perform it. If for any cause a feast to Brahmans shall be given in this village, the people shall give a dinner according to their means to the members of the college. By the [illegible] (*Chaturvedin*) fifty nivartanas of rent-free land and a rent-free house within this college are given to the lecturer.

The earth has been enjoyed by many kings commencing from Sagara. To whomsoever the land belongs for the time, to him belongs the fruit for that time. This bridge of religion is common to all kings. It should be protected by you from time to time. This Râma entreats again and again of all kings that will reign in future. Whoever shall take away land whether given by himself or by others, lives as an insect in filth for sixty thousand years.

FOLK-LORE OF ORISSA.

BY JOHN BEAMES, B.C.S.

(Continued from p. 179.)

No. II.

Witches object to be disturbed when in possession of a victim, and are apt to turn on the exorciser and revenge themselves on him. To prevent this it is advisable to repeat the following mantra before attempting that mentioned in the last number:—

> Bajra kilant bajra dwar
> Chau kali chau dwar
> Dahâne Dihâuchandi bâme bhairavi
> Age Narsinghâ, pachhe [illegible] bagal
> [illegible] pinda [illegible]
> Koti ... [illegible]!
> Kâhâr âgyâ?
> Kâmâkhyâ Kâmâkhyâr koti âgyâ.

Thunder-bolt bar, thunder-bolt door
Four sides, four doors.
On the right Dahanchandi, on the left Bhairâvi,
In front Narsingh, behind eight demons,
The great seal, the thunder door, has fallen
  on my body,
If a myriad come, do not allow one to enter!
By whose order?
The myriad orders of Kamâri Kâmâkhya.

I do not attempt to make sense of all this rubbish. It is sufficient to observe that there are human beings who believe in its efficacy.

Kamâri Kâmâkhyâ, Dahânchandi and some others are deities who specially preside over incantations, and have power over spirits, hobgoblins, demons, and witches. The first named is said to reside in Assam.

The following rather difficult mantra is infallible as a cure for snake bites. It is not quite such nonsense as the others:—

> [illegible] [illegible] jyoti,
> Kamal [illegible] prabhu Dâsaratha.
> Kathak [illegible] Krishna Kalambar mâla,
> [illegible] Jamunâr jale.
> Jamunâ jale [illegible] maya [illegible].
> [illegible] kila [illegible]
> [illegible] dwarika [illegible],
> Kanak [illegible] jhapila [illegible]
> [illegible] prabhu chakradhar.
> [illegible]
> Kâlîa [illegible]
> [illegible]
> Khâilâr [illegible] lâgila [illegible]
> Tâhar [illegible] jagila
> [illegible] prabhu,
> [illegible] Himagiri [illegible],
> [illegible] amrut [illegible]
> [illegible]
>   thila.
> [illegible]
> Dele amritâ [illegible] bhagawânâ.
> [illegible]
> Dubi Bisti Mûka [illegible] koti [illegible].

* [illegible] | The words [illegible] might also mean 'twenty-seven and a half.'

† [illegible] | [illegible] [illegible]. The translation of [illegible] 'five flowers,' given above, is literal.

‡ [illegible] etc. That is half of what shall be given at the time of a marriage and half of that which shall be given at a thread ceremony. The sum is five.

Light of the sun on the mountain at night,
The lord Dasaratha went holding a lotus.
Krishna put his sandals at the root of the
Kadambari tree,
Slowly slowly he advanced his feet in the
Jamuná's water.
In the Jamuná's water was a snake foolish
with illusion,
Bharata informed him; Sankat-kihat-kili;
He bit holding him the poison went twelve
fingers deep,
The exorcist swept many incantations
Then the lord Chakradhar did not move,
The gods began to consult
Where art thou, ho! Garur come ho! they said.
Garur was feeding in the Ramyak island
His food tasted to him like poison.
His history I will tell, conqueror of the world!
I tell thee O lord of birds,
Rushing enter the Himalaya mountain;
In the mountain there was a pot of nectar
With swords and maces ten thousand Gan-
darbas and Yakshas surround it
Garur spread his wings a little
He gave the nectar, the lord Bhagwan arose.
Student bring in thy hand a gift to the good
guru.
I salute a myriad myriad times Debi Bisti Má.

"Sankat, kihat, kili" are nonsense words, which though they are just translateable are stated to be here used in some mystic sense. Garur is the Uriya pronunciation of Garuda. Debi Bisti is another of the goddesses who have power over demons. The short ŏ is the equivalent of अ and is so pronounced in open unaccented syllables, though it sounds a in accented or closed ones.

This spell for snakes is firmly believed in, while it is being uttered the part affected must be tightly rubbed by the hand of the exorcist, and this is what is meant by the expression "the exorcist swept many spells." The continued belief in the efficacy of this spell may be due to the fact that several of the Orissa snakes are not deadly, though their bites cause pain and swelling. This is particularly the case with the grass-snakes, as well as with the blue and yellow snake found on the sea-shore which is only really dangerous when in the water.

LEGEND OF THE ORIGIN OF THE TUNGABHADRA RIVER.

Once upon a time in the remote past, the earth was carried away bodily to Pátála, or the nether regions of the world, by the powerful giant Hiranyaksha. The Devas, ever noted for their pusillanimity, were in consequence deprived of their legitimate perquisites in the shape of havis, or sacrificial food, and, unable to redress their own wrongs, went to Kshíra Ságara, or the milky ocean, and laid their complaint at the feet of Vishņu, who was living on an island called Śvéta Dwípá. Vishņu was graciously pleased to grant their petition, and, incarnate in the form of a boar, conquered the giant, and rescued the earth from his grasp. When the earth was unrolled, the deliverer found that Váráha Parvata was the land's end, and therefore rested on its summit for a while. While in this posture, the right tusk of the boar broke [for some unexplained reason], and presently there gushed forth from it the river Bhadrá. From the left tusk, which was longer than the other, sprang at the same time the sister river Tungá. Simultaneously, a third stream issued from the eyes of the boar, called Netrávati. The two former, taking different courses towards the east, unite at Kúdli, about eighty miles from the source, and become thenceforward the compound river of Tungabhadrá. The last named stream goes in an opposite direction below the ghâts, and unites with another sea-going river called Kumáradhárá.

In this manner, the aforesaid rivers, being of divine origin, exist in the world for the spiritual (as well as temporal) benefit of sinful mankind.

The foregoing history, contained in the Bhavishyóttara Puráņa, and related to Shaņmukha by his father Rudra, was repeated by Krishņa to Dharmarája, as having been inculcated to Kurukula Mahárája by Nárada.

The rival rivers Tungá and Bhadrá take their rise in the same alpine tract of country, in the extreme west of the province of Maisúr, about 150 miles as a crow flies from Bangalor. The source is called Ganga Múla, and is scarcely accessible for two or three months in the hot weather. It is however frequented by pilgrims, who seek to wash off their sins by bathing in the rivers at their sources. It is certainly no easy task to unravel the tangled mass of mystery and superstition involved in the above legend. But it is suggested that the early Brahmans, wishing to secure for the region a special celebrity and holiness, have endowed the rivers with a divine origin, in imitation of the myth which connects the Ganges with the foot of Vishnu. The hill from which the rivers flow has, from a distance, the faintest possible resemblance to the form of a boar, and Vishnu manifested himself, according to the Purânas, in one of his avatârs as a boar. These two circumstances being put together, can it be possible that the mystery of the legend is solved? The name Gangâ Mâta is certainly suggestive.

V. N. N.

THE SACRED FIRE OF THE PARSIS AT UDWÂḌÂ.

By W. RAMSAY, Bo. C.S.

The ancient followers of the religion of Zoroaster had been reduced by years of persecution to a comparatively small band of fugitives; giving up all hope of better times in a land in which they had once reigned supreme, they took refuge on board ship, and sailing from Ormasdbandar eventually landed on the isle of Diu, off the coast of Kâthiâwâḍ, where they remained for some years; but they were not to remain in peace even here, so again embarking* on board ship the "Colony" steered for the shores of the Konkan. A great storm overtook them, and the pilgrims in their fear vowed a vow that, if spared to reach the land, they would set up again the sacred fire which had been lost in their first flight from their old home. The storm ceased, the sky cleared, and under a bright sun the wanderers landed on the shores of what was then the kingdom of Sanjân, ruled over by a Râja of Rajput lineage. The prince received them favourably, and gave a kaul or charter defining their future rights and liabilities. By this they were debarred from the use of arms; their apparel was fixed after the fashion ever since in vogue among them; and their various rites and ceremonials, religious and social, were recorded, and as it were stereotyped. For 674 years† the Parsi community went on multiplying and thriving as they do at the present day, when a Subah of the then Pâdshah, one 'Mâhmud Beg,'‡ invaded the kingdom of Sanjân, and pressed the Râja hard. In his distress, he applied to the Parsis, and put arms into their hands. Three times did the latter under a heroic leader named Ardeshir beat back the ill-disciplined levies of Mahmud, but a fourth invasion was successful, and the Zoroastrians were again compelled to fly in search of fortune. This time, however, they managed to preserve their sacred fire, which, in accordance with the vow of their ancestors, had been kept ever burning during their sojourn in Sanjân. The fugitives reached Bhârat, in the hills above Wânsda, and there cherished the holy flame for some years. The fire had been borne somewhat after the manner of the ark of the Israelites in the desert; it was carried by the priests in a sort of a litter, by night to hide it from the rays of the sun, the touch of which would be a catastrophe to be averted by all means, and so covered up as to be safe from the possible profane gaze of the outer and uninitiated world. But the fire was not to burn on in peace, and soon it was moved to Wânsda, where it remained 14 years, and thence to Nausâri, where for 318 years§ the flame burned peacefully and without interruption.‖ But internal dissensions arose, and again a move was made to Surat, thence after three years, back again to Nausâri, and thence again to Balsâr, the mystic and sacred fire being ever borne in the dead of night by the trusty guardians of its mysteries. After a sojourn of two years at Balsâr, the priests had an interview with the Râja of Mândvi, Durgam Singhji, then residing in his fort at Pârdi. Protection was implored and promised, and a choice given of certain villages on the sea coast for a residence. At Udwâḍâ was found a small band of Parsis and a Tower of Silence, and here the fugitives fixed their choice of a resting place. A sanad was given them conferring certain privileges and immunities. This is stated to have been in the Samvat year 1799, (A.D. 1742,) or about 130 years ago. A small temple was erected to shelter the fire; some years after a larger temple was built on the same site which was subsequently enlarged, and finally about 43 years ago the present edifi-

* About A.D. 717. See the *Kissah-i-Sanjân*, of Bahman Kaikobad (A.D. 1600) in the *Jour. Bomb. B. R. As. Soc.* Vol I. pp. 167 191.

† The first Atash-Behrâm is said to have been erected by the Anjuman of Sanjân, and consecrated by Neryosang Dhaval in Samvat 777, or A.D. 721. See Wilson, *Parsi Religion*, p. 557.—Ed.

‡ This is doubtless Mâhmud Begada of Ahmadâbâd, who invaded this district in A.D. 1507. See *Notes of a Visit to Gujarât*, p. 15. Wilson, *Sermon to the Parsis* (1862), p. 14.

§ There is probably an error of 100 years in this period. Nausâri is the *Nausaripa* of Ptolemy.—Ed.

‖ Fryer mentions the Fire-temple at Nausari in 1675, *New Account of East India, &c.* p. 117. The present temple at this place was consecrated by Dastur Sorabji Rustamji in [illegible], and to it all the young *Mobeds* from Bombay and elsewhere are sent for confirmation.—Ed.

tal building was erected by the liberality of Dâdâbhâî Pestanji Wâdia of Bombay.

Such is the story as told by the old Dastur or Chief Priest of Udwâdâ, a lineal descendant, as he avers, of the priest who revived the sacred flame in the kingdom of Sanjân. Udwâdâ has a considerable population of this priestly caste, but not all of them actually hold any sacerdotal office. The priests are divided into nine *Bêdys* or families, who serve the fire by turns for a month at a time, the members of the *body* specially sanctified to the office taking their turns to feed the flame, which burns in a large brazen pot, with sandal and babul wood, their only fare.

Udwâdâ has its Parsi school which is well attended, and where among other things the *Zend Avesta* is taught; but neither teacher nor scholars know aught of the meaning of what they read and recite, nor is there a single Mobed in all the place who knows anything more. As is well known, with comparatively few exceptions, the Parsis know nothing of the meaning of the prayers they recite, or of the quotations they make from their sacred books. The original Zend, I am told, and not any translation into Pahlvi, is in use at Udwâdâ.

THE SANJAN S'LOKAS.

(From 'Notes of a Visit to Gujarat,' by the Editor.)

In connexion with the landing of the Parsis at Sanjan, in the early part of the 8th century, there still exist copies of the sixteen Sanskrit *S'lokas*, in which their Mobeds explained their religion to Jâdi Râṇâ,* the Raja of the place, and the reply he gave them. These *S'lokas* form the oldest document relating to the Parsis in India,† and the following version of them may interest some readers; it is compiled principally from a translation prepared by Dastur Hoshang Jamasp, the learned High Priest at Puna, and has been compared with an old version in the possession of Dr. Wilson. The last two distichs have been taken from the latter version—the Dastur's MSS. being unintelligible. I am informed by Dr. Wilson that he has not found "any two independent copies, either in Sanskrit or in the Gujarati translations, that agree in words, though they conform to one another in their general scope."

Translation of the Sanjân S'lokas.

1. They who thrice a day worship the sun, the elemental fire—fire, wind, earth, ether, water,—the three worlds, through the *Naiah Mantras*, and the divine Hormazd the chief of the *Suras* (or angels), the highly endowed, the exalted, the merciful one,—are we—the fair, the bold, the valiant, the athletic, the Parsis.‡

2. We observe silence, according to our religious precepts, in these seven situations—in making the fire-oblation,§ bathing, contemplating the divinity, reading the sacred books, eating, and performing the functions of nature. The best among us always give liberally in alms, and adore the splendid fire with various scented woods, sweet flowers, and the best fruits. Such are we—the fair, the courageous, the brave, the strong, the Parsis.

3. They who wear the shirt (*sadra*), and who have raised their loins, of good woollen thread, the sacred *kusti* with equal ends, and who cover the crown of the head with a cap of two folds, are we—the fair, the fearless, the valiant, and athletic Parsis.

4. On marriage and other festal days, and on usual holidays, we rejoice with song and the sound of instruments. Our maids at such times, perfume their persons with *Srikhanda Sandal* and sweet scents; we are firm in our pure religion, which abounds in good and perfect precepts, and is of advantage in all its observances: such are we—the fair, &c., the Parsis.

5. We keep our houses clean, with plenty of food, and what is pleasing to the taste; and water from tanks or wells we always offer in charity with clothes and money to deserving mendicants. Such are we, &c.‖

6. As pleasure and pain, ease and trouble, knowledge and ignorance, virtue and vice, uprightness and baseness, health and sickness, light and darkness, existence and destruction, are double and opposite in the system of the world, so we have opposites in our belief. Such are we, &c.

7. Drinking thrice of *gaumutra*, consecrated with mantras and carefully preserved, we purify our insides; and then, after outward and inward purification, we replace the *kusti* on our waists; and without this girdle we may not engage in silent meditation, in offerings, or other good acts. Such is our custom which is ever pleasing; and such are we, &c.

8.¶ Intercourse with women of ill-fame is forbidden. Our parents and ancestors we honour and

* He is called *Jâdi Rânâ* by the Parsis, and Dr. J. Wilson suggests he may have been Jayasinha or Vana Râja of Anahillawâda Pattan, who ruled in Gujarat A. D. 746-806.—Ed.

† As Dr. J. Wilson suggests, these s'lokas were perhaps composed ex post facto.

‡ Wilson, *Parsi Religion*, p. 210.

§ The fire-oblation is called *hom* or the performance of *Atash Nyaish*, in which the Parsis feed the sacred fire with sandal wood, &c., five times a day.

‖ There are considerable differences among the readings of different copies in the 5th and 6th *S'lokas*.

¶ The 8th, 9th, 10th, 11th, and 12th in this version, are the 10th, 11th, 8th, 13th, and 9th respectively of the older version.

celebrate their *Sráddhas*; we pay due respect to fire; we do not use meat without sacrificing it; our females lately delivered or in their courses spread their bedding on the floor; our marriages are celebrated at the most propitious hours, and the widow who has lost her husband is not considered pure.* Such are we, the Parsis,—observing daily these religious rites.

9 Till a Parsi woman who has borne a child has passed forty days, she cannot cook victuals, she should be moderate in her talk and sleep; nor ought she to bathe (*snána*) for forty days, to pray or adore the sun. We always venerate the æther, fire, earth, water, the moon, the sun, and *Yazad*. So is our tribe ever esteemed and acceptable.

10. Only with fuel six months dried (do we feed the sacred fire); and sandal wood, aloe-wood of *Malaya*, and benzoin, we use five times a-day to perform the *Homa* (fire oblation), uttering appointed words and formulas [in the *Avesta Vendid*]; The fire is kept under a dome in shade from the sun's rays. We are ever true and just in our motives, and never addicted to young women. Such are we Parsis, &c.

11. As spoken by our *guru* (teacher) and enjoined by our writings, we preserve round the waist above the sadra, a woollen band, neat, of golden colour, long and entire like a *mekhla* (or zone); the many advantages of wearing it are equal to snána (ablution) in the Ganges. Such are we, &c.

12. In our minds we ever reflect upon the æther, the moon, fire, the earth, the sun, and worship Hormazd as the bestower of victory, religion, and natural desires. We especially observe graces (*âfrîns*) before and after meals to render them wholesome. Such are we, &c.

13. Our females are held pure only after passing seven nights from the commencement of their menses, and a month from childbirth, when only they are pure. We are beautiful in our dress, fair and of golden colour, vigorous, and strong: Such are we, &c.

14. For expiation of sin we make *confession* (?) and as *panchagavya* (five products of the cow) is used, we first anoint our persons with *gomutra*, before washing them with water, and after nine days we are clean. We constantly keep all the sayings of our *guru*, and are happy in observing his directions for the ablution of our sins. Such are we—the fair, the bold, the brave, the athletic Parsis.

15. The inspired sage who appointed these religious observances for the guidance of men, promised eternal bliss to those who walked according to them. And we believe their supporters have found places in heaven. To their sacred memories devout Parsis strew sandal and pulse upon the ground. Such, &c.

16. (*The Rana's Reply*:) Welcome to those who walk faithfully in the way of Hormazd! May their race increase! May their prayers obtain the remission of their sins, and the smile of Heaven; also may abundance of wealth, and the fulfilment of their desires flow from the liberality of *Lakshmi*; and may the ornaments of person and of mind which now adorn them continue to distinguish them among people for ever!

NOTES ON THE RASAKALLOLA, AN ANCIENT ORIYA POEM.

BY JOHN BEAMES, B.C.S., M.R.A.S., BALASOR.

THE Rasakallola or "Waves of Delight" is the most popular poem in Orissa. Its songs are sung by the peasantry in every part of the country, many of its lines have passed into proverbs, and have become "household words" with all classes. It owes this great popularity in some measure to its comparative freedom from long Sanskrit words, being for the most part, except when the poet soars into the higher style, written in the purest and simplest Oriya vernacular.

The great religious revival in India in the fourteenth and fifteenth centuries, with which the name of Chaitanya is inseparably connected throughout Orissa and Bengal, turned the current of popular thought in the direction of the worship of Vishnu, under his newly-invented, or perhaps I should say, recently popularised, manifestation of Krishna. It is to the Vaishnavas in all parts of India that we owe the earliest and most copious outpourings of poetic thought. In the majority of instances these poems are monotonous, childish, and indescribably indecent variations on the leading features of the Bhagavata Purána. The Rasakallola is one of this class, and superadds to the usual impurity of Indian poems on this subject, that special and peculiarly revolting obscenity which is the distinguishing characteristic of the Oriya mind.

Fortunately, however, the earlier parts of the poem, relating as they do to incidents in the childhood of Krishna, are free from this objection, and from them we may be able to reproduce extracts which will exhibit the nature and style of this popular work without offending against propriety.

* For menstruation ?

The author of the Rasakallola, Dín Krishna Dás, was a Vaishnava or quasi-religious idler at the great temple of Jagannáth at Puri. He is popularly believed to be the son of the god. His mother was one of the female devotees who live in the temple, and are, theoretically, chaste and virtuous. The lady in question, however, one fine morning, was delivered of a son, to the great scandal of the highly virtuous society. Being asked how she came to do such a reprehensible thing, she related a long and somewhat confused story to the effect that one night as she was worshipping in the temple while all the others were asleep, the god himself descended from his shrine, and honoured her with his society. This story so effectually accounted for the birth of Dín Krishna, and so ingeniously removed all scandal from the sacred community, that it was eagerly taken up and trumpeted abroad. The boy was brought up as a Vaishnava, and, as far as the Pandits of the present day know, spent the whole of his uneventful life at Puri, composing poetry and dawdling about the courtyards and gateways of the temple. His date is ascertained approximately by the fact that some verses of his in praise of the reigning sovereign Purushottam Deb (A.D. 1478-1503) are still extant. These verses must have been written after that monarch's celebrated expedition to Conjeveram, and we may therefore place Dinkrishna Dás and his poem, the Rasakallola, at the close of the fifteenth century, that is a little less than four hundred years ago; three hundred years later than Chand the earliest Hindi poet. Dinkrishna is contemporary with the first Gujarati poet Narsingh Mehta of Junagarh, with Nanak Shah the Panjabi reformer, with Kabir and Keshab Dás of Hindustan, and with Vidyapati of Bengal. Most of these authors were followers of the new Vaishnava doctrines, and though Vishnu, under his form of Jagannáth, had long been worshipped in Orissa, yet the restoration of his temple, and we may suspect, his complete identification with Vishnu as the supreme being, only date from two hundred years earlier, if the annalists of the province may be believed. There is some doubt about the point, as many other signs seem to show that the ancient Siva worship was prevalent in Orissa till a much later date, in fact until Chaitanya himself, by his visit to the province, introduced his distinctive tenets.

Be this as it may, and the subject is one which cannot be entered into here, it is evident that in the poem before us we have the earliest fruit of the literary instincts which the Vaishnava creed awakened in Orissa, as it did in all other parts of Aryan India.

We now turn to the poem itself. It consists of 34 cantos (chhándas) varying in length from 50 to 150 lines. I have not counted the whole poem, nor in fact have I as yet finished reading it all through, but from a cursory examination I should estimate it to contain about four thousand lines. The metres are generally very light and graceful, and the poem was intended, as most of these poems are, to be sung. Indeed the Pandits strongly object to our English habit of reading poetry, and affirm that the full beauty of the metres cannot be appreciated unless they are sung, i. e. chanted through the nose in a droning sing-song. To our years the lugubrious whining, with the harsh voices which all Uriyas unfortunately possess, varied by an insane howl and accompanied by the dulcet tom-tom and the harmonious penny-whistle of the country, is not on the whole pleasing or enjoyable. *Sed de gustibus, &c.*; when read, the poem is certainly very pretty, and trips as lightly off the tongue as an Irish melody or a French chansonette.

The first canto is in a metre called Rág Gujari; and in reading poetry the final short a of Sanskrit words, which is usually dropped in prose or in speaking, must invariably be pronounced. It sounds however like a very short ŏ. In this metre no account is taken of long or short syllables; each consonant with the vowel attached to it is regarded as an *instant* or unit of the verse (mátrá), at the eighth instant there must be a caesura (jati), and after the caesura five more instants, the whole verse (charana) thus consisting of thirteen instants, and the couplet (pada) of twenty-six. Thus in the two first lines we must scan them (I mark off each instant by | and the caesura by ‖):—

Ka | ru | ṇá | dhu | ja | na | má | na° | ná | ga | ra | ná |
ya | ka | ka°

Ka | ra | dhi | ra | dhya | na | ni | na° | cha |
la | ná | ya | ka | .

This first canto opens with an invitation to all good men to meditate on Krishna whose praises are then set forth. He is declared to be the supreme god, and even Siva and Brahmá worship him. The last six lines invoke the protection of the god on the poet and his poem. They run thus:—

Karuṇá nágara nágaraja-náyaka,
Kara dhyána dhyánadhara-dáyaka |
Kashṭa-nashiddhara nashiddhara-kaṇṭaka

Kalasha-bárapara bárana-antaka
Kara ágyá Kansa-nisudana ! etaka
Kahe Dinakrishna Krishna kathá aneka.
Iti.

Ocean of mercy, lord of the ocean-born,
Make me fearless, O granter of the gift of boldness!
Thou art as lightning to the mountain of woe,
As a lion to the elephant of sin.
Give the order, O slayer of Kansa! thus saying,
"Tell Dinakrishna, many a tale of Krishna."

This extract exemplifies the taste for playing on words so much cultivated by Indian poets. Thus in the first line ságaraja, a name of Lakshmi, is introduced to jingle with the preceding ságara; in the third mahidhara-kuntaka or the "mountain-splitter" for lightning, and in the fourth bárananta or the "destroyer of elephants," for the lion,—are considered great beauties of style.

The first canto, consisting chiefly of religious ideas and invocations, naturally bristles with Sanskrit words, but in the second canto we get to business, and drop a good deal of the highflown style. It begins by relating how the earth, oppressed by demons, sought assistance from Brahma, who in order to keep up the idea of his subordination to Vishnu, is made to intercede with the supreme being on behalf of the earth. The metre (Rág chokhi) is one of the prettiest in the whole poem.

Kansa-jana kulara bhár[illegible] hoi dhartrí sundari,
Binaya kari Brahmanka áge kahilá,
"Kansa pratápare mora hoilá ati dukkha,
Ki karibi ebe kaha," boli boilá
Kamalásana sunì se katha,
Kahile Jagannáthaku dharani byathá.

Kamalamukhi Kamalákantha marakata málá
Agyá dele karuná katákhyo anái
Kichhi na bhábiba tumbhe Jadukula jái ambhe
Játa heba Kansa-jibana ghenibá páin
Kara tumbhe ebe gamana,
Karibáku gope keli ambhara mana.

Oppressed by the demon race, the beautiful earth
Making supplication before Brahma said—
"From the splendour of Kansa my body has become intolerable;
What shall I do? tell me now" speaking she said,
Kamalásana (Brahmá) hearing this speech,
Told to Jagannáth the grief of the earth.

The lotus faced, he who is a sapphire necklace on the neck of Lakshmi
Looking with pitying glance, thus gave order—
"Take thou no care; going into the race of Jadu, I
Will be born in order to take the life of Kansa.
Go thou now away,
On sporting in Gope my mind is bent."

Then follows a description of the birth of Krishna and his transfer to the house of Nand. Durgá, taking the shape of a female infant, is given to Basudeb, who brings her back from Nand's house to his own. Kansa, warned by his guards, comes and demands the child from the father. Basudeb alleges that as it is a girl it can do him no harm, and begs to be allowed to keep it. Kansa refuses to listen, and quotes from Indian mythology several instances in which Vishnu taking a female form has destroyed members of his own demon race. Here the poet indulges in a rather strikingly expressed remark on the character of bad men in general and Kansa in particular.

Karpúra chandana deí, rasuna rupile mahí,
Kebe ki chhádiba ki kutsita bása
Kutila dushta mánaba manku [illegible] abhilákhi
Lakhaku asambhaba nahi [illegible] ;
Kokila bachana madhura
Kaká kigrapa jana tanara bidhura.

In planting garlic, though it be covered with camphor and sandal,
Will it ever lose its disgusting smell?
Of crafty, wicked, unbelieving, sinful, unreflecting
Persons the nature is exactly like this.
Even the sweet voice of the bird,
Disturbs the mind of a sick man.

Kansa therefore takes the child and dashes it against a stone. As he does so it changes into the goddess Durgá, flies up into the air, and vanishes having pronounced a curse on Kansa. The rest of the canto is occupied by a description of how Nand took care of the child Krishna and his brother Balaráma.

Every line in the poem begins with the letter क; this is a favourite conceit in Oriya poetry, and is found in several other poems. It does not seem to hamper the poet at all, as a very large number of common words begin with that letter.

The language of this second canto is pure vernacular colloquial Oriya. It is only here and there that an antiquated or obsolete word occurs. This fact supplies an argument, which cannot be refuted, against the pretensions of the Bengalis, who claim the Oriya language as merely a dialect of their own, because at the time Dinkrishna wrote the Bengali language did not exist in its present form. In the writings of Dinkrishna's contemporary Bidyapati the language is far from being identical with modern Bengali; it is in fact merely a dialect of Eastern Hindi.

(To be continued.)

BENGALI FOLKLORE—MORE LEGENDS FROM DINAJPUR.

BY G. H. DAMANT, B.C.S.

(*Continued from page* 172.)

THE FOURTH STORY.

The Prince and the Sages.

THERE was once a king whose wife bore him a son, and in the night the creator came to write on the child's forehead. The nurse was lying asleep in front of the door, and she awoke and asked who it was that had come. The creator said it was he, and he had come to write on the child's forehead. The nurse said she would open the door for him if he would promise to tell her what he wrote. He refused for a long time, but when she told him that she would not admit him, and he saw that he could not step over her body, he consented. So she opened the door, and he went in, and sat down to write on the child's forehead. He sat behind the child, and wrote three times with his left hand, writing the same words each time, saying that the child should be married when he was twelve years old, and be killed in the following year by the stroke of a thunderbolt. When the creator came out from the room he told the nurse all that he had written, and how the child should be married and die, and then he went away. The nurse brought up the child, and sent him to school to learn reading and writing, but when he was nearly twelve years old she used always to cry when she saw him. One day the king saw her, and said to her, "you have always nursed my child, why do you cry whenever you take him in your arms? you cry every day, he is the only child I have, and if you want anything I will give it you, but tell me why you cry, or I will kill you." She said it was better left untold, but the king insisted on hearing it, so she told him the whole story how the creator had come when the child was five days old, and what he had written on his forehead. The king was very much distressed at what he heard.

After a short time the boy also heard the story of his fate, and he went to the king, and said, "I have come to take leave of you, for there is no use in my remaining here. I will go to another country, and if I escape, I will come back again." So he took some money and a horse and went away, and travelled through the countries of many kings till the day of his marriage arrived. In the evening of that day he fastened his horse to the root of a tree, and began to walk about. Now it happened that the daughter of the king of the country was to be married, and she had adorned the bridegroom, and come to that place with him. He ordered the palkee to be put down there, and then went into the jungle. His servants waited some little time, and then finding that he delayed in coming, began to search for him. At last they found the other king's son, and thinking he was the bridegroom they seized him and put him in the palkee. They then took him away and married him to the princess. In the mean time the real bridegroom came out of the jungle, and found that the palkee and his servants had disappeared, so he went back to the king's palace, and asked who it was that they had taken in his stead and married to the princess. The king said he did not know, but ordered the man to be brought, as he wished to see him. So the prince went, and called him, but he said he could not come that day, but would come and introduce himself early the next morning. About three o'clock in the morning the princess said to the prince, "Who are you, where do you live, whose son are you, and how did you contrive to come here and marry me? tell me all about it." The prince replied, "I shall tell you nothing to-night, for I am now going away, but I will give you this lamp, and when it goes out, you will know that I am dead, and so long as it remains alight so long I shall be alive." With these words he took leave of the princess, and went back to the place where he left his horse, and mounted him and rode from country to country till he reached an impenetrable forest where nothing was to be seen but jungle on every side. He travelled on through it till he came to a tank full of lotuses in which the saints and sages who worshipped in the forest used to bathe. Now there was a great quantity of mud all round the tank, which they were forced to pass through every time they went to bathe. The prince seeing this thought that they must be put to great inconvenience, so he determined to have the tank cleaned, and to build a stone ghât, and save them from further annoyance. Accordingly he collected a number of men and proceeded to clean the tank and build the ghât.

When the saints and sages came to bathe they saw what had been done, and were so much pleased that they said the man who had done it deserved to be immortal. The prince heard what they said, and putting his cloth over his face came forward with folded hands, and said that he had built the ghât and cleaned the tank. The sages replied, "We have nothing that we can give you in return for the favour you have done us, yet we will grant you a boon, you shall be immortal." The prince answered that he could not be immortal, for it was fated that he should die the next day. The sages enquired how that came to pass, and the prince told them all about it. They replied, "you shall not die to-morrow, we will see to it," so they went away. On the following day all the sages came to the tank, and said to the prince, "O Prince, come with us," so the prince went to them, and they all sat on his body. In the mean time the hour of his death had come, and a great storm of thunder and lightning and rain arose, but the sages were sitting on the prince's body, and concealed the whole of it, so that the lightning could not touch it. The creator was exceedingly disturbed at this, and went to the sages, and told them to let the prince go. They asked why they should do so? and he told them that the prince was fated to die by lightning, and the hour of his death had come, but they replied that they would not let him go, as they had granted him the boon of immortality. The creator was speechless at first, and then said, "You have spoiled everything, how can Brahma exist if you act in this way?" They answered that they would never allow the prince's life to be taken whatever might happen. The creator said, "If you will not allow his life to be taken, at all events let one finger of his left hand remain unprotected, so that the lightning may strike it, and he shall not die but merely become unconscious for a little time." The sages agreed to do so, and put out the little finger of his left hand, and the lightning struck it, and he became senseless, but recovered in a short time, and rose up and saluted all the saints and sages. He then mounted his horse and rode back to his wife. She asked him where he had been, and wished to hear the story of his adventures which he had promised to tell her the night they were married. He told her everything, and early the next morning went to her father's court, and related his whole history. The king was excessively surprised and pleased when he heard it, and sent his daughter and son-in-law with a great many attendants to their own country. When the prince reached home he told his father all that had befallen him, and the king was very glad to see his son's face again after so long an absence, so he gave him the management of the kingdom, and himself lived at ease for the rest of his life.

THE FIFTH STORY.

King Dalim and the Apsarases.

There was once a king who was married but for many years had no son, till at last his wife planted a pomegranate tree, which grew and grew till at last it bore fruit, of which the queen ate and became pregnant, and in ten months she bore a son. When the king saw him, he named him Dalim (*i. e.* *pomegranate*), and he was so rejoiced at having a son after so many years waiting, that he ordered all his musicians and cymbal-players to play. When the child had eaten his first rice, and his ears had been bored, and he was grown up, his father gave him in marriage, but in a short time he died. After his death his mother would not allow his body to be burned, but built a house and there deposited it, and every day came weeping to see it. In a few days some Apsarases came from heaven and placed a silver wand and a golden wand near Prince Dalim's pillow. The next day they came again and touched his face with the golden wand, and he came to life. Then all the Apsarases came from heaven, and gave him sweetmeats to eat, and when he had eaten they went back to heaven again; but before they departed they touched his face with the silver wand, and he again became dead. In this way a long time passed till one day his wife came to see him and happened to touch his face with the golden wand. He instantly came to life, and said, "who are you, and why have you come here? the Apsarases will kill you when they come." His wife told him who she was, and asked him how it was that he was restored to life. So he told her all about it, and they passed some time talking together. Some months after this his wife bore a son, and then she went to her husband, and enquired how she could restore him to life. King Dalim told her that she must invite all the Apsarases to see the child eat his first rice, and when she had saluted them they would say, "Act like Savitri," and then she must say, "I have no husband, you must give me one," and if she did this, the Apsarases would tell her how to bring him to life. His wife did as he told her, and obtained her husband again, and they lived happily for the rest of their lives.

ROCK INSCRIPTION IN GANJAM DISTRICT.

(Abridged from the Proceedings of the Madras Government, 22nd Feb. 1872.)

We have been favoured with a report by Mr. W. F. Grahame, Principal Assistant to the Collector of Ganjam, on some ancient inscriptions at Jugada Naugam in the Ganjam district.

The site of rock is north latitude 19° 13′ 15″, east longitude 84° 58′ 56″, on the north bank of Kohlbalya river, 3 miles 1,930 yards, to the west of Purshotapuram, the Kasba town of Palakonda, and close to the modern village of Pandya. It is situated in what appears to have once been an extensive but now deserted town, surrounded by the debris of a lofty wall. The remains of the ramparts can be traced round the whole enceinte, forming a square with two gateways in each face. The line of ramparts is now covered with jungle shrubs. A little removed from the centre, towards the east, rises the group of granitic gneiss rock, on the face of which, at a considerable height from the ground, are three smoothed tablets filled with inscriptions. Numerous coins have been found in the place from time to time.

Mr. Grahame reports:—The rock is part of a large mass of rock or rocks, rising to various heights, and covering a large space of ground, I should say many thousand square yards. It is inside the enclosure which is called the "loo fort," and if the latter was really a fortification, must have been of considerable use as a watch-tower. Mr. Minchin and I could not climb up to the highest point of the rocks, probably 150 feet above the plain, but we climbed to the top of the inscription rock. From that we could see to the north-east and west, as far as the foot of the distant hills all around. Mr. Minchin pointed out villages which he said he knew to be ten miles off, and there could be no doubt that in the event of an attack on the fort, its defenders would have known of the approach of their enemies as soon as the latter passed the hills, and must thus have gained several hours for preparation. The horizon is bounded by hills all round. We could not see to the north, because immediately to the north of the rock, to the top of which we had climbed, rose another peak, the highest of the mass, and to the top of which we did not climb, chiefly because we had no time while we were there, but partly also because the thickets all round the base and the grass were always wet, and rendered a thorough soaking a matter of certainty. The view from the inscription rock, which I suppose to be 120 feet above the plain, is exceedingly pretty, and much more like a view in a hilly district at home than what one would expect to see in India. From the rock we could distinctly trace all round the line of the mound or rampart of earth enclosing the so-called 'the fort.' It is irregular in outline, for I think I made out six distinct faces, though there were far longer than the others. The distance round this rampart is about 2½ or 3 miles. The inscription is cut on the side of a large block of rock, about the centre of the mass of rocks, and faces pretty nearly north. There was once a large open space immediately in front of the inscription-rock. Some twenty years ago a Brahman Bairagi or mendicant beggar took advantage of this to build himself a very substantial two-storied house right in front of the inscription. Some years ago, I think in 1858, when Mr. Minchin, and, if I remember rightly, Sir Walter Elliot (then Mr. Elliot and Commissioner of the Northern Sircars) visited the place and saw the inscriptions, this Bairagi made himself objectionably obstructive, and prevented them from turning their visit to as great advantage as they might have done, although, indeed, Mr. Minchin even then took a photograph of the rock. Mr. Minchin having a lively recollection of the obstructiveness of the Bairagi on his former visit, told Mr. Carr and me that he was afraid we should be able to do nothing unless the Bairagi was turned out of his house, and that even then, he thought, we should find the man a nuisance and a hindrance to the taking of copies of the inscriptions. This fear on the part of Mr. Minchin, I am happy to say, was falsified by the result. I was quite prepared to make use of 'moral suasion,' and to try the influence of a little bribery, if necessary, and if that failed to tell the man he must allow us to do what we wanted, and retire for a few days. To my surprise he never spoke a word of remonstrance. I do not know what the Sub-Magistrate said to him, or what arguments he used; but the Bairagi voluntarily, I was told, not only left his house while we were there, but gave it up to our use! The dark room of the photographer was made in the lower story of the house, and all the chemicals, etc., were kept there. When we were coming away the Bairagi came to me, and said that it would cost him Rs. 25 or Rs. 30 to purify his house, not, as one would suppose, because Mr. Minchin and I had been in it, but because he thought certain of Mr. Minchin's followers (dog-boys by caste, I think) had been in it. I may remark, *en passant*, that, whereas Mr. Carr and I had heard that the gentleman always goes about with rather less clothing on him than the proverbial fig leaf, in fact, stark naked, he thrice made his appearance before me, clothed in very fine white garments. To his modest request for the sum aforementioned for purification I demurred. I said I was not prepared to pay so much for that purpose, and that, although if he wished I would apply to Government for it on his account, I doubted if they would grant it. I then casually, as it were, asked him who was the owner of the land upon which he had built his house. "Sarkar" was his reply. "You have no doubt a title-deed?" I asked. "No" was the answer. "Then some Collector or other officer gave you permission to build the house here?" was my next question. He still replied "No." I then asked him if he did not think it possible that his right to be there at all and to have a house there might be called in question, when he began to claim Rs. 25 or Rs. 30 to purify the house. He thought over this a little, and then said that as those people (dog-boys) had not gone into the house, it would not require purification.

Mr. Minchin brought with him a man who very easily made the characters as plain as they could well be, and rendered a photograph of them as distinct as a page of print. He mixed chunam and water into a rather thick white-wash of the consistency of cream. With this he smeared the whole face of the inscription, thus obliterating every trace of a letter. Then he wiped the surface of the stone with an oiled cloth. By this method he removed all the white-wash which was on the surface of the rock, but left that which was in the incisions and in the inequalities of the letters. The oil smeared over the rock also enabled the white-wash in the letters to resist rain to a considerable extent, but not altogether, as I saw in the case of the fourth inscription. When the white-washing and cleaning with the oiled cloth were over, the photograph could be taken.

With regard to the tracings, Mr. Graham found some difficulty in carrying out Mr. Burnell's plan, owing principally to the unfavourable weather, which was very wet. Mr. Burnell's plan consists in pressing a sheet of damp paper over the inscription, and thus taking a moulding of the characters. The paper used by Mr. Graham was cartridge paper. He first soaked it well, then applied it to the rock and beat it into the interstices "by means of a hard clothes brush." The impression took well, and the most favourable results were anticipated, but after the paper was taken off the impression faded either from defects in the paper or from damp. Mr. Grahame does not consider cartridge paper well adapted for moulding, as it gets pulpy in some places while in others it remains quite stiff. He recommends a thinner and tougher paper—a paper which can be more easily beaten into the irregularities of the letters, and yet be tough enough not to disintegrate under the pressure of blows. Altogether the mouldings do not appear to have been very successful. However both Mr. Grahame and Mr. Harris were successful in making tracings of the inscriptions. Mr. Grahame also copied the whole of the inscriptions, letter for letter, so far as he could make them out.

It is much to be regretted, says the Report, that these inscriptions were not long ago looked after, and some steps taken to preserve them from destruction. As they exist now, for the greater part of the first and second inscriptions have disappeared bodily, the rock having lost large fragments upon which the missing parts of these two inscriptions were engraved. There is a story told by the inhabitants of Jaugada, repeated, too, by the Sub-Magistrate, that about twenty years ago a European gentleman went to the place, threw a quantity of hot tamarind juice and water on the rock, and then beat it with cammers, the result being that he broke off a large portion of the rock on which the inscription was carved. This tale reminds one of the story told of the way in which Hannibal cut his way through the rocky barriers of the Alps. It may be true, but I, for one, cannot believe that any one who would take an interest in going to see an old inscription would act in so foolish and barbaric a way. I am more inclined to think that the rock has been gradually eaten away by the action of the elements, having been continually for many ages baked by the fierce, hot, tropical sun, and lashed by furious rains. Mr. Minchin, indeed, says that when he first saw the inscriptions, there was then far more of the first and second than now exists. The third and fourth inscriptions are regularly worm-eaten away, evidently by rain and atmospheric effects. A good deal of the right hand edges of both has been almost totally obliterated, with here and there a letter, or the suggestion of one remaining. If these remains of inscriptions are to be preserved, it is high time that something was done. The only step which I think would really preserve the face of the rock from the corroding effects of rain and sun is the building of a shed, the roof of which should slope back well over the top of the rock so as to throw rain off to the back, and which should slope forward in front of the rock far enough to keep rain from beating on it. Mr. Minchin suggested that a deep rim should be cut in the rock running all round the inscriptions, with the idea that it would act as a channel to carry off rain. I apprehend that it would act very imperfectly as an escape channel for rain running down from the top and not at all for rain beating on the inscription. The rock must be roofed in to protect it properly. The roof would come over the top of the Bairagi's house, unless like a pent-house, it came down at a very sharp angle from the brow of the rock over the inscription; but as the Bairagi has no title to have a house there at all, he should be required either to remove from the place altogether, or to acquiesce in the measures which may be taken. Mr. Minchin made another suggestion worthy of consideration, which was, that if a roof be put over the rock, the Bairagi should be required to look after it on condition of his house being allowed to remain there, or he might even receive a rupee or two monthly to look after it. He would, in the latter case, have an interest in seeing that the roof was kept in good order, and that the inscriptions suffered no damage.

I have carefully compared my transcript with the photographs, and I am certain that in one, at any rate, of the latter certain letters are wrong. This probably arose from the chunam having run in consequence of rain, and of Mr. Minchin's man not having attended as carefully as he might have done to wiping off the superfluous chunam. Owing to this he has left one or two letters with their tails turned the wrong way, and altered others. I carefully compared the moulding of the second inscription with my transcript. The two are identical.

The characters in the first and second inscriptions are cut much more deeply and distinctly, and are larger than those of the third and fourth. The first two seem to have been much more carefully carved than the third and the fourth, in which not only are the characters smaller but there is not apparently the same careful division of the words.'

I have been informed that there are several old inscriptions in this division. One is on a stone at the back of a mosque in Chikakol. I have seen it, but owing to the rains which prevailed for two months after my return to Chikakol, and to my absence from head quarters, have been unable to take a copy of it. The mosque was built in Anno Hej. 1051, about 230 years ago. Formerly there was a Hindu temple in the place where the mosque now stands. This temple was destroyed by Sher Muhammad Khan, and from its materials the mosque was built. The other inscriptions are in different parts of the Chikakol Taluq. I shall examine and report on them afterwards.

NOTE ON THE GANJAM ROCK INSCRIPTION.

By PROF. R. G. BHANDARKAR.

The Ganjam inscription is in four large tablets, and each of the four sheets of lithographs published by the Madras Government represents one. On comparing them with the published transcripts of the Aśoka inscriptions, I find that the first two sheets contain the celebrated edicts discovered at Girnar, Dhauli, and Kapur di Giri. Wherever there are differences in the copies of the inscriptions from these three places, this agrees, as might be expected, with that at Dhauli. It is much to be regretted that it is worn away in many places; still it will be of use in clearing up some of the many difficulties attending on a correct interpretation of the Aśoka inscriptions.

The Girnar copy of the edicts consists of fourteen tablets. In the present inscription, each line of which contains on an average about 58 letters, the first tablet is entire, and occupies four lines and a quarter. The second, of four lines, has lost about twelve letters towards the end in each line. The third extends over three lines and a quarter, but of these nearly one half of each line is effaced. Each of the first five lines of the fourth tablet has lost one half, while the sixth and seventh have lost more, and in the eighth line, which ends the tablet, three words are wanting. What remains of the fifth tablet is from two to seven letters in the beginning of each of the seven lines of which it consists. This ends the first sheet. The sixth tablet at the head of the second sheet is nearly entire, and consists of six lines and three quarters, the seventh occupies two lines, the second of which has got only twenty letters in the middle, but the first is nearly entire, having lost only some two or three letters. Each of the first three lines of the eighth tablet has got a few letters in the beginning, in the middle, and at the end. The fourth line ought to consist only of eleven letters, of which we have ten. But the transcriber puts down dots after the tenth letter up to about the end of the line, where he gives the letters ... which are the first letters of the first line of the next tablet, and consequently do not belong to the eighth; and in the sheet before me they occur at the end of that line also. This may be a mistake either of the original engraver or of the transcriber. The ninth tablet consists of six lines all mutilated; about one-third only or a little more in one or two cases, being preserved. The tenth tablet has lost the first halves of the three lines composing it. The eleventh, twelfth, and thirteenth Girnar tablets are wanting both in the Dhauli inscription and in the present one. The fourteenth however, occurs here though apparently it is wanting at Dhauli; but more than half of each of the two lines of which it consists is effaced.

The inscriptions in the third and fourth sheets correspond to the separate edicts at Dhauli translated by Prinsep and after him by M. Burnouf. The readings in these have been so unsatisfactory that the discovery of the same or nearly the same edicts at Ganjam cannot but be welcome to all students of Indian Antiquities. But we fear these sheets will not be of much use in clearing up the difficulties. The letters in them are in many cases ill formed and imperfect; for instance, where we ought to have D e v â n a m p i y e h e v a m â h a,—we have in the third sheet, D e v a l a m p i y a p a v a m h a and in the fourth, D e v â n a m a s y a h e v a m a h a. The first *d* in this latter is unlike the usual *d* or any other known letter. The small strokes which mark the vowels and distinguish in a few cases one letter from another are not so carefully copied as is desirable. Mr. Graham says:—"The third and fourth inscriptions are regularly worn away, evidently by rain and atmospheric effects. A good deal of the right hand edge of both has been almost totally obliterated with here and there a letter or the suggestion of one remaining." The transcript on the third sheet, however, is more legible than that on the fourth. And with greater care it is perhaps not impossible to obtain still better transcripts. It is to be hoped the Madras Government, which has already exhibited so laudable a zeal in this matter, will again attempt to secure better copies.

ASIATIC SOCIETIES.

Proceedings of the Bengal Asiatic Society, April and May 1872.

At a meeting of the Bengal Asiatic Society on 3rd April, Mr. Blochmann read a paper on 'Koch Bihár, Koch Hájo, and Asám in the 16th and 17th centuries according to the *Akbarnámah*, the *Pádisháhnámah* and the *Fathiyah i 'Ibriyah*,' in which he traced the Eastern frontier of Bengal at the time of the Mughuls from the Phaní River, east of Bhaluah and Nawákhálí, along the western portion of Tipárah over Silhat and Lát́ú (or Lódú, so spelt by Muhammadan historians) to the southern part of Pargánah Karíbárí, from where the Brahmaputra formed the boundary as far as Pargánah Báhirband; from thence the boundary passed westward to Pátgáon and the north of Púrniah. Morang, Koch Bihár, Koch Hájo, Kámrúp, and Asám did not belong to the empire under Akbar.

During the reign of Jahángír, Koch Hájo, which coincides with the modern districts of Gwálpárá, was conquered and annexed; and under Sháhjahán Kámrúp, or lower Asám between Gwálpárá and Gauhátí, was also occupied. Towards the end of Sháhjahán's reign, the Koch Bihár and Asám Rájahs attacked Koch Hájo, and forced the Imperialists to withdraw from the province. This repulse was the cause of Mír Jumlah's expedition to Asám in 1662.

Mír Jumlah invaded Koch Bihár, reconquered Koch Hájo, and occupied Central and Eastern Asám for fourteen months. The most eastern part to which he advanced is marked by the intersection of Long. 93° and Lat. 27°, or the districts east of Sibsagar and Nazirah. In the expedition to Rakhang (Arakan), which was undertaken immediately after Mir Jumlah's death, the most southern part which the Mughals reached, is Rámú or Ramúh, half way between Chátgánw (Chittagong) and Akyab. Beyond these two points the Muhammadans did not advance.

Mr. Blochmann has collected all notes regarding Kuch Bihar, Kuch Hájo (the 'kingdom of *Ass*' of early European travellers in India) and Asám, from the Akbarnámah, the Tuzuk i Jahángírí, and the Pádisháhnámah. He then gives a free translation of the *Fathiyah i Ibriyah*, or, as the book is sometimes called, *Taríkh i Fath i Ásham* (Conquest of Asam), in 1662 by Mir Jumlah. The author of this work, a native of Persia, was a clerk in the employ of Mir Jumlah, and wrote the book in 1662-63, because the official reporters, in Mir Jumlah's opinion, did not send correct accounts of the progress of the expedition to court. The author of the *Álamgírnámah* appears to have used the *Fathiyah i Ibriyah* for his history.

Shiháb's work contains many interesting remarks on Asám and the Assamese, and on several of the aboriginal tribes. The book ends with the death of Mir Jumlah, on the 2nd Ramazán, 1073, at Khizrpúr near Dháká.

Journal Asiatique, No. 24, Jan. 1872.

The first part of tome XIX. is chiefly occupied with the 'Report on an Archæological Mission to Yemen,' by M. Joseph Halévy. The Académie des Inscriptions et Belles-lettres, having presented a scheme for the publication of a *Corpus Inscriptionum Semiticarum* to the Minister of Public Instruction, M. Halévy was charged with a mission to seek for and copy the Sabæan or Himyaritic inscriptions in Yemen.

From Aden he proceeded first to Hodeyda, whence he started for the *Nejrán*, one of the three provinces governed by the Dái, a viceroy of the race of the Makáramis, the religious and political chiefs of Nejrán, who have made large conquests in Arabia during the last two centuries. After much dangerous investigation in this Arabic Switzerland he was disappointed in finding a single veritable Himyaritic inscription. On arriving at Saná he fell ill, and was confined to his couch for a month. Saná, he says, is the most beautiful and most characteristic city of Arabia. It is half in ruins. The quarter *Bir Azab*, where were the pleasure houses and gardens of the late imáms, as well as the famous Qasr Ghumdán, contain almost no inhabitants, and have been despoiled of inscriptions. Some stones in certain buildings and on the chief gates of the city had inscriptions, usually very short, of which he enumerates twelve. At Ghaymán, five hours S.E. from Sána in the territory of Bani Bahlul, he found vestiges of an ancient surrounding wall and 34 fragments of inscriptions. He left Saná, and for three days explored the beautiful plains of Hamdán, Zubayrát, and Hababa, forming part of the Beled Hárith, where he found some fragments of inscriptions. At Sirwáh, a large ruin in the territory of Beni Jebr (Khaulán), a day's journey to the west of Mareb, he found a great number of *Stelæ*, part standing and others overturned, and bearing long inscriptions. The principal colonnade is called by the Arabs '*Arsh Bilqis*—' the throne of Bilqis,' the supposed Queen of Saba, which tradition makes the wife of Solomon. Here and on a hill near by, he secured parts of 31 inscriptions, but after his arrival at Mareb in the territory of the Beni Ashab, he was imprisoned by the Sheikh, who confounded him with a personage passing himself off as the Messiah among the Jews of Yemen. He was, however, set at liberty, and found Mareb to abound in ancient monuments, though very many of the inscriptions have already perished through the carelessness of the inhabitants who largely prepare lime and burn whatever stones fall into their hands. From this place he obtained 33 inscriptions and position. His next halt was at El-Medid in Beled Nehm, fully a day's journey east of Saná, in the neighbourhood of which he found many inscriptions. The vicinity of this place forms the rallying point for the nomad tribes, who bring their flocks to graze at certain times of the year. The district between Awidhm and *Jauf* is dangerous and arid, and M. Halévy had some difficulty in obtaining a guide, and had to content himself with an Arab of no reputation, who from the inoffensive appearance of the traveller and his assumed character of a Qudsi (inhabitant of Jerusalem) was rather won towards him. On the way they passed many ruins destroyed by the Arabs, and called 'Adiyyát—belonging to the '*Ad*, an ancient people to whom are attributed all the ante-islamic buildings. The Arabs see in the advanced arts of the ancients a sign of pride and rebellion against heaven, so that in place of being pleased to have for their ancestors so civilised a people, the inhabitants of Yemen are vain enough to consider themselves as the true descendants of Ishmael, and he who would dare to tell an Arab he was sprung from 'Ad might pay for it with his life. Even the name of Himyar is hated in the country, and the epithet Yahud Himyar—a Himyaritic Jew, is the last insult that one of the faithful in his rage can level at the follower of Moses when he wishes to overwhelm him with opprobrium and shame. Near Jebel Yam he came upon many tombs; then he reached Wadi Haba, a cultivable tract a day's march in width, on the confines of the great desert El-Ahqáf.

At Mejzer he was asked by the Arabs if he had seen the stone called Hajarat el-Waqá'a, which they believe is suspended in the air above the mosque of Omar. This stone descends insensibly but with in-

ascend regularly, and the moment it shall touch the minaret of the mosque, the earth will shake and the resurrection take place, and with it the end of the world. He replied that the holy Ulema alone had the privilege of seeing the stone which was invisible to all the profane; and that consequently he did not know the exact moment of the end of the world. His auditors ejaculated "There is no power but what comes from God."

Proceeding to the north-east, he visited El-Ghayl in Lower Jauf, near which he came upon a river abounding in fish. He had seen it in the plain of the Beni Arhab, Belad Arhab, thence it flows to Mount Jeera where it disappears at El-'Ish. Near the village of Hazm, half a day's journey from Jauf, it re-appears, and joined by the torrent from Hirran, it flows towards the ruins of Es-Saud, El-Beyda, and Kamna, and then continues more in an easterly direction towards El-Hazm and Haidrah, where its waters are utilised in watering the fields.

In the Wadi Saba at Medinat Haram or El-Fer, El-Hazm, and Ma'in, the old capital of the Minaeans, he obtained 125 inscriptions. In Lower Jauf he got upwards of 300; and in Belad Nejran he believes he discovered in Medinat el-Khudud (for *El-Ukhdud*) the Nagera Metropolis of ancient times. According to the information M. Halévy was able to obtain in this region, the famous Wahabis are by no means Islamite puritans, but belong to the orthodox sect of Shawáfi, to which many of the tribes of Nejrán belong, though the prevailing doctrine is that of Hanifa.

He now returned southwards to Ez-Záhir in Upper Jauf, where, though ruins were very numerous, except in the neighbourhood of Mount Salyán, he found very few inscriptions. Returning to El-Ghayl he was led by some Jews to Berâqish, where he found the imposing remains of a Sabean city, parts of its walls still standing and covered with inscriptions beautifully engraved. In the inscriptions it bears the name Ytil, or Itil. Among other places visited in the same neighbourhood was Inabba, which naturally recalls the Inapha of Ptolemy.

He next went by the Wadi Raheba, in which, at Kharibat-Sa'ud, he found another deserted town, but was not allowed by his guides to obtain many inscriptions. At Marib he was also closely watched, and the Arabs now persecuted him so persistently that his labours came to an end at Sana. The total collection numbers 685 inscriptions and fragments,—many of them of course very short, and but few of any considerable length. J. B.

REVIEW.

PHILOSOPHIA INDICA EXPOSITIO. Ad Usum Scholarum. Bangalori 1872.

We are not sure that this valuable little work has been as yet noticed by scholars in this country, though it is well deserving of their acquaintance. It is a compilation in Latin by the Rev. A. Bottero of the Roman Catholic Mission at Bangalore, from the larger work by Colebrooke on the "Philosophy of the Hindus," but translated through the medium of *Pauthier's* French version of Colebrooke's Essays, and the author consequently complains of his inability to remove all the obscurities of the French version on which he had to depend in compiling his own work. The book is a small 8vo. of 186 pp., and following the arrangement of the original consists of five parts, with a vocabulary of philosophical terms appended, giving their equivalents in Canarese as well as in Sanskrit, in Roman characters.

The author has supplied foot-notes all through the volume, in most cases explanatory of terms and expressions used in the text, and in some few others illustrative or corrective of the statements to be found in it. Thus in p. 39 there is an interesting note from Taylor's *Lilavati*, indicating on the authority of *Bhaskara Achárya*, that the true laws of *Gravitation* were known to the Hindus from the twelfth century after Christ. So again the note at the foot of p. 60 calls attention to the wonderful similarity between the logical process of the *Mimansa* and that adopted by *S. Thomas Aquinas* in his great *Summa*. At p. 72 the author gives a brief account of the controversy between *Vans Kennedy* and *Haughton* regarding Colebrooke's assertion that the *Vedanta* affirms that "the Supreme Being is the material, as well as the efficient cause of the universe." Other notes of equal interest are interspersed.

Sometimes indeed we miss a note where it is needed. For instance, we find the expression *ekâ mûrtis trayo devâh* (being one person and three gods), in Colebrooke's Essay on the Sankhya, under the head of the first product of nature. He attributes this idea to the Mythological Sankhyas, and quotes the expression from a *Purána*. Yet in a passage further on, in the account he gives of Patanjali's *Iswara*, he shows that Kapila himself acknowledged a similar *Iswara* as the first shape of intelligence. But it is more than is to be expected perhaps that such a point should claim a place in the little volume. Not so however as to another point. In treating of the *Pásupatas*, whom Colebrooke describes under the northern appellation of the sect, it was of importance, as it seems to us, that notice should have been taken of their existence and their tenets as found in South India. The Tamil development of the sect is marked by very peculiar features, and, in a manual for use principally in this part of the country, information regarding it, however briefly given, might attract attention to the subject which is well deserving of investigation.

We trust, however, that we have said enough to commend this unpretending work to the notice of our readers. It is published anonymously, but may be obtained, we suppose, on application at the Roman Catholic Mission Press, Bangalore, at a trifling price.

C. E. K.

MISCELLANEA, NOTES, AND QUERIES.

TIPERA AND CHITTAGONG KUKIS.

The Kukis of the Tipera hills are divided into five great tribes, the Uarui, the Chuthang, the Halam, the Baryni, and the Kochuak Kukis. In their marriages, the bridegroom is expected to show his gratitude for the bride he has won, by making a present of money to the girl's father. In the case of every fatherless girl marrying, the Raja claims the usual money consideration for himself, on the plea, we suppose, of his being the father of his people, and especially of all Kuki young ladies left fatherless. The Tipera Kukis bury their dead, but in the case of Rajas and men of distinction, not before the corpses have undergone the process of smoking and drying. When a Raja dies, his household places the corpse on a platform of wood, or bamboo, elevated from about four to five feet above the ground; a moderate fire is kept up underneath in order to dry up all the humours. After the corpse has been kept in this wise for at least three months it is interred, in a horizontal position, in a grave seven or eight feet deep. The Tipera Kukis worship only one deity, whom they call Lochi. Their worship consists in fixing in the ground a number of perpendicular strips of bamboo, about two feet long, in a rude circle, and one in the centre having a coarse basket suspended from its head. Within this basket are placed a little cotton, thread, paddy, chillies, and other produce of the soil, as offerings of propitiation, and petitions for plenty. At times a low strong and covered enclosure is constructed with the view to keep off wild animals, and within this the offerings are left. The neck and head of a cock are often offered to the deity, whilst the body of the bird is eaten by the people as a treat. But, of all offerings, a young monkey, killed with one dash against the ground, and left on the spot, is considered the most acceptable that can be made. There appear to be no priests among the Tipera Kukis.

Their messages and orders are communicated in a curious manner. Several peeled strips of bamboo, between eight and nine inches long, are tied together, and this bundle is called a *Parui*. The upper portion of the central strip is then split in two, resembling the two prongs of a fork, to which a cross piece is tied at right angles. If the prongs be aligned by holding the *Parui*, so that the two shall appear as one, the missive will be seen to resemble a cross. The tips of the prongs and the cross piece being turned in breaks, indicate black mail to be levied—a rupee for every such break. If an additional piece having its ends charred be attached, it implies that the people to whom the *Parui* is sent are to come on even at night with torches. If a chillie is fixed at the intersection of the cross, it signifies literally that disobedience to the summons will meet with punishment as severe as the chillie is hot. If both the burnt bit of bamboo and chillie are attached together, the indication is that the requisition is extremely urgent and imperative and must be forthwith complied with; whilst, if a piece of plain bamboo or stick is added to the cross, it means that disobedience to the order will entail corporal punishment. It will be seen that the manner of indicating the varying urgency of requisitions, and the different modes of punishment for their disobedience, is simple but highly suggestive. With the poor Tipera Kukis there appears no torment so great as that of a hot chillie, and no fear so potent as that induced by the exhibition of the rod. We cannot help also observing in their manner of conveying royal mandates a characteristic resemblance to the *phool*, *chupatis*, &c., which are for ever troubling the timid-minded of our population in India. The practice of representing their wishes by means of symbols is common to all uncultured tribes, and as the chillie means a tremendous warming by way of corporal punishment, and a stick a standing argument of the mode of application of that punishment, so the circulation of the *phool* may simply be an intimation to householders that the approach of the revolutionary storm is at hand, and that of the *chupati* an intimation that there is a fear of an approaching scarcity of food.

The Chittagong Kukis are divided into four great tribes, the Chukmas, Tiperas, Mroongs and Kumi, and have but little affinity to the Tipera Kukis. On the contrary, they are more closely allied to the Bengalis of the plains than are the savages of the Tipera hills. The Chukmas speak a sort of mongrel Bengali, and assimilate more in manners and features to the Bengalis than the other Hill tribes. The Tiperas speak Burmese, and are evidently of Burmese descent. They profess a corrupt form of the Buddhist faith, and are the only Hill tribe who have any religious belief. The Chittagong Kukis are of middle height, and strongly built. They have no caste or religion, and they do not believe in a future state. Marriage is performed by mutual consent, and the payment of a rather large sum of money to the relations of the bride. The Dewan of the tribe has also to be heavily paid, the whole expense seldom falling short of a hundred rupees, even for the poorest among these Kukis. When a death takes place, the whole village turns out weeping, the corpse is washed, flowers are put on his breast, a dish of rice is prepared, and the wife or nearest female relative raises the dead man to a sitting posture, and embracing him places a few grains of rice between his lips; this done, the body is carried to the banks of the river, and burned. A piece of cloth, curiously punctured in fine holes, giving it at a distance the appearance of fine damask work, is suspended on a long bamboo, and the ceremony of cremation is over. But by far the worst and most offensive feature of the Kuki people, especially of those of the Tipera hills, is the amount of disease with which they are almost universally infected, and its hideous variety. Hill tribes, generally, are notoriously filthy in their habits and entire mode of life, but the Tipera Kukis surpass them all in this respect. Their excessive filthiness generates numerous diseases, of which the cutaneous affections constitute the mildest type. Most of them are more or less infected with leprosy, elephantiasis, ulcers, or some other inveterate skin disease. The elephantiasis prevalent among them is generally accompanied with [illegible] at the angle between the foot and the leg. The universal prevalence of disease of some sort or other, besides being attributable, as we said, to want of cleanliness and indiscriminate feeding, is also due, though only secondarily, to foul air and bad water. Dogs, elephants, snakes, poisonous insects, and poisoned fish are regarded as legitimate food, and even coveted. There is a certain tree in the jungles, the branches of which are cut down and thrown into the first pool of water, natural or artificial, having fish; these in a little time die, and both the fish and the poisoned water are used by the Kukis and the Tiperas. Although we have no accurate data to go upon, yet we may safely assume that with a people like the Kukis, whose filthy habits produce such loathsome and hideous disease, it is not likely that the rules of morality are strictly observed. For, daring as savage nations generally are, and conscious of their physical superiority to the frail inhabitants of the contiguous plains, the Kukis are, nevertheless, a degenerate race, and it is not, therefore, difficult to understand how vice should prevail among them to so fearful and unblushing an extent, as to re-act, with deadly power, upon the entire population. Nor has any systematic attempt, that we are aware of, been made to bring civilizing influences to bear upon their savage state. A great drawback to any such attempt, we suppose, is the restless, roving disposition that is constantly urging them to shift from place to place; and the very crude and unsatisfactory mode of cultivation common among them, is but in keeping with their migratory tendencies. For instance, here stands a Kuki village to-day; its relative position is ascertained; it is surveyed, and its name carefully noted in the map of the country. Two years hence you look for the village, and it is not to be found. The twenty, or two hundred souls that formed it have gone miles away, and built dwellings for themselves in some new and unknown spot. Grass and bamboos are plentiful everywhere in the hills, and a new village requiring little else may be run up in two or three days. The nature of the cultivation among these people is quite in keeping with the uncertain mode of their location. The bamboo jungle is first felled, and allowed to dry in the sun; this takes about a fortnight; it is then set on fire, after which the stumps are removed. No sooner has a good clearance of [illegible] fallen than men, women, and children proceed with [illegible] and seed to these plots, which are generally at long distances from their hamlets. Their principal tools are *daos*, with which oblique cuts are made by single strokes, and in the pits so formed, which rarely exceed three to four inches in depth, the seeds are dropped, either paddy by itself, or paddy, cotton, and maize altogether, in the same pit, just as the cultivators feel disposed to grow, or may happen to require. It is our firm conviction that, to bring these people within the range of civilized influences, we must begin, not with an attempt to teach them to read and to write, but to instruct them and persuade them to adopt a certain and remunerative style of cultivation, and then we may be sure that, the [illegible] on which care is bestowed will not be readily abandoned for new and untried spots as now, and the adoption of a settled mode of life will follow as a matter of course. Our friends the Lushais have a dialect of their own which is more or less intelligible all over the hills of Tipera and Chittagong.—*Bengal Times.*

THE TRIVYAR FESTIVAL.

At the annual festival, known as the *Saptasthanam* thousands upon thousands of people, taking advantage of the cheap return-tickets granted by the Great Southern of India Railway, crowd to Trivyar, a place about eight miles from Tanjor, to take part in the festivities in honour of [illegible], the presiding deity. To estimate the number of visitors and devotees on such an occasion would be next to impossible, for not only from Tanjor itself and its suburbs, but from places far distant do these worshippers come, to bathe in the sacred waters known as the *Pancha nadi*, rendered ten times more sacred by the occasion, and superstitiously believed to possess all healing qualities. The sacred temple at Trivyar, in the court-yard of which the sacred tank containing the *Pancha nadi* is situated, was built by a Rishi named Nyaminar, at the divine [illegible]. This Rishi, we are told, was once doing penance before a Siva Lingam situated beneath a *Vilva maram*, supposed to have existed from eternity, as no one knew how it came there, for planted it was not. During his severe penance the Rishi contemplated building a costly temple in honour of his tutelary deity, but one serious impediment lay in his way: he had not the means of carrying his pious intention into effect. The gods, however, ever ready to encourage piety of such a description, came to his help, and while he was racking his brains as to where, and how, he could raise the wind, a voice was heard to tell him that in the vicinity of the Lingam, towards the north there were three hoof prints. If he dug up the ground in these three places, he would find what he required. He obeyed the divine injunction, and to his joy, he found in one place bricks, in another lime and mortar, and in the third gold. With these he built the temple now the centre of attraction at Triyar.

The legend given us of the origin of the Sabathanam we shall briefly relate. Once upon a time there lived a Brahman named Tiruvali? When he was a child of a few years old, he happened to be playing in a forest when a Rishi came round begging. Tiruvali in a playful mood and ignorant of the mendicant's great rank and sanctity, threw a stone into his vessel in lieu of money. The Rishi said nothing, but enduring the insult with wonderful meekness and humility departed. Tiruvali, when he attained to manhood, forgot this simple occurrence of his childish days, and in course of time entered, like other men, into the business of the world and a married life. For years, however, he was childless; and becoming apprehensive at what he could not but regard as an indication of the deity's displeasure, he devoted his whole time to the exercises of religion, and the performance of severe penance and bodily mortification. One night, in a dream, the form of the insulted Rishi appeared to him, and something within him rebuked him for what he had done when he was a child, and told him that in his present misfortune he was reaping the fruits of his wicked behaviour towards the saintly mendicant. When Tiruvali awoke he was an altered man. The Jackdaw of Rheims did not exhibit greater signs of contrition than the repentant Brahman. His course of life was changed, his daily habits were of the most austere character, and, to punish himself for the wicked stone he had cast into the Rishi's vessel, his diet was changed, and he lived upon stones! Hence his name was altered also from Tiruvali to Silathanan?, or the stone-eater. It was to be expected, of course, that such acts of virtue would meet with due reward; and so one day the god appeared to him, and told him that, in a certain place indicated he would find a chest underground, in which was the child he had so long and so anxiously desired. This child, in whose honour the festival at Triyar is now observed, was no other than Tirumanthi. The child who had the head of a cow on a human body, the father dedicated to Siva, and the god appointed the monster as captain of his guard of goblins.

In representations of Siva, Tirumanthi is generally included, as upon him the deity is supposed to ride on great occasions. Tirumanthi was supposed to the [illegible] of Vasistan the Rishi. The *Pancha nadi*, or five sacred rivers, took their origin at the coronation of Tirumanthi as chief of the goblins. On his head were poured (1) water from the sacred vessel in the hand of Siva, (2) the waters of the Ganges supposed to flow from Siva's head, (3) the froth from the mouth of a cow, and (4) water from the moon? These four flowed from his head into the sacred tank, where they were speedily joined by a *fifth* stream, thus forming the *Pancha nadi*. Where this fifth stream came from must be explained. Near the site of the present town of Shiali, Indra, in days of yore, had a forest of choice trees. From want of rain and excessive heat the forest suffered accordingly. Indra was afflicted with much sorrow, and, though a god, was powerless to call down the elements to his aid. In his distress Narada came to him, and said that, on Mount Pothyum, Agastiar the Rishi had the waters of the Ganges in a sacred vessel, and if he applied to Pillyar the god would send the water down to refresh the forest. Indra besought Pillyar, and the latter deity, assuming the form of a crow, and, ascending to the summit of Mount Pothyum, upset the vessel, and the water flowing down from thence mixed first with the *four* rivers in the sacred tank at Triyar, and then became the majestic river now called the Kâveri. After his coronation Tirumanthi was, according to the prevalent custom, carried in procession to seven sacred places. The seven Rishis are said to have been doing penance, as the god, in procession, visited them severally. Very large donations, we are told, were given towards the expenses of this annual festival by a king named Surula? Maharaja of the Solar race, who lived many years ago.—*Madras Mail.*

To the Editor of the 'Indian Antiquary.'

SIR,—In reply to Babu Rajendralal I must point out that he has given no authority for taking glâni to mean *three*; or if it did so, for taking the expression *three eights* to represent 888, and not 8 + 8 + 8 or even 8 × 8 × 8. He says he thinks his interpretation is 'not forced;' but is the word glâni, which is very indefinite, ever used to signify figures in this way? If the writer meant to express *three*, would he not have used one of the many symbolical expressions for it, instead of a word which simply means 'a collection'? And according to the usual way of expressing numbers in this symbolic way, and to the rule 'Ankânâm vâmato gatih,' if glâni means three, would not the expression bhanjara-glâni mean 38? And what is the necessity of restricting the 'collection' to three. It may mean any number, even 9, in which case, though a row of nine nines, according to Babu Rajendralal's way of taking it, may not refer to any era, still the expression may mean 98. Altogether the supposition that the expression represents the date appears to be extremely improbable. The grammatical difficulty the Babu thinks I have myself solved, when I admit the alternative interpretation that "the temple took the 98th year to be constructed." But what one would naturally expect to find in an inscription is that such and such a building was constructed in such and such a year, and not that it took such and such a year to be constructed. And the phrase that a temple took the twentieth or any such year to be constructed is not Sanskrit as it is not English. I admitted the interpretation only so far as the grammar was concerned. The writer has not sinned against grammar in using bhûshaṇa as masculine, for though verbal nouns ending in ana, only are necessarily neuter, but others signifying the instrument or place of an action, generally take the gender of the noun qualified. This is clear from the [illegible] (Sid. Kaum. Calc. edn. Vol. II [illegible] page). This appears to be made especially the case when the verbal noun has what may be called an Upapada, or another noun depending on it. In the Sid. Kaum. under Pân. 3-3-116 and 3-3-117 the instances given are râja-bhojanâḥ śâlayaḥ, [illegible] and godohanî sthâlî, in which nouns in ana take the gender of the nouns they qualify. Bhûshaṇa as an abstract noun is neuter, but in the sense of Bhûshayati anena it may take any gender. Many verbal nouns in ana are used by Sanskrit authors in this way. In the present case [illegible] is [illegible], and hence it is masculine.

Babu Rajendralal supposes a double entendre on the expression in question, but such a double entendre appears to be purposeless. For the syntactical connection of a word on which a play is intended is generally the same in both senses, but here in the one sense the compound becomes an epithet of [illegible], and in the other it stands independently.

Babu Rajendralal calls the compound awkward when interpreted in the way I have done, but he takes it to be a bahuvrîhi, which it is not. It is what may be called an Upapada compound; and is to be dissolved thus:—Kunjarâṇâm ghaṭâ—Kunjara-ghaṭâ, kunjara-ghaṭâm varshati, kunjara-ghaṭâ-varshaḥ. Pân. 3-2-1. Neither is it farther from the noun qualified than such epithets are even in such a simple kâvya as Raghu.

R. G. BHANDARKAR.

Note on Tap.

Allow me to point out a little slip of the pen in the Rev. K. M. Banerjea's article "Bhavabhûti in English garb." On p. 1[illegible] the learned writer connects the Sanskrit root tap with the Greek [illegible]. Mr. Banerjea specially "invites discussion," I therefore beg to point out that Bopp and other philologists agree in assigning to तप् the original meaning of "to burn."

Bopp quotes *na tatra sûryas tapati* from Bhagavad-gîtâ 11-12, and similar passages. The next meaning is that of *pain* in general.

We can readily conceive that to the Aryan race, natives originally of a cold climate, the excessive heat of the plains of India would be very distressing, and the idea of heat and pain would thus grow out of the same root. In the other Aryan languages the Latin gives us *tepeo, tepidus*, the Greek [illegible] which originally meant to burn dead bodies, but, as the practice of burying gained ground, was applied to it, and so lost its first meaning. The Greek [illegible] means 'to bend,' and is connected with a different Sanskrit root [illegible]. *Tapas* therefore, like *penance*, is originally merely "pain," subsequently self-inflicted pain in hope of expiating sin; or, in the case of already sinless beings, of adding to their merits. And there is therefore no word which so accurately renders the Sanskrit *tapas* as the Latin-English *penance* from *poena*.

[illegible], June 11, 1872. JOHN BEAMES.

Query 9—Derivation of Elephant.

Is the word *elephas* of Dravidian descent? Professor Bopp in his Comparative Glossary seems inclined to think that it is composed of the Semitic article and Sanskrit *ibha*. Professor Weber in his Indian Sketches favours the view of its being *aleph hindi*, i.e. Indian ox. Of further guesses I do not know; but my own impression is that the word is Dravidian as regards its first part. In the South Indian languages âne (often pronounced yâne, sometimes changed into âle) means *elephant*. This âne I consider to be the *ele*. Do we find this in Sanskrit? I believe it is the airâ in airâvata. The interchange of the liquids n, l, r (cf. Sanskrit [illegible]) is not uncommon. Initial yâ is not seldom changed into e in Dravidian, and in the middle of words the vowel â is generally pronounced as yâ. Further, the Sanskrit eḍa, sheep, for instance, is derived from Dravidian âḍu (yâḍu). The visible vowel in airâ ought to raise no serious obstacle. Initial vowels are sometimes changed without any apparent necessity. Thus airâ-vata means also "an orange tree"; here the airâ is the Dravidian [illegible], orange. When airâ-vata conveys the meaning "lightning," the airâ is probably the Dravidian iḍi (iḍe), thunderbolt. The vata, vant (*plural*) would be a secondary addition, and from the secondary composite form airâvata (airâ-vant) *elephant* may have been introduced into the Western languages. To me it would be most strange, if âne had not entered the Sanskrit language at a remote time; and I have not been able to discover it in another word but airâ. F. KITTEL.

TABLE of the ALPHABET used in the JEWISH and SYRIAN INSCRIPTION at COCHIN.

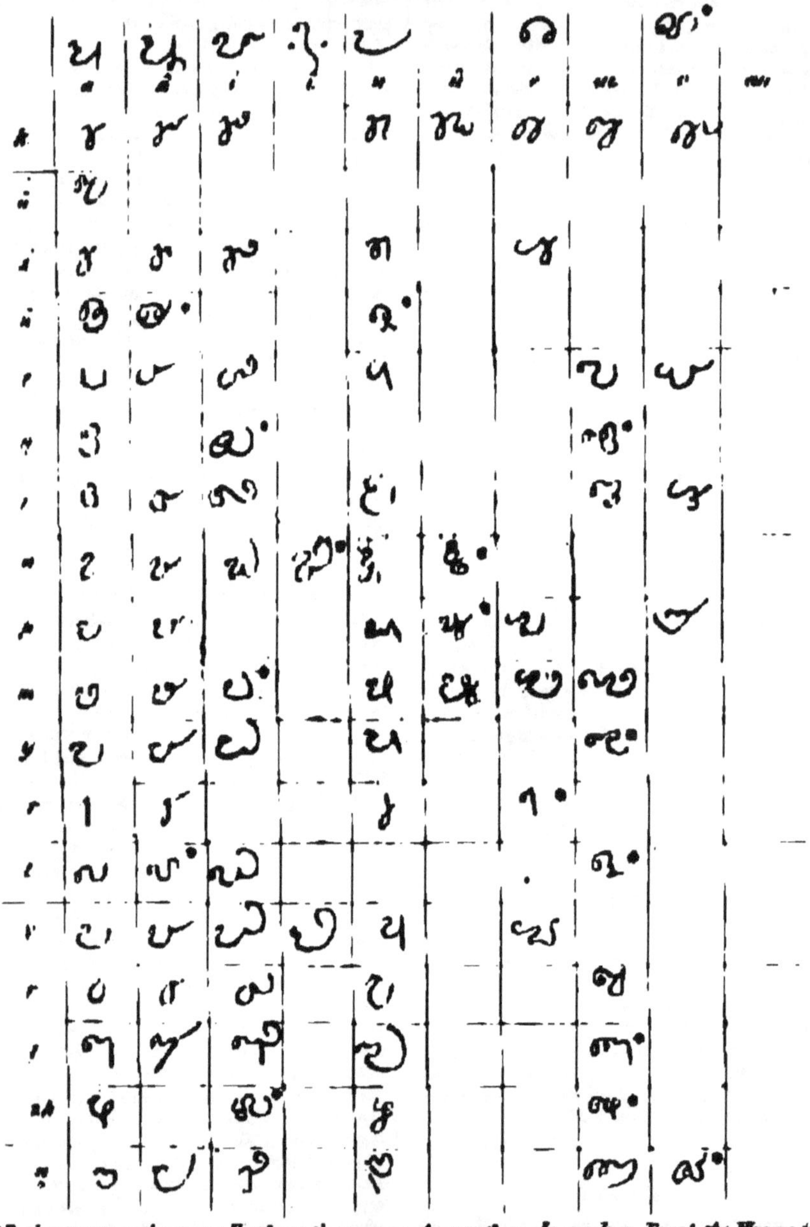

N.B. Consonants without any Vowel are the same as those with a. In modern Tamil the Virama is marked by a dot over the letter.

Govt. Litho Press, Bombay
18??

THE OLDEST KNOWN SOUTH INDIAN ALPHABET.

By A. C. BURNELL, M.C.S., M.R.A.S., MANGALORE.

THE alphabet shown in the accompanying table is that used in the Tamil-Malayalam inscriptions on copper in possession of the Jews and Syrians at Cochin. There are three of these:

A. A single copper-plate containing a grant by Vira Rāghava to Iravi Korttan of Koḍungalūr (Cranganore of the maps). In possession of the Syrians.

B. A document on five plates also in possession of the Syrians. By this one Maruvān Sapīr Īsō transfers some ground to a church (?)—Tarisāpaḷḷi—built by one Isodātaviras, and constitutes the Jews and Syrians trustees.

C. Two plates in possession of the Jews, by which Bhāskara Ravivarmā grants a principality to Iouppu (Yusuf) Rabban.

A great deal of vain speculation as to the dates* has been wasted, but I think the question may be easily settled. A and C are clearly the oldest, being the documents by which the Jews and Syrians were originally established. Now the style of writing and language shows that these are of nearly the same date, and about the date of A there can be little doubt. It is said to have been executed when "Jupiter was in Capricornus, the 21st of the Mīna month, Saturday, Rohiṇī asterism." Strange as it may seem, no one has as yet taken the trouble to get the necessary calculation worked out, even though this date is expressed in usual and intelligible terms. Some time ago I showed the passage to the ablest native astronomer† in Southern India, and in two days he brought me the calculation worked out, proving that A. D. 774 is the only possible year.

The date of C has been much discussed; it was executed by Perumāḷ Bhāskara Ravi Varmā, "in the 36th year against (*scil.* opposite) the 2nd year." Reference has generally been made to the Quilon Cycle (or rather era) used in Malabar in order to explain this date, but always with preposterous results. I can only suggest (after comparing Tamil inscriptions in which two years are mentioned) that it means in the 36th year of the king's age and second year of his reign.‡

B is not dated, it is however remarkable for two pages of attestations by witnesses which are in Kufic-Arabic, Pahlavi (Sassanian), and Chaldæo Pahlavi. Dr. Haug attributes these to the early part of the 9th century.§

Thus all the means for fixing the date of these documents point to the latter half of the 8th and early part of the 9th century, during which time the glorious rule of the early Abbasside Khalifs caused Arab trade and enterprise to spread in a way before unknown, and which therefore is the earliest‖ and most likely period for such settlements as those of the Jews and Syrians near Cochin. These colonies must soon have extended; the Syrians (rather Manichæans than Nestorians) are still very numerous in Travancore and Cochin, and there is a considerable society of ancient proselytes near Cochin, called "Black" Jews; but western missionaries and bigotry have long done their worst and ruined the good feeling which once existed among these different persuasions.

The inscriptions have been critically translated and explained by F. W. Ellis (1819) and Dr. Gundert.¶ Unfortunately they chiefly consist of lists of privileges, mostly obscure and without importance. Palæographically they are, however, of the greatest value, for they are the oldest inscriptions in Southern India that have been as yet discovered, and give the oldest form of the ancient Tamil alphabet. This alphabet was once used over all the South Tamil and Malayalam country, but chiefly in the extreme South. It appears to have fallen into disuse in the Tamil country about the 11th century, but was generally in use in Malabar up to the end of the 17th. It is still occasionally used for deeds in Malabar, but in a more modern form,* and still more changed, it is the character used by the Māppilas of North Malabar and the Islands off the coast.†

Its origin may be guessed with great probability rather than proved. From the earliest historical times we find a trade with the east by way of the Red Sea conducted by Phœnicians and Sabæans,‡ perhaps by Egyptians, and later by

---

* e.g. *Madras Lit. Soc. Jour.* vol. XXI. pp. 30ff.

† K. Krishna Jośyar.

‡ Conf. Caldwell's *Dravidian Grammar*, p. 69, for another explanation.

§ In a paper on the Pahlavi language read before the Royal Bavarian Academy at Munich.

‖ Taking into consideration the Kufic-Arabic attestations.

¶ *Jour. Madras L. S.* vol. XIII. I believe these inscriptions were first noticed by Anquetil Duperron.

* Given in the 1st edition of Dr Gundert's Malayalam Grammar (in Malayalam).

† See M. D'Abbadie's note, ante p. 52—54.

‡ Conf. Renan's remarks in *Orient und Occident*, III. p. 138. I have heard it asserted that there are Indian inscriptions in the Wadi Mukatteb (near Sinai), but when I was there in 1868, I looked in vain for them. The natives of India probably stayed at home always as now.

Greeks and Romans. Now taking into consideration the prevailing winds and currents, sailing ships from the Red Sea would most naturally touch on the Malabar coast below Mount Dilli.* Again at a later period we find intercourse through Persia and Baktria by land. Now in the earliest Indian inscriptions we possess—those of *Piyadasi* (*Aśoka*), we find two characters used. In the extreme North we find an alphabet evidently derived directly from the Phœnician, but with peculiar vowel marks added. In the other parts of India we find a perfectly distinct alphabet used for the Aśoka edicts but which has the vowels marked according to a regular system, and which the Northern alphabet has copied. It must therefore be the older of the two. Now if the Aśoka alphabet be compared with that given in the plate, it is evidently nothing more than an extension of this last, though derived from a slightly different, because older, form. The origin of this Tamil alphabet will perhaps never be conclusively proved by older inscriptions being discovered, but the only possible theory is that it is an importation brought by traders from the Red Sea, and thence from Phœnicia, and is therefore of Egyptian origin eventually.† In many respects the old Tamil alphabet resembles that of the Himyaritic inscriptions found in Yemen. In one respect it differs remarkably from that (Himyaritic) alphabet, but agrees with the Ethiopic, in that the consonants are modified by the addition of the vowels. Whatever may be the origin of the similar peculiarity in the Ethiopic alphabet,‡ it is scarcely possible to doubt that in the old Tamil alphabet this is not a relic of a syllabic system of writing but has arisen from a practice of writing the character for the following vowel on that of the preceding consonant (except perhaps with ŭ), and that the resulting combinations have been in the course of time abridged. This becomes very plain if the characters for *e* and *o* be compared with those for ke, ko, &c. The existence of a distinct character for cerebral letters may also point to a Semitic origin. Such sounds certainly existed in Egyptian and Hebrew, but not originally in Sanskrit.

A Phœnician origin of the Indian alphabets has already been suggested by Lepsius and Weber, but I have not been able to see their articles; Prof. Pott, is however unwilling to admit it,§ though Prof. Benfey considers it most probable‖ Prof. Westergaard also appears to accept this theory.¶

I have taken the letters given in the plate chiefly from C, as the more extensive and better preserved of the two older inscriptions. Those marked with * are from B, which is not so carefully written as the others. I have given every letter which clearly occurs in the inscriptions, and besides the indifferent lithographs in the *Madras Literary Society's Journal*, vol. xiii, I have been able to use reverse impressions of C and part of B.

SKETCHES OF MATHURA.

BY F. S. GROWSE, M.A., OXON, B.C.S.

III.—GOBARDHAN.

GOBARDHAN, *i.e.*, according to the literal meaning of the Sanskrit compound 'the nurse of cattle,' is a considerable town and famous place of Hindu pilgrimage, 15 miles to the west of Mathurā.* It occupies a recess in a narrow sand-stone range some 4 or 5 miles in length, and with an average elevation of 100 feet, which rises abruptly from the alluvial plain, and runs

* It is surprising that it has never been suggested that Ophir was somewhere in Travancore or Malabar. Lassen's *Abhira* at the mouth of the Indus is most improbable in every way. On the other hand, Dr. Caldwell has proved that the Hebrew name for peacock is a purely Tamil word, and that it cannot be derived from the Sanskrit *śikhin*. In Malabar we find all the products Solomon imported. Sea gold is yet found at Nilambur. And this (or rather Mysore) is the only part where sandal grows, if *algum* really have that meaning; but it is impossible to believe that such small trunks as the sandal has, and so useless for everything but perfumery, could have been used for pillars. The wood is too brittle and not even handsome enough for such a purpose, could it be had in sufficient size.

† The Egyptian origin of the Phœnician alphabet has been almost conclusively proved by the Vte. de Rougé, but Ewald, *Geschichte des Volkes Israel*, I. p. 79, doubts it. Renan appears to accept the Phœnician origin of the Sabæan alphabet (*Histoire Générale des Langues Sémitiques*, pp. 319 and 320). The difficulty about the direction of the writing no longer exists since Arnaud's discovery of boustrophedon Himyaritic inscriptions now amply confirmed, vide von Maltzan's letter in *Allg. Zeit.* March 1st 1871, p. 10-11. Lassen, *I. A. K.* vol. I (2nd Edn.) repudiates a foreign origin for the Indian alphabets.

‡ Dillmann thinks it an Ethiopic invention; Weber that it came from India to Ethiopia (Semen).

§ *Etymol. Forschungen*, W. W. II. 2, p. 116.

‖ *Orient und Occident*, III. 170.

¶ Does not the fluctuating and irregular spelling of the Aśoka inscriptions point to the recent introduction of writing? and that the alphabet was borrowed from a Semitic race? In Tamil the difficulty of distinguishing several letters continued till the beginning of the 18th century, when the famous Jesuit Beschi made some improvements; v. *Grammatica Fam. Tamulic*, p. 5.

* Its position is thus marked with unusual accuracy in the Mathurā Māhātmya—

Asti Govardhano nāma kshetram parama-durlabham
Mathurā-paśchime bhāge adhikam yojana-dvayam.

Math. Mahāt. xiii.

north-east and south-west. This is the hill which Krishṇa is fabled to have held aloft on the tip of his finger for seven days and nights to cover the people of Braj from the storms poured down upon them by Indra when deprived of his wonted sacrifices. In pictorial representations it always appears as an isolated conical peak, which is as unlike the reality as possible. It is ordinarily styled by Hindus of the present day, the Giri-ráj, or Royal Hill, but in earlier literature is more frequently designated the Anna-kúṭ. There is a firm belief in the neighbourhood that, as the waters of the Jamna are yearly decreasing in body, so too the sacred hill is steadily diminishing in height; for in past times it was visible from Aring, a town 4 or 5 miles distant, whereas now a few hundred yards are sufficient to remove it from sight. It may be hoped that the marvellous fact reconciles the credulous pilgrim to the insignificant appearance presented by the object of his adoration. It is accounted so holy that not a particle of the stone is allowed to be taken for any building purpose; and even the road which crosses it at its lowest point, where only a few fragments of the rock crop up above the ground, had to be carried over them by a paved causeway.

The ridge attains its greatest elevation towards the south between the villages of Jatipura and Ánaur. Here on the summit was an ancient temple dedicated to Śri-náth. In anticipation of one of Aurangzeb's raids, the image of the god was removed to Nathdwara in Udaypur territory, and has remained there ever since. The temple on the Giri-ráj was thus allowed to fall into ruin, and the wide walled enclosure now exhibits only long lines of foundations and steep flights of steps, with a small, unornamental, and quite modern shrine. The plateau, however, commands a very extensive view of the neighbouring country both on the Mathurá and the Bharatpur side, with the distant hills of Nand-gánw, Barsána and Dig. At the foot of the hill on one side is the little village of Jatipura with several temples, of which one, dedicated to Gokul-náth, though a very mean building in appearance, has considerable local celebrity. Its head is the Gosáin of the temple with the same title at Gokul, and it is the annual scene of two religious solemnities both celebrated on the day after the Dip-dán at Gobardhan. The first is the adoration of the sacred hill, called the Giri-ráj Pújá, and the second the Anna-kúṭ or commemoration of Krishṇa's sacrifice. The right to take the lead in the procession has been vehemently disputed by the priests of the two rival temples, Śri-náth and Gokul-náth; and it is generally found desirable, a little before the anniversary, to bind both parties over in heavy sums to keep the peace. Immediately opposite Jatipura, and only parted from it by the intervening range, is the village of Ánaur—literally 'the other side'—with the temple of Śri-náth on the summit between them. A little distance beyond both is the village of Puchhri, which, as the name denotes, is considered 'the extreme limit' of the Giri-ráj.

Kártik, the month in which most of Krishṇa's exploits are believed to have been performed, is the favourite time for the *pari-krama* or perambulation of the sacred hill. The dusty circular road which winds round its base has a length of 7 kos, that is about 12 miles, and is frequently measured by devotees who at every step prostrate themselves at full length. When flat on the ground, they mark a line in the sand as far as their hands can reach, then rising they prostrate themselves again from the line so marked, and continue in the same style till the whole weary circuit has been accomplished. The ceremony, called *Dandauti pari-krama*, occupies from a week to a fortnight, and is generally performed for wealthy sinners vicariously by the Brahmans of the place, who receive from Rs. 50 to Rs. 100 for their trouble, and transfer all the merit of the act to their employers. The ceremony has been performed with 108 prostrations at each step; but in that case it occupied some two years, and was remunerated by a donation of 1,000 rupees.

About the centre of the range stands the town of Gobardhan, on the margin of a very large irregularly shaped masonry tank, called the Mánasi Gangá, supposed to have been called into existence by the mere action of the divine will (*mánasa*). At one end, the boundary is formed by the jutting crags of the holy hill, on all other sides the water is approached by long flights of stone steps. It has frequently been repaired at great cost by the Rájás of Bharatpur; but is said to have been originally constructed in its present form by Rájá Mán Sinh of Jaypur, whose father built the adjoining temple of Harideva. There is also at Banáras a tank constructed by Mán Sinh, called Mán Sarovar, and by it a temple dedicated to Mánesvar. Unfortunately there is neither a natural spring, nor any constant artificial supply of water, and for half the year the tank is always dry. But ordinarily at the annual illumination, or Dip-dán, which occurs soon after the close of the rains, during the festival of the Diwáli, a fine broad sheet of water reflects the light of the innumerable lamps ranged tier above tier, along the ghâts and adjacent buildings, by the 100,000 pilgrims with whom the town is then crowded.

In the year 1871, as there was no heavy rain towards the end of the season, and the festival of the Diwáli also fell later than usual, it so happened that on the bathing-day, the 12th of November, the tank was entirely dry, with the exception of two or three green and muddy little puddles. To obviate this mischance, several bores were made and wells sunk in the area of the tank, with one large pit, some 30 feet square and as many deep, in whose turbid waters many thousand pilgrims had the happiness of immersing themselves. For several hours no less than 75 persons a minute continued to descend, and as many to ascend the steep and slippery steps; while the yet more fœtid patches of mud and water in other parts of the basin were quite as densely crowded. At night the vast amphitheatre, dotted with groups of people and glimmering circles of light, presented a no less picturesque appearance than in previous years when it was a brimming lake. To the spectator from the opposite side of the broad and deep expanse, as the line seemed to be precipitous which parts the steep flights of steps from the irregular masses of building which immediately surmount them, the town presented the perfect semblance of a long and lofty mountain range dotted with fire-lit villages, while the clash of cymbals, the beat of drums, the occasional toll of bells from the adjoining temples, with the sudden and long-sustained cry of some enthusiastic band, reiterating the praises of mother Gangá, the clapping of hands that began scarce heard but was quickly caught up and passed on from tier to tier, and prolonged into a wild tumult of applause,—all blended with the ceaseless murmur of the stirring crowd in a not discordant medley of exciting sound. According to popular belief the ill-omened drying up of the water, which had not occurred before in the memory of man, was the result of the curse of one Habib-ullah Sháh, a Muhammadan fakir. He had built himself a hut on the top of the Giri-ráj, to the annoyance of the priests of the neighbouring temple of Dán Rai, who complained that the holy ground was defiled by the bones and other fragments of his unclean diet and procured an order from the civil court for his ejectment. Thereupon the fakir disappeared, leaving a curse upon his persecutors; and this has borne fruit in the drying up of the healing waters of the Mánasi Gangá.

Close by is the famous temple of Hari-deva, erected during the tolerant reign of Akbar, on a site long previously occupied by a succession of humble fanes. It consists of a nave 68 feet in length and 20 feet broad, leading to a choir 20 feet square, with a sacrarium of about the same dimensions beyond. The nave has five arches on either side with clerestory windows above, and is about 30 feet high to the cornice, which is decorated at intervals with large projecting heads of elephants and sea-monsters. The centre of the roof is flat, but as it is deeply coved at the sides, and the width of the building is inconsiderable, it has all the effect of a vault, and no doubt suggested the design of the true radiating vault, which we find in the temple of Govind Deva built by Bhagwán's son and successor, Mán Sinh, at Brindában. The construction is extremely massive, and even the exterior is still solemn and imposing, though the two towers which originally crowned the choir and sacrarium have been levelled with the roof of the nave. The material employed throughout is red sandstone from the Bharatpur quarries. The reputed founder was Rájá Bhagwán Dás of Multán. His father Bihári Mall, the first Rájpût who attached himself to the court of a Muhammadan Emperor, was chief of the Rajáwat branch of the Kachhwáhá Thakurs seated at Ambér, and claimed to be 18th in descent from the founder of the family. The capital was transferred to Jaypur in 1728 A.D., the present Mahárájá being the 34th descendant of the original stock. In the battle of Sarnál, Bhagawán Dás had the good fortune to save Akbar's life, and was subsequently appointed Governor of the Panjáb. He died about the year 1590 at Láhor. His daughter was married to Prince Salím, who eventually became Emperor under the title of Jahángir; the fruit of their marriage was the unfortunate prince Khusru. The temple has a yearly income of some Rs. 2,300, derived from the two villages Bhagosa and Lodhipura, the latter estate being a recent grant, in lieu of an annual money donation of Rs. 500, on the part of the Rájá of Bharatpur, who further makes a fixed monthly offering to the shrine at the rate of 1 rupee per diem. The hereditary proprietors, 17 in number, devote the entire income to their own private uses, and are constantly wrangling about its partition, completely neglecting the fabric of the temple and its religious services. In consequence of this short-sighted greed, the votive offerings at this, one of the most famous shrines in upper India, have dwindled down to about Rs. 50 a year. Not only so, but some months ago a great part of the nave roof suddenly fell in, and unless repaired, the remainder must follow before very long. Accordingly to prevent accidents and probable loss of life, the customary order was issued to the guardians of the building, requiring them, within a certain fixed time, either to restore it or pull it down. As the nave is not considered sacred, the shareholders are quite indifferent as to its fate; and so long as the actual cella stands and contains an image of the god, before which some brief daily services are performed, they have no qualms of conscience about appropriating the endowment. But the European antiquary can scarcely regard with equal nonchalance the destruction of so interesting an architectural monument. A very large sum of money has been lately expended by the Imperial Government in taking photographs of the Mathurá temples. But when the work was completed, it was found that the points of view had been so badly selected, and the letter-press was so meagre, that both were worthless for the purposes of the student; and to save the Government the discredit of appearing as patron of such an abortive production, steps were taken most judiciously to ensure its absolute suppression. Now that the actual building is in imminent danger of falling, no grant can be made towards its repair, on the ground that it would be an encouragement of idolatry. Yet it seems somewhat inconsistent to incur the most reckless expenditure in publishing illustrations of a temple, as a model for architects to follow, and then to condemn the original to ruin as an unclean and unholy thing. And the more so, since there is no doubt that the priests, for a small consideration, would gladly erect on some adjoining spot, a new and more commodious shrine for the reception of the ejected Thákur, and vacate the ancient building in favour of the Government. It would then remain a national monument, and at some day in the future golden age, might be to Gobardhan what the Pagan Pantheon is now to Christian Rome; for though originally consecrated to idolatrous worship, it is in all points of construction equally well adapted for the public ceremonial of the purest religious faith.

On the opposite side of the Mánasi Gangá are two stately cenotaphs, or chhatris, to the memory of Randhir Sinh and Baldeo Sinh, Rájas of Bharatpur. Both are of similar design, consisting of a lofty and substantial square masonry terrace with corner kiosks and lateral alcoves, and in the centre the monument itself, still further raised, on a richly decorated plinth. The cella, enclosed in a colonnade of five open arches on each side, is a square apartment surmounted by a dome, and having each wall divided into three bays, of which one is left for the door-way, and the remainder are filled in with reticulated tracery. The cloister has a small dome at each corner, and the curious curvilinear roof, distinctive of the style, over the central compartments. In the larger monument, the visitor's attention is specially directed to the panels of the dome, painted in miniature with scenes from the life of Krishna, and to the [illegible], a flowered design of some vitreous material executed at Delhi. This commemorates Baldeo Sinh, who died in 1825, and was erected by his son and successor, the late Rája Balavant Sinh, who was placed on the throne after the reduction of the fort of Bharatpur by Lord Combermere in 1826. The British army figures conspicuously in the paintings on the ceilings of the pavilions. Rája Randhir Sinh, who is commemorated by the companion monument, was the elder brother and predecessor of Baldeo and died in the year 1823.

A mile or so from the town, on the borders of the parish of Rádhákund, is a yet more magnificent architectural group erected by Jawáhir Sinh in honour of his father Suraj Mal, the founder of the family, who met his death at Delhi in 1764. The principal chhatri, which is 57 feet square, of precisely the same style as the two already described, is flanked on either side by one of somewhat less dimensions, commemorating the Rájá's two queens, Hansiyá* and Kishori. The lofty terrace upon which they stand is 460 feet in length, with a long shallow pavilion serving as a screen at each end, and nine two-storied kiosks of varied outline to relieve

* Hans-ganj, on the bank of the Jamuna, immediately opposite Mathurá, was founded by this Rání; in consequence of a diversion of the road which once passed through it, the village is now that most melancholy of all spectacles, a modern ruin; though it comprises some spacious walled gardens, crowded with magnificent trees.

the front. Attached to Rani Hansiyá's monument is a smaller one in commemoration of a faithful attendant. Behind is an extensive garden, and in front, at the foot of the terrace, is an artificial lake, called the Kusum-Sarovar, 460 feet square; the flights of stone steps on each side being broken into one central and four smaller side compartments by panelled and arcaded walls running out 60 feet into the water. On the north side, some progress had been made in the erection of a chhatri for Javáhir Sinh, when the work was interrupted by a Muhammadan inroad and never renewed. On the same side the gháts of the lake are partly in ruins, and it is said were reduced to this condition, a very few years after their completion, by the Gosain Himmat Bahádur, who carried away the materials to Brinda-ban, to be used in a house that he was building for himself there. Subsequently he established an independent sovereignty over a considerable portion of Bundel-khand, and in 1803 entered into a special treaty with the British Government.

Other sacred spots in the town of Gobardhan are the temple of Chakreswar Mahadeva, and four ponds called respectively Go-rochan, Dharm-rochan, Páp-mochan and Rin-mochan. But these latter, even in the rains, are mere puddles, and all the rest of the year are quite dry; while the former, in spite of its sanctity, is as mean a little building as it is possible to conceive.

The break in the hill, traversed by the road from Mathurá to Dig, is called the Dán Ghát, and is supposed to be the spot where Krishna lay in watch to intercept the Gopis and levy a toll (dán) on the milk they were bringing into the town. A Bráhman still sits at the receipt of custom, and extracts a copper coin or two from the passers-by. On the ridge overlooking the Ghát stands the temple of Dán Ráe.

Of late years the paramount power has been repeatedly solicited by the Bharatpur Raja to cede him Gobardhan in exchange for other territory of equal value. It contains so many memorials of his ancestors that the request is a very natural one for him to make, and it must be admitted that the Bharatpur frontier stands greatly in need of rectification. It would, however, be most impolitic for the Government to make the desired concession, and thereby lose all control over a place so important both from its position and its associations as Gobardhan.

The following legend in the Harivansa (cap. 94) must be taken to refer to the foundation of the town, though apparently it has never hitherto been noticed in that connection. Among the descendants of Ikshváku, who reigned at Ayodhya, was Haryaswa, who took to wife Madhumati, the daughter of the giant Madhu. Being expelled from the throne by his elder brother, the king fled for refuge to the court of his father-in-law, who received him most affectionately, and ceded him the whole of his dominions, excepting only the capital Madhuvana, which he reserved for his son Lavana. Thereupon Haryaswa built, on the sacred Giri-vara, a new royal residence, and consolidated the kingdom of Ánarta, to which he subsequently annexed the country of Arúpa, or as it is otherwise and preferably read, Anúpa. The third in descent from Yadu, the son and successor of Haryaswa, was Bhima, in whose reign Ráma, the then sovereign of Ayodhya, commissioned Satrughna to destroy Lavana's fort of Madhuvana, and erect in its stead the town of Mathurá. After the departure of its founder, Mathurá was annexed by Bhima, and continued in the possession of his descendants down to Vasudeva. The most important lines in the text run thus:

Haryaswasya mahábhuja divye Girivarottame
Nivesáyá mása puram vásártham amaropamah
Anartam náma tadráshtram suráshtram Go-dhanáyutam
Achirenaiva kálena samriddham pratyapádyata
Anúpa-vishayam chaiva vela-vana-vibhúshitam.

From the occurrence of the words Giri-vara and Go-dhana, and the declared proximity to Mathurá, it is clear that the capital of Haryaswa must have been situate on the Giri-ráj of Gobardhan; and it is probable that the country of Anúpa was to some extent identical with the more modern Braj. Anúpa is once mentioned, in an earlier canto of the poem, as having been bestowed by king Prithu on the bard Súta. The name Ánarta occurs also in canto X, where it is stated to have been settled by king Reva, the son of Śaryáti, who made Kusasthali its capital. In the Rámáyana IV. 43, it is described as a western region on the sea-coast, or at all events in that direction, and has therefore been identified with Gujarát. Thus there would seem to have been an intimate connection between Gujarát and Mathurá, long anterior to Krishna's foundation of Dwáraká.

ON THE DRAVIDIAN ELEMENT IN SANSKRIT DICTIONARIES.

By THE REV. F. KITTEL, MERKARA.

Letters a, â.

There is not the slightest doubt that a great number of true Dravidian words have been introduced into the Sanskrit language and dictionaries. But native grammarians often try to convince us of the contrary. Thus, for instance, they say that the Dravidian Kô*l*i, fowl, is derived from the Sanskrit kukkuṭa. The Dravidian root for kô*l*i,* however, is kû, the loud cry of a bird, of which the root kûg or kûk is formed, the base for Kôgil, Kôkil (kokila), the crier, cuckoo; kô*l*i means crier, crower. How natural it was for the Indian Aryas to appropriate, among many others, the following Dravidian words:

âḍu (ajâ), sheep, goat, Root,—âḍ, to play. Erume, emme (herambha), buffalo. Mîn (mîna), fish, star,—R. mîn, to glitter. Bêr, vêr, (vera), root,—R. vir, to expand, go into parts. Balli, valli (valli), creeper,—R. bal, val, to be curved, bent; to surround.† Mogul (mukura, mukula), bud,—R. mug, to be shut up. Ûr (ûra), village,—R. ûr, to settle. Haḷḷi (haṭṭa), hamlet,—R. haḷ, to settle down. Kuṭi, guḍi, hut; either R. kuḍ, to take in, gather in; or, though improbable, R. kuḍ, to bend (a bending, a building made of bent canes or twigs). Koḍa (kuṭa), a very common earthen vessel,—R. kuḍ, to take in, receive; cf. No. 64. Koḍli (kuṭhâra), axe,—R. kaḍ, to cut, R. kuṭ, to beat. Peṭṭe, peṭṭige (peṭa, peṭaka), basket, box,—R. piḍ, to hold, contain. Kaṭla (khaṭvâ), bedstead,—R. kaṭ, to join together, bind. Maṇi, precious stone,—R. maṇ, earth (maṇal, sand). Mutta (mukta) pearl, originally: foremost, best,—R. mun, to be before.

In giving the following list of Dravidian words that occur in Sanskrit dictionaries under the letters a and â, completeness is beyond our reach, and the rules which underlie certain formations have not been adduced, though due regard has been paid to them. We begin with a combination of some so-called Sanskrit words:—

Aka, aga, sin. Anka, anga, place, side, body. Anka, heart, mark, cipher, sin. Ankura, shoot, intumescence, hair (—growth), water, blood (—flowing). Anga, portion, depending part; angana, angana—place or yard of a house.

These find their explanation in the following Dravidian roots:—

ak, ok, ag (âg), og.

(1) to go in, enter (aga, inside, house, place, side, mind, soul, body);‡ to be in, be hidden, (agaḍa, inside, belly; ugulu, middle; agara, village); to enter into, to dig (cf. agal, to dig, dive; aga, agate, ogate, depth); to enter, to fill, prevail, overflow, flow; to make go in, to fix into (anke, mark, cipher; certainty, trust; command; aga, agadu, self-will, pride, sin).

(2) to beat (angaṭa, a goad); to chew; to tremble for joy, fear, or grief.

(3) to be born (age, shoot, young plant, generally explained by "ankura"; aga, auga, agul, grain, corn; conf. angâḍi, angaḍi, corn-selling, provision shop).

A derivative root is agal (agal) to be wide become separated; to make loose (angala, angal, separated, widely apart; agala, breadth, breast).

The following so-called Sanskrit words are numbered, and after a sign of equation the corresponding Dravidian terms introduced:

1. agni—Vindu—bindu, drop; R. bil, to fall.

2. Anch, ank, ang, to go; to bend—R. ach, to move, walk; to bend; anchal, achu, usually explained by "pathabhedu," running point; anchu—border, shore. The connection of ach with ag, to enter, seems to be shown by achchu, receptacle, mould.

3. Aṭ, aṭh, aṭṭh—R. aṭ, aṭṭ, aṭṭ, to run after; resort to; cf. R. âḍ, to move, play; aḍi, foot.

4. Aṭavi=aḍavi, a wood; R. aḍ, to be close, thickest, obstructed, plentiful, etc.; conf. aḍavu, thickset, as corn or trees.

5. Aṭṭ, to transgress; kill=R. aṭṭ, to drive; R. aḍ, to strike, rap.

6. Aṭṭa, excess—R. aḍ, to be plentiful; cf. aḍḍaḍavi, an impervious jungle.

7. Aṭṭa, upper-loft=aṭṭa, R. aṭ, to put one thing upon the other.

---

* In Dravidian languages the vowels e and o, unlike Sanskrit, are also short; we have therefore: e, ê; o, ô. The italic *l* represents a letter resembling in sound the Vedic ळ.

† The signification "to appear" given under this root in Sanskrit dictionaries, belongs to R. bel, vel, bil to appear; the signification "to increase" to R. bal, bal, to grow; the signification "to move," to R. bal, to be current; etc.

‡ Cf. akrangu, enangu=R. ale, to melt meat, and anga, hands.

8. Aṭṭa, haṭṭa, haṭṭi*—haṭṭa, hamlet; R. aḍ, haḍ, to be, to settle; h—p; cf. therefore paṭṭaṇa, though also written pattana.

9. Aṭṭa, food—aṭṭa, cooked substance; R. aḍ, to cook, mature.

10. Aṭṭa, dried—aṭṭa, cooked (by the sun); cf. aṭṭa tengu, dried cocoa-nut.

11. Aṭṭa, loft—R. aḍ, No. 7. The upper loft is often used as a dormitory. The Tamil, however, has also aḍukku mecce, a couch with piled up pillows. (If aṭṭa originally has been haṭṭa, conf. No. 8, we have: paṭṭa, haṭṭa, bed; R. haḍ, to lie down.)

12. Aṭṭana, aḍḍana, shield—aḍḍaṇa; R. aḍ, to obstruct; aḍḍa, obstacle, fence, covering.

13. Aḍ, aḍḍ, to strive, occupy—R. aḍ, No. 3; R. aḍ, No. 4.

14. Aṇ, to sound—R. aḷ, to cry, weep.

15. Aṇi, border, frontier—aṇe, dam; R. aṇ, to strike against.

16. Aṇi, âṇi, nail—âṇi, a nail for fastening together; R. aṇ, to join.

17. Aṇu, small—aṇu; R. aṇ, aṇuge, to decrease, disappear.†

18. Aṇḍa, âṇḍa—testicle (the sign of a male), egg,—aṇḍa—R. âṇ, âl, to be manly, strong.

19. Attâ (conf. attikâ, elder sister)—atte, a maternal uncle's wife, etc.; perhaps R. al,—to love (alti, arti,—love).

20. ana-Guṇa—guṇa, rope, quality, further degree;—R. kuḍ, to join, be joined, to add.

21. Anḍu, chain—anḍu;—R. aṇḍ, end,—to join, to reach.

22. Andolay, to swing—R. al, to swing,—and R. âl, to move about; The and is a participle of al.

23. a-Pogaṇḍa (not-) not full grown; (not-) having a defective member—R. pô, to go, absent; and gaṇḍa, manliness;—R. pô, to go; and gaṇṭu, knot, joint. See No. 53.

24. Amb, bamm, to go—R. bamb, barb,—to run, spread; cf. No. 6.

25. Amb, to sound—R. an, to speak (ambade, speaking).

26. Ambary, to carry together—om, together, and R. bar, to come, of which the transitive is baru?

27. Ayi, aye, oh—ayyô.

28. Aya-Guḍa—guṇḍu,—a mass, ball, stone;—R. kuḍ, to come together.

29. Ara—ara, are,—a moiety, little.

30. Arapi, word for attrition—ure, a file;—R. ar, to grind.

31. Arara—ore, orre, sheath‡;—R. ar, to be, settle in.

(32. Arâla—either aril, aral, mud; orvâla, resinous exudation; (râḷi, turbid stuff, dregs.)

33. Ari—ari, enemy. R. ar, ad, to cut, destroy; R. ar, are, to strike with a sword; R. aḷ, aḷi, to ruin.

34. Arka, elder brother—akka. The gender of this word is, now feminine—elder sister; its form, however, allows also the meaning "elder brother." Akkare, love. Root, therefore, probably aḍ, to love; or ar, to love; cf. No 37.

35. Arka, a learned man—R. ar, to know. It is not impossible that No. 34 is to be referred to this root.

36. Arah—R. arach, to roar.

37. Arti—arti, pain; R. al, to weep, sorrow.

38. Ardha-Bhakshâ—piḷige, a cake. This word is considered by Dravidian grammarians to be a Tadbhava of aphâṭaka; but we have the true Dravidian puḷgi, a mixed mess, of which piḷige is but another form.

39. Arb, to go—R. barb; see No. 24.

40. Arb, arv, to kill—R. ar, arambh; see No. 33.

41. Arbuda, swelling—R. el, eḷu, to rise; ubbu, ubbuḷa, swelling (e at the beginning written and pronounced as ye).

42. Al, to be sufficient, proper—R. al, ditto, and to knit.

43. Al, to keep off—R. al, to despise.

44. Alavâla, alavâla—ale-vâḷu, a basin round a tree; ale, depth, R. al, to be deep; vâḷa, curve, R. vaḷ, to bend.

45a. Alasa—alasa, weary, lazy; R. also to be weary; see Supplement to Al, No. 1.

45b. Alarka, a certain flower—R. alar, to open, blossom.

46. Alaṇḍu, a kind of insect—alâḍu, allâḍu, the shaker, oscillator; conf. Nos. 22,72.

47. Alâta, firebrand—olale, olale, burning; R. ol, to shine, burn; ole, fire-place.

48. Alîka, displeasing, false—R. aḷi, aḷ, to perish, be out of order, effaced.

49. Alika, small—yalya, elya, small. Root perhaps that of No. 46.

50. Alpa, little—hala, halav, some.

51. ava-Khaṇḍana—R. kaḍ, to cut.

* Aṭṭa (hamlet) —haṭṭa, paṭṭa, cloth; cf. Tamil—aṭṭu, Canarese—Kannada—haggu; etc. See Supplement.

† It may be remarked that Dravidian homonymous roots are sometimes lengthened, and sometimes receive the terminations u, a, i, etc. to distinguish them from each other.

‡ The italic r is an r that is pronounced somewhat like ḍ.

52. ava-Gaṇa—gaṇa, mass; R. gaḍ, kaḍ to be thick, strong, excessive.

53. ava-Gaṇḍa—gaṇṭu, knot, joint; also kaṇ, kaṇṇu mean the same; R gaḍ, kaḍ, No. 52 gaṇḍa, hero, best—gaṇḍa, manly.

54. ava-Guṇṭhana, hiding, veiling; sweeping.

a, guṇḍ, guṇṭh, guj, to cover, protect, sweep; R. kuḍ guḍ, 1, to join, gather, assemble, keep together, contain, (kuḍuke, receptacle, shell; kuḍike—guṇḍaka, small oil-vessel); 2, to take in, protect, cover (koḍe, koḍe, umbrella); 3, to take covering (gûḍu, nest); 4, to be covered (guṭṭu, secret); 5, to take in, to drink; 6, to cause to join or meet, to give; 7, to join together make a heap, to sweep.

b, guṇḍ—R. kuṭṭ, pound.

55. ava-Ghaṭṭa, a pit; and ava-Ghaṭṭana, rubbing off. Both perhaps from the R. keḍ, to fall; or R. kaḍ, to cut off, cut into, hew down; cf. kaḍe, end. We may introduce here the following roots of the Sanskrit dictionary:

a, ghaṭ, to work—R. kaṭṭ, to build, perform; to join together.

b, ghaṭ, to be possible—R. kaṭṭ in an intransitive sense, in which it also is found; or R. kiḍ to be obtained.

c, ghaṭ, to be joined—R. kaṭṭ, as under *b* (or R. kiṭṭ, to approach).

d, ghaṭṭ, to stir, churn—R. kaḍ, to stir, churn.

e, ghaṭṭ, to slip over—R. kaḍ, to pass over, cross.

56. ava-Piḍa, pressure—pîḍu; R. piḍ, to press; to milk; piṇḍe, piṇṭe (puṇḍe), mass, lump; piṇḍu, that which is milked, herd, flock.

57. a-Vichi, without waves—vichi, wave; perhaps from R. vis, bis, to wave, swing about.

58. a-Vela, denial—probably R. pêl, speak; a-pêl, in the sense of saying "no."

59. a-v-ela, chewed betel. Betel is belle, creeper, and ele, leaf—leaf of the creeper. a-v-ele, betel that is no longer fit for use.*

60. As (though partly valid)—R. is, es, yas, to throw; to shine.

61. As, to take—R. is, to take. This is perhaps the causative of R. î, to give—to cause to be given to one's self, to take; but cf. the secondary R. aṅg, to take into one's hands, to begin.

62. asthi-Tuṇḍa, bone, bill—tuṇḍa, bill; R. tuḍ, to beat; cf. tuḍi, drum.

63. Ah, aḍ, to pervade, fill—R. aḍ, see No. 4.

64. (Ahallika, prattler?—perhaps from hall, tooth; toothless?)

65. Ākheṭa, hunting—if of a root khiṭ, this would probably be R. kiḍ, to destroy.

66. Āñjika, a certain Dânava—terrifier? R. añj, to fear.

67. Āṭa, a certain serpent—player; R. âḍ, to play; cf. 72.

68. Āṭi, âḍi, a certain fish and bird—player.

69. Āṭikara, ball—play-maker.

70. Āḍambara—âḍum-vare, drum. This is composed of R. âḍ, to play, and pare, drum; pareya, a Pariah, a man of the drum.

71. Āḍambara, eye-lash—âḍum, playing, and pare, feather. (pare, web)

72. âḍa (as a suffix)—playing with, tending after; also in the form âṭa; cf. vâchâṭa, talkative.

73. Āḍû, âlu, float, raft. The two forms may have arisen from negligent pronunciation. As roots may be given âl, to dive; âḍ, to play (on the water); âṇ, to join; to recline on (participle âû).

74. Āḍhya, rich—âḍhya; R. âl, to be strong, rule, possess.

75. Ādi, beginning—âdi. This may be a formation of âda, participle of âg, to become; for a Dravidian, when adducing a number of things in succession, always uses âda together with modal, beginning, or munna, first, at their end. For instance: houses, trees, gardens, modal âda (at first-being) things. In the same manner âdi is used. Why should it not be a conventional abridgment for modal âda?

76. â-Bilam—bila, opening; R. bir, to split, open.

77. âm, yes—âm, which is a contraction of âgum, it will happen; R. âg, to happen.

78. âr, to praise—R. âr, to cry aloud, call.

79. âra-kûṭa, brass—a joining or combination of metals; kûṭa, union; R. kuḍ, kûḍ to join.

80. âru, crab—âḍu, crab.

81. âla, great—âḷa, possessing, great; No. 74.

82. âla, possessing (as suffix, for instance, in vâchâla, malayâla, mountain-possessing, aivarâla)—âla, possessing.

83. âli, impure or deceitful disposition—âḷi, deceit; perhaps R. âḷ, to be deep (hidden).

* After this ought to have come: ava-ḍaḍava, stallion and mare. Baḍavâ, mare, is probably connected with maḍadi, woman; R. maḍ, to lie down, sink, be submissive. The vaḍaba in vaḍabâgni is—maḍavu, depth; R. maḍ, to sink, be deep.

84. âḷi, ditch—âḷi; R. âḷ, to be deep.

85. âḷu (=âḷa, as suffix), possessing—âḷu. No. 82.

86. âḷu=âḷu, water-vessel; R. âḷ, to possess, contain.

87. Avuka, father—avva+ka. Avva, avva, now means "mother," although its form allows also the meaning "father;" cf. No. 34. The R. av means, 1, to hide, put close together, press; 2 to shake; 3, to excel (?)

Supplement to Al.

A very rich Dravidian root (the branches of which appear, as it seems, in ir, il, ul, el, ell, ël, hal, pal, kr, al, el) is al (âl, an, ad):

I. To go from place to place; to flow; to be dissolved; move about, play, be occupied, wander about; to be shaken, beaten; to be fatigued (in body or spirit); to be bewildered, poor, distressed; (medial: alas, to fatigue one's self, to be weary.)

II. To sound, cry; (medial: âlis, to make sound for one's self, to listen.)

III. To be complete, sufficient, useful, neat bright, full, blown, large, extended, abounding (covering?), powerful, violent.

IV. (to cover?), to be dark (or shady? conf. Al-mara or âla mara, extending, outspread or shady tree, the Banian tree.)

V. (to be agitated or expanded with mental emotion,) to rejoice, be glad, (to be fond of).

VI. (to go into, be attached to,) to join, connect, knit, net, (to make meshes or stitches); to be entangled.

VII. (to be located.)

1. Ala, âla, spawn, or fluids spattered out by venomous creatures*—Tamil âla, water, etc., (Canarese—âll, âle, âne), poison. cf. Tamil—âla poison; and Sanskrit—hala, halâhala, hâlâ, hâlahâla, hâlâhala, hâlahala.

2. Ala, sting of a scorpion; scorpion (also ali, alin)—the beater or stinger. Here, however, al may have the meaning "to be pointed," which meaning may be inferred from alag, alug, blade or point of a weapon; cf. ala.

3. Alakâ, young girl—the playful, bright or rejoicing female. Alaka, curl—what is knit.

4. Alasa, âlasa, fatigue, indolence.

5. Ali, [illegible]; crow=crier.

6. Ali, bee—hummer; or wanderer (conf. bhramara.)

7. Alika, alika, forehead; heaven=expanse (cf. vîsâla-bhâla).

8. Alipaka, dog—wanderer, or barker; conf. the forms under No. 11.

9. Alipaka, cuckoo=crier.

10. Alipaka, bee—No. 6.

11. Alimaka, alimpaka, alimbaka, frog=crier; or player.

12. Alimaka, the stamina of a lotus flower—Tamil alli. For these two words R. al may be R. il=R. ul, to be placed, stand. Cf. Tamil [illegible], there—Canarese al, alli; Tamil il, there—Canarese (i) illi, here; Tulu il, house. A mass of Dravidian roots is formed by adding to a root al, ana, apa, probably meaning "state," the German "anstand." For the possibility of l being changed into p, cf. also pul—alimbaka.

13. Alpa, little—being humbled, depressed (past-present of al); the possibility, however, of the word being related to halava I should not like to exclude; see No. 31 above.

14. âla—No. 1 (cf. aliphin?)

15. Alâvartana (al=âla + âvartana), an umbrella that is used always a fan—ala-pattala, [illegible] (shade-fan). The translation is given as if avartana (vartana) were the synthesis of pattala and patta.

16. âlâsya, alligator—large-mouth; or (according to Dravidian al pilivam, man-catcher) man-mouth (a mouth that takes a man in)

17. Ali=âli, âli, extension, line, lineage. Cf. Dravidian âli, line, mass, of which âvali, âvali may have been derived.

18. Ali, bee—âli, âli, No. 6.

19. Ali, scorpion—âli, âli, No. 2.

20. âli, female friend—âli, âli. The first meaning probably "a play-mate." Cf. No. 3.

21. Alina, alinaka, lead (though being explainable by â + lîna—âla, fluid, (what easily goes into the state of a fluid), lead. cf. No. 1.

22. Alu, owl—sounder, howler.

23. âlu, bulbous root. In Canarese potatoes are called âlu-gadde, gadde—lump, bulbous root; the meaning of this âlu, though certainly Dravidian, I have not been able to ascertain. People say it is hâlu, juice, milk; and the reason for their saying so is their knowledge, that Tamulians, when using a Canarese word beginning with h, often drop this letter, though they have the letter p as substitute in their own language. I am, however, inclined to think that âlu is, as the Sanscrit goes to show, in its meaning equal to vir, root, from R. vir, to extend itself—R. al, Nos. I. and III. âlu-gadde—

* Has the Dravidian hal (cf. colour), had any influence upon the meaning? In Tulu pâr milk.

big bulb, fine-bulb, although "root-lump" is not to be rejected.

Is it not perhaps possible, that hâlu, hâl, pâl, juice, milk, is the same word as the hâlâ, etc., water, vinous or spirituous liquor poison, under No. 17 and that a spirit of hatred (caste) against the Anâryas, combined with the fact that the milky or vinous juice of many trees, called hâl, is obnoxious and poisonous, has given it also a bad signification? From pâl the Sanskrit pâlana, milk of a lately calved cow, is derived, but this is probably a recent formation. The aspirate does not appear at the beginning of the Tamil and Canarese words under No. 1, and in the Tamil of the present day "milk" is pâl (Canarese hâl, pâl); but the word without the h (p. v.) may be the original one. It would, certainly, be strange if hâl, pâl, the only word for "milk" in Dravidian, should not have entered into Sanskrit at an early age.

It is curious that initial h and p, as in Dravidian, so also in Sanskrit Tatsamas or Tadbhavas are used promiscuously. Thus Dravidian halli, palli, village—Sanskrit palli (which is not at all connected with puri); Dr. hallu, pallu, tooth—S. hâla; Dr. halli, palli, house-lizard—S. hâlini; Dr. horage (hurage), purage (puRage), without—S. bâhya; Dr. hoḍ, hûḍ, poḍ, pûḍ, to join together—S. hoḍ, huḍ, poḍ; Dr. hul, hûl, pul, pûl, to cover—S. hul; Dr. hoḍ, puḍ, huḍ, puḍ (hoḍ, huḍ), to beat (powder)—S. puṭ, (puḍ) etc.

Sometimes an aspirate is used in a Sanskrit Tadbhava where there is none in the original. Thus Sanskrit heramba, buffalo=Dravidian erume; S. hrîvera, many-branched root of the grass Andropogon muricatus—Dr. iruvêli, iruvêl (S. ir, to go into parts); S. hingu, Assafoetida—Dr. hingu: (ingu may be a foreign word: if not, we have the Dravidian root ing, to dry up, evaporate, decoct, which fully explains it). On the other hand Sanskrit agni, fire, has received the form haggi in Canarese.

We have continued above to find al again in hal, pal (pul), to unite, join; cf. al, al and pal (pal), to mend; ôl, vôl, pôl, hôl, to resemble, liken; âli, ôli, pâli, line; remember also that an initial a sometimes, and an initial o generally are written and pronounced as if there were a v at the beginning (vonda, one—vondu or vondu). If our supposition is right, a spirit must, here and there, have originally occurred where we have now a spiritus asper; and thus the comparison of âla and hâlu, milk, would become the more justifiable. We could adduce further instances in favour of this supposition. It is we think worth being well tested.

ON THE RÂMÂYANA.

BY PROF. ALBRECHT WEBER, BERLIN.

Translated from the German by the Rev. D. C. Boyd, M.A.

(*Concluded from page 182.*)

If the preceding considerations have made it sufficiently clear that there is nothing either in the substance or in the form of the Râmâyana distinctly inconsistent with the idea that it was composed at a time when Greece had already exercised a considerable influence on India, that on the contrary it is necessary to strike out of the poem important passages* which clearly indicate such an influence,—the *external* testimonies to the existence of the work, which we are able to produce from the rest of Indian literature, are in complete harmony with this result. If, indeed, Gorresio is right in supposing that the passage in the Râja-Tarangiṇî I. 116, according to which king Dâmodara was condemned to wear the form of a serpent "until he should have heard the whole of the Râmâyana in one day," decides in favour of at least the "remota antiquità del poema," (Introd. to Vol. I. p. xcvii-xcviii), inasmuch as king Dâmodara lived about the beginning of the 14th century B. C.,—then, of course, nothing further need be said! But it is well known that the Râja-Tarangiṇî itself dates only from the beginning of the twelfth century of our era (composed about 1148, see Lassen, *Ind. Alt.* I. 473; II. 18); and we should certainly hesitate to ascribe such a "remota antiquità" to this epic, merely on the ground that in it the Râmâyana is brought into connection with the bewitchment of a king, who is presumed to have reigned 2,400 years before the date of the poem! And besides, the

* Which would be a work of some difficulty with regard to the numerous passages in which the planets are mentioned.

Dámodara of the Rája-Taranginí has nothing whatever to do with the fourteenth century before Christ. On the contrary he is spoken of in the poem as having sprung from the race of Aśoka I* (I. 153.); the Indo-Scythian (Turushka) kings Hushka, Jushka, and Kanishka† are mentioned as his immediate successors; and consequently he must have reigned (see Lassen, *Ind. Alt.* II. 278, 408) "after the overthrow of the Greek rule, sometime in the beginning of the first century B. C." But however little importance we may attach to this notice in the Rája Taranginí as determining the question at issue, it is certainly a singular circumstance that the earliest time to which the Rámáyana is referred, and then it would seem as a work that had not yet been completed, is just a period that lies exactly in the middle between the rule of the Yavana and that of the Śaka—both, with their victorious hosts, well-known in the Rámáyana (vide supra, p. 178, 179.)

If we take the testimonies to the existence of a Rámáyana in their chronological order, the first that I have as yet met with is the mention of a poem of this name in the Anuyogadvára-sútra of the Jains (see my Treatise on the *Bhagavatí*, I. 373, 374; II. 248,) in which it takes its place with (though after) the *Bhárata* at the summit of profane literature. This sútra is indeed considerably later than the Bhagavatísútra itself; it is not reckoned among the twelve sacred angas of the Jains, though it undoubtedly belongs to their earlier texts, standing somewhat on the same footing with the Súryaprajnapti; and it is, beyond all question, considerably older than the Kalpasútra, composed in the beginning of the seventh century. We cannot, it is true, assign to the work any definite date. We are unable therefore to determine with certainty whether it would not be more correct to give it the second place in our list, the first place belonging rather to the *Bhárata* referred to in conjunction with the Rámáyana in the Sútra, to the various episodes namely, and allusions to the Rámáyana which are found in the Mahábhárata, and specially to the history of Ráma as that is treated in the Rámáyana. The difficulty in determining this question lies in this, that it cannot be ascertained whether that text of the *Bhárata* which existed at the time of the Anuyogadvárasútra really contained these episodes and allusions.

At the head of the testimonies to be taken from the Mahábhárata we have to name the *Rámopákhyána*, that lengthy episode introduced near the end of the third book (15872-16601), in which the story of Ráma is told almost precisely in the way that Válmíki represents it, but at the same time without his name being mentioned, or even the remotest allusion being made to the existence of a Rámáyana. The entire episode is placed rather in the mouth of Márkandeya who, after the happy restoration of Krishná (Draupadí) whom Jayadratha had carried away, narrates it by way of consolation to Yudhishthira as an example taken from the olden time to show that his was not a singular experience. The substantial agreement, however in the course of the narrative, frequently even in the form of expression, is so very marked that we are involuntarily led to regard it as a kind of epitome of the work of Válmíki. On the other hand it must be admitted that there are also striking points of difference, partly arising from the fact that various passages which are contained in our present text of the Rámáyana are altogether wanting in this episode, partly on account of numerous actual deviations, some of them very important, from the story as told by Válmíki. Thus, the narrative begins with the circumstances that preceded the incarnation of Vishnu; and it treats with much fulness of detail of what is mentioned in the Rámáyana first in the *Uttarakánda* only, though with material variations from the representation there given,—namely, the early history of Rávana and his brothers. The sacrifice of Daśaratha, the education of Ráma, his winning of Sítá as his bride, and indeed the entire contents of the *Bálakánda*, are left alto-

* If—let me say in passing—the notices regarding Aśoka's son Jaloka in the *Rája-Taranginí* did not so directly characterize him as an enemy of the Mlechha, a friend of the Śiva-worship, &c., it would be very reasonable to recognise in his name just a misunderstood reminiscence of the name of Seleukos. And indeed I find it difficult, in spite of these notices, to refrain from looking for the Indian name in the Greek one.

† It is singular that among their successors the following names re-appear (I. 192 ff.) immediately after one another:—(Gonarda III.) Vibhíshana, Indrajit, Rávana, Vibhíshana; see Lassen, vol. II. p. 881; and this circumstance, taken in connection with the Buddhist persecution (partial as it was) of these kings of Kashmir, furnishes a curious incidental support to Wheeler's theory, according to which these names occurring in the *Rámáyana* are to be considered as indicating the Buddhist princes of Ceylon. Regarding Gonarda III., indeed, it is stated that he persecuted the bhikshus (I. 188); but regarding his son Vibhíshana I. we have nothing of the kind. Rávana worshiped Vateśvara (Śiva?).

gether unnoticed. The narrative really begins, after the mention of Râma's birth and a few brief words regarding his youth (15917—50), with the wish of Daśaratha to inaugurate him as heir-apparent to the throne. Even the *Ayodhyâkâṇḍa* and a great part of the *Araṇyakâṇḍa* are despatched in a few verses (15950—90). The more detailed account begins, in accordance with the purpose for which the story is told, with the appearance before Râvaṇa of the mutilated Śûrpaṇakhâ (=*Râm.* III. 36, Gorresio); but from this point onward the various incidents of the Râmâyaṇa are related in essentially the same order as in that poem, although with many variations in details. The putting of Kabandha to death is told without the alleviating balm of his restoration to life (*Râm.* III. 75, 93). The story of Śavarî is wanting. Equally so is the account of the dream sent by Brahman to comfort Sîtâ. The dream of Trijaṭâ (*Râm.* V. 21) and Râvaṇa's visit to Sîtâ (*Râm.* V. 27) are inserted between the installation of Sugrîva (*Râm.* IV. 26) and the subsequent summons addressed to him four months afterwards to come forth and take part in the battle (*Râm.* IV. 33); inserted here, no doubt, because the discovery of Sîtâ by Hanumant, in connection with which these incidents are narrated in the Râmâyaṇa, is only slightly touched on in this episode, and indeed merely in the brief report of it which Hanumant himself gives to Râma.* The god of the Ocean consents here at once to the building of a bridge under Nala's direction (16300), without waiting, as in the Râmâyaṇa, V. 98, to have that consent forced from him by the arrow of Râma. Vibhîshaṇa comes over as a deserter only after the bridge is finished (16314), not before (*Râm.* V. 92). Kumbhakarṇa is killed by Lakshmaṇa (16420), not by the arrow of Râma. The twice-performed sacrifice of Indrajit in Nikumbhilâ (*Râm.* VI. 19, 30; 52, 18) is wanting. The striking down of Râma and Lakshmaṇa by the śarabandha (*arrow-charm*) of Indrajit occurs only once (16468), not twice, as in the *Râm.* VI. 19, 76; 52, 51; and consequently their revival is necessary only once, not twice (*Râm.* VI. 24, 2; 53, 28.) The herb that has the power of healing wounds is not fetched even once (much less twice, *Râm.* VI. 55 and 83)† by Hanumant from Gandhamâdana, but is found in the hand of Sugrîva (16470). Sîtâ does not pass through any fire ordeal, but the gods summoned by her as witnesses, Vâyu, Agni, Varuṇa, Brahma, all come of their own accord, and bear testimony to her chastity. Without doubt, then, this narrative in the Mahâbhârata is in many respects more primitive than that of the Râmâyaṇa;‡ and in fact we are now and then tempted to ask, whether, instead of an epitome of the later work, we may not rather have before us the original out of which the Râmâyaṇa has been developed?§ Or ought we to assume only that the Mahâbhârata contains the epitome of an earlier recension of our text of the Râmâyaṇa? an assumption, however, which would imply, with regard to the latter, an alteration so serious in the interval, that we could no longer speak with any propriety of the identity of the work; as there would in that case be rather two distinct texts treating of the same subject, and agreeing substantially in the main, but with important variations in detail. Or, thirdly,

* It is worthy of notice that a portion of this report recalls the story of Icarus—that, namely, which tells that the vulture Sampâti singed his wings when, in a race with his brother Jaṭâyus, he flew too near the sun (16286). Cf. *Râm.* VII. 58, 78.

† In the Bombay edition the fetching of the herb occurs only once (VI. 74, 33ff.); while, on the second occasion of its being used, Sushena immediately applies the herb which is already by this time in his possession (VI. 92, 41ff.). And so it is also in A (fol. 36a and 79a) and in C (fol. 258b and 287b).

‡ Thus, the circumstance that Râma is satisfied with the oath of Sîtâ and the testimony of the gods to her innocence especially appears to me to be more ancient than the representation in the Râmâyaṇa, where she is not purified until she has first passed through the ordeal of fire (VI. 111, 25ff.). It is singular enough that in the *Uttarakâṇḍa* also, however (48, 67; 104, 5), Râma speaks only of the oath of Sîtâ and the testimony of the gods to her purity, not at all of the ordeal; so that the latter could hardly have existed in the Râmâyaṇa at the time when the *Uttarakâṇḍa* was composed? In the course of time, even the ordeal was felt to be no longer satisfying; and the constantly growing feeling of fastidiousness and scrupulosity on the part of the people with reference to this matter sought to satisfy itself by supplementing the story with the repudiation of Sîtâ, as we find this related in the *Uttarakâṇḍa*, in the *Raghuvaṃśa*, in the *Uttararâmacharita*, &c. But if they went unquestionably a great deal too far in their punctiliousness, yet it must be allowed that in this respect they show throughout a higher moral tone than we find among the Greeks, in whose epic Menelaus without any hesitation takes back the beautiful Helen as the wife of his bosom, after she has spent years with her paramour, Paris!—in the Mahâbhârata the Pâṇḍavas do not make Draupadî herself suffer on account of her being disgraced by Duḥśâsana, or of her being carried away by Jayadratha, as she was quite innocent in the matter (just as Sîtâ was), but they vent their fury exclusively upon the offender; and in this respect the Mahâbhârata unquestionably occupies a more primitive and more chivalrous stand-point, even as compared with what is contained in this episode.

§ Though of course this would not hold good for the entire narrative in the Râmâyaṇa, but only from III. 36 onward, as the preceding incidents in Râma's history, which were of no importance so far as the purpose was concerned for which the episode was introduced into the Mahâbhârata are accordingly almost entirely wanting in that poem.

should these differences be perhaps regarded as merely emendations which were to be found in the epitomiser's text of the Rāmāyaṇa, and which he selected by way of preference?*—this consideration only being opposed to such an idea, that a large proportion of these variations bear the impress of a greater simplicity and antiquity.† Or lastly, as a fourth possibility that may be advanced, should both texts, the *Rāmopākhyāna* and the Rāmāyaṇa, be regarded as resting alike upon a common groundwork, but each occupying an independent stand-point,‡ and therefore representing the incidents of the story in accordance with different purposes? I am unable at present to commit myself to any decision. One thing is certain: with all the admitted differences, there yet remains a mutual connection so evident that we are justified in regarding this episode of the Mahābhārata as at all events furnishing a proof of the existence at that time of *some* form of the Rāmāyaṇa. It is true that we have not succeeded in gaining hereby a chronological datum, as we do not know when this episode became a part of the Mahābhārata; this only we can say, that whether or not we attribute, with Muir (*Orig. Sansk. T.* IV., 410-11) the Vaishṇava introduction, the admission of the episode undoubtedly belongs to a time in which the *Rāmāyaṇa* was made use of for Vaishṇava—in other words for anti-Buddhist purposes.

Nor is the testimony of the Mahābhārata to the existence of poetical representations of Rāma's history restricted merely to this one episode; other passages also of the same work furnish similar testimony.§ Thus in an earlier portion of this same third book, a description is given of a meeting between Bhīma and the Monkey Hanumant, in which the latter is directly mentioned (11177) as: 'Rāmāyaṇe 'bhikhyātaḥ,' and in which he himself gives (11197—11220) a brief sketch of that portion of the Rāmāyaṇa which follows the rape of Sītā.|| Regarding Rāma it is said in the same place that he Vishṇur mānushavigraha charchāra vasudhātalam; he is thus regarded as an incarnation of Vishṇu (compare on this point *Mahābhārata* XII. 12940, 12958, where he appears as the eighth of the ten avatāras of Vishṇu).—In the seventh book also (2221-40, amplified from XII. 914—935) the story of Rāma is given as one of sixteen proofs¶ taken from the olden time that even the noblest are overcome by death, his contest with Rāvaṇa for the ravished Sītā being briefly told, the chief stress being at the same time laid on the wonderful happiness of the people under his reign. The earlier version of this episode, contained in the twelfth book, is perfectly silent regarding Sītā and Rāvaṇa, and describes only the happiness enjoyed during the time of Rāma's reign, and indeed represents it to be the Brahman-golden age, truly Golden Age. The Brahmanical representation of the Rāma-Saga is therefore that which comes nearest to the version found in the *Daśarathajātaka*. Since, however, it is also perfectly silent concerning the exile of Rāma, we should certainly be in error if we were to employ it as a proof that, at the time when it was composed, the version of Vālmīki was not yet in existence. It is evidently not at all intended to give a detailed account of the incidents of Rāma's life, but only to describe the splendour of his brilliant reign; and in point of fact it does this (as does also the enlarged form in Book VII) in essential, partly even in verbal agreement with the Rāmāyaṇa, I. 1; VI. 110. And besides, there is nothing said in either of the versions of this episode (either in Book XII. or in Book VII.) regarding Rāma's being an incarnation of Vishṇu.—In the twelfth book there is quoted also a śloka (2196) regarding the indispensableness of royalty, which runs thus: "purā gītaḥ Bhārgaveṇa bhūshitena | ākhyāne Rāmacharite." And this is evidently a direct reference to the

* Compare, for instance, the considerable alterations which the histories of Śakuntalā, Daśaratha, &c. have undergone in the *Kathāsaritsāgara*!

† We can hardly be expected to recognise as original all the useless repetitions and re-touchings, which he has judiciously avoided (the space at his command of course was limited!), and which served only to increase unnecessarily the extent of the Rāmāyaṇa.

‡ It is noteworthy that the Rāmopākhyāna contains as its starting-point the incarnation of Vishṇu in Rāma, but yet treats the latter throughout as a merely human hero.

§ We remark, however, in passing that such testimony affords no materials for deciding the question, which of the two epics is the earlier; for most of these passages belong to the substance of the *Mahābhārata* proper, but they are all found in the overgrowth of episodes with which the original body of the work (Bhārata-kathā, according to I. 81) is enveloped. Compare on this point my *Vorles. über Ind. L. G.* p. 181 and *Indische Skizzen* p. 38.

|| It is worthy of notice that here, as in the *Rāmāyaṇa* and the *Rāmopākhyāna*, the history of Rāma closes with his return to Ayodhyā (where he enjoyed a prosperous reign of 11,000 years), and that no mention is made of the putting away of Sītā (on account of the suspicion of the citizens of Ayodhyā), which is not found even in the *Rāmāyaṇa* until we come to the *Uttarakāṇḍa*.

¶ These are sometimes very interesting: see *Ind. Stud.* I. 276-77. The putting to death by covetous robbers of the prince Suvarṇashṭhīvin, who was continually dropping gold about, recalls the hen or the goose that laid the golden eggs of our nursery tales, and their similar fate.

work of Válmíki, who in the *Uttarakáṇḍa* Cl. 26, is expressly designated as Bhárgava* (compare also *Verz. der Berl. S. H.* p. 121). The verse is as follows:—

"rájánam prathamam vindet tato bháryám tato dhanam |
rájany asati lokasya kuto bháryá kuto dhanam ||"

and it occurs, if not in these exact words, yet with identically the same sense, in the Serampore edition, II. 62, 9, and also in the Bombay one, II. 67, 11 (after II. 67, 24, Schlegel), as follows:—

"arájake dhanam násti násti bháryá 'py arájake |"

while the corresponding sections in Schlegel (II. 67), in Gorresio (II. 69), and in A (fol. 86b) present nothing directly answering to this. (This identical verse occurs also in the *Hitopadeśa* I. 194, see Böhtlingk, *Sprüche*, 2010.)

And in this connection we may subjoin the following. In the seventh book, v. 4018 seqq., there occurs, placed in the mouth of Sátyaki, a direct quotation from a work of Válmíki. In that passage we find these words:—

"Api chá 'yam purá gítaḥ śloko Válmíkiná bhuvi:"

and then follow three hemistichs—

"Na hantavyáḥ striya iti yad bravíshi plavaṃgama | 19 |
(then I answer thee:) sarvakálam manushyeṇa vyavasáyavatá sadá |
píḍákaram amitráṇáṃ yat syát kartavyam eva tat || 20 ||"

I cannot indeed recall any passage in the Rámáyaṇa similar to this, nor can I remember any situation in which such words addressed to a Monkey would have been appropriate (the affair with Táḍaká, I. 27, 28, has of course nothing to do with what is here quoted); but yet the passage seems to afford sufficient evidence of the existence at that time, and indeed for a long time previous (purá), of a work composed by Válmíki, in which Monkeys played a part; and in all probability this was just a Rámáyaṇa! In addition to this, Válmíki is also frequently mentioned in the Mahábhárata, and invariably with great honour as belonging to the old maharshi, but yet without any further reference to his being the author of a poetical work; so that it remains doubtful whether these passages refer to the author of the Rámáyaṇa, to the grammarian of the *Taittiríya-Prátiśákhya* (vide supra, p. 123n.), or to some other sage of the same name. Thus (in I. 2110), his skill is extolled to Janamejaya:—'Válmíkivat te nibhṛitaṃ svavíryam'; he belongs to the *sabhá* of Indra (II. 297), as Nárada informs Yudhishṭhira (Válmíkiś cha maháṭapáḥ), but also to the worshippers of Kṛishṇa, XII. 7381 (Asito Devalas táta Válmíkiś cha mahátapáḥ | Márkaṇḍeyaś cha Govinde kathayaty adbhutaṃ mahat) and V 2946, where he is called Válmíkaḥ† (Śukra-Nárada-Válmíki-namitaḥ Kuśiko Bhṛiguḥ | deva-brahmarshayaś chaiva Kṛishṇaṃ Yudhishṭhira-vikaṃ | pradakshiṇam avartanta sahitá Vásavánujam ||).

Lastly there are some passages that refer to the Rámáyaṇa to be found also in the Harivaṃśa, which is regarded as a supplement (*khila*) to the Mahábhárata. The authority of this work has recently gained increased importance‡ from the circumstance that it has been ascertained that Subandhu, the author of the *Vásavadattá*, who in all probability lived about the beginning of the seventh century, was even then in possession of a recension of it, which actually contained at least a portion of the work as we now have it (see *Ind. Streifen*, I. 380); and the same may be said also with regard to the mention made of this work in the Kádambarí of Báṇa, who is to be assigned to a date not long after that of Subandhu; see, for instance, *Kádambarí*, I. 45, 46§. In the first passage, then, of the Harivaṃśa that bears on our subject (2320—59), mention is made along

* Válmíki is usually designated as Práchetasa; see Muir, Introduction, v. 1, Schol. *Uttarakáṇḍa*, Cl. 19; 111. 12, *Raghuvaṃśa*, XV. 63; Prachetas is a surname of Varuṇa, father of Bhṛigu. In the *Bhágavata Puráṇa*, VI. 18, 4 Válmíki appears as a son of Varuṇa by a valmíka (Charshaṇí Varuṇasyásíd yasyáṃ játo Bhṛiguḥ punaḥ | Válmíkiś cha maháyogí valmíkád abhavat kila). In the *Arundhatí Kaumudí*, 1868, Válmíki is represented as belonging (with Páṇini, but after him) to the race of the Bhṛigavas (in an account which purports, as it would seem, to be borrowed from Sambhayana). In the passage from the *Mahábhárata* quoted above, the designation of Válmíki as Bhárgava is perhaps selected also because here directly afterwards, in v. 2664, a verse is quoted from the Manu Práchetasa. Perhaps it was thought that the quoting of two Práchetasas, one after the other, would cause some misunderstanding.

† Under this form of the name he appears in a modern work among the sons of Viśvámitra; see Aufrecht, *Catal.* 215b. In the *Mahábhárata* itself (V. 3761) Válmíki is also found among the names of the sons of Garuḍa; see the *Petersburger Wörterbuch*, s. v.

‡ The Kavi translation of the work appears to be of modern origin; see *Ind. Stud.* II. 143.

§ harivaṃśa-kathá-sakalabálajanaramaṇíyá, p. 45,—yaduvaṃśam iva ... p. 46 (or, is what is spoken of here not the work, but the race itself?)

with the other nine avatâras of Vishṇu, of his incarnation also as Râma, and of this hero's childhood, exile, contest with Râvaṇa, &c., (exactly as in the Râmâyaṇa); and then, after the return from Ceylon, the splendour of his reign is described (from v. 2348 onwards) in essentially the same fashion as in the episode of the sixteen ancient kings in the Mahâbhârata, Books VII. and XII., and consequently in similar harmony with the Râmâyaṇa, I. 1, and VI. 113. The author states that he relies for his materials upon "ancient ballads" which treated of his subject (2352 gâthâś chα 'py atra gâyanti ye purâṇavido janâḥ | Râme nibaddhâḥ...). A very special testimony to the existence of the Râmâyaṇa is borne also by the second passage (8672-4), in which direct mention is made of a dramatic treatment (nâṭakîkṛitam) of the râmâyaṇam mahâkâvyam, without indeed connecting therewith the name of Vâlmîki, but with statements so definite as clearly to show that, so far as regards its main elements, our present text of the Râmâyaṇa existed even at that time, and already in its Vaishṇava form. We are informed, namely, that the renowned actor, to the eulogizing of whom the passage in question is devoted,* represents in a drama "the birth of the immeasurable Vishṇu for the purpose of fulfilling his wish to put to death the prince of the Râkshasas. Lomapâda (and) Daśaratha (in the drama) caused the great muni Ṛishyaśṛiṅga to be fetched, by means of Śântâ and the courtesans. Râma, Lakshmaṇa and Śatrughna, Bharata Ṛishyaśṛiṅga and Śântâ were personated by actors characteristically dressed" (read 'kṛitâḥ' instead of 'kṛitaiḥ'). A third passage occurs at the close (16232), where, among the verses that extol the sublimity of the Mahâbhârata we read: "In the Veda, in the pure Râmâyaṇa, in the Bhârata, Hari's (praise) is everywhere sung, in the beginning, at the end, and in the middle;" the attributive puṇya shows the high estimation in which the work was held at the time when this concluding section was composed, though it may no doubt have been only a later addition. Eulogistic mention of Vâlmîki, associated with Vyâsa, and therefore most probably as the author of the Râmâyaṇa, occurs also in v. 5:—tal labhyate Vyâsavachaḥ pramâṇam gîtam cha Vâlmîkimaharshiṇâ cha; and in v. 2265:—"Thou (O Âryâ!) art: sarasvatî cha Bâhuka(ḥ?) muniś cha Dvaipâyano tathâ."

The Vaishṇava complexion of the greater part of these passages from the Mahâbhârata affords unmistakable evidence that they belong to a time in which the banner of the national gods had been raised in opposition to Buddhism. But whether they reach so far back as to the beginning of this period is, to say the least, doubtful; or rather we may say that there is no manner of doubt that it cannot have been the case with regard to those passages in which a fixed system of ten avatâras is assumed. Nor does the circumstance that the existence of a *Harivaṁśa* in the sixth century seems to have been ascertained furnish any proof that the whole of what we at present find in the poem (which extends, as is well known, to 16374 ślokas) actually belonged to it at that time.

We descend now from the region of the Epic which has always been regarded as sacred (puṇya), into that of profane literature. The earliest text of this nature in which the story of Râma is referred to in such a manner as to furnish certain evidence the existence of a Râmâyaṇa is, so far as yet known,† the Mṛichchhakaṭikâ, purporting to be the work of a king Śûdraka. It is true that the date of this work is also by no means definitely fixed;‡ but so much at least is

* The entire narrative in the passage in question is deeply interesting in its bearing upon the history of dramatic art in India. The same frenzied enthusiasm which celebrated actors awaken in our own day appears, from the narrative, to have been common in India also, with all its seductive allurements and effects on the female portion of the audience, &c.

† No help in this direction is to be got from Pâṇini (cf. *Ind. Stud.* I. 147-148); but what about the *Mahâbhâshya* I have been able to find nothing bearing on our subject in the portion of this work published by Ballantyne.

‡ For there were several kings who bore the name Śûdraka: cf. *Râja-Taraṅgiṇî*, III. 343, and the notices in Râma, Daṇḍin, Somadeva (*Ind. Streifen*, I. 314) Lassen, II. 508. In Îśvarachandra Vidyâsâgara's essay on the "Marriage of Hindu Widows," Calc. 1856, there is a passage (p. 41) quoted from the "chapter of prophecies in the *Skanda Purâṇa*," according to which king Śûdraka reigned 3290 years after the beginning of the Kali (3101 B.C.; corresponding therefore with 190 A.D.) twenty years before the Nandas (3310 Kali; therefore 209 A.D.) whom Châṇakya wished to destroy; while in the same passage Vikramâditya is assigned to the year 4000 Kali, corresponding to 899 A.D.!

trishu varshasahasreshu Kaler yâteshu pârthiva |
triśate cha daśanyûne hy asyâṁ bhuvi bhavishyati |
Śûdrako nâma vîrâṇâm adhipaḥ siddhasattamaḥ |
nṛipân sarvân pâparûpân varddhitân yo hanishyati ||
Charvitâyâṁ (?) samârâdhya (worshipping the divinity at Charvita," Îśvarachandra) lapsyate bhûbhṛito 'pahaḥ |
tatas trishu sahasreshu daśâdhikaśatatraye |
bhavishyaṁ Nandarâjyaṁ cha Châṇakyo yân hanishyati |
Śuklatîrthe sarvapâpanirmuktiṁ yo 'bhilapsyate |
tatas trishu sahasreshu sahasrâbhyadhikeshu cha |
bhavishyo Vikramâdityo râjyaṁ so 'tra prapsyate ||

The above passage had previously been quoted in the *Asiatic Researches*, IX. 107, from the *Kumârikâkhaṇḍa* of the *Skanda Purâṇa*; but it is remarked there that some MSS read Śûraka instead of Śûdraka.

certain, that it was composed at a time in which Buddhism was flourishing in full vigour, and Râma-worship or Krishṇa-worship had not yet come into existence.—I have not been able to find any similar reference to the Râmâyaṇa in the dramas of Kâlidâsa;* but allusions to it occur in his *Meghadûta* (vv. 1. 99) and in the *Raghuvaṃśa*, in which latter work direct reference is made to the 'Prâchetasopajnam Râmâyaṇam', and even to Vâlmîki (XV. 63, 64). Unfortunately, however, we are met here also by the difficulty that arises partly from the uncertainty that still exists regarding the date we should assign to Kâlidâsa (third or sixth century of our era: see my *Abh. über Krishna's Geburtsfest*, p. 319; *Z. D. M. G.* XXII. 726ff.), partly with reference to the Raghuvaṃśa, about which there exists at least some amount of doubt whether we are right in ascribing it to the author of the dramas and of the Meghadûta.† We have to mention besides, in this place, still another work which undeniably assumes, as its very groundwork, the existence of a Râmâyaṇa, and which at least in recent times (see Höfer, *Z. für die W. der Spr.*, II. 500ff., *Verz. der Berl. S. H.*, p. 156, 369) has been ascribed to Kâlidâsa, namely the Setubandha; for the more recent editors and scholiasts have endorsed the statement that Kâlidâsa composed this work by the command of king Vikramâditya for a king Pravarasena, that it had been begun by the latter himself, and that the ambiguous words 'abhinavarâârûḍhâ .. meti vva .. pivvedhuṃ hoi dukkaraṃ kavvakahâ' in v. 9 of the introduction refer to this beginning of the work by the "new king," Pravarasena.§ In accordance with this latter statement, Bâṇa (in all probability at the beginning of the seventh century), in the opening of the *Harshacharita*, ascribes the composition of the setu to Pravarasena:|| see (Hall, *Vâsavadattâ*, p. 13, 14, 54, and my *Ind. Streifen*, I. 357.) There is a strong temptation to identify this royal author with the renowned Kashmir king, Pravarasena II, who appears in the *Râja-Taraṅginî*, III. 109, 123, 293 ff. as a contemporary of two Ujjayinî kings, Harsha surnamed Vikramâditya and Pratâpaśîla surnamed Śilâditya, and as successor of the poet Mâtṛigupta,¶ whom Harsha placed on the throne in Kashmir. And according to this supposition, if this king really reigned, as Lassen (*Ind. Alt.* II. [402] 770, 910 ff., xxiv) holds, from 241-266 of our era, the composition of the *Setubandha* would in fact date as far back as the third century! Since, however, Bhâu Dâji has directed attention, in the *Journ. Bombay Branch R. A. S.* VII. 208 ff. (1861 Jan.) 223 ff., VIII. 248-51 (1864 Aug., published in 1868), to the relations that probably existed between Pravarasena and Hiwen Thsang, and especially to the contemporaneousness of Harshavardhana, Śilâditya, and Hiwen Thsang,* it certainly seems more reasonable to

* In the *Vikramorvaśî*, the subject of which is also the carrying off of a beautiful woman by a demon, there would have been an excellent opportunity, especially in Act IV (see LIV. 8, 12; LV. 1) for alluding to the rape of Sîtâ. The words Tumhâ [illegible], *Śâkuntala* XXIX. 12, ed. Böhtlingk (XLII. 15 ed. Premachandra), refer also indeed to the Saga which is found in the *Râmâyaṇa*, I. 90, 24 (Schlegel); but the reference is not necessarily just to that version of it in the Râmâyaṇa.

† Compare also *Z. D. M. G.* XXII. 710; *Ind. Streifen*, I. 312; II. 373. According to the notices in the *Pandit*, No. X, p. 161, the work has twenty-six Sargas in the *Dhârâdeśapracârita Kâlidâsavaṃśa*, but merely nineteen. Is this local difference to be regarded as due to influences that at least date far back, and as favouring the idea that the work should be ascribed to Kâlidâsa, who lived at the court of the Dhârâ-king, Bhoja? It is greatly to be desired that Shankar Pandit, whose edition of the *Raghuvaṃśa* (Bombay, 1869, Cantos I—VI; containing, besides the text and Mallinâtha's Commentary, 36 pages of notes and 8 pages of various readings taken from MSS. and from the Commentaries of Vallabha and Dinakara) we have to welcome as the first really critical work of this kind for which we are indebted to a native of the country,—would furnish us with some further and fuller information regarding this point.

‡ Abhinavarâja rabdhâ or abhinavarâgârabdhâ.

§ Bhojadeva iti kecit, says the scholiast.

|| At least it is stated there "that by means of the setu, the fame of Pravarasena had extended to the further shore of the sea." And as the words:—"or who would not be charmed with the admirable... language of Kâlidâsa," do not immediately follow, but are separated by a verse, from the foregoing, they cannot be understood as continuing the ground-work of Pravarasena's fame.

¶ Mâtṛigupta reigned only five years (*Râja-Taraṅginî* III. 264), during which Bhartṛimeṇṭha (placed by Râjaśekhara between Vâlmîki and Bhavabhûti, see Aufrecht, *Catalogus*, 140a) composed the *Hayagrîvavadha*, and presented it to the king (v. 261 ff.). He abdicated the throne on hearing of the death of his patron, Harsha, retired to Vârâṇasî, and in consistency with the gentleness of his disposition (see vv. 248 ff.), became a Buddhist ascetic (prîtyâ kâshâyam grahaṇa . . . pâlih, v. 321; see Lassen, *Ind. Alt* II. 897-909). Nothing is known regarding Mâtṛigupta's poetical works (Bhâu Dâji's identification of him with Kâlidâsa does not rest on any reasonable foundation); on the other hand, the scholiasts occasionally quote passages from a rhetorical work in ślokas bearing his name.

* When Bhâu Dâji, in the same essay, connects the *Setubandha* with the building of a bridge of boats which Pravarasena, according to the *Râja-Taraṅginî*, III. 354 (Lassen, II. 915), threw across the Vitastâ, and accordingly asserts (p. 229) "that the construction of this very bridge is the subject of the *Setu Kâvya*," he falls into serious error. That circumstance, however, whether the poem is to be attributed to the king himself (as Bâṇa has it) or to Kâlidâsa (as the tradition goes; see also Bhâu Dâji's reference l. c. to Râmacharaṇa's commentary on the *Vâsavadattâdarpaṇa* of Sundara), might well have furnished an opportunity for celebrating by song the corresponding bridge-building by Râma, especially as the Râja-taraṅginî expressly mentions (III. 363) that the king had direct relations with Ceylon.—From inscriptions, unfortunately undated, which have been found in Seoni

regard king Pravarasena II.* as contemporary with, or perhaps as the immediate predecessor of the Chinese pilgrim, and therefore as belonging to the beginning of the seventh or the second half of the sixth century.† Besides, we do not need this identification in order to make good that the Setubandha belongs at the latest to this period, seeing that besides being referred to by Bâṇa, it is expressly mentioned also in Daṇḍin's *Kâvyâdarśa*, I. 34; and the date of Daṇḍin's works ought no doubt also to be assigned to the sixth century (see *Ind. Streifen*, I. 312 ff.)

Now, for this period the testimonies to the existence of the Râmâyaṇa flow in upon us in great abundance. Passing over the mention of Râma as a demi-god in Varâhamihira (505—587), which takes for granted at least that he was at that time specially honoured (see my *Abh. über die Râma Tâp. Up.* p. 279), we instance the following as referring to the poem itself:—the *Bhaṭṭikâvya*, written‡ in Valabhî under king Śrîdharasena (530—545 according to Lassen); the *Śatruñjaya-Mâhâtmya*, written in the same place under king Śîlâditya about 598§; the *Vâsavadattâ* of Subandhu, written about the beginning of the seventh century,|| in which, among other evidence, express mention is made of the Sundarakâṇḍa as even then known as a section of the Râmâyaṇa; and lastly the *Kâdambarî* of Bâṇa, which dates from about the same time or rather a little later,¶ and in which also repeated reference is made to the Râmâyaṇa (see I. 34, 45, 61). The *Saptaśataka* of Hâla (see v. 35, 316) may perhaps be also mentioned in the same connection (see my Treatise on the same, p. 6 ff.). —And in the last place, last not least, we have to mention here also the name of Bhavabhûti, whose date appears to be fixed by the *Râjataraṅgiṇî*, IV. 144, as belonging to the reign of Yaśovarman, the contemporary of Lalitâditya, and therefore, according to Lassen, 695—732.** It is well known, that he has taken for the subject of two of his dramas the story of Râma with special reference to Vâlmîki's Râmâyaṇa (see my *Abh. über die Râma Tâp. Up.* p. 279). And indeed one of these, the *Uttararâmacharita*, possesses in this respect a deep and special interest from the circumstance that it directly quotes some verses from the Râmâyaṇa, and thus provides a means of critically verifying the then existing text of the work. There are three passages in which this test can be applied. The first of these occurs in the second Act (ed. Calc. 1831, p. 27; ed. Cowell, Calc. 1862, p. 29), where the Râmâyaṇa I. 2, 18 (Schl., Ser., 17 Gorr. 15 Bomb., also in ABC), is quoted word for word, and as being (just as in that passage) the verse which prompted Vâlmîki to enter upon the composition of the entire work:—

mâ nishâda pratishṭhâṃ tvam agamaḥ śâśvatîḥ samâḥ |
yat krauñchamithunâd ekam avadhîḥ kâmamohitam ||

The other two passages occur in the sixth Act (p. 115-116; Cowell, p. 157-158), the one closely following the other. The first consists of two verses which, according to the statement there given, should be found—Bâlakâṇḍasyâ 'nte ('ntye?) 'dhyâye (sic! not sarge!), consequently at the close of the Bâlakâṇḍa; they read thus:—

prakṛtyaiva priyâ Sîtâ Râmasyâ "sîn mahâtmanaḥ |
priyabhâvaḥ sa tu tayâ svaguṇair eva vardhitaḥ ||
tathaiva Râmaḥ Sîtâyâḥ prâṇebhyo 'pi priyo 'bhavat |
hṛdayaṃ tv eva jânâti prîtiyogaṃ parasparam ||

And corresponding herewith, the last chapter of the Bâlakâṇḍa in BC, in Schlegel's and in the Bombay editions, and the last chapter but one in the Serampore edition, contain respectively two verses (LXXVII. 26, 27, Schl., LXXIII. 72. 73, Ser., LXXVII. 26-28, Bombay).

on the upper Narmadâ valley, we learn that there were besides two other kings called Pravarasena who reigned there over a region that bore the name Vâkâṭaka; see Prinsep, *Journ. As. S. B.* 1836, p. 727, ff. Lassen, *Ind. Alt.* III. 63-4. Pravarasena II. appears in these inscriptions as the grandson, by his mother's side, of a Mahârâjâdhirâja Devagupta, whom Lassen places at about 400-401. The seal impressed upon the corresponding copper-plate grant bears the inscription (in śloka):—

Vâkâṭakalalâmasya kramaprâptanṛpaśriyaḥ |
râjñaḥ Pravarasenasya śâsanaṃ ripuśâsanam ||

* The grandfather of the same name, Pravarasena I., died according to the Râja-Taraṅgiṇî thirty-six years before the king mentioned in the text ascended the throne.

† In Bâṇa's Harshacharita, Pratâpaśîla appears as the father of Harshavardhana; and the king who, according to Hiwen Thsang, corresponds with the latter himself bears the name Śîlâditya; see Hall, Vâsavadattâ, p. 17, 51; *Ind. Streifen*, I. 354-6.

‡ See Lassen, *Ind. Alt.* III. 512.

§ See my *Abh. über das Śatruñjaya-Mâhâtmya*, p. 6, 13 ff., 20.

|| See *Ind. Streifen*, I. 370, 380.

¶ See *Ind. Streifen*, I. 354 ff.

** It is not clear what reason Hall has for placing Bhavabhûti before Subandhu (Introduction to the Vâsavadattâ p. 27, 51); see *Ind. Streifen* I. 356. † vide B. (fol. 59)

which are the same in substance at least, and correspond to some extent also in expression; they read as follows:—

priyâ* tu Sîtâ Râmasya dârâḥ pitṛikṛitâ† iti |
guṇâd rûpaguṇâch châ 'pi prîtir‡ bhûyo vyavardhata§ |
tasyâś cha bhartâ dviguṇam|| hṛidaye parivartate¶ |
antargatam** api vyaktam âkhyâti†† hṛidayam hṛidâ ‡‡ |

In Gorresio there is nothing at all corresponding (see I. 79, 45–48); and the chapter in which the two verses now quoted occur in Schlegel, &c. is not the last in Gorresio, but (as in the Serampore edition) the one before the last of the Bâlakâṇḍa. There is, on the other hand, one text at least, namely A, that gives the two verses quite identically with Bhavabhûti's text, with only trifling variations: "abhivardhitaḥ, hṛidayam, "yogam pṛichchhanam"; and in fact they appear in this text also immediately before the close of the Bâlakâṇḍa; after them there follow, just as in BC. Schl., only two other verses, the second of which likewise closes the book in BC. Schl.§§

The second of the two passages from the sixth Act (being the third we cite from the Uttararâmacharita) reads thus:—

"tvadartham iva vinyastaḥ śilâpaṭṭo 'yam agrataḥ |
yasya 'yam abhitaḥ pushpaiḥ pravṛishṭa iva kesaraḥ |"

The corresponding verse, however, reads thus in Schlegel (II. 96, 9), in Carey-Marshman (Ser., II. 70, 5), and in the Bombay edition (II. 96, 5. 6):—

"tvadartham iha vinyastâ tv iyam âśoka-mamâlikâ |
yasyâḥ pârśve*|| taruḥ pushpaiḥ pravṛishṭa¶¶ iva kesaraḥ*|

in Gorresio (II. 105, 6) on the other hand:—

"tvadartham iha vinyastaḥ śilâpaṭṭo 'yam agrataḥ |
asya pârśve taruḥ pushpaiḥ pravṛishṭa iva kesaraḥ |."

and in A. fol. LXXVIII^{a} (unfortunately the second book exists here only in one MS.):—

"tvadartham iha vinyastaḥ śilâyâm sukhasamstaraḥ |
yasyâḥ pârśve taruḥ pushpai(r) vibhrashṭa iva kesaraiḥ |."

If, then, we are to draw any conclusion regarding the rest of the text from the differences in these three examples, it must be allowed that the result as regards its authenticity, in the form in which we possess it, will be very far from encouraging. But with respect to this matter we are entitled to ask, whether, as matter of fact, Bhavabhûti made his quotations with such accuracy as that they really represent the text then in existence? And when we remember the extremely unreliable way in which Indian authors are accustomed to make their quotations, we are fully justified in asking such a question. But it ought to be considered, on the other hand, that the quotations here in question were made from a work that was universally known and esteemed, that any considerable deviations from it would therefore have certainly been noticed by the public before whom the drama was represented, even though they might not have been possessed of any great critical acumen, and that consequently the poet would not be likely to lay himself open to the charge of mis-quoting.† It must, however, in my opinion, be allowed that the diversity in the above quotations does not on the one hand permit us, by reason of their limited range, to pronounce any decisive verdict on the question at issue, and that on the other hand it is not after all so very serious—but in

---

* [illegible] BC.—† [illegible] priyatayâ° B.—‡ [illegible] rûpaguṇâc cha 'pi [illegible] BC.—§ [illegible] 17 C., pi vyavardhata (!) R. 'bhivardhitaḥ, Ser. Bomb.

|| [illegible] Râmam C.—¶ [illegible] BC.—** [illegible] BC.—†† vyâkhyâti BC.—‡‡ hṛidi BC.

§§ These read as follows:—

Sîtayâ tu tayâ Râmaḥ prîtyâ saha samgataḥ |
priyo 'bhichakame tayâ vijânadâ 'nantaguṇaḥ |
tayâ sa râjarshisuto 'nurûpaya, (1) samyivâs (2) [illegible] [illegible]
śiva Râmaḥ s'arvabhir [illegible], (3) yathâ [illegible] Vishṇur ivâ 'parâjitaḥ | (4)
1 [illegible] C. Schl.—2 samayivân BC. Schl.—3 [illegible] BC., [illegible] Schl.—4. [illegible] Vishṇur ivâ 'marasvaraḥ Schl., [illegible] C, s'as'iva [illegible] D.

|||| pâśva. Ser. ¶¶ pravrishṭa, Ser. Bomb. * [illegible] kesaraih, Bomb.

† And we learn from the beginning of the Mâlatîmâdhava that Bhavabhûti had some bitter antagonists to face, probably from among the circle of his own Brâhmanical relations, who reproached him, the Brâhman, for not having given himself "to the study of the Vedas, and to acquiring a knowledge of the Upanishads, of the Sânkhya and Yoga," and for turning his attention instead to the dramatic art. He treats these opponents of his with lofty disdain, and appeals from their judgment to the verdict of futurity and to the world at large:—"Those who are here seeking everywhere to depreciate us, do they really know anything? This work of ours is not for them" | "There will arise, yea, even now there lives many a one like-minded with myself (who is able to appreciate me)! | for time is boundless and the world is wide" | Bold words reminding us of Ovid: quaque patet domitis Romana potentia terris . . . !

any great degree exceeding the difficulties which we have already encountered, namely, the variations in the different recensions, the notices in the scholia regarding interpolations, and the contradictions and repetitions within individual texts. These quotations in Bhavabhûti, in fact, furnish rather a most valuable guarantee that the Râmâyaṇa, taking it as a whole, really existed at that time in essentially the same form as that in which we at present possess it.—And indeed this further conclusion may be drawn from what we find in the *Uttararâmacharita*, that at that time the stories also which are contained in the Uttarakâṇḍa were already thoroughly established, in so far at least as they refer to the repudiation of Sîtâ by Râma after his return, to the birth of her two sons, Kuśa and Lava, in the hermitage of Vâlmîki, to the latter's educating of the two boys in an acquaintance with the Râmâyaṇa which he had himself composed, and to the re-uniting of Râma and Sîtâ.* The same remark holds good for the Raghuvaṁśa. But in the telling of these stories Bhavabhûti deviates in some degree from the version of them given in the Uttarakâṇḍa (as also from that of the Raghuvaṁśa). He cannot find it in his heart, for instance, immediately to separate again the newly re-united pair, but leaves them in their state of restored union;† while in the *Uttarakâṇḍa*, CIV. 11; *Raghuvaṁśa*, XV. 81, (and in the *Adhyâtmarâmâyaṇa*, according to Wheeler) Sîtâ is obliged to adduce this further proof of her innocence, that in answer to her prayer the ground opens, the earth-goddess ascends out of the chasm, and takes Sîtâ down with her into the Rasâtala.‡ And then, further, the first meeting of Râma with his two sons, which in the *Uttarakâṇḍa*, C. 1ff. *Raghuvaṁśa*, XV. 63 ff. (and *Adhyâtmarâmâyaṇa*) follows only upon their chanting, at Râma's sacrifice, of the Râmâyaṇa which Vâlmîki had taught them, is much more poetically introduced in Bhavabhûti, namely, by Lava's defeating of the army sent out for the protection of the sacrificial horse;§ the prowess of the son proves his legitimacy, and confirms the innocence of his mother. Whether these variations in Bhavabhûti are to be credited to himself, or whether the responsibility of making them rests on some other recension‖ of the Uttarakâṇḍa less precise and possibly more wanting in reverence for the poet of the Râmâyaṇa, must in the meantime be left an open question. The circumstance that the version given by Wheeler, equally with that in the Jaimini-Bhârata, harmonises in part with that of Bhavabhûti, certainly tells against the theory that these variations owe their origin to the latter; but yet it wants the force of direct evidence, inasmuch as both of these versions may really have a later date than his, a supposition which is in fact decidedly favoured by the exaggerations which they exhibit (vide infra n. §)

* Neither the Râmâyaṇa itself, the Râmopâkhyâna, the notices in the third, seventh and twelfth books of the Mahâbhârata, nor those in the Harivaṁśa (vide supra p.) make any mention of these incidents; on the other hand, they are all unanimous in relating that Râma, after his return, daśa Varshasahasrâṇi [illegible] (*Râmopâkhyâna*, *Mahâbhârata* XII. [illegible] *Harivaṁśa*, [illegible]), or, as we find it in an amplified form in *Mahâbh.* VII. 2243 —[illegible] [illegible].

† Just as in the recension of the Râmâyaṇa followed by Wheeler (p. 440), and in the *Jaimini Bhârata*, adhy. 67.

‡ Very different therefore both from our version of her "wishing to sink into the earth with shame," and from the versions of the Buddhists. For in a Buddhist legend (Fausböll, *Dhammapada*, p. 341), the earth opens, the flames of Avîchi (the hell under the earth) burst forth, and the slanderess sinks down into them; and in Bigandet (p. 139) several other instances are given of falsehood being similarly punished. Compare also Fausböll, l. c. p. 419, Wilson, *Select Works*, I. 69, and Bigandet, *Life of Gaudama* (1866), p. 231, according to which Suprabuddha, the father-in-law of Buddha, seven days after he had calumniated the latter, sank down through the earth into hell, as a punishment for his offence. A similar fate befell Devadatta, Fausböll, l. c. p. 148, Bigandet, p. 262. According to Bigandet, p. 93, it was a universal custom among the Buddhists to call upon the Earth as a witness "of the good works they have done or are about doing," and the custom is said to have arisen from the circumstance that Buddha himself, in his contest with Mâra, appealed to the Earth to bear witness in his favour.

Our "wishing to sink into the earth with shame" occurs in *Pañchatantra*, LXVII. 7, ed. [illegible], where [illegible] [illegible] by the [illegible] [illegible] bhagavati [illegible] [illegible] [illegible] [illegible] [illegible], *Pañchatantra*, p. 156, 17). So also in Bhavabhûti's *Mahâvîracharita* p. 56, where Jâmadagnya (Paraśurâma), after being defeated by Râma, cries out:—bhagavati vasundhare prasîda [illegible]

§ This idea is still more fully developed in the *Jaimini Bhârata* (Chap. 31—35); and the recension of the Râmâyaṇa followed by Wheeler (p. 449) also agrees with this version of the story. In the Jaimini Bhârata, Kuśa is victorious over his three uncles and even over Râma himself, after Lava has been taken prisoner by Śatrughna; the story is somewhat differently told in Wheeler.

‖ From the *Sâhityadarpaṇa* § 504 (p. 184; see also p. 280) it appears that the rules of rhetoric not only permitted the dramatic poets, but even required them both to omit anything objectionable in the traditional legends which they made use of, and to adopt such variations in the stories as good taste might seem to demand. Thus we are told that Râma's slaying of Vâli by means of a stratagem, in the Râmâyaṇa, is not mentioned at all in the drama Udâtta-Râghava; and that in the Vîracharita the incident is modified to this extent that Vâli goes forth to kill Râma, and then is killed by Râma. This last reference is probably to Bhavabhûti's *Mahâvîracharita* (p. 70-72, Wilson, *Hindu Theatre*, II. 328, 331) which among other deviations from the version given in the Râmâyaṇa, contains as a matter of fact, also the one here mentioned.

—With reference to this matter, I remark in passing, that the whole of this later story about Kuśa and Lava as sons of Râma seems to me to have been invented merely by the bards and minstrels, kuśîlava, in order to avert from themselves the odium attached to the name kuśîlava (see my *Akad. Vorles. über Ind. Lit.* G. and the *St. Petersburg Lexicon*, s. v.), and to obtain, on the other hand, the highest possible consideration for their order.

And, as bearing upon this part of our subject I draw attention to the additional fact that, according to the account given by Friederich in his treatise *Ueber die Sanskrit und Kawi-Literatur auf der Insel Bali* (see my notice of this work in the *Ind. Stud.* II. 133-136), the Uttarkâṇḍa, represented too as having been composed by Vâlmîki, appears also among the Sanskrit works translated into the Kavi language; and likewise that the *Arjunavijaya*, an independent Kavi poem (see *ibid.* p. 142), is borrowed, so as far as its substance is concerned, from the same work (see *Uttara-kâṇḍa*, 21, 22). We are, however, in the meantime prohibited from drawing any chronological conclusion from this circumstance, so long as we are unable to fix exactly the time at which the work found its way into Java. The relations of India to this island have evidently not been restricted to the circumstances of merely one immigration, but they extend in all probability over several centuries; and consequently the work may have passed over from the mainland at any particular date during that period. Lassen has indeed entered his protest (*Ind. Alt.* II. 1046ff.) against Friederich's view that the earliest of these relations does not go further back at all events than the year 500 A.D.; but whether his own views are so perfectly trustworthy has yet to be proved. In any case, what Friederich himself states regarding the Kavi translation of the Râmâyaṇa—see my remarks thereon in the place already referred to—is not brought forward with the view of making out that a high antiquity ought to be assigned to it; on the contrary, the conjecture which I have there expressed, to the effect that the poem referred to is probably not the Râmâyaṇa itself, but only a Bâlarâmâyaṇa, into which were interwoven the latest incidents in the story of Râma, narrated for the first time in the Uttarakâṇḍa—this conjecture seems to be borne out by the fact that recently, and just in Southern India, quite a number of similar works bearing the name Bâlarâmâyaṇa have been brought to light: see Taylor, *Catalogue of Oriental MSS. of the College, Fort St. George* (Madras 1857) I. 205, 296, 299, 419, 450, 455. These are, to be sure, designated for the most part thus:—"A Brief Epitome for Schools (106 ślokas);" but besides these, mention is also made, (p. 456), of two separate Saṅgraha Râmâyaṇas,—a short one in seven sargas, and a longer one of uncertain extent (the MS. is defective; it contains about fifty sargas); and similarly, (p. 169), of a prasanna-Râmâyaṇa in twenty-one sargas.* If we add to these the numerous translations of the Râmâyaṇa that are referred to in the Catalogue, with or without the Uttarakâṇḍa, in almost all the languages of the Dekhan, in Tamil, (p. 360, 420), 531), in Telugu, (p. 495), in Malayalam, (p. 670), in Uriya, (p. 675), in Canarese, both in prose and in verse (p. 595, 597, 604, 605, 645, 666, 602 bâlarâmâyaṇa, 603, 606 Râmâyaṇasaṅgrahanâtha), we are furnished, even from modern times,† with a sufficient number of analogues of the Kavi translation of the Râmâyaṇa, so that we are under no necessity, from the mere fact of its existence, to carry it back to any early date, as long as it cannot be shown from other sources that it really has any claim to such an antiquity.

To go beyond Bhavabhûti, in order to obtain testimonies for the existence of the Râmâyaṇa, is evidently unnecessary; but yet, considering the importance of the work with reference to the history of literature, there is a certain interest in such an investigation. And therefore I will also exhibit here in one view, at least briefly, such other laudatory notices of the Râmâyaṇa and such works directly assuming its existence or based thereupon, as I find ready to my hand. As instances of the former class, I mention the notice of and panegyric upon the Râmâyaṇa, and indeed upon Vâlmîki, by Râjaśekhara‡ who lived about the end of the tenth century. In the opening of

* In the Kavi-Râmâyaṇa, according to Friederich, the contents of the first six books of the Râmâyaṇa are also divided into twenty-five sargas.

† The translation in Kanarese (with the Uttarakâṇḍa) must certainly date, according to Wilson, *Mackenzie Collection*, I. 333, 104, as far back as Saka 1170=A.D. 1248. The Canarese version of the Râmâyaṇa dates, according to Weigle (*Z. d. M. G.* II. 278) from about the 14th century.

‡ Regarding the time at which he lived, cf. *Ind. Streifen*, I. 313, 314. Râjaśekhara lived both before Bhojadeva, who quotes him in his *Sarasvatîkaṇṭhâbharaṇa* composed after Muñja's time; see Aufrecht, *Catal.* p. 208a, and before

his Prachaṇḍapâṇḍava (Aufrecht, *Catal.* p. 140a.),—by Dhanaṃjaya, who belongs to the same period,* in his Daśarûpa, I. 61 (Râmâyaṇâdi cha vibhâvya Bṛihatkathâṃ cha),—by Govardhana, who also lived somewhere in the tenth or twelfth century,† in the opening of his Saptaśatî (v. 32, śrî-Râmâyaṇa-Bhârata-Bṛihatkathânâṃ kavîn namaskurmaḥ; v. 33, ati kâkutsthakulonnatakâriṇi Râmâyaṇe kim anyakâvyena?),—by Trivikramabhaṭṭa in the opening of his Damayantîkathâ (v. 11, namas tasmai kṛitâ yena ramyâ Râmâyaṇî‡ kathâ),—by the Râja-taraṅgiṇî (I. 166, *vide supra* p. 250) —finally, by Śârṅgadhara§ (kavîndraṃ naumi Vâlmîkiṃ yasya Râmâyaṇîṃ kathâm | chandrikâm iva chinvanti chakorâ iva sâdhavaḥ || see Böhtlingk, *Ind. Sprüche*, 3665; and Aufrecht, *Catal.* p. 124a). In the Brahmavaivartapurâṇa also: 'itihâsaṃ Bhâratañ cha Vâlmîkaṃ kâvyam eva cha' are mentioned after the eighteen *Upapurâṇas*, (see Burnouf, *Introduction to the Bhâgavata Purâṇa*, I. 72.) In the *Vishṇupurâṇa*, III. 3 "Ṛiksha, the descendant of Bhṛigu, who is also known by the name Vâlmîki" appears as the Vyâsa (reviser) of the twenty-fourth dvâpara—which unquestionably refers to Vâlmîki's authorship of the Râmâyaṇa; (see Wilson, p. 274; Hall, III. 35.)

In the latter class, we have first of all to consider the later epic literature to which the two great epics gave rise. The literature of the Purâṇas, however, which calls for the earliest attention here, yields comparatively little that bears on our subject (see my *Abh. über die Râma Tâp. Up.* p. 281). I take from Aufrecht's *Catalogue* the statement that the Agnipurâṇa in seven chapters, quae singulorum Râmâyaṇa librorum nomina gerunt, contains an epitome of the seven books of the Râmâyaṇa‖ (Aufrecht, p. 7a); and that in the Padmapurâṇa several sections are occupied with the history of Râma (ibid. p. 13, 14). The Skandapurâṇa too appears to contain a short section on the same, introduced in connection with the account of the Râmanavamîvrata.¶ Regarding the section of the Vishṇupurâṇa that relates to this matter (IV. 4), see Wilson, p. 385, and Hall, in his edition of Wilson's translation, III. 317. In addition to these, I have only been able to get from the Brahmâṇḍapurâṇa a *Râmâyaṇamâhâtmya* (Aufrecht, *l. c.* 8ba), and the *Adhyâtmarâmâyaṇa*.* But we have still to mention here that singular work which bears the name: Ârsham (or Ârsheyarachitam) Vâsishṭham mahârâmâyaṇa (see *Verz. der Berl. S. H.* p. 187—194; Aufrecht, *Catalogue*, p. 354ab.), which is placed in the mouth of Vâlmîki, and which against the 24,000 verses of the ordinary Râmâyaṇa, seems to represent a redaction in 100,000 verses,† but really contains only an exhortation addressed by Vasishṭha to the youthful Râma regarding true blessedness and the means of attaining to it, accompanied by numerous narratives, that are quoted as illustrative examples.‡ We have next, directly connected herewith, the artificial-epic (dating [illegible] even from the eleventh century§), *Râghavapâṇḍavîya* of Kavirâja, which sums up at the same time and in the same words the contents of the Râmâyaṇa and of the Mahâbhârata, and which has served as a model for a whole series of similar artificial works.‖ And lastly, as occupying the same ground, though quite modern, we have to mention also:—the *Râmachandracharitasâra* of Agniveśa,

[illegible], see Hall, *Introduction to the Daśarûpa* p. 3. The verse in the opening of the *Prachaṇḍapâṇḍava*, which has in view the self-laudation of the poet, occurs again, in precisely the same words, in the beginning of another drama by the same author, the *Bâlarâmâyaṇa* namely (I. 10 p. 2, vide infra p. 251), and reads thus:—
babhûva Valmîkabhavaḥ purâ kaviḥ, tataḥ prapede bhuvi Bhartṛimeṇṭhatâm |
sthitaḥ punar yo Bhavabhûtirekhayâ, sa vartate samprati Râjaśekharaḥ ||

* See Hall in his edition (Calc. 1865) Introd. p. 2, 3.

† See my *Abh. über Hâla's Saptaśatakam*, p. 8, 16.

‡ Vyâsa with the *Bhârata*, Bâṇa and Guṇâḍhya are mentioned further on.

§ According to Hall, Introd. to the *Vâsavadattâ* p. 49 A. D. 1363.

‖ And before that of the Harivaṃśa and the Mahâbhârata.

¶ In a passage quoted in the *Sarvadarśanasaṃgraha*, LXXII 10 from the Skanda, the mûla-Râmâyaṇa "original Râmâyaṇa," is designated, after the four Vedas, the Bhârata and the Pâñcharâtra, as also possessing the character of a śâstra. And this evidently presumes the existence of various later versions of the Râmâyaṇa.

* On this work see Wheeler, in vol. II. We already know, from Friederich (*Ind. Stud.* II. 161, 162), that this Purâṇa is found in Java, on the island Bali, and it would be interesting to learn whether the Javanese text contains also these two pieces.

† When Târanâtha (Schiefner, p. 8) speaks of a Râmâyaṇa in 100,000 verses, as little weight is to be attached to the statement as when (ibid.) he ascribes 10,000 verses to the *Raghuvaṃśa*!

‡ For the sake of these stories, a more thorough investigation of the work would certainly be very desirable. It is quoted so early as by Ujjvaladatta (see Aufrecht, *Catalogue*, p. 126a), and it was probably composed in Kashmir.

§ See *Ind. Streifen*, I. 352, 370, 371 and my *Abh. über das Saptaśatakam des Hâla*, p. 8.

‖ [illegible] in his *Bhârata-Râmâyaṇa-Bhâgavata*[illegible] treats of the history of these three works at the same time and in the same words; see Taylor, *Catalogue*, p. 176, 114 (each verse is therefore "capable of three renderings"). An analogous literary conceit is the *Râmakṛishṇakâvya*, probably composed by Sûryadâsa, whose date falls about 1500; see Aufrecht, *Catalogue*, 132a.

(Aufrecht, *Catal.* p. 121b),—the *Rāghavavilāsa* of Viśvanātha, author of the *Sāhityadarpaṇa* (p. 208 ed. Roer)—two works bearing the name *Rāmavilāsa*, the one composed by Rāmacharaṇa, (see Aufrecht, 214b); the other (an imitation of the *Gītagovinda*) by Harinātha, (*ibid.* 132a),—the *Raghunāthābhyudaya* of Śrī Rāmabhadrāmbā, see (*Verz. der Berl. S. H.* p. 154),—the *Abhirāmamaṇināṭaka* of Śrī Ra-lamanātha, (*ibid.* p. 156),—the *Rāmakutūhala* of Govinda, from the middle of the seventeenth century, (Aufrecht, 198b),—finally, the revision of the *Setubandha* in the *Setusarasi*, from the beginning of the same century, (see *Verz. der Berl. S. H.* p. 154-156.)

The dramatic literature, too, that has a bearing on this matter is peculiarly rich.* At the head of the list we may name the *Prasannarāghava* of Jayadeva, son of Mahādeva;† at the head, because according to Hall (Preface to the *Daśarūpa*, p. 36),‡ a verse from this drama is quoted in Dhanika, and it must therefore be placed before the middle of the tenth century. The *Mahānāṭaka* ascribed to Hanumant himself, belongs also to this period; for, according to Aufrecht, (*Catal.* 208a), it is quoted by Bhojadeva, the author of the *Sarasvatīkaṇṭhābharaṇa* which dates probably from the end of the tenth, or it may be from the beginning of the eleventh century: Śārṅgadhara also (Aufrecht, 123a) quotes it occasionally; and with this, too, accords exactly the venerable tradition (see Wilson, *Hindu Theatre*, II. 372-3), which ascribes the composition of the work to the Monkey Hanumant himself,‡ who first "engraved or wrote it on the rocks"§ and then, to please Vālmīki, cast it into the sea, lest his Rāmāyaṇa should be thrown into the shade; in Bhoja's time, however, some portions came again to the light, and at his request, were arranged by Miśra-Dāmodara; (see further Aufrecht's notices in the *Catalogue*, 142b, 151a; Taylor's *Catalogue*, I. 146). In Taylor (I. 11) mention is made also of a second drama of this name, but as having been composed by "Bodhāyanachari" (*vide supra*, p. 125 note). The Champurāmāyaṇa, by Vidarbharāja, "otherwise Bhojarāja" in five kāṇḍas, also claims (Taylor, I. 175, 456) to date from the time of Bhoja. Similar claims to belong to the middle or the end of the tenth century are set up by the Bālarāmāyaṇa, a somewhat tasteless drama by Rājaśekhara,‖ and by two dramas that are also quoted by Dhanika in the scholium to the

* Cf. *supra* p. 124, the earliest notice of the kind that bears upon the subject from the Harivaṃśa. According to the *Sāhityadarpaṇa*, § 277 p. 124 the [illegible] of the Rāmāyaṇa forms a particularly suitable subject for drama.

† Aufrecht 148b. It is certainly doubtful whether this Jayadeva is identical with the author of the *Gītagovinda*, as Hall believes; see my *Abh. über Hāla's Saptaśataka*, p. 15. According to the account in Bholanath Chunder's *Travels of a Hindu*, (Lond. 1869) I. 57, the author of the *Gītagovinda* lived as late as the end of the fourteenth, or rather the beginning of the fifteenth century, and was an adherent of Rāmānanda. Compare also the account in Wilson, *Select Works*, I. 65 ff. Now, considering the strong bias of the *Gītagovinda* in favour of Krishṇa worship, we should not readily infer that its author belonged to the Rāma sect.

‡ Hanumant appears also in the *Pañcharātra*, XL. 14, as a great grammarian. According to the account of the [illegible] Kaiyaṭa, he was the ninth vyākaraṇakarttā (see Muir, *Sanskrit Texts*, IV. 417, 418). It is possible that a grammarian actually bore this name and that his work was then regarded by the illiterate as the first bearer of the name (and there is a work ascribed to him, on the ten avatāras of Vishṇu: see Aufrecht, *Catalogue*, p. 23a).—Quite analogously, the name of Rāvaṇa is quoted as that of a king of Kashmir (*vide supra* p. 200 n.); and it is told of the latter prince himself (see *Ind. Stud.* V, 161, *Ind. Streifen*, II. 202), that on one occasion, on the [illegible], he wrote upon stone the bhāshya of Patañjali &c., and by that means preserved it from being lost. According to Hall's communications in M. Müller, *Rigveda*, vol. III p. xiii, there are also ascribed to Rāvaṇa, or at least to some one of that name, a Ṛigvedabhāshya and a commentary "on one of the *Kāṭhakas* of the *Yajurveda*," both of which are said still to exist. Similarly a Rāvaṇabhāshya to the *Sāmaveda*" (Hall in *Ind. Stud.* IX. 176). A pariśishṭa belonging to the *Sāmaveda* bears the name, [illegible]: see Burnell's valuable Catalogue of his Vedic MSS. in Trübner's *Record*, Jan 1870 p. 601.

§ In this writing "on the rocks" (see also the preceding notice) we have evidently a testimony to the existence of the "rock inscriptions" of Piyadasi, and specially the [illegible] of that fact. Compare with this also the account in the *Fo Kue Ki*, Chap. 38, regarding the forty-two questions which were addressed by Śakra to Buddha and written with his finger on a rock. As regards moreover the well known tradition of Hanumant's having given to Vālmīki, is it not possible that we should look for its origin in the fact that the Rāma legend was chanted in the dialects of the people before it was clothed in Sanskrit by Vālmīki? As a matter of fact the first account that we have of Rāma is in Pāli, and even then composed in a partially metrical form. The statement too in the *Adhyātma Rāmāyaṇa* (*vide supra* p. 121n.) that Vālmīki was "of low caste" may perhaps be considered as pointing in the same direction. Compare as analogous with this the statement that the Bṛihatkathā was originally composed in Paiśāchī, in the language of the Piśāchas (Brockhaus's *Kathāsarit*, I. 36 see *Ind. Streifen*, I. 315).

‖ See Hall, Preface to the *Daśarūpa* p. 30, 31. The *Bālarāmāyaṇa* has recently been published in Benares (1869) by Govinda Deva Śāstrī, first in the *Paṇḍit* newspaper, and afterwards in a separate form. It consists of ten acts (pp. 312), and exhibits a remarkable absence of poetic feeling. There is much that is interesting, however, in the account contained in the opening of the poem regarding Rājaśekhara. From this it appears that Mallinātha was quite in error when he described him, in the [illegible], as king of Kerala (see Aufrecht *Catal.* 138b, *Ind. Streifen*, I. 314). According to the account given here, he sprang from a Yāyāvara race (see the St. Petersburg Lexicon, s.v.), and was the guru, or rather upādhyāya of a king Nirbhaya or Mahendrapāla, of the Raghu family, who is designated as his pupil. The same verse in laudation of the poet which, according to Aufrecht (*vide supra* p. 219, n. §), is found in the opening of his drama *Prachaṇḍapāṇḍava*, and which extols him as a newly arisen Vālmīki, Bhartṛimeṇṭha and Bhavabhūti, turns up again here, being put in the mouth of a Pāripārśvika; and this is immediately followed by another similar laudatory estimate of the poet's talents, which is given as that of a

Daśarúpa, namely, the *Udátta-Rághava** and the *Chhalita-Ráma* (Hall, p. 36). All three are quoted also in the *Sáhityadarpaṇa*. In addition to these we have still to mention the following dramas that bear upon our subject:—the *Anargharághava* of Murári (quoted as early as by Sárṅgadhara, Aufrecht, 124b; according to Wilson, II. 375, dating from the thirteenth or fourteenth century),—the *Kṛtyá-Rávaṇa*,—the *Jánakí-Rághava*,—the *Bálacharita*,—the *Rághavábhyudaya*,—the *Rámánanda* (or is Bhavabhúti's work here meant?),—the *Rámábhinanda*,—and the *Rámábhyudaya*.† The *Rámachandrachampú* of Kavichandra was not composed till after the date of the *Sáhityadarpaṇa* (Aufrecht, 211a). The *Abhirámamaṇinátaka* dates (according to Wilson, II. 395, Aufrecht, 137b), from the year 1599 A.D. The *Dútángada* of Śrí-Subhaṭa appears also (Wilson, II. 390; Aufrecht, 139b) to be a modern production, composed by order of the Mahárájádhirája of Tribhuvanapáladeva for the pilgrimage to the temple of Devadatta-Kumárapála. Hall (*Introduction to the Daśarúpa*, p. 30) mentions also a drama called *Anargha-Rághava*, which he had found quoted from, and one called Chhabhandhi's *Jánakípariṇaya*, which he had himself looked into. The *Rámavarmavilása* of Purushottama (Aufrecht, 201a) probably also belongs to this category.

I might now mention also, in conclusion, those works which, in a greater or less degree, treat of the worship of Ráma as a god. But I will not go into this part of the subject, partly because I am able to refer, for information on it, to my *Abh. über die Ráma-Tápaníya Upanishad* (Berlin, 1864),‡ and partly because a full treatment of the quite modern literature of this description, which is connected with the names of Rámánuja§ and Rámánanda‖ would certainly lead me too far afield. I will mention here only the *Adbhutottarakáṇḍa* (see *Verz. der Berl. S. H.* p. 123—127), since it clearly makes a direct reference to the Rámáyaṇa.

Let us briefly sum up the results of our investigation.

1. The earliest indigenous testimonies to the existence of a Rámáyaṇa date from about the third or fourth century of our era.

2. Considering the present extent of the work (about 24,000 ślokas), and the great diversity found in the numerous recensions, it is impossible to pronounce a judgment, with anything approaching to certainty, regarding the original condition of the text. In the existing condition of the text, however, we find unmistakeable indications that the influence of Greece upon India was already firmly established.

3. Seeing that the earliest form of the story told in the Rámáyaṇa, as we find it, namely, in the Buddhist legend,¶ knows nothing of the abduction of Sítá by Rávaṇa, or of the siege of Laṅká, it is possible that, in the addition of these two elements by Válmíki, we should recognize the influence of an acquaintance with the Homeric saga-cycle, just as other stories belonging to this cycle have found their way into the Buddhist legend.

4. It is uncertain whether the Vaishṇava bias which characterizes the Rámáyaṇa, as we possess it, and which has done so, according to the testimony of the literature on the subject, for a long time back, belonged to the poem originally; but it is clear that the presence of this bias is due to the endeavour of the author to avail himself of national legends and the heroic figures of national tradition, and to make use of these, in the interest of the Brahmanical theology, as an antidote to Buddhism.

5. It is certainly at least possible that Wheeler is right when he refers the conflict with

---

[illegible] Svayamvaravarṇana. In the third Act there is inserted a drama of Bharata, called [illegible] (p. 68—69), which is represented by Kohala's troupe in presence of Rávaṇa, with the object of diverting his mind from the contemplation of his love sorrows. Regarding the [illegible], see the account in the *Sáhityadarpaṇa*, [illegible] p. 1[illegible].

* Quoted also by Hemachandra in his *Prakrit Grammar*, IV. 264; see Aufrecht Catal. p. 201b.

† The *Rámábhyudaya* is quoted as early as by Dhanika (*Daśarúpa*, p. 42) along with the *Bálarámáyaṇa* (*ibid.* p. 51), which, however, is perhaps only another name for the *Mahánáṭaka*. There is still one less of the dramas quoted in the *Sáhityadarpaṇa* that must be included in our list, namely the *Bálacharita*, as in the quotation made from it in that work (§ 384, p. 180, according to the account in Ballantyne's translation (301)), Daśaratha speaks to Ráma.

‡ In that treatise (147) the version of the *Rámacharita* closes with the return from Laṅká to Ayodhyá, as being [illegible] taken of the last incidents in Ráma's history till his final entrance into heaven with all that belonged to him (p. 76; conf. *Uttararámacharita*, 138 and 1161.

§ About the middle of the twelfth century (previous date 1127 A.D.), according to Wilson, *Select Works*, I. 46; Aufrecht, *Catalogue* p. 126, 199a.

‖ End of the fourteenth century, Wilson, *Select Works*, I. 46.

¶ The circumstance that in this legend Sítá appears as the sister of Ráma, and becomes his wife only at the close of the exile, probably finds its counterpart in the Rámáyaṇa in its representation that during the entire period of the exile (and in fact throughout the poem) she remains without children. It is only when we come to the Uttarakáṇḍa that we hear of her being a mother.—For a different and singular view of this circumstance see Wheeler, p. 312.

the Sâkyas in Ceylon to anti-Buddhist tendencies.

6. It is uncertain in how far the story of Râma and Sîtâ, as contained in its earliest form in the Daśaratha-Jâtaka, may have a historical germ, or whether even that earliest version may not also have had as its ground work, in addition to such a germ, what Vâlmîki has undoubtedly interwoven into his representation of the story, namely, the adoration of a demi-god, bearing the name of Râma, and regarded as the guardian of agriculture, but hindered in his beneficent activity by a temporary exile (possibly the Winter?), and also of the field-furrow deified under the name of Sîtâ.

7. The extreme mildness, which is the prominent feature in Râma's character as represented by Vâlmîki, is in this form an inheritance from the Buddhist legend.* It is possible that, in the course of time, Christian elements may also have found their way into the representation (Śabarî, Śambûka &c.)

8. Vâlmîki appears to have belonged to a school of the Yajurveda, the sages of which he has interwoven into his narrative (Rishyaśringa, Janaka, Aśvapati); and we may conclude that his birth-place was probably somewhere in the neighbourhood of Ayodhyâ.

Note.

Professor Weber contributes to the *Literarisches Centralblatt* of 30th Dec. last, a notice of "*The Daśaratha-Jâtaka* being the Buddhist story of King Râma, the original Pâli text, with a translation and notes by V. Fausböll, Kopenhagen, 1871." In this notice, referring to the fact that the account furnished by D'Alwis had already shown that one of the verses of the *Daśaratha-Jâtaka* was reproduced in the Râmâyana, Weber quotes his own conjecture (*ante* p. 124), that "an acquaintance with the whole of the Pâli text might bring to light still further coincidences of a similar nature." This conjecture, he here says, has been fully confirmed. According to Fausböll, there are two other verses in this Buddhist version which are found also in the *Râmâyana*; for although the parallel is not so close as to be a word for word reproduction, yet the verses are identically the same in substance as those in the Pâli text. These are, v. 5 of the *Daśaratha-Jâtaka* found in *Râmâyana*, II. 106, 16 (Schlegel and also in the corresponding chapters in Gorresio and Carey-Marshman); and v. 10 in *Râm.* II. 106, 8 (Schlegel, and in both the other editions). And it is further worthy of notice that both the remaining portion of *Râm.* II. 106 contains several additional distinct allusions to the words of the Pâli text, and that the verse of the *Râmâyana* which corresponds to the 10th verse of the *Daśaratha-Jâtaka* is put into the mouth of Jâbâli, who is represented in the Brahmanical poem as the representative of the atheistic wisdom, and whose words give occasion to Râma's sharp retort and to his well-known attack upon Buddha—

yathâ hi corah sa tathâ hi Buddhas, tathâgatam nâstikam atra viddhi.

It is true, says Weber, that Schlegel has cast suspicion upon the authenticity of this passage; but whether he was justified in doing so appears at least questionable in the light of the new information we have on the subject. At all events the whole of this section of the *Râmâyana* has now acquired special importance; and a collation of all the available manuscripts of the same is therefore greatly to be desired.

ARCHÆOLOGY IN BOMBAY PRESIDENCY.

(*Extract from the Administration Report for* 1870-71.)

The materials collected from an examination of the ancient temple of Ambernâth, by the party of artists sent to that place in 1868, and mentioned in the Administration Report of that year, have been utilised. Six sets of the casts and photographs of the temple have been completed, and one set of architectural drawings made. One of each of the former and the single set of drawings were sent to England for the last International Exhibition, to be eventually handed over to the Secretary of State for India. Out of the remaining photographs and casts, two sets have been already ordered to be sent to England and one to each of the museums at Calcutta and Madras. It has been proposed to cause copies of the architectural drawings to be made in England, by the carbon or other process for distribution among learned persons and institutions and museums.

At the request of Government Mr. Burgess drew up, in August 1870, a Memorandum on the Survey of the Architectural and other archæological remains in the Bombay Presidency and surrounding territories, appending amongst others "a list of places chiefly in the Nizam's territory, at which Hemâdpanti or other remains are said to exist." At a subsequent date the same gentleman addressed

* The circumstance, too, that the Râma-worship has never degenerated, either like that of Krishna into sensual excesses, or like that of Śiva into bloody orgies, is undoubtedly due to the earnest moral tone which, as a [illegible] of origins, it preserves as a heritage from the same source.

a letter suggesting that enquiries be made as to the description and extent of the remains mentioned in the lists, and that "lists be collected of all remains, rock temples, ancient shrines, monasteries, wells, forts, &c. &c., with such accounts of each, however fragmentary, as informants may be able to supply." A copy of Mr. Burgess' letter with the Memorandum and lists referred to, and extracts from despatches from the Secretary of State bearing on the subject have been forwarded to the Resident at Haidarabad, with a request that he will move the Nizam's Darbar to collect and communicate such information as it may be able to obtain regarding the archæological remains in His Highness the Nizam's territory. Intimation has been received that this information has been called for from the local authorities by the Nizam's minister.*

A grant of Rs. 2,000 from one per cent Income-tax balances was made during the year under report for the conservation and restoration of the Muhammadan buildings at Ahmadabad, and the money was expended on the palace at Sarkhej: the total expenditure from first to last at Sarkhej has been Rs. 10,231. The Masjid, which was half ruined and fast becoming wholly so, has been restored as far as is apparently necessary to retain the original architectural effect. Much attention has been paid to make the new portions an exact copy of the old work. All the fallen stones that could be found have been replaced in their proper position, and the new carving has been accurately copied from the old.

The municipality of Bijapur have expended in the past year a sum of Rs. 460 in repairs to the following old architectural buildings of the place,—Ibrâhim Rozah, Gôl Gumbaz, Bhagi Mahal, and Taj Baodi.

General Tremenheere, Political Resident, Aden, having reported that an Arab had brought to him from the interior a very interesting inscribed stone, orders were given to purchase the stone for the sum of Rs. 150; and the stone has been forwarded to the British Museum from Aden.

ASIATIC SOCIETIES.

Bengal Asiatic Society.

At the meeting of the Society on 4th June, Capt. W. L. Samuells, Assistant Commissioner, Mânbhûm, read a paper on the legend of Bâghesar, current among certain clans of Gonds, descended from a family of five brothers named Kûsrû, Sahi, Markam, Netâ, and Marâvi, that once upon a time a tiger cub was born to Kûsrû. As it grew up, the young tiger made itself very useful in keeping predatory animals from its father's crops, and in consequence the greatest affection existed between them. To Kûsrû's intense grief the cub died, but shortly afterwards his wife gave birth to a daughter who in due time became marriageable. The marriage ceremonies had been completed, and the party were about to enjoy themselves with feasting and dancing, when suddenly a frightful sound is heard proceeding from one of the company who had become possessed with a demon. On interrogation by an exorcist the demon is recognized by Kûsrû to be the spirit of his lost tiger-son. The demoniac is appeased with the sacrifice of a live kid which he tears in pieces after the manner of a tiger, and after being presented with three cupfuls of liquor and some mouthfuls of fine ghî, disappears. The appearance is considered a most happy omen, and Kûsrû's tiger-son is thenceforth deified, and worshipped under the name of Bâghesar by the five clans.

To this day among the descendants of the five brothers, during their marriage ceremonies it is usual for one or two of those present, generally the officiating priest and a looker on, to feign being possessed with the soul of a tiger, and in that state to kill and tear to pieces a live kid. The demons are afterwards appeased by the bride's father with an offering of three cupfuls of liquor and a mouthful of ghî. No marriage ceremony in these five clans is considered complete without the appearance of Bâghesar and the attendant rites.

Journal of the Asiatic Society of Bengal Nos. 174, 175, 176, for 1873.

Nos. 174 and 175 contain the papers on Physical Science. These are:—Part IV of a 'Monograph of Indian Cyprinidæ,' by Surgeon F. Day; 'Zoology of Sikkim,' by W. T. Blanford, F.G.S., C.M.Z.S.; 'Notes on the Ornithology of Kashmir,' by W. E. Brooks, C.E.; 'Note on various new or little known Indian Lizards,' by Dr. F. Stoliczka; 'On the Osteology of Trionyx Gangeticus,' by G. E. Dobson, B.A., M.B.; 'Third list of Birds from the Khasi and Garo Hills,' by Major H. H. Godwin-Austen, F.R.G.S.; 'On Differential Galvanometers,' by Louis Schwendler, Esq.; and 'On Birds from Sikkim,' by W. T. Blanford, Esq.

The first paper in No. 176 is a 'List of Words of the Nicobar language as spoken at Kamorta, Nankauri, Trinkut, and Katchal,' by E. H. Man, Esq. The next is on 'Buddhist remains in Orissa,' by J. Beames, B.C.S., Balasor. At Chhatiâ 16 miles north of Katak, the writer says "I came to a flat surface of laterite closely resembling that at Kupari. At the foot of a small hill was a square platform, about 40 feet square, of hewn laterite stones, from which rose twelve pillars, octagonal and with

* Since the report was published a 'Translation of a List of Old buildings in Indur, Bir, Yalgandal and Nagarpur' has been received; but it contains no 'remains' but what are classified to be "in good condition"—genuine ruins have been carefully excluded, and it is a mere list, no descriptions of even the briefest sort are attempted.—Ed.

rounded capitals, but much worn by the action of the elements, and covered with grey lichen. To the west of this was a rude square building composed of the same stones, roughly put together without mortar. This had evidently been constructed from the stones of the older structure, as there were pieces of mouldings, capitals of pillars and sculptured stones, some upside down, and all evidently out of place. Inside, smeared with vermilion and turmeric, were numerous portions of statues, heads, arms, a mutilated trunk or two, few of which bore any resemblance to the traditional figures of Hindu mythology.

"The images unfortunately are so smeared with vermilion and oil, that it is difficult to make out all the details. There seems to be a serpent's hood over the head of one, but it is too much worn to admit of any certainty."

Again at Dharmsala on the Brahmani, 31 miles north of Katak. "One mile to the west of the road, at the foot of a little hill, on a small promontory jutting out into the river, stands a temple of Siva, under the name of Ooharineswara Mahádeva, or as the peasants call it, Ooh'na'r Mahadeb. This is one of the usual Siva temples of the modern or sikarpin shape, so common in Orissa. It faces the east, and in front of it is a square platform of laterite stones, surrounded by pillars exactly similar in design to the Kupari ones; they are twelve in number, three at each corner of the platform.

"The Mahadeb temple has been built of stones taken from some part of this ancient structure, though the fact is concealed by its being entirely covered with a smooth coating of plaster. The Hindu statues of late date surrounding this temple are of remarkable beauty and fineness. The principal figure is called by the people Saraswati, and represents a smiling woman with four arms holding a conch and lotus, with many female attendants with laughing faces grouped round the principal which is not in relief, but has the stone cut away at the back of the figure.

"This image was found in the river some years ago, and the others were found in the jungle close by, or as the attendant Brahman states, suddenly appeared out of the rock, and ordered themselves to be worshipped!"

From 'Notes on a Visit to the Tribes inhabiting the Hills south of Sibsagar, Assam, by S. E. Peal, Esq., we make the following extracts:—

"Our ignorance of these various tribes, their many languages, customs, and internal arrangements, seems to be only equalled by their complete ignorance of us, our power and resources. The principal of clanship is here carried to the extreme; not only are there numerous well marked tribes inhabiting considerable tracts, as the Duflas, the Abors, Singphos, Nagas, but these again are cut up into small, and usually isolated, communities, who, among the Nagas at least, are constantly at war with each other. Their isolation is often so complete, that their resources lie wholly within their limited area.

"There seems good reason to suppose that the present state of things has existed for a considerable period. Not only are the languages spoken by contiguous tribes often mutually unintelligible, but the still better evidence of strongly marked physical variation holds good. And to these inferences of a long period must be added that tangible fact, that at their villages, or 'chungs,' and not elsewhere in the hills, there are numerous Jack trees, many of them very large, and not less than 400 years old, I should say, as the Jack is a slow growing wood."

"We now saw for the first time how they weed the 'dhán,' commencing at the bottom of the slopes and working upwards, in parties of ten to twenty. The dhán stalks seem far apart, and they use a bamboo loop to scrape up the earth, removing the weeds with the left hand and throwing them in little heaps. Each house or family seems to have its dhán marked out by sticks, stones, or weed heaps, and neighbours combine to work in batches. The rate at which they got over the ground was astonishing, the work being well done. The dhán was not in ear, and this was their second weeding. I was told, it was enough for the year.

"The labour they are put to for a scanty crop is almost incredible. They seldom cultivate the same piece of land for more than two years in succession, as grass comes up rapidly the second year, and they have no way of eradicating it, the only implement used in cultivation being the dhao. After the second year, they let the land go into jungal, and make fresh clearances for their dhán. The hills are thus in all stages of jungal and forest, now all grass, as Birata, Ulú, and Hamará; or ground deserted for three years, all in small tree jungal (for the trees kill the grass in that time); on other patches again larger trees may be seen, five and six years old, or eight and ten, and no grass at all. In about ten years all the available rice-growing land has had a turn, and they can clear the young forest again. They thus require far more land than the ryots in the plains, especially if the smallness of the crop yielded is taken into account."

A little beyond Longlang "we passed some small raised changs, on which we saw bodies tied up in Toccopalm leaves, and roofed in. We heard it was the way in which they disposed of their dead."

"We were taken to the highest point in the village from whence we had a fine view of the surrounding changs. To the east, nearest to Longlang and the plains, lay the Hâtí Mûtons' chung on its peak, which is wooded to the top. With the binoculars the houses could be clearly seen in detail, they seemed the same as in Longlang. The Hâtí Mûtons are the deadly enemies of the Banpara tribe, though so close. Next to the south lie the Kulan

Mûtons, also on a hill, and next to them again the Bor Mûtons, on a conical hill with the village on the apex. More to the south and in the extreme distance was the chang of the Naynwinng Nágás, or, as they are called, Abors; and due south was Unéghon, one of the four Banpara villages. Several small ranges ran behind these, all inhabited by Abors, up to the foot of the Deoparbat due east. This mountain is uninhabited, and called 'Deoparbat' from an idea that it is haunted by a Deo, or devil. Hollow noises are said to be heard on the summit, where a lake is believed to exist. It is wooded to the top, and the western face is rather precipitous; here and there large masses of rock stand out clear of the forest and so light as to look like quartz. From behind Unéghon a large hill rose shutting in the view; on it are the so-called Abors, who can never get into the plains, though in sight, as the border tribes would "cut" them, as it is called. In the foreground of this hill lay a series of small hills, all Banpara territory, and on one of them we were shown the village of that name where the Rájah resides. Nearly due south-west, Jaboka rises, and is as conspicuous here as from the plains, having a gradual slope on its southern face, and a very steep one to the north. It is the hill of the Jaboka tribe, with whom the Banparas are constantly at war, with varying success."

"We saw at Banpara some Abor women as girls, wives of the [illegible], one of whom, we were told, had cost five buffaloes, and was the daughter of an Abor Rájah. They seemed far more sprightly and intelligent and good-looking than Nágánis, and could, we thought, understand us far better [illegible]; whether they were exceptional cases, I cannot say. They wore the hair in a long queue, tied up with beads and wire, and in many cases it was long, not cropped at all, as is common among Nágánis. Costume as usual was at a discount, and as is often said "a pocket handkerchief would make four suits;" yet with all this, I doubt if we could beat them in either real modesty or morals, and this applies to Nágánis too.

"The Morang (deadhouse), or place where the skulls taken in their wars are put, was next visited. It also contained the great drum cut out of a tree stem and hollowed like a boat. I had reason to think that they might have scruples to take us in, and as I had often tried to get a skull, I did not show my interest in it outwardly. Roughly estimated, there were about 200 skulls. About half of them hung up by a string through a hole in the crown and in the open gable end, the other half lying on a heap on the ground. No lower jaws were to be seen, nor hands and feet, as I had expected. The latter are always cut off with the head when a man is killed, and confer another kind of 'ák' or decoration. None seemed fractured by a dhao, and a large number were of young people, or children, being small and smooth.

"We were conscious of being face to face with the great cause of this tribal isolation, constant warfare, evidently a custom of great antiquity. As long as social position depends on tattooing as here, and can only be got by bringing in the head of an enemy, so long shall we have these wars, and consequent isolation of clans. The man who brings in a head is no longer called a boy or woman, and can assist in councils of state, so called. And his [illegible] goes out as a man again, I hear. The head he brings, is handed to the Rájah, who confers the 'ák,' or right of decoration by tattoo, at which there is great feasting, and pigs, cows, or even buffaloes are killed and an amount of 'madh,' or fermented rice water is drunk. Those who are not tattooed, when old enough, make a party and lie in wait for stragglers, men, women, or children, anybody in fact with a head on him; and as cover is plentiful, they can get on the enemy's land and lie in ambush along side his paths, never breaking cover unless certain of success and getting clear off. All those who get heads, get the ák on the face; those who get hands and feet, get marks accordingly, for the former on the arms, for the latter on the legs. No two tribes, however, have the marks alike, and some even do not tattoo the face. The worst of this kind of warfare is that women and children are as often killed as men, and without any compunction."

"Besides the skulls, the Morang also contains the big drum which is nothing more than a "dug-out." It is beaten by short heavy sticks, and can be heard a great distance. The drum from the Mûton Chang can be heard here, at least six or seven miles in a direct line. Some are made of a hollow tree with the inside gradually burned out, and open at the ends, some 20 feet long by 3 to 4 in diameter."

The Banpara tribe consists of four villages, Banpara, Longhong, Unâ, and Nokrong, and Mr. Peal estimates them at 600 houses, and the able-bodied men at 1,000 to 1,200. The Jaboka Nágás have five villages, Jaboka, Kamlong, the [illegible], and Longting, and may have 1,000 to 1,200 houses and 2,000 able-bodied men. The Mûtons have four villages,—Bor Mûton, Horu Mûton, Kolen Mûton, and Nungbam—a 'new village' at least 60 years ago. "Whether these are separate tribes or simply different villages of one, I cannot say. A Rájah is at each, but they never go to war with one another, but fight on the contrary together, I believe, against any enemy. Their ák also is the same.

"Of the Bor Dúarias, Pani Dúarias, and Namsangias, I cannot give an estimate, but I think that they have not less than 1,000 to 2,000 houses, each tribe. Some of the Abor tribes again are very small, and consist of but one village, and that a small one; as the village and tribe of Bánfeang (Bamboo-chang)."

"Between the Desang on the east and the Dikho, there are as many as 8 or 10 tribes having a frontage to Asam. From Desang to Lafiry alone, only

36 miles, there are six tribes, *i. e.*, Bor Duarias, Métons, Banparas, Jobokas, Sangloys, and Lakmas, and this gives but six miles average frontage. They do not extend far into the hills, so that each may safely be said to occupy about 40 or 50 square miles. In some cases a tribe is more extensively placed; but again in others, as Banyong, the entire tribe consists of but one village. I know of no cases where one tribe has conquered and become possessed of the lands of another, hence the *status quo* seems of long continuance. The oldest 'Nuguans,' or new villages, are not less seemingly than 40 or 50 years.

"As a consequence of the above noted custom of head-cutting, and its isolating influence, few Nagas reach the plains, but those living on the border. We thus see a community of some hundreds perched on a hill, and depending almost exclusively on their own resources, constantly fighting others similarly isolated, on all sides, yet thoroughly able to maintain themselves. Perhaps in no other part of the world can so complete a tribal isolation be seen, and subdivision carried to such an extreme. The available land, too, seems all taken up. To every 40 or 50 square miles there are about four villages, of perhaps one hundred families each; yet from the nature of the case, as before stated, not more than an eighth or tenth of the land available can be cultivated at one time, and the population would seem to have reached its maximum.

The Banparas, like most Nagas, use the 'Jathi' or spear, and the 'dhao.' "They also use the cross bow. (Hop in Naga). It is not, I hear, of recent date. In the use of the jathi they seem clumsy and bad shots; I have tried batches of several tribes at a mark for prizes, but found them unable to reach 80 yards. Nor could they touch a sack of straw for half an hour at 60 yards, but at 40 yards one did succeed.

"They use their jathis for close work, usually from ambush, and never attack in the open. The dhao is used as a hatchet or mace, and held by both hands. One blow is usually enough, if fairly given in a fight, as they can cut with tremendous force. The jungle is so thick and continuous, that their warfare is wholly by ambush and surprise, and this gives the dhao great advantage. The bow is chiefly used for game and pigs."

"Their religion seems confined to the fear of a legion of deotas or devils, and has no system, and their devils are of course on a par with their limited ideas. Whatever they do not understand, is the work of a 'deota.' Every tree, rock, or path has its 'deo,' especially big trees and waterfalls. If a man is mad, a deo possesses him, who is propitiated by offerings of dhan, spirits, or other eatables. Deos in fact are omnipresent, and are supposed to do little else than distress human beings. The only remedy is presents and counter witchcraft." "There are no regular priests, though they have 'deoris,' men whose office it is to bury or attend to the dead. Two or more such men are in each village. They tie up the corpse in kaon leaves, and put it on the 'rik thân,' where it is left till sufficiently decayed when the skull is put in the Morang."

(To be continued.)

CORRESPONDENCE, &c.

AGE OF INDIAN CAVES AND TEMPLES.

To the Editor of the Indian Antiquary.

SIR,—In the XXVIth number of the Proceedings of the Bombay Branch of the Royal Asiatic Society which has just reached this country, I perceive that Dr. Bhau Daji adheres to the assertion made by him at the meeting in July 1869, to the following effect:—"I have personally," he says, "visited "many of the oldest Uriya Temples, with inscriptions "in many of them, and have also examined almost "every cave in this Presidency, as well as many in "Behar and Eastern India. I have sometimes "found Mr. Fergusson in error to the extent of one "to three centuries in respect to the age of Temples "and Caves. He generally postdated them." (No. XXVI. p. cxxxix).

Nothing would surprise me less than that this assertion should, in some cases, at least, prove correct. As I stated in my "History of Architecture" (vol. ii, p. 591), "when I visited Bhubaneswar "the subject was new to me, and I had had no "practice in inferring the dates of Hindu buildings "from their styles." Indeed when I last had an opportunity of personally inspecting those buildings, more than thirty years ago, the whole subject was in its infancy, and nothing had then been published that was of any real value or assistance. Since then numberless inscriptions have been published and translated, and almost all the buildings I then knew have been visited and described by others. Under these circumstances, I would naturally expect that, with all the increased knowledge and facilities now available, any one might detect errors in my determinations. It would hardly, however, be in Uriya temples. I only ascribed dates to three of them:—Bhubaneswar, Kanarak, and Jagannath. These dates I took, not from their style, but from Stirling's Essay in the XVth volume of the *Asiatic Researches*; where they are recorded in evidence that seemed so clear that it will be very interesting to know how Dr. Bhau Daji can upset it. Dr. Hunter, I see, tumbles into the same pit, and it is high time we were both rescued.

With regard to Temples and Caves in Western India, Dr. Bhau Daji may be in possession of information not now available to the general public; but I have seen nothing yet in print that shakes my faith in the general correctness of the data on which I have proceeded; but there is nothing I desire more than that any mistakes I may have committed should be rectified, and that others may thus be prevented from falling into the same errors. Actuated by these feelings, as soon as I saw a report of the discussion in the Bombay papers, I wrote a private letter to Dr. Bhau Daji, in which I explained to him that I was preparing for the press a second edition of my "History of Architecture," and how undesirable it was for the good cause we both had at heart that these errors should go uncorrected, and promising the fullest acknowledgment of any assistance he might give me in ascertaining the truth. That letter he has had in his possession now for a twelvemonth at least, but he has not yet condescended to take the slightest notice of it; and I am therefore induced to ask him publicly to make good his statement; inasmuch as by doing it in print and in the form of an answer to this letter, he will secure to himself, without dispute, all the credit due to his superior knowledge and sagacity.

London, 5th July 1872. Jas. Fergusson.

NOTE ON THE "GAULI RAJ."

I am glad to see this subject noticed by Mr. Sinclair, (p. 204), and I should wish to see more contributions to our stock of information on the subject. If every reader of the *Indian Antiquary* who knows anything, however small, bearing on the question would but contribute his mite, our store of knowledge might be considerably increased. I have come across many traces of the so-called Gauli Râj in Gondwâna, but the subject has never emerged out of the phase of misty tradition in which it is enveloped. The usual solution of the mystery is to refer to it an ante-Aryan period,—easiest, I say, as being incapable of contradiction by actual proofs, but this cannot be accepted for many reasons. All over the Betul and Chhindwara districts are found groups of monumental stones, three or four feet high, and sculptured over with equestrian and other figures. On enquiry, these are always referred by the people to the Gauli Râj; at most these stones cannot be above a century or two old. The modern race of Gaulis and Ahirs do not erect such monuments, but the Gollas or goatherds and the analogous tribe of "Bharwars" in Gujarat do erect somewhat similar monuments, only of wood instead of stone. It is quite clear that the villagers of the Sâtpura highlands fully believe in the existence in former times of a Gauli Râj, but they can throw no further light on the subject. The following is the only tale I have ever heard making any definite allusion to the rule of the Gaulis, and it is curious inasmuch as it seems to bring the râj within the range of a comparatively recent historical epoch. The Chaudris or hereditary Patels of Chhindwara are a well-to-do family of Rahbunsis, an offshoot of the Rajput stock, and the pedigrees which they show go back to a very remote period. The story told me by the present representative of the eldest branch of the family is, that his ancestors were formerly in the service of the Gond Râjas as military retainers, and that on some occasion of want of means to pay their dues the Râja gave them permission to take and plunder the fort of Chhindwara then held by Gauli chiefs. This they proceeded to do, and they have lived in the fort to this day. I could get no documentary corroboration of the story, but if true it makes the Gauli Râj contemporary with the Gond Râj. It may be quite possible that the term Gauli Râj expresses nothing more than that at some past day the upland plains of the Sâtpuras and adjoining lands were chiefly occupied by shepherd tribes who monopolized all the wealth of the country, and who no doubt carried arms to save their herds from being harried. The aborigines of the country would be in a state of serfdom to them, and look up to them as their rulers, and talk of their "raj." I think this is a more rational solution than to conjure up the ghost of some lost dynasty—a task almost as hopeless as that of identifying the lost ten tribes of Israel. This however is but a humble suggestion, and I shall feel happy if I can succeed in provoking further enquiry and eliciting some interchange of ideas on this ethnological problem.

Bombay, 22nd July 1872. W. Ramsay.

THE KHAJUNA LANGUAGE.

Sir,—I have lately confirmed some observations formerly made by me as to the classification of the Kajunah language, of which Dr. Leitner has been a chief exponent.

This language has hitherto remained unclassified, and the reason is a simple one, because it has no neighbouring congeners. It certainly has no connection with those languages with which it is intermixed in Dr. Leitner's vocabularies.

The group of languages which furnish the key to it is that of the Agaw, [illegible], Falashas (Black-Jews), [illegible], [illegible], and Shankalla of Abyssinia; but with these are also connected those of the Abkhass in Caucasia, of the Rodiya of Ceylon, of the [illegible], &c., of the Indian Archipelago. A Siberian class and two American classes are also related.

The Rodiya, the language of the Pariahs of Ceylon, was also unclassified. It will be seen that it belongs to the same general family as the Kajunah. There is little direct resemblance between the Kajunah and the Abkhass, or between the Kajunah and the Rodiya, but the relationship of each is rather with the Abyssinian class. One chief reason for calling the attention of the readers of the *Indian Antiquary* to the subject is for the purpose of inviting their attention to these sources for the early philology, ethnology, and history of India. The group which I have named at present —the Siberio-Nubian—must have had possession of the whole of India before the Dravidians.

St. George's Sq., 24th Feb., 1872. Hyde Clarke.

BIOGRAPHICAL NOTICES OF GRANDEES OF THE MUGHUL COURT.

By H. BLOCHMANN, M.A., CALCUTTA MADRASAH.

(Continued from p. 70.)

ON TITLES.

I SHALL say, by way of introduction, a few words about the titles that were in use at the Dihli Court.

The kings up to the time of Bábar had the title of Sulṭán; with the Mughuls the higher title of 'Pádisháh' came into use. In fact we find that the Mughul dynasty brought a new court ceremonial to India. The word 'sulṭán' is an Arabic noun and means 'power.' It then became, like other abstract nouns, a title; but it is still used in the sense of 'salṭanat,' or 'rule.' 'Salaṭ' is an old Shemitic root. In Chaldee we have 'shallīṭ,' in the books of Daniel and Ezra, which is used in the sense of 'strong,' and as a substantive, 'a prince,' whilst in Hebrew it occurs in Ezekiel in the sense of 'a hard, impudent woman.' In Arabic, the root 'salaṭa,' like its cognates 'ṣalada' and 'ṣaluba,' means 'to be hard,' and its secondary meaning 'to rule' is generally ascribed to Syriac influence. The word *sulṭán* occurs very often in the Qorán; but it has there the meaning of *burhán*, and refers chiefly to that power which a prophet as such has over men. The meaning will become still clearer when we compare *Act. Apost.* VIII. 19, where the ἐξουσία, or power communicated by laying the hands on any one, is translated in Syriac and Arabic by 'sulṭán.' Among the Arabians the use of the word 'sulṭán' as a title belongs to the times after Muhammad. The pre-Islamitic Arabians used *al-amír*, *malik*, *shaikh*, and later *al-wálí*, in the sense of 'a king.' Some Arabian chiefs had peculiar titles. Thus '*tubba'*' was the title of the kings of Yaman; and foreign kings were called by their foreign titles, as *kisrá* (king of Persia), *qaiṣar* ('Cæsar', Emperor of Constantinople), &c. The first clear case of 'sulṭán' having been used as a title belongs to the time of Ruknuddaulah deputy over Fárs under the Khalifah al-muttaqí 'billah, who bestowed it, according to Abulfidá, in A.H. 338, or A.D. 949, upon his nephew 'Imád-uddaulah. A later, though better known, example refers to the reign of Maḥmúd of Ghazni, who in 393 A.H., or 1002 A.D., dignified Khalf ibn Aḥmad, the governor of Sijistán, with the title of 'Sulṭán.'

From this time the title of 'Sulṭán' becomes common, and is occasionally interchanged with the Persian *Sháhinsháh* or *Pádisháh*, or the Turkish *Khágán* or *qáán*. The idea of dependence on the Khalifahs of Baghdád was always implied, and the early Sulṭáns of Dihli, Jaunpur, &c., tried to confirm their claims as reigning princes by calling themselves *náṣir amíril muminín*, helper of the commander of the Faithful, or *mu'ín-i khalífatullah*, assister of the Khalifah (vice regent) of God, &c., and sending embassies to Baghdád, and later, to Egypt with presents to obtain the coveted acknowledgment (*taqlíd*) as lawful rulers. Bábar, however, and his descendants based their right upon conquest, and from his time the emperors of Dihli are styled *Pádisháh* or *Pádisháh i Ghází*.

That the title of 'Pádisháh' was looked upon as a higher title than 'Sulṭán,' is best seen from the fact that from the time of Bábar the word Sulṭán, and in two instances the word 'Sháh' also, became the title of the Imperial princes, and 'Sulṭán Begum' that of imperial princesses, whilst the sons of princes, i.e. the grandsons of the reigning emperor, were called 'Sháhzádahs.'* Immediately after the conquest of Dihli under Iltutmish (Altamsh), we find that the princes also were called 'Sulṭán,' and the grandees 'Maliks,' a title which was only abolished by Bábar. From the time of Balban, we observe that the princes get the title of 'Khán,' or higher titles as Khánkhánán, Ulugh Khán (great Khán) and Ikit Khán (young Khán). Under Bábar and Humáyún we also see the word 'Mírzá' applied to them, which is a Persian usage, and later we find that two Princes, Khurram (Sháhjahán) and Muḥammad Mu'azzam (Bahádur Sháh), got the title of Sháh, which they even retained after accession.

The queens had the titles of '*Malikah*,' '*Malikah i Jahán*,' '*Makhdúmah Jahán*' (*pr.* served by the world), &c. Under the Mughuls the title of *Pádisháh Begam* appears (Núr Jahán

---

* In the title of the Princesses, the name was inserted between Sulṭán and Begum; thus Sulṭán Zebunnisá Begum. The word *Sháhzádah* is occasionally employed in histories for the sons of the emperor; but the word is then used as an epithet rather than a title.

and Mumtáz Mahall); other wives had the titles of Begum, Ráni, Khánum, Gúlibah, and Bibi, and were by outsiders and at court often geographically distinguished as Akbarábádí Mahall (the Ágrah Lady), Aurangábádí Mahall, &c. Within the haram the principal queens held darbárs and conferred titles. Standing epithets were also common; thus Akbar's mother is invariably called *Mariam Makáni* (holding the rank of the Virgin Mary); Jahángír's mother, a Hindú princess, *Mariam uzzamáni* (the Mary of the age); Mumtáz Mahall, *Mahdi 'ulyá* (the high cradle); Ūdham Bái, the mother of Ahmad Sháh, *Ṣáhibah Zamáni* (the lady of the age), &c.

The grandees, as mentioned above, had the title of *malik* before the Mughuls. The early kings of Dihli rarely conferred titles as personal distinctions. There were, of course, titles attached to offices, as *wazír*, finance minister; *ákhurbeg* (for *ákhurbeg*), master of the horse; *dád beg*, chief justice; *bárbeg*, master of ceremonies; *'áriz*, presenter of applications; *mír-bakhshí*, quarter-master general; *shiḥnah-i-píl*, master of the elephants; *dabír*, councillor; *barid* (the Latin *veredus*), the court intelligencer; *kotwál-bak*, the commandant of the capital and the palace; the *Ṣadr-i-jahán*, who conferred lands as *madad-i-ma'ásh*, ranking as highest authority in law matters and higher than all Maliks and Princes; *Vakíl-dar*, or *Vakíl-i-dar*, the Vukíl of the 'Porte,' and many more; but with the exception of titles conferred on princes, I think but few Maliks in the beginning of the Dihli empire got titles. It was as if the idea still lingered among the courtiers that the Khalífah alone was the fountain of honours. This did not prevent the Maliks from assuming titles as Zafar Khán (a favourite title), Nuṣrat Khán, &c., and poets and flattering dependents may have given currency to such assumptions. The power of the Maliks was almost absolute, and inscriptions shew that they even assumed the epithets of royalty, leaving the emperors nothing but the *khuṭbah* and *sikkah*, the honour of the Friday prayer and the right of striking coins. From the time of 'Aláuddín and Fírúz-sháh titles became more common, and are a recognised institution under the Lodís and the Afgháns, when the royal power was on a firmer basis. The title of '*khánkhánán*' was the highest, and '*Khán Jahán*' was the second in rank. Under the Mughuls, the Pádisháh was considered the sole fountain of honours, and the power of the nobles being limited and confined, they were anxious to obtain personal distinctions for which formerly there had been no need.

The Mughul emperors considered themselves the lawful rulers of the whole of India. The existing dynasties in the Dak'hin, or Hindú rájas, were invariably ascribed to the fact that Tímur left India; and the founders of dynasties were only successful rebels. Thus there was a constant reason for attacking and reducing independent states and restoring the empire to its old limits. The titles and rights of independent kings were never acknowledged by the Mughul emperors; the kings of the Dak'hin are never even called 'Sulṭán,' and had to be satisfied with general epithets as *ḥákim*, *wálí*, *marzbán*, or *dunyádár* (holders of worldly property—a word successfully coined by Abulfazl), and no Hindú Rájah was called otherwise than *zamíndár*, until he had made his submission, when he received the title of Rájah from the emperor and entered the service of the Mançabdárs. From the time of Akbar, the succession in Hindú reigning families required the sanction of the emperor, and the *tíka*, (or *qashqah*, as the Muhammadans called it) was, in the case of great Rájahs, put on by the Emperor himself. Aurangzíb, from religious motives, abolished the custom.*

The Hindús had different titles from the Muhammadans, viz.: Ráṇá, Maháràjah, Ráo, Ráwal, Rájah, Rái, Rai Ráyan, Jám, &c. These titles were *conferred*. 'Mahárájah' occurs rarely and only in later times; but Rájahs often assumed it or were so called by their subjects. There is no case on record that the title of Khán was ever conferred on a Hindú, though many assumed it or made it part of their names; and similarly, the title of Rájah was never 'conferred' on Muhammadans, though now-a-days there exist a few Muhammadan Rájahs.† Epithets also occur; thus—Mán Singh was called 'Farzand', or 'son'; several

* It had formerly been customary with the emperors to put the *qashqah* with their own hands on the foreheads of great Rájahs, and in the present reign [Aurangzíb's] Asad Khán had been ordered to put it on Rám Singh; but now the custom was abolished, and Rájahs were directed to make the *taslím*.—*Ma'ásir i 'Álamgírí*, p. 178.

The *taslím* or salám, usual at the Dihli court, consisted in placing the upper surface of the right hand near the ground, the body being bent forward, and then raising the hand slowly to the forehead. When *sijdah*, on the contrary, abolished the prostration, which Akbar had introduced and Jahángír retained, the *taslím* was performed 4 or times.

† An older example is Rájah 'Alí Khán of Khándesh under Akbar. In MSS. his name is often corrupted by well-meaning copyists to *Rají 'Alí Khán*—*rají* in Arabic means 'hoping'.

Jaipur Rájahs were called 'Mirzá Rájah', or *Sarámad-i-Rájahái Hind*,* Bahádur, &c. But the Hindús were worse off as regards titles than the Muhammadans.

In treating of Muhammadan titles, we must carefully distinguish those which were conferred from such as were assumed. First of all, the title of 'Nawáb' was never conferred. The word is said to be a corruption of *nuwwáb*, the plural of *náib*, a deputy. The singular occurs in *náib vazír*, *náib bárbak*,† and other ante-Mughul titles attached to offices. But 'Nawáb' and 'Nawáb Çáhib' occur as epithets on inscriptions and in prefaces to books as early as Akbar's reign. Again, the word 'Bahádur,' a Turkish word meaning 'brave,' was only used as an epithet. Ahmad Sháh used it as title and ordered his name to be read in the Friday prayer as 'Mujáhid uddín Muhammad Abú naçr Ahmad Sháh Bahádur.' Hence also '*Kampaní bahádur*,' the name by which the E. I. Company is still known in India. The modern 'Khán Bahádur' is, in Bengal, by permission assumed by Muhammadan Deputy Magistrates, whilst Hindú Deputy Magistrates assume 'Rái Bahádur'; it stands, of course, for 'Khán-i-Bahádur,' 'the courageous Khán.' The compound, however, is a modern abnormal one; for 'Khán' was conferred by the Dihlí emperors, and so also 'Bahádur' and 'Bahádur Khán,' but not 'Khán Bahádur.'

The word 'Khán' is a Turkish word, meaning 'king,' 'prince.' Thus we still say *Khán-i-Bukhárá*, the King of Bukhárá, for 'Sultán-i-Bukhárá,' which is also used. The title when conferred, had a high reputation. The word occurs also, as is well known, as part of names, especially in Afghán names, and in many parts of India it is looked upon as hereditary. In fact, according to Sher Sháh I think, the Afghans and their descendants are all Kháns. But the title of Khán which the emperors conferred was the Turkish title and ranked above Beg or Be (the abbreviated form of Beg). There are no cases on record to show that the Mughul emperors ever conferred 'Beg' or 'Be,' but many instances can be cited where foreigners with the title of Beg, after several years of service, received the title of Khán and then dropped the 'Beg.' I am not sure whether 'Beg' was ever conferred by the early Dihlí emperors, or whether the Turks looked upon it as hereditary; but it was often used, though chiefly in official titles and in the form 'Bak.'‡

The chief facts which we have to remember in connection with Muhammadan titles are, (1) no title conferred by the Mughul emperors was hereditary; and (2) with the exception of the title of Khán, no title was held by more than one grandee at the same time. Thus the title of Bahádur Khán would only be conferred on a grandee, when the former holder had died, or had, through misconduct, lost it. Hence such titles, from their limited range, were much valued; in fact they ranked so high that they gradually brought the real name of the owner into oblivion. Akbar's third Khánkhánán is generally known in history as 'the Khánkhánán,' but his real name Mirzá 'Abdurrahím is rarely mentioned. There were many titles to which, from historical recollections, an unusual estimation attached, such as Khán Jahán, Khán Zamán, Vazír Khán, Açaf Khán, A'zam Khán, Islám Khán, Sher Khán, Rustam Khán, Bahádur Khán, &c., and the emperors only conferred them for most distinguished services. As these titles recurred in different reigns, distinguishing epithets were used; thus we find a Khán Jahán-i-Akbarsháhí and a Khán Jahán-i-Sháhjahání. With the increasing number of the grandees after Akbar's reign the emperors had to invent new titles, and often availed themselves, for this purpose, of events or peculiar circumstances connected with the service of a grandee. Thus Jahángír rewarded a deserving officer who had first brought him the good news of a victory with the title of Khushkhabar Khán, and another with that of Muarrikh Khán, for his knowledge of history; and Sháhjahán conferred descriptive titles as Qal'ahdár Khán, Muhallidár Khán, Díndár Khán, &c. Doctors received titles as Masíh uzzamání (the healing Messiah of the age), Masíhulmulk, Hakím ulmulk, and so on, and many a court doctor rose to high military commands. Geographical titles were also in use, as Rúmí Khán, Ghaznín Khán, Khafí Khán (from Kháf, or Khawáf, in Khurásán), Habshí Khán, &c. Most of the titles have 'Khán' as the second word; but there are a few with 'mulk,' as Saifulmulk, Tájulmulk, and Im-

* I have seen in modern times the barbarous *sarámadah* for *sarámad*.

† Observe that in many titles the Persians leave out the *izáfat*. Besides the above examples, we have to say Khán Khánán, Khán Jahán, Khán 'A'zam, Khán Daurán, Khwájah Jahán, Qilen ... &c., all without the izáfat. But 'Khán-i-A'zam' is used with the izáfat.

‡ I believe that the Uzbak Pai, mentioned in Mr. Thomas's valuable *Chronicles of the Pathán Kings*, (p. 93), should be called *Uzbak Be*.

'ádilmulk. Compounds with 'daulah,' which had been in common use under the Khalifahs and the Ghaznawis, and later with the Dihli kings, were revived by Jahángir, who dignified his father-in-law Ghiás Beg, father of Nur Jahán, with the title of I'timád uddaulah, and by Sháhjahán who gave the father of Mumtáz Mahall the title of Yamin uddaulah. In the 18th century, however, compounds with 'daulah' became common. In general, the titles became high sounding when the emperors had become puppets and derived an unexpected revenue from the sale of titles both personal and indicative of duties that were never to be performed, or from presentations at court and the bestowal of robes made of sprigged calico as dresses of honour. The power of conferring honours, and the general belief that only the Emperor of Dihli could confer them, remained for years after the last silver-plating of the audience hall and of the throne itself had been put into the melting pot; the E. I. Company reigned and ruled in the name of the 'great Mogul;' the Nawáb Vazirs of Audh did not dare, before 1819, to assume the title of Pádisháh; and till within the last ten years, or even now, some independent rulers coin in the name of Sháh 'Álam.

Another class of titles may be mentioned. Jahángir introduced compounded adjectives ending in *jang* as Firuzjang, Nusratjang, Ghálibjang, Mahábatjang,* &c., which were placed after the principal title. These additions, also, became common in the 18th century, and were often assumed. Thus in the early (Bengal) history of the E. I. Company, we hear of Colonel Clive Bahadur Sabatjang,† and Mr. Verelst, Mons. Law, and other distinguished Europeans were similarly honoured.

Turkish titles as Tarkhán, and Ulugh Khán and Afghan titles, as Ulugh Majlis, Majlis-i-Ikhtiár, Majlis ulmajális, Masnad i 'Ali, &c., disappeared entirely under the Mughal emperors. The 'Malik ulumará,' or principal grandee of the courts of the early Dihli kings became, under the Mughals, the 'Amir ulumará,' and the title was, after the reign of Akbar, generally given to the Khánkhánáns.

The right of displaying a flag and beating the kettledrum (*naqqárah*) was as much valued as a title. Vazirs, or Diwans generally received on appointment, a golden penbox or a golden inkstand. The Khánkhánán also, as commander of the emperor's contingent, *i. e.* the standing army, received insignia. What they were is not quite certain; but flags of a peculiar kind formed part of them. All insignia were returned to the Emperor on death or dismissal.

I now proceed to the biography of—

VAZIR KHAN HAKIM 'ALIM UDDIN.

He was born at Chiniot, in the Rechnà Duáb,‡ a town to which Shaikh Sa'dullah the renowned Sa'dullah Khan also belonged. 'Alimuddin entered the service of Prince Sháhjahán as a doctor, but he was often in civil employ and accompanied the prince in the war with the Rána. He was the constant attendant of his master, even during his rebellion, and assisted him with 10 or 12 lakhs of rupees of his own property. When Sháhjahán stayed at Junar, he was treasurer to the prince, and was, after Mahábat Khán, the most influential officer.

On Sháhjahán's accession, he was made a commander of 5000, received a flag and a kettledrum, and five lakhs of rupees as a present. In the 5th year of the reign, he received the title of Vazir Khán, and marched with 10,000 horse from Burhánpur upon Daulatábád; but as Fath Khán, the governor, sent to him his eldest son with the peshkash, which Fath Khán had hesitated to pay, Vazir Khán returned to court. He was now appointed governor of the Panjáb, an office which he held for seven years. In the 14th year of Sháhjahán's reign, he was appointed Súbahdár of Ágrah. He held this office for ten months, when he died (21st Jumáda I. 1051, or 18th August 1641, A. D.) It is said that a short time before his death, on passing one day into Ágrah over the Hathipul Bridge, his horse fell. The fright seems to have proved injurious to him, for on his return home he made an inventory of his property and sent it to the Emperor to whom, according to custom, the property of every Amir lapsed. He died immediately afterwards.

He is said to have been simple in his mode of living and in dress; his faithfulness towards his master was proverbial. "Loyalty and piety," he used to say, "are twin sisters."

Vazir Khán's name is well known up to the present day in Láhor and Chiniot. In Láhor,

* Meaning either victorious, or dreadful in war.

† *i. e.* hard in war.

‡ The Duábs of the Panjáb are said to have been called by Akbar, (1) Bist Jálandhar or Bist Jálandhar, (2) Bári Duáb, (3) Rachna Duáb; (4) Chanhat Duáb. These names were invented to indicate the rivers which bound the Duábs; thus *Bist* stands for *Biáh* and *Satlej*; *Bári* for *Biáh* and *Rávi*; *Rachna* for *Rávi* and *Chenáb*; *Chanhat* for *Chenáb* and *Jhelam*.

he built a bath, a bázár, and several houses, and also the Jámí' Masjid, which is still known at Láhor as the Vazír Khán's mosque. The inscriptions on it show that it was built in A. H. 1044, or 1634-35 A.D.—

Sál i táríkh iń bináe Masjide 'Álímakán,

Az khirad justam, bagufta "sijdahgáhe ahl i fazl."

'I pondered to find a chronogram for the building of this noble mosque, and discovered the words '*sijdahgahe ahl i fazl*', a place of worship for the good.'

The other chronogram is better—

Táríkh iń bináe pursídam az khirad,

Gufta bigo bih "báni i masjid Vazír Khán"

in which the words *báni i Masjid Vazír Khán*, 'the builder of the Mosque Vazír Khán,' will be found to give 1044. Like other buildings in Láhor, the mosque was desecrated by the Sikhs, who are said to have killed swine in it and used the interior as a stable.

Vazírábád, in the neighbourhood of Láhor, was also founded by Vazír Khán. In Chiniot, his birth place, he built the brick wall of the town, erected many houses which he gave away to the inhabitants, as also a bázár with shops, a mosque, an inn, a Madrasah, an hospital, and besides he dug several wells. "In fact, he adorned his native town as no other Amír in India has done." (*Maásir ul-Umará.*) Though he was anxious to revisit his native town he found no suitable opportunity for doing so.

Vazír Khán's son, Saláh Khán, served under Aurangzib as Mír Tuzuk. In the 23th year, he received the title of *Anwar Khán*, was appointed Dárogah of the establishment of servants, and died in the 30th year of Aurangzib's reign.

The title of *Vazír Khán* was first held, under Akbar, by the brother of 'Abdul Majíd Áçaf Khán, the conqueror of Gondwánah. His biography will be found in my Áin translation (p. 353). Under Jahángír, the title of Vazír Khán was again conferred, namely, on Muqím, who served as Assistant Finance Minister and as Díwán of Bengal, but he rose to no importance. Under Sháhjahán, as we saw above, the title was conferred on 'Alímuddín of Chiniot. In order to complete the series, I shall now give a short biography of the grandee who held the title of *Vazír Khán* under Aurangzib.

VAZIR KHAN, MUHAMMAD TAHIR KHURASANI.

Muhammad Táhir was born at Mashhad in Khurásán. He served Prince Aurangzib as treasurer, and had the reputation of being a good soldier. In the 10th year of Sháhjahán's reign, Aurangzib ordered him to invade, together with Máloji, the Dak'hani, the district of Baglánah, which the emperor had given Aurangzib as an *altamghá* tenure. Muhammad Táhir invested Mulher, the stronghold of the Bharji of Baglánah, and forced him to submit. The district received a financial settlement, and Táhir remained as governor in Mulher.

In 1062 (A.D. 1652), he was appointed by Prince Aurangzib as his *náib*, or vice-governor of Khándesh, where he remained for several years. When Aurangzib, in 1068, left Burhánpúr to march against Dárá Shikoh, he left Táhir in Khándesh, gave him the title of *Vazír Khán*, and conferred upon him 'the right of a flag and a kettledrum.' After Aurangzib's accession (Ramazán, 1068), Vazír Khán was called to court, Mír Jumlah having been appointed governor of Khándesh, and was made, in the first year, *çúbahdár* of Agrah. In the 6th year, he accompanied Prince Muhammad Mu'azzam to the Dak'hin, and was again sent to Khándesh as governor. In the following year, he was appointed to Málwah* and received a full command of 5,000. He died in Málwah in 1082 A. H., or A.D. 1672.

"There is a spot in Aurangábád, still called after his name, where he had a villa. The part of Aurangábád between the 'Little Tank' and the tomb of Islám Khán of Mashhad, was founded by his elder brother Mírzá Mahmúd and is hence called *Mahmúdpúrah*. His son, Muhammad Taqí Khán, was Bakhshi and Wáqi'ahnawís, or intelligencer, and died in the 10th year of Aurangzib. He built a palace at the Little Tank in Mahmúdpúrah "which still stands."

Another nephew of Vazír Khán is Rafí' Khán, who was for some time Faujdár of Báns Barelí (Rohilkhand). He was a poet and wrote under the *nom-de-plume* of *Bázil* (liberal). His large

* Or Málvá, as Aurangzib spelt it. In the present agitation regarding the best system of spelling of Indian names, it may be of interest to refer to Aurangzib's order, by which Indian names ending in long á, as rája, Málwá, &c., were forbidden to be spelt rajah, Málwah, &c. In Persian there are but few names ending in long á, but a large number ending in a short a; but as words in Persian generally) end in a consonant, words with final short a were written as ending in ah, the h being silent. This peculiarity of spelling was mechanically transferred by Muhammadan writers to Indian names, and thus we have an explanation for Rájah, Koreah, Málwah, Ramah, instead of Rájá, Korá, &c. However, the order of the emperor only referred to the final ah (Kháfí Khán, II. 396). Of course, it would be wrong to spell Persian words ending in ah with a final á, as Khájah, banda, &c.

work, entitled *Hamlah i Haidari*, contains 40,000 verses in Mutaqárib metre, and describes the wars of the Prophet.

THE RÁJAHS OF NÚRPÚR (DISTRICT KÁNGRAH).

Núrpúr lies north-west of *Kángrah*, on the Jabbarkhad, a small tributary of the Chakki, which flows into the Biáh. Its old name, *Dhameri*, the "Temmery" of old travellers, was changed to Núrpúr by Rájah Bású in honour of Jahángír, whose first name was Núruddín. The Rájahs of Núrpúr are generally called in Muhammadan histories 'the zamindárs of Mau and Paithán.' Mau was one of their strongholds and was destroyed by Sháhjahán, and Paithán is the same as Pathánkot, west of Núrpúr. Paithán or Pathán is mentioned in the Áín as a parganah of the Bári Duáb, containing 199,672 bíghahs, yielding a revenue of 7,297,015 dáms (40 dáms = 1 Akbarsháhí Rupee), and furnishing 250 horse and 2,000 foot; and Dhameri is quoted as yielding 1,000,000 dáms, and furnishing 60 horse and 1,300 foot.

The zamindárs of Mau and Paithán are first noticed in the very beginning of Akbar's reign, when Rájah Bakht Mall is mentioned as a supporter of Sikandar Súr whom Akbar, in 963 A. H., besieged in Mánkot. When Bakht Mall saw that Sikandar's cause was hopeless he paid his respects in the imperial camp, and after the surrender of Mánkot, accompanied the army to Lahor, where Bairám Khán had him executed on the ground that he had supported Sikandar Súr. As his successor Bairám appointed his brother Takht Mall. I am not sure whether the names of these two Rájahs of Dhameri are correct, or whether the first ought not to be Takht Mall and the second Bakht Mall; for in every MS. of the Akbarnámah that I have seen, the two names are continually interchanged.

Nearly thirty-two years later we hear of Rájah Bású as reigning zamindár of Mau and Paithán. It is not stated how he was related to Bakht Mall and Takht Mall; but the historians of the reigns of Sháhjahán and Aurangzib look upon him as the founder of a new line, and give the following genealogical tree:—

Rájah Bású of Núrpúr. (Dies 1022.)

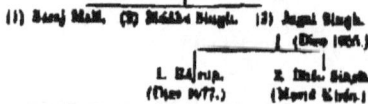

(1) Súraj Mall. (2) Mádho Singh. (3) Jagat Singh. (Dies 1056.)

1. Rájrúp. (Dies 1077.) 2. Bháo Singh. (Murid Khán.)

The last Bháo Singh in the beginning of Aurangzib's reign turned Muhammadan and received the name of Murid Khán. His descendants, according to the *Maásir*, still hold Sháhpúr, north-west of Núrpúr, near the Rávi, and "he who becomes Rájah, takes the name of Murid Khán."

Rájah Bású.—When Rájah Bású became zamindár, he made his submission to Akbar. But when Akbar, after the death of his brother Mirzá Muhammad Hakim, King of Kábul, (A.H. 993) made Láhor the capital, Bású did not pay his respects as he was expected to do, and the Emperor ordered Hasan Beg Shaikh Umari[*] to invade Mau. But when he had moved as far as Paithán, Bású, advised by Todar Mall, made his submission and went with Hasan Beg to court. In the 31st year, however, he rebelled again, and Akbar appointed Mirzá Rustam and Áçaf Khán[†] to reduce the district; but as the commanders did not agree, Akbar recalled them and gave the command to Jagat Singh, son of Rájah Mán Singh. Mau surrendered to him and peace was restored. In the 47th year, Bású rebelled a third time, and when an imperial corps was again despatched to Paithán he requested Prince Salím (Jahángír) to intercede on his behalf with the emperor. He waited on the prince, and accompanied him, in the 49th year, to court. Before he had reached the capital, Akbar heard that Bású was with Salím, and ordered an officer to seize him. But Bású was informed of this and escaped to his hills.

On the accession of Jahángír, in 1014 (A. D. 1605), Bású paid his respects and was appointed Rájah and commander of 3500. In the 6th year, he served in the Dakhin, and died, two years later, in 1022. He was succeeded by his eldest son—

Súraj Mall.—He is said to have been so unruly that Bású, from fear, imprisoned him. Jahángír after some hesitation, appointed him Rájah and commander of 2,000, and left him in possession of his paternal estates. Súraj Mall served with Shaikh Faríd in the siege of Kangrah; but when he saw that the fort was on the point to surrender, he created disturbances in the camp, and Faríd reported him to court as a rebel. Súraj managed to obtain Prince Sháhjahán's intercession, and was pardoned. In the 11th year, Faríd died and Kángrah still held out. Súraj then served with

* Vide A'ín translation, p. 454.

† A'ín translation, pp. 310, 411.

* For a biography of this excellent man, vide A'ín, translation, p. 413.

Sháhjahán in the Dak'hin. The prince, on his return, was sent to Kángrah, and though it was not advisable that Súraj should accompany him he was allowed to join the expedition and marched to Kángrah with Sháh Qulí Khán Muhammad Taqí, Sháhjahán's Bakhshí. Sháh Qulí was soon compelled to complain of Súraj Mall, but was recalled, and Rájah Bikramájít was sent instead. The time which elapsed before Bikramájít could join his command was used by Súraj Mall for mischief. He allowed a large number of imperial soldiers to return to their jágírs on the plea that the war had lasted a long time and their outfits was bad, but told them to return when Bikramájít should arrive. He then plundered the whole district at the foot of the hills, which was the jágír of Núr Jahán's father, and when Sayyid Safí Bárha opposed him with some of the troops that had not yet left, he killed him. Bikramájít arrived in the end of the 13th year, and Súraj Mall tried in vain to gain his favour by flattery. He therefore openly attacked Bikramájít, but was repulsed, and Mau and Núrpúr, and the whole district, were occupied by the Imperialists. Súraj Mall fled to the hills and perished miserably soon after. Fort Katlah also, which lies between Núrpúr and Kángrah, was taken, and Mádhú Singh, brother of Súraj Mall, who commanded it, together with his son, was sent to court (A. H. 1029).

(*To be continued.*)

ON THE BHAR KINGS OF EASTERN OUDH.

By W. C. BENETT, B.C.S., GONDA.

Three years ago I wrote of Dal and Bal, the great Bhar heroes of eastern Oudh, that they constantly appeared in the legends of any time between 1000 A. D. and 1400 A. D., and that though they had eluded all my attempts to saddle them with a date, they probably lived at the beginning of the thirteenth century. I have since succeeded in hunting them down, and the partial elucidation of a dark chapter of middle Indian history may prove interesting.

The ancestors of the great Kanhpuria clan of Rajputs, Sahas and Rahas, are said to have completed the conquest of the western half of the Pratábgarh district in Oudh by inflicting a decisive defeat on the Bhars, whose kings *Tiloki* and *Biloki* were left dead on the battle-field. A tradition of the Bais of Dhundhia Khera relates that Abhaichand, the founder of that house in Oudh, defeated *Dal* and *Bal* on the banks of the Ganges in the Roy Barrilly district. In my report on the chief clans of the Roy Barrilly district I have proved beyond reasonable doubt that Abhaichand and Sahas and Rahas were contemporaries and lived early in the 13th century.* A third tradition states that Dal and Bal fell fighting with Ibrahim Shah Sharki of Jaunpur at Dalman on the Ganges, and near the boundary of the Roy Barrilly and Pratábgarh districts. The locality is fixed by the fact that a large crowd of Ahirs collects once a year at a mound, the reputed tomb of the chieftains, about a mile from the fort, and offer milk to their manes. Leaving legend for history, we find that Firishtah, probably drawing from the Tabakát-i Násiri, records that "in 645 (1246-47 "A. D.) Sultán Násiruddín marched through the "centre of the Doáb, and took the Tilsandah(?) "fort, and in the same year advancing to- "wards Karra laid waste the villages of *Dalki* "and *Malki* and took prisoners a number of "their family and servants. This *Dalki* and "*Malki* were kings in the neighbourhood of the "Jamná, and had formerly royal stations at "Kalinjar and Karra."

Dalman is about thirty miles to the west of Karra, the similarity of the names Dalki, Malki, of Firishtah, Dal and Bal of the Bais and general tradition, and Tiloki and Biloki of the Kanhpurias, the identity of the dates in the Bais, Kanhpuria, and Firishtah's accounts, and the identity of locality in all, place it beyond doubt that the Dalki and Malki of history are no others than the great Bhar Kings of tradition who fell in the desperate fight with the Muhammadans under the walls of the Dalman fort. The date of their death is therefore 1247 A. D. That the local account should have substituted Ibráhim Sharki for the earlier Muhammadan conqueror presents no difficulty, as such mistakes in tradition are of constant occurrence.

So much for the date. The next question is who were these Bhar Kings? We are helped some way towards an answer by two inscriptions discovered at Kálanjar, and criticized by Lassen

* *Report on the Family History of Roy Barrilly Clans*, pp. 3, 17, and appendix, p. [illegible].

Ind. Alt. III. 706 *seq.*) From these we find that a man whose name is not given, but who is described as the first of his race (Pravaṇṇa) rose to distinction among the Kâyasths of Kauśâmbî, and took the fort of Ajaygarh. He was followed in succession by Jahnu or Hâraka, Jalhaṇa, Gangâdhara, Kamala, and lastly Mâlika. The last of this dynasty of six is identified by Lassen with Firishtah's Malki, and him I have just proved to be the Bal of Bhar legend. The inscriptions, therefore, furnish us with the information that this Bhar dynasty lasted for six generations, and we may place its commencement at about 1100 A. D. or 150 years before its destruction by Nasiruddin.

Mr. Sherring in his new book on Castes has given a tolerably accurate account of the popular idea of what the Bhars were, an idea which is confirmed by the condition of the Bhars still existing in this district of Gonda. They were aborigines and closely connected with the Cheru stock, and they were, and are still lovers of the forest, great hunters and gross feeders, with a passion for pork and wine, peculiar and mysterious religious rites, and a special aptitude for sorcery. Mr. Sherring may be in the right when he identifies them with the bearded figures found in middle Indian sculptures, though it is strange that he should have fallen into the mistake of attributing to them old cities of the Buddhist period, such as Sahet Mahet (Srâvasti).

I am inclined to translate the unmeaning "Chandâl Bhor" of Al 'Utbi (Elliot's *Hist. Ind.* by Dowson, II. 46) by the words "Chandela Bhawar" (Bhawar—Bhar; v. Lassen, *Ind. Alt.* I. 648, note*) and to conjecture that, even at the time of Mahmud's conquest, a Bhar chieftain flourished at a few marches to the south of Kanauj. We are told that the Chandal Bhawar was always at war with the Hindus of that place.

Lassen goes on to state that he has no hesitation in identifying Paramaldrahman, the founder of the Chandel clan with Mâlika and the synchronism, and similarity of names may together be held to justify the identification.

Thus much may be deduced from the above evidence,—at the time of the Ghori conquest an aboriginal tribe held a fortress not far south of Kanauj, and at about the end of the same century a chieftain of the same tribe took Kalanjar, and established a powerful kingdom, stretching from Malwa to Mirzapur and Palamau, and with its principal strongholds at Kalanjar and Karra. The Bhar king did what aborigines in his position always do, and got himself admitted as a Kayath into the Hindu caste system. His dynasty reigned for a century and a half and was overthrown in 1247 A. D. His descendants were promoted to be Chhatris, and are now known as Chandels. The rise of the aboriginal tribes is paralleled in the contemporaneous history of Kashmir, and was probably due to the action of some general cause. Of the change of caste I could easily bring other instances, but refrain from straying into quite a new subject.

A SPECIMEN OF KASHMÍRI.—THE DÁSTÁN SHEIKH SHIBLI.

IN KASHMIRI VERSE.

WITH AN INTERLINEAR AND A LITERAL TRANSLATION.

By G. W. LEITNER, Ph. D.

1. *Os asurai Sheikh Shibli dar zamâ*
   Was Righteous Sheikh Shibli upon time
   Dardi lada ak wuchhan gris wadda.
   Disease afflicted one he saw much wept.

   Dapâs Sheikhan: dard lobit dapâ ba
   Said Sheikh disease-afflicted† may them
   Dardo khoda yut wadân tahak yo tri
   Affliction from whom so much weeping is this there

* Cf. 2nd Ed. vol. I, p. 636, also Fr. (Buchanan) Hamilton (1819) says:—"The chiefs of the low tribe called Bhawar trace their origin to a Kanyakubja, who brought the [illegible] of the king of Dilli to [illegible] in the plains of Mithila, then entirely waste. Certain it is, that the Bhawars, about that time, extended their dominion over the Gorakhpur district as well as Tirahut, and that many petty chiefs of that tribe continued to occupy the parts adjacent to the hills until long after; and many of them continue to this day to be objects of worship among the low tribes. These may have been the descendants of collateral branches of the Raja's family, or of the chief officers of their government; and it must be remarked, that many of these assumed the title of Deva, as all the princes descended from Nanyup [king of Tirahut etc. A.D. 1130] had done." *Nepal*, pp. 47, 48. And again,—"I have mentioned that the tribe called Bhawar or Bhar has many territories, which had been subject to a powerful chief, whose capital was [illegible] in Tirahut, and the dominion of these Bhawars extended once all over Gorakhpur. [illegible] was destroyed in 1322 by the Muhammadans, and in its vicinity a state of anarchy, under petty chiefs, prevailed for twenty-four years, while the Muhammadans moved on the parts towards the Ganges." —*ib.* pp. 129, 130; [illegible]; also his *Eastern India*, vol. II. pp. 342, 346, 366; and Elliot's *Races of the N. W. Prov.* vol. I pp. 3, 167.—Ed.

† Should be "disease-affliction", *dard* is really 'tyranny,' 'oppression.'

Tire dupnas tshans sich rdo-wat tar
From there said: he to me lost beloved
ydr
friend
Dupnas Shekhan: tshnd wafadar ydr
Said the Shaikh: find out a faithful friend
Sui ydr tshnd yus na-rawi ta abid
That mistress seek who not be lost till eternity
Ydr wafadar watshinn ba-hazur,
Mistress faithful see thou in God,
Tsi dzaki rowmut; sui tshui na dûr
Thou wilt be lost. He is not far
Tsky basharat maanas smih tálibas
In good-news meaning of this to the pupil
Asil travit ghair pazshà tsân-dzunia?
Reality quitting another was it proper to seek?
3. *Shaba akh Shekh bemar dardo-sità*
Night one Shaikh ill pain with
Dardo sitin ashik harsa paye tal
Pain with tear-drops fell several
Dardi sitin dilf rdwan pat kundi
Pain with swollen back side
Na gahi Shekhas tshrdr aasawi
Suddenly? to the Shaikh objection was
Hatifi awdz lagnis purghazab
Angel's voice struck full of wrath;
Hay Shekha! yit kih tshukh bey adab
Alas! O Shaikh! so much why art ill-behaved
Yá tu dzoho na dawdi-bandagi
Or thou make not claim of devotion
Nate hirahe rat-doh sharmandigi
Nor dost thou take night-day shame
Tore aásia bodi balaw tálibas
From there he sent great calamities to the pupil
Tore dupus hamd-u-thana zulm sajt.
From here, he said thanks & praise tyranny self.
5. *Shekh Zunun Misrin dûth arifa*
Shaikh Zunun* of Egypt saw a believer
O's wadan dard-ted ahli-sajd
Was weeping pain-afflicted pious man
Dupnas Shekhan: tshukh ta wasil aminna
Said Shaikh: art thou arrived for certain
Wasl kho-tai,† myuyj Kamuk tshui
Union has become now of what thing is
tamanna
wish?
Tore dupnas:‡ ay Zunun wutshta
The other said: oh Zunun see
Zati mashirl gûs beytshagûn
Essence creator, colour incomparable

O's Azazil nishe-arshas pas ba-dja
Was the devil nigh to throne foot on place
Malkut tshas-malkan-hund pathraw
Worlds of angels of the guide (leader)
Kibri sitin gûs Azazil lânati
Pride with became Azazil accursed
Girio sitin Baba Adam Djanati
Weeping with Father Adam of Paradise
Qahri sitin kit wdsil dûrgas
Wrath with how many who had reached far became
Mihr sitin kit ghafil manzûr gas
Grace with how many ignorant accepted became!
Shakl Balamas gas qabulas na-qabul
The form Balaam to, became accepted not accepted
Sage Ashab Kahf gas majd qabul.
Dog of the Ashab Kahf became there was accepted.
4. *Shabe-akh wod djenabi sarwarân*
Night one wept His Highness the Chief
Tshus ba khitsan sata-sandes mashârân
Am I fearing essence of him the Creator
Wuhis bayata tshum nubuwate paighambari
To this time to is me of prophecy the mission.
Andil watsun nai tshum mlt
Till the last if has reached, this is to me then
barkhari.
success.
5. *Sabiri Ayub Yûnus Zakaria*
Patient Job, Jonas, and Zacharias
Tsala aasan dûkh zahmat tay bald
To bear caused pain of fatigue and calamity.
Wutshta pith kat dûw hazrat sabiras
See thou before what came saint "the Patient" to
Mal u daulat sihat bada niwalas
Property and goods, health, body took from him
Darba tulard payim tshala bodanas
Leech wasps worms he threw to his body
Dard-tadan wati zonun na
The afflicted strength (place) he knew not
wadanas
to weep
Doh akh ak ta dona wuyat pidh
Day one one two worm fell came.
Bey tasûna trahida tayyn mdz kûs
Again lifted up from rage it flesh ate
Ah! kadun bey-kasi ta-tshur gûs
Ah! fetched out deserted helpless was
Malkutas malkan para para gûs
Of heavens angels torn torn were

* The name refers to the miraculous story of a fish presenting the Shaikh, who was travelling in a boat, with a lost jewel, which he had been falsely accused of stealing, after it had fallen into the water by accident.

† Or 'khotai—then.'

‡ Azizas should be put here to complete the metre.

Khás- páńsis da nadá an rahi
To himself especially came voice from the Lord
Náma Sábir mandi tabhávach, ay
The name of "patient" shame you have made
   nabi!
   Prophet!
Sená sitás sabr ay ná at yút bil!
Us from patience came not hand so late!
Kóna [illegible] *wasáhi mazhárí**
Why not endured, seeing the manifestation of
   zu-l-jalál!
   the Glorious!
Os dapán, ya Ilahi, bozhum
Was he said, Oh God, hear thou
Sabr-e- takat, meherbánó an tam
Patience strength by kindness, send thou
Táhár [illegible] *ant andre* [illegible]
Thy grace with patience I am taking
Zivo [illegible]
Tongue my keep thou praise from thee not I may
   fall.
Tithin sabiron thin kalamas [illegible]
Such to patients such words for fall a falling
Timannsaben [illegible] *Ahmad bisabur!*
On that account what is Ahmad impatient?

Translation.

1 Once there lived a holy man, called Shaikh Shibli, who on one occasion saw a man weeping bitterly from excessive grief. The Shaikh said:— "tell me O thou who art plunged in sorrow, why is it that has caused all these tears?" The man replied: "because I have lost my beloved friend." The Shaikh rejoined,—"seek [another] faithful friend, seek such a friend as thou mayest never lose, and find this faithful friend only in God. Thy fault only will it be if thou lose him, for he is never far." By this good-news the meaning to the seeker of truth is, that he should not abandon the reality of God's love for human friendship.

2. One night the Shaikh was suffering from pain. The pain caused some tear drops to fall. He reclined on his back with the pain, and unconsciously gave vent to an expression of impatience, when an angel's voice struck his ear full of wrath; saying "why alas! O Shaikh! art thou so ill-behaved: either thou shouldst make no claim to be a servant (of God), or thou shouldst accept with resignation continual suffering. On the one part great calamities He sends to his servant, on the other the servant should give thanks and praise, considering his sufferings to be the consequence of his own sins."

3. Shaikh Zunun of Egypt once saw a believer—a possessor of goodness, who was weeping and afflicted. Said the Shaikh "'union with God' assuredly thou hast already attained. than such union what higher desire canst thou have?" The other said,—"Oh Zunun! consider thou Him the manifester, the incomparable. I do not weep on account of bodily pain, but lest I should, after all, be rejected of God. [How many are those who have fallen.] Azazil himself once was near the throne of God, and the leader of angels who were residents of angelic worlds, yet, in consequence of pride, he became accursed, whilst by means of the weeping of repentance, Father Adam was [restored] to Paradise. How many Walis [who had already attained to union with God] have not been rejected in consequence of the Divine wrath! and how many ignorant have not been accepted! Balaam was first accepted and then rejected, while the dog of the Ashab Kahf* was accepted in His sight."

4. One night His Highness [Muhammad] wept, and said I fear Him the Creator, for though till this time he has continued to me the gift of prophecy, yet will the result only be blessed if it be continued to the last.

5. God caused patient Job, Jonas, and Zacharias, to bear the pain of trouble and misfortune. For what happened to the holy Job. God took from him health and wealth and made his body a prey to leeches, worms, and vermin; yet the afflicted Job did not think it becoming to weep. One day a worm fell to the ground; he replaced it, when it bit his flesh with double rage. Deserted by his friends and helpless as he was, he fetched a sigh which pierced the hearts of the angels of heaven. Then came a voice to him from the Lord. "Oh prophet! thou hast disgraced thy name of 'the Patient', for thou hast not learnt patience, though thou hast been so long with me. Why hast thou not endured seeing [that thy sufferings were only] the manifestations of the Almighty?" Job said "Oh Lord! hear thou me and send me patience and strength. It is only by thy grace that I can be patient; keep thou my tongue lest it cease to praise thee."

If such words were considered reprehensible in such patient saints, what will happen to me, [the author] impatient Ahmad?

"This story of Shaikh Shibli was composed by the poet Ahmad; in it there is the mention of the sorrows and patience of Saints and advice for finding one's true friend. It is ancient, and has not much Persian in it." (Note of copyist found in the above poem called "Dastan Shaikh Shibli.")

Note.

Many of the vowel sounds in Kashmiri cannot be rendered by any known alphabet. Our transliteration is merely an approach. Kashmiri is generally written in the Persian character, which still more feebly represents the sounds of that very

---

* Is read both *mazhir* "one who comes to appear," and *mazhar* "theatre, manifestation, contest" by the Kashmiris.

* *i.e.* the companion of the cave, otherwise known as the seven sleepers of Ephesus.

interesting language. The pronunciation of Kashmiri is different in different parts of Kashmir, but, on the whole, the above attempt, which was made in 1865, to commit to Roman letters a connected specimen of the Kashmiri language, may be considered as fairly successful.* At any rate, the readers of the "Antiquary" are now offered the first instalment of Kashmiri Literature, no portion of which has been hitherto published in Kashmiri for European readers.

TRANSLATION FROM THE FIRST BOOK OF THE PRITHIRÁJA RÁSAU.

By KAVI CHAND BARDÁI.

The following pages are a paraphrase of the whole of the first book of Chand's vast poem, with the exception of the introductory portion, that is the first 136 stanzas containing about 1,000 lines.

The book opens with invocation to Vishnu and Siva and their wives. Then Chand holds a long conversation with his wife, in which he recites the names and number of verses in the eighteen Puráṇas, then follow some more hymns to gods.

At stanza 18 begins the well known legend of Parikshita, and the serpent sacrifice of his son Janamejaya, after which comes the story of the foundation of Mount Abu by the Rishi Vasishtha, and the celebrated sacrifice thereon, which led to the preparation of the fire-fountain (अनल कुंड anal kund), from which sprang in succession the Pratihár, Chálukya, and Pawár, and finally, as these were unable to cope with the demons, the Chauhán.† The first of the race was called Anal because he sprang from the fire; and after recounting his victories over the Daityas, Dánavas, Rákshasas and objectionable beings in general, the bard briefly recounts the list of his descendants, saying nothing particular about any of them until he comes to Bísal Deo, the twenty-third in descent from Anal.

Here the present version begins, and I leave it to tell its own tale.‡ It is not in all cases a literal word for word translation. To those who read Chand for the sake of the historical, legendary, and geographical information which his poem contains, the following rendering will be highly useful and satisfactory; on the other hand, it is much less useful to the philologist, who, while caring comparatively little for the facts related, scrutinises minutely every noun and verb in order to detect the ancient forms of inflexion, and the archaic phonesis of the language.

It is properly speaking a paraphrase. All Chand's repetitions, his long-winded and rambling style, his unnecessary heaps of epithets are ruthlessly cut short. Here and there descriptions of scenery or of festivals are omitted. In all narrative parts, however, the paraphrase is close and exact, almost approaching to a literal translation.

I have compared it with the original as contained in a fairly correct manuscript in my possession, and made such alterations as were necessary to bring it into more accurate correspondence with the original.

J. Beames.

PRITHIRÁJA RÁSAU.

The cause of calamity in the world was Bísal Rái [the son of Bálan Rái],—a great sinner, fond of riches: he did things that ought not to be done and things that ought to be done; terrible as an Asura, from mines he dug up wealth, he was blinded by lust (*kám*), he regarded not death (*kál*); right and unright he regarded as equal; he acted not according to Rájnít, in many places, though a king he fixed customs not sanctioned; he paid no respect to religion; he abandoned the Vedas and followed the Tantras. Abandoning the bounds of right he abandoned also the bounds of good fame. He abandoned justice and followed injustice. No Atith (mendicant) was to be seen in his darbár. He heard his own ill name among men. For sixty-four years he ruled. He enjoyed not the happiness of a son. His body was subjected to age; he became like a stalk of poison. All his life was devoted to the desire of wealth and to *kám*. He was possessed by an evil spirit, he became Dhundhá the Asura. The Yogis worshipped him, riding in a lofty chariot with four wheels, he had swords in both hands, fire issued from his mouth. Stamping on the earth he shook it. His shout was like the shout of

---

* Most of the explanatory words and phrases have been omitted in the interlinear translation, in order to bring each line of the original within the width of our column and thus present a complete specimen of rhymed Kashmiri.—Ed.

† Conf. Tod, *Rajasthan*, vol. I. pp. 94, 95, where an extract from this part of the book is given.—Ed.

‡ This version is taken partly from the *Rás Málá* of the late Hon. A. K. Forbes, (vol. I. pp. 74-79), and partly from his notes written down from a viva voce translation into Gujarati, read off from the Hindi by the well-known Dalpatrám Dáyábhai, the Kavíshwar, who was five years in his service. Some verbal changes were made in copying the notes five years ago.—Ed.

Indra* in the cities and towns. The nine (*khands*) sections of the earth began to tremble as a ship reels under the force of the wind. The Devas who protect the world trembled, and the Diggajas groaned. He seemed a foremost Dânava, as Vishnu in the form of Vairat. Birds, deer, men, and snakes fled from him,—he roared so horribly.† . . .

This Chahuvân daitya destroyed Abu. The country became void of living beings. In the jungal of Ajmer he lived many days, and ate up all things movable and immovable.‡ . . .

Gauri, the queen of Sârang, went in her pregnancy to Rimthambh. She was of the race of Jâdava, on her mother's side a Chahuvân. She had a son Anala Râja; he dwelt in Devagâm, and was of great bashfulness. He was continually studying religion. Sambhari Devi loved him, and he communicated with her. Though absent he beheld Ajmer in his mind. Skilled was he in all sciences, a wrestler and fighter, he learnt many spells. Day and night he enjoyed himself in hunting. Sleep never overtook him. His two arms were long. Such was Anâ Râup: very strong and majestic; on foot he hunted deer, antelopes, and hares; blue bulls he bound and brought in. In the jungal, in the mountains, among the streams, the Rai wanders with bows. He learnt music, singing, and languages; divine language he utters from his heart. When he gives away horses or elephants he thinks nothing of it. He wears his blood-stained sword in the way. The head ornament of the Chahuvân race in many kinds of qualities (*lit.* colours) Anâ lived. Believing the earth to be his own, abandoning the wisdom of childhood, angry at some sayings of an enemy he asked his mother the story. The skill of archery is good, there is none like it—that skill Anâ learned without fail with mantras too.§

He went to Gauri the wife of the king: "In whose race was I born that tell to me mother!" Mother Gauri says to her son—"O son! do not ask that question, from fear of which the tears start to my eyes, son do not ask for thy father." The son exclaimed to his mother,—"I know not the race of my father's race. My father's name the bards mention not. I have never performed shrâddh or presented handfuls of water (*tarpan*) to my father. O mother! from whose body am I sprung? Whoever mentions my name speaks of me by the mark of my mother's family. Should anyone have slain my father I wish to take up the *bair* (to seek revenge). If you will not tell me my father's name I will quit the body, or throw off the load of this world's affairs." Thus spoke Anâ Narind. His mother, when she heard him, fell to the earth. "O son, this matter should not be told, in my mind doubt arises. From the commencement even the Dânavas have been powerful,—the Asuras, powerful to shake the earth. With such you desire to contend. You are a man in mortal body. I am like Gandhârî,|| but I see your face alone. The race of your maternal uncle you should receive as peculiarly your own. He had ten sons. Reflecting, he built there the town of Sambhari: he dwelt himself in Ajmer in peace." "Bali Rai abandoned the whole earth and seized on fame. O mother! Pandu's sons abandoning the earth left calamity and attained delights. Srî Ram left the earth (his kingdom), Sitâ was lost, his strength obscured. Nal Rai left the earth; on his head a stain fell. Harischandra abandoned the earth, in the house of the low he filled water. Know a king to be the adorner of the earth, the earth the adorner of a king,—the Devs the adorners of the heavens, the heavens the adorners of the Devs,—fame is the destroyer of infamy, infamy the destroyer of fame,—wisdom is the destroyer of bad qualities, bad qualities the destroyers of wisdom,—death (*kâl*) is the destroyer of Dharm, Dharm the destroyer of death. Parents and teachers are the adorners of children, children the adorners of parents,"—thus Anal Râja spoke; the old tale of Sambhari he asked,—"How did Dhundhâ Râkshasa arise? How did Sârang Deva fight? This tell to me, explaining it, O! mother. How did a man become a Dânava, this seems strange to me. If you do not tell me the truth I will abandon my body. This certainly know."¶ "This story is not fit to be told, it is death producing, no hope is left of life. O son! from hearing this story of the Dânavas the mind is destroyed, calamity was caused to your father and your father's father."

"So saying you try to frighten me. You have no pity on me. The tales of the *Râmâyana* and *Mahâbhârata* I have heard throughout, O mother! No one asks the way to a place

* Some MSS. read [illegible] for [illegible].

† Four lines omitted.

‡ A long piece omitted.

§ Six lines omitted.

|| The mother of the Kauravas.

¶ Four lines omitted.

he does not wish to go to. How can one see a thing that is out of sight? How can one repeat that which he never heard? How can one seize what has no body?"

"This story so great and unequalled you must not press me to tell: the ear that hears it is pained, nor is any advantage derived."

And said "Mother hear my words: What happens to a man who hears a tale? In old times, how many Rishis, Raos, Suras, and Dânavas have existed: well known are the stories of them. Their fights and contests men sing in Śâstra and Veda. This understand O mother! Why should I not hear? from speaking no calamity occurs: that which fate has fixed upon assuredly happens."

(*St.* 102) O Son! Hear this tale of old, in reciting which my voice trembles.* The sages made at Abu a fire-pit; a man came forth to whom he entrusted royalty. Of his race sprung a great and religious king, named Bâlan.† His son was Bisal Deva, who possessed all the kingdom. In the year of Vikrama 821‡ Bisal mounted the throne. It was Friday the first day of the month, the light half of the month, the month Baisakh; the thirty-six races assembled—Brahmans, bards, and all men; Bisal was presented with the royal umbrella (*chatra*); he received the mark (*tilak*) of sovereignty on his forehead; the Brahmans repeated Vedas and verses of power (*mantras*).

Bisal enjoyed as happy a state as that of Indra; he restored *dharma* and fame. In Ajmernagar dwelling—his enemies subduing—Bisal reigned a pure reign. Many mighty cities he took; in his reign the world seemed to be covered by one umbrella.

When the umbrella was placed over the head of Bisal, and he was seated on his throne like an Indra, the Brahmans prepared a *Vedi*, they offered a sacrifice of the five flowers. The smoke issued—the flame burst forth; the Brahmans repeating charms (*mantras*) performed his enthronement, and gave him their blessing.

The king divided the lighted wick into three parts:
Two of the cups were overturned on the ground;
Seeing the offering before (them, they) whispered together.
From the three cups smoke arose.
Knowing the Vedas, they remained silent;—
At an auspicious time, who would say aught inauspicious?*

The assembly cried 'Jay! Jay! Bisal Bhûpâla (earth-protector)!' Thus ruled Bisal Deva over Ajmer.

He adorned the city as if it had been adorned by Vishvakarma (the architect of the gods). Abandoning irreligion, he caused religion to flourish; sinful deeds he sought not to perform. He exacted only his rights; without right he indulged not his avarice; the four castes were subservient to the Chohuân; the thirty-six races served him. Bisal Râjâ, the religious, shone resplendent as a Deva upon the earth.

His Pat Rânî was of the race of Parmâr. From her sprung Sârang Deva,—she died in giving him birth. The child he gave to a merchant (*bania*); the bania's daughter, whose name was Gauri, was brought up with Sârang. From the same breast they drank milk, they had one seat, one bed. When the maiden (*kanya*) became nine years old, Bisal Deva caused her marriage to be performed. After the marriage the bridegroom went into the forest, there a lion slew him. Then the bania's daughter took a vow of virginity, abandoning the world she began to perform penance. Very grieved was Sârang Deva. Constantly he performed the worship of the Arihant; the Buddhist religion he adopted; he wore no sword. The Raja hearing it became sorrowful. He sent for the prince (*Kumar*).

---

* The following passage is given in the *Ras Mala*, Vol. I. pp. 93-95, and is altered in minor points to bring it into accordance with Mr. Beames's MS.—Ed.

† This is Balanga the "liear Bealundor or Dharmaraj" of Colonel Tod, who defended the [illegible] Hill or hill-fortress of Ajmer against Mahmud of Ghazni. (*Rajasthan* vol I. p. 71b; vol. II. p. 451-[illegible].) On the pillar of Firuz Shah (vide *As. Res.* vol. I. p. 379; vol. VII. p. 180; vol XI. p. 443) is an inscription beginning "in the year 1220 (A. D. 1164), on the 15th day of Vaisakh sudi (this monument) of the fortunate Visala Deva, son of fortunate Vella Deva, King of Sakambhari." The date belongs to the reign of Vigraha Râja, whom Tod identifies with Prithiraja, and "Vesla Deva" or Vel Dev with Bisa. Conf. Prinsep, *Essays*, vol. I. pp. 324-25; Forbes, *Ras Mala*, vol. I. p. 93 note.—Ed.

‡ Forbes's MS. seems to have read 811. Tod says the date S. 821 is "interpolated—a vice not uncommon with the Rajput Bard." (*Rajasthan*) v. II. p. 448) Tod's date for Bisal's birth is S. 1066 or A.D. 1010, corresponding to Sak 931, and his death A.D. 1075. He must have ascended the throne about A.D. 1031; Wilford places his accession in 1016.—Ed. The words in these MSS which I have collated are '[illegible] sau ra thâda.'—J. B.

* The meaning of these lines is very obscure. I suppose it to be thus the king had to light three lamps consisting of wicks floating in cups filled with oil, and that some omen was drawn from the way these lamps burned. Two of the cups appear to have been upset and the wicks did not burn properly. The attendant Brahmins appear to have observed that the omen was bad, but from prudential motives did not say anything about it.

The lines have a special significance when taken in connexion with the disastrous close of King Bisal's reign and the poet has probably introduced them with this intent, though from ignorance of the ceremonies usually observed at coronation services I am unable to explain what it was that really took place.—J. Beames.

and received him with respect. "Why did you adopt this religion? Abandoning shame, tell me the truth. Is it because you are grieved at the death of the Rana's son? Such evil doctrine should not be listened to, which is destructive of manhood and fame. You are of royal race. Remaining with Rájas in the far-stretching forest, hunt the deer. Abandon this delusion; let the Puranas be your guide; listen to the Mahábhárata and the Rámáyana. Pride, generosity, the field of battle, protection of the fallen,—this is our Dharma, these are the four attributes of royalty." The Prince confessing his error attended to the advice of the Rája: that moment he called for, and bound on his sword. The Rája, pleased, made him a present. "Go thou to Sambhar and rule there." He gave also a great elephant, clothes, a powerful horse, and a throne studded with jewels. "Go, Kunwar, to Sambhar." Kayath Kirpal he made his minister, Mukund his purohit—and Sárang Chohán the lord of Sambhar, like to Narsingh. He gave with him from Kandhár and Lár, mighty Bilochis, servants (*kaskam*) with robes of many colours, horses, elephants, men, carriages, chamowars and chariots.

At that time he sent for Sárang: "you must not go with the Kunwar—you have made my son a great fool." He exclaimed in anger—"why do you thus punish me? Sambhar is close to Ajmer." "If you go there I will take your life." So saying the king went with the prince, four chariots there told were filled with arms. At the distance of a yojan they made a halt. They enjoyed there all sorts of viands; when it was morning the son fell at his feet. Asking his blessing he went, and arrived at Sambhar. When he arrived at the lake of Sambhari, with good mind, body and speech, ten buffalo calves he sacrificed; offering the Hom sacrifice he pleased the goddess. Bending his head to the Devi, he entered the town; garlands and water-vessels were placed at the gates of the palace. Entered Sárang Deva into Sambhari the strong place; there assembled many Vaisyas and Kshatriyas; bending they touched the feet of the prince. Then Kayath Kirpal gave leave to the whole. To some he gave arms, to others [illegible], according as they deserved and dismissed them with compliments. Then Jálavant (Gauri) came and touched the feet of the Parmár; the skilled in omens pronounced that a good omen had occurred, and that the Kunwar would have a good son. The daughter of the Rának, Deva Rája, by name Gauri the Jálavant* slowly by the side of Sárang Deva on Hati beside Kama.

Then returning Bisal the king hunted deer in the forest. Seeing a place well adapted for the purpose, the desire of constructing a tank arose in his mind. He examined the good place, where the streams flowed from the mountains, where the forest was good. He sent for his principal minister; "cause a lake to be made here, such as that of Pushkar."† Having given this order he returned home; joy without limit arose in his mind. Upon a throne he sat like Yudishthira, the son of Dharma,—did Bisal the king of men, the Indra of the world. Over his head an umbrella, on each side stood chámara holders very beautiful to the sight,—like the two Ashwins. The thirty-six races then assembled—from head to foot nobly equipped. The king called them into his presence; he presented them with betelnut. The minstrels in their verses celebrated his praises; the king, smiling, bent his head; the assembly shone like a constellation; the Chohán in the midst like a moon. With compliments he dismissed them all. As they retired the bards pronounced a blessing. When a watch and five pals of the night had passed, the raja entered within the palace. Camphor, agar, sandal, musk, and other perfumes scented the place. It was redolent of precious essences which had been showered upon it. An apartment well coloured, fit to inspire pleasure, therein rested the Rája. He sent for actors, for singers, and other amusements. He enjoyed the society of the Parmár's daughter the (*Pat Rani*) favourite queen, who in beauty and youth resembled an Apsaras, who was dear to him as his life, whom he forgot not for one moment. With her the delights of love always he enjoyed, and no other fair one did he ever look upon. The other wives being angry, met together, and all conspired to take from the king his virility. Then they sent maidservants to the Devi. Promising presents and rewards they called the Yogini on Monday, they changed her dress, and caused her to enter the King's door. Taking arms she gave them to the Darwán, thus she entered and went among the Queens. "Done, done, be your work," she exclaimed. They worshipped her, standing before

* That is, he married Gauri, a princess of the Jádav clan.—J. B.

† Or 'square or oblong in shape.'

her with joined hands. "For what cause have you called me hither to-day. What woman taught you to call upon me." All the rival wives said, "Hear our grief. The Raja does not see our bodies. O! mother, except you, who can know the pain of a childless woman! The arrow of having a rival wife pierces our hearts."

"If you please I will deprive him of life, if you please I will make the women averse to him, if you please I will destroy desire within him, I will make the man's body like a woman's. All the wives approved of this plan. "At once, O mother! perform this work," they said.

Sending for fire she performed *hom*, throwing therein the flesh of dogs and cows, and pronouncing charms. At that moment his desire (*kām*) became extinct. Making her presents, the wives dismissed the mother. "Abandoning this city, go to another." The Raja became much grieved at the loss of his virility. He took the vow of chastity* for four months. In Kartik month he went to Pushkar to bathe. He heard mention of the greatness of Gokaran. He called for Jait Sing the Gohwāla and said to him, "you are expert (*nāgar*) in the knowledge of all countries; tell me all about the country of Gokaran, its mountains, rivers, tanks and jungles.

"Maharaja there is the temple of Mahādev (Śiva), the river Banas, shy as a virgin is there. There is a great mountain three kos in height, they who eat the water which flows from it are delighted." "How far is it from Ajmer?" "In a journey of two days a man may arrive there." The Rāja mounted and went off to Gokaran. He took great elephants with him, nobats (drums), and banners. The noise was heard in the ten directions. Enemies in various places, abandoning their own residences, fled into the jungle. In other kingdoms the noise sounded. Then the Rāja reached Tuchhitpura in the direction of Gokaran. There is a lofty mountain there, a swift river, many birds, gardens, and places sacred to Śiva; sandal streams, creepers entwining the trees with leaves and flowers of various colours, plantains, and fruits, Koils, Chakors, peacocks, Sarasas, beautiful to behold. Bears, lions, companies of deer:—the Rāja seeing them was astonished. The place was very good; a place of rest. Worshipping Śiva, all were happy. In the mountain was a cave where resided a Kinnara. Drops of water fell on his head from the roof, a company of lions were his attendants. The Rāja coming suddenly and touching his feet entreated him: "Hara! I praise Śiva, I praise him of the great wisdom."

Fruits, flowers, and other articles, *panchāmrita*, incense, and lamps he placed before him. Bathing (the idol) and offering gifts the Chahuan prayed: "I praise the lord of Bhutas, dwelling in terrible places, in whose locks the Ganga is visible, from whose three eyes brightness like fire issues, on whose forehead is the moon, in whose throat is poison, on his neck the (*mundamāla*) necklace of skulls,—the great All, whose voice is as the roaring of a lion, who is attended by Siddhas and Devas, whose body is smeared with the ashes of the funeral pile; I praise thee! I praise thee! I praise thee! I praise thee! He who wears an elephant's hide, who is surrounded by Vīrs and Bhairavas in a crowd, resting his feet on Nandi, attended by the four Vedas, and sixty-four Yoginis, round whom sound the drum and the battle-drum (*damaru*)† at the sound of whose footsteps Meru mountain shakes, the atmosphere thunders; who holds the bow Pināka in his left hand. I praise thee! I praise thee! I praise thee! I praise thee! Him whom the liberated Siddhas and the Sādhakas, who seek liberation, worship; who holds in his hand a trident, whose name is repeated by men, Kinnaras, Gandharvas, serpents and Yakshas, by Suras and Asuras, by Apsarases and Rishis, whom Janaka and other Rishis from childhood worship. The earth, the whole, the air, the fire, the water, the sun and moon, the nine constellations, were created by thee. I praise thee! I praise thee! I praise thee! I praise thee! If thy name be called to mind, difficulties of the road, of the resting place, are removed, a host of calamities is dissipated. Whose charms and spells bind all that travel in the sky, and in the earth, and disarm incurable diseases; worshipping thee whose sin would not be destroyed, the half of whose body is Gauri, who dwellest in Kailās? I praise thee! I praise thee, I praise thee! I praise thee!"

So much praise the king uttered, worshipping touching the god's feet. The Siddha seeing it was astonished. "This Raja is a vessel of wisdom." The Siddha asked—"From what city do you come? of what family (*gotra*) are you? What is your name? Are you come here on pilgrimage, or have you business with any one?"

* Under the circumstances one would think this vow somewhat superfluous: the meaning probably is that he became an ascetic for the period mentioned.—J. B.

† This description is in close accord with the representations of Śiva at Elephanta and Elora. conf. my Elephanta, §§ 62, 64, 66, 68-72, and notes.—Ed.

"I dwell in Ajmerpur, I am of the renowned race of Chauhan; Bisal Deva is my name. O Siddha! I am come to perform ablutions." The Siddha answers,—"Hear O Rája, my words. Since you have come to this land from your home,—in this place is the unrivalled shrine of Mahádeva; always Apsarasas descend in the night. This place four men discovered; their names will I relate, explaining,—Bhasmaket, Mávasu, Mádhu, Kalava,—these dwelling here pleased the Deva. The greatness of this Tírtha they sang; they washed the Deva, bringing the milk of a cow, and attained whatever they desired." Thus saying the Siddha arose and disappeared. The Rája was amazed in his mind hearing the story of the place. As much as he desired to ask the Siddha had told him at once. The Rája sent for a thousand cows with calf, spending money and cleansing the land. A thousand vessels of milk he poured upon Śiva, and took a vow to fast for three days. For three days the Rája fasted, he abandoned water and *fruit*,* eating air only. The night an Apsaras came; all the Apsarasas were dancing and singing. After a long while Hur spoke. "Apsaras go and raise that mortal." The Apsaras came to see him, and perceived that he was asleep. "Śiva is pleased with you, as the husband of Mohini (Durgá) has sent this request. Go to your own home, Śiva's residence abandoning. Śiva is pleased with you, the desire of your heart has reached Śiva on high." Thus saying, Mohini raised up the Rája. It was the last watch of the night. The king returned to his tent; desire increased in his mind; virility returned to him. In the morning, bathing, he presented the thousand cows to Brahmans. With *Panchamrita*, incense, and lights, he worshipped Śiva. At that time he gave orders for the erection of a temple and the construction of a town called Bisalpur. Calling for an elephant he seated himself upon it. Hastily he returned to his own home. Travelling two days' stages in one, Bisal returned to his home; he entered the city; there was joy in every house. In his lofty mansion he rested, in the coloured hall of four colours:† in the apartment of the women of middle age, he told to the Parmari all that had occurred. Excited by *love*, he sent for all his wives; the whole night he passed awake. All the wives were agitated, asking when before did Sambhu give such a gift? Night and day all alike the desire of his mind found increase. Young, middle-aged, and old, all began to tremble at him. Sending for other men's wives, for one *place* no one could restrain him; if any attempted it, he would run to slay him. The wives were terrified that he never rested from *love*; even on hearing his name all trembled; in Ajmer city king Bisal burned when he saw a woman.‡ . . Losing control over his mind, he surrendered himself to *love*. He began to lose respect for the distinction between lawful and unlawful; with women, in pleasure, he spent his time; he listened not to the advice of any. Whatever women asked for, he would give them. The wives of Brahmans, Vaishyas or Sudras—he leaves none on whom he casts his eyes. Great Narind became of this mind; neither day nor night could anyone take rest. Many people of the city thronged together to the house of the minister (pradhán) 'Calamity falls upon all, both men and women—we will not remain here—we will depart in anger.' The minister soothed the enraged people, and with the counsel of their head men and the wives of the rája, approached Bisal.‖

'On the earth,' said they, 'there are many rájas; a great sovereign should attack and subdue their cities and territories to destroy such thorns. To protect the land, a prince should travel about it.' Such was the advice the ministers gave him, and also the counsel (*panch*) of the city. Such advice also the wives gave him. The Rája understood the object of what they were saying: "The flame of love which has been excited in me singes you, that I know, but my mind submits not to control, it remains within itself as the shadow within a well, continues within it. Well, I will do as you say, assuredly. Send for Kirpál, and whatever countries you attack, I will mount and accompany you."

He gave the order to the ministers; they sent for Kirpál. From Sambhar he came to the city (Ajmer). When Kirpál came and touched the feet of the king, he placed two swords before him,¶ studded with jewels and bars. The rája

* When the Hindus fast on the 11th day of the month, it is allowed to them to eat fruit. The Shrawaks are not allowed.

† Red, black (or blue), yellow, and green. Usually the five colours are used, the fifth being white.

‡ Four lines of no consequence omitted.

§ The passage that follows with a few corrections is taken from the *Rás Málá*, vol. I. p. 23.—Ed.

‖ These last two sentences condense the substance of a much longer piece.

¶ As a hint that he ought to take warlike exercise.

bound a sword on his loins. The skilful in calculation pronounced the omen to be good. As he who extends wisdom improves his own, so he who uses the sword gains territory. The rája said —"As this omen has now happened to me, I will draw my sword in all the nine divisions (*khands*) of the earth. The whole world (*bhúkhand*), I will subdue; I will conquer the earth from Meru to Meru—(from pole to pole). Hear, O Kaymás, my speech;—Providing treasure prepare to accompany me. At the Bísal Sarovar* (lake) firmly pitch our tents."

In writing, to the ten directions, he sent summons: 'Let all come and meet me at Ajmer.' Mahansi† Parihár came and joined him; the chief of Mandovar came and touched his feet; all the [illegible] collected, like the crows of the assembly‡; the Tuar§ armed from head to foot; [illegible]; Mahesa the lord of Mewát too came; the Malik of Jaunpur came with his followers; the Baloch came all on foot together. The king of [illegible] came and joined him; the [illegible] king came to meet him; the vassal chiefs of Multán and Thatta came. The order went to Jesalmer. All the Bhumias and Bhatias were submissive. The Yádava, the Bághela, the dwellers in Malwa, the Mori, the Raghuvansi responded to his call. From Antarved came the Kurambh. All the Meos submissively touched his feet. Jait Singh, obeying the order, came; the chief of Tarbhitpur¶ he brought with him. Udaya** the Puár mounted and came. The Dors came to follow him from Lar, the Chandelas,†† the Dáhimas‡‡ went up at his foot (*cf. Judges* iv. 10). Shaking his sword, he made all the Bhumias submissive. No Chálukya came to pay obeisance, they stood aloof, sternly grasping the sword. Hearing the [illegible] spoke, "Leaving a force to protect our honour and city, give them charge of Ajmer.§ The Chálukya cannot escape." Stage by stage, long while marched the warriors; by the way of the mountains the rája advanced, drying up the rivers at their sources, to strike his first blow at the Solankhi.|| Many forts he levelled with the earth. He took Jhalor and destroyed its castle; to the mountains and the forest the enemy retreated. Ascending Abu he beheld Achaleswar. Immediately he took the land of Girnar, Wágar, Sorath, the fifty-six cities: paying [illegible] they met him, they did not meet him in fight. In the country of Gujarat seventeen thousand warriors were with Bhola Rai¶ the Chálukya. Hearing this matter he mounted and came full of pride, he worshipped Siva and Sakti (Durgá); his spear he took upon his shoulder. With him he had thirty thousand horsemen of Lar, seventy elephants streaming with juice (*mad*)*, at a yojana's distance he made a halt. The Chauhán heard the noise—heard the noise, did Bísal the king,—of the advance of Bhola Rao. Calling for a charger, he mounted; he caused the kettledrums to sound; setting his army in order, Bísal moved onwards. The sound of his approach reached the camp of the enemy. With seventy thousand soldiers he came on; it seemed like the [illegible] in some rainy season raising their booming noise. With swinging shields and glittering spears, the warrior was full of joy, the coward full of sorrow. [illegible] the tide of the ocean [illegible]

---

* 'This lake,' says Tod, 'still bears the name of Bísal Sar, notwithstanding the changes that have occurred during the lapse of one thousand years, since he formed it by damming up the springs. It is one of the sources of the Loni river. The emperor Jahangir erected a palace on the banks of the Bísal Sar, in which he received the ambassador of James I. of England.'

† So in the old Walpot transcription of Sirke[illegible].

‡ This somewhat mentions [illegible] 'the [illegible] of the throng,' clearly proves that the Chauhán prince came as an ally,' an inscription found amidst the ruins of a city of Mewar, alludes to this very [illegible]. The inscription is a record of the friendship [illegible] by their [illegible] in the 12th century,—Samarsi of Chitor, and Prithiraja the last Chauhán king of India—on their combining to chastise the king of Pattan Anhalwara, "in like manner as did Hamira and Tejsi of old unite against the foe," &c. &c. Now Tejsi was the grand-father of Rawal Samarsi, who was killed in opposing the final Muslim invasion, on the Kagar, after one of the [illegible] reigns in their annals: from which we calculate that Tejsi must have sat on the throne about the year A.D. 1[illegible]. His youth and inexperience would account for his acting subordinately to the Chauhán of Ajmer. The name of [illegible] further confirms this date.' (See *Trans. R. Asiat. Soc.* vol I. p. [illegible]).—Tod.

§ 'The Tuar must have been one of the Dehli vassals, whose monarch was of this race.'—Tod.

|| The name of a [illegible] of [illegible] [illegible] taken in 'the great league,' [illegible] *Ras Mala*, vol. I p. [illegible]; also my edition of Elliot's *Races of the N. W. Provinces*, vol. I, p. [illegible].—J. B.

¶ The western Sinde, near Tatta, where there are fine ruins.—Tod.

** See note ‡ above.

†† 'The Dors and Chandels were well known tribes: the latter contended with Prithiraja, who deprived them of Mahoba and Kalinjar, and all modern Bundelkhand.—Tod. The war with Parimal the Chandel forms the subject of the [illegible] book of Chand's poem.—J. B.

‡‡ 'The renowned Dahima was lord of Biana; called also Durgasthan.'—Tod.

§ The preceding part of this paragraph is given by Tod (*Raja-sthan*, vol II. pp. 448–49) but with considerable variations from this version.—Ed.

|| That is the Chálukya.

¶ This was Bhima Deva I., the son of Nága Ráia, and grandson of Chámunda Deva. He is the 'Brahma Dev' of Ferishtah, and succeeded his uncle Durlabha Rája in A.D. 1021, and ruled till 1072. Bhola Rao is a title rather than a name, and may possibly be the origin of Balhara—the title applied by the Arabs to the sovereigns of Gujarat.—Ed.

* *Mad* here is the fluid that exudes from the temples of the elephant when in rut. Forbes translates it honey. *Ras Mala*, vol. I. p. 96.

destroying the country of the Chálukya, on roll-ed the army, taking many, Bhoomias with them, destroying the lands of those who opposed them. Throwing forward a guard of a thousand* ele-phants in rut, when the light half of Mágh arriv-ed, he made his camp at ten kos distance. Cities, towns, and villages, all that came in their way, they plundered.

Báluk heard the news. Angrily at once he started up, as when flame starts up in a forest, without smoke. Bálak Rao, the Chálukya war-rior, calling for water, laved his body; he drank a handful (*anjali*) of water which had washed the feet of Vishnu. Hari he placed on his throat. "To-day I go forth to conquer, or to meet death. If I fly, may dishonour fall on my race. In all this land is there no warrior (*Kshatri*), that this man has traversed it without being debarred by weapons?"

Arming his horses with plates of steel, he placed armour on his elephant. The warriors got on their armour and weapons (*Sillah*). When the king mounted his horse he sent word:—"'Bálak Rao has come without fear.' O Srikant Bhát go to the Chohán and thus declare."

Srikant Bhát went to the enemy; he met Bisal Deo Chohán; raising his hands, he gave him the salutation; he told him the message of Bálak Rao. "Your business lies with kings, what have you to do with subjects, you have done ill in that you have injured the subjects. No Hindu monarch would do so. Ceasing to molest the peasants, now return to your home; to Ajmír depart and there reign. Bálak Rao has said I am the Brahma Rai, inured to war, to fly were great grief to me, but the day of my death is a day of holiday. Of noble race are the chiefs that are around me. I have never had any quarrel with you; knowing this, turn back then, and abandon war. I and thou have to meet to-gether in the field to-day. Who shall remain in the field, who shall fly." When the Chohán received this message, he at once gave orders to sound the kettledrum. Armour they placed on horses and on elephants; the warriors clad them-selves in their armour; the two armies met shield to shield in their ranks; they seemed like two billows of the ocean bending their crests toward each other. The Chohán made a phalanx (*chakrávyúh*). Bálak Rao, like Abhimanyu,† may break it or remain in the middle. What destiny has determined will come to pass.

In the morning the two armies met as waves of the ocean. Elephants stood firm; the war-riors struck at their trunks; arrows flew darken-ing the light of the sun. Good warriors with spear on shoulder set their horses at speed; with-out fear, putting their lances as they charged; each was like a drop of water in the ocean. Wounds were apparent on men's bodies. The Chálak's army gave back; then Bálak Rao encour-aged them. They cried "brother, brother, strike, strike!" Both armies fight and wound each other. Bálak shook the Chakrávyúh. The Parihar and Gahilot turned their backs; the Gahilot fled in the direction of the Tunr; the Chakrávyúh was broken in one place;‡ then the other warriors acted nobly and like heroes; they closed up like lions. Corpses fell to the earth; the warriors fought locked in each other's embraces; they displayed such strength as surpasses description. At that time the Kundilis and Balochs advanced against Bálak boldly, nothing regarding. Ele-phants roar; in the field of battle are strewn heads and trunks. The warriors' garments (*bágo*) were stained red, as if they played together at the Holi; they were bathed in gore. The ele-phants, streaming with blood, showed brilliantly as the palása§ flowering in the spring (*basant*) season. Bálak, and Bisal the king perceived each other. It was as if the moon grew dim from being opposed to the sun. The Chálak urged on his horse, the Chohán his elephant; the two rájas fought a terrible fight staying on horse and elephant, they crossed weapons with each other, when to the teeth of the elephant Bálak urged on his steed. "Hear, king," said the Chálak, patting his horse, "it is night, let us break off the fight, and in the morning again resume it." They returned each to his own tent, and bound up the wounds of all who were wounded.

All the ministers of the Chálak came toge-ther; they forged a false paper. Having made it, they brought it to the king:—"Do you go home; the Chálak has fled, we, all his ministers,

---

* My copy reads [illegible] probably [illegible] i.e. 1,000.—J. B.

† The chakravyúh is a phalanx of peculiar form de-scribed in the Mahábhárata as having been formed by the Kaurava army. Abhimanyu, the son of Arjuna, broke through one rank of it, and was slain in front of the seventh. The figure is also used as a charm when a woman finds difficulty in delivery.—Forbes. *Ras Mála*, p. 97, *note*.

‡ i.e. by the Gahilots running away and leaving their place empty. For the curious legend by which cowardice is said to be an inherent vice of the Gahilots, see my Edn. of Elliot's *Races of N. W. P.* Vol. I. p. 84.—J. B.

§ The *Butea frondosa*, which bears scarlet blossoms.

have come to meet you and to seek your protection. Call for what property you will." Pawasur hearing this, went to the Rája, he sent for Kirpal. The Châluk's ministers came to meet him "Whatever property you may demand we will place it at your feet." The king replied "Listen, I will place a *thâna* here; in a month, I will build a city. Pawasur the Tuar said, "bring the tribute." They sent for property; he founded a city there. The Chahuván king gained the field, the Châluk was wounded. Bisal returned home again, having founded Bisalnagar.* In Samvat 986,† Bisal the king founded a royal city, handsome to behold.

Bisal Rája entered his city Ajmer. A Bania dwelt there; at his house the Rája prepared to marry beholding the maid to be like an Apsaras. The earth exclaimed "Jay! Jay!" the sons of the Mágadhas; grain and wealth the king rained on the earth as Indra pours rain.‡ In this way at Ajmer the king performed as it were a *yajna* at the bania's house. The bride was not yet thirteen: the whole city ridiculed it. In Asárh month in the light half, on the second day, Monday, much rain came from the north, the sun was not seen for five days, at this time the Rája enjoyed his bride.§ One night she said, "O Rája I have a boon to beg. At Pushkar is a woman of great beauty, you should go to see her." On the second day after the Dasera the king went there and beheld a bania's daughter named Gauri performing austerities. Bisal Rája seeing her became excited by lust, when the day came to an end he committed what should not have been committed. Every one who heard it was sorrowful. They declared that the king was never to be satisfied.‖

The girl fumed in the midst of her penances, to the Deva pronounced a curse. "Become an Asura, King Bisal, an eater of the flesh of men." The king hearing this trembled, and touching her feet, asked how his restoration would be effected. She said his son's son who would be an ornament of the earth and a great warrior would effect his liberation.¶

O! son (says the relater to her son Ana) by the strength of her penances he became an Asura. The *bania's* daughter continued her penances standing in the heat between fires, in the cold water in winter, saying, "My sin has been very great, if I perform an amount of penance then I may get pardon."* The king determined not to return to Ajmer, but to repair to Gokarna, the shrine of Hara. He halted at the Bisal Sarovar. [On Sunday the seventh of the month, as he was about to proceed with chariots, horses, and elephants]† the king saw a snake in his tent and shot at it with an arrow. It escaped and hid in his boot (*mojari*). When he was putting on his boots to mount his horse the snake bit him [the Rája laughed and said "that which is fated will happen." They tried medicines and spells in vain; the Rája's pain increased. Hearing the Rája was dead the Parmári became a *Sati*:—dying she said—"The son of the Jadavani will rule the country, may my blessing be on him"]. In that same place Bisal became an Asura, always hungry, vomiting flames of fire, eating men where there was a town or an army; as many as he could obtain he ate.

(Ana's mother says) "When your father heard this story he sent me to Bhuthaniah, I being then pregnant. He prepared himself to fight the Dánava. [His fate and mine were one, or rather, our ill fortune was alike, to stop disgrace we endured trouble. This was his desire and mine.] With a thousand men sounding the kettledrum, the Chahuván set forth: he reached Ajmer. He found all the gardens waste and the fort broken down: Sárang Deva saw this. He [thought of the bania (his foster father) and] reflected that it was a female ascetic of his race that had destroyed his family. He lamented [his eyes filled with tears as he thought on his father]. Three days he remained in the fort, but he saw not the Asura. Then Sárang Deva began to take heart and think of again building the city. In the morning of the 11th the Dánava entered the city. The whole army snatching their weapons ran to fight him. They fought with swords, he seized them in his mouth and broke them as a monkey breaks fruit from trees and creepers, father and son were fighting. Sárang Deva

* Colonel Tod, *Western India*, p. 173, mentions that one stipulation of this treaty was, that the Chalukya should give a daughter in marriage to Bisal Deva. He also mentions, quoting the Komár Pála, a work relating the exploits of a Chaulukya prince of that name, that Bisal Deva took prince Rama, son of Rája Bhim, prisoner.—*Rás Mála*, vol. I. p. 1[illegible], note.

† This battle was probably fought about A.D. 1046, or Samvat Bikho 986.—ED.

‡ Much condensed.

§ Twelve lines left out and the rest condensed.

‖ About 100 lines are here compressed.

¶ About 40 lines are compressed into this passage.

* About 40 lines here omitted expressive of the king's evil life and remorse.

† In what follows the longer additions made by Mr. Beames have been put within brackets.—ED.

fell as falls a mountain; knowing him to be an Asura, all the men remained hidden in the city. Searching he ate the men, thence his name Dhundhâ.* He ruined the city of Ajmer which was like a Deva's city." "O mother, listen! the austerity-practising Rishi has promised,—the Parmâri too has given a blessing. I will go to Ajmergarh and return having slain the enemy." Gauri did not agree to this matter, she advised the Kumar to remain quiet: thus Gauri-mâ persuades but her son refuses to listen. She said "A man may fight with a man but not with a Dânav. Much time has passed away, the roads are broken up, he destroys the elephants and the deer of the jangal. In this house of your maternal uncle (*mosâl*) you are living, he will come and destroy it." Before his mother Anâ exclaimed, "I will either live or die there, I will perform his service or take an opposite course." "I see that you have conceived a bad desire, from which my mind is destroyed. Dhundha seeks men to eat them, and do you think of going to serve him." Then replied Anâ thus; "To me this seems good,—to give to him my head, or to return with a *chhatra* raised over me. By service the Devas may be pleased; by service the Râkshasas may be subdued; by service a lion may be tamed; by service snakes may be deprived of their poisonous powers; by service is much property acquired." His mother urged that enemies were not to be served, but Anâ determinedly went to the forest of Ajmer.† Long had that Dânava remained in the Ajmer forest; there he had destroyed all: there was neither Siddha nor Sâdhak; neither beast nor bird.‡ He had many powers with him. When Anâ went thither, the Râkshasa was surprised at seeing a man. "Here is a good meal for me to-day: destiny provides for us mortals' food without our toil." Anâ saw the Râkshasa, having five hundred hands each holding a sword, roaring with his mouth, yawning, up he rose. Anâ concealing his sword in his breast made obeisance. Firm stood his feet, but in mind much he trembled.§ The Râkshasa began to enquire of him "Who is your mother? who your father? what is your name? what lord do you follow?" Anâ [reflecting in his mind,—"If this Dhundha should swallow me, as Indra did to Vritra, so will I do, ripping open his belly from within with my sword"] said—"Gauri was the mother who bore me in her womb. My father (or ancestor) Bisal, strong in *kâm*, I have longed to come hither to see with these eyes your form." "What! has poverty fallen to your lot, or has disease afflicted your body, has an enemy taken your land, or has your wife deserted you, has some calamity been thrown upon you by destiny, have men driven you from them, or has your Guru cursed you, or your mother died?" "None of all these have happened. It is to serve you that I come hither. Until I met you I had disease and poverty,|| until then I was of no repute."

The Râkshasa took him in his embrace, and placed his hand on his head. "The world and desire to live abandoning, now have you come hither." "For this reason, I care not to live that I have no land or home. Therefore I am come to serve you. It is alike to me to live or to die. I will either give you my head or place above it an umbrella. This land from long bygone times belonged to my fathers, to ask it from you I am come."

The Dânava was pleased beholding his son, he himself longed to assume human form.

"Your descendants from father to son shall reign." Thus saying he rose into the sky taking his sword with him. "On Sunday pay me worship."¶ The royalty he gave to Anâ the Chauhan; he went by the way of the air to Gangâ, being afflicted by thorns. A Rishi named Sim[illegible] was seated there, the Râkshasa paid him obeisance. He asked him who he was, and why he had come. Dhund told his whole tale,—"I have with force [illegible] how shall my sins be effaced?" "You are a Kshatri, your sins cannot here be effaced, you should go to Kasi. Many are the sins you have committed, there they will be washed away, and you will become sinless." Hearing this, the Râkshasa rose into the air, he arrived at Dilli, where is the place of Devas,—Nigambodh, where is Yamuna river—pure and clear are its waters. Thither the demon (*nishâchar*) went. He was very thirsty and wearied. In his doubled hands he drank water. His body became cooled, he walked up and down. A Rishi named Harit was performing penance there in a cave. Hearing the noise he came out to see. Beholding him he asked his story. The Râkshasa detailed the whole matter.

* From Hindi ढूंढना to search.

† A few lines here omitted.

‡ Rather a fine description of the utter desolation of Ajmer is here omitted.

§ The preceding three sentences are much condensed.

|| This sentence is very much compressed.

¶ He became the Kul Deva.

"In the neighbourhood of Yoginipur,* on the banks of the river, I have come and drunk water. I am called Dhundha and Bisalarupala. By a curse I have assumed a Daitya's body. To abandon it and to behold Gangâ I am desirous, to wash away my sins, and again to rule in Ajaypur.† O Rishi Râja! going to Gangâ I will destroy this body with my sword. Will my release be thus effected? O Râja Rishi! instruct me that I may accomplish it."

The Rishi smiling said,—"Without penance royalty cannot be obtained. Food, wealth, wife, and children, all the happiness of the world, may be obtained by penance." The Râkshasa, receiving this instruction, began to call Hari to mind. In the Rishi cave he continued performing austerity. The Rishi went away to a tîrtha, saying—"Until I return, having visited all tîrthas, do you remain here penance performing."

The demon, performing penance, continued for three hundred and eighty years. His body began to be without pain in consequence of meditating on Vishnu. At this time Anang of the race of the Pândavs ruled at Hastinapur. On the banks of the Yamunâ he founded a city. Anang Pâl Tuar founded there Dilli. The King, the subjects, men and women, dwelt there, all of them in peace. Anang Pâl Tuar Sulakh the virtuous King: his daughter was very beautiful, eight years of age. With her companions, chaste and full of good qualities like Sîtâ, she came in Shrâwan and Bhadrapad‡ to worship Gauri. At Nigambodh on the banks of Kâlindî (Yamunâ) they all went to worship the Gauri. At that time the rain fell with great violence, the maidens began to be wet. Anang Pâl's daughter, with five hundred maidens and a daughter of a Purohit, went all together to bathe on Yamunâ's banks. They entered the cave where Dhundha was performing penance, looking the image of death. All of them worshipped him. He enquired of them who they were, and for what purpose they had come. They answered—"We seek as a boon from you that we may all have good warriors for our husbands, and may dwell in one place." The Dânava Râja made them this promise; and rising in the air he flew towards Kâsî; he reached the banks of Gangâ to perform sacrifice. Of his body making a hundred and eight fragments, he offered them in burnt sacrifice. He asked for a boon from Siva. "May the fragments of my body become a hundred and eight men upon earth." Thus his body being burned with fire, his splendour (jyoti, soul) went to Brahmaloka. Amidst the Apsarasas he began to sing. Thus obtaining the restoration of his body, he took birth upon the earth: that matter says Kavi Chand relating I will describe.

To the cave of Nigambodh, the daughter of Anang Pâla and her maidens again having gone, found there an image of stone, which they washed with water and worshipped with pure souls, with sandal, incense, and lamps, with pure bodies. Siva gave a boon, "you shall give birth to a great warrior, with whom no man shall be able to fight, also to a Bhat powerful in tongue." From the boon granted by Dhundha Rakhas, and his having cut his body into fragments at Kâsî,—from his fragments sprang a Bhat, twenty Kshatris were born at Ajmer, of whom one was Someswara, whose son was Prithirâja; the others arose in other places. Kähar arose in Kanoj, Jait and Salakh in Abugarh, in Mandovar the Parihâr; in Karnâl Kangra Hâhuli; in Nagar Balibhadra; Chand arose in Lahor;§ in Dilli Attatâya; in other places arose Samanta. At Jhalu, Rama Deva; at Gorkhpura Dham; [the Dahima arose at Biyana.] In Prithirâja's service, they all remained.

[The birth and dwelling of the nobles, Chand sings severally in the Paddhari metre]:—In Jesalmer, dwells Achalesa like the sun; Pajjun dwells in Chittaur; Hari Sing arose in Sambhal Bayana; in Kulikanth arose Jangale Bhim; in Sambhargarh, Narsing Râo. Jaisar Bhim who dwelt in Junagarh and fought many days with Bhim who was wounded; Nârung Rai rose, the Mori King, Rânad-Râi, who dwelt in Asigarh and fought with Kanhai Rai the Chahuvân warrior—the servant of Prithirâja. Tejpâl of the Dor race lived at Jummu; Kaluda, a very powerful warrior, who did obeisance to the Chahuvân; Mahâ Chandel of Ujjain, who, when wounded, was protected by a Samant, and who afterwards did good service here. When Arsi Chandel was slain, the royalty was given to Dhuda. The Râja of Dilli gave to Maha Chandel a country by the sea road. With the Râja of Kanoj fighting, he kept his name in the Kaliyug. On the throne of the

* An old name of Delhi.

† Ajmer, the old name of which is Ajayameru.—J. B.

‡ That is the last half of Shrawan and first of Bhadrapad—a month.

§ This is the poet himself, and this passage is usually quoted to prove that he was a native of Lahor.—J. B.

Chaluk was Bhola Bhim; in the Dekhan country [illegible]; the Bargujar Rai was Aliya, who day by day destroyed the Khan's country Mard Khan Ali . . . .
Hada Hamir, Khatal Khangar, two brothers, when a famine occurred in their own country they came to Dilli. Parmar Kanak who brought a courtesan from Jayachand's house to the country of Prithiraja;* he received six *[illegible]* in *pasáyo* (present). In the year 1115, in five places the Rajas were burnt† . . . .

Anal came and embraced his mother. He told her all that had happened. The people, taking the *mahájans* with them, re-inhabited the country. When Anal Narind founded Ajmer and made Sambhar as it were a heap of gold, he began to raise and punish his enemies. [From village to village people bound garlands of flowers] he dug out the treasures buried among the ruins of wasted towns. The voices of birds and animals began to be heard, the country was restored, poverty was destroyed; [bathing in water, and giving gifts to Brahmans, he ruled sixty-four years, did Anal the King.] Taking the country by his sword, he delivered it to his son, Jaisingh Deva, who mounted the throne. Jaisingh Deva discovered much property which had been buried by Anal, and in the Bisal tank. He found so much to it [The wealth of Anal was a mere drop compared with it;] then he adorned his house with gold, and gave the gold to three Brahmans who had charge of his granaries and wealth.] He, the Chahuván, of good conduct, listened to the Vedas and Puráṇas. Abandoning pride, he did not mistake the custom of his family. For eight years he reigned. Anand Deva, his son, received the umbrella: while he ruled, he saw one day the Deva in the Varaha avatára. He built a temple in Pushkar, called the Dharni Vihára. [He reigned for a hundred years.] His son Som received the umbrella; he, Somesa the hero, conquered with his sword the Rájas of Gurjara and Malwa. In Maru, where the Bhattis ruled, the Chahuván took the desert country. He married in the house of the Dilli lord; and from this marriage arose Pithal.‡ Anand Raj's son Somesa defeating the army of the Moriyás, made a fire sacrifice. [In his own city making oblations to the gods,] he enjoyed himself in Ajmer, did Someśwar. [This is that hero Somes] who conquered the Khorasani [warrior. This is that hero Somes] who laid waste the Gurjara land. This is that hero Somes who took the Parihar Nahar [of exceeding strength. Kavi Chand compares him to Rahu seizing the moon. The valiant hero, merciful, powerful, wealthy] . . . . .

When Anang Rája was ruling in Dilli the Kamdhuj§ prepared a four-armed army. Vijaypál followed it,‖ he came to Antarved. Anang heard this, he prepared his army and crossed the Kalindi. The Sambhar Raja heard that the Kamdhuj and the Tuar were about to engage. He considered that it was not the duty of a Kshatri to sit at home, and that he should either increase the fame of the house of Anal or seek Kailása, or Indra's abode (*swarga*).¶ He sounded the kettle-drum (*nisán*)* and advanced to succour Dilli, as a snake puts the jewel first. The banners (*[illegible]*), chowries, and all the other paraphernalia of war, taking with him,—he reached Dilli. He met Anang Rái and entered into friendship with him; they ate together *pán*, full of strong flavour.† Anang told the state of affairs concerning the Kamdhuj.‡ Someśwara biting his lip, [full of anger, seizing his sword, and twisting his moustache in his hand] declared that he would destroy the presumptuous Kamdhuj [and arranged the plan of the battle with the Rája.] At the last watch of the night the *nisán* began to sound; the noise of the drums was like drops of rain. Somes and Anang Rája set off together, in much joy, love, and friendship. The white umbrella borne above them, shone amidst the standards like the sun amidst clouds; the warriors armed and eager for the fight. The news was brought of Vijay Pál's army having arrived, drawn up in the form of a serpent (*sarpaqunha*). Of the host of his servants he formed the fangs, himself formed the tail. Anang Pál consulted with Somes. They resolved to form their army in the (*Garud*) form, to swallow up the serpent; Someśwar Rai formed the beak and neck, in whose aid was Sambhar

* The whole of this passage about the courtesan differs from my MS.—J. B.

† This date should probably be 1245 or A.D. 1188.—Ed. Ten lines omitted.

‡ This is a familiar name for Prithiraj, he is also called Rai Pithora (राय पिथौरा)

§ Sprung from a headless corpse,—a name of the Rahtores; or from Kamadhvaj whose standard was Káma.

‖ Four lines omitted.

¶ A long description of the army is here omitted. There is nothing new in it.—J. B.

* The small drum with the banner.

† So I translate 'ghana-sára pána' which is the reading in my copy. Dalpatrám had read "with camphor."—J. B.

‡ The preceding three sentences are a very condensed outline.—J. B.

Devî. The right wing was led by Chaunang the hero, a victorious warrior of the Chauhân race, the left wing by the hero Birang Deva. The feet of the eagle were formed by Anang Raja—the tail by the Kuramish Jai, conqueror in many fights.

[The armies joined, a cloud of dust arose, the earth shook, banners and standards waved, drums and trumpets sounded.] The battle raged, the arrows darkened the sun, the dagger (*jamdad**) plied its trade, the Chauhân was the victor, the enemy fled. When the army of Narsingh fled, the Rathor having drunk liquor (crazed) came on; he drove back Viram and Hipmal Vâghelâ. Vijaypâl then attacked Somes, who was supported by the princes of the Moon-race and Anang-pâl. The Kanauj-râj sounded like the thunder of the *Pralaya*. Anang-pâl repulsed the Kamdhaj; but retreating a hundred paces he came on again. Som advanced against him, he struck him down with his sword, giving him many wounds.† One thousand and five fell in the Kamdhaj army. Bijay Râja fled shamefully, leaving horses and elephants. [The bards utter the cry of "victory, victory!"] Someswar acquired great fame in Dilli city from repulsing the powerful Kamdhaj. Bijaya Râj returned home. Anang Pâl Tuar gave his daughter to Someswar with much gold, horses, elephants, maidservants, necklaces of jewels. The king went to Ajmer, bearing a strict alliance with him. Adorning his elephants, he returned home sounding the instruments of victory. He made presents to his relations. Old and young sang songs of the Chauhân's fame. The women, with faces like the moon, were looking at him from the windows. They praised his fame.

I now tell how the Chahuvân Râi conquered territory: how Anang Râja made him his heir at Dilli. [Then will I tell of the descendants of the Chahuvân], how they took forts impregnable, raising their fame in the world, how they destroyed a Mlechha army, many times binding the Shâh and releasing him; how he defeated the Kamdhaj; how he disturbed the sacrifice, and took away Sanyogitâ; how the king protected Abu, and destroyed the power of the Chalûk—the lord of Pattan; how he defeated the lion-like Parihâr and married his daughter; how he gained the fort of Devagiri with the hoof of his horse; how he married the daughter of the Jâdav lord of [illegible], and protected his country; how many wild [illegible] fled from Mewâr.—such an avatar of [illegible] never was or will be.

Som Râja in Ajmer and Anang Tuar in Dilli lived in great happiness. Anang had two daughters but no son; one he married to the Kamdhaj, one to the Chauhân,‡ he was the [illegible] of the race of Mânik Râi. Anangpâl married his daughters—one to Bijay Pâl, another to Somes, one was named Surasundari, the other Kamalâdevi.§ After a certain time, Someswara's wife became pregnant, she gave birth to Prithirâja of the Dânava race of Kshatris. Someswara made many gifts.| The destruction of Kanauj, Gazni, and Pattan, began to be proclaimed. The day Prithirâja was born, Anang Pâl sent for a Vyâs named Jagjyoti. He enquired the signs of the auspicious moment; placed flowers, pân, and incense before him. He said 'this is as it were an avatar of Sri Krishna in the Kaliyuga, to slay the lord of horses like Kans' [Kavi Chand says for the safety of Dilli this incomparable avatar was born]. In his delight, Anangpâla presented many gifts and caused songs of joy to be sung at his house.

The mother of Jaychand of Kanauj, hearing that her sister had a son, sent congratulations (*vadhâvano*). Jaychand presented robes of honour (*pahirâvani*) to the Brâhmans; Someswar too presented gifts [illegible] with joy. In the year of Vikrama 1115¶ (A.D. [illegible]) Prithirâja was born. The king caused Someswar, from the virtues of his former birth [illegible] a son Prithirâja. He gave, as congratulatory presents, a thousand horses and a village with gold. He gave dresses of honour also to his relations. The drums sounded aloud. When the King beheld the face of his son he felt that he had attained the reward of his virtues in a former birth. Calling for a Brâhman, he caused the *jâtakarm* to be performed as described in the Vedas. With dance and song he caused the *jâtakarm* to be made. It was predicted that he would be a great Râja, would reign forty years in Dilli, and in the Panjâb, in Indraprastha, and Sambhar; that he would often conquer the Gajni lord and release him.

Anangpâl felt anxiety hearing that he was to reign at Delhi.

Prithirâja learns all martial exercises, to read

---

* *Jamdad*, the dagger *Jambia*.—*Yam-dant* or *yama dâḍh* Yama's tooth.

† The preceding five sentences are a very brief summary.

‡ Twenty lines omitted.

§ Two lines omitted.

| Very much compressed.

¶ Perhaps 1215 or A. D. 1158.—Ed.

poetry, to swim, to hunt. Rámgáru was his teacher. He learned to sing, to play, to dance, to examine omens, to draw, to fence, to ask questions, to answer them, grammar, prosody, &c. He learned six languages, Sanskrit, Prakrit, Mágadhi, &c. He wore a *pagri* ornamented with jewels, with a splendid turá.* In his ears he wore pearls; on his neck a pearl necklace.†

THE BHÚTÁS OF NAGARA MALNÁD IN MAISÚR.

By V. N. NARASIMMIYENGAR, BANGALOR.

The fertile kingdom of Maisur, as constituted on the fall of Seringapatam, in 1799 A.D., forms a conspicuous table-land of various altitude over the surrounding plains of Southern India. The Western Ghâts from Sorabs on the north to Manserabad on the south form its western boundary. Excepting two or three Taluqas which are territorially in another Division, the Eastern slopes of the Ghâts are in the Nagara Division. It will be convenient to retain in the present paper the names of the existing political sub-divisions, or Taluqas, which constitute the Malnad section of the Division. They are—

1 Sorabs.	2 Ságara.	3 Anantapura.
4 Nagara.	5 Kaulédurga.	6 Koppa.
7 Vastárá.	8 Chickamagalúru.	9 Lakavalli.

The term Malnád is etymologically of Dravidian origin; from Malé *hill*, and nád *country*, Malnád thus means 'hilly country.' A strict application of the term would exclude some of the above Taluqas, such as Sorabs, as they have no hills of importance to justify their being considered as hilly, and contain only lofty and thick forests. But contiguity to the Malnád proper, affinity of climate, land tenures, ethnology, manners and customs, as well as similarity of the flora, have conduced to include these Taluqas likewise in popular estimation in the western highlands of the province.

The beauties of this favoured locality in scenery, as well as its natural fertility and romantic seclusion, have been sufficiently glorified, both in prose and verse. The present object is to show, as far as can be done in so narrow a compass, the strong grip which demonology has obtained over the credulous masses inhabiting these regions. It will be perceived that facilities of intercommunication between different parts of the same land, and their natural configuration, have a considerable and direct influence over the faith prevailing therein, and that whilst the monstrous lies and deceptions which do duty in the Malnád for articles of religion, would be laughed at by the most superstitious pariah in the open country; the scoffer who dared refuse them on the spot would be hooted as a downright blasphemer. It would certainly be a profitable study for the antiquary to trace the history of Bhuta worship in earlier times.

Mr. Garrett in his Classical Dictionary, and quoting Thompson defines the Bhutas as "evil "spirits said to proceed from Bramha, children of Krodha, malignant spirits, goblins or "ghosts, haunting cemeteries, lurking in trees, "animating dead bodies, and deluding and de-"vouring human beings. They are generally "coupled with the Prétas, and in this character "belong to the ogre period. In the Puránas "period, they are personified as demi-gods of a "particular class, produced by Bramha when in-"censed, and their mother is considered in the "Padma Purána as Krodha or 'anger,' and "their father Kásyapa." In the Amara Kosha the Bhutas, Vidyádharás, Apsarasas, (celestial frail beauties), Yakshas, Rákshasas, Gandharvas (celestial musicians), Kinnaras, Pisáchas, Guhyakas and Siddhas are all grouped together under the comprehensive but seemingly heterogeneous class of "Déva Yónis," meaning the offspring (illegitimate?) of the Dévas. Bétála, the mythic vampire, whose exploits in conjunction with Vikrama have been popularly illustrated by Burton, was the chief of the Bhutas.

For the sake of simplicity, we shall call these fetishes 'demons.' There seems to be no authority in the Hindu sacred writings for their worship as practised in these parts.

The Bhutas are divided into two major classes, viz., male and female; and each Bhuta has a particular name. The following are some of the most common‡:—

Male.	*Female.*
1. Bramha.	1. Chaudi.
2. Raga.	2. Mátangi.
3. Jattiga.	3. Uri Kumári.
4. Kappina Bhuta.	4. Panjurali.
5. Kshétrapála.	5. Raga Panjurali.
&c.	6. Dhumávati.
	7. Kallurali.

From the physical configuration of these

* Turrá, the border—the end of a turban with gold edge.

† Ten pages of about 170 lines are condensed into this para.—J. B.

‡ The Nágara or serpent is not unfrequently associated with them.

regions, the villages are almost always embedded in the valleys between the hills and rising grounds. They consist of only a few straggling hovels, in the midst of which there is to be found a house of substantial structure, sheltered by jungal, and by the stately and graceful betel palm plantations. The cultivation extends in terraces along the length of these narrow valleys, called Kúgu, Kôva, Hora, &c. Each of these valleys has its tutelary Bhúta, which is supposed to be its guardian. Lest the direst calamities befal the defaulter, the insatiable Bhúta should be appeased periodically by sacrifices and worship. Is it the gathering in of the harvest? or the liquidation of the ryot's long-standing debt? or the celebration of a wedding? or the occurrence of an eclipse? or a new moon-day? or is it a social gathering? The Bhúta must invariably be propitiated. It is however a rule that, except in rare instances, the jurisdiction of one Bhúta is never invaded by another; and in no case can the Bhúta pursue its victim beyond the hills which form the natural barriers on all sides of the Malnád country.

The Brahma is by some stated to be the ghost of a deceased Bráhman, which, for some reason or other, haunts the valley where his homestead was originally established. In fact, it is supposed to be an abbreviation of Brahma Rákshasa. No animal sacrifices are as a rule offered to it, but only half-boiled rice in large heaps mixed with turmeric or saffron. The Bhútas are represented by small pieces of stone, seldom covered by any building or temple, but generally placed in the midst of clumps of trees, called Bana. In very rare instances a metallic image is set up. Two or three of them are often to be met with in the same place, the Brahma, the Chaudi and the Jattiga. While the former is restricted to its "bread and water," the two latter receive all other sacrifices, called collectively Harike. They are not worshipped daily, but only at stated periods. The Bráhman jóyis or astrologer is called upon to perform the pújá in the day, and towards nightfall the villagers congregate in the locality, and commit all sorts of abominations in the name of the Bhúta, such as the slaughtering of pigs, sprinkling the village with rice mixed with their blood, dancing around the stones, &c. the toddy and arrak going a great way towards rendering the debauch unusually prolonged. Sheep, pigs, fowls, &c. are slaughtered, and if buffaloes are wanting, it is only from the difficulty of procuring them, and the forbidding price which is demanded for them by the drovers who periodically bring their cattle for sale to the Malnád. All persons residing or holding land in the valley to which the Bhúta belongs are obliged, for fear of the direst calamities, to contribute to the feast. If the popular impression is correct, woe betide the heterodox recusant, who rebels against the demoniacal sway. Either his cattle will be killed by beasts of prey, which are nothing but the Bhúta transformed; or some member of his family will fall sick; or the bundles of new clothes secured in his strong box will be found reduced to rags; or the pots in which the food is dressed in his house will be filled with filth and excrement at meal time; or the most impossible stones will be found in his vessels, which could not have got in in a natural way; or a large boulder will roll upon his house from the adjoining hill; or his crops will wither away most unaccountably; or some other equally serious mishap will fall on his devoted head. In the midst of his distractions, his only remedy is to consult the jóyis or astrologer, who, in the orthodox fashion, divines the cause of the misfortune by means of cowries, grains of rice, &c., and after making, or seeming to make the necessary calculations, says it is the Bhúta. Forthwith vows are made, and sacrifices offered to the angry Bhúta, who assures the penitent of his satisfaction, generally by means of pújáris, or other persons, who work themselves up to a state bordering on frenzy ([illegible]), and whatever they may utter whilst in that condition is considered to be a supernatural revelation:—without miracles, it would seem that Bhúta worship would have waned away long ago. An instance of it is the ceremony called "hendárchana," in which the idol is carried over a layer of live coals, the bearers and others treading upon it barefooted, and the operation never hurts them, it is said, through the might of the Bhúta.

It was formerly the custom to import from a shrine below the Gháts in the South Canara District, called Dharmasthala, or K[illegible], blocks of stone of various sizes, generally of a globular shape, which have a fixed price, and which were supposed to become from the moment of purchase, the ghostly servitors of the purchaser. The Bhúta received, and still receives, the daily dole of prepared rice and curds, and whenever the owner had reason to be dissatisfied with, or had a grudge against, any one, it was believed that he had only to set the Chaudi or Bhúta at his enemy, and the poor fellow would become speechless, or his house would suddenly be set fire to, or some other catastrophe would befal him. His only remedy was in falling at the feet of the offended devil-owner, who, if satisfied, would give him a handful of ashes in token of peace, and the Bhuta at once returned to its lithic abode. When verbal directions did not produce obedience from his ghostly slave, the owner treated the stone with a preparation of chillies and mustard, and it was supposed that the doom of the victim was sealed. And when even this failed of effect, the Bhuta stone was plucked off its bed, and turned upside down. This extreme measure is supposed to excite the homicidal and incendiary proclivities of the demon to the highest pitch. It was further an item of the popular belief till recently that if a thief were to put his hand to the betel-nut or other crop of his neighbour with dishonest intentions, the guardian Bhuta would invisibly chain him to the tree, and would only deliver him red-handed to the owner. This trait of the devil-worship is not altogether devoid of its redeeming points. It is easy to conceive that in a sparsely populated and jungly country like the Malnad, the inefficient police were supplemented by a supernatural force which, as a rule, had more influence on evil-minded superstitious individuals than the real policeman of the state. The spread of intelligence, increased facilities of communication, the slow advance of education, the fear of certain punishment at the hands of the authorities, the frequent inroads of travellers attracted by the natural beauty and plenty of the country, the free sprinkling of European planters, and above all forty years of British rule, have all conspired together gradually to weaken the influence of the Bhuta, if not altogether to unseat him from the pedestal which he had occupied for centuries. If the superstition still clings to the land, it is more from the mere force of habit, and the depredations of the beasts of prey, especially of the tiger, that lord it over the poor ryot's cattle with impunity, and which are supposed by them to be messengers, if not avatars, of the neglected Bhuta.

These village demons are endowed with Inam lands in order to ensure the better performance of their vile rites which are supposed to be indispensable to the well-being of the community.

As if the density of the popular darkness was not enough, the subordinate native officers of the Government were themselves victimised by the Bhuta tyranny. It was customary till very recently for the Taluq Amildars and Shekdars (the former is the Tahsildar of H. M.'s country, and the latter is a revenue officer in charge of a division of a Taluq) to issue notices and orders to the Bhuta not to molest a particular individual, or to quit a tree which it was supposed to haunt, and which was required to be felled, or to do, or to cease doing any particular act required! It is stated that the Bhuta never disobeyed the behests of the Government officers. Only about 30 years ago, a certain Amildar who longed to have a son and heir, was told by the inspired follower of a Bhuta that his wish would be realised if he would give away to devotees the whole of his property. The credulous man almost prepared himself to follow the commands of the Bhuta, but he was fated not to become a father to the last.

It is not to be denied that demon-worship is known in the open country. The Mari, and her ever-smiling compeers and followers, are familiar enough. But the sway of the supernatural and malignant spirits seems to possess its chief stronghold in the Malnad, and it is the object of the writer to direct attention to it.

It may not be out of place here to state that as a large preserve of game, large and small, the Nagara Malnad is almost unrivalled. Here the tiger, the cheeta, the panther, the elephant, and other beasts of prey roam in comparative safety, devouring the poor ryots' cattle, and otherwise rendering themselves obnoxious. Birds too are to be found in countless varieties, and taken as a whole, the amateur or professional sportsman will have to go many hundreds of miles before an equally plentiful field can be met with. Where European planters are settled, and where an exceptionally good sportsman is in charge of the district, the large game are fast disappearing; but as a rule most of the notorious haunts of the tiger in the Malnad remain to the present day uninvaded by the venturesome Shikari. It will be a gala day for the Malnad ryot when he can graze his costly cattle in the adjoining natural paddocks, without the dread of the tiger.

BENGALI FOLKLORE—LEGENDS FROM DINAJPUR.

By G. H. DAMANT, B.C.S.

(Continued from page 219.)

THE SIXTH STORY.

The Four Friends.

There was once a king's son, a wazir's son, a kotwal's son, and a barber's son, they were all great friends, but none of them knew how to read and write, and they would not work for their living but spent all their time in amusing themselves. One day their guardians determined that when they came home to dinner they would give them nothing to eat but ashes. The four friends, seeing this, met together and agreed to forsake their own country and go elsewhere. As they were on their way one of them said "a camel has passed along this road," another said "it was blind," "it was a female" said a third, and the fourth said "it was in foal." Now it happened that just as the four friends were saying this, the king of that country had come out to hunt, and was concealed near, so that he heard what they said, and immediately sent persons to fetch them.

When the four friends came before the king he asked them how they knew that a camel had passed by that way, and how they had discovered all its qualities, for a camel of his own which answered to the description had gone astray, and he said further that if they would not tell him, he would punish them as thieves. They replied, "We knew it was a female because it stopped while the left foot [illegible], and from the shape of its foot prints we could tell that it was a camel, and we saw that it only ate the grass on one side of the road, so that it must have been blind." The king said, "very good, but how could you tell that it was in foal?" One of them answered, "We saw that the hind feet were more deeply impressed in the ground than the fore feet, and so we knew." On hearing this the king began to think that they were no ordinary men and must be possessed of rare qualities, so he enquired where they were going, and they told him they were travelling to seek for service. He then enrolled them among his own guards. One night when the king's son was on guard, he saw a snake hissing terribly and going into the house where the king and queen were sleeping. He followed it and found it just about to bite the king, so he instantly cut it in pieces with his sword but a drop of its blood fell on the queen's breast. He considered that he had saved the life of the king, but did not at first see how he could preserve the queen. At last he cut the snake in small pieces, and put it in a cup. And hid it under the king's bed, he then put a piece of cloth on his tongue and licked the drop of blood from off the queen's breast. She woke up, and said to the king, "You have taken a great deal of trouble to find these men, and now one of them has touched me with his hand." The king at once dismissed them all from his service without hearing a word of what they had to say. When they saw that he acted in such a hasty manner, they told him that they would rob his palace, and annoy him in every possible way, but he paid no attention to what they said. So they continued to live in the city, and began to rob the king's palace until he lost nearly all his property, and although he made many attempts he could not detect them.

One day the king's eldest son said that he would undertake to catch the thieves; the king was very glad to hear him say so, and provided him with everything that was necessary and he started on his way. Meanwhile the four friends consulted together, and agreed that they must show the king's son something that would astonish him. So they disguised themselves and changed their dress, and went out to meet him. They contrived to separate him from his companions, and took him a little way, and left him to walk on by himself. In the meantime the barber's son, pretending that he was going to shave some one in the neighbouring village, passed near the king's son, and he being a very effeminate person admired the barber's beautiful hair, and asked him how he obtained it. The barber replied, "Sir if you will agree to suffer a little pain, I will make just as beautiful hair grow on your own head. I do not wish you to pay me anything, but if you get a good crop of hair, you can make me a little present." The king's son believed all that he said, and asked what was to be done; so the barber made him sit down, and cut off all his hair with a razor, and then began to scrape off all the skin from the front part of his head, so that the blood flowed all over his body, but still he made no objection. The barber then rubbed some salt on his head, and told him to go to a pond, and dip his head in it, saying that the virtue of the charm was such that the deeper he dipped the longer his hair would grow. So the prince went into the water, and began to dip his head, but in the meantime the barber took his clothes, and went away. The prince continued to dip his head and each time looked to see if his hair was growing or not. After some time he saw that no good came of his dipping, and began to think that he had been deceived, and found that both his clothes and the barber had disappeared. As he could not go home without any clothes, he stopped all day in the jangal, and when it was night, went towards home; but as he did not come by the road, but through the jangal, all the people thought he was a thief, and laid hold of him, till they saw that he was the kings' son, when they took him into the house.

The king again asked how the thief was to be caught, and a man said there was a soothsayer who could tell where the thief was by his magical arts.

The next morning the king summoned the magician and he came and began his incantations. Every one was crowding round him to see what would happen, and the four friends came and stood there with the rest. The magician soon discovered that the thieves were there, but he could not say precisely who they were, so he made further calculations, and discovered that they were on the north side, but they moved round to the south, so that he arrived at no result. The magician then went home, saying that he would make further calculations, and point out the thieves to-morrow, but it was too late to do any more that day.

That night the friends went to the magician's house, and called out to him, saying that the king had sent him a present. He believed what they said, and stretched out his hand to take it, but they cut his hand off with a sword, and took it away. They then went to the house where the king slept, and put the severed hand through the window, and touched him with it. He thought the thieves had come, and drew his sword to cut the hand, at that very moment they dropped it, and ran away. The king thought he had cut off the thief's hand, and was very much pleased, because he [illegible] that next day he would find the man whose hand had been cut off and punish him. The magician was summoned to come next day; so the king sent people to bring him, but he kept his right arm concealed and began to perform his incantations with the left hand. Now the four thieves were present, and one of them said, "Incantations which are performed by the left hand are never correct." The king replied "Quite true, he must use the right hand." When the magician heard that his mouth grew dry, for when he rose in the morning he had heard that the king had cut off the thief's hand and kept it, so he would not put forth his right arm, but they lifted up his cloth, and discovered that the hand which the king had cut off belonged to him, and then they began to think that it must be the work of the thieves; and the king promised on the spot that he would give half his kingdom to any one who could catch them.

On hearing that the four friends agreed that one of them should assume the dress of a Sanyasi, and perform worship, and in the meantime another of them should dress himself like Siva, and come to the place riding on a bull. When this was settled, the weaver's son put on the dress of a Sanyasi, and went to the king, who treated him with great respect and offered him food, and told him that thieves had come into his kingdom, but although he had made many attempts he could not catch them. The Sanyasi said he would catch them, and the king was very glad to hear it, and enquired what he was to do.

The Sanyasi replied, "Nothing very difficult, I will perform worship, and then Siva will come in riding on a bull, you must ask a boon of him, and he will grant it." So the Sanyasi began his worship, and beat his cymbals saying "dum, dum," and the barber's son dressed like Siva came in riding on a bull. Directly he came the Sanyasi put out the candle, and every one was struck with amazement at the sight. The Sanyasi said "Now Siva has come in person, ask whatever boon you please." The king thought that since Siva had come himself, he would not ask for the capture of the thieves, but would ask to go to heaven, so he said, "My Lord, I wish to see heaven." The barber's son who was dressed like Siva replied, "How can any mortal go there? but still I have been very much pleased with your worship, therefore I will not refuse your request, catch hold of my bull's tail, and let the Sanyasi fasten your hands very carefully to it, for the bull will go very swiftly, and you must follow him." So the king consented, and the Sanyasi bound his hands firmly to the bull's tail, and told the king that whenever he felt any pain he must say "Bham, bham, I am going to heaven," and nothing else. With this the [illegible] Siva and the Sanyasi struck the bull, and started him off, and he took the king, and began to run through the woods, and the thorns tore the king's body, and caused him much pain, yet he did nothing but repeat, "bham, bham, I am going to heaven," and the bull continued to run faster and faster, and whenever any one asked the king how he had fallen into such a plight, he gave no answer but repeated the same words as before. So he suffered pain all that night, and in the morning his subjects recognized him, and unfastened the rope by which he was tied to the bull's tail, and took him home, and then he knew that he had been unjust to his servants, and therefore this misfortune had befallen him, for the thieves had come to his kingdom just as his servants had left it; so he thought it would be proper to search for them, inasmuch as he was now reaping the fruit of the unjust action which he had committed, and if he could find them he would hear their story, and give them justice. So the four friends came into the king's presence, and confessed that they were the thieves, and that they had acted thus because the king had driven them out without giving them justice. The king asked what injustice he had done, and the man who killed the snake told him all about it, he then ordered them to show him the snake's body, and they said they had buried it under the bed, so he had it dug up, and brought, and finding that their story was true, he asked them kindly who they were and their whole history. After they had told him everything he let them go free, so they returned to their own country, and spent their time in amusement as before.

(To be continued.)

REVIEW.

HINDU TRIBES AND CASTES as represented in Benares. By the Rev. M. A. SHERRING, M.A., LL.B. Calcutta, Bombay and London, 1872.

MR. SHERRING has already proved himself to be a careful inquirer into Hindu customs; and in his "Sacred City of the Hindus" he amassed much valuable information regarding the place of his residence, Benares. We welcome the present contribution from his pen on a subject of very great interest and no less complexity.

Mr. Sherring does not enter at any length into antiquarian discussions. His object is not to investigate the origin or history of the various divisions of Hinduism, but to describe them as he finds them now existing in the city of Benares. This limitation of range enables him to speak with the authority of an eye-witness of many, or most, of the facts which he brings forward; while, on the other hand, as representatives of nearly all the divisions of Hindus visit the sacred city, there is ample room and verge enough to include a very tolerable survey of the subject of Indian castes as they now are. Mr. Sherring writes in a very kindly spirit. His favourite motto seems to be *Homo sum; humani nihil a me alienum puto*. He speaks in terms of commendation of all that to a dispassionate mind can appear praiseworthy. Of the caste system as a whole, however, he has no admiration; on the contrary, it is his "intense conviction" that the absolute renunciation of caste would be an unspeakable blessing to India.

The work is divided into four parts, treating of 1st, the Brahmanical tribes; 2nd, the Kshatriya or Rajput tribes; 3rd, mixed castes and tribes; and 4th aboriginal tribes and inferior castes. Prefixed to the whole is an introduction which deals chiefly with the views of Manu regarding caste. To our mind this, which is the least original, is also the least valuable part of the book. The laws of Manu in their present form cannot be safely held to be older than the third century B. C. The Sanhita of the Rig Veda was probably collected a thousand years before that date, and how much earlier composed, it would be hard to say. Without discussing the very difficult question of the date at which the caste system was introduced, we cannot doubt that it was long before Manu's day; and the views of the legislator regarding its origin are amusing, and little more.

Mr. Sherring's tread is far firmer—like the Macgregor's on his native heath—when he comes in Chapter I to speak of the Brahman as he is. Here is a lively sketch of his physical appearance and character:—

"Light of complexion, his forehead ample, his countenance of striking significance, his lips thin, and mouth expressive, his eyes quick and sharp, his fingers long, his carriage noble and almost sublime, the true Brahman, uncontaminated by European influence and manners, with his intense self-consciousness, with the proud conviction of superiority depicted on every muscle of his face, and manifest in every movement of his body, is a wonderful specimen of humanity walking on God's earth...... Endowed with an extremely subtle rather than with a powerful mind, which by long habit perpetuated from age to age and from family to family, he has trained to the utmost keenness; dogmatic, self-willed, pertinacious, and supremely arrogant and vain."

Mr Sherring goes on to tell us that this remarkable being has lived his day, that his *prestige* is rapidly declining; and that the lower classes have availed themselves of European schools and colleges more than the highest have done. We accept the statement on his authority as true regarding Benares and the North-West Provinces; but it hardly holds good of Calcutta, and still less of such places as Poona, Nasik, and other cities in Maharashtra.

From the great mass of valuable information with which the author supplies us, we can only make an extract here and there. Here is his description of an important class of Brahmans with whom he has often been brought into contact, the *Gangaputras, or sons of the Ganges*:—

"The name is given to those Brahmans who preside over the religious ceremonies performed on the banks of the Ganges. At Benares their number is very large. The ghats, or stairs leading down to the river are apportioned out to them; and they watch over their several boundaries with much jealousy. Moreover, they lay claim to the entire bank between high and low water-mark, which is considerable, seeing that the difference is upwards of fifty feet. As a class, they are notorious for coarseness of manners, licentiousness and rapacity. Yet the tens of thousands who every year visit Benares are entirely at their mercy. Many of these come from remote parts of India, and not a few are females. Most of them arrive tired and worn out by travel, yet full of joy at the thought of having at length reached the sacred city. Unsuspectingly, they entrust themselves to the care of the Gangaputras, who with all their wickedness at home, have a reputation abroad for sanctity. These enfold them within their toils, fleece them of their money, and otherwise behave towards them in a shameless manner, while the poor pilgrims, being generally utter strangers, having no means of redress, patiently submit to maltreatment. It would be well if the Government authorities exercised control not only over the Gangaputras but also over all the priests of the temples in Benares, so as to ensure their good behaviour and the comfort of pilgrims and other worshippers."

Of the Marathi Brahmans, Mr. Sherring speaks thus—

"The Mahratta Brahmans are a very distinguished race among the Brahmanical tribes of India. For quickness of intellect, for energy, practical power, and learning, they are unsurpassed. In Benares itself, which is famous for its Pandits deeply read in Sanskrit literature, they are highly respected for their intelligence and knowledge. As a people they seem to possess, wherever they are found, those great mental gifts which formerly made the Mahrattas so formidable."

On the question why the Marathi Brahmans—particularly the Konkanasth division of them are so fair,—our author is opposed to the view adopted by Mr. Campbell, (Lieutenant Governor of Bengal,) in his work on Indian Ethnology—that they came by sea from the north and so have received less admixture of aboriginal blood. Mr. Sherring maintains that in the North-Western Provinces—

"The Brahman is quite as fair, and exhibits quite as strongly the physical characteristics of his race as the Mahratta Brahmans of the Konkan. He is occasionally as fair as the lightest

Kanojias half caste, and in his face the red blush is seen to come and go as in that of the Englishman. The remarks of Mr. Campbell would go to prove an almost tribal distinction between the Maharatas and all other Brahmans, consisting in a far greater purity of Brahmanical blood. I, suspect that these tribal distinctions among the Brahmans are in the main of a provincial character, and to be accounted for on geographical grounds rather than ethnological."

A very interesting question, this—and one which merits fuller investigation than it has yet received. For ourselves, we see no difficulty in believing that the Brahmans in, and near, the Panjab may have crossed the Indus, or, for that matter, the Sarasvati, which in Vaidik times was a copious river flowing either into the Indus or the ocean. We also doubt whether climatic differences will sufficiently explain the striking diversities of colour among Brahmans. Still we express no decided conviction; we are happy to hear Mr. Sherring's pleading, and in the meantime, we take the matter, as the Scotch judges say, *ad avizandum*.

We cannot follow Mr. Sherring into the endless ramifications of Brahmanism, which he sets down with wonderful minuteness. For example, he enumerates all the eighty-four divisions of Gujarâtî Brahmans; and fourteen of Maithila Brahmans, with names in numbers without number.

In Part II he speaks of the Rajputs in Benares. Including the district and province of that name, he finds twenty-nine Rajput tribes, and of all these an account is given longer or shorter account. All this we are compelled to pass over. As, however, Mr. Sherring is no dry-as-dust collector of [illegible], but a man who steadily views the past in its bearing on the present and the future, we must in justice quote some of his opinions on the condition-of-India question as affected by caste changes that have come already or are fast coming. First, however, let us hear what he thinks of the Rajputs' physique and morale.

"In ancient times the two functions of this race were ruling and fighting. Only one of these, the latter, still remains. A large proportion of the sepoys of the Indian army have ever been, and still are, Rajputs. The number, I imagine, has somewhat diminished since the mutiny. Yet this occupation is regarded by all classes as a legitimate and natural one for the members of this caste. The physique of the Rajputs, in the opinion of military men, peculiarly adapts them for the life of a soldier. He is generally tall and well made, with a good development of muscle, but with a smaller proportion of bone. He is of somewhat larger build than the Brahman, yet does not display in his countenance the Brahman's high intelligence and commanding dignity, nor has the Brahman's thinness of skin and delicacy of complexion."

Now as to their condition—

"Formerly, they could command armies or divisions and sub-divisions of armies, and were employed as rulers over provinces and districts, or else governed in their own right. Such occupations gave scope to their ambition, and an object on which their intelligence and energy might expend themselves. But all this has been changed. Not being employed now in such offices, or in any other of great material or social interest, life is to many of them without a purpose. The majority of the higher classes of course are satisfied with an existence of luxurious indolence; yet not all. They feel, however, that it is useless to be ambitious, for that there is nothing for them to do, and very little for them to gain. A few make themselves conspicuous by their liberality and public spirit, in laying out vast sums of money on colleges, schools, hospitals, asylums, and the like. Yet their secret personal ambition is mostly directed to very inferior objects. To secure a higher place in the Governor-General's Durbar, or more frequent salutes, or a greater number of guns at each salute, some will devote years of time, and lacs of rupees, and will engage in a course of intrigues of the most intricate character.

'This is pitiful, but by no means surprising. The truth is, that want of employment is the great bane of the aristocracy of India in the present day. It is not a healthy condition nor a safe and satisfactory one."

True and weighty words; although we think the shading is, just by a shade, too deep. All Rajputs did not rule; only princes and chiefs did so. Now, although "the pride, pomp, and circumstance of glorious war" have happily to a great extent passed away in India, and so one half of the Rajput chieftain's occupation is gone, what hinders him from continuing the other half, and with double diligence? He may find a noble sphere in governing his subjects; and if he governs them well, he will not be molested by the British authorities. Even were his powers reduced, which they are never likely to be, to the dimensions of those of an English nobleman, why could not the Rajput chief find, like the nobleman, honourable employment in managing his estates? It is true all this requires that he be educated and so fitted to bear his part in the improved régime of peace. Let the British Government look to that prime requisite.

So much for the chiefs. As for the mass of the Rajputs, they can beat their swords to ploughshares. They make bad traders, and would be driven out of the market by cunning Vaisyas; but they take kindly to agriculture. Let them go in for farming, it is no hardship, and no disgrace. "He who cultivates barley, cultivates purity," was said—or, at least, is said to have been said—by Zoroaster, the great and wise; and over India, so far as our experience goes, with the exception of Lower Bengal, the occupation of tillage is deemed perfectly honourable.

A question, however, of an interesting kind emerges here. If, in these halcyon days of peace the races in India that are by descent and profession fighting men, can find few fields in which to exercise and augment their hereditary valour, will they not gradually sink into a timorous herd quite unequal to stand, in the shock of arms, before the warlike races of the extra Indian North? If aught should once more precipitate these on the fertile plains of Hindustan, where is our security? Can we hold India with British bayonets alone, that is, can we supply them in sufficient numbers?

The other point. In Britain you pick up any lad at the corner of a street, say a shoemaker, or the ninth part of a man, a tailor; and in a few weeks or months you manufacture that very raw material into an erect, martial looking man, who meets the hurtling shot and shell as steadily as if he had been trained to it all his days. We apprehend you cannot do this with an Indian tailor or shoemaker. The question then is a very serious one—where are the fighting men to come from? who shall recruit our native army? But we are getting beyond our depth, and shall wisely return to civilian themes.

In Part III. Mr. Sherring treats of the mixed castes and tribes—Vaiśyas, Śudras, and others. He compares the position of these in the social scale to that of the middle classes in England. He has several pages of thoughtful writing as to the effects of our rule—slow, but certain as the action of gravitation—in depressing the sacerdotal class and the warlike nobility of the past, and in elevating a great body intermediate between them and the ignorant helpless masses. As we proceed with our educational scheme, we shall affect even the lowest. A stupendous revolution is thus in progress; and much wisdom is required to secure that it be quiet and successful. Probably none of us realizes the magnitude of the changes that are impending, or the dangers that accompany the transition period. Mr. Sherring says that "the wisdom of the course we have adopted has hardly yet been ever properly tested. The test will have to be applied on any occasion of great political disturbance in the country, involving the social status and dignity of the castes." Yet we doubt not Mr. Sherring would admit that it was imperative to move in the direction we have taken. There may be a question as to what the rate of progress ought to be,—whether it is better to walk or run; but it is impossible to go back—impossible to stand still. And after all, Europe has witnessed civil and religious revolutions on quite as vast a scale as any that we can witness here. The curtailment of the powers of the Mediæval Church—the abolition of the feudal system—the rise of free cities and the commercial classes generally—the emancipation of the serfs in Russia; what reforms in Indian society can surpass these revolutions in magnitude?

In Part IV. Mr. Sherring treats of the aboriginal tribes and inferior castes. The most interesting point which he has dwelt upon is the Bhar tribe—once of great importance in the regions around Allahabad and Benares. Mr. Thomason said of them: "The inhabitants were a powerful and industrious people as is evident from the large works they have left behind them." They seem to have been skilled in the arts both of peace and war. We are too ready to think of the races that preceded the Hindus in the possession of India as having been savages or semi-savages; yet even amidst all the passionate invectives of the Veda against them, we cannot glean from its pages such a notion of the Dasyus. Black-skinned they were, probably flat-nosed, and inferior in physical appearance to the worshippers of the "beautiful nosed" (*susipra*) Indra; but barbarians—at least in many cases—they certainly were not. We agree with Mr. Sherring—"I know not why we should be so ready always to ascribe to successive troops of Hindu immigrants all the ancient civilization of India. The more I investigate the matter, the stronger do my convictions become that the Hindu tribes have learned much from the aboriginal races."

We regret that we must stop. We part from Mr. Sherring with much respect for him as a painstaking, conscientious and intelligent investigator. His book is a repository of very important information; and the spirit in which it is written is very genial—friendly to all that is good—and worthy of a Christian minister. So far as the castes in Benares are concerned—and these are largely representative of India generally,—we do not know that this work leaves anything to be desired. J. M. M.

CORRESPONDENCE.

THE KHATTRIS.

To the Editor of the Indian Antiquary.

SIR,—Perhaps some of your readers may be able to throw some light on the origin of the caste of Khattris in Hindustan. I have attempted, whenever I have had the opportunity, to discover what I could from members of the caste themselves; but their accounts are various and conflicting. As it is highly desirable that we should know as much as we can about the history of Hindu castes, I am sure you will be ready to admit such a discussion to a place in your columns.

I will therefore briefly state what I have been able to discover on the subject, and ask your readers to aid in elucidating the matter as far as possible. The Khattris are divided into four sub-divisions, viz., the Panjâbî, the Lahori, the Dilliwâlî, and the Pûrbî, and these *four sorts* are separate from each other and have not the *jus connubii* or the custom of eating and drinking in common with each other. They deny being anything but pure Hindus and are reputed especially religious, worshipping the ordinary deities of Hindustan. There are no Saráogis (Shrâvaks) amongst them. They are without doubt immigrants into Hindustan at a comparatively late period. Their Purohits are invariably Sârsut (Sarasvati) Brahmans and they have the peculiar custom among them of the Purohit eating with his Jajmans (Yajamâns). If you ask them concerning their origin, nine out of ten will reply that they are the offspring of Rájputs: they generally say *Kshatri* Rájputs, and one account is that they are sons of a Rájput woman by a Sûdra father. I am not inclined to place any reliance on statements like this for the simple reason that every caste which cannot explain its origin, invariably invents the Kshatriya theory of paternity. A more detailed legend concerning their origin runs as follows:—When *Paras-Ráma* was exterminating the Kshatriyas, a pregnant girl escaped from the massacre and took refuge with a Sarsut Brahman. He gave her shelter, and when asked by the pursuers concerning her, replied that she was his cook (*Khatrâṇi* खत्री ?) and to prove it ate bread from her hand. The tradition is deserving of notice as attempting to explain the meaning of the name Khatri and the peculiar custom of the Purohit and Jajmans eating in common. But I do not think the internal evidence of truth is intrinsically worth much. My own opinion is, that this question of the origin of the Khatris is intimately connected with the, at present, unknown history of the arrival of the Jats in India. I mean that there will be found to exist some close analogy between the histories of the two races. The Khatris themselves allow that they have comparatively lately come westwards, and this is conclusively proved by the distribution of their sub-divisions. Ignorant village Jats (*Pachhâdi or Dhê*) have incidentally compared to me the history of the Khatris with their own, and the facts shewing that both races were very considerably influenced by the Musalman propaganda are numerous. Thus the *sehra*, not the *mor*, is used in marriages by both races; the Khatri women alone of Hindus wear shoes though this custom down east here is dying out and the only observance of it is in the sending of a pair of shoes among the wedding presents of the bride. The Khatris deny that they ever had the custom of *ekhâh khânâ* (viz., eating from vessels) or that their women ever wore *turki lopas*; while the Pachhâdi Jats still openly practise both customs at marriage feasts. The connexion of the Khatris with the great reformer Nânak Shâh is curious: their own account is that Nânak Shâh was a Khatri who attempted to reconcile Hinduism and Islam together, and to this day travelling Nânakshahi fakirs are much respected and well taken of in all Khatri households. It is stated in the Ajâib-i-Makhlûkât that the successor of Nânak Shâh was a Khatri disciple named *Lahna*.

The question of the origin of the Tagas—another subject of controversy—is connected again without doubt with the history of the Khatris. Sir Henry Elliot gives a quotation from the *Mirat-i-Sikandari* in his Supplementary Glossary, page 109, which states that the Tagas were expelled from their caste by the Khatris for drinking. The Tagas ridicule the theory, but the tradition is still held by the Khatris. I hope that some of your Panjâbi correspondents will be able to illustrate these points of difficulty with facts which have come under their own notice.

The *Koh-i-Nûr* (vernacular journal) of 15th June 1872 has a classification of Khatri sects, I believe, but I have not been able to examine it.

Futtehpur, N.W.P. J. White,

6th August, 1872. Assistant Collector.

Query 10, Concerning Chaturanga.

In my paper on Chaturanga, I have identified (p. 61) the 'Radhacant' on whose information the treatise of Sir W. Jones *On the Indian Game of Chess*, in the *As. Res.* vol. II pp. 159-165, is based, with Radhakanta Deva, the author of the *Sabdakalpadruma*. But after more mature consideration, I have become more than doubtful of the correctness of this identification, or, I should rather say, I am convinced already of its impropriety.

As Sir W. Jones speaks of his Radhacant as "my friend" (p. 161), acknowledges that the passage "was copied for me by Radhacant and explained by him" (p. 163), and says that, "Radhacant and his preceptor Jagannâth are both employed by Government in compiling a digest of Indian laws (p. 165),—we are led to assume, that this Radhacant was already a young man of distinction when the paper was written (about 1790). Now Râja Râdhâkânta Deva died on the 19th of April 1867. To have been the same person with the friend of Sir W. Jones, he ought to have been more than a hundred years old at the time of his death; but we have the distinct statement in the preface to the Parisishṭa-vol. of his *Sabdakalpadruma* that he was born Śaka 1706 i. e. A. D. 1785 ([illegible] Śake bhûpateḥ | [illegible] mahîpateḥ | *Srîrâdhâkânta* [illegible] putro 'bhyajâyata). And H. H. Wilson, in the preface to his *Sanskrit Dictionary* (1819), speaks of the author of the *Sabdakalpadruma* as "a young gentleman of fortune and family"—words which might well apply to a man of 35 years, but not to one who was the "friend" of Sir W. Jones (ob. 1794).

But now the question remains,—who was *the* Radhacant of Sir William? are there any other traces of his literary achievements? They ought not to have been small after what Sir William says of his accomplishments.

I take this occasion to express beforehand my deep obligations to any one who may be able to point out:—

1. The passage in "an ancient treatise of Law," in which Colebrooke (*Asiat. Res* vol. vii. p. 204) found mentioned,—"the elephant, horse, and *chariot* as pieces of the game of Chaturanga";

2. The very passage on Chaturanga given in Raghunandana's *Tithitattva* (ed. Serampore, I. 88, 89), and stated by the Radhacant of Sir W. Jones to be a part of the Bhavishya Purâṇa;" or

3. Any other passage on Chaturangakrîḍâ on the occasion of the Kojâgara of the Kaumudî festival, or at any other festivity.

Berlin, 4th July 1872. A. Weber.

STONE MONUMENTS IN THE DISTRICT OF SINGHBHUM—CHOTÁ NÁGPUR.

BY V. BALL, B. A., GEOLOGICAL SURVEY OF INDIA.

IN Mr. Fergusson's *Rude Stone Monuments* there is no allusion to the practice of certain of the Chotá Nágpur Kols to erect monuments to their deceased friends. It would appear that the brief accounts of the custom hitherto published have escaped notice.

Referring to the geographical distribution of Dolmens, Mr. Fergusson has written—"They do not exist in the valley of the Ganges or any of its tributaries." This is not strictly accurate, as the tributaries of the Ganges which drain Chota Nagpur* pass through a country in parts of which both ancient and modern Dolmens or tables, and Menhirs abound.

The following notes and accompanying sketches were made a few years ago in the district of Singhbhum. The facts described will, I trust, prove sufficient to draw attention to the rude stone monuments of that district.

The Chota Nagpur division, as is well known to those interested in Indian Ethnology, is the present home of numerous aboriginal races, nearly, if not quite all of which have been assigned by Col. Dalton to positions under the two great family groups of Kols, known as Mundas and Uráons.

Various customs with regard to the final disposal of the dead are practised by these different races; but it is with Múndás, and among them a particular race only—the Hos, that we have to do at present.

The Hos with a few exceptions are now to be found only in a portion of Singhbhum known as the Kolehan, or Hodesum as it was called by Col. Tickell. There they live shut out from all Aryan influences, observing a most rigid conservatism with regard to the traditional customs of their race. Notable among these customs, as being one that must force itself on the attention of any traveller in the district, is the erection of stone tablets and slabs (Menhirs and Dolmens) over the graves and to the memory of the deceased. Although it is only in the Kolehan that these monuments are erected at the present day, they are to be found scattered throughout Chota Nagpur and to some extent in the Orissa tributary mehals; in some cases in localities upwards of one hundred miles distant from the Kolehan, and which, according to Col. Dalton, cannot have been inhabited by the Hos for centuries.

There are few parts of the Kolehan, where an extensive view of several villages can be obtained, which do not include several groups of upright monumental stones. These groups may include any number, from a single stone upwards, and there is no restriction to odd numbers, as is said to be the case in the Khasia Hills.

The stones selected for erection are generally more or less rectangular or cylindrical in form, but sometimes they are of very fantastic shapes. These latter, however, it is important to observe, are not due to either freak or design upon the part of the people. They are the natural forms of the flags which they assume in their exposed positions in the rivers. Beyond being prised from the beds by means of crowbars, they are not, as a rule, touched with any tools. I have often come across the spots in the river sections whence stones for this purpose and also larger ones intended for dolmens or tables had been raised. The geological formation in the Kolehan consists partly of slates and schists, which supply an abundance of flags suited to the purpose. When these rocks contain an appreciable quantity of carbonate of lime, the chemical action of the water produces honey-combed surfaces and more or less irregular outlines.

In portions of the country not now occupied by the Hos, where the rocks are granitic, and flag-like masses of rock can seldom be obtained, the ancient monuments are more massive in shape and of smaller size. I cannot help thinking that the geological formation may have had something to do in determining the selection of the Kolehan as the final resting place of the race.

The rivers, where the stones are raised, are not unfrequently several miles distant from the villages near which the Menhirs and Dolmens are erected. The transport of the stones is effected in the following manner. Partly according to the estimation in which the deceased was held, partly according to the amount of refreshments—chiefly rice-beer—which the surviving members of the deceased's family are prepared to stand, a greater or less number of men assemble and proceed to the spot where the stone

* The Damúdá and Kosái, &c. which join the Húgli. The Subanrikha pursues an independent course to the sea.

is to be raised. If the flag selected is not very heavy, it is placed on a wooden framework, and so carried on the shoulders of the men to its destination. When however the stone is of large size, it is placed on a kind of truck with enormously massive wheels, specially constructed for the purpose. Sometimes it is necessary to make a road for the passage of such a truck; at others the number of men pushing and pulling with ropes is sufficient to carry it over all the obstacles which are encountered on the way.

No. I.

Group of Cenotaph stones or Menhirs, at a village near Chaibassa, in Singhbhum.

The history of the group of stones figured in sketch No. 1 is as follows: The stone on the left was erected to the memory of Kundapather, Munki, or local head of the village of Pukaria, a few miles south of the station of Chaibassa. The next two stones were erected to Kowali and Sumari, daughters, and the fourth to a son of Pasingh, the present Munki. This was in 1869, since that time others may have been added; possibly Pasingh himself, having lost father, wife and children, has also died.

For some reason there is no memorial stone here to Pasingh's wife Seni. I rather think however, there was one standing by itself somewhat nearer the village. But in the centre of the village, under the shade of some glorious old tamarind trees, a stone, conspicuous among many others from its uncommon size, covers her remains, and affords practical evidence that respect for her memory was not wanting. Its dimensions are 17 feet 2 inches × 9 feet 2 inches × 10 inches.

No. II.

Menhirs—Cenotaph stones, Singhbhum.

The second sketch represents a group of stones situated in a plain a few miles to the south-west of the other. Of its history I do not know the particulars.

The groups of Menhirs which occur scattered throughout the Kolehan are, so far as my observation went, in no way limited as to the number of stones. I have counted as many as 30 stones in one group, and my impression is that I have seen more than that number. A circular arrangement is seldom seen, generally the stones are either ranged along a straight line or an arc.

Only one instance can I remember of seeing in Chuta Nagpur any attempt at sculpture on stone monuments; this was in the district of Hazaribagh. The stones had the appearance of great antiquity and, whether rightly or wrongly, they were attributed by the people of the neighbourhood to an ancient settlement of Kols.

Though not rich in ancient temples or other Hindu remains—as compared with some other parts of India—the Chuta Nagpur division with its stone monuments of the aborigines and its cave temples, mines,* and other traces of the early Jains is for the Antiquarian, as it is well known to be for the Ethnologist, a noble field for research.

NOTES ON THE RASAKALLOLA, AN ANCIENT ORIYA POEM.

By JOHN BEAMES, B.C.S., M.R.A.S., &c., BALASOR.

No. II.—Continued from p. 217.

A noticeable feature in this poem is the readiness with which the poet's native language bends itself to the metres which he employs. Consequently there are very few of those arbitrary lengthenings and shortenings of vowels, elisions of case and tense-endings which in the oldest Hindi and Gujarati poems so much obscure the real language of the period. In reading

* See "on the ancient copper mines of Singhbhum,"—Proc. As. Soc. Beng. for June 1869.

the latter class of poems we are never sure that we are being presented with a real living picture of the language as it was actually spoken by the contemporaries of the author; we have to allow for so many licenses of form and construction that it is only by observing the shape taken by a particular word, in places where no metri causa occurs to change it, that we can feel even tolerably certain that we have at length lit upon its genuine colloquial guise. No such difficulty confronts us in Dinkrishna's flowing and facile verse. If we except an occasional diaeresis such as [illegible] for [illegible], [illegible] for [illegible] and a few other easily recognized licenses, the language is the same as that in which the gentle and refined Oriya clodhopper of to-day fondly curses his wife or his bullocks, or grumbles over his daily pill of adulterated opium.

In the third canto the Gopis hear that a son has been born to Nand and rush tumultuously to Nand's house to see the infant. Here occurs one of those absurd pieces of exaggeration which so frequently, to European taste, spoil the beauty of Indian poems. The Hindu never knows when to stop. Starting from the generally accepted opinion that the female form is most symmetrical and beautiful when the waist is slender and the parts immediately below it large and round, the poet proceeds to make the waists of the Gopis so absurdly thin and their continuations so enormously large that they become, instead of the ideals of loveliness he intends them to be, monsters of deformity. One charming creature who appears to have combined in her own person every possible disproportion, is thus addressed by the girdle round her waist—

Kâhâ katire ḍâki kânchi mâlâ
Kahu achhi, "dhire are abalâ!
Kâma mada re hoï matta, bholâ
Karu majhâ thâre jâ ere holâ,
Ki! tu jâna nâhiṅ e jeṇe saru
Kucha jugala tora jeṇe garu?
Karu achhu jâhâ druṭha gamana
Kâle chhâku hoi achhi âmana.
Ki to sâhasa jâyâjiba prâye,
Ki bâ ehâ thâre eṇe nirdaye?
Ki ki hoi e jebe jiba bhangi?
Kâle tu hi maribu ehâ lâgi.

From the waist of one the girdle calling
Says, "gently, gently, O maiden!
Thou, intoxicated with the wine of love,
Forgettest thy waist of what sort it is.
What! knowest thou not how slender it is
And thy twin breasts how heavy?
The swift pace which thou maintainest
Shortly will be its destruction.
What, is thy boldness like the spider's,
Or why on this (the waist) art thou so pitiless?
What will happen when it shall break?
At that time thou too wilt die."

The poet seems rather proud of this tasteless trifling for he specially remarks that this is to be regarded as a metaphor, and is elegant and fanciful (âtiśayâkâra).

The Gopis crowd round the two infants, and examine them with every mark of delight. The sun, the moon, night, lotuses, the sea, and all sorts of plants and animals are called into comparison, and are pronounced inadequate to rival the beauty of Krishṇa's black skin, or Balarâma's white one. The Gopis then go home looking back and lingering and loth to depart, and the canto ends.

The metre of the second canto, which I omitted to describe before, consists of four lines to the pada or stanza. The first and third are very long consisting of 29 mâtras each. There are cæsuras at the eighth and sixteenth mâtras, the syllables of which generally rhyme with each other. The last syllable of the first line rhymes with that of the second. Owing to the great length of the lines it is customary to write the first sixteen mâtras as one line and the remaining thirteen as a second line. The third line has nine mâtras with cæsura at the fourth, and the fourth line thirteen with cæsura at the eighth mâtra; thus:

1. ka | ra | â | ha | ra | dhu | ja | na[illegible] | ne |
na | na | e | ka | ti | na |
ka[illegible] | na | de | i | ku | ma | la | na | ya |
na | ka | thâ | kuḷ
2. The same.
3. ka | la | ka | rañja | dhâ | ra | pra | paḷ
4. Krish | ṇa | ka | thâ | âra | va | na | ra |
du | ri | ta | kha | pa |.

The rhyme-syllables are in italics.

The metre of the third canto is very simple. It is the *Rág kedár chakrakeli*, and consists of two charans to the pada, each containing nine mâtras with no cæsura. The charans rhyme.

The fourth canto is in the Ahâri metre with 12 mâtras to the charan and two rhyming charans to the pada. There is a cæsura at the sixth mâtra. Thus—

ka | na | de | i | âs | na | â | ha | [illegible] | ja | na.
ka | mâ | ran | ka | jan | mi | la | ke[illegible] | di | na.

It relates how Krishṇa in his cradle destroyed

various demons sent against him by Kans. In the description of the Nâg Putanâ, who turned herself into a beautiful female, we see what sort of dress and adornment was considered *chic* in Dinkrishna's time; for this reason it is worth quoting,—

Kalâ kutila kuntale khosâ khosi,
Kamaniya phula mâlâ achhi misi;
Kapâlare sindûra marujala chitâ,
Katâkshare mohu achhi ardhi areta;
Karne tâmkha, bhramari, phula sohe;
Kanthe kantha-âbharana mana mohe;
Kari tâmbûla-bolare ochtha ranga,
Karu achhi purushanka dhairja bhanga;
Kanthi nâsa-âbharana nâsâ pute,
Kajrale paripurita netra-tate;
Katane suri jâe jâi achhi lâgi,
Kâmi dekhile hele kâma ganji;
Kare tara, chuti, kanâli râje;
Kwaun-kwaun pâinjâ padare bâje;
Kantha-tale jhuntia-mâle bândhi
Kalâ-megha sâdhi eka achhi pindhi.

Her black wavy hair knotting in a knot
A garland of lovely flowers she has mingled in it;
On her brow a round mark of vermilion;*
With her glance she is ravishing Shiva;
In her ear the *tâmkha*,† *bhramari*,‡ and flowers shine;
On her neck the necklace fascinates the mind;
Dyeing her lip with betelnut juice;
She is breaking down the composure of men;
In her nostril the *nolakh*§ and nose-jewel;
The lampblack completely surrounds her eye,
The streak of it extends as far as her ear,‖
Amorous men seeing it would go mad with love;
On her hand shines the *târa*,¶ bracelet, and armlet;
"Twang twang" sounds the anklet on her foot;
On the pit of her neck she has bound a *jhuntia**;
A dark-blue *sâdhi* she has put on.

It will be seen that then, as now, the wearing of gewgaws and ornaments was highly popular. In spite of all the profusion of jewellery, however, the lady's dress consists of nothing but a *sâdhi*.

The *sâdhi* is a broad and long cloth wound tightly round the waist in such a way as to expose the right leg half way up the thigh, the end is then brought round over the head. In the present instance, however, it must have been worn only over the shoulders as we have the head decorated with flowers. The wearing of the *sâdhi* over the shoulders only is customary among the non-Aryan hill-tribes to this day, and may possibly have been the custom among the Aryan population also in former times. It is so worn also by the Telingas. As the connection of the Uriyas, until recent times, was greater with their neighbours to the south than it was with those on the north, we may suppose that the habit of wearing the *sâdhi* on the head is of late introduction from Bengal.

The fifth canto relates the childish sports of Krishna, and is itself very childish and tedious. Krishna seems to have spent his time principally in stealing and devouring curds, cream, and butter, of which articles his diet appears to have chiefly consisted. He also makes jokes with the *Gopis*, and indulges in *double entendres* of a very unpalatable character. The sixth canto continues the same subject *ad nauseam*.

One or two passages a little more sensible than the rest may be quoted. Here is a description of Krishna's roguishness:

Kandhâi hasâe kete kânde;
Kanuri châhânte se nayana kone,
Kilakila bhâbaku badhâi,
Kahun kahun anubhâbaka pâi.
Kâlita nandana âgare jâta,
Kahun sikhilâ e ete charita?
Ke bole dine se kahili dhire,
Kâhâki gola hara gopapure?
Kiyâ se panchu hâje na hara?
Kete khâila dadhi, dudha, sara.
Krushna tumi bole kaî
Kete phal to dudha achhi misi;
(Gopî *Ingitam*).

Having made me cry he makes me laugh for nothing.
How he looks out of the corner of his eye!
He increases one's playful disposition,
From time to time meeting answering glances.
Only yesterday he was born in our presence,
Whence has he learnt such conduct?

* The vermilion on the forehead denotes a married woman, but is now generally smeared as a great patch across the parting of the hair.

† तांवकु is a small earring worn in the outer edge of the ear; sometimes eight or ten of them are worn one below another all round the ear.

‡ भ्रमरी a large earring hanging from the lobe of the ear, so called from its resemblance to a bee (भ्रमर).

§ नोळखि worn suspended to the cartilage between the nostrils, the other kind is worn on the side of the nose.

‖ This is considered a great beauty.

¶ These are various kinds of rings and bracelets.

* झुंटिआ small ornament shaped like a flower and usually enamelled in various colours.

One says "one day I said softly,—
'Why do you make such a disturbance in Gop?
Why do you not honour my house with a visit?
How much curds, milk, and cream you shall eat.'"
Kanhá hearing said laughing,
"How much water has been mixed in your milk?"

This last line is a *double entendre* whose second meaning may be left to be guessed.

A second passage represents the Gopis as indignant with Nand for sending Krishna to tend the cattle.—

Kena sukha nahin Nanda ghare, ehi
putra jáe brindábana ke ;
Karuṇa hridaye nahanti nirdaya,
dhika ehánkara dhanaku !
Kena bidhátá kalá emanta abichára
Koti lakshmí jáhá sebáku bánchhanti
Se bane banaku sanchára,

What happiness is there not in Nand's house,
Yet this boy goes to the wilderness ;
They are not merciful in heart, but pitiless ;
Fie on their wealth !
What god has made this mistake ;
He whom a myriad Lakshmis desire to worship
Tramps about the forest.

The metre is that of the Ráy Kesari containing four lines to the stanza. The first two lines consist of twenty-one instants each with cæsuras at the sixth, twelfth and eighteenth instants, the first two of which rhyme. The third line is of fourteen instants with a single cæsura at the fifth ; the fourth line is the same as the two first except that the cæsuras do not always rhyme.

In the matter of grammatical peculiarities it is noticeable that Dinkrishna uses frequently the old plural in *e* as *kumára*, a boy ; pl. *kumáre*. This is very seldom heard in modern Oriya, and never in the classical style. An old-fashioned peasant from the interior of the country may now and then use it. In the modern language the analytically formed plural by the addition of *mane* is always used as *rájá*, pl. *rájámane*,—kings ; in inanimate objects, however, the final *e* of the termination is dropped, as *kántha*, wall, *kánthamána*, walls.

There occurs also the old universal Aryan locative in *e* as *gope*, in Gop ; *pure*, in the town. The moderns affix *re* and would say *gopa-re* instead of *gope* ; the affix *re* is already in use, as are also *ku*, *ru*, and the *ar* or *ara* of the genitive in this poem.

With regard to the short final *a*, it must be remembered that it is necessary to express it in writing poetry for the sake of preserving the rhythm, but that in common conversation it is hardly ever heard, and when heard is a short ŏ.

Dinkrishna knows only the old forms of the personal pronouns which our high-flying modern writers condemn as vulgar. These are—

	I	*thou*
Nom.	mui	tu
Acc.	[illegible]	[illegible]
Gen.	mor	tor
	&c.	&c.

The plural of *mu* is *ámbhe* (pronounced *ámbhe*) and that of *tu* is *tumbhe* (*tumbhe*) but as the learned have taken *ámbhe* and *tumbhe* into use as equivalents for I and thou, they have had to make fresh plurals *ámbhemáne*, and *tumbhemáne*. Dinkrishna uses only the two first, and always in their proper ancient signification.

(*To be continued*)

THE CAVES OF THE BRAZEN GLEN AND OTHER REMAINS ABOUT MAUJE PÁTNA, TALUKA CHALISGAUM.

BY W. F. SINCLAIR, ASSISTANT COLLECTOR IN CHARGE KHANDESH FORESTS.

About ten miles south-west of the Chalisgaum Station of the Great Indian Peninsula Railway (N. E. extension) the Sátmála Hills open into a curious valley, included in the limits of the deserted village of Pátna.

The nearest camping-place is at the village of Warthán, 8 miles on the way, but it is a poor little place, and any visitor who had not bespoken the assistance of the district authorities 10 or 12 days before, would get nothing in it. Two miles from Warthán is the gateway of the valley, flanked on the left by steep rocks passable only by a single foot path, called the Gai Ghát, and on the right by the old hill fort of Kanhár. In the sides of the latter are four caves which I have not had time to examine closely, but I believe them to be all viháras, and of the sort having stone lotus-headed pillars. They are called by the natives the houses of Nâg Arjuna, his wife Dûrpada, and his son Abhimân, and the fourth the Singhâl Chauri,—names not unsuggestive. For although Dûrpada (*Draupadi*) and Abhimân belong to Arjuna the Pândava, I have never heard that hero called Nâg Arjuna elsewhere. But Nâgârjuna is the name of a Buddhist author of some repute, and I believe common among that sect. The name "Singhal Chauri" too, seems to point to a connection with Ceylon. There are, I believe, other caves on the top of the fort and beyond it, but of more doubtful character.

Immediately below the fort are the remains of the village of Pâtna, the more recent of which indicate a place of about 300 houses; but much older mounds, enclosing a large area, show that in times before the population first dwindled and then disappeared altogether, there must have been a considerable town here, which is not to be wondered at, considering the water supply, the security of the place, and its position, on what was one of the chief passes of the Sâtmala Hills. Near the village is a small temple of Bhawânî, supposed to be very old. It contains some of the most obscene sculptures in Western India, which appear to me to indicate a more recent date. Above the village is the wider valley called the Bhawânî Khorâ, and half a mile up it is a very ancient temple of the goddess, said to have been built either by a Râkshasa or by Hemâd Panth, who is as misty an architect here as elsewhere. The legend of the place is that the goddess, usually called here "*Âi*," was shikaring the *Daityas* (Râkshasas) in these parts, shortly after she slew the buffalo devil further south. She "flushed" a Daitya in the precipices above the Ucl Ghât, (which we passed on our left in entering the valley), and hunted him round the cliffs till they came to a ravine called the Gaon Dhara, where the poor Daitya, being hard pressed, dived into the solid rock, and burrowed to a fabulous depth, as easily as a mole in an English tulip-bed. However, the goddess was not to be easily beat, and she got him out somehow, and finished him with her trident. In honour of which event Hemâd Panth built the little temple in the valley and devout Hindus make pilgrimage there twice a year, and present iron trisulas to the goddess, some of them as big as cart axles, and nail horse-shoes to her door, a practice curiously analogous to our Western custom of nailing them to stable-doors and boats' sterns. The Hole which the *Daitya* made is shown to this day, and is neither more nor less, to my thinking, than the remains of a ruined Chaitya cave. There is a long inscription on the west face of the temple which the Pandit whom I sent to copy it failed to decypher,* and the stone is too much covered with oil and other beastliness for rubbing off.

Above the temple the main valley of Bhawânî Khorâ splits into several lesser glens. The most westerly terminates in a fine waterfall and pool somewhat like that in *Lenapur* of Ajanṭâ. The next is a pass, of which I forget the name, and the third is a long deep glen, containing nothing but a teak and bamboo plantation, which the visitor had just as well keep out of. The remains of several ruined caves appear in the face of the cliff between this and the next ravine, the Gaonda Ghât, up which there is a pass to the Dakhan formerly of considerable importance; above it is the *Unarda Tîrth* a curious underground cistern, possibly as old as the caves. The fifth is the Gaon Dhara, or village glen, before referred to; and the sixth is the Pital Khorâ or Brazen Glen, the stream of which falls over an impassable cliff, a little behind the temple of Âi Bhawânî. There is however a pass over a spur between these two last, by steps cut in the rock, which, although they were perhaps not actually cut by the Buddhist monks, appear to me to be the successors of an earlier stairway probably of their making. This ladder is called the Sâtpâyarî Ghât or pass of seven steps, but there are really about eighteen.

Having got to the top of this very steep and tiresome but not dangerous pass, we go up the Pital Khorâ for about a mile to where the ravine opens out a little, below a waterfall under and to the right of which are the caves. The first cave is a vihara, cut right under the fall (in flood) and of considerable size, but not otherwise remarkable. The next called the Rang Mahâl is a Chaitya about the size of the Chaityas at Ajanṭâ. The roof has been supported by timber horse-shoe rafters, long gone, and two rows of polygonal pillars without capitals, separate the nave from the side-aisles.

* Dr. Bhau Dâji found an inscription here recording a grant of certain privileges to a College established by Changadeva, the son of Lakshmîdhara, the son of the celebrated Bhâskarâchârya. The donor was Sonhadeva, a chief subordinate to Râja Singhana, and the grant is dated Śaka 1128, A.D. 1206. A transcription and translation are given by Dr. Bhau: see *Jour. R. As. Soc. N. S.* Vol. I. pp. 414, 416, 418.—Ed.

These pillars are partly hewn *in situ*, and partly built up of separate pieces, and on their plastered surface and that of the side walls are several paintings of Buddha, either seated or standing, always supported by the lotus, crowned with an aureole, and overshadowed by a triple umbrella. The colours are brighter than any now at Ajaṇṭâ. I could find no inscriptions but some scratches on the plaster, which I do not believe to be ancient, and some daring red paint letters recording the visit of Dr. Bhau Daji and Mr. Somebody (Jardi) of Dhoolia. The next cave is a vihara and very curious. The cells are divided by pilasters having each a capital something like a wool sack or a ship's rope fender, carved in so intricate a pattern that at first I mistook them for inscriptions. Above this capital each pilaster has a separate pair of animals. The first are humped bulls, the second winged griffins, the third winged dogs, the fourth winged horses, the fifth winged antelopes, the sixth elephants and the seventh winged tigers. There are one or two more, destroyed and unrecognizable.

In the large Chaitya I had in vain tried to persuade my Bhil guard that the caves were built by men like themselves, which they stoutly declared to be impossible, disputing among themselves whether the five Pândus or the Daityas could have done it. However in this vihâra they held a fresh palaver on the subject, and finally the naik came forward and said that after all they thought the saheb was right. "For these cells were obviously made to sleep in, like those in the lock-up, and no man will presume to say that the Daityas and the Pândavas could squeeze themselves into such holes as these." Next to this cave is another vihâra the entrance to which is blocked up, but after ascertaining that there was no wild beast inside, I crept in through a breach in the wall of the sculptured vihara, my men following. However this, and two more beyond it, are similar in character to the first cave under the fall.

These caves must have had a fine façade, and probably there were one or two small ones above, approached by passages the remains of which still exist, but the whole front of the cliff has come down in a common mass of ruins, destroying the upper caves, and blocking up the lower ones.

I heard of an inscription near here, but was unable to find it. I believe these caves were in former days reported on by Mr. Rose, C.S., a copy of whose report is given in Dr. J. Wilson's "Second Memoir on the Cave Temples" in the *Bombay Asiatic Society's Journal* (vol. IV. p. 357-359). They have been visited by Dr. Bhau Daji, but that learned Orientalist has not, I think, published the result of his researches. The local legend of Bhawâni hunting the Daityas into the rock points, I think, to a Brahmanical raid upon the Buddhists, and it may be noted that the Dim Ghât is the only pass by which a force from the plain could turn the flank of the whole group of caves and block up all avenues of escape, without being easily perceived.

The whole Sâtmâla range is full of promise for the archæologist. Two years ago Mr. Campbell, C.S., discovered a new group in the old fort of Wasgarh, which I believe Major Gill has further explored, and Mr. Pottinger, C.E., found what I believe to be a large vihâra near the Gotala Ghât. Caution, however, and a double gun loaded with ball are necessary in all these places. In one cave in the Pital Khora I found fresh traces of a panther, and in the next some gnawed bones that told their own story.

THE DATE OF THE NYÂYAKUSUMÂNJALI.

By KASHINATH TRIMBAK TELANG, SENIOR DAKSHINA FELLOW, ELPHINSTONE COLLEGE.

In the preface to his edition of the Nyâyakusumânjali, Professor E. B. Cowell has endeavoured to fix the age of Udayanâchârya, the author of that work. The result of his reasoning he thus states:—"Perhaps, therefore," he says, "we may without fear of much error fix Vâchaspati Miśra in the tenth and Udayanâchârya in the twelfth century." This conclusion, Prof. Cowell bases on the fact, that while on the one hand Udayanâchârya is mentioned with expressions of high respect by Mâdhavâchârya, he has, on the other, commented on a work of Vâchaspati Miśra, who is himself one of the commentators of the great Śankarâchârya. Now as the dates of Śankarâchârya and Mâdhavâchârya may be taken with tolerable safety to be respectively in the eighth and fourteenth centuries of the Christian era, we have, according to Prof. Cowell, "a *terminus a quo* as well as a *terminus ad quem* to limit our chronological uncertainty."* And the Professor then divides the interval between the two *termini* as stated above.

Now we think that, plausible as this reasoning appears, there is a flaw in it. What proof have we that the Udayana who has commented on Váchaspati Misra is the same with the Udayana who wrote the Kusumánjali? Independently of any light which may be thrown upon this question by other considerations, the fact itself cannot be assumed as beyond controversy. On the contrary, we think there is positive evidence calculated to upset such a conclusion, and we propose here to set forth that evidence.

In the introduction to his edition of Váchaspati Misra's Sánkhyatattvakaumudi, Professor Táránáth Tarkaváchaspati of Calcutta mentions that Váchaspati Misra has written a work in answer to the Khandanakhandakhádya of Śri Harsha, entitled Khandanoddhára.† We do not know from whence this information is derived: it may be from the enumeration of his own works said to be given by Váchaspati Misra in his Bhámatínibandha, to which we have not access, and the Khandanoddhára has no place in the list reproduced by Dr. Hall.‡ If, therefore, Dr. Hall's list omits nothing that is in the list as given in the Bhámati, and if that list includes all the works written by Váchaspati Misra, the statement made by Prof. Táránáth ceases to have any weight. We find it difficult, however, to understand how the statement could have been made without some sufficient authority, and if there is such authority, it is possible that the Khandanoddhára, if Váchaspati Misra really wrote it, was written after the Bhámati had been finished. It is unfortunate that Prof. Táránáth has not given the authority for his statement; for reasoning in the absence of such authority must be merely hypothetical.

Now if we adopt Prof. Táránáth's statement, the results we arrive at deprive Prof. Cowell's arguments of all weight. The series of authors appears to stand thus:—1st Udayana; 2nd Śri Harsha; 3rd Váchaspati Misra. This clearly appears to result from the following words of the author of the Khandana. "Therefore," says he, "in this matter, it is not impossible for us to adopt your own verses with only some letters altered." And he then proceeds as follows:

"Vyágháto yadi śankásti, na chechchhanká tatastarám.
Vyághátávadhiráśanká tarkaśankávadhih kutah."

Now these verses are distinctly and expressly a parody of the verses in the Kusumánjali,—

"Sankáchedanumástyeva na chechchhanká tatastarám.
Vyághátávadhiráśanká tarkaśankávadhirmatah."§

We have thus (1) Udayana's Kusumánjali; (2) Śri Harsha's Khandana which quotes it; and (3) Váchaspati Misra's Khandanoddhára, which is an answer to (2).

Now it will be observed that this series reverses the chronological relations of Udayana and Váchaspati as laid down by Prof. Cowell. And this leads to the further result that Prof. Cowell's *terminus a quo* is lost, whatever may be said of the *terminus ad quem*; for if Váchaspati comes after Udayana, we have no link to connect Udayana and Sankara.

If, then, Prof. Cowell's argument must be given up, the question arises—What can we substitute for it? The age of Báṇa's Harsha, as fixed by Dr. Hall, will not help us in this matter; for while Báṇa's Harsha is a royal personage,‖ the Harsha of the Khandana is a mere dependant of a king of Kányakubja. And in this case, the supposition that some writer at the king's court gave to his work the king's name is also negatived by the fact that Śri Harsha is stated at the close of the Khandana to be the name of the author himself—who is further described as a "kavi."¶ One hint, however, we get from Dr. Hall's catalogue. At page 26, we find a work noted, which is there said to have been composed in 1252, and which quotes or mentions Udayana. Who this Udayana is, however, does not appear from Dr. Hall's note. A further circumstance, which will throw some light on this matter, and which is less open to question, is to be found in Dr. Hall's preface to the Vásavadattá. We there learn, that the Naishadhiya is quoted in the Sarasvatíkanthábharaṇa—which work, according to Dr. Hall,

* Kusumanjali, pp 9 & 10.

† Vide Introduction, p. 3.

‡ p. 67 of Dr. Hall's catalogue. Dr. Hall's language implies that his list omits nothing that is in the list in the Bhámati.

§ See the Khandana (Calc. edition), p 91, and the Kusumánjali, p. 22.

‖ Vásavadattá, Pref. p 17.

¶ Khandana, 152.

"is unquestionably more ancient than the Harsha of Kâshmir."* Now the author of the Naishadhîya is the same with the author of the Khandana,† and the Harsha of Kashmir reigned from 1113 to 1125.‡ The Kusumâñjali, at the latest then, cannot be later than the eleventh century, and may go back into the tenth or even an earlier period. And this conclusion we arrive at, be it remembered, independently of the circumstance about Vâchaspati's having answered Śrî Harsha, the authority for which is at present unknown to us.

If we take Vâchaspati Miśra as coming after Śrî Harsha, the results seem to point towards the same date. Vâchaspati is quoted in the Sarvadarśanasangraha of Mâdhavâchârya, as an authority on the Sânkhya philosophy,§ and allowing a sufficient interval between these two writers—Udayana, at the latest, might come in the eleventh century. Furthermore, we find a writer of even earlier date than Mâdhava quoting both Vâchaspati Miśra and Udayanâchârya. We allude to Bhatta Râghava who wrote his work entitled Nyâyasâravichâra in A. D. 1252.‖ We thus confirm from three different sources the conclusion that at the latest, Udayanâchârya flourished about the eleventh century, and that, for aught that appears to the contrary, he may have flourished even at an earlier period.

One more fact may perhaps be added. According to Mâdhavâchârya's Sankaravijaya, Śrî Harsha, Bâṇa, Mayûra, Udayana, and Sankarâchârya were contemporaries, and all the first four philosophers were vanquished in controversy by the last. Śrî Harsha, it may be added, is here particularized as the author of the Khandana¶; Bâṇa and Mayûra are represented as having flourished in the districts of Avanti**; about Udayana, there is nothing less vague than that he was an opponent of a dualism, and that he was unable to vanquish Śrî Harsha.† He is called Kavîndra.

There is one stanza in this work of Mâdhavâchârya's which seems to make some allusion to Vâchaspati Miśra. We cannot, however, be sure of this, and will therefore leave the reader to judge for himself. Sankara tells Sarvavarâchârya that the latter will become "Vâchaspati" in his next birth in the world, and that he will write an excellent commentary on his Bhâshya, which will live to the end of time. The words of Mâdhava are—"Vâchaspatitvamadhigamya vasundharâyâm

Bhavyâm vidhâsyasitamâm mamabhâshyatîkâm."‡

The word Vâchaspatitvam may, and probably does mean only "the quality of being a master of style or language." But the "ṭîkâ" alluded to is probably the Bhâmatî of Vâchaspati Miśra, and there may possibly be an oblique reference to the name of its author in the word "Vâchaspatitvam." But we do not feel sure of this and the commentary affords no help. It may be added, that there does not seem to be any historical objection to this account of Mâdhava. Śrî Harsha in the Khandana alludes to Sankara,§ but that would not by itself negative the possibility of their having been contemporaries. Of course, this must not be understood as equivalent to an admission that Mâdhava's account is wholly trustworthy. Bâṇa and Mayûra, and Daṇḍin who is mentioned with them, are now hardly known as philosophers. But if that account is accepted as meaning that, according to Mâdhava, Vâchaspati Miśra flourished in the next generation, or the next generation but one, after Sankarâchârya, it may corroborate the other statement made by Mâdhava, about Udayana's having been confuted in controversy by Sankara.

* Vasavadatta, Pref. p 16 and 17.

† So stated by the author himself in the Naishadhîya. See Dr. Hall's Vâsavadattâ, 16, and in the Khandana, p. 23.

‡ Prof. Wilson quoted in Dr. Hall's Vasavadatta, 15.

§ See the new Calcutta edition by Taranath, p. 168.

‖ Dr. Hall's catalogue, p. 23, referred to above.

¶ Madhav, xv. 157.

** Ibid 141.

† XV. 72, 157

‡ XIII. 73.

§ See the Khandana, Calc. ed., p. 2.

ON THE DATE OF PATANJALI AND THE KING IN WHOSE REIGN HE LIVED.

By RAMKRISHNA GOPAL BHANDARKAR, M.A., ELPHINSTONE COLLEGE, BOMBAY.

In Patanjali's Mahâbhâshya or great commentary on Pâṇini, a rule (vârtika) laid down by Kâtyâyana, is given, teaching that the Imperfect should be used to signify an action not witnessed by the speaker but capable of being witnessed by him and known to people in general. Of this rule Patanjali gives two instances; "The Yavana besieged [aruṇat] Sâketa" and

"The Yavana besieged [arunat] the Mâdhyamikas." The siege of Sâketa, therefore, must be considered to have been an event capable of being witnessed by the speaker, *i. e.* by Patanjali himself, in other words, some Yavana king must have besieged Sâketa in Patanjali's time. Sâketa is the usual name for Ayodhyâ. Reasoning in this way, the late Prof. Goldstücker arrived at the conclusion that the Yavana here spoken of must have been Menandros, King of Bактria, who is said to have pushed his conquests in India to the river Yamunâ. Menandros, according to Prof. Lassen, became king about 144 B. C. Patanjali therefore must have lived about that time.

But there is another passage in Patanjali not noticed by Prof. Goldstücker, in which the name of the king of Pâṭaliputra, during whose reign he flourished, is given, and which enables us to arrive at the date of the author of the Mahâbhâshya in another way and from other data. In his remarks on Pân. III 2-123, Patanjali quotes a *vârtika* of Kâtyâyana, the meaning of which is "A rule should be made teaching the use of the present tense [*laṭ*] to denote an action or undertaking which has been begun but not finished." The examples given by Patanjali are:—"Here we study;" "Here we dwell;" "Here we perform (as priests) the sacrifices (instituted) by Pushpamitra." Then Patanjali asks "How is it that Pâṇini's rule III. 2-123, (*Vartamâne laṭ*), which teaches that the present tense should be used to denote present time, does not extend to these cases?" The answer is, "the time here involved is not present time." How not? This question is answered by Kaiyaṭa, whose gloss upon this runs as follows:—"The phrase 'here we study' means that study has begun but not ended. When the students being engaged in eating and doing such other things do not study they cannot then properly say 'we study' [according to Pân. III. 2-123, *i. e.*, they cannot use the present tense, for it is not study that is then going on, and consequently the time is not present:] hence the rule by Kâtyâyana."* The sense of the whole is, that when an action, such as that of studying or performing the great sacrifices, spreads over many days, the present tense should be used to denote it, if the action has begun but not ended, even though at the time of speaking the speaker may not be actually performing the action. "Here we sacrifice for Pushpamitra," is Patanjali's example. Now this cannot be an imaginary instance, for such a one would not bring out the distinctive sense that Patanjali wishes to convey, namely, that the action has begun but not ended. This example then expresses a fact; *i.e.*, that at the time Patanjali wrote, there lived a person named Pushpamitra and a great sacrifice was being performed for him and under his orders. If he employed priests to perform the great sacrifices for him he must have been a king; for in the olden days it was Indian kings that propitiated the gods and patronised the Brâhmans in this way. The sacrifices were always expensive, and were treated rather as extraordinary festivals than ordinary religious performances. But in another part of the Mahâbhâshya we are actually told who this Pushpamitra was. Pâṇini (in I 1, 68) tells us that any grammatical change or operation that he may lay down in his work prescribed in the case of a certain word ought to be made applicable to that word alone and not to what it signifies, or to its synonyms. This, however, does not hold in the case of his own technical terms. Thus, for instance, to form derivatives in a certain sense from the word *agni* (fire) the termination *ḍhak* should, he says, be applied to *agni*. The meaning of this rule should not be stretched so as to make it applicable not only to *agni*, but to other words also, having the sense of *agni*. *Vahni* for instance also means fire but does not take that termination. But in the case of the technical terms of grammar, the change or operation should be effected in the case of the things (which of course are words) signified by that term. Thus, for instance, when he tells us to apply a certain termination to *ghu*, it is to be applied, not to *ghu* itself, but to the roots to which the name *ghu* is given by him. Now Patanjali, after a long discussion of this rule, in the course of which he

* Pâṇini वर्तमाने लट् III. 2, 123. Kâtyâyana प्रवृत्तस्या-विरामे शिष्या भवन्तीवर्तमाना॥ Patanjali प्रवृत्तस्या-विरामे शासितव्या भवन्ती। इहाधीमहे। इह वसामः। इह पुष्य-मित्रं याजयामः। किं पुनः कारणं न सिध्यति। वर्तमानत्वात्॥ Kaiyaṭa प्रवृत्तस्येति। इहाधीमहे इत्यादौ प्रारब्धस्य कर्मणः समाप्तिर्न कृता। भोजनादिना परस्परं व्यवधाने वर्तमानत्वे त्वतिप्रसङ्गः इति वचनम्॥ Patanjali then proceeds to say that the sense is conveyed by Pân. III-2-123 and no new rule is required, but this has no bearing on the present question.

shows that it is not wanted, though out of respect for the great Âchârya he does not distinctly say so, tells us that there are some sûtras in which the rules given are applicable,—1, sometimes to the synonymes of the words,—2, sometimes to the individuals comprised under the species denoted by the words,—3, sometimes to the words alone, and, sometimes to any two of these three. In these cases some indicatory letters ought, he says, to be attached to the words to show to which, or to which two, of the three categories the rule is to be applied. Then in such rules as II. 4, 23, which teaches that a Tatpurusha compound ending in the word *sabhâ* (court or assembly) preceded by *râjan* (king) becomes neuter he tells us that *j* should be attached to *râjan* and others, to show that the rule is applicable only to the synonymes of *Râjan* and others, and not to *râjan* or others themselves, or to the individuals comprised under the species denoted by *râjan* and others. And the instances he gives to show that it is not applicable to individual *râjâs* or kings are *Pushpamitrasabhâ* (the assembly or court of Pushpamitra) and *Chandragupta-sabhâ** (the assembly or court of Chandragupta) in which we see that the compound is not neuter but feminine. We thus come to the conclusion that Pushpamitra was the name of a king.

Now we know that the most powerful kingdom during a few centuries before Christ, the sovereigns of which extended their sway over a large portion of India, was that of Magadha, the capital of which was Pâṭaliputra. And Patanjali so often speaks of this city in his work† that we must infer that he had a great deal to do with Pâṭaliputra, and perhaps lived there for sometime, and that so that account the city and things concerning it were uppermost in his thoughts. The Pushpamitra then that he speaks of in the two cases here pointed out, must have been king of Pâṭaliputra in his time. And the fact of his being mentioned along with Chandragupta in one of the two cases strengthens this inference. For Chandragupta the Maurya was king of Magadha, and there was no other Chandragupta till several centuries afterwards when the Gupta dynasty came into power.

Now looking into the Purâṇas we find that there was only one king of Magadha of the name of Pushpamitra, the founder of the S'unga dynasty, which succeeded the Mauryas.‡ He was the Commander-in-Chief of Bṛihadratha, the

* [illegible Devanagari passage]

† [illegible] comments on I-2-2, II-1-16, II-4-[illegible], III-3-[illegible], and [illegible] and V-3-57. In the second of these, one of the examples given is [illegible Devanagari]. 'Pâṭaliputra was situated on the banks of the S'oṇa.'

‡ And I may say the Purâṇas do not mention another king of the same name of any country whatever. The name Pushpamitra does occur elsewhere, but in that case there is no agreement among the Purâṇas. The Vishṇu and the Vâyu make it the name of a dynasty and according to the former it was a [illegible] of foreign dynasty. The Bhâgavata only mentions it as the name of an individual, but this Purâṇa, from the manner in which it has corrupted several names and [illegible], is not much to be depended on. See Wilson Vish. Pur. [illegible] p. 478.

This Pushpamitra is spoken of in the Mâlavikâgnimitra of Kâlidâsa. Prof. Wilson calls him a general, and Prof. Lassen the general of his son, who is represented in the drama as king of Vidis'â. Prof. Lassen, *Ind. Alterthumsk.* (Vol. II. p. [illegible] and 406) is constrained however by other evidence to admit that he was king; but he thinks he reigned at Vidis'â, and that his son was co-regent with him. Prof. Wilson supposes that he usurped the throne for his son rather than for himself. But the first portion of the passage on which they seem to base their conclusions is this:—Devasya senâpateḥ Pushpamitrasya [illegible] [illegible] lekhaḥ prâptaḥ. Professor Lassen understands this to mean "a letter has been received from Pushpamitra, the general of the lord (i. e. Agnimitra)." But who ever heard of a father being Commander-in-Chief to his son? And immediately after, Pushpamitra is represented as about to perform an As'vamedha sacrifice, which none but kings who pretended to paramount supremacy could perform. In other authorities also it is Pushpamitra that appears as the [illegible] and not the son. Pushpamitra therefore could not have been his son's general; and [illegible] may be [illegible]. Agnimitra's commander-in-chief was Vîrasena, to whom he is more than once represented in the play as sending orders. The words above quoted are to be thus interpreted. "A letter has been received from the lord senâpati (general), Pushpamitra" i. e. the genitive [illegible] might be taken as an epithet of Pushpamitra, and not as connected with [illegible] by [illegible]. Indeed the title [illegible] shows that Pushpamitra was king, for it is applied in the dramatic works to kings only, and there is even a rule to that effect (see Sâhitya Darpaṇa, p. [illegible]—[illegible]). And Senâpati (general) must have become a distinguishing epithet of Pushpamitra, for he was the general of Bṛihadratha, the last Maurya king. And even in the Vishṇu Purâṇa the epithet senâpati seems to have been applied to him somewhat in this way. "[illegible] Pushpamitraḥ Senâpatiḥ [illegible] [illegible] râjyam karishyati." The first two kings of the [illegible] dynasty in Mahârâshṭra, were called Senâpatis; nor does it follow from this passage that Vidis'â was the capital of Pushpamitra but rather the opposite. For in the letter which he sends to Agnimitra, he invites the latter to come with his wife to be present at the As'vamedha sacrifice. If Vidis'â had been his capital, the sacrifice would have been performed at that city, and no such invitation would have been necessary. It follows, therefore, that some other city was Pushpamitra's capital, and what other could it have been but Pâṭaliputra, the capital of the Mauryas whom he had supplanted, and which in the Buddhist account given by M. Burnouf is mentioned as his place of residence. Agnimitra too may probably have been appointed by him Governor or King of Vidis'â, while he himself reigned as supreme monarch at Pâṭaliputra; for the practice of appointing sons to govern remote provinces existed in the time of the Mauryas. May not Patanjali be alluding to this As'vamedha sacrifice in the instance quoted in the text?

last Maurya king, and usurped the throne after having killed his master.* The ten Mauryas are said to have ruled the kingdom for 137 years.† The accession of Chandragupta, the first of these ten, has been fixed about 315 B.C. Pushpamitra, therefore, must have raised himself to the throne about 178 B.C. The Mātsya Purāṇa assigns him a reign of 36 years,‡ *i.e.* from 178 B.C. to 142 B.C. It follows then that Patanjali wrote his comments on Pāṇ. III. 2, 123 some time between these limits. The limits assigned by Dr. Goldstücker, reasoning from the one example he considers, are 140 and 120 B.C. But there is apparently no reason why he should not take into account the earlier years of Menandros's reign. For, according to Prof. Lassen, Menandros must have become king about 144 B.C.§ The passage in the Mahābhāshya, on which I base my conclusion, is not far from the one noticed by Dr. Goldstücker. The latter occurs in the comments on III. 2, 111, while the former in those on III. 2, 123. We thus see that when this portion of the Bhāshya was written, a Yavana king (who must have been Menandros) had laid siege to Sāketa or Ayodhyā, and Pushpamitra was reigning at Pāṭaliputra; and if we adhere to Lassen's chronology these two things could have happened only between 144 B.C. and 142 B.C.; for there is, I think, no reason to distrust the chronology of the Purāṇas here, since the date arrived at from the statements contained in them coincide in a remarkable degree with that determined from the evidence of coins. And even supposing that Prof. Lassen's date is not quite accurate, it must be admitted that it cannot be very far wrong.

We thus see that Patanjali lived in the reign of Pushpamitra, and that he probably wrote the third chapter of his Bhāshya between 144 B.C. and 142 B.C. And this agrees with the conclusion drawn by Prof. Goldstücker from a statement in another part of the work that the author of the Mahābhāshya flourished after the Maurya dynasty was extinct. Since all the passages then, and the different historical events they point to, lead us to about the same period, the date of Patanjali so derived must be regarded as trustworthy, and in the History of Sanskrit Literature it is of great importance.

ON THE VṚIHATKATHĀ OF KSHEMENDRA.

By Dr. G. BÜHLER.

Amongst the numerous Indian collections of fables the Kathāsaritsāgara of Somadeva takes the first place. With its 24,000 stanzas, it surpasses the Hitopadeśa, the Panchatantra, the Vetālapanchaviṁśati, the Siṁhāsanadvātriṁśati and the Śukasaptati not only in bulk, but it actually includes abstracts or versions of several of these works, as well as of other romances. This latter circumstance would make the Kathāsaritsāgara one of the most important tools for determining the age and development of Indian fables, were it not that peculiar difficulties connected with questions regarding the origin of the 'Ocean of fable-streams,' obliged Sanskritists to use it with great caution.

Somadeva, who according to his own statement, composed his work about the beginning of the 12th century A. D. for the amusement or consolation of Queen Sūryavatī or Sūryamatī, the mother of King *Harsha* of *Kashmir* declares that it contains the essence of the Vṛihatkathā, written by one Guṇāḍhya in the Paiśāchī Prakrit

---

* The Buddhist work *Aśoka Avadāna* erroneously makes him the successor of Pushyamitra, and the last of the Mauryas.—See Burnouf, *Introd. à la Hist. du Bud.* I. p. 432; Lassen, *Ind. Alt.* II. pp. 271, 272, 345, 346.—Ed.

† *Vish. Pur.* IV. 24, or Wilson's translation.

‡ Wilson's *Vish. P.* 1st Edn. p. 471. The Brahmāṇḍa Purāṇa agrees with the Mātsya. (See Dr. Hall's note in his edition.)

§ Various dates have been assigned to the accession of Menandros from B.C. 200 to B.C. 126. But the facts here brought forward may be used as a corrective. The manner in which Patanjali in the passage alluded to in the next part of the text contrasts the times in which the Mauryas lived with his own shows that when he wrote, the new polity had completely superseded the old. This may have taken twenty years or more. He could not have said "the Mauryas did such and such a thing, but in these days it is not so," if he wrote only five or six years after they were displaced. Patanjali therefore may have written the passage as early as B.C. 158. Now in order that about this time Pushpamitra and Menandros should be contemporaries, it is necessary that the date of the accession of the latter should not be pushed higher than about 178 B.C., nor lower than 162 B.C. for Menandros reigned for about 20 years according to all the writers; and the only two dates that fall within these limits are those assigned by Genl. Cunningham (B.C. 160) and Prof. Lassen. If we take that of the former, the limits between which the third chapter of the Mahābhāshya was written will be about 160 and 142 B.C. But I have adopted Prof. Lassen's date as it agrees sufficiently with all the facts.

—literally the dialect of the goblins—and that it differs from its original only in the language and by a condensation of the too prolix narrative.*

After this statement the Kathâpîṭha, or introduction to the work, gives the wonderful origin of the tale at great length. (Kath. I. 1-13—I. 8) Śiva, we are told, once narrated to Pârvatî the marvellous history of the seven Vidyâdhara Chakravartins. He was overheard by one of his attendants, Pushpadanta, who communicated it to his wife Jayâ, a servant of Pârvatî. The latter again spread it amongst her fellows and the indiscretion of Pushpadanta soon became known to the divine pair. Pârvatî, filled with anger, then cursed Pushpadanta and condemned him, in punishment of his fault, to be born as a mortal. His brother Mâlyavân, who dared to intercede for him, received a like sentence. But when Pârvatî saw Pushpadanta's wife, her faithful attendant, overwhelmed by distress, she relented so far as to set a term to the effects of her curse. She decreed that, when Pushpadanta, on meeting a goblin or Paiśâcha called Kâṇabhûti, in the Vindhyas, should remember the great tales and his former birth and should tell them to Kâṇabhûti, he should be delivered from his mortal body. Mâlyavân also should be allowed to return to heaven, when he had heard the Vṛihatkathâ from Kâṇabhûti and had spread them on the earth. Agreeably to this order, Pushpadanta was born in Kauśâmbî, as Vararuchi-Kâtyâyana, and became a great grammarian and the minister of Yogananda, the last of the Nandas. After an eventful life he retired into solitude and on a pilgrimage to the temple of Pârvatî Vindhyavâsinî, he met Kâṇabhûti in the forest. He remembered his former life and communicated to the Piśâcha the seven 'great tales.' Having accomplished this he re-obtained his celestial nature, according to Pârvatî's prediction.

Mâlyavân, also, who in his human birth had become Guṇâḍhya of Pratishṭhâna and had served King Śâtavâhana† as minister, came accompanied by his two pupils Guṇadeva and Nandideva, to the dwelling place of Kâṇabhûti. He received from him the seven stories in the language of the Piśâchas and wrote them down in 100,000 Ślokas each, with his own blood. By the advice of his pupils, he sent the whole to Śâtavâhana, hoping that the king being a man of taste, might preserve and spread them. But that monarch rejected with disgust a work that was written in the language of the goblins and with blood. On receiving this news Guṇâḍhya burnt six of his stories; the seventh was preserved with difficulty through the entreaties of his pupils. King Śâtavâhana, who accidentally learned that the recitation of the remaining book charmed even the beasts of the forest, repented of his former conduct, repaired to Guṇâḍhya's habitation and obtained the MS. of the remaining story. He studied it with the help of Guṇadeva and Nandideva, and wrote the introduction, detailing its origin, likewise in the language of the Piśâchas.‡ The book then became one of the stories that are famed in 'the three worlds.'

This account of the composition of Somadeva's original, which traces the story from Śiva, through Vararuchi and Kâṇabhûti, to Guṇâḍhya, his pupils and Śâtavâhana, looks as if it were purely legendary. Its nature has led Professor H. H. Wilson,§ who first made known Somadeva's work by an analysis of its contents, Professor H. Brockhaus,‖ the editor of the Kathâsaritsâgara, and Professor Lassen,¶ to doubt Somadeva's assertion, that he worked up an older Prakrit poem. These three scholars are, on the contrary, of opinion that Somadeva collected various works of fiction and digested them into a harmonious whole. Their view was certainly defensible twenty or even ten years ago, when the number of Sanskrit works, generally accessible to European Sanskritists, was not very large. But it is no longer tenable since Dr. F. E. Hall collected, in the introduction to his Vâsavadattâ,* a considerable mass of trustworthy evidence, which proves that a Vṛihatkathâ in the Paiśâcha Prakrit† existed, many centuries before Somadeva. The most important witnesses there adduced, are Daṇḍî who mentions a Vṛihatkathâ composed in the Bhûtabhâshâ, in his Kâvyâdarśa, I. 38, and Subandhu who, in the Vâsavadattâ, speaks of a Vṛihatkathâ, divided into sections called Lambas.

* Kathâsaritsâgara, ed. Brockhaus, I. 1. 3.
Vṛihatkathâyâḥ sârasya saṁgrahaṁ rachayâmyaham || and I. 1. 10.—
Yathâ mûlaṁ tathaivaitan na manâg apy atikramaḥ | granthavistarasaṁkshepamâtraṁ bhâshâ cha bhidyate ||
Compare for the last line Hall, *Vâsavadattâ*, Introd. p. 23.

† Alias Sâtavâhana or Śâlivâhana.

‡ Tâbhyâṁ saha sa tâṁ kathâṁ [illegible] [tavâdya ?] sa Sâtavâhanas tasyâ | [illegible] vakshyan chakre kathâpîṭhaṁ tataḥ || Brockhaus, *Kath.* I. 8. 37.

§ *Collected Works* III. 160 sqq.

‖ *Kathâsaritsâgara*, I. p. viii.

¶ *Indische Alterth.* III. 1024 & IV. 811.

* p. 22–24.

† Regarding the Paiśâcha dialect, see Lassen, *Instit. Prakrit.* pp. 377 and 439.

The former of these two poets is at least as old as Bâṇabhaṭṭa, the protégé and court-poet of King Harshavardhana who lived in the first half of the 7th century, and the latter is certainly older, since Bâṇa praises his work in the Harshacharita.* It appears to me incontestable, that both Daṇḍi and Subandhu speak of the Vṛihatkathâ, which, according to Somadeva's statement, was the basis of his Kathâsaritsâgara. For Daṇḍi says that the Vṛihatkathâ was composed in the dialect of the goblins, and the Vṛihatkathâ which Subandhu knew was divided into *Lambas*, just as Somadeva's work is made up of *Lambakas*. On this evidence it may, therefore, be safely asserted, that Somadeva's statement, that he translated and abbreviated a Vṛihatkathâ written in the low popular dialect, to which the writers on Alaṅkâra and grammar give the name Paiśâchî, deserves full credit,† and it is highly probable that Somadeva's original was in existence at least 1,200 years ago. But it remains an open question whether Guṇâḍhya was really the author of the old Vṛihatkathâ and whether he was a contemporary of Śâtavâhana or Śâlivâhana‡ of Paiṭhân. It also remains undecided, in what manner Somadeva treated his original, whether he merely contented himself with abridging it, or whether he embellished it by additions of his own—a point which is of the highest importance in determining the value of his book for the history of the Sanskrit fable books.

It gives me great satisfaction, that by the recovery§ of the *Vṛihatkathâ* of Kshemendra, I am able fully to corroborate the above conclusions, which are based on Dr. F. E. Hall's researches, and to determine more accurately the value of Somadeva's book. I lately acquired for the Government of Bombay a MS., the colophon of which runs as follows: "iti vyâsadâsaparâkhyakshemendraviracitâ vṛihatkathâ sampûrṇâ, granthasaṅ [khyâ] 7080, Samvat 1742 varshe bhâdrapadamâse śuklapakshe 11 guruvâre samâptam | śrîrastu | śrîrâma, i.e.—'Thus the Vṛihatkathâ composed by Kshemendra called Vyâsadâsa is completed. Number of granthas (16 syllables) 7080, Samvat 1742 (A.D. 1685) etc. According to the Anukramaṇikâ or Index, which apparently was made by the poet himself, it should contain the following Lambhakas or sections:‖

1. Kathâpîṭha.
2. Kathâvaktra.
3. Lâvâṇaka.
4. Naravâhanajanma.
5. Chaturdârikâ.
6. Sûryaprabhâ.
7. Madanamanchukâ.
8. Velâ.
9. Śaśâṅkavatî.
10. Vishamaśîlâ.
11. Madirâvatî.
12. Padmâvatî.
13. Panchalambhaka.
14. Ratnaprabhâ.
15. Alaṅkâravatî.
16. Śaktiyaśas.
17. Mahârâjyâbhisheka.
18. Suratamañjarî.

Actually however I find only lambhas I—IX. and XIV-XVIII. and among these lambha IX. is incomplete.¶

The names of the Lambhas of Kshemendra's story, though the order is changed, correspond exactly to those of the Lambakas of the Kathâsaritsâgara and the contents of the sections of the Vṛihatkathâ, as far as I have compared them, are almost identical with those of the corresponding chapters of the Kathâsaritsâgara. Kshemendra writes in the Anushṭubh metre like Somadeva. But he does not know the division of the Lambas into Taraṅgas. His style is not so flowing as Somadeva's and in his excessive eagerness for brevity, he sometimes becomes obscure. In order to give an idea of Kshemendra's manner of narrating, I subjoin the part of the Kathâpîṭha, which corresponds to Kathâsaritsâgara, I. 4, 1-92.*

---

* Hall, l. c. p. 14.

† I may mention that Paṇḍit Premachandra Tarkavâgîśa, the editor of the Kâvyâdarśa, holds the same opinion, vide his gloss on K. I. 38.

‡ Regarding the identity of Śâtavâhana and Śâlivâhana, see Wilson, *Coll. Works*, III. 183, note. Weber, *Saptaśatakam*, p. 2 seq.

§ If I speak of the recovery of this work, I mean simply that, as far as *I know*, no other copy of the book is accessible to European Sanskritists. The work seems to have been in the hands of Prof. Wilson's pandits. See Aufrecht, *Oxford Catalogue*, p. 36a.

‖ Anukramaṇikâ—
kathâpîṭhaṁ kathâvaktraṁ lambho lâvâṇakastathâ |
naravâhanajanmâkhyaś chaturdârikâ tataḥ |
sûryaprabhâ [illegible] madanamañchukâ |
velâ [illegible] śaśâṅkavatî tataḥ |
lambho vishamaśîlâkhyo madirâvatî |
Padmâvatî [illegible] pañchalambhakaḥ |
ratnaprabhâ cha [illegible] alaṅkâravatî [illegible] |
tataḥ śaktiyaśâ [illegible] |
mahârâjyâbhishekaś cha pañcha [illegible] mañjarî—fol. 2b (99a) line 2 seqq.

¶ Kathâp. fol. 1-22; Kathâv. 22-44; Lâvâṇ. 44-63; Naravâh. 63-73; Chaturd. 73-83; Sûryap. 83-98; Madanam. 98-130; Velâ 130-154; Śaśâṅkav. 154-206, where a break occurs; Ratnap. 1-26; Alaṅk. 26-43; Śakti. 43-78; Mahârâjyâbh. 78-81; Suratamañjarî, 81-92. The last page 91 is again numbered 206.

* Vṛihatkathâ, fol. 3a, l. 2:—
iti śrutvâ garor vidyâṁ [illegible] sarvâṁ [illegible] |
[illegible] ॥ 1 ॥
[illegible] |
[illegible] ॥ 2 ॥
[illegible] sarvaiśca mayi [illegible] |
[illegible] ॥ 3 ॥
[illegible] |
[illegible] ॥ 4 ॥
[illegible] |
[illegible] ॥ 5 ॥

Having heard this (story of the origin of Pâṭaliputra) and having received all sciences from my teacher, I, (Vararuchi) who dwelt at my ease, obtained in marriage the daughter of then Upavarsha, called Upakośâ. After I married *Upakośâ*, whose eyes resembled blue lotuses, I became the empire over which Cupid rules and a vessel of all happiness. Whilst I, living in the company of Vyâḍi and Indradatta acquired the fame of omniscience, a pupil of Varsha, Pâṇini by name, who was formerly a blockhead, obtained by virtue of his austerities, keeping his senses in subjection, a new grammar from Śiva. Disputing with me for eight days, he proved himself an opponent of equal force. When I conquered him at the end of that period, *Hara*, bewildering me by a growl, bereft me, through anger, of the recollection of *Indra's* grammar. After I had suddenly forgotten that work, I resolved to perform austerities in order to obtain the sight of *Bharga* who is the destroyer of Cupid and the wish-fulfilling husband of *Pârvati*, and I placed money for the household expenses in the hands of a neighbour, a Vâṇiâ called Hiraṇyagupta. After I was gone my faithful Upakośâ, though left alone in the beauty of her fresh youth, being versed in the Vedas, performed the vow which is becoming for wives whose husbands are absent. Time passed on and once the young foujdar of the king* the domestic priest, and the minister saw that beauty with the swan like gait, who bathed daily and played with the thick spray which had the appearance of a thin and transparent garment, whose broad hips resembled sandbanks, who was dark-blue in colour, whose eyes had the appearance of newly opened lotuses and who was a bud of Cupid, going like Yamunâ to the Ganges.† Gazing at her all three fell in love with her and stood apart from each other. First amongst them

upakośâ vimarśite [illegible] kṛtânte'bhayaṁ |
[illegible] vasudevaṁ pârvatîpatim ‖ 6 ‖
hiraṇyaguptasaṁsthe [illegible] vaṇijaḥ prativeśmanaḥ |
[illegible] gate mayi ‖ 7 ‖
upakośâ [illegible] |
[illegible] ‖ 8 ‖
[illegible] |
[illegible] ‖ 9 ‖
[illegible] |
[illegible] ‖ 10 ‖
yuvâ [illegible] |
purohitaś cha mantrî cha dadṛśur [illegible] ‖ 11 ‖
iti vihasya [illegible] prâbhṛtî-
thaḥ |
tasho [illegible] ‖ 12 ‖
[illegible] |
[illegible] ‖ 13 ‖
[illegible] |
[illegible] ‖ 14 ‖
dvitîyayâme [illegible] |
[illegible] ‖ 15 ‖
tṛtîyaṁ [illegible] |
[illegible] ‖ 16 ‖
[illegible] |
[illegible] ‖ 17 ‖
hiraṇyaguptasya gṛhe [illegible] |
tṛtîyaṁ [illegible] ‖ 18 ‖
ityuktvâ [illegible] |
tataḥ prâpte [illegible] ‖ 19 ‖
[illegible] niśi —
upakośâ [illegible] (?) [illegible] ‖ 20 ‖
[illegible] |
[illegible] ‖ 21 ‖
[illegible] |
[illegible] ‖ 22 ‖
[illegible] |
[illegible] ‖ 23 ‖
[illegible] (?) [illegible] |
[illegible] purohita [illegible] ‖ 24 ‖
[illegible] iti [illegible] kṛtaḥ |
[illegible] ‖ 25 ‖
[illegible] vijṛmbhitaḥ |
purohito'pi [illegible] ‖ 26 ‖

[illegible] kṛtaḥ |
[illegible] ‖ 27 ‖
[illegible] |
[illegible] ‖ 28 ‖
[illegible] |
hiraṇyagupta [illegible] ‖ 29 ‖
[illegible] |
[illegible] ‖ 30 ‖
[illegible] |
[illegible] ‖ 31 ‖
[illegible] |
[illegible] ‖ 32 ‖
[illegible] |
[illegible] ‖ 33 ‖
[illegible] |
[illegible] ‖ 34 ‖
[illegible] |
[illegible] ‖ 35 ‖
hiraṇyaguptena [illegible] |
[illegible] ‖ 36 ‖
upakośâ [illegible] |
[illegible] ‖ 37 ‖
[illegible] |
[illegible] ‖ 38 ‖
[illegible] |
[illegible] ‖ 39 ‖
[illegible]
sthitam —
[illegible] ‖ 40 ‖
[illegible] |
[illegible] ‖ 41 ‖
[illegible] |
[illegible] ‖ 42 ‖
[illegible] |
[illegible] ‖ 43 ‖
[illegible] |
upakośâ [illegible] ‖

* Daṇḍavâsika is elsewhere explained to mean 'door keeper,' but Kshemendra always has it where Somadeva gives daṇḍâdhipati.

† It seems to me impossible to express in English the puns contained in each of the epithets given to Upakośâ. They are chosen in such a manner that with a different interpretation they apply to Yamunâ also.

the son of the minister said to her—'Love me.' She, who had finished bathing, seeing that night had come, became afraid and spoke to him. 'Be it so, on the third day at night-fall I will meet you secretly.' Speaking thus to him, she went. After leaving him she addressed the domestic priest to this effect, 'On the third day hence, in the second watch of the night, I shall be at your disposal.' Turning away from him she said to the foujdar 'On the third day hence, in the third watch of the night I am ready to do your will.' After she had made this assignation, he let her go and she went home, filling as it were, by her frightened glances, the sky with lotuses.

Being in want of her husband's money she tried to remedy its concealment (by the banker). But Hiraṇyagupta asked her for an assignation in her house. She said to him 'On the third day hence, at the end of the night, I will obey thee, what harm is there (in my doing it).' She told that story to her domestics. When the third day had come, the excellent minister, trembling and having lost all control over himself, entered in the night her house, where the lamps had been extinguished. Upakośá called him by his name and said 'On you I have placed my affection.' At her order he entered a dark room in the interior of the house. There the servant-maids smeared for a long time the limbs of the lover with a soft unguent consisting of oil and lamp-soot. But, when in the second watch of the night the domestic priest came in haste, Upakośá showed to the (first lover) an open wooden box, said 'Enter, enter quickly here comes the master of the house,' and made him enter it. Closing it with an iron bolt, she said to the domestic priest 'You must not touch me without having bathed.' He also was treated in the same manner (as the first lover). When he had been anointed with oil and soot, the third also came. Forsooth, who escapes being deceived and made a fool of by the rogue Cupid! After the priest, overwhelmed with fear, had been disposed of in the same box (as the first lover), the third also, in his turn, was made to resemble a goblin. At the end of the night the excellent Váṇiá Hiraṇyagupta arrived, and the foujdár was concealed likewise in the wooden-box. Then Upakośá, facing the box, spoke to the Váṇiá, who was sitting at his ease on an excellent seat, 'Give me the deposit.' Hiraṇyagupta replied 'Love me, sweet smiling one. I have the money, fair-browed one, which your husband deposited with me.' Hearing this she exclaimed in a loud voice, 'Hear ye deities of the house, be witnesses, ye goblins: he has my property.' Speaking thus she defaced him also with lamp-soot. Then she said 'The night has passed, go.' Quickly the Váṇiá went forth, covering his face from fear of the people who are about early. Bereft of his garments, he was hooted on the road by the people. Wise Upakośá who had thus protected her virtue, after his departure, started early for the audience-hall of King Nanda. The king was informed, that the daughter of Upavarsha, the faithful wife of Vararuchi had come, and he honoured her there. She said 'O king, the Váṇiá Hiraṇyagupta conceals great wealth which my husband deposited with him. It is now for you, Lord, to give orders.' After that, when that liar had been summoned and come, Upakośá said 'Lord, at home I have witnesses; order my household-gods to be brought, who are kept in a box, they will declare the truth.' The basket-box was brought at the king's command and placed by the bearers in the midst of the assembly. Then the faithful wife spoke again: 'Ho ye deities, who are worthy of constant worship, tell the truth for my sake. If you remain silent in this matter of evidence, I shall quickly burn the basket.' Hearing this, they said, full of fear, 'Forsooth, thy property is in the hands of Hiraṇyagupta, we three are witnesses to that.' All present in the assembly, who heard this miraculous answer, were astonished; they opened the basket and saw the naked men smeared with soot. When the king had been informed of the circumstances of the case, he punished them by a fine and honoured Upakośá as his spiritual sister. About this time I (Vararuchi), by the grace of Sambhu, remembered the grammar, learned with joy the news about my house and went to visit my teacher. The story of Upakośá."

This sample of Kshemendra's style will fully bear out the strictures passed on him. His brevity sometimes makes him unintelligible and his style is far from being easy and flowing.

But I must return to the chief point in question, viz. what light Kshemendra's work throws on the origin of the Vṛihatkathá. In this respect the concluding verses of his poem are of the greatest importance. After enumerating, in the Anukramaṇiká, the contents of his work, he gives the following information regarding his predecensors.* 'Sarva proclaimed it first; Kâṇabhûti heard it from the Gaṇas (Pushpadanta-Vararuchi) and told it to Guṇâḍhya who delivered it in his turn to his pupils and to Sâtavâhana. The story which thus had come to be written in the Paiśâcha language, gave trouble to the readers. For this reason it has been rewritten in Sanskrit." From these verses we learn nothing new beyond the fact that *Kshemendra actually had before him the Vṛihatkathâ, attributed to Guṇâḍhya* and written in the Paisâchî dialect. The remaining statements are merely a recapitulation of the contents of the Kathâpîṭha, which I have given above according to Somadeva. But in the concluding ślokas the poet gives some further information regarding himself which is highly important. He says† that his father was a wealthy *Kashmirian* called [illegible] who fed numberless Brahmans, who gave on the occasion of an eclipse of the sun three black-buck skins with a lakh [illegible], who dedicated statues in the temple of Siva, spent 35 lakhs on 'gods, Brahmans, and Maths,' and finally died whilst hearing Śambhu's wisdom. He further informs us that he studied Alaṅkâra under *Abhinavagupta*, and that, 'intent on the worship of Nârâyaṇa he received the highest happiness through the dust of the lotus feet of Soma, the illustrious Âchârya of the *Bhâgavatas*.' He further narrates the particular circumstances which led to his taking the Vṛihatkathâ in hand, in the following manner:—

'Once, whilst fasting, on the twelfth day of the month, he who was possessed of taste was asked by the pure-minded Brahman Râmayaśas, and thinking over the story in his mind, he composed for the delight of clever persons this river flowing with nectar. He composed this amusing story at the order of the omniscient [illegible], who had obtained royalty over the Brahmans."

Though Kshemendra is fuller in his statements about himself than Sanskrit poets usually are, still it is difficult to fix his age even approximately. His Vṛihatkathâ is quoted in Dhanika's commentary on the Daśarûpaka and by [illegible] on the [illegible].‡ If we could trust the quotation in Dhanika's Avaloka, we should obtain a respectable age for Kshemendra. For, as Dhanika lived under Muñja, it would follow that Kshemendra lived not later than in the beginning of the 10th century. But unfortunately, the passage of the Avaloka in which the quotation occurs, is given by only one of Dr. Hall's MSS. The other two omit these verses. It may therefore be an interpolation. The quotation by [illegible] and another in the Śârṅgadharapaddhati do not carry us beyond the 14th century.§ None of the personages mentioned by Kshemendra are known except his teacher Abhinavagupta. The latter is cited as an authority on Alaṅkâra by Mallinâtha and Mammaṭa and Śârṅgadeva. He therefore appears to have been known in the 12th century.‖

Whilst it is thus impossible to decide with certainty the question of priority between the

* Vid. MSS. (Vol.) l. 6—
[illegible]
[illegible]
[illegible]
[illegible]
[illegible]
[illegible]
[illegible]
[illegible]
[illegible]
[illegible]
The word '[illegible]' ought to stand immediately after the enumeration of the [illegible] given above.

† Vid. MSS. (Vol.) f. 2, immediately after the passage quoted above.—
[illegible]
[illegible]
[illegible]
[illegible]
[illegible]
[illegible]
[illegible]
[illegible]
[illegible]
[illegible]
[illegible]
[illegible]
[illegible]
[illegible]
[illegible]
[illegible]
[illegible] (ibidem MS.)
[illegible]
I am far from considering the emendations in the text of [illegible] as certain.

‡ See F. E. Hall, Vâsavadattâ, Introd. p. 51 and Daśarûpa, p. 81. The lines quoted by Hall are thus rendered by my MS. fol. 17b l. 6.—
[illegible]
[illegible]
[illegible]
[illegible]
The reading [illegible] in the last line for [illegible] is evidently the better one. Chhâpilya for [illegible], is a mistake of the copyist who, being a [illegible], saw no difference between [illegible] and [illegible].

§ A śloka by Kshemendra's [illegible] is quoted by Purushottama, the son of Vallabhâchârya (16th century). Aufrecht, Oxf. Cat. p. [illegible]. This work may possibly be the [illegible], written by a Kshemendra, pupil of Vyâsa; vide Hall's Catalogue p. [illegible].

‖ An Abhinavagupta is also known as one of the teachers of a sect of Śaivas. A work of his is mentioned by Hall, Catal. p. 199 as well as several works by a pupil of this Śaiva called *Kshemarâja*. It is not unlikely that Kshemarâja may be the same as Kshemendra. But as the works quoted by Dr. Hall, are not accessible to me, I leave the question undecided.

Vṛihatkathâ and the Kathâsaritsâgara, I think we shall be more fortunate in regard to the clearing up of another point, viz., whether either of the two poets used the other's composition, or whether they both worked up independently the lost poem attributed to Guṇâḍhya. On this point we have first their statements, which affirm distinctly that each had before him a Prakrit original, not a Sanskrit one. A number of other circumstances corroborate the truth of this assertion. In the first place it seems to me impossible that Somadeva could have used Kshemendra's work. In very many passages the latter gives so short and condensed an outline of the narrative, that it would go beyond the power of anybody to construct out of that the connected and clear story given by Somadeva. One example of this kind is contained in the portion of the Vṛihatkathâ, translated above, where all details about Upakośâ's and Vararuchi's first acquaintance and marriage are left out. Other instances from the Kathâpîṭha —the only portion of the two poems which I have carefully compared—are,

1. Kathâsaritsâgara I. 2, 8-23, gives a full account of how Kâṇabhûti learned the reason why, in consequence of a curse, he became a Yaksha, by overhearing a conversation between Śiva and Pârvatî; the Vṛihatkathâ states briefly, that Kâṇabhûti heard Śiva, who haunts burial places, tell the reason of his being cursed, but omits to mention with whom Śiva conversed,* nor does it give the story explaining why Śiva dwells in burial-places.

2. The Kathâsaritsâgara, (I. 3, 4-22), gives a full account of the descent of Putraka, the founder of Pâṭaliputra, how his father and uncles were born at Kanakhala, migrated to Râjagṛiha, and thence to Chinchinî, married the three daughters of Bhojika and finally left them, and how one of the forsaken wives was delivered of Putraka. Instead of this story the Vṛihatkathâ states drily, 'During a great drought, three brothers, Brahmans, forsook their three wives and went to another country. In time one of the wives, who was pregnant, bore a son.†

3. Further on in the same story of Putraka, the legend of Brahmadatta is left out by Kshemendra.

4. In the same story the Kathâsaritsâgara relates that Putraka puts up in the house of an old woman, during his stay at Âkarshikâ. The Vṛihatkathâ calls the town Âyajñikâ and leaves out the particular circumstance alluded to. But it gives a long description of Mahendravarman's daughter and the embarrassment and doubts experienced by Putraka, when he first saw her asleep. The conversation of the two watchmen, whose stanza decides him to awake the sleeping beauty is given, but differs from that of the Kathâsaritsâgara.‡

I could easily add a dozen other instances, where particulars given in the Kathâsaritsâgara, are *hinted at* but *not developed* in the Vṛihatkathâ. It seems to me, however, that those adduced will suffice to show that Somadeva worked up something else than Kshemendra's poem.

On the other hand, it is not likely that Kshemendra used Somadeva's Kathâsaritsâgara. For he differs from the latter work frequently in a manner which seems to indicate that his statements are not mere fanciful alterations of Somadeva's narrative. In several passages, where such differences occur, Kshemendra's statements are more sober and simpler than Somadeva's. Thus, whilst in the passage regarding Pâṇini's and Vararuchi's disputation, Somadeva says that 'Śiva standing in the clouds gave a great growl and thereby the grammar of Indra (defended by Vararuchi) disappeared from the world,'§ Kshemendra contents himself with saying 'that the growl of Śiva confused Vararuchi and made *him forget* the grammar of Indra.' Further on in the same story Somadeva tells us, that 'Vararuchi obtained a revelation of Pâṇini's grammar from Śiva and the permission to complete it by adding the

* Vṛihatkathâ fol. 4.—
[illegible] |
[illegible] |
[illegible] |
[illegible] |
[illegible] |
[illegible] |
[illegible] | [illegible]

† Vṛihatkathâ, fol. 4.—[illegible] kâle bhrâtaro brâhmaṇâs trayaḥ |
[illegible] parityajya [illegible] ||
[illegible] kâle [illegible] garbhiṇî |
[illegible] ||

[illegible] |
kâlena [illegible] prâpya râjyaṃ [illegible] | [illegible] ||

‡ Vṛihatkathâ, fol. 4.—
[illegible]
[illegible]
[illegible] |
yaḥ [illegible] svayaṃ na [illegible]
[illegible]
[illegible] |

§ *Kathâsaritsâgara*, I. 4, 24-25.

Vārttikas.* Kshemendra merely states, that 'Vararuchi, through the grace of Sambhu, recollected the grammar (i.e., that of Indra).' Again in the story of Putraka, Somadeva states (I. 3-22,) that the new-born child, by the grace of Śiva, obtained a daily present of a *lakh* of pieces of gold; Kshemendra contents himself with *one thousand* coins. Now it is invariably the rule that the later Sanskrit poets, especially if they treat of the same subject as their earlier brethren, try to efface the latter by exaggerating, not by toning down too glaring absurdities. Hence it is not likely that, when writing such passages, Kshemendra had before him the Kathāsaritsāgara. Finally, there are other differences in the two works which, it seems to me, find a sufficient explanation only if we assume that either author worked on a Prakrit original. Thus Śātavāhana's adoptive father's name is given as *Dīpakarṇi* by Somadeva† and as *Dīpakarṇa* by Kshemendra. These two forms look like transliterations of a Paiśāchī 'Dipakanna or Tipakanna.'‡ Again the teacher of Pushpadanta is named in the Kathāsaritsāgara (I. 7, 96) *Vedakumbha*, in the Vṛihatkathā *Vedagarbha*. According to the Prakrit grammarians the Paiśāchī form of *Vedagarbha* would be *Vetakabbha*, and that would explain the different forms used by the two Sanskrit poets.

Another curious discrepancy occurs in the story 'Why the fish laughed' (Kathāsaritsāgara I. 5. 14, 27.) In the first śloka, Somadeva states that 'Yogananda saw his queen asking a Brahman guest§ (about what is not said) and became jealous.' Kshemendra says that the queen asked a Brahman about the lunar day (tithiprishṭāṁ dvijanmānam bhāshamāṇām). Now this looks exactly as if Somadeva had had before him a bad MS. which contained the syllables '*tithim*' and as if, not understanding their real meaning he had made the word *atithim* out of them and referred that to the Brahman.

All these circumstances make the statements of Somadeva and Kshemendra, that they remodelled a Prakrit original, perfectly credible. But if that is granted, the recovery of Kshemendra's work furnishes us with a powerful instrument for determining the exact contents of the old Paiśāchī Vṛihatkathā. The old Vṛihatkathā once being reconstructed, we shall further obtain important results for the history of those works, which like the Panchatantra the Vetālapanchaviṁśati are embodied in it. For Guṇāḍhya's Vṛihatkathā possessed certainly a higher antiquity than the Persian or Mongolian translations of those fable-books. I must defer the exploration of the portions of Kshemendra's work, which contain these stories books, until later; but I may state now that the Vṛihatkathā includes them just as well as the Kathāsaritsāgara.

* Kath. I. 4–22.

† Kathā. I. 6, 66.

‡ According to the conflicting statements of the grammarians either form is possible. See Lassen, *Inst. Prak.* 439 & 448.

§ 'Prichchhantam brāhmaṇam atithim.'

AN INTERESTING PASSAGE IN KUMÁRILA BHAṬṬA'S TANTRAVÁRTTIKA.

By A. C. BURNELL, M.C.S., M.R.A.S., MANGALORE.

The most famous Mímáṅsá treatise existing in India, is Kumárila Bhaṭṭa's Tantravárttika, a commentary on the Jaimini-sútras, but supplementary to Śabara's Bháshya. It seems uncertain if this work exists in a complete form, but the examination of a number of MSS. leads me to the conclusions arrived at by Dr. F. E. Hall, that the chief divisions bear distinct names, improbable though this may seem.‖

Granted the premisses, it is a very subtle and well-reasoned treatise, but since Dr. Goldstücker is no more, it is little likely to attract attention in England or India. Among a mass of arguments which are neither interesting nor of any importance, there are however casual notices of customs, races, and languages, that certainly deserve excerpting. Prof. Max Müller¶ has already given one relating to the Buddhists, but the following which, I believe, is the earliest known mention (in Sanskrit) of the Dravidian languages has passed unnoticed. Kumárila Bhaṭṭa lived at the end of the seventh century A.D.* so it is interesting to remark that the words he mentions are still good current Tamil words, and his evident acquaintance with

‖ *Contributions towards an Index*, p. 178.

¶ *Ancient Sans. Lit.* pp. 79 and 88 (note).

* See the reasons for this given in the preface to my edition of the Sámavidhána Bráhmaṇa, and elsewhere from Tibetan texts.

this South Indian dialect is worth notice, as he is said to have been a native of the South.* The passages which follow are from the annotations on sûtra 10th of the 3rd pâda of the first lecture, and the subject of discussion is:—

ये शब्दा न प्रसिद्धाः स्युरार्यावर्तनिवासिनाम्।
तेषां म्लेच्छप्रसिद्धोऽर्थो ग्राह्यो नेति विचिन्त्यते॥

'It is now considered:—(as regards) words which are not known to the inhabitants of Âryâvarta, if they have a meaning known to the Mlechchhas is that to be accepted or not?'

Kumârila suggests (but only to reject the notion) that by application of affixes, &c. it may be possible to convert them into Sanskrit words, and he gives the following examples:—

आन्ध्रद्राविडभाषायामेव तावद्व्यञ्जनान्तादि-
देषु भाषास्वरान्तविभक्तिस्त्रीप्रत्ययादिकल्पनादिभिः
स्वभाषानुरूपानर्थान् प्रतिपद्यमाना दृश्यन्ते तद्यथा।
ओदनं चोर् इत्युक्ते चोरपदवाच्यं कल्पयन्ति।
पन्था नडैर् इत्युक्ते नन्तर इति कल्पयित्वाहुः।
सत्यं दुस्तरत्वान्नन्तर इति। पाप् शब्दं पकारान्तं सर्प-
वचनमकारान्तं कल्पयित्वा सत्यं पाप एव।
अपायेति वदन्त्येवम् आल् शब्दं स्त्रीवचनं कल्पा-
यित्वा मालेति सत्यमाहुः।
वैर् शब्दं च ऐकारान्तमुदरवचनं वैर् शब्देन प्रत्याम्ना-
य वदन्ति सत्यं सर्वस्य क्षुधितस्याकार्ये प्रवर्तनादुदरं
वैरिकार्ये प्रवर्तत इति तदेवं द्राविडादिभाषायामी-
दृशी स्वच्छन्दकल्पना सदा पारसीकबर्बरयवनरो-
मकादिभाषासु किं विकल्प्य किं प्रतिपत्स्यन्त इति न
विद्मः (v. l. विद्यः)
तस्मान्म्लेच्छप्रसिद्धेऽपि यत्पदं यद्विकल्प्यते न कश्चि-
त्तत्र विश्वासो युक्तः पदपदार्थयोः॥

The first word chor, in the Tamil ćôṟu, and means (as Kumârila states) 'boiled rice;' naḍar = way, is the Tamil naḍai; so pâmp† = snake, is perfectly correct, and âl = person,‡ and vair = vayiṟu, the belly—are common Tamil words and their meanings are correctly given. It must however be remarked that the consonantal terminations of chor, pâmp, and vair, have now assumed a vowel ending, which is written u, but is pronounced in a vague and indeterminate manner.

There can be little doubt that Bhaṭṭa Kumârila regarded the South Indian (Dravidian) dialects as Mlechchha or unbrahmanic, uncivilized languages; he does not say so expressly, but his words imply that he thought so. It is not to assume too much therefore if we infer that about 700 A.D. brahmanical civilization had but little penetrated the South of India. Brahmans had, no doubt, begun to find the South a promising field of labour, but there could have been very few settlers. Hiwen Thsang, who visited the Telugu and Tamil countries in 639-40 A.D., mentions that the inhabitants were chiefly Nirgranthas (i. e. Digambara Jains),§ he mentions a few Buddhists, but has not a word about Brahmans.‖

The vague term by which the Tamil language is mentioned—Ândhradrâviḍabhâshâ is remarkable, as it indicates that a systematic study of the so-called Dravidian languages can hardly have begun in the 8th century. The Sanskrit grammar of Telugu (there called Ândhra) by Nannaya (a Brahman) is to be attributed to the 10th century,¶ and the Śabdamaṇidarpaṇa, a Canarese grammar which displays a very large acquaintance by its author with Sanskrit grammar is to be attributed to about the same time.* All earlier civilization in Southern India, so far as it is known, is connected with the Jains. Drâviḍa is not in use as the name of a language; since Dr. Caldwell's Comparative

* Târanâtha, History of Indian Buddhism p. 162. "At this time in the country of the South, among the leaders (lit. bulls of the herd) of the non-Buddhist doctrine was the famous Brâhman Kumaralila or gzhon-nu-rol-pa." The perversion in the form of the name is owing to the wrong etymology, as the Tibetans always translate Sanskrit names, and, as may be imagined, are often hard up for a way of doing so. So here we have "boy's play" translating Kumâralila i. e. as if Kumâralîla.

† The MSS have pâmp. In Tamil it is written pâmpu but pronounced pâmbu.

‡ An affix also of the feminine form of the 3rd person singular in verbs.

§ The Nirgranthas are generally asserted to be naked Brahman mendicants (Böhtlingk and Roth, St. Petersburg Lex. s.v.; Lassen, Ind. Alterthumsk. III. 682, IV. 257) but as the Mîmâṃsists oppose them, it is difficult to see how they could be Brahmans. Stan. Julien says cautiously as usual—"hérétiques qui vont nus." (Mém. II. 461, and conf. I. 4), 216; II. 42, 94.) That they were really Digambaras is, I think, proved by the Aṭṭhapâhuḍaka gâthâ in which niggantha is continually used as an epithet of true Jains; e. g. iv. 10 (niggantha vîyarâyâ jiṇamagge erisâ paḍimâ); ii 14: hoi khandaṇiyâ niggantha saṃjadâ...; 14; 30 (niggantha ......) and in several other places. Of the age of this work I have however no information.

‖ Stanislas Julien, Voyages des Pèlerins Bouddhistes, III. pp. 72, 106, 110, 115, 118 and 122.

¶ C. P. Brown, Telugu Grammar, p. 1.

* See Mr. Kittel's preface to his edition, p. xxiii. I find that the author has even taken some technical terms from the Prâtiśâkhyas!

Grammar appeared, it is technically used to designate the South Indian family of languages.

The last few words mention the Pâraśika Yavana, Romaka and Barbara languages. The first three, it is almost unnecessary to remark, are *Persian*, *Greek*, and *Roman* (Latin); what language is intended by Barbara is not easy to say. The Greek word [illegible] is here not to be thought of*; it may perhaps be intended for *Bod-pa*, Tibetan, or for Burmese, which (if I recollect rightly) is called properly *Mranma*. At all events, in addition to the proofs furnished by the Astronomical treatises, this list of languages will show that the Brahmans knew much more of foreigners than is commonly supposed, or they indeed have ever been willing to admit.

There is another reason for believing that Southern India was brahmanized but comparatively recently, and this is taken from the Nibandhanas or law-digests. In most of these we find a chapter termed [illegible], and in the Smṛitichandrikâ which belongs to about the 13th century A.D. this is pretty full. The country of the Brahmans, as is well known, originally comprised but a small part of the vast peninsula now known by the name of India, (conf. Mânava-Dh. S. ii, 17 and flg.), and at the time the Digests were compiled the lawyers had to determine how far the laws of Âryâvarta and Brahmâvarta held good in other countries. In the end they are obliged to admit that people must follow the customs that prevail where they live; the question had evidently arisen very recently. I do not mean to deny for a moment that a few Sanskrit names are found some centuries earlier in South India, such as are preserved to us by classical writers, but they occur only in the fertile deltas or important seaports of the South, and were probably introduced by Buddhist missionaries. Indeed the process is so slow that the brahmanization of wild tribes in Central and South India is going on to this day, and is yet far from complete.

Mangalore, 11th August 1872.

SKETCHES OF MATHURÁ.

BY F. S. GROWSE, M.A., OXON, B.C.S.

IV.—BARSANA AND NANDGAON.

Barsana, according to modern Hindu belief the home of Krishna's favourite mistress Rádhá, is a town which enjoyed a brief period of great prosperity about the middle of last century. It is built at the foot and on the slope of a ridge, originally dedicated to the god Brahma, which rises abruptly from the plain, near the Bharatpur border of the Chhátá Pargana, to a height of some 200 feet at its extreme point, and runs in a south-westerly direction for about a quarter of a mile. Its summit is crowned by a series of temples in honour of Lâdlî Jî, a local title of Rádhá, meaning 'the beloved.' These were all erected at intervals within the last 200 years and now form a connected mass of building with a lofty wall enclosing the court in which they stand, each of the successive shrines was on a somewhat grander scale than its predecessor, and was for a time honoured with the presence of the divinity. But even the last and largest, in which she is now enthroned, is an edifice of no special pretension; though seated, as it is, on the very brow of the rock, and seen in conjunction with the earlier buildings, it forms an imposing feature in the landscape to the spectator from the plain below. A long flight of stone-steps, broken about half way by a temple in honour of Rádhá's grandfather, Mahábhán, leads down from the summit to the foot of the hill, where is another temple-court, containing a life-size image of the mythical Brikhbhán robed in appropriate costume and supported on the one side by his daughter Rádhá, and on the other by Sridâma, a Pauránik character, here for the nonce represented as her brother.

The town consists almost entirely of magnificent mansions all in ruins, and lofty but crumbling walls now enclosing vast, desolate, dusty areas, which once were busy courts and markets, or secluded pleasure grounds. All date from the time of Rúp Rám, a Katára Brahman, who having acquired great reputation as a pandit in the earlier part of last century, became Purohit to Bharatpur, Sindhia, and Holkar, and was enriched by those princes with the most lavish donations, the whole of which he appears to have expended on the embellishment of Barsána and the other sacred places within the limits of Braj, his native

* Though Fick (*Indogerm. Wörterb.*) and others consider that the *Sanskrit* word is borrowed from the Greek.

country. Before his time Barsána, if inhabited at all, was a mere hamlet of the adjoining village Unchá-gánw, which now under its Gújar landlords is a mean and miserable place, though it boasts the remains of a fort and an ancient and well endowed temple, dedicated to Baldeva. Rúp Rám was the founder of one of the now superseded temples of Lárlí-Jí, with the stone staircase up the side of the hill. He also constructed the largest market-place in the town with as many, it is said, as 64 walled gardens; a princely mansion for his own residence; several small temples and chapels and other courts and pavilions. One of the latter, a handsome arcaded building of carved stone, has for some years past been occupied by the Government as a police station without any award of compensation, though the present representative of the family is living on the spot and is an absolute pauper. Three chhatris, commemorating Rúp Rám himself and two of his immediate relatives, stand by the side of a large stone tank with broad flights of steps and flanking towers, which he restored and brought into its present shape. This is esteemed sacred and commonly called Bhánokhar, that is, the tank of Brikhabhán, Rádhá's reputed father. In connection with it is a smaller reservoir, named after her mother Kírat. On the margin of the Bhánokhar is a pleasure-house in three stories, known as the Jal-mahall. It is supported on a series of vaulted colonnades which open direct on to the water, for the convenience of the ladies of the family, who were thus enabled to bathe in perfect seclusion, as the two tanks and the palace are all enclosed in one court-yard by a lofty bastioned and embattled wall with tower-like gateways. Besides these works, Rúp Rám also constructed another large masonry tank for the convenience of a hamlet in the neighbourhood, which he settled and called after his own name Rúp-nagar; and on the opposite side of the town, in the village of Ghásipur, faced with octagonal stone gháts, the sacred lake called Prem Sarovar. Opposite the latter is a walled garden with an elegant domed monument in the form of a Greek cross to his brother Hem-ráj.

Contemporary with Rúp Rám, two other wealthy families resided at Barsána and were his rivals in magnificence. The head of the one family was Mohan Rám, a Lavániya Bráhman; and of the other Lálji, a Jatiá Thákur. It is said that the latter was by birth merely a common labourer, who went off to Lakhnau to make his fortune. There he became first a Harkára, then a Jamadár, and eventually the leading favourite at court. Towards the close of his life he begged permission to return to his native place and there leave some permanent memorial of the royal favour. The Nawáb not only granted the request, but further presented him with carte blanche on the State Treasury for the prosecution of his designs. Besides the stately mansion now much dilapidated, he constructed a large *báolí* still in excellent preservation, and two wells sunk at great expense in sandy tracts where previously all irrigation had been impracticable.

The sacred tank on the outskirts of the town called Priya-kund, or Píri-pokhar, was faced with stone by the Lavaniyas; who are further commemorated by a large *Katra*, or market place, the ruins of the vast and elaborate mansion where they resided, and by elegant stone chhatris at the foot of the hill. They held office under the Rája of Bharatpur, and their present representative, Rám Naráyan, is now Tahsíldár of Kámán in that territory.

Barsána had scarcely been built, when by the fortune of war it was destroyed beyond all hope of restoration. In 1774 A.D., the Játs, who had advanced upon Dehli in support of the cause of Zábita Khán, and in consequence of ill-success were returning to their own country, were met at Hodal in Gurgáon by Najaf Khán hastening up from Agra. Dislodged from their position, they fell back upon Kotban and Kosi, where they remained for nearly a fortnight, and then finally withdrew towards Dig, but at Barsána were overtaken by the Vazír and a pitched battle ensued. The Ját infantry, 5000 strong, were commanded by Sumroo, or to give him his true European designation, Walter Reinhard, a celebrated adventurer who had first taken service under Súraj Mal, and was still with his son Naval Sinh, the then Rája of Bharatpur. The ranks of the Imperialists were broken by his gallant attack, and the Játs feeling assured of victory were following in reckless disorder; when the enemy rallying from their sudden panic turned upon their pursuers, who were too scattered to offer any solid resistance and effectually routed them. They contrived however to make good their retreat to Dig; while the town of Barsána was given over to plunder and the stately mansions, so recently erected there, were reduced to their present state of ruin in the search for hidden treasure. Naval Sinh died some twenty days after the battle, but whether in consequence of wounds there received is not certainly known. He was succeeded by his brother Ranjit Sinh; but the whole country had been so thoroughly subjugated, that the title was at first merely a barren honour. It was only at the intercession of Suraj Mal's widow, the Rání Kishorí, that the conqueror allowed the new Rájá to retain the Fort of Bharatpur with an extent of territory yielding an annual income of nine lakhs. Barsána never recovered from this blow, and in 1812 sustained a further misfortune, when the Gaurua Thákurs, its Zamindárs, being in circumstances of difficulty, and probably distrustful of the stability of British rule, then only recently established, were mad enough to transfer their whole estate to the oft-quoted Lálá Bábú for the paltry sum of Rs. 602 and the condition of holding land on rather more favourable terms than other tenants. The parish now yields Government an annual rental of Rs. 2109, and the absentee landlords about as much, while it receives nothing from them in return, though their donations for charitable purposes in the neighbourhood of their own home in Bengal are often on a magnificent scale. Thus the appearance now presented by Barsána is a most forlorn and melancholy one.

The hill is still to a limited extent known as *Brahmá-ká-pahár* or Brahmá's hill and hence it may be inferred with certainty that Barsána is a corruption of the Sanskrit compound *Brahma-sánu*, which bears the same meaning. Its four prominent peaks are regarded as emblematic of the four-faced divinity and are each crowned with some building; the first with the group of temples dedicated to Lárlí Jí, the other three with smaller edifices, known respectively as the Mán-Mandir, the Dán-garh and the Mor-Kuṭí. A second hill of less extent and elevation completes the amphitheatre in which the town is set, and the space between the two ranges gradually contracts to a narrow path which barely allows a single traveller on foot to pass between the shelving crags that tower above him on either side. This pass is famous as the Sánkari-khor, literally "the narrow opening" and is the scene of a *mela* in the month of Bhádon, often attended by as many as 10,000 people. The crowds divide according to their sex, and cluster about the rocks round two little shrines erected on either side of the ravine for the temporary reception of figures of Rádhá and Krishṇa, and indulge to their heart's content in all the licentious banter appropriate to the occasion. At the other mouth of the pass is a deep dell between the two high peaks of the Mán-Mandir and the Mor-Kuṭí with a masonry tank in the centre of a dense thicket called the Gahwarban: and a principal feature in the diversions of the day is the scrambling of sweetmeats by the better class of visitors, seated on the terraces of the Peacock-Pavilion above, among the multitudes that throng the margin of the tank some 150 feet below.

The essentially Hindi form of the title Lárlí, equivalent to the Sanskrit Lalitá, may be taken as an indication of the modern growth of the local cultus. Even in the Brahma Vaivarta, the last of the Puráṇas, and the one specially devoted to Rádhá's praises, there is no authority for any such appellation, though it gives a professedly exhaustive list of her titles, which are 16 in number and as follows:—

Rádhá, Rásesvari, Rásavásini, Rásikesvari,
Krishṇa-pránádhiká, Krishṇa-priyá, Krishṇa-svarúpiṇí,
Krishṇá, Vrindá-vaní, Vrindá, Vrindávana-vinodiní,
Chandrávalí, Chandra-Kántá, Sata-chandra-nibhánaná,
Krishṇa-vámánga-sambhútá, Paramánanda-rúpiṇí.

Nandgánw, as the reputed home of Krishṇa's foster-father, with its spacious temple of Nand Ráe Jí on the brow of the hill overlooking the village, is in all respects an exact parallel to Barsána. The distance between the two places is only 5 miles, and when the *naubat* is beaten at the one, it can be heard at the other. The temple of Nand Ráe, though large, is in a clumsy style of architecture and apparently dates only from the middle of last century. Its founder is said to have been one Rúp Sinh, a Sinsinwár Ját. It consists of an open nave, with choir and sacrarium beyond, the latter being flanked on either side by a Rasoí and a Sej-mahall, and has two towers, or sikharas. It stands in the centre of a paved court-yard, surrounded by a lofty wall with corner kiosks, which command a very extensive view of the Bharatpur hills and the level expanse of the Mathurá district as far as Gobardhan. The village which clusters at the foot and on the slope of the rock is for the most part of a mean description, but contains a few handsome houses, more especially one erected by

* A similar use of the local form *Khor*, for *Khol*, may be observed in the village of Kháiro, where is a pond called Chandr-Khol Kund, corresponding to the more common Sanskrit compound Chandra-kunda.

the famous Rûp Râm of Barsâna. With the exception of one temple dedicated to Mânasî Devî, all the remainder bear some title of the one popular divinity, such as Nar-siñha, Gopînâth, Nritya-Gopâl, Giri-dhâri, Nanda-nandan, Râdhâ-Mohan and Jasodâ-nandan. This last is on a larger scale than the others, and stands in a court-yard of its own, half way up the hill. It is much in the same style and apparently of the same date as the temple of Nand-Rai, or probably a little older. A flight of 114 broad steps, constructed of well-wrought stone from the Bharatpur quarries, leads from the level of the plain up to the steep and narrow street which terminates at the main entrance of the great temple. This staircase was made at the cost of Babu Gaur Prasâd of Calcutta in the year 1818 A.D. At the foot of the hill is a large unfinished square with a range of stone buildings on one side for the accommodation of dealers and pilgrims, and at the back is an extensive garden with some fine khirni trees, the property of the Râjâ of Bharatpur. A little beyond this is the sacred lake called Pân Sarovar, a magnificent sheet of water with noble masonry ghâts on all its sides, the work of one of the Râjâs of Bardwan. This is one of the four lakes of highest repute in Braj; the others being the Chandra-sarovar at Parsoli by Gobardhan, the Prem-sarovar at Gahvarban near Barsâna, and the Mân-sarovar at Arua in the Mât Pargana. According to popular belief there are within the limits of Nand-gânw no less than 56 kunds, though it is admitted that in this degenerate age all of them are not readily visible. In every instance the name is commemorative of Krishṇa and his pastoral occupations. Like Barsâna and so many other of the holy places, Nand-gânw is part of the estate of the representatives of the Lâla Bâbû, who in 1811, A.D., acquired it in free gift from the then zamindârs.

The above sketch has entered rather largely into details regarding two comparatively unimportant places. But such minutiæ are the most trustworthy exponents of provincial customs, speech and traditionary ideas; and their recital in the present case has been further intended as an attempt—first to rescue from oblivion the name of a local worthy, who has been somewhat hardly treated by posterity; and secondly, to illustrate by a view of the fortunes of one small town, a curious transitional period in Indian history. After a chequered existence of 500 years, there expired with Aurangzeb all the vital energy of the Muhammadan empire. The English power, its fated successor, was yet unconscious of its destiny and all reluctant to advance any claim to the vacant throne. Every petty chieftain, as for example Bharatpur, scorning the narrow limits of his ancestral domains, pressed forward to grasp the glittering prize; and spared no outlay in the attempt to enlist in his service the ablest men of any nationality, either like Samru to lead his armies in the field, or like Rûp Râm to direct his counsels in the cabinet. Thus men, whatever their rank in life, if only endowed by nature with genius or audacity, rose in an incredibly short space of time from obscurity to all but regal power. The wealth so rapidly secured was as profusely lavished; nor was there any object in hoarding, when the next chance of war would either increase the treasure ten-fold, or transfer it bodily to a victorious rival. Thus a hamlet became in one day the centre of a princely court, crowded with magnificent buildings, and again, ere the architect had well completed his design, sunk with its founders into utter ruin and desolation.

ON SOME EMINENT CHARACTERS IN SANSKRIT LITERATURE.

By M. SASHAGIRI SASTRI, B.A., ACTING PROFESSOR OF SANSKRIT, MADRAS.

Vikramâditya.—This name is applied to several kings and consequently causes considerable confusion. The first sovereign that is known by it was the Vikramâditya from whom the well known era takes its name. He is said to have been the son of a Brahman named Chandragupta, who married four wives, one of the Brahman caste, another of the Kshatriya, the third of the Vaisya, and the fourth of the Sudra caste. They were called Brahmani, Bhânumati, Bhâgyavati, and Sindhumati respectively. Each of the four bore him a son. Vararuchi was born of the first wife, Vikramârka of the second, Bhaṭṭi of the third, and Bhartṛihari, of the fourth. Vikramârka became king while Bhaṭṭi served him in the capacity of the prime minister. After an incredibly long reign he is said to have been killed by a prince of the potter caste, named Śâlivâhana in 56 B.C. and in that year commences his era. He is considered one of the greatest of the sovereigns of India. He was distinguished for his learning, his patronage of Sanskrit literature, and liberality to the poor. Several marvellous stories are related of him in the account of him called the Vikramárkacharita. He is there figured somewhat as Charlemaigne and Arthur are in the romances of the Middle Ages. Whatever may be the authenticity of the Vikramacharita and other books which give accounts of him, they prove beyond all doubt, that this sovereign was most popular, that his reign was a long one and was distinguished by many great deeds and that he was very religious and protected the Varnasramadharma or duties of caste and the religious orders. He is said to be the author of a kosha or lexicon; but of what kosha, we cannot ascertain. From a catalogue of books sent by a Brahman from Kadappa, it would appear that this book is the Sabdaravarta; but this statement is contradicted by Medinikara,* who in a list of lexicographers, enumerates most of the koshas which are prior to his book, and there mentions the kosha of Vikramárka as a separate book. While from the Haravali it appears that the Sabdaravarta was written by Vikramárka†

He is also said to be the author of a treatise on music.

The name of Vikramáditya was assumed by several kings and this, as remarked above, occasions some confusion. Subandhu in his Vasavadattá says—

> Sárasvatá vigatá navaká vilasanti
> charati no kankah. Sarasiva kirtiseshum
> gatavati bhuvi Vikramáditye

Now Subandhu quotes the Brihatkathá which is believed to be the same as the Kathásarit-Ságara. But the author of this book says he compiled it for the recreation of the grandmother of Harshadeva; and this prince is said in the Rájatarangini to have been the son of Kalasa, the son of Ananta, the son of Sangrámarájá. From a reliable source it has been ascertained that Sangráma ascended the throne in 1027 A.D., and his son Ananta in 1058, and Harsha the grandson of the latter in 1059. This last prince reigned only twelve years and consequently Somadeva must have written the Kathásarit Ságar between 1059 and 1071. (Wilson on Hindu Fiction). From this it may be inferred that the Vasavadatta was posterior to the Brihatkatha and that its author must have flourished in the twelfth century. We learn the following from tradition. Subandhu, the author of the Vasavadatta, wrote the poem with a view to be rewarded by Vikramárka, and before he completed it that sovereign died. The author finding a new sovereign on the throne who was destitute of the learning, taste, and judgment necessary to appreciate his poem, became hopeless and vented his despair in the stanza quoted above. From this it follows that Subandhu was a contemporary of Vikramárka. Who this Vikramárka was we cannot determine.

According to Major Wilford's Essay on Vikramárka and Saliváhana, there were three Vikramárkas who were all alike celebrated for their power, greatness, and good government. The first of them was the Vikramárka who flourished before Christ and is said to have been killed by Saliváhana. The second was the same with Sriharsha Deva. This prince is said to have reigned A.D. 191. The third Vikramáditya commenced his reign in 441. The second of these three princes was also called Súdraka. In the Skanda Purána, Kumarika Khanda it is said that a great king named Súdraka will reign in the year of Kaliyuga 3290, that is in 190 A.D. This agrees well with the former date. But we are not certain about the identity of these kings, for the Skanda Purána does not specify the Sudraka of whom it speaks.

There is a short grammatical treatise in Sanskrit containing about 700 anushtup stanzas divided into four chapters, and called Prayogachandrika. The author calls himself Vemalabhupati, the ornament of the Chogen dynasty.

---

* [illegible Devanagari] | 1. |
[illegible Devanagari] | 2. |
[illegible Devanagari] | 3. |
[illegible Devanagari] | 4. |
[illegible Devanagari] | 5. |
Medini.

† [illegible Devanagari]
Haravali.

In the beginning of the book there is a stanza which runs as follows :—

Chandravatî vadana chandra chakora vikramâditya bhûpatitanayasya tautravatâ.

"The son of Vikramârka who was as fond of the face of (his wife) Chandravatî as the Chakora is of the moon." I think that there is a stanza at the end of the book concerning the age of the author, but as the book is not at hand I cannot quote it.

BHOJA.

This prince was the son of Sindhula, King of Dhârâ in Malwa, and his uncle was called Munja. While he was very young his father died, and on account of his minority his uncle ascended the throne. The young prince made great progress in learning various arts and sciences. His popularity gradually increased and excited the envy of his uncle, who apprehended that the young king would soon dethrone him. He wanted therefore to secure his position and contrived how to put his nephew to death. He sent for Vatsarâja, one of his tributary princes and, having communicated to him his design, asked him to murder the young Bhoja in a solitary wood. The latter, though unwilling to execute such an odious commission, could not refuse, and accordingly he took the young prince to the place appointed. But when he went there and contemplated what he was going to do, he was seized with horror and his own conscience prevented him from doing it. Instead of murdering the prince he took him privately to his house and presented to the king his sword besmeared with the blood of some wild animal which he had killed. When the king asked him what his nephew said before his death Vatsarâja gave him a leaf on which the young king had written a verse. He read as follows :—

Mândhâtâ samahîpatiḥ kritayugâ lankâra bhûtu gataḥ. Seturyena mahodadhau viruchitaḥ kwâsau daśâsyântakaḥ. Anyechâpi yudhishṭhira prabhritayo yâtâdivam bhûpate Naikenâpi samangatâ vasumatî nûnam twayâ yâsyati.

"Mandhâta, that king who was the ornament of the kritayuga died. Where is the enemy of Râvaṇa (Râma) by whom a bridge was built to the ocean? Others such as Yudhishṭhira went to heaven. The earth followed none of them; but it will certainly follow you." No sooner did the king read this verse than he fell down thunderstruck, but was soon consoled by Vatsarâja, who told him that he did not murder his nephew as he was ordered to do, but took him to his house and concealed him there. As soon as Bhoja was brought before him he embraced him and humbly asked his pardon. Soon after this the king placed his nephew on the throne and retired to the woods to perform ascetic ceremonies. The young Bhoja having thus got the throne of his father, invited poets and philosophers from all parts of India. The book from which I have taken the foregoing account makes the following poets his contemporaries :—

Karpûra	Dhanapâla	Harivaṃśa
Kalinga	Bâṇa	Lakshmîdhara
Kâmadeva	Bhavabhûti	Vidyâvinoda
Kâlidâsa	Bhâskara	Viśvâvasu
Kokila	Mayûra	Vishṇu Kavi
Śrîdachandra	Mallinâtha	Śankara
Gopâladeva	Maheśwara	Sâmbadeva
Jayadeva	Mâgha	Śuka
Târavendra	Muchakunda	Sîtâ
Dâmodara	Râmachandra	Vasanta
Somanâtha	Râmeśwarabhaṭṭa	Subandhu

There are gross anachronisms here, but the author, Vallâlasena who is said to have written the work in the 19th century, did not perceive them, and his object was to eulogize the patronage of Sanskrit literature by this prince. This King of Dhârâ is said to be the author of the Champurâmâyaṇa. There is internal evidence at least to show that it is not the work of a Brahman.

It contains a stanza in the beginning which is as follows :—

Uchairgatirjagati siddhyati dharmataschet
tasya pramâcha vachanaiḥ kṛita ketaraischet
teshâm prakâśana daśâpi mahî suraischet.
Tenântarena nipatet kwanu matpraṇâmaḥ.

"If salvation comes from virtue, if the authority for virtue (is given) by words not composed (the Vedas) and if the work of spreading them is (to be done) by the Brahmans, whither will my homage go but to them? This verse could not have proceeded from the mouth of a Brahman. At the end of each Kaṇḍa it is said to have been written by Bhoja. Other works are ascribed to him, viz., the Sarasvatî Kaṇṭhâbharaṇa, a treatise on rhetoric, a commentary on the lexicon of Amarasiṃha, a treatise on music, Râjavârtika, a commentary on the Patanjali sutra, and the Charuchârya. But there is no mention of these works in the Bhojacharitra. In the Vikramârka charitra it is said that Bhoja who was the King of Ujjayani and was the descendant of Vikramârka wanted to ascend the throne of that celebrated sovereign, which he discovered under the ground. While he was abroad on a hunting excursion he came to a field of growing corn. A Brahman was watching over the ground from an eminence and while there he invited every passenger to reap the rich corn. But when he got down he began to abuse severely every one who, tempted by his invitation, entered the field. This struck the king, who with a view to find out the cause ordered the Brahman to come down from the eminence and sat himself there. But no sooner did the king do this than he was inspired with a degree of liberality which his mind never before felt. But when he came down he began, as the Brahman did, to censure the freedom of the people whom he called to reap the corn. He then thought there must be something under the ground below the eminence; and accordingly he dug out the earth and found a throne or Sinhasana, adorned with thirty-two putlis. He brought it home on a propitious day appointed by the Brahmans and wanted to ascend it; but he was interrupted by one of the putlis, which having assumed the form of a maiden, related to him one of the great achievements of Vikramárka and asked him whether he was so great as that sovereign and on his acknowledging his inferiority to him the speaker disappeared. The next time he came to ascend the throne he was interrupted by another putli in the same manner and at a third time, by a third and so on. He tried to sit on that throne 32 times and was prevented every time by a putli; and at last the throne itself disappeared. It is difficult to ascertain who this Bhoja was. But this is evident that the author wanted to show that the king was inferior to Vikramárka in respect of power, greatness and liberality.

ASIATIC SOCIETIES.

Journal of the Asiatic Society of Bengal No. 170.

(*Continued from p.* 307).

The fourth paper is a 'Note on Gharghon, Assam,' by J. M. Foster, F.R.G.S., containing somewhat lengthy extracts from Robinson's *Descriptive Account of Assam* (1841), from Bernier's *Particular Events in the Empire of the Great Mogul*, and from the 'Loss of the Ter Schelling' in *Tales of Shipwrecks and Adventures at Sea* (London, [illegible]).

In 'Translations of Selected Portions of Book I of Chand Bardai's Epic,' by J. Beames, B.C.S. M.R.A.S., &c. the opening 15 stanzas are thus rendered :—

1. *Gátha metre.* Om !—

First reverently bowing, bowing, the poet adores the feet of the Guru.

(Taking) refuge at the feet of the highest, the afforder of support,* the husband of the opulent Lachhi ;

(Who) stands the lord of vice and of virtue, consuming the wicked, the lord of heaven, blessing with success ;

(Who is as) sandalwood to the life of living beings moving on the earth, lord of all, bestower of blessings.

2. *Paddhari metre.*

First the very auspicious root is to be celebrated.†
Irrigated with the water of the truth of tradition,
Religion, (like) a fair tree with one trunk sprung up
With the six branches rejoicing the three worlds
Leaves (of various) colours, leaves (like) mouths three words‡
Colour of flowers, and weight of fruit (it had)
Speech unfailing, princely,
Rejoicing with fragrance the sight and touch§
A'ma tree of hope to the parrot (like) poet.

3. *Kavit*

First having indeed proclaimed a blessing
Having honoured the sacred writings, (whose) beginning (is) the Veda, [those
(Whose) three-fold branches, in (all) four directions
(Are) possessed of colour, and leaves (like) letters
Religion having sprouted (out through) the bark
Flowered fair in (all) four directions
Its fruit, (virtuous) deeds, springing out
Immortal, dwelling amidst mortals
(Firm as) counsel of kings, (or as) the earth, the wind shakes it not
Giving to life the flavour of nectar,
The Kali (yuga) affixes no stain to it
Containing truth, wisdom, and (perpetual) freshness.

4. *Kavit.*

Taking possession of the earth (like) a garden plot
Irrigating it with the fullness of the Veda, as with water
Placing in it good seed‖
Upsprung the shoot of knowledge

---

* Or "supporting the earth," if [illegible] be meant for [illegible] which is quite possible.

† This line is extra-metrical, and is probably meant as a note.

‡ A conjectural rendering, which does not satisfy me.

§ I read [illegible]. Another reading is [illegible], which seems to have arisen from an omission of the vowel by the copyist.

‖ This strange line I read as if for [illegible].

Combining branches of three qualities
With leaves of many names, red on earth
It flowered with good deeds, and good thoughts
Complete deliverance, union of substances
The twice-born of pure mind have experienced
the flavour of perfect wisdom
A banian tree of delight, spreading abroad virtues
The branches of (this) excellent tree in the three
worlds
Unconquered, virtuous, diffusing virtues.

5. *Bhujanga prayáta metre.*

First in the well adorned Bhujangi* taken
Whose name this one, is spoken in many ways
Second, he takes the god, the lord of life
Who placed the universe by powerful spells on
Sesháng.
In the four Vedas by the Brahmans the glory of
Hari is spoken,
Of whose virtue, this unvirtuous world is witness.
Third, the Bhasati Vyása spake the Bhárata,
Who bore witness to the more than human cha-
rioteer.†
Fourth Suka dove at the feet of Paríkhit
Who exalted all the kings of the race of Kuru
Fifth * *‡
Who placed a six-fold necklace on the neck of
King Nala.
Sixth Kálidása, fair of speech, fair of wit,
Whose speech is that of a poet, a master-poet
fair speaking,
Who made the pure fragrance of the mouth of
Kali,
Who firmly bound the dyke of three-fold enjoy-
ment.
Seventh, Dandamali's charming poem,
The wave of whose wit is as the stream of Gangá.
Jayadeva eighth, poet, king of poets
Who only made the song of Govinda;
Take all these poets as thy spiritual guide, Poet
Chand,
Whose body is as a sacrifice inspired by Devî.
The poets who have uttered praises and excellent
speech,
Of them Poet Chand has spoken highly.

6. *Dohá.*

The speech in verse of Chand, excellent.
Hearing him utter, his wife (says)
Purifier of the body, O poet,
Uttering excellent speech.

7. *Kavit.*

Saith the wife to her husband:
Purifier of offspring, great poet,
Uttering spells and charms,
Like an oblation offered to Hari,
Hero of spells, very terrible,
Giving pleasure to kings by thy poetry;
The childish sports, one by one,
Of the gods having extolled in thy poems,
Having uttered unlimited speech,
From which to me (comes) wisdom,
That word which is the visible form of Brahm,
Why should not the best of poets speak it?

8. *Kavit, Chand's speech.*

To his wife (saith) the bard
Chand, muttering soft and low,
That true word of Brahm,
Purifier of (all) others itself pure,
That word which has no form,
Stroke, letter, or colour,
Unbroken, unfathomable, boundless,
Purifier of all things in the three worlds,
That word of Brahm, let me expound
The glory of the Gunas, pleasing to Sarasvati,
If in the arrangement of my phrases I should
succeed,
It will be pleasing to thee, O lotus-faced one.

9. *Kavit, Chand's wife's speech.*

Thou art the poet, the excellent bard,
Gazing on the heavens with unclouded intellect,§
Skilful in the arrangement of metres
Having made the song of the Peacock-youth.||
The wave of thy wit is like Gangá,
Uttering speech immortal, soft.
Good men hearing it are rejoiced,
(It) subdues like a spell of might.
The incarnation King Prithiraj the lord,
Who maintained the happiness of his kingdom,
Hero, Chief of heroes, and all his paladins,
Of them speak a good word.¶

10. *Kavit Chand's speech.*

To her of the elephant-gait, Chand
Singing a pleasant rhyme (said),
Ravisher of the soul, tendril of enjoyment,
Possessing the fragrance of the ocean of the gods.
(Thou) of the glancing eye, in the flower of thy
youth,
Beloved of my soul, giver of bliss,
Wife, free from all evil qualities,
(Thou) who hast obtained the fruit of the worship
of Gauri.
As many poems as there have been from first to
last

---

* I do not know what the allusion is here.

† These words are probably a corruption. [illegible] being for [illegible], more than earthly, from उद्, over, and पृथ्वी, earth, and [illegible] charioteer. It is an allusion to Krishna's acting as charioteer to Arjuna in the great war.

‡ I cannot understand this line.

§ Of the many senses of [illegible], the one here given is the only one that will yield any meaning.

|| This seems to be an allusion to the Sanskrit poem called Kumara Sambhava, or the "Birth of the Wargod" Kartikeya, whose vahan is the peacock. Chand may have written a paraphrase of that work, as he seems to have been well acquainted with Sanskrit literature.

¶ [illegible] is still the common Panjabi for a "word." Many of these Panjabi words occur in Chand, which is natural, as he was a native of Lahor.

Consider how endless a string (there are) of them.
The description of this matter (is in) many books,
Then having taken in the [illegible] [illegible].*

11. *Padāvali* [illegible].

First [illegible] my first of gods
Who uttered the imperishable word [illegible]!
Who made the [illegible] of the [illegible],
The will of his mind [illegible] and [illegible] fruit,
The [illegible] of the three qualities, inhabiting the three worlds,
Shining as gods in heaven, men on earth, serpents (in hell).
Then in the form of Brahma leaving the Brahma-[illegible].†
The lord, the essence of truth said the four Vedas,
The creator uttered them, unwritten,
Without qualities, having neither form nor [illegible],
He who made the heaven, earth, and hell,
Yama, Brahma, Indra, the Rishis, and guardians of the worlds,
Winds, fire, clouds, ether,
Rivers, oceans, earth, mountains, and their inhabitants,
He created eighty-four lakhs of living beings
I cannot come to an end of the description of them
He made a [illegible] of eighteen colours,
Of various kinds, mixed of all qualities,
No one can avoid his [illegible],
Placing the order on his head (the) [illegible] great in the body.
Day by day the sun-god [illegible] night [illegible] dawn‡
[illegible]; this comes to pass by force of the lord's command.
The moon every night obedient to order
[illegible] in the sky, being without [illegible].§
The guardians of the regions remain patiently pressed down by the earth,
Their [illegible] do not [illegible] though they remain heavily pressed.
He appoints to the wind its measure and the place of its going.
It [illegible] remains nor falls short, makes joy to the body.
Indra's heaven, clouds, and sky (obey his) orders
He makes the rain to rain joyfully.
Firm and immoveable remains the earth (like) the glory of the lord,
It cannot shake or move for an instant in distress.
The wave rising touches the sky,
On the brink of the ocean there remains no trace of it;
Having obtained its limit, not one (wave) passes it,
It advances only so far as the lord's command (allows)
[illegible] no one can refute,
Neither in the past, nor in the future, nor in the present.
The Veda describes Brahma as [illegible],
Filling the water and land he remains in every material object.
Then spake Vyasa eighteen Puranas
Arranging the incarnations in various order
He describes with clear intellect every god,
He searched out all of them, he did not confound their characters.
Then Valmiki, the incarnation of Ram,
[illegible] in a [illegible] of a hundred [illegible] (of lines) [illegible] of truth.

* * * *||

The mighty [illegible], the story of the friendly monkey.

Again five [illegible] five poets made,
Placed a light in the breasts of ignorant men,
In a few words wisdom is shown,
I might make a [illegible], then you would laugh.

12. *[illegible].* *Hearing the [illegible] Chand.*

[illegible] in her mind, his wife [illegible],
Then not the [illegible], the [illegible],
Longing being [illegible].

13. *[illegible].* *[illegible] the intelligent wife.*

Thou who hast spells on thy tongue—ocean of spells
Excelling in the description of [illegible]
Like the [illegible] moon
Thou [illegible] of heavenly blessings,
Grant a gift to me, O poet!
The eighteen Puranas
Thou [illegible] all;
Thou telling the tale, joy (will be) to me,
Past and future existences will be purified,
The darkness of ignorance is destroyed by hearing them,
The [illegible] of (spiritual) blindness is removed from the heart.

Mr. Blochmann's paper on Koch Bihár, &c., has been already noticed (p. [illegible]). The last paper is 'Notes on Arabic and Persian Inscriptions from [illegible], [illegible], [illegible] (N. of Dhákă), [illegible] and [illegible] (E. of [illegible])' by the same.

At the last meeting of the Asiatic Society, Mr. Blochmann exhibited a rubbing of an inscription made by Mr. W. M. Bourke from a ruined mosque at [illegible] near Hugli. The inscription states that the mosque was founded during the reign of Ala-uddin Abul Muzaffar Firuz Shah, son of Nusrat

---

* I do not pretend to understand what the poet means by these four lines, which I have translated as literally as I [illegible]

† I read ब्रह्मपुर चारि (for चारि), but there is another reading ब्रह्मा पुरारि which is not intelligible. [illegible] and [illegible] are often written for one another in the MSS.

‡ रजनी भोर, literally 'dawn of night,' which would convey a different meaning to our minds.

§ [illegible], having no kalas, or the 16 digits into which the moon is divided.

|| This line is not intelligible, it contains some allusion to [illegible] cups, but the meaning is not clear.

Shah, A.H. 896. Mr. Blochmann stated that the reign of this king could not have been of long duration, and he might probably have only reigned in Western Bengal. The reign of Nusrat Shah ended, according to the historians, in 940 A.H., and his successor was called Mahmud Shah, no mention ever having been before discovered either in an inscription or on a coin of Firuz Shah of this date. It is intended, if possible, to secure the stone with this inscription on it for the Indian Museum.—*Englishman.*

Bombay Br. Asiatic Society.

At the monthly meeting of the Society held 8th August, 1872.

Dr. Bhau Daji read the following report on 19 gold coins received from the Collector of Belgaum—3 larger and 16 smaller.

The larger three are circular, flat pieces weighing 58 grains. On one side each has a circular line very near the rim which is beaded. Within the circle is the figure of a lion passant, face to the left. In front of the neck is a short inscription in Devanagari characters comparatively modern, mentioning the name of one of the years of Brihaspati Chakra, or sixty years cycle of Jupiter. In that year the coin was probably struck.

In one the name of the year is Subhakrita, the 36th in the cycle. The second has Pramoda, the 4th in the cycle, the third has Pingala, the 51st in the cycle.

A little above the ear of the lion and close to the circular line is a small circle and the crescent, evidently to represent the sun and the moon.

The coin having the name of the year Pingala, has the Svastika symbol just behind the raised tail, whilst that with the name of the year Pramoda has the same symbol under the raised front foot.

The form of the lion has a general resemblance to the lions found in the caves of Elephanta and in the ruins of Mathura.

On the obverse of the coin with the Subhakrita year, is an inscription of five lines within a circle; the first line is in modern Devanagari characters, and may be read Siva Chitta. The line under has the same name but in a different character, probably the old Dravidian alphabet. The third line has the name of Sri Siva Chitta in Devanagari.

The fourth line reads exactly as the third, but the character is the old Canarese.

The fifth line has again Siva Chitta in Devanagari.

The coins having the name of Pramoda and Pingala have on the obverse inscriptions in five lines.

1st. Sri Sapta ko.
2nd. tisa labdha vara vi
3rd. ra Jaya ke.
4th. Siva Malava.
5th. ra mari.

In the coin with the name of the year Pingala, the letter vi is at the commencement of the third line, and instead of [illegible] there is [illegible], which is equivalent to [illegible] in Sanskrit.

The legend may be translated—

"The brave Jayakesi who obtained the favour of Sri Saptakotisa and was the enemy of Malavaras."

The temple of Saptakotisa (Siva) is in Narvem in Goa. In my paper on Madhavacharya, I have stated that Madhava Mantri established the shrine in the time of Hari-Hara.

The sixteen coins are all alike, being 58 grains in weight. On one side is the representation of an elephant with trappings, badly carved and never entire in any one of the coins.

On the obverse is a conventionalized [illegible]. These coins appear to be cast and not die-struck.

The age of the coins, judging by the alphabets, is later than the thirteenth century of the Christian era. We have the name of a King Jayakesi and his enemy Malavaras, but I am unable to find at present their exact position in the dynasties of Southern and Western India.

MISCELLANEA.

NOTES.

1. In the *Indian Antiquary*, p. 174, Prof. Weber mentions that an *Æsopic fable*,—that of the flight of the tortoise through the air, is found in Buddhism. This reminds me that the story is represented in a small panel sculpture at the entrance to the Mundut (Buddhist) temple in Java, near Boro Budor. The fact is mentioned by me in the *J. As. S. Ben.* of 1862, p. 20.

2. Sultan Baber mentions (p. 146) a curious superstition in the hill country north of the Kâbul River (Kunar, Nurgil, Swât, &c.): "It is the custom, when a woman dies, to place her on a bier which they lift up by the four sides. If the woman has lived virtuously, she shakes the bearers to such a degree that even when they are upon their guard, and attempting to prevent it, the corpse falls from the bier."

In an annual procession where I write (at Palermo) in honour of the Patron Saint of the City, St. Rosalia, a bier containing her bones, real or supposed, is carried through the streets. The bearers are always masons. At intervals they stagger as if involuntarily, and shake the bier till the bones rattle. I cannot give the reason assigned, and the procession has this year been abolished or suspended, but the circumstance is curious in juxtaposition with Baber's story.*

3. I know not if the *Maramut* Department at Madras still flourishes by that name. But it is worthy of note that a standing commission for the maintenance and repair of the ancient Cathedral here bears the name of Maramma. It is a curious trace of the former extent of Muhammadan power to find the same official phrase thus current in Palermo and Madras.

4. It seems to me all but certain that the Semylla of Ptolemy and the Periplus, the Saimûr or Taimûr of the Arab geographers, is *Chaul*. I should be glad to learn the oldest known native spelling of the latter name. *Chaumal*, *Chêmul*, or *Chamwar* would easily run into Semyl-

* Since writing the above I am told that the shaking is intended to commemorate the bringing of the bones down from the precipitous Mount Pellegrino, on which they are believed to have been discovered in a miraculous way. But this may be a *post-factitious* reason.

la or Jaimur on one hand, and into Chaul on the other. And Ptolemy says the natives called it Timulla (*Tiamula?*).

It was probably also the Simor of Cosmas, as the order of his names indicates, rather than Supara.

Supâra, on the other hand, appears to correspond exactly to the *Swally* of our old traders, the *Bandar* of Surat, north of the Tapti. Supâra is represented by Lassen to be a corruption of (Sanskrit) Sûrpâraka "Fine shore." Is *Swally* a Hindu name, in which case it might be a surviving trace of Supâra, or is it only the Arabic *Sawâhil*, "shores"? I have seen the latter suggestion somewhere, but on the other hand Supâra is called *Sufâlah* by Abulfeda, which comes near *Swally*. And Langlois quoted by Reinaud, says that Supâra or Sufâlah "answers to the place called by the Sanskrit writers *Subâhlika*," which comes nearer still. Gildemeister says of Sufâlah "*de cujus situ nondum interiit memoria*." But if *Swally* is Sufâlah, its memory is not clean perished. Supara is mentioned by Friar Jordanus, a contemporary of Abulfeda's, who was there as a missionary. This is perhaps the latest mention of the name in that form.

5. Perhaps few readers of the *Antiquary*, though it is published at Bombay, know that four Franciscan missionaries, comrades of the said Jordanus, suffered martyrdom at Thana, at the hands of the Musulman "Melic", or Governor, in 1321. The story is told at length by Friar Odoric a few years later.

6. Cosmas mentions as exported from Kalliana (near Bombay) sesamin logs (*ξύλα σησάμινα*). The Periplus also names among exports from Barygaza "spars of sesamin and ebony" (*φάλαγγες σησάμιναι καὶ ἐβένιναι*). And Kazwini (in Gildemeister, p. 209) quotes some verses on the products of India by one Abulzhali of Sind, in which are mentioned "*arbor Zingitana et shisham et piper*." No commentator to my knowledge has explained what this timber is. But is it not manifestly *sisú*, or as it is more usually called (at least in upper India) *shisham*? If I am right in supposing the *blackwood* of Bombay to be a kind of *sisú*, we may now add the query is, What is the *Arbor Zingitana* (*shajar-al-Zanj*) in the last quotation? Can it be *ginger*? A Sanskrit etymology is assigned to the word *zingiber*, but the mediæval map of Marino Sanuto (circa 1320) connects the name and article with Zinj or Zanzibar.

H. Yule, Colonel.

Palermo, August 28th, 1872.

SUPARA.

Alberuni says, from Bahruj to Sindan is 50 parasangs; from thence to Subarah 6 parasangs; and from thence to Tanah is 5 parasangs.* Had he given these distances as 40, 16, and 5 respectively they would have agreed remarkably well with the distances from Bharuch to Sanjân 108 miles in a direct line, Sanjân to Supârâ near Wasâi (N. Lat. 19° 25'; E. Long. 72° 50') 41 miles, and from Supârâ to Thânâ 17½ miles. The last distance, however, is so nearly 5 parasangs, and the distance from Bharuch to Supârâ so nearly 50, that it can scarcely be doubted that Supârâ is the *Subarah* of the Arabs and the *Souppara* of Ptolemy.†—Editor.

THE GAULI RAJ.

I see in the *Indian Antiquary* page 250, some remarks by Mr. Ramsay on my suggestions about the Gâuli Râj. Monuments similar to those that he mentions are very common in that corner of Khandesh which lies on the head waters of the Panjara River west of Pimpalnair. I believe that the Bhills erect them both of stone and wood at this day, but had no time when I was there to go into the subject. The favourite figures are horsemen and warriors, and a curious symbol like "the young moon with the old one in her arms." I do not know whether it represents that or the Sun and Moon.

With reference to Mr. Ramsay's concluding remarks I must point out that I have "conjured up the ghost of some lost dynasty" with more success, as I have induced him to contribute the Ahirwâdâ legend to the stock of published information on the subject. And when he guesses "that at some past time the upland plains of the Satpuras and adjoining lands were chiefly occupied by shepherd tribes," I think he is more open than I am to chaff about the ten lost tribes of Israel.

Tribe or dynasty, they are gone, and it is the totality of their disappearance that leads me to believe that they cannot have been a nation, for that seldom perishes utterly, while it has been often seen in Europe and Asia that a mighty dynasty can collapse.

> "And like the baseless fabric of this vision
> Leave not a wrack behind."

W. F. Sinclair.

ON GOMUTRA.

The remarks recently made before the Asiatic Society of Bengal by Bâbu Râjendralâla Mitra with regard to the use of beef among the Hindus of ancient days, seem to have startled a good many, and have suggested an inquiry as to the period at which the cow came to be regarded as a sacred animal in this country. As a contribution to this enquiry, it is perhaps worthy of note that one of the "products of the cow" appears to have been held sacred in the days of Patanjali. In his commentary on Pânini I., 4, 96, occurs the sentence: "Gomûtrasyâpi syât" which may be rendered,—"Might there be [a drop] at least of Gomûtra?" This looks very like an inquiry by one who holding the "mûtra" sacred, required it for purposes of purification.

Now the date of Patanjali has been ingeniously fixed by the late Dr. Goldstücker in the middle of

* Reinaud, *Frag. Arab. et Pers.* p. 121.

† See my *Notes of a Visit to Gujarat*, p. 16.

the second century B.C.; and Professor R. G. Bhandarkar has, I understand, been able to find a further confirmation of Dr. Goldstücker's conclusion. It would seem therefore that the cow must have been revered at as early a period at least as the second century B.C.

KASHINATH TRIMBAK TELANG.

PUBLICATION ON CHAND.

We learn that Mr. J. Beames is preparing for the Bibliotheca Indica, published for the Bengal Asiatic Society, the text of Chand's Prithirâja Râsau, with the words divided, from a collation of several MSS., and that Dr. Hoernle, Professor of Sanskrit at Jaynarayan's College, Benares, will prepare the second part, beginning with book XXIII. The two parts will be carried on simultaneously, and the first fasciculus containing about 2,000 lines will appear immediately.

JAGANNATH.

Though there is nothing positively indecent in the festival of Jagannâth itself, the Pandas or priests, who have the management of it, are notoriously immoral men, and many females who go on pilgrimage to Puri return no more to lead chaste lives. Nor is that all. The sculptures on the temple from top to bottom and the paintings on the car are the foulest and the most abominable possible. Even those who have every faith in Jagannâth cannot help being disgusted by them.—*Indian Mirror.*

CAR AT SRIRANGAM.

From actual observation I am compelled to endorse what you say of the frightful immorality and obscenity of some of the religious rites of actual, living, and popular Hinduism. Benâres is bad enough, with its myriad Lingas continually worshipped. But I have seen nothing in Benâres so beastly and corrupting as the band of sculptures that encircle the new car of the great god of Srirangam. You may be aware that this granite god Rangaswâmi-Iyengar, with his twelve or fifteen hundred thousand rupees' worth of trumpery in gold, silver, pearls, emeralds, and diamonds, sits and lies in the most splendid temple of Southern India; seven-walled, and with the outer wall measuring half a mile on the side, or two miles in circuit. On three sides of each of these seven walls are richly ornate pyramidal gateways, called Gopuras, which show finely in photographs, and are so captivating to the eye of an artist.

Let the visitor of Seringam, insist as I did, on seeing the latest edition of old Brahmanism, in the newly constructed and freshly painted rath (carriage) of the presiding deity. He will see nothing so vile as this in the Naples Museum, among objects which the fearless student of history and life sees there, just as they were taken from the darkest Roman times and the brothels of unburied Pompeii. Rangam-Iyengar once a year leaves his angry Juno, Rangam-Iyengari in the temple and is dragged in his giant car, by a thousand Brahmans and their deluded users, with songs and shouting, to spend three nights in the pretty little temple of Nachi-aramma, the dancing goddess.—*Mrs. C. H. Dall in the 'Indian Mirror.'*

HILL OR ABORIGINAL TRIBES IN THE DEKHAN.

I am indebted to the learned Dr. Carter, the Civil Surgeon of Satara, for the short account that I propose to give on the above points. According to his opinion, the aboriginal tribes in the District are either settled or wandering. In the first class he places (1) the Ramosis, who inhabit the eastern parts of the District; (2) the Mangs and Berads, who occupy the parts which lie adjacent to the Kolhapur state; (3) the Kolis, who live in small numbers in the hilly tracts near the Ghats; and (4) the Dhangars, who live either on the top of the hills which form the offshoots of the Sahyadri, or on the plains of the eastern part of the District, where they find sufficient room to pasture their flocks. In the other classes he places the Wadars, Vanjaris, Kaikadis, and Dombaris. The last, however, do not wander only in this Collectorate, but pass and repass through it in the course of their migrations to other Zillas. They have no distinct grammar or vocabulary of their own; but the settled tribes speak the Marathi language with a mixture of a few words peculiar to each tribe, and the wandering tribes those of the districts from whence they come. The Wanjaris, the Doctor thinks, come from Khandesh, but I am humbly of opinion that they are Vanacharas, that is, wanderers in the forests on the slopes of the tracts which lie at the foot of the Sahyadri range of hills. They are also found in large numbers in the Madras and Western Ghâts. The Kaikadis and Dombaris, the Doctor believes, came from Telinga, as the dialects which they speak resemble the Telugu. I have had no time to make inquiries of them, and can therefore offer no opinion of my own.

The Dhangars (Shepherds) are the quietest and most peaceful race of people. They wander in the district in search of pasture for their herds and flocks, but often return to their settled homes on the plains or mountains. Their religion, language, and manners, are to a great extent like those of the Kunbis. But the temples in which they worship their deities are mere piles of large unhewn stones, which Captain M. Taylor in one of his works remarks resemble the places of worship of the old Druids. These people render great service to the cultivators, who invite them with an offer of a reward to pen their flocks in their fields, so that they may leave behind them valuable manure. The founder of the Holkar family in Malwa sprang from this race.

The Wadars, a rude and hardy race of people, wander over all parts of the Dekhan. They speak a dialect which I think neither resembles the Maharashtra nor the Telugu. They are principally engaged in cutting large stones and rocks, and working stone quarries; they work very hard and spend money as fast as they get it in drinking and other vices. They have a distinct system of religion of their own, and their manners and customs differ widely from those of the general mass of the Hindus.

There is another race of people in this District which cannot properly be called a hill tribe. They inhabit the Murhas, or low valleys at the foot of the Sahyadri, and are known under the appellation of the Kunbis of the Mawals. They are a very peaceful race of men, extremely ignorant, simple, and superstitious. For six months in the year they subsist on coarse corn, which they grow on the sides of their mountains, and pass the remaining half of the year either in hunting or obtaining roots and bark of trees which serve them as food.—*Bombay Educational Record.*

MERKARA COPPER PLATES

I

II

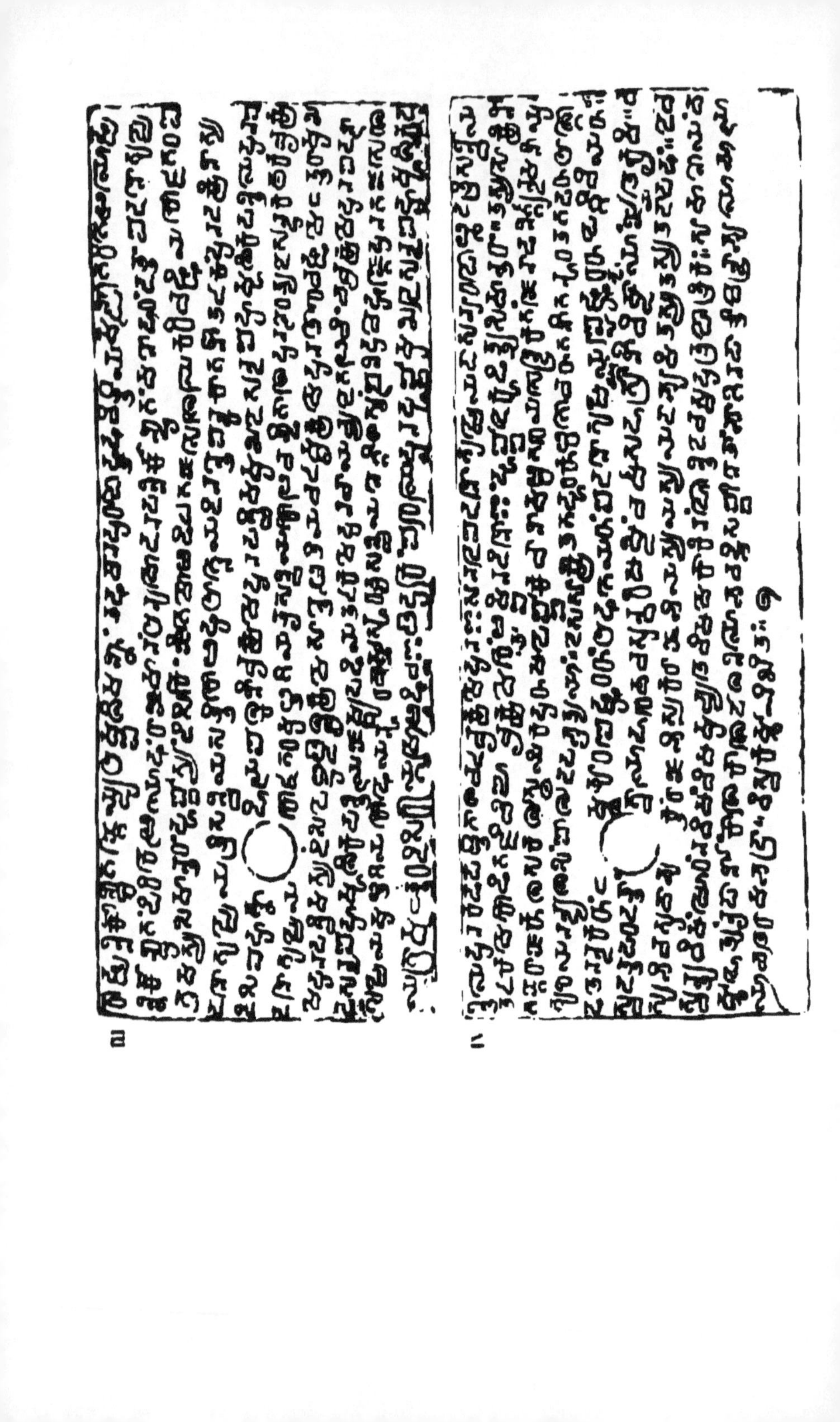

KÍRTANS, OR HYMNS FROM THE EARLIEST BENGALI POETS.

By JOHN BEAMES, B.C.S., &c. &c.

A special interest attaches to the six short hymns which I now lay before the public for the first time. Not only do they represent a large and widely popular class of compositions hitherto almost unknown to European scholars, but they are at the same time absolutely the earliest known specimens of Bengali literature, and thus present to the philologist a means of solving many very obscure and difficult problems, while to the student of Indian philosophy they exhibit to the fullest extent the natural and unrestrained sentiments of a follower of the Vaishnava creed in its first and purest stage.

These hymns are still sung in every village in Bengal. I believe there are some thousands of them living on the lips and in the hearts of the peasantry which have never been reduced to writing. Collections have been made, and I believe a few have been published in Bengali, but not in such a way as to be generally accessible to English readers. From their internal structure and from historical considerations they may be ascribed to the end of the fourteenth and beginning of the fifteenth century, and are therefore genuine representatives of the speech of Bengal five hundred years ago.

I.

Rág Sindhúra [illegible]-tála.

Anjana ganjana, jagajjana ranjana,
  meghapunja jini* baraṇa;
Tarunáruna,† sthalakamala dalāruna,
  manjira ranjita charaṇa;
Dekha sakhi nágara rája birāje‡;
Sudhal sudhámaya háre bikasita,
  [illegible] malina [illegible]§ láje;
Indibara garaba [illegible] [illegible],
  manasija [illegible];
Bhánga [illegible] [illegible] [illegible],
  [illegible] [illegible] [illegible] [illegible] [illegible];
Anukula [illegible] bhramara karambita,
  keli kadamba [illegible];
[illegible] [illegible] [illegible] [illegible] [illegible],
  [illegible]¶ [illegible] [illegible].

Translation.

Behold, beloved,
Surpassing collyrium (in blackness) delighter of human kind,
  Conquering in hue the cloud-masses;
Tender as the dawn, redder than the red lotus,
  His feet adorned with anklets;
See, dear friend, shines the king of youths;
  (His face) expanded with nectared smiles is fair
  (so that) the moon has become dim from shame;
Annihilating the pride of the lotus with his eyes,
  Love's snare;
Binding with his eyebrow's snake-like curve,
  The race of women, distress of [illegible];
Made musical by bees hangs the beautiful
  Garland of keli and kadamba flowers;
In the heart of Gobind Das is ever firmly fixed
  that gracious form.

The lines being very long I have divided each one into two with the exception of the third, which is a sort of chorus, and shorter than the rest. The whole piece thus consists of eight lines. The end of each line is marked by a colon (:).

II.

Lalit [illegible].

Sun, Sun! Mádhava, [illegible] [illegible]!
[illegible] [illegible] [illegible] [illegible]* [illegible]!

* *Jini*—having conquered, an old form of the aorist participle.

† *Aruṇa* has two meanings. In the first place it means "the dawn," in the second "red."

‡ *Birāje*. This form of the simple indefinite present is common to all the languages of the Aryan group, though its meaning as a present is somewhat obscured by modern usage in Marathi and Hindi; the older form is in -ai as in [illegible], [illegible], and is contracted from the Sanskrit ending -ati. In the forms like [illegible] [illegible], we have the old oblique case of the noun which expresses both instrumentality and location. In the poems of the mediaeval period of all the seven languages this form occurs though in the modern development of each of them it has met with a different fate.

§ *Bhal* is still used in the Bhojpuri dialect of Hindi, but is no longer current in Bengali, which uses instead the more modern form *bhál*.—Grotlaus, [illegible], &c.

‖ [illegible]—[illegible]. The [illegible] written as -ng.

¶ [illegible]—Hindi, [illegible]; Bhojpuri, [illegible]; (from Skt. through Prakrit).

* This poem contains more grammatical forms than the preceding one: and those who are acquainted with the Bengali of the present day will see how little these forms have as yet acquired of the distinctive characteristics of that language. Thus—

तोहारि 'of thee,' Bengali, तोर; Bhojpuri Hindi, [illegible]: old Hindi (Chand) तुव, तेरो also तेरी; Marwari [illegible], Panjabi, तुहाडा; Gujarati, तारो; &c.

It would seem that *Tohari* is almost as closely allied to any one of these forms as to the modern Bengali.

[illegible] "may it remain! be it!" The termination agrees with Uriya in [illegible], [illegible], but not particularly with Bengali. It resembles more the [illegible], [illegible] of old Hindi. It is in fact Sanskrit [illegible] [illegible], [illegible] imperat.; which becomes in Prakrit [illegible] [illegible], and the hiatus is in Hindi filled up by [illegible], while in our text the *a* is dropped. Whence the Bengali gets its final *é* in *hauk*, *rahuk*, I do not yet know.

Kâhe kahasi* tahari sakhiyâ bâta!
Jâmini [illegible] [illegible] ânta?
Rajata [illegible] kari Râika [illegible],
Âna ramani [illegible] karaha bilâsa.
Kahaha rasika dekhara bara Kâna?
Tohe sama [illegible] jagata [illegible] âna.
Mânika [illegible] kâchahi [illegible],
Chhiya! chhiya! tohari [illegible] bhâsha;
Bidyâpati [illegible] bhâna,
Râi nâ heraba tohari bayâna.

Translation.

([illegible])

[illegible] ;
Hear, hear! Mâdhava, [illegible] lady!
Fie on such love as this of thine!
Why didst thou say a word of meeting,
At night thou [illegible] with another?
Having made deceitful love to Rái (Râdhikâ)
Thou makest sport with another woman.
Who says that Kânh is the crown of lovers?
Like thee another [illegible] there is not in the world.
Leaving the diamond thou delightest in glass;
Fie! fie! on thy [illegible] words.
Bidyâpati says—O thou who [illegible] the champak
Rái will not look on thy face.

III.

Rág: [illegible].

Râika [illegible] Mâdhaba,
[illegible] dharanî [illegible]:
Dui kare dui pada [illegible] Mâdhaba,
[illegible] Rai:
[illegible] kari Kâna:
[illegible] sangata, [illegible] jânat,
[illegible] prâna:
[illegible] ni herbi,
[illegible] prâna:
[illegible] rakhaba,
[illegible] prâna:
[illegible] Kâna [illegible],
[illegible] bayâna:
Gobinda Dâsa [illegible],
[illegible] Kâna:

TRANSLATION.

(*[illegible]*)

Mâdhav [illegible] the [illegible] of Rái,
at her feet rolling on the earth:
Mâdhav [illegible] holding her two feet in his two hands,
still Rái was averse:
Again making entreaty Kânh (says):

---

* [illegible] may be also [illegible], as a [illegible] to Bengali [illegible]. It is 2 sing. [illegible] the original (कहसि—[illegible] + [illegible]). It is the same as [illegible], Bengali, [illegible].

† [illegible] Bhojpuri [illegible] is the nearest form, Bengali [illegible] for [illegible] is further removed. A few lines further on we get the still more Bhojpuri form [illegible].

‡ [illegible]—a pure Sanskrit form 2 sing. [illegible]. In modern Bengali the [illegible] has leapt backwards over the [illegible] making [illegible], as in [illegible], [illegible].

§ [illegible]—[illegible], says, as in [illegible] and many other dialects.

‖ [illegible]—[illegible]. [illegible] and [illegible].

¶ [illegible] [illegible]. The old present participle, still retained in Uriya, though disused in modern Bengali.

* [illegible] This is a curious formation, the [illegible] is probably shortened from [illegible] and represents a feminine past participle such as still subsists in Hindi [illegible], [illegible]. [illegible] [illegible], [illegible], but which has died out in Bengali.

† [illegible] plur. of personal pron. 1st person. Hindi [illegible]. This is a peculiarly instructive form. The origin of this word in all the seven languages is the Prakrit [illegible] [illegible]. The Uriya with its usual fondness for archaisms still retains this form almost unchanged in [illegible] where the [illegible] is merely the natural thickening of the pronunciation after [illegible]. Hindi has thrown the [illegible] backwards to the beginning of the word making [illegible]. In [illegible] we have the tendency, natural to Bengalis, towards lengthening the short vowel, so that this form may be regarded as transitional between middle Hindi and the modern Bengali [illegible].

‡ [illegible] is a [illegible] [illegible] oblique singular of [illegible] [illegible] as in Bengali [illegible] is generally pronounced [illegible], we are perhaps justified in transliterating this word [illegible] when it will be an [illegible] form to [illegible] in the [illegible]. [illegible] a little lower down, the dropping of the [illegible] of the [illegible] is one step in the transition from the [illegible] form [illegible], [illegible] to the Bengali [illegible].

§ [illegible] this is pure Hindi and has no representative in Bengali.

‖ [illegible] like [illegible], [illegible] in the next line is the first person singular of the future. There is a singular want of agreement between the terminating vowels of this tense in the three languages which use the form in [illegible] for the future. Thus—

		Bhojpuri	Bengali	Uriya
Sing.	1.	[illegible]	râkhiba (o)	[illegible]
	2.	[illegible]	[illegible]	[illegible]
	3.	[illegible]	[illegible]	[illegible] ([illegible])
Pl.	1.	[illegible]	[illegible] ([illegible])	[illegible]
	2.	[illegible]	[illegible]	[illegible]
	3.	[illegible]	[illegible]	[illegible] (and -[illegible])

The words in the text agree with the Bhojpuri of Behar better than with the modern Bengali in one respect, namely, in that they retain the [illegible] in the second syllable, or in other words they [illegible] the terminating syllable to a [illegible], not as in Bengali to a [illegible] base [illegible]. The curious variations of the terminal vowel in the several persons may perhaps be referred to successive corruptions of the [illegible] [illegible], [illegible], etc. in which for reasons not yet fathomed one vowel has acquired the ascendant in one case, another in another. Thus in the 3 sing. the -o is probably for -ai [illegible], and Uriya has changed [illegible] as it has in the genitive sing. of the noun where it has -ar for the Bengali -er.

¶ [illegible] this should also like [illegible] be read [illegible], being the common Prakrit form for [illegible].

I am obedient to thee, thou knowest it well,
Why dost thou burn my soul? :
If thou wilt not look on my face,
to what place shall I go?
Without thee to what end shall I preserve my life,
I will abandon my own life :
When Kánh had made all this entreaty,
and still she looked not on his face :
Gobind Dás says vain was hope,
weeping sadly then went Kánh.

IV.

Rág : Dhyánesri.

Hari! Hari! [illegible] dharaṇi dhari [illegible]
[illegible] [illegible] [illegible] :*
Níla gagana heri táhári bhavana† [illegible]
[illegible]‡ [illegible]§ [illegible] :
Ki karabo chandra [illegible] [illegible] lepana
kamalaye dharaṇi [illegible] :
Ána [illegible], [illegible] [illegible], [illegible]
Gobinda Dása nahi jáne :

TRANSLATION.

(Radha repents of her sulkiness.)

"Hari! Hari!" she calls, lying on the ground
she rises up,
Speaking trembling words.
Looking at the blue sky thinking of his wandering,
Her sobs from the [illegible] [illegible].
"What avails the moon, thick smearing of sandal-paste,
Kamalaye leaves, or lying on the ground?
Bring him, friend, bring him to my feet," [illegible]
Gobind Das knows not.

V.

Sri Rág.

[illegible] all [illegible] rahaṇa [illegible] gel,¶
[illegible] [illegible]* ná [illegible];
[illegible] náhi [illegible] karana jo [illegible],
[illegible] [illegible] jana [illegible] [illegible];
[illegible] [illegible] [illegible] [illegible] [illegible],
Tabhu [illegible] hiya majhu† nahi [illegible].

Hamári [illegible] [illegible] [illegible] [illegible] bhági‡
[illegible] [illegible] [illegible] [illegible] [illegible] [illegible].
Vidyápati kaha [illegible] kaha [illegible]
[illegible] [illegible] [illegible]§ [illegible]

(Radha's regrets at the long absence of Krishna.)

I have remained in much fear enduring this body
Not having been near that source of delight;
No one of my companions has been in my power;
As the [illegible] [illegible] stinging the heart;
Again how many entreaties have I made humbly
Kṛishṇa the [illegible] in my heart understands not the [illegible].
What fortune was mine in a former life?
Again I have come to attain this reward.
Vidyápati says, speak not this grief,
Thus has occurred the first separation.

There is a mystic meaning in all these kirtans which it is worth while to draw out more clearly.

The old Aryan element-worship had led to the creation of a multitude of gods between whose varying attributes and powers a considerable amount of confusion must necessarily have existed. In the long centuries of depression under which the Brahmanical religion languished during the supremacy of Buddhism, the necessity of introducing some order into the grotesque and crowded Pantheon of the Hindus must have forced itself upon the mind of the Brahmans.

The monotheism of Buddha, affording as it did one definite person upon whom the popular mind might fix itself, led to the idea of elevating either Siva or Vishnu into the supreme place. The shadowy [illegible] *Brahma* of an earlier age became personified in one or other of the rival gods, and gradually the incarnation of Kṛishṇa, an Indian rendering of the great Christian fact received through the medium of later Buddhist legends, shaped itself into a distinct creed and won an immense and ever increasing popularity.

A further development awaited it when the Muhammadans came to India. The emotional or unphilosophical monotheism which they profess-

* [illegible] It is a distinctly Hindi peculiarity to pronounce this 'bhakha.' [illegible] is in Hindi regularly [illegible], but not in Bengali. That it must be so pronounced here is evident from the rhyming with [illegible], a wing.

† *[illegible]* : my authorities are not in accord about this word, one writes it '[illegible],' a second, '[illegible],' while a third suggests '[illegible]'; the above seems the more probable reading.

‡ [illegible] i. e. [illegible].

§ [illegible] seems a sort of double formation, [illegible], i. e. [illegible] would have been sufficient, the additional syllable is perhaps of [illegible].

[illegible] etc. The meaning is not clear. I have rendered it as though [illegible] was for [illegible] and supposed Rádhá to be addressing her [illegible] or [illegible], but I am not satisfied with this. Babu [illegible] thinks [illegible] [illegible] to [illegible] word for [illegible] 'i. e. without resource,' he then translates [illegible] by 'without the lover,' but I cannot get this meaning out of the words.

‡ [illegible] Here again comes the Hindi type with [illegible] for [illegible] unknown to modern Bengali.

¶ *gel* probably corrupted from [illegible] a [illegible] from root [illegible], meaning "having caused to go," that is, having borne or endured.

* *Thor* perhaps from [illegible].

† *Majhu* a form of [illegible] i. e. [illegible].

‡ *[illegible]* for [illegible], &c.

ed made a deep impression on the philosophical minds of the Hindus, and led to that outbreak of new religious theories which was reduced to system by Chaitanya in Bengal, by Râmânand and his disciple Kabîr in Hindustan and by Nânak in the Panjâb. Vishnu is the supreme being; the whole Hindu Pantheon sinks into the position of ministers to his will; by a further extension of the same line of thought the supreme being is in everything—is everything. We must love him, for we are a part of his essence. He has provided us with a concrete expression of this love, in his sports with Râdhâ and the gopis. Let us then meditate on these, let our hymns and songs be of these. Let Râdhâ typify the human soul and Krishna the divine essence. But in man's nature the divine and the animal are strangely mingled—he is half god, half beast. The glowing temperament of the Indian poet, unrestrained by any of those curbs and checks which Europe has agreed to obey, led him into the wildest excesses. The love at first intended to be purely spiritual soon degenerated into mere earthly lust, and the scenes between Râdhâ and her lover are often more suggestive of the brothel than of the temple.

I give as an example of the least offensive of this class a short hymn.

VI.

Sâjá samaya samaya nâhi sikha,
Ati mre madana dui diguna dukhike;
Sab sakhi mili saïta jâen
Chumbi chumbi dhali chibuka je nâwâen
Kanaite hain [illegible] sage
Mantra na [illegible] jaise [illegible] bhujanga
Dori ekha kara dhali mudita nayana,
[illegible] karaye jaise [illegible] pâna.
Tila ek dukha janam bhari sukha,
Ither kâhe dhali [illegible] mukha!
Bhanaye Bidyâpati suna he Murâri

Trembles even [illegible] nárí.
To a young girl in love there is no pleasure,
In her heart Madana causes double pain;
All her companions assembling lay beside her
[illegible], the girl is [illegible],
When taking her into his arms she contorts all her body,
As spells are disregarded by the young serpent
Covering her closed eyes with her hands,
As a sick man takes medicine;
For a moment is the pain, for life is the joy:
From this O girl! why do you turn your face?
Vidyâpati says, hear, O Murari!
These are the senses of love, the girl is but young.

This is Horace's

"Nondum subacta ferre jugum valet
Cervice; nondum munia comparis
Aequare, nec tauri ruentis
In venerem tolerare pondus."*

But it is at first sight rather startling to see the metaphor applied as it is in this case to the first effect upon the soul of the awakening influence of divine love. Accustomed as we are to keep the flesh and the spirit widely apart and to regard them as antagonistic to one another, it is strange and revolting to be brought face to face with a phase of thought in which the fleshly serves as a type of the spiritual. Unaided human nature has in Vaishnavism soared high and nearly touched the goal of truth, but for lack of revelation it has fallen back and lies grovelling in the mire.

In conclusion, I must acknowledge the source whence I obtained these interesting hymns. I have to thank Babu Jagaddishnath Rai for his kindness in procuring them for me, for assisting me with his advice in translating and making notes on them.

He has promised to endeavour to procure for me some more of them, which if the specimens herein given should prove interesting to any class of readers, I will publish in due course hereafter.

THE CELTS OF TOUNGOO.

BY FRANCIS MASON, D. D.

Mr. W. Theobald, of the Geological Survey, in the Proceedings of the Asiatic Society of Bengal for July 1865, and again in the Proceedings for July 1869, first brought to public notice the existence of stone implements in Burmah "both of the palæolithic and neolithic types."

In the latter number of the Proceedings he furnished a very full and interesting article, illustrated with figures of the principal types, and remarked:—"The entire number of all types which I have observed in Burmah amount to 30 or thereabouts."

* Carm. II. v.

At the March meeting of the Asiatic Society of Bengal for the present year, Capt. Fryer exhibited more than one hundred specimens of celts which he had collected in Burmah, the largest collection ever made; but no detailed description has yet been published of them.

In the *Rangoon Times* of April 16, 1872, the Curator of the Phayre Museum acknowledges the reception of twenty-five specimens from Capt. Fryer with tabular notices of "Implement—Rock Material—weight—where found."

All the specimens collected by Mr. Theobald and Capt. Fryer are from the Tenasserim Provinces, Pegu, or Arakan. It is here proposed to notice a few which have come under my own observation in the Toungoo district.

One of the most common forms of the small stone implements is given in Fig. 1 *a*.* The edge is bevelled down on both sides, but more on one side than the other, as may be seen by the form of the border given in *Fig.* 1 *b*. The specimen from which these tracings were taken is made of basalt, as most of this type are; occasionally they are met formed of schistose rock. Some specimens have the corners at the cutting edge more angular, and others more rounded than the one figured. A second form has a cutting edge on three sides, and is even slightly sharpened behind. A sketch of one is given in Fig. 2 and is formed of a schistose rock, as are all of this type that I have seen. A third form is that of a small adze with shoulders. A tracing of one is given in *Fig.* 3 *a*. and its side in *Fig.* 3 *b*. The specimen was formed of basalt, as are most of the specimens I have seen in Toungoo.

But the most remarkable stone instrument, which I have seen or heard of in Burmah is a curved two-edged sword or dagger, but the point is broken off. It is nearly ten inches long by three and a half broad, at its widest part, and is six tenths of an inch thick. Three inches of the lower part is narrowed down to two inches and a half in width for a handle, leaving the blade on each side to form a shoulder. It is made of basalt, but where the stone has not been recently chipped or ground down, it has a soft whitish incrustation, owing to the decay of the rock from exposure to the atmosphere. On this surface some regular cross lines have been drawn, some of which are nearly obliterated; but for what object is not clear.

A tracing of the instrument is given in Fig. 4 *a*, and of the end, to show the thickness, in Fig. 4 *b*.

All the celts collected by Capt. Fryer are of stone, as are also all those collected by Mr. Theobald excepting the "fragment of a bronze celt which was shown me near Maulmain, and was regarded by me of doubtful authority."

In the Toungoo district copper celts are not uncommon. They are sometimes little wedges of the same size and shape as the most common of the stone celts. Fig. 5 is the tracing of one. It is 1·8 inches long by 1·7 broad, and 6 thick at the end; and weighs 10 tolas. It is bevelled down on both sides at the edge and has evidently been cast in a mould with, I think, some admixture of metal not copper.

Another, but rarer form, is that of a small spade, cast with a hollow socket in which to insert a wooden handle, such as are used in cultivation by both Burmese and Karens and other tribes at the present day, but made of iron. A tracing of one is given in Fig. 6. It is 3·2 inches long by 1·7 wide at the broadest part. In the specimen figured, a portion of the upper side of the socket has been broken off.

A third form is that of the hollow spearheads. A figure of one is given in *Fig.* 7 *a*. The length is 4·4 inches hollow with a depth of 3·9, leaving 0·5 solid at the margin. The width of the broadest part is 3·2. The lines in the figure are on one side only, and are raised above the surface, showing that they were in the mould when the instrument was cast. Fig. 7 *b*. is a tracing of the end, showing a hollow space 1·6 inches long by 0·5 wide. The chevron is hardly pre-historic. Another spearhead of the same general outline but smaller, with sharper barbs, and one larger than the other, was brought me by a Shan who said it came from the borders of China. A sketch of it is given at Fig. 8. It was 3·4 inches long by 2·6 broad at the blade.

Besides the forms usually recognised as celts, the Karens associate with them a miscellaneous collection of circular articles both of stone and bronze. The most notable among them is a stone quoit, 4·5 inches in diameter, with a hollow in the centre 2·2 across, leaving the stone circle 1·1 broad; and which is 0·5 thick on the inner side, but is bevelled off to a sharp edge on the margin. I have heard of several specimens, but the one I examined is a fine polished instrument made of striped jasper, and before the edges

* The lithographs are 2-3ths of the scale of Dr. Mason's tracings.—Ed.

were chipped off for medicine, was a perfect circle. A tracing is given in Fig. 9.

The figure of a fragment of a smaller but similar instrument is given in Fig. 10 *a*. It is 0·5 of an inch thick on the inner margin, like the former one, but only 0·8 or 0·9 broad and is bevelled down on both sides to form an edge on the outer margin. A section is represented in Fig. 10 *b*. It is made of reddish brown compact rock which is scratched with a knife, and looks like magnesian limestone.

A small circular pebble with a hole bored through the centre had evidently, by the wear of the rock, been used at some period of its history, for a spindle whirl, and among the numerous non-descripts brought me for examination was a small article made of jade, of which a tracing is given in Fig. 11. It is only ·15 of an inch thick. The material is unquestionably Chinese and there can be no doubt but it is of Chinese workmanship. It is said that the inhabitants of Manchuria used jade-tipped arrows as late as the twelfth century.

In regard to the use of the implements noted, some of the copper ones appear to have been used for spades and spearheads, and some of the stone ones for adzes and knives or cleavers or daggers; while others are doubtful. There is no reason however to believe that any of them were ever used for such purposes in Burmah. The material of which nearly all are made shows conclusively that they were not made here but have been imported. The far larger proportion of the stone ones are made of basalt or other rock foreign to Burmah, and have probably been introduced from Hindustan. In the northern parts of Burmah, they are usually made of jade and undoubtedly come from China; as do the copper ones, for there is no copper in Burmah, but it is constantly imported from China. The reason they have been introduced into Burmah, both by sea and by land is that they are regarded by all the native tribes as thunderbolts fallen from heaven, and that they are talismans or amulets, protecting from evil and curing disease. Hence they have a fictitious value, and a trade is carried on with them at enormous prices. The solid copper wedges are rated at their weight in silver, and for the smallest of the copper spear-heads, Fig. 8, thirty rupees were demanded. Thirty rupees had been paid for the stone quoit Fig. 9, and in payment for Fig. 10, fifteen were demanded. These high prices necessarily lead to their manufacture. In America when fossil giants are in demand, they can be found almost anywhere by digging. In Yunan, celts principally of jade are so abundant, that Dr. Anderson found them for sale in the bazars of Momein.

It will not be disputed but the celts of Burmah have the *form* of pre-historic implements, but all I have seen appear to me of comparatively modern manufacture, and I think Mr. Theobald, who knows most about them, is of the same opinion. The natives say they are picked up in the streams, or found on the mountain sides, or dug out of the ground, but their representations are utterly untrustworthy and deserve no more credence than their assertions that they came down originally from heaven with the lightening, or that they have power to cure disease.

But supposing for the sake of argument, that these spades and hoes were formerly used in Burmah for agricultural purposes, their use necessitated the existence of means to cut down trees and clear the forest, and, therefore, of iron instruments, for all the celts in Burmah would not cut down a single teak tree; so we are forced to the conclusion that these stone and copper implements coexisted with iron, when we may suppose iron was scarce and not sufficiently abundant for all purposes; a state of things which it is not necessary to go down to before seen in the Mosaic chronology to find.

Not many days walk from Balmoral, where the Queen eats off gold and silver, I have seen, in the latter half of the nineteenth century people dining on wooden dishes. Now were these people, with their wooden platters in the pantry, sunk by a sudden catastrophe into the mud of the lake by which they dwell, they might, before the century closes, be dug up again a veritable "cran-'nog," and by the reasoning now applied to celts, it might be proven that they lived in a "wooden age" before crockery was known.

Many people stand masticating the truths of the Bible as an ox does his fodder, lest they should incontinently swallow a myth, but at sight of such trumpery shams as these Hindu and Chinese "Brummagem" wares, they instantly read us marvellous dissertations on pre-historic times, long before Moses was born or thought of, on this wise—"These stone instruments clearly prove that there was a period in pre-historic times when the Burmese or the inhabitants of Burmah, of whatever race they were, were wholly unacquainted with the arts of fabricating iron, steel, and metal instruments for cutting, and they resorted to the more difficult work of fashioning stone into adzes and axes, and other cutting instruments."—*Credat Judæus Apella, non ego.*

CELTS FROM TOUNGOO

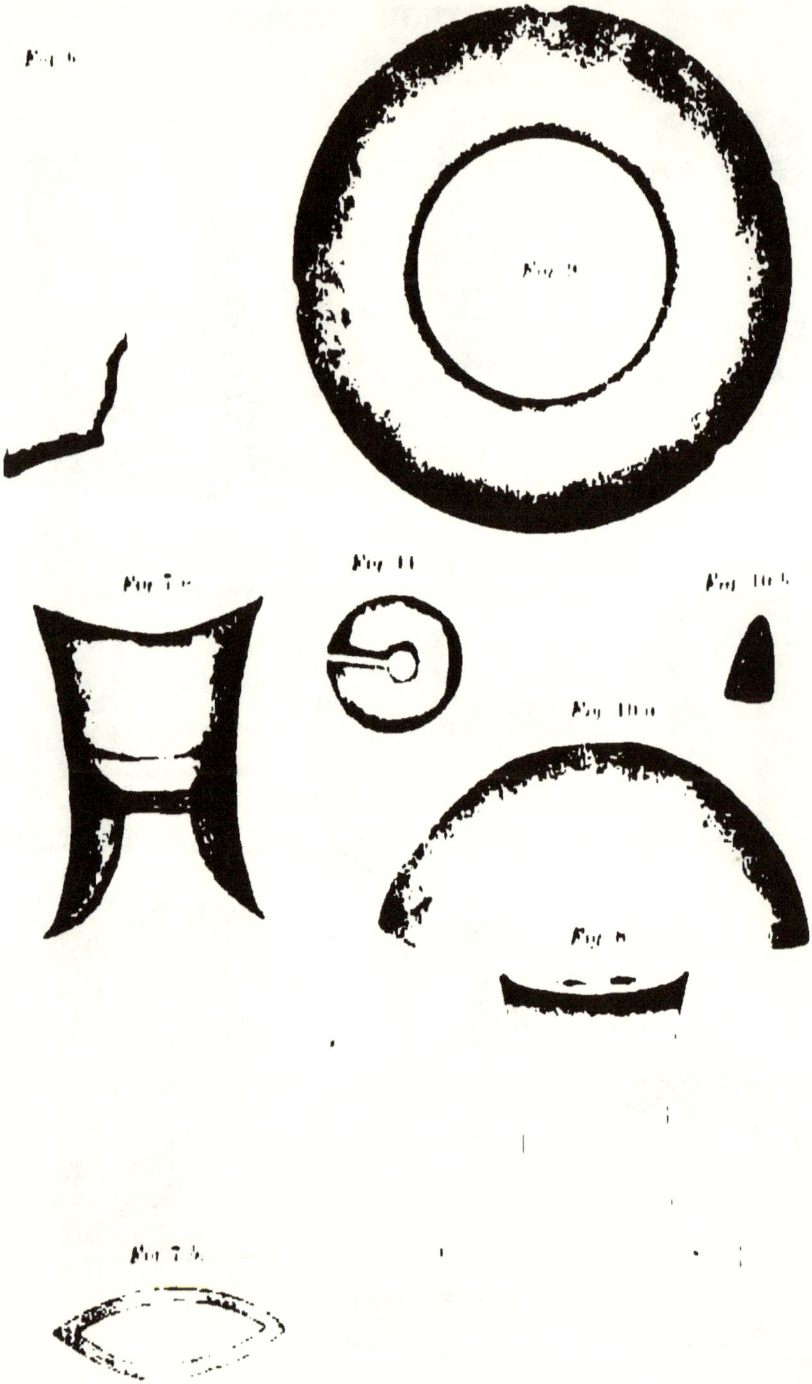

Fig. 6

Fig. 9

Fig. 11

Fig. 7a

Fig. 10b

Fig. 10a

Fig. 8

Fig. 7b

DONDRA INSCRIPTION.

By T. W. RHYS DAVIDS, C.C.S., ANURADHAPURA.

Like Cape Kamorin on the continent of India, Dondra Head on the island of "Happy Lanka," has always been a place of pilgrimage, and seems to have derived its sanctity from its being the extreme southerly point of land, where the known and firm earth ceases, and man looks out upon the ocean—the evermoving, the impassable, the infinite.

The worship of Neptune is no modern cultus, but even now when standing on these points, or on Śiva's rocky headland at Trinkomali, who does not feel a touch at least of the grand afflatus that inspired Byron's hymn to the "far-sounding sea!" It is at least acknowledged that no one who cannot enter in some degree into the feelings which gave rise to the worship of nature can hope to understand the history of the religious movements of the world.

The history of the temple on the headland at Dondra is at present quite unknown. Sir E. Tennent* describes its destruction as follows:—

Dondera Head, the Sunium of Ceylon, and the southern extremity of the island, is covered with the ruins of the temple, which was once one of the most celebrated in Ceylon. The headland itself has been the resort of devotees and pilgrims, from the remotest ages. Ptolemy describes it as Dagana, "sacred to the Moon," and the Buddhists constructed there one of their earliest dagobas, the restoration of which was the care of successive sovereigns. But the most important temple was a shrine which in very early times had been erected by the Hindus in favour of Vishnu. It was in the height of its splendour when, in 1587, the place was devastated in the course of the marauding expedition by which De Souza d'Arronches sought to create a diversion during the siege of Columbo by Raja Singha II. The historians of the period state that at that time Dondera was the most renowned place of pilgrimage in Ceylon, Adam's Peak scarcely excepted. The temple they say was so vast, that from the sea it had the appearance of a city. The pagoda was raised on vaulted arches, richly decorated, and roofed with plates of gilded copper. It was encompassed by a quadrangular cloister, opening under verandas, upon a terrace and gardens with odoriferous shrubs and trees whose flowers were gathered by the priests for processions. De Souza entered the gates without resistance; and his soldiers tore down the statues, which were more than a thousand in number. The temple and its buildings were overthrown, its arches and its colonnades were demolished, and its gates and towers levelled with the ground. The plunder was immense—in ivory, gems, jewels, sandalwood, and ornaments of gold. As the last indignity that could be offered to the sacred place, cows were slaughtered in the courts, and the car of the idol, with other combustible materials, being fired, the shrine was reduced to ashes. A stone door-way exquisitely carved, and a small building, whose extraordinary strength resisted the violence of the destroyers, are all that now remain standing; the ground for a considerable distance is strewn with ruins, conspicuous among which are numbers of finely cut columns of granite. The dagoba which stood on the crown of the hill is a mound of shapeless debris.

I have not been able to find Sir Emerson Tennent's authority for stating that the Buddhists constructed there one of their earliest dagobas; and the statement is in itself so unlikely that a good authority for it is all the more needful; and again—what can be the derivation of the name Ptolemy gives to Dondra, namely, *Dagana*? is it Dāgaba? or is it *Dêva-nagara*? which becomes in Elu *Dewu-nuwara*, in modern Sinhalese *Dewundara*,† and in the English corruption *Dondra*? No attempt has been made to repair the temple since its destruction by the Portuguese and Major Forbes‡ thus describes its state in 1840:—

"Dondera or Dewinuwara (city of the god), is situated four miles from Matura, on a narrow peninsula, the most southerly point of Ceylon, latitude 5° 55′ N. and longitude 80° 40′ E. Here, interspersed amongst native huts, gardens and cocoanut plantations, several hundred upright stone pillars still remain: they are cut into various shapes, and exhibit different sculptures; amongst others, Râma, with his bow and arrows, may be discerned in various forms. A square gateway, formed of three stones elaborately carved, leads to a wretched "mud edifice," in which four stone windows of superior workmanship are evidences that a very different style of building had formerly occupied the site of this hovel. It is now, however, the only temple of Vishnu at Dewinuwara; a station reckoned particularly sacred by his votaries, as being the utmost limit which now remains of his conquests when incarnate in that perfect prince and peerless warrior Râmachandra. Although his temple is so mean, the place still retains much of its sanctity; and an annual festival, which takes place at the full moon in the month of July, continues to attract many thousands of the worshippers of Vishnu. From the

* *Ceylon*, Vol. II. pp. 112, 114.

† Accented on the second syllable which is short.

‡ In his now rare book *Eleven Years in Ceylon*, vol. II. pp. 170-172.

temple, a broad road, overshadowed by cocoanut trees, leads to a group of plain stone pillars near the sea-shore; but from these my attention was attracted by a single pillar, situated on a low rocky point, over which the sea breaks amidst hewn stones, the remains of some ancient building.

If Râma's expedition and conquest of Lanka existed in any form, or had any foundation more material than a poet's fancy, this lone pillar may be considered as an index which has resisted the waste of ages, and now battles with the waves of ocean to maintain its position, and mark the utmost limit which remains of Vishnu's conquest and religion. The pillar is of a form alternately octagonal and square, and exactly resembles columns* that are to be seen on the sacred promontory of Trinkomali.

Near the temple of Vishnu stand a Buddhist wihara and dâgoba; and a quarter of a mile farther inland is situated a stone building called Galgeha, consisting of two rooms; the roof as well as the walls are of the hewn stone, and exhibit excellent specimens of masonry. On the top there appears formerly to have been a dâgoba; but the ruin is now covered with shrubs and creeping plants that find root in the interstices of the building. These remains of Buddhism were completed or restored in the reign of Dapulu the Second, A.D. 686. A stone, which had been removed from the rubbish near one of the ruins, was pointed out to me at the house of my friend, Mr. H——, the cultivator of the district, with whom I was residing. It owes its preservation and present place of safety to Mrs. H——, to whom I am indebted for much information regarding the antiquities in this part of the island. In the inscription on this slab I recognised the name and sounding titles of the King Prâkrama Bahu, a zealous restorer of religious buildings, and a most persevering recorder of his own virtues and power. he reigned from A.D. 1155 to 1186.

On an upright stone, near the temple of Vishnu, is cut an inscription in the ancient Cingalese character: although considerably decayed, by perseverance it might probably be deciphered.

The inscription on the latter stone I have succeeded in completely deciphering with the exception of one line† and the one engraved on the front and two sides of the former I would transliterate thus—

	Śrí.	
	Śiri sanga	go para-
	Bo Śrí Parâkrama Bâ-	mparâwa-
	hu chakrawartti swâ-	n pawat
yutayi	min wahanseta	wí sagu
minise	10 warusha *tiara*	mok sa-
lautan	Bhûmi-mahâ-wihârayata	mpat sa
mehi	*era tan be rasata* ga-	dhiya yutu
prayojana	ta etikala da pol wa-	megas pra-
ekkota	tayi pilima geta	yojana wi-
Nila sela	gas 200yi llew ra-	ndinawun
siya yu	jjuru-âmintat	matu matu
tu	warddhana kalawanta *ta*	pala i-
	yi me ime mekuna-	ndawa

which written continuously is "Siri Sanga-Bo Śrí Parâkrama Bâhu Chakrawartti swamin wahanseta 10 warusha *tiara* Bhûmi-mahâ-wihârayata *era tan-be rasata* gata etikala da pol wattayi pilima-geta gas 200 (desiyayi) llew-rajjuru-âmintat warddhana-kalawanta *tayi me ime* mekunge paramparâwen pawat wí sagu mok sampat sadhiya yutu. Me gas prayojana windinawun matu matu pala indawa yutayi minisu (? minisen) *lautan* mehi prayojana ekkota Nila selasiya yutu."

The words in italics are doubtful and give no sense: (and though unfortunately the grammatical construction is not clear without them) yet their being so scarcely impairs the value of the inscription whose importance lies in the *name of the king*, the *name of the god*, and the *numerals* used.

I would translate:—

"In the tenth year of the overlord (Chakrawarti) Siri Sanga Bo Śrí Parâkrama Bâhu . . . . . near to the Bhûmi-mahâ wihâra and . . . cocoanut tope to the image house, and 200 cocoanut trees to the lord Dewa Râja (Vishnu). Let those who increase these gifts, and maintain their unbroken succession obtain the bliss of release in heaven (swarga-moksha sampatti). Those who enjoy the fruit (prayojana) of these trees ought from time to time to plant seedlings. People who pick up the fruits ought to present them to Nila (Vishnu)."

First as to the name of the king: Sanga-Bo (for Bodhi) and Parâkrama Bâhu (for Bhoja) are both common epithets of Ceylon kings. The first came into use after the martyrdom, 246 A.D. of the first king and Buddhist devotee of that name, and nine kings are given by Turnour with the name of Parâkrama Bâhu: but no king is given with the name mentioned in the text.

Forbes states that the temples were completed or restored by Dâpulu the second A. D. 686, and Tennent‡ has copied the statement, but I find nothing to support this in the books.§ The

* There is only one column, on which is no inscription.—T. W. R. D.

† It is published with text translation and notes in the last number of the Ceylon Asiatic Society; and the facsimile will be found in the *Proceedings* of the C. A. S. published in July 1871. [See *Ind. Antiquary*, p. 59.—Ed.]

‡ Note p. 118 loc. citat.

§ Turnour gives in his list two kings under the name of Dâpula. The second one began to reign 650 and the other 795 A. D.!

earliest mention of Dew-nuwara that I have found is in the *Rája Ratnákara* (verse 83 of my MS.) where it is said:—Ohu hè nàla Siri Sanga-bo raja Piyangal-wehera àdi wihàra karawà Dew-nuwara Dew-rajun pihituwà lo sàsana-ta sela baleya:—

'His nephew the younger Siri Sanga-bo, the king, built the Piyangal and other wiháras, *established the king of the gods* at Dewanuwara, and showed favour to the world and to religion.'

This is confirmed by Upham's extracts from the *Rájávaliya*,* and is probably correct, and the "establishment" referred to may be the same act as the building of the image house, and the dedication to it and to Vishnu of the lands referred to in our inscription.

If so the inscription would date from about 713 A. D., the king referred to having reigned from 702 A. D. to 718 A. D. according to Turnour.

The form of the letters would favour this view; they are a good deal older (especially the *e* and *m*, which are test letters in the Elu corruptions of the old Páli alphabet) than those of the long inscription of Nissanka Malla Parákrama Báhu the Great at Dambulla; and there is no other Sangabo between the one who came to the throne in 702 and the 4th of the name crowned A. D. 1071, whose epithet is known to have been Wijayabáhu and not Parákrama Báhu.

Secondly, as to the *name of the god*. Vishnu is commonly called in this (Anuradhapura) district, 'Utpala warna diwya rájayan wahanse,' and is always represented in the temples as of a blue colour. The Buddhists think Brahma the highest god, the next to be Sakra, and the third Vishnu. Brahma is too exalted to receive much worship. Sakra is sometimes painted on vihára walls, but I have never seen his image. Vishnu is both painted and his image sculptured with Maitri Diwya rája's (for so they call the coming Buddha) near to the sacred image of Sákya muni. But I have never heard the title Diwya rája used alone of any one god, nor the word Nila applied as a name to Vishnu.

Thirdly, *as to the numerals*: the Elu numerals are given by Prinsep as far as 10† and by Alwis as far as 1000.‡ These numerals have never, I believe, been noticed in any inscriptions, or in any books,—in Páli and Elu books, the words being always given in full; and neither Prinsep nor Alwis give any authority for their lists. In this inscription, however, the character before the warsh (varsha) is clearly that for 10 and the signs following the word gas (trees) and succeeded by yu, (used for cardinals like our -th after ordinals) are certainly figures: the second seems to be the 8 of the lists; the preceding figure probably represents, therefore, either tens or hundreds: it is very like the figure for 100 minus the last part. Is it possible that the figure showing the number of hundreds, instead of being written before the figure for 100 was sometimes written after it, and that then the last stroke of the 100 figure may have been omitted? If so our figures would represent 208: but in the absence of any examples with which to compare them, no certain decision can be arrived at. It only remains to be noted that the sign for two hundred is very like the figure of the Valabhi plates, stated by Prof. Bhandarkar§ to represent 200.

* Upham, Vol. II p. 246. I regret that writing away from my library, I cannot refer to the Mahawansa or to the original Rájávaliya.

† Thomas's edition, Vol. II. p. 79, Plate XL.

‡ Sidat Sangaráwa, p. 111.

§ *Indian Antiquary*, p. 60.

NÁRÁYAN SWÁMI.

COMPILED BY THE EDITOR.

One of the most numerous of the modern Hindu sects in Western India is that of Náráyan Swámi in Gujarát and Káthiáwád.‖ The facility with which multitudes have been led to regard this impostor as an incarnation of the deity is an average specimen of Hindu credulity. The Sikshápatra or book of instructions, provided by the Swámi for his disciples, and which may be regarded as the creed of the sect, is written in Sanskrit, and a translation of it will be given hereafter.

Swámi Náráyan is supposed by his followers to have been an incarnation of the god Náráyana and the following legend is told to account for this avatar:—On a certain day in the Dwápara Yug, while Náráyana was engaged in the performance of the rite tapascharyá surrounded by eighty-eight thousand Rishis, who were

‖ This and some subsequent paragraphs are taken, with little alteration from a paper in the *Dnyánodaya*, Vol. VIII. pp. 276 278.

also similarly employed, the irritable old Rishi Durvása* approached them. The god was absorbed in the contemplation of the invisible *Brahm*—and the rishis in that of his visible representative before them; so that no one noticed the approach of Durvása, who was thus indignant at their total want of civility and vented his rage in a curse upon Náráyana, saying, "For your disrespectful treatment of me you shall become incarnate in the *Kaliyuga*."—Then, turning to the Rishis, he said, "you also shall become men at the same period." The god not only acquiesced in the sentence, but received it with joy, observing that he had long been desirous of becoming incarnate at that time for the salvation of sinful mortals. The Rishis also rejoiced that they would have the opportunity of becoming the worshippers of Náráyana among men. In consequence of this curse, Sahajánand appeared, an avatára of Náráyana. Sahajánand or Náráyana Swámí was born at Chhapyá, a small town 8 miles north from Ayodhyá (Oudh) on the 9th Chaitra *sudha* S. 1837 (A.D. 1780). According to the *Bhakti Chintámaní* of Nishkulánand a Sádhu of the sect, his father's name was Hariprasád and his mother's Bálá; but another account gives their names of his parents as Dharmadeva and Premavatí, "but the people called his mother Bhaktí." He was named Ghanasyám, and belonged to the Sarvaryá class of Brahmans and the Sávarní *gotra*, and was a student of the Kauthumí Shákhá of the Sáma Veda. He was the second of three brothers, the elder, called Rámapratáp, was three years older, and the younger was named Ichhárám. When Ghanasyám, according to another account named Harikrishnaji, was a year old, his parents removed to the town of Ayodhyá.

Sahajánand and Rámapratáp were both invested with *jáneo* on the same day—the former having attained the age of eight years. According to custom, both the boys were on that occasion, ordered to run off, to intimate their unwillingness to enter the world, and their desire to devote themselves wholly to religious observances; and their maternal uncle, whose duty it was to bring them back and compel them to enter the world, started off after them. Rámapratáp was easily caught. But Sahajánand completely outran his uncle. Having run, it is said, twelve kos, he turned round and said to his pursuer, 'Are you so stupid as not to understand that it is not my fate to return to the world?' From that day the boy attached himself to a guru from whom he learned the principles and practices of religion.†

His parents dying when he was eleven years old, Ghanasyám, according to the *Bhakti Chintámaní*, at the age of twelve, started to perform pilgrimages, and having visited Badrikedar, Kásí, Calcutta, Jagannáth, and travelled thence through Southern India to Rámesvar, he retired into a forest where he devoted himself with undivided attention to the worship of the Sun. Súrya was accordingly greatly pleased and blessed him saying, "Whatever you undertake you will succeed in." He travelled about from place to place as a Brahmachári calling himself Nílakantha Brahmachári. "He wore nothing on his head but his matted hair, and nothing on his body but his *langoti*; he carried with him the skin of a deer and a book. The Bhagavat Gítá he knew by heart; as also the thousand names of Vishnu. He also carried the things required in Sháligrám worship, a staff of *palas* wood and an earthen waterpot."‡ In the round of his pilgrimages to sacred places (*tirthas*) he came to Ahmadabad, and after a while travelled through Káthiáwád, visiting the shrine of Bhimnáth Śiva, and proceeding by way of Gopnáth to the port of Mangrol. In the year S. 1856 (A.D. 1799), being 19 years of age, he arrived in the attire of a *tapasa* at the village of Loj or Aslíve, near Junágadh, where lived about fifty *sádhus* of the sect of Rámánand, the chief among whom was Muktánand, and with him Nílakantha formed a friendship and soon became a convert to the doctrines of his sect. Muktánand then wrote to his Guru, Rámánand, who was at Bhuj in Kachh, and he returned to Loj and gave *Upadesh* to Nílakantha on the 11th Kartik *sudha* S. 1857 (A.D. 1800) and changed his name to Sahajánand Swámí. Thereupon, at the age of about twenty years, Sahajánand began to propagate his tenets and preach the doctrines of his sect. He affected also miraculous powers before his disciples, en-

* Throughout the whole range of literature the name of Durvása is always at hand to account for every mishap or misadventure. He is represented as the son of Atri and Anasúyá, under the special influence of Śiva, or as a portion of Śiva. He is figured as sitting on a fire stretching his arms upwards. He cursed Indra for having disrespectfully treated a garland of celestial flowers which he had given him; in consequence of which disconformed the three worlds and Śakra lost their vigour, all vegetable products withered and died; this led to the war between the Dánavas and the gods and finally ended in the churning of the ocean. In the drama Durvása is represented as cursing Śakuntalá for a slight delay in opening her door to him, which led to her sorrow and disgrace.

† *Dnyánodaya*, Vol. VIII. p. 277.

‡ *Dnyánodaya*, Vol. VIII. p. 291.

trancing whomsoever he cast his eyes upon and causing them in this mesmeric state (*samâdhi*) to imagine they saw Sahajânand as Krishṇa with yellow robes, weapons of war and other characteristics of the god, and to behold him seated as chief in an assembly of *devatâs*.* The story of his working this supposed miracle reached the ears of Râmânand who discredited it and put Sahajânand to the test, but he was thrown into the same state, and thus convinced, placed him at the head of his disciples, and at his death, six months afterwards, left the *gâdi* of Achârya to him. He then went to Kachh where he made many disciples of the Mâlî caste, among whom were the Râjâ Rao Kachh's carpenters, also many of the Mumna class of Kaulis, respecting whom one of the priests of the sect gives the following account:—

"These people professed the Musalmân religion. It seems that about 370 years ago, the principal men of the class set out on a pilgrimage to Benâres, to the number of about [illegible]. As they were going through the Gujarât country, they came to Pirâna, a famous Musalmân place, where there was a distinguished *fakir* living, and there they stopped to spend the night. The fakir enquired of them whither they were going. They answered 'We are going to Kâśî.' The fakir then said, 'If I bring your Kâśî here, will you do all I tell you?' They said they would. Then, on the following morning, in the place where they had passed the night, what should they behold but Kâśî itself! They then all bathed in the Ganges. After remaining there three days, Kâśî became invisible. The fakir then commanded them all to become Musalmâns. They accordingly complied, agreeing to worship after the Musalmân fashion, to bury the dead, and to ratify their marriage contracts in presence of a *fakir*, only they would not break caste. When these people saw the marvellous acts of Swâmi Nârâyan, many of them embraced the Hindu religion as taught by him. From that time they have performed their marriage ceremonies under the direction of Brahmans, have performed *Śrâddhas* in honour of ancestors, and burned the bodies of their dead."†

When he first arrived at Ahmadâbâd about 1804, he was accompanied by his *gurubhâi* Râmânand, and several other *Sâdhus*; and for a time he continued to make disciples, and disseminate his principles. It is said that he first forbade the worship of idols; and exhorted to the service of only one god Nârâyaṇa. In consequence of such teaching, opposition was raised against him by the Brahmans, who so stirred up against him the Peshwâ's government that he was obliged for a time to leave Ahmadâbâd.

Sahajânand performed the *yajna* called Mahârudra—or sacrifice to Agni at Gûmadbhâm, at Kâriyâni, and at Jetalpur near Ahmadâbâd, and repeated it at Dabhâṇa near Vadtâl a few miles from Nadiyâd. At Jetalpur, says the last quoted authority, "Nârâyaṇ became the subject of obloquy for inducing some to forsake their wives and homes and become Sâdhus."

In S. 1868 (A.D. 1811) he went to Gadhaḍâ, in the Bhaunagar state, and there converted Dâdâ Khâchar a Kâṭhi who owned the fourth part of the revenues of that village. Here the Swâmi lived in the house of his Kâṭhi disciple and made about 800 converts among whom were 300 *Sâdhus* and Brahmachâris, 300 *pâlas* attendants in the temple, and about 150 females called *Sânkhyayogni* (female devotees).

In the year S. 1876 (A.D. 1819) he sent a Sâdhu named Brahmânand to Ahmadâbâd, and had a temple built there in which was placed an image of Naranârâyaṇ. This is a large temple and is reckoned one of the principal ones of Swâmi Nârâyan. Afterwards temples were built (S. 1878) at Bhuj in Kachh, at Vadtâl near Nadiyâd in Gujarât, and at Junâgaḍh in Soraṭh, and images were placed in them: these received the names of Rādhâ and Krishṇa. Then a temple was built at Dholerâ, containing an image called Madan Mohan. Domed temples were also erected at Jetalpur, Dholkâ, and Muliyâ; and "temples without domes are to be seen everywhere throughout the provinces of Kâṭhiâwâḍ, Kachh, and Gujarât."

It was at Kaira on the 26th March 1825 that Bishop Heber learnt from the Collector, Mr. Williamson, that some good had been done among the wild Kulis "by the preaching and popularity of the Hindu reformer, Swâmi Nârâyan." We give the greater portion of his account in his own words:—

"His morality was said to be far better than any which could be learned from the Shastras. He preached a great degree of purity, forbidding his disciples so much as to look on any woman whom they passed. He condemned theft and bloodshed; and those villages and districts, which had received him, from being among the worst, were now among the best and most orderly in the provinces. Nor was this all, inasmuch as he was said to have de-

* Conf. a 'memorandum' extracted from the *Bombay Courier* in the *Asiatic Journal*, Vol. XV. (1823) p. 348.

† *Dayânandaya*, [illegible] p. 221.

stroyed the yoke of caste,—to have preached one God, and in short, to have made so considerable approaches to the truth, that I could not but hope he might be an appointed instrument to prepare the way for the Gospel.

"While I was listening with much interest to Mr. Williamson's account of this man, six persons came to the tent, four in the dress of peasants or lumbardars, one, a young man, with a large white turban, and the quilted lebada of a Kuli, but clean and decent, with a handsome sword and shield, and other marks of rustic wealth; and the sixth, an old Musalman, with a white beard, and pretty much the appearance, dress, and manner of an ancient serving-man. After offering some sugar and sweetmeats as their nazar, and, as usual, sitting down on the ground, one of the peasants began, to my exceeding surprise and delight, 'Pandit Swámi Náráyan sends his salám,' and proceeded to say that the person whom I so much desired to see was in the neighbourhood, and asked permission to call on me next day. I, of course, returned a favourable answer, and stated with truth, that I greatly desired his acquaintance, and had heard much good of him. I asked if they were his disciples, and was answered in the affirmative. The first speaker then told me that the young man now in company was the eldest son of a Kuli Thákur, whose father was one of the Pandit's good friends, but he was himself a Rájput, and also that the old man in green was a Musalman sipáhi to the Thákur's ancestors, and sent to attend on his young master. He added, that though of different castes, they were all disciples of Swámi Náráyan, and taught to regard each other as brethren. They concluded by asking me where I was to go next day, and appointed, in their teacher's name, that he would visit me at Nadiad in the forenoon; they then took leave, I having first embraced the Thákur, and sent my salám back to his father and his Guru."*

March 30, 1825 (*Nadiad*).—"About 11 o'clock, I had the expected visit from Swámi Náráyan, to my interview with whom I had looked forward with an anxiety and eagerness which, if he had known it, would perhaps have flattered him. He came in a somewhat different style from all which I had expected, having with him near 200 horsemen, mostly well armed with matchlocks and swords, and several of them with coats of mail and spears. Besides them he had a large rabble on foot, with bows and arrows. . . .

The armed men who attended Swámi Náráyan were under the authority, as it appeared, of a venerable old man, of large stature, with a long gray beard and most voluminous turban, the father of the young Thákur who had called on me the day before. He came into the room first, and after the usual embrace, introduced the holy man himself who was a middle-sized, thin, and plain looking person, about my own age, with a mild and diffident expression of countenance, but nothing about him indicative of any extraordinary talent. I seated him on a chair at my right hand, and offered two more to the Thákur and his son, of which, however, they did not avail themselves without first placing their hands under the feet of their spiritual guide, and then pressing them reverently to their foreheads. Others of the principal disciples, to the number of 20 or 30, seated themselves on the ground, and several of my own Musalman servants, who seemed much interested in what was going on, thrust in their faces at the door, or ranged themselves behind me. After the usual mutual compliments, I said that I had heard much good of him, and the good doctrine which he preached among the poor people of Gujarat, and that I greatly desired his acquaintance; that I regretted that I knew Hindustani so imperfectly, but that I should be very glad, as far as my knowledge of the language allowed, and by the interpretation of friends, to learn what he believed on religious matters, and to tell him what I myself believed, and that if he would come and see me at Kaira, where we should have more leisure, I would have a tent pitched for him and treat him like a brother. I said this because I was very earnestly desirous of getting him a copy of the scriptures, of which I had some with me, in the Nágari character, and persuading him to read them; and because I had some further hopes of inducing him to go with me to Bombay, where I hoped that by conciliatory treatment, and the conversations to which I might introduce him with the Church Missionary Society established in that neighbourhood, I might do him more good than I could otherwise hope to do. I saw that both he and, still more, his disciples, were highly pleased by the invitation which I gave him, but he said, in reply, that his life was one of very little leisure, that he had 5,000 disciples now attending on his preaching in the neighbouring villages, and nearly 50,000 in different parts of Gujarat, that a great number of these were to assemble together in the course of next week, on occasion of his brother's son coming of age to receive the brahmanical string, but that if I staid long enough in the neighbourhood to allow him to get this engagement over, he would gladly come again to see me. 'In the meantime,' I said, 'have you any objection to communicate some part of your doctrine now?' It was evidently what he came to do, and his disciples very visibly exulted in the opportunity of his, perhaps, converting me. He began, indeed, well, professing to believe in one only God, the maker of all things in heaven and earth, who filled all space, upheld and governed all things, and, more particularly, dwelt in the hearts of those who dili-

* Heber, *Journal* (8vo ed.) Vol. II. pp. 143-44.

gently sought him; but he alarmed me by calling the god whom he worshipped Krishna, and by saying that he had come down to earth in ancient times, had been put to death by wicked men through magic, and that since his time many false revelations had been pretended, and many false divinities set up. . . . I observed, that I had always supposed that Hindus called the God and Father of all, not Krishna but Brahm, and I wished, therefore, to know whether his god was Brahm, or somebody distinct from him? The name of Brahm appeared to cause great sensation among his disciples, of whom some whispered with each other, and one or two nodded and smiled as if to say 'that is the very same.' The pandit also smiled and bowed, and with the air of a man who is giving instruction to a willing and promising pupil, said, 'a true word it is that there is only one God who is above all things and in all things, and by whom all things are. Many names there may be, and have been, given to him who is and is the same, but whom we also as well as the other Hindus call Brahm. But there is a spirit in whom God is more especially, and who cometh from God, who hath made known to man the will of the God and father of all, whom we call Krishna and worship as God's image, and believe to be the same as the Sun, Sûrya. . . .'"

After detailing some further conversation the bishop continues:—"The Pandit replied that their belief was, that there had been many avatârs of God in different lands, one to the Christians, another to the Musalmans, another to the Hindus, in times past, adding something like a hint, that another avatâr of Krishna, or the Sun, had taken place in himself. . .

"I then asked in what way he and his followers worshipped God? . . I found, however, that he supposed me to ask in what form they worshipped God, and he therefore unrolled a large picture in glaring colours, of a naked man with rays proceeding from his face like the Sun, and two women fanning him; the man white, the women black. I asked him how that could be the God who filled everything and was everywhere? He answered that it was not God himself, but the picture or form in which God dwelt in his heart; I told him, as well as I could, . . . what Christians and Musalmans thought as to the worship of images; but did not decline receiving some paltry little prints of his divinity in various attitudes, which I said I would value as keepsakes. I asked about caste, to which he answered, that he did not regard the subject as of much importance, but that he wished not to give offence; that people might eat separately or together in this world, but that above, upar, pointing to heaven, those distinctions would cease, where we should be all *ek ekhi jat*, (one like another). . . On the whole it was plain that his advances towards truth had not yet been so great as I had been told, but it was also apparent that he had obtained a great power over a wild people, which he used at present to a good purpose."*

To return to our narrative: In the year S. 1886 (A.D. 1829) the Swâmi began to build a temple on one side of what is known as the Darbâr of Dâdâ Khâchar, the residence of the Kâthi chief of Gaḍhaḍâ, mentioned above; and there he died on the 10th of Jeshth suddha in the same year. His body was burned, and his disciples placed in the great domed temple they erected there, a stone bearing his **p â d u k â**, or representation of his feet.

Since his death his followers have become very numerous throughout Gujarat and Kâṭhiâwâḍ. Notwithstanding the vigorous opposition they met with in some places, they continued zealously to propagate and practise their religion. "Some of his followers," says the priest quoted above, "were denied admission to the towns; some were buried alive; some sâdhus even were put to death." In Surat an attempt was made some twenty-five years ago to procure their expulsion from their several castes—but without success. They manifest a most bigoted attachment to their doctrines and rites.

"His **Śikshâpatra**, or book of instructions," continues the priest,† "contains 212 *ślokas*, and the **ṭ î k â** or commentary 500 *ślokas*. He also composed in Sanskrit a book of 24,000 *ślokas*, containing a more full account of his doctrines, under the title of **Satsangijîwan**. He was the author also of seventy-five works in the Gujarâtî and Hindusthânî vernaculars; also of two small Sanskrit works. Swâmi Nârâyan had a number of Sanskrit poets in his train, for instance Satânand Swâmi, Dinanâth Bhat, Shâstrî Nityânand, Gopâlânand, Bhagawadânand, and Wâsudevânand. And among vernacular poets that followed him, were the following: Brahmânand, Muktânand, Premânand, Devânand Dâyânand, Nishkulânand, Bhumânand, and Purnânand.

"After the death of Swâmi Nârâyan, his disciples erected **c h h a t r î s** or stopping places, and monuments to his memory, in all the villages, and beneath all the trees where he had at any time made any stay. There they worship him; they worship also the trees.‡ And they perform all religious rites in his honour, just as

* Heber, *Jour.* ut sup. supp.

† *Dayânandaya*, u. s. p. 282.

‡ This reminds us of the respect paid to Buddha, especially by Aśoka, who erected so many stûpas to commemorate his visits to different places. Tree Worship, so closely connected with Buddhism, may have had an origin similar to that indicated here.

they would in honour of the Gujarâti guru Gosâînji Mahârâj. At the death of Nârâyan, there were about 100,000 heads of families holding his tenets, and about 500 Sâdhu ascetics."

In 1821, when his religion had taken a firm hold among the people, he called his elder brothers Râmapratâp and Ichhârâm with their wives, sons and cousins from Ayodhyâ. Râmapratâp had three sons named Nandarâma, Thâkurarâma, and Ayodhyâprasâd, of whom Ayodhyâprasâd succeeded to the *gâdi* of Ahmadâbâd. The villages and temples attached to it are called *Uttarji* as distinguished from those attached to the Wartâl gâdi which are known as *Dakshina Bhâg*. The river Watrak near Kheda separates the two sees; all that portion of Gujarat lying to the north of this stream, with Dhandhukâ, Dholkâ, Wadhwân, Limdi, Nawanagar, Râjkot, Morbi, and Kachh, and in the east of India all to the north of Ujjain, Kâsi, Calcutta, and Jagannâth belongs to the Ahmadâbâd gâdi. The Wartâl gâdi includes Kaira, Kâthiâwâd proper, Gadhada in (Gohelwâd), Junâgadh, Dwârka, Dholera, Baroda, Bharoch, Surat, Bombay and the Dakhan.

Ichhârâm had five sons, of whom Raghuvîrji the second succeeded to the *gâdi* of Wartâl. Sahajânand in his life-time had adopted Ayodhyâprasâd and Raghuvîr as his children, and invested them with authority as his vicars on earth. Ayodhyâprasâd installed his son the present Mahârâja Keśavaprasâd on the Ahmadâbâd gâdi in S. 1922 (A.D. 1865) and died in A.D. 1867 at the age of 58 years. The Wartâl gâdi is now occupied by Bhagvatprasâd Mahârâja, now about 35 years old, who succeeded his uncle Raghuvîrji in 1863. The latter died at the age of 51 years.

"These representatives of Nârâyan Swâmi," says the *Dnyanodaya*, "alone have the power of fully initiating disciples into the faith. The initiatory rite is performed as follows:—The person to be admitted takes a little water in his right hand, and casts it on the ground at the feet of the High Priest, saying, 'I give over to Swâmî Sahajânand (*man, tan, dhan aur sare janmon ka pap*) mind, body, wealth, and the sins of all my births.' He then receives the following *mantra*, by employing which, he is on all occasions to be preserved from evil and made prosperous and happy, viz.:—'*Sri Krishna twam gatir mama*.'—'O Krishna I desire only thee.'

"Under the authority of either of the High Priests, others commissioned by them are able to admit followers as candidates for perfect discipleship, by giving them what is called the *Panch vartmân mantra*, consisting of prohibitions against theft, adultery, intoxicating substances, the use of flesh as food, and lying. But no one can become a perfect bhagat but by receiving the *mantra* from one or other of the High Priests. Five places are recognized as principal seats of authority, viz. Wartâl, Ahmadâbâd, Gadhada, Surat, and Junâgadh. In each of these places, and in many others, there is a temple,—or rather there are two temples,—one for males, and one for females. Women are made disciples by the wives of the High Priests, and always worship in a separate temple from that of the men. In their temples, the chief images are those of Krishna, Râdhâ, and Swâmî Nârâyan himself.

"The followers of Swâmî Nârâyan are chiefly of the lower castes. But there are many also of the very highest. It is said that Gaikwâd Sayaji became a disciple—and also the Râja of Gadhada. It is thought that about one fourth of the Hindu population of Surat are followers of Swâmî Nârâyan.

"Two reasons may be assigned for the spread of this sect. First, and perhaps chiefly, the strict prohibition of the taking of animal life, which completely falls in with the prejudices of the whole Hindu community. True, there are many castes who eat flesh, but this is always considered rather in the light of a *tolerated sin* than a lawful practice, and abstinence is considered meritorious. Among the Mâlis, Kolis, &c. this is the chief difference between the followers of Sahajânand, and other Hindus. Again Sahajânand promises to take away sin: he is regarded by his disciples as the surety of sinners." In Kâthiâwâd and Gujarât, when Christianity is preached, "the hearers frequently remark that this is very similar to their own faith respecting Swâmî Nârâyan."

SOME ACCOUNT OF THE PÁLIS OF DINAJPUR.

BY G. H. DAMANT, B.C.S.

The Koch and Pális or Páliás as they are indifferently called, are a race of people peculiar to the districts of Dinajpur, Rangpur, Purniyâ, Koch Behâr and Mâldâ: in the latter district they are never found south of the river Mahânandâ, which seems to be their limit to the south; towards the east they are found commonly as far as Gowalpâra.

They can be distinguished at a glance from all other Bengalis by their broad faces, flat noses, and projecting cheekbones, and also by their sturdy appearance and different style of

dren. They profess to be Hindus, but while they follow the Hindu religion in the main, they also practise some ceremonies borrowed from Musalmans and others, which are apparently remnants of an older superstition. Their own tradition of their origin, as communicated to me by an old Pali of this district, is as follows:—

"The whole country of Behar, from whence the Palis and Koch are supposed to have come, was once governed by a celebrated king named Jarasandha; his subjects used to fight for him with sticks as they had no weapons of iron. He claimed to be a Khatriya, and the descendants of his subjects, believing themselves to be of the same family, call themselves Rajvansi to this day.

"Now there was a poor old man living in the country (his name I learn from other sources was Haju) who had two daughters, unmarried virgins; the name of the elder was Hira and of the second Jira. The god Siva used to visit them, and at last Hira became pregnant by him. Their old father discovered it, and became very angry with them, and used to reprimand them continually; but still they used to meet Siva every day in secret, till it happened that their father had gone away on some business, and they ventured to bring him into the house, and began to talk with him, and Hira said 'I have become pregnant by you and my father is angry with me; all his caste are my enemies, and my time of delivery is approaching.' Siva replied, 'Take courage, the son which shall be born to you must be concealed and brought up secretly; you must call him Kagendra and by my favour he shall become king, and thirty-six of his descendants shall reign after him.' While they were talking thus Hira's father appeared at the door with a stick in his hand: they were all three frightened and the old man lifted up his stick to strike Siva, and he seeing no other means of escape, began to retreat underground. As he was disappearing the old man attacked him with his stick, but by that time all his body had disappeared except his feet which the old man struck, and from that circumstance Śiva is still known and worshipped by the name of Jalpesvarnath.* Sometime after this Hira, although she was still a virgin, bore a beautiful boy, and as she was afraid of her father and kinsfolk, she made a ring (koch- [illegible]†) of kusa grass and concealed him in it, and brought him up secretly and gave him the name of Kagendra.

"In course of time this child became king of Behar, and although king Jarasandha was a Khatriya, yet because Kagendra was brought up in a koch, his tribe is still known by the name of Koch, and because the five ceremonies‡ were not used at his birth, the Koch do not use them to this day.

"Some time after this Parasurám, son of Jamadagni, cleared India of Khatriyas twenty-one times, for he fought with them as hereditary enemies. In the course of his travels he came to Behar, and the king and his Rájvansis took sticks in their hands, and went forth to meet him, but he was no ordinary warrior, and moreover used a battle-axe. The Rájvansis could not withstand him, and some by fording, some by swimming, crossed over to the west bank of the Tista. The king saved himself by telling Parasurám that he was a Koch. From that time forth those who escaped by fleeing into this country have been called Pallis (from पलाय), and as the Khatriyas boast that they have never been defeated, and these men were routed by Parasurám, they are also called Bhangakhatriyas, and the few men of the Koch caste who inhabited the country before the battle are called Desis." This tradition must be taken for what it is worth, but there can be no doubt that the Palis and Koch are a people of Mongolian race who migrated into this district from the North-east. The story they tell of their ancestors being conquered by Parasurám probably refers to their conquest by the Aryans, and that they came from the east side of the Tista seems almost certain.

They live under an almost pure patriarchal system, each family has its head and each village has its mandal; while again four or five villages are placed jointly under a patwari, the mandal and patwari are generally appointed by the zamindar, of whom they are the local representatives. The greatest respect is paid to the older members of the family in every household; there is a headman who is called, if the elder brother—darbáriya bhai (दरबारिया भाइ), or if he is any other relative—dewániyá (दिवानिया); the other members of the family are absolutely

* Worshipped at [illegible] in Jalpaiguri: the image is enclosed in a pukka wall, a large mela is held there every year.

† Probably connected with the Sk. root कुच् or कुञ्च् to contract.

‡ जातकर्म, नामकरण, चूडाकरण, [illegible], अन्नप्राशन

subject to him, they can do nothing unless his consent is first obtained, no marriage can be solemnised or suit instituted unless he agrees. He is looked up to with respect second only to that shown to the zamindar: all the business of the family is conducted through him, he pays the rent and manages all money matters. He is excused from labour in the fields and is allowed to eat salt while the other members of the family must content themselves with the saline matter extracted from the ashes of plantain and other trees. He is also allowed to have two or more wives, while no other person is allowed to have more than one, and his favourite wife is excused from working in the fields and allowed to eat salt.

The dress of the Palis is very different from that worn by ordinary Hindus; in the hot weather the men wear nothing but a thread round the loins which is called ([illegible]) *sikikal* and on it a piece of rag called *pâjhal* ([illegible]), on great occasions they also wear a cloth on their heads or round their body, and in the cold weather a piece of cloth is given them by the head of the family and returned to him again at the beginning of the hot season. They all wear a necklace of wooden beads, their head is shaved all round, and the hair which is left is tied in a knot at the top. The women wear a cloth of jute called *mekhri* ([illegible]), which is their only dress. It is about three hâths in length and two in breadth and coloured with red, black, and white stripes. This cloth is not worn across the shoulder as is usual amongst Hindu women, but in a straight line across the breasts under the armpits falling down as low as the knees. The use of these mekhris is gradually being discontinued, and cotton cloths are being introduced, coloured in the same way, and worn in the same manner; they are called *pâthal* ([illegible]). The women attend *hâṭs* and markets and carry burdens on their heads; they carry their children hanging in a cloth at their backs, and help the men to work in the fields; very few of them wear silver or metal ornaments, but all have bangles of conch shell.

They have no fixed age for marriage; some of the women remain unmarried till they are grown up, while others are married when they are three or four years old. In an ordinary marriage the amount of the dower to be paid by the bridegroom is fixed by the mediation of a Ghatak, called by the Palis '*kamiya*' ([illegible]). After this is settled the bridegroom's relatives go to the bride's house and give her family betelnut and pay part of the money: this is called ([illegible]) *duegnyâ*. When all the money has been paid, the marriage day is fixed and a procession is formed consisting principally of women who go to the bride's house; after they have been welcomed by the girl's family, her sister's husband or some other relative takes her on his back and carries her to the bridegroom's house; the bride is now often brought in a doli; no music or dancing is used at the procession; the women of both the bride and bridegroom's party clap their hands as they go along and pretend to quarrel with each other and repeat the following mantra—

" We have been to the ploughed field
We have come to the bridegroom's house
Where is your water pot to wash our feet."

When the bride reaches the bridegroom's house, his friends plant four plantain trees in the courtyard and connect them with a thatched roof, covering a gunny-cloth spread on the ground on which the bride and bridegroom are made to sit. The bridegroom first of all stands under the roof and the bride makes a *pradakshin* round him five times, they then sit down facing the east. The bride sits at the right hand of the bridegroom, no priest is required for this marriage, but if a priest is employed, he sits facing the north to the right hand of the bride and bridegroom and recites some mantras. The bride's guardian then gives her to the bridegroom and joins their hands and pours water over them and says, " From this day the honour of the family is in your hands." An offering is then made which is called an " Arghya," though the word seems to be used with a meaning different to that usually ascribed to it; it consists of rice, cowdung, vermilion, a hair comb, and a candlestick with five branches, and two pots of water each containing a mango branch, with a garland of flowers made of sola.

The father and mother of the bridegroom then come and the father places the garland on the bridegroom's head and the mother places it on the bride's head, and then they both make them a present, and throw the pots of water with the mango branches over them. After that they take the arghya and invoke blessings on them, all the friends do the same, and the bride and bridegroom present each other with betelnut, and the bride will distribute rice among the guests. The guardian of the bridegroom then washes the feet of the mahant, or principal per-one present, and gives him betelnut, and all the assembled guests repeat this mantra—

"Take rice and eat,
Let the thorns of time be far away,
Let that which is empty be refilled
Victory to Jagannáth, let there be peace,
The name of Hari is sweet as honey."

The bride and bridegroom then go to the house of the bride's father, he makes them presents and the next day they return home.

Widow marriage is commonly practised both by the Palis and Koch, they call it kâhin ([illegible]); it nearly corresponds to the Musalman nika. If an elder brother dies leaving a widow, his younger brother has a right to marry her; if he refuses to take her she can marry into another family, but in that case a dower is usually paid by the bridegroom. In this form of marriage, five or six widows or married women go by night and take the widow who is to be married to a place where three roads meet; in the meantime the bridegroom takes some vermilion and mixes it with oil and puts it on a plantain leaf and goes to the place, one of the women puts the vermilion on the bride's forehead and another washes it off again, saying that the name of her old husband is obliterated while that of a new husband has taken its place. This is done three times, and the woman is then taken home and made to sit with her husband on a piece of cloth, they then present each other with water, and a flower made of sola is tied on the bridegroom's knee and another on the pot containing the vermilion; the friends who are present are then feasted, this is all done privately so that no one can see, no purohit is required for this ceremony, and no unmarried person is allowed to be present.

Another form of marriage is the ghârjiyâ ([illegible]). In this the guardian of a virgin settles with a man to give him the woman in marriage, this is arranged through a kamyâ. After the terms are agreed on, the kamyâ takes some parched rice and curds and goes to the man's house, and presents them to him, and then brings him back to the woman's house. The man is called gharjamai, because he lives in his father-in-law's house, he occasionally lives there two or three years before the marriage is completed.

When the marriage ceremony takes place, the gharjamai is made to sit in the court yard, and sprinkled with water from a mango branch, and after that he presents all the friends who have assembled with betel.

There is another form of marriage called dângiyâ ([illegible],) which is perhaps the most curious of all. If a widow is rich she selects a husband for herself, and settles with him through a kâmyâ, the man is called a dângiyâ ([illegible]). When all is arranged he goes to the widow's house at night, and strikes against the wall with a láthi; on hearing this she comes with a dao, and cuts the string round his loins, and catching his hand takes him in and feasts him. He says with tears, "Rice boiled from uncleaned grain and pulse for vegetables is the food of a dângiyâ, he has lived all his life in his father's house;" he is then considered to be married to her, and takes all the property her former husband had.

The ceremonies performed after a death are very similar to those common to all Hindus, and need not be described at length. The Pális remain impure for thirteen days afterwards, some of them burn and others bury their dead, this depends on the custom of the family.

At the birth of a child the whole family remains unclean for five days, which is called Pânchi ([illegible]). Neither the gharbhardhân [illegible] or panchâmrita ([illegible]) ceremonies are known to them. On the third day after the birth a fire is lighted in the house where it took place, and the nurse a Hariani scatters the ashes on the ground, the house itself is thoroughly cleaned, this is called Dhyulamni ([illegible]). On the fifth day the whole house and its furniture and all the clothes of the family are cleaned, and a barber is brought who shaves the whole family; the mother is then made to sit down in the courtyard and the child's umbilical cord is put on it, and covered with khâir ([illegible]—alkali ashes of plantain leaves). Some turmeric ([illegible]) and five cowries are also put with it. The woman faces the east and the barber the west, and the plantain leaf is put between them. The barber first cuts the woman's nails, and puts the parings on the plantain leaf, and then washes the child, and shaves the father's head, and after that the child is again bathed and shaved, this is called dokâmâ ([illegible]). The hair which is shaved from the head of the father is collected and put on the plantain leaf, and the whole is afterwards burnt. The barber and father then bathe together, and the father distributes food to all the people who are assembled, and gives the barber some rice and curds, he also makes him and the nurse a present. The mother next places her child in a winnowing fan ([illegible]) and puts it in front of a tulsi tree, which she salutes, after that five or six women take the child to a well, and draw water five times in a lota, in which a mango branch has been placed, the water is poured out as a libation, and the god to whom it is offered is invoked by name. This is called (पुआ पुर्वा) chayáchhuyá; no purohit is required for these ceremonies. The Palis are not acquainted with the usual Hindu ceremonies of shaving the head, boring the ear, and naming a child. Both the Palis and Koch worship the usual Hindu gods, but they have also deities of their own to whom they seem to pay greater respect. The tutelary goddess of the Tista river is almost universally worshipped by them under the name of "barni Thakurani" in the month of Chait. Some of the ceremonies they practise are very curious and appear to be quite unknown to the common Hindus; amongst them is an annual festival held in honour of Durgá, who is worshipped under the name of Bamáhira. The head of a dead man is taken, or if that cannot be procured, a skull which is painted to resemble life and offered before the goddess with singing and dancing.

When the land is suffering from want of rain, the women assemble at night, and covering their bodies with red powder go naked through the village with swords in their hands dancing and singing indecent songs; notice is given beforehand, and no man is allowed to leave his home that night. The ceremony is called hudmdyan (हुद मार्गी) an expression of which I have not been able to find the exact meaning but मार्गी may possibly be the Sanskrit root धु or दिव् the heaven and I am told that हुद means "open" but it resembles no Bengali word with which I am acquainted. I should be glad of suggestions on this subject. This interpretation would afford a good meaning, as the women might well be supposed to call on the heavens to open in time of drouth.

The Palis are subdivided into three classes—the Shadu, Bábú, and Desi Palis. The Bábú Palis, or Byabahari, as they are also called, eat pigs and fowls and drink spirits, and the Desi Palis will eat shellfish. Both the Shadu and Bábú Palis use cows in ploughing. The Shadu Palis for the most part follow the tenets of Chaitanya, the founder of the Bairaghi sect. The Koch are the palki bearers of the district; they seem to be about on an equality with the Palis in respect of caste, no Brahman will take water from either Koch or Palis. I am informed that a few Koch are to be found in Dakka and one or two other districts, but the Palis I believe are peculiar to the districts mentioned above.

ON SOME EMINENT CHARACTERS IN SANSKRIT LITERATURE.

BY M. SASHAGIRI SASTRI, B.A., ACTING SANSKRIT PROFESSOR, MADRAS.

(Continued from page 315.)

KÁLIDÁSA.

Of this great poet nothing is known except his works; nor does he say anything of himself. Some place him at the court of Bhoja, while others say that he was a contemporary of Vikramárka of whose court he is said to have been one of the nine sages. An inscription found by Mr. Wilkins at Buddha Gaya, of which he published a translation, alludes to "the nine gems" (Wilson's preface to the Sanskrit Dictionary.) According to Bhoja charitra he was a contemporary of Bhoja; but this book forfeits all its claim to an authority since it enumerates Bána Mayúra Bhavabhúti, Mágha and Mallinátha as the contemporaries of that prince. Kálidása is said to have been the author of Raghuvansa, Kumára Sambhava, Meghasandesa, Ritusamhára, Nalodaya, Setuprabandha,* Śakuntalá, Vikramorvasí, Málavikágnimitra, Jyotirvidábharana, Śruta-bodhini, Vrittaratnávali, Śringáratilaka, Prasnottaramálá, and Hásyárnava. We cannot believe that the author of Śakuntalá was the same as the author of Nalodaya. But there is a tradition that there was a poet at the court of Bhoja, inferior to Kálidása, who, grudging the great poet the reputation he had acquired by his excellent works, observed that he could not produce a poem with yamakas and prásas or puns of

---

* The author of a commentary on the Setuprabandha named Rámadása says in the beginning of the work, that Kálidása was induced by Vikramáditya to write the poem— [illegible Devanagari verse]

various kinds nor a poem with a subject invented by himself. To remove this reproach Kâlidâsa, it is said, wrote Nalodaya and Meghasandesa. Who the opponent of Kâlidâsa was, we cannot ascertain, but there is one stanza in the Meghasandesa which runs—

Adrehśringam harati pavanah kimsvidityunmukhîbhih Drishtotsâhaśchakitachakitam mugdhasiddhânganâbhih Sthânâdasmât sarasanichulâdutpatodaṅmukhah kham Diṅnâgânâm pathi pariharan sthûla hastâvalepân.

From this it follows that the banishment of Yaksha from the court of Kubera, and his residence in Râmagiri was a pure invention of Kâlidâsa's, but the Kathâsaritsâgara alludes to a Yaksha doomed by Kubera to live in the Vindhya Mountains. As the author of this book flourished in the eleventh century A.D., he may have borrowed it from Kâlidâsa and consequently there is no inconsistency in the tradition. Besides the ordinary meaning there is one which the commentator gives at the end of his commentary on that stanza, from which it is learnt that Nichula was a friend, and Diṅnâga an opponent of Kâlidâsa's, that the latter out of envy condemned this work notwithstanding its merit, and that the poet addressing himself to Megha, i. e., (the Megha Sandesa) says "you go aloud from this place in which there is a friend of mine called Nichula and spread in the world putting down, as you proceed, the gestures which Diṅnâga makes with his hands, expressive of his pride and his disapproval of you and other works of mine."

There is a work in the Oriental Manuscript Library in Madras called Nânârthaśabdaratnam, the 'Gem of Homonymous words.' It is divided into three nibandhanas, and at the end of each it is said to have been written by Kâlidâsa.

Iti śrîkâlidâsavirachite nânârthaśabdaratne kâdikshântavarṇâdyantârthavarṇachhalabijaprakaraṇe chakitabhâvârthavichâraramaṇîye prathamam nibandhanam samâptam. "Thus ends the first nibandhana in the Gem of Homonymous words" composed by Kâlidâsa, a great poet, which contains words that have (all) the letters from ka to ksha (arranged in order) at their end and which is interesting on account of its discussing (or more properly referring to) the meaning of each dhâtu or root. There is also another book called Tarala. This is a commentary on the above book. The author says that his name is Nichula Yogîndra, and that he wrote the work at the request of the king Bhoja.

If this be genuine it will no doubt reduce Kâlidâsa's antiquity and place him at the court of Bhoja, and thus authenticate all the accounts given of him and the king in the Bhojacharitra. From a philological point of view it will be a very important work demanding the attention of literary students. Now if this had been the work of Kâlidâsa who is believed to have been versed in every branch of Sanskrit literature, we might expect that it would be quoted as the Amara, the Viśvaprakâśa, the Śabdârṇava, and other lexicons. But if we look into the various commentaries of Amara, and Mallinâtha's commentaries on the Raghuvaṁśa and other poems, we nowhere find the name of this book; nor is Kâlidâsa ever quoted as a lexicographer. If he was an author of a Kosha surely his name, or the name of his work would be mentioned by Medinikâra in his list of lexicographers, for Medinikâra mentions the name of each lexicon which he knew or the name of its author. The following is a list enumerating nearly all the authors that have written lexicons:—

Author's names.	*Names of their works*
Kâtyâyana	....
Vyâḍi	Utpalinî.
Vâsuki	....
Vararuchi	....
Vikramâditya	Saṁsârâvarta.
Amara	Nâmalingânuśâsanam.
Dhanañjaya	Nâmamâlâ.
Dhanvantari	....
Śâśwata	....
Vopâlita	....
Rantideva	....
Hara	....
Śubhânga	....
Halâyudha	Abhidhânaratnamâlâ.
Pratâpa	....
Mahendra	....
Ardhanârîśwara	....
Bhoja	....
Bhaṭṭachandra	....
Vâchaspati	Śabdârṇava.
Madanapâla	....
Govardhana	....
Rabhasapâla	....
Rudra	....
Amaradatta	....
Ajaya	Nânârthasaṅgraha.
Gangâdhara	....
Dharaṇîdhara	....

Hemachandra	Nâmamâlâ and Anekârthasangraha.
Vâgbhaṭṭa	....
Mûlhara	....
Dharma	....
Târapâla	....
Chandragomi	....
Vâmana	....
Keśavaswâmi	Kalpadru.
Yâdava	Vaijayantî.
Maheśwara	Viśwaprakâśa.
Brihaṭa	Vanavilâsa Dwirûpakosha.
Rûpadeva	....
Purushottamadeva	Trikâṇḍaśesha Hârâvali.
Bhâmaha	....
Mahîpa	Śabdaratnâkara Nânârthatilaka.
Medinikara	Medinî.
Dundubhinâtha	Nânârtha Ratnamâlâ.
Râmeswaraśarmâ	Śabdamâlâ.
Padmanâbhabhaṭṭa	Bhûriprayoga.
Madhava	Śabdaratnâvali.
Jaṭâdhara	Abhidhânatantram.
Hemadatta	Śivakosha.
Chakrapâṇidatta	Śabdachandrikâ.
Jayabhaṭṭa	Avyayârṇava.
Rajana	Nânârthapadapeṭikâ, Śabdalingârtha Chandrikâ.
Harshakîrti	Paryâyapada Manjarî.
Vallabhamiśra	Saraswatî Vilâsa.
Saraswata Miśra	Viśwa Medinî.
Dhananjayabhaṭṭâraka ..	Paryâyaśabda Ratnam.*

Here we find neither the name of Nânârtha Śabdaratnakosha nor of Kâlidâsa. To come to the internal evidence:—The work is divided into three chapters each containing a set of homonymous words without any arrangement except its combining into one group words which have the same termination or *Pratyaya* which are strung together in one *Uṇâdisûtra*. The object of the Kosha appears to be to illustrate the *Uṇâdisûtras*, and in this respect it is like the Uṇâdikosha of Râmaśarmâ. As a specimen I quote two passages one from the book and the other from its commentary.

[illegible]
[illegible] ॥ १ ॥
[illegible]
[illegible] ॥ २ ॥
[illegible]
[illegible] ॥ ३ ॥
[illegible]
[illegible] ॥ ४ ॥
[illegible]
[illegible] ॥ ५ ॥
[illegible]
[illegible] ॥ ६ ॥
[illegible]
[illegible] ॥ ७ ॥
[illegible]
[illegible] ॥ ८ ॥
[illegible]
[illegible] ॥ ९ ॥
[illegible]
[illegible] ॥ १० ॥
[illegible]
[illegible] ॥ ११ ॥
[illegible]
[illegible] ॥ १२ ॥
[illegible]
[illegible] ॥ १३ ॥
[illegible]
[illegible] ॥ १४ ॥
[illegible]
[illegible] ॥ १५ ॥
[illegible]
[illegible] ॥ १६ ॥
[illegible]
[illegible] ॥ १७ ॥
[illegible]
[illegible] ॥ १८ ॥
[illegible]
[illegible] ॥ १९ ॥
[illegible]
[illegible] ॥ २० ॥
[illegible]
[illegible] ॥ २१ ॥
[illegible]
[illegible] ॥ २२ ॥
[illegible]
[illegible] ॥ २३ ॥
[illegible]

* See Wilson's preface to his *Sanskrit Dictionary*, Aufrecht, *Catal. Cod.*, Fitzedward's *Catalogue of Sanskrit books in the Madras Presidency.*

The commentary on this runs as follows:—

[illegible]

In the Uṇâdisûtra, 3rd chap. we have the following:—

[illegible]

In the order of these sûtras, he has taken [illegible] (the last three being nipâtas or words irregularly formed from the roots [illegible]), [illegible].

At the end of each chapter the concluding words of the author are as follows:—

[illegible]

There is not much merit in the commentary; it simply gives the root of every word and quotes the Uṇâdisûtra in a mutilated form. If Nichulayogîndra, the friend of Kâlidâsa, was a sage under Bhoja he should be mentioned in the Bhoja Charitra, but he is not, nor do we know anything of him from other sources. The internal evidence however is not strong against their being the works of Kâlidâsa and Nichulayogîndra respectively. The subject requires more investigation. There was another Kâlidâsa, viz., the author of the Bhagavata Champu. He calls himself Abhinava Kâlidâsa (the new Kâlidâsa) and thus distinguishes himself from his illustrious namesake; some of the works mentioned above may be his.

ŚRÂVAṆA SATURDAYS IN SOUTHERN INDIA.

By V. N. NARASIMMIYENGAR, MAISUR.

Few Europeans in India are aware that one of the most lucrative vows made in honour of Śrînivâsa Svâmî of Tirupati consists of an eleemosynary excursion on Saturdays in the month of Śrâvaṇa (August-September). People, especially young lads, who do not ordinarily wear the three marks affected by the followers of Râmânujâchârya put on these emblems of Vaishnavism on these days, and adorning themselves with tinsel and silk clothes, go from house to house begging alms, and exclaiming "Śrî Venkaṭeśâya Mangalam." At each door, they receive a handful of raw rice, the aggregate of which they give away in alms, or lay apart for the purpose of giving a feast to the Brahmans in honour of the god they specially adore. It is immaterial whether the observer of this vow be rich or poor, beg they must, and that too in an ignominious manner. It is firmly believed by those that the non-observance of this vow is sure to excite the wrath of the angry god, while on the other hand chronic fevers and other distempers are got rid of, and riches and prosperity secured by the observance of this religious rite.

It does not appear that this custom is supported by any Purâṇic authority. I do not know whether the Tirupati Sthala Purâṇa enjoins it. But even tradition fails to explain its origin or rationale. It is followed exclusively by those families whose tutelary god is the Tirupati Venkaṭaramaṇasvâmî. They imagine that they become the Dâsas or servitors of that deity on the particular Saturdays alluded to, which are always sacred to his worship, and when feasts are frequently given to Brahmans in his honour. Although it is very difficult to discover the cause of this peculiar observance, it would not be very hazardous to trace it to the cardinal character of the god Śrînivâsa Svâmî. His legendary origin, his insatiable greed, and the heartless manner in which his dues, even to one's lock of hair, are exacted, all tend to serve the same primary object of squeezing as much as possible from his deluded worshippers and fear-inspired victims.

* The manuscript from which the above passage has been quoted is so full of mistakes that any attempt at translating or explaining it is entirely useless. Nor do we require a translation or explanation. The quotation serves our purpose so far as it shows the manner in which the author has handled his subject.

BENGALI FOLKLORE.—LEGENDS FROM DINAJPUR.

By G. H. DAMANT, B.C.S.

(*Continued from page 287.*)

THE SEVENTH STORY.

The History of a Rogue.

Once on a time a great friendship existed between a king's son and a barber's son, they were always together, and could not bear to be separated. One day each of them promised that he would do whatever the other asked him. After a little time the king's son became anxious to know whether the barber's son would be faithful to his promise, so he sent a man to him to say that a dog of which he was very fond was dead and it was necessary to burn him, he therefore wished the barber's son to cut down his beautiful large mango tree and send it to him for fuel. The barber's son cut the tree, but at the same time was rather annoyed, and in order that he might retaliate on him he sent him a message saying, "I want a piece of wood to clean my teeth, so unfasten the beam which is in the middle of the roof of your house and send it me." The king's son did so, but they both saw that by continuing to act in this way they would ruin each other and gain nothing, so they agreed to travel into some other country and try what they could gain by their cleverness. They started together, and in the course of their journey came to a king's palace. They were very tired of travelling, and lay down to rest, and the king's son went to sleep. The barber's son thinking it a good opportunity went to the king, and said, "Your Majesty, I have kept a slave for a long time, but as I am now in want of money I wish to sell him, perhaps you will buy him from me." The king agreed to do so, and they fixed on a price. Then the barber's son said, "I love my slave very much, and if I wake him from his sleep I shall not be able to part with him, so you must let me go away whilst he is asleep." With these words he took the money and went away. Thus the king's son became a slave, and the barber's son went away to the country of another king. Whilst he was there he saw some labourers working in a field, one of them was advising the rest to buy a cow, thinking that this opportunity was not to be neglected he went to them, and said, "Brother I have a very good cow which I will let you have for sixty rupees," the labourer agreed and the barber's son took the money and went away with him. After they had gone some little distance the barber's son saw a fine cow tied in front of a Musalman's house, so he said to the labourer, "you stop here, and I will bring you the cow directly, the cow which you see in the can." The labourer sat down, and the barber's son went to the house, and said to a woman who was there, "Aunt, your husband has ordered me to show the cow to this man, you show it to him, and I will be with you directly," so saying he ran away with the money. The woman showed the cow to the labourer as she had been told, but when he wished to take it away, she called her neighbours and hindered him; he then discovered that he had fallen into the hands of a swindler, and left the place in tears.

Meanwhile the barber's son went to the country of another king, and there he heard that a merchant was just dead, and his son was making preparations to perform his funeral ceremonies. On hearing this news he went to the house of a poor woman, and said, "Aunt, you are suffering great hardships, do as I tell you, and you will soon become very rich. A merchant of the place is just dead, you must pretend to be his wife, and I will pretend to be your son, and then follow my instructions exactly, and you will obtain great wealth." So he made the woman put on a widow's dress, and he himself put a mourning cloth round his neck and went crying to the merchant's house, and said, "The merchant who is dead was married to this woman, and I am her son, now that he is dead I have come to perform his funeral ceremonies, and my mother will perform *sati* with him, if you will give us the needful money." The merchant's son believed his story, and gave him the money for performing *sati*. When all the preparations were completed, and the woman was seated on the funeral pile, and the fire was lighted, she grew frightened, and began to say, "I am a Yogi I am a Yogi." The merchant's son enquired what she was saying and the barber's son answered, "My mother loves me very much, and wishes that I may live for many Yugs." So the woman died, and the barber's son and the merchant's son went home, and began to prepare for the funeral ceremonies, and the barber's son said, "Brother, our father suffered much hardship for our sakes, let us sell all we have to celebrate his funeral." The merchant's son agreed and put all his property on board a boat in order that he might take it away and sell it; they both started together, and when they had come to a certain place, the barber's son said, "Brother, I have never visited this place before. You go and choose what is necessary, and I will remain here and take care of the boat." So the merchant's son went, and as soon as he was gone, the barber's son ran away with the boat and all the property.

He became very rich by this stratagem, and determined to visit some other country, but he considered that it would be very wrong to go away and leave his friend a slave, so he went back to the country of the king to whom he had sold him.

When he arrived there he heard that the son-in-law of a gentleman had been missing for a long time, so he enquired of another person how the man used to dress, and one day went to the gentleman's house, and told him that his son-in-law had returned; as it was a very long time since the people of the house had seen the son-in-law they had forgotten his appearance, and seeing that the barber's son was dressed like him, they believed his story, and let him into the house. In the middle of the night, when everybody had gone to bed, and his wife was fast asleep, he took all her ornaments and jewellery and cut off her nose and went away.

The next morning he made some noses of gold and went from place to place to sell them till at last he reached the gentleman's house, and said, "I know a charm by which I can fix on a new nose. I put on a golden nose which will unite with the old one, all persons who have such noses can obtain good ones instead." So the woman whose nose had been cut off came and bought a nose, and the barber's son fixed on the one which he had cut off the night before. Now the wives of the gentleman's neighbours all had such noses and were very anxious to get good ones, so they cut theirs off and bought gold noses, but the woman whose nose had been first cut off, had obtained a real nose, and it remained fixed firmly, while the noses of the other women which were only made of gold dropped off as soon as they were touched by water. After this happened a rumour arose that a rogue had come into the country and many petitions on the subject were presented at the king's palace and he was exceedingly troubled at it.

There was a sorcerer living near the palace, who by his calculations discovered the whole history of the rogue, and the barber's son saw that if the sorcerer was not put out of the way, there was every probability of some misfortune befalling him. As he thought over the matter, one night he went to the sorcerer's house, and called out, "Bhattacharjya Thakur, Bhattacharjya Thakur." Now the Brahman was an old man and did not wish to get up, so the barber's son said, "The king has sent you a very urgent letter, stretch out your hand and take it." The Brahman stretched his hand out through the door, and the barber's son, immediately cut it off, and went away with it, and as he knew that the sorcerer could practise no more magical arts now that his hand was cut off, he gained increased confidence and began to cheat the people on every side in a terrible way.

At last the king being unable to hit on any other plan proclaimed through the city by beat of drum that if the man who was doing all this roguery would come forward, he would give him his daughter in marriage. When the barber's son heard of the news he went to the king, and as a proof that he was the rogue, produced the hand of the Brahman. The king was amazed, but nevertheless kept his promise and gave him his daughter in marriage. He was overwhelmed with joy, and obtained the release of his friend, and went away with his wife to his own country.

THE EIGHTH STORY.

The Merchant and the Demon.

In the country of Bhuj Rája there lived a merchant named Kinu Shaha. Now Bhuj Rája and the merchant were great friends, and when the latter was going away to carry on his trade, he asked Bhuj Rája to take care of his house in his absence. Sometime after he had gone a demon assumed his shape and came into the presence of the rája and said, "I have neither son nor daughter, what then is the use of my trading any more?" With these words he went to the merchant's house and lived with his wife, and in the course of time three or four children were born. After twelve years the merchant returned from his trading, but when he went to his house the demon refused to admit him saying that he was the true merchant. At this the merchant went and complained to Bhuj Rája; the rája summoned both parties before him, but as they were both exactly alike he could not decide which was the true merchant. In this state of doubt he determined to go to another rája and tell him the whole story and let him decide the matter. Now while the true Kinu Shaha was going crying along the road he saw some shepherds who had climbed up on a mound of earth and were playing at a game, some of them pretending to be kings, others ministers, and others attendants. When the shepherds heard his cries they called him and enquired how he came in such a plight and after he had told them all that had befallen him, the shepherd who was acting the part of a king and was throned on the mound of earth, said— "If your rája will bring both parties before me and allow me to give a decision I am sure I can give a very good one." When Kinu Shaha heard this he went back to Bhuj Rája and told him what the shepherd king had said, and Bhuj Rája ordered his attendants to take both parties before him. He heard what each party had to say and then took a long reed and bored it through and placed it upright in the ground and said, "Whichever of you can pass through the hollow of this reed, is the true Kinu Shaha."

The real Kinu Shaha knowing that he was a man and could not by any means pass through the hollow of the reed, began to cry, but the false Kinu Shaha, saying that he could easily do it, was in the act of passing through the hollow reed, when the shepherd king, knowing that he was an impostor, stopped both ends of the reed with mud and killed him and let the real Kinu Shaha go back to his own house.

MANGA RÁJA'S OR KAVI MANGA'S ABHIDÁNA.

By THE REV. F. KITTEL, MERKARA.

Last year when searching after certain Canarese manuscripts in the Rája's Library at Maisur, I happened to meet with a Canarese Dictionary entitled "Manga Rája's Nighantu." Having read a few pages I felt convinced that the work was of considerable value as it explained, whenever possible, the Sanskrit vocables either by Canarese terms or Tadbhavas, and Tadbhavas, which are in common use amongst the Canarese. I had never seen such a work before, and anxious to get a copy (by the kind permission of J. D. Gordon, Esq., C. S. I.,) I took the manuscript with me to Merkara where I copied it as it was with its thousands of mistakes.

It is composed in Canarese verse, the so-called Vārdhika Shatpadi. Its introductory words are literally as follows:—"Bhāguri, Halāyudha, Surahari, Dhananjaya, Nāgavarma, Vaijayanti, Vararuchi and others having been, the modern (abhinava) Manga Rāja (mangārya-ra) uttered this modern Abhidhāna (with long initial) on earth." And verse 4 is: "The modern Manga having fully made ready the wisdom of Vararuchi, the novelty of Gopālika, the mystery of Bhāguri, the arrangement of Dhananjaya, the nice division (suvibhakti) of Surahari, the cleverness of Viśvaprakāśa, the Canarese of Nāgavarma,* the elegance of the great Vaijayanti, the extensiveness of Halāyudha and the propriety of Dhānambria, uttered the Abhidhāna (with short initial) in such a manner that females and boys can understand it."

CONTENTS

I Svarga Kānda			
1. Svarga Varga,	verses	2- 22	
2. Vyoma V.	"	23- 30	
3. Dig. V.	"	40- 60	
4. Kāla V.	"	60- 75	
5. Nātya V.	verses	76- 83	
6. Śabdādi V.	"	84- 90	
II Bhū Kānda			
1. Bhū Varga,	"	91- 95	
2. Śaila V.	"	96-102	
3. Vanaushadhi V.	"	103-152	
4. Mriga V.	"	153-166	
5. Pakshi V.	"	167-178	
6. Go(Paśu) V.	"	179-188	
7. Purushavilepakarana V.	"	189-214	
8. Āhāra V.	"	215-222	
9. Manushya V.	"	223-240	
10. Brāhmana V.	"	240-262	
11. Kshatriya V.	"	263-301	
12. Strī V.	"	302-315	
13. Bhūshālankāra	"	316-344	
14. Vaiśya V.	"	344-369	
15. Śūdra V.	"	370-375	
16. Tāli V.	"	376-383	
17. Vāhya V.	"	384-391	
III Pātāla Kānda			
1. Matsya Varga,	"	392-398	
2. Uraga V.	"	399-413	
3. Vāri V.	"	414-423	
IV Sāmānya Kānda	"	424-465	
V Nānārtha Kānda	"	466-530	

The author thus promises much, and I think he has executed his work in a fair manner. It would be very desirable to critically prepare, by the help of some further manuscripts, the work for the press.

* I possess Nāgavarma's Chhandas and a part of his Kāvyāvalokana.

ARCHÆOLOGY IN THE KRISHNÂ DISTRICT.

Extracts from a letter from Sir Walter Elliot to the Under-Secretary of State for India, dated Wolfelee, Hawick, 18th Feb. 1871.

(From 'Proceedings of the Madras Government,' 7th June 1871.)

I HAVE no doubt that the further investigation of the Buddhist remains, described in Mr. Boswell's interesting report,† will lead to important discoveries, and I therefore strongly recommend that the excavation of the Amravati mound should be resumed under competent supervision.

The present aspect of the site is that of an extensive earthen knoll or hillock. When I began my operations in 1845, I fortunately hit upon one of the four entrances, and from sculptures that turned up, I was enabled to form a tolerable idea of the plan and purpose of the edifice. The first remarkable objects were the two lions which had been seated on the wall of the outer enclosure at the entrance, a miniature dahgop which had surmounted a detached monolithic column in the space between "the inner and outer rail" of Mr. Fergusson; the shaft of the column itself;‡ the shafts of the smaller pillars at the ends of the entrance wing-walls, with their circular-ribbed bases and capitals; and portions of the five upright pilasters or "stela" on the dome, over the principal image opposite the entrance. Several of the tall upright slabs sculptured on both sides were still standing in situ, with the coping stones bearing figures of animals lying below.

These correspond so exactly with the sculptured representations of a dahgop, repeated again and again on the excavated stones, that I felt persuaded the latter were, in fact, representations of the edifice itself.§ Mr. Fergusson, to whom I communicated my notes and sketches, with a restored elevation of the dome, drawn in conformity with this conclusion, did not agree with me. He supposes that a dahgop occupying the area of the mound implies too vast a structure; and he imagines therefore that the enclosing walls, or, as he terms them, "the outer and inner rails" surrounded an open space, in the centre of which a small "dagoba, say 40 or 50 feet in height and 30 or 40 in diameter," had been erected.‖

† See *Indian Antiquary*, pp. 149 & 182.—ED.

‡ *Tree and Serpent Worship*, plate LXXXIX.

§ See *Journal Royal Asiatic Society*, N. S. Vol. III. woodcut on page 132, and *Tree and Serpent Worship*, plates LXXV to LXXXI.

‖ *Journal Royal Asiatic Society*, N. S. Vol. III. page 164.

From this theory I feel compelled, with the greatest diffidence, to dissent. The character and position of the sculptures discovered in 1845 impress me strongly with the conviction that my conjecture will prove correct; and this point will, I trust, be satisfactorily cleared up if the Government shall be pleased to sanction a thorough investigation of the locality.

The edifice which occupied the site of the mound still known as the *Dipal-dinna*, or "hill of lights" was probably one of the most magnificent dagobas ever constructed. It seems to have suffered serious damage at an early period, probably during the great Buddhist persecutions in the sixth and twelfth centuries. When the mound was first seen by Captain (afterwards Colonel) Mackenzie in 1797, it was much in the condition in which I found it. He states that, in the year preceding his visit, Venkatadrie Naidu, the Venerable Zemindar, in removing a large stone from it for a pagoda he was then building, came on the brick work of the original edifice, and dug a circular trench 10 feet wide by 12 feet deep, in hopes of finding additional building material. The central area was still untouched and a mass of rubbish thrown out of the trench prevented any observation of its original state; but he "conjectured that the whole had, previous to its opening, formed a solid circular mound."* The sculptures then visible were few and insignificant." The most remarkable, representing a serpent, had been removed to some distance, where it served as a covering or roof to one of the small temples frequent on the outskirts of Hindu villages, and appears to have been the same referred to by Mr Fergusson.†

After Captain Mackenzie's visit the zemindar, seized with the idea that the mound contained treasure, sank a shaft down the centre, but only found the covered stone vessel containing a crystal casket with the relic of Buddha. Disappointed in this expectation, he determined to enlarge the excavation, and convert it into a tank or hauz; and in doing so, covered the walls still deeper with the earth thrown out. Of Colonel Mackenzie's operations in 1816 no record remains,‡ but I could not learn that any extensive explorations had been made by his orders. His surveyors probably ascertained the lines represented in his plan by running shafts into the mound at various points. A few stones only were sent by him to Calcutta. I did not see more than four or five in the Asiatic Society's Museum in 1861. A few more that remained exposed were taken to Masulipatam, by direction of Sir Frederick Adams, in 1835-36, for the purpose of ornamenting a proposed chuoltry or town well, but it never was built, and the sculptures were appropriated by Mr. Alexander, the Master Attendant, after whose death the Collector was ordered to claim them as public property, and they were sent, I believe, to the Central Museum in 1855-56. I observed some more built into walls in Amravati, but not many. These should be examined and reported upon. . . . .

It is probable that the other three entrances will be found in a more or less perfect state and that much of the outer wall or "rail" will also be discovered to be erect and in situ, especially on the west half of the circle; whilst the sculptures of the "inner rail," or what I should term the base of the dagoba proper, are probably buried deeply under the sides of the excavated tank. Most of the upright slabs laid open by me had never been disturbed, but, as I explained to Mr. Fergusson, a few only had been re-arranged to form a small chamber or shrine in the gate-way; perhaps after the injuries done to the building in the sixth century, and may be due to a later local family, professing Buddhist tenets which is referred to in inscriptions extant in the neighbouring temples, as flourishing in the eleventh or twelfth century.

Some of the stones transported to Madras in 1846 should still remain in the Government Museum, and ought to be carefully preserved as illustrative of the original architecture. Among these I may mention the other lion (regardant), the shafts of the columns immediately under it in the entrance wing-wall, the ribbed melon-shaped base and capital,§ the miniature dagoba of sand-stone that had surmounted the amandakle pillar,‖ etc. The stone vase and the crystal reliquary, which I recovered from the zemindar's sequestrated property in 1860, should also be figured in any future description of the ruins . . . . .

The Krishna division contains many other Buddhist remains which ought to be explored. About 1840 the Collector, to obtain material for repairing the high road between Bejwada¶ and Bandar, demolished a mound of brick-work, in which were found four stone-vases, each containing a crystal reliquary, not deposited in the centre of the mound as at Dipal-dinna, but in the four sides. The country people called the place Langa-dibba, and ascribed it to a courtesan (*langa*), the favourite mistress of

* They are described in the *Asiatic Researches*, Vol. IX. pages 272-8.

† *Tree and Serpent Worship*, p. 102. note.

‡ There is an account of the 'Ruins of Amravati, Depaldinna and Darnakota' in the *Asiatic Journal*, Vol. XV. (1823) pp. 464–478, taken from a "Calcutta Journal." And as it appears from internal evidence (see p. 470) to have been written in 1819, when Col. Mackenzie was in Bengal, and two years before his death, it is probable that it was from his pen. It contains no details of explorations however.—Ed.

§ See Captain Tripe's photographs of the Elliot Marbles, p. 21, No. 72.

‖ No. 74 in the same photographs represents the pillar, and plate 85 in *Tree and Serpent Worship*.

¶ A similar deposit was found some years ago by the zemindar of Pittapur in the Rajahmundri District.

The four stone-vases, each containing a crystal box, were seen by Sir Henry Montgomery in 1843, who induced the Raja to send them to the Government Museum where they now are. They were figured in the *Madras Journal of Literature and Science*, Vol. XV. and Plate 2. but without any description, *Madras Journal*, Vol. XIX. p. 225.

a former Rája, who built it and several others of a height to enable her to see the lights of Sripúdúma. Two of these were said to be at Gudivádá* and Bhattiprolu, and I ascertained that a remarkable mound did exist at the latter place, but I had no time to visit it. Mr. Boswell indicates other sites promising to repay examination.

Mr. Boswell alludes in Section VI. (*I. A.* p. 154) of his paper to a collection of inscriptions:—These, I regret to say, came to an unfortunate end. I had obtained copies of almost all the inscriptions of any value throughout the Northern Sarkars, amounting to several hundreds and filling two large folio volumes. These, with three volumes of translations, were despatched by my agents in a vessel laden with sugar which encountered a gale in the Bay of Bengal, and shipped a great deal of water. Although enclosed in tin-cases, the combined action of the sea-water and sugar completely destroyed them, together with many books, drawings, and other manuscripts. I have still a number of Copper Sâsanams which I hope to utilize.

I embrace this opportunity of drawing attention to two other remains of Buddhist supremacy worthy of further notice. The first is the site of the city of Vegi, the capital of Vegidesam, and the residence of a Buddhist dynasty anterior to the foundation of the Eastern Chálukyan kingdom about the end of the sixth century. Some notice of Vegi will be found in the *Madras Journal*.† I afterwards identified the site between the modern villages of Vegi and Pedavegi near Ellore. A good survey of this ancient city is very desirable. The second place is a rock-inscription in the Ganjam district, exhibiting another version of Asoka's celebrated edicts. Some account of the place is also given in the *Madras Journal*.‡ At my request Mr. Minchin of the Aska Factory took a photograph of it, but at too great a distance and on too small a scale to be of use. A better photograph or rubbing on cartridge paper would be much prized by Orientalists here.§

ON THE GONDS AND KURKUS OF THE BAITUL DISTRICT.

(From the Report on the Land Revenue Settlement of the Baitul District.)

BY W. RAMSAY, B.C.S.

The Gonds are found in all the wild and jungal villages, and also in some of the more open ones, where they live chiefly by manual labour in the fields, following the plough or tending cattle.

The Kurkus are almost entirely confined to a few taluqas of the Sawligarh Pargana, which belongs to a Kurku proprietor, Ganda Patel. Some of the Kurkus are very industrious in the cultivation of rice, but the majority of them are very similar to the Gonds in character and disposition; these latter have no idea, and no wish, beyond living from hand to mouth, taking no thought for the morrow, and consequently obliged to put up with little food and scanty clothing. Their favourite mode of livelihood is by cutting grass and firewood, which they sell in the nearest market, but they also carry on a certain amount of agriculture, chiefly by that method termed Dhya. They are thoughtless and improvident beyond measure, and greatly addicted to drink, to obtain which they will put up with any sacrifice; on the other hand, they possess that great merit of most rude and savage tribes, *viz.*, truthfulness, which is developed in them in a remarkable degree, the more so when compared with the opposite character of the Hindus generally in that respect.

The Gonds are found more or less over the whole of the range of the Sátpura hills as far as Amarakantak to the east and also north of the Narmadá in Bhopal. The Kurkus are found more to the west as far as Borhánpur, westward of that they are called Mowásis and are intermingled with the Bhils. There can be little doubt, I think, that all these tribes, though now perfectly distinct in religion, language, and ceremonial observances, are the representatives of the aboriginal people who inhabited India prior to the times from which authentic history commences. The short, but well-built figures, the flat features, dark complexion and abundant locks, of almost all the various hill tribes of India, mark them as the descendants of a common stock, though history and tradition alike fail to give any satisfactory clue to the many changes which time, and the many convulsions to which the country has been subjected, must have wrought before the various tribes had fallen into their present shapes.

The Gonds themselves, and especially the higher class of them, who pride themselves on the name of Ráj Gond, the branch of the race from which the reigning family of the old Gond kingdom was sprung, are said to be of Rájpút descent, and their Thákúrs or chiefs many of them even at this day affect the bearing of Rájpúts; but little trace however of the Rájpút origin can be seen either in their language, their customs, or their physical features.

The Kurkus at the present day are an essentially different race, speaking a different language, and

---

* P.S.—23 Feb. Since the foregoing was written I find that the Langa-dibba mound, demolished by the Collector for the repair of the road, was at Gudivádá itself. *Madras Journal*, Vol. XIX. (or new Series, Vol. III.), page 226.

† *Madras Journal of Literature and Science*, Vol. XI. page 302.

‡ *Madras Journal of Literature and Science*, Vol. XX. (or new Series Vol. IV.) pages 70 and 72.

§ See *Ind. Antiquary*, pp. 219, 222.—Ed.

|| Pp. 43–47, or *Selections from the Records of the Govt. of India, Foreign Dept.* No. LVII. pp. 28–31.

having a perfectly different religion; they also however claim a Rájpút origin, and I believe that some of their chiefs on the hills adjoining Berar still arrogate to themselves the title and privileges of Rájpúts. It is popularly believed that the Gonds are divided into 12½ gots or tribes, corresponding to the 12½ castes into which the Hindus have been divided; but I believe this to be a mere invention of modern times, put forward by some of the Pradháns, or the priest class of Gonds, in affectation of Hinduism. The gots of the Gonds are properly family distinctions, marking different branches of the original stock; as a proof of which I record the fact that only members of different gots are allowed to intermarry, the wife being adopted into that of her husband. I believe that originally there were but two well recognised gots, termed "Dhurwa" and "Wika;" from the former the royal race and the chief Thákurs or Chiefs are said to have sprung; and from the latter, the remainder of the population. At the present day, the number of recognised gots is very great, so much so, that I have failed in meeting any person who pretended to know the names even of all of them.

As far as I have been able to discover, there are 22 gots belonging to the "Wika" branch of the race, and 20 to the "Dhurwa." Besides the gots there are a number of "Jats" as they term them; such are the Pongudyas, Pradháns or priests, Dhobyas, Dubaryas—makers of liquor to be used at ceremonies,—Chirkyas and Ojhas—musicians employed on similar occasions,—Koilyas, who make images of deities, and various other professional divisions; these again are sub-divided into the gots. The whole subject is involved in great obscurity, owing to the want of any records, and the utter ignorance and want of education among even the better educated Chiefs and Thákurs.

The Gond religion is a peculiar one. Besides the subdivision of the race into gots, the gots themselves are again divided into classes according to the gods they worship. There are three classes generally recognised, worshipping seven, six, and three gods respectively. The first class comprises, I believe, the Ráj Gonds, the priest caste, and perhaps some others; the second class comprises the bulk of the gots as its followers, while the three god worshippers are termed "Murnakobas;" there are said to be some gots that worship five, and some four gods, but this is a matter of some doubt. This is the theory of the religion as expounded by their "wise men;" but the great bulk of the nation know little of these distinctions. They follow in the steps of their fathers in the ceremonies attending marriages, births, and deaths, some of which are very peculiar, all involving more or less outlay on drink, and they all know some god to whom they make their customary offering at stated times. The religious generally of the Gonds may be divided into two heads, which for want of better terms, I would call "precative" and "deprecative;" the one addressing itself to the powers of good, and calling for blessing; the other addressed to the powers of evil, and intended to avert calamity; the latter rites frequently involve the shedding of animal blood as an expiation; of course with such an ignorant race, almost every object of external nature is made at times to serve as the visible symbol of the divinity. The lowest class of Gonds, a sort of outcaste tribe, called "Dhuryam," are even said to worship the dung of pigs! It is hardly possible for the imagination to carry one lower than that.

It is worthy of remark that one of the ceremonies after a death consists in killing a cow and sprinkling its blood over the grave; in default of this it is said that the spirit of the departed refuses to rest, and returns upon earth to haunt its relatives in life. From my own experience I am convinced that this ceremony is by no means universally acted upon, and not at all in the case of Gonds, living in the open country, and in contact with the Hindus. The Gonds as a rule bury their dead; but I have been informed that in the case of Gonds who, as it is expressively termed "die in their beds," that is in easy circumstances and better position than the mass, they are burned after the manner of Hindus. Another peculiar custom of the Gonds is that of serving for a wife in her father's house precisely as Jacob did for Rachel, the period varies from 7 to 10 years.

The language of the Gonds is quite peculiar to themselves, and, so far as I know of it, contains no element of Sanskrit or other roots of the present Hindu languages. The language and religion of the Korkus are perfectly distinct; the former has a decided affinity to Telugu; their religion consists chiefly in the worship of Mahadeva, whose symbol is the "Linga;" they also worship the sun. Altogether they are much more allied to the Hindus than the Gonds both as regards their language and their religion.

There are but few wandering tribes, and professional criminals are but a handful; this would naturally be the case in a purely agricultural district, possessing no large towns; all have employment, more or less, and consequently the chief incentives to crime are wanting; occasionally dacoities are committed by Banjáras, but these occurrences are few and far between. Formerly the Gonds were the chief offenders in this respect, but they have now been greatly reclaimed from their former habits, and now seldom break out into crime except under pressure of want. As I have said before they live entirely from hand to mouth; during the intervals of the harvests they subsist mostly on jangal produce; during seasons of failure they are utterly dependent on the bounty of the Malguzar, and if the bountiful hand be withheld, want will necessarily drive the sufferers to extremes.

Education must be pronounced to be still in a low state throughout the district generally, though improvement is gradually taking place in this respect.

As yet education has not found its way among the Gonds, and I see little prospect of its doing so for many years to come, or until they have made further advances in general civilization.

ASIATIC SOCIETIES.

Bombay Br. R. Asiatic Society.

At the monthly meeting of the society held on Thursday, the 12th September 1872. Professor Ramkrishna Gopal Bhandarkar, M.A., read a paper on the date of the Mahâbhârata, of which the following is an abstract:—

There is a notice by Colebrooke, in the 9th vol. of the Asiatic Researches, of a copper-plate grant in the possession of some Brahmans in Southern India, purporting to be from Janamejaya, of the race of the Pândavas. This king is described in the grant in the same terms as in the Mahâbhârata. The grant was pronounced to be spurious by Colebrooke, since it appeared to be very modern. From the solar eclipse mentioned in the grant its date has been determined to be the 7th of April 1521 A.D.

The earliest literary date is that of Patanjali. Prof. Goldstücker places him in the second century B.C., and the writer of this has recently discovered that he lived in the reign of Pushpamitra, the founder of the Sunga dynasty, who reigned from B.C. 178 to B.C. 142. Pânini must have preceded him by about three centuries, and the Srauta and Grihya Sûtras of the three Vedas must have preceded Pânini, or some of them were probably written about the same time with him. The Sûtras again presuppose the Brâhmanas, between which and them a considerable interval must have elapsed. Now the Aitareya Brâhmana mentions Janamejaya, the son of Parikshit and Bharata, the son of Dushyanta, as very powerful kings (VIII. 21, 23). This shows at least that some of the elements of the story in the Mahâbhârata run far into antiquity. In the Grihya Sûtra of Âśvalâyana the name of the Mahâbhârata occurs. It is questioned whether the Mahâbhârata here referred to contained the story of the Kurus as the epic now known by that name does. But the question does not appear reasonable, since another author (Pânini), who probably lived soon after, or at about the same time, mentions the names of some of the characters in the story, and the name of the poem also. Pânini in his *Sûtras*, not *Ganas*, mentions Vâsudeva and Arjuna (IV. 3. 98), Yudhishthira (VIII. 3. 95) and the Mahâbhârata, (VI. 2. 38). The first is a remarkable rule, for it teaches the formation of derivatives from these names signifying persons devoted to or worshipping Vâsudeva or Arjuna. And the manner in which they are mentioned together, reminds one of the great friendship which, according to the Mahâbhârata, existed between them, and looks like a reference to the representation of these heroes contained in that poem. Patanjali, in his comments on this Sûtra, asks no reason why Vâsudeva should have been mentioned in this Sûtra, since the same derivative from the name is taught in another rule. He says this Vâsudeva is the name of the great god Vâsudeva, thus showing that in his time, and even in those of Pânini, the heroes of the Mahâbhârata had come to be worshipped as gods. Patanjali gives the names of Bhîmasena, Sahadeva, and Nakula, whom he calls Kurus (IV. 1.4 also), and of Duryodhana, and Duhśâsana (III. 3. 1 also) mentions that Yudhishthira was the elder brother of Arjuna (under *Pân.* II. 2. 34), and tells us (under *Pân.* VIII. 1.15) that these persons were popularly known in his time. As an instance of III. 2. 118 he gives *Dharmena sma Kuravo yudhyante*, 'the Kurus fought with fairness,'—in which *yudhyante* with *sma* has the sense of the perfect, i.e., remote past. It thus appears that there was in his time a work describing the war of the Kurus, that the war was considered to have taken place at a remote time, that Bhîmasena, Nakula, Sahadeva, Yudhishthira and Arjuna were heroes of the Kuru race, and that they were popularly known. The Mahâbhârata therefore existed in Patanjali's time, though it is not denied that the poem must have undergone a great deal of transformation in the course of ages and many episodes have been introduced into it. The main story, however, appears to have been substantially the same as it is now. Perhaps the Mahâbhârata story was even made the subject of new poems in Patanjali's time, for under III.2.34 he quotes, as if from such a work, *Asidvitîyo 'nusasâra Pândavam*, 'he followed the Pândava, sword in hand.' This forms a regular line in the [illegible].

The Nasik inscriptions date probably from the 1st to the 3rd century A.D. In one of them Gautamiputra's exploits are compared to those of Bhîmasena, Arjuna, and Janamejaya, all of whom are Mahâbhârata characters (*Jour. B. B. R. A. S.* No. xxiii. p. 41). The Châlukya copper-plate grant translated by Prof. Dowson (*Jour. R. A. S. N. S.* Vol. I. p. 268-[illegible]), and one of the Gurjara dynasty, translated by the author last year, contain verses, quoted as from the work of Vyâsa, one of which is addressed to Yudhishthira. The date of the former is 472 A.D. and of the latter 480 A.D. An inscription in a temple at Aivalli in the Dharwad district is dated in the 3735th year of the Bhârata war. The Śaka date in the inscription is 556, corresponding to 634 A.D. (*Jour. B. B. R. A. Soc.* Vol. IX. p. 315.)

Kâlidâsa lived before Bâna, as he is mentioned as a famous poet by the latter in his Harsha-Charita. Bâna flourished in the first half of the seventh century. For he tells us that he was patronized by Śrî Harsha the same as Harshavardhana (the contemporary of Hiouen Thsang,) who was conquered by Satyâśraya, a Châlukya prince mentioned in the Aivalli inscription as then reigning, and whose great-grandson was on the throne in 700 A.D. (Dr. Hall's ed. of *Vâsavadattâ* p. 14, 17, notes, and *Jour. B.B.R.A.S.* Vol. III. p. 203-11). Kâlidâsa mentions the war of the Kurus that took place in the Kurukshetra, and Arjuna, one of the heroes, in his Meghadûta. Bâna himself in his Kâdambarî makes Vilâsavatî, the queen of Târâpîda, go to the temple of Mahâkâla in Ujjayinî and hear the Mahâbhârata read. The people of Ujjayinî are represented in another place as fond of the Mahâbhârata, Râmâyana, and the Purânas. There are equivokes on the name of the Bhárata, and the death of Pándu, by the curse of Kindama Muni, his wife Prithá having remained a widow all her life, the death of Abhimanyu, the widowhood of Uttará, Arjuna's being killed by Babhruváhana, and afterwards restored to life by Ulupí, and several other incidents are alluded to in different parts of the work. (*Bad.* Cal. edn. of Samv. 1919, p. 57, 128, 108, 196, 197.) The Mahábhárata there existed in a form, complete so far as concerns the main story, in the first half of the 7th century A.D. Bána mentions a work called Vásavadattá, in the Harsha Charita, (Dr. Hall's *Vásavadattá*, p. 12), which is very probably a tale of that name by Subandhu. Subandhu is mentioned in a verse by Rájas'ekhara, from whose works there are quotations in the Sarasvatí-Kanthábharana (Dr. Aufrecht's *Oxf. Cat.* p. 208a) attributed to King Bhoja, and consequently to be referred to the early part of the 11th century A. D. Subandhu's Vásavadattá contains allusions to Bhíma's having killed the giant Baka, to the skill of the Pándavas in gambling, to the Kíchakas, the officers of king Viráta, Arjuna, Duhs'ásana and others. The name of the Mahábhárata also occurs several times (Dr Hall's edition, p. 15, 21, 97, 98, 70, 166, 167.) One of the characters in the Mrichchhakatika, a very old dramatic play, mis-quotes the Mahábhárata. According to him Draupadí is dragged by the hair by Ráma instead of Duhs'ásana, Subhadrá becomes the sister of Vis'vávasu and not Krishna, and she is carried away by Hanumán, instead of Arjuna. There are also many allusions in other parts of the play (Calc. edition of S'aka 1792, p. 28, 31, 110, 120). Mrichchhakatika is mentioned in Dhanika's commentary on the Das'arúpa.

There is a commentary by S'ankaráchárya on the Bhagavadgítá, an episode of the Mahábhárata. In his principal work the Bháshya on the Vedánta Sútras there are quotations from the Bhagavadgítá. (*Bibl. Ind. Sanskr.* 64, Vol. I. p 273, 184, &c.) A verse from the Maitreyopákhyána, an episode in the Vanaparva of the Mahábhárata, occurs in the comments on Sútra 1,3, 24 (Ib. p. 276.) S'ankaráchárya is considered to have lived in the 8th century. In a Tamil chronicle he is spoken of as having converted a king of Chera of the name of Vira Vikrama from Jainism to the S'aiva faith. From a copperplate grant by a successor of Vira Vikrama, recently discovered, it appears that this king probably reigned in 846 A.D., and another of the same name in 828 A.D. The drama of the Venísamhára by Bhatta Náráyana is based on the latter part of the story of the Mahábhárata. In the prologue Náráyana speaks of Krishna Dvaipáyana, the author of the Mahábhárata, in terms of reverence. The Kirátárjuníya of Bháravi and the S'is'upálavadha of Mágha are also based on parts of the Bhárata story. There are quotations from these works in Dhanika's commentary on the Das'arúpa by Dhananjaya (Dr. Hall's edn. pp. 118, 142, 143, 145, 146, 150, 151, 162 &c., &c.) Dhanika was possibly the brother of Dhananjaya, who was patronized by Munja, uncle of Bhoja. A copperplate grant of the latter part of the 10th century mentions a Dhanika, who is very probably the same as the commentator of the Das'arúpa. (Dr. Hall's *Das'arúpa*, p. 3, notes.) These authors are also quoted in the Sarasvatí Kanthábharana.

Hemádri tells us that he was a minister to Mahádeva, a Yádava king of Devagiri, who, according to Mr. Elliot, ascended the throne in 1182 S'aka, *i.e.*, 1260 A.D. (*Jour. R. A. S.* Vol IV. p. 28.) In the Dánakhanda of this author there are many quotations from the Mahábhárata. The Jnánes'varí, a Marathi commentary on the Bhagavadgítá, was written, as the author tells us, in 1212 S'aka, *i.e.*, 1290 A.D. Jnánes'vara speaks of the Mahábhárata in terms of reverence, and we are told that the Bhagavadgítá is an episode occurring in the Bhíshmaparva of that work, as it does in our existing copies. Sáyana was a Minister of Bukka, king of Vijayanagar, whom he mentions in all his works. Bukka was on the throne in 1354 A.D. (Prinsep's *Chron. Tab.*) Sáyana mentions the Mahábhárata, and quotes from the work in the Sarvadars'ana Sangraha (*Bibl. Ind.* p. 64, 128,) in the commentary on Paras'ara and other works (Prof. Aufrecht's *Oxf. Cat.* p 264a, 286b.) In the Sarvadars'ana Sangraha (p. 177) there are quotations from the Kávyaprakás'a and this latter quotes from the Venísamhára. S'árngadhara, in his Paddhati tells us that his grandfather was patronized by Hammira, a Chauhán prince, who came to the throne, according to Col. Tod, in [illegible] A.D. (Dr. Hall's *Vásavadattá*, p. 44 notes.) S'árngadhara's work contains verses from the Venísamhára, Kirátárjuníya, S'is'upálavadha, Bhagavadgítá and other parts of the Mahábhárata.

REVIEW.

A Tract on Sacrifice ([illegible]) by Revd. F. Kittel, Basel M. Soc. Mangalore, 1872. 12mo. pp. 184.

The west coast of India has been for nearly three centuries the seat of a very considerable literary activity. By the end of the 16th century the Goa Jesuits had introduced printing and published many Konkani works in the roman character, which they first used in a scientific manner. In the 17th and 18th centuries they and the Carmelites continued the work of research chiefly in the Cochin territory. At the end of the 18th and beginning of the 19th centuries all enquiry seems to have died out, but since 1836 the Basel Missionaries have amply made up for previous deficiencies, and both by the importance and also by the number of their works, they have surpassed already all that had been done before. Dr. Gundert's Malayalam Grammar and Dictionary are well known to every philologist as proof of German patient labour and true science. The little work now noticed is by a well known member of the same society, and though essentially a Missionary work, it deserves being brought to the attention of all interested in India on account of the mass of information it contains on the ancient Vedic sacrifices. The use to which this is applied does not come within the scope of the *Indian Antiquary*, but many persons will be glad to know that they can here find a thoroughly trustworthy and accurate, though brief, account of all the ancient Vedic rites. Information of this nature has hitherto been obtainable only from rare Sanskrit MSS. or scattered and, to the general public, inaccessible, articles in scientific German periodicals. In pp. 20-48 the learned author gives the essential parts of each of the twenty-one sacrifices according to the usual arrangement, and he also gives copious reference to the Śrautasûtras printed and MSS. the Brâhmaṇas and Saṁhitâs, with very appropriate explanations of the meaning and purpose of the rites.

The Indian sacrificial rites are very numerous and often exceedingly complex; they therefore form a very uninviting object of study. But some knowledge of them is necessary to all who would understand even the modern Sanskrit literature and Hindu ideas, and Mr. Kittel's tract will, I think, be found the most useful aid to be had at present by students who cannot have recourse to the original texts. The object of this "Tract" is purely Missionary, but the description of the Vedic rites is of general interest, and is throughout well done.

A. B.

CORRESPONDENCE AND MISCELLANEA.

WAS SIHARAS THE SAME AS ŚRÎ HARSHA?

Sir,—I do not know whether the Siharas of the *Chachnâma*, (Sir H. Elliot's *Hist. of India*, p. 138) has ever been explained to mean Śrî Harsha, but it appears to me that it would be a very natural Prakrit form of that name. The loss of the R and the change of Ś into S are very common phenomena, illustrated by the conversion of the Sanskrit Śrâvasti into the Prakrit Sâvatthi. I therefore venture to suggest that Siharas of Kanauj is really Śrî Harsha as pronounced in the local dialect with which the author of the *Chachnâma* was brought into connection. Now if this Śrî Harsha was Harshavardhana the second, the predecessor of Hiwen Thsang's Śilâditya (and the name of his father as given in the *Chachnâma*,—Rasal, looks suspiciously like a corruption of Râjyavardhana, whom we know to have been the father Harshavardhana II.,) it is obvious that the *Chachnâma* is guilty of a gross anachronism in making him fight with an uncle of Rai Dâhir of Sindh.

The date of the composition of the *Chachnâma* is involved in obscurity, but it appears to me that this argument makes it very unlikely that it could have been before the death of Muhammad Kâsim. There are other facts tending to throw suspicion on the book, such as its romantic stories, and the *Hindu-ized* name of Budhiman for the prime minister of Chach. The only possible way out of the difficulty that I can suggest is that Śrî Harsha might have been used as a family name for the Rais Kings of Kanauj, and refers to the last of the series Jayâditya, but there is nothing whatever to show that this was the case, and the name Rasal, as well as the existence of another family name Aditya, makes the supposition unlikely.

This anachronism relates to an event which at the outside could not have occurred more than thirty years before the Arab conquest of Sindh, and I have invariably found oral tradition pretty accurate in its chronology for at least eighty or a hundred years. Beyond that, of course, it gets wild in the extreme. It is not likely that the author of the Chachnâma, if he was co-temporary with the events he describes could have been so grossly misinformed about quite recent occurrences.

W. C. Benett.

Gondah, Oudh, 20th January 1872.

GINGER.

As regards *Ginger*, the derivation of which Col. Yule asks about (*I. A.* p. 231),—it is supposed to be from the Sanskrit Śṛiṅgavera (see Colebrooke, *Amarakosha*, II. ix. st. 37), but this is derived from the Malayâlam name of the plant, and the Greeks probably took it direct from the same. In Malabar green ginger is called inchi and inchiver is from inchi, 'root.' Inchi was probably in an earlier form of the language singi or chinchi, as we find it in Canarese called śuṇṭi. Ginger is chiefly exported even now from Malabar, and in earlier times the Greeks procured it almost exclusively from that province, so that there is every probability that the name is Dravidian and not Sanskrit. If we look at the form of the Sanskrit word, it is impossible to doubt that it is a foreign word altered by the Brahmans, who, by their pedantry, disguise all they meddle with.

A. C. Burnell.

Mangalore, Oct. 17th, 1872.

BELGAM FAIR.

Fairs in honour of Lakshmî are very common in the Southern Marâṭhâ Country. They are celebrated once in two years in almost all large places. The fair of Belgâm however surpasses all the others. It takes place every twelfth year. The goddess Lakshmî is held in great veneration by the common people; but this goddess is not the same as that celebrated in Purâṇas. The tradition about the origin of this fair is as follows:—

A son of a Mâhâr left his home and went to a village where he used to pass through a street, on one side of which was the house of a Brâhman who taught boys to recite the Veda. The Mâhâr's son took this opportunity of learning by heart some part of the Vedas and made himself acquainted with all the duties of a Brahman. When this lad had accomplished this he put on a sacred thread and gave out that he was the son of a Brahman and easily passed for a such because he had learned everything that a Brahman is expected to know. He then went to the house of the Brahman who taught the Vedas and asked his permission to learn with the other boys. This the Brahman readily gave; for his strong memory and intelligence gave promise that he would turn out a celebrated Vaidika (one who knows Vedas by heart.) The boy soon gained the favour of his teacher, who gave him his daughter in marriage. After residing for a few months after his marriage with his father-in-law he went back to his native place and made his parents acquainted with all his adventures. He built a separate house that he might live in it with his wife, and after binding the people of his caste by a promise that they would not divulge the secret of his caste to his wife, he went again to his father-in-law's house and took her to his newly built house. Notwithstanding the precautions, the Brahman girl heard enough of his low caste. No words can describe her indignation when she learned that she was wedded to a Mâhâr. Immediately she returned to her father's house and poured a torrent of abuse on him. After this she returned to her husband and attempted to kill him, but he escaped from her grasp and entered the body of a buffalo which was killed by her. She also set fire to the house in which her mother-in-law was residing, and finally became a devî or goddess after her death. It is in honour of this goddess that the fairs are celebrated and buffaloes killed.

I have given the substance of what I was able to gather from inquiries among the common people of this place. In Belgaum a large car of the height of about fifty feet is prepared every twelve years, and a statue of the goddess is placed on it and carried in procession through the thoroughfares of the town. The car of this year was so heavy that it required three days to draw it through the town though some two hundred men were pulling it. When the car reached the green between the town and the fort of Belgaum, twelve buffaloes and hundreds of goats were killed. A large concourse of people was assembled on the green. There was a dispute as to who should kill the first buffalo between two Patels, each of whom claims the right. Everywhere on the green the work of slaughtering went on on the 16th July last. The head of the buffalo which was borne in procession before the car was carried round the town and buried in the ground and over it a small hut was built. During the twelve days on which Lakshmî remains in a temporary shed on the green no mills are allowed to grind.

THE NYAYA'KUSUMA'NJALI.

SIR,—Since I wrote my paper on the age of the Nyâyakusumâñjali which appeared in the *Indian Antiquary* p. 297, I have come across some additional information which appears strongly to corroborate the conclusions at which I arrived. One of the principal arguments there adduced was, that Udayana being older than Srî Harsha, and Srî Harsha older than the Sarasvatîkanthâbharana, and the Kanthâbharana in its turn older than the beginning of the twelfth century of the Christian Era, Udayana at the latest must be placed in the eleventh century. I now find that the date of the Sarasvatîkanthâbharana has been fixed with somewhat greater precision than it was in the sentence quoted by me from Dr. F. E. Hall. I find that the Sarasvatîkanthâbharana "dates probably from the end of the tenth, as it may be from the beginning of the eleventh century."* It clearly follows from this that the *terminus ad quem* for the date of Udayana may safely be transferred back from the eleventh century into at least the close of the ninth century, if not even to an earlier date. It will be observed that we are thus making some approaches to that contemporaneity of Udayana and Śankara which, as I have shown, Mâdhava takes for granted.

I have also recently observed the bearing on this investigation of the conclusion as to the age of Srî Harsha at which Dr. J. G. Bühler arrived in the paper which he read before the Bombay Branch of the Royal Asiatic Society on the 9th of November last, a summary of which appears in the *Indian Antiquary*,† viz., that Srî Harsha flourished somewhere about the middle of the twelfth century. This evidently conflicts with that in which the foregoing argument is made, and the question comes to one of the balancing of evidence on either side. Now I take it that the only vulnerable point in my argument, is the age of the Sarasvatîkanthâbharana—while on the other hand, Dr. Bühler's argument rests primarily first upon the assumption that Râjasekhara, the Jaina biographer of Srî Harsha, is a perfectly trustworthy guide, and secondly, on the assumption that the identification of Râjasekhara's Jayantachandra, the son of Govindachandra, with Jayachandra "who reigned over Kanyakubja and Benares in the latter half of the twelfth century," is fully established. The correctness of this last date (supposing the identity proved) would also require consideration. But that question is common to both the arguments, and on striking a balance, it results that the one argument involves two assumptions, while the other involves none at all.

The other argument corroborative of the position which I based upon the circumstance of Vâchaspati Misra's having answered Srî Harsha has also received additional confirmation. I was aware, that Vâchaspati Misra is stated by Professor

* See *Indian Antiquary* p. 251 and Aufrecht's *Catalogue* 207b there cited.

† P. 39. Prof. Cowell's Preface to Mr. Boyd's *Nâgânanda* also mentions some other dates to which Srî Harsha has been assigned. [illegible], if I remember rightly, corresponds [illegible] to mine.

Tārānāth,* to be quoted from by Gangeśopādhyāya, one of the greatest of the Naiyāyikas of Bengal. But I was not till lately aware of the century in which that great logician flourished, and Dr. Hall's catalogue gave no help in that direction. I have since found it stated, however, in the second number of Mookerjee's Magazine, (following apparently the statement to the same effect in Bābu Rājendralāla Mitra's *Notices of Sanskrit Manuscripts*, Vol. I. Part III.) that Gangeśopādhyāya lived seven centuries ago. This date, I take it for granted, either originates in, or is confirmed by, the traditions belonging to the school of Nuddea with which Gangeśopādhyāya's name is connected. And assuming it to be correct, it follows that Vāchaspati Miśra should be assigned to somewhere about the eleventh century, and the dates of Harsha and Udayana as based upon his, should undergo a corresponding modification. With that modification it will be seen that this argument also as now developed supports the conclusion of the foregoing one in the more precise form which it has assumed.

KASHINATH TRIMBAK TELANG.

17th October 1872.

AJANTA FRESCOES.

Lovers of art all over the world are growing keenly alive to the importance of preserving accurate and careful records of the old works while there is yet time, before each image has wholly escaped the plaster. They will be glad to know that Mr. Griffiths, of the Bombay School of Art, goes with a few of his students to the Caves of Ajanta at the end of November, to copy the very beautifully painted decoration which still clings to the walls in spite of damp, neglect, bats, and the relentless tooth of time.—*Pioneer*.

ELEPHANTA CAVES.

On the representations of Mr. Burgess to the Government of Bombay regarding the conservation of the Caves at Elephanta, the Government of India has sanctioned a monthly expenditure of Rs. 50 for their protection, and the Public Works Department is directed to carry out, in communication with Mr. Burgess, the improvements he has suggested. These include fencing at the entrance to keep out cattle, proper drainage to prevent water standing in the caves during the rains, and the removal of the earth accumulated at the main entrance of the great cave.

CONCLUDING VERSES OF THE PRITHIRAJA RASAU.

By the son and successor of Chand, relating to the sack of Dehli and the death of Prince Rainasi, the son of Prithirája.

"Glory to Prithivirāja! Renown to the Chauhān. Renown to Prince Rainasi who gave his head for the land, watered with his blood. Unfading be the wreath of praise. He, whose wisdom is blind, cannot understand this story. Should princes not reward you† in reading it, murmur not, Hingalaj‡ will reward you. To hear the renown of Prithwiraja, the jackal would assume the part of the lion. To hear the renown of Prithwirája, the miser would unlock his stores. To hear the renown of Prithwirája, the dumb would shake his head in delight; for its relation is a sea of virtues. The ignorant, on hearing it, will become stored with wisdom. In hearing it, the coward will become a hero. It is not the bard who says this, it is Sarasvati herself; for Uma delights to hear it; and the lord of the lyre§ dwells in its praise. The ills of life it can remove, it will remove even your foes. It can bestow offspring and riches; and, though death it cannot remove, it can cause it to be envied."—(*Trans. R. As. Soc.*, Vol. I., pp. 153, 154.)

Honour to Prithvirája's name!
To Rainsi of eternal fame,
Who for his sinking country fell!
Let bards in verse their glory tell,
In strains that with their martial fire,
May every mortal breast inspire,
Instruct the dullest, rudest boor,
Make misers open their hoarded store,
The dumb gesticulate delight,
And cowards rush into the fight.
Such strains as soothe immortal ears,
And Umá's self enraptured hears.
What can ensure such rich reward,
As eulogy from tongue of bard?
It cures all ills, subdues all foes,
Wealth and posterity bestows;
And, though death's sting it cannot heal,
Makes others wish the sting to feel.

Asiatic Journal, Vol. XXI. (1826.)

THE ORIGIN OF THE WORD 'LUSAI.'

Having been frequently asked the origin of the word "Lusai," I endeavoured, in my last interview with the chief Dumbum (Poiboi's governor and present minister), to obtain this information from him, and, as far as the imperfect means of communicating with him through a rude interpreter permitted, ascertained that the word was derived from "Lusai Kot," the name of a place at present inhabited by the Sailu and Haingro Howlongs, probably the Bhangies mentioned by Mr. St. John of Arracan. This country is said to lie between the Lusais and Poeis east of the head of the Koladyne river. The Lusais were at one time a weak and unimportant tribe, but the country alluded to being healthy and productive, they increased to a great extent, and then took the name of their place of residence, and thus became Lusais, just as the people of Wales are called Welshmen.—Major-General W. F. Nuthall, in the *Englishman*.

* See the Sânkhyatattvakaumudi Introduction p. 5. It is much to be wished that Professor Tārānātha would give us the authority for this statement.

† Addressed to his brother, and future bards.
‡ The patroness of bards.
§ Narada.

COPPER-PLATE GRANT OF PURUSHOTTAM DEB.

A. D. 1483.

Obverse.

ON A COPPER-PLATE GRANT FROM BALASORE (A. D. 1483.)

By JOHN BEAMES, B. C. S., &c.

THIS plate is in the possession of the Bhuyāns of Gaḍhpaḍā, an ancient and respectable family of zamindars. Their estate of Gaḍhpaḍā is situated on a rocky spur of the Moharbhanj hills about 13 miles north of the station of Balasore. The plate records the grant of the estate to their ancestor, Poteswar Bhat, a Brahman by Rāja Purushottam Deb, King of Orissa. This monarch ascended the throne in A. D. 1478 and the 5th year of his reign, the date of the grant, would be therefore 1483. The Bhuyāns however read it the 25th year of his reign which would make it 1503. This I shall show presently is incorrect. The text in Roman characters is as follows:

Obverse.

" Śrī jaya durgāyai namaḥ | vīra Śrī gajapati gauḍeśwara nava koṭi karṇāṭakala-vargeśwara Śrī purushottama deva mahārājānkar | poteswara bhaṭanku dāna śāsana paṭā | e 5 anka mesha di [illegible] somabāra grahaṇa-kāle gaṅgā-garbhe purushottamapura śāsana bhūmi chalisaśa aṭhaṅgaṭera [illegible] dāna deluṅ e bhūmi yāvachchandrārke putra pautrādi paramparā kramena bhoga karu [illegible] jalasama [illegible] likhita dela.

Reverse.

Yāvach chandraś cha sūryaś cha yāvat tiṣṭhati medinī |
Yāvat [illegible] mahī maya | yukta [illegible] dharā ||
Swadattam paradattām vā brahmavṛittim harel yaḥ |
Shashṭir varshasahasrāṇi vishṭāyām jāyate kṛimiḥ ||
Śrī madanagopālaḥ | śaraṇam mama.

Translation.

Reverence to Śrī Jaya Durgā. Of the hero, the illustrious Gajapati, lord of Gaur, lord of the tribes [of the country] of the nine forts, Karnāta and Utkala Śrī Purushottam Deb Mahārāja to Poteswar Bhat a deed of gift of a śāsan. In this fifth year of my reign the tenth day of Mesh, Monday, at the time of an eclipse, in the womb of Gangā, I have given Purushottampura Śāsan land fourteen [hundred] and eight besides, ie 1408 [illegible], as a gift. This land as long as the moon and sun, son, grandson and the rest, generation after generation enjoying remain! I have given the land together with its tanks and gardens.

(The above is in Oriya; the rest is in Sanskrit.)

Reverse.

As long as the moon and the sun, as long as the earth shall stand,
So long be the gift upheld of this rich grain-bearing land;
Whoso of his own or another's gift a Brahman shall deprive,
For sixty thousand years a worm in dung shall be born and live.
Śrī Madangopal my protection.

The marks at the end are; first, the dabusi or elephant goad, the special sign manual of the kings of Orissa, referring to their ancient title of Gajapati or lord of elephants; second, the śankh or conch-shell of Vishnu (Jagannāth), third and fourth the khandā or straight sword, and the katar or dagger, both emblems of the warrior-caste, the khandā belonging especially to the hill-people, and the katar to those of the plains.

With regard to the wording of the deed one or two points may perhaps stand in need of explanation.

Gaureshwara or lord of Gaur i.e. Bengal, is a constant empty boast of the kings of Orissa, who claimed to rule from the great to the little Gangā, i.e. from Gangā to Godāvari. Their kingdom did frequently stretch as far as the latter river, and even beyond it, but only twice in all their annals did they reach the Ganges and then only for a brief period each time.

" Karnāṭa kala" is a mistake of the engraver for karṇāṭa-utkala "Karnata and Utkala," the form which occurs in all the deeds and inscriptions of the monarchs of Orissa. This very Purushottam Deb conquered Kanjikaveri or Conjeveram and spent the greater part of his reign on the Godavery. The expression later on in this plate "Gangāgarbhe" probably refers to that river the "Sāngangā" or little Ganges of the Oriyas as there is no record of this king's having ever visited the great Ganges.

" Śāsan" in Orissa is a patch of rent-free land with a village inhabited and cultivated exclusively by Brahmans, generally on behalf of some god, whose temple is in their village and whose worship they are theoretically bound to keep up. As a rule the poor thakur gets very little worship and the money goes into the Brahman's bellies or on to their backs. These Brahman's Śásans are scattered all over the country and are detected at once by the large comfortable homesteads, the groves of cocoa-palms and fruit trees and the generally superior style of cultivation. The cocoa-palm flourishes well in Orissa, but is not grown except by Brahmans owing to the popular superstition that if a man of another caste plants them, he or his children will die in a year and a day.

"e b anka." The letter which I read e 'this' was read by the Bhuyáns as a ꠀ which it only very distantly resembles.

"Mesha"—the sign Aries, and technical name for the month Baisákh (see my note at p. 64 *Indian Antiquary.*)

"Dittam" and "bá1406tí." This is the Oriya fashion of writing figures, the name of the article is divided in two and the numbers written in between, the above forms stand for 10 diam, and 1406 báti respectively. Thus they would write 10 rupees, ṭa10nka = 10 tanka; 5 maunds would be ma5ṇa, 30 years ba30rsara, and so on.

"Chaüdasa sabtatiara" here again the engraver has omitted the letter *t* he should have written "Chauda *sata*"—fourteen hundred. As the grant is in Oriya and not in Sanskrit perhaps he meant the *sa* to do duty for *sata*, as the short vowel is pronounced *a*, and Oriyas often carelessly write *sa*, as for *sata*, *sata*. The grant of so vast a tract of country to a single Brahman (1106 bátis = 28,150 acres) seems to support the native tradition that Harbipada and the adjacent country was at that time uninhabited, or at least only sparsely peopled, and this idea is further countenanced by the fact that the king gives his own name to the grant, calling it "Purushottampur Śásan."

The reverse contains merely the usual Sanskrit formula observed in all such grants.

The subsequent history of the Śásan is singular and interesting. Potosur Bhat obtained possession and he and his descendants held the estate for some generations. In the reign of the bigoted Emperor Aurangzeb, however, Harbeswar Bhat, the then proprietor, was ousted by the Rája of Moharbhanj whose territories adjoined the grant. The Bhat applied to the Subah of Bengal who sent a small force and drove away the Rája's troops. Before restoring the land however to the Brahman, he demanded payment of the expenses of the expedition. The Brahman in vain represented that having been dispossessed of his land, he was unable to pay; the Subah refused restitution. Harbeswar then journeyed all the way to Agra where he laid his case before the Emperor. Aurangzeb was no lover of the Brahmans and paid very little attention to him, and at last to get rid of him tauntingly told him he should have his land back and be let off paying the costs of the expedition if he would turn Musulman. The Brahman resisted for a long time, but finding that the Emperor was deaf to remonstrances, he eventually consented, embraced Islam and returned to Orissa with an order for his restitution to his estates. Since that time the family has been Muhammadan, and the present head of it, Ghulam Mustafa Khan, and his brothers are men with quite a Mughal type of countenance, probably derived from frequent intermarriages with Mughul and Pathan ladies.

The archaic form of the letters in this grant renders it very valuable as showing the gradual development of the modern Oriya alphabet from a southern variety of the Kutila type. I would call attention to the two forms of the [illegible], also to the double [illegible], and the [illegible]; The appended [illegible] and [illegible] are also very antiquated and singular, showing especially the absence of all distinction between the long and short [illegible] and the gradual growth of the now somewhat abnormal [illegible].

ON THE DERIVATION OF SOME PECULIAR GAUḌIAN VERBS.

By Rev. A. F. RUDOLF HOERNLE, D. Ph. TÜBINGEN,
PROF. SANSK. JAYNARAYAN'S COLLEGE, BENARES.

By the term *Gauḍian* I understand the Sanskritic vernaculars of North India.

The Gauḍian languages possess a class of verbs which, though, as a rule, easily traceable to a Prákrit or Sanskrit origin, they have not received from either the one or the other language, but have formed by a process peculiar to themselves.

All Sanskrit and Prákrit verbs can be divided into their component parts, viz., the *conjugational affix*, the (*verbal*) *base*, and the *root*; e. g., 'kathayati' consists of the affix *ti* of the 3rd pers. sing. pres., of the base 'kathaya,' and of the root 'kath' (which last is obtained by separating the *affix of verbal derivation* 'aya' from the *verbal base* 'kathaya'). Similarly the Prâkrit 'kahei' consists of the *affix* i, the *verbal base* 'kahe,' and the *root* 'kaha.' Now in most cases the Sanskrit verbs have passed through the Prâkrit on to the Gaurian, merely subject to certain phonetic modifications; as Sanskrit 'kathayati' becomes in Prâkrit 'kahei,' and in Gaurian (Hindi) 'kahe,' where the affix, being a final short vowel, has been dropped according to a general Gaurian phonetic law [compare Sanskrit (Vedic) 'chalya' Prâk. 'chalia,' Gaur. 'chali' or 'chal.'] In some cases, however, the Gaurian has lost the original *base* of the verb, and replaces it by a new base of its own formation. This new base is the participle perf. pass. formed from the *root* of the verb of which the original verbal *base* has been lost; and to this new or secondary verbal base all the conjugational *affixes* are added, exactly as they would have been added to the original verbal base, if it had not been lost.

The verbs formed in this manner may be considered as a kind of nominal verbs; only that these secondary verbs, being substitutes for the lost original verbs, are in meaning identical with the latter. If we should suppose that the English language had lost the verb "to draw" with its whole conjugation excepting the past part. pass. "drawn," and had formed from this participle a new verb "to drawn," but with the same meaning as "to draw," and conjugated regularly, thus pres. "he drawns," past "he drawned," fut. "he will drawn," &c., we should have an exact parallel of what has actually happened in Gaurian. A few examples will fully illustrate this.

In Sanskrit there is a root 'vis' which with the prefix 'pra' (*i.e.* 'pravis') means "to enter"; and with the prefix 'upa' (*i.e.*, upavis) "to sit." Their respective *verbal bases* (adding the *derivative affix* a) are 'pravisa' and 'upavisa.' The 3rd pers. sing. pres. (adding the *inflexional affix* ti) are 'pravisati' and 'upavisati.' In Prâkrit these forms are found in the modified form 'pavisai' and 'uvavisai.' In Gaurian, on the other hand, not only these forms but the whole conjugation of 'pravis' and upavis have disappeared altogether; and in their place we find substituted the two verbs 'paiṭhanâ' and 'baiṭhanâ' with a regular and complete conjugation, *e.g.*, the 3rd pers. sing. pres. of 'paiṭhanâ' and 'baiṭhanâ' are 'paiṭhe' and baiṭhe,' just as 'paise' and 'baise' which would be the regular Gaurian modification of the Prâkrit forms 'pavisai' and 'uvavisai,' if they had passed into the Gaurian. It is not difficult to recognise the principle and method of formation of these two new verbs. Their *verbal bases* are 'paiṭha' and 'baiṭha'; and these, as can be very easily shown, are identical with the past part. pass. of the roots 'pravis' and 'upavis,' viz., with 'pravishṭa' and 'upavishṭa', of which they are merely phonetic modifications according to regular phonetic laws, namely, Sanskrit 'pravishṭa' becomes in early Prâkrit 'paviṭṭha,' in later Prâkrit 'paiṭṭha,' in Gaurian 'paiṭha.' Similarly Sanskrit 'upavishṭa' becomes in early Prâkrit 'uvaviṭṭha,' in later Prâkrit 'uaiṭṭha,' in Gaurian 'vaiṭha' or 'baiṭha.' The general phonetic laws involved in these changes are the following:—1. The early Prâkrit changes all Sanskrit compound consonants, if initial, to simple consonants, and if medial and dissimilar, to similar compound consonants; and 2. it turns all medial single surds into sonants. 3. Gaurian makes *sandhi* of all vowels placed in hiatus by the second Prâkrit law, changes all similar compound consonants into single consonants, and, by way of compensation, lengthens a preceding short vowel and turns into a triphthong (aï, aü) a preceding diphthong (e, o). For details and exceptions from these laws, so affecting the Prâkrit, I must refer the reader to Prof. Cowell's excellent edition of the Prâkrita Prakâśa.

To the secondary bases 'paiṭha' and 'baiṭha,' thus formed, the conjugational affixes are added exactly as they are added to original bases. The affix of the infinitive is nâ (or rather anâ, for Sanskrit *aniyam*), hence 'paiṭhanâ' and 'baiṭhanâ,' just as 'kahanâ' or 'chalanâ' (for Sanskrit 'kathaniyam' 'chalaniyam'). The affix of the 1st pers. sing. pres. is 'ûn' (*Skr. âmi*) hence 'paiṭhûn' and 'baiṭhûn' just as 'kahûn, chalûn' for Skr. 'kathayâmi,' 'chalâmi.' The affix of the 3rd pers. sing. pres. is e (Skr. *ati*); hence 'paiṭhe' and 'baiṭhe,' just as 'kahe,' 'chale' (for 'kathayati,' 'chalati'). The form 'paiṭhe' transliterated into Sanskrit would give us a form 'pravishṭati,' separable into *pra* (prefix) *vish* (root) a (verbal derivative affix) *ti* (conjugational affix); similarly the form 'paiṭhanâ' would represent a Sanskrit form 'pravishṭaniyam,' separable into *pra* and *vish* (root) and *aniya*. That is, they would postulate a root or *dhâtu* 'vishṭ,' and this may perhaps illustrate the origin of not a few *dhâtus* of similar phonetic construction (as 'cheshṭ' *to move*,' 'gushṭ' *to accumulate*, which are now enumerated among the primary roots, but which doubtless are really secondary roots derived from original verbal bases.

A few more examples of this kind of secondary Gaurian verbal bases or verbs are the following:—'Uṭhanâ' *to rise, to stand up*, from the secondary base 'uṭh' for 'uṭhya,' Prâkrit 'uṭṭhia,' Sanskrit 'utthita' (from the prefix 'ut' *up* and root 'sthâ' *stand*). Again 'ugnâ' *to spring up*, from the secondary base 'uga,' Prâkrit 'uggaa,' Sanskrit 'udgata' (from 'ut' *up* and 'gam' *to go*). Again 'ubhanâ' *to be erect, to rise*, from the secondary base 'ubha,' Prâkrit 'ubbhia,' Sanskrit 'udbhṛita' (from 'ut' *up*, and 'bhṛi' *to hold*). The Prâkrit form 'ubbhia' becomes in the first instance 'ubhya,' which we have in the low Hindi participle and adjective 'ubhyâ' *erect or reared up*. Next 'ubhya' is contracted into 'ubha,' which we have in the Marâṭhî adjective 'ubhâ' *erect* (see Col. Vans Kennedy's *Marâṭhî Dictionary*). And from this form 'ubha' the secondary verb 'ubhanâ' is derived. The original verb would be 'ubhâranâ' from the Sanskrit 'udbharaṇîyam;' just as 'chalanâ,' from Sanskrit 'chalanîyam.' This original verb, indeed, has not altogether disappeared from the Gaurian; for it exists with a very limited meaning and in a slightly modified form in the verb 'ubhalanâ' *to boil, to bubble up*.

There is a peculiarity about the verb 'ubhanâ.' It has an apparently irregular causal. According to the regular Gaurian manner of forming causals, the causal of 'ubhanâ' should be 'ubhânâ.' This form, indeed, is probably used in low Hindi when the verb is employed in its literal meaning *to cause to be erect*. But when it is used metaphorically (as applied to the mind) in the sense of *cheering* or *providing*, it forms the causal 'ubhâranâ.' This irregularity, however, is only apparent, for 'ubhâranâ' is only the Gaurian phonetic modification of the Sanskrit causal of the original verb; that is, 'ubhâranâ' represents a Prâkrit form 'ubbhâraṇiaṁ', and Sanskrit 'udbharaṇîyam', which is the past part. pass. of the verbal base 'udbhâri' (or udbhâraya), the causal of the original base 'udbhara'; and 'udbhara' is the base of the root 'udbhṛi' from which the past part. pass. 'udbhṛita' is derived, which in its turn gives rise to the Gaurian secondary base 'ubha' and secondary verb 'ubhanâ.' The Sanskrit original base 'udbhara' with 3rd pers. sing. pres. 'udbharati', &c. would be in Gaurian 'ubhare', ubhare', &c.; but all these forms have disappeared in Gaurian (except, as already noticed, in the form 'ubhalanâ'), and have been substituted by the secondary base 'ubha' with its conjugation 'ubhe', &c. But fortunately, the Sanskrit causal of the original base has been preserved in Gaurian; and thus a clue is afforded us for tracing the (otherwise somewhat obscure) origin of the verb 'ubhanâ' and the adjective 'ubhâ,' *e. g.* the 3rd pers. sing. pres. of the verb 'ubhâranâ' is 'ubhâre', Prâkrit 'ubbhârei' or 'ubbhârai', Sanskrit 'udbhârayati;' just as Sanskrit 'kathayati,' becomes Prâkrit 'kahedi' or kahei, Gaurian 'kahe*.'

The case of the two verbs 'ubhanâ' and 'ubhâranâ' serves to illustrate the origin of another group of verbs, viz., 'pagnâ' and 'pahârnâ', 'chanâ' and 'pahunchnâ'. The verb 'pagnâ' means *to arrive*, and occurs in low Hindi (Marwâṛî), and in Naipâlî. The same word occurs in Panjâbî as 'pajnâ' (or 'pujjaṇâ') and in Marâṭhî as 'pochaṇeṁ'. The Marâṭhî form 'pochaṇeṁ' has an alternative form 'pohoṁchaṇeṁ.' The latter form is the only one preserved in high Hindi where it is 'pahuṁchnâ.' It occurs also in Panjâbî as 'pahuṁchṇâ.' It follows from this comparison, that the low Hindi 'pagnâ' and the high Hindi 'pahuṁchnâ' are identical. From this again it follows that the syllable 'pa' of 'pagnâ' is identical with the element 'pahuṁ' of 'pahuṁchnâ', being merely a contraction of two syllables into one, such as is not uncommon in the modern vernaculars; and further that the element 'gnâ' is identical with the element 'chnâ.'

The next question is, what is this 'gnâ' and chnâ? In the first place we observe, that in Naipâlî, as a rule, the initial *k* of the root 'kara' (Prâkrit *kar* *kṛi*) is *chø* softened to *g*; and, second, that the two verbs 'ubhanâ' and 'pagnâ' are conjugated identically; *e. g.*, in Naipâlî, as 'ubhikana' *having risen*, as 'pagikana' *having arrived*; as 'ubhyo' *risen*, as 'pagyo' *arrived*, etc. Putting this together we must conclude, that as 'ubhanâ' is derived from 'ut' and the root 'bhara' (or bhṛi), so 'pagnâ' is derived from 'pa' and the root 'kara' (or kṛi); that, in fact, the element 'gnâ' is a phonetic modification of kanâ and is a verb formed from a secondary base derived from the past part. passive of the original verb 'kara.' This participle in Sanskrit is 'kṛita,' in Prâkrit 'kida' or 'kia,' in Gaurian 'gyo' (or kyo), a form which we

* The same Sanskritic or Prakritic causal is preserved in the Gaurian verb 'sambhâlanâ,' *to keep, to support*. For 'sambhâlanâ' is the Skr. 'sambhâlanîyam,' Prâk. 'sambhâlaṇiaṁ,' the 3rd pers. sing. pres. is 'sambhâle,' Prâk. 'sambhârei,' or 'sambhâledi,' Skr. 'sambhârayati,' etc.

have in the Naipálí past tense, 'pugyo.' This form 'pugyo', then stands for an original form pa + kṛita. From the past part. passive 'pugyo', the secondary base 'pugo' is derived, as 'ubho' from 'ubhyo;' and from the secondary base 'pugo' the verb 'puganá' is derived. In the next place, this result is confirmed by an examination of the verb 'pukárná.' We have seen that the causal of 'ubhaná' is 'ubhárná'. On the assumption, that the element 'ganá' of 'puganá' be identical with 'kaná' and a derivative of the root 'kara' (or kṛi), if we form a causal of 'puganá' (or its original form 'pukaná') analogous to the causal 'ubhárná' of 'ubhaná,' we obtain the form 'pukárná.' Now this assumed causal really exists, and is, in fact, nothing else but the verb 'pukárná,' mentioned above. For 'pukárná' means *to call*, and "to call some one" means really nothing else but "to cause some one (by means of the voice) to arrive." The verb 'pukárná' originally must have had a wider meaning, *i.e.* in general "to cause to arrive." In course of time its use and meaning was restricted to a particular mode of causing to arrive, viz., by means of the voice.

Having thus discovered the origin of the element 'ganá,' the next question is what is the origin of the other element 'pa' or 'pahun.' We have already seen that the Naipálí past tense 'pugyo' represents a Sanskrit form pa + kṛitaḥ; just as 'ubhyo' a Sanskrit form 'ud' + 'bhṛitaḥ.' The element 'ud' is a prefix; but there is none among the Sanskrit prefixes, which could have been phonetically modified to 'pa,' and still less to 'pahun.' But there is another way of accounting for this element. It may be an adverb qualifying the participle 'kṛitaḥ.' In that case, since the verb 'puganá' means *to arrive*, and the element 'ganá' *to make*, it must be an adverb meaning "near;" for *to make near* is the same as *to come* or *to arrive*; if, *e.g.*, I make near a town, I arrive at it. This is well illustrated in the well known prayer,

सान्निध्यं कुरु मे देव प्रसन्नो भव सर्वदा।

i.e., come to me, God, and be gracious to me always; or literally 'make near to me, O God, etc.' Now there is a Sanskrit adverb 'párśvaḥ' or 'párśve' meaning near, which still very commonly occurs in Gaurian poetry in the form 'pásaṅ' or 'pahuṅ.' The original Sanskrit past participle from which the secondary verb 'puganá' is derived, must have been párśvakṛita or párśvekṛita. I think, for reasons which it would take too long to detail here, that it was the latter párśvekṛita. This form would be represented in Prákrit by passammi kia or pahammi kia. The latter form would change in old Gaurian to 'pahámkya' or 'pahoṅkya;' and of these again the latter would change in Modern Gaurian to pahoṅkya.* And finally from this form, a secondary base 'pahoṅka' and a secondary verb 'pahoṅkaná' would be derived. This form 'pahoṅkaná' or slightly modified 'pahúṅkaná' or 'pahuṅkaná,' must have been (at all events ideally) the form of the verb on which all the different Gaurian modifications of it are founded. These modifications most probably took place very early. In Maráṭhí, Hindí, and Panjábí the guttural क changed to the palatal च, thus we obtain the forms, Maráṭhí — 'pahoṅchaṇeṃ,' Hindí — 'pahuṅchaná,' Panjábí 'pahuṅchaṇá' which are also sometimes met with in a slightly corrupted form without the anuswára 'pahuchaná' and 'pahuchaṇá.' Next the element 'pahoṅ' (*pahá*) or 'pahuṅ' (*pahu*) was contracted to *pa* or *pu*, and at the same time the hard guttural क was in Naipálí and (low) Hindí softened to ग, and the hard palatal च in Panjábí to ज, thus we obtain the Maráṭhí form 'páhuṇeṃ,' the Hindí 'puganá,' Marwárí also 'pugaṇo,' the Naipálí 'pugnu,' and the Panjábí 'pujaṇá' or 'pujjaṇá.' The change of gutturals to palatals is rather common in the Aryan family of languages (see Bopp, Comp. Gramm. §. 14, 15); and it is not without example in the Indo Aryan branch of it itself; *e.g.*, the Sanskrit 'kiráta' a savage, becomes in Prákrit 'chiláda'; the Prákrit 'kio' (for Sanskrit 'kṛitaḥ') becomes in Gaurian 'chiyo' (for kiyo which is the old Maráṭhí postposition of the genitive); to the Hindí (gen. postposition) ká corresponds in Maráṭhí chá, in Sindhí jo. In all these instances as well as in the original form (pahoṅ kia) of the base 'pahoṅcha,' the guttural क is immediately followed by the palatal vowel इ. This circumstance naturally accounts for the transformation of the guttural क into the palatal च. Very similarly a Sanskrit dental, followed by a palatal semivowel य or palatal vowel इ, changes in Prákrit and Gaurian

* This Gaurian o must not be confounded with the Sanskrit diphthong ओ, with which it shares the same letter. It is a pure vowel, the long o, the Greek Omega (Ω), and like it equivalent to the Sanskrit á. Gaurian possesses also the corresponding short vowel o, the Greek omikron, and like it equivalent to the Sanskrit a, from which it is not distinguished in writing. For this statement as well as for the numerous phonetic changes given in the text, there is abundant evidence. But this paper has already run to such a length, that I must refrain from entering into them here.

into a palatal; as *tya*, *dya*, *dhya*, etc, become resp. *chcha*, *jja*, *jjha*; *e.g.*, Skr. 'satya' *true*=Prâk. and Gaur. 'sachcha'; Skr. 'adya' *to-day*—Prâkrit 'ajja,' Gaur. 'âja'; Sanskrit 'madhya' *middle*,—Prâk. and Gaur. majjha. The Panjâbî form 'pajaṇâ' has the same relation to the Marâṭhî form 'pâchaṇaṇ' as the Sindhî genitive postposition 'ju' to the Marâṭhî 'châ.'

There is another theory of the origin of the verb 'pahuñchanâ' and its group of modifications. According to this theory, it is derived from the Sanskrit noun 'praghâṇa' *guest*, or from the Sanskrit past participle passive 'praghûrṇita,' also meaning *guest*. The first of these two words may be set aside at once, as it does not account for the consonants *ch*, *j*, *ṇ*, which are the distinguishing feature of that group of verbs. In the other word 'praghûrṇita,' the dental *t* is supposed to be the original of the palatal *ch*. It is not proved that the word occurs in Sanskrit. Still this need not be an insuperable objection. But it is fatal to this theory that the Sanskrit dental *t* is always elided in such words, in their passage through the Prakrit to the Gauṛian, and therefore cannot have originated the palatal *ch*; and 2, that a dental never changes by itself into a palatal, but only if followed by a palatal sound (as in *ty*, *dy*, etc.); and 3, that the theory does not account for the verb 'pahûṇnâ,' and not easily for 'paûṇâ.'

THE MERKARA PLATES.

I. NOTICES OF THE CHERA DYNASTY.

The inscription of which the accompanying plate presents a facsimile is engraved on three copper plates 6 inches by 2·2, and varying in thickness from 0·125 to 0·1 inch. They are strung on a ring 0·25 inch in thickness and about 3 inches diameter inside, closed by an elephant in relievo with its trunk down, and measuring 0·87 by 0·66 inch. They were first brought to my notice by Mr. Graeter who gave me a transcript of them, and called my attention to their age and the names of the kings mentioned in them. Through the kindness of the Rev. G. Richter of Merkara, I have been able to obtain the use of them in order to prepare the facsimiles.

As illustrative of the history of the Chera dynasty, the following extracts are given from Wilson's *Mackenzie Collection*:—

"CHERA.—Another political division of the south of India which may be traced to periods of some antiquity, is that of the Chera kingdom, which is always enumerated along with the Pândyan and Chola states, by original authorities. The boundaries of this principality seem to have been of little extent, and it was probably most commonly feudatory to its more powerful neighbours except where it had extended its northern limits so as to interpose a mountainous barrier between it and its enemies. The northern limit of Chera varied at different periods, being originally placed at Palini near Dharapura, whilst at a subsequent period the capital, Dalavanpur or Tâlkâd above the Maisur Ghâts, indicates a considerable extension of the boundary in this quarter, and the Chera principality probably included the greater portion of Karnata. Its eastern limits were the possessions of Chola and Pandya, and the western those of Kerala. In its early state, however, it comprehended the extreme south of the Malabar coast or Travankur, and consisted of that province, Wynâd, the Nilgiri mountain district, the southern portion of Koimbatur, and part of Tinnevelli. In this tract we have in Ptolemy the people called Caréi, and not far from it Carura regia Cerobothra in which, making an allowance for inaccuracies of sound and expression, we have the Cheras and Karûr still a city in this district, and Cherapati, the sovereign of Chera.

"It seems probable, therefore, that in the commencement of the Christian era, Chera, or as it is also called Konga, was an independent principality. Of its history, either before or since, little satisfactory occurs, until periods comparatively modern. Lists of princes, one of thirty, and another of twenty, who, it is said, ruled in the *Dwapar* and beginning of the *Kali* age, are given but they are unaccompanied by details: another series of twenty-six princes while the political events of their reigns, and closing with the conquest of the province by Aditya Varmâ, a Chola prince in A.D. 894, it enables us to place the commencement of the dynasty in the fifth century. The occupation of the country by the Chola Râjas was not of very long continuance, and in the course of the tenth century the capital Tâlkâd was that of the first or second sovereign of the Hoysala or Belâla dynasty of the sovereigns of Karnâta. The name of Chera appears to have been discontinued from this period, and the districts were annexed to the neighbouring principalities of Karnâta, Madura, or Tanjor."*

The *Kongadesa Rájakal*, a palm leaf MS. referred to above, he describes as "an account of the princes of the country known as Konga or Chera," corresponding "nearly with the modern

* Wilson, *Mackenzie Coll.* Intr., pp. xcii-xciv.

districts of Salem and Koimbatur, with additions of parts of Tinnevelli and Travankor. The boundaries, according to the *Tamil* authorities, are the Palini river on the north, Tenkâśi in Tinnevelli on the east, Malabar on the west, and the sea on the south.

"According to this work, the series of Kongu or Chera princes, amounted to twenty-six from Vîrarâya Chakravarti to Râja Malladeva, in the time of whose descendants the kingdom was subdued by the Chola Râja, in the year of Sâlivâhan 816 or A. D. 894."

"From the Tanjor sovereigns, Chera passed under the dominion of the Bellâla Râjas of Maisur, and finally under that of the princes of Vijayanagar, of whom some account is also given in this work."*

Professor Dowson gives an abstract from a MS. translation of the *Kongadesa Râjâkal* at the India House,† from which the following account of the Chera kings is taken :—

1. "Śrî Vira Râya Chakravarti was born in the city of Skandapura, and was of the Reddi‡ or Ratta tribe (kulam) and of the Sûryavansa (solar race); he obtained the government of the country and ruled with justice and equity.

2. Govinda Râya, son of Vira Râja, was the next king.

3. Krishna Râya, son of Govinda Râya, ruled next.

4. Kala Vallabha Râya, son of Krishna Râya, was next in succession.

Of these kings nothing more than their equity, justice, and renown is recorded.

5. Govinda Râya, son of Kala Vallabha, was the 5th in succession; he conquered the hostile râjas, exacted tribute from them, and ruled his country with justice and renown. This king made a grant of land to a Jaina Brahman, named Arinemi, for the performance of worship in the Jaina basti (temple) of Kongani Varma, in Vakakkiva, A. Sâl. 4,—year of the cycle Bahudhana (A. D. 82.)

6. Chaturbhuja Kanara Deva§ Chakravarti succeeded, he was of the same race, but his parentage is not mentioned. He is stated to have had four hands;|| he was versed in the art of archery and various sciences, and ruled with equity and renown, 'obtaining the honorary insignia of all the other rajas.'

A Jaina named Nâga Nandi, a learned and venerable man, was minister to the three last named râjas.

7. Tiru¶ Vikrama Deva Chakravarti I., son of Chaturbhuja Kanara, succeeded, and was installed in A. Sal. 100 (A. D. 178), at Skandapura. The celebrated Sankarâchârya (called in the MSS. Sankara Deva) came to this king and converted him from the Jaina to the Saiva faith. After his conversion he marched into the southern country and conquered the Chola, Pandya, Kerala, and Malayâlam countries, after which he returned. He made many grants in charity and in encouragement of the learned; a deed of grant, dated Vaisâkha-śuddh A. Sâl. 100,—year of the cycle, Siddharthi (A.D. 178), to Narasimha Bhatta, Guru, of the Bharadwaja gotra, is stated to be in the temple of Sankara Deva, at Skandapura. This king governed the Karnâta as well as the Kongadeśa.

8. Kongani Varma Râya succeeded; he was of the Kanâvas or Kanvâyana tribe and Ganga-kula, and was installed at Vijaya Skandapura in A. Sâl. 111,—year of the cycle Pramâthi (A.D. 189), and reigned for fifty-one years; he exacted tribute from many râjas whom he conquered, and 'by his munificence and charity cleared away the sins of his predecessors of the Ganga race'; his title was Srîmat Kompati Kongani Varma Dharma Mahâdhi Râya.

9. Srîmat Madhava Mahâdhi Râya, son of Kongani Varma, succeeded, and was installed in the government of the Konga deśa, at Skandapura; he was learned in all the sciences and maxims of justice, ruled with equity, and was renowned for his munificence to the learned and the poor.

10. Srîmat Hari Varma Mahâdhi Râya, son of Madhava Râya, succeeded; he was installed at Skandapura, but 'resided in the great city of Dalavanpura, in the Karnâta desa.' He exacted tribute from many different râjas, and was renowned as an eminent hero among all kings; he ruled according to the maxims of polity, and being very wealthy made many grants of land, one of which is recited, viz., a grant of land in Tagadur, a pollu (subdivision) of Talakad to the Brahmans for the worship of Mahâlinga Iśwara in that place, dated Pravaru A. Sâl. 210,—year of the cycle, Saumya (A.D. 288).

11. Vishnu Gopa Mahâdhi Râya, son of Hari Varma, succeeded, and was installed at Talakad or Dalavanpura; he conquered the *Pûrva-deś* (eastern country) and was renowned as a great warrior; he made many grants to Brahmans and to the poor, and being a zealous votary of Vishnu erected many temples to that deity; hence he derived his name of 'Vishnu Gopa.' 'The Konga and Karnâta deśas were both under his command;' having no children he adopted a lad of his own race, named him Madhava, and resigned the crown to him.

* Wilson, *Mack. Coll.*, Vol. I, pp. 198-9.

† Dowson "on the Chera kingdom of Ancient India," *Jour. R. As. Soc.*, Vol. VIII., pp. 1-9.

‡ A Telugu tribe, see Elliot's *Numismatic Gleanings*, p. [illegible]

§ Wilson, *Mack. Coll.*, p. 198, has Kandara Deva, and apparently intended for the 5th king. He omits the names of the 12th and 16th in the list, and his series ends with Gunottama Deva.—Ed.

|| The writer of the MS. has evidently understood the title *Chaturbhuja*, "four armed," as having a personal and literal reference to the prince; it is however a title of Vishnu, which is frequently assumed by his followers.

¶ Dowson says (*Jour. RAS.* [illegible]) the word Tiru preceding this name is Tamil, and is to be regarded as a translation of the Sanskrit Śrî.—Ed.

12. Mâdhava Mahâdhi Râya, adopted son of Vishnu Gopa, was installed at Dalavanpura, and ruled for some time under the orders of his father; but a son being born to Vishnu Gopa, that son was installed in the government.

13. Krishna Varma Mahâdhi Râya, son of Vishnu Gopa, was installed at Dalavanpura, and on that occasion he granted some countries near the Kanavâi and the mountains to his adoptive brother, Mâdhava Mahâdhi Râya, who had lately ruled; he governed the kingdom equitably; he was a zealous votary of Śiva, and having set up a Linga at Dalavanpura granted some lands for its support: he had no son.

14. Dindikâra Râya, son of Kêlari Râya, of the family of Vishnu Gopa's adopted son Mâdhava ruled for some time, but was deposed by the Mantri Senâpati of the late râja, who installed

15. Srimat Kongani Mahâdhi Râya, son of Krishna Varma's younger sister, in A. Śâl. 288*—year of the cycle, Parâbhava (A.D. 366). This prince was learned in sciences and in languages, 'he conquered all the deśas and took tribute from their rajas,' and granted many charities. A person named Yavachandra Dindikâra Râya, who had some duties under his charge during the reign of this king, made a grant of the village of Paruls-kondr near Alergrama.

16. Durvaniti Râya, son of Kongani Râya II. succeeded and ruled the Konga and Karnata deśas. This prince is represented to have been deeply versed in magic and the use of mantrams; by repeating the mystical word om when his enemies were drawn up against him, they were enervated and dispirited, so that he obtained easy victories over them. He conquered the countries of Kerala, Pandya, Chola, Dravida, Andhra, and Kalinga, and exacted tribute from the rajas thereof; all hostile kings were afraid of him, and hence he was called Dunny Vanrosta Râya (Dharma viruddi, or Punya viroda) the unjust Râya.

17. Mushkara Râya, son of Durvaniti, succeeded, he was learned in the military art, and took tribute from those râjas whom his father had conquered, keeping them in subjection and fear. He resumed the grants which had been made to the Brahmans and the poor; and hence he obtained the title of Brahmahatya Râya.

18. Tiru Vikrama II. son of Mushkara, succeeded; he was a learned man and well versed in the science of government; 'he obtained possession of all the deśas,' and ruled them with justice.

19. Bhû Vikrama Râya, son of Tiru Vikrama succeeded, and was installed in A. Śâl. 461,—year of the cycle, Siddhârthi (A.D. 539). He ruled the two countries of Konga and Karnata, and conquered many other countries. From the great number of elephants which he procured, the title of Gajapati was given to him; he had several weapons made of ivory which he kept by him as trophies of victory. He maintained all the charitable and religious grants which had been made by his ancestors in the countries which they had conquered, as well as in the Chera and Karnata countries.

20. Kongani Mahâdhi Râya III. succeeded his father Bhû Vikrama, and governed the countries with justice and equity. He made his brother commander of his armies, and several râjas having refused to pay tribute, he collected his armies and conquered the Chola, Pândya, Drâvida, Andhra, Kalinga Varada, and Maharashtra deśas, as far as the Narmada river, and took tribute from them; he then returned to his capital, Dalavanpura, which he strongly fortified, and made many benefactions. The title of Bhû Vikrama Râya was taken by him. He acted in these campaigns, and in the government of the country under the advice of his youngest brother Vallavagi Râya.

21. Râja Govinda Râya succeeded his father, and ruled the country with equity and renown, subduing all the hostile rajas. He was 'esteemed a most pure person in the Gangakula,' and from his attachment to the Lingadhari sect, was called Narali Varma. This prince resided for some time at the city of Maganda-pattana.

22. Sivaga Mahâ Râya, brother of Govinda Râya succeeded; he was installed at Dalavanpura, but resided for some time at Maganda-pattana, ruling the kingdom justly. In A. Śâl. 591,—year of the cycle, Pramadhita (A.D. 669), he made a grant of the village called Mallahalli to a learned Brahman of Drâvida deśa.

23. Prithivi Kongani Mahâdhi Râya, grandson (son's son) of Sivaga, succeeded; his commander-in-chief, Paruchu Râya, conquered the hostile rajas, and the king conferred upon him a grant of twelve villages near Skandapura, and the title of Chavarya Parama Narendra Senâdhipati, in Chaitra, A. Śâl. 668,—year of the cycle, Pârthiva (A.D. 746). This king ruled the country in felicity, and was known by the title Siva Mahâ-râja.

24. Râja Malla Deva I. son of Vijayâditya Râya, younger brother of Prithivi Kongani Râya, succeeded, and ruled the Konga and Karnâta deśas. This prince always dressed with magnificence and elegance. He is recorded to have made a grant to his Senâdhipati 'of twelve villages belonging to Vijaya Skandapura situated above the Kanavâi along with Vijaya Skandapura. The mantris of his tribe, the nobility, and the Mallikârjuna Swâmi, were declared witnesses to the grant.'

25. Ganda deva Mahâ-râya, son of Malla-deva, succeeded; he was a powerful prince, and obtained the different insignia of all the râjas. He fought with the Drâvida Râja in Kânchi deśa, defeated him and exacted tribute from the country; he fought also with the Chola Râja, 'into whom he carried terror, and afterwards established amity with him.' He maintained a friendship with the Pândya Râja,

* Compare this date with that given in the grant, viz. 288.—Ed.

and was renowned among the Gangá-kula for protecting the kingdom.

26. Satya Vâkya Râya succeeded his father Ganda-deva, and ruled the kingdom in equity and justice, punishing the wicked and protecting the good. He was never failing in truth, hence he obtained the title of Satya Vâkya Râya (the truth-speaking king).

27. Gunottama Deva, brother of Satya Vâkya, was installed at Dalavanpura; he ruled the kingdom in an equitable manner, allowing many charities, and maintained friendship with the other rájas.

28. Malla Deva Râya II., younger brother of Gunottama, succeeded during the life-time of the latter, whom he is stated to have kept at Vijaya Skandapura. This king was a very valiant man and defeated the Pândya Râja, who had attacked him.

In the reign of this prince, his brother Gunottama made a grant of land in Aid, A. Sál. 800,—year of the cycle, Vikari (A.D. 878), to a Jaina, for the performance of worship to a Jaina deity.

On the 7th Vaisákha sud. A. Sál. 816,—year of the cycle, Ananda (A.D. 894), a person named Tirumalayan, built a temple, and to the west of it erected an image of Vishnu, which he called Tirumala Deva, upon some land "in the midst of the Kâvéri," where in former times the western Ranganâth Swâmi had been worshipped by Gautama Rishi, but which was then entirely covered with jungle. This place he called Srî Ranga pattana (Seringapatam)."

Prof. R. G. Bhandarkar's remarks given below will show the importance of the inscription in connection with this abstract. And Mr. Rice's transcription* will aid those unacquainted with the original character in reading it. The Canarese ḷ has been rendered by l, ḻ—equivalent to ळ—by ḷ, ಱ by ḻ, and by l. ರ by r, and the second form by ṟ.

There is a difficulty connected with the date. Finding that Mâgh Suddha 5th, S. 388, fell on Wednesday, I submitted the question to Prof. Keru Lakshuman Chatre. He finds the day to fall on "Wednesday—Budhavâra or Saumyavâra, Nakshatra—Uttara Bhadrapada," and considers that the engraver, being careless, has written स्वति for शुद्ध." Nakshatra Svâti never falls near 5th Mâgh Suddha, but the astrologer consulted, he thinks, may have carelessly taken Mâgh vadha, and given Svâti, which falls only a day in advance of the 5th, for S. 388.

Badaneguppe, mentioned in the last line of the second plate, appears on Arrowsmith's map as Budunagoopy or Padanagoopa, and in the Atlas sheet of the Gt. Trigonometrical Survey maps as Baddanagupa* in N. Lat. 11° 59', E. Long. 76° 56'. It is therefore 10 geographical miles S. W. from the old capital of Tâlakâd on the Kâveri.—J. B.

II. TRANSLITERATION AND TRANSLATION.

By B. LEWIS RICE, EDUCATIONAL INSPECTOR, MAISUR.

[I.] Svasti jitam bhagavatâ gata-ghana-gaganâbhena Padmanâbhena śrîmaj-jâhnaviya [ku] lâmala-vyomâvabhâsana-bhâskaraḥ sva-khaḍgaika-prahâra-khaṇḍita-mahâ-śilâ-stambha-labdha-bala parâkramo dâraṇârigaṇa - vidâraṇopalabdha - vraṇa - vibhûshaṇa - vibhûshita Kaṇvâyana-sa gotrasya śrîmân Koṅguṇi mahâdhirâjaḥ tasya putra pitur anvâgata-guṇa-yukto vidyâ vinaya-vihita-vṛittaḥ samyak-prajâpâlana-mâtrâdhigata-râjyâ-prayojana vidvat-kavi-kâñchana-nikashopala-bhûto nîti-śâstrasya vaktri-prayoktri-kuśalo Dattaka-sûtra vṛitti-praṇetâ śrîmân Mâdhava-mahâdhirâjaḥ tasya putra pitṛi-paitâmaha guṇa-yukto 'nêka-châturdanta-yuddhâvâpta-chaturudadhi-salila-svâdita-yaśa śrîmad Hari Varmma mahâdhirâjaḥ tasya putra dvija guru devatâ-pûjana-para Nârâyaṇa charaṇânudhyâta śrîmad-Vishṇu-Gopa-ma-

[II.] hâdhirâjaḥ tasya putra Tryambaka-charaṇâmbhoruha-rajaḥ-pavitrîkṛitottamâṅga sva-bhuja-bala-parâkrama-kraya-krîta-râjya kaliyuga-bala-paṅkâvasanna-vṛishoddharaṇa-nitya-sannaddha śrîmân Mâdhava-mahâdhirâjaḥ tasya putra śrîmat Kadamba-kula-gagana-gabhastimâlina Kṛishṇa Varmma-mahâdhirâjasya priya-bhâgineyo vidyâ-vinayâtiśaya-paripûritântarâtma niravagraha pradhâna-śauryya vidvatsu prathama-gaṇya śrîmân Koṅguṇi mahâdhirâja Avinîta-nâmadheya-Dattasya deśiga-gaṇa Koṇḍakundânvaya-Guṇachandra-Bhaṭâra-śishyasya Abhayanandi Bhaṭâra tasya śishyasya Śîlabhadra-Bhaṭâra-śishyasya Jaṇanandi-Bhaṭâra-śishyasya Guṇanandi-Bhaṭâra-śishyasya Vandaṇandi Bhaṭârarggê ashṭa aśîti uttarasya trayo śatasya saṁvatsarasya Mâgha-mâsaṁ somavâraṁ svâti nakshatra śuddha pañchami akaja.

* A transcription was also prepared by Prof. Bhandarkar, but as he was doubtful about the Kanarese portion of it, I have used Mr. Rice's, transliterating it from Devanagari into Roman characters.—J. B.

varsha prithuvi vallabha mantri Tajavana nagara árivijaya jinálaske Púnáda 600 sahasra Kijenádu saptari madhye Badaṇeguppe náma Aviuita mahádhiráje bhadattena paḍiye ároḷaṅ úra-

[III.] [ko]pennikkoṇḍugañgeyalu ambalimaṇṇaṅ Tajavanapuradu] taḷa vittiyamaṇ voguri geleyo]pa-nnikkoṇḍugaṅ Pirikereyoḷaṅ rájamánaṅ anumodana pannikkoṇḍugeṅ manoharaṅ dattaṅ Badaṇeguppe-grámasya simántaraṅ púrbbasyáádimi kaḍjige moraḍiü Gajaseleye Karivaḷḷiya koṭṭagara Ba-daṇeguppeya trisandhiya satti koraḷu ágneyadinante bandudá guṇi taṭakaṅ puna dakshiṇasyáṅ disi bahu ána biye balkaṇi vrikshame puna paschima mukhadu sanda bahumúlika paniiye puna Ba-daṇeguppeya koṭṭagara maḷtagiya trisandhiya kaṭe Chaṇḍigále puna nairatyadesadu kaḷaka vriksha me puna paschimasyáṅ disi paḍiaidelvrikshame sánteretiya vaṭa vrikshame puna tere vaḷḷame ut-tará mukha-

de sanda bahumúlika paniiye jambú paḍiya taṭakame puna váyavyade gaḷechilúcha vrikshame puna Badaṇe-

guppeya maḷtagiya Koḷeyanúra Dásanúra trisandhiya neggila gumbe nilduveḷuñige puna Gajasele-ya gráma uttara disi kayga moraḍiü | ilade kaḷasaraye puna púrbba mukhade sanda bahumúlika pa-

[IV.] niiye puna kuḷuṇaṭigále vaṭa vrikshame puna isánade Badaṇeguppeya Dásanúra poṇṇala trisandhiya

taṭakame koḍigadili chiñcha vrikshame kottarambina diṇṇe púrbbade kúḍitta simántaraṅ | tasya sákshiṇa

Gaṅga rájakula sakalásthávyaka purusha Prabhakaraṇa Marugareya senábika Gaṅjenáḷa nirgguṇḍa maṇiya

Gareya Nandála sisbáládaya bhriṭyáyádiṇḍina tahal Tagadúra kaḷugavaru Gaṇigaṇúra tagadara Ála-dese sandaharaṅ U maṇaṭúra haḷḷararaṅ Álageyaraṅ Badaṇeguppeya iheḷḷarara duggiviyaruṅ | evaluttu paradattáṅ gráyo haretha vasundharaṅ shashṭiṁ varsha-sahasráṇi vishṭáyáṅ jáyate krimiḥ va sabhi vasudhá bhu ktá rájabhi Sakarádibhi yasya yasya yadá bhúmi tasya tasya tadá phalaṅ | deva svantu vishaṅ ghoraṅ na vishaṅ visham uchyate vishamekákinaṅ hanti devasva putra-pautrikaṅ | sámá-nayaṅ dha

rmma hetuṅ nripáṇáṅ kále kále pálaniyo bhavadbhi sarbbánetán bhávino párthivendrá bhúyo bhúyo yáchate Rámabhadra | Visva-Karmmaṇa likhitaṅ.

Translation.

May it be well. Success through the adorable *Padmanábha** resembling (in colour) the cloudless sky. A sun illuminating the clear firmament of the *Jáhnavi race*† distinguished for the strength and valour attested by the great pillar of stone divided with a single stroke of his sword, adorned with the ornament of the wound received in cutting down the hosts of his enemies, was Kongaṇi Mahádhirájá, of the Kaṇváyanasa gotra. His son, inheriting all the qualities of his father, possessing a character for learning and modesty, having obtained the honours of the kingdom only through his excellent government of his subjects, a touchstone for (testing) gold, the learned, and poets, skilled both in expounding and practising political science, the donor of lands to the *Dattaka* line,‡ was Mádhava Mahádhirájá. His son, possessed of all the qualities inherited from his father and grandfather, having entered into war with many elephants (so that) his fame had tasted the waters of the four oceans, was Hari Varmma Mahádhirájá. His son, devoted to the worship of Bráhmans, *gurus* and gods, having humbled himself at the feet of Náráyaṇa,§ was Vishnu Gopa Mahádhirájá. His son, with a head purified by the pollen from the lotuses—the feet of Triyambaka,‖ having by personal strength and valour obtained his kingdom, daily eager to extricate merit from the thick mire of the *Kali Yuga*, in which it had perished, was Mádhava Mahádhirájá. His son, the beloved sister's son of Krishṇa Varmma Mahádhirája, who was the sun to the firmament of the auspicious Kadamba race, having a mind illuminated

* Vishnu.

† Jáhnavi Kula. The same as Gangá Kula or Vansa.

‡ May also be rendered 'the author of a treatise on the law of adoption.' § Vishnu. ‖ S'iva.

with the increase of learning and modesty, of indomitable bravery in war, reckoned the first of the learned, was K o n g a ṇ i M a h â d h i r â j a.

To Vandaṇandi Bhaṭâra, the disciple of Guṇanandi Bhaṭâra, who was the disciple of Jainanandi Bhaṭâra, who was the disciple of Silabhadra Bhaṭâra, who was the disciple of Abhayanandi Bhaṭâra, who was the disciple of Guṇachandra Bhaṭâra, of the Kondakunda race,* the line of gurus to the Datta named Avinita;† in the year 388,‡ the month Mâgha, Monday, the nakshatra being Svâti,§ the fifth day of the bright fortnight. (The village) named B a d a ṇ e g u p p e, situated in the middle of the seven of Edenâḍ in the............thousand of Pûnâḍ, having been obtained by Avanita Mahâdhirâja Bhaṭâra, minister of the sovereign of all the continents,‖ conqueror of the city of T a l a v a n a,¶ for war on the Jains.** (He) plundering and taking possession of the six associated villages, obtaining by friendship (or flattery) Uyambali†† and the town lands of the city of Talavana, procuring the enjoyment of royal rights in Pirikere—presented the charming (village).‡‡ The boundaries of the village of B a d a ṇ e g u p p e :—east, a red stone, Gôṇasale, the sâlti post at the junction of the three paths of the Karivalli rest-house and Badaṇeguppe: south east, a bank covered with the tumbudas :§§ again to the south, a thicket of milk-hedge,‖‖ a kaltani tree: again to the west, a line of many medical plants,¶¶ then the pond at the junction of the three paths of the Badaṇeguppe rest-house and Chandigala: again south west, a clearing-nut tree:* again to the west, a [pedahled] tree, a [nâsteroli] banyan tree, thence the bed of the stream: again to the north, a line of many medical plants, and a bank covered with the rose-apple:† again north west, the temple tamarind tree, the group of nagalu‡ at the junction of the three paths of the Badaṇeguppe [maltagi] Kadaysudra and Dâsanûra§ [nâlavâdanga], thence the hill which protects the north of the village of Gajaeria and the descent to the large stone; again east, a line of many medical plants, then a [halapaltugala] banyan tree: again north east, the bank at the junction of the three paths of Badaṇeguppe and Dâsanûra [palmasla], the [kodigalli] tamarind tree, and so the mound of [kontaramba] which joins the eastern boundary.

Witnesses thereto;—Perbba Kavaṇa, the man who is a friend in all things to the line of the Gangâ râjâs,‖ Mara Gereya Sendraka, Ganjenâḍ Nirgguṇḍa¶ Mapiya, Gereya, servants** of Nandâla Sinabaladapa.

Country witnesses††:—Tagadûru‡‡ Kolagere, Gaṇigenûru Tagada, Âlgoḍaṭe§§ Nandaka, Ummaṭûru‖‖ Bellura Alageya Badaṇeguppe Bellura Deggiriya. (Signature (?) of three letters.)

Whoso by violence takes away land presented by himself or by another shall be born a worm in ordure for sixty thousand years. The earth has been enjoyed by Sâgara and other kings. According to their (gifts of) land so was their reward. Poison is no poison, the property of the gods that is the real poison. For poison kills a single man, but a gift to the gods (if usurped) destroys sons and descendants. Merit is a common bridge for kings. This from age to age deserves your support, O kings of the earth. Thus does Râmabhadra beseech the kings who come after him.—Written by V i s v a K a r m m a.

III.—REMARKS ON THE MERKARA COPPER-PLATE GRANT.

BY PROF. RAMKRISHNA GOPAL BHANDARKAR, M.A.

The genealogy of the kings of C h e r a as given in the grant is :—

1. Kongaṇi I.
 |2. Mâdhava I.
  |3. Hari Varmma.
   |4. Vishṇu Gopa.
    |5. Mâdhava II.
     |6. Kongaṇi II.

These names agree with the 8th to 12th and 13th given by Prof. Dowson from the Tamil

* Koṇḍakundânvaya.
† [illegible] gaṇam—i.e. the gaṇam.
‡ Aṭita saka [illegible] kâle [illegible].
§ Svâtiyum.
‖ [illegible] (pṛithvî) [illegible].
¶ T a l a v a n a—T a l a k â ḍ u Sanskritised. Kâḍu (Kan.) —man. Talkâḍ is on the Kâvêri, about 30 miles S. E. of Seringapatam.
** Jinâla.
†† Or Avambali; Uyamballi is a village a few miles south of Badaṇeguppe. Ambali is to the west of the same.
‡‡ i. e. Badaṇeguppe.
§§ Pterospermum phoeniceum.
‖‖ Euphorbia tirucalli.
¶¶ Bahu sâlila.
* Strychnos potatorum.
† Jambu.
‡ Small nelvage.
§ Dâsanûru, a village to the south of Badaṇeguppe.
‖ Gangâ râja kula sarvakâryâdhikâri.
¶ N i r g g u ṇ ḍ a,—perhaps n i r g a ṇ ḍ a, the village servant who distributes water to the irrigated fields.
** Dârigoppina.
†† Nâḍa sakshi.
‡‡ Tagadûru, a village N. W. of Badaṇeguppe.
§§ Â l g o ḍ u, a village near Badaṇeguppe.
‖‖ Ummaṭûru, a village N. of Badaṇeguppe.

chronicle in the Mackenzie collection. But the fifth in the above list is represented in the chronicle as Vishṇu Gopa's adopted son, and a very short tenure is assigned to him, for he had to give place to Krishṇa Varmma, a son afterwards born to Vishṇu Gopa. This Krishṇa Varmma and the next king Dindikâra, son of Kulati Râya of the family of Vishṇu Gopa, are not given in the grant. The sixth king Kongaṇi is placed after Dindikâra in the Tamil chronicle, and is mentioned as the son of Kṛishṇa Varmma's younger sister. As his relationship with any other king of the dynasty is not given, it is to be understood that the Krishṇa Varmma here meant is the one who is represented in the list as the son of Vishṇu Gopa. But in the grant before us he is mentioned as the son of Mâdhava, represented in the chronicle as the adopted son of Vishṇu Gopa, and the Krishṇa Varmma whose nephew he was, is spoken of distinctly as "the sun in the sky of the prosperous race of the Kadambas." In this place therefore the grant gives us information, while the chronicle as appears from the abstract is silent.

The date of the grant is 388. What era is meant we do not know. The dates in the chronicle are in the Saka era, from which it appears likely that this is also to be referred to that era. If so the date is 466 A.D. Krishṇa Varmma of the Kadamba race is very likely the second in Mr. Elliot's list; since there is no other of that name in the list. His date also is thus fixed by this grant to be 466 A.D. or thereabouts. Mr. Elliot assigns to the predecessor of this king the date 500 or 520 Śaka, *i.e.* 578 or 598 A.D., but his sources of information regarding this dynasty were so scanty that very little faith can be placed in the date.

Prof. Dowson's abstract assigns to Kongaṇi II. the last king in the above list, 288 Śaka, that is, he is placed a hundred years before he actually flourished according to the grant. But whether this is a mistake of the chronicle itself I cannot say. The accession of the fourth king after Kongaṇi II. is represented to have taken place in 461 Śaka. The four kings then beginning with Kongaṇi II. reigned according to the chronicle for 173 years, *i.e.* each reign lasted for 43 years, which is very improbable, since each of them was his predecessor's son. But if 388, the date given in the grant be taken, the duration would be at least 73 years, which would give 18 years to each king. The first date in Prof. Dowson's abstract must therefore be considered to be an error, while the second may be depended on. The Professor considers all the dates to be too early and proposes new ones. But Prof. Lassen inclines to defend the chronology of the chronicle,* which is supported by this grant.

* Lassen (*Alterthumskunde*, II. p. 1017-1021) says, "With reference to the chronology it must be remarked that, besides quoting the years in which grants of land were made by the princes whose acts are narrated, there is also mention of the years according to the cycle of sixty years in use in the Dekhan, which may be regarded as evidence that the unknown writer of the work in question found a well arranged chronology for the reigns of the kings whose acts he has described. According to the dates of his land-grants Malladeva, the twenty-eighth king of Chera, reigned in the years [illegible] and [illegible]. The seventh, Vikramadeva I., in the year 178. These dates give a total sum of more than seven hundred and twenty years for twenty-two princes,—for these dates cannot be regarded as the first and last years of the reigns of the two kings. Hence each sovereign would have ruled on an average about thirty-three years, a period which certainly seems inadmissible, because the utmost average length of the reigns of Indian kings amounts only to twenty-five years (Thomas, *Jour. R. A. Soc.*, Vol. XII, p. [illegible]). From this difficulty we have two ways of escape. The first is by supposing that the reigns of the Chera kings have been lengthened in order to give them a higher antiquity, and starting from the fixed dates of the subjugation of the Chera sovereigns about 900, to shorten the period so that Vikrama I. should reign (as Dowson supposes) only in the 4th century. Against this hypothesis it may be observed that in such a case the supposition would have to be made, that the author of the history of these kings had wilfully falsified the numbers of the inscriptions, or had read them wrongly, which, considering the acknowledged accuracy of his work does not appear to me admissible. It should also be remarked further that the contemporary of Vikrama I. of Chera, was the Pâṇḍya king Vamśaśekhara, who probably reigned in the second century [see Wilson, *Jour. R. As. Soc.*, Vol. III., p. [illegible]]. I considered it proper therefore to follow a different course and to support the traditional chronology as being upon the whole correct. My reasons for this are as follows:—Of the Ballâla kings it has already been noticed [Dowson, in *Jour. R. As. Soc.*, Vol. VIII., p. 34], that they reigned on an average nearly [illegible] years, so that a somewhat longer duration appears admissible in this case. Secondly, it must be remarked that it is true that of the Chera princes only two (the 13th and 14th) had short reigns, and two others (the 11th and 27th) abdicated the throne, but one (the 5th) reigned fifty-one years and one (the 19th) was the great grandson of his predecessor, so that to him a tolerably long rule may be allowed. Only against the commencement of the dynasty and against the first date can a valid objection be raised. The 4th king, Govinda, is said to have made a grant of land in the [illegible] year of the Śaka or in [illegible] A.D., it may, however, be legitimately doubted whether this chronology had come into use in the southern districts of India so soon after its establishment. To the insecurity of the chronology of the earliest period of the kings of Chera also, the circumstance that of the 6th it was only known that he was of the same descent as his four predecessors but that his father was not known—bears testimony. We can scarcely go far wrong, however, if we place the rise of the Chera dynasty back in the commencement of our era, because at that time the two adjoining kingdoms of the Pâṇḍyas and Cholas already existed."

Lassen's notices of the Chera kings, (both in II. pp. 1017-1020, and IV. pp. 243-246) are founded almost exclusively on Dowson's article above referred to.—Ed.

THE LADY AND THE DOVE:

A BENGALI SONG, COMPOSED BY A HINDU FEMALE.

TRANSLATED INTO ENGLISH VERSE,

BY REV. J. MURRAY MITCHELL, LL.D., CALCUTTA.

FEMALE education has now made such progress in Bengal, that the writings of women both in prose and verse are beginning to appear not unfrequently in print. A very interesting collection of female compositions was given to the public a few months ago by the adjudicators of the Hare Prize Fund,—the fund having for its special object the production of works in Bengali fitted for the instruction of women. The adjudicators seem to have made a very good selection of papers written not only for, but by, women. The volume extends to 267 pages, and it is interesting throughout.

I have selected for translation the piece which, on the whole, appears to me the most spirited in the book. If I do not over-estimate its merits, it is possessed of much life and colour. It is said to have been composed by a lady of Dhâkâ (Dacca).

I am far from thinking the rendering of verse into verse an easy task—I almost assent to the dictum of Voltaire, *Les poètes ne se traduisent pas.* If, then, any of my readers maintain that my lines but poorly represent the vivacity of the original, I certainly shall not dissent from the judgment. In one thing I hope I have succeeded—I mean, in reproducing the tone of the Bengali. The poem is sad throughout; and the sadness deepens as the strain proceeds. I have done my best to make the version a faithful echo of the plaintive note of the unhappy Hindu woman.

The measure in the original is Trochaic; the first two lines of each stanza are octo-syllabic, the last two decasyllabic. I have also used Trochaic metre; each line containing seven syllables.

The original has double (generally called female) rhymes always; but I do not possess a sufficient mastery over our somewhat intractable language to imitate the poetess in this respect.

I give the original in Roman character, with the hope of attracting a much larger number of readers than would attempt Bengali letters. The relation between Bengali and most of the dialects of Northern India is such that no person who has a good knowledge of one of these will find serious difficulty with the lady's composition.

Hardly anything as yet has been done towards the use of Romanized Bengali; and several questions in orthography thus remain undetermined. Initial *y* in Bengali sounds like *j* in Sanskrit; and I have written it *j*, though with hesitation. *Ksh* sounds *kh* in Bengali; but I have not had courage to throw out the *s*. For the most part *v* sounds like *b*; and I have so given it, as 'subarṇa' for suvarṇa. But when the word occurs in the contracted form 'svarṇa,' I have not dared to write 'sbarṇa,' the Bengali pronunciation—though corrupt enough—having then no sound of *b* in it.

PÁLITA KAPOTINI'S PRATI.

Bala ogo kapotini
Kena eta bishádini
Haráyechi kabáre tomáya
Prakáśiyá bala ná ámáya.

Eta dukhi kena dukhe
Áchha sadá adhomukhe
Netranire kara sambaraṇa
Sudháo ámáya bibaraṇa.

Subarṇa ábása pade
Basá ácchha ati bahumade
Mithaṇna pinjare abasthána
Ithe ki bhábe ná go prána?

Tomára santosha tare
Apurba bicharaṇa
Nadyá prahárane bichare
Tabe tumi kena go chhaila hala?

Bala kari kichhu karaṇa
Kari ichchhá dhara manosthira
Tátal bhi bata sukhodaya
Bala more haiye sadaya.

Suna go kapotápriye
Balite bidare hiye
Ámi go pinjarabásini,
Kibá sukhe báñcheo ekadehinî.

Áchha tumi je sukhete
Svarṇamaya pinjarete
Ámádera nahi eta sukha.
Tumi kena bhao go bimukha?

Ná deya gañjaná keha
Dásitva bhidra ná laha
Annajale nábhika abhába
Tabe kena bhábo nána bhába

Chhile jabe svechchhádhiní
Bhrami bane ekákiní
Kata sukha labhichhile táya !
Ki duḥkha bá áchha go kotháya !

Beŗáite náná bane
Śákhá kari árohaṇa
Kata kashte jápichha jáminí !
Eta sukhe áchha bishádini ?

Bujhhiláma etakshaṇe
Taba bhába daraśane
Tomará-i bujhhiyáchha sára
Náhi taba adhínatá bhára.

Śuna ogo bihaginí
Morá ati abhágini
Antaḥpura pińjaranibásí
Áchhi sadá adhínera dásí.

Chiradina ekamate
Hitáhita jñánahate
Jnána dharama diye bisarjjana
Eka bháve kariláhi jápana.

Tumi nao chiradásí
Kichhu dina tare ási
Heritechha duḥkhera bayána.
Habe punaḥ duḥkha abasána.

Hŕdayera sabera duḥkha
Balite bidare buka
Ena cheye pákhi jadi hai
Tabu bujhhi manasukhe rai.

Dhanya ogo kapotiní
Mánabiní hatamání
Haye áchhe dekhe taba sukha
Tái ḍháke ghomaṭáte mukha.

Ki balibo bidhátáre ?
Balite práṇa bidare.
Morá bujhhi taba banyá nai
Tái sadá eta duḥkha pái.

Ná balye dharmmasádhiní
Áchhi sadá parádhíní
Sadá thákí kríta dásí práya.
Ei kibe taba abhipráya ?

Pái kata marama byathá
Tathápi ná bali kathá.
Sadá mukha ḍháki ghomaṭáya.
Ei kibe taba abhipráya ?

Haye deśáchára dásí
Ajnána salile bhási
Káṭiláma e durlabha káya.
Ei kibe taba abhipráya ?

Translation.

TO A TAME DOVE.

1 Pretty dove, oh tell me now,
Why so sorrowful art thou ?
As I stand and look at thee,
All thy case explain to me.

2 Sure, thou hast some secret woe,
When I see thee drooping so ;
Speak, my bird,—and dry thy tears—
All thy troubles, all thy fears.

3 On thy foot a chain of gold,
Then thy perch on high dost hold,—
And in golden cage dost dwell ;
Should not that content thee well ?

4 For thy comfort, all around,
See what pretty cups abound,
Which all dainty morsels fill !
Yet thy heart is heavy still.

5 Say, when thou abroad didst fare,
Pecking, picking, here and there,
Was thy life a life of bliss ?
Do, kind birdie, answer this !

6 Nay, my cherished darling, nay,
Hear what else I only say,—
I too am caged like thee—
(Blessed, doubtless, are the free.)

7 But the solace that is thine
In that golden cage so fine,
Never comes to such as I ;
Why then pine my darling, why ?

8 Words ungentle vex not thee,
Nor great load of slavery ;
Every want at once supplied,—
Why art thou not satisfied ?

9 And when thou at liberty
Flitting wert from tree to tree,
Was thy happiness so great ?
And so wretched now thy state ?

10 Wandering ever, ill at ease,
Perching but on forest trees,
Lonely was thy life and sad :—
Surely, now thou might'st be glad !

11 But I can discover now—
As I watch thy feelings—thou
Scout the truth, that this can be
Hardly called captivity.

12 Listen then to what I say,—
Think how miserable they,
Captives in Zenana drear,
Lowest thralls, and crushed by fear.

13 Still the same, we drag along,
Ignorant of right and wrong,
Knowledge and religion, none!
Life a dreary monotone!

14 Thou art not a slave always;
Thou but comest a few days,
Just to look on misery;
Then away thy sorrows flee.

15 But the heart will die, before
Half our trials it counts o'er;
Oh were I a dove like thee,
Then, methinks, I'd blessed be!

16 Bird! thy happier lot to see
Makes a woman envy thee;
Filled with shame she hides her face,
So to cover her disgrace.

17 Shall I speak to God on high?
But I tremble as I try!
We are not Thy daughters, sure,
Who must woes like these endure!

18 All untrained in truth, the soul—
Swayed alone by harsh control—
On, like purchased slaves, we go;
Ah! dost Thou then mean it so?

19 Still, although the heart is broken,
Must the pang remain unspoken;
Veil the face, and hide the woe!
Ah! dost Thou then mean it so?

20 Wretched custom's helpless slaves—
Whelmed in superstition's waves—
Thus our precious life doth go;
Ah! dost Thou then mean it so?

FAC-SIMILE OF A PERSIAN MAP OF THE WORLD, WITH AN ENGLISH TRANSLATION.

By EDWARD REHATSEK, M.C.E.

In ancient times our globe was divided into various portions, and so early as the Vendidad, (Fargard XIX. 46) "The earth consisting of seven Keshwars" is mentioned. These divisions the Greeks named *klimata* (from 'klima' inclination) the number of which was also considered by them to amount to seven. Muhammadan writers do not agree on the breadth of the climates. Zakriyah Qazviny in his *Ajáyb-almakhlúqát* or "Wonders of creation" assumes every climate to be 23½ Farsakhs broad; making 1 farsakh = 12,000 cubits, 1 cubit = 24 fingers, 1 finger = 7 barley-grains, whilst other writers agree with occidental geographers in assuming exactly half an hour's difference of time between each climate. The number of climates has gradually been so much increased, that we have at present 24 hourly and six monthly climates on each side of the equator. In the absence of more accurate means to ascertain the latitude of a place it was sufficient to know the longest day, to tell immediately in what climate it belonged. Thus for instance, supposing the longest day of a town to be 15 hours, and subtracting 12 from this number, we have three hours, and as the difference between each climate is 30 minutes, the town will be situated in the 6th climate.

The ancient geographers who believed only that portion of the earth to be inhabited which was known to themselves, were quite contented with seven climates; but Ptolemy during the second century of our era added seven more, and thus made the whole world to extend from the equator 63 degrees northwards and 20 southwards, according to our present reckoning. The subjoined table shows the first 17 climates, with the breadth of each and also the degrees of geographical northern latitude answering to each:—

Climates.	Longest day.		Latitude.		Breadth.	
	h.	m.				
1	[illegible]	[illegible]	[illegible]	[illegible]	[illegible]	[illegible]
2	[illegible]		[illegible]	[illegible]	[illegible]	[illegible]
3	[illegible]	[illegible]	[illegible]	[illegible]	[illegible]	[illegible]
4	[illegible]		[illegible]	[illegible]	[illegible]	[illegible]
5	[illegible]	[illegible]	[illegible]	[illegible]	[illegible]	[illegible]
6	[illegible]		[illegible]	[illegible]	[illegible]	[illegible]
7	[illegible]	[illegible]	[illegible]	[illegible]	[illegible]	[illegible]
8	[illegible]		[illegible]	[illegible]	[illegible]	[illegible]
9	[illegible]	[illegible]	[illegible]	[illegible]	[illegible]	[illegible]
10	[illegible]		[illegible]	[illegible]	[illegible]	[illegible]
11	[illegible]	[illegible]	[illegible]	[illegible]	[illegible]	[illegible]
12	[illegible]		[illegible]	[illegible]	[illegible]	[illegible]
13	[illegible]	[illegible]	[illegible]	[illegible]	[illegible]	[illegible]
14	[illegible]		[illegible]	[illegible]	[illegible]	[illegible]
15	[illegible]	[illegible]	[illegible]	[illegible]	[illegible]	[illegible]
16	[illegible]		[illegible]	[illegible]	[illegible]	[illegible]
17	[illegible]	[illegible]	[illegible]	[illegible]	[illegible]	[illegible]

This Persian Map of the world (of which I have made a fac-simile, keeping everything exactly as it was drawn in the original, and translating only the writing or transcribing it in Roman characters) was in a dilapidated state and is of no great value except as a curiosity, since documents of this kind must make way to correct geographical notions, and must very soon disappear altogether; the only way of rescuing them from total oblivion is to insert them in some journal. The owner of it was a Muhammadan from Junnar in the Bombay presidency, but could give no clue as to who drew the map and when. Maps of this kind remind us of our own ancient European geographical delineations which were as crude as the present one, and contained analogous superstitious descriptions of unknown and remote countries.

It may be presumed that the draftsman was an Indian Musalman, because he has inserted in no other country so many names of towns and rivers as in India, but he has strangely enough omitted Calcutta and Madras; neither is any European country mentioned by name except Portugal. *Feringi* and *Rûs* are only general denominations; the former designating all Europeans, and the latter all the Slavonic nations; and it is only within the last few decades since the Russian conquests in Asia that the name has been applied to them specially. Rûm formerly designated the Byzantines who are called by this name in all the Arabic books treating on the conquest of Syria, A. H. 13; now however it means Turkey.

In this map the climates were intended to be equal according to Qazviny's scheme, but the execution is not very accurate; especially in the 4th climate, which is so convergent and narrowing towards the West as to catch the eye. Qazviny takes 25 Farsakhs to a degree and makes each climate 235 Farsakhs, *i.e.*, 9·4 degrees broad, or according to another reading 285, *i.e.*, 11·4°. The climates of this map begin at the equator, in which case according to the first reading it would extend to 65·8° N. Lat. and according to the 2d to 79·8°.

The representation of Africa—for that is evidently meant by Habsh or Abyssinia—is rather small, and its termination does not fall even as far south as the equator; it is in the first climate, like the southern extremities of Arabia and of India. All the other countries are just as much out of proportion as these.

The mountains are coloured brown, and a belt of them equal in breadth to one climate, runs across the whole earth occupying a portion of the 4th and the 5th climate, due East and West. "And He hath thrown on the earth mountains firmly rooted, lest it should move with you." (Qurân xvi, 15.)

The traditions about Alexander and his doings are endless and contradictory, but all agree with the historical fact of his having founded Alexandria. In this map also the tower of Alexander, which may have been a lighthouse, (and is in other documents stated to have reflected in mirrors, events which took place at distant places, such as Constantinople) is laid down, but the extraordinary circumstance is added, that it is built of Qahqah stone, and that everyone who looks at it dies laughing, laughing. This addition induces me to conclude that the spelling *Qaqah* is a blunder, and that the projector of the map wrote *Qahqahah* which, though occurring in dictionaries, must be considered to be only an onomatopoeia or imitation of a natural sound, like *cachinnation*; hence the tower was built of the *Ha-ha-ha stone*.

The word *Qalmaq* does not occur in dictionaries, its sound is like that of *Kalmuck*, but it is not possible to translate it otherwise than by "slave" or some analogous word according to the context.

Gog and Magog are two savage nations not defined by tradition except in vague terms, they are said to be descendants of Japhet, the son of Noah; also that the Gog are a Turkish and the Magog a Gilány tribe; some say they were anthropophagi, and this appears also from the statement on the map. They are twice mentioned in the Qurân, *i.e.* Surah xviii and xxi. It may also be observed that the draftsman has omitted to insert the regions of the *Dawal-pâpâ*, the timber-legged men, and of the *Kelym-push* the carpet-eared tribes, and other monstrous beings which occur in old Arabic and Persian books, and may easily be recognized as having been taken from Ktesias, or his imitators and embellishers.

In the Qurân, Surah xviii., v. 91-96, the following words occur about Dhulqarnyn: "And he prosecuted his journey [from south to north] until he came between the two mountains, beneath which he found a certain people, who could scarce understand what was said. And they said, O Dhulqarnyn, verily Gog and Magog waste the land; shall we therefore pay thee tribute on condition that thou build a rampart between us and them? He answered, The [power] wherewith my Lord has strengthened me is better [than your tribute]; but assist me strenuously and I will set a strong wall between you and them. Bring me iron in large pieces, until I fill up the [space] between the two sides [of these mountains]. He said [to the workmen] blow [with your bellows] until it make [the iron red hot as] fire. He said [further] bring me molten brass that I may pour upon it. Wherefore [when this wall was finished, Gog and Magog] could not scale it, neither could they dig through it." (*Sale*, p. 247).

This Dhulqarnyn, *i.e.*, two-horned is by the commentators said to be Alexander the Great; but at present scarcely any doubt can remain that the rampart* placed here and called the rampart of Gog and Magog is the great wall of China, it was built about the end of the first century of the Christian era, and is still called *wan-li-chang-ching*, ten-thousand-li-long-wall.

The state of ignition in which the rampart appears on the map is in conformity with the verses of the Qorân just quoted.

* Caussin de Perceval (vol. I., p. 66) tries to indentify it with [illegible] which extended from the west shore of the Caspian Sea to the Pontus Euxinus, built, it is said, by Alexander the Great, and repaired by Yazdegird II. [illegible] (*[illegible]*, II. 39) makes Gog the same as the [illegible] *Ghef* or *Ghogh*, and the syllable *ma* in Magog, the Sanskrit *Maha*, great. Conf. Rodwell's *Koran*, pp. 191, 228.—Ed.

ON SOME KOCH WORDS IN Mr. DAMANT'S ARTICLE ON THE PALIS OF DINAJPUR.

By JOHN BEAMES, B.C.S., M.R.A.S., &c.

I beg to offer the following solution of the curious phrase *hudu dyao* applied as stated in Mr. Damant's interesting paper on the Koch tribes, to a ceremony observed by them to procure rain.

The Koches (if I may be pardoned the expression) are, as the writer justly observes, a non-Aryan tribe and belong to that section of the southern or sub-Himalayan Tibetans of which so many scattered fragments are to be found on our northern frontier. Having been for four years Collector of Purneah,* I took much interest in this tribe who, together with the Mechis and Dhimâls occupy many villages in the Kaliaganj Thânâ of that district. The best account of them is to be found in Brian Hodgson's *Aborigines of India*, published by the Bengal Asiatic Society in 1847, and still procurable from the Society. Hodgson laments that he was unable to pick up many words of *bond fide* Koch, as that people have for some time past abandoned their original speech for Bengali, and accordingly in the long list extending over 102 pages, which he gives of their vocabulary, hardly a word is to be found which is not pure Bengali. It is well known however that some expressions of their ancient Tibetan dialect do still survive among them, and Mr Damant has I think been fortunate enough to pick up one of them.

I was led to study Tibetan during a residence at Darjiling in 1863, when I made a tour into the heart of independent Sikkim, and again in 1867, when as Collector of Champaran, I drew up a grammar of the Magar language, another of these semi-Tibetan dialects.† The principal peculiarity in the phonetics of Tibetan is that through the isolation into which the different tribes of its ancient race have fallen, owing to the rugged and difficult nature of the country which they inhabit, a great change has taken place in the pronunciation. It was reduced to writing in a character which is a correct reproduction of the Sanskrit character of the period, by Buddhist emigrants from India in the 7th century. They expressed in writing all the sounds then in use, but as many of these sounds have dropped out of pronunciation since then, while the traditional method of spelling has remained unchanged, it follows that the written language contains many letters which are not used in speaking. There exist however rules by which it may be easily ascertained which letters are mute and which are to be pronounced.

The first thing which led me to think of the possible Tibetan origin of these words *hudu dyao* was the *o*. In Tibetan *mo* is the sign of the feminine, and is added to verbs, participles and all other parts of speech in that monosyllabic language to denote that the thing or action is done by or refers to a female being or thing.

I am disposed, if not absolutely certain, to refer these words to the following Tibetan origin. The word *rgyug* pronounced *dyu* means the act of running. When a final consonant in eastern Tibetan is rejected, the preceding word is often lengthened, we thus get *dyo* or *dyao*. *shod*,‡ pronounced in eastern Tibet *hod* or *hod*, means first, 'open,'§ then 'shameless,' 'licentious,' 'loose,' and *mo* is the feminine affix. The whole phrase then would roughly mean 'the running of the licentious or shameless women,' an interpretation which corresponds fairly enough to the state of the case. Of course in a rude and only semi-Tibetan dialect like Koch, and after the lapse of ages, we cannot expect to find all the signs of case and tense faithfully preserved, but I think the similarity is still sufficiently striking to carry conviction to most minds. It will be interesting if Mr. Damant can recover for us some more words of this hitherto lost dialect.

* Purniyâ, from Sanskrit purâna old; it was the oldest Aryan settlement in these parts.

† It has been printed in the *Journal of the Royal Asiatic Society*, Vol. IV., N. S., for 1870 p. 178.

‡ This *sh* is not to be pronounced like the *sh* in 'shall,' but as two distinct sounds *s-hod*.

§ This agrees with what Mr. Damant was told by the Palis, and it is possible that with them the original meaning 'open' may have been used for 'naked,' so that the word might be rendered 'naked women.'

ARCHÆOLOGY IN THE KRISHNA DISTRICT.

Extracts from a Report by the late J. A. C. Boswell, M.C.S.

('*Proceedings of the Madras Government*,' 14th *Dec.* 1871.)

We generally find that the conception of a divine being is associated, among most races, with the power of destruction, before men's minds attain the idea of beneficence or wisdom. Hindus readily admit that the worship of Siva is of much greater antiquity than the worship of Vishnu. And now we see how the serpent is brought into the worship of Siva. One of his great titles is Nâgabhûshana, the snake-adorned one. The serpent, worshipped originally as a fetish, becomes naturally, and appropriately, like the Greek idea of the snaky locks of the Gorgon, a symbol in the representation of Siva, the destroyer. With this power of adaptation, we can readily imagine how the religion of the Scythians was calculated to find acceptance with the aborigines in this country, the Dasyus, or whatever name they went by; and we see how the worship of the snake instead of ceasing became naturally an accessory and development of a more advanced system.

In connection with this I may here mention the recent discovery of a very interesting stone at Inkol in the Bapatla Taluk. There is a temple here dedicated to Siva under the designation of 'Bhîmes'-vârasvâmi. Close to the temple there are two very ancient sculptured stones. Upon one there is a large representation of the Nâga, and on the other side of the same stone there is a male figure in what I venture to call the ancient Scythic costume, the cap and the tunic. On the second stone there is another figure sculptured in the same costume in the same style of art. Now, this serpent is to this day an object of worship. It is painted with vermilion and turmeric, and receives offerings of fruits and flowers; but in regard to the Scythian figures even Hindu imagination in for once failed. It is not often that the natives of this country are at a loss to give the name of some one of their gods to any piece of sculpture that may turn up; but with regard to these figures the people confess utter ignorance. There they stand among their objects of veneration, but they do not worship them; they do not know what they are. If we can really identify these figures with the Scythic period, the age of the cromlechs and tumuli, then we shall have gained an important step.* The style in which these works are executed, though the stone used is very coarse, is considerably in advance of the mode of sculpture employed in many of the serpent stones.

On the other hand, I have been informed by Mr. M. J. Walhouse, Civil and Session Judge of Mangalor, that such, or somewhat similar stones, abound in Korg and all through Maisur, and are called *Kulle kallu*, slaughter-stones, usually set up to commemorate the deaths in battle or by wild beasts of some chief; sometimes to commemorate boundaries or grants. There is one, he states, by the roadside within a mile of Mangalor, bearing a male and a female figure, side by side, standing with crossed legs, both with high caps and tunics which, he takes it, are nothing but the old Hindu or Palygar costume coming down to recent times and exhibited on numberless temples of known date. Offerings are made to some of these sculptured figures whose deeds are still remembered. We have here a very interesting subject of ethnological research. We know what the dress and appearance is of modern Tartars. In the Amravati sculptures, nearly 2,000 years old, we have these Scythic Tartars clearly portrayed in their characteristic costume, almost invariably in connection with horses, and then we have occasional allusion to the Sakas, *Shakas*, in ancient classical records that have come down to us. A careful and systematic examination and comparison of the contents of the cairns and barrows all over the country will probably afford much useful material from which to draw deductions as to the stage of civilization reached by that early race, and the influence they exerted upon succeeding generations. But at present private individuals open these ancient tombs and ransack the contents in a most reckless manner. Curiosity satisfied, the few articles found may be kept, or, more probably, are thrown aside as useless, and no record is preserved of the result. If this state of things goes on, the remaining Scythic remains in the country will, in a few years, be entirely destroyed. I would strongly urge that Government issue orders for the protection of all such ancient remains and that the research be made by qualified persons under official authority, and let all that is found be brought together to one Indian Museum to be carefully preserved, where those who take an interest in such matters may be able to examine them.

To return to the Krishna. In another Sivalayam, in the same village of Inkolu, there are built into the wall parts of a frieze, apparently taken from an older temple, representing animals, &c., with figures. There are portions of similar friezes to be seen in a choultry at Vinukonda and in a temple at Pârchur in the Bapatla Taluk. This is what we find, indeed, in many of the old temples in the district. Stones have been used in their construction which are evidently the relics of more ancient buildings.

I have briefly adverted to what I conceive to have been the order of transition from a fetish to the *Linga* as a symbol, up to the representation or ideal embodiment of the thing symbolized in Siva, the destroyer. The next stage seems to have been the adorations paid to the *Sakti* as the symbol of

* Mr. Boswell unfortunately adopted and advocated a very unsound hypothesis respecting these remains, and it vitiates much of his reasoning. Mr. Walhouse's views are well deserving of development.—Ed.

female energy and creative or productive power, as a part and distinct from, and yet intimately connected with, Almighty power. I have found several images of this kind which appear to be of considerable antiquity, and the form represented is the same in each, a female figure with four arms holding in each hand a sword, a mallet, a trident, and a chakra. These figures have been turned out of the temples. They are not regarded as the consorts of Vishnu and Siva, and the people call them village goddesses, and give them the names of Ankamma in one village, and Polerammа in another, and so on. I have met with two in Bapatla (one in the chief street, the other near the kacheri), another at Dachépalli near the kacheri, and the fourth at Tenali in the Weavers' street, beside a collection of snake stones and sculptured figures which recall their Scythic costume. There are four stones near the kacheri at Bapatla, one the female figure, a second represents a full length female figure with a glory round its head; on the third there are a few Telugu letters sculptured of forms now obsolete; on the top of the fourth stone there is represented a circle depicted by a serpent having its tail in its mouth, and within the circle are portrayed two pairs of footprints. The circle is only about a foot in diameter; on the side of the same stone are sculptured four standing figures in striking attitudes. The people say these are Palnati Viralu, or Palnad heroes. The Viralu, I may remark in passing, have a temple dedicated to them at Karempudi in the Palnad. The hundred heroes are here represented each by "smooth stones of the stream" well waterworn, and these are ranged round the temple. There are also some [illegible] [illegible] in the temple. There is an annual festival held in November, which is very numerously attended. It is observed exclusively by the lower castes of the people. Whether there is any connection really between these Viralu and the sculptures at Bapatla, I cannot say; but in the enclosure of a Sivalayam, dedicated to the title of Agastesvarasvami, on the bank of the [illegible] tank at [illegible], there is a stone which has a striking resemblance to the one at Bapatla. On the top are portrayed two pairs of footprints, and on the side there are standing figures. The stone has been broken. Near it there are several snake stones and other stones with figures which appear to belong to a pre-Brahmanic age.

Connected with the worship of the snakes, as the female personifications of creative power, fecundity, and fertility, we have the worship of Bhu Devi, the earth goddess, so general throughout Central and Southern India, celebrated by the Khonds with human sacrifices, and by other classes with slaughter of cattle. We find the worship prevalent among many wild tribes and among the Pariahs. It is evidently a very ancient form of religion.

Among the lowest orders, where the densest ignorance prevails, the idea of deity is still intimately associated with fear and dread, and so they have taken the personifications of female energy, the *Saktas*, and linked them as consorts of the deities, and invested them with all the attributes most calculated to terrify and alarm. Such are Kali, Durga, and Bhavani in the north. Such are the village goddesses throughout Southern India. In nearly every village we find some special female divinity of the kind; a Polerammа, or Ankamma, or Gangamma. And if Brahmans and Vaisyas frequent Vaishnava and Saiva shrines, the great bulk of the lowest classes confine their religious services to the propitiation of evil in the offerings made at the temple of some local female divinity.

It may not be out of place to mention here an experience of my own. It will show how superstitions gather, and also how the popular mind delights to associate the human element with its rude conceptions of a Supreme Power. In the village of Nandigama in the Krishna District, one early morning I was visiting the temples as I often do, and looking for antiquities, when I came upon a new shed in a line with two others. On inquiry I was informed that this was a temple dedicated to a new village goddess named, I think, Polerammа. I was further informed that she was, in fact, a raiyat's wife who lately lived in the village, and was murdered by her husband. He was tried for the offence, but was acquitted. The popular rustic mind at once conceived the idea of adopting the unhappy woman as the personification of unsatisfied vengeance. An image was made to represent her, and in her hands was placed a sword, and she was installed henceforth as the village goddess. Strange to say, an image of her husband, who is living to the present day in the village, was added and placed by her side.

Perhaps the worship paid to the spirits of murdered persons, or those who have left behind them an evil memory, is analogous to the belief in Europe of ghosts haunting particular spots. It appears a common notion among all nations in all ages. Mr. Walhouse, Judge of Mangalore, South Kanara, informs me that Bhuta worship is the really prevalent cult in that district, and half the Bhutas are the spirits of murdered or notoriously evil-lived persons. It assumes the character of propitiatory worship. New village deities are thus continually springing up. Mr. Walhouse mentions a curious instance which came under his own observation in Trichinopoli. A much dreaded dacoit was killed, and after his death became a fashionable Bhuta, and half the children born were named after him. So, too, Dr. Caldwell, in his *Comparative Grammar of the Dravidian Languages*, relates a very curious illustration of the same sentiment. In some lonely wild spot of the Tinnevelli District there is the grave of a European Officer. In life, he appears to have made himself obnoxious to the natives, and to have been greatly dreaded. To this date it is a custom to offer spirits and cigars upon his grave.

But to return to the idea of serpent worship, and its connection with the several phases of religion in India:—To this day the serpent may be still found all over the country worshipped purely and simply as a fetish among the lowest classes, as well as under the more refined personification of Nâgeśvarasvâmi. For instance, there is a well at [illegible]-palli, it contains the best water in the place, but a cobra, it was discovered, frequented the spot; a temple was built over the well, and it was totally abandoned to the serpent divinity. In Saivism, I have suggested that the serpent found a place as a fitting symbol and adornment of the power of evil. But when the Aryans brought with them conceptions of the Supreme Being as invested with what we may call the powers of nature, the serpent assumed a new character. Conquered and subdued, it became the protective guardian of Vishnu. Over his head is represented the seven-headed snake. And so again, in the Aryan scheme of cosmogony there is a remarkable scene represented,—the Devatas and Rákshasas (the powers of good and evil) churning the ocean of milk with the great serpent Vasuki employed as a churning-string. This is a scene continually represented in the most ancient sculptures of the district. For instance, it is one of the scenes depicted on one of the stones dug up at [illegible], and used to form what is a comparatively modern monument. It is found on Buddhist remains at Amravati, and it is still sculptured on [illegible] cars of quite recent construction. The mode of treatment is always the same, the Devatas and Rakshasas are always pulling different ways, the contending powers of good and evil; and a serpent is a subject power,—a mere instrument to give effect to the purposes of the divine mind through the very opposing forces. He employs "rain and sunshine, heat and cold, fire and hail, snow and vapours, stormy wind fulfilling his word."* It is thus I apprehend that Buddhism borrowed the Aryan symbolization of the serpent as a protective power. The conquered enemy is made a captive slave, and employed to watch and guard; the serpent, as the emblem of evil to man, is subdued by Almighty power, and instead of receiving divine honours, serves simply to represent the fear and dread naturally associated in the human mind, with any idea of a divine being. It is possible also that the over-shadowing serpent above the representations of Vishnu and Buddha may be employed in another sense to convey the idea of wisdom,—this being a characteristic attribute of the serpent.

Now with regard to the Nâgas; we find them to have been in existence in various parts of India, immediately prior to the Buddhist era. The dahgop at Amravati was erected by a Nâga population. Everywhere we find the Nâgas represented as worshipping and doing homage to Buddhism, and Buddha is represented as supported by the Nâga's folds or shaded by his protecting hood, while the two systems seem to have coalesced so far that alternate reverence is paid to the relic casket, the wheel, the sacred fig-tree, and the five-headed snake.

With regard to Buddhist remains, I would mention that I have come across another colossal image of Buddha at Tenali. It is in the enclosure of a Sivalayam, dedicated to the name of Râmalingeśvarasvâmi. This image is placed in the open air under some trees entirely neglected. The figure is in the usual sitting position, naked, protuberant lips, wooly hair, and pendant ears. This makes the third similar image I have met with in this district, the others being at Bezwâda and Gudivâda. The latter image has the Nâga overshadowing the head.

I may mention here that a very interesting sculpture of a female figure has just been discovered at Bezwâda in digging a channel. It is the only instance I have met with in this district of a female figure with wooly hair, thick lips, and long pendant ears. It is loosely draped from the loins downwards, and was found at a considerable depth below the surface. In the Amravati sculptures there are many representations of the Nâga type, as well as other ethnological varieties. A careful study of these might throw some light on the communications between India and other countries in early times.

I have already addressed Government with reference to the desirability of issuing instructions for the protection of the interesting Buddhist remains in the Krishna district, as the Department Public Works have been making excavations at Bhattiprolu and Gudivâda I am informed, and using the old bricks for road materials and other purposes. In the case of Bhattiprolu I am told that Captain Vibart found a stone casket, inside of which was a crystal vial with some small pearls, &c. The natives say that another bottle was broken in digging, which contained the secret of alchemy, the substance capable of turning all other metals to gold. They also firmly believe these structures cover some hidden treasure, and from the fact of a five-headed Nâga being discovered, this has been taken to fix the actual amount at five crores. It is very desirable that whatever excavations are to be made, they should be conducted under competent supervision. These remarkable structures have been entirely covered up and buried with a mass of earth, which has preserved them through long centuries, during which their history and purpose have almost perished, and have certainly become forgotten in the neighbourhood where they were originally raised. With all the interest that attaches to the Buddhist era of Indian history, it becomes us to deal reverently with these relics that time has spared. They are the evidences of a past age of civilization. When we have carefully disinterred them and brought once more to light the symmetry and proportions of their architectural designs, we shall probably find that they are worthy of a better fate than to make district roads.

There is only one other point to which I wish to allude. In writing in my former report of the *Frengula Dibbalu* near the coast at China Ganjam,

* Conf. Ind. Antiq., pp. 347-48.—Ed.

I suggested that these might be the remains of an early Portuguese Settlement.* It has been suggested in an article in the *Madras Mail*, that they are more probably the remains of the early Venetian or Genoese traders, who penetrated to India by the land route long before the Portuguese visited the country. I have heard of the discovery of old Italian coins in the district, which might throw some light on this matter. I have not, however, been able to trace any. Sir Walter Elliot, who was a most successful collector of coins, may, perhaps, have been more fortunate, and may be in a position to afford some information that may assist in clearing this doubt.

THREE MAISUR COPPER GRANTS.

Memo. on Certain Copper Grants found during the Settlement of the Inams in the Malnâd or Hill-tracts of the Nagar Division.

During my investigation into the Inams located in the Malnâd talukas of the Nagar division, I had occasion to inspect the copper grants held by the Agrahârdârs of the villages of—1. Kuppagadde, Soraba Taluka; 2. Gauja, Anantapura Taluka; 3. Bhîmanna Katté Matha of the Kâvaledurga Taluka.

It will be observed in the translations of the grants for the Gauja and Kuppagadde Agrahâras, which have been rendered by my Personal Assistant, that these grants are said to have been made during the great "Sarpa Yâga," or sacrifice of serpents, though the allusion to the solar eclipse is only made in the grant for the Gauja Agrahâra. A copy of this grant was sent some years ago by Sir Mark Cubbon to Colonel Elliot, who was then Political Agent at Bundelkhand. Colonel Elliot asserted that the solar eclipse alluded to in the grant was that of 1521 A.D.,† and drew the conclusion that the Janamejaya alluded to must have been one of the Vijayanagar kings. Colebrooke denounced this grant as a forgery, and declared that the writing was modern, and that the errors in the composition betrayed gross ignorance.‡

The grant of the Bhîmanakatte Matha is dated in the 89th year of the era of Yudhishthira, who was the eldest of the five brothers, the sons of Pându by his wife Kunti or Pritha. This Matha is situated on the banks of the Tunga and takes its name from a Katte, or dam, partly natural and partly composed of huge blocks of stone, which Bhîma, another of the five sons of Pându, is alleged to have hurled across the bed of the river so as to form the dam. I have begun the translation of the legendary account of the origin of this Matha, but as pointed out by Mr. Narasimhaiyengar, the doctrine of Madhvâchârya was only promulgated between 5 and 600 years ago. Whatever may be the origin of the Matha, the dam bears undoubted traces of the wondrous magnitude of the works of those days.

Rob. Cole,

Supt. of Inam Settlements, Mysore.

5th *August*, 1872.

I. TRANSLATION OF THE COPPER GRANT PRODUCED BY THE AGRAHARDARS OF KUPPAGADE, SORABA TALUKA.

Śloka I.—Jayatyâvishkritam Vishnor,
Vârâham kshobhitârnavam;
Dakshinonnata damshtrâgra,
Vishrânta bhuvanam vapuh.

The body of Vishnu, incarnate in the form of a boar, on the edge of whose lofty right tusk the earth rested, and which agitated and troubled the ocean, exists in transcendent glory.

Emperor Janamejaya; the refuge of the whole universe; the master of the earth; the Mahârâja of Râjas; the arbiter of Râjas; the great Mahârâja; the master of Hastinâpura, the Queen of cities; the bestower of widowhood on the wives of the hostile princes of Aruba and Bangaluru; the sun of the lotus of the Pândava race; the skilful in warfare; whose sword-like bow overwhelmed the Kalinga emperor; the single-handed hero; the unconquered in battle; the slayer of 'Asvapatirâya' and 'Nârapati Gajapatirâya'; the smiter of the head of Narapatirâya; the terror of Kâmbhoja, Mriga, Chaturas, Konkana and the four quarters of the globe; the famous in Bharata Varsha,§ consisting of pure Kshatriyas, Brahmans, Vaisyas, sprung from the mouth of Brahma; possessed of many Sâstras, the celebrated professor of the three worlds (charms) of Karnâtaka Vyâla Nâga, &c., whose lotus-like feet are universally saluted; the lion of the elephants of inimical dynasties; the ever-bright; the son of others' wives‖; the bearer of the flag of the golden boar; the most refulgent in the circle of Râjas; who is daily adorned; the descendant of the blessed lunar race; and the son of the emperor Parikshit was reigning at Hastinâpura in the midst of happy and virtuous amusements. During an expedition of conquest, at the confluence of the Tungabhadra and Haradra, at the shrine of Harihara Deva, in the dark half of the month of Chaitra of the year 111, on Monday combined with¶ Bharani Nakshatra, Sankrânti and Vyatipâta Nimitta, on the occasion of Sarpa Yâga

---

* Conf. *Ind. Antiq.* pp. 101-2. † Vide note p. 356.—Ed.

‡ See Colebrooke, *Essays*, Vol. II, p. 260.—Ed.

§ Tracts of many possessions. ‖ Chaste.

¶ Astronomical symbols.

(serpent sacrifice) when the púrnáhuti or the rite of consummation was being performed, in the midst of 2000 Brahmans, the Emperor granted in due form, as an offering of blessing to Brahmans, of whom the principal were Mádhava Pattavardhana of Atréyagótra of Karnátaka race; Sankara ghaláura of Vasishtagótra of the same race; Yogís'vara Pattavardhana of S'rívatsagótra, and Vishnu Díkshita, of Vis'vámitragótra of the said race; the village of Pushpagaddé, situated in the midst of Kampanaya Nádu, Teppatin and Basavéh Sahasra, together with the nine subordinate villages of Hosamahalli, Nittakki, Nechó, Kurukódu, Amangadde, Kudalihara, Ilemalena kaluvalli, and Kaimetiyahalli, inclusive of the items of revenue comprehended by the terms Chakravarti unechi, Panchánga Pasaya, Chatra Sukhásana, Balidaganidige, Ankadonda khandana, and Ashtabhóga tejasámya.

The boundaries thereof are:—On the north-east, a nala at which the limits of Pushpagaddé, Haya and Kantapura villages converge. To the south of the above, a watercourse near which the boundaries of Pushpagaddé and Haya meet. South of the above, the bend of a stream at which the limits of Pushpagaddé, Haya and Vaddaré meet. To the south of the above, the boundaries of Pushpagaddé and Vaddaré terminate near a feeder. To the south-west, a hollow at which the boundaries of Kadalige, Pushpagaddé and Vaddaré converge. To the west of the above, Mathéya kola or pond, so called, near the boundaries of Kadalige and Pushpagaddé. To the west of the above, Háláya kola or pond, so called, where the boundaries of Pushpagaddé, Kadalige and Tavanidhi meet. To the west of the above, the boundaries of Tavanidhi and Pushpagaddé meet, at a place called Lavadukatta. To the south-west, the limits of Pushpagaddé, Tavanidhi and Tukkúru meet at a rising called Mulya Maradi. To the north of the above, a turn of a nala, at which the boundaries of Pushpagaddé and Tukkúru terminate. To the north of the above, Mágára or mark, so called, defining the boundaries of Pushpagaddé, Tukkúru and Kulaga. To the north of the above, Vayangadde marking the limits of Pushpagaddé and Kulaga. To the north-west, a water course, where the limits of Pushpagaddé, Kulaga and Basúru meet. To the east of the above, a water-course marking the boundaries of Pushpagaddé, and Basúru. To the east of the above, Pálagolla at which the boundaries of Pushpagaddé, Basúru and Tánaguppé terminate. To the east, a bend of a nala, marking the limits of Pushpagaddé and Tánaguppé. To the east, a stream, marking the boundaries of Pushpagaddé, and Tánaguppé, as also the boundary of Kántapura. The boundaries from the east to the north-east are complete.

II.—Sámányoyam dharmasetur nripánám
Kálé kálé pálaníyó bhavadbhih :
Sarvánetan bhávinah párthivéndrán,
Bhúyobhúyo yáchate Rámachandraha.

Rámachandra again and again entreats all future kings and rulers. "This (grant) which is a bridge of charity common to all rulers, should be protected from time to time by you."

III.—Svadattám paradattám vá.
Yóharéta vasundharám :
Shashtir varsa sahasráni.
Vishtáyám jáyaté krimihi.

Whosoever usurps (or takes away) land, which has been granted either by himself or others, will be born a worm in human offal, (and will suffer there) for sixty thousand years.

IV.—Bramhasvatvam visham ghóram.
Navisham vishamuchyate :
Vishamekákinam hanti.
Bramhasvam putra pautrakam.

Brahman's property is a virulent poison, and poison is not called poison, (because) poison kills a single person, but Brahman's property slays the whole race, inclusive of the sons and grandsons.

Note by the Translator.

Kuppagadé is an Agrahára about 8 miles from Sorabe, and situated in that taluka. It is called Pushpagaddé in the grant. The present occupants do not seem to be lineally descended from the original grantees, as their respective gotrás are different. The village, though styled Agrahára, was to all intents and purposes Sarkár, but the result of the settlement will restore to it the status of an alienated village. The boundaries described in the s'ásanam are not, with a few exceptions, identifiable.

The grant is engraved on three sheets of copper, protected by two more, one underneath and the other on the top, the whole clasped together by a massive ring of the same metal impressed with the seal of a boar at the point of soldering. The last sheet of the writing is broken towards the right-hand side, thereby rendering some of the s'lokas at the end unreadable.

The characters of the s'ásanam are said to be 'Nandi Nágara,' and resemble those of the modern 'Bálabandh,' although there are several differences, which mark the writing in the s'ásanam as a separate dialect. The Sanskrit portion of the composition is not very creditable to the original composers, and abounds with inaccuracies. In the translation, they have been as far as possible rectified in the 's'lokas' at the commencement and termination. The Kanarese words used in the body of the grant do not impress one with its alleged antiquity when compared with those to be met with in old stone inscriptions, whose genuineness is guaranteed by their not being portable.

At the commencement, in reciting the titles of Janaméjaya, the words (*chacha pata chácha pata*) are inserted. It is not known to what they refer, and what is their meaning.

Certain eminent astrologers, who have been consulted on the subject, doubt the truth of the astronomical combinations said to have occurred on the day of the grant....The year of the grant is denoted by the letters *ka, ta, ka*, being the first letters of two series in the Sanskrit alphabet. It is therefore, if true, 4861 years old, being executed in the year 111 of the Kaliyuga, or 2990 years B. C. Janamejaya flourished at the commencement of the Kali age. It is mentioned however, in a sannad confirming the village issued by Chennammáji a female occupant of the gádi of Nagar in 1745, A. D.

V. N. Narasimmiyengar.

Anantapura, 2nd January 1872.

II. TRANSLATION OF THE COPPER GRANT BELONGING TO THE GATUA AGRA'HARA, ANANTAPURA TALUKA.

Sl. I.—Jayatyávishkritam Vishnu várdham kshóbhitárnavam,

Dakshinónnata damshtrágra vishránta bhuvanam vapuha.

The body of Vishnu, incarnate in the form of a boar, which troubled and agitated the ocean, and on the edge of whose lofty right tusk the earth rested, exists in transcendent glory.

The Emperor Janamêjaya; the refuge of the whole universe; the master of the earth; the king of kings; the Paramés'wara of rulers; the great Mahárája; the sovereign of Hastinápura, the finest of cities; the bestower of widowhood on the wives of the hostile kings of Anga, and Magadha; the sun of the lotus of the Pándava race; most skilled in warfare; whose bow controlled the Kálinga serpent; the unrivalled hero; the dauntless in battle; the slayer of Asvapatiráya, Dhrupata and Gajapatiráya; the stalker on the head of Narapatiráya; the most accomplished equestrian; the terror of the [illegible] of Konkana, [illegible], Nunnala, [illegible], &c.; the very brilliant; the sun of [illegible] virtue; the bearer of the flag with the emblem of the golden [illegible]; the most glorious of Rajas; the adorned; the descendant of the great lunar race; the son of the Emperor Parikshit; was reigning at Hastinápura, (attended) by happy [illegible] amusements.

On a certain occasion, during an expedition of conquest in the south, at the shrine of Harihar s'wara, at the confluence of the rivers Tungabhadra and Haridra, in the dark fortnight of the month of Chaitra, in the year 111, on new moonday, which was a Monday, coupled with "Bharani Nakshatra, and Kimstughna karana,"† (astrological terms denoting particular constellations, &c.,) in Uttaráyana (when the sun is in the tropic of Capricorn) and in Simhabali, governed by Vyatipáta, on the occasion of a solar eclipse, when the sun was half obscured; when the snake sacrifice was performed, and when the principal rite of consummation was being conducted; the Emperor after duly saluting the Brahmans of various Gotras; co-adjutors in the sacrifice, who had arrived to the number of 32,000 from Banavase, Kuntalige Gautamagráma and other villages; notably Góvinda Pattavardhana, Karnátaka Brahman, of Gautama Gotra; Vámana Pattavardhana, Karnátaka Brahman, of Vasishtha Gotra; Keshava Yagnadikshita, Karnátaka Brahman of Bharadvája Gotra; and Náráyanadikshita, Karnátaka Brahman of Srivatsa Gotra; granted (to them) with water, &c. in due form the twelve villages of Gautamagráma, and those therein contained, viz., Nadavalli; Bidalavalli; Chikka Hiraku; Taralagura; Buralaguda; Tagaregunji; Aldúra; Nadúrahalli; Champaguda; and Kiri Champagúdu‡; together with the items of Chakravarti Mudhiri; Panchága Pasaya, Chatra Sukhásana, Balada Gaddige; Aneha Bandia Khandara; Nadu Bitti; Gadi Banda, and the eight qualifications known as "Ashtabhóga Téjas Sámya."

The boundaries thereof are:—On the north-east, a stream at which the joint boundaries of Gautamagráma, Hunasyúru, and Saliyúru converge. To the south of the above, Amlagudda is the boundary of the villages of Gautamagráma and Saliyúru. On the west of the above, the boundaries of Saliyúru and Gautamagráma extend as far as a stream. To the south of the above, proceeding from the boundary of Saliyúru and Gautamagráma, up to a tank near a hill called "Yengudda." Towards the south, up to a stream on the limits of Gautamagráma, and Saliyúru. On the south-west, the meeting of the boundaries of Gautamagráma, Kesavapura, and Saliyúru, also a ravine called "Vyágranagundi," or tiger's ravine, between two hills. On the west of the above, a stream flowing on the boundaries of Gautamagráma and Kesavapura. On the west, a bank of "Kubbige tank," at which the limits of Gautamagráma, Malludure and Kesavapura terminate. On the west, a hillock called "Kaggale Mardi," where the boundaries of Malandúru, Gautamagráma and Ambalesára converge, near which there is a saline stream, (Lavana vanti.) On the north-west, as far as the salt river (Lavana nadi) flowing at the junction of the limits of Gautamagráma, Hosagunda, and Ambalesára. Towards the north, up to a stream which flows on the confines of Gautamagráma and Hosagunda and a hill near Bidaragunji; and also 'Kshírakuda,' or milky pond. On the north a watercourse at which the boundaries of Trigarta (Tagarta) Bidaragunji and Gautamagráma meet. From north to north-east the boundary line between Trigarta, and Gautamagráma is marked by a stream called "Oshiyahalla." On the east of the above, a 'kitaki' bush, and a white Matti (tree) between the boundaries of Gautamagráma and Trigarta. On the east, a mound of red-earth marks the boundaries between Gautamagráma, Trigarta and Billuru; as also a hill. On the east Sirakuda to the north of a hill at which the boundaries of Billúru, Gautamagráma and Maraba meet: also a bamboo bush. On the east, a hillock marking the limits of Gautamagráma and Bannúru.

* [illegible]. † Conf. Colebrooke, *Essays*, Vol. II. p. 294.—Ed. ‡ One is omitted.

The boundaries from the east to the north-east have thus been completed.

II.—Sámányoyam dharma setúrnrupánám.
Kálé kálé pálaniyó bhavadbhihi.
Sarvánétán bhávinaha párthivéndrán.
Bhúyó bhúyó yáchaté Rámachandraha.

Rámachandra again and again entreats all future great kings:—This (grant) which is a bridge of charity common to rulers should from time to time be protected by you.

III.—Dánapálanayor madhyé.
Dánáchhréyóna pálanam.
Dánát svarga mavápnóti.
Pálanádachyutam padam.

Between giving and saving (of charities) it is more meritorious to save than to give. By giving (the donor) attains svargam, or Indra's paradise, but by saving, everlasting position (bliss) is attained.

IV.—Madvamsajáha paramahipati vamsajává.
Yé bhúmipáa satata mujvala dharma chittáhá.
Maddharma méva paripálana múcharanti
Tatpádapadma yugalam sirasá namámi.

I salute with my head the lotus-like feet of those rulers, whether descendants of my own race or of other dynasties, who always with a resplendent love of virtue, uphold and confirm my charity.

Note by the Translator.

The first sloka is an invocation used by most grantors of lands, because in the third incarnation, Vishnu is supposed to have released the earth from the grasp of Hiranyaksha, a demon who had usurped, and carried it away.

The year is denoted by the letters *ka*, *ta*, *ka*, which are the first letters of two different sets of letters in the alphabet. It is usual to read the figures thus expressed from right to left. In this case, the era is not mentioned. . . .

The characters in which the grant is embodied are called by the Inamdars the "Nandi Nágari." But they resemble the modern "Balaband" more than any other. The language is a mixture of Sanskrit and Kanarese, the *former* disfigured by a great many inaccuracies, whose existence cannot be accounted for except under the supposition, not improbable, that the engraver was ignorant of Sanskrit, and the original composer of the grant did not revise his work.

The grant is engraved on three sheets of copper, the edges of two of which are broken, clasped by a solid ring of the same metal which is stamped with a seal bearing the inscription of a boar.

In translating the slokas which are written at the commencement and termination of the grant, the grammatical mistakes found in the original have been rectified.

V. N. Narasimmiyengar.

III. TRANSLATION OF A BALABAND COPPER GRANT IN THE POSSESSION OF THE BHIMANAKATTE MATHA, KAVALEDURGA TALUKA.

Prostrations to Ganapati, Remover of Obstacles.

I.—Pántu vó jalada shyámaha,
Shárnga jyá gháta karkashaha.
Trailókya mantapa stambháha,
Chatváró hari báhavaha.

May the four arms of Hari (Vishnu), which are as dark as the water-laden clouds, which are hardened by the scars caused by the blow of the string of the Shárnga bow, and which are as the foundation pillars of the Mantapa of the three worlds, save ye.

In the year Plavanga, in the [illegible] year of the era of Yudhishthira, in the month of Pushya, on new-moonday, on Wednesday, King Janamêjaya, the arbiter of the Mahárájas, the master of the rajas, the possessor of the valour of heroes, the descendant of the race of Kuru, who is seated on the throne of the city of Kishkindha, the protector of all professions and castes, made this grant for the pújá of Sitarama, worshipped by Kaivalyanátha, disciple of Garudaváhanatírtha Sripáda, of the Munibrinda Matha, in Vrikodara (Bhíma) Katte, situated in the western town of [illegible]. The boundaries of the Munibrinda Katte, in which my great grandfather Yudhishthira remained are:—

On the East.—Western bank of the Tungabhadra, flowing towards the north. *On the South.*—North of the confluence near Agastya Ashram. *On the West.*—East of the Dána Nadi. *On the North.*—South of the Khâma Nadi.

Munibrindakshetra, situated within these boundaries, is granted by me, with offerings of the Tungabhadra water and money, in the presence of Harihara, on the occasion of an eclipse, into the hands of the yati or sanyasi, with my free consent, in view to obtaining Vishnu's heaven for my parents, to be enjoyed by you and the line of your disciples, as long as the sun and the moon last, inclusive of the items of hidden wealth, treasure-trove, water, trees, minerals, future acquisitions and improvements, &c.

The witnesses of this deed of charity are—

II.—Aditya chandravanaló nalascha,
Dyur bhúmirápó hridayam Yamascha.
Ahascha rátrischa ubhécha sandhye.
Dhármascha jánáti narasya vrittam.

A man's conduct and actions are known to the sun, moon, air, fire, firmament, earth, water, heart, Yama, day, night, morning, evening, and duty.

III.—Dánapálanayór madhye.
Dana chchréyónu pálanam.
Dánátsvargámavápnóti.
Pálanáddachchyutam padam.

Between giving and protecting, it is more meritorious to protect. By giving (the donor) attains svarga, but by protecting, immortal station (Heaven) is attained.

IV.—Svadattâd dviguṇam puṇyam,
Paradattânupâlanam.
Paradattâpahâreṇa,
Svadattam nishphalam bhavet.

The act of saving another's gift is productive of twice as much merit as giving one's self. By taking away another's gift, one's own grants become unfruitful of merit.

V.—Maddattâ putrikâ dhâtri,
Pitrâ dattâ sahodarî.
Anya dattâ tu jananî.
Dattâm bhûmim parityajêt.

The land granted by me is my daughter; and that granted by my father is my sister. But the one granted by another is like my mother. Therefore land granted (away) should not be relinquished.

VI.—Annaistu charitam bhangâ,
Sahleva charitam nata.
Tasaha kashtântarâ nichaha.
Svayam dattâpahârakaha.

The same person, who revokes his own gifts will, in the time of retribution, eat what was thrown up by others, but not his own.

VII.—Svadattâm paradattâm vâ,
Bramha vrittim harettaha.
Shashtivarsha sahasrâṇi.
Vishṭhâyâm jâyate krimihi.

Whoever usurps, or takes away Brahman's land, whether given by himself or by others, will be condemned to the life of a worm in human offal for sixty thousand years.

Note.

The original copper grant is not in the office, and I have not seen it. The copy is full of inaccuracies, both orthographical and grammatical. They cannot be rectified, lest the nature of the grant be altered. The translation is as near the original meaning as can be rendered under the circumstances. The ślokas are given here as accurately as possible, but they have been sadly mutilated in the process of transcription. There is a sentence in the copy as follows:—

[illegible]

This being unmeaning, it is omitted in the translation.

The Gauja and Kappagadde grants of Janamejaya are estimated to be dated in 111 of the era of Yudhishthira. This grant, if genuine, is 92 years older, but it is a question whether the Matha to which the grant is alleged to have been made, is so ancient, seeing that the teachings of Madhavâchârya are only between 5 and 600 years old. The words made use of in the grant, viz., Tîrtha [illegible], seem to be still peculiar to the [illegible] of the Madhava persuasion.

V. N. Narasimmiyengar.

2nd *July* 1872.

Dr. BÜHLER'S REPORT ON SANSKRIT MSS. IN GUJARAT.

From Dr. Bühler's Report to the Director of Public Instruction, Bombay, dated 30th August 1872, we give the following abridgment:—

During the last year two fascicles of the catalogue of Sanskrit manuscripts from Gujarat, comprising a little more than three thousand manuscripts of Vedic books, purâṇas, and poetical works, have been published. The third fascicle, which contains works on grammar, glossaries, works on rhetoric, metre, and law, is ready for issue, and the fourth number, which gives the remaining Śâstras, is in the press. With the publication of the fourth fascicle, all the materials collected in 1869, so far as they refer to Brahmanical literature, will be exhausted. But, as since 1870 I have received a large number of new lists, a supplementary fascicle will have to be prepared, which should also contain an alphabetical index to the preceding parts. Besides, the lists of Jaina books remain unpublished; I have, however, made preparations for the publication of a fascicle containing Jaina works, and hope to bring it out early in 1873.

A number of fresh lists comprising uncatalogued Brahmanical libraries in Lunawara, Olpâr, Baroda, &c., have been prepared. Considerable progress has been made in catalogueing the Jaina libraries at Rânder, Surat, Limdi and Khambay. Several large Bhandars at Ahmedabad, Wadwan, and the largest collection of all at Patan have, as yet, not been touched. Something in this direction will, I hope, be done during 1872-73. But I am persuaded that the work cannot be finished before the end of 1874-75.

The number of manuscripts purchased during the year (up to June 30, 1872) amounts to [illegible]. Among these 120 belong to the Brahmanical literature, the remainder to that of the Jainas. In the former class poetical and philosophical books are most numerously represented. Particularly valuable, are the complete old manuscript of Patanjali's Mahâbhâshya with Kaiyata's commentary, the [illegible] of [illegible], the two manuscripts of the [illegible], the Âdityapurâṇa, the fragment of the Sarasvatîpurâṇa, the Jaina commentary on the Meghadûta, the commentary on the [illegible], &c. Our collection of Jaina books is now larger than any other public collection, of which I have ever heard. We have copies of nearly all the sacred works and commentaries, both old and new, or most of them, so that there would be no difficulty in editing the more important ones. There are also fresh materials for the history of the Jaina religion, of the political history of Gujarât, and above all for the history of the Gujarâtî language. I have bought a large number of Râsâs and other legendary works, simply, in order to obtain specimens of the ancient Gujarâti. The oldest pieces in that language are some verses preserved in Ratnaśekhara's Prabandhakośa written A.D. 1347, one of which is ascribed to a Chāraṇ, belonging to Rājavīradhavala's camp, A.D. 1235. As I hope to give in my catalogue of Jaina manuscripts an account of the most interesting works bought, I omit here the enumeration of important acquisitions.

My operations since July have had even more important results than those of last year. I have already acquired several manuscripts, which are fully 600 years old, and have full confidence that I shall obtain others which exceed that age by 200 years. The more I become acquainted with Gujarât, the more offers of old and valuable books I get, and I trust that Government will see fit to allow the grant for Sanskrit manuscripts also for next year.

CORRESPONDENCE.

'HULLE MUKKALU.'

It came officially before me that the goldsmiths of a certain village laid claim to the property of some men of the "Hulle Makkalu" (old sons) caste who had died intestate. That one caste should claim the property of another caste on the grounds that they had performed the burial-service, &c., seemed so strange that I made enquiries. It appears that the "Hulle Mukkalu" is a caste grafted on to the goldsmiths. The term "Hulle Maga," an old son, is now a term of reproach among the Canarese. The following story of the rise of this caste I have had confirmed by different members of the goldsmith caste:—

"About 300 years ago in the kingdom of Chikbunda lived a person of the Kumti merchant caste who held some high Government appointment but had embezzled large sums of money entrusted to him. This having come to light the king ordered the Kumti to be impaled unless he would grant the money. None of his caste people would assist him. In the same village lived the widow of a goldsmith. She had gone to the well to get some water, and on her way back she met the Kumti being led out to execution. She asked and was told all the circumstances of the case. The amount embezzled was about two lakhs of rupees which she offered to pay provided the Kumti would bind himself and his descendants to become the sons of her caste. On being formally resigned by his own caste, the convert received a copper grant which created him the "old son" of the goldsmith caste. This caste is now said to be of 1,000 families: they live by begging and from the realisation of the following fees which the Panchalas pay them:—

(1) One pagoda for every goldsmith's workshop.

(2) One fanam = 4 an. 8 pie for every blacksmith's shop.

(3) One fanam for every marriage ceremony.

Admissions to the caste which is performed by granting the neophyte a copy of the grant together with a peculiarly shaped knife are still made. The convert's children become "Hulle Mukkalu."

It appears that a similar caste is to be found both among the Komatis and the Chakliers. I have not however yet had an opportunity of learning anything about them. I have never read or heard of anything of this sort among the castes. An outcaste might create a new caste, but I never thought they could be grafted one to another.

Hassan, 1872. J. H. F. Mackenzie.

COROMANDEL COAST.

It is now I believe pretty generally accepted that the first word in the phrase 'Coromandel Coast' is derived from the name of a village between Madras and Pulicat called Coromandel, but how it came to be applied to so long a line of sea-board is another matter. The words 'Kari manal,' known to the merest tyro in Tamil, means 'black sand,' and at this very village there is found the glittering black sand used so much by native clerks instead of blotting paper. My theory is that one of the early explorers landed at this spot and, being ignorant of the language, went through what appears to me a very natural way of solving the difficulty by taking up a handful of this black sand and pointing to it. The answer he would receive would be 'Kari manal,' which he would take to be the name of the country instead of simply the sand grains in his palm. The mistake has, I consider, been propagated, and on this supposition we have, what appears to me, a very simple solution of the question.

J. B. J.

Palconda, Vizagapatam, March, 17th 1872.

HÂSYÂRNAVA.

Sir,—In the *Indian Antiquary* p. 340, I find an article on Kālidāsa by Pandit Hanhagari Sastri, B.A., who cites Hāsyārnava among the works of Kālidāsa. It is a comparatively modern work of a Bengal Pandit, Jagadīśvara Tarkālankāra. Prof. Wilson gives a short account of this work in his *Theatre of the Hindus*, Vol. II., where he says, "It is the work of a Pandit named Jagadīśa, and was represented at the vernal festival." Hāsyārnava is a *prahasana* or farce in two acts. There is a modern commentary on it by Mahendra Nāth, son of Taraka Nāth Tarkavāgīśa.

Ram Das Sen.

Berhampur, Bengal, 11th Nov. 1872.

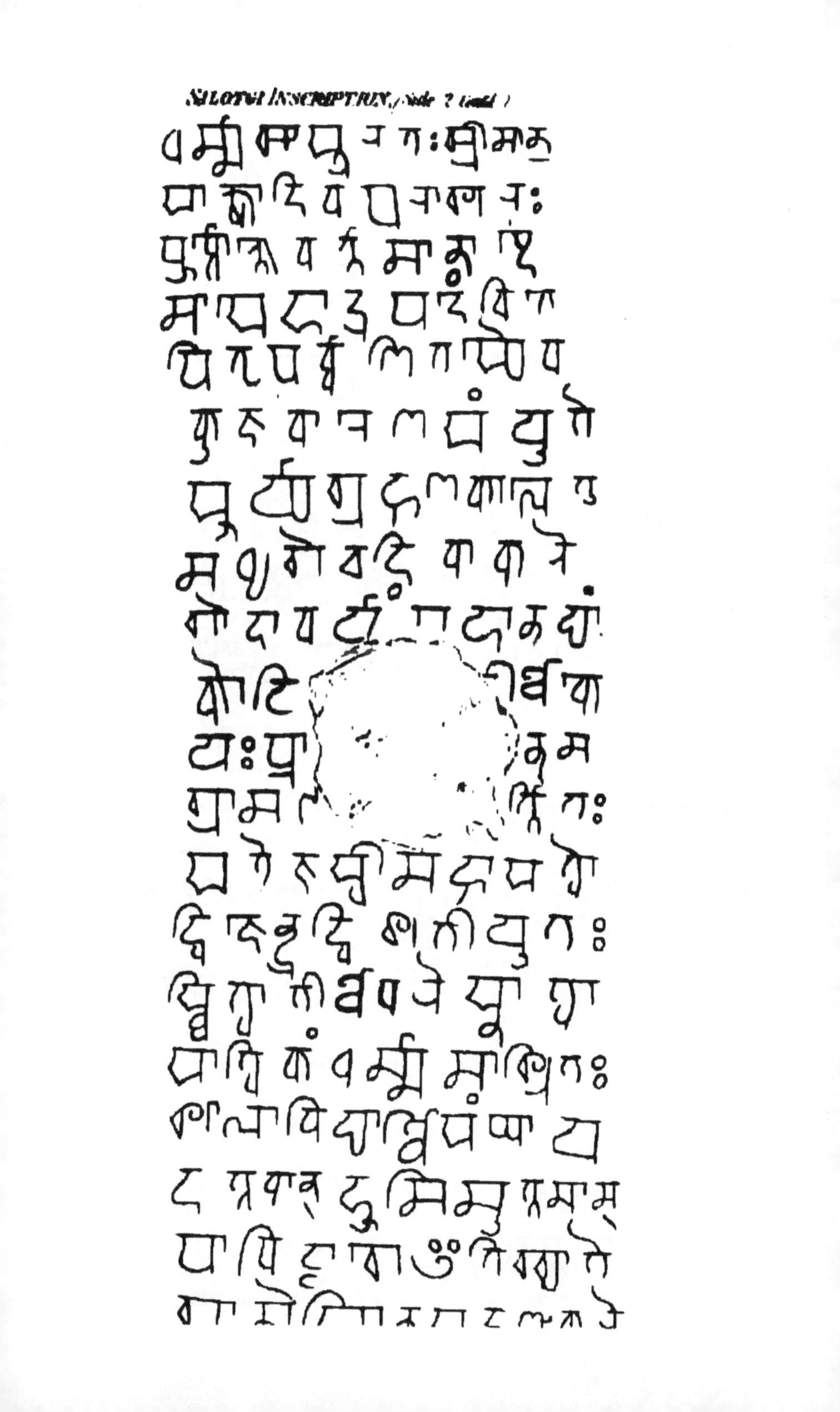

SILOTGI INSCRIPTION, (Side 2 Contd.)

निवर्त्तनानि पंचाशद्भूमेर्म्मोन्यानि तानिच

व्या ग्व्या तुरस्यां शाल्यां मान्यमेकं निवेशनम्

वहु भिर्व्वसुधा भुक्ता राजभिः सगरादिभिः

यस्य यस्य यदा भूमिस्तस्य तस्य तदा फलम.

Of five lines more only a transcription was taken.

INDEX.

ERRATA AND CORRIGENDA.

[illegible]

www.ingramcontent.com/pod-product-compliance
Lightning Source LLC
Chambersburg PA
CBHW032316280326
41932CB00009B/828

* 9 7 8 3 7 4 2 8 3 7 5 6 1 *